This Day in American History
THIRD EDITION

This Day in American History

THIRD EDITION

Ernie Gross and
Roland H. Worth, Jr.

McFarland & Company, Inc., Publishers
Jefferson, North Carolina, and London

ALSO BY ERNIE GROSS
AND FROM MCFARLAND

*Advances and Innovations in American
Daily Life, 1600s–1930s (2002)*
This Day in Sports (2001)

ALSO BY ROLAND H. WORTH, JR.
AND FROM MCFARLAND

Shapers of Early Christianity (2007)
Messiahs and Messianic Movements through 1899 (2005)
Congress Declares War (2004)
Alternative Lives of Jesus (2003)
Biblical Studies on the Internet (2002)
World War II Resources on the Internet (2002)
Secret Allies in the Pacific (2001)
Church, Monarch and Bible in Sixteenth Century England (2000)
No Choice but War (1995)
Pearl Harbor (1993)
Bible Translations (1992)

LIBRARY OF CONGRESS CATALOGUING-IN-PUBLICATION DATA

Gross, Ernie.
This day in American history / Ernie Gross and Roland H. Worth, Jr.— 3rd ed.
p.   cm.
Includes bibliographical references and index.

ISBN-13: 978-0-7864-3192-2
illustrated case : 50# alkaline paper ∞

1. United States— History— Chronology.   2. United States—
History— Miscellanea.   I. Worth, Roland H., 1943–
II. Title.
E174.5.G76   2008   973 — dc22   2007044163

British Library cataloguing data are available

On the cover: Space shuttle *Challenger* lifts off Pad 39B at
Kennedy Space Center, Florida, at 11:38 a.m., EST, January 28, 1986.
The entire crew of seven was lost in the explosion 73
seconds into the launch(AP Photo/NASA)

Manufactured in the United States of America

McFarland & Company, Inc., Publishers
Box 611, Jefferson, North Carolina 28640
www.mcfarlandpub.com

TABLE OF CONTENTS

PREFACE

In selecting entries for this detailed compilation, the late author of its first two editions (Ernie Gross) and his successor (Roland H. Worth, Jr.) have attempted to provide not only the "important" events, but also those which pique the human curiosity and interest. Since history consists not only of "hard phenomena"—that is, such-and-such happened on a certain date—but also changes in the broader society that require years to occur, a variety of statistical data that summarize these transitions have been included as well. Usually these concise entries are to be found on the date the material was released to the public (since the compilation of data generally requires a considerable period past the last date covered). Occasionally these have been placed at the end of a calendar year or month, when that seemed more appropriate.

The subject matter covered is vast — scientific discoveries (and recantations), wartime battles, elections, notable births and deaths, natural and manmade disasters, legislative decisions, "firsts" by women athletes, events in the struggle over homosexual rights and traditional views of marriage and human sexuality, the more than a century-old conflict between Darwinists and creationists (and the newest challenge to the dominant opinion in the scientific community, intelligent design), Supreme Court decisions and a wide range of other occurrences that would register as significant in American history. Praise them; condemn them. Either way these events *are,* and the knowledge of them provides not only the bare facts of our ever-changing society but also the flavor of sentiments and attitudes at any given moment in our history.

When Ernie Gross originally began this compilation, he did so as a tool to add interest to the script of the daily radio broadcast he was responsible for preparing. He explained it thus:

This Day in American History had its beginnings years ago when as a young radio news writer I tried to include a topical historical item in each day's newscast. In selecting items for inclusion, I considered, first, the impact of certain persons on American life, and, second, a broad spectrum of events — scientific inventions and geographical discoveries, landmark government actions, and man-made and natural disasters.

It was not always easy to find the information I needed. Biographical references tended to focus on military or government officials, along with some educators, clergy, and industrialists. Calendrically oriented data on sports and entertainment personalities were especially difficult to find, despite their impact on and interest for the American people. Information on events not associated with a particular person was scattered in numerous reference works. In short, there was no single source back then to which I could turn for a good overview of the events of a specific day in American history.

In spite of the multiplication of many varied reference works, a surprising amount of this frustration occasionally still remains for the contemporary researcher. For example, while compiling the more than 950 new entries to cover the period 2000 to 2006, I discovered that a certain well-known Washington political figure commonly had his name spelled two different ways. One would think that in this era of vast news resources such discrepancies would not occur, yet (somehow) they do, and the compiler can only do his best to

1

go with the most reliable or at least dominant usage found at the moment.

When Ernie Gross left news work, he continued to expand this volume in the hope of making it of maximum use to a variety of individuals: "It is my hope that *This Day in American History* will be of repeated use to media specialists, speechwriters, events planners, teachers, librarians, students, and the general reader who is simply curious about what happened on a particular day in American history."

For some the interest will arise in that a surprising number of significant events have all coincidentally happened on a specific day; for others, in that these are events that happened on their birthday or that of a loved one.

The ongoing purpose continues to be to provide a concise, easily used, and reliable source of information on what has happened on every day of the calendar year. Your personal inter-est or need may vary from that of others, but whatever it may be, this work intends to meet it in a readily usable manner.

Finally, in being given the privilege of updating the third edition with material from the most recent years, I faced the major problem of what do with the "war on terrorism," since an entire volume could easily be compiled just documenting the daily events belonging in that category alone. Instead, we have opted for including a selective sampling of key and representative incidents connected with that ongoing conflict. In short, though it is an important and vital part of our contemporary history, it still remains only one segment of the vast panorama of contemporary American life and culture. Just as during World War II, "life went on," so it does during this contemporary conflict.

Roland H. Worth, Jr.

JANUARY

1

1673 First regular mail service between Boston and New York inaugurated on monthly basis.

1705 Charles Chauncy, Congregational clergyman, born in Boston; served Boston's First Church 60 years; opposed George Whitefield's revival movement, effort of British to impose Church of England's doctrine, practices (died 1787).

1735 First American fire insurance company (The Friendly Society for the Mutual Insurance of Houses Against Fire) began in Charleston, SC; lasted five years, fire destroyed half the city and company.

1735 Paul Revere, silversmith/express rider, born in Boston; remembered as one of trio who alerted New England countryside of British attack in 1775; designed, printed first Continental money; designed, engraved first official seal of Colonies, Massachusetts seal; discovered process for rolling sheet copper (died 1818).

1745 Anthony Wayne, Revolutionary officer known as "Mad Anthony," born in Waynesboro, PA; represented Georgia in House (1791–92); led American troops to victory over Indians at Fallen Timbers, OH (1794) (died 1796).

1750 Frederick A. Muhlenberg, colonial legislator, born in Trappe, PA; represented Pennsylvania in House, serving as first Speaker (1789–91, 1793–95) (died 1801).

1752 Gregorian calendar officially adopted by Great Britain and colonies.

1752 Betsy Ross, flagmaker, born in Philadelphia; made first American flag reputedly at request of George Washington and others (died 1836).

1772 Thomas Jefferson married Martha Wayles Skelton in Williamsburg, VA.

1776 George Washington announced forma-tion of Colonial Army and raised for first time flag of the united colonies in Cambridge, MA (flag was 13 alternate red and white stripes and crosses of St. Andrew and St. George).

1776 Norfolk, VA, burned on orders of Governor Dunmore because city refused demands for provisions.

1779 Universalist Church of America organized in Gloucester, MA.

1780 Settlers led by James Robertson arrived at site of Nashville, TN.

1781 Pennsylvania troops mutinied at Morristown, NJ, killing several officers; grievances resolved before mutineers reached Congress in Philadelphia.

1782 Juan Crespi, Spanish missionary/ explorer, died at 61; co-discoverer of San Francisco Bay.

1783 Public debt of United States reported at $42 million.

1785 *Falmouth Gazette and Weekly Advertiser*, first Maine newspaper, begun by Benjamin Titcomb and Thomas B. Wait.

1788 Etienne Cabet, socialist, born in Dijon, France; created utopian settlement of Icarians in Nauvoo, IL; served as its president (1849–56) (died 1856).

1800 Constantine Hering, homeopathic physician, born in Oschatz, Germany; organized first homeopathic school (North American Academy of Homeopathic Healing Art, Philadelphia 1836), first such medical college (1848), Hahnemann Medical College (1867) (died 1880).

1808 Federal law went into effect which penalized forfeiture of ship and cargo if vessel was involved in slave trade; disposition of seized slaves left to states where seizure occurred.

1810 Charles Ellet, civil engineer, born in Penn's Manor, PA; built suspension bridges—first important American suspension bridge over Schuylkill River near Philadelphia (1842) and then world's longest (1,900 ft.) over Ohio River near Wheeling (died 1862).

1813   John Kling, physician, born in New York City; founder of eclectic school of medicine, introduced to general use podophyllin, hydrastic, and sanguinaria (died 1893).

1817   Second Bank of United States began operations as depository for federal funds, with authorized capitalization of $35 million.

1818   Restored White House opened for a public reception; was burned by British in 1814.

1824   James K. Polk and Sarah Childress married in Murfreesboro, TN.

1827   William C. Cabell, Confederate general, born in Danville, VA; active in trans–Mississippi area (died 1911).

1831   William Lloyd Garrison began publishing *The Liberator* in Boston, continuing the anti-slavery paper until December 29, 1865; he set tone in first issue, stating: "I am in earnest, I will not equivocate, I will not excuse, I will not retreat a single inch, and I will be heard."

1833   *Knickerbocker Magazine* began publication in New York City.

1842   First illustrated weekly magazine (*Brother Jonathan, a Weekly Compend of Belles Lettres and the Fine Arts, Standard Literature, and General Intelligence*) was issued by Benjamin H. Day and Nathaniel Parker Willis.

1843   Thomas J. Foster, educator, born in Pottsville, PA; founder, International Correspondence Schools (1891), helped educate about one million persons (died 1936).

1848   Willis S. Paine, lawyer/banker, born in Rochester, NY; compiled, revised New York state banking laws; state banking superintendent (1885–89); president, State Trust Co. (1889–1927) (died 1927).

1855   George H. Bissell and Jonathan J. Eveleth, New York City law partners, formed first American oil company (Pennsylvania Rock Oil Co.), discovered eight products extractable from oil from a spring in Venango County, PA.

1856   Use of adhesive postage stamps, available since 1847, made mandatory by Congress.

1857   Tim(othy J.) Keefe, baseball pitcher who won 344 games in 14 years, born in Cambridge, MA; named to Baseball Hall of Fame (died 1933).

1858   Albert Gleaves, World War I naval officer, born in Nashville, TN; led Atlantic convoy operations (1917–19); commanded Asiatic station (1920–21) (died 1937).

1859   Michael J. Owens, inventor/manufacturer, born in Mason County, WV; invented bottle blowing machine; an organizer, officer of Libby-Owens Glass Co. (1916) (died 1923).

1860   First state insurance department began operating in New York; William Barnes was first superintendent.

1860   Clarence R. Edwards, Army officer, born in Cleveland; commanded troops in Canal Zone (1915–17); organized, commanded 16th Division in France (1917–18), (died 1931).

1861   John L. Long, author, born in Hanover, PA; wrote *Madame Butterfly*, which became a play, opera (died 1927).

1862   Federal income tax went into effect with a 3 percent tax on income over $800; lasted until 1872.

1862   James M. Mason and John Slidell, Confederate diplomats, were released and put aboard a British sloop at Provincetown, MA; sailed to Halifax.

1863   Emancipation Proclamation, announced by President Lincoln September 22, 1862, went into effect; provided that all slaves in areas still in rebellion were "then, henceforward, and forever free."

1863   Homestead Act went into effect providing that anyone over 21 could get title to 160 acres of public land by living on it for five years, making certain improvements, and paying fees of about $18; first homesteader was Daniel Freeman, a Union soldier who staked out a claim near Beatrice, NE.

1864   Alfred Stieglitz, photographer/editor, born in Hoboken, NJ; often called father of modern photography (died 1946).

1867   Lew(is M.) Fields, entertainer, born in New York City; half of Weber & Fields comedy team; managed several theaters (died 1914).

1874   Frank (William F.) Knox, publisher/public official, born in Boston; publisher, *Chicago Daily News* (1931–40); Republican vice presidential candidate (1936); Secretary of Navy (1940–44) (died 1944).

1876   Philadelphia Mummers Parade officially got under way; similar parades held sporadically for 100 years.

1878   Edwin Franko Goldman, bandmaster/composer, born in Louisville; led summer band concerts in New York City's Central Park 38 years (died 1956).

1879   William Fox, pioneer movie executive, born in Tulchva, Hungary; built multi-million dollar empire, had virtual control of movie production, distribution during silent film era (died 1952).

1879   Knights of Labor, predecessor of American Federation of Labor, organized.

1880 Thomas A. Edison demonstrated the first experimental overhead line for incandescent lights.

1883 William J. Donovan, attorney/public official, born in Buffalo; World War I Congressional Medal of Honor winner; organized, directed, Office of Strategic Services (OSS) (1942–45), predecessor of Central Intelligence Agency (died 1959).

1883 Roy W. Howard, editor/publisher, born in Gano, OH; served with United Press, Newspaper Enterprise Assn. and Scripps-Howard chain (1906–64), as board chairman (1921–36), president (1936–52); president, *New York World Telegram* (1931–62) (died 1964).

1886 First Tournament of Roses parade held in Pasadena, CA; staged by Valley Hunt Club.

1887 Harry Scherman, Book of the Month Club founder, born in Montreal (died 1969).

1888 John C. Garand, firearms inventor, born in St. Remy, Canada; ordnance engineer, U.S. Armory, Springfield, MA (from 1919); developed 30 caliber M1 semiautomatic rifle, World War II basic shoulder weapon (died 1974).

1892 Ellis Island in New York Harbor became receiving station for immigrants; operated 62 years, processing about 20 million persons.

1895 J(ohn) Edgar Hoover, head of Federal Bureau of Investigation (FBI) (1924–72), born in Washington, DC (died 1972).

1897 Catherine Drinker Bowen, author, born in Haverford, PA; works included *Yankee from Olympus* and *The Lion and the Throne* (died 1973).

1898 City of Greater New York inaugurated with ceremonies, making it (then) world's second largest city with a population of 3,438,899.

1900 Xavier Cugat, band leader, born in Barcelona, Spain (died 1990).

1902 First Rose Bowl football game held, with Michigan defeating Stanford 49–0; first regular annual game held in 1916.

1903 Pacific cable went into operation, connecting San Francisco and Hawaii.

1907 Food and Drug Administration began operating.

1908 Statewide prohibition went into effect in Georgia.

1909 Barry M. Goldwater, legislator, born in Phoenix; represented Arizona in Senate (1952–64, 1968–86); Republican presidential nominee (1964) (died 1998).

1911 Hank (Henry B.) Greenberg, baseball player, born in New York City; with Detroit Tigers (1930–46), .313 career batting average; named to Baseball Hall of Fame (died 1986).

1913 Parcel Post Service began throughout country; estimated six million parcels sent the first week.

1914 Seasonal commercial air passenger service begun between St. Petersburg and Tampa, with two daily round trips at $10 each.

1914 Dayton, Ohio, became first large American city to adopt commission-city manager form of government.

1915 Panama-California Exposition opened in San Diego.

1915 Prohibition went into effect in Arizona and Idaho.

1918 Federal government took over railroad operations with Treasury Secretary William G. McAdoo director general; returned to private operations March 1, 1920.

1919 J(erome) D. Salinger, author, born in New York City; best known for *Catcher in the Rye*.

1927 Massachusetts adopted compulsory auto insurance, first of its kind; required $5,000/10,000 liability coverage.

1934 Dr. Francis E. Townsend of Long Beach, CA, announced his Old Age Revolving Pension Plan, providing every applying American citizen 60 or older with an annuity not exceeding $200 a month from the U.S. Treasury; money to be spent in United States within a month.

1936 National Recovery Administration (NRA) ended after 2½ years when Supreme Court found parts of Act unconstitutional.

1942 United Nationals declaration signed in Washington by 26 nations, affirming the principles of the Atlantic Charter.

1947 Atomic Energy Commission, with David E. Lilienthal chairman, took over control of national atomic energy program; succeeded January 19, 1975, by Nuclear Regulatory Commission.

1961 Merger of American Lutheran Church, Evangelical Lutheran Church, and United Evangelical Church became effective; created church of nearly 2.5 million members.

1966 New York City's first transit strike began; ended January 13.

1970 President Nixon signed bill creating Council of Environmental Quality.

1971 Three-day holiday weekends became effective for Washington's Birthday, Memorial Day, Columbus Day, and Veterans Day.

1974 Supplemental Security Income (SSI) program began as phase of Social Security.

1975 Former Attorney General John N. Mitchell and former presidential aides John D. Ehrlichman and H.R. Haldeman were found guilty of Watergate cover-up charges.

1975 New state constitution went into effect in Louisiana.

1976 New minimum wage law went into effect, setting rate at $2.30 a hour.

1978 First phase of increased minimum wages went into effect, providing for $2.65 an hour, rising to $2.90 on January 1, 1979; $3.10 on January 1, 1980; and $3.35 January 1, 1981.

1979 China and United States established full diplomatic relations as U.S. severed diplomatic relations with Taiwan.

1984 Largest American corporate reorganization occurred when American Telephone & Telegraph Co. divested itself of 22 wholly-owned local Bell telephone companies as a result of 1982 consent agreement with Justice Department.

1988 Evangelical Lutheran Church in America began functioning as nation's fourth largest Protestant denomination; 5.3 million member body created by merger of Lutheran Church in America, the American Lutheran Church, and Association of Evangelical Lutheran Churches.

1991 Minimum wage was increased to $4.25 an hour.

1994 North American Free Trade Agreement went into effect.

1998 Helen Wills (Moody), early tennis star who won 31 Grand Slam tournaments, died at 92.

2000 The vast bulk of computer systems made the transition into 2000 without the general electronic collapse many feared.

2001 Ray Walton died at 86; had Broadway successes but in popular mind most identified as the television star of *My Favorite Martian*.

2002 Open Skies treaty went into effect, which permits signatory nations to fly unarmed reconnaissance flights over territory of each other (including the U.S.) to verify for themselves what is happening militarily in the concerned nations; first proposed by President Eisenhower in 1955.

2

1608 Christopher Newport arrived at Jamestown with food and 110 new settlers.

1752 Philip M. Freneau, "poet of American Revolution," born in New York City; founder/editor, *National Gazette* (1791–93); poetry included *The British Prison Ship*, *The Wild Honeysuckle*, *Indian Burying Ground* (died 1832).

1781 Virginia ceded western lands to Federal Government opening way for Maryland to ratify Articles of Confederation (February 27); Maryland would not ratify until all western lands ceded.

1788 Georgia convention unanimously ratified Constitution, entering Union as fourth state.

1830 Henry M. Flagler, oil executive/land developer, born in Hopewell, NY; a cofounder of Standard Oil, vice president (1870–1908); organized Florida East Coast Railway and coastal resort area (died 1913).

1856 Edward S. Martin, editor/writer, born near Auburn, NY; a founder, *Harvard Lampoon* (1876); first editor, editorial writer (1887–1933), *Life Magazine*; columnist, *Harper's Magazine* (1920–36) (died 1939).

1857 Frederic B. Opper, pioneer cartoonist ("Happy Hooligan"), born in Madison, OH (died 1937).

1860 Louisiana State University opened.

1861 Helen Herron Taft, wife of President Taft, born in Cincinnati (died 1943).

1863 Three-day battle of Stone River or Murfreesboro, TN, ended without definite decision.

1865 William Lyon Phelps, educator, born in New Haven, CT; early specialist in teaching modern literature (Yale U. 1893–1933) (died 1943).

1871 Tex (George L.) Rickard, boxing promoter, born in Kansas City, MO; first to promote million dollar gate (died 1929).

1871 Construction began on Brooklyn Bridge over East River in New York City.

1872 Albert C. Barnes, drug manufacturer, born in Philadelphia; created, produced the antiseptic, argyrol (died 1951).

1875 David H. Miller, lawyer who helped draft League of Nations covenant, born in New York City (died 1961).

1876 William H. Jeffers, railroad executive, born in North Platte, NE; president, Union Pacific (1937–46); rubber production administrator (1942–43) (died 1953).

1878 Frederic J. Fisher, auto body manufacturer, born in Sandusky, OH; principal founder/head, Fisher Body Co. (1908) (died 1941).

1887 Jewish Theological Seminary of America founded in New York City by Alexander Kohut and Sabato Morais.

1889 Roger Adams, chemist, born in Boston; headed U. of Illinois chemistry department (1926–54); a foremost organic chemist who did important research on composition of many natural substances (died 1971).

1890 Tito Schipa, operatic tenor (Metropolitan and Chicago 30 years), born in Lecce, Italy (died 1965).

1892 Artur Rodzinski, musician/conductor, born in Split, Yugoslavia; symphony conductor at Los Angeles 1929–33; Cleveland 1933–42; New York 1943–47; Chicago 1947–48 (died 1958).

1900 Lake Michigan waters diverted into Chicago Drainage Canal, a major engineering project; canal is 40 miles long, 22 feet deep; cost $45 million.

1904 Sally Rand, entertainer, born in Elkton, MO; her exotic fan dance was sensation of 1933 Chicago World's Fair (died 1979).

1920 Government agents in 22 cities made simultaneous raids on Industrial Workers of the World (IWW) and Communist Party members; resulted in deporting 516 aliens.

1920 Isaac Asimov, biochemist/author, born in Petrovichi, Russia; wrote 200+ books, including some of best science fiction (*Foundation Trilogy*, *Nightfall*) (died 1992).

1929 United States and Canada signed convention to preserve Niagara Falls.

1933 American Marines were withdrawn from Nicaragua, ending forceful intervention in Latin America.

1935 Trial of Bruno Hauptmann, charged with kidnapping/murder of son of Charles A. Lindbergh, held in Flemington, NJ; found guilty, electrocuted April 3, 1936.

1936 Electron tube, enabling man to see in dark, invented by Vladimir Zworykin and George A. Morton; device sensitive to ultraviolet and infrared rays.

1942 Manila and Cavite captured by Japanese; American and Philippine forces strengthened positions on Bataan Peninsula, holding out until April 9.

1949 Puerto Rico inaugurated Luis Munoz-Marin, its first elected governor.

1963 Sixteen persons died in an explosion in a packing plant in Terre Haute, IN.

1974 President Nixon signed legislation limiting highway speed to 55 miles per hour.

1988 President Reagan and Canadian Prime Minister Mulroney signed landmark trade agreement that would eliminate tariffs and lower other barriers to trade and investment before the end of the century.

1988 Collapse of a new storage tank poured about one million gallons of diesel fuel into Monongahela River at West Elizabeth, PA; threatened drinking water at Pittsburgh.

1990 Dow Jones industrial average reached 2810.15, its highest level ever.

2000 Gary Adams, golf innovator, died at 56.

3

1711 Richard Gridley, military engineer, born in Boston; Continental Army chief engineer, fortified Bunker (Breed's) Hill, Dorchester Heights (died 1796).

1777 George Washington secretly moved his pinned-down troops against a large British force, routing them at Princeton, NJ; this and the Trenton victory restored American morale.

1787 People of Maine in convention voted to separate from Massachusetts.

1793 Lucretia C. Mott, women's rights activist, born in Nantucket, MA; active in anti-slavery movement, associated with Elizabeth Cady Stanton in calling, directing first women's rights convention (Seneca Falls, NY, 1848); her home was sanctuary for runaway slaves (died 1880).

1814 President Madison ordered court martial of General William Hull for surrendering Detroit to British without resistance; found guilty.

1825 First secular utopian society founded in New Harmony, IN, by Robert Owen; lasted only a few years.

1831 First building and loan association (Oxford Provident Building Association) organized in Thomas Sidebotham's tavern in Frankford, PA; first loan was $500.

1834 Stephen Austin arrested in Mexico City, where he had gone to protest Mexican restrictions on Texas colonization; imprisoned for eight months.

1835 Larkin G. Mead, sculptor, born in Chesterfield, NH; sculpted Lincoln Monument in Springfield, IL, Ethan Allen in Montpelier, VT (died 1910).

1840 Henry Holt, publisher/author, born in Baltimore; founder (1873)/head of Henry Holt & Co.; wrote several novels (died 1926).

1861 Delaware legislature unanimously rejected secession from the Union.

1861 Fort Pulaski in Savannah seized by Georgia troops.

1871 U.S. Weather Service began; Weather Bureau organized in 1890.

1872 Hugh K. Moore, chemical engineer, born in Andover, MA; invented unsubmerged diaphragm cell, new method for making calcium arsenate, and other improvements (died 1939).

1879 Grace A. Goodhue Coolidge, wife of President Coolidge, born in Burlington, VT (died 1957).

1886 Raymond A. Spruance, World War II admiral, born in Baltimore; led forces in Battle of

Midway victory; commander, 5th Fleet (1944–45), commander-in-chief, Pacific Fleet (1945–46); headed Naval War College (1946–48); ambassador to Philippines (1952–56) (died 1969).

1909 Victor Borge, entertainer, born in Copenhagen; noted for his humor and piano artistry.

1911 First American postal savings banks opened in 48 cities; system ended in 1966.

1915 Jack Levine, artist, born in Boston; a protest painter, he sought to depict social and political ills.

1918 U.S. Employment Service established as separate unit in Department of Labor.

1919 Herbert Hoover named head of international relief organization to help liberated and enemy countries.

1924 Explosion in food plant in Pekin, IL, killed 42 persons.

1939 Bobby (Robert M., Jr.) Hull, probably best left wing in ice hockey, born in Pointe Anne, Canada; played 16 seasons with Chicago Blackhawks (1957–73).

1949 Supreme Court ruled that states have right to ban the closed shop.

1953 Lyndon B. Johnson elected minority leader of Senate.

1959 President Eisenhower signed proclamation admitting Alaska as the 49th state.

1961 President Eisenhower announced the United States had broken diplomatic relations with Cuba after a long series of harassments.

1961 Experimental reactor exploded at a federal installation near Idaho Falls, ID, killing three workers.

1967 Jack Ruby, Dallas night club owner charged with killing Lee Harvey Oswald, President Kennedy's alleged assassin, died in Dallas before he could be retried for the murder.

1985 California Institute of Technology and U. of California announced they would build world's largest telescope on Mauna Kea on island of Hawaii; scheduled for service in 1992.

1993 Presidents Bush and Boris Yeltsin (of Russia) signed START II to reduce long-range nuclear weapons by a third in ten years.

2000 Seventy couples signed up on the first day of California's new registry for unmarried couples; applies primarily to homosexuals but also to "straight" couples over 62 years of age. Designed to encourage providing of marriage-style benefits to such individuals.

2001 Double-header economic boost: First half-point reduction in interest rate by Federal Reserve this month; second on 31st.

2003 Sid Gillman, American Football League coach, died (b. 1911); pioneered the running game when passes dominated and substituted long-distance passes for the short distance ones usually used.

2005 Ex-presidents George W. H. Bush and Bill Clinton to lead fund-raising effort to assist those hit by the massive Pacific tsunami of the previous month.

2006 Major Washington lobbyist Jack Abramoff agreed to plead guilty to lobbying related felonies and to provide testimony against those he influenced.

4

1679 Roger Wolcott, early Connecticut leader, born in Windsor, CT; deputy governor (1741–50), governor (1751–54) (died 1767).

1789 Benjamin Lundy, abolitionist, born in Sussex County, NJ; organized one of first anti-slavery organizations, Union Humane Society (1815) (died 1839).

1804 Samuel M. Isaacs, orthodox rabbi, born in Leeuwarden, Netherlands; served New York City congregations from 1839; founder/editor, *Jewish Messenger* (1857–78); a founder, Mt. Sinai Hospital, United Hebrew Charities, Hebrew Free School Association (died 1878).

1818 Service on Black Ball Line, first transatlantic packet line, began between New York City and Liverpool.

1831 Edward P. Dutton, publisher, born in Keene, NH; founder (1858)/head, family publishing firm; co-publisher, *Everyman's Library*, series of inexpensive reprints (died 1923).

1836 Convention in Little Rock adopted Arkansas state constitution.

1838 Charles S. Stratton, midget, born in Bridgeport, CT; known as General Tom Thumb, exhibited by P.T. Barnum (died 1883).

1858 Carter Glass, legislator/public official, born in Lynchburg, VA; publisher, *Lynchburg News*; represented Virginia in House (1902–18) and Senate (1920–46); Secretary of Treasury (1918–20) (died 1946).

1859 Senate moved into its newly-completed chambers in the Capitol.

1861 Alabama troops seized Fort Morgan in Mobile.

1866 Niels E. Hansen, horticulturist, born near Ribe, Denmark; with South Dakota State College (1895–1937), originated hybrid plums, hybridization of alfalfa (died 1950).

1874 Thornton W. Burgess, children's author, born in Sandwich, MA (died 1965).

1883 Max Eastman, author/editor, born in Canandaigua, NY; editor, *New Masses, Liberator*; a leader of liberal opinion (died 1969).

1887 Edwin E. Witte, .economist, born in Jefferson County, WI; economics professor, U. of Wisconsin (1920–57); wrote Social Security Act (1935) (died 1960).

1893 President Benjamin Harrison proclaimed amnesty for past offenses against the anti-polygamy law.

1895 Leroy R. Grumman, airplane designer/manufacturer, born in Huntington, NY; founder, Grumman Aerospace Corp. (1929); designer of fighter planes (died 1982).

1896 Utah entered Union as 45th state.

1896 Everett M. Dirksen, legislator, born in Pekin, IL; represented Illinois in House (1933–49) and Senate (1951–69); Senate minority leader (1959–69) (died 1969).

1904 Supreme Court held that Puerto Ricans are not aliens and are not subject to immigration restrictions.

1930 Don(ald F.) Shula, retired football coach whose professional teams won record 347 games, born in Painesville, OH.

1935 Floyd Patterson, world heavyweight boxing champion (1956–59, 1960–62), born in Waco, NC.

1951 United Nations forces in Korea gave up Seoul in their retreat.

1974 President Nixon refused to surrender 500 tapes and documents subpoenaed by Senate Watergate Committee.

1988 Secretary of Health & Human Services planned to request $1.1 billion to fight AIDS.

1989 Defense Secretary Frank Carlucci approved recommendations of commission to close 86 military installations, partially close five, and revise 54; Congress to make final decision.

1989 Two F-14 Tomcats shot down two Libyan jets which threatened them and acted in a hostile manner about 70 miles north of Tobruk over the Mediterranean.

1995 Senator Daniel Moynihan of New York introduced legislation to repeal baseball's 73-year-old exemption from antitrust laws.

2000 Alan Greenspan nominated by President Clinton to serve fourth term as chairman of the Federal Reserve.

2004 Success on Mars: *Spirit* rover landed and

took first photographs of nearby area; continued to operate long beyond estimates of how long it would remain functional.

5

1665 New Haven formally submitted to union with Connecticut.

1776 New Hampshire voters in convention in Exeter adopted first written state constitution.

1779 Stephen Decatur, naval officer, born in Sinepuxent, MD; commanded vessels in Tripolitanian and War of 1812 naval battles; a toast attributed to him was: "Our country! may she always be right; but our country right or wrong;" killed in duel in 1820.

1779 Zebulon M. Pike, Army officer/explorer, born in Lamberton, NJ: explored Mississippi River headwaters and Southwest; a mountain is named for him; killed while leading troops in fighting at York (now Toronto) April 27, 1813.

1781 Benedict Arnold, leading 2000-man British force into Virginia, occupied Richmond; forced Governor Thomas Jefferson to flee.

1794 Edmund Ruffin, agriculturist, born in Prince George County, VA; developed system to revitalize soil; publisher, *Farmers' Register* (1833–42) (died 1865).

1811 Cyrus Hamlin, missionary/educator, born in Waterford, ME; missionary to Turkey; founder/first president, Robert College, Istanbul (1863–77) (died 1900).

1835 Olympia Brown, first American woman ordained in a regularly-constituted religious organization (Universalist 1863), born in Prairie Ronde, MI; president, Wisconsin Woman's Suffrage Association (1887–1917) (died 1926).

1838 John C. Moss, photoengraver, born in Bentleyville, PA; established photo engraving as a commercial enterprise in United States (died 1892).

1838 President Van Buren issued neutrality proclamation in dispute between Great Britain and Canada.

1847 George F. Becker, head of U.S. Geological Survey for 40 years, born in New York City (died 1919).

1855 King C. Gillette, inventor/manufacturer, born in Fond du Lac, WI; invented safety razor, blade; headed company named for him (1901–32) (died 1932).

1871 Frederick S. Converse, composer of first American opera performed at the Met, born in

Newtown, MA; dean, New England Conservatory of Music (died 1940).

1873 Charles F. Burgess, chemical engineer/inventor, born in Oshkosh, WI; invented electrolytic process for purifying iron, various alloys (died 1945).

1874 Joseph Erlanger, physiologist, born in San Francisco; shared 1944 Nobel Physiology/Medicine Prize for discoveries "regarding the highly differential functions of single nerve fibers" (died 1965).

1876 William J. Hale, sometimes called the father of chemurgy, born in Ada, OH; patented processes for making phenol, aniline, acetic acid (died 1955).

1877 Henry Sloane Coffin, Presbyterian clergyman, born in New York City; pastor, Madison Ave. Church, New York City (1905–26); president, Union Theological Seminary (1926–45) (died 1945).

1879 Jack Norworth, vaudevillian/lyricist (*Take Me Out to the Ball Game; Shine On, Harvest Moon*), born in Philadelphia (died 1959).

1882 Herbert Bayard Swope, journalist/editor, born in St. Louis; war correspondent, (1914–16), executive editor, *New York World* (1920–29) (died 1958).

1886 First "piggy back" operations began on Long Island Railroad when a produce train consisting of eight flat cars for carrying farmers' wagons, eight cars for horses, and a coach for drivers, went from Albertson's Station to Long Island City, then by ferry across the East River to New York City.

1887 First American library school opened at Columbia U. through efforts of Melvil Dewey; moved to Albany (1889), became the New York State Library School.

1887 Courtney H. Hodges, World War II Army general, born in Perry, GA; led 1st Army through most of European campaign (died 1966).

1893 Last spike driven at the east-west junction of the Great Northern Railroad in Cascade Mountains, completing another transcontinental rail line.

1913 Kemmons Wilson, hotel executive, born in Osceola, AR; founded Holiday Inn in Memphis (1952); board chairman, Holiday Inns Inc. (1953–79).

1914 Ford Motor Co. raised basic wage rate from $2.40 for nine-hour day to $5 for eight-hour day.

1915 Supreme Court sustained lower court in Danbury hatters case, holding the union guilty of restraint of trade; ordered to pay $252,130 in fines against 186 union members.

1920 Supreme Court upheld constitutionality of Volstead (prohibition) Act.

1925 Mrs. Nellie Tayloe Ross sworn in as Wyoming governor, the first woman state governor; she was the widow of Gov. William B. Ross, who died three months before.

1925 John R. Opel, IBM executive (president 1974–83, CEO 1981–85, chairman 1983–86), born in Kansas City, MO.

1928 Walter F. Mondale, Vice President (1977–81), born in Ceylon, MN; represented Minnesota in Senate (1964–76); 1984 Democratic presidential candidate; ambassador to Japan (1993–97).

1931 Alvin Ailey, dancer/choreographer, born in Rogers, TX; combined modern, jazz, and classical dance forms; founder, American Dance Theater (1958) (died 1989).

1932 Chuck Noll, football coach (Pittsburgh Steelers 1969–91), born in Cleveland.

1933 Construction began on Golden Gate Bridge in San Francisco.

1933 Former President Coolidge died in Northampton, MA, at 60.

1940 Static-less FM (frequency modulation) radio, developed by Edwin H. Armstrong, introduced.

1943 George Washington Carver, agricultural chemist, died at 79; headed agricultural research at Tuskegee Institute, leading shift from one-crop (cotton) Southern economy by developing more than 400 peanut and soybean by-products.

1946 Diane Keaton, screen actress (*Annie Hall*), born in Santa Ana, CA.

1948 Mary L.S. Harrison, widow of President Benjamin Harrison, died at 89.

1955 Lyndon B. Johnson elected Senate majority leader.

1957 President Eisenhower told Congress that the United States would use its military and economic power to protect Middle East against Communist aggression.

1970 United Mine Workers official Joseph A. Yablonski, his wife, and daughter were found shot to death in Clarksville, PA; UMW President W.A. (Tony) Boyle later convicted of the killing.

1972 President Nixon approved plans for development of a space shuttle.

1987 An Amtrak train crashed into three locomotives which slid onto the main track near Baltimore; 15 persons were killed and 176 injured.

1987 President Reagan submitted the nation's first trillion dollar budget.

1996 Lincoln Kirstein, cofounder of the New York City Ballet, died at 88.

1998 Rep. Sonny Bono, 62, of California, a former television entertainer, died after hitting a tree while skiing at South Lake Tahoe, CA.

2000 Labor Secretary Alexis Hermann repudiated his Department's earlier decision that week that an employer is responsible for the home safety of its telecommuting employees since they are at computer "work" though not on company property.

2002 Fifteen-year-old teenager stole small plane in Miami and crashed into a 40-story office building in Tampa, Florida, killing self.

6

1702 Jean Baptiste Bienville established the capital of Louisiana on Mobile Bay, the first settlement in what became Alabama.

1730 Thomas Chittenden, first governor of Vermont (1778–89, 1791–97), born in East Guilford, CT (died 1797).

1759 George Washington and the widow Martha Dandridge Custis were married in New Kent County, VA, by the Rev. David Mossom, rector of St. Peter's Church.

1776 The Alexander Hamilton Provincial Company of Artillery of the Colony of New York founded, marking the beginning of the oldest Army unit (now known as Battery D, 5th Field Artillery).

1779 British troops captured Sunbury, GA.

1793 James M. Porter, public official/railroad executive, born in Norristown, PA; Secretary of War (1843–44); first president, Lehigh Valley Railroad; a founder of Lafayette College (died 1862).

1799 Jedediah S. Smith, explorer, born in Bainbridge, NY; first white man to cross Great Salt Lake Desert and Sierra Nevada Mountains; killed by Indians 1831.

1807 Joseph Holt, public official, born in Breckenridge County, KY; Postmaster General (1859–61), Secretary of War (1861), Army Judge Advocate General (1862–75), prosecuted assassins of President Lincoln (died 1894).

1811 Charles Sumner, legislator, born in Boston; represented Massachusetts in Senate (1851–74); violent opponent of slavery, his attacks led Rep. Preston S. Brooks of South Carolina to assault him; a leader in effort to impeach President Andrew Johnson (died 1874).

1842 Clarence King, geologist, born in Newport, RI; first head of Geological Survey (1879–81) (died 1901).

1859 Hugh S. Rodman, World War I admiral, born in Frankfort, KY; commander, battle squadron, North Sea (1918–19); commander, Pacific Fleet (1919) (died 1940).

1859 Lucius L. Van Slyke, agricultural chemist, born in Centerville, NY; known especially for his milk research (died 1931).

1861 Florida state troops captured the federal arsenal at Appalachicola.

1864 Ban (Byron B.) Johnson, baseball official, born in Norwalk, OH; organized, headed American League (1900–27); organized World Series; named to Baseball Hall of Fame (died 1931).

1878 Carl Sandburg, author/poet, born in Galesburg, IL; poetry (*Chicago Poems, Corn Huskers, Smoke and Steel*), author of six-volume biography of Abraham Lincoln (died 1967).

1879 Joseph M. Patterson, publisher, born in Chicago; grandson of Joseph Medill (4/6/1823) and brother of Eleanor M. Patterson (11/7/1884); co-editor, *Chicago Tribune* (1918–25); founder/publisher, *New York Daily News* (1925–46) (died 1946).

1880 Tom Mix, screen actor, born in El Paso, TX; appeared in more than 400 western films, silent and sound (died 1940).

1882 Sam T. Rayburn, legislator, born in Roane County, TX; represented Texas in the House (1913–61), Speaker (1940–46, 1949–53, 1955–61) (died 1961).

1882 Ferdinand Pecora, jurist, born in Nicosia, Italy; helped create Securities & Exchange Commission, an original member (1934–35); New York State Supreme Court Justice, presided over racketeering trials (1935–52) (died 1971).

1883 Kahlil Gibran, artist/author, born in Bsherri, Lebanon; best remembered for *The Prophet* (died 1931).

1886 Russell R. Waesche, first Coast Guard admiral, born in Thurmont, MD; Coast Guard commander (1936–46) (died 1946).

1889 Most of Seattle's business district destroyed by fire.

1892 Ted Lewis, musician, born in Circleville, OH; clarinetist/bandleader, remembered for phrase, "Is everybody happy?" and battered top hat (died 1971).

1896 Abram N. Pritzker, founder of Hyatt Hotels, born in Chicago (died 1986).

1906 Clarence H. Graham, psychophysiologist, born in Worcester, MA; contributed much to understanding various aspects of vision (died 1971).

1911 "Flying Fish," first successful hydroplane, flown by Glenn Curtiss, its inventor, at San Diego.

1912 New Mexico entered Union as 47th state.

1919 Former President Theodore Roosevelt died at Oyster Bay, Long Island, at 60.

1921 Louis Harris, pollster, born in New Haven, CT; began with Elmo Roper pollsters, developed method useful in political campaigns.

1931 E.L. Doctorow, author (*Ragtime*), born in New York City.

1936 Supreme Court found Agricultural Adjustment Act of 1933 unconstitutional; ruled against paying cash benefits to farmers from tax money to restrict production.

1941 President Franklin Roosevelt defined his goals for world peace in the "Four Freedoms"— Freedom of speech, Freedom of worship, Freedom from want, Freedom from fear.

1942 First round-the-world commercial flight completed by Pan American Airways.

1950 Louis J. Freeh, director, FBI (since 1997), born in Jersey City, NJ.

1957 Nancy Lopez, champion golfer, born in Torrance, CA; LPGA player of year four times.

1961 Fire in Thomas Hotel in San Francisco killed 20 persons.

1986 Cylinder of nuclear material burst after being improperly heated at Kerr-McGee plant at Gore, OK; one worker died, 100 injured.

1989 President Reagan approved independent commission report to increase pay of top federal officials and Congress by about 50 percent

1993 Rudolf Nureyev, Russian-born renowned ballet dancer, died at 54.

1995 Lenny Wilkens, Atlanta basketball coach, became winningest regular season pro basketball coach (939), passing Red Auerbach of Boston.

2000 The Commission on Presidential Debates adopted criteria that would effectively rule out third-party participation; required average 15 percent approval of a candidate in five specified nationwide polls.

2003 For the first time in its history, the Republican Party selected New York City to hold its presidential nominating convention; the Democrats had met there five times.

2006 Lou Rawls (b. 1933) died of lung cancer at 72; won 3 Grammies; recorded over 70 albums in a variety of styles.

7

1608 Jamestown Fort burned.

1658 Theophilus Eaton, colonial leader, died at 68; an original member of Massachusetts Bay Colony, he established new colony at New Haven; named governor 1638 and re-elected annually till his death.

1699 Treaty signed by Massachusetts Bay Colony and Abenaki Indians at Casco Bay, ME, ending French and Indian War on New England border.

1718 Israel Putnam, Revolutionary leader, born in Danvers, MA; an active military leader (Bunker Hill, Long Island); reputedly warned Bunker Hill troops, "Don't fire until you see the whites of their eyes;" incapacitated by stroke (1779) (died 1790).

1751 William Penn Academy opened; later became U. of Pennsylvania.

1782 First American commercial bank (Bank of North America) opened in Philadelphia; organized by Robert Morris, original depositors included Thomas Jefferson, Alexander Hamilton, Benjamin Franklin, James Monroe, John Jay, Stephen Decatur.

1789 First national election for president held, with electors selected variously by different states; all 69 votes cast for George Washington on February 4; Senate counted vote April 6.

1795 Yazoo Land companies fraudulently sold 30 million acres of land at 1½ cents an acre after being revived by Georgia legislature.

1800 Millard Fillmore, 13th president (1850–52), born in Locke, NY; represented New York in House (1833–35, 1837–43); Vice President (1849–50), succeeding to presidency on death of President Taylor (7/9/1850); a founder, U. of Buffalo (died 1874).

1826 Oliver H. Kelley, farm organization founder, born in Boston; organizer (1867) of National Grange of the Patrons of Husbandry (died 1913).

1829 James B. Angell, educator/diplomat, born near Scituate, RI; president, U. of Vermont (1866–71), Michigan (1871–1909); minister to Chile (1880–81), to Turkey (1897–98) (died 1916).

1830 Albert Bierstadt, painter, born in Solingen, Germany; noted for huge scenes (*Discovery of Hudson River, Settlement of California*) which hang in Capitol (died 1916).

1830 Baltimore & Ohio Railroad, first American railway system, began operations.

1839 Georgia Female College (later Wesleyan) opened in Macon; first college in world chartered to give degrees to women.

1849 LaVerne Noyes, inventor, born in Genoa, NY; invented wire dictionary holder, improved steel windmill, tractor wheel, harvester reel, cord knotter for grain binders; organized Aeromotor Co. to build windmills (died 1919).

1851 Bernard E. Fernow, forester, born in Posen, Germany; first chief, Forestry Division, Agriculture Department (1886–98); organized, headed, first forestry school, Cornell U. (1898–1903) (died 1923).

1867 House passed resolution by James M. Ashley of Ohio calling for investigation by Judiciary Committee of accusations against President Andrew Johnson.

1872 Trial of "Boss" William M. Tweed of New York began with Tweed defended by David Dudley Field and Elihu Root; first trial ended in hung jury, second found him guilty of taking millions in graft.

1873 Adolf Zukor, movie executive, born in Riese, Hungary; president, Paramount Pictures (1916–35), chairman (1935–76) (died 1976).

1879 Melvin Jones, Lions Club founder (1917), born in Ft. Thomas, AZ; secretary-general, Lions (1917–61) (died 1961).

1881 Gene Carr, cartoonist, born in New York City; created several comic strip series (*Lady Bountiful, All the Comforts of Home, Little Nell*) (died 1959).

1890 Maurice E. McLaughlin, early tennis great, born in Carson City, NV; on Davis Cup team (1909–14); started tennis on way to becoming a national sport (died 1957).

1894 First motion picture, showing 47 successive frames of Fred Ott sneezing, copyrighted; known as the *Edison Kinetoscope Record of a Sneeze.*

1910 President Taft removed Gifford Pinchot as Forest Service head because of a letter from Pinchot criticizing Interior Secretary; rules forbade such letters to a congressman.

1910 Orval Faubus, Arkansas governor (1954–67), born in Combs, AR; defied Federal Government (1957) blocking integration of Little Rock high school; impasse ended with arrival of federal troops (died 1994).

1911 Woodrow Wilson inaugurated as governor of New Jersey.

1914 First passage through the Panama Canal was made by a self-propelled crane boat *Alex LaValley*; canal officially opened August 15.

1917 Ulysses S. Kay, composer of neoclassical music, born in Tucson, AZ (died 1995).

1918 Supreme Court upheld constitutionality of Selective Service Act.

1927 Transatlantic commercial telephone service opened between New York and London; 31 calls made the first day at cost of $75 for three minute conversation.

1933 Supreme Court held that a section of National Industrial Relations Act was unconstitutional; entire Act invalidated May 27.

1941 Office of Production Management created by executive order to supervise defense production; headed by William S. Knudsen, General Motors president, and Sidney Hillman, Amalgamated Clothing Workers president.

1942 American and Philippine forces completed withdrawal from Bataan Peninsula.

1944 Lou H. Hoover, wife of President Hoover, died in New York City at 68.

1949 Drs. Daniel Pease and Richard Baker announced photographing a gene in experiments at U. of Southern California; they magnified tissue sections by 120,000 diameters.

1950 Fire in Mercy Hospital in Davenport, IA, killed 41 persons.

1955 Marian Anderson performed as Ulrica in Verdi's *Masked Ball* becoming first black to perform at Metropolitan Opera.

1963 Cost of first class postage increased to five cents an ounce.

1968 Cost of first class postage increased to six cents.

1996 One of worst blizzards deposited up to three feet of snow in Mid-Atlantic and New England states in two days; most operations shut down, damage estimated at $1.5 billion.

1997 Newt Gingrich (R-GA) re-elected House Speaker; reprimanded for possible political use of tax-exempt donations.

8

1682 Jonathan Belcher, colonial governor, born in Cambridge, MA; governor, Massachusetts and New Hampshire (1730–41), New Jersey (1747–57) (died 1757).

1732 First South Carolina newspaper, *South Carolina Gazette*, published in Charleston by Thomas Whitmarsh.

1735 John Carroll, first American Catholic bishop, born in Upper Marlboro, MD; bishop (1790), first archbishop of Baltimore (1808–15); accompanied Benjamin Franklin on mission to get Canadian support for Revolution (died 1815).

1771 Elisha North, physician, born in Goshen, CT; pioneer in smallpox vaccination (died 1843).

1777 First price regulation law went into effect in Rhode Island "to prevent monopolies and oppression by excessive and unreasonable prices for many of the necessaries and conveniences of life, and for preventing engrossers, and for the better supply of our troops in the army with such necessaries as may be wanted."

1786 Nicholas Biddle, president, Bank of the United States (1822–39), born in Philadelphia; President Jackson refused to issue new charter, bank became a state bank (1836) (died 1844).

1790 President Washington delivered first annual message to Congress, the first State of the Union address.

1791 Jacob Collamer, legislator/public official, born in Troy, NY; Postmaster General (1849), served in House (1843–49), Senate (1855–65) (died 1865).

1792 Lowell Mason, music educator, born in Medfield, MA; devised system of musical education for children, directed such education in Massachusetts public schools; founder, Boston Academy of Music (1833); composer of hymn, "Nearer My God to Thee" (died 1872).

1798 The 11th Amendment, by which judicial powers are construed, was ratified.

1800 Edward M. Robinson, merchant/financier, born in Philadelphia; leader in shipping, whaling industries; left fortune to daughter, Hetty Green (11/21/1835) (died 1865).

1802 Commission settled British Revolutionary War claims against United States at $2,664,000.

1810 John J. Thomas, agriculturist, born in Ledyard, NY; editor, *Rural Affairs* (1869–81); author of *The American Fruit Culturist*, which launched American systematic study of fruit (died 1895).

1815 Gen. Andrew Jackson led 6,000 American troops in victory over 12,000 British at New Orleans; neither side knew that peace had been reached two weeks earlier; British had 2,000 casualties; Americans eight killed, 13 wounded.

1821 James Longstreet, Confederate general, born in Edgefield District, SC; his delay in carrying out Lee's orders blamed for defeat at Gettysburg; minister to Turkey (1880–81); U.S. railroad commissioner (1898–1904) (died 1904).

1830 Gouverneur K. Warren, Union general, born in Cold Spring, NY; saved day (July 2) at Gettysburg by seizing, holding Little Round Top position, where his statue stands (died 1882).

1831 Charles H. Morgan, invented automatic bag-making machine, born in Rochester, NY; also invented continuous rolling mill for wire making (died 1911).

1840 House passed resolution refusing to accept resolutions or petitions concerning abolition of slavery, the first "gag rule."

1847 Col. Stephen Kearny and his forces defeated rebellious Californians in battle of San Gabriel River.

1857 Augustus Thomas, playwright, born in St. Louis; wrote many plays (*Alabama, In Mizzoura, The Copperhead*) (died 1934).

1862 Frank N. Doubleday, publisher, born in Brooklyn, NY; founder, Doubleday & McClure publishers; ran chain of bookstores; headed several successor companies (died 1934).

1867 Blacks were given right to vote in Washington, DC, by a bill passed over President Andrew Johnson's veto of the previous day.

1867 Emily G. Balch, economist/pacifist, born in Jamaica Plain, MA; secretary, Women's International League for Peace (1919–21), shared 1946 Nobel Peace Prize (died 1961).

1870 Burton Holmes, traveler/lecturer, born in Chicago; noted for his travelogues (died 1958).

1871 Walter T. Swingle, agricultural botanist, born in Canaan, PA; helped make growing figs, dates, and Egyptian cotton possible in U.S.; head of crop physiology and breeding research in Agriculture Department (died 1952).

1872 Charles W. Hawthorne, artist, born in Lodi, IL; remembered for such works as *The Trousseau, The Mother, Fisherman's Daughter* (died 1930).

1873 Harvey W. Corbett, architect, born in San Francisco; worked with Raymond Hood to design Rockefeller Center's Radio City (died 1954).

1881 William T. Piper, aircraft designer, born in Knapp's Creek, NY; first mass producer of small, inexpensive planes; designed Piper Cub (1931) (died 1970).

1881 John G. Neihardt, editor/author, born in Sharpsburg, IL; literary editor, *St. Louis Post Dispatch*; poet ("A Cycle of the West," "Black Elk Speaks") (died 1973).

1883 Patrick J. Hurley, public official, born in Oklahoma; Secretary of War (1929–33); special representative to several countries, ambassador to China (1944–45) (died 1963).

1889 Patent issued for first tabulating machine,

invented by Herman Hollerith of New York City; used punched cards and electrical counters; used in 1890 census.

1891 Willard M. Kiplinger published magazine *Changing Times* and various newsletters, born in Bellefontaine, OH; (died 1967).

1904 Peter Arno, cartoonist, born in New York City; his satire of cafe society appeared mostly in *The New Yorker* (died 1968).

1912 National Monetary Commission, headed by Sen. Nelson W. Aldrich, proposed legislation which ultimately led to forming Federal Reserve system.

1912 Jose Ferrer, actor/director, born in Santurce, Puerto Rico; made many hit films (*Cyrano de Bergerac, Caine Mutiny, The Shrike*) (died 1992).

1914 Thomas J. Watson, industrialist/diplomat, born in Dayton; president, IBM (1952–79); ambassador to Russia (1979–81).

1917 Supreme Court upheld prohibiting liquor shipments to dry states.

1918 President Wilson outlined 14-point peace program to Congress; later became basis for peace treaties and League of Nations.

1919 First transatlantic flight by Navy seaplane began at Rockaway, NY; ended May 27, in Lisbon.

1935 Elvis Presley, entertainer, born in Tupelo, MS; screen actor/popular singer ("Love Me Tender," "King Creole") (died 1977).

1968 President Lyndon Johnson broke ground for Joseph H. Hirschhorn Museum and Sculpture Garden in Washington, DC, to house extensive collection donated to Federal Government.

1971 President Nixon signed acts establishing Voyageurs National Park in Minnesota and Chesapeake & Ohio National Historic Park along 184-mile stretch between Washington and Cumberland, MD.

1971 Annual pensions of former presidents raised from $25,000 to $60,000 and for presidential widows from $10,000 to $20,000.

1982 Federal lawsuit against American Telephone & Telegraph settled after 13 years; ATT will give up 22 Bell system companies and permitted to enter previously-prohibited areas such as computers and telephone equipment; court approved settlement August 5, 1983.

1982 Justice Department dropped its antitrust case against IBM.

1985 The Rev. Lawrence Jenco, Catholic priest, abducted in Beirut; released July 26, 1986.

1986 President Reagan by executive order froze all Libyan government assets in U.S. and American banks abroad.

1987 Dow Jones industrial average closed above 2,000 (2,002.25) for first time.

1988 Presidential task force investigating 1987 Wall Street crash blamed it on two types of computerized program trading.

1988 Stock prices plunged 140.58 points, sharpest drop since 1987, because of rising interest rates and computerized stock trading.

1988 Arizona Governor Evan Mecham indicted on six felony counts, including perjury, and filing of a false contribution report.

1991 President Bush asked Congress to support the use of force against Iraq if it does not withdraw from Kuwait by January 15.

1992 President Bush collapsed during a state dinner in Japan; later diagnosed as suffering from intestinal flu.

2001 Former Louisiana Governor Edwin W. Edwards fined and given ten years in jail for extorting money from casino industry.

2001 Outgoing President Clinton's Forest Service chief prohibited cutting of "old-growth timber" found on federal lands.

2001 After new California law went into effect allowing mothers of unwanted newborns to legally "abandon" them at a hospital within 72 hours of birth, first mother took advantage of new statute, designed to save lives of babies that would otherwise perish.

2002 Founder of the world's third-largest hamburger chain, Wendy's, Dave Thomas (1932–2002), died at 69; in addition to hard work and astute business acumen, he became publicly recognizable to millions through the hundreds of television ads that used him as salesman for his chain.

2006 First-class stamp went up to $.39, 2-cent increase.

9

1745 Caleb Strong, colonial leader, born in Northampton, MA; member of Constitutional Convention, one of first Massachusetts senators (1789–96) and its governor (1800–07, 1812–16) (died 1819).

1781 Lemuel Shaw, chief justice, Massachusetts Supreme Court (1830–60), born in Barnstable, MA; drew up Boston city charter (1822), in effect until 1913; as judge, handed down more than 2,200 decisions (died 1861).

1788 Connecticut legislature ratified Constitution 128–40, becoming fifth state.

1789 Treaty of Ft. Harmar signed by Ohio Indians and Gen. Arthur St. Clair.

1793 First American balloon flight made by 39-year-old French pilot, Jean Pierre Blanchard, from courtyard of Walnut St. Prison, Philadelphia, to near Woodbury, NJ; 15 mile trip took 46 minutes, reached altitude of 5,812 feet.

1803 Christopher G. Memminger, Confederate Secretary of Treasury (1861–64), born in Nayhingen, Germany (died 1888).

1817 Nathan S. Davis, medical educator/physician, born in Greene, NY; founder, Lind U. medical department (1859), which later became Northwestern U. Medical School; a founder, American Medical Association (died 1904).

1839 John Knowles Paine, composer/organist, born in Portland, ME; first music professor in United States (Harvard 1862–1906) (died 1906).

1856 James F. Bell, Army officer in Spanish-American War, born in Shelbyville, KY; Army chief of staff (1906–10), commander, 77th Division (1917) (died 1919).

1859 Carrie Chapman Catt, women's rights leader, born in Ripon, WI; president, National American Women Suffrage Association (1900–04, 1915–47); founder/president, International Woman Suffrage Alliance (1904–23); founder, League of Women Voters (died 1947).

1861 *Star of the West*, unarmed federal supply ship, fired on by South Carolina batteries in Charleston Harbor, bringing Civil War closer; ship sent to supply and reinforce garrison at Ft. Sumter.

1861 Mississippi seceded from Union by a convention vote of 84 to 15.

1865 Tennessee convention adopted antislavery constitution amendments, ratified by popular vote February 22.

1870 Joseph B. Strauss, bridge designer, born in Cincinnati; designed the Golden Gate, George Washington, Columbia River at Longview bridges (died 1938).

1878 John B. Watson, psychologist, born in Greenville, SC; founder, behaviorist school of psychology; professor, Johns Hopkins U. (1908–20) (died 1958).

1879 Emory S. Land, naval officer/public official, born in Canon City, CO; chief, Naval Bureau of Construction (1932–37); U.S. Maritime Commission (1937–46), chairman (1938–46) (died 1971).

1900 Richard Halliburton, explorer/author, born in Brownsville, TN; books include *Royal Road to Romance*, *The Glorious Adventure*; lost in a typhoon sailing a Chinese junk in the Pacific 1939.

1901 Chic (Murat B.) Young, cartoonist ("Blondie"), born in Chicago (died 1973).

1902 Sir Rudolf Bing, British manager, Metropolitan Opera (1950–72), born in Vienna; cofounder, Edinburgh Festival (died 1997).

1903 Wind Cave (SD) National Park established.

1904 George Balanchine, choreographer, born in Leningrad; a founder, School of American Ballet (1940), head of New York City Ballet (1948–83); choreographed 100 ballets, musicals (died 1983).

1908 East River Tunnel from New York City's Battery to Brooklyn opened.

1913 Richard M. Nixon, 37th president (1969–74), born in Yorba Linda, CA; represented California in House (1947–50) and Senate (1950–53); Vice President (1953–61); Republican presidential candidate (1960); elected 1968; became first president to resign (August 9, 1974) after Watergate revelations (died 1994).

1914 Gypsy Rose Lee, entertainer, born in Seattle; American burlesque queen in 1940s; musical, *Gypsy*, based on her life (died 1970).

1922 Har Gobind Khorana, chemist, born in Raipur, India; shared 1968 Nobel Physiology/Medicine Prize for working out most of genetic code.

1928 Judith Krantz, author (*Scruples*, *Mistral's Daughter*), born in New York City.

1941 Joan Baez, folk singer, born in New York City; active in 1960s civil rights, antiwar movement; founder, Institute for Study of Non-Violence.

1945 American soldiers fulfilled promise of Gen. Douglas MacArthur, "I shall return," when they invaded Luzon in the Philippines.

1951 Crystal Gayle, country music singer, born in Paintsville, KY.

1964 Violence in Panama Canal Zone resulted in death of 21 Panamanians and four American soldiers; Panama severed diplomatic relations with U.S., asked for "complete revision" of canal treaties.

1990 Space shuttle *Columbia* launched from Cape Canaveral, deployed a communications satellite.

1991 Former Senator Lowell P. Weicker became Connecticut governor; launched effort to impose state income tax for first time.

1991 Secretary of State James A. Baker met for six hours in Geneva with Iraqui foreign minister without reaching agreement.

1997 Conair plane approaching Detroit airport crashed, killing 29 persons.

1998 State of Texas and tobacco industry reached agreement on lawsuit brought by state; industry agreed to pay state $15.3 billion over 25 years.

2001 By narrow 5–4 decision, Supreme Court decided that federal power to regulate isolated marshland does not exist.

2002 In addition to already announced investigations by Security Exchange Commission and various Congressional committees, the Justice Department began criminal queries of Enron over the billions lost by its investors.

2003 The Transportation Security Administration issued order prohibiting baggage and human screeners at American airports from engaging in collective bargaining, effectively banning all unionization at most locations.

10

1740 Loammi Baldwin, engineer, born in North Woburn, MA; planned, supervised construction of Middlesex Canal; developed Baldwin apple (died 1807).

1744 Thomas Mifflin, Revolutionary War general, born in Philadelphia; served in Continental Congress (1774, 1783–84), governor of Pennsylvania (1790–99) (died 1800).

1776 Thomas Paine published pamphlet, "Common Sense," in Philadelphia, urging colonies to separate from Great Britain, form own nation; published as anonymous two-shilling pamphlet of 47 pages.

1781 Office of Secretary of Foreign Affairs established by Continental Congress.

1791 Vermont ratified Constitution, admitted as 14th state on May 4.

1804 Oakes Ames, builder of Union Pacific Railroad, born in Easton, MA; represented Massachusetts in House (1863–73), where he was censured for trying to block investigation of his role in construction deals; made original fortune manufacturing shovels (died 1873).

1805 U. of South Carolina, chartered in 1801, opened at Columbia.

1810 Jeremiah S. Black, Attorney General (1857–60), born near Stony Creek, PA; exposed California land title frauds; nominated for Secre-

tary of State but Senate refused to confirm him (February 5, 1861) (died 1883).

1835 Harry (William H.) Wright, baseball pioneer, born in Sheffield, England; organized Cincinnati professional team (1868), first team to tour (1869); manager (Boston N, Philadelphia N); named to Baseball Hall of Fame (died 1895).

1841 George W. Melville, naval officer, born in New York City; modernized Navy ships, streamlined administration as chief of Bureau of Steam Engineering (died 1912).

1843 Rep. John M. Botts of Virginia introduced resolution to impeach President Tyler for corruption, malconduct of office, high crimes, misdemeanors; rejected 127–83.

1847 Col. Stephen Kearny and 600 troops captured Los Angeles from the Mexicans, concluding hostilities in California.

1850 John W. Root, architect, born in Lumpkin, GA; helped design Montauk Building, an early skyscraper and the Monadnock Building, which broke with tradition (died 1891).

1855 Albert W. Marquis, founder/publisher of *Who's Who in America* and related publications, born in Brown County, OH (died 1943).

1861 Louisiana state troops seized the arsenal and barracks in Baton Rouge.

1861 Florida legislature voted 62 to 7 to secede from the Union.

1867 John A. Lejeune, Marine Corps commandant (1920–29), born in Pointe Coupee Parish, LA; served in Mexico and World War I; superintendent, Virginia Military Institute (1929–37) (died 1942).

1870 Standard Oil Co. incorporated in Cleveland with $1 million capital; original stockholders were John D. Rockefeller, William Rockefeller, Henry M. Flagler, Stephen V. Harkness, O.B. Jennings, and firm of Rockefeller, Andrews & Flagler.

1873 Howard C. Christy, painter, born in Morgan County, OH; best known for his *Christy Girl* and the *Signing of the Constitution* in the Capitol (died 1952).

1877 Frederick G. Cottrell, inventor of electrostatic precipitator used in air pollution control, born in Oakland, CA (died 1948).

1883 Francis X. Bushman, leading man in 400 silent films (1911–18), born in Baltimore (died 1966).

1883 Fire destroyed Newhall House in Milwaukee, killing 71 persons.

1887 Robinson Jeffers, author, born in Pittsburgh; among his plays were *The Cretan Woman* and *The Tower Beyond Tragedy* and poems "Tamar," "The Roan Stallion" (died 1962).

1889   John Held, Jr., illustrator, born in Salt Lake City; leading graphic interpreter of Jazz Age (died 1958).

1892   Dumas Malone, historian/editor, born in Goldwater, MS; editor-in-chief, *Dictionary of American Biography* (1931–36); director, Harvard U. Press (died 1986).

1898   Katherine B. Blodgett developed non-reflecting "invisible" glass, born in Schenectady, NY (died 1979).

1901   Texas oil boom began with drilling of Spindletop well near Beaumont, which delivered 25,000 barrels daily; owned by Anthony F. Lucas.

1904   Ray Bolger, actor/dancer, born in Dorchester, MA; stage plays (*Where's Charley?*, *By Jupiter*); played scarecrow in movie, *Wizard of Oz* (died 1987).

1911   Garrett Birkhoff, mathematician, born in Princeton, NJ; made important contributions to abstract theory of structures, or lattices.

1917   White House picketed by Congressional Union for Woman Suffrage.

1918   House passed resolution 274–136 calling for a constitutional amendment to provide woman suffrage.

1920   League of Nations was established; but despite President Wilson's urging United States failed to become a member.

1923   Executive order by President Harding ended American occupation of the Rhine in Germany.

1927   President Coolidge, in special message to Congress, outlined reasons for intervention in Nicaragua; resulted in sending 5,000 Marines.

1936   Robert W. Wilson, physicist, born in Houston; shared 1978 Nobel Physics Prize for co-discovery of cosmic radiation background, helping support "big bang" theory of the origin of universe.

1940   Mine disaster at Bartley, WV, claimed 91 lives.

1946   First man-made contact with moon occurred when radar signal from New Jersey Signal Corps installation echoed back from moon in 2.4 seconds (round trip of 477,714 miles).

1946   United Nations General Assembly held first meeting in London.

1949   George Foreman, Olympics and professional heavyweight boxing champion (1973–74, 1994–95), born in Marshall, TX.

1966   Georgia legislature refused to seat Julian Bond, 25-year-old black pacifist and civil rights leader; later re-elected and Supreme Court ruled unanimously he must be seated.

1967   President Lyndon Johnson nominated Alan S. Boyd as first Secretary of Transportation.

1984   Full diplomatic relations with the Vatican were resumed after 117 years.

2000   Largest merger in American history agreed to as AOL paid $165 billion to buy Time Warner.

11

1755   Alexander Hamilton, first Secretary of the Treasury (1789–95), born in Nevis, Leeward Islands; served as aide to George Washington in Revolution; member of Continental Congress (1782–83, 1787–88); killed in duel with Aaron Burr (1804).

1759   First American life insurance company incorporated in Philadelphia: "Corporation of Poor and Distressed Presbyterian Ministers..." and their widows and children.

1760   Oliver Wolcott, colonial leader, born in Litchfield, CT; Comptroller of the Treasury (1791–95), Secretary of the Treasury (1795–1801), Connecticut governor (1817–27) (died 1833).

1775   First Jewish person in New World elected to public office was Francis Salvador, plantation owner, named to serve in South Carolina provincial congress; also was first Jew to die for American independence, being killed in skirmish July 31, 1776.

1785   William W. Seaton, journalist, born in King William County, VA; an editor, *National Intelligencer* (1812–64); helped make shorthand reports of congressional debates (1812–56); these and state papers published (1832–61) (died 1866).

1785   Congress convened in New York City.

1793   Cave Johnson, Postmaster General (1845–49) who introduced use of stamps, born in Springfield, TN; represented Tennessee in House (1829–37, 1839–45) (died 1866).

1803   James Monroe named minister extraordinary to France to help buy Louisiana.

1805   Michigan Territory created by Congress, effective as of July 1.

1806   Moses Taylor, financier, born in New York City; president, City Bank of New York (1855–82), involved in first transatlantic cable attempt (died 1882).

1807   Ezra Cornell, founder of Western Union, born in Westchester Landing, NY; worked with Samuel F.B. Morse on starting telegraphy; cofounder, benefactor, Cornell U. (1868) (died 1874).

1825   Bayard Taylor, most widely-known travel writer/lecturer of time, born in Kennett Square, PA; translated Goethe's *Faust*; minister to Germany (1878) (died 1878).

1836   Alexander H. Wyant, landscape painter, born in Evans Creek, OH; one of Hudson River School of painters (died 1892).

1842   William James, psychologist/philosopher, born in New York City; created first psychological research laboratory; author (*The Principles of Psychology*, *The Varieties of Religious Experience*) (died 1910).

1843   Henry Y. Satterlee, Episcopal prelate, born in New York City; bishop of Washington, DC (1896–1908); planned, began work on National Cathedral (died 1908).

1861   Alabama legislature voted 61–39 to secede from the Union.

1863   Ft. Hindman (Arkansas Post), which protected Little Rock, surrendered to Admiral David D. Porter's fleet of Union ironclads.

1864   Thomas Dixon, Baptist clergyman/author, born in Shelby, NC; wrote *The Clansman* from which came the screen play, *The Birth of a Nation* (died 1946).

1870   Alice Hegan Rice, author (*Mrs. Wiggs of the Cabbage Patch*), born in Shelbyville, KY (died 1942).

1880   John W. Greenslade, World War II naval officer, born in Bellevue, OH; commander, Western Sea Frontier (died 1950).

1885   Alice Paul, women's rights leader, born in Moorestown, NJ; a founder, National Woman's Party (1917), World Women's Party; early proponent of equal rights constitutional amendment (died 1977).

1889   Calvin B. Bridges, geneticist, born in Schuyler Falls, NY; made contributions to study of heredity (died 1938).

1895   Laurens Hammond, developer of electric organ, born in Evanston, IL; developed electronic organ (Hammond Novachord) (died 1973).

1897   Bernard A. DeVoto, author/editor, born in Ogden, UT; columnist, *Harper's* ("Easy Chair") (1935–55); editor, *Saturday Review* (1936–38); author (*Mark Twain's America*, *Across the Wide Missouri*) (died 1955).

1899   Eva LaGallienne, actress, born in London; founder, director, Civic Repertory Theater, New York City (1926); cofounder, American Repertory Theater (died 1991).

1904   President Theodore Roosevelt appointed William Howard Taft as Secretary of War, effective February 1.

1905   Frederic Dannay, writer, born in Brooklyn; with Manfred B. Lee (10/20/1905) formed team which was Ellery Queen, mystery writer (died 1982).

1909   National Conservation Commission, headed by Gifford Pinchot, submitted report which for first time tried to inventory nation's natural resources.

1909   Canada and United States signed waterways treaty, creating an international joint commission to handle disputes, set limits on water diversion at Niagara Falls.

1912   Strike of 15,000 textile workers began against American Woolen Co., Lawrence, MA; Industrial Workers of the World (IWW) succeeded in getting wage gains and better working conditions; strike ended March 14.

1916   Pancho Villa, in effort to discredit new Mexican government stopped a Mexican train, removed 17 Americans, killing all but one.

1924   Roger C.L. Guillemin, physiologist, born in Dijon, France; shared 1977 Nobel Physiology/Medicine Prize for research in role of hormones in body chemistry.

1926   Grant A. Tinker, television executive born in Stamford, CT; chairman, National Broadcasting Co. (1981–87).

1940   American Ballet Theater gave first performance in New York City.

1964   Surgeon General Luther L. Terry issued report that cigarette smoking is a definite health hazard.

1995   National Hockey League lockout ended after 103 days with a six-year contract agreement.

2000   Over a million acres are added to the National Park System, primarily on the north rim of the Grand Canyon.

2001   Federal Communications Commission approved AOL-Times Warner mega-merger but sets conditions.

2003   Governor George Ryan of Illinois commuted 167 death sentences to life imprisonment; challenged concept of capital punishment.

2003   Richard ("Dick") Simmons died at 89; had small roles in 50 movies, but made his reputation in the pioneer color television series *Sergeant Preston of the Yukon* (1955–58), which continued to be syndicated for decades.

12

1588   John Winthrop, first governor of Massachusetts Bay Colony, born in Suffolk, England; served 12 one-year terms, attempted to make colony a theocratic society; presided at trial which banished Anne Hutchinson (died 1649).

1662   Samuel Shute, governor of Massachusetts and New Hampshire (1716–27), born in London (died 1742).

1682   New set of Fundamental Constitutions issued for Carolina.

1687   Sir Edmund Andros dissolved Rhode Island government, changed it to English county status.

1737   John Hancock, first governor of Massachusetts (1780–85, 1787–93), born in Braintree, MA; first signer of Declaration of Independence; member of Continental Congress (1775–80, 1785–86), president (1775, 1777) (died 1793).

1773   First American museum established in Charleston, SC, by the Library Society.

1777   Hugh Mercer, Revolutionary War general, killed at Battle of Princeton; Mercer County, NJ, named for him.

1828   Treaty with Mexico established American-Mexican boundary in accord with Adams-Onis Treaty of 1819; agreement effective in 1832.

1837   Thomas Moran, painter, born in Bolton, England; landscapes and etchings of Yellowstone region best known work (died 1926).

1846   Rasmus B. Anderson, Wisconsin businessman/writer, born in Albion, WI; his major contribution was work on Scandinavian life, history and contributions to America (died 1936).

1856   John S. Sargent, one of greatest portrait painters, born in Florence, Italy, of American parentage; did murals for Boston Public Library (died 1925).

1861   Fort Barrancas and Navy Yard at Pensacola seized by Alabama and Florida troops.

1864   Benjamin G. Lamme, inventor, born in Clarke County, OH; developed various electrical machines (rotary converter, induction motor, AC generator) (died 1924).

1869   National convention of African-American people held in Washington, DC; first national attempt to organize.

1873   Frank Gerber, manufacturer who headed baby-food company (1917–45), born in Douglas, MI (died 1952).

1876   Jack (John G.) London, author of adventure novels (*The Call of the Wild, The Sea Wolf*), born in San Francisco (died 1916).

1880   Ellen L. Arthur, wife of President Chester Arthur, died in New York City at 42.

1884   Texas (Mary Louise) Guinan, night club hostess, born in Waco, TX; personified 1920s flappers, hostess at several speakeasies, greeting customers with "Hello, sucker" (died 1933).

1903   General Education Board, funded by John D. Rockefeller, incorporated to promote education in United States, regardless of race, creed, or sex.

1907   Tex (Woodward M.) Ritter, singer/screen actor, born in Murvaul, TX; starred in 60 films, on radio (died 1974).

1908   José (A.) Limon, dancer/choreographer, born in Culiacan, Mexico; exerted strong influence on contemporary dance (died 1972).

1909   Mine disaster at Switchback, WV, killed 67 persons.

1920   President Wilson announced recall of troops from Russia.

1920   James L. Farmer, civil rights leader, born in Marshall, TX; cofounder, CORE (Congress of Racial Equality), national director (1961–66) (died 1999).

1921   Judge Kenesaw M. Landis began 23 years as first baseball commissioner following the "Black Sox" scandal.

1932   Mrs. Hattie W. Caraway of Arkansas became first woman to be elected to the Senate, serving from 1931 to 1945 (originally appointed, then elected).

1942   National War Labor Board, with William H. Davis as chairman, created by President Franklin Roosevelt to settle labor disputes by mediation and arbitration; successor to National Defense Mediation Board; terminated December 31, 1945.

1951   Rush Limbaugh, news commentator, born in Cape Girardeau, MO.

1955   Secretary of State John Foster Dulles announced policy of "massive retaliation," whereby the United States would "depend primarily upon a great capacity to retaliate instantly by means and at places of our choosing."

1980   United States offered $400 million in aid to Pakistan in the face of the occupation by Soviets of neighboring Afghanistan.

1991   Congress authorized use of force against Iraq — the Senate by a 52–47 vote, the House 250–183.

1994   Orbiting Hubble Space Telescope

repaired by astronauts in space, restoring it to full operations.

1995   President and Congress agreed on an economic bailout package for Mexico, which included as much as $40 billion in loan guarantees.

1997   Two of four female cadets at the Citadel, South Carolina military academy, resigned from the school because of alleged harassment.

2000   U.S. Supreme Court unanimously affirmed that a person's flight upon seeing a police officer constituted legitimate grounds for stopping and searching, but divided 5–4 against the principle having been properly applied in the case at hand.

2002   Cyrus Vance (b. 1917) died; secretary of state under Jimmy Carter; quit post after policy disagreements concerning the rescue of American diplomatic hostages imprisoned in Iran.

2003   Founder of Internet provider pioneer America Online resigned; Stephen Case undone by customer dissatisfaction and declining stock prices.

2005   By 5–4 Supreme Court rejected mandatory federal sentencing guidelines as giving judges too little power but also upheld their validity if changed to being discretionary in nature.

2005   Deep Impact launched from Cape Canaveral: "impactor" segment designed to blow hole in comet and a "flyby" segment to visually record what happens; purpose to learn more about how comets come into existence, what they consist of, and origin of solar system.

2006   California Public Utilities Commission to encourage use of alternative energy sources by giving $2.9 billion in rebates over 11 years to those who install solar panels to produce electricity; to be paid for by surcharge on electric bills.

13

1630   Plymouth patent granted to William Bradford and others by the Council for New England, defining the limits of the June 1, 1661, patent.

1733   James Edward Oglethorpe, with 130 colonists, arrived at what is now Charleston, SC, with a charter to establish a settlement in Georgia.

1808   Salmon P. Chase, public official/jurist, born in Cornish, NH; Secretary of the Treasury (1861–64), originated national banking system;

served Ohio as governor (1855–60) and in the Senate (1849–55); chief justice Supreme Court (1864–73), presiding at the President Johnson impeachment trial (died 1873).

1832   Horatio Alger, Unitarian clergyman and author, born in Revere, MA; wrote more than 100 boys' books emphasizing pluck and honesty, hard work; most popular writer of his time (died 1899).

1840   Steamboat *Lexington* caught fire near Eaton's Neck, NY; 140 died.

1847   Treaty of Cahuenga signed ending California portion of the Mexican War.

1865   Union forces launched successful two-day assault on Ft. Fisher, NC, opening Cape Fear River to Union troops; Confederate General Whiting killed in battle.

1867   Francis E. Townsend, social reformer, born in Fairbury, IL; developed plan to help elderly, proposing $200 monthly pension, financed by 2 percent tax (died 1960).

1868   Edwin M. Stanton reinstated as Secretary of War; President Andrew Johnson dismissed him again February 21, but he refused to vacate office.

1870   Ross G. Harrison, biologist, born in Germantown, PA; developed method of culturing animal tissue, vitally important to biology; headed Yale Biology Department (1907–38) (died 1959).

1874   Police charged meeting of unemployed laborers, injuring hundreds, in what has been called the Tompkins Square riot in New York City.

1884   Sophie Tucker, entertainer, born in Russia; last of the "red hot mamas," she is remembered for her theme song, "Some of These Days" (died 1966).

1884   Roy Cross, chemist, born in Ellis, KS; co-inventor of petroleum cracking process; designer of oil refineries (died 1947).

1885   Alfred C. Fuller, founder of brush company bearing his name, born in Kings County, Nova Scotia; invented twisted wire brush, developed door-to-door sales method (died 1973).

1887   Holger Cahill, director, Federal Art Project (1933–43), born in Snaefellsnessysla, Iceland (died 1960).

1890   Elmer H. Davis, journalist, born in Aurora, IN; with *New York Times* (1914–39), radio commentator (1939–42); director, Office of War Information (1942–45) (died 1958).

1905   Secretary of State John Hay proclaimed

American policy is "to maintain the integrity of China and the Open Door in the Orient."

1908 More than 100 persons were killed in a fire in Rhoades Opera House in Boyertown, PA; fire started by explosion of motion picture projector.

1908 Earle G. Wheeler, World War II Army general, born in Washington, DC; Army chief of staff (1962–64); chairman, Joint Chiefs of Staff (1964–70) (died 1975).

1926 Bituminous coal mine disaster at Wilburton, OK, killed 91 persons.

1933 Philippines Independence Act, giving the Philippines right to establish an independent government, passed over President Hoover's veto.

1982 An Air Florida Boeing 737 crashed into Potomac River after taking off from Washington, DC, National Airport killing 78 persons.

1988 Supreme Court ruled 5–3 that public school officials have broad powers to censor school newspapers in case involving a Hazelwood, MO, school.

1989 Major charges against Oliver L. North dismissed because national security might be jeopardized by highly-classified information used in trial; 12 criminal charges remain.

1997 President Clinton awarded Medal of Honor, highest bravery award, to seven black World War II veterans, the first blacks receiving the medal.

2000 F.D.A. advisory panel unanimously approved use of laser surgery to correct farsightedness.

2002 Presidential embarrassment: George Bush passed out while watching football on television due to choking — on a pretzel.

14

1638 Fundamental Orders of Connecticut drawn up by freemen of Hartford, Windsor, and Wethersfield, first written constitution that created a government.

1730 William Whipple, member of Continental Congress (1776–79), born in Kittery, ME; a signer of Declaration of Independence (died 1785).

1741 Benedict Arnold, colonial leader turned traitor, born in Norwich, CT; led unsuccessful campaign to capture Quebec (1775); helped force Burgoyne surrender at Saratoga; court martialled for minor irregularities as Philadelphia commander, reprimanded; as West Point commander

(1780) arranged to surrender to British, plot discovered and he fled to British (died 1801).

1745 Gershom M. Seixas, rabbi, born in New York City; led drive (1783) to amend Pennsylvania constitution to eliminate barring Jews from holding public office (died 1816).

1772 Duncan McArthur, War of 1812 general/public official, born in Dutchess County, NY; in command at Sackett's Harbor, NY (1813), Northwest (1814); served Ohio in House (1823–25), governor (1830–32) (died 1839).

1778 James Madison elected to Virginia's eight-man Council of State.

1780 Henry Baldwin, legislator/jurist, born in New Haven, CT; represented Pennsylvania in House (1817–22); associate justice, Supreme Court (1830–44) (died 1844).

1784 Continental Congress, meeting in Annapolis, MD, ratified 1783 Treaty of Paris, officially ending American Revolution.

1790 Treasury Secretary Hamilton issued first report on public credit to Congress.

1799 Senate concluded impeachment trial of Sen. William Blount of Tennessee (1796–97), first such trial; charges dismissed for lack of jurisdiction; charged with conspiring with British to divert part of Louisiana from Spain.

1806 Matthew F. Maury, pioneer oceanographer, born in Fredericksburg, VA; with Naval Observatory, produced wind, current chart of North Atlantic; his *Physical Geography of the Sea* was first modern oceanography work (died 1873).

1825 Robert G. Harper, represented South Carolina in House (1794–1801), died at 60; remembered for toast he proposed: "Millions for defense, but not a cent for tribute."

1863 Richard F. Outcault, pioneer cartoonist ("Yellow Kid," "Buster Brown"), born in Lancaster, OH (died 1928).

1867 Supreme Court ruled in *Cummings v. Missouri* that a state oath excluding Confederate sympathizers from professions violated the law; same applied to federal test oath.

1871 Felix M. Warburg, banker, born in Hamburg, Germany; with Kuhn, Loeb & Co.; renowned philanthropist (died 1937).

1878 Supreme Court in *Hall v. DeCuir* ruled unconstitutional state law requiring equal accommodations to all passengers regardless of race and creed, because of its bearing on interstate travel.

1881 Joseph A. Green, World War II general, born in Cherokee, IA; chief, Coast Artillery (from 1940) (died 1963).

1881 Francis G. Pease, astronomer, born in

Cambridge, MA; with Mt. Wilson Observatory, known for direct photographs, spectrograms of nebulae, star clusters, moon, planets; developed method for grinding mirror for 200-inch Caltech telescope (died 1938).

1862 Hendrik Van Loon, historian/author (*Story of Mankind, The Arts, Geography*), born in Rotterdam (died 1944).

1886 Hugh Lofting, author of the *Dr. Doolittle* stories, born in Maidenhead, England (died 1947).

1892 Hal Roach, pioneer moviemaker, born; produced early screen comedies in 1920s, 1930s (died 1992).

1893 Pope Leo XIII established apostolic delegation in Washington, DC, with Archbishop Francisco Satolli as the first delegate.

1896 John Dos Passos, author (*Manhattan Transfer, 42d Parallel, Big Money, 1919*), born in Chicago (died 1970).

1902 Alfred Tarski, mathematician, born in Warsaw; made important studies in general algebra, mathematical logic, set theory.

1914 Henry Ford revolutionized automobile industry by inaugurating an assembly line, cutting assembly time for auto from 12½ hours to 93 minutes.

1914 Jane Wyman, screen actress (*Johnny Belinda, The Lost Weekend, My Man Godfrey*), born in St. Joseph, MO; first wife of President Reagan.

1932 Loretta Lynn, country and western music singer, born in Butcher Hollow, KY.

1940 Julian Bond, legislator/civil rights leader, born in Nashville; a founder, Student Nonviolent Coordinating Committee; served in Georgia legislature (1967–78).

1942 President Franklin Roosevelt ordered registration of all aliens.

1943 President Franklin Roosevelt and Winston Churchill began 10-day conference at Casablanca to plan Allied offensive aimed at unconditional surrender of Axis.

1949 Lawrence E. Kasdan, screen writer/director (*The Empire Strikes Back, Raiders of the Lost Ark*), born in Miami Beach, FL.

1949 Justice Department filed antitrust suit against American Telephone & Telegraph Co.

1951 The *Today* show began on National Broadcasting Co.

1986 President Reagan signed compact with Micronesia, giving Pacific islands region limited autonomy.

1986 Supreme Court ruled 6–3 to upset 23-year-old murder conviction of a defendant because he was indicted by a grand jury from which members of his own race had been excluded unconstitutionally.

1987 Supreme Court upheld California law that grants pregnant employees four months leave to have the child and guarantees their job afterward.

2000 David Letterman, host of *Tonight* show, hospitalized; undergoes quintuple heart-bypass.

2000 Dow Jones industrial average hit record 11,722.98, propelled to peak by overpriced enthusiasm for dot-coms, which then began to decline.

2001 Outgoing President Clinton sent final Congressional letter; urged racial harmony.

2004 President Bush proposed new manned moon mission to be completed by 2020; also embraced Mars mission for astronauts.

2006 Jim Gary, sculptor, died at 66; most famous works were those he welded from old cars, transforming them into metallic dinosaurs.

2006 Shelley Winters, nominated for four Academy Awards over an acting career of decades, died of heart failure.

15

1716 Philip Livingston, colonial leader, born in Albany; member, Continental Congress (1774–78), signer of Declaration of Independence; a founder, King's College (later Columbia U.) (died 1778).

1777 Vermont, which had been claimed by both New York and New Hampshire, declared its independence, calling itself New Connecticut.

1780 Congress established Court of Appeals.

1783 William Alexander (also known as Lord Sterling), Revolutionary general, died at 57; a leader in battles of Long Island, Trenton, Monmouth; served on court which tried John André, British officer involved with Benedict Arnold.

1786 Thomas Nuttall, botanist/ornithologist, born in Settle, England; known for discoveries of numerous North American plants; published North American bird manual (1832) (died 1859).

1800 Moses Yale Beach, newspaper pioneer, born in Wallingford, CT; invented rag cutting machine (still in use); joined *New York Sun* (1834), bought it in 1838; originated syndicated news story, first European edition of an American paper (died 1868).

1810 Abigail K. Foster, equal rights leader,

born in Pelham, MA; pioneer in women's suffrage movement, also an ardent abolitionist (died 1887).

1811 Congress authorized president to take temporary possession of East Florida to prevent its falling into foreign hands.

1815 American frigate *President* taken by a British squadron off Sandy Hook.

1821 Lafayette McLaws, Confederate general, born in Augusta, GA; saw action at Harpers Ferry and Antietam; in command of Savannah (1864–65) (died 1897).

1831 James B. Thayer, legal educator, born in Haverhill, MA; law professor, Harvard (1874–1902), cofounder of case method of teaching law (died 1902).

1841 Charles A. Briggs, Presbyterian leader, born in New York City; espoused "higher criticism," suspended following heresy trial; Union Theological Seminary, where he taught (1874–1913), broke with Presbyterians, becoming independent; Briggs became Episcopal clergyman (1900) (died 1913).

1845 Ella F. Young, Chicago school superintendent (1909–15), born in Buffalo; first female president, National Education Association (died 1918).

1861 Robert L. Bullard, World War I general, born in Youngsboro, AL; led 2d Army in Argonne Forest offensive (died 1947).

1862 Loie Fuller, dancer who made innovations in theater lighting, born in Fullersburg, IL; invented the "serpentine" dance (died 1928).

1870 Donkey as an emblem of the Democratic Party first appeared as a cartoon by Thomas Nast in *Harper's Weekly*.

1870 Pierre S. DuPont, industrialist, born in Wilmington, DE; headed, DuPont (1909–20); bought into General Motors, president (1920–24) (died 1954).

1876 Eliza McCardle Johnson, widow of President Andrew Johnson, died in Greenville, TN, at 65.

1877 Lewis M. Terman, psychologist, born in Johnson County, IN; known for Sanford revision of Binet-Simon intelligence test; coined term IQ (intelligence quotient) (died 1956).

1897 Stringfellow Barr, educator, born in Suffolk, VA; president, St. John's College, Annapolis; abolished elective course system, required study of great books, emphasized science, mathematics (died 1982).

1899 The poem, "The Man with the Hoe," by Edwin Markham, a school teacher, appeared in the *San Francisco Examiner*.

1908 Edward Teller, physicist, born in Budapest; worked on Manhattan Project; sometimes called the father of the hydrogen bomb; administrator of H-bomb project (1949–52).

1909 Gene Krupa, jazz drummer/band leader, born in Chicago; with Benny Goodman (1935–38), then formed own band (died 1973).

1915 Alan Lomax, folk song collector, born in Austin, TX; with father, John A. Lomax (1867–1948), collected, recorded thousands of folk songs.

1926 Chuck (Charles E.A.) Berry, a major shaper of popular music in 1950/60s, born in St. Louis; remembered for "Maybellene," "Roll Over, Beethoven," "Memphis."

1929 Senate ratified Kellogg-Briand treaty wherein 49 governments agreed to abolish war as an instrument of national policy.

1929 Martin Luther King, Jr., civil rights leader, born in Atlanta; awarded 1964 Nobel Peace Prize; founder, president, Southern Christian Leadership Conference; assassinated in Memphis 1968.

1936 Ford Foundation, designed to administer funds for scientific, educational, and charitable purposes, incorporated.

1943 The Pentagon, home of the Defense Department, completed.

1960 United States and Japan signed a mutual cooperation and security treaty in Washington, DC; provided for American defense of Japan, American military bases in Japan, and "economic collaboration"; treaty ratified in June.

1967 First Super Bowl football game played in Los Angeles Coliseum with the Green Bay Packers winning 35–10 over Kansas City Chiefs.

1973 President Nixon ordered a halt to military actions against North Vietnam.

1987 Supreme Court ruled 5–4 that the nation's three million tenants of low-income housing projects have the right to sue over alleged housing law violations.

2003 Legality of Congress' 1998 extension of current copyrights upheld by Supreme Court by 7–2 vote.

2006 Linton Brooks, who was running the National Nuclear Security Administration, told press that the new "Reliable Replacement Warhead" program that Congress had authorized would involve almost a total redesign of existing nuclear weapons in the hope of making them more reliable and efficient rather than the more limited redesigns some anticipated.

2006 NASA's mission Stardust successfully

parachuted into Utah carrying dust from comet Wild 2, successfully ending a three-billion-mile, seven-year journey.

16

1754 George Washington returned from what is now western Pennsylvania with a French refusal to the Virginia demand they leave the area.

1782 Nicholas Longworth, horticulturist, born in Newark, NJ; known as the father of American grape culture, experimented with wine grapes and strawberry culture (died 1863).

1786 Virginia adopted statute for religious freedom drafted in 1779 by Thomas Jefferson; he ranked its authorship as important as that of the Declaration of Independence and founding of the University of Virginia.

1815 Henry W. Halleck, Union general, born in Westerville, NY; commanded Union Army (1862–64), chief of staff to Grant; active in developing California (died 1872).

1845 Charles D. Sigsbee, Spanish-American War naval officer, born in Albany; commander, *Maine* when it was blown up in Havana harbor (2/15/1898); invented special apparatus for deep-sea exploration (1875–78) (died 1923).

1864 Frank Bacon, actor/playwright, born in Marysville, CA; starred in numerous plays (*The Miracle Man, The Fortune Hunter*), co-author, star of *Lightnin,'* which ran for three years (died 1922).

1883 Civil Service Commission (now Office of Personnel Management) established when Pendleton Act went into effect; Dorman B. Eaton headed three-man commission.

1896 Mathew B. Brady, photographer, died at 74; noted for his Civil War pictures.

1909 Ethel Merman, actress/singer, born in Astoria, NY; starred in musicals (*Anything Goes, Call Me Madam, Annie Get Your Gun*) (died 1984).

1911 Dizzy (Jerome) Dean, baseball pitcher, born in Lucas, AR; with St. Louis (NL), won 150 games; later a baseball broadcaster; named to Baseball Hall of Fame (died 1974).

1919 Nebraska became 36th state to ratify 18th Amendment, establishing prohibition.

1920 The 18th Amendment went into effect, limiting use and sale of alcoholic beverages; launched era of bootlegging and speakeasies.

1934 Marily B. Horne, mezzo-soprano noted for roles in operas (*Norma, Carmen, Barber of Seville*), born in Bradford, PA.

1935 A(nthony) J. Foyt, Jr., automobile race driver who won Indianapolis 500 four times, born in Houston.

1935 FBI agents and local lawmen conducted four-hour shootout in Oklawaha, FL, killing Donnie Clark, known as Ma Barker, and her son Fred, ending years-long spree of bank robberies, kidnappings, and ten murders.

1942 Carole Lombard, screen actress, and her mother were among 22 passengers killed in plane crash near Las Vegas; she had been on a bond sale promotion tour.

1942 War Production Board established by executive order to run entire war production effort, with Donald M. Nelson as head; terminated October 4, 1945.

1944 Gen. Dwight D. Eisenhower arrived in Great Britain to assume duties as Supreme Commander, Allied Expeditionary Force.

1968 Two teams of scientists working independently for Merck Laboratories and Rockefeller University synthesized an enzyme for first time.

1975 U.S. District Court in Washington, DC, awarded $12 million in damages for false arrest and infringement of rights of 1,200 protestors who had been jailed in 1971 May Day antiwar demonstration.

1997 Bomb exploded at Atlanta abortion clinic, which was damaged; a second bomb exploded later injuring six investigators and reporters.

17

1524 Giovanni de Verrazano, Italian-born explorer for the French, sailed from Madeira, arriving three months later off the Carolina coast.

1700 Sieur d'Iberville built fort on Mississippi River, about 38 miles below present New Orleans and 54 miles above the river delta.

1706 Benjamin Franklin, author/scientist/diplomat, born in Boston; editor of *Poor Richard's Almanac* for 25 years; known for his work in electricity; publisher, *Pennsylvania Gazette* (1730–48); helped establish first American subscription library, volunteer fire department, paid police force; a founder, American Philosophical Society, U. of Pennsylvania; invented an improved heating stove; member, Continental Congress (1775–76); signer of Declaration of Independence (died 1790).

1766 London merchants, hurt by American

nonimportation policy, petitioned Parliament to repeal Stamp Act.

1768 Smith Thompson, jurist/public official, born in Armenia, NY; Secretary of Navy (1819–23), associate justice, Supreme Court (1823–43) (died 1843).

1771 Charles B. Brown, early novelist, born in Philadelphia; first American novelist to gain international reputation; wrote *Ormond*, *Wieland*, *Edgar Huntly* (died 1810).

1781 At Battle of Cowpens, SC, 1,150 British cavalry were defeated by 800 Americans under Gen. Daniel Morgan in what has been described as "one of the most brilliant tactical operations" fought on American soil.

1781 Robert Hare, chemist, born in Philadelphia; invented oxyhydrogen blowpipe (1801), much other laboratory apparatus; studied electricity (died 1858).

1794 Andrew Jackson and Rachel Donelson Robards married in Nashville (their second ceremony).

1796 Thaddeus Fairbanks, inventor of platform scale (1831), born in Brimfield, MA; headed company which made many types of scales (died 1886).

1800 Caleb Cushing, legislator/public official, born in Salisbury, MA; special envoy to China (1843–45), opening five ports to American trade; Attorney General (1853–57); nominated for Supreme Court chief justice but not confirmed; minister to Spain (1874–77) (died 1879).

1806 James Madison Randolph, grandson of President Jefferson, born in the White House, first child born there.

1821 American settlement of Texas began when Moses Austin secured charter from what later became Mexico, granting land for colonization by 300 American families; Austin died soon thereafter; colonization carried out by son, Stephen Austin.

1832 George H. Babcock, inventor/manufacturer, born near Otsego, NY; invented several printing presses, improved boiler design, headed boiler-making company (Babcock & Wilcox 1881–93) (died 1893).

1849 Charles R. Miller, newspaper editor, born in Hanover, NH; editor, *New York Times* (1883–1922) (died 1922).

1851 Arthur B. Frost, illustrator, born in Philadelphia; noted for illustrating Joel Chandler Harris books (*Bre'r Rabbit*, *Uncle Remus*) (died 1928).

1853 Alva E.S. Belmont, women's rights leader, born in Mobile; president, National Woman's Party (1920–33) (died 1933).

1856 Charles V. Chapin, public health officer, born in Providence; health superintendent Providence (1884–1932); a public health leader, applying bacteriological discoveries, establishing administrative procedures (died 1941).

1861 Former President Tyler, in letter to *Richmond Enquirer*, recommended that border states meet to try to resolve North-South differences.

1867 Carl Laemmle, pioneer movie maker, born in Laupheim, Germany; organized, headed Universal Pictures; made first full length picture (*Traffic in Souls*) 1912; first million dollar movie (*Foolish Wives*) 1922; many others (*All Quiet on the Western Front*) (died 1939).

1870 Alexander Grossett, publisher, born in Windsor Mills, Canada; with George T. Dunlap formed publishing company (1900), president (1900–34) (died 1934).

1876 Frank Hague, mayor of Jersey City (1917–47), born in Jersey City (died 1956).

1878 Treaty of amity and commerce signed with Samoan Islands, giving United States nonexclusive rights to naval station at Pago Pago.

1886 Mack Sennett, pioneer movie producer, born in Richmond, Canada; made early comedies, including the *Keystone Kops* (died 1960).

1886 Glenn L. Martin, pioneer airplane builder, born in Macksburg, IA; built his first plane 1909, built World War I planes, a twin-engine bomber (1919), became the "clipper" of 1920s (died 1955).

1886 Harold O. Rugg, author of high school science texts, born in Fitchburg, MA; education professor, Columbia U. (died 1960).

1892 James David Zellerbach, president, Crown-Zellerbach Corp. (1928–45, 1952–56), born in San Francisco; ambassador to Italy (1956–61) (died 1963).

1893 Provisional government created in Hawaii; American minister helped depose Queen Liliuokalani; Hawaii proclaimed a protectorate.

1893 Former President Hayes died in Fremont, OH, at 70.

1898 Commodore Edward D. Taussig of USS *Bennington* raised American flag over Wake Island, taking formal possession for United States.

1899 Robert M. Hutchins, president, U. of Chicago (1929–51), born in Brooklyn; dean, Yale Law School (1927–29); headed Ford Foundation, Fund for the Republic, Center for Study of Democratic Institutions (died 1977).

1899 Al Capone, gangster, born in Naples, Italy; well-known "Scarface" in Chicago; imprisoned for income tax evasion (died 1947).

1904 Sidney Waugh, architectural sculptor, born in Amherst, MA; works include Pulaski Monument, Philadelphia; Mellon Memorial Fountain, Washington; foremost glass designer (died 1963).

1910 Sidney Catlett, all-time great jazz drummer, born in Evansville, IN (died 1951).

1911 George J. Stigler, economist, born in Renton, WA; with U. of Chicago; awarded 1982 Nobel Economics Prize (died 1991).

1917 American purchase of Virgin Islands from Denmark for $25 million ratified; the islands were transferred March 31, 1917.

1922 Nicholas deB. Katzenbach, public official, born in Philadelphia; Attorney General (1964–66), Undersecretary of State (1966–69).

1949 Trial of top-ranking American Communists for plotting overthrow of the government began before Judge Harold R. Medina in New York City; found guilty after 169 days.

1950 Masked bandits robbed Brinks Express office in Boston of $2.8 million ($1.2 million cash); case solved in 1956, eight men sentenced to life imprisonment.

1961 Canada and United States signed Columbia River Treaty, a 60-year water power and water storage agreement; ratified by Senate March 16.

1966 Senate confirmed Robert C. Weaver as first secretary of Department of Housing & Urban Development; became first black cabinet member.

1969 President Lyndon Johnson signed act increasing salary of the president from $100,000 to $200,000 beginning with his successor; also provided $100,000 travel allowance, $12,000 entertainment allowance.

1977 Convicted murderer Gary M. Gilmore executed by firing squad in Utah State Prison, first American executed in nearly 10 years.

1986 President Reagan signed secret order authorizing direct American arms shipments to Iran; order instructed Central Intelligence Agency not to inform Congress.

1989 Gunman shot and killed five Stockton, CA, elementary students, wounding 30 others; then took his own life.

1991 Desert Storm, the war in Iraq, began with U.S.-led air units striking Iraqi targets.

1994 Pre-dawn earthquake struck Los Angeles area; claimed 61 lives, caused more than $13 billion in damages.

1996 Ten Muslims were convicted of conspiracy to bomb the United Nations and other New York City landmarks and to assassinate public figures; sentenced leader, Sheik Rahman and one other to life imprisonment, others to 25 years.

2001 In 8–1 decision, Supreme Court ruled that dangerous sexual predators could be sent into civil confinement after their jail terms completed.

18

1770 British soldiers, who had cut down the Liberty Pole in New York City two days earlier, clashed with the Sons of Liberty on Gold Hill (near William St. above Wall St.); liberty poles were symbols before which the Sons assembled and pledged "their fortunes and their sacred honor in the cause of liberty."

1782 Daniel Webster, legislator/public official, born in Salisbury, NH; one of America's greatest orators; represented New Hampshire in the House (1813–17) and Massachusetts in House (1823–27) and Senate (1827–41, 1845–50); Secretary of State (1841–43, 1850–52) (died 1852).

1803 President Jefferson sent special secret message to Congress proposing exploration of the West; subsequently led to Lewis and Clark expedition.

1813 Joseph F. Glidden, inventor, born in Charleston, NH; invented barbed wire, which was vital in settlement of the West (died 1906).

1850 Seth Low, merchant/public official/educator, born in Brooklyn; mayor of Brooklyn (1882–86), reform mayor of New York City (1901–03); president, Columbia U. (1890–1901) (died 1916).

1854 Thomas A. Watson, electrical engineer who worked with Alexander Graham Bell, born in Salem, MA; involved in phone conversation (March 10, 1876) when Bell said, "Mr. Watson, come here, I want you"; later into shipbuilding, manufacture of engines (died 1934).

1858 Daniel Hale Williams, surgeon, born in Hollidaysburg, PA; founder, Provident Hospital, Chicago (1891), to provide opportunity for black women to become nurses; also with Freedman's Hospital, Washington, DC; performed first successful open heart surgery, closing a heart wound and pericardium (1893); only black charter member, American College of Surgeons (1913) (died 1931).

1862 Former President Tyler died in Richmond, VA, at 71.

1874 Myron C. Taylor, industrialist, born in Lyons, NY; board chairman, chief executive, U.S. Steel (1932–38); presidential representative to Vatican (1939) (died 1959).

1892 Oliver Hardy of Laurel and Hardy comedy team, born in Atlanta; team turned out more than 200 short films (died 1957).

1904 Cary Grant, screen actor, born in Bristol, England; starred in many films (*North by Northwest, The Awful Truth, Philadelphia Story*) (died 1957).

1911 Eugene Ely, civilian pilot, landed plane on platform built on quarterdeck of battleship *Pennsylvania* in San Francisco Harbor; ropes attached to sandbags served as arresting gear; Ely then took off from same ship.

1913 Danny Kaye, actor/entertainer, born in New York City; starred in many stage/screen plays (*Up in Arms, Secret Life of Walter Mitty*) (died 1987).

1919 Versailles Peace Conference opened with 70 delegates from 27 countries attending, including President Wilson, who addressed opening session.

1942 Muhammad Ali, boxing champion born in Louisville as Cassius Clay; world heavyweight champion three times (1964–67, 1974–78, 1978–79); stripped of title after refusing military induction, reinstated after Supreme Court ruled in his favor.

1942 Office of Civilian Defense, headed by Fiorella LaGuardia, created.

1943 Supreme Court ruled that American Medical Association was guilty of violating antitrust laws by preventing activities of cooperative health groups.

1969 Peace talks to end war in Vietnam got under way.

1985 United States formally announced it would not participate in International Court of Justice proceedings brought against it by Nicaragua.

1990 Eastern Airlines ceased flying operations to sell its planes and other assets.

1997 Clyde W. Tombaugh, astronomer who discovered planet Pluto in 1930, died at 90.

2000 Michael J. Fox, long-time television star, announced retirement due to Parkinson's disease; to lobby on behalf of its cure.

2000 Kaiser Family Foundation reported that only 61 percent of American businesses provide health insurance; national average cost of family coverage was $145, 32 percent of total cost.

19

1750 Isaiah Thomas, colonial printer, born in Boston; founder, Massachusetts Spy (1770–75), driven out by British; moved to Worcester (1775–1802); turned out many books noted for beautiful typography and music; founder, first president, American Antiquarian Society (1812) (died 1831).

1789 Pierre Chouteau, fur trader, born in St. Louis; operated along Missouri River; Pierre, SD, named for him (died 1865).

1807 Robert E. Lee, Confederate general, born at Stratford (Westmoreland County), VA; served in Mexican War; superintendent, West Point (1852); commanded detachment which retook Harpers Ferry and captured John Brown; commander of Virginia forces in Civil War, later of all Confederate troops; president, Washington College (now known as Washington & Lee) (died 1870).

1808 Nathaniel M. Hayward, inventor, born in Easton, MA; invented process of treating rubber with sulphur creating partial vulcanization; assigned patent to Charles Goodyear (died 1865).

1809 Edgar Allan Poe, author/poet, born in Boston; known for his short stories ("Gold Bug," "Fall of the House of Usher," "Murders in the Rue Morgue"); poetry ("The Raven," "Ulalume," "Annabel Lee") (died 1849).

1837 William W. Keen, physician, born in Philadelphia; first American brain surgeon (died 1932).

1840 Lt. Charles Wilkes and his expedition sighted/discovered Antarctic continent; a portion is named in his honor.

1842 George T. Ladd, psychologist/philosopher, born in Painesville, OH; helped found experimental psychology in U.S.; author (*Philosophy of the Mind, Philosophy of Religion*) (died 1921).

1848 Minor C. Keith, railroad executive, born in Brooklyn; also founder, United Fruit Co. (1899) (died 1929).

1851 David Starr Jordan, biologist, born in Gainesville, NY; probably world's outstanding ichthyologist; president, Indiana U. (1885–91); first president, then chancellor, Stanford U. (1891–1916) (died 1931).

1856 Rollo Ogden, journalist, born in Rensselaer County, NY; editor, *New York Evening Post* (1903–20), *New York Times* (1922–32), (died 1937).

1861 A Georgia convention voted 208 to 89 to secede from the Union.

1862 Union troops under Gen. George H. Thomas defeated a Confederate force at the Battle of Mill Springs, KY, the first important Union victory in the West; Confederate Gen. Felix K. Zollicoffer was killed.

1864 Convention in Arkansas adopted an anti-slavery constitution; ratified by popular vote March 14.

1869 American Equal Rights Association met in Washington, DC, to discuss woman suffrage.

1874 President Grant nominated Morrison R. Waite as Supreme Court chief justice; confirmed two days later.

1881 Western Union Telegraph Co. formed by Jay Gould and William H. Vanderbilt by consolidating three companies.

1886 Presidential Succession Act signed, providing that in the event of death, resignation, or inability of both the president and vice president, the heads of the executive departments in order of their creation would succeed to office; remained in effect until 1947.

1887 Alexander Woollcott, author/critic, born in Phalanx, NJ; drama critic, author (*Shouts and Murmurs*, *While Rome Burns*); acted in *The Man Who Came to Dinner*; "Town Crier" on radio (1929–39) (died 1943).

1888 Millard F. Harmon, Jr., Air Force general, born in San Francisco; commander, Army Air Forces in Southern Pacific, (1942–45); died when his plane was lost in the Pacific (1945).

1905 Oveta Culp Hobby, newspaper publisher/public official, born in Killeen, TX; published *Houston Post* (from 1931); director, Women's Army Corps (WAC) (1942–45); first secretary of Health, Education and Welfare (1953–55) (died 1995).

1918 John H. Johnson, publisher, born in Arkansas City, AR; founder/publisher, *Negro Digest* (1942), *Ebony* (1945), *Tan* (1950), *Jet* (1951).

1931 Robert MacNeil, television reporter (*MacNeil-Lehrer Report*), born in Montreal.

1946 Dolly Parton, singer/screen actress (*Nine to Five*), born in Sevierville, TN; gained fame in country music.

1949 Salary of the president raised from $75,000 to $100,000; vice president from $20,000 to $30,000.

1955 First filmed (television and newsreel) presidential press conference held in State Department Treaty room; President Eisenhower took questions for half an hour.

1975 Nuclear Regulatory Commission established to regulate civilian nuclear facilities, assuming all functions previously assigned to Atomic Energy Commission.

1982 Brig. Gen. James L. Dozier was found unharmed by anti-terrorist police in Padua, Italy, 42 days after he was abducted by the Red Brigades.

1990 Mayor Marion Barry of Washington, DC, arrested on narcotics charge; found guilty on one misdemeanor charge.

1994 Skater Tonya Harding's ex-husband, Jeff Gilooly, arrested, charged with planning attack on Nancy Kerrigan, figure skating champion; later four men were convicted of the attack and jailed.

1997 Two bombs exploded at Tulsa, OK, abortion clinic, causing building damage but no injuries; site also bombed January 1.

1998 Carl Perkins, singer/songwriter ("Blue Suede Shoes"), died at 65.

2000 Federal Communications Commission loosened rules to permit major expansion of small-scale broadcast stations in hope of broadening diversity of viewpoints on the airwaves.

2001 President Clinton agreed to five-year suspension of his law license for misleading statements under oath about sexual relationship with an employee; independent counsel agreed not to indict if penalty accepted.

2005 Number one death cause among Americans 85 or younger was now cancer rather than heart disease.

20

1724 Isaac Backus, Baptist clergyman, born in Norwich, CT; organizer/pastor, New Light Church (1748–56), then the Middleburg (MA) Baptist Church (1756–1806); champion of religious liberty (died 1806).

1775 William Pitt (the Elder) — Earl of Chatham — proposed to Parliament that British troops be withdrawn from Boston; motion defeated by three to one vote.

1781 Mutiny of New Jersey troops quelled by Gen. Robert Howe.

1783 Preliminary articles of peace were signed by John Adams and Benjamin Franklin and the commissioners from Great Britain, Spain, and France, ending hostilities in the American Revolution.

1801 President John Adams nominated John

Marshall of Virginia to be Supreme Court chief justice; took seat January 31 and served for 34 years; one of greatest chief justices, participated in 1,106 opinions, writing 519 majority opinions.

1806 Nathaniel P. Willis, writer/publisher, born in Portland, ME; one of most prominent writers of his time; co-publisher/editor, *New York Home Journal* (1846–65) (died 1867).

1814 David Wilmot, legislator, born in Bethany, PA; remembered for his legislation (Wilmot Proviso) which brought slavery question to head; a founder, Republican Party; represented Pennsylvania in House (1845–51) and Senate (1861–63) (died 1868).

1874 Congress in face of public opposition repealed a portion of the "Salary Grab" Act of 1873, which raised congressional salaries from $5,000 to $7,500; raise of president's salary to $50,000 retained.

1877 Ruth St. Denis, dancer, born in Newark, NJ; worked with husband, Ted Shawn, in organizing Denishawn Dancers (died 1968).

1887 Hawaiian Reciprocity Treaty ratified by Senate; gave United States exclusive right to establish a fortified naval base at Pearl Harbor.

1891 Mischa Elman, violin virtuoso, born in Talnoye, Russia; made American debut in 1904, numerous worldwide concert tours (died 1967).

1892 Students at the International YMCA Training School in Springfield, MA, played first official basketball game, invented by Dr. James Naismith, teacher at the school.

1894 Harold L. Gray, cartoonist ("Little Orphan Annie"), born in Kankakee, IL (died 1968).

1894 Walter H. Piston, composer/educator, born in Rockland, ME; composer ("Symphonic Piece," "The Incredible Flutist," various symphonies); author of several widely-known music texts (died 1976).

1896 George Burns, entertainer/screen actor, born in New York City; part of Burns and Allen vaudeville/radio comedy team; later television and movies (*The Sunshine Boys, Oh God!*) (died 1996).

1902 President Theodore Roosevelt sent Panama Canal Commission report to Congress; report recommended purchase of land rights for canal at $40 million.

1933 The 20th Amendment, which set dates for terms of president, vice president, and congressmen, ratified.

1937 President Franklin Roosevelt inaugurated for second term; first president inaugurated in January under 20th Amendment, which called

for federal officials to take office in January rather than March.

1940 Carol Heiss (Jenkins), champion figure skater, born in New York City; national champion (1957–60), world champion (1956–60), and 1960 Olympics gold medalist.

1946 President Truman issued an executive order creating the CIA (Central Intelligence Agency).

1949 President Truman proposed Point Four Program to help world's backward areas by making "the benefits of our scientific advances and industrial programs available for the improvement and growth of underprivileged areas."

1954 Senate approved construction of St. Lawrence Seaway.

1981 Iran released American hostages after a year of captivity.

1986 United States officially observed Martin Luther King, Jr., day for first time.

1993 Audrey Hepburn, movie star, died at 63.

1994 Attorney General Janet Reno appointed Robert Fiske independent counsel to investigate Whitewater affair in which President Clinton and his wife were involved in a real estate venture with James McDougal. (Fiske later replaced by Kenneth Starr)

1995 President Clinton announced that the trade embargo in effect against North Korea since the Korean War will be eased.

2000 Johns Hopkins School of Public Health and the Center for Health and Gender Equity issued first worldwide study examining anti-female violence; asserted that one-third of women had been severely abused, including beatings and rapes.

2001 In last-minute actions of term in office, Clinton granted 140 pardons; some bitterly controversial, including one for wealthy fugitive Marc Rich.

2001 President George W. Bush sworn in as new president, America's 43rd.

2003 Al Hirschfeld (b. 1903) passed away at 99; drew 7,000 whimsical drawings of Hollywood and Broadway personalities, with many published in the *New York Times* and *The New Yorker;* continued to practice his craft, literally until the day before he died.

2004 Salvation Army received $1.5 billion from estate of Joan Kroc.

2005 President George W. Bush sworn in for second term as president.

21

1621 Mayflower company gathered on shore of New England for first preaching service.

1738 Ethan Allen, commander of Green Mountain Boys, born in Litchfield, CT; with Benedict Arnold, seized Ft. Ticonderoga; captured at Montreal, held prisoner (1775–78); active in seeking recognition of Vermont (died 1789).

1743 John Fitch, inventor, born in Windsor, CT; built steamboat, successfully launched (1787) first vessel on Delaware River (died 1798).

1784 Andrew Stevenson, legislator/diplomat, born in Culpeper County, VA; represented Virginia in House (1821–34), serving as Speaker (1827–34); minister to Great Britain (1836–41) (died 1857).

1785 Wyandot, Chippewa, Delaware, and Ottawa tribes ceded most of what is now Ohio to the United States.

1786 Virginia legislature invited representatives of all states to meet in Annapolis "to consider how far a uniform system in their commercial regulations may be necessary to their common interest and their permanent harmony."

1813 John C. Fremont, explorer/political leader, born in Savannah; explored, mapped much of the West; known as "the Pathfinder"; one of California's first senators (1850–51); Republican presidential candidate (1856); governor of Arizona Territory (1878–83) (died 1890).

1815 Horace Wells, pioneer dentist, born in Hartford, VT; pioneer in use of nitrous oxide (laughing gas) in tooth extraction (died 1848).

1815 Daniel C. McCallum, engineer, born in Johnson, Scotland; invented an arch-truss bridge (1851); military director and superintendent of railroads for Union in Civil War (died 1878).

1821 John C. Breckenridge, Vice President (1857–61), born in Lexington, KY; represented Kentucky in House (1851–55) and Senate (1861); served as Confederate secretary of war (1865) after serving in its army (1861–65) (died 1875).

1824 Stonewall (Thomas J.) Jackson, Confederate general, born in Clarksburg, WV; led Confederate troops in Shenandoah Valley campaign (1862); accidentally wounded by own men at Chancellorsville (May 1, 1863), died nine days later.

1842 Former President John Quincy Adams, as a congressman, presented petition from citizens of Haverhill, MA, asking for peaceful dissolution of the Union; resolution censuring him for the resolution was introduced, tabled then refused.

1853 Helen H. Gardener, suffragist, born in Winchester, VA; associated with Susan B. Anthony and Elizabeth Cady Stanton in woman suffrage movement; first woman member, Civil Service Commission (1920) (died 1925).

1855 John M. Browning, inventor/manufacturer, born in Ogden, UT; invented automatic pistol, machine gun, and automatic rifle (died 1926).

1874 Frederick M. Smith, religious leader, born in Plano, IL; son of Joseph Smith (11/6/1832), succeeded father as president, Reorganized Church of Latter Day Saints (1915–46) (died 1946).

1884 Roger N. Baldwin, lawyer/civil rights activist, born in Wellesley, MA; director, American Civil Liberties Union (1917–50), national chairman (1950–55) (died 1981).

1888 Amateur Athletic Union (AAU) formed.

1889 Pitrim A. Sorokin, sociologist, born in Turya, Russia; founder, head, Harvard U. sociology department, which became major center of social sciences (died 1968).

1901 Carry A. Nation, temperance crusader, first used a hatchet in smashing a saloon in Wichita, KS; act soon became widespread.

1908 Smoking by women in public places was made illegal in New York City.

1909 Statewide prohibition was passed by Tennessee legislature over governor's veto.

1911 National Progressive Republican League organized by Robert M. LaFollette.

1912 Konrad Emil Bloch, biochemist, born in Silesia, Germany; traced construction of cholesterol out of two-carbon compound acetic acid; shared 1954 Nobel Physiology/Medicine Award.

1915 Kiwanis International founded in Detroit; there now are about 8,000 clubs in more than 70 countries.

1930 London Naval Conference opened with United States, Great Britain, France, Italy and Japan participating; resulted in treaty regulating submarine warfare, limiting tonnage and size of submarines and other warships.

1940 Jack Nicklaus, one of world's greatest golfers, born in Columbus, OH; won Masters tournament six times; leader in winning major tournaments (20).

1941 Placido Domingo, opera singer, born in Madrid, Spain.

1947 President Truman named former President Hoover to study food and economic conditions in Germany, Central Europe; on February 27, Hoover recommended $475 million aid program.

1950 Alger Hiss, former State Department official, found guilty of perjury and sentenced to five years, bringing to an end long, spectacular court trial.

1954 World's first atomic-powered submarine, *Nautilus*, launched in Groton, CT.

1968 Restored Ford's Theater in Washington, DC, dedicated.

1977 President Carter pardoned Vietnam War draft resistors.

1985 Lockheed charter airliner carrying 71 persons crashed on takeoff at Reno, NV, airport; all aboard killed.

1994 Dow Jones industrial average closed above 3,900 (3,914.48) for first time.

2000 U.S. negotiators in Geneva agreed to raise minimum combat age for soldiers from 15 to 18; had preferred 17.

2001 Three Americans appointed cardinals by John Paul II out of group of 37 selected for office.

2002 Jazz, blues, and popular songs singer Peggy Lee died at 81 (1920–2002); wrote many songs and recorded over 600; hallmark songs of hers included "Fever" and "Is That All There Is?"

2005 After 80 years on the west coast, the East-West Shrine (football) Game was played in the East, in San Antonio, Texas; the annual affair was the first sports event created to gain recognition and financial support for a specific cause (in this case, support of the Shrine hospitals).

22

1758 Elkanah Watson, experimental farmer, born in Plymouth, MA; considered father of county, state fairs; organized Berkshire Agricultural Society, which sponsored first county fair (about 1810) (died 1842).

1789 First American novel published in Boston — *The Power of Sympathy, or The Triumph of Nature Founded in Truth* by Philenia (said to be Mrs. Sarah Wentworth Morton and William H. Brown).

1797 John Harper, publisher, born in Newtown, NY; with brother, James (4/13/1795), founded family publishing business; firm first to use steam-run presses, to introduce electrotyping on large scale (died 1875).

1802 Richard Upjohn, architect, born in Shaftesbury, England; known for Gothic revival churches (Trinity Episcopal, New York City; St. James, New Haven); a founder, head (1857–76), American Institute of Architects (died 1878).

1804 Charles O'Conor, lawyer, born in New York City; as special deputy State Attorney General, successfully prosecuted Boss Tweed and associates (1871–75) (died 1884).

1807 President Jefferson officially informed Congress of Burr conspiracy.

1812 Convention in New Orleans adopted Louisiana state constitution.

1813 Captured American troops slain by Indians at Frenchtown (now Monroe), MI, in what was called the Raisin River massacre.

1849 Terence V. Powderly, labor leader, born in Carbondale, PA; head, Knights of Labor (1883–93), instrumental in getting several states to create labor bureaus; general commissioner, Immigration Service (1897–1902) (died 1924).

1850 Robert S. Brookings, industrialist/philanthropist, born in Cecil County, MD; helped rebuild Washington U., St. Louis; successful in wooden ware business; a benefactor/founder (1926), Brookings Institution (died 1932).

1855 Iowa enacted statewide prohibition; nullified in 1858.

1874 Edward S. Harkness, philanthropist, born in Cleveland; benefactor of Metropolitan Museum of Art, Presbyterian Hospital in New York City, Harvard U. to which he donated $12 million to start a house system (died 1940).

1875 D(avid) W. Griffith, pioneer movie producer, born in LaGrange, KY; developed many moviemaking techniques; produced hundreds of films in 23 years, including *The Birth of a Nation* (died 1948).

1890 Frederick M. Vinson, public official/jurist, born in Louisa, KY; represented Kentucky in House (1924–29, 1931–38); director, Office of Economic Stabilization (1943–45); Treasury Secretary (1945–46); chief justice, Supreme Court (1946–53) (died 1953).

1891 Franz Alexander, physician, born in Budapest; often called father of psychosomatic medicine (died 1964).

1895 National Association of Manufacturers (NAM) held first meeting in Cleveland.

1897 Rosa Ponselle, opera soprano, born in Meriden, CT; leading dramatic soprano with the Met for 20 years (died 1981).

1903 Hay-Herran Treaty signed, allowing new Panama Canal Co. which held an option on

23

a canal route, to sell land to the United States; also provided that Colombia would lease a strip of land across the Isthmus for a canal.

1917 President Wilson called on World War I belligerents to accept "peace without victory."

1932 Reconstruction Finance Corporation, first government agency to provide direct credit to business in need, approved by President Hoover; set up February 2, with Charles G. Dawes president; abolished June 30, 1957.

1935 Pierre S. DuPont, IV, Delaware governor (1976–84), born in Wilmington; represented state in House (1970–76).

1944 Allied offensive began in Central Italy with costly amphibious landing at Anzio Beach.

1952 Airliner crashed in Elizabeth, NJ, killing 30 persons.

1973 George Foreman celebrated his 25th birthday by knocking out Joe Frazier in second round to win world heavyweight boxing crown in Kingston, Jamaica.

1973 Former President Lyndon Johnson died near Johnson City, TX, at 64.

1973 Supreme Court ruled 7–2 in *Roe v. Wade* that a state may not prevent a woman from having an abortion during the first six months of pregnancy.

1976 Seminole Indians accepted $16 million payment for Florida after 25 years of litigation.

1991 U.S. Postal Service approved an increase of four cents (to 29 cents) for first class postage, effective February 3.

1995 Rose Fitzgerald Kennedy, mother of a president and two senators, died at 104.

1998 The so-called Unabomber (Thaddeus Kaczynski) pleaded guilty to various mail bombings; was spared death penalty, sentenced (May 4) to life imprisonment.

2000 In first caucus of the presidential election cycle, Vice President Al Gore won on the Democratic side and Texas governor George Bush on the Republican.

2001 Bush prohibited foreign aid grants to groups providing or facilitating abortions.

2002 K-mart filed for bankruptcy; sunk by $2.38 billion in debt and refusal of suppliers to give further credit; stores remained open as plans made to consolidate and close many.

2004 Ann Miller (b. 1923) died; often considered Hollywood's second-best female tap dancer; from 1937–1946 did work in low-budget films and then moved on into more prestigious ones, which included *Easter Parade* (1948) and *Kiss Me Kate* (1953).

1730 Joseph Hewes, colonial leader, born in Princeton, NJ; member of Continental Congress (1774–77, 1779); a signer of Declaration of Independence (died 1779).

1765 Thomas Todd, jurist, born in King and Queen County, VA; associate justice, Supreme Court (1807–26) (died 1826).

1775 London merchants petitioned Parliament for reconciliation with American colonies as exports from England dropped sharply.

1789 Georgetown College, the first Catholic college in the United States, formed in Washington, DC.

1845 A uniform election day — the first Tuesday after the first Monday in November — established by Congress and signed by President Tyler.

1849 Elizabeth Blackwell became first American woman physician, graduating from Geneva (NY) Medical Institute (now Syracuse U. College of Medicine).

1869 Susan B. Anthony and Elizabeth Cady Stanton spoke for woman suffrage before a Senate committee, first congressional hearing on women's rights.

1869 Herbert D. Croly, editor, born in New York City; founder, editor, *The New Republic* (1914–30) (died 1930).

1881 New York State enacted law making way for cooperative apartments by permitting tenants to purchase their apartments; first was the Rembrandt House, 152 West 57th St.

1884 George McManus, cartoonist, born in St. Louis; drew "Bringing Up Father" (Maggie and Jiggs) (died 1954).

1884 Ralph DePalma, automobile race driver, born in Troia, Italy; pioneer American driver, won 2,557 of 2,889 races (1908–34) (died 1956).

1915 Potter Stewart, jurist, born in Jackson, MI; justice, U.S. Court of Appeals (1954–58), associate justice, Supreme Court (1958–81) (died 1985).

1916 David Douglas Duncan, photojournalist, born in Kansas City, MO; with *Life* (1946–56); produced several books (*I Protest, Goodbye Picasso*).

1917 North Dakota granted women limited suffrage.

1918 Gertrude B. Elion, research scientist, born in New York City; shared 1988 Nobel Physiology/Medicine Prize.

1919 Ernie Kovacs, entertainer, born in Trenton, NJ; one of first major television stars; made several films (died 1962).

1944 Allied forces made a second landing on Italian coast, south of Rome at Anzio Beach, in effort to outflank Germans.

1955 United States signed treaty with Panama increasing the canal annuity to $1,930,000; agreed to curtail certain businesses in canal zone which compete with local merchants.

1964 The 24th Amendment ratified, eliminating the payment of poll tax as a prerequisite for voting.

1968 American intelligence ship, *Pueblo*, seized by North Korea; 83 men aboard were held as spies, released 11 months later.

1987 Trading volume on New York Stock Exchange topped 300 million shares when it soared to 302,390,000 shares; previous record was 253,120,000 set a week earlier.

1995 President Clinton signed bill extending various protections to congressional employees already enjoyed by most Americans.

1997 Madeleine Albright sworn in as the first woman Secretary of State.

2000 Worst ice storm in almost 20 years hit Georgia, South Carolina, and North Carolina, shutting down much of the highway system.

24

1639 Fundamental Orders, a frame of government, ratified by Hartford, Windsor, and Wethersfield, CT; these Orders, adopted a year earlier, generally declared that authority should rest upon the free consent of the people.

1733 Benjamin Lincoln, Revolutionary general/public official, born in Hingham, MA; commanded army in South (1778–79); captured at Charleston (1779), exchanged and served in Yorktown campaign; Secretary of War (1781–83) (died 1810).

1754 Andrew Ellicott, surveyor, born in Bucks County, PA; surveyed continuation of Mason-Dixon Line, many state boundaries, the plan for Washington, DC (died 1820).

1791 President Washington issued the Federal District proclamation, the first presidential proclamation, directing commissioners to lay out exact location of 10-mile square District of Columbia.

1811 Henry Barnard, educator, born in Hartford, CT; improved Connecticut, Rhode Island public schools; president, U. of Wisconsin (1858–60), St. John's College, Annapolis (1866–67); the first U.S. commissioner of education (1867–70) (died 1900).

1820 Henry J. Raymond, editor, born in Lima, NY; a founder, editor, *New York Times* (1851–69); a founder, Republican Party; represented New York in House (1865–67) (died 1869).

1830 John M. Thayer, legislator, born in Bellingham, MA; one of first Nebraska senators (1867–71) and its governor (1887–91); governor, Wyoming Territory (1875–79) (died 1906).

1832 Joseph H. Choate, lawyer/diplomat, born in Salem, MA; involved in several major cases — the Tweed Ring prosecution, Standard Oil antitrust case; ambassador to Great Britain (1899–1905) (died 1917).

1835 Charles K. Adams, educator, born in Derby, VT; president, Cornell U. (1885–92), founded its law school, and U. of Wisconsin (1892–1901) (died 1902).

1848 Gold discovered by James W. Marshall, working to build a mill race on American River near Coloma, CA, for John Sutter; discovery started gold rush which brought more than 200,000 persons to California in four years.

1860 Bernard H. Kroger, founder of a grocery chain (1876), born in Cincinnati (died 1938).

1861 Georgia state troops seized federal arsenal in Augusta.

1862 Edith Wharton, author, born in New York City; wrote several novels (*Ethan Frome*, *The Age of Innocence*) (died 1937).

1881 Supreme Court in *Springer v. United States* held that the 1862 federal income tax law was constitutional.

1885 Charles H. Niehaus, sculptor, born in Cincinnati; did numerous portrait busts, the John Paul Jones monument in Washington, DC (died 1935).

1895 Eugene V. Debs and associates placed on trial in Chicago for interfering with the Pullman strike; new trial ordered February 12.

1899 Hoyt S. Vandenberg, Air Force general, born in Milwaukee; held various commands in World War II, chief of staff (1948–53) (died 1954).

1903 Alaska-Canada boundary dispute commission of three Americans, two Canadians, and one Briton created; the Briton, Lord Albertson, later voted with the Americans, thus deciding in their favor.

1913 Norman Dello Joio, composer, born in New York City; known for his neoclassical music (*Triumph of St. Joan*, *Psalms of David*).

1915 Robert Motherwell, painter/art teacher, born in Aberdeen, WA; a founder of abstract expressionism (died 1991).

1916 Supreme Court upheld constitutionality of federal income tax law.

1918 Oral Roberts, evangelist, born in Ada, OK; built up Pentecostal Holiness Church to millions of members through radio, television evangelism; founder, Oral Roberts U., Tulsa, OK (1963).

1940 Ronald W. Reagan married Jane Wyman in Glendale, CA; ended in divorce (1949).

1941 Neil Diamond, composer, born in New York City; wrote numerous popular hits ("Sweet Caroline," "Song Sung Blue").

1942 Allied naval forces sank five Japanese transports in three-day engagement in Macassar Straits, severely damaging invasion fleet.

1946 United Nations General Assembly created commission to study control of atomic energy.

1957 Angela Morgan, poet, died; wrote numerous poems, best known of which was "The Unknown Soldier," read over bier of unknown soldier in Capitol Rotunda.

1968 Mary Lou Retton, gymnast who won 1984 Olympic gold medal, born in Fairmont, WV.

1977 President Carter restored gasoline price controls.

1980 House passed resolution endorsing President Carter's call for an international boycott of Olympic Games in Moscow because of the Russian invasion of Afghanistan; Senate did likewise January 29.

1989 American Episcopal bishops approved election of first woman bishop in the 2,000 year history of the Anglican/Episcopal church; Barbara Harris elected September 24, 1988, by the Massachusetts Diocese to become suffragan bishop of the Boston Diocese.

1992 J. Carter Brown, 57, announced his retirement as director of the National Gallery of Art after 22 years.

2000 Emory O. Cunningham passed away at 78; built a fortune by helping reinvent the Southern image and popularizing it through his *Southern Living* magazine.

2001 With his rival for the office now in power in the White House, Al Gore announced he would teach on the college level.

2002 Philosopher Robert Nozick died at 63; in political theory, his *Anarchy, State, and Utopia* (1974) helped lay the philosophical groundwork for opposition to the modern welfare state as needlessly and excessively repressive of individual rights; argued that instead of eliminating inequality, welfare state actually imposed it.

25

1615 Ezekiel Cheever, educator, born in London; headed various New England schools for 70 years, including the Boston Latin School (1670–1708) (died 1708).

1715 Thomas Walker, explorer, born in King and Queen County, VA; discovered the Cumberland Gap (died 1794).

1783 William Colgate, manufacturer/philanthropist, born in Hollingsbourn, England; founder of soap/toiletries business which became Colgate-Palmolive (1806); benefactor of Colgate U.; founder, American Bible Society (died 1857).

1787 Daniel Shay, leading 2,000 debt-ridden, discontented colonists, marched on the federal Springfield, MA, arsenal to overthrow government in what became known as Shay's Rebellion; effort failed.

1807 William Adams, Presbyterian theologian, born in Colchester, CT; a founder (1836) president, Union Theological Seminary (1873–80) (died 1880).

1812 Charles G. Page, physicist, born in Salem, MA; developed principle of modern induction coil, small reciprocating electromagnetic engine, an electric locomotive (died 1868).

1813 James M. Sims, physician, born in Lancaster County, SC; an originator of operative gynecology; a founder, Women's Hospital, New York City (1855) (died 1883).

1823 Dan Rice, entertainer, born in New York City; foremost clown of mid–19th century (died 1900).

1825 George E. Pickett, Confederate general, born in Richmond, VA; led 4,500 men in charge at Cemetery Ridge at Gettysburg, losing three-fourths of them; fought brilliantly at Battle of Five Forks (died 1875).

1832 House passed resolution calling for annexation of Texas; Senate approved on February 27.

1860 Charles Curtis, Vice President (1929–33), born in North Topeka, KS; represented Kansas in House (1893–1907) and Senate (1907–13, 1925–29); majority leader (1925–29) (died 1936).

1861 William C. Bobbs, publisher, born in Montgomery County, OH; founder, president, Bobbs Merrill Co. (died 1926).

1863 Rufus M. Jones, a founder (1917) of American Friends Service Committee, born in South China, ME; shared 1947 Nobel Peace Prize (died 1948).

1863 President Lincoln removed Gen. Ambrose E. Burnside as commander of Army of the Potomac, replacing him with Gen. Joseph Hooker.

1871 Maud Park, women's rights leader, born in Boston; active suffragist; first president, League of Women Voters (1920–24) (died 1955).

1871 William McKinley married Ida Saxton in Canton, OH.

1875 John F. Noll, Catholic bishop of Ft. Wayne, IN, and founder of *Our Sunday Visitor*, born in Ft. Wayne (died 1956).

1878 Ernst F. W. Alexanderson, engineer/inventor, born in Upsala, Sweden; invented high frequency alternator, making transoceanic radio communication possible; pioneer in television, electric ship propulsion, railroad electrification (died 1975).

1882 Charles J. Guiteau found guilty of assassinating President Garfield in 1881; hanged June 30, 1882.

1885 Roy S. Geiger, World War II general, born in Middlebury, FL; served with Marine Corps in South Pacific (died 1947).

1890 United Mine Workers organized in Columbus, OH, by William B. Wilson, who later became the first Secretary of Labor.

1890 Nellie Bly (Elizabeth Seaman), a *New York World* reporter, arrived in New York City, completing round-the-world trip in 72 days, six hours, 11 minutes, beating record of Phineas Fogg in Jules Verne's *Around the World in 80 Days*.

1891 William C. Bullitt, first American ambassador to Soviet Republic (1933–36), born in Philadelphia; ambassador to France (1936–42) (died 1967).

1900 House refused 268 to 50 to seat Rep. Brigham A. Roberts of Utah because of his plural marriages.

1903 Francis M. Flynn, publisher of *New York Daily News* (1947–73), born in Mt. Ayr, IA (died 1974).

1904 Disaster in a bituminous coal mine at Cheswick, PA, killed 179 persons.

1915 First transcontinental telephone conversation was held by Alexander Graham Bell in New York City and his assistant, Thomas A. Watson, in San Francisco; call cost $20.70 for first three minutes, $6.75 for each minute thereafter.

1939 Dr. George B. Pegram of Columbia U. helped carry out first successful American demonstration of nuclear fission; advised President Franklin Roosevelt of this in March.

1946 United Mine Workers returned to the AFL, which they had left in 1936.

1961 First live presidential televised news conference held in State Department auditorium with President Kennedy answering 31 questions in a half hour.

1988 Justice Department charged that Hertz Co. billed rental car customers and their insurance carriers higher prices to fix vehicles damaged in accidents than it actually paid for repairs.

1993 President Clinton appointed his wife, Hillary, to head a task force on health care reforms.

2000 The Conference Board reported that consumer confidence had risen to 144.7 in January, the highest since the survey was begun in the 1960s.

2004 NASA's second Mars rover, *Opportunity,* safely lands inside a crater; has similar mission with *Spirit,* to investigate landscape and send back pictures; it also continued to operate long beyond pre-landing estimates of how long it would remain functional.

2004 Texas in midst of considering unusual means to meet projected teacher and other school employees retirement deficit of $1.7 billion in future three years: state may buy insurance policies on retirees and collect the benefits. As news of proposal spreads, general response was hostile, that proposal was morbid and did nothing to directly benefit retirees.

26

1780 A court martial sentenced Benedict Arnold to public reprimand on two charges — acting without authority permitting a vessel to enter Philadelphia port and using state wagons to transport private property.

1810 Joseph R. Brown, inventor, born in Warren, RI; devised precision instruments, calipers, protractors; cofounder, Brown & Sharpe (1853) (died 1876).

1826 Julia Dent Grant, wife of President Grant born in St. Louis (died 1902).

1831 Mary E.M. Dodge, author/editor, born in New York City; editor, *St. Nicholas Magazine* (1873–1905); author of children's books, best-known of which is *Hans Brinker or The Silver Skates* (died 1905).

1832 Rufus H. Gilbert, developer of elevated railway in New York City (1876–78), born in Guilford, NY (died 1885).

1832 George Shiras, associate justice, Supreme Court (1892–1903), born in Pittsburgh (died 1924).

1837 Michigan entered the Union as the 26th state.

1837 Daniel S. Tuttle, Episcopal prelate, born in Windham, NY; missionary bishop of Montana (1869–86), of Missouri (1886–1923); presiding bishop of church (1903–23) (died 1923).

1846 Benjamin F. Keith, theater operator, born in Hillsboro Bridge, NH; a founder of vaudeville circuit (died 1914).

1847 John B. Clarke, economist, born in Providence, RI; taught at various schools (1877–1923 — Smith, Amherst, Columbia); editor, *Political Science Quarterly* (1895–1911); author (*Philosophy of Wealth, Distribution of Wealth*) (died 1938).

1861 Louisiana legislature voted 113–7 to secede from Union; popular vote ratified action 20,448 to 17,296.

1870 Virginia readmitted to the Union by an act of Congress.

1871 Samuel Hopkins Adams, author, born in Dunkirk, NY; books included *Canal Town, The Incredible Era, Night Bus*— which became the movie *It Happened One Night* (died 1958).

1880 Douglas MacArthur, Army general, born in Little Rock, AR; commanded Rainbow Division, World War I; superintendent, West Point (1919–22); Army chief of staff (1930–35); commander, American forces in Far East (1941), Allied Supreme Commander, Southwest Pacific (1942–45); commander, American forces in Japan (1945–51); supreme commander, UN forces in Korea (1950–51); dismissed when he publicly challenged President Truman's conduct of the war (died 1964).

1881 Walter Krueger, World War II general, born in Flatow, Germany; commanded 6th Army in Pacific (died 1967).

1884 Roy Chapman Andrews, naturalist/explorer, born in Beloit, WI; headed Asian expeditions of American Museum of Natural History (1916–30) with their many discoveries; Museum director (1935–41) (died 1960).

1884 Edward Sapir, anthropologist/linguist, born in Lauenburg, Germany (now Poland); known for studies of Indians in Pacific Northwest (died 1939).

1887 Marc A. Mitscher, naval officer, born in Hillsboro, WI; headed Task Force 58 in Pacific, the principal carrier strike force (1944–45); headed Atlantic Fleet (1945–47) (died 1947).

1907 Congress passed law prohibiting campaign contributions by corporations to candidates for national office.

1911 Polycarp Kusch, physicist, born in Blankenburg, Germany; shared 1955 Nobel Physics Prize for atomic measurements (died 1993).

1913 James Van Heusen, composer of screen musicals (*Going My Way, Our Town*), born in Syracuse, NY (died 1990).

1915 Rocky Mountain (CO) National Park established.

1918 Americans were asked to observe wheatless Mondays and Wednesdays, meatless Tuesdays, porkless Thursdays and Saturdays, and the use of Victory bread.

1925 Paul Newman, screen actor, born in Cleveland; starred in many films (*Judge Roy Bean, Exodus, The Sting, Butch Cassidy and the Sundance Kid*).

1936 Samuel C.C. Ting, physicist, born in Ann Arbor, MI; shared 1976 Nobel Physics Prize for co-discovery of the J-(psi) particle.

1942 First Europe-bound American forces arrived in Northern Ireland.

1961 Wayne Gretzky, one of greatest hockey players, born in Brantford, Canada; National Hockey League most valuable player (1980–86); with Edmonton Oilers till 1988, then Los Angeles, St. Louis, New York.

1969 Week long floods in Southern California ended; caused 100 deaths.

1990 Jetliner from Colombia crashed on Long Island approaching Kennedy Airport, 72 persons were killed.

1996 Legislative budget battle between President Clinton and Congress ended when the president signed a stopgap bill to keep government operating into March.

1996 Henry Lewis, first black conductor of a major American orchestra (New Jersey Symphony 1968), died at 63.

1996 Senate ratified Second Strategic Arms Reduction Treaty (START II) which had been signed three years earlier by Presidents Bush and Yeltsin.

2003 Tampa Bay Buccaneers defeated Oakland Raiders 48–21 in Super Bowl XXXVII.

2004 A sea of red ink predicted: Congressional Budget Office estimated total deficit for next decade to hit $2.4 trillion, nearly $1 trillion higher than its estimate of six months earlier; figure could top $5 trillion if recent tax reductions made permanent.

2005 Worst U.S. train wreck in six years: 11 killed and 200 injured in Glendale, California; man arrested for causing accident to occur by deliberately parking and abandoning his sports utility vehicle on the track.

27

1785 U. of Georgia chartered; opened in 1801 in Athens.

1788 William Tryon, colonial governor, died at 59; governor of New York (1771–78); commanded Loyalist forces (1778–80) raiding Connecticut towns.

1795 Eli W. Blake, inventor, born in Westborough, MA; invented stone, ore crusher, still being used (died 1886).

1814 William H. Appleton, publisher, born in Haverford, MA; expanded family publishing business; originator of *Popular Science Monthly* (died 1899).

1818 Congress fixed its compensation at $8 per day; House Speaker and Senate President to receive $16 per day.

1826 Richard Taylor, Confederate general, born in Jefferson County, KY, son of President Taylor; served in Shenandoah Valley campaign, Louisiana, Alabama (died 1879).

1850 Samuel Gompers, founder/head, American Federation of Labor (1886–1924, except 1895), born in London; a union cigar maker (died 1924).

1862 President Lincoln issued General War Order #1, directing that all Union forces advance on February 22—"the day for a general movement of all the land and naval forces ... against the insurgent forces."

1872 Learned Hand, jurist, born in Albany; U.S. district judge (1909–24), U.S. Court of Appeals (1924–51), chief justice (1939–51); considered one of nation's greatest judges (died 1961).

1880 A patent for an electric incandescent lamp granted to Thomas A. Edison.

1885 Jerome D. Kern, composer, born in New York City; dean of American musical comedy composers (*Sally, Sunny, Show Boat, Roberta, The Cat and the Fiddle*) (died 1945).

1888 National Geographic Society founded in Washington, DC.

1895 Harry Ruby, composer, born in New York City; remembered for "Three Little Words," various stage, screen musicals (died 1974).

1896 Buddy (George G.) DeSylva, lyricist, born in New York City; lyricist for many hits ("April Showers," "California Here I Come") (died 1950).

1900 The first convention of the Social Democratic Party held in Rochester, NY; Eugene V. Debs nominated for president.

1900 Hyman G. Rickover, admiral, born in Makov, Poland; considered father of atomic-powered naval vessels; retired 1982 (died 1986).

1901 Art(hur J.) Rooney, professional football pioneer who purchased Pittsburgh Steelers franchise (1933), born in Coulterville, PA (died 1988).

1924 President Wilson signed executive order establishing permanent civil government for Panama Canal Zone, effective April 1.

1918 Skitch (Lyle) Henderson, band leader, born in Halstad, MN; long-time musical director of *Tonight* television show.

1920 Philip Caldwell, auto manufacturer, born in Bournesville, OH; president, Ford Motor Co. (1978–84).

1922 Two-day snowstorm began in Washington, DC, resulted in collapse of Knickerbocker Theater roof and death of 100 persons.

1926 Senate approved 76 to 17 American adherence to Permanent Court of International Justice.

1938 Honeymoon Bridge over Niagara River at Niagara Falls collapsed under strain of a massive ice jam.

1943 The 8th Air Force bombed Wilhelmshaven in first attack on Germany.

1967 Three Apollo astronauts—Virgil L. Grissom, Edward H. White, II, Roger B. Chaffee—killed in a spacecraft fire in a simulated launch at Cape Canaveral.

1967 United States, Great Britain, and Russia signed treaty limiting use of outer space for military purposes and outlawing claims for national sovereignty.

1973 Defense Secretary Melvin R. Laird announced end of military draft.

1973 Henry Kissinger and LeDuc Tho of North Vietnam agreed on a cease fire in Vietnam.

1988 Senate approved bill to reverse the impact of a 1984 Supreme Court ruling that federal funds should be denied only to programs that practice discrimination and not to entire colleges.

1989 Political cult leader Lyndon H. LaRouche, Jr., sentenced to 15 years in prison for scheming to defraud the IRS and deliberately defaulting on more than $30 million in loans from his supporters.

2000 In Clinton's final state of the union message, he lauded strength of economy and called for major new programs.

2003 Federal Aviation Authority ordered 24 air carriers using small planes to question a cross-section of passengers as to their weight; FAA feared that a January 8th crash might have been caused by plane carrying too heavy a load; current guidelines for estimating weight: 180 pounds for adults (175 in summer), 20 pounds in carry-ons; children 2–12, 80 pounds regardless of season.

2004 Jack Paar passed away at 85; pioneer talk show host from 1957–65; helped create traditions of late-night talk shows.

28

1712 North and South Carolina militias, aided by Indian allies, killed 300 Tuscaroras on the Neuse River.

1754 John Wheelock, president of Dartmouth College (1779–1817), born in Lebanon, CT (died 1817).

1760 Matthew Carey, publisher, born in Dublin; founded book publishing company and *Pennsylvania Herald* (1785); helped establish first American Sunday school (died 1839).

1818 George S. Boutwell, legislator/public official, born in Brookline, MA; first commissioner of internal revenue (1862–63), Secretary of Treasury (1869–73); represented Massachusetts in House (1863–67) and Senate (1873–77) and served as its governor (1851–52); a leader in move to impeach President Andrew Johnson (died 1905).

1821 William T.H. Brooks, Union general, born in New Lisbon, OH; served in Mexican War; saw action at Antietam, various other battles (died 1870).

1841 Henry M. Stanley, journalist/explorer, born in Denbighshire, Wales; with *New York Tribune*, assigned to find missionary David Livingstone in Africa; found him in 1871; later in service of Belgium, opening up the Congo; then repatriated as Briton and member of Parliament (1895) (died 1904).

1855 William S. Burroughs, inventor, born in Rochester, NY; invented first practical, successfully-marketed adding machine (died 1898).

1861 U. of Washington founded in Seattle.

1864 Charles W. Nash, pioneer automobile manufacturer, born in DeKalb County, IL; president, Buick Motor Co. (1910–16), General Motors (1912–16); founder, head, Nash Motor Co. (later Nash-Kelvinator) (1916–48) (died 1948).

1865 Confederate President Jefferson Davis named three commissioners for informal peace talks.

1866 Charles S. Barrett, a founder, president, National Farmers Union (1906–28), born in Pike County, GA (died 1935).

1878 First commercial telephone switchboard installed in New Haven, serving 21 subscribing customers.

1884 Twin atmospheric scientists, Auguste and Jean Piccard, born in Switzerland; Auguste studied radioactivity, atmospheric electricity in balloon flights, developed airtight gondola; Jean designed new type of balloon for stratospheric flights; Auguste died in 1963, Jean 1963.

1887 Arthur Rubinstein, pianist, born in Lodz, Poland; made formal debut at 11; famed for international concerts, interpretation of Chopin (died 1982).

1893 Abbe Hillel Silver, rabbi, born in Neinstadt, Lithuania; chief spokesman for Jewish agency in UN debate on founding of Israel; rabbi, Cleveland Temple (1917–63) (died 1963).

1902 Carnegie Institution in Washington, DC, founded by $10 million endowment from Andrew Carnegie; designed to promote original research.

1902 Alfred H. Barr, Jr., museum director, born in Detroit; first director, Museum of Modern Art, New York City (1929–43) (died 1981).

1912 Jackson Pollock, a leading abstract expressionist painter, born in Cody, WY; initiator of pop art movement in 1950–60s (died 1956).

1915 President Wilson signed legislation creating the Coast Guard by combining the Life Saving Service (established 1871) and Revenue Cutter Service (founded 1790).

1915 American vessel, *William P. Frye,* loaded with wheat for Great Britain was sunk in South Atlantic by a German cruiser.

1916 Louis D. Brandeis was named to the Supreme Court by President Wilson, the first Jewish justice; confirmed June 1, served until 1939.

1922 Robert W. Holley, biochemist, born in Urbana, IL; shared 1968 Nobel Physiology/Medicine prize for contributing to understanding genetic mechanism and protein synthesis (died 1993).

1929 Claes Oldenburg, sculptor, born in Stockholm; creator of happenings, pop art.

1932 Wisconsin enacted first unemployment insurance act.

1936 Alan Alda, actor, born in New York City; starred in television (*M*A*S*H*), screen (*Paper Tiger, Seduction of Joe Tynan*).

1942 Foreign ministers of 21 American republics voted to sever relations with Germany, Italy, and Japan at the conclusion of their Rio de Janeiro conference.

1945 First truck convoy carrying war material over the Ledo (later the Stillwell) and Burma roads reached China; 400 mile Ledo Road ran from India to the Burma Road, which ran 717 miles into China.

1948 Mikhail Baryshnikov, ballet dancer/choreographer, born in Riga, Latvia; with American Ballet Theater from 1980 on; was member of Kirov Ballet until he defected in 1974.

1978 Coates House Hotel in Kansas City burned, 16 persons died.

1986 Space shuttle Challenger exploded 74 seconds after liftoff at Cape Canaveral, killing its crew of seven.

1995 United States and Vietnam agreed to exchange low-level diplomats and open liaison offices in each other's capital city.

2001 Super Bowl XXXV won by Baltimore Ravens over New York Giants, 34–7.

29

1656 Samuel Andrew, Congregational clergyman, born in Cambridge; pastor, Milford (CT) Church (1685–1738); a founder, rector, Yale U. (1707–19) (died 1738).

1677 Three commissioners from London arrived to investigate conditions in Virginia; Governor Berkeley recalled April 27.

1737 Thomas Paine, pamphleteer, born in Norfolk, England; issued "Common Sense," 47-page pamphlet urging immediate declaration of independence and 12 issues of *Crisis*, upholding American cause during Revolution; also wrote pamphlet to help French Revolution and "The Age of Reason," about deist beliefs (died 1809).

1751 Joseph B. Barnum, public official, born in Dracut, MA; represented Massachusetts in House (1795–1811), serving as Speaker (1807–11), and in Senate (1811–17) (died 1821).

1754 Moses Cleaveland, colonial leader, born in Canterbury, CT; led group in founding Cleveland, OH (1796); served Virginia as governor (1792–95) and represented it in House (1799–1801); in eulogy of George Washington, he coined phrase: "First in war, first in peace, first in the hearts of his countrymen" (died 1806).

1761 Albert Gallatin, legislator/public official, born in Geneva, Switzerland; Secretary of Treasury (1801–14); minister to France (1816–23), to England (1826–27); represented Pennsylvania in House (1795–1801) (died 1849).

1779 British captured Augusta, GA.

1795 Naturalization Act passed requiring five years residence and renunciation of allegiance and titles of nobility.

1801 Virginian John Beckley, clerk of the House, named first librarian of Congress, serving until 1807; library set up in a Capitol room; salary not to exceed $2 a day for every day of necessary service.

1834 Federal troops first used in labor dispute when President Jackson ordered War Department to put down "riotous assembly" among laborers building Chesapeake & Ohio Canal near Williamsport, MD.

1838 Edward W. Morley, chemist/physicist, born in Newark; professor, Western Reserve U. (1869–1906), known for experiments on atmospheric oxygen content, ether drift, thermal expansion of gases; helped start modern physics (died 1923).

1840 Henry H. Rogers, financier/oil industry leader, born in Mattapoisett, MA; devised machine for separating naphtha from crude oil, originated idea of pipeline transportation; chief executive, Standard Oil interests (died 1909).

1843 William McKinley, 25th president (1897–1901), born in Niles, OH; served Ohio as governor (1891–95) and represented it in House (1877–91); fatally wounded in Buffalo at Pan-American Exposition (1901).

1845 "The Raven," a poem by Edgar Allan Poe, appeared in *New York Evening Mirror* over pseudonym "Quarles."

1845 Charles F. Crisp, legislator, born in Sheffield, England, of American parents; represented Georgia in House (1883–96), serving as Speaker (1891–95) (died 1896).

1850 Henry Clay suggested series of resolutions to Senate in effort to resolve issues of sectional strife; wound up as five separate proposals known as the Compromise of 1850; passed September 9 and 18.

1861 Kansas entered the Union as the 34th state.

1864 Whitney Warren, architect, born in New York City; co-designer of many New York City hotels (Ritz Carlton, Biltmore, Commodore) and Grand Central Terminal (died 1943).

1869 Kenneth McKellar, Tennessee legislator (Senate 1916–53), born in Richmond, AL (died 1958).

1874 John D. Rockefeller, Jr., banker/philanthropist, born in Cleveland; restored Colonial Williamsburg, planned the Rockefeller Center, donated land for United Nations building in New York City (died 1960).

1874 Owen Davis, playwright, born in Portland, ME; wrote many plays, best remembered for *Icebound* (died 1966).

1875 Anton J. Carlson, physiologist, born in Svarteborg, Sweden; at U. of Chicago, conducted many experiments on self, providing many contributions to understanding human body (died 1958).

1877 Commission composed of five senators, five representatives, and five Supreme Court justices (eight Republicans, seven Democrats) created to judge presidential election; on March 2, Rutherford B. Hayes awarded 20 electoral votes, giving him necessary 185 votes to defeat Samuel J. Tilden by one vote.

1878 Walter F. George, legislator, born near Preston, GA; represented Georgia in Senate (1922–56), ambassador to NATO (1956–57) (died 1957).

1878 Barney (Berna Eli) Oldfield, auto racer, born in Wauseon, OH; first to drive car 60 miles per hour (1903); by 1910 reached 131.724 miles per hour (died 1946).

1880 W(illiam) C. Fields, screen actor, born in Philadelphia; starred in many films (*David Copperfield, Poppy, Little Chickadee*) (died 1946).

1892 Ernst Lubitsch, movie director, born in Berlin; directed Mary Pickford in films, worked with several companies (died 1947).

1895 Adolf A. Berle, public official, born in Boston; member of New Deal "brain trust"; special counsel, Reconstruction Finance Corp. (1933–38); Assistant Secretary of State (1938–44), helped carry out "good neighbor policy" (died 1971).

1900 Baseball's American League formed but not recognized by National League and others until 1903.

1901 Allen B. DuMont, inventor, born in New York City; television pioneer; perfected first commercially-practical cathode ray tube (died 1965).

1905 Barnett Newman, abstract expressionist painter, born in New York City (died 1970).

1907 Bituminous coal disaster at Stuart, WV, killed 84 miners.

1919 The 18th Amendment (prohibition) ratified; effective January 16, 1920.

1923 Paddy Chayefsky, screen writer/playwright, born in New York City; best remembered for plays about urban working life (*Marty, The Bachelor Party*) (died 1981).

1936 Baseball Hall of Fame established in Cooperstown, NY; first five named to Hall were Ty Cobb, Walter Johnson, Christy Mathewson, Babe Ruth, Honus Wagner.

1945 Tom Selleck, television actor (*Magnum PI*), born in Detroit.

1960 Greg Louganis, champion diver, born in San Diego, CA; won gold medals in 1984, 1988 Olympic Games.

1980 Six Americans who avoided capture by Iranian terrorists were smuggled out of Iran by the Canadian embassy.

1998 A bomb exploded outside an abortion clinic in Birmingham, AL, killing a security guard, seriously injuring a nurse.

2003 Setting unwanted record: AOL Time Warner announced 2002 annual loss of $98.7 billion; figure larger than annual budget of Russia.

30

1649 Virginia announced its allegiance to the House of Stuart after execution of Charles I; gave refuge to more than 300 prominent Cavaliers; Parliament imposed a blockade and sent two armed vessels to put down insurrection, which ended March 12, 1652.

1672 John Mason, colonial leader, died at about 72; one of first settlers of Windsor, CT (1653); magistrate in Connecticut colony (1642–60), deputy governor (1660–69), assistant governor (1669–72).

1797 Edwin V. Summer, Union general, born in Boston; acting governor, New Mexico (1852); saw action at Antietam and Fredericksburg (died 1863).

1801 Pierre-Jean DeSmet, Jesuit missionary, born in Termonde, Belgium; worked 30 years among American Indians, who called him "Black Robe" (died 1873).

1815 Library of Congress, which was destroyed by invading British troops, restored when government purchased Former President Jefferson's library of 7,000 volumes for $23,950.

1816 Nathaniel P. Banks, Union general and

legislator, born in Waltham, MA; led capture of Port Hudson (1863); represented Massachusetts in House for about 20 years between 1853 and 1891, Speaker (1855–57); served state as governor (died 1894).

1835 First attempt to assassinate a president occurred when Richard Lawrence, a demented painter, shot at President Jackson in the Capitol; both his shots misfired; committed to mental hospital for life.

1836 Joseph W. Kiefer, Army officer and legislator, born near Springfield, OH; served in Civil and Spanish-American wars; represented Ohio in House (1876–84, 1905–11), serving as Speaker (1881–83) (died 1932).

1840 Father Damien, Catholic missionary, born in Tremeloo, Belgium, as Joseph Damien de Veuster; served leper colony on Molokai Island, Hawaii; died of leprosy 1888.

1862 Walter J. Damrosch, conductor, born in Breslau, Germany; directed New York Symphony (1903–27); founder, conductor of radio concerts for schools; composer (*Cyrano, Man Without a Country*) (died 1950).

1862 Ironclad steamer, *Monitor*, launched at Greenpoint, Long Island, NY.

1863 Gen. U.S. Grant assumed command of troops besieging Vicksburg, MS.

1866 (Frank) Gelett Burgess, humorist/illustrator, born in Boston; author of classic "Purple Cow" jingle; illustrated many books (died 1951).

1875 President Grant signed reciprocity treaty with Hawaii, providing for free access of sugar and other products into American ports.

1882 Franklin D. Roosevelt, 32d president (1933–45), born in Hyde Park, NY; a distant cousin of President Theodore Roosevelt; Assistant Secretary of Navy (1913–20); governor of New York (1929–33); died suddenly in Warm Springs, GA, 1945.

1882 Sosthenes Behn, industrialist, born in St. Thomas, Virgin Islands; a founder, president/chairman, International Telephone & Telegraph (ITT) (1920–56) (died 1957).

1885 John H. Towers, naval officer, born in Rome, GA; pioneer Navy flier; commander, Pacific Fleet air force (1942–44); deputy commander, Pacific area (1944–45) (died 1955).

1891 Walter H. Beech, aircraft manufacturer, born in Pulaski, TN; founder, president Beech Aircraft Corp. (1936–50) (died 1950).

1894 New York Legislature named Lexow Committee to investigate alleged corruption in New York City.

1899 Max Theiler, epidemiologist, born in Pretoria, South Africa; awarded 1951 Nobel Physiology/Medicine Prize for discoveries about yellow fever and vaccine (died 1972).

1905 Supreme Court ruled that "beef trust" (Swift & Co. et al) was illegal; forbade agreements not to bid against each other, price fixing, blacklists.

1908 Ray Milland, screen actor (*Lost Weekend*), born in Neath, Wales (died 1986).

1909 Saul D. Alinsky, social reformer, born in Chicago; developed local leadership to meet local problems through self-help (died 1972).

1928 Mitch (Irwin S.) Leigh, composer, born in Brooklyn; best remembered for *Man of La Mancha*.

1928 Harold S. Prince, producer/director, born in New York City; had numerous Broadway hits (*Pajama Game, Damn Yankees, West Side Story, Fiddler on the Roof, Cabaret*).

1934 Gold Reserve Act was passed, nationalizing all gold; all Federal Reserve banks received gold certificates as reserves against deposits and Federal Reserve notes.

1934 First balls observing President Franklin Roosevelt's birthday held; President accepted $1 million for Georgia's Warm Springs Foundation to combat polio and infantile paralysis.

1939 Supreme Court upheld Tennessee Valley Authority in competition with private firms.

1941 Richard B. Cheney, Secretary of Defense (1989–93) born in Lincoln, NE.

1942 Price control bill signed, giving Office of Price Administration power to fix all prices, except on farm products.

1968 The Tet offensive launched by Communist forces against numerous Allied centers in Vietnam, including the American Embassy in Saigon.

2000 Super Bowl XXXIV won by St. Louis Rams 23–16, defeating Tennessee Titans.

2003 Richard Reid convicted and given life imprisonment; had been charged with 2001 attempt to blow up an airplane with explosives in his shoes.

2006 Coretta Scott King, wife of Dr. Martin Luther King, Jr., died while under siege by multiple ailments; had continued as an energetic proponent of her husband's civil rights views after his murder.

2006 Muslim demonstrations and threats of violence over Danish political cartoons depicting prophet Muhammad grew abroad; most American papers refused to reprint any of them.

31

1583 Peter Bulkeley, Puritan clergyman, born in Bedfordshire, England; founder of Concord, NH, its first minister (1635) (died 1659).

1732 Richard Henry Lee, colonial leader, born in Westmoreland County, VA; member of Continental Congress (1774–79, 1784–89), introduced resolution (6/7/1776) to make colonies free of England; signer of Declaration of Independence; represented Virginia in Senate (1789–92) (died 1794).

1734 Robert Morris, financier of American Revolution, born near Liverpool, England; finance superintendent (1781–84); founder, Bank of North America (1782); signer of Declaration of Independence; delegate to Constitutional Convention; represented Pennsylvania in Senate (1789–95) (died 1806).

1737 Jacob Duché, Anglican clergyman, born in Philadelphia; chaplain of Continental Congress (1774); had change of heart, asked George Washington to have Declaration of Independence withdrawn; left with Loyalists, returned 1792 (died 1798).

1752 Ceremony for the Profession of Sister St. Martha Turpin, the first American-born Catholic nun, held in Ursuline convent in New Orleans.

1752 Gouverneur Morris, diplomat/financier, born in New York City; helped devise American decimal coinage system; commissioner to England (1790–91), minister to France (1792–94); represented New York in Senate (1800–03) (died 1816).

1774 Parliament dismissed Benjamin Franklin as colonial deputy postmaster general because of his patriotic sympathies, considered him subversive.

1801 John Marshall began his 34 years as Supreme Court chief justice.

1812 William H. Russell, express business pioneer, born in Burlington, VT; founder, Pony Express (1860) between St. Joseph, MO, and Sacramento, CA (died 1872).

1817 Massachusetts Peace Society asked Congress to call an international meeting for settlement of controversies.

1830 James G. Blaine, public official, born in West Brownsville, PA; served Maine in House (1863–76), Speaker (1869–75), and in Senate (1876–81); Secretary of State (1881–82, 1892); 1884 Republic presidential nominee (died 1893).

1831 Rudolph Wurlitzer, musical instrument manufacturer, born in Schoneck, Germany; began making trumpets, drums (1860), pianos (1868); introduced first automatically-played, electric, coin-operated instruments (1892) (died 1914).

1842 President and Mrs. Tyler's daughter, Elizabeth, married in White House to William N. Wall; marked only public appearance by Mrs. Tyler, who was paralyzed; died eight months later.

1843 Virginia Minstrels, first such troupe, made debut at benefit in New York City's Chatham Theater; organized by Daniel D. Emmett, who went on to write "Blue Tail Fly," "Dixie," and "Old Dan Tucker."

1846 Stephen D. Field, inventor, born in Stockbridge, MA; inventions included a multiple call district telegraph box, stock ticker, and an electric locomotive (died 1913).

1848 John C. Fremont found guilty by a court martial of mutiny and disobeying orders; charges brought by Gen. Stephen Kearny; dismissed from service but punishment cancelled by President Polk; Fremont resigned March 15.

1848 Nathan Straus, merchant, born in Rhenish, Germany; active in Macy's department store with brothers Isidore and Oscar until 1914; spearheaded national drive for milk pasteurization (died 1931).

1862 President Lincoln authorized to take over railroads and telegraph lines when public safety was involved.

1862 George W. Perkins, businessman, born in Chicago; as officer of New York Life Insurance Co. revolutionized insurance and other businesses which depended on direct sales by agents; with J.P. Morgan & Co. (from 1901), helped organize various large companies (died 1920).

1866 William W. Atterbury, railway executive, born in New Albany, IN; with Pennsylvania Railroad (1886–1935), president (1925–35); directed construction, operation of American military railroads in France (1917–19) (died 1935).

1868 Theodore W. Richards, chemist, born in Germantown, PA; awarded 1914 Nobel Chemistry Prize for determining atomic weight of many chemical elements (died 1928).

1872 Rupert Hughes, author of biographies, plays, and about 25 novels, born in Lancaster, MO (died 1956).

1875 Zane Grey, author of romantic Western novels (*Riders of the Purple Sage, Last of the Plainsmen*), born in Zanesville, OH (died 1939).

1881 Irving Languir, chemist, winner of 1932

Nobel Chemistry Prize, born in Brooklyn; developed cloud-seeding technique, a gas-filled tungsten lamp, high vacuum pump; with Gilbert N. Lewis developed atomic theory (died 1957).

1881 Alfred Harcourt, publisher/founder, Harcourt Brace (1919), born in Ulster County, NY (died 1954).

1891 Paul R. Hawley, medical director of Veterans Administration, born in West College Corner, IN; chief surgeon, European theater in World War II (died 1965).

1892 Eddie Cantor, entertainer, born in New York City; starred in vaudeville, burlesque, musical comedies (*Kid Boots, Whoopee*) (died 1984).

1894 Isham Jones, bandleader of 1930s, born in Coalton, OH; composer ("I'll See You in My Dreams," "It Had to Be You") (died 1956).

1895 (Samuel) Ward McCallister, social leader, died at 68; coined phrase "the 400" in shortening an invitation list to a New York ball, saying only that number was worthy of an invitation.

1903 Gardner Cowles, editor/publisher, *Des Moines Register, Look Magazine* (1937–41), born in Algona, IA (died 1985).

1903 Tallulah Bankhead, stage actress, born in Huntsville, AL; starred in many plays (*The Little Foxes, The Skin of Our Teeth*) (died 1968).

1905 John O'Hara, author, born in Pottsville, PA; wrote many short stories, novels (*Appointment in Samara, Butterfield 8, Pal Joey, A Rage to Live*) (died 1970).

1908 Statewide prohibition enacted in North Carolina.

1910 Mine disaster in Primero, CO, claimed 75 lives.

1915 Thomas Merton, Trappist monk, born in Paris; spiritual writer (*The Seven Storey Mountain*) (died 1968).

1919 Jackie Robinson, first black baseball player in major leagues, born in Cairo, GA; played with Brooklyn (1947–56); named to Baseball Hall of Fame (died 1972).

1919 Nat(haniel G.) Goodwin, stage star of 1880/90s (*The Gilded Fool, Rivals, Oliver Twist*), died at 62.

1923 Carol Channing, actress (*Hello, Dolly!, Gentlemen Prefer Blondes*), born in Seattle.

1923 Norman K. Mailer, author, born in Long Branch, NJ; best known for *The Naked and the Dead, An American Dream, The Executioner's Song*.

1925 Benjamin Hooks, first black Securities & Exchange commissioner (1972–76), born in Memphis; executive director, NAACP (1976–82).

1934 Federal Farm Mortgage Corporation created to help refinance farm debts, guarantee principal and interest of bonds exchanged for consolidated loan bonds.

1944 American forces invaded the Marshall Islands; Roi and Namur secured February 3, Kwajalein February 6, Eniwetok February 22.

1947 Nolan Ryan, baseball pitcher 27 years (New York NL, California AL, Houston NL), born in Refugio, TX; pitched seven no-hit games, won 324 and lost 292; recorded 5,714 strikeouts, 2,795 walks.

1949 United States granted de jure recognition of Israel when it created a permanent government.

1950 President Truman ordered development of the hydrogen bomb; initial objective reached in November 1952.

1958 Army's Jupiter-C rocket fired first American earth satellite, Explorer I, into orbit from Cape Canaveral; side benefit was discovery of the Van Allen radiation belt.

1966 United States resumed bombing raids on North Vietnam; 27-day pause ended when North Vietnam and China rejected a peace drive.

1994 Dow Jones industrial average closed at an all-time high of 3,978.36.

1995 President Clinton invoked emergency powers to extend a $20 billion loan to help Mexico avert financial collapse.

2000 Alaska Airways plane crashed in Pacific off Oxnard, California, on flight northward to Seattle; 88 dead; no survivors.

2006 Samuel Alito became 110th Supreme Court Justice after Senate confirmation; 58–42 vote.

FEBRUARY

1

1682 William Penn and 11 other Quakers purchased East New Jersey from the Carteret heirs.

1716 John Bard, pioneer physician, born in Burlington, NJ; helped introduce practice of dissecting human bodies for instruction in United States (died 1799).

1753 George Washington named adjutant of the counties of the James River; officially became a major.

1763 Thomas Campbell, church cofounder, born in Scotland; helped son, Alexander, and Barton W. Stone found the Disciples of Christ Church (died 1854).

1775 A second Massachusetts Provincial Congress met in Cambridge; framed measures to prepare colony for war.

1781 Gen. William L. Davidson was killed in battle at Cowans Ford, NC.

1790 Supreme Court met for first time (in Royal Exchange Building, Broad Street, New York City) but did not organize until February 2 when all five appointees were present.

1801 Thomas L. Cole, painter, born in Bolton-le-Moors, England; a founder, Hudson River School of landscape painting; best known for allegorical cycles (*The Course of Empire, The Voyage of Life*) (died 1848).

1819 Supreme Court ruled in *Dartmouth v. Woodard* that a college charter was a contract which could not be altered by the state without consent of the college trustees.

1828 George F. Edmunds, legislator, born in Richmond, VT; regarded as an authority on constitutional law while representing Vermont in Senate (1866–91); author of anti-polygamy law, wrote most of Sherman Antitrust Act (died 1919).

1828 Meyer Guggenheim, financier/industrialist, born in Langnau, Switzerland; founder of worldwide copper industry, controlled American Smelting & Refining Co. (died 1905).

1838 Joseph Kepper, caricaturist/publisher, born in Vienna; a founder of *Puck* in German (1875), in English (1877) (died 1894).

1839 James A. Herne, author/playwright, born in Cohoes, NY; numerous successful plays (*Hearts of Oak, Shore Acres, Sag Harbor*) (died 1901).

1840 Baltimore College of Dental Surgery, first dental school, incorporated.

1844 G(ranville) Stanley Hall, psychologist/educator, born in Ashfield, MA; established one of first psychology laboratories; founder, American experimental psychology (1883); first president, Clark U. (1888–1920); American Psychological Association (1891) (died 1924).

1859 Victor Herbert, conductor/composer, born in Dublin; composed light operas (*Babes in Toyland, The Red Mill, Naughty Marietta, Sweethearts*); cofounder, American Society of Composers and Performers (ASCAP) (1914) (died 1924).

1860 Henry J. Miller, actor, born in London; theater manager/star (*The Great Divide, The Servant in the House, The Faith Healer*) (died 1926).

1861 Texas legislature voted 166–7 to secede from the Union; ratified by popular vote (34,794 to 11,255) on February 23.

1861 Mint and custom house in New Orleans seized by Confederate troops, $536,000 taken.

1865 President Lincoln signed 13th Amendment outlawing slavery; day now observed as National Freedom Day.

1885 Alcan Hirsch, chemical engineer, born in Corpus Christi, TX; a founder, Molybdenum Corp. (1920); started American pyrophonic alloy industry (died 1938).

1887   Charles B. Nordhoff, author, born in London of American parents; co-author with James Norman Hall of several books (*Mutiny on the Bounty, Pitcairn Island, Botany Bay*) (died 1947).

1895   John Ford, movie director, born in Cape Elizabeth, ME; directed many hits (*The Informer, Tobacco Road, Stagecoach, Grapes of Wrath*) (died 1973).

1901   Clark Gable, screen actor, born in Cadiz, OH; starred in many films (*Gone with the Wind, Mutiny on the Bounty, It Happened One Night*) (died 1960).

1902   Langston Hughes, author, born in Joplin, MO; wrote *Not Without Laughter*, known as the poet of Harlem (died 1967).

1904   William Howard Taft became Secretary of War, served until June 30, 1908.

1904   S(idney) J. Perelman, author, born in New York City; humorist (*Dawn Ginsburgh's Revenge; Parlor, Bedlam and Bath, Westward Ho!*); movie script writer (died 1979).

1905   President Theodore Roosevelt appointed Gifford Pinchot as first chief of Forest Service in Agriculture Department.

1905   Emilio G. Segré, physicist, born in Tivoli, Italy; shared 1959 Nobel Physics Prize for demonstrating existence of anti-proton; discovered element 43, technetium, first artificially-produced element (died 1989).

1913   Senate adopted 47–23 recommendation of President Taft for a constitutional amendment limiting presidency to one six-year term; House did not act.

1917   German submarine assaults against all neutral and belligerent shipping renewed.

1926   Gen. Billy Mitchell, air advocate, resigned from Army after court martial found him guilty of insubordination in his outspoken views.

1929   Bok Singing Tower near Lake Wales, FL, dedicated by President Coolidge.

1940   Hervé Filion, probably greatest harness racing driver, born in Angers, Canada; won 10,000th race in May 1987.

1942   Pacific Fleet attacked Japanese bases on Marshall and Gilbert Islands.

1944   American forces landed on Kwajalein in Marshall Islands.

1949   Consolidated city-county (parish) government went into effect in Baton Rouge, LA.

1960   Four black students sat in at a lunch counter in Greensboro, NC, resulting in organization (April 1961) of Student Non-violent Coordinating Committee (SNCC) and a wave of sit-ins.

1979   President Carter commuted sentence of Patricia Hearst, who had been kidnapped by the Symbionese Liberation Army and later joined them in a series of robberies.

1988   Army and Shell Oil Co. agreed to share cost of $1 billion toxic waste cleanup at Rocky Mountain Arsenal.

1991   U.S. Air plane landing at Los Angeles collided with a Sky West commuter plane on runway; 18 persons were killed.

1994   Twelve Eastern states from Virginia to Maine agreed to adopt California's more stringent auto emission standards.

2000   In first presidential primary of year in New Hampshire, Al Gore squeaked through a serious challenge by Senator Bill Bradley while George Bush went down by a decisive margin to Senator John McCain.

2001   U.S. Senate approved John Ashcroft for Attorney General by 58–42 vote; he had been intensely criticized for conservative views.

2003   Major blow to manned U.S. space exploration: shuttle *Columbia* disintegrated on reentry; seven astronauts perished.

2004   New England Patriots chalked up 32–29 victory over Carolina Panthers in Super Bowl XXXVIII.

2

1619   Patent granted to Puritans at Leyden, Holland, for a settlement in North America.

1651   Sir William Phips, colonial leader, born in Maine; first royal governor of Massachusetts (1692–94); knighted after recovering sunken treasure off Haiti (about 1683) (died 1695).

1653   New Amsterdam proclaimed a municipality by director-general of the Dutch West Indian Co.; municipal officials appointed.

1800   William Gregg, industrialist, born near Carmichaels, WV; launched textile industry in South (died 1867).

1803   Albert S. Johnston, Confederate general, born in Washington, KY; surprised, defeated Union forces under Grant at Shiloh (1862); killed in that action.

1804   George Walton, colonial leader, died at 63; member of Continental Congress from Georgia (1776–81), signer of Declaration of Independence; served Georgia as governor (1779–80, 1789–90).

1827   Supreme Court in *Martin v. Mott* declared the President was final judge on when to call out the militia.

1843 Knute Nelson, legislator, born in Evanger, Norway; represented Minnesota in Senate (1895–1912), served state as governor (1893–95) (died 1923).

1846 Francis M. Smith, prospector/financier, born in Richmond, WI; co-discoverer of metal from which borax is extracted; gained control of area and virtual world monopoly (Pacific Coast Borax Co.) (died 1931).

1848 Treaty of Guadalupe Hidalgo signed, ending two-year Mexican War; ratified May 30, 1848; added 1,193,061 sq. miles to United States (Arizona, Nevada, Utah, and parts of New Mexico, Colorado, Wyoming).

1854 Stephen H. Horgan, photoengraver, born in Norfolk, VA; pioneer in developing photoengraving process for newspapers (died 1941).

1875 Fritz Kreisler, violinist/composer, born in Vienna; composed, arranged music for violin, the operetta *Apple Blossoms* (died 1962).

1881 Christian Endeavor Society organized in Williston Congregational Church in Portland, ME, by its pastor, the Rev. Francis E. Clark.

1882 Knights of Columbus founded in New Haven by the Rev. Joseph M. Givney.

1886 William Rose Benet, poet/novelist, born in Ft. Hamilton, NY; a founder, *Saturday Review* (1924); author (*The Dust Which Is God, The First Person Singular*) (died 1950).

1890 Charles J. Correll, entertainer, born in Peoria, IL; played Andy in *Amos 'n' Andy* radio show (died 1972).

1895 George S. Halas, football player/coach, born in Chicago; with Chicago Bears as founder, owner, coach (1922–83); a founder, National Football League (died 1983).

1901 Jascha Heifetz, one of world's greatest violinists, born in Vilna, Russia (died 1987).

1905 Ayn Rand, author, born in Leningrad; developed philosophy of self-interest or objectivism (*The Fountainhead, Atlas Shrugged*) (died 1982).

1912 Burton Lane, composer (*Three's a Crowd, Finian's Rainbow*), born in New York City (died 1997).

1914 Renato Dulbeco, molecular biologist, born in Catanzaro, Italy; shared 1975 Nobel Physiology/Medicine Prize for study of animal viruses.

1917 Desi(derio) Arnaz, musician/television personality, born in Santiago, Cuba; co-star of *I Love Lucy* show (died 1986).

1923 James Dickey, poet/author (*Deliverance*), born in Atlanta; poetry consultant to Library of Congress (1966–68) (died 1997).

1925 Diphtheria epidemic in Nome, Alaska, broken by arrival of antitoxin brought 650 miles by dogsled.

1926 Bob (the Rev. Robert E.) Richards, Olympics (1952, 1956) pole vault champion, born in Champaign, IL.

1927 Stan Getz, tenor saxophonist/orchestra leader, born in Philadelphia (died 1991).

1980 Two days of rioting began in New Mexico state prison, resulting in 33 deaths.

1988 Defense Department ordered military services to enforce rules against sexual discrimination and harassment more vigorously and to open more positions for women.

2000 "Oxygen" began broadcasting, originating first strictly women-orientated cable television network.

2006 Livermore (California) National Laboratory showed press its new Gatling (machine) guns to protect its plutonium samples from terrorist theft; each had six barrels that could fire up to 4,000 rounds a minute; installation to come later in year.

3

1748 Samuel Osgood, public official, born in Andover, MA; member of Continental Congress (1781–84); first commissioner, U.S. Treasury (1785–89), Postmaster General (1789–91) (died 1813).

1777 Felipe de Neve, Spanish governor, arrived at Moneterey, which he made the capital of California.

1807 Joseph E. Johnston, Confederate general, born in Farmville, VA; helped win at first Bull Run, commanded troops at Vicksburg, then in Tennessee; represented Virginia in House (1879–81); commissioner of railroads (1887–91) (died 1891).

1811 Horace Greeley, journalist/political leader, born in Amherst, NH; founder/editor, *New York Tribune* (1841–72); important influence on North before and during Civil War; Democratic presidential candidate (1872) (died 1872).

1821 Elizabeth Blackwell, pioneer doctor, born in Bristol, England; first woman to receive medical degree in modern times (from Geneva NY Medical School 1849); started New York Infirmary (1857), women's medical college; returned to England (1869) (died 1910).

1823 Spencer F. Baird, naturalist, born in Reading, PA; secretary, Smithsonian Institution

(1878–87); his collection formed nucleus of Smithsonian natural history museum; established marine laboratory at Woods Hole, MA (died 1887).

1834 Edwin Adams, actor, born in Medford, MA; one of most popular American actors of his day; one of his successes was *Enoch Arden* (died 1877).

1836 Whig Party held its first convention in Albany; nominated William Henry Harrison for president.

1842 Sidney Lanier, poet, born in Macon, GA; a leading Southern poet ("Corn," "Song of the Chattahoochee," "Marshes of Glynn") (died 1881).

1844 Tolbert Lanston, inventor of typesetting machine (Monotype), born in Troy, OH (died 1913).

1853 Hudson Maxim, inventor/explosives expert, born in Orneville, ME; developed high power explosives, machine gun ammunition (died 1927).

1855 Michigan enacted a prohibition law; repealed in 1875.

1862 George C. Tilyou, amusement rides inventor, born in New York City; developed Coney Island, other amusement parks (died 1914).

1862 James C. McReynolds, attorney/jurist, born in Elkton, KY; special government counsel in tobacco antitrust suit; Attorney General (1913–14); associate justice, Supreme Court (1914–46) (died 1946).

1865 Three Confederate commissioners, headed by Vice President Alexander H. Stephens, met with President Lincoln aboard the *River Queen* in Hampton Roads without result because President demanded union as basis for peace, Confederates wanted independence.

1869 Giulio Gatti-Casazza, opera manager, born in Udine, Italy; manager, Metropolitan Opera (1908–35) (died 1940).

1872 Sam H. Harris, theatrical producer, born in New York City; worked with George M. Cohan (1904–20), then alone (1920–40), produced many hits (*Music Box Revue, Rain, Dinner at Eight, Of Mice and Men*) (died 1941).

1874 Gertrude Stein, expatriate author, born in Allegheny, PA; lived in Paris, concerned with words, sounds, rhythm ("A rose is a rose is a rose," "Pigeons in the grass, alas"); author (*Three Lives, Autobiography of Alice B. Toklas*) (died 1946).

1883 Clarence E. Mulford, author, born in Streator, IL; author of westerns, including the *Bar 20* and *Hopalong Cassidy* series (died 1956).

1884 Frank M. Andrews, World War II Army general, born in Nashville; early proponent of air power; organized, commanded Air Forces in Europe in 1930s and in 1943; killed in plane crash in Iceland (1943).

1887 Electoral Count Act passed to prevent a disputed national election such as the 1876 Tilden-Hayes election; each state was made absolute judge over the appointment of electors and state vote returns.

1890 Larry (Leland S.) MacPhail, baseball executive with various clubs, born in Cass City, MI; named to Baseball Hall of Fame (died 1975).

1894 Norman Rockwell, artist who did about ten covers a year for *Saturday Evening Post* (1916–59), born in New York City (died 1978).

1907 James A. Michener, author, born in New York City; wrote numerous best sellers (*Hawaii, Iberia, Centennial, Space, Chesapeake, Texas*) (died 1997).

1907 Hodding Carter, editor, born in Hammond, LA; crusading liberal editor of *Greenville* (MS) *Delta Democrat Times* (died 1972).

1908 Supreme Court ruled that antitrust laws cover labor combinations and prohibit boycotts by unions (*Danbury Hatters* case).

1913 The 16th Amendment to the Constitution, authorizing the income tax, was ratified.

1917 United States severed relations with Germany after the latter announced intensified submarine activity; President Wilson said, "we do not desire any hostile conflict ... we proposed nothing more than the reasonable defense of the undoubted rights of our people."

1920 Henry J. Heimlich, surgeon, who developed the "Heimlich maneuver" to save persons from choking to death, born in Wilmington, DE.

1924 Former President Wilson died in Washington, DC, at 67.

1930 Chief Justice William Howard Taft resigned from the Supreme Court for reasons of health; President Hoover nominated Charles Evans Hughes to succeed him; confirmed February 13.

1941 Supreme Court in *United States v. Darby* upheld Fair Labor Standards Act.

1943 Four chaplains aboard the *Dorchester*— Alexander Goode, John P. Washington, George L. Fox, Clark V. Poling — gave up their life jackets to others and went down with the ship.

1944 United States and Mexico signed agreement for use of water from the Rio Grande, Colorado, and Tiajuana Rivers.

1959 Airliner crashed into East River in New York City killing 65 persons.

1984 Anne Townsend, leading American field hockey player, died in Bryn Mawr, PA, at 84.

1988 New Jersey Supreme Court ruled 7–0 that paying a woman to have a baby amounts to illegal baby selling in the landmark *Baby M* case, finding surrogate agreements illegal when arranged for profit.

1988 Senate unanimously confirmed Anthony M. Kennedy to the Supreme Court to succeed retired Justice Lewis F. Powell; sworn in February 18.

1988 National Religious Broadcasters, representing most radio/television evangelists, voted 324–6 for self-regulation by requiring members soliciting tax exempt donations to meet certain standards.

1989 National League baseball club owners named former player Bill (William D.) White as National League president, effective April 1 to succeed A. Bartlett Giammati, who will become commissioner.

1992 Bert Parks, host of television game shows and Miss America pageant, died at 77.

1994 President Clinton announced the United States was lifting its trade embargo against Vietnam.

1995 Discovery space mission resulted in first American and Russian space rendezvous.

1996 Audrey Meadows, actress who portrayed Jackie Gleason's wife on TV's *The Honeymooners*, died at 71.

1998 Texas executed its first female convict in 135 years; Karla Faye Tucker was convicted of participating in two murders.

2002 New England Patriots defeated St. Louis Rams 20–17 in Super Bowl XXXVI.

2005 Ernst Mayr passes away at 100; regarded as one of the pivotal creators and popularizers of the modernized form of Darwinian evolutionary theory which is now scientific orthodoxy; he adapted and modified the original premises with the fruits of later scientific study.

2006 Betty Friedan, whose *The Feminine Mystique* inspired the modern feminist movement in 1963, died of congestive heart failure at 85.

4

1789 With only four absent, 69 electors unanimously voted for George Washington as the first President; John Adams received 34 votes for vice president.

1792 James G. Birney, antislavery leader, born in Dansville, KY; executive secretary, American Anti-Slavery Society (1837–57); presidential candidate, Liberal Party (1840, 1844) (died 1857).

1802 Mark Hopkins, educator/author, born in Stockbridge, MA; president, Williams College (1836–72); inspirational teacher, wrote many books on moral, religious topics (died 1887).

1848 Francis W. Ayer, pioneer advertising executive, born in Lee, MA; founder, N.W. Ayer Co. (1869), first company to do market research, pioneered in use of trademarks, slogans, ad copy (died 1923).

1860 William L. Rodgers, World War I admiral, born in Washington, DC; served in Atlantic Fleet (1917–18); commander, Asiatic Fleet (1918–19) (died 1944).

1861 Convention of Confederate states opened in Montgomery, AL; adopted provisional constitution February 8, elected Jefferson Davis president and Alexander H. Stephens vice president (only six of 15 slave states represented).

1861 Peace convention of states (13 northern, seven border) met in Washington, DC, with Former President Tyler serving as chairman in effort to avoid war; conference unsuccessful because recommendations satisfied no one.

1869 William D. Haywood, Socialist labor leader, born in Salt Lake City; a founder, Industrial Workers of the World (IWW) (1905); acquitted of charge of murdering Idaho governor Frank R. Steuenberg; charged with sedition (1917), fled to Russia while on bail (1921), died there 1928.

1870 John Mitchell, labor leader, born in Braidwood, IL; president, United Mine Workers (1898–1908); chairman, New York State Industrial Commission (1915–19) (died 1919).

1886 Edward B. Sheldon, playwright, born in Chicago; wrote numerous hits (*Salvation Nell, Romance, Song of Songs*); coauthor of *Lulu Belle* (died 1946).

1887 Interstate Commerce Act signed by President Cleveland, setting up federal regulation of commerce.

1899 Filipino guerilla war began in an effort to get independence from United States; ended with capture of the leader, Emilio Aguinaldo (1901).

1902 Charles A. Lindbergh, aviator who made first solo nonstop flight across the Atlantic Ocean (May 20–21, 1927), born in Detroit; known as the "Lone Eagle" (died 1974).

1904 MacKinlay Kantor, author, born in Webster City, IA; books included *The Voice of Bugle Anne, Arouse and Beware, Andersonville, Long Remember* (died 1977).

1912 Byron Nelson, golfer, born in Ft. Worth, TX; a leading golfer of 1930/40s; won 11 consecutive tournaments in 1945.

1912 Erich Leinsdorf, conductor, born in Vienna; conductor of Metropolitan Opera (1930–43, 1957–61), Rochester Philharmonic (1947–56); musical director, Boston Symphony (1962–68).

1913 National Institute of Arts & Letters incorporated, designed to further literature and fine arts.

1921 Betty Friedan, women's rights activist, born in Peoria, IL; her book, *The Feminine Mystique* accelerated the movement; a founder, president, National Organization of Women (NOW) (1966–70).

1928 President Coolidge dedicated the National Press Club in Washington, DC.

1932 Winter Olympics Games opened in Lake Placid, NY.

1945 President Franklin Roosevelt, Prime Minister Churchill and Premier Stalin met in Yalta through February 11; reaffirmed the unconditional surrender policy.

1947 J. Danforth Quayle, elected Vice President in 1988, born in Huntington, IN; represented Indiana in House (1979–83) and Senate (1983–89).

1962 Clint Black, popular country singer, born in Katy, TX.

1985 State Department announced that New Zealand denied request to allow port call by Navy destroyer because U.S. refused to say whether or not the ship had nuclear arms.

1997 Civil trial jury found former football star O.J. Simpson liable in deaths of his former wife and a friend; ordered to pay $21 million in damages; he had been found not guilty in 1995 criminal trial.

2000 Carl B. Albert, Speaker of House 1971–76 and career Democratic Congressman (1947–76) died. Due to vacancies in post of vice president in 1973 and 1974 he was twice next in line to become president if the president died.

2004 No alternative permitted: Massachusetts Supreme Judicial Court again ruled that "gay unions" or any other approach than allowing homosexuals to marry violated their rights; removed other options in reaffirming their November 2003 ruling extending marriage privilege to that group.

5

1631 The Lyon from Bristol, England, arrived in Massachusetts with 26 passengers, including Roger Williams, and provisions to end long famine; Williams served in Salem and Plymouth churches; he attacked validity of the charter, questioned the right of civil authorities to legislate in matters of conscience; urged Salem Church to separate from rest; he was later (September 13) banished.

1703 Gilbert Tennent, Presbyterian clergyman, born in County Armagh, Ireland; one of the leaders of the "Great Awakening" in United States (died 1764).

1723 John Witherspoon, Presbyterian leader, born in Yester, Scotland; an organizer of Presbyterian Church along national lines; president, College of New Jersey (later Princeton) (1768–94); a signer of Declaration of Independence; member of Continental Congress (1776–79, 1780–81, 1782) (died 1794).

1725 James Otis, colonial leader, born in West Barnstable, MA; brilliant speaker, writer for colonial cause, developed powerful legal rationale for colonial rights (died 1783).

1745 John Jeffries, physician/balloonist, born in Boston; practiced medicine in Boston, moving to England after the Revolution; made first balloon crossing of English Channel (1785) (died 1819).

1777 Georgia voters ratified their state constitution adopted by convention in 1775.

1783 Sweden recognized the independence of United States.

1817 First gas light company incorporated in Baltimore.

1819 Hannah Hoes Van Buren, wife of President Van Buren, died in Albany at 35.

1826 Millard Fillmore and Abigail Powers were married in Moravia, NY.

1837 Dwight L. Moody, foremost evangelist of 19th century, born in Northfield, MA; organized North Market Sabbath School, Chicago (1838); made several American and English evangelistic tours (1873–83); founded Northfield Seminary for girls (1879), Mt. Hermon boys school, Chicago (1881), Chicago (now Moody) Bible Institute (1889) (died 1899).

1840 Sir Hiram S. Maxim, machine gun inventor, born in Sangerville, ME; moved to England (1881), invented automatic machine gun, illuminating gas equipment; knighted 1901 (died 1916).

1846 *The Spectator*, first Oregon newspaper, published in Oregon City.

1858 Mahlon Pitney, jurist, born in Morristown, NJ; represented New Jersey in House (1895–99); justice, New Jersey Supreme Court (1901–12); associate justice, Supreme Court (1912–22) (died 1924).

1871 Maxine Elliott, actress, born in Rockland, ME; starred in Shakespearean and other plays in United States and England (died 1940).

1872 Lafeyette B. Mendel, psychological chemist, born in Delhi, NY; discovered Vitamin A (1913), function of Vitamin C; did research on digestion, nutrition (died 1935).

1900 Adlai E. Stevenson, public official, born in Los Angeles; served Illinois as governor (1949–52); delegate to United Nations founding conference (1946); Democratic presidential candidate (1952, 1956); UN ambassador (1961–65) (died 1965).

1900 First Hay-Pauncefort Treaty signed, providing for joint protectorate by England and United States of any transisthmian canal, would permit construction and operation of canal by United States.

1915 Robert Hofstader, physicist, born in New York City; shared 1961 Nobel Physics Prize for measurements of proton, neutrons, and atomic nuclei (died 1990).

1917 American troops were withdrawn from Mexico.

1918 British ship *Tuscania*, carrying 2,000 American troops, sunk by a submarine off Irish coast, 210 lives lost.

1926 Arthur Sulzberger, publisher, born in New York City; publisher of *New York Times* (1963–92).

1933 Addison Mizner, architect, died at 61; designed many of the Florida mansions.

1934 Hank (Henry L.) Aaron, baseball player, born in Mobile, AL; broke Babe Ruth's home run record (714) in 1974, reaching 755 by retirement; played with Milwaukee, Atlanta (1954–74); named to Baseball Hall of Fame.

1937 President Franklin Roosevelt in message to Congress recommended increasing Supreme Court from 9 to 15 justices; the so-called "packing" court bill went to Senate Judiciary Committee, where it died.

1979 Three thousand farmers drove campers, tractors, and trucks into Washington to dramatize their demand for price supports.

1988 General Manuel Noriega, Panama military ruler, indicted by Miami office of Justice Department on charges of turning Panama over to drug traffickers and making Panama the capital of international cocaine smuggling.

1988 Arizona's Governor Evan Mecham impeached by the State House of Representatives; faces trial in Senate in April.

1997 Morgan Stanley Group Inc. announced it will merge with Dean Witter, Discover & Co. to form the largest American securities company.

1997 Pamela Harriman, ambassador to France, died at 76.

2005 New York City Mayor Michael Bloomberg said he will appeal local court decision approving of gay marriages: says he supports the concept but that that does not give him the right to authorize unions that have no legal foundation in existing law.

2006 Pittsburgh Steelers defeated Seattle Seahawks by 21–10 in Super Bowl XXXX.

6

1682 Sieur de LaSalle reached the mouth of the Illinois River in his Mississippi Valley exploration.

1733 James Duane, legislator/jurist, born in New York City; represented New York in Continental Congress (1774–84), helped draft Articles of Confederation; mayor of New York City (1784–89), U.S. district judge (1789–94) (died 1797).

1756 Aaron Burr, Vice President (1801–05), born in Newark; represented New York in Senate (1791–97); in 1800 election was tied with Thomas Jefferson in electoral vote, Congress voted for Jefferson as president, Burr as vice president; killed Alexander Hamilton in duel; tried for treason in trying to form separate nation, acquitted (died 1836).

1778 Franco-American treaties were signed; one was treaty of amity and commerce, the other a treaty of alliance if and when war broke out between France and England (which it did June 17); ratified by Congress May 4.

1785 Elizabeth P. Bonaparte, socialite, born in Baltimore; married to Jerome Bonaparte (1803), brother of Napoleon I; marriage nullified (1805) (died 1879).

1788 Massachusetts legislature ratified Constitution by vote of 187–168 to become sixth state in the Union.

1802 War was declared against Tripoli.

1807 Hiram Sibley, a founder of Western Union, born in North Adams, MA; president,

Western Union (1856–69); an incorporator, benefactor, Cornell U. (died 1888).

1811 Samuel McIntire, the "architect of Salem," died at 54; designed, constructed great mansions of Salem shipping merchants, churches, and public buildings.

1813 Joseph R. Anderson, industrialist, born near Fincastle, VA; owner, head Tredegar Iron Works in Richmond, which supplied heavy artillery for Confederacy (died 1892).

1814 Edward F. Sorin, Catholic leader, born in Laval, France; founder, president Notre Dame U. (1844–65); superior general, Congregation of the Holy Cross (1869–93) (died 1893).

1814 James Craik, physician, died at 84; served with George Washington on expedition to Ft. Duquesne; chief physician, surgeon, Continental Army.

1818 William M. Evarts, lawyer, born in Boston; as Attorney General (1868–69), he was chief counsel for President Andrew Johnson in his impeachment trial; led fight against Tweed Ring; Secretary of State (1877–81); represented New York in Senate (1885–1901) (died 1901).

1820 Thomas C. Durant, railroad organizer, born in Lee, MA; helped organize, complete Union Pacific Railroad (1863–67) (died 1885).

1833 J.E.B. (Jeb) Stuart, Confederate general, born in Patrick County, VA; engaged in numerous battles, succeeded Stonewall Jackson as corps commander; wounded in action (May 11, 1864), died the next day.

1845 Isidor Straus, merchant, born in Otterberg, Germany; with father, Lazarus, founded crockery firm (1866), took over department at Macy's (1874); with brother, Nathan, became Macy partners (1888), sole owners (1896); made store world's largest; also developed Abraham & Straus store; represented New York in House (1893–95); with his wife, he died in *Titanic* disaster April 15, 1912.

1847 Henry J. Hardenberg, architect, born in New Brunswick, NJ; designed many leading hotels (Waldorf and Plaza, New York City; Copley Plaza, Boston; Willard, Washington) (died 1918).

1857 Ernest Flagg, architect, born in Brooklyn; designed St. Luke's Hospital and Singer Bldg., New York City; Naval Academy buildings, Corcoran Art Gallery, Washington (died 1947).

1862 General Grant's Union troops assisted by Andrew H. Foote's gunboats captured Ft. Henry, TN.

1865 Robert E. Lee appointed commander in chief of all Confederate armies.

1867 Eldridge R. Johnson, manufacturer, born in Wilmington, DE; inventor, founder, Victor Talking Machine Co. (1901) (died 1945).

1868 George A. Dorsey, anthropologist, born in Hebron, OH; anthropology curator, Field Museum, Chicago; author (*Why We Behave Like Human Beings*) (died 1931).

1878 Walter B. Pitkin, author best remembered for *Life Begins at Forty*, born in Ypsilanti, MI (died 1853).

1887 Ernest Gruening, editor/legislator, born in New York City; served Alaska as governor (1939–53) and senator (1959–69) (died 1974).

1892 William P. Murphy, medical researcher, born in Stoughton, WI; shared 1934 Nobel Physiology/Medicine prize; codiscoverer of liver treatment for pernicious anemia (died 1987).

1895 Babe (George H.) Ruth, baseball home-run hitter who helped popularize sport in 1920/30s, born in Baltimore; played with Boston AL, New York AL (1914–34); an original member of Baseball Hall of Fame (died 1948).

1900 President McKinley appointed William Howard Taft chairman of commission to establish civil government in the Philippines.

1911 Ronald Reagan, 40th President (1981–89), born in Tampico, IL; popular screen actor; served California as governor (1967–74).

1915 Prohibition law, effective January 1, 1916, signed by Arkansas governor.

1919 First American general strike occurred in Seattle when most unions and businesses shut down to protest elimination of western cost of living differential; strike lasted six days.

1923 Federal Judge Harold H. Green, who gave final approval (1983) of consent decree breaking up AT&T, born in Frankfurt, Germany.

1940 Tom Brokaw, television news reporter, born in Webster, SD; with *Today* show, then became (1980) anchorman for *NBC Nightly News*.

1951 A commuter train plunged through a temporary overpass in Woodbridge, NJ; 85 were killed, 500 injured.

1974 House of Representatives authorized its Judiciary Committee to conduct an impeachment inquiry of President Nixon.

1990 Los Angeles school board voted to put all city schools on a year-round basis.

1998 Three-day blizzard in Kentucky and West Virginia ended; killed 10 persons.

2000 Hillary Rodham Clinton became first ex-president's spouse to run for U.S. Senate by announcing candidacy for New York seat.

2003 Journalist Robert St. John died at age

100; covered world events as varied as Al Capone and the London Blitz of World War II. On NBC radio, he logged 117 straight hours covering D-Day and 72 for Japan's surrender, which he scooped competitors on — by 20 seconds.

2005 Super Bowl XXXIX resulted in 24–21 victory by New England Patriots over Philadelphia Eagles; second Patriots victory in as many years.

7

1688 Cadwallader Colden, colonial administrator, born in Ireland of Scottish parents; lieutenant governor of New York (1761–76); upheld British policy; a botanist of note (died 1776).

1784 Massachusetts Bank of Boston chartered.

1794 Sidney E. Morse, journalist/inventor, born in Charlestown, MA; a founder, editor *New York Observer* (1823–58); invented method of making stereotype plates from inscribed wax sheets, a bathometer to explore depths (died 1871).

1795 The 11th Amendment, spelling out judicial powers, went into effect.

1796 Tennessee adopted its state constitution.

1799 Federal marshals arrested John Fries, leader of a taxpayers rebellion, in Bethlehem, PA; twice convicted of treason, he was sentenced to death but was pardoned by President John Adams.

1804 John Deere, manufacturer/inventor, born in Rutland, VT; invented steel plow; founder, president, Deere & Co. (1868–86) (died 1886).

1814 George P. Putnam, publisher, born in Brunswick, ME; founder (1848), president of family publishing firm (died 1872).

1817 Frederick Douglass, human rights leader, born in Tuckahoe, MD; one of most eminent rights leaders; editor, *North Star*, abolitionist newspaper (died 1895).

1821 First documented landing on the Antarctic continent occurred when men from Capt. John Davis' shallop, *Cecilia*, from New Haven, went ashore.

1827 First ballet in America (*The Deserter*) presented in Bowery Theater, New York City.

1827 Richard W. Johnson, Union general, born in Smithland, KY; saw action at Murfreesboro, Chickamauga, the march through Georgia (died 1897).

1849 Thomas W. Symons, military engineer, born in Keeseville, NY; advocated New York State Barge Canal, served as consulting engineer in its construction (died 1920).

1854 Thomas Fitzpatrick, frontier guide and Indian agent, died at about 55; guide for John C. Fremont, negotiated several Indian treaties.

1864 Union troops occupied Jacksonville, FL, restoring state to federal status.

1870 Supreme Court in *Hepburn v. Griswold* ruled Congress did not have power to make treasury notes contracted before the legislation legal tender.

1874 Louis A. Fuertes, illustrator of bird books, born in Ithaca, NY (died 1927).

1874 William L. Hutcheson, president of Carpenters Union (1915–52), born in Saginaw, MI (died 1953).

1882 John L. Sullivan beat Paddy Ryan in nine rounds in Mississippi City, MS, to win world's heavyweight boxing championship.

1883 Eubie Blake, jazz pianist, born in Baltimore; composer ("I'm Just Wild About Harry") (died 1983).

1885 Sinclair Lewis, author who was first American to win Nobel Literature Prize, born in Sauk Centre, MN; wrote many popular novels (*Main Street, Babbitt, Arrowsmith, Elmer Gantry, Dodsworth*) (died 1951).

1886 Riot occurred in Seattle when group of extremists tried to deport Chinese workers and volunteer home guards interceded; five persons hurt, one killed.

1886 George H. Brett, World War II general, born in Cleveland; deputy supreme commander, South Pacific (1942); head, Caribbean Defense Command (1942–45) (died 1963).

1904 Fire wiped out most of Baltimore's business district; lasted 30 hours; destroyed 2,600 buildings, did $125 million damage.

1910 Buster (Clarence L.) Crabbe, Olympics winning swimmer and later a movie star, born in Oakland, CA (died 1983).

1939 John S. Reed, chief executive officer, Citicorp (1984–), born in Chicago.

1942 War Shipping Administration established by executive order.

1962 Garth Brooks, popular country music singer, born in Tulsa, OK.

1964 Beatles singing group arrived at Kennedy Airport for first American tour.

1972 President Nixon signed Federal Election Campaign Act requiring the reporting of all campaign contributions.

1973 Senate established the Watergate Select

Committee headed by Sen. Sam J. Ervin of North Carolina.

1984 Astronaut Bruce McCandless, II, crew member of the shuttle *Challenger*, became first person to go into space with no ties to the mother ship, using a powered back pack for motive power.

1986 Federal district court held a key provision of Gramm-Rudman budget deficit bill unconstitutional because it vested executive power in an official removable by Congress; decision upheld by Supreme Court July 7.

1989 Congress voted overwhelmingly to turn down its 51 percent pay increase; President Bush signed the measure before midnight when the raises would have gone into effect without action.

2000 Mildred (Wiley) Dee died; participated in Olympics first year women were permitted in field and track competitions (1928) and returned with a bronze medal for the high jump.

2001 Dale Evans died at 88; co-starred in 38 movies, 2 television series and composed 25 songs, including "Happy Trails," which became the theme song she and her husband Roy Rogers used.

2001 Anne Morrow Lindbergh passed away, wife of first man to fly across the Atlantic alone; her child was victim of famous kidnapping/murder in early 1930s; first woman certified as glider pilot in U.S.

8

1689 King William and Queen Mary granted charter to the Rev. James Blair to found a college in Virginia — the College of William and Mary in Williamsburg.

1791 Congress passed a bill establishing a national bank; signed by President Washington February 25.

1794 First fire insurance policy was issued, marking the beginning of the insurance business in Hartford.

1802 James W. Webb, editor/diplomat, born in Claverack, NY; owner/editor, *Morning Courier* and *New York Enquirer* in New York City (1829–61); minister to Brazil (1861–69) (died 1884).

1817 Richard S. Ewell, Confederate general, born in Washington, DC; led forces through Shenandoah Valley to Pennsylvania, took part in Gettysburg battle and Wilderness campaign; in charge of Richmond defense (died 1872).

1820 William T. Sherman, Union general, born in Lancaster, OH; led march to sea after razing Atlanta; credited with two famous quotes — "War is hell" and "If nominated, I will not accept; if elected, I will not serve" (died 1891).

1839 Aroostok "war" broke out between Maine frontiersmen and Canadian trespassers; settled in March without hostilities.

1861 Harry W. Leonard, electrical engineer, born in Cincinnati; worked with Edison on city central electric stations; invented first electric train lighting system, a system of motor control, electric elevator controls, and others (died 1915).

1861 Arkansas state troops seized federal arsenal in Little Rock.

1861 Jefferson Davis elected president of newly-formed Confederate States government, with Alexander H. Stephens as vice president; inaugurated February 18.

1862 Union troops took Roanoke Island, NC, key to rear defenses of Norfolk, VA.

1866 Moses Gomberg, chemist, born in Kirovograd, Russia; isolated first free radical, triphenylmethyl (died 1947).

1867 Harcourt A. Morgan, educator, born in Strathroy, Canada; president, U. of Tennessee (1919–33); member, Tennessee Valley Authority (1933–41); chairman (1938–41) (died 1950).

1879 Maude Slye, pathologist, born in Minneapolis; director of cancer laboratory, U. of Chicago (1919–44); known for extensive research (died 1954).

1887 Dawes Act passed, reforming the treatment of Indians and marking end of 25 years agitation for reform.

1895 King Vidor, screen director, born in Galveston; among his many films were *War and Peace* and *The Big Parade* (died 1982).

1906 Chester F. Carlson, inventor of xerography, born in Seattle; invention led to development of copying machines (died 1968).

1910 Boy Scouts of America founded and incorporated.

1918 First issue of *Stars & Stripes*, official American Expeditionary Force weekly published.

1921 Thornton A. Wilson, president, Boeing Co. (1968–), born in Sikeston, MO.

1923 Mine disaster at Dawson, NM, claimed 120 lives.

1924 President Coolidge signed joint resolution charging Interior Secretary Albert B. Fall and Navy Secretary Edwin Denby with fraud and corruption in handling of 1922 oil leases.

1925 Jack Lemmon, screen actor, born in Boston; numerous starring roles (*Mr. Roberts, The Odd Couple, Irma LaDouce*).

1931 James Dean, screen actor, born in Marion, IN; symbol of social rebellion for entire generation (died 1955).

1955 John Grisham, author (*The Firm, The Client, The Chamber*), born in Jonesboro, AR.

1965 President Lyndon Johnson ordered air strikes against North Vietnam in retaliation for Viet Cong attacks.

1996 President Clinton signed Telecommunications Reform Act which deregulates in large measure telephone, mobile phone, and cable television services.

2000 President Clinton issued executive order prohibiting all federal agencies from using genetic data on individuals as basis for promoting, hiring or firing them.

2001 Clinton administration's Mideast peace proposals officially scuttled by new president, asserting that the regional situation had dramatically changed.

2002 Nineteenth Winter Olympics began at Salt Lake City; with 77 nations competing, Germany won 36 gold, silver, or bronze metals, with U.S. coming in second with 34 (12 gold, 16 silver, and 8 bronze).

2006 Bush signed into law a provision requiring Medicaid recipients to prove U.S. citizenship to receive benefits effective July 1st; official estimated that of 50 million in program only 35,000 negatively affected; critics feared wider impact due to difficulty of some very elderly and sickly U.S.-born individuals to document their status.

9

1690 French and Indians led by Sieur d'Iberville destroyed Schenectady.

1744 Luther Martin, attorney, born near New Brunswick, NJ; member of Continental Congress (1785) and Constitutional Convention; successfully defended Supreme Court Justice Samuel Chase in impeachment trial; a defense attorney in Aaron Burr treason trial (died 1826).

1768 William King, colonial leader, born in Scarborough, ME; advocated separate state of Maine, its first governor (1819–21) (died 1852).

1773 William Henry Harrison, ninth President, born in Charles City County, VA; governor of Indiana Territory (1801–13) and represented Ohio in House (1816–19) and Senate (1825–28); was first president to die in office; a month after his inauguration (1841) he died of pneumonia he contracted during inauguration ceremonies.

1775 British Parliament declared Massachusetts in a state of rebellion.

1802 Horatio Potter, Episcopal prelate, born in Beekman, NY; served as bishop of New York (1854–87) (died 1887).

1814 Samuel J. Tilden, political leader, born in New Lebanon, NY; governor of New York (1875–76); Democratic presidential candidate in 1876 receiving 250,000 more popular votes than Rutherford B. Hayes and 184 to 163 in electoral votes; an electoral commission gave 22 missing electoral votes to Hayes and the election by one vote; Tilden bequeathed fortune to Tilden Trust to establish public interest in New York City (died 1886).

1818 John Milledge, legislator and public official, died at 61; governor of Georgia (1802–06) and represented state in House three times between 1792 and 1802 and Senate (1806–09); donated land on which U. of Georgia was built; state capital (1807–67) was Milledgeville, named for him.

1820 Moses G. Farmer, inventor, born in Boscawen, NH; invented machine to print paper window shades, co-inventor of electric fire alarm system; paved way for Edison with numerous inventions (died 1893).

1825 House decided 1824 presidential election in which no candidate received a majority of electoral votes; gave John Quincy Adams the votes of 13 states, Andrew Jackson of seven, William H. Crawford four; made final electoral vote: Adams 87, Jackson 71, Crawford 54.

1826 John A. Logan, Union general and legislator, born in Jackson County, IL; represented Illinois in House (1859–62, 1867–71) and Senate (1871–77, 1879–86); helped establish Memorial Day; Republican vice presidential candidate (1884) (died 1886).

1840 William T. Sampson, Spanish-American War admiral, born in Palmyra, NY; allegedly claimed victory over Spanish fleet in Cuba when victory belonged to W.S. Schley (died 1902).

1861 Provisional Confederate Congress declared that all laws of United States not inconsistent with Confederate constitution continued in force.

1861 Public referendum in Tennessee turned down proposed secession convention by vote of 68,202 to 59,449.

1866 George Ade, playwright and humorist, born in Kentland, IN; remembered for his *Fables in Slang* (died 1944).

1869 George H. Moses, legislator, born in

Lubec, ME; minister to Greece (1909–12); represented New Hampshire in Senate (1918–33), serving as president pro tem (1925–33) (died 1944).

1870 Weather Bureau began operations.

1871 Howard T. Ricketts, pathologist, born in Findley, OH; discovered cause of typhus, Rocky Mountain spotted fever (died 1910).

1874 Amy Lowell, poet/critic, born in Brookline, MA; a leading poet of Imagist school ("Men, Women and Ghosts," "Patterns," "The Bronze Horses"); a leading exponent of American modernist movement (died 1925).

1889 President Cleveland signed act creating Department of Agriculture as an executive department; first secretary was Norman J. Colman of Missouri, who had been serving as commissioner.

1891 Ronald Colman, screen actor, born in Richmond, England; starred in many films (*Lost Horizon, Random Harvest, A Tale of Two Cities*) (died 1958).

1899 Max Miller, author, born in Traverse City, MI; best remembered for *I Cover the Waterfront* (died 1967).

1901 Frederick H. Harvey, restaurateur, died at 66; opened restaurants in railroad stations, later adjacent hotels, and began operating railroad dining cars (1890).

1909 Dean Rusk, Secretary of State (1961–69), born in Cherokee County, GA; president, Rockefeller Foundation (1952–60) (died 1995).

1911 Arizona voters ratified their state constitution.

1912 Thomas H. Moorer, admiral, born in Mt. Willing, AL; chief of naval operations (1967–70); chairman, Joint Chiefs of Staff (1970–74).

1914 William J. Veeck, baseball executive, born in Chicago; served with Cleveland, St. Louis, Milwaukee, Chicago; introduced firecracker scoreboards, use of midget as pinch-hitter (died 1986).

1917 Indiana governor signed prohibition bill, effective April 2, 1918.

1928 Roger Mudd, television newsman, born in Washington, DC; served with CBS and NBC.

1942 French liner *Normandie*, being converted for transport service, capsized and burned in New York City berth.

1943 President Franklin Roosevelt decreed that for war's duration, the minimum work week was to be 48 hours.

1955 An agreement to merge was reached by the American Federation of Laborland the Congress of Industrial Organizations.

1971 Earthquake rocked San Fernando Valley in California with a death toll of 64 and damage of $1 billion.

2001 USS *Greeneville*, a nuclear submarine, accidentally sank Japanese fishing vessel near Hawaii as civilian personnel at the controls; on February 15th Navy issued new regulations limiting civilian activities aboard submarines.

10

1665 Lord John Berkeley and Philip Carteret signed the "Concessions and Agreements of the Lord Proprietors of New Jersey," the first constitution of the colony; Carteret was commissioned governor.

1763 Treaty of Paris ended French and Indian (Seven Years) War, with France ceding all land east of the Mississippi River, except New Orleans and Canada.

1766 Benjamin S. Barton, physician and botanist, born in Lancaster, PA; wrote first elementary botany text in America (1803) (died 1815).

1786 John Cadwallader, Revolutionary general, died at 44; led Pennsylvania troops at Trenton, Princeton, and various Philadelphia area battles.

1807 Coast and Geodetic Survey began as Coast Survey; became Coast and Geodetic Survey June 20, 1878; transferred to Environmental Science Services Administration July 13, 1965; then became part of NOAA (National Oceanic and Atmospheric Administration) October 3, 1970.

1837 Harrison G. Otis, publisher, born in Marietta, OH; owner/publisher, *Los Angeles Times* (1886–1917) (died 1917).

1846 Ira Remsen, chemist/educator, born in New York City; chemistry lab head, Johns Hopkins U. (1876–1906), then president (1901–13); founder/editor, *American Chemical Journal*; co-discoverer of saccharin (died 1927).

1851 Indiana adopted its state constitution, effective November 1.

1855 Congress enacted a law guaranteeing citizenship to children born abroad to American citizens and to alien women married to American citizens.

1857 Henry DeL. Clayton, legislator, born in Barbour County, AL; represented Alabama in House (1897–1915), author of Clayton Antitrust Act (died 1929).

1858 Millard Fillmore, widowed former president, married Caroline C. McIntosh in Albany.

1865 Frank M. Colby, editor, born in Washington, DC; editor, *International Year Book* (1898–1925) (died 1925).

1867 Charles W. Bryan, Nebraska governor (1923–25, 1931–35), born in Salem, IL; 1924 Democratic vice presidential candidate (died 1945).

1868 William Allen White, editor, born in Emporia, KS; owner/editor, *Emporia Gazette* (1895–1944) (died 1944).

1872 John A. Hartford, merchant, born in Orange, NJ; a developer/executive, A&P food chain (died 1951).

1893 Jimmy Durante, entertainer, born in New York City; starred on stage, screen, and television (died 1980).

1893 William T. ("Big Bill") Tilden, tennis great, born in Germantown, PA; one of greatest players of all time; world champion in 1920s–30s (died 1953).

1897 John F. Enders, bacteriologist, born in West Hartford, CT; shared 1954 Nobel Physiology/Medicine Prize for producing polio virus; led to development of Salk vaccine (died 1985).

1898 Dame Judith Anderson, actress, born in Adelaide, Australia; starred in many plays on American stage (*Mourning Becomes Electra, Strange Interlude*) (died 1992).

1899 Herbert C. Hoover married Lou Henry in Monterey, CA.

1902 Walter H. Brattain, physicist, born in Amoy, China; co-inventor of transistor; shared 1956 Nobel Physics Prize for that (died 1988).

1914 Larry Adler, generally considered world's greatest harmonica player, born in Baltimore.

1915 American note to Germany stated that United States would hold Germany to strict accountability for acts at sea; note to Great Britain protested use of neutral flags on British vessels.

1916 German note announced that beginning March 1 armed enemy merchant ships would be treated as war vessels.

1927 Leontyne Price, operatic soprano, born in Laurel, MS; appeared as Bess in *Porgy and Bess* (1952–54), starred with Metropolitan Opera (1961–85).

1938 Federal National Mortgage Association (FNMA) created; after being moved to various agencies, became a government-sponsored private corporation (1968).

1950 Mark Spitz, champion swimmer and first athlete to win seven gold medals in a single Olympics (1972), born in Modesto, CA; won two in 1968.

1959 A tornado in St. Louis killed 21 persons.

1967 The 25th Amendment, which set procedures for presidential succession, went into effect.

1988 U.S. Circuit Court of Appeals in California ruled 2–1 that the Army regulations barring homosexuals from military service violate the constitutional guarantee of equal protection; on June 9, the court reversed itself.

1998 The Office of Surgeon General, vacant for three years, was filled by Dr. David Satcher; confirmed by Senate 65–35.

2000 Publisher Steve Forbes dropped out of bid for Republican presidential nomination after second primary loss; had spent $66 million of own money to finance campaign.

2005 Following 7-month trial and 12 days of jury deliberations, well-known defense lawyer Lynne Stewart convicted in New York City on charges of aiding terrorism by smuggling messages from convicted terrorist Sheik Omar Abdel Rahman to his compatriots outside jail.

11

1766 Northampton County (VA) Court declared the Stamp Act unconstitutional and therefore not binding on the colonies.

1768 Massachusetts Circular Letter, written by Samuel Adams, outlined the steps taken by the colony's assembly and solicited proposals for united action; British ministry demanded the letter be rescinded and when the Massachusetts General Court refused, it was dissolved; other colonies endorsed the letter.

1780 Eight thousand British troops under Sir Henry Clinton landed at St. John's Island, south of Charleston, SC.

1801 A count of electoral votes for the presidency resulted in a tie between Thomas Jefferson and Aaron Burr with 73 each; the House resolved the issue in favor of Jefferson February 17.

1802 Lydia Maria Child, author/social reformer, born in Medford, MA; author of practical books (*The Frugal Housewife*, which went through 21 editions; *The Mother's Book*); founder, *Juvenile Miscellany*, the first monthly children's magazine; active abolitionist (died 1880).

1812 Alexander H. Stephens, Confederate

Vice President (1861–65), born near Crawfordville, GA; represented Georgia in House (1843–59, 1873–82) and served state as governor (1883) (died 1883).

1812 Massachusetts legislature, during Elbridge Gerry's second term as governor, passed a bill re-districting the state for partisan advantage; this gave rise to term "gerry-mandering."

1833 Melville W. Fuller, jurist, born in Augusta, ME; chief justice, Supreme Court (1888–1910) (died 1910).

1836 Washington Gladden, Congregational clergyman, born in Pottsgrove, PA; moderator, National Council of Congregational Churches (1904–07); pastor, First Church, Columbus, OH (1882–1918); preached practical application of religion to current social problems; called "father of American social gospel" (died 1918).

1839 Josiah Willard Gibbs, physicist/mathematician, born in New Haven; considered greatest American theoretical scientist; established basic theory of physical chemistry (died 1903).

1839 U. of Missouri at Columbia chartered; opened in 1841.

1847 Thomas A. Edison, inventor, born in Milan, OH; patented more than 1,000 inventions, including the electric light bulb, phonograph, electric pen, various telegraphic devices, alkaline storage battery; produced talking motion pictures (1913), improved dynamos, motors (died 1931).

1861 President-elect Abraham Lincoln left Springfield, IL, for Washington, DC, telling his neighbors he did not know "when or whether I ever may return, with a task before me greater than that which rested upon Washington."

1887 Henry K. Hewitt, World War II naval officer, born in Hackensack, NJ; directed amphibious landings at Casablanca, Sicily, Southern France (died 1972).

1898 Leo Szilard, physicist, born in Budapest; helped devise chain reaction system; developed first method of separating isotopes of radioactive elements (died 1964).

1900 Thomas Hitchcock, Jr., considered the greatest polo player ever, born in Aiken, SC (died 1944).

1907 William J. Levitt, builder/developer, born in New York City; mass producer of housing after World War II; built about 140,000 in Northeast (died 1994).

1917 Sidney Sheldon, author/playwright, born in Chicago; also noted for several screen and television plays.

1920 Senate began reconsideration of the League of Nations, the Versailles Treaty.

1921 Lloyd Bentsen, legislator, born in Mission, TX; represented Texas in House (1948–54) and Senate (1971–89); 1988 Democratic vice presidential candidate; Secretary of Treasury (1993–95).

1946 Burt Reynolds, screen actor, born in Waycross, GA; starred in many films (*Smokey and the Bandit, The Longest Yard*).

1949 President Truman named Dwight D. Eisenhower chairman of Joint Chiefs of Staff; Eisenhower took leave of absence from Columbia U. presidency.

1952 Third airline crash in Elizabeth, NJ, in less than two months killed 33 persons.

1988 Lynn Nofziger, former President Reagan aide, found guilty of illegally lobbying former colleagues within a year of leaving the government; sentenced April 8 to 90 days and $10,000 fine.

1988 Federal appeals court in San Francisco found unconstitutional requirement that rail workers be tested for drugs or alcohol after being involved in an accident or a rules violation.

1989 The Rev. Barbara Clementine Harris, 55-year-old black priest, became first woman consecrated as a bishop in the Episcopal Church.

1998 Casey Martin, who had difficulty walking, was permitted by a Eugene, OR, court to use a cart in PGA-sponsored tournaments; the first such use.

2000 WebMethods (an integrated computer-software applications firm) had Nasdaq's fourth largest ever Initial Public Offering; soared from $30 at beginning of first trade day to $212 at end.

2001 In 50th annual NBA All Stars game, western conference eked out 111–110 victory.

2003 NFL 49ers hired Oregon State's Dennis Erickson for coach: $12.5-million, 5-year contract.

2005 U.S. Justice Department disclosed January 7th agreement with Wal-Mart: Giant chain pays $135,540 to have government drop charges of violating child labor laws in three states; charges centered on operation of potentially dangerous equipment by those 17 or younger.

2006 Vice President Dick Cheney accidentally shot hunting companion, causing non-fatal injuries.

12

1606 John Winthrop, colonial leader, born in Suffolk, England; leader of a group which settled in Ipswich; served as governor of Connecticut (1636, 1657, 1659–76); obtained new liberal charter for Connecticut (died 1676).

1663 Cotton Mather, most famous Puritan cleric, born in Boston; assisted father, Increase Mather, at Second Church (1685–1723), succeeded him as pastor (1723–28); helped establish New England as cultural center; originally led drive against Salem "witches," later felt trials were unfair (died 1728).

1733 Settlers, led by Gen. James E. Oglethorpe, founded Savannah after making a treaty with Indians.

1746 Thaddeus Kosciuszko, Polish general, born in Lithuania; fought with Americans in Revolution, later fought for Polish freedom (died 1817).

1775 Louise C. Johnson Adams, wife of President John Quincy Adams, born in London (died 1852).

1781 *Vermont Gazette*, first newspaper in that state, published at Westminster.

1785 Alden Partridge, soldier/educator, born in Norwich, VT; founder of elementary and secondary grades military academies (died 1854).

1789 First newspaper in District of Columbia, *Times and Patowmack Packet*, began publication in Georgetown under Charles Fierer.

1791 Peter Cooper, businessman/inventor, born in New York City; designed, built first American steam locomotive; a leader in iron milling, steel production; promoted, financed first Atlantic cable; founded Cooper Union (1857–59) in New York City for the "advancement of science and art" (died 1883).

1792 William Smallwood, Revolutionary general, died at 60; served at Long Island, White Plains, and Camden; governor of Maryland (1785–88).

1783 Fugitive Slave Act passed, empowering an owner or agent to bring a fugitive before a magistrate to order his return.

1809 Abraham Lincoln, 16th President (1861–65), born in Hardin County, KY; assassinated while sitting in a box in Ford Theater in Washington, DC, by John Wilkes Booth, the actor, in 1865.

1813 James D. Dana, geologist/zoologist, born in Utica, NY; at Yale U. (1855–92), wrote basic mineralogy and geology texts; editor, *American Journal of Science* (1840–90) (died 1895).

1815 Martin B. Anderson, educator, born in New Brunswick, ME; first president, U. of Rochester (1853–88) (died 1890).

1822 James P. Anderson, Confederate general, born in Franklin County, TN; saw action at Corinth, Murfreesboro, Chickamauga (died 1872).

1830 Stephen Wilcox, inventor, born in Westerly, RI; invented safety water-tube boiler and steam generator; helped organize (1867) Babcock, Wilcox & Co. to manufacture inventions (died 1893).

1849 Mass meeting in San Francisco established temporary government for area.

1852 Frank W. Very, astronomer, born in Salem, MA; confirmed existence of water vapor and oxygen in Mars atmosphere, proved that white nebulae are galaxies (died 1927).

1862 Siege of Ft. Donelson, TN, began by Union forces under General Grant; attack repulsed February 14 but Union troops succeeded February 16.

1870 A Utah law gave full suffrage to women.

1873 Coinage Act passed, demonetizing silver and making gold the sole monetary standard.

1880 John L. Lewis, labor leader, born in Lucas, IA; president, United Mine Workers (1920–60); helped organize CIO, its first president (1935–40) (died 1969).

1893 Omar N. Bradley, World War II general, born in Clark, MO; commanded 12th Army Corps, led ground forces in Normandy invasion; administrator, Veterans Administration (1945–47); Army chief of staff (1948); first permanent chairman, Joint Chiefs of Staff (1949–53) (died 1979).

1896 Isaac Murphy, jockey who rode three Kentucky Derby winners (1884, 1890, 1891), died at about 35; first jockey named to Racing Hall of Fame.

1896 Oscar M. Charleston, one of first great black baseball players, born in Indianapolis; named to Baseball Hall of Fame (died 1954).

1896 Roy E. Harris, composer, born in Lincoln County, OK; among his works were *Third Symphony, Challenge, Folk Song Symphony, Kentucky Spring* (died 1979).

1898 David K.E. Bruce, diplomat, born in Baltimore; ambassador to France (1949–52), to Great Britain (1961–69), to NATO (1974–76); headed American delegation to Paris Vietnam peace talks (1970–71); head, American liaison office in Peking (1973–74) (died 1977).

1909 National Association for the Advancement of Colored People (NAACP) created.

1914 Tex (Gordon) Beneke, tenor saxophonist/band leader, born in Ft. Worth, TX; leader of Glenn Miller band.

1918 Julian S. Schwinger, physicist, born in New York City; shared 1965 Nobel Physics Prize for research in quantum electrodynamics (died 1994).

1934 Bill (William F.) Russell, basketball player/coach, born in Monroe, LA; starred with San Francisco U., Boston Celtics; first black to coach a major professional sports team (Celtics); named to Basketball Hall of Fame.

1934 Export-Import Bank created by executive order to facilitate trade with Russia.

1979 First Susan B. Anthony dollar struck at the Philadelphia mint.

1980 Winter Olympics opened in Lake Placid, NY.

1983 Coal freighter *Marine Electric* sank during storm off Chincoteague, VA; 33 died.

2000 For almost 50 years Charles Schulz's "Peanuts" was daily comic-page reading for millions of Americans; Schulz died at 77.

2001 Bush endorsed a $5.7 billion increase in pay and benefits for U.S. military personnel; to be paid for by shifting funds from other military programs.

2001 After a year in orbit around asteroid 433 Eros, NEAR Shoemaker space probe became first to land on an asteroid.

2004 San Francisco Mayor Gavin Newsom ordered that marriage licenses be issued to homosexuals as well as heterosexuals; over 85 couples promptly took advantage of opportunity; California courts later ruled that mayor overstepped his authority.

2006 As result of two-day snowfall, Central Park, New York City, broke its snow record with 26.9 inches of accumulation.

13

1741 First American magazine, *The American Magazine*, published by John Webbe.

1805 David Dudley Field, attorney, born in Haddam, CT; led in codification of New York laws, worked up code of international law (died 1894).

1812 Samuel P. Lee, Union admiral, born in Fairfax County, VA; saw action on the Mississippi River at New Orleans, Vicksburg (died 1897).

1844 *Louisville* (KY) *Courier* established.

1867 Mississippi repealed many of its restrictions, giving blacks nearly full civil rights.

1870 Joseph C. Lincoln, author, born in Brewster, MA; known for Cape Cod stories (died 1944).

1877 Sidney Smith, cartoonist ("The Gumps"),

born in Bloomington, IL; on staff of *Chicago Tribune* (1911–35) (died 1935).

1885 Bess (Elizabeth V.) Wallace Truman, wife of President Truman, born in Independence, MO (died 1982).

1892 Robert H. Jackson, jurist, born in Spring Creek, PA; Attorney General (1940–41); associate justice, Supreme Court (1941–54); served as American prosecutor at Nuremberg Trials (1945–46) (died 1954).

1892 Grant Wood, artist, born in Anamosa, IA; noted for realistic work (*American Gothic, Dinner for Threshers, Woman with Plants*); often called America's "painter of the soil" (died 1942).

1904 Erwin D. Canham, editor of *Christian Science Monitor* (1941–74), born in Auburn, ME (died 1982).

1910 William B. Shockley, physicist, born in London; shared 1966 Nobel Physics Prize for co-invention of transistor (died 1989).

1918 Patty Berg, golfer who won 83 tournaments in about 30 years, born in Minneapolis.

1919 Tennessee Ernie Ford, entertainer, born in Bristol, TN; starred on television (1955–65); recordings; remembered for song, "16 Tons" (died 1991).

1919 Edward G. Robinson, football coach with more than 400 wins, born in Baker, LA; coached Grambling College 1941–97.

1920 President Wilson accepted the resignation of Secretary of State Robert Lansing, whom he had accused of attempting to usurp presidential powers by calling meetings of the cabinet during his (Wilson's) illness.

1923 Charles E. Yeager, test pilot who broke the sound barrier for first time (October 14, 1947), born in Myra, WV.

2000 Tiger Woods lost first golf tournament after six consecutive prior wins, more consecutive wins than anyone in over 50 years.

2002 Waylon Jennings (1937–2002) died at 64; recorded 60 albums even though he routinely boycotted awards events, even when he was likely to win.

2003 Walt W. Rostow, foreign-policy adviser to JFK and Special Assistant for National Security Affairs to Lyndon Johnson, died at 86; known for strong advocacy of on-going American intervention in Vietnam War.

14

1760 Richard Allen, church leader, born in Philadelphia; a founder, bishop of African

Methodist Episcopal (AME) Church (1816–31); first black ordained as American Methodist minister; founded first Negro church (died 1831).

1790 Thomas Jefferson appointed as first Secretary of State.

1802 John White, legislator, born near Middlesboro, KY; represented Kentucky in House (1835–45), serving as Speaker (1841–43) (died 1845).

1819 Christopher L. Sholes, inventor, born in Mooresburg, PA; invented, perfected typewriter; sold patent rights to Remington (died 1890).

1824 Winfield S. Hancock, Union general, born in Montgomery Square, PA; held key defense positions at Gettysburg; 1880 Democratic presidential candidate (died 1886).

1834 First newspaper published in Hawaii by Lorrin Andrews missionary school; Andrews later became first justice of Hawaii's Supreme Court.

1838 Edwin Ginn, publisher, born in Orland, ME; founder, Ginn & Co. (1867), which specialized in textbooks (died 1914).

1847 Anna Howard Shaw, women's rights activist, born in Newcastle-on-Tyne, England; president, National American Woman's Suffrage Association (1904–15) (died 1919).

1859 Oregon admitted to Union as 33d state.

1859 George W. Ferris, engineer, born in Galesburg, IL; built the Ferris wheel for the Columbian Exposition (1893) (died 1896).

1864 Robert E. Park, sociologist, born in Luzerne County, PA; one of world's leading race relations experts; author (*Race and Culture, Human Communities, Society*) (died 1944).

1864 Union troops occupied Meridian, MS, followed by destruction of railroads, supplies.

1865 Carl T. Anderson, cartoonist ("Henry"), born in Madison, WI (died 1948).

1878 Julius A. Nieuwland, chemist/botanist, born in Hausbeke, Belgium; taught at Notre Dame U. (1904 on); known for synthesis of organic compounds, especially artificial rubber, from acetylene (died 1936).

1882 George Jean Nathan, editor/author, born in Ft. Wayne, IN; most widely read American drama critic of his time; co-editor, *Smart Set* (1914–23); cofounder, editor, *The American Mercury* (1924–30) (died 1958).

1890 William Howard Taft named Solicitor General by President Benjamin Harrison.

1893 Treaty of annexation of Hawaii submitted to Senate, but withdrawn later (December 18) by President Cleveland.

1894 Jack Benny, entertainer, born in Chicago; starred on radio (1932–55), television (1956–65); acted in several movies (died 1974).

1903 Department of Commerce and Labor created, with George R. Cortelyou as the first secretary; divided into two departments in 1913.

1907 Johnny Longden, jockey, born in Wakefield, England; rode more than 6,000 winners in 40 years; including "triple crown" with Count Fleet.

1912 Arizona entered Union as the 48th state.

1913 James R. Hoffa, labor leader, born in Brazil, IN; president, Teamsters Union (1957–71); disappeared mysteriously July 30, 1975.

1919 President Wilson returned from France to seek approval of League of Nations; went back to France March 14 to seek some changes.

1921 Hugh Downs, radio/television personality, born in Akron, OH; headed *Today* show (1962–72).

1929 St. Valentine's Day "massacre" occurred in a Chicago garage when seven gangsters were executed by a rival gang.

1935 Mickey (Mary Kathryn) Wright, golfer who had 82 career victories, born in San Diego, CA; won the LPGA (1958, 1960) and U.S. Women's Open (1958–59, 1961, 1964); named to LPGA Hall of Fame.

1941 Donna E. Shalala, Secretary of Health and Human Services (since 1993), born in Cleveland.

1979 Adolph Dubs, American ambassador to Afghanistan, was shot and killed after being kidnapped in Kabul by Muslim extremists.

1996 Juliet Prowse, dancing star of stage and screen, died at 59.

2000 Crude oil broke $30-a-barrel price for first time since 1991 and the Persian Gulf War.

2000 NEAR Shoemaker became first space probe to go into orbit around an asteroid, 21-mile wide 433 Eros; sent back photographs; was launched February 17, 1996.

2003 Liberalization of Bush anti-abortion policy: Agencies treating those with AIDS in Africa and the Caribbean who receive American government financial assistance may continue to receive it so long as any family planning or abortions provided are not financed with the funds.

15

1643 Swedish settlers arrived at Ft. Christina (now Wilmington), DE.

1726 Abraham Clark, surveyor, born in Roselle, NJ; member of Continental Congress (1776–78, 1779–83); a signer of Declaration of Independence (died 1794).

1730 Thomas Bray, English clergyman, died at 74; organized Anglican Church in Maryland (1699).

1764 St. Louis was founded by Pierre Laclede, a French trader from New Orleans.

1776 Continental Congress named Benjamin Franklin, Catholic Bishop John Carroll, and Samuel Chase to go to Canada to try to enlist its help.

1782 William Miller, clergyman, born in Pittsfield, MA; preached about Second Coming, which he predicted for 1843 or 1844; though his movement died after his failed predictions, they led to formation of Adventist Church (1845) (died 1849).

1797 Henry E. Steinway, piano manufacturer, born in Wolfshagen, Germany; founded Steinway Co. (1853) in New York City (died 1871).

1802 John A. Sutter, California pioneer, born in Kandern, Germany; owned area where gold was discovered (1848); during gold rush, his workmen deserted, his cattle and sheep were stolen, his land was occupied by squatters; went bankrupt, was given $250 monthly pension by California (1864–78) (died 1880).

1804 New Jersey enacted law calling for gradual abolition of slavery, granted freedom to all blacks born in state after July 4.

1809 Cyrus H. McCormick, inventor/manufacturer, born in Rockbridge County, VA; developed first successful reaping machine, founded company which became International Harvester Co. (1848) (died 1884).

1812 Charles L. Tiffany, jeweler, born in Killingly, CT; jewelry manufacturer; cofounder of firm bearing his name (1853) (died 1902).

1820 Susan B. Anthony, suffragist, born in Adams, MA; organized (1869) National Woman Suffrage Association; president, National American Woman Suffrage Association (1892–1900) (died 1906).

1822 Henry B. Whipple, first Episcopal bishop of Minnesota, born in Adams, NY; led successful fight to reform government handling of Indians (died 1901).

1827 Francis A. Pratt, industrialist, born in Woodstock, VT; cofounder, Pratt & Whitney (1864), pioneered in production of machine tools (died 1902).

1829 S(ilas) Weir Mitchell, physician, born in Philadelphia; with Philadelphia Orthopedic Hospital 40 years; did much work on nerves, physiology of cerebellum, toxicology (died 1914).

1834 Henry B. Hyde, founder (1859) of Equitable Life Assurance Co., born in Catskill, NY; company president (1874–99) (died 1899).

1835 Alexander S. Webb, Union general/educator, born in New York City; chiefly responsible for turning back Pickett's charge at Gettysburg; president, City College of New York (1869–1902) (died 1911).

1842 Adhesive postage stamps used for first time in New York City.

1843 Russell H. Conwell, educator, born in South Worthington, MA; revived Philadelphia Baptist Church, began night school (1884), which became Temple College; served as its first president; as lecturer he gave his "Acres of Diamonds" speech more than 6,000 times (died 1925).

1845 Elihu Root, public official, born in Clinton, NY; War Secretary (1899–1904), Secretary of State (1905–09); represented New York in Senate (1909–15); president, Carnegie Endowment for International Peace; awarded 1912 Nobel Peace Prize (died 1937).

1850 Albert B. Cummins, Iowa governor (1902–08) and Senator (1908–26), born in Carmichaels, PA (died 1926).

1858 William H. Pickering, astronomer, born in Boston; discovered a Saturn satellite, predicted existence of and helped locate planet Pluto (1919) (died 1938).

1861 Alfred North Whitehead, philosopher, born in Ramstage, England; author (*Principia Mathematica, Adventures of Ideas, Science and the Modern World*) (died 1947).

1863 James A. Farrell, steel executive, born in New Haven; began work at U.S. Steel at 16, rose to president (1911–32) (died 1943).

1869 U. of Nebraska chartered, opened on September 7, 1871.

1876 Patent issued for manufacture of barbed wire by Joseph F. Glidden, a significant factor in settling the Great Plains.

1879 President Hayes signed act permitting women to practice before Supreme Court.

1882 John Barrymore, actor, born in Philadelphia; starred in many stage and screen plays (*Beau Brummel, Don Juan, Grand Hotel, Dinner at Eight*); his *Hamlet* was considered one of greatest (died 1942).

1884 Alfred C. Gilbert, toymaker, born in Salem, OR; developed Erector set, expanded operations with various kits (died 1961).

1884 Alice H.L. Roosevelt, 23-year-old wife of Theodore Roosevelt, died of Bright's disease in New York City and his mother, Martha B. Roosevelt, died of typhoid fever.

1892 James F. Forrestal, first Secretary of Defense (1947–49), born in Beacon, NY; president, Dillon, Read & Co. (1937–40); Undersecretary of Navy (1940–44), Secretary (1944–47) (died 1949).

1893 Walter Donaldson, composer, born in Brooklyn; wrote many Broadway musicals, hit songs ("My Buddy," "Yes, Sir, That's My Baby," "My Blue Heaven," "Little White Lies") (died 1947).

1897 Earl (Red) Blaik, Army football coach (1941–59), born in Dayton, OH (died 1989).

1898 USS *Maine* mysteriously blown up in Havana harbor with the loss of 260 lives, led to Spanish-American War.

1898 Fritz Zwicky, physicist, born in Varna, Bulgaria; became a Swiss citizen; known for studies of cosmic rays; invented many essentials of jet engines (died 1974).

1905 Harold Arlen, composer, born in Buffalo, NY; wrote many musicals, movies (*The Wizard of Oz*), many hit songs ("Stormy Weather," "That Old Black Magic") (died 1986).

1911 Leonard F. Woodcock, labor leader/diplomat, born in Providence; president, United Auto Workers (1970–77); representative, later ambassador, to China (1977–81).

1916 Ian K. Ballantine, publisher, born in New York City; head of Bantam Books (1945–52), pioneer in publishing paperbacks; president, Ballantine Books (1952–75) (died 1995).

1917 Wyoming enacted a prohibition law.

1929 James R. Schlesinger, public official, born in New York City; chairman, Atomic Energy Commission (1971–73); director, CIA (1973); Secretary of Defense (1973–76), Secretary of Energy (1977–79).

1933 Assassination attempt made on President-elect Franklin Roosevelt in Miami by Giuseppe Zangara; Chicago Mayor Anton J. Cermak fatally wounded; Zangara was convicted, electrocuted March 20, in Raiford, FL.

1934 Civil Works Emergency Relief Act signed for a civil works and direct relief program through 1935; about 2.5 million unemployed were assisted before program was returned to state and local agencies.

1936 President Franklin Roosevelt proposed a conference for Latin America peace keeping; scheduled for Buenos Aires in December.

1953 Tenley Albright of Newton Centre, MA, became first American woman to win world figure skating title.

1958 Two-day blizzard in northeastern United States resulted in 171 deaths.

1961 Maribel Vinson (Owen), champion American figure skater nine times in 1928–37 and U.S. pairs champion five times in that period, died in a plane crash at 50.

1978 Leon Spinks defeated Muhammad Ali in 15 rounds in Las Vegas to win world heavyweight boxing championship; Ali reversed the decision in September.

1997 Fourteen-year-old Tara Lipinski became the youngest American national figure skating champion.

2000 Intel announced new computer chip with 1.5 gigahertz operating speed, nearly doubling any currently in production.

2002 Howard K. Smith (1914–2002), died at 87 of pneumonia and congestive heart failure; foreign correspondent for radio who made the transition to decades of television work with great success; although considered generally a political liberal, he was a strong supporter of doing whatever necessary to successfully win the war in Vietnam.

16

1724 Christopher Gadsden, colonial leader, born in Charleston, SC; member, Continental Congress (1774–76); general, Continental Army, leading South Carolina troops (1776–78) (died 1805).

1783 First proposal for a new federal government appeared in "A Dissertation on the Political Union of the 13 United States of North America" by Pelatiah Webster.

1786 James Monroe and Elizabeth Kortright were married in New York City.

1804 Stephen Decatur and 80 officers and men in a daring raid recaptured the *Philadelphia*, which had been held by Tripolitans in Tripoli Harbor.

1812 Henry Wilson, Vice President (1873–75), born in Farmington, NH; represented Massachusetts in Senate (1855–73); a founder, Free Soil (1848) and Republican parties (died 1875).

1825 Crosby S. Noyes, journalist, born in Minot, ME; editor, *Washington Star* (1861–1908) (died 1908).

1838 Henry Brooks Adams, historian/educator, born in Boston; initiated summer teaching at Harvard; editor, *North American Review* (1870–77); author (*The Education of Henry Adams*) (died 1918).

1840 Henry Watterson, editor, born in Washington, DC; editor, *Louisville Courier-Journal* (1868–1919); considered one of America's greatest editors; represented Kentucky in House (1876–77) (died 1921).

1843 Henry M. Leland, pioneer automaker, born in Danville, VT; founder, president, Cadillac Motor Co. (1902–17); president, Lincoln Motor Co. (1917–22); developed eight-cylinder motor (1914); co-developer of electric starter (1911) (died 1932).

1852 Charles Taze Russell, religious leader, born in Pittsburgh; founder, International Bible Students Association, which later became Jehovah's Witnesses; founder, *The Watchtower* (died 1916).

1860 Samuel S. Fels, soap manufacturer, born in Yanceyville, NC; partner with brother of Fels-Naphtha, president (1914–50) (died 1950).

1861 Texas state troops seized federal arsenal in San Antonio.

1862 Ft. Donelson (TN) and 14,000 Confederate troops under Gen. Simon Buckner fell to Union forces under General Grant; victory brought Grant to national attention.

1880 Charles T. Fisher, an organizer (1908) and administrator (1908–34) of Fisher Body Corp., born in Sandusky, OH (died 1963).

1884 Van Wyck Brooks, author/critic, born in Plainfield, NJ; author (*The Flowering of New England, New England Indian Summer*) (died 1963).

1898 Katherine Cornell, actress, born in Berlin to American parents; starred in many stage plays (*Barretts of Wimpole Street, A Bill of Divorcement, Candide*) (died 1974).

1901 Wayne King, musician/orchestra leader known as the "Waltz King," born in Savannah, IL (died 1985).

1903 Edgar Bergen, entertainer who gained fame as a ventriloquist (Charlie McCarthy), born in Chicago (died 1978).

1904 George F. Kennan, diplomat, born in Milwaukee; influential in devising Russian containment policy; ambassador to Russia (1951).

1915 South Carolina established statewide prohibition.

1938 President Franklin Roosevelt signed Agricultural Adjustment Administration Act "for the conservation of national soil resources" and to replace the 1933 Act which had been declared unconstitutional by the Supreme Court.

1959 John McEnroe, tennis star of 1970/80s, born in New York City; won Wimbledon singles title three times, U.S. Open title four times.

1970 Joe Frazier knocked out Jimmy Ellis in fifth round in New York City to win vacant world heavyweight boxing championship.

1988 Firestone Tire & Rubber Co. agreed to sell 75 percent of its tire operations to Bridgestone Corp. for $1 billion; said to be largest Japanese investment in American manufacturing.

1992 William Schuman, founding president of Lincoln Center and president, Juilliard School of Music, died at 81.

1995 Margaret Wade, basketball coach (Delta State in 1970s) and first woman named to Basketball Hall of Fame, died at 82.

2000 Chemist Andreas Toupadakis resigned from Lawrence Livermore National Laboratory to protest development of nuclear weapons; laboratory responded it did much other work as well.

2000 Genetic Savings and Clone of Texas became first company to provide cloned animals for pet owners as replacements for their dead animals.

2001 U.S. and British aircraft destroyed Iraq radar stations in retaliation for recent "provocations."

2005 After teams locked out players for 153 days and the two sides were unable to come to terms, the National Hockey League cancelled the entire season. Though fourth major sport in U.S., interest already was in decline as television coverage had slipped from regular networks to cable.

17

1621 Miles Standish made a captain with military authority over Plymouth Colony.

1692 Thomas Neale received royal patent to establish colonial post offices for 21 years.

1708 William Rittenhouse, Mennonite clergyman and industrialist, died at 64; chosen first pastor of Germantown, PA, church and first American Mennonite bishop (1703); built first American paper mill (1690).

1718 Matthew Tilghman, member of Continental Congress (1774–76), born in Queen Anne County, MD; did not sign Declaration of Independence because he was called home to help draft first Maryland constitution (died 1790).

1740 John Sullivan, colonial leader, born in Somersworth, NH; Revolutionary War general (served at Trenton, Princeton); member, Continental Congress (1774, 1780–81); "president" (governor) of New Hampshire (1786–89) (died 1795).

1801 House on 36th ballot elected Thomas Jefferson president, with 10 states voting for him, four for Aaron Burr, who became vice president; votes of two states were nullified when their delegations divided equally; Jefferson and Burr had each received 73 electoral votes.

1805 New Orleans incorporated as a city.

1807 William L. Dayton, public official, born in Basking Ridge, NJ; represented New Jersey in Senate (1845–51); was first Republican vice presidential candidate (1856); ambassador to France (1861–64) (died 1864).

1817 United States formally ratified Treaty of Ghent ending the War of 1812.

1837 Francis J. Herron, Union general, born in Pittsburgh; youngest major general in war; awarded Congressional Medal of Honor (died 1902).

1843 (Aaron) Montgomery Ward, merchant, born in Chatham, NJ; cofounder with George F. Thorne of mail order dry goods business in Chicago (1827); began with one page catalog of 30 items, capital of $2,400 (died 1913).

1845 Charles McBurney, surgeon, born in Roxbury, MA; pioneer in antiseptic surgery, an authority on appendectomy (died 1913).

1855 Congress authorized construction of telegraph line from Mississippi River to the Pacific Ocean.

1856 Frederick E. Ives, inventor, born in Litchfield, CT; invented various photographic development processes; his half-tone process (1886) is essentially unchanged (died 1937).

1857 Samuel S. McClure, editor, born in County Antrim, Ireland; founder (1884) of first American newspaper syndicate; founder (1893), editor, *McClure's Magazine* (died 1949).

1864 Confederate submarine *R.I. Hunley* sank Union ship, USS *Housatonic* and sank with her; the 35-ft. submarine was propelled by a screw worked from the inside by eight men.

1865 Columbia, SC, captured by Union forces; city was burned but cause of the fire never determined; Charleston evacuated by Confederates.

1866 David F. Houston, educator/public official, born in Monroe, NC; headed several universities (1902–16); Secretary of Agriculture

(1913–20), of Treasury (1920–21); chairman Federal Reserve Board (died 1940).

1872 William Duane, biophysicist, born in Philadelphia; with Harvard U. (1917–35), developed methods, apparatus for using x-rays and radium in medicine (died 1935).

1874 Thomas J. Watson, industrialist, born in Campbell, NY; president, Computing-Tabulating Recording Co., which became International Business Machines (IBM) (1924); IBM president, chairman (1924–49) (died 1956).

1879 Dorothy Canfield Fisher, author (*The Brimming Cup*, *The Deepening Stream*, *The Bent Twig*), born in Lawrence, KS (died 1958).

1888 Otto Stern, physicist, born in Sohrau, Germany; awarded 1943 Nobel Physics Prize for detecting magnetic momentum of protons; developed molecular beams as tool for studying structure of molecules (died 1969).

1889 H(aroldson) H. Hunt, oil/natural gas producer, born in Vandalia, IL; became one of world's richest men (died 1974).

1893 State University of Montana established.

1895 Charles T. Jay, World War II admiral and Allied naval commander in Korean War, born in St. Louis (died 1956).

1902 Marian Anderson, opera/concert singer, born in Philadelphia; one of world's greatest contraltos; first black to perform in major opera role (died 1993).

1906 Three men were arrested in Colorado for murder of former Idaho Gov. Frank Steuenberg; one was William D. Haywood, head of Industrial Workers of the World.

1908 Walter (Red) Barber, renowned baseball announcer (1934–66), born in Columbus, MS (died 1992).

1909 Geronimo, Apache chief who led raids against the Americans and Mexicans, died at about 80.

1913 New York Armory Show brought modern art to the United States.

1923 A(lden) W. Clausen, president of World Bank (1981–86), born in Hamilton, IL; chief executive officer, Bank of America (1970–81).

1925 Hal (Harold R.) Holbrook, actor, born in Cleveland; best known for portrayals of Mark Twain.

1936 Jim Brown, football great, born in St. Simons, GA; starred with Syracuse U., Cleveland Browns (1957–65); rushing record of 12,312 yards stood for 20 years.

1957 Fire in a Warrenton, MO, home for aged killed 72 persons.

1963 Michael Jordan, college/professional star basketball player, born in New York City; one of greatest basketball players of all time.

1964 Supreme Court ruled that congressional districts should have equal populations.

1988 Two executives of Beech-Nut Co. convicted of violating federal law by intentionally distributing bogus apple juice intended for babies.

1988 Lt. Col. William R. Higgins, Marine officer, kidnapped in Beirut while on temporary duty as chief of a UN international truce observer group.

2000 Microsoft's Windows 2000 officially released to the public.

2002 U.S. government took over responsibility for airport security; private security agents currently working to be retrained or replaced; U.S. citizenship now a prerequisite.

18

1688 Germantown (PA) Mennonites adopted resolutions against slavery, the earliest known protests against the practice in America.

1735 *Flora, or Hob in the Well* was performed in Charleston, the first recorded opera performance in America.

1783 James Biddle, naval officer in War of 1812, born in Philadelphia; negotiated treaty between United States and China (1846) (died 1848).

1792 Jabez Gorham, silversmith, born in Providence; founded Gorham Manufacturing Co. (died 1869).

1793 Supreme Court in *Chisholm v. Georgia* ruled that a state could be sued by citizens of another state; this led to 11th Amendment.

1795 George Peabody, financier, born in South Danvers, MA; endowed Peabody Institutes in Baltimore and Peabody, MA, museums at Harvard and Yale, and Peabody Education Fund to advance education in the South (died 1869).

1797 John Bell, legislator, born in Nashville; represented Tennessee in House (1827–41), serving as Speaker (1834–35), and Senate (1848–60); 1860 Constitutional Union Party presidential candidate (won in Tennessee, Kentucky, Virginia) (died 1869).

1804 Elizur Wright, insurance reformer, born in South Canaan, CT; led fight to require insurance companies to establish adequate untouchable reserves with which to pay claims; called the father of legal reserve life insurance (died 1885).

1805 Louis M. Goldsborough, Union naval officer, born in Washington, DC; commanded fleet that captured Roanoke Island, destroyed Confederate fleet (1862) (died 1877).

1817 Lewis A. Armistead, Confederate general, born in New Bern, NC; killed in Pickett's charge at Gettysburg July 3, 1863.

1818 Simon Girty, the "great renegade," died at 77; American who led British and Indian raiding parties along northern, western frontiers; fled to Canada (1796).

1832 Octave Chanute, pioneer aviator, born in Paris; experimented with gliders, designed biplane glider; his data of value to Wright brothers (died 1910).

1848 Louis C. Tiffany, painter/designer who developed Tiffany glass, born in New York City (died 1933).

1861 Jefferson Davis inaugurated as provisional president of Confederacy in Montgomery, AL, the first Confederate capital; re-elected in October under the Confederate constitution; inaugurated February 22, 1862.

1862 Charles M. Schwab, steel industry leader, born in Williamsburg, PA; president, Carnegie Steel Co. (1897–1901); first president, U.S. Steel (1901–03); organized, headed Bethlehem Steel Co. (1903–13), board chairman (1913–39); director of shipbuilding in World War I (died 1939).

1865 Charleston, SC, captured by Union troops.

1869 The "Chicago Protest" of Episcopal Church launched by Charles E. Cheney, who helped organize and head Reformed Episcopal Church; brought to trial for heresy, deposed; refused to leave Christ Church, Chicago (where he served 1860–1916); court held that church property belonged to parish, not diocese; Cheney was bishop of Reformed Church (1878–1916).

1884 O(scar) O. McIntyre, journalist, born in Plattsburg, MO; wrote syndicated column, "New York Day by Day" (died 1938).

1885 Richard S. Edwards, World War II admiral who was vice commander of American fleet (1942–46), born in Philadelphia (died 1956).

1890 Adolf Menjou, screen actor, born in Pittsburgh; many supporting roles (*The Front Page, A Farewell to Arms, A Star Is Born*) (died 1963).

1892 Wendell L. Willkie, lawyer/industrialist, born in Elwood, IN; general counsel, president, Commonwealth & Southern Corp. (1933–40); 1940 Republican presidential candidate; author (*One World*) (died 1944).

1896 Dimitri Mitropoulos, conductor, born in Athens; conductor (Minneapolis 1937–49); musical director (New York Philharmonic 1950–58) (died 1960).

1898 Luis Munoz-Marin, Puerto Rican leader, born in San Juan, PR; founder of Popular Democratic Party; Puerto Rico governor (1948–64) (died 1980).

1915 Oregon enacted statewide prohibition, effective January 1, 1916.

1922 Helen Gurley Brown, editor/author, born in Green Forest, AR; editor, *Cosmopolitan* (1965–96); author (*Sex and the Single Girl*).

1924 Edwin Denby, Navy Secretary, resigned because of his involvement in the Teapot Dome scandal.

1931 Toni (Chloe A.M.) Morrison, educator/author, born in Lorain, OH; awarded 1993 Nobel Literature Prize.

1939 Golden Gate Exposition opened in San Francisco; closed October 29.

1942 U.S. destroyer *Truxton* and cargo ship *Pollux* ran aground and sank off Newfoundland, 204 men lost.

1954 John Travolta, screen actor, born in Englewood, NJ; starred in many films (*Saturday Night Fever, Urban Cowboy*).

1976 Pesticides containing mercury were banned.

1995 The NAACP named Myrtle Evers Williams, widow of slain civil rights leader Medger Evers, as chairman, replacing William Gibson.

1998 Harry Caray, popular Chicago Cubs baseball announcer for more than 50 years, died at 78.

2000 New York Stock Exchange trading of Aurora Foods, Inc., stopped. Manufacturer of Duncan Hines cake mixes and Aunt Jemima Syrup, among other products, being investigated due to accounting practices; four top executives resign.

2001 Racing legend Dale Earnhardt died at 49; killed in accident during Daytona 500.

2001 Career FBI agent Robert Hanssen, a supervisor in counterintelligence, arrested on charges of being Russian spy for 15 years.

2005 "Class Action Fairness Act" signed into law; transferred large percentage of class-action lawsuits to an exclusively federal jurisdiction, thereby eliminating the ability to choose whichever individual state offered the greatest opportunity for large cash awards.

19

1674 Treaty of Westminster restored the New York Province to England from Dutch occupation; Dutch formally surrendered to Sir Edmund Andros.

1766 William Dunlap, painter/playwright, born in Perth Amboy, NJ; known as the father of American drama (*Leicester, Andre, Father of an Only Child*); founder, National Academy of Design (died 1839).

1792 John Locke, scientist/inventor, born in Lempster, NH; investigated terrestrial magnetism and electricity; invented surveying instruments and an electro-magnetic chronograph to determine longitude (died 1856).

1802 Leonard Bacon, Congregational clergyman, born in Detroit; sometimes called the Congregational "pope"; served First Church, New Haven (1825–66) (died 1881).

1807 Aaron Burr arrested in Alabama on charge of forming an expedition against Spanish territory; charge later changed to treason.

1819 Lydia E. Pinkham, patent medicine manufacturer, born in Lynn, MA; developed a herb medicine ("Vegetable Compound") to remedy "woman's weakness" (died 1883).

1821 Francis P. Blair, Jr., legislator, born in Lexington, KY; represented Missouri in House (1857–59, 1860–64) and Senate (1871–73); 1868 Democratic vice presidential candidate (died 1875).

1855 William Crozier, Army officer/inventor, born in Carrollton, OH; co-inventor of disappearing gun carriage; chief of Army ordinance (1901–17) (died 1942).

1866 Thomas J.J. See, astronomer/mathematician, born in Montgomery City, MO; established wave theory of solid bodies and the cosmic ray; headed naval observatories (Flagstaff, AZ; Mare Island) (died 1962).

1881 Kansas adopted a prohibition law.

1884 Sixty tornadoes, most of them in the South, killed 800 persons.

1887 Oregon passed first law recognizing Labor Day as a holiday; begun by Knights of Labor in New York City in 1882.

1908 Statewide prohibition enacted in Mississippi.

1911 Merle Oberon, screen actress (*Wuthering Heights*), born in Tasmania (died 1979).

1912 Stan Kenton, musician, born in Wichita, KS; conducted own band (1941–79), featuring screaming "walls of brass" (died 1979).

1915 American steamer, *Evelyn*, sunk by a German mine off Borkum Island.

1916 Eddie (George E.) Arcaro, jockey, born in Cincinnati; rode 4,779 winners in 24,000+ races, winning Kentucky Derby five times, Preakness and Belmont six times each; rode two Triple Crown winners (*Whirlaway, Citation*) (died 1997).

1917 Carson McCullers, author, born in Columbus, GA; wrote popular novels (*The Heart Is a Lonely Hunter, A Member of the Wedding, The Ballad of the Sad Café*) (died 1967).

1924 Lee Marvin, screen actor, born in New York City; starred on television, several films (*Cat Ballou, Ship of Fools*) (died 1987).

1942 President Franklin Roosevelt by executive order authorized War Department to evacuate 112,000 West Coast Japanese, two thirds of them American citizens, to relocation centers; terminated January 2, 1945.

1945 Month-long battle for Iwo Jima began.

1986 Senate by a vote of 83–11 ratified the 1948 United Nations treaty outlawing genocide.

1988 Pope John Paul II in an encyclical letter condemned rivalry between the superpowers which subjected poor nations to imperialistic "structures of sin" that deny them freedom and development.

1996 Charles O. Finley, owner of the Oakland A's baseball team (1960–80), died at 77.

1997 Leo Rosten, writer on Jewish culture and language, died at 88.

2001 At 87, Stanley Kramer passed away; made popular films for decades; nine Oscar nominations, but no victories.

2003 Johnny Paycheck died of respiratory failure; his country music tale of worker resentment, "Take This Job and Shove It," tapped a widely shared sentiment; had a career repeatedly burdened and hurt by run-ins with the law.

20

1528 Pamphillio de Narvaez, Spanish soldier/explorer, sailed from Havana for Florida; landed at Tampa Bay April 14 for overland journey to Mexico.

1620 Thomas Weston, a London ironmonger, and John Peirce, a London clothmaker, received patent from the Virginia Co. and persuaded the Separatists (who also had a patent) to join with them.

1726 William Prescott, Revolutionary commander, born in Groton, MA; led troops at Battle of Bunker Hill (died 1795).

1772 Isaac Chauncey, War of 1812 naval officer, born in Black Rock, CT; commanded naval forces of Lakes Erie and Ontario (1812–15) (died 1840).

1781 Robert Morris named head of newly-created Department of Finance, responsible to Congress, in effort to correct colonies' worsening financial state.

1794 Debates of the Senate were opened to the public.

1803 Henry Stanberry, Attorney General (1866–68), born in New York City; chief counsel for President Andrew Johnson in his impeachment trial (1868) (died 1881).

1805 Angelina Emily Grimké, social reformer, born in Charleston; with sister, Sarah, became Quakers, took active role in abolitionist, women's rights movements (died 1879).

1809 Supreme Court in *United States v. Peters* sustained power of national over state authority.

1811 Senate refused to recharter Bank of the United States, leading to creation of many local banks.

1815 U.S. Frigate *Constitution* captured two British sloops off Lisbon.

1829 Joseph Jefferson, actor, born in Philadelphia; best known for his role of Rip Van Winkle (died 1905).

1831 Patrick J. Ryan, Catholic archbishop (St. Louis 1883–84, Philadelphia 1884–1911), born in Thurles, Ireland (died 1911).

1840 Congress outlawed practice of dueling.

1844 Leonidas Merritt, mining prospector, born in Chautauqua County, NY; discovered Mesabi iron ore deposits in Minnesota (1890) (died 1926).

1874 Mary Garden, operatic soprano, born in Aberdeen, Scotland; starred with Chicago Civic Opera (1910–31) (died 1967).

1893 Russel Crouse, playwright/librettist, born in Findley, OH; collaborated with Howard Lindsay (*Life with Father, Anything Goes, Call Me Madam*) and with Rogers and Hammerstein (*The Sound of Music*) (died 1966).

1901 Rene J. Dubos, microbiologist, born in St. Brice, France; pioneer in study of antibiotics and tuberculosis (died 1982).

1901 Louis I. Kahn, architect, born in Saaremia, Estonia; influenced late 20th century architecture (Yale Art Gallery; Salk Institute, LaJolla, CA) (died 1974).

1902 Ansel Adams, photographer, born in San Francisco; a foremost photographer, specializing in landscapes, nature (died 1984).

1905 Supreme Court in *Jackson v. Massachusetts* held that states have the police power to enact a compulsory vaccination law.

1905 Mine disaster in Virginia City, AL, killed 116 persons.

1907 Senate by vote of 42–28 confirmed election of Reed Smoot of Utah, defeating proposal to unseat him because of membership in Mormon Church.

1915 Panama Pacific International Exposition opened in San Francisco; closed December 4.

1927 Sidney Poitier, screen actor, born in Miami; starred in several films (*Porgy and Bess, The Defiant Ones, Guess Who's Coming to Dinner*).

1942 Phil(ip A.) Esposito, a leading hockey player, born in Sault Ste Marie, Canada; National Hockey League most valuable player (1969–74) and league's leading scorer (1971–74).

1946 Congress passed the 1946 Employment Act which set up a Council of Economic Advisors to study economic trends and to recommend to the President policies to alleviate the negative effect of business cycles.

1962 Lt. Col. John H. Glenn, Jr., became first American to orbit earth, circling it three times in four hours, 55 minutes in a *Friendship 7* capsule.

1982 Construction began on $20 million renovation of Carnegie Hall in New York City.

1996 Former U.S. Representative Kweisi Mfume sworn in as president and chief executive officer of NAACP.

2000 Weekend meeting ends in Carmel, California, of three dozen top health leaders from around world; discussed ways to make modern Western medicines economically feasible in third world.

2002 Colossal U.S. government agencies' misjudgment — in retrospect: massive American bankrupt business Enron Corp. received $544 million in loans from Overseas Private Investment Corp., plus $204 million political-risk insurance; $675 million went to Enron-related companies from Export-Import Bank. Figures from agency officials and congressional investigators. Aid began in 1992.

2002 Willie Thrower, dead of a heart attack at 71; on October 18, 1953, he was the first black quarterback to play in a pro game; following year

and for remainder of career played with the Canadian Football League.

2005 Hunter S. Thompson dead at 67; inventor of "gonzo journalism," which blurred line between fact and fiction, reality and imagination.

21

1787 Continental Congress called for a meeting in May in Philadelphia "for the sole and express purpose of revising the Articles of Confederation."

1792 House passed Presidential Succession Act, which provided that in case of removal, death, resignation, or disability of both the president and vice president, the president pro tempore of the Senate would succeed; if there was no president pro tempore, the House Speaker would succeed; the Senate had previously passed the measure which was in effect until 1886.

1807 Martin Van Buren and Hannah Hoe were married in Catskill, NY.

1821 Charles Scribner, publisher, born in New York City; cofounder of family publishing firm (1846); founder, publisher *Scribner's Monthly* (1870) (died 1871).

1822 Oliver W. Gibbs, chemist, born in New York City; laid foundation for American chemistry; pioneer in spectroscopy; a founder (1863), president (1895–1900), National Academy of Sciences (died 1908).

1848 John Quincy Adams, former president, suffered cerebral stroke on the House floor, where he had been representing Massachusetts; died two days later at 80.

1855 Alice F. Palmer, pioneer educator, born in Colesville, NY; president, Wellesley College (1882–87), dean of women, U. of Chicago (1892–95) (died 1902).

1863 Rudolph J. Schaefer, brewery executive, born in New York City; with family-owned, F&M Schaefer Brewing Co. (1882–1923); introduced first bottled beer (1891) (died 1923).

1867 Otto H. Kahn, banker/art patron, born in Mannheim, Germany; with William K. Vanderbilt bought (1907) financially-troubled Metropolitan Opera; later became sole owner, serving as president or chairman (1911–31); probably nation's greatest art patron (died 1934).

1868 President Andrew Johnson removed Edwin M. Stanton as Secretary of War, leading to presidential impeachment proceedings; motion to impeach made by Rep. John Covode of Pennsylvania.

1885 Washington Monument dedicated in Washington, DC.

1907 W(ystan) H. Auden, poet/playwright, born in York, England; librettist for Stravinsky's *Rake's Progress* (died 1973).

1917 Women's suffrage went into effect in Ohio.

1922 American dirigible *Roma* exploded over Hampton, VA; 34 were killed.

1927 Erma Bombeck, author/humorist, born in Dayton, OH; syndicated columnist and television commentator (died 1996).

1936 Barbara Jordan, legislator who was first black woman to serve in Texas legislature, born in Houston; represented state in House (1972–78) (died 1996).

1965 Malcolm X, black leader, was assassinated in New York City by Black Muslims.

1971 Tornadoes in Mississippi delta area caused 110 deaths.

1972 President Nixon began week-long visit to China, the first president to visit a nation not recognized by United States.

1988 The Rev. Jimmy Swaggart, television evangelist, confessed to sins before his congregation of 8,000 in Baton Rouge, LA; said he would absent himself from his pulpit for "an indeterminate time."

2000 American Academy of Science heard evidence that nicotine patches can help at least partially with Alzheimer's and Parkinson's; evidence hinted at impact on certain psychiatric problems such as depression and schizophrenia.

2001 In narrow 5–4 decision, Supreme Court decided that the federal Americans with Disabilities Act did not give state employees the right to sue over discrimination.

2002 U.S. reduced recommended age to begin yearly mammograms for women by a decade; now age 40 urged.

2006 Lawrence Summers announced he would resign as president of Harvard University effective at the end of the current academic term; had aroused passionate opposition from much of staff for ideological reasons and because of how he handled administrative matters.

22

1732 George Washington, first president (1789–97), born in Westmoreland County, VA; commanded American forces in Revolution (died 1799).

1778 Rembrandt Peale, artist, born in Bucks County, PA; painter of portraits, historical scenes (died 1860).

1784 *Empress of China* sailed from New York to Canton, opening trade with China.

1819 James Russell Lowell, author/poet, born in Cambridge; wrote *The Vision of Sir Launfall*; a founder, editor, *Atlantic Monthly* (1857–61); minister to Spain (1877–80), to Great Britain (1880–85) (died 1891).

1819 Under Adams-Onis Treaty, Spain ceded Florida to the United States after long negotiations; ratifications exchanged February 22, 1821.

1820 William F. Channing, inventor, born in Boston; co-inventor of electric fire alarm telegraph system (died 1901).

1831 William N. Byers, surveyor/pioneer, born in Madison County, OH; founder (1859), editor, *Rocky Mountain News*, first Colorado newspaper; mineral byerite named for him (died 1903).

1838 Anson P. Stokes, financier, born in New York City; partner in Phelps Dodge & Co.; successful in New York City building construction, management; a founder, Metropolitan Museum of Art (died 1913).

1855 Pennsylvania State College chartered as Farmers' High School.

1857 Frank L. Stanton, lyricist, born in Charleston, SC; remembered for "Mighty Lak a Rose" and "Going Home" (died 1927).

1865 Union troops captured Wilmington, NC.

1865 Tennessee ratified its constitution; provided for abolition of slavery.

1871 George O. Smith, geologist, born in Hodgdon, ME; with Geological Survey (1896–1930), director (1907–30); chairman, Federal Power Commission (1930–33) (died 1944).

1873 Samuel Seabury, attorney, born in New York City; conducted investigation of New York City administration (1931–32), led to resignation of Mayor Jimmy Walker (died 1958).

1874 William J. Klem, baseball umpire, born in Rochester, NY; first umpire named to Baseball Hall of Fame (died 1951).

1877 Bedloe's (now Liberty) Island in New York Harbor approved by Congress as site for Statue of Liberty.

1879 Frank W. Woolworth opened his first 5-and-10 cents store in Utica, NY; only lasted a short time, moved to Pennsylvania.

1892   Edna St. Vincent Millay, poet/playwright, born in Rockland, ME; poet ("The Harp Weaver," "Wine From These Grapes," "Huntsman, What Quarry?"); playwright (*The Lamp and the Bell, Aria da Capo*) (died 1950).

1892   David Dubinsky, labor leader, born in Brest-Litovsk, Poland; president, International Ladies Garment Workers (ILGWU) (1932–66); a founder, American Labor Party (1936) and Americans for Democratic Action (1947) (died 1982).

1896   Nacio Herb Brown, composer ("Singin' in the Rain," "You Were Meant for Me"), born in Deming, NJ (died 1964).

1900   Paul Kollsman, aeronautical engineer, born in Freudenstadt, Germany; invented the altimeter (died 1982).

1901   Charles E. Whittaker, associate justice, Supreme Court (1957–62), born near Troy, KS (died 1973).

1904   Peter Hurd, painter, born in Roswell, NM; did portrait of President Lyndon Johnson, who called it "the ugliest thing I ever saw" (died 1984).

1907   Robert Young, screen and television actor, born in Chicago; noted for role of Dr. Marcus Welby (died 1998).

1926   (Nelson) Bunker Hunt, financier, born in El Dorado, AR.

1932   Ted (Edward M.) Kennedy, legislator, born in Brookline, MA; represented Massachusetts in Senate since 1963.

1955   Congress received a special message from President Eisenhower calling for the expenditure of $101 billion over 10 years for interstate highways.

1973   China and the United States agreed to set up permanent liaison offices in each other's country.

1983   United States government purchased town of Times Beach, MO, for $33 million because dioxin level in soil posed threat to the health of 2,400 residents.

1988   Navy Secretary James H. Webb, Jr., resigned citing differences with Defense Secretary Frank C. Carlucci over the Navy's budget and Defense Department management; William L. Ball, III, later nominated for post.

1997   Albert Shanker, longtime president of American Federation of Teachers, died at 68.

2002   Chuck Jones (1912–2002) dies; pioneer animator, who did more than 300 animated films and won three Oscars (one for Lifetime Achievement) in the process; did sustained work first for Warner Bros., then MGM, and finally for his own production company.

23

1665   Col. Richard Nicolls, head of a British commission, confiscated all properties of Dutch West India Co. in New York area as result of second Anglo-Dutch war, which began December 1664.

1680   Jean Baptiste LeMoyne, Sieur de Bienville, colonial governor, born in Longueuol, Canada; governed Louisiana colony (1701–12, 1718–26, 1733–43); founder of New Orleans (died 1768).

1744   Josiah Quincy, colonial leader, born in Boston; with John Adams, he defended British soldiers accused in Boston Massacre, winning acquittals for most (died 1775).

1751   Henry Dearborn, soldier/public official, born in Hampton, NH; served in Revolution (Ticonderoga, Saratoga, Yorktown); Secretary of War (1801–09), during which he ordered a fortification at "Chicago," which began as Fort Dearborn; minister to Portugal (1822–24) (died 1829).

1778   Baron Friedrich von Steuben arrived at Valley Forge and began to organize and discipline the troops.

1781   George Taylor, Irish-born colonial leader, died at 65; member of Continental Congress from Pennsylvania (1776–77), signer of Declaration of Independence.

1784   Rhode Island General Assembly authorized freeing of slaves; declared all blacks, mulattoes free who were born in state after March 1.

1787   Emma Willard, educator, born in Berlin, CT; pioneer in higher education for women; founder, Middlebury Seminary (1814) and other New York schools to prepare women for college (died 1870).

1823   James G. Batterson, insurance executive, born in Bloomfield, CT; founder, president, Travelers Insurance Co. (1863–1901), first American accident insurance company (died 1901).

1832   John H. Vincent, religious educator, born in Tuscaloosa, AL; helped organize school for Methodist Sunday School teachers; Methodist bishop (1888–1904); a founder, Chautauqua Assembly (1874) (died 1920).

1835   Thomas W. Phillips, petroleum industry executive, born near Mt. Jackson, PA; an early developer of Pennsylvania oil fields; represented Pennsylvania in House (1893–97); member, U.S. Industrial Commission (1878–1902) (died 1912).

1836 Siege of the Alamo in San Antonio began with 27-year-old Col. William B. Travis in command of 145 men facing 6,000–7,000 Mexicans; ended March 6.

1844 James F. Babcock, chemist who established 3 percent limit in defining intoxicating liquors, born in Boston; Massachusetts assayer of liquors; invented a fire extinguisher (died 1897).

1846 William Horlick, originator of malted milk, born in Ruardeen, England; headed company named for him (1883–1936) (died 1936).

1847 Zachary Taylor led 4,600 American troops to victory over Mexicans at Buena Vista, ending fighting in northern Mexico; Americans had about 600 casualties, Mexicans under Gen. Antonio Santa Ana 1,600 casualties, 1,900 missing.

1861 Henry B. Wilson, World War I admiral, born in Camden, NJ; commanded Atlantic patrol forces and naval forces in France (1917–18); commander-in-chief, Atlantic Fleet (1919–21); superintendent, Naval Academy (1921–25) (died 1954).

1861 President-elect Lincoln arrived in Washington, DC, after secret night trip because of a warning of an assassination plot in Baltimore.

1868 William E.B. DuBois, editor/civil rights leader, born in Great Barrington, MA; a founder, NAACP and editor of its journal, *Crisis* (1909–32); later joined Communist Party, moved to China (died 1963).

1870 Mississippi was readmitted to the Union, but continued under reconstruction government until 1875.

1871 George T. Moore, botanist, born in Indianapolis; in charge of botany at Woods Hole (MA) Marine Laboratory (1909–19), discovered way to prevent water pollution by algae, certain bacteria (died 1956).

1880 Roy D. Chapin, auto manufacturer, born in Lansing, MI; president, Hudson Auto Co. (1910–23, 1933–36), board chairman (1923–32); Secretary of Commerce (1932–33) (died 1936).

1881 William S. Farish, oil industry leader, born in Mayersville, MS; founder (1917), president (1922–32), Humble Oil Co. (died 1942).

1882 U. of North Dakota founded at Grand Forks.

1884 Casimir Funk, biochemist, born in Warsaw; known for his work in vitamins and hormones (died 1967).

1886 Charles M. Hall, after a year's research for a solvent to purify aluminum, found it in molten cryolite (sodium aluminum flouride); formed company which became Aluminum Company of America.

1889 John G. Winant, public official/diplomat, born in New York City; first chairman, Social Security Board (1935–37); director, International Labor Organization (1939–41); ambassador to Great Britain (1941–46) (died 1947).

1902 Ellen Stone, American missionary captured by Turkish brigands in September 1901 was released on payment of $72,500 ransom, raised by public subscription.

1904 William L. Shirer, journalist, born in Chicago; foreign correspondent/author (*Berlin Diary, Rise and Fall of the Third Reich*) (died 1993).

1905 Rotary Club formed in Chicago; there now are about 18,000 clubs in 152 countries with 850,000 members.

1906 Thomas Burns defeated Marvin Hart in 20 rounds in Los Angeles to win world heavyweight boxing championship.

1915 American steamer *Carib* sunk by a mine off Germany in the North Sea.

1927 Federal Radio Commission created.

1945 American flag raised on Mt. Suribachi on Iwo Jima by Marines.

1954 First mass inoculation of Salk polio vaccine began in Pittsburgh.

1975 Ten year embargo on arms trade with Pakistan lifted.

1988 Texas Co. agreed to pay $1.25 billion to government to settle accusation that it overcharged customers for crude oil and refined oil products in 1973–81 period.

1995 Dow Jones industrial average passed the 4,000 point mark for the first time.

1998 Tornadoes struck Florida for two days; killed 42, injured 260. Torrential rains February 23 and 24 in San Francisco and Los Angeles washed out roadways, caused mud slides; nine killed, damage put at $475 million.

2000 Capt. Chester ("Chet") Lee served as Mission Director for six Apollo moon missions; dead at 80.

24

1750 Theophilus Parsons, jurist whose decisions led to universal adoption of the English common law tradition, born in Byfield, MA; chief justice, Massachusetts Supreme Court (1806–13) (died 1813).

1772   William H. Crawford, legislator/public official, born in Amherst County, VA; represented Georgia in Senate (1807–13); minister to France (1813); Secretary of War (1815–16), of Treasury (1816–25) (died 1834).

1785   John Adams named the first minister plenipotentiary to Great Britain.

1803   Supreme Court in *Marbury v. Madison* overturned a law for first time, declaring a section of the 1789 Judiciary Act unconstitutional; set precedent of authorizing federal courts to review legislation for constitutionality.

1808   John Wise, pioneer aeronaut, born in Lancaster, PA; made first ascent in balloon of own design (1835), carried mail for first time (1859) (died 1879).

1813   American sloop *Hornet* sank the British sloop *Peacock*.

1824   George W. Curtis, editor/author, born in Providence; editor of *Harper's* and author of its "Easy Chair" column, strongly influenced opinions of his day (died 1892).

1836   Winslow Homer, artist of seascapes (*The Gulf Stream, Maine Coast, Northeaster*), born in Boston (died 1910).

1843   Miles A. Seed, inventor of process for making photographic dry plates, born in Preston, England; organized company (1882) to manufacture, sold out to Kodak (1902) (died 1913).

1855   President Pierce signed act creating first Court of Claims; before that citizens had to get congressional approval of claims against the government.

1860   Daniel B. Updike, printer, born in Providence; founder, Merrymount Press (1893); did much to improve American typography (died 1941).

1860   Alabama legislature resolved that the state would not submit to a "foul sectional party" and called for a convention in the event of the election of a "black Republican" president.

1863   Territory of Arizona established.

1868   House voted 126–47 to impeach President Andrew Johnson; set up a committee of two to lead impeachment proceedings in the Senate.

1874   Honus (John Peter) Wagner, baseball player considered the greatest all-around player, born in Carnegie, PA; called the "Flying Dutchman," he played with Pittsburgh (1900–17), getting 3,415 career hits and a batting average of .327; one of the original five in Baseball Hall of Fame (died 1955).

1885   Chester W. Nimitz, World War II admiral, born in Fredericksburg, TX; commander-in-chief, Pacific Fleet (1941–45); chief of naval operations (1945–47) (died 1966).

1887   Mary Ellen Chase, educator (Smith College 1918–55), born in Blue Hills, ME; author (*Mary Peters*) (died 1973).

1908   Supreme Court in *Miller v. Oregon* upheld the Oregon ten-hour day for women in industry.

1919   War Revenue Act levied taxes on incomes, excess profits, estates, and products of child labor.

1931   Supreme Court upheld constitutionality of 18th (Prohibition) Amendment.

1942   National Housing Agency created by presidential executive order.

1955   Steven P. Jobs, cofounder of Apple Computers, born in Mountain View, CA.

1977   Securities & Exchange Commission adopted rules to prevent foreign buyers from secretly gaining control of American companies.

1988   Federal AIDS Panel Chairman James D. Watkins urged $2 billion a year national effort to expand drug treatment programs.

1988   Supreme Court ruled unanimously that public figures who are victims of satirical attacks may not sue for damages; decision rejected $200,000 judgment won by the Rev. Jerry Falwell against *Hustler Magazine*.

1991   Ground fighting in Iraq began; virtually ended five days later.

1996   Cuban jets shot down two unarmed planes owned by Cuban exiles in Miami; four persons in planes presumed killed; charter flights between Cuba and United States suspended; downing of planes said to be in international waters.

2000   Public Policy Institute of California reported that, in spite of massive additional expenditures for public education in the state over prior decades, poorer students still tended to have less skilled teachers and educational opportunities.

2004   President Bush embraced a federal constitutional amendment to assure that right to marriage continued to be limited to heterosexual couples.

2006   Don Knotts, winner of five Emmys for playing Barney Fife on the *Andy Griffith Show*, passed away at 81.

2006   Dennis Weaver (b. 1924) died; famous for his role as Chester on the long-running Western classic *Gunsmoke*; did a series of television movies (*McCloud*) in which he played a 20th-century sheriff.

25

1643 Gov. Willem Kieft of New Netherlands began war against Indians at Pavonia and Corlaer's Hook because of their refusal to surrender murderer of a colonist.

1673 Charles II granted Virginia to Lords Arlington and Culpeper as proprietary province for 31 years.

1710 Daniel G. Duluth, French explorer, died at 74; explored Lake Superior region, was responsible for French control of the area; Minnesota city named for him.

1746 Charles C. Pinckney, colonial leader, born in Charleston, SC; minister to France (1796–1800); unsuccessful Federalist candidate for president (1804, 1808); a founder, U. of South Carolina (died 1825).

1779 Col. George Rogers Clark with 127 men captured Vincennes, IN, from a British-Indian force.

1781 John Adams named minister plenipotentiary to the Netherlands.

1783 Denmark recognized independence of the United States.

1791 Bank of the United States incorporated as a national bank, given a 20-year charter with a capital of $10 million.

1799 First federal forestry legislation approved to acquire timber for the Navy.

1805 Thomas Pownall, colonial governor, died at 83; governor of Massachusetts (1757–59); served in Parliament (1767–80), tried to prevent Revolution by urging changes in colonial taxation.

1807 George A. Trenholm, Confederate Secretary of Treasury, born in Charleston, SC (died 1876).

1809 George A. Collum, Union general, born in New York City; served in Army from 1833 to 1874; endowed construction of Memorial Hall at West Point (died 1892).

1828 John Adams, son of President and Mrs. John Quincy Adams, married in White House, the first and only wedding of a president's son there.

1833 John P. St. John, temperance leader/politician, born in Brookville, IN; governor of Kansas (1879–83); presidential candidate, National Prohibition Party (1884); drew enough votes in New York to give state to Democrats; thereby he is sometimes credited with President Cleveland's election (died 1916).

1836 Samuel Colt received patent for revolver, an important link in the development of arms; the revolver played important role in development of West.

1848 Edward H. Harriman, financier/railroad executive, born in Hempstead, NY; owner, director, Union Pacific and other railroads; lost control of Northern Pacific in battle with J.P. Morgan and James J. Hill, which touched off stock market panic of 1901; organized first boys clubs (1876) (died 1909).

1856 Charles L. Freer, industrialist/philanthropist, born in Kingston, NY; amassed fortune in railroad car manufacturing; donated 8,000 art works to Smithsonian for display in Freer Gallery (1906) (died 1919).

1862 Confederate forces evacuated Nashville after fall of Ft. Donelson; Union troops occupied the city.

1863 President Lincoln signed national banking system act, which included creation of office of Comptroller of the Currency.

1864 Anna T. Harrison, widow of President William Henry Harrison, died in North Bend, OH, at 88.

1873 Enrico Caruso, opera tenor, born in Naples; one of greatest tenors, was top star at Metropolitan Opera (1908–21); first opera singer to make phonographic recordings (died 1921).

1881 William Z. Foster, American Communist leader, born in Taunton, MA; secretary-general, U.S. Communist Party (1921–30), chairman (1945–56); Communist Party presidential candidate (1924, 1928, 1932) (died 1961).

1883 Charles A. Dykstra, educator, born in Cleveland; president, Wisconsin U. (1936–45), provost, California U. (1945–50); director, Selective Service (1940–41) (died 1950).

1888 John Foster Dulles, public official, born in Washington, DC; Secretary of State (1953–59), prime architect of American policy of Communist containment (died 1959).

1894 Bert (DeBenneville) Bell, professional football commissioner (1946–59), born in Philadelphia; co-owner, Philadelphia team (1933–45) (died 1959).

1896 John L. McClellan, legislator, born in Sheridan, AR; represented Arkansas in House (1935–39) and Senate (1942–77); conducted televised hearings on labor unions (died 1977).

1900 Jed Harris, theater producer (*Front Page, Our Town*), born in Vienna (died 1979).

1901 U.S. Steel Co. incorporated in New Jersey with capitalization of $1.3 billion.

1904 John J. Bittner, biologist, born in Meadville, PA; work at Minnesota U. Medical School contributed to theory that cancer is caused by a virus (died 1961).

1907 First Hudson River tunnel between New York and New Jersey completed.

1907 Mary C. Chase, playwright (*Harvey, Mrs. McThing*) born in Denver (died 1981).

1913 The 16th Amendment creating the federal income tax went into effect.

1918 President Wilson ordered the construction of Muscle Shoals Dam on the Tennessee River to produce power for the manufacture of explosives and nitrates.

1933 First American aircraft carrier, *Ranger*, was launched at Newport News, VA.

1964 Muhammad Ali (then Cassius Clay) won world heavyweight boxing championship for the first time, knocking out Sonny Liston in seven rounds in Miami Beach.

2000 California public health officials defended sexually explicit anti–HIV ads as means to shake potential victims out of their complacency.

2003 Although many places were adopting computer screen voting, Santa Clara, California, became the first to purchase a system that also provided voters a printed record of how they voted.

2003 Environmental Protection Agency approved Monsanto's genetically modified corn to be grown and sold; rationale: more disease resistant and reduced amount of pesticides needed to grow crop; since most corn is fed to animals the EPA assumed this would be primary means of it [the corn] reaching humans.

2004 Right of states to provide low-income college scholarships to those majoring in religious studies upheld by Supreme Court 7–2.

2004 Mel Gibson's *Passion of the Christ* opened to huge box office even though it was entirely in Aramaic and used English subtitles; hostile critics had accused it of anti–Semitic overtones.

2006 Darren McGavin (b. 1922) died; found success on stage, in the movies, and on television; perhaps best remembered as the star of *Kolchak: The Night Stalker* (1974), which became a cult classic even though surviving on TV only one year.

26

1732 First Catholic church in the colonies finished in Philadelphia and first mass celebrated.

1775 Col. Alexander Leslie ordered to go to Salem, MA, to seize American stores and cannons collected there; detained at the bridge while material was moved.

1785 Thomas Mason, colonial leader, died at 53; while serving in Virginia Assembly he wrote nine letters of a "British American," upholding the colonial position.

1795 Francis Marion, Revolutionary commander, died at about 63; known as "The Swamp Fox," he commanded troops in South Carolina.

1832 John G. Nicolay, private secretary to President Lincoln (1860–65), born in Essingen, Germany; author of Lincoln biography, edited Lincoln works (died 1901).

1833 Supreme Court in *Barron v. Baltimore* held that the Bill of Rights does not protect against state actions.

1844 Horace H. Lurton, associate justice, Supreme Court (1910–14), born in Newport, KY (died 1914).

1846 William F. Cody ("Buffalo Bill"), hunter/showman, born in Scott County, IA; Pony Express rider and scout; Cody, WY, named for him (died 1917).

1852 John H. Kellogg, physician, born in Battle Creek, MI; founder, director of sanitaria; invented medical instruments and apparatus, helped develop breakfast cereals (died 1943).

1957 Charles M. Sheldon, Congregational clergyman, born in Wellsville, NY; his novel, *In His Steps*, was a best seller; editor, *Christian Herald* (from 1920) (died 1946).

1858 William J. Hammer, electrical engineer/inventor, born in Cressona, PA; associated with Edison, established first central station for incandescent electric lighting (in London), invented luminous radium preparation for watch and clock dials; first to suggest and use radium for cancer and tumor treatment (died 1934).

1866 Herbert H. Dow, chemist who developed process for removing bromine from brine, born in Belleville, Canada; founder, president, Dow Chemical Co. (1897); developed, patented 100+ chemical processes (died 1930).

1869 The 15th Amendment was enacted, providing that the right to vote must not be abridged because of "race, color, or previous condition of servitude"; ratified in 1870.

1877 Rudolph Dirks, cartoonist ("Katzenjammer Kids"), born in Heinde, Germany (died 1968).

1890 Chance M. Vought, airplane designer/manufacturer, born in New York City; built training planes for British in World War I; formed Lewis & Vought (1917), became Chance Vought, merged with Pratt & Whitney Co. (died 1930).

1896 Evans F. Carlson, Marine Corps general, born in Sidney, NY; led raids in South Pacific; his force was known as Carlson's Raiders (died 1947).

1907 Gen. George W. Goethals named chief engineer for Panama Canal construction.

1916 Jackie Gleason, entertainer, born in New York City; starred on television 20 years; screen actor (*The Hustler, Gigot*) (died 1987).

1917 Mt. McKinley, Alaska National Park established; renamed the Denali National Park in 1980.

1917 President Wilson asked Congress for emergency powers, including arming American merchant vessels; approved by House (403–13) March 1, filibustered in Senate.

1919 Grand Canyon (AZ) National Park established.

1920 Tony Randall, entertainer, born in Tulsa; screen actor (*Mating Game, Pillow Talk*), television (*The Odd Couple, Sidney*).

1929 Grand Teton (WY) National Park established.

1932 Johnny Cash, country/western singer, born in Kingsland, AR; composed many hit songs ("I Walk the Line," "Folsom Prison Blues").

1972 More than 118 died when a slagpile dam collapsed at Man, WV, flooding a 17-mile long valley.

1984 U.S. Marines withdrawn from Beirut, Lebanon.

1986 Robert Penn Warren, poet/novelist, named the country's first official poet laureate by Daniel J. Boorstin, Librarian of Congress.

1993 Powerful bomb exploded in parking garage under World Trade Center in New York City; six persons were killed, more than 1,000 injured.

1998 Oprah Winfrey, television star, was acquitted in a $12 million damage suit brought against her for some comments on beef by Texas cattle ranchers.

27

1659 Henry Dunster, English-born first president of Harvard (1640–54), died at 50; had to resign post because of his views on infant baptism; became Baptist pastor in Scituate, MA (1655–59).

1720 Samuel Parris, Salem Village (now Danvers), MA, clergyman, died at 67; credited with starting witchcraft trials when he supported accusations brought against his West Indian slave.

1773 Christ Church in Alexandria, VA, completed after six years construction at the cost of $4,070; George Washington purchased his family pew for $100.

1775 Lord North's conciliation plan adopted by Parliament, exempting any colony from taxation if it contributed to support of civil officials and troops; at same time, the New England Restraining Act was passed, forbidding New England from trading with any nation but Great Britain and the British West Indies after July 1; barred New Englanders from North Atlantic fisheries after July 20.

1776 American troops defeated a British force, mostly Loyalists, led by Gen. Donald McDonald, at Moore's Creek Bridge, NC, near Wilmington.

1782 House of Commons urged King George III to end American Revolution.

1801 Congress assumed jurisdiction over District of Columbia.

1801 Thomas Jefferson's *Manual of Parliamentary Procedure* published; code still substantially governs American deliberative bodies.

1807 Henry Wadsworth Longfellow, author, born in Portland, ME; modern language professor (Bowdoin 1829–35, Harvard 1835–49); wrote many well-known poems (*The Wreck of the Hesperus, Evangeline, Hiawatha, Paul Revere's Ride, The Village Blacksmith*) (died 1882).

1823 William B. Franklin, Union general, born in York, PA; saw action at first Bull Run, Antietam (died 1903).

1830 Henry E. Huntington, railway executive/noted philanthropist, born in Oneonta, NY (died 1927).

1836 Russell A. Alger, public official, born in Lafayette, OH; governor of Michigan (1884–88) and represented it in Senate (1902–07); Secretary of War (1897–99), resigned at request of President McKinley because of criticism of War Department operations (died 1907).

1860 Abraham Lincoln made his Cooper Union speech in which he defended the rights of the Federal Government to prohibit slavery in the territories.

1867 Irving Fisher, economist who pioneered in monetary economic theory, born in Saugerties, NY (died 1947).

1869 Alice Hamilton, toxicologist who

investigated occupational poisons, born in New York City; served in Bureau of Labor Statistics (1911–21), with Harvard U. Medical School (1919–35) (died 1970).

1872 Ellery Sedgwick, editor, *Atlantic Monthly* (1908–38), born in New York City (died 1960).

1873 Congress censured two of its members, Oakes Ames and James Brooks, for their role in Credit Mobilier affair — Ames for selling Union Pacific stock at low prices to congressmen to influence votes, Brooks for corruption.

1882 Burton K. Wheeler, who represented Montana in Senate (1923–47), born in Hudson, MA; Progressive Party vice presidential candidate (1924) (died 1975).

1886 Hugo L. Black, associate justice, Supreme Court (1937–71), born in Harlan, AL; represented Alabama in Senate (1927–37); led activists in Court, wrote opinion forbidding prayer in public schools (died 1971).

1888 Lotte Lehman, soprano, born in Perleberg, Germany; considered one of greatest singers of German repertory (died 1976).

1888 Arthur M. Schlesinger, historian, born in Xenia, OH; edited 13-volume series *A History of American Life* (died 1965).

1891 David Sarnoff, radio/television pioneer, born in Uzlian, Russia; invented radio set (1915); with RCA (1919–71) as president (1930–47), chairman (1947–71); a founder, National Broadcasting Co. (died 1971).

1896 Arthur W. Radford, World War II admiral, born in Chicago; chairman, Joint Chiefs of Staff (1953–57) (died 1973).

1902 Gene Sarazen, an outstanding golfer of 1920/30s, born in Rye, NY; won PGA tourney three times, U.S. Open twice.

1902 John Steinbeck, author, born in Salinas, CA; wrote many popular novels (*Grapes of Wrath, Of Mice and Men, East of Eden, Cannery Row*); awarded 1962 Nobel Literature Prize (died 1968).

1904 James T. Farrell, author (*Studs Lonigan* and *Danny O'Neill* series), born in Chicago (died 1979).

1907 Mildred Bailey, singer, born in Tekoa, WA; vocalist with Paul Whiteman orchestra (died 1951).

1910 Joan Bennett, screen actress (*Little Women, Woman in the Window*), born in Palisades, NJ (died 1993).

1910 Peter DeVries, author/short story writer for *The New Yorker*, born in Chicago; books include *Tunnel of Love*; *Reuben, Reuben*.

1913 Irwin Shaw, popular novelist (*The Young Lions*; *Rich Man, Poor Man*; *Two Weeks in Another Town*), born in Brooklyn (died 1984).

1922 Supreme Court upheld constitutionality of women's suffrage (19th Amendment).

1926 David H. Hubel, medical scientist, born in Windsor, Canada, of American parentage; shared 1981 Nobel Physiology/Medicine Prize for research on brain's function in vision.

1930 Joanne Woodward, screen actress (*Three Faces of Eve, Long Hot Summer*), born in Thomasville, GA.

1932 Elizabeth Taylor, screen actress, born in London; starred in many films (*National Velvet, Butterfield 8, Cleopatra, Who's Afraid of Virginia Woolf*).

1934 Ralph Nader, consumer advocate, born in Winsted, CT; work led to passage of National Traffic and Motor Vehicles Safety Act.

1939 Supreme Court in *NLRB v. Fansteel* outlawed sit-down strikes.

1942 Two-day battle of Java Sea and Sunda Strait resulted in loss of four Allied cruisers and four destroyers.

1943 Mine disaster at Red Lodge, MT, killed 74 persons.

1950 United States and Canada signed 50-year treaty for the power output increase of Niagara River, protection of Niagara Falls beauty.

1951 The 22d Amendment, limiting presidency to two terms, went into effect.

1973 Two hundred members of American Indian Movement seized Wounded Knee on the Oglala Sioux Reservation in South Dakota; held town until May 8.

1987 Tower Commission, which studied the Iran Contra affair, issued its report castigating President Reagan and some top aides for making serious mistakes in selling arms to Iran and diverting profits to the Nicaraguan Contras.

1991 President Bush ordered a cease fire in the Desert Storm operation.

2000 After over two decades of rivalry, the son of Elijah Muhammad and Louis Farrakhan of the Nation of Islam publicly embraced and declared reconciliation; Farrakhan avowed growing unity with traditional Islam.

2001 Bush proposed $1.6 trillion tax cut to help taxpayers and encourage more private spending; on following day sent to Congress a $1.96 trillion budget for next fiscal year.

2003 Fred Rogers, host of *Mister Rogers' Neighborhood*, died of stomach cancer at 74. Program ran on PBS from 1968 to 2000, with almost 700 episodes filmed.

2004 The Rev. Kenryu Takashi Tsuji, the first American-born bishop of the Buddhist Churches of America, died at 84; interned by Canadians during World War II.

28

1610 Patent was granted to Lord De la Warre as lord governor and captain general of Virginia; arrived with three ships and provisions (June 10), just as settlers were about to abandon Jamestown.

1787 Pittsburgh Academy founded; became U. of Pittsburgh 1908.

1797 Mary M. Lyon, pioneer in providing advanced education for women, born in Buckland, MA; founder, Mt. Holyoke Seminary (later College), first women's college in the United States; president (1837–49) (died 1849).

1799 Samuel S. Schmucker, religious leader, born in Hagerstown, MD; founder, first president, Gettysburg (now Lutheran) Seminary (1826–64); founder, first president, Gettysburg College (1832–34); leader of American low-church Lutherans (died 1873).

1822 George Vasey, botanist who headed National Herbarium (1872–93), born in Scarborough, England; specialized in grasses, Vasey grass named for him (died 1893).

1825 Quincy A. Gillmore, Union general, born in Lorain County, OH; served throughout war; commander, Department of South (1865); president, Mississippi River Commission (1879) (died 1888).

1827 Baltimore & Ohio Railroad chartered in Maryland; on March 8 in Virginia.

1844 President Tyler, his cabinet, and 350 dignitaries were aboard the frigate, USS *Princeton*, when a bow gun exploded; eight men including Secretary of State Abel P. Upshur, Navy Secretary Thomas W. Gilmer, and Senator David Gardiner of New York, were killed; President was below decks at the time of the explosion.

1847 Col. A.W. Doniphan and his troops, on a march from New Mexico to California, defeated a Mexican force at the pass of Sacramento.

1849 First band of gold seekers arrived in San Francisco aboard the *California.*

1854 Anti-slavery forces met in a schoolhouse in Ripon, WI; recommended formation of a "Republican Party."

1860 Carl G.L. Barth, mechanical engineer, born in Oslo; pioneer of scientific management in the United States (died 1939).

1860 Victor L. Berger, editor/legislator, born in Nieder Rehbach, Austria; first Socialist elected to Congress, representing a Wisconsin district in House (1911–13, 1923–29) (died 1929).

1861 Congress created the Colorado Territory and President Lincoln appointed William Gilpin as the first governor.

1861 Missouri state convention rejected secession 89–1.

1867 U. of Illinois at Urbana incorporated; opened March 2.

1869 William V. Pratt, naval officer, born in Belfast, ME; assistant chief of naval operations (1917–19); commander-in-chief, U.S. fleet (1929–30); chief of naval operations (1930–33) (died 1957).

1878 Bland-Allison Act passed, the first of several government subsidies to silver producers during depressed times; law required government to purchase $2–4 million in silver bullion monthly to be coined.

1882 Geraldine Farrar, dramatic soprano, born in Melrose, MA; sang at the Metropolitan Opera (1906–22) (died 1967).

1894 Ben Hecht, journalist/author, born in New York City; author (*Erik Dorn, The Egoist*); co-author with Charles MacArthur of plays (*The Front Page, Twentieth Century*) (died 1964).

1896 Philip S. Hench, physician, born in Pittsburgh; shared 1950 Nobel Physiology/Medicine Prize for discoveries about hormones of adrenal cortex (died 1965).

1901 Linus C. Pauling, first to win two unshared Nobel prizes, born in Portland, OR; won 1954 Chemistry Prize for describing the forces holding together proteins and other molecules and 1962 Peace Prize (died 1994).

1907 Milton A. Caniff, cartoonist ("Terry and the Pirates" and "Steve Canyon"), born in Hillsboro, OH (died 1988).

1915 Zero (Sam) Mostel, actor, born in Brooklyn; starred in several plays, including *Fiddler on the Roof* (died 1977).

1917 Woman suffrage became effective in Indiana.

1920 Transportation Act passed by Congress, ending the war-time government operation of railroads and providing for their return to private ownership.

1923 Gyo Obata, architect who designed the National Air & Space Museum and Dallas-Ft. Worth Airport, born in San Francisco.

1924 Christopher G. Craft, aeronautical engineer who was flight director of American manned space program (1959–70), born in Phoebus, VA.

1927 Supreme Court ruled that oil contracts and leases granted to Edward L. Doheny by former Interior Secretary Albert B. Fall were illegal, fraudulent, and corrupt.

1930 Leon N. Cooper, physicist who shared 1972 Nobel Physics Prize for theory of superconductivity of metals, born in New York City.

1931 Dean Smith, basketball coach who established new winning record, born in Emporia, KS; coached U. of North Carolina team (1961–97).

1940 Mario G. Andretti, automobile race driver, born in Trieste, Italy; won numerous championships, including Indianapolis 500, Daytona 500, and Formula One world championship.

1945 President Franklin Roosevelt appointed delegates to United Nations Conference in San Francisco.

1987 President Reagan appointed former Senator Howard H. Baker, Jr., as the White House chief of staff, replacing Donald T. Regan.

1993 Four federal agents were killed in gun battle with members of the Branch Davidian cult outside Waco, TX; two cult members also died.

1995 New Denver International Airport opened after 16 months' delay.

2001 Most powerful earthquake in 52 years in Seattle, Washington, inflicted serious damage on Seattle, Washington, and nearby area.

2002 Mary Stuart (1926–2002) died at 75; had starred on *Search for Tomorrow* from its beginning in 1951 through its end in 1989.

2003 San Jose, California, Post Office celebrated a level of service never reached anywhere else in country: 97 percent next-day delivery of local mail; handles two million pieces of mail daily.

2004 Daniel J. Boorstin, best-selling historian and winner of the 1974 Pulitzer prize, died at 89; had served as Librarian of Congress.

29

1704 Deerfield (MA) massacre occurred when 50 French soldiers and 200 Indians attacked a sleeping settlement, killing about 50 and taking 111 prisoners (17 of whom died on the march to Canada); 137 escaped.

1736 Ann Lee, religious leader, born in Manchester, England; founder of American Shakers; began first Shaker colony (1776) at what is now Watervliet, NY (died 1784).

1784 John E. Wool, Mexican War general, born in Newburgh, NY; second in command at Buena Vista; various commands until Civil War (died 1869).

1820 Lewis A. Sayre, first American orthopedic surgeon, born in Morris County, NJ; an organizer, surgeon at Bellevue Hospital Medical College (1861) (died 1900).

1840 John P. Holland, submarine developer, born in County Clare, Ireland; launched successful submarine (1898), sold it to Navy (1900) (died 1914).

1844 Colby M. Chester, Union naval officer, born in New London, CT; saw action at Mobile Bay; commandant, Naval Academy (1891–94); commander, South Atlantic squadron (1897–98); superintendent, Naval Observatory (1902–06) (died 1932).

1860 Herman Hollerith, tabulating system inventor, born in Buffalo; invented punch card tabulating system, used in 1890 census; formed Computing-Tabulating Machine Co. (1896), which became International Business Machine Co. (IBM) in 1924 (died 1929).

1904 Jimmy Dorsey, musician, born in Shenadoah, PA; saxophone player and important orchestra leader in Big Band era (died 1957).

1996 Television executives, meeting with President Clinton, agreed to implement use of v-chip (v for violence) that could be installed in sets and enable TV owners to block out programs with high violence ratings.

MARCH

1

1543 Expedition of Juan Cabrillo, who died January 3, 1543, reached mouth of the Rogue River in Oregon at Cape Mendocino.

1625 John Robinson, Separatist clergyman, died at about 50; led his Pilgrim congregation from England to the Netherlands, built up congregation, planned voyage to America; stayed behind with the majority.

1732 William Cushing, jurist, born in Scituate, MA; chief justice, Massachusetts Supreme Court (1777); first associate justice appointed to the Supreme Court, served from 1789 to his death in 1810.

1780 Pennsylvania legislature adopted act calling for gradual emancipation of slaves.

1781 Articles of Confederation, before the states since November 1777, formally ratified with the approval of Maryland; the name United States began to be used the next day.

1784 Bill presented by Thomas Jefferson to the Continental Congress on governing the western territory; approved April 23 but was superseded by the Northwest Ordinance of 1787.

1790 President Washington signed an act providing for the first census.

1794 William J. Worth, Mexican War general, born in Hudson, NY; involved in most major battles; commander, Department of Texas; commandant of cadets, West Point (1830–38) (died 1849).

1803 Ohio admitted to the Union as the 17th state.

1805 Associate Supreme Court Justice Samuel Chase, impeached for trial conduct, was acquitted after a two-month trial; impeachment sought because of high-handed conduct in a 1799 trial; first impeachment proceedings against a Supreme Court justice.

1807 William Woodruff, president, Mormon Church (1889–98), born in Avon, CT; with first Mormons arriving at Salt Lake (1847) (died 1898).

1809 Illinois Territory formed by dividing the Indiana Territory.

1837 Senate by 23–9 vote recognized independence of Texas; approved by President Jackson March 3.

1837 President Jackson signed Judiciary Act which increased the Supreme Court from seven to nine justices.

1837 William Dean Howells, author/editor, born in Martins Ferry, OH; an editor, *Atlantic Monthly* (1866–81), *Harper's* (1866–1920), where he wrote "Easy Chair" column (1900–20); author of *The Rise of Silas Lapham* (died 1920).

1841 Blanche Kelso Bruce, first black to serve full Senate term, born in Farmville, VA; represented Mississippi (1875–81) (died 1898).

1845 President Tyler signed joint resolution of Congress annexing Texas.

1848 Augustus Saint-Gaudens, sculptor, born in Dublin; among best known works are Adoration of the Cross, Admiral Farragut, General Sherman (all New York City), Abraham Lincoln (Chicago), The Puritan (Springfield, MA) (died 1907).

1867 Nebraska admitted to Union as 37th state.

1872 Yellowstone National Park established in Wyoming, Montana, and Idaho.

1875 Congress passed Civil Rights Act providing for equal rights for blacks in public places and in jury duty; law invalidated by Supreme Court in 1883.

1880 Supreme Court in *Stander v. West Virginia* held the West Virginia law excluding blacks from jury duty unconstitutional.

1882 Gaston Lachaise, sculptor, born in Paris; did decorative sculptures for the Rockefeller Center, the Chicago World Fair (died 1935).

1896 Harry Winston, founder of gem dealership (1932), born in New York City; purchased many renowned jewels, including Hope Diamond, which he gave to the Smithsonian (1958) (died 1978).

1899 Edmund Duffy, editorial cartoonist, born in Jersey City; with *Baltimore Sun* (1924–62) (died 1962).

1904 Glenn Miller, orchestra leader, born in Clarinda, IA; a leading figure of Big Band era; died when plane in which he was flying disappeared enroute to France in 1944.

1910 Rockefeller Foundation established by John D. Rockefeller for the benefit of humanity.

1910 Railroad disaster at Wellington, WA, killed 96 persons.

1914 Ralph W. Ellison, author (*Invisible Man*), born in Oklahoma City (died 1994).

1914 Prohibition went into effect in Tennessee under a new law.

1914 Statewide prohibition law enacted in Idaho; effective January 1, 1916.

1917 Robert T. S. Lowell, poet/translator, born in Boston; poet ("Lord Weary's Castle," "The Dolphin," "Life Studies"); translated Aeschylus, Baudelaire (died 1977).

1920 Railroads and express companies were turned back to private operators after being operated by the government during World War I.

1921 Terence J. Cooke, Catholic Archbishop of New York (1968–83), born in New York City; elevated to cardinal 1969 (died 1983).

1921 Dinah Shore, screen/television actress and singer, born in Winchester, TN; (died 1994).

1926 Pete (Alvin R.) Rozelle, professional football commissioner (1960–89), born in South Gate, CA; general manager, Los Angeles Rams (1957–60) (died 1996).

1927 Harry Belafonte, singer/screen actor, born in New York City; noted for calypso songs; films included *Carmen Jones* and *Island in the Sun*.

1932 Son of Charles and Anne Lindbergh was kidnapped from their New Jersey home; found dead May 12.

1943 Point rationing system set up for processed foods.

1954 Five congressmen were wounded in the House by four Puerto Rican independence supporters firing from the spectators gallery.

1961 Peace Corps created by executive order; put on permanent statutory basis September 22; R. Sargent Shriver named director March 4; functions of agency transferred to ACTION July 1, 1971.

1962 Plane crashed into Jamaica Bay after taking off from Idlewild Airport, NY, killing 95 persons.

1967 Rep. Adam Clayton Powell of New York was denied his seat in the House because of charges of misusing government funds; re-elected in 1968, seated but fined $25,000.

1971 The Capitol bombed by radical Weather Underground; device was planted in a Senate wing restroom; did $300,000 damage, no one was injured.

1997 Tornadoes in central Arkansas killed 26 people.

2000 U.S. House of Representatives voted unanimously to remove earnings cap on those receiving Social Security.

2001 Census Bureau rejected proposal to increase U.S. population figures by estimated number of individuals who had been missed.

2003 INS (Immigration and Naturalization Service) ceased to exist as its 35,000 employees were divided among different bureaus of Homeland Security; enforcement and service responsibilities separated; critics feared that bureaucratic rearrangements would not solve operational problems found in the past

2005 Supreme Court by 5–4 ruling outlawed executing anyone under 18.

2

1643 Virginia Assembly passed act denying the governor and council the right to impose taxes without its consent; voted to banish nonconformist clergymen.

1685 Colonial post office established in New York with Edward Randolph as postmaster.

1769 Dewitt Clinton, public official, born in Little Britain, NY; served New York City as Mayor (1803–15) and New York state as governor (1817–23, 1824–28); sponsored construction of Erie Canal (died 1828).

1779 Joel R. Poinsett, legislator/diplomat, born in Charleston; represented South Carolina in House (1821–25); first minister to Mexico (1825–29), Secretary of War (1837–41); an amateur botanist, he introduced plants from Mexico; poinsettia was named for him (died 1851).

1780 Massachusetts constitution, adopted by convention, was ratified; a clause prohibited slavery.

1793 Sam Houston, frontiersman and Texas leader, born in Rockbridge County, VA; represented Tennessee in House (1823–27) and served state as governor (1827–29); became a founder of Texas, led troops against Mexico (1836); president of Texas Republic (1836–38, 1841–44), one of its first senators (1846–59) and its governor (1859–61); deposed when he refused to take oath of allegiance to Confederacy (died 1863).

1807 President Jefferson signed an act prohibiting importation of slaves after January 1, 1808; passed House 63–49, agreed to by Senate.

1819 Arkansas Territory created from part of Missouri Territory.

1824 Supreme Court in *Gibbons vs. Ogden* gave Congress power to regulate commerce with foreign nations and among the states.

1824 Henry B. Carrington, Union general, born in Wallingford, CT; fought in Indian wars on the Plains, negotiated treaties and helped create reservations (died 1912).

1829 William B. Allison, legislator, born in Perry Township, OH; represented Iowa in House (1862–70) and Senate (1872–1908), where he chaired Appropriations Committee (1881–1908), a most influential legislator (died 1908).

1829 Carl Schurz, soldier/public official, born in Liblar, Germany; Union general (Bull Run, Gettysburg); Interior Secretary (1877–81), minister to Spain (1861–62); represented Missouri in Senate (1869–75); editor, *New York Evening Post* (1881–84) (died 1906).

1829 First school for the blind, the New England Asylum for the Blind, incorporated in Boston; became the Perkins Institute in 1839.

1833 President Jackson signed compromise tariff act designed to placate the South and an act authorizing collecting tariffs by force if necessary.

1836 Henry B. Brown, associate justice, Supreme Court (1890–1906), born in Lee, MA (died 1913).

1836 Convention in Washington, TX, adopted a declaration of independence, drew up a constitution; two days later formed a provisional government, named Sam Houston commander of its army.

1836 John W. Foster, diplomat, born in Pike County, IN; minister to Mexico (1873–80), to Russia (1880–81), to Spain (1883–85); Secretary of State (1892–93); American agent in establishing Alaska-Canada boundary (died 1917).

1847 American forces under Col. Alexander Doniphan occupied Chihuahua, Mexico.

1853 Territory of Washington created from the northern part of Oregon.

1861 Territories of Nevada and Dakota were created.

1861 Resolutions of a peace convention promoted by Former President Tyler were rejected by the Senate 28–7; House did not vote on them.

1865 Union cavalry force defeated Confederate troops near Waynesboro, VA.

1867 Congress passed first Reconstruction Act, dividing the South into five military districts subject to martial law; adopted over veto of President Andrew Johnson.

1867 Louisiana convention completed work on a constitution; ratified August 17–18.

1867 Congress created the Department of Education, headed by a commissioner; made an office in the Interior Department July 1, 1889.

1867 Congress passed act strengthening international exchange of official publications; Library of Congress the beneficiary; voted $100,000 for purchase of Peter Force Collection of Americana.

1887 Hatch Act passed providing funds for establishing agricultural experiment stations.

1890 Paul de Kruif, bacteriologist/author (*Microbe Hunters, Hunger Fighters*), born in Zeeland, MI (died 1971).

1899 Mt. Rainier (WA) National Park established.

1900 Kurt Weill, composer of musicals (*Threepenny Opera, Lady in the Dark, One Touch of Venus, Street Scene*), born in Desau, Germany (died 1950).

1902 Edward U. Condon, physicist who made important contributions to quantum mechanics, born in Almagordo, NM; director, Bureau of Standards (1945–51) (died 1974).

1904 Theodore S. Geisel, better known as Dr. Seuss, author, born in Springfield, MA; writer and illustrator of many popular children's books (died 1991).

1905 Marc Blitzstein, composer, born in Philadelphia; translated, adapted Brecht-Weill's *Threepenny Opera* (died 1964).

1907 H(aakon) I. Romnes, industrialist, born in Stoughton, WI; president, Western Electric Co. (1953–63); chief executive officer, president, AT&T (1967–72) (died 1973).

1909 Mel(vin T.) Ott, baseball player, born in Gretna, LA; with New York Giants (1926–44); first National Leaguer to hit 500 home runs; named to Baseball Hall of Fame (died 1958).

1915 Mine disaster at Layland, WV, resulted in 112 deaths.

1917 President Wilson signed act making Puerto Rico an American territory and its inhabitants American citizens.

1937 U.S. Steel Corp., to avoid strike, recognized Steelworkers Organizing Committee, predecessor of United Steelworkers.

1949   Air Force B-50 Superfortress landed at Ft. Worth, TX, completing first nonstop around-the-world flight in 94 hours, one minute.

1955   President Eisenhower signed act raising vice presidential salary from $30,000 to $35,000, congressmen from $15,000 to $22,500, Supreme Court chief justice from $25,500 to $35,000 and associate justices from $25,000 to $35,000.

1968   National Advisory Commission on Civil Disorder, chaired by Illinois Gov. Otto Kerner, reported that nationwide riots were due to unemployment, underemployment, and white racism.

1972   *Pioneer 10* was launched, the first spacecraft to explore the asteroid belt, and to fly by Jupiter.

1973   Ambassador Cleo A. Noel, Jr., and Chargé d'Affaires George C. Moore were killed by Palestinian guerillas in Khartoum, Sudan.

1974   Cost of first class postage increased to 10 cents.

1995   Senate failed to vote necessary two-thirds for a constitutional amendment requiring a balanced federal budget; House had approved the measure; a later Senate attempt in June also failed.

2000   For first time a major executive of America's largest cigarette manufacturer, Philip Morris, referred to nicotine as a "drug" and conceded right of Federal Drug Administration to at least partially regulate it.

2004   By winning Super Tuesday primary/caucus victories in nine out of ten states, John Kerry locked up Democratic presidential nomination.

2004   Marge Schott (b. 1928) died at 75; bought limited interest in Cincinnati Reds baseball team in 1981 and bought additional interests in 1984 to make her general partner; after heavy censure for her 1999 ethnic and racial remarks, she sold the club.

3

1513   (Juan) Ponce de Leon, Spanish conqueror of Puerto Rico, sailed to Florida, landing somewhere between St. Augustine and the St. John's River; after short stay (April 2–8), explored most of Florida coastline.

1540   Hernando de Soto, continuing exploration across South, entered what is now Georgia and reached present Talladega County, AL, July 26.

1636   Massachusetts General Court granted powers of government to freemen of the town; required its consent for establishing new churches.

1768   Francis Fauquier, colonial governor, died at about 64; was Virginia lieutenant governor (1758–60), acting governor (1760–68).

1776   Continental Congress voted to send Silas Deane to Europe to purchase war material.

1779   American force was defeated by British at the Battle of Brier Creek, near Savannah, strengthening British position in South.

1791   Congress established the District of Columbia.

1803   Senate began impeachment hearings of U.S. District Judge John Pickering of New Hampshire; removed March 12, 1804, for drunkenness and profanity on bench; this was first impeachment of a federal judge.

1805   Territory of Louisiana-Missouri created; in 1812, Louisiana became a state, Missouri a separate territory.

1817   President Madison signed act creating Alabama Territory.

1819   Congress enacted law providing a $50 bounty to informers for every illegally imported black person seized in the United States or at sea.

1820   Missouri Compromise went into effect when Maine was admitted as a free state and Missouri as a slave state; slavery excluded from Louisiana Purchase territory north of the line 36°30'.

1823   Congress passed first National Harbor Improvement Act.

1824   George T. Anderson, Confederate general, born in Georgia; saw action at Gettysburg, Chattanooga, Knoxville (died 1901).

1826   Joseph Wharton, industrialist, born in Philadelphia; developed process for making pure malleable nickel; a founder, Bethlehem Steel Co., Swarthmore College; benefactor of Wharton School of Finance (died 1909).

1831   George M. Pullman, inventor/manufacturer of railway sleeping car, born in Brocton, NY; invented sleeping car with folding upper berth (1865); founder, head, Pullman Palace Car Co. (1867–97); also developed dining, chair cars (died 1897).

1839   President Van Buren sent Gen. Winfield Scott to take charge of bloodless Aroostok "war," a dispute between Maine and New Brunswick; truce arranged, finally settled by Webster-Ashburton Treaty (1842).

1842   Massachusetts law passed requiring a minimum education for every child, a maximum ten-hour work day for those under 12.

1843 Congress appropriated $30 million to aid Samuel F.B. Morse in building first telegraph line between Washington and Baltimore.

1845 Florida admitted to Union as the 27th state.

1845 Congress for first time overrode a presidential veto — President Tyler's veto of construction of revenue cutters, steamers for defense.

1845 Congress reduced postal rates to five cents for a half ounce for up to 300 miles.

1847 Alexander Graham Bell, telephone inventor, born in Edinburgh; also invented the photophone, which transmitted first wireless telephone message (1880), a recorder for Edison's phonograph; helped solve problem of balance stability in a flying machine; founded Volta Bureau to increase knowledge about the deaf (died 1922).

1848 Territory of Minnesota created.

1849 Department of Interior created; originally called the Home Department, including the Census, General Land, and Indian Affairs offices; Thomas Ewing of Ohio the first secretary.

1851 Congress reduced postal rates to three cents for a half ounce for up to 300 miles.

1853 President Fillmore signed an act increasing salary of vice president from $5,000 to $8,000.

1859 First newspaper in Arizona, *Weekly Arizonan*, published in Tuber by William Wright.

1862 Union troops occupied Columbus, KY.

1863 National Academy of Sciences, created by Congress, was incorporated.

1863 Territory of Idaho created.

1863 First conscription act passed, making all men 20 to 45 liable for military service; service could be avoided by payment of $300 or procuring a substitute to enlist for three years.

1865 Freedmen's Bureau created as part of War Department to care for war refugees, freedmen, and abandoned lands; Maj. Gen. Oliver O. Howard named commissioner; Bureau went out of existence June 30, 1872.

1865 Congress passed act requiring the deposit in the Library of Congress of all books and other materials on which a copyright was claimed.

1867 James G. Rogers, architect, born in Bryants Station, KY; designed buildings at Yale U., Columbia-Presbyterian Medical Center, New York City (died 1947).

1868 House completed adoption of the 11 articles of impeachment against President Andrew Johnson.

1871 Congress created Civil Service Commission, with George William Curtis named to head

agency; Curtis resigned (1875) when his recommendations were ignored and the commission died.

1873 President Grant signed act increasing the salaries of president to $50,000, vice president to $10,000, and congressmen from $5,000 to $7,500.

1873 William Green, president, American Federation of Labor (1924–52), born in Coshocton, OH (died 1952).

1877 Congress passed the Desert Land Act, under which the government would sell up to 640 acres at $1.25 an acre to anyone who would reclaim the land in three years.

1879 Elmer V. McCollum, biochemist, born near Ft. Scott, KS; played fundamental role in developing knowledge of nutrition as a government consultant, educator (Wisconsin, Johns Hopkins); co-discoverer of Vitamin A, discovered Vitamin D (died 1967).

1879 U.S. Geological Survey established.

1883 Cost of first class mail reduced to two cents for a half ounce.

1885 Maximum weight for first class mail raised to one ounce for two cents.

1891 Immigration and Naturalization Service created.

1891 Forest Reserve Act approved; authorized president to set apart forest reserve lands anywhere on public lands.

1893 Free postal delivery extended to rural communities.

1895 Matthew B. Ridgway, World War II general, born in Ft. Monroe, VA; commander, 81st Airborne, UN troops in Korea (1951–52); supreme Allied commander in Europe (1952–53); Army chief of staff (1953–55) (died 1993).

1899 Alfred M. Gruenther, World War II general, born in Platte Center, NE; led troops in Italy; supreme Allied commander in Europe (1953–56) (died 1983).

1901 National Bureau of Standards established.

1901 Roger F. Turner, American men's champion figure skater (1928–35), born in Milton, MA.

1911 Jean Harlow, screen actress, born in Kansas City, MO; starred in many films (*Hell's Angels, Dinner at Eight, Platinum Blonde*) (died 1937).

1915 National Committee for Aeronautics created; terminated July 29, 1958, when its functions were transferred to National Aeronautics & Space Administration (NASA).

1915 Colorado adopted a prohibition law.

1918 Arthur Kornberg, biochemist, born in New York City; shared 1959 Nobel Physiology/ Medicine Prize for discoveries related to compounds within chromosomes, which play vital role in heredity.

1923 Henry R. Luce, with Britton Hadden, published first issue of *Time* magazine.

1931 "The Star Spangled Banner" officially adopted as national anthem by Congress.

1933 Frances Perkins, the first woman cabinet member, assumed her duties as Secretary of Labor; served until June 30, 1945.

1943 Two-day Battle of Bismarck Sea resulted in destruction of 10 Japanese warships, 60 Japanese planes.

1952 Ronald W. Reagan married Nancy Davis in Los Angeles.

1962 Jackie Joyner-Kersee, Olympic gold medalist in heptathlon (1988, 1992) and long jump (1988), born in East St. Louis, IL (died 1998).

1963 Two-day protest march begun by thousands of blacks in Birmingham, AL.

1966 Tornadoes in Jackson, MS, and Alabama caused 118 deaths.

1987 President Reagan nominated FBI Director William H. Webster to be director of Central Intelligence Agency to succeed the late William Casey; kept on by President Bush (1989).

1987 Supreme Court ruled 7–2 that people with contagious diseases are handicapped and are covered under civil rights laws; this was seen as protection for AIDS patients from job discrimination.

2000 First rise in unemployment reported since June, 1999: up 1/10 of 1 percent; factory production dropped 1.1 percent, sharpest decline since April 1999.

2004 Bush administration proposed to permit public school gender segregation if participation voluntary and equivalent classes provided for both sexes; underlying hope: to improve student performance by removing distractions.

2005 Steve Fossett completed flying the *GlobalFlyer* around the world alone without stopping or refueling, setting a world record.

2006 Former Congressman Randy Cunningham of California convicted of receiving $2.4 million in bribe money while in office.

4

1629 Royal charter granted to Massachusetts Bay Co.; territory previously had been granted to Council of New England; company able to transform itself into a self-governing commonwealth.

1681 William Penn, in return for a debt of 16,000 pounds owed his father, secured a royal charter to land which became Pennsylvania; began to organize a colony by selling shares to those who wanted to join the enterprise.

1747 Kazmierz (Casimir) Pulaski, nobleman who fought with the Americans, was born in Winiary, Poland; commanded a cavalry unit, mortally wounded at siege of Savannah October 9, 1779.

1754 Benjamin Waterhouse, physician, born in Newport, RI; first professor of theory, practice of "physic," Harvard Medical School (1783–1812); pioneered vaccination (died 1846).

1776 Gen. John Thomas led 2,000 troops of Continental Army to occupy, fortify Dorchester Heights, which overlooked Boston; British evacuated Boston (March 7–17), sailed to Halifax.

1777 Fourth Continental Congress began meetings in Philadelphia.

1789 The first Congress met in New York City; House did not have a quorum until April 1, Senate April 6.

1791 Vermont entered Union as the 14th state.

1793 President Washington delivered his second inaugural address — the shortest on record — 135 words.

1801 Thomas Jefferson became the first president inaugurated in Washington, DC, the new capital; called for a government of limited powers, economy in the national administration, support of state governments in all their rights, preservation of civil liberties, and "peace, commerce, and honest friendship with all nations, entangling alliances with none."

1806 Ephraim W. Bull, horticulturist who developed the Concord grape, born in Boston (died 1896).

1826 John Buford, Union cavalry commander who fought at Antietam, Gettysburg, born in Woodford, KY (died 1863).

1837 Chicago was incorporated as a city with William B. Ogden as first mayor.

1849 State of Deseret (Utah) founded at a convention in Salt Lake City, which became its capital.

1851 University of Minnesota founded.

1853 Frederick B. Power, chemist, born in Hudson, NY; dean, U. of Wisconsin Pharmacy School (1883–92); director, Wellcome Labs, London (1896–1914); with Department of Agriculture (1916–27); known for research in constituents of plant products (died 1927).

1855 Luther E. Holt, who wrote standard childhood text, born in Webster, NY; author (1894) of *The Care and Feeding of Children*, which went into 75 printings, and *The Diseases of Infancy and Childhood* (died 1924).

1861 A flag of seven stars and three stripes was raised over Confederate capital in Montgomery, AL.

1862 President Lincoln appointed Andrew Johnson, Tennessee senator and former governor, as military governor of the state; served until he became vice president in 1865.

1864 David W. Taylor, naval architect, born in Louisa County, VA; developed, operated testing basin for ship models; devised "Standard Series," matching engine power to hull design (died 1940).

1867 Charles P. Summerall, World War I general, born in Blount's Ferry, FL; commanded 1st Division (1918), later corps commander; Army chief of staff (1926–30); president, The Citadel (1931–53) (died 1955).

1869 Brand Whitlock, minister to Belgium (1913–22), born in Urbana, OH; a leader in postwar Belgian relief work (died 1934).

1873 Congress amended an act of the previous day to make their pay increase ($5,000 to $7,500) retroactive for two years; public outcry resulted in repealing amendment January 20, 1874.

1880 Channing Pollock, novelist/playwright, born in Washington, DC; play co-author (*Clothes, The Red Widow, 1915 Ziegfeld Follies*); author (*Behold the Men, Footlights*) (died 1946).

1884 Iowa adopted statewide prohibition; a previous law was in effect 1855–58.

1886 U. of Wyoming in Laramie chartered; opened in 1887.

1888 Knute Rockne, legendary football coach of Notre Dame (1918–31), born in Voss, Norway; teams won 105, lost 12, tied five; killed in plane crash (1931).

1889 Pearl White, silent screen actress, born in Green Ridge, MO; starred in early film series (*Perils of Pauline*) (died 1938).

1897 Robert A. McClure, Army officer who was first chief of psychological warfare, born in Mattoon, IL; helped plan North Africa and Normandy invasions (died 1957).

1901 Charles H. Goren, bridge expert who won two world and 26 American championships, born in Philadelphia; his point count bidding system became very popular (died 1991).

1902 American Automobile Association formed in Chicago by representatives of nine auto clubs; Winthrop E. Scarritt of New York was first president.

1904 George Gamow, nuclear physicist, born in Odessa, Russia; a major formulator of "big bang" theory of the origin of the universe; author (*Mr. Tompkins Explores the Atom*) (died 1968).

1908 School fire in Collinwood, OH, near Cleveland killed 161 children and teachers.

1909 President Theodore Roosevelt signed act increasing salary of the president from $50,000 to $75,000, with his successor (Taft) as first recipient; vice president's salary raised to $12,000.

1912 W. Willard Wirtz, Labor Secretary (1962–69) born in DeKalb, IL.

1913 Department of Commerce and Labor divided into two separate departments, with William B. Wilson as Labor Secretary and William C. Redfield as Commerce Secretary.

1913 John Garfield, screen actor (*Body and Soul, Gentleman's Agreement*), born in New York City (died 1952).

1918 Margaret Osborn duPont, one of greatest women tennis players, born in Joseph, OR; won French singles (1946, 1949), U.S. (1948–50) and Wimbledon (1947); with Louise Brough won U.S. doubles 12 times, Wimbledon five times, French three times.

1918 Bernard Baruch appointed chairman of the reorganized War Industries Board by President Wilson.

1921 Hot Springs (AR) National Park established.

1921 President Harding appointed Herbert Hoover as Secretary of Commerce.

1922 Bert (Egbert A.) Williams, popular comedian/song writer, died at 48; starred in vaudeville, musical comedy, and Ziegfeld Follies.

1923 Interior Secretary Albert B. Fall resigned in the wake of developments in Teapot Dome scandal.

1925 Executive and legislative salaries were increased with the vice president, cabinet members, and Speaker going from $12,000 to $15,000; congressmen were raised from $7,500 to $10,000.

1930 Coolidge Dam in Arizona dedicated.

1933 In his first inaugural address, President Franklin Roosevelt initiated the term "good neighbor policy."

1940 King's Canyon (CA) National Park established.

1944 First American air raid was made on Berlin.

1971 President Nixon declared South Vietnamese drive into Laos was successful, promised continued withdrawal of American troops.

1987 President Reagan said he accepted "full responsibility" for the Iran-Contra affair even though he was "angry" and "disappointed" with the actions of subordinates who carried out the policy.

1987 U.S. District Court Judge W. Brevard

Hand banned 31 textbooks from Alabama public schools, saying they illegally promoted "the religion of secular humanism"; U.S. Circuit Court of Appeals on August 27 reversed the decision.

1991 Iraqi military leaders accepted Allied terms for formally ending the Desert Storm fighting.

1997 For the third time in three years, the Senate rejected a proposed constitutional amendment for a balanced federal budget.

1997 President Clinton banned the use of federal funds for human cloning research; action came shortly after a British report of a successful cloning of an adult animal.

2000 Twelfth-annual Black Church Week of Prayer for the Healing of AIDs begins: a series of meetings and seminars in churches designed, among other things, to discourage moral condemnation of victims and to encourage free distribution of needles and condoms.

2001 Former Minnesota Governor Harold E. Stassen died at 93; after gaining widespread public attention giving the keynote address to the 1940 Republican National Convention, he became a perennial candidate for the nomination himself— nine times unsuccessfully attempting to obtain it.

2002 U.S. Supreme Court ruled that utilities companies must permit competitors to move electricity over their networks.

5

1707 Abraham Pierson, first rector of Yale U., died at about 62; Congregational clergyman who helped found Yale, was named rector in 1701.

1770 An early afternoon fight between a soldier and a citizen resulted in the Boston Massacre at about 9 P.M.; three citizens were killed, eight wounded by Customs House guards.

1788 Guy Johnson, Loyalist leader, died at 48; superintendent of Indian affairs in North America (1774–82); tried to organize Indians against Americans.

1794 Robert C. Grier, associate justice, Supreme Court (1846–70), born in Cumberland County, PA (died 1870).

1817 John Quincy Adams was named Secretary of State by President Monroe.

1819 Anna C. Mowatt, playwright/actress best known for play, *Fashion*, born in Bordeaux, France; also wrote books on etiquette, cookbooks and novels (died 1870).

1824 James M. Ives of Currier & Ives prints, born in New York City (died 1870).

1835 William Steinway, piano manufacturer/public official, born in Seesen, Germany; headed family-owned company (1876–96); first chairman, Rapid Transit Commission, which planned New York City's first subway; subway tunnel under East River named for him (died 1896).

1853 Howard Pyle, illustrator/author of children's books, born in Wilmington, DE; books depicted characters, events of early American history (died 1911).

1870 Frank Norris, author (*The Pit, The Octopus*), born in Chicago (died 1902).

1875 Former President Andrew Johnson took his seat in the Senate representing Tennessee.

1882 Egbert Van Alstyne, composer, born in Chicago; known for "In the Shade of the Old Apple Tree," "Goodnight, Irene," "Drifting and Dreaming" (died 1951).

1891 Daniel R. Fitzpatrick, editorial cartoonist with *St. Louis Post-Dispatch* (from 1913), born in Superior, WI (died 1969).

1918 James Tobin, economist, born in Champaign, IL; awarded 1981 Nobel Economics Prize for analysis of investments and financial markets.

1946 British Prime Minister Winston Churchill, accompanied by President Truman, made his "iron curtain" speech at Westminster College in Fulton, MO; called for Anglo-American association to deter Russian ambitions.

1979 *Voyager I* spacecraft relayed a wealth of information after it came within 172,500 miles of Jupiter.

1984 Supreme Court ruled 5–4 that public financing of a Nativity scene did not of itself violate the doctrine of separation of church and state.

2001 Santee, California 15-year-old Charles A. Williams killed two fellow high school students and wounded thirteen others.

2002 Tariffs as high as 30 percent placed on imported steel products; intended to protect U.S. manufacturers; 178 items removed from list on August 22nd.

2003 California's "three strikes and you're out" (life imprisonment or extremely long sentence for third conviction regardless of its seriousness) upheld by Supreme Court in two 5–4 decisions.

6

1724 Henry Laurens, colonial leader, born in Charleston, SC; president of first Continental Congress (1777–78); captured by British (1780) while enroute to negotiate a treaty with the Dutch; held in Tower of London until exchanged (1782) for Lord Cornwallis (died 1792).

1797 Gerrit Smith, abolitionist/philanthropist, born in Utica, NY; founder of Liberty Party (died 1874).

1809 John Quincy Adams named minister to Russia by President Madison; served until 1814.

1812 Aaron L. Dennison, watchmaker, born in Freeport, ME; devised machine-made interchangeable parts, thus increasing accuracy, lowering costs; known as the father of American watchmaking (died 1895).

1819 Supreme Court ruled in *McCulloch v. Maryland* that Congress had the power to charter the Bank of the United States, could set up branches in the states without their consent; Chief Justice Marshall held that the national government, while limited in its powers, is supreme within its sphere of action.

1820 Horatio G. Wright, Union general, born in Clinton, CT; served at Gettysburg, the Wilderness Campaign, Shenandoah Valley; chief of engineers (1879–84) (died 1899).

1829 Martin Van Buren named Secretary of State by President Jackson, serving until 1831; resigned as New York governor after three months to take post.

1831 Philip H. Sheridan, Union general, born in Albany; headed Army of the Shenandoah Valley, cut off Lee's line of retreat at Appomattox; commander-in-chief, Army (1884) (died 1888).

1833 Abraham Lincoln received a saloon license to dispense liquor in Springfield, IL (Berry and Lincoln); never used it.

1836 The Alamo in San Antonio fell after 12 days siege; 187 Americans led by William B. Travis and including Davy Crockett and James Bowie, and 1,544 Mexicans were killed; 145 original American defenders were reinforced by men who crept through Mexican lines to join the besieged.

1838 John Stevens, inventor/developer of steamships, died at 89; built the *Phoenix* (1808), which made trip (1809) from New York to Philadelphia, becoming the first working steamship.

1844 Mexican government severed diplomatic relations with United States following passage of a joint resolution annexing Texas.

1848 People of Illinois ratified their state constitution, effective April 1.

1857 Supreme Court announced the controversial Dred Scott decision, which sharpened differences over slavery; majority ruled blacks were not citizens and therefore Scott could not sue in federal court, that residence on free soil did not make him a free man on returning to slave territory, and that the Missouri Compromise of 1820 was unconstitutional.

1861 Provisional Confederate Congress established the Confederate Army (a corps of engineers and artillery, five regiments of infantry, one of cavalry); called for 100,000 men to serve 12 months.

1862 President Lincoln sent special message to Congress recommending compensated emancipation of slaves in states that adopted gradual abolition; Congress adopted a joint resolution for federal assistance (April 10).

1862 Three-day battle of Pea Ridge (or Elkhorn Tavern), AR broke the Confederate hold in Arkansas and Missouri; Confederate gens. McCulloch and McIntosh were killed.

1871 Benjamin R. Harney, pianist who popularized ragtime music, born in Middleboro, KY; was a vaudeville headliner (died 1938).

1885 Ring(gold) Lardner, sports writer and humorist (*You Know Me, Al*; *Gullible's Travels*), born in Niles, MI (died 1933).

1886 The Gould system of railroads was struck by 9,000 members of the Knights of Labor; strike ended May 4 without benefit to the strikers.

1897 John D. McArthur, president of Bankers Life Insurance Co. (1936–78), born in Pittston, PA (died 1978).

1899 Richard L. Simon, publisher, born in New York City; cofounder (1924), partner, Simon & Schuster; introduced Pocket Books (1939), first inexpensive reprints (died 1960).

1900 Lefty (Robert M.) Grove, one of greatest left-handed pitchers, born in Lonaconing, MD; played with Philadelphia AL (1925–33) and Boston AL (1934–41); named to Baseball Hall of Fame (died 1975).

1902 Permanent Census Bureau created, effective July 1.

1906 Lou Costello of the Abbott and Costello comedy team born in Paterson, NJ; starred in films and radio (died 1959).

1924 Sarah Caldwell, conductor/opera producer, born in Marysville, MO; founder of Boston Opera Company.

1926 Alan L. Greenspan, chairman of Federal Reserve Board (1987–), born in New York City; chairman, Council of Economic Advisors (1974–77).

1929 Thomas S. Foley, House Speaker (1989–94), born in Seattle, WA; represented Washington in House (1965–94).

1933 Chicago Mayor Anton J. Cermak died in Miami at 60, the victim of an assassination attempt on President-elect Franklin Roosevelt February 15.

1933 Four-day bank holiday begun by proclamation of President Franklin Roosevelt.

1937 Ivan Boesky, investment banker, born in Detroit; his illegal insider trading in stocks led to his paying $100 million fine and a ban on further Wall Street dealings.

1945 Inter-American Conference on the Problems of the War adopted the Act of Chapultepec, which in essence agreed that an attack on one was an attack on all.

1984 Senate confirmed William A. Wilson 81 to 13 as ambassador to the Vatican, thus resuming diplomatic relations after a more than 100-year gap.

1986 Commission investigating the bombing of a violent radical group in May 1985 in Philadelphia in which 11 people died and 61 homes were destroyed found Philadelphia Mayor W. Wilson Goode "grossly negligent."

2000 Supreme Court ruled 7–2 that a defendant's rights are not violated if a prosecutor asserts that he may have tailored testimony to fit that of other witnesses.

2001 Senate repealed President Clinton's workplace injury "liberalization" rules by 56–44; next day House concurred by 223–206.

2002 An issue of the *Journal of the American Medical Association* printed most in-depth study yet of heavy marijuana use impact on brain function: impedes it for hours after last joint; study involved patients in three cities and over 150 individuals.

2003 Report: Air Force internal investigation of the Air Force Academy indicated 54 claims of rape in a ten-year period; several top officials at school removed on March 25.

2005 Teresa Wright (b. 1918), actress in movies and television beginning in 1940s, died; only performer to receive Oscar nominations for each of first three films; one of only ten to receive Supporting and Best Actor nominations the same year.

7

1590 Roger Ludlow, one of Connecticut's early leaders, baptized in Dinton, England; headed Massachusetts Bay Colony (1635); believed to have been author of the Fundamental Orders of Connecticut; codified Connecticut laws and presided over first court held there; returned to England (died 1664).

1638 Anne Hutchinson banished from Massachusetts for her religious opinions; she, William Coddington, and 17 others founded Pocassat, RI (later named Portsmouth).

1644 Samuel Gorton (1592–1677), founder of a religious sect (Gortonians), banished from Massachusetts; settled in Rhode Island, founding Warwick; his sect rejected outward religious ceremonies, held that Christ was both human and divine, that heaven and hell exist only in the mind.

1707 Stephen Hopkins, colonial official, born in Providence; Rhode Island governor eight years between 1755 and 1767; member of Continental Congress (1774–80); a signer of Declaration of Independence; wrote *The Rights of the Colonies Examined* (1765) (died 1785).

1766 British Parliament enacted the Declaratory Act a day after repeal of the Stamp Act; declared that any colonial legislature which denied Parliament the right to pass laws affecting the colonies "are hereby declared to be utterly null and void to all intents and purposes whatsoever."

1814 John H. Raymond, educator, born in New York City; an organizer, professor, U. of Rochester (1850–55); first president, Brooklyn Polytechnic Institute (1855–64); president, Vassar College (1865–78) (died 1878).

1832 Orlando M. Poe, Army engineer, born in Navarre, OH; with Sherman's march to the sea; had charge of many waterway improvements, building locks at Sault Ste. Marie canals (died 1895).

1837 Henry Draper, physiologist/astronomer, born in Prince Edward County, VA; devised methods of photographing skies, did unique work in stellar spectroscopy; physiology professor, dean of medical faculty, New York U. (1866–82) (died 1882).

1844 Anthony Comstock, reformer who conducted spectacular raids on publishers, vendors, born in New Canaan, CT; cofounder, New York Society for the Suppression of Vice (died 1915).

1845 David D. Palmer, pioneer chiropractor, born in Toronto; began "magnetic healing," which became chiropractic; opened school in Davenport, IA (1898) (died 1913).

1849 Luther Burbank, plant breeder, born in Lancaster, MA; experimented, developed more and better varieties of plants — plums, berries, tomatoes, corn, squash, lilies, the Burbank rose, poppies, the Shasta daisy (died 1926).

1850 Champ (James Beauchamp) Clark, legislator, born in Lawrenceburg, KY; represented Missouri in House (1893–95, 1897–1921), serving as minority leader (1907–11) and Speaker (1911–19);

led successful fight against arbitrary control by House Speaker Joseph Cannon (died 1921).

1866 Mark A. Carleton, plant pathologist who founded durum wheat industry, born in Jerusalem, OH; introduced Kubanka wheat from Asia (died 1925).

1876 Alexander Graham Bell granted a patent on his telephone.

1913 Dynamite exploded in Baltimore Harbor killing 55 persons.

1930 Stanley L. Miller, chemist, was born in Oakland, CA; noted for a key experiment related to the chemical origins of life.

1938 David Baltimore, microbiologist, born in New York City; demonstrated existence of "reverse transcriptase," a vital enzyme that reverses normal DNA-to-RNA process; shared 1975 Nobel Physiology/Medicine Prize for that work.

1945 American forces crossed the Rhine River, the first foreign crossing since Napoleon; the 9th Armored Division seized the Rhine bridge at Remagen.

1965 Marchers from Selma to Montgomery, AL, were met at the Alabama River Bridge outside Selma by state police and a sheriff's posse; marchers were turned back by force, 50 injured.

1984 Jeremy Levin, television news reporter, and William Buckley, CIA station chief, were kidnapped in Beirut; Levin escaped February 14, 1985; Buckley was killed.

1995 Gov. George E. Pataki signed a bill restoring the death penalty in New York State after 32 years.

2000 California Proposition 22 restricting marriage to heterosexual couples passed with 61 percent of the vote and a sweep of 53 of state's 58 counties.

2001 Census Bureau issued report that Hispanic population of U.S. had increased over 60 percent from 1990 census.

2003 Broadway musicians went on strike, closing many theaters; settlement agreed to on March 11.

8

1752 William Bingham, banker/legislator, born in Philadelphia; founder, director, Bank of North America (1781), first bank in U.S.; served in Continental Congress (1786–89), represented Pennsylvania in Senate (1795–1801); founded Binghamton, NY (died 1804).

1765 Stamp Act passed by the House of Lords (Commons passed it February 27) to go into effect November 1; British hoped to raise 60,000 addi-tional pounds in the colonies, with stamps to be put on commercial and legal documents, pamphlets, newspapers, almanacs, playing cards, dice; met by unanimous opposition in the colonies, as feelings mounted against taxation without representation.

1783 Hannah Hoes Van Buren, wife of President Van Buren, born in Kinderhook, NY (died 1819).

1796 Supreme Court in *Hylton v. United States* upheld for first time the constitutionality of a congressional act.

1799 Simon Cameron, public official/diplomat, born in Lancaster County, PA; Secretary of War (1861–62); minister to Russia (1862); represented Pennsylvania in Senate (1845–49, 1957–61, 1867–77) (died 1889).

1803 James Monroe, named special minister to France to clear up Mississippi Valley situation, sailed for France.

1804 Alvan Clark, astronomer, born in Ashfield, MA; produced telescope lenses for major observatories with son, Alvan G. (died 1887).

1813 Russia offered to mediate war between United States and Great Britain; offer turned down by British.

1817 New York Stock Exchange formally chartered; had been operating informally since 1791 when brokers met in the shade of a buttonwood tree on Wall St.

1821 Morgan L. Smith, Union general, born in Mexico, NY; served at Ft. Donelson, Shiloh, Vicksburg, Missionary Ridge (died 1874).

1839 James M. Crafts, organic chemist/educator, born in Boston; while doing research in France he was co-discoverer of Friedel-Crafts reaction, which paved way for hundreds of new carbon compounds; MIT professor (1892–98), president (1898–1900) (died 1917).

1841 Oliver Wendell Holmes, Jr., associate justice, Supreme Court (1902–32), born in Boston; justice, Massachusetts Supreme Court (1883–1902); a towering figure in Supreme Court where he was known as the "Great Dissenter" (died 1935).

1862 Joseph Lee, social worker known as the "father" of American playgrounds, born in Brookline, MA; president, Playground Association of America (1910–37) (died 1937).

1865 Frederick W. Goudy, printer/type designer, born in Bloomington, IL; designed more than 90 type faces; established Village Press (1903) (died 1947).

1874 Former President Fillmore died in Buffalo at 74.

1886   Edward C. Kendall, biochemist, born in South Norwalk, CT; shared 1950 Nobel Physiology/Medicine Prize for discoveries about hormones of adrenal cortex (died 1972).

1924   Mine accident at Castle Gate, UT, claimed 171 lives.

1930   Former President Taft died in Washington at 72.

1948   Supreme Court ruled that religious training in public schools is unconstitutional.

1954   United States and Japan signed a mutual defense treaty.

1965   First American combat troops landed in South Vietnam when two battalions of Marines arrived to defend the Danang air base.

1993   Dow Jones industrial average hit a new high of 3469.42.

1996   Dr. Jack Kevorkian, retired pathologist who was present at the suicide of 27 persons, was acquitted in Michigan of violating a law against doctor-assisted suicide.

1998   Groundbreaking held for Safeco Field, future home of Seattle Mariners; to be located on site of old Kingdome parking lot; scheduled to open 1999.

2002   Kmart announced the 284 stores it would close in an effort to shed unprofitable operations and to stay competitive with rivals; leaves over 1,800 stores in operation.

9

1454   Amerigo Vespucci, Italian explorer, born in Florence; made several trips to New World (1497–1503); made maps of area; America named for him (died 1512).

1679   Zabdiel Boylston, physician, born in Brookline, MA; first to use inoculation to combat smallpox epidemic, inoculating his son Thomas and two slaves first; many more later (died 1766).

1764   George Grenville, chancellor of Exchequer, introduced American Revenue Act (generally known as the Sugar Act), the first law specifically passed to raise money for Britain in the colonies; in retaliation, colonies began program of nonimportation.

1773   Isaac Hull, War of 1812 Navy officer, born in Shelton, CT; commander of the *Constitution* ("Old Ironsides") when it defeated the British frigate, *Guerriere*, August 19, 1812 (died 1843).

1781   Spanish fleet of 38 ships began siege of Pensacola; British surrendered city and all of West Florida.

1791   George Hayward, first American surgeon to use ether anesthetic in a major operation (1846), born in Boston (died 1863).

1806   Edwin Forrest, actor, born in Philadelphia; his feud with fellow actor, William C. MacReady, led to riot in Astor Place Opera House, New York City (1849), in which 22 were killed when militia fired on crowd (died 1872).

1814   John Evans, educator/public official, born in Waynesville, OH; a founder, Northwestern U.; Evanston, IL, named for him; territorial governor of Colorado (1862–65); founder, Colorado Seminary which became U. of Denver (died 1897).

1815   David Davis, legislator/jurist, born in Cecil County, MD; represented Illinois in Senate (1877–83), serving as president pro tem (1881–83); associate justice, Supreme Court (1862–77) (died 1886).

1820   Maria Hester Monroe, daughter of President and Mrs. Monroe, married in the White House, first presidential daughter married there.

1820   Samuel Blatchford, associate justice, Supreme Court (1882–93), born in New York City (died 1893).

1824   (A.) Leland Stanford, railroad executive/public official, born in Watervliet, NY; governor of California (1861–63) and represented state in Senate (1885–93); a founder, president, Central Pacific Railroad (1853–83) which was absorbed by Southern Pacific, of which he was president (1884–90); founder, Stanford U. (1885) in memory of his son (died 1893).

1829   Postmaster General became member of president's cabinet.

1830   Charter issued to New York Life Insurance & Trust Co., first company to specialize in life insurance.

1834   Henry A. Ward, naturalist who sold natural history items collections, born in Rochester, NY; sold collections to colleges, museums, etc; a major collection was purchased by Marshall Field (1893), formed nucleus of Field Museum of Natural History (died 1906).

1841   Supreme Court freed blacks taken from the Spanish ship, *Amistad*, after they had seized the ship; former President John Quincy Adams defended the blacks.

1847   First large scale amphibious operation in American military history took place when 2,595 American troops landed on the beaches of Vera Cruz, Mexico; occupied the city March 29.

1856   Edward G. Acheson, discoverer of silicon carbide (carborundum), born in Washington,

PA; served as assistant to Thomas A. Edison (died 1931).

1856 Eddie (Edward F.) Foy, entertainer, born in New York City; popular song-and-dance man with his children ("the seven little Foys") (died 1928).

1862 Ironclad vessels *Merrimac* and *Monitor* met in Hampton Roads, an epoch-making development in naval warfare; battle indecisive but considered a Union victory because the *Merrimac* was disabled.

1863 Confederate raiding party, led by John S. Mosby, captured Union General Edwin H. Stoughton and his staff behind Union lines at Fairfax Court House, VA.

1864 President Lincoln commissioned Ulysses S. Grant a lieutenant general, then highest rank in the Army; assumed command of Union forces.

1867 Lillian D. Wald, social worker, born in Cincinnati; founder (1893), head, public health nursing in Henry St. Settlement, New York City; suggested the Children's Bureau, which was created in 1908 (died 1940).

1900 Howard H. Aiken, mathematician who invented an early computer, born in Hoboken, NJ; invented the Mark I, forerunner of digital computer (1944); weighed 35 tons, was 51 ft. long, had a memory but did only arithmetic (died 1973).

1902 Edward Durrell Stone, architect, born in Fayetteville, AR; designed American Embassy, New Delhi; American Pavilion at Brussels World Fair; Kennedy Center in Washington (died 1978).

1903 Albert G. Meyer, Catholic archbishop (Milwaukee 1953–58, Chicago 1958–65), born in Milwaukee; named cardinal (1959) (died 1965).

1910 Samuel Barber, composer, born in West Chester, PA; wrote ballets (*Medea*), operas (*Varessa*), and other compositions (died 1981).

1916 Band of 1,500 men led by Pancho Villa attacked Columbus, NM, setting the town afire and killing 19 Americans.

1917 President Wilson announced that American merchant vessels would be armed.

1918 Mickey (Frank M.) Spillane, mystery story writer, born in New York City; began as comic book writer (*Captain Marvel*); best known for Mike Hammer stories.

1933 President Franklin Roosevelt signed emergency Banking Relief Act authorizing the Treasury Secretary to call in all gold and gold certificates; banned hoarding and exporting gold; bill submitted to opening session of Congress at 1 P.M.; passed both houses by 7:30 P.M., signed by president 8:36 P.M.; Act also empowered the president to reorgan-

ize all insolvent banks, permitted sound banks to reopen.

1957 Congress endorsed Eisenhower Doctrine, which provided economic aid to any Middle East country threatened by Communist aggression.

1964 Supreme Court in *New York Times v. Sullivan* provided protection to newspapers against libel suits.

1975 Construction of the Alaska oil pipeline began.

1977 Restrictions were lifted on American travel to Cuba, Vietnam, North Korea, and Cambodia.

1977 Twelve Hanafi Muslim gunmen seized three buildings in Washington and held 139 persons prisoner for 39 hours before surrendering; had demanded release of imprisoned Muslims; one person killed in ordeal.

1987 Piedmont Aviation accepted bid of USAir Group of $1.59 billion to take over line.

1987 Chrysler Corporation announced it planned to buy American Motors Corp. for more than $1.5 billion in a deal that would reduce to three the number of American car manufacturers.

1989 Senate by 53–47 vote rejected nomination of former Texas Senator John G. Tower as Defense Secretary; 52 Democrats were joined by Republican Senator Nancy Kassenbaum of Kansas against the nomination.

1995 Edward Bernays, father of public relations, died in Cambridge, MA, at 103.

2000 Path to presidential nomination of Bush (Republican) and Gore (Democrat) cleared as their respective rivals, Senators McCain and Bradley, withdraw from the race.

10

1775 Daniel Boone and 30 men began to clear the Wilderness Road for access to Transylvania County land in Kentucky.

1783 Last naval battle of the Revolution fought in the Gulf of Florida, when an American ship under John Barry beat back three British frigates.

1785 Thomas Jefferson was elected by Congress as minister to France for three years, succeeding Benjamin Franklin.

1804 Upper Louisiana formally transferred to United States when Capt. Amos Stoddard took command of the area at St. Louis.

1810 John McCloskey, Catholic prelate, born in Brooklyn; archbishop of New York (1864–85); was first American cardinal (1875) (died 1885).

1818   George W. Randolph, Confederate general and Confederate Secretary of State (1862), born in Goochland County, VA (died 1867).

1824   Thomas J. Churchill, Confederate general who served in Trans-Mississippi theater, born in Jefferson County, KY (died 1905).

1848   Senate by vote of 38–14 ratified treaty ending Mexican War.

1865   Union forces occupied Fayetteville, NC, destroying the arsenal and iron works.

1869   Charles W. Eliot inaugurated as president of Harvard U.; he contributed to all American higher education with the elective system and other reforms.

1876   Alexander Graham Bell transmitted the first intelligible sentence on a telephone to his assistant, Thomas A. Watson, saying "Mr. Watson, come here, I want you."

1880   Max Thorek, surgeon, born in Hungary; founder, International College of Surgeons; cofounder, American Hospital in Chicago (died 1960).

1888   Oscar G. Mayer, president of meat company named for him (1928–55), born in Chicago (died 1965).

1900   Peter DeRose, composer ("Deep Purple," "Wagon Wheels"), born in New York City (died 1953).

1902   First antitrust suit was filed by United States against the Northern Securities Co., a railroad holding company organized by James J. Hill.

1903   Bix (Leon B.) Beiderbecke, jazz trumpeter who had influence on later jazz musicians, born in Davenport, IA; first white musician considered a jazz innovator (died 1931).

1913   Harriet Tubman, organizer of the underground railroad, died at about 93.

1915   German cruiser, *Prinz Eitel Friedrich*, arrived in Newport News, VA, after sinking an American vessel, *William P. Frye*, January 28; cruiser interned.

1916   President Wilson ordered American troops into Mexico in an effort to capture Pancho Villa, whose troops raided Columbus, NM, the day before, killing 19 Americans; 4,000 troops under Gen. John J. Pershing entered Mexico March 15.

1919   Supreme Court unanimously upheld conviction of Eugene V. Debs under the Espionage Act.

1923   Val L. Fitch, Princeton physicist, born in Merriman, NE; shared 1980 Nobel Physics Prize for research in big bang theory of universe formation.

1942   Gen. Joseph Stilwell was made chief of staff of Allied armies in China.

1945   American troops landed on Mindanao in the Philippines.

1971   Senate approved constitutional amendment lowering the voting age to 18 by a vote of 94–0; House approved 400–19 on March 23; ratified by June 30.

1994   Centers for Disease Control reported that the number of new AIDS cases had more than doubled in 1993 to 103,500.

2000   Mother Katharine Drexel, who devoted her fortune to promoting black and Indian education, approved for October 1 canonization by pope.

2000   Nasdaq Composite Index hit record 5048.62.

11

1731   Robert T. Paine, colonial leader, born in Boston; member of Continental Congress (1774–78), signer of Declaration of Independence; Massachusetts attorney general (1777–90), judge (1790–1804) (died 1814).

1779   Continental Congress authorized creation of Corps of Engineers; disbanded in 1783, but restored permanently March 16, 1802.

1781   Anthony P. Heinrich, composer known as the Beethoven of America, born in Schönbüchel, Austria (died 1861).

1785   John McLean, associate justice, Supreme Court (1829–61), born in Morris County, NJ; represented Ohio in House (1813–16); Postmaster General (1823–29) (died 1861).

1818   Henry Jacob Bigelow, surgeon, born in Boston; made many important contributions to surgery, published first account of using ether in an operation (died 1890).

1824   Bureau of Indian Affairs created in the War Department.

1860   Thomas Hastings, architect (New York Public Library, Senate Office Building), born in New York City (died 1929).

1861   Representatives of Confederate states met in Montgomery, AL; adopted their constitution, closely resembling the U.S. Constitution; later ratified by the seceding states.

1862   President Lincoln relieved Gen. George B. McClellan of command over all military departments, except the Army of the Potomac.

1868   State convention adopted new Georgia constitution.

1888 Tremendous three-day blizzard began in Midwest; took 400 lives.

1890 Vannevar Bush, builder of first analog computer, born in Everett, MA; his computer designed to solve differential equations; director, Office of Scientific Research and Development, which laid groundwork for uranium research (died 1974).

1890 Eugene F. McDonald, Jr., founder (1923), head, Zenith Radio Corp., born in Syracuse, NY; founder, National Association of Broadcasters (died 1958).

1898 Dorothy Gish, early screen actress, born in Massillon, OH; starred in *Orphans of the Storm*, *Romola*, *Nell Gwynn* (died 1968).

1903 Lawrence Welk, accordionist and orchestra leader, born in Strasburg, ND; formed own band 1927 (died 1992).

1903 Dorothy Schiff, publisher *New York Post* (1939–77), born in New York City.

1920 Nicolaas Bloembergen, physicist, born in Dordrecht, Netherlands; shared 1981 Nobel Physics Prize for work in developing laser spectroscopy technique.

1923 (Althea) Louise Brough, star doubles tennis player, born in Oklahoma City; with Margaret Osborne duPont won American doubles 12 times, Wimbledon five, French three; also won Wimbledon singles three times.

1926 Ralph D. Abernathy, a founder, president (1968–77), Southern Christian Leadership Conference, born in Linden, AL (died 1990).

1931 Rupert Murdoch, newspaper publisher (New York, London, Australia), born in Melbourne, Australia.

1936 Atonin Scalia, associate justice, Supreme Court (1986–), born in Trenton, NJ.

1941 Lend Lease Act signed, making defense material available to any country vital to the defense of the United States; provided military credit to Great Britain, and later to Soviet Russia.

1977 Brazilian Government, angered by what it called intolerable interference in its internal affairs (criticism of human rights), cancelled the 15-year-old military aid treaty with the U.S.

1996 Vince Edwards, actor who starred on television as Dr. Ben Casey, died at 69.

1996 National Football League owners approved move of Cleveland Browns to Baltimore.

2004 Sidney L. James, first managing editor of *Sports Illustrated* in 1954, died at 97; in 1960 moved up to publisher.

12

1773 Virginia House of Burgesses named a committee to keep in touch with other colonies on matters of mutual interest; five other colonies did likewise by July.

1790 William Grayson, colonial leader, died at about 54; aide to George Washington (1776), commissioner of Board of War (1779–81); member, Continental Congress (1784–87), represented Virginia in Senate (1789–90).

1801 Joseph Francis, inventor of wooden and metal lifeboats, born in Boston (died 1893).

1806 Jane M. Appleton Pierce, wife of President Pierce, born in Hampton, NH (died 1863).

1818 John L. Worden, Union naval officer who commanded the *Monitor* in its historic battle with the *Merrimac*, born in Westchester County, NY (died 1897).

1831 Clement Studebaker, pioneer automaker, born near Gettysburg, PA; cofounder with brothers of wagon company (1852), president (1868–91); company produced 750,000 wagons before switching to automobiles (died 1901).

1835 Simon Newcomb, a foremost mathematician/astronomer, born in Wallace, Nova Scotia; mathematics professor, Naval Observatory (1861–97); Johns Hopkins U. (1884–1900) (died 1909).

1854 Andrew Furuseth, president, International Seaman's Union (1903–38), born in Romedal, Norway; helped raise working standards and conditions for American sailors (died 1938).

1858 Adolph S. Ochs, publisher, born in Cincinnati; publisher, *Chattanooga Times* (1878–1935), *New York Times* (1896–1935), *Philadelphia Times and Public Ledger* (1902–12); originator, Chattanooga-Lookout Mountain Park (died 1935).

1862 Jane A. Delano, organized American Red Cross nursing service, born in Townsend, NY; she made possible the enlistment of 20,000 nurses (1911–18) (died 1919).

1864 Gen. U.S. Grant named general-in-chief of Armies of the United States, the first to attain rank of full general.

1885 U. of Arizona chartered.

1886 Robert Hallowell, painter/publisher, born in Denver; illustrator, *Century Magazine* (1910–14); a founder/publisher, *New Republic* (1914–25) (died 1939).

1888 Great Blizzard struck the Atlantic Seaboard, centering on New York City; killed about 400 people and did $25 million damage.

1901 Andrew Carnegie offered New York City $5.2 million for 65 branch libraries, the city to provide the sites.

1907 Russell Sage Foundation created by Mrs. Margaret Olivia Sage with a $10 million endowment "for the improvement of social and living conditions in the United States."

1912 Girl Scouts of the United States (originally Girl Guides) founded in Savannah by Juliette G. Low.

1917 An executive order authorized the arming of merchant vessels bound for submarine zone.

1922 J. Lane Kirkland, president, AFL-CIO (1979–96), born in Camden, SC; secretary-treasurer, AFL-CIO (1969–79).

1922 Jack (Jean-Louis) Kerouac, author of the Beat Generation, born in Lowell, MA; wrote several novels (*On the Road, Big Sur, The Dharma Burns*) (died 1969).

1928 Edward F. Albee, playwright, born in Washington, DC; wrote several hits (*Who's Afraid of Virginia Woolf?, A Delicate Balance, Tiny Alice*).

1932 Andrew Young, legislator/public official, born in New Orleans; represented Georgia in House (1973–77); United Nations ambassador (1977–79); mayor of Atlanta (1982–89).

1933 President Franklin Roosevelt made his first "fireside chat," addressing the nation by radio; urged people to return savings to the banks, which were now safe.

1942 American troops landed on New Caledonia.

1946 Liza Minelli, entertainer/actress, born in Los Angeles; starred in *Cabaret* and *New York, New York*.

1947 President Truman, in what came to be known as the Truman Doctrine, asked for $400 million in aid for Greece and Turkey against Communism; approved May 22.

1978 Theresa W. Blanchard, leading American competitive figure skater between 1914 and 1927, died in Brookline, MA, at 85; won women's title five times (1914, 1920–24) and with Nat Niles, the pairs championship title nine times (1918, 1920–27).

1985 Disarmament talks began between the United States and Soviet Russia in Geneva.

1993 Janet Reno, a Florida state attorney, became first woman U.S. Attorney General.

1996 President Clinton signed bill strengthening U.S. economic embargo against Cuba.

2001 Robert Ludlum died (1927–2001); pioneered modern thriller-style novels, which he developed through over two dozen works; over 210 million copies printed in 32 languages.

2003 Lynne Thigpen, African-American actress (b. 1948), unexpectedly died; appeared on Broadway in musicals, and then in over three dozen movies, usually in powerful dramatic supporting roles.

13

1639 Massachusetts General Court named the new school at New Town for John Harvard, who had left books and money for the school.

1798 Abigail Powers Fillmore, first wife of President Fillmore, born in Stillwater, NY (died 1853).

1813 Lorenzo Delmonico, restaurateur who helped found, operated famous New York restaurant, born in Marengo, Switzerland (died 1881).

1815 James C. Hepburn, Presbyterian medical missionary, born in Milton, PA; one of first missionaries to Japan, compiled first Japanese-English dictionary, supervised translation of Bible into Japanese (died 1911).

1833 William F. Warren, Methodist clergyman/educator, born in Williamsburg, MA; president, Boston Theological School (1867–73), a cofounder, Boston U. of which Boston Theological became part; first president, Boston U. (1873–1903), instrumental in making it the first university to grant doctoral degree to women (died 1929).

1848 Wisconsin residents ratified state constitution, which prohibited slavery.

1855 Percival Lowell, astronomer, born in Boston; created observatory near Flagstaff, AZ (1893–94); best known for studies of Mars, mathematical work predicting discovery of planet Pluto (died 1916).

1868 Impeachment trial of President Andrew Johnson formally began before Supreme Court Justice Salmon P. Chase, presiding in the Senate.

1872 Oswald G. Villard, editor/owner, *New York Post* (1897–1918), born in Wiesbaden, Germany; also editor, *The Nation* (1918–32); champion of minority rights, pacifism (died 1949).

1883 Clifford M. Holland, engineer of tunnels in New York City area, born in Somerset, MA; directed tunnel building under East and Hudson Rivers (1914–24); one under Hudson named for him (died 1924).

1887 Alexander A. Vandegrift, Marine Corps commandant (1944–48), born in Charlottesville,

VA; led Marine landings at Guadalcanal, Bougainville; first Marine to hold rank of general (died 1973).

1899   John H. Van Vleck, physicist, born in Middletown, CT; shared 1977 Nobel Physics Prize for work underlying computer memories and electronic devices (died 1980).

1901   Former President Benjamin Harrison died in Indianapolis at 67.

1908   Walter H. Annenberg, publisher/diplomat, born in Milwaukee, WI; president, Triangle Publications (*Racing Form*, *TV Guide*) ambassador to Great Britain (1969–76).

1911   L. Ron (Lafayette R.) Hubbard, religious leader, born in Tilden, NE; founder of Scientology, a religious movement based on dianetics, a method of achieving mental and physical health (died 1986).

1913   Sammy Kaye, orchestra leader noted for his "swing and sway" music, born in Lakewood, OH (died 1987).

1922   Walter Byers, first executive director of National Collegiate Athletic Association (1951–88), born.

1924   Temporary injunction issued by a Wyoming federal judge against further exploitation of Teapot Dome by Sinclair Oil interests; similar injunction issued March 17 in California on naval reserves and the Doheny interests.

1928   St. Francis Dam on Santa Clara River, 40 miles north of Los Angeles, gave way, destroying much property and killing 450 persons.

1930   Astronomers at Lowell Observatory at Flagstaff, AZ, photographed for first time the ninth planet (Pluto).

1939   Neil Sedaka, composer/entertainer, born in New York City; wrote and recorded many hit songs ("Breakin' Up Is Hard to Do," "Laughter in the Rain").

1961   President Kennedy offered a ten-year Alliance for Progress program to raise living standards in Latin America.

1981   President Reagan ordered a grant of $1.5 million to help city of Atlanta finance an investigation of the murders of black children.

1986   Barber B. Conable, Jr., former New York congressman, named president of the World Bank; he had served in the House from 1964 to 1984.

1988   Gallaudet College (Washington, DC) Board of Trustees selected a deaf president, Dean I. King Jordan, to head the only American institution for the hearing-impaired after several days of student protests.

1988   American Conservative Judaism issued its first statement of principle, rejecting fundamentalism in all religions.

1989   Justice Department settled its racketeering case against the Teamsters Union after it agreed to let members vote directly for national officers and to create a review board to guard against organized crime.

1996   Liggett Group, Inc., broke ranks with other tobacco companies in a class-action suit against the industry; Liggett agreed to contribute 5 percent of annual pre-tax income, up to $50 million, for 25 years to programs to help smokers give up the habit.

2000   Federal Census forms scheduled to arrive in all American homes within next few days; for first time citizens could fill them out via the Internet.

2001   European meat imports banned due to outbreak of foot-and-mouth disease abroad.

14

1761   George Washington inherited Mt. Vernon when his sister-in-law, the widow of his half-brother Laurence, died.

1782   Thomas Hart Benton, legislator, born in Hillsboro, NC; represented Missouri in Senate (1821–51) and House (1853–55); defender of sound money (died 1858).

1794   Patent issued to Eli Whitney for the cotton gin.

1800   James Bogardus, inventor, born in Catskill, NY; among his inventions were a dry gas meter and a method of manufacturing postage stamps, for which he won a $2,000 prize from England (died 1874).

1813   Joseph P. Bradley, associate justice, Supreme Court (1870–92), born in Berne, NY (died 1892).

1837   Charles A. Cutter, librarian who developed dictionary catalog for libraries, born in Boston (died 1903).

1840   David B. Henderson, legislator, born in Old Deer, Scotland; represented Iowa in House (1883–93), serving as Speaker (1899–1903) (died 1906).

1854   Thomas B. Marshall, Vice President (1913–21), born in North Manchester, IN; Indiana governor (1909–13); memorable quote attributed to him: "What this country needs is a really good five cent cigar" (died 1925).

1859   William G. Sharp, ambassador to France (1914–19), born in Mt. Gilead, OH (died 1925).

1862 New Madrid, MO, on the Mississippi River abandoned when Union forces under Gen. John Pope maneuvered Confederate forces into a cul-de-sac.

1862 Union land and naval forces captured New Bern, NC; threatened advance on Richmond, VA.

1877 Edna W. Chase, editor-in-chief (1914–54), *Vogue*, born in Asbury Park, NJ; organized first American fashion show (died 1957).

1879 Albert Einstein, physicist who enunciated theory of relativity and unified field theory, born in Ulm, Germany; awarded 1921 Nobel Physics Prize for discovery of photoelectric law (died 1955).

1880 George V. Strong, World War II general, born in Chicago; commanded 8th Army Corps; chief of military intelligence (1942) (died 1946).

1886 Hattie Carnegie, fashion designer, born in Vienna (died 1956).

1891 A group of New Orleans citizens shot and killed 11 Italians accused of murdering Police Chief David C. Hennessy in October 1890; trial of nine of 11 resulted in acquittal of four, mistrial of three, and dismissal of charges against two.

1895 Robert F. Loeb, medical researcher whose studies of salt metabolism led to control of Addison's disease, born in Chicago (died 1973).

1897 Polish National Catholic Church of America was organized in Scranton, PA.

1898 Reginald Marsh, artist, born in Paris to American parents; painter of New York City scenes (died 1954).

1898 Richard L. Strout, journalist who wrote "TRB" column in *New Republic* (1943–83), born in Cohoes, NY (died 1990).

1900 Gold Standard Act passed and signed after agitation for free silver died down and an agreement for bimetallism failed; gold dollar became standard of value.

1903 Executive order created pensions for Civil War veterans over 62 years old — a minimum of $6 a month, a maximum of $12 at 70; increased gradually over time.

1918 Lucretia R. Garfield, widow of President Garfield, died at Pasadena, CA, at 85.

1920 Hank (Henry K.) Ketcham, cartoonist (*Dennis the Menace*), born in Seattle.

1928 Frank Borman, astronaut who took part in first manned flight around moon, born in Gary, IN; board chairman, Eastern Airlines (1976–86).

1933 Quincy Jones, composer and arranger, born in Chicago.

1964 Jack Ruby, Dallas nightclub owner, found guilty of murdering Lee Harvey Oswald, alleged assassin of President Kennedy; sentenced to death but conviction overturned, new trial ordered; Ruby died before new trial.

1993 Two-day blizzard ravaged eastern United States, causing about 200 deaths.

1995 American astronaut Norman B. Thagard became part of MIR space station crew in flight with Russian crew in spacecraft.

1997 President Clinton suffered serious knee injury in Palm Beach, FL; after successful surgery, he used crutches or cane while recovering.

2000 Pacific Stock Exchange, U.S.' fourth largest, announced it would close its trading floors and go to an entirely electronic trading system.

2003 NASA announced that full safety review of space shuttle and launch procedures might require up to two years before another launch could occur.

15

1665 John Endicott, colonial governor, died at 76; first governor of Massachusetts Bay Colony (1628–30); at various times served as assistant, deputy governor, and governor until his death.

1767 Andrew Jackson, seventh president (1829–37), born in Waxhaw, SC; represented Tennessee in House (1796–97) and Senate (1797–98, 1823–25); judge, Tennessee Supreme Court (1798–1804); in War of 1812, successfully led defense of New Orleans against British; governor of Florida Territory (1821) (died 1845).

1781 In Battle of Guilford Court House, NC, Gen. Charles Cornwallis claimed a British victory in repulsing Americans; a British legislator said, "Another such victory would ruin the British army."

1800 James H. Hackett, actor noted for role as Rip van Winkle, born in New York City (died 1871).

1820 Maine admitted to the Union as the 23d state.

1827 Michael C. Kerr, legislator, born in Titusville, PA; represented Indiana in House (1864–72, 1874–76), serving as Speaker (1875–76) (died 1876).

1838 Alice C. Fletcher, anthropologist, born in Cuba of American parents; specialized in Plains Indians culture, pioneered in study of Indian music (died 1923).

1858 Liberty H. Bailey, horticulturist, born in South Haven, MI; founder, head, New York State College of Agriculture, Cornell U. (1903–13); organized world's first botanical institution devoted to cultivated plants (died 1954).

1874 Harold L. Ickes, Secretary of Interior (1933–46), born in Franktown Township, PA; headed, Public Works Administration (died 1952).

1875 Archbishop John McCloskey of New York became the first American Catholic cardinal; invested April 27 in St. Paul's in Rome.

1875 Lee Shubert, theater manager/producer, born in Syracuse, NY; with brothers, J.J. and Sam, controlled 37 theaters at one time (died 1953).

1907 A convention adopted Oklahoma's constitution.

1913 First regular press conference held in White House, with about 125 accredited correspondents in attendance.

1916 Harry James, noted trumpeter and orchestra leader, born in Albany, GA (died 1983).

1916 Gen. John J. Pershing led 4,000 American troops across Mexican border to pursue Pancho Villa, who was responsible for many American deaths in various raids; troops were withdrawn in January 1917.

1919 An informal organizational meeting of American war veterans held in Paris to form the American Legion; formally created May 8–10, 1919.

1930 USS *Constitution* (Old Ironsides) was reconditioned by public subscription, relaunched in Boston; originally launched in 1797.

1937 First blood bank created in Cook County Hospital in Chicago.

1948 Soft coal miners (360,000) struck over the demand for $100 monthly pensions at 62; strike ended April 12 with agreement on a pension plan.

1985 Raymond Donovan, first sitting cabinet member to be indicted, resigned as Secretary of Labor; replaced by William Brock, American trade representative and former Tennessee senator.

1988 Catholic Bishop Eugene A. Marino elevated to Archbishop of Atlanta by Pope John Paul II, becoming first black American archbishop; had previously served as secretary of National Conference of Catholic Bishops.

1989 Former Illinois Representative Edward J. Derwinski sworn in as first Secretary of Veterans Affairs, the 14th cabinet department.

1995 Stockholders of Lockheed Corp. and Martin Marietta Corp. overwhelmingly approved $10 billion merger of the companies into a new company, Lockheed Martin Corp.

2000 In first major effort to make ATMs generally available to blind, Bank of America announced intention to systematically upgrade all of its 14,000+ ATMs in 20 states to provide verbal instructions.

2001 Ann Southern died (1909–2001); had her own comedy show, *The Ann Southern Show* (1958–61); acted in movies from 1930s to 1980s and as guest on many television series.

2004 Discovery of "planetoid" Sedna announced: three-quarters the size of Pluto and twice as far from the sun, with an orbit of 10,500 years.

2006 U.S. in small dissenting minority as U.N. voted 170–4 in favor of establishing a new Human Rights Council; U.S. feared that membership requirements so loose that even extreme human rights violators could remain members.

16

1641 General Court declared Rhode Island a democracy and a new constitution was adopted granting freedom of religion for all citizens.

1679 John Leverett, colonial leader, died at 63; served Massachusetts as colonial agent in England (1655–62), on General Court (1663–65) and council (1665–70), lieutenant governor (1671–73), governor (1673–79).

1696 William Greene, colonial administrator, born in Warwick, RI; deputy governor of Rhode Island (1740–43), governor (1743–45, 1746–47, 1748–55) (died 1758).

1739 George Clymer, merchant and legislator, born in Philadelphia; member, Continental Congress (1776–78, 1780–83), a signer of Declaration of Independence (died 1813).

1750 Thomas Walker sent by Virginia Council to survey western public lands; crossed mountains at Cumberland Gap, entering Kentucky; completed first house built in Kentucky (April 25), near present Barbourville.

1751 James Madison, fourth president (1809–17), born in Port Conway, VA; sometimes called father of the Constitution; with Alexander Hamilton and John Jay wrote *The Federalist Papers*; served in Continental Congress (1780–83) and represented Virginia in House (1789–98); Secretary of State (1801–09); rector, U. of Virginia (1826–36) (died 1836).

1802 U.S. Military Academy at West Point authorized by Congress; opened July 4.

1802 Corps of Engineers created.

1822 John Pope, Union general, born in Louisville, KY; commanded Army of the Mississippi; was defeated at second Bull Run (died 1892).

1827 John B. Russworm and John Cornish published *Freedom's Journal*, the first American black newspaper.

1836 Andrew S. Hallidie, engineer who invented cable railway, born in London; built wire suspension bridges, then cable railway, first used in San Francisco (1873) (died 1900).

1840 John A. Howell, naval officer/inventor, born in Bath, NY; served in Civil War, Spanish-American War; invented gyroscope steering torpedo, disappearing gun carriage, certain high-explosive shells (died 1918).

1845 Alexander McDougall, shipbuilder, born on Islay Island, Scotland; designed "whaleback" Great Lakes freighter (died 1923).

1855 Nebraska enacted a prohibition law; repealed 1858.

1861 Confederacy sent delegation (William L. Yancey, Pierre A. Rost, A. Dudley Mann) to Europe to explain Southern position and seek support.

1878 Henry B. Walthall, pioneer screen actor, born in Shelby City, AL; best remembered for *The Birth of a Nation* and *The Scarlet Letter* (died 1936).

1880 William B. Stout, builder of first all-metal airplane in United States, born in Quincy, IL; formed company (1922) to build planes (sold to Ford), founded passenger airline (sold to United); active in developing stainless steel planes, welded steel aircraft engines (died 1956).

1884 Eric P. Kelly, author of children's books, born in Amesbury, MA; his works included *The Trumpeter of Krakow*, *The Blacksmith of Vilno* (died 1960).

1889 Elsie Janis, actress who starred in various plays, born in Columbus, OH; gained fame entertaining American troops in France (1917–18) (died 1956).

1889 Hurricane sank six warships in the Samoan harbor of Apia.

1902 Charles D. Jackson, administrative vice president, Time-Life, born in New York City; publisher, *Fortune* (1949–54), *Life* (1960–64) (died 1964).

1903 Mike (Michael J.) Mansfield, legislator/diplomat, born in New York City; represented Montana in House (1945–53) and Senate (1953–77), serving as majority leader (1961–76); ambassador to Japan (1977–89).

1903 Roy Bean, legendary frontier lawman, died; known as "the law west of the Pecos."

1912 Pat (Thelma C.) Ryan Nixon, wife of President Nixon, born in Ely, NV (died 1992).

1926 Dr. Robert H. Goddard demonstrated the practicability of rockets at Auburn, MA, with the first liquid fuel rocket traveling 184 ft. in two and a half seconds.

1926 Jerry (Joseph L.) Lewis, entertainer/screen actor in many comedies, born in Newark, NJ; conducts annual fund raising telethon for Muscular Dystrophy Association.

1927 Daniel P. Moynihan, legislator/diplomat, born in Tulsa, OK; ambassador to India (1973–74), to United Nations (1975–76); represented New York in Senate (1977–).

1940 St. Clairsville, OH, was scene of a mine disaster which killed 72 persons.

1942 Tornadoes in central and northeast Mississippi killed 75.

1961 Senate ratified treaty which made United States a member of the Organization for Economic Cooperation and Development (OECD).

1978 By vote of 68–32, just one above the required two-thirds, the Senate approved first two Panama Canal treaties, turning the facility over to Panama by the year 2000.

1985 Terry Anderson, Associated Press correspondent in Lebanon, abducted in Beirut.

1988 Federal grand jury indicted former National Security Advisor John M. Poindexter, Lt. Col. Oliver L. North, retired Air Force Major Richard V. Secord, and Albert Hakim on charges they conspired to divert to the Nicaraguan Contras profits from arms sales to Iran.

1988 President Reagan vetoed a civil-rights bill passed by Congress but the veto was overridden March 22 by the Senate (73–24) and House (292–133).

2000 Under judicial pressure, Vermont House approved civil unions between same-sex couples, with bulk of same legal rights of heterosexual married couples. Senate voted 79–68 to accept on April 25.

2000 Natural Heritage Network releases cumulative results of 25-year study: more than 200,000 species of animals, plants, and other living things in the U.S.; one-third endangered to some extent.

2005 Robert Blake — television's "Baretta" — acquitted by jury of murdering his wife and of one of two charges of soliciting someone else to commit the murder; on second solicitation charge jury deadlocked: wanted to acquit 11–1, so judge threw out that count as well.

17

1725 Lachlan McIntosh, Revolutionary War general, born in Badenoch, Scotland; was at Valley Forge with Washington; captured by British at

Charleston (1780); killed Button Gwinnett in a duel (1797) (died 1806).

1737 First American celebration of St. Patrick's Day staged by the Charitable Irish Society of Boston.

1764 William Pinkney, legislator/diplomat, born in Annapolis; represented Maryland in House (1795, 1815–16) and Senate (1819–22); minister to Great Britain (1807–11), to Russia (1816–18); Attorney General (1811–14) (died 1822).

1766 House of Lords passed law repealing Stamp Act, effective May 1, following example of House of Commons.

1776 Ten thousand British troops accompanied by 1,000 Loyalists, evacuated Boston; troop ships took them to Halifax, Nova Scotia.

1777 Roger B. Taney, chief justice, Supreme Court (1836–64), born in Calvert County, MD; Attorney General (1831–33), Secretary of Treasury (1833–34), but Senate refused to confirm appointment; nominated as associate justice, Supreme Court (1835), but Senate again refused confirmation (died 1864).

1804 James Bridger, trapper/guide, born in Richmond, VA; discovered Great Salt Lake (1824) (died 1881).

1806 Norbert Rillieux, sugar refiner, born in New Orleans; developed technology which revolutionized sugar refining, established modern industrial evaporation (died 1894).

1828 Patrick R. Cleburne, Confederate general, born in County Cork, Ireland; died in a charge at Franklin, TN, November 30, 1864.

1832 Walter Q. Gresham, public official, born in Harrison County, IN; Postmaster General (1883–84), Secretary of Treasury (1884), Secretary of State (1893–95) (died 1895).

1837 Republic of Texas adopted constitution.

1843 Henry W. Lawton, Army general, born in Manhattan, OH; served in Civil War and Indian frontier fighting; captured Geronimo (1886); commanded troops in Cuba, Philippines (1898–99) (died 1899).

1849 Charles F. Brush, electricity pioneer, born in Euclid, OH; invented electric arc light, storage battery; installed first electric arc street lighting (Cleveland 1879); first electric store lighting (Wanamakers, Philadelphia 1878) (died 1929).

1866 Pierce Butler, associate justice, Supreme Court (1923–39), born in Dakota County, MN (died 1939).

1874 Stephen S. Wise, rabbi and Zionist leader, born in Budapest; founder, Zionist Organization of America; a leader in efforts to make Palestine the Jewish homeland (died 1949).

1884 Frank Buck, animal hunter/collector, born in Gainesville, TX; author of *Bring 'Em Back Alive, Wild Cargo* (died 1950).

1894 Paul E. Green, playwright (*In Abraham's Bosom, The Lost Colony, Trumpet in the Land*), born in Lillington, NC (died 1981).

1902 Bobby (Robert T.) Jones, golfing great, born in Atlanta; one of greatest golfers of all time, starred in 1920s; helped found Masters Tournament (died 1971).

1905 Franklin Delano Roosevelt married Eleanor Roosevelt in New York City.

1910 Bayard Rustin, civil rights leader, born in West Chester, PA; helped organize first freedom rides in South, the march on Washington (1963) (died 1987).

1914 Sammy Baugh, one of greatest football quarterbacks, born in Temple, TX; starred with Texas Christian U., Washington Redskins (1936–52).

1919 Nat "King" Cole, popular singer, born in Montgomery, AL; pianist and singer with numerous hit records (died 1965).

1941 President Franklin Roosevelt dedicated the National Gallery of Art.

1942 Gen. Douglas A. MacArthur named commander of Allied forces in Southeast Pacific and Australia; left besieged Bataan for Australia.

1943 American Second Corps began offensive in Tunisia.

1960 A Lockheed Electra on Chicago-Miami flight exploded over Tell City, IN; 63 killed.

1985 Canadian Prime Minister Brian Mulroney and President Reagan met in Quebec; appointed joint team to examine problems of acid rain; signed agreements on security, fishing rights, trade, and law enforcement.

1988 Three thousand American soldiers began arriving in Honduras as a show of support to the Honduran government after 10 days of border clashes with Nicaraguan troops; began leaving 10 days later.

1988 Federal regulator pledged to provide $1 billion to the First Republic Bank Corp. of Dallas in an effort to halt widespread withdrawals.

1989 Richard B. Cheney, congressman from Wyoming and former White House aide, was sworn in as Secretary of Defense after being confirmed by Senate 92–0.

2000 In exchange for the dropping of lawsuits, Smith & Wesson agreed to new rules on how it manufactures and sells its handguns.

2004 Third-largest U.S. bank created as $47 billion merger approved by FleetBoston Financial Corp. and Bank of America Corp.; expected to cost employees 13,000 jobs.

2005 Congress held open hearings on steroid use and abuse in professional baseball; major players testified: Mark McGwire refused to discuss whether he had used them during his career; Sammy Sosa and Rafael Palmeiro denied utilizing them.

18

1747 William Duer, Assistant Treasury Secretary (1789), born in Devonshire, England; sued by government for irregularities (land speculation, government contracts); imprisoned and financial panic followed (1792), died in prison 1799.

1782 John C. Calhoun, Vice President (1825–32), born near Calhoun Mills, SC; represented South Carolina in House (1811–17) and Senate (1832–33, 1845–50); Secretary of War (1817–24), Secretary of State (1844–45) (died 1850).

1795 Demetrius A. Galitzin, Dutch-born priest, was ordained, the first Catholic priest who received all his training, orders in United States.

1800 Francis Lieber, influenced development of American social sciences, born in Berlin; edited first American encyclopedia (*Encyclopedia Americana* 1829–33) (died 1872).

1813 Joshua B. Lippincott, founder (1836) of publishing company bearing his name, born in Juliustown, NJ (died 1886).

1818 Congress approved pension bill for veterans of the Revolutionary War — $20 per month for life for officers, $8 for soldiers.

1834 James B. Herreshoff, inventor, born in Bristol, RI; invented sliding seat for rowboats (later used in racing shells), a fin keel for racing yachts; improved process for making nitric acid and hydrochloric acids (died 1930).

1837 (Stephen) Grover Cleveland, 22d and 24th president (1885–89, 1893–97), born in Caldwell, NJ; mayor of Buffalo, NY (1881–82), governor of New York (1883–85) (died 1908).

1837 U. of Michigan organized in Ann Arbor, opened to students September 20.

1848 Nathanael G. Herreshoff, boat designer, born in Bristol, RI; developed first Navy torpedo boats, designed five yachts which successfully defended six America's Cup races (died 1938).

1857 Henry Berkowitz, one of the first rabbis ordained in United States (1883), born in Pitts-burgh; served Rodolph Sholem Congregation, Philadelphia (1892–1922) (died 1923).

1861 An Arkansas convention rejected secession from the union.

1861 Texas legislature deposed Gov. Sam Houston for his refusal to take oath to support the Confederacy.

1862 Dorr E. Felt, inventor of calculating machine, born in Beloit, WI; invented first wholly key-operated calculator, first practical adding, listing machine (died 1930).

1864 Arkansas constitution, abolishing slavery, ratified by the people.

1864 John H. Kinealy, mechanical engineer, born in Hannibal, MO; invented air purifying apparatus, damper regulator, thermal valve (died 1928).

1869 Congress passed Public Credit Act, calling for payment in gold of government obligations.

1892 (Robert P.) Tristram Coffin, author/poet, born in Brunswick, ME; poetry (*Strange Holiness, Golden Falcon*), biographies and novels (died 1955).

1898 Lawrence J. Shehan, Catholic Archbishop of Baltimore (1961–74), born in Baltimore; named cardinal in 1965 (died 1984).

1911 Roosevelt Dam on Salt River in Arizona dedicated.

1925 Eight Midwest and Southern tornadoes killed 792 persons.

1927 John Kander, musical composer (*Cabaret, Chicago, Funny Lady*), born in Kansas City, MO.

1932 John H. Updike, novelist (*Rabbit, Run; Rabbit Redux, The Centaur, Couples*), born in Shillington, PA.

1937 Natural gas explosion destroyed a school in New London, TX, killing 294 children and teachers.

1963 Supreme Court ruled that all criminal defendants must have counsel, that illegally acquired evidence is not admissible in state, federal courts.

1964 Bonnie Blair, speed skater who was only American woman to win five Olympic gold medals (1988, 1992, 1994), born.

1869 Strike of nearly 200,000 postal employees began in New York City, the largest strike against the Federal Government; spread throughout nation, except South, ended March 24–25.

1974 Ban on oil exports to the United States by Arab oil-producing countries was lifted after five months.

1985 Capital Cities Communications Inc. purchased ABC (American Broadcasting Co.), the first time that any of the nation's three major networks changed hands.

1986 President Reagan and Canadian Prime Minister Brian Mulroney began two-day session in Washington in which they agreed on a plan to reduce acid rain.

1988 Lt. Col. Oliver L. North, indicted in the Iran-Contra affair, resigned from the Marine Corps

2004 In its first ever formal trade accusation against China, the U.S. accused it before the World Trade Organization of imposing excessive taxes on semiconductors purchased from America in order to minimize imports from that source.

19

1590 William Bradford, Pilgrim leader, born in Austerfield, England; arrived on Mayflower, where he was a framer, signer of Mayflower Compact; governor of Plymouth Colony 28 years between 1621 and 1657 (died 1657).

1628 New England Company formed by the Rev. John White, a Dorsetshire Nonconformist; given patent to land between the Merrimack and Charles Rivers; company succeeded by the Massachusetts Bay Company (March 14, 1629).

1687 Sieur de LaSalle, Mississippi Valley explorer, was shot and killed during a mutiny.

1734 Thomas McKean, colonial leader, born in New London, PA; member of Continental Congress (1774–83), president (1781); signer of Declaration of Independence; Pennsylvania chief justice (1777–89), governor (1799–1808) (died 1817).

1778 General Assembly of South Carolina adopted a state constitution.

1816 Compensation of congressmen changed from per diem to $1,500 annually plus mileage; Senate President and House Speaker $3,000; repealed February 6, 1817.

1835 James E. Scripps, cofounder of newspaper chain (Scripps-Howard), born in London; founder, editor, *Detroit News* (1873) (died 1906).

1847 Albert P. Ryder, artist, born in New Bedford, MA; noted for landscapes, seascapes, and allegorical scenes; hang in Metropolitan Museum of Art and National Gallery of Art (died 1917).

1848 Wyatt Earp, legendary frontier lawman, born in Monmouth, IL (died 1929).

1855 David Todd, astronomer, born in Lake Ridge, NY; designed, erected college observatories at Smith, Amherst; first to photograph solar corona from plane (1925); invented automatic device to photograph eclipses (died 1939).

1860 Elizabeth Cady Stanton spoke on woman suffrage to New York Legislature.

1860 William Jennings Bryan, public official, born in Salem, IL; known as "the Commoner," he was Democratic presidential candidate (1896, 1900, 1908); Secretary of State (1913–15); a prosecuting attorney in Scopes "monkey" trial (1925); died a day after trial ended.

1883 Joseph W. (Vinegar Joe) Stilwell, World War II general, born in Palatka, FL; commanded American forces in Burma-China Theater (1942–46) (died 1946).

1891 Earl Warren, chief justice, Supreme Court (1953–69), born in Los Angeles; served California as Attorney General (1939–43) and governor (1944–53); 1948 Republican vice presidential candidate; headed investigation of Kennedy assassination (died 1974).

1899 Henry I. Hodes, World War II and Korean War Army general, born in Washington, DC; commander-in-chief, U.S. Army in Europe (1956–59) (died 1962).

1901 Jo Mielzner, stage designer for more than 360 Broadway productions, born in Paris; with Eero Saarinen, designed the Vivien Beaumont Theater in Lincoln Center (died 1976).

1903 Paul J. French, executive director, CARE (1945–55), born in Philadelphia (died 1960).

1904 John J. Sirica, judge who presided over Watergate trials (1972–74), born in Waterbury, CT (died 1992).

1917 Supreme Court upheld constitutionality of the Eight Hour Day Act, directed primarily at the railroads.

1918 Daylight savings time established by Congress, to be in effect March 31 to October 27.

1920 Senate by a 49–35 vote refused to ratify the League of Nations Covenant and the Versailles Treaty; the vote was short of required two-thirds.

1925 Brent Scowcroft, National Security Council chairman (1975–77), born in Ogden, UT; served again 1989–93.

1933 Philip Roth, author (*Goodbye, Columbus*; *Portnoy's Complaint*), born in Newark, NJ.

1941 National Defense Mediation Board created by executive order to settle labor disputes affecting defense production.

1988 General Manual Noriega rejected an American offer to leave Panama in return for a promise that the United States would not seek his extradition.

1997 Ten members of the anti-government paramilitary group Freemen, in Phoenix, AZ, were sentenced to prison terms on various counts.

1998   Baseball owners approved sale of Los Angeles Dodgers to media tycoon Rupert Murdoch for reported $311 million.

2000   By an infrared photographed recreation of part of the events of the bloody climax to the 1993 Waco Branch Davidian siege (80 dead), federal judge hoped to obtain conclusive evidence whether the federal government had knowingly lied about the events of that day.

2002   Report to the Atlanta, Georgia, meeting of the American College of Cardiology: widespread implantation of cardiac defibrillators could cut heart deaths 24,000 a year; biggest problem to general use: $20,000 cost of unit and $40–60,000 price of operation to install.

2003   "Operation Iraqi Freedom" began: U.S. invasion of Iraq to topple Saddam Hussein; April 9, Baghdad fell; regime considered ousted as of April 14; bitterly and violently contested reconstruction/occupation stage soon began.

2004   U.S. Army dropped all espionage-related accusations against Capt. James J. Yee, who had served as chaplain at Guantánamo Bay, Cuba.

20

1702   Streets were laid out in Mobile, the new capital of the Louisiana Colony by Sieur d'Iberville.

1760   Boston was swept by a disastrous fire.

1777   Edmund F. Gaines, War of 1812 general, born in Culpeper County, VA; distinguished self at Ft. Erie, Canada (died 1849).

1782   With the defeat of Cornwallis at Yorktown, VA, the government of Lord North fell, succeeded by Lord Rockingham, who decided to open negotiations with the American peace commission.

1804   Neal Dow, temperance reformer, born in Portland, ME; helped found Maine Temperance Union (1838); responsible for enactment of Maine prohibition law (1851) (died 1897).

1823   Edward C. Judson, author under pseudonym of Ned Buntline, born in Stamford, NY; pioneered the dime novel, producing about 400 such works (died 1886).

1830   Eugene A. Carr, Union general, born in Concord, NY; served at Vicksburg, in Missouri; later led troops in many battles against Indians (died 1910).

1834   Charles W. Eliot, president, Harvard (1869–1909), born in Boston; organized graduate school of arts and sciences (1890), made divinity school nonsectarian; helped establish Radcliff

College (1894); edited "five foot shelf" of classics (died 1926).

1844   Robert Dollar, founder of shipping companies, lumber company in San Francisco, born in Falkirk, Scotland (died 1932).

1852   *Uncle Tom's Cabin* by Harriet Beecher Stowe published; had been serialized earlier in newspaper (*National Era*); by mid–1853, about 1.2 million copies were sold.

1856   Frederick W. Taylor, industrial engineer who pioneered scientific management, born in Germantown, PA; invented largest steel hammer in United States (1890); co-developer of heat treating steel; developed "time and motion" studies (died 1915).

1856   David Conner, naval officer in War of 1812 and Mexican War, died at 64; was in charge of landing American troops at Vera Cruz, Mexico, the first large scale amphibious operation.

1883   Wilfred J. Funk, president of Funk & Wagnalls (1925–40), born in Brooklyn; editor, *Literary Digest* (1936–37) (died 1965).

1890   Lauritz Melchior, operatic tenor at Metropolitan (1926–50), born in Copenhagen; starred in Wagnerian roles (died 1973).

1903   Vinni (Vincent) Richards, tennis star of 1920s, born in New York City (died 1959).

1904   B(urrhus) F. Skinner, behavioral psychologist, born in Susquehanna, PA; invented teaching machine (died 1990).

1908   Frank N. Stanton, president CBS (Columbia Broadcasting System) (1946–71), born in Muskegon, MI; instrumental in developing CBS television.

1909   Edward F. Knipling, entomologist who developed new agricultural pest control methods, born in Port Lavaca, TX.

1912   Mine disaster killed 73 at McCurtain, OK.

1920   Lenore Hershey, editor of *Ladies Home Journal* (1968–97), born in New York City.

1933   Economy Act passed, reducing federal salaries and veterans payments.

1948   Bobby (Robert G.) Orr, one of best hockey defense men, born in Parry Sound, Canada; played with Boston, was National Hockey League Most Valuable Player (1970, 1971, 1972).

1987   Dow Jones industrial average climbed over the 2,300 mark for first time, closing at 2,333.52.

1987   American Lutheran Church congregations approved merger with Lutheran Church in America and Association of Evangelical Lutheran Churches; new 5.3 million member Evangelical

Lutheran Church in America became effective January 1, 1988.

1997 Liggett Group, fifth largest American tobacco company, agreed to admit that smoking is addictive and harmful to health.

1998 Tornado in northeast Georgia killed 12 persons, injured at least 120.

2000 Fifty-five "Oscars" stolen from loading dock of Roadway Express on March 10; 52 found in dumpster on March 20 and finder given $50,000 reward for returning them. On June 2, $40,000 of reward was stolen from the recipient.

2001 Bill Clinton's EPA had ordered major reduction in permissible arsenic level in America's water supply; Bush's EPA announced reversal of policy.

2002 Republican candidate for California governorship Bill Simon dropped Phil Sheldon (a religious opponent of abortion and homosexuality) as campaign consultant in response to criticism of his presence on advisory staff.

2005 Congress voted to require a federal court review of whether Terri Schiavo of Florida was so brain-damaged that her feeding tube should be removed; based upon a review of existing record rather than a new examination of all data, decision to remove tube was ultimately upheld.

21

1699 John Bartram, America's first important botanist, born near Darby, PA; his park, now part of Philadelphia's park system, was a favorite resort of Franklin and Washington (died 1777).

1713 Francis Lewis, colonial leader, born in Llandaff, Wales; member of Continental Congress (1775–79), a signer of Declaration of Independence (died 1802).

1843 The first date set by William Miller, sectarian leader, for the second coming of Christ; marked as "first disappointment"; although again disappointed, his movement led to formation of Adventist Church.

1857 Hunter Liggett, World War I general, born in Reading, PA; commander, First Army (1918–19), Army of Occupation on the Rhine (1919) (died 1935).

1865 George O. Squier, military and electrical engineer, born in Dryden, MI; chief signal officer, Army (1917–23); numerous inventions included nine-wave system of cable telegraphy and multiplex telephony and telegraphy (died 1934).

1866 James G. Harbord, World War I general,

born in Bloomington, IL; served at Belleau Wood, second battle of the Marne; president/chairman, RCA (1930–47) (died 1947).

1869 Florenz Ziegfeld, theatrical producer who introduced the "revue," born in Chicago; produced annual Follies, *Show Boat, Rio Rita* (died 1932).

1869 Albert Kahn, architect who pioneered modern factory design, born in Rhaunen, Germany; designed Detroit auto plants; Fisher, GM buildings; Willow Run plant (died 1942).

1880 Hans Hofmann, painter and art teacher, born in Weissenberg, Germany; introduced modern European painting styles in United States (died 1966).

1885 Raoul V.G. Lufbery, World War I aviator, born in Clermont, France, to an American father; became ace in Lafayette Escadrille (17 victories 1916–18); transferred to American service, killed in combat May 19, 1918.

1885 Joseph Pulitzer, publisher of *St. Louis Post-Dispatch* (1912–55), born in New York City (died 1955).

1896 Ballington Booth, who had resigned as head of Salvation Army in America, formed new organization, Volunteers of America.

1898 Naval court of inquiry ascribed destruction of the battleship *Maine* to an external cause; a Spanish inquiry blamed an internal explosion.

1905 Phyllis McGinley, author/popular poet, born in Ontario, OR; wrote *A Pocketful of Wry, On the Contrary, One More Manhattan* (died 1978).

1910 Railroad disaster at Green Mountain, IA, caused 55 deaths.

1913 Floods in the Miami Valley of Ohio killed more than 400 persons.

1916 Fire in Paris, TX, burned 1,400 buildings, with damage of $11 million.

1917 American steamer *Healdton* sunk by a German submarine off the Netherlands with a loss of 20 lives.

1918 President Wilson signed Railroad Control Act which set the compensation to be paid during government operations, which would end no later than 21 months after peace treaty ratification.

1932 Walter Gilbert, molecular biologist, born in Boston; shared 1980 Nobel Chemistry Prize for pioneering research in genetic engineering.

1932 Series of tornadoes in Alabama killed 168 persons.

1952 Tornadoes hit six Mississippi Valley states, killing 239, injuring 1,200.

1965 The 54-mile march from Selma to Montgomery, AL, led by the Rev. Martin Luther King, Jr., began with Alabama National Guard escort; 3,200 marchers started and crowd grew to 25,000 by end of March.

1989 Supreme Court ruled 7–2 to uphold mandatory blood and urine tests for railroad workers involved in accidents; voted 5–4 to uphold urine tests for Customs Service employees seeking drug enforcement jobs.

1991 The 21-weeks-old union strike at the *New York Daily News* ended when agreements were reached on the paper's sale to Robert Maxwell, British publisher.

2000 Although unanimous as to the severe health danger of smoking, Supreme Court ruled 5–4 that the FDA lacked any legal authority to regulate it as if a drug.

2000 Diabetes drug Rezulin removed from pharmacies by Federal Drug Administration due to documentation of liver failure side-effect.

2001 Study released linking increased danger of ovarian cancer with being on estrogen for a decade or longer.

2002 Democratic Party leaders announced two largest known donations to any political party: $7 million from Haim Saban, chairman of Saban Capital Group, and $5 million from Steve Bing, another Hollywood entertainment executive; both are classified as "soft money" and would have been illegal if donated November 7 or later due to campaign finance law changes.

2002 Former senator Herman E. Talmadge died at 88. As two-term governor of Georgia he launched massive new school construction program to move state into modern era. Four-term U.S. Senator; in 1950s advocated closing public schools rather than permitting them to be integrated; major participant in questioning Nixon Administration figures during Watergate hearings.

22

1621 Massassoit, chief of the Wampanoag Indians, came to Plymouth to "treat of peace."

1622 Nearly 350 Virginia colonists were massacred by Indians.

1687 First Anglican service was held in Boston's South Meeting House on Good Friday; on Easter Sunday, the Anglican service was held from 11 A.M. to 2 P.M. and Congregationalists had to wait until the Anglicans had finished before having their service.

1765 Virginia House of Burgesses adopted five of seven resolutions introduced by Patrick Henry,

a new member from Louisa County, against the Stamp Act.

1790 Thomas Jefferson, returning from France, assumed office as the first Secretary of State, to which he had been named September 26, 1789.

1794 Congress passed law prohibiting slave trade by American citizens from one country to another.

1799 Joseph Saxton, inventor of many things, born in Huntington, PA; inventions included a fountain pen, locomotive differential pulley, deep sea thermometer, self-registering tide gauge; designed, built balances to check weights of government assay and coinage offices; superintendent of weights and measures, U.S. Coast Survey (1843–73) (died 1873).

1813 Thomas Crawford, sculptor known for the Statue of Freedom on Capitol dome, born in New York City (died 1857).

1817 Braxton Bragg, Confederate general, born in Warrenton, NC; led victory at Chickamauga, unsuccessfully besieged Chattanooga (died 1876).

1819 William W. Adams, Confederate general, born in Frankfort, KY; served at Shiloh, in Mississippi and Alabama (died 1888).

1820 Commodore Stephen Decatur was killed in duel with James Barron, who had accused Decatur of leading intrigue to block his promotion; Barron had been found guilty of negligence (1807) as commander of the *Chesapeake*.

1868 Robert A. Millikin, physicist credited with being first to isolate, measure the electron, born in Morrison, IL; awarded 1923 Nobel Physics Prize for elementary charge of electricity and photoelectric phenomenon; coined term cosmic ray (died 1953).

1874 First Young Men's Hebrew Association (YMHA) met in New York City.

1876 Robert Fechner, director, Civilian Conservation Corps (CCC) (1933–39), born in Chattanooga (died 1939).

1880 Kent Cooper, Associated Press general manager (1925–43)/executive director (1943–51), born in Columbus, IN (died 1965).

1882 Congress adopted Anti-Polygamy Act, which imposed penalties for the practice, forbade polygamists from voting, holding public office, serving on juries; placed Utah elections under supervision of a five-man presidential board.

1884 Arthur H. Vandenberg, legislator, born in Grand Rapids, MI; represented Michigan in Senate (1928–51), serving as president pro tem (1947–49); a leader in bipartisan foreign policy (died 1951).

1896 Joseph Schildkraut, silent screen actor, born in Vienna; played in several films later (*Emile Zola, Diary of Anne Frank*) (died 1964).

1897 Supreme Court in Trans-Mississippi Freight case held 5–4 that railroads are subject to antitrust laws.

1914 William E. Miller, legislator, born in Lockport, NY; represented New York in House (1950–65); 1964 Republican vice presidential candidate (died 1983).

1918 Texas enacted a prohibition law, effective June 26.

1924 Allen H. Neuharth, newspaper publisher, Gannett Newspapers (from 1970 on), born in Eureka, SD; founder, *USA Today* (1983).

1930 Stephen J. Sondheim, composer/lyricist, born in New York City; among his compositions were *A Little Night Music, Sweeney Todd, A Funny Thing Happened on the Way to the Forum*; lyricist for *West Side Story, Gypsy*.

1931 Burton Richter, physicist, born in New York City; co-discoverer of J-(psi) particle (1974); shared 1976 Nobel Physics Prize for the discovery.

1933 President Franklin Roosevelt signed bill legalizing 3.2 percent alcoholic content in beer; first beer in 15 years sold beginning April 7.

1955 Navy plane crashed into a cliff near Honolulu; 66 killed.

1972 Senate adopted Equal Rights Amendment (84–8); requires ratification by 38 states to become effective.

1975 Fire causing $100 million damage occurred at Brown's Ferry nuclear reactor in Decatur, AL, after a technician checked leaks with a lighted candle.

1981 Cost of first class postage increased to 18 cents.

1989 Pete Rozelle resigned as National Football League commissioner after 30 years service; will stay on to help train a successor.

1992 USAir jet crashed while taking off from LaGuardia Airport in a snowstorm; 27 were killed, 24 injured.

1997 Immense Hale-Bopp comet made its closest approach to earth — about 122 million miles away.

2000 U.S. Senate voted unanimously to remove outside earnings cap for Social Security recipients; president announced he would sign it.

2000 In settlement of sex-discrimination charges at the U.S. Information Agency that spanned the decade beginning in 1974, government agreed to pay out a record $508 million.

2001 Long-standing custom reversed: American Bar Association no longer to be requested to provide a judgment on legal credentials of proposed federal judges.

2001 Co-creator of made-for-television cartoons, William Hanna, died at 90; won first Emmy ever given to a cartoon series.

23

1662 Virginia passed severe laws against the Quakers.

1713 South Carolinians captured Indian stronghold, Ft. Nohucke, ending the Tuscarora War.

1775 Speaking at a Virginia convention in St. John's Church, Richmond, Patrick Henry declared: "Is life so dear, or peace so sweet, as to be purchased at the price chains and slavery? Forbid it, Almighty God! I know not what course others may take, but as for me, give me liberty or give me death."

1818 Emperor Napoleon ordered the seizure, sale of American ships in French ports.

1823 Schuyler Colfax, Vice President (1869–73), born in New York City; represented Indiana in House (1855–69), serving as Speaker (1863–69); his involvement in Credit Mobilier scandal ended his career (died 1885).

1823 Aaron French, inventor of railroad springs, born in Wadsworth, OH; invention of coil and elliptical railroad car springs revolutionized industry (died 1902).

1824 Samuel S. Laws, educator, born in Ohio County (now West Virginia); president, Westminster College, Fulton, MO (1855–61), Missouri U. (1876–89); president, New York Gold Exchange, invented stock ticker (died 1921).

1831 Edwin Reynolds, engineer/inventor, born in Mansfield, CT; developed Corliss-Reynolds triple expansion pumping engine for water works; improved boilers, air compressors, ore crushers, hoists (died 1909).

1842 Clemens Herschel, hydraulic engineer who invented Venturi tube for measuring water flow in pipes, born in Boston (died 1930).

1857 Fannie M. Farmer, cooking expert, born in Boston; conducted cooking school for housewives, produced cookbook which is still in use; introduced standard level measurements in recipes (died 1915).

1867 U. of California chartered; had been College of California since 1855.

1868 Senate sitting as impeachment court heard President Andrew Johnson reply to charges, that removal of War Secretary Edwin M. Stanton was legal, that Tenure of Office Act was unconstitutional (Supreme Court agreed in 1926).

1884   Florence E. Allen, first woman state supreme court justice, born in Salt Lake City; served in Ohio courts (1922–34) (died 1966).

1887   Sidney Hillman, president, Amalgamated Clothing Workers (1914–46), born in Zagare, Lithuania; co-director, Office of Production Management (1941–43) (died 1946).

1888   Supreme Court Chief Justice Morrison R. Waite died in Washington, DC, at 72.

1899   Louis Adamic, author of novels about immigrants' lives, born in Blato, Czechoslovakia; novels include *The Native's Return, My America* (died 1951).

1900   Erich Fromm, psychoanalyst/author (*The Sane Society, The Art of Loving*), born in Frankfurt, Germany (died 1980).

1901   Emilio Aguinaldo, leader of Philippines independence movement against United States, was captured; freed after taking oath of allegiance to U.S.

1908   Joan Crawford, screen actress (*Mildred Pierce, Humoresque, Our Dancing Daughters*), born in San Antonio, TX (died 1977).

1912   Wernher von Braun, rocket scientist, born in Germany, where he helped develop V-2 bomb in World War II; later, with United States, he was director of missile research facility, Hunts-ville, AL; deputy NASA administrator (1970–72) (died 1977).

1932   Norris-LaGuardia Anti-Injunction Act was passed; forbade injunctions in labor disputes except under defined conditions.

1982   President Reagan sent Congress plan to revitalize declining urban areas through creation of "enterprise zones"; businesses would receive tax relief for investments creating jobs.

1982   Supreme Court upheld Federal Trade Commission order requiring American Medical Association to permit doctors to advertise, compete for business, and enter into non-traditional arrangements for practice of medicine.

1988   Smoking on all Northwest Airlines flights in North America banned by the airline, effective April 23.

1989   Largest oil spill in North American history occurred when Exxon tanker ran aground on a reef off Valdez, Alaska; spill killed thousands of animals, damaged thousands of miles of beaches, endangered fish.

1998   The movie *Titanic* tied a record in winning 11 Academy Awards; record set 1959 by *Ben Hur*.

2000   First Roman Catholic chaplain of the House of Representatives appointed (the Rev. Daniel Coughlin).

2003   Fighting for audience share with those closely following the American-Allied invasion of Iraq, the audience for the Oscar Awards shrank to about 33 million, lowest figure since 1955, 21 percent reduction from 2002.

2006   Cindy Walker (b. 1918) passed away at 87 in Texas after decades of successfully writing popular country music songs: about 500 were composed, many of which became on-going standards of the genre; hits included "Take Me in Your Arms and Hold Me" and "Warm Red Wine."

24

1754   Joel Barlow, poet/diplomat, born in Redding, CT; consul to Algeria (1795–96), arranged treaties with Tunis, Algiers, Tripoli; poetry includes The Vision of Columbus, Advice to a Raven (died 1812).

1755   Rufus King, colonial leader, born in Scarborough, ME; member of Continental Congress (1784–87), in Constitutional Convention (1787); one of New York's first senators (1789–96, 1813–25); minister to Great Britain (1796–1803, 1825–26); unsuccessful candidate for vice president (1804, 1808), president (1816) (died 1827).

1765   Quartering Act went into effect in the colonies requiring that barracks, supplies be made available to British troops.

1771   William Shirley, governor of Massachusetts colony (1741–49, 1753–56), died at 78; led victorious expedition against Cape Breton Island.

1781   Anson G. Phelps, a founder of Phelps, Dodge & Co. copper producer, born in Simsbury, CT (died 1853).

1783   Spain recognized independence of the United States.

1788   Popular referendum in Rhode Island rejected (2,945–237) new federal constitution; not ratified until May 29, 1790.

1820   Fanny (Frances J.) Crosby, blind hymn writer of about 6,000 hymns, born in Southeast, NY; her hymns include "Soft in the Arms of Jesus," "Blessed Assurance," "Sweet Hour of Prayer," "Jesus Is Calling" (died 1915).

1825   Texas, part of a state in the new Mexican republic, opened to colonization.

1828   Pennsylvania legislature approved financial aid to the Pennsylvania Railroad, first railroad undertaken by a government anywhere in the world.

1828 Horace Gray, associate justice, Supreme Court (1882–1902), born in Boston; justice, Massachusetts Supreme Court (1864–73) (died 1902).

1832 Creek Indians ceded all lands east of the Mississippi to the United States.

1834 John Wesley Powell, explorer and geologist, born in Mt. Morris, NY; explored in the Rockies; first director, Smithsonian Bureau of American Ethnology (1879–1902); director, U.S. Geological Survey (1881–94) (died 1902).

1853 Oath of office administered to William R.D. King, who was elected Vice President, in Cumbre, Cuba, because he was too ill to make trip to inauguration; died April 18 without assuming office.

1855 Andrew W. Mellon, industrialist/public official, born in Pittsburgh, PA; extensive interests in coal, steel; Secretary of Treasury (1931–32); ambassador to Great Britain (1932–33); donated funds, art collection for National Gallery of Art (died 1937).

1884 Peter J.E. Debye, physical chemist, born in Maastricht, Netherlands; awarded 1936 Nobel Chemistry Prize for work in dipole movements, x-ray diffraction (died 1966).

1886 Edward Weston, photographer noted for nature studies, born in Highland Park, IL (died 1958).

1890 John Rock, physician, born in Marlborough, MA; helped develop oral contraceptive — the pill — with Gregory Pincus (died 1984).

1893 George Sisler, considered greatest first baseman (St. Louis AL 1915–27), born in Manchester, OH; had .340 lifetime batting average; named to Baseball Hall of Fame (died 1973).

1893 Walter Baade, astronomer who redetermined size, age of the universe, born in Schröttinghausen, Germany (died 1960).

1902 Thomas E. Dewey, public official, born in Owosso, MI; "gangbusting" district attorney, New York City (1935–38); New York governor (1942–54); Republican presidential candidate (1944, 1948) (died 1971).

1907 Lucia Chase, ballet dancer/manager, American Ballet Theater more than 40 years, born in Waterbury, CT (died 1986).

1919 Lawrence Ferlinghetti, poet who was a founder of "beat" movement, born in Yonkers, NY.

1924 Two Catholic archbishops were elevated to cardinal by Pope Pius XI — Patrick J. Hayes of New York and George W. Mundelein of Chicago.

1930 Steve McQueen, screen actor (*Bullet, LeMans, Papillon, The Reivers*), born in Indianapolis (died 1980).

1935 President Franklin Roosevelt signed the Tydings-McDuffie bill, providing independence for the Philippine Islands.

1976 President Ford proposed an immunization program against swine flu; program halted December 16 after 58 persons suffered paralysis from the shots.

1981 Supreme Court ruled that a state may require a doctor to notify the parents of a teenage patient before performing an abortion on her.

1988 DuPont Co. promised to phase out all production of chemicals suspected of destroying the ozone shield.

1998 In Jonesboro, AR, two boys aged 11 and 13, fatally shot four students and a teacher, wounded 10 others outside their middle school.

2000 Pentagon released survey of treatment of closet homosexuals in the military: during the preceding year, 80 percent had heard an anti-gay statement; 37 percent had seen or endured harassment.

2001 Unexpected downside of cloning efforts revealed by scientific report: random changes in genetic structure.

2003 Deputy Associate NASA administrator Michael C. Kostelnik informed agency personnel that existing space shuttles might remain in use as late as 2015 or 2020; one possibility is a new "space plane" for astronauts alone and adapting shuttles to carry only cargo.

25

1584 Queen Elizabeth I granted a charter to Sir Walter Raleigh to colonize North America; sent out five expeditions to New World, including the "lost colony" on Roanoke Island, NC.

1634 Leonard Calvert, the colony's first governor, led 200 English colonists to Maryland, landing first at St. Clemens (now Blakiston) Island, then establishing a settlement at St. Mary's two days later.

1687 An Episcopal church was established in the Old South Meeting House in Boston, formerly a Congregational church, by order of Gov. Edmund Andros.

1775 George Washington selected by the Provincial Congress to be a member of the second Continental Congress.

1797 John Winebrenner, founder of Church of God (1830), born in Walkerville, MD (died 1860).

1805 George H. Evans, published first important American labor paper, born in Bromyard, England; the paper was *Working Man's Advocate* (died 1856).

1825 U. of Virginia opened.

1827 Stephen B. Luce, president of Naval War College (1884–89), born in Albany, NY; the college was world's first such institution (died 1917).

1837 *Philadelphia Public Ledger* began publication.

1838 Elwell S. Otis, Civil War and Spanish-American War general, born in Frederick, MD; military governor of Philippines (1898–1900), suppressed insurrection (died 1909).

1839 William B. Wait, pioneer in education of blind, born in Amsterdam, NY; devised a variation of Braille, a machine for its printing (died 1916).

1862 George Sutherland, associate justice, Supreme Court (1922–38), born in Buckinghamshire, England; represented Utah in House (1901–03) and Senate (1905–17) (died 1942).

1863 Simon Flexner, pathologist, born in Louisville, KY; isolated dysentery bacillus, developed serum for cerebrospinal meningitis (died 1946).

1867 Arturo Toscanini, one of world's greatest orchestra conductors, born in Parma, Italy; conducted LaScala (1898–1905), Metropolitan (1908–15), New York Philharmonic (1928–36) (died 1957).

1871 Gutzon Borglum, sculptor known for the Mt. Rushmore presidential heads, born in Bear Lake, ID; the heads in the Black Hills were first federally-authorized national memorial (died 1941).

1879 William S. Knudsen, auto manufacturer, born in Copenhagen; executive vice president, General Motors (1933–41); co-director, Office of Production Management (1941), production director, War Department (1942–45) (died 1948).

1881 Béla Bartók, noted composer of contemporary Hungarian music, born in Nagyszentmiklos, Hungary (now Rumania) (died 1945).

1891 Byron Price, newspaper editor/public official, born; with Associated Press (1912–41), executive editor (1937–41); director of censorship (1941–45); assistant secretary general, United Nations (1947–54) (died 1981).

1903 Frankie Carle, pianist and orchestra leader, born in Providence, RI.

1911 Triangle Shirt Waist factory fire in New York City resulted in death of 145 women workers; led to sweeping reforms in building and factory laws.

1914 Norman E. Borlaug, agronomist who was awarded 1970 Nobel Peace Prize, born in Cresco, IA; developed new strains of wheat, rice and practices in Mexico and elsewhere to help ease world hunger.

1917 President Wilson issued executive order calling up the National Guard of the Eastern states; made nationwide July 3.

1918 Third Liberty Bond sale was conducted with the issuance of $412 billion in 4.5 percent gold convertible bonds.

1920 Howard Cosell, abrasive and controversial sports reporter, born in Winston-Salem, NC; with ABC television network (1956–85) (died 1995).

1934 Gloria Steinem, feminist leader and editor, born in Toledo, OH; cofounder, editor *Ms* magazine (1972); cofounder, Women's Political Caucus.

1942 Aretha Franklin, popular singer, born in Memphis, TN.

1947 Explosion in a Centralia, IL, coal mine killed 111 miners.

1982 Wayne Gretzky of Edmonton became first National Hockey League player to surpass 200 points in one season; he later became first unanimous choice for most valuable player of the year.

1988 Catholic bishops refused to set aside controversial policy statement on AIDS; voted to hold broad discussions on subject in June.

1990 Arson fire in an illegal Bronx social club killed 87 persons; club had been ordered to close 16 months earlier.

1996 FBI began a confrontation with about 20 Freemen, an antigovernment antitax group, near Jordan, MT; they were charged with defrauding banks and other firms of $1.8 million, held seminars on how to conduct fraud, threatened a judge.

26

1740 Jonathan Trumbull, legislator and public official, born in Lebanon, CT; first Comptroller of the Treasury (1778–80); represented Connecticut in House (1789–95), serving as Speaker (1791–93), and in Senate (1795–96); governor of Connecticut (1797–1809) (died 1809).

1749 William Blount, legislator, born in Edgecombe County, NC; member of Continental Congress; was one of first Tennessee senators (1796–97); expelled (July 8, 1797) on charge of plotting to aid British in getting control of Spanish Florida and Louisiana (died 1800).

1753 Benjamin Thompson, engineer, born in Woburn, MA; made many improvements in home heating, cooking, lighting; a Loyalist, he went to England during Revolution, became Count Rumford (died 1814).

1773 Nathaniel Bowditch, navigator who wrote seaman's "bible"—*New American Practical Navigator*, born in Salem, MA (died 1838).

1784 John W. Taylor, legislator, born in Charlton, NY; represented New York in House (1813–33), serving as Speaker (1820–21, 1825–27) (died 1854).

1788 Slave trade was forbidden in Massachusetts.

1789 William C. Redfield, a founder/first president (1848) of American Association for the Advancement of Science, born in Middletown, CT; was a saddler, harness maker, railway developer; made study of gales and hurricanes (died 1857).

1804 District of Orleans created; became Territory (1805) and State of Louisiana (1812).

1814 Court martial sentenced Brig. Gen. William Hull to death for surrendering Detroit to the British without resistance; sentence remitted because of his Revolutionary War record.

1820 George H. Williams, legislator and public official, born in New Lebanon, NY; a framer of Oregon's constitution and one of its first senators (1865–71); Attorney General (1871–75); nominated for Supreme Court chief justice but not confirmed by Senate because of an apparent involvement in an Oregon vote fraud (died 1910).

1850 Edward Bellamy, founder of movement to nationalize industry, born in Chicopee Falls, MA; author of *Looking Backward 2000–1887* (died 1898).

1863 Amended West Virginia constitution ratified by popular vote; provided for gradual emancipation of slaves.

1874 Robert L. Frost, noted for New England poems, born in San Francisco; poems included *North of Boston, A Further Range, A Witness Tree* (died 1963).

1874 Condé Nast, publisher (*Vanity Fair, House and Garden, Vogue*) born in New York City (died 1942).

1878 William P. Hobby, Texas lieutenant governor (1915–17)/ governor (1917–20), born in Moscow, TX; owner/publisher, *Houston Post* (1924–64) (died 1964).

1879 Othmar H. Ammann, bridge designer, born in Schaffhausen, Switzerland; designed George Washington and Verrazano Bridges, New York City, and Golden Gate, San Francisco (died 1965).

1880 Duncan Hines, food critic and writer, born in Bowling Green, KY; author of *Adventures in Good Eating* (died 1959).

1893 James Bryant Conant, educator/diplomat, born in Dorchester, MA; president, Harvard (1933–53); high commissioner, later ambassador, to West Germany (1952–57) (died 1978).

1905 Maurice Barrymore, noted actor, died at 58; starred with Modjeska, Lillie Langtry, Mrs. Minnie Maddern Fiske.

1911 Tennessee (Thomas L.) Williams, playwright, born in Columbus, MS; among his hit plays were *The Glass Menagerie, Cat on a Hot Tin Roof, Streetcar Named Desire, Night of the Iguana*) (died 1983).

1912 Mine accident at Jed, WV, resulted in 83 deaths.

1914 William C. Westmoreland, Army commanding general in Vietnam (1964–68), born in Spartanburg County, SC; Army chief of staff (1968–72).

1916 Christian B. Anfinsen, biochemist, born in Monessen, PA; shared 1972 Nobel Chemistry Prize for pioneering studies in enzymes (died 1995).

1917 Texas gave women the right to vote in primary elections.

1918 An Allied conference named French General Ferdinand Foch as supreme commander of Allied forces.

1930 Sandra Day O'Connor, first woman named to Supreme Court, born in El Paso, TX.

1944 Diana Ross, singer/screen actress, born in Detroit; sang with The Supremes; starred in film, *Lady Sings the Blues*.

1961 President Kennedy conferred with British Prime Minister Harold Macmillan at Key West, FL, about the Laos crisis.

1962 Supreme Court backed the one-man, one-vote apportionment of seats in state legislatures in the case of *Baker v. Carr*.

1972 SALT I (Strategic Arms Limitation Talks) agreement signed in Moscow by American and Soviet representatives.

1979 Egyptian President Anwar Sadat and Israeli Prime Minister Menachem Begin signed a peace treaty on the White House lawn after the historic Camp David accord which was arranged by President Carter.

1988 Donald J. Trump bought New York City's Plaza Hotel for $390 million, saying he planned to convert it to "the most luxurious hotel in the world."

1997 Thirty-nine members of Heavens Gate religious cult were found dead in their California compound after a ritual suicide.

2000 Academy Awards show—in many ways upstaged by the saga of the stolen Oscars (see March 20)—resulted in expected films taking most awards, including *American Beauty* as Best Picture.

2000 80-year-old Richard Farnsworth attended Academy Awards where he was the oldest person ever nominated for a Best Actor Award; loses though profusely praised during ceremonies; died October 6, 2000.

2002 Supreme Court by 8–0 decision, agreed it's reasonable to expel tenants of public housing if they or any-one else present by their permission uses drugs — even if tenant is unaware of it happening.

2003 Anti-Defamation League report on anti–Jewish incidents during 2002: 1,559 ranging from nuisance telephone harassment to cemetery desecrations to synagogue arson; increase fueled by near doubling of incidents in California.

27

1797 John D. Fisher, pioneer in education of the blind, born in Needham, MA; responsible for establishing Perkins Institution and Massachusetts School for the Blind (1829) (died 1850).

1813 Nathaniel Currier of Currier & Ives fame born in Roxbury, MA; founded firm in 1835, joined by Ives in 1857 (died 1888).

1814 Most important engagement of Creek War occurred at Horseshoe Bend, AL; Andrew Jackson's victory was a major step in his military career.

1840 George F. Baker, banker, born in Troy, NY; a founder (1863), First National City Bank, New York City, chief operating officer (1865–77), president (1877–1909), board chairman (1909–31); benefactor, Harvard School of Business Administration (died 1931).

1844 Adolphus W. Greely, Army officer and explorer, born in Newburyport, MA; chief, Army Signal Service (1887–1907); in charge of establishing chain of circumpolar stations (1881), headed San Francisco earthquake relief (died 1935).

1848 Frederick C. Beach, editor, born in Brooklyn; founder/editor, *American Photography*; editor-in-chief, *Encyclopedia Americana* (1902–18) (died 1918).

1861 Benjamin Purnell, organizer (1903), head of House of David, born in Mayville, KY; founded communistic religious group in Benton Harbor, MI (died 1927).

1865 Union Gen. Philip Sheridan and 10,000 cavalrymen arrived before besieged Petersburg, VA, after successful raid through the Shenandoah Valley.

1865 William S. Graves, World War I general, born in Mount Calm, TX; commanded American expeditionary force to Siberia (1918–20) (died 1940).

1866 Civil Rights Bill was vetoed by President Andrew Johnson because it conferred citizenship on blacks when 11 of 36 states were not represented in the legislation; act passed over his veto April 9.

1879 Edward Steichen, photographer, born in Luxembourg; pioneer in photography as an art form (died 1973).

1886 Ludwig Mies van der Rohe, architect who developed first glass and steel skyscraper, born in Aachen, Germany; headed Illinois Institute Architecture School (1938–58); also designed chairs (died 1969).

1892 Ferde Grofé, composer/arranger best known for his *Mississippi Suite* and *Grand Canyon Suite*, born in New York City (died 1972).

1896 William Lescaze, architect, born in Geneva, Switzerland; designed various office buildings in New York City and Philadelphia, the Swiss Embassy in Washington (died 1969).

1899 Gloria Swanson, screen actress (*Sunset Boulevard, Sadie Thompson*), born in Chicago (died 1983).

1905 Hal (James Harold) Kemp, orchestra leader of 1930s, born in Marion, AL (died 1940).

1910 John R. Pierce, considered the father of the communications satellite, born in Des Moines, IA; an engineer with Bell Laboratories.

1912 The wife of President Taft and of the Japanese ambassador planted the first of 3,000 cherry trees at the Tidal Basin in Washington, DC, inaugurating the annual cherry blossom festival; trees donated by city of Tokyo.

1914 Budd Schulberg, author and film producer, born in New York City; author of *What Makes Sammy Run?*, *The Disenchanted*.

1917 Cyrus R. Vance, Secretary of State (1977–80), born in Clarksburg, WV; Army Secretary (1962–64), Deputy Secretary of Defense (1964–67).

1924 Sarah Vaughan, vocalist with Earl "Fathah" Hines and Billy Eckstine bands, born in Newark, NJ (died 1990).

1940 Cale(b) Yarborough, a winning stock car driver, born in Timmonsville, SC; grand national champion NASCAR (National Association for Stock Car Auto Racing) (1976–78); won Daytona and Southern 500 four times each.

1952 President and Mrs. Truman moved from Blair House back to the White House, which had been undergoing extensive renovation since November 1948.

1964 Good Friday earthquake 80 miles east of Anchorage, Alaska, killed 131 persons.

1986 Augustine Volcano in Cook Inlet, Alaska, began erupting for first time in 10 years.

2000 Gas pump fuel prices jumped drastically from preceding March: up to $1.79 (regular) in California; unprocessed price per barrel had jumped from $14.69 to $31.66; per-gallon profit of refineries had tripled from 21 to 66 cents since Valentine's Day.

2002 Milton Berle dead at 93; vaudeville star and pioneer of early television comedy.

28

1638 Willem Kieft, new governor of New Netherlands colony, arrived in New Amsterdam; recalled after launching a war against the Indians; died in shipwreck on way back to Netherlands.

1652 Samuel Sewall, judge at the Salem witch-draft trials, born in Bishopstroke, England; condemned 19 persons to death; later (1697) confessed error of his decisions; justice, Massachusetts Superior Court (1692–1728), chief justice (1718–28) (died 1730).

1674 William Byrd II, colonial leader, born in Westover, VA; member of Virginia council of state (1709–44), president (1743–44); known for his diaries (died 1744).

1706 Andrew Oliver, colonial official, born in Boston; secretary, Massachusetts Bay Company (1756–71); appointed stamp officer after Stamp Act passed (1765) and lieutenant governor (1771–74), unpopular in both posts (died 1774).

1811 John N. Neumann, Catholic bishop who was later canonized, born in Prahatice, Bohemia; Bishop of Philadelphia (1852–60), built schools and seminaries, helped establish Sisters of Notre Dame (1877) and Sisters of the Third Order of St. Francis (1855); beatified 1963, canonized 1977, the first American prelate so honored (died 1860).

1814 USS *Essex* captured by British ships in Valparaiso, Chile, port.

1818 Wade Hampton, Confederate general and political leader, born in Charleston, SC; cavalry commander, associated with Jeb Stuart; served South Carolina as governor (1877–79) and in Senate (1879–81) (died 1902).

1834 Senate censured President Jackson for removing federal funds from Second Bank of the United States; censure expunged from record January 16, 1837.

1836 Roger B. Taney became chief justice of Supreme Court, succeeding John Marshall; served until 1864.

1845 Mexico broke off relations with United States over Texas annexation.

1878 Arthur B. Springarn, civil rights leader who headed NAACP (1940–65), born in New York City (died 1971).

1878 Herbert H. Lehman, headed UNRRA (United Nations Relief and Rehabilitation Administration) (1942–46), born in New York City; served New York as governor (1932–42) and in Senate (1949–56) (died 1963).

1890 State College of Washington founded at Pullman.

1891 Paul Whiteman, known as the "King of Jazz," born in Denver; innovative orchestra leader (died 1967).

1893 Spyros P. Skouras, founder, 20th Century–Fox (1935), born in Skourchourian, Greece; served as president of movie company (1942–62) (died 1971).

1895 Christian A. Herter, Secretary of State (1959–61), born in Paris of American parentage (died 1966).

1897 Frank M. Hawks, pioneer aviator, born in Marshalltown, IA; set transcontinental speed records (1930) and nonstop transcontinental record (13 hours, 27 minutes, 15 seconds) (1933) (died 1938).

1903 Rudolf Serkin, concert pianist of world renown, born in Eger, Austria; was with Curtis Institute of Music, Philadelphia (died 1991).

1905 Marlin Perkins, zoo director (Buffalo, Chicago, St. Louis), born in Carthage, MO; best known for television series, *The Wild Kingdom* (died 1986).

1908 Explosion and cave-in at Union Pacific Coal Co. mine at Hanna, WY, killed more than 60 persons.

1914 Edmund S. Muskie, Secretary of State (1980), born in Rumford, ME; served Maine as governor (1955–59) and in Senate (1959–79) (died 1996).

1924 President Coolidge asked for resignation of Attorney General Harry Daugherty for his role in Teapot Dome scandal; Daugherty charged with malfeasance; acquitted.

1969 Former President Eisenhower died in Washington, DC, at 78.

1979 A major nuclear accident occurred at Harrisburg, PA, when a reactor cooling system at the Three Mile Island nuclear power plant malfunctioned; no deaths or injuries.

1984 Tornadoes in North and South Carolina caused 57 deaths.

1989 New York Supreme Court ruled that America's Cup, yachting's major prize, belonged to New Zealand, disqualifying American boat, *Stars and Stripes*, for violating spirit of the race; ruling was appealed.

1994 Series of tornadoes over two days in Southeastern states caused 52 deaths.

2000 Scientists announced that their tests indicated that amino acids (the building block of life) could have survived earth impact within comets rather than being destroyed, thereby providing an origin for life on earth.

29

1630 Puritans sailed from Southampton for New England in 11 ships.

1638 Ft. Christina (now Wilmington) established by Peter Minuit and Swedish settlers in what became the first permanent white settlement in Delaware.

1790 John Tyler, 10th president (1841–45), born in Charles City County, VA; represented Virginia in House (1817–21) and Senate (1827–36), and as governor (1825–27); elected vice president and became first to succeed to the presidency on death of president William H. Harrison (died 1862).

1799 New York legislature enacted law providing for gradual freeing of slaves.

1812 First wedding held in White House when Mrs. Lucy Payne Washington, widowed sister of First Lady Dolley Madison, married Supreme Court Justice Thomas Todd.

1813 John Tyler and Letitia Christian were married in New Kent County, VA; Mrs. Tyler died during his presidency.

1819 Isaac H. Wise, Jewish leader, born in Steingrub, Bohemia; a founder, American Reformed Judaism; a founder/president, Hebrew Union College, Cincinnati (1875–1900) (died 1900).

1819 Former President Jefferson named rector of U. of Virginia.

1821 Frank Leslie, magazine publisher, born in Ipswich, England; magazines included *Popular Monthly*, which became *The American Magazine* (died 1880).

1823 Leopold Eidlitz, architect who led Gothic revival, born in Prague; designed many American homes and churches, redesigned state capitol in Albany (died 1908).

1847 Gen. Winfield Scott, with 12,000 soldiers and marines, occupied Vera Cruz, Mexico.

1853 Elihu Thomson, electrical engineer and inventor, born in Manchester, England; had more than 700 patents for electrical inventions; cofounder, Thomson-Houston Co. which merged with Edison General Electric to form General Electric (1892) (died 1937).

1859 Oscar F. Mayer, who developed meat packing company from small market, born in Kaisinger, Germany; president, board chairman of company (1919–55) (died 1955).

1865 Gen. U.S. Grant began Appomattox campaign.

1867 Cy (Denton T.) Young, all-time winningest pitcher (511 games), born in Gilmore, OH; pitched in 906 games, completing 751; named to Baseball Hall of Fame (died 1955).

1869 Ales Hrdlicka, who helped establish American physical anthropology, born in Humpolec, Czechoslavakia (died 1943).

1874 Lou Henry Hoover, wife of President Hoover, born in Waterloo, IA (died 1944).

1878 Albert von Tilzer, composer, born in Detroit; hits included *Take Me Out to the Ball Game, Put Your Arms Around Me, Apple Blossom Time* (died 1956).

1881 Raymond M. Hood, architect, born in Pawtucket, RI; designed part of Rockefeller Center, New York Daily News, and Chicago Tribune buildings (died 1934).

1889 Howard Lindsay, actor/playwright, born in Waterford, NY; played Father in *Life with Father*, which he co-authored with Russel Crouse; also co-author of *State of the Union, Anything Goes, Call Me Madam* (died 1968).

1894 George W. Merck, head of pharmaceutical company (1925–50), born in New York City; company produced streptomycin, vitamins (died 1957).

1916 Eugene J. McCarthy, legislator, born in Watkins, MN; represented Minnesota in House (1945–59) and Senate (1959–71); independent presidential candidate (1976).

1918 Pearl Bailey, popular singer/actress (*Hello, Dolly!*), born in Newport News, VA; also played in several movies (died 1990).

1937 Supreme Court upheld constitutionality of minimum wage law of Washington state and the right of collective bargaining on the railroads.

1951 Julius Rosenberg, his wife Ethel, and Morton Sobell were found guilty of conspiracy to commit wartime espionage; Rosenbergs executed June 19, 1953; Sobell sentenced to 30 years.

1953 Fire in a Largo, FL, nursing home killed 35 persons.

1961 The 23d Amendment went into effect, giving voters of Washington, DC, right to vote in presidential elections.

1988 New American-Japanese agreement allows American construction companies to work with Japanese contractors in building large public works projects in Japan.

1988 Deputy Attorney General Arnold L. Burns and five other department officials resigned because of concern over Attorney General Edwin Meese's legal problems and his leadership.

1995 House of Representatives failed to approve a proposed constitutional amendment to set limits on congressional terms.

1996 House completed congressional action on sharply curtailing the farm subsidy program; farmers would receive declining transition payments and end in seven years; President Clinton signed the measure.

2000 By a 6–3 vote, Supreme Court upheld local laws that required exotic dancers to wear at least minimum clothing rather than dancing nude.

2004 Massachusetts legislature passed ban on homosexual marriage but approved civil union status for such cases; requires a second approval in next legislative year and then voter approval.

2005 Johnnie L. Cochran, Jr. (b. 1937), died of brain tumor at 67; prominent black lawyer whose effective representation created a nationwide reputation for his skills and effectiveness.

30

1624 About 30 families, mostly Walloons, sailed from Amsterdam under the leadership of Cornelis Jacobsen May, who was the colony's first director; on arriving in New York Bay, several families were left on Governor's Island, several went on to what is now Gloucester, NJ; the rest went to Ft. Nassau (present day Albany).

1691 An assembly of New York communities was called, a date which marked the beginning of representative government in New York.

1775 Great Britain enacted the New England Restraining Act, which forbade Massachusetts from trading with any nation but Britain and the British West Indies; later, widened to other colonies.

1814 A new American attack on Montreal was turned back; Gen. James Wilkinson retreated to Plattsburgh, NY, and was relieved of his command.

1822 President Monroe signed an act creating the Territory of Florida.

1842 First anesthesia was used in an American operation by Dr. Crawford W. Long; used sulfuric ether on a patient in Jefferson, GA, to remove a tumor from his neck.

1853 Abigail P. Fillmore, first wife of President Fillmore, died in Washington at 55, about three weeks after the presidential term ended.

1858 DeWolf Hopper, actor in light operas, born in New York City; remembered for his recital of *Casey at the Bat* (died 1935).

1865 Union troops won a decisive victory in three days of fighting at Five Forks, VA.

1867 Alaska purchase from Russia for $7.2 million was signed by President Andrew Johnson; sale became final June 20.

1868 Trial of President Andrew Johnson began before the Senate with a speech by Benjamin F. Butler for the prosecution.

1870 The 15th Amendment, declaring that race is no bar to voting, became effective.

1870 Congress re-admitted Texas to the Union.

1876 Clifford W. Beers, public health pioneer, born in New Haven, CT; hospitalized with a mental breakdown, he studied his recovery; helped found Connecticut Society for Mental Hygiene (1908), first group of its kind; a founder, of national group (1928), international mental hygiene organizations (1931) (died 1943).

1880 Metropolitan Museum of Art in New York City opened.

1881 Boston Symphony Orchestra founded, with George Henschel as the first conductor; principal backer was Henry L. Higginson.

1883 Jo Davidson, sculptor/painter, born in New York City; among his many famous sculptured persons were Woodrow Wilson, Clemenceau, Anatole France, Marshal Foch (died 1952).

1888 James R. Williams, cartoonist (*Out Our Way*), born in Halifax, Nova Scotia (died 1957).

1891 Arthur W.S. Herrington, engineer who developed military vehicles including the World War II jeep, born in England (died 1970).

1893 Thomas F. Bayard, Delaware public official, was named the first ambassador to Great Britain.

1913 Frankie Laine, popular singer ("The Wild Goose," "Mule Train"), born in Chicago.

1919 McGeorge Bundy, public official, born in Boston; special presidential assistant involved in Cuban missile crisis, Vietnam policies; president, Ford Foundation (1966–79).

1938 Warren Beatty, screen actor, born in Richmond, VA; starred in many films (*Bonnie and Clyde, Shampoo, Reds*, which he also directed).

1972 Gabriel Heatter, radio commentator, died at 82; national newscaster whose opening words, "Ah, there's good news tonight" became a catch phrase.

1981 The assassination of President Reagan was attempted in Washington, DC; he suffered a chest wound, Press Secretary James S. Brady and two others were wounded; 25-year-old John W. Hinckley was charged with the attempt.

2000 Army's highest-ranking woman officer — Lieut. Gen. Claudia J. Kennedy — filed sexual harassment charges against a superior; on April 14 charges rejected by military reviewers.

2001 President Bush rejected Kyoto anti-global warming treaty on grounds it's unfairly burdensome to American economy; European officials deeply outraged at rejection.

2002 Medicare coverage expanded to include Alzheimer's.

2005 By 5–3 vote U.S. Supreme Court decided that age discrimination is prohibited even when it is only the result rather than direct intent; backs "adverse impact" standard in determining whether discrimination has occurred.

2005 Fred Korematsu (b. 1919) died at 86; Nisei (second-generation Japanese-American) whose lawsuit against internment of West Coast Japanese during World War II was most famous of several cases on the matter; internment upheld by Supreme Court 6–3.

2006 U.S. journalist Jill Carroll released after 82 days as hostage of Iraqi insurgents.

31

1774 British Parliament passed Boston Port Act, effective June 1; designed to punish city for Tea Party by closing the port until East Indian Co. was paid for its loss; seat of government moved to Salem, MA.

1808 James P. Henderson, first governor of Texas (1846–48), born in Lincolnton, NC; represented state in Senate (1857–58) (died 1858).

1810 James Alden, Union naval officer, born in Portland, ME; as commander of the *Brooklyn* at Mobile Bay, he was target of Farragut's classic order, "Damn the torpedoes! Go ahead!" (died 1877).

1817 New York adopted law prohibiting slavery, effective in 1827.

1833 Treasury Building in Washington, DC,

and many records were destroyed by fire.

1835 John LaFarge, church muralist, born in New York City; developed opalescent glass for church use; did murals for various New York City churches (died 1910).

1840 President Van Buren issued executive order setting a 10-hour day for government employees without a reduction in pay.

1850 Charles D. Walcott, secretary, Smithsonian Institution (1907–27), born in New York Mills, NY; director, Geological Survey (1894–1907) (died 1927).

1854 Commodore Matthew C. Perry negotiated treaty opening Japanese ports to American commerce.

1862 Claude A. Swanson, Navy Secretary (1933–39), born in Swansonville, VA; served Virginia in House (1893–1906) and Senate (1910–33) and as governor (1906–10) (died 1939).

1863 Caleb H. Baumes, legislator, born in Bethlehem, NY; as a New York state legislator he wrote statute calling for life imprisonment after fourth felony conviction (died 1927).

1870 James M. Cox, public official and publisher (Springfield, Dayton papers), born in Jacksonville, OH; represented Ohio in House (1909–13) and as governor (1913–15, 1917–21); Democratic presidential candidate (1920) (died 1957).

1882 President Arthur signed act providing $5,000 annual pension to widows of presidents; first eligibles were the wives of Presidents Polk, Tyler, and Garfield.

1895 Vardis Fisher, author of novels about Mormon life, born in Annis, ID (died 1968).

1895 John J. McCloy, banker and diplomat, born in Philadelphia; president, World Bank (1947–49); first American commissioner of Western Germany (1949–52); board chairman, Chase Manhattan Bank (from 1953) (died 1989).

1917 General Munitions Board created by Council of National Defense effective April 9, with Frank A. Scott chairman.

1917 United States took formal possession of Danish West Indies (Virgin Islands).

1918 Daylight savings time went into effect.

1928 Gordie (Gordon) Howe, greatest hockey forward, born in Floral, Canada; played 26 years with Detroit (1946–71), named National Hockey League most valuable six times.

1931 Knute Rockne, Notre Dame football coach, died in a plane crash.

1933 Civilian Conservation Corps. (CCC) created to promote 250,000 jobs for unemployed males (18–25) in reforestation, road construction, erosion control, park and flood control projects; paid $30 a week, of which $25 was sent home to their family.

1934 Philippine Independence Act signed, providing for independence in 1944, after formation of a transitional government with a Filipino head.

1935 Herb Alpert, trumpeter and orchestra leader (Tiajuana Brass), born in Los Angeles.

1935 Richard Chamberlain, screen/television actor (*Dr. Kildare, Shogun, Thorn Birds*), born in Beverly Hills, CA.

1948 Albert A. Gore, Jr., Vice President (1993–), born in Washington, DC; represented Tennessee in Senate.

1968 President Lyndon Johnson announced he would not seek reelection.

1972 Representatives of Major League Baseball Players Association voted to strike over a pension; this, the first strike, lasted 13 days.

1988 Senate approved $47.9 million Contra aid package a day after House approval for food, clothing, medicine, and housing assistance.

1995 United States transferred its peace-keeping responsibilities in Haiti to a United Nations force.

1995 Baseball players strike ended after 232 days although all differences had not been resolved.

1998 Bank One Ballpark, home of the Arizona Diamondbacks, opened in Phoenix.

2000 Carl S. Shoup of Columbia University died; oversaw the writing of the post-war Japanese tax code; pioneer advocate of value-added tax in several countries.

2004 Air America Radio inaugurated first openly avowed liberal talk-show network; humorist Al Franken: "We're liberals, and we say that without apology."

2005 Terri Schiavo, subject of a prolonged and bitter right-to-live case between parents and husband, died after feeding tube removed.

APRIL

1

1742 Samuel Bard, pioneer physician, born in Philadelphia; physician to George Washington after the Revolution; a founder, medical school at King's (later Columbia) College; a founder, New York Hospital; author of book on midwifery (died 1821).

1764 Henry Ware, divinity professor whose courses at Harvard led to creation of its Divinity School (1816), born in Sherborn, MA (died 1845).

1789 House of Representatives organized with Frederick A.C. Muhlenberg the first Speaker; sessions began April 8.

1811 James McCosh, president, Princeton U. (1868–88), born in Ayrshire, Scotland (died 1894).

1823 Simon B. Buckner, Confederate general, born in Hart County, KY; served in Mexican and Civil wars; served Kentucky as governor (1887–91) (died 1914).

1827 Thomas S. Hall, inventor of electric automatic signal devices for railroad and highway uses, born in Upper Bartlett, NH (died 1880).

1834 James Fisk, considered the epitome of the "robber baron" financier, born in Bennington, VT; called the Barnum of Wall St.; helped raise price of gold, reaping a fortune but causing a depression (died 1872).

1852 Edwin A. Abbey, painter/illustrator, born in Philadelphia; illustrated numerous books; did murals for Boston Public Library, Pennsylvania State Capitol (died 1911).

1865 Gen. Robert E. Lee led last assault of Civil War trying unsuccessfully against the Union left flank at Five Forks, near Petersburg, VA.

1883 Lon Chaney, screen actor called "the man of a thousand faces," born in Colorado Springs, CO; starred in *The Hunchback of Notre Dame* and *The Phantom of the Opera* (died 1930).

1884 Laurette Taylor, stage and screen actress, born in New York City; starred in *Peg o' My Heart*, *The Old Lady Shows Her Medals*, and some Shakespeare plays (died 1946).

1885 Eli Lilly, headed family pharmaceutical firm (1932–66), born in Indianapolis (died 1977).

1886 Wallace Beery, screen actor (*The Champ*, *Min and Bill*, *Dinner at Eight*), born in Kansas City, MO (died 1949).

1888 Clarence D. Batchelor, editorial cartoonist with *New York Daily News* (1930–69), born in Osage City, KS (died 1977).

1900 William Benton, advertising agency head/public official, born in Minneapolis; co-founder, Benton & Bowles agency; U. of Chicago vice president (1937–45) where he founded Chicago Round Table, published *Encyclopedia Britannica*; Assistant Secretary of State (1945–47), founding Voice of America; served Connecticut in Senate (1949–52) (died 1973).

1908 Abraham Maslow, humanistic psychologist, born in New York City; altered ways of thinking about human needs, motivations, neurosis, and health (died 1970).

1917 Armed American steamer, *Aztec*, torpedoed off French coast with loss of 28 lives.

1920 The 14th Census reported population of 105,710,620, excluding outlying possessions; population center 8.3 miles southeast of Spencer, IN.

1922 William Manchester, author (*Portrait of a President*, *Death of a President*, *American Caesar*), born in Attleboro, MA.

1922 Wage reduction led to strike of 500,000 coal miners; ended in September with union concessions.

1930 The 15th Census showed population rise of 17,064,426 in 10 years to a total of 122,775,046.

1932 Debbie Reynolds, screen actress (*The

Unsinkable Molly Brown, Singin' in the Rain), born in El Paso, TX.

1939 Embargo on sale of arms and ammunition to Spain was lifted and United States recognized Franco regime.

1943 Rationing of meat, fats, and cheese began.

1945 Marines invaded Okinawa, gained complete control by June.

1946 Strike of 400,000 bituminous coal miners began.

1948 Soviet Russia set up land blockade of Allied sectors of Berlin; British and American planes airlifted 2.3 million tons of food and coal into city; blockade lifted September 30, 1949.

1953 President Eisenhower signed act creating Department of Health, Education and Welfare; nominated Oveta Culp Hobby April 11 to be Secretary.

1954 Air Force Academy created.

1960 First weather satellite, *Tiros I*, launched.

1965 Helena Rubinstein, Polish-born beauty expert and cosmetics manufacturer, died at 94.

1986 Supreme Court ruled 6–3 that police could not interrogate a defendant at his arraignment without his lawyer present once the defendant had requested a lawyer.

1988 A 60-day cease fire began in the Nicaraguan fighting.

1988 Campeau Corp. of Canada won right to take over Federated Stores for $6.6 billion.

1996 John McSherry, veteran umpire, collapsed behind home plate as the opening day baseball game began in Cincinnati; died an hour later.

1998 Federal judge dismissed sexual harassment suit brought against President Clinton by Paula Jones.

2003 Report: Unexpected cultural side effect of war on terror: museum insurance up as much as 50 percent since 9/11.

2006 January-March bankruptcies dropped to lowest level in two decades.

2

1513 Ponce de Leon anchored off coast of Florida, which he named; the landfall probably was near present St. Augustine.

1683 The Great Charter and Frame of Government for the province of Pennsylvania was issued; province was taken from William Penn (1692) when he fell into disfavor, returned in 1694; new frame of government drafted and adopted in 1699.

1689 Arthur Dobbs, colonial governor, born in County Antrim, Ireland; purchased 400,000 acre estate in North Carolina (1745), named governor (1754–62) (died 1765).

1720 Joseph Dudley, governor of Massachusetts Bay Colony (1702–15), died at 73.

1775 Boonesboro, on the south side of Kentucky River in what is now Madison County, founded by Daniel Boone.

1787 Thomas Gage, British general and colonial administrator, died at 66; served with Braddock and in conquest of Canada; headed British troops in colonies (1763–73); last royal governor of Massachusetts (1774–75).

1792 Mint of the United States established; replaced by Bureau of the Mint (February 12, 1873).

1811 James Monroe named Secretary of State, took office April 6.

1814 Erastus B. Bigelow, inventor of loom for making lace, figured fabrics, carpets (1851), born in West Boylston, MA; founded Bigelow carpet mill (about 1850); a founder of MIT (1861) (died 1879).

1833 Thomas H. Ruger, Union general, born in Lima, NY; served at Gettysburg, suppressed draft riots in New York City (1863), served in Tennessee and North Carolina campaigns (died 1907).

1844 George H. Putnam, publisher, headed George P. Putnam & Sons (1872–1930), born in London (died 1930).

1850 James L. Laughlin, economist who helped set up Federal Reserve System, born in Deerfield, OH (died 1933).

1862 William B. Wilson, labor leader and first Secretary of Labor (1913–21), born in Blantyre, Scotland; secretary-treasurer, United Mine Workers; represented Pennsylvania in House (1907–13) (died 1934).

1862 Nicholas Murray Butler, president, Columbia U. (1902–45), born in Elizabeth, NJ; a founder, first president, New York Teachers College (later Columbia Teachers); president, Carnegie Endowment for International Peace (1925–45); shared 1931 Nobel Peace Prize; Republican vice presidential candidate (1912) (died 1947).

1865 Both Richmond and Petersburg, VA, evacuated by Confederate troops, following battle before Petersburg in which Confederate Gen. A.P. Hill was killed.

1866 President Andrew Johnson issued a proclamation of peace ending the "insurrection."

1866 Francis Hodur, founder, Polish National Church of America (1897), born in Zarki, Poland; the church's prime bishop (1907–53) (died 1953).

1869 Clifford K. Berryman, editorial cartoonist (*Washington Post 1896–1907, Washington Star 1907–49*), born near Versailles, KY; originated "teddy bear" in cartoons of President Theodore Roosevelt (died 1949).

1873 Sergei Rachmaninoff, composer, pianist, conductor, born near Novgorod, Russia; gave concerts throughout the world; composed many piano concertos, short operas (*Francesca da Rimini*), symphonies, cantatas (*The Bells*) (died 1943).

1875 Walter P. Chrysler, auto manufacturer, born in Wamego, KS; president, Buick Motors (1916–20), reorganized Willys Overland and Maxwell into Chrysler Corp. (1924), of which he was board chairman (1924–35) (died 1940).

1908 Buddy (Christian R.) Ebsen, stage, screen, television actor, born in Belleville, IL; best remembered for TV roles (*Beverly Hillbillies*).

1914 Assemblies of God, one of largest Pentecostal churches, organized in convention in Hot Springs, AR.

1917 President Wilson, addressing a joint session of Congress, called for declaration of war against Germany; called submarine warfare attack on mankind, said the United States was joining the fight for ultimate world peace and "the world must be made safe for democracy." (Declaration of war passed April 4).

1927 President Coolidge issued executive order returning the naval oil reserves to the Navy Department from the Interior Department, where they had been since 1921.

1958 President Eisenhower, in special message to Congress, called for creation of NASA (National Aeronautics & Space Administration).

1980 President Carter signed Crude Oil Windfall Profit Tax, believed to be the largest single tax ever imposed on an industry; expected to bring in about $227 billion in 10 years.

2001 Chinese fighter hit American spy plane in international waters; American craft emergency landed on Hainan Island; U.S. personnel released on April 12.

2001 New census report for 2000 showed increase of 32.7 million residents since 1990 survey of population.

2002 IRS help in losing weight: It announced that in future weight-loss programs would be deductible on taxes; theoretically applicable to any 5-foot, 5-inch person weighing more than 180 pounds, the current federal definition of overweight.

2003 Without dissent, Supreme Court ruled that states may require HMOs to use "any willing provider" rather than limit doctors under their policies.

2005 Success at older age survey: Of Fortune 500, only 11 corporate top executives were over 70; of 100 U.S. senators, however, 22 are over 70, and on Supreme Court only Clarence Thomas young enough not to qualify for Social Security.

3

1737 Arthur St. Clair, Revolutionary general at Princeton, Trenton, born in Thurso, Scotland; member of Continental Congress (1785–87), president (1787); governor of Northwest Territory (1787–1802) (died 1818).

1753 Simon Willard, clockmaker who developed the "banjo" clock, born in Grafton, VA; specialized in church, hall, and gallery clocks (died 1848).

1755 Simon Kenton, frontiersman associated with Daniel Boone, born in Fauquier County, VA; served as a scout in Kentucky, Northwest Territory (died 1836).

1782 Alexander Macomb, War of 1812 general who defended Plattsburgh, NY, against British, born in Detroit; commanding general, Army (1828–41) (died 1841).

1783 Washington Irving, first American author admired abroad, born in New York City; wrote several classic short stories, "Rip van Winkle," "Legend of Sleepy Hollow"; minister to Spain (1842–46) (died 1859).

1798 Charles Wilkes, Navy officer who commanded exploration of Antarctic islands (1838–42), born in New York City; Wilkes Land in Antarctica named for him (died 1877).

1814 Lorenzo Snow, president of Mormon Church (1898–1901), born in Mantua, OH; after passage of Anti-Polygamy Act, he was convicted, imprisoned (1886); decision reversed by Supreme Court (1887) (died 1901).

1822 Edward Everett Hale, Unitarian clergyman and author, born in Boston; pastor, South Congregational Church, Boston (1856–1901); remembered for short story, "The Man Without a Country" (died 1909).

1823 William M. Tweed, political boss in New York City, where he was born; controlled Tammany Hall; he and his ring swindled the city treasury of about $30 million; concerted campaign led to his conviction, imprisonment (1873) (died 1878).

1837 John Burroughs, author who developed nature essay as a literary form, born in Roxbury, NY (died 1921).

1848 Chicago Board of Trade organized; incorporated by special act of Illinois legislature February 18, 1859.

1859 Reginald DeKoven, composer, born in Middletown, CT; composed light operas (*Robin Hood, Rob Roy*); also the classic "Oh, Promise Me" (died 1920).

1860 First pony express between St. Joseph, MO, and Sacramento, CA, began; ended October 24, 1861, with completion of first transcontinental telegraph line.

1870 Sara A.M. Conboy, first woman elected to a national labor office, born in Boston; named secretary-treasurer, United Textile Workers (1915–28) (died 1928).

1882 Jesse James, notorious bandit and outlaw, was shot and killed by two members of his band in St. Joseph, MO.

1884 Bud (Harry C.) Fisher, cartoonist of first widely syndicated comic strip (*Mutt and Jeff*) (1908), born in Chicago (died 1954).

1888 Thomas C. Kinkaid, World War II admiral, born in Hanover, NH; commander of Seventh Fleet (1943–45) (died 1972).

1888 John H. Hammond, engineer/inventor, born in San Francisco; invented radio-controlled torpedo for coastal defense, system of selective radio telegraphy carrying eight simultaneous messages on one carrier wave (died 1965).

1893 Leslie Howard, stage and screen star, born in London; in numerous hit plays (*Petrified Forest, Berkeley Square*) and films (*Scarlet Pimpernel, Of Human Bondage, Gone with the Wind* (died 1943).

1898 Henry R. Luce, magazine founder/publisher, born in Tenghchow, China, of American parentage; cofounder, *Time* (1923); founder, *Fortune* (1930), *Life* (1936), *Sports Illustrated* (1954) (died 1967).

1898 George Jessel, entertainer known as the toastmaster general of United States, born in New York City (died 1981).

1924 Marlon Brando, screen actor, born in Omaha, NE; starred in many movies (*A Streetcar Named Desire, On the Waterfront, The Godfather, Last Tango in Paris*).

1926 Virgil I. Grissom, one of the original astronauts, born in Mitchell, IN; second to travel in space; killed in a capsule fire with two others in 1967.

1935 Robert C. Marshall, a witness at a New York City hearing on relief administration, said he taught workers "boondoggling"; he said "boondoggles" were gadgets or useful articles of scrap material.

1940 Isle Royale (MI) National Park established.

1948 A. $6.1 billion foreign aid act under the Economic Cooperation Administration went into effect; Paul G. Hoffman named administrator.

1972 President Nixon devalued the dollar by 8.57 percent and raised the price of gold from $35 to $38 an ounce.

1988 First-class postage rates increased three cents to 25 cents for the first ounce.

1996 Ronald Brown, Secretary of Commerce, died in a plane crash with 34 others while on a trip to the Balkans.

1996 Federal agents seized Theodore Kaczynski, a former professor, in western Montana; later determined he was "Unabomber," being sought since 1978 for sending mail bombs which killed three, injured 23.

2000 Evelyn Irons died at 99; was a pioneer woman combat correspondent in the European theater during World War II.

4

1748 William White, Episcopal prelate who led move to Americanize the Anglican Church, born in Philadelphia; rector, Christ Church, Philadelphia (1776–1836); helped create Protestant Episcopal Church of America, named first bishop of Pennsylvania (1787), presiding bishop (1795–1836) (died 1836).

1778 William Bard, founder of first company making life insurance its primary business, born in New York City; founder, president, New York Life Insurance & Trust Co. (1830–47) (died 1853).

1782 Sir Guy Carleton made general-in-chief of British forces in America, commissioned to negotiate peace.

1792 Thaddeus Stevens, legislator who led move to impeach President Andrew Johnson, born in Danville, VT; represented Pennsylvania in House (1849–53, 1859–68); managed impeachment trial (died 1868).

1800   First federal bankruptcy law enacted, making possible the release of Robert Morris from prison; law repealed December 19, 1803.

1802   Dorothea L. Dix, social reformer, born in Hampden, ME; improved care of insane, disturbed; prompted building of care institutions in United States and abroad; superintendent of women nurses in Civil War (died 1887).

1809   Benjamin Peirce, mathematician and astronomer, born in Salem, MA; superintendent, U.S. Coast Survey (1867–74), renowned for many astronomical computations; author of mathematical textbooks (died 1880).

1818   American flag was established as 13 alternate red and white stripes, representing the original states, and one star for each state on a blue field.

1821   Linus Yale, lock manufacturer, born in Salisbury, NY; cylinder-type lock he developed is basically the lock used today (died 1868).

1841   President William Henry Harrison died of pneumonia at 68, a month after his inauguration, the first president to die in office; had ridden horseback to Capitol without a hat or coat despite the cold rain, then delivered speech lasting an hour 45 minutes (8,578 words); Vice President John Tyler became president.

1843   William H. Jackson, pioneer photographer, born in Keeseville, NY; one of first to photograph the American West (died 1942).

1850   Los Angeles incorporated as a city.

1859   "Dixie," written by Daniel Emmett for Bryant's Minstrels, was first sung in Mechanics Hall, New York City.

1861   President Lincoln ordered a supply expedition to Ft. Sumter in Charleston Harbor, notified the South Carolina governor of the shipment.

1863   Samuel S. Childs, founded nationwide Childs restaurant chain (1888), born in Basking Ridge, NJ; introduced use of waitresses, calorie counts on menus (died 1925).

1865   Jefferson Davis made final appeal to Confederacy to continue war; appeal was not supported by Gen. Robert E. Lee.

1866   George P. Baker, drama teacher ("47 Workshop") at Harvard, born in Providence, RI; his students included Eugene O'Neill, Philip Barry, John Dos Passos, Thomas Wolfe (died 1935).

1870   George A. Smith, president, Mormon Church (1945–51), born in Salt Lake City (died 1951).

1875   Pierre Monteaux, symphonies conductor, born in Paris; led the Boston (1919–24), Paris (1930–38), of which he was also the founder, and San Francisco (1934–52) orchestras (died 1964).

1875   Louis K. Liggett, founder, president, United Drug Co., born in Detroit; board chairman, Liggett Drug Co. (died 1946).

1876   Claude W. Kress, cofounder with brother of S.H. Kress & Co. dime-store chain, born in Slatington, PA (died 1940).

1876   Senate began impeachment hearing on charges against William W. Belknap, accused of selling privileges at Indian trading posts while Secretary of War (1869–76); acquitted August 1.

1888   Tris(tram) Speaker, baseball player Boston AL (1907–15), Cleveland (1916–26), born in Hubbard, TX; lifetime batting average of .344; named to Baseball Hall of Fame (died 1958).

1896   Robert E. Sherwood, author/playwright, born in New Rochelle, NY; chief speech writer for President Franklin Roosevelt; author (*Roosevelt and Hopkins*); plays (*Reunion in Vienna, Petrified Forest, Idiot's Delight, Abe Lincoln in Illinois*) (died 1955).

1917   Declaration of war against Germany passed by Senate 82–6, by House 373–50.

1932   Richard G. Lugar, political leader, born in Indianapolis, which he served as mayor (1968–75); served Indiana in Senate (1977–).

1933   American dirigible, *Akron*, broke up in a violent storm off Barnegat Bay, NJ; 73 persons killed.

1938   A(ngelo) Bartlett Giamatti, Yale U. president (1976–86), born in Boston; president, National (baseball) League (1986–89); baseball commissioner (1989) (died 1989).

1949   North Atlantic Treaty signed in Washington, DC, by United States, France, Belgium, Canada, Denmark, Iceland, Italy, Luxembourg, Netherlands, Norway, Portugal, and United Kingdom; ratified by Senate July 21.

1961   Gen. Dwight D. Eisenhower established Supreme Headquarters, Allied Powers in Europe (SHAPE) in Paris.

1968   The Rev. Martin Luther King, Jr., civil rights leader, assassinated in Memphis by James Earl Ray, who was captured in London January 8, 1969; sentenced to 99 years in prison.

1969   World's first totally artificial heart implanted in a human being in Houston by Dr. Denton A. Cooley; patient died April 8.

1974   Two days of tornadoes in Alabama, Georgia, Tennessee, Kentucky, and Ohio killed 315.

1975   Air Force plane carrying Vietnamese children crashed near Saigon killing 172.

1981 First Mexican-American mayor of an American city, 33-year-old Henry G. Cisneros, elected in San Antonio, TX; later became Secretary of Housing & Urban Development (1993–97).

1988 Arizona Gov. Evan Meacham convicted 21–9 by state Senate in first impeachment trial of a governor in almost 60 years; former Secretary of State Mofford was sworn in as governor to succeed Meacham.

1991 Sen. John Heinz of Pennsylvania and six others were killed when his chartered plane collided in the air with a helicopter in Merion Township, PA.

1994 Northrop Corp. acquired Grumman Corp. for $2.1 billion.

1994 New baseball stadium in Cleveland, Jacobs Field, opened.

1995 Francisco Duran, who had fired shots at the White House, convicted of trying to assassinate the president; sentenced to 40 years in prison.

2003 First embedded U.S. journalist died in Iraq war: Michael Kelly perished in accident when his Humvee ran into canal.

5

1621 John A. Carver, colonial leader and first governor of Plymouth (1620–21), died at about 45; chartered and arrived on the Mayflower.

1649 Elihu Yale, philanthropist who made fortune with East India Co. (1671–99), born in Boston; donated books, goods to Collegiate School, which was moved from Branford, CT, to New Haven and renamed in his honor (died 1721).

1684 Oloff S. Van Cortlandt, Dutch leader in New Amsterdam, died at 84; burgomaster (1655–60, 1662–63); Van Cortlandt Park in New York City named for him.

1726 Benjamin Harrison, colonial leader, born in Berkeley, VA; member of Virginia legislature (1749–75), Continental Congress (1774–78); signer of Declaration of Independence; governor of Virginia (1782–84) (died 1791).

1764 Britain passed Sugar Act, modifying the Molasses Act of 1733 by raising duty on sugar, lowering it on molasses.

1792 President Washington vetoed bill to apportion representatives according to the first enumeration; this was first presidential veto.

1793 District of Columbia commissioners accepted design of the Capitol by William Thornton; President Washington approved July 25.

1816 Samuel F. Miller, associate justice, Supreme Court (1862–90), born in Richmond, KY (died 1890).

1822 President Monroe appointed Gen. Andrew Jackson military governor of Florida.

1822 Theodore R. Timby, invented revolving gun turret, born in Dutchess County, NY; the revolving turret first used on the *Monitor*, the Union ironclad vessel (died 1909).

1838 Alpheus Hyatt, a leading invertebrate paleontologist, born in Washington, DC; played major role in establishing Woods Hole (MA) Marine Biology Laboratory; a founder, editor, *American Naturalist* (1867–71) (died 1902).

1856 Booker T. Washington, educator, born a slave in Franklin County, VA; established, first principal, Tuskegee (AL) Institute (1881–1915); at his death (1915), school had 100+ buildings; faculty of 200; 1,500 students.

1858 W. Atlee Burpee, plant seed merchant, born in Sheffield, Canada; began seed business (1876), developed huge mail order business (died 1915).

1871 Pop (Glenn S.) Warner, football coach (1896–1942), born in Springville, NY; coached at Cornell, Pittsburgh, Stanford, and Temple (died 1954).

1871 Winchell Smith, playwright (*Brewster's Millions, The Fortune Hunter*), born in Hartford, CT; co-author of *Lightnin'* (died 1933).

1872 Samuel C. Prescott, bacteriologist who discovered method for making canned food entirely sanitary, born in South Hampton, NH (died 1962).

1874 Jesse H. Jones, bank and public official, born in Robertson County, TN; publisher, *Houston Chronicle*; chairman, Reconstruction Finance Corp. (RFC) (1933–39); administrator, Federal Loan Agency (1939–45); Secretary of Commerce (1940–45) (died 1956).

1894 Lawrence D. Bell, aviation pioneer, born in Mentone, IN; founder, president, Bell Aircraft Corp. which produced P-39 fighters in World War II; built first commercially-licensed helicopter and the X-1A, first plane to break sound barrier (died 1956).

1897 President McKinley appointed Theodore Roosevelt as Assistant Secretary of Navy; served until May 6, 1898.

1899 Alfred Blalock, chief surgeon, Johns Hopkins Hospital (1941–63), born in Culloden, GA; a developer of technique to save "blue babies" (died 1964).

1900 Spencer Tracy, screen actor, born in

Milwaukee, WI; starred in many films (*Boys Town, The Old Man and the Sea, Guess Who's Coming to Dinner*) (died 1967).

1901 Chester B. Bowles, advertising executive and public official, born in Springfield, MA; cofounder, Benton & Bowles, ad agency; governor of Massachusetts (1949–51); ambassador to India (1951–53, 1963–69) (died 1986).

1901 Melvyn Douglas, stage and screen actor, born in Macon, GA; leading roles in many films (*Hud, Ninotchka, Sea of Grass*) (died 1981).

1908 Bette Davis, screen actress (*Jezebel, Of Human Bondage, The Petrified Forest*), born in Lowell, MA (died 1989).

1915 Jess Willard knocked out Jack Johnson in 26th round in Havana to win world's heavyweight boxing championship.

1917 Gregory Peck, screen actor (*The Yearling, To Kill a Mockingbird, MacArthur*), born in La Jolla, CA.

1920 Arthur Hailey, author (*Airport, Wheels, Hotel, The Money Changers*), born in Luton, England.

1929 Ivar Giaever, physicist, born in Bergen, Norway; made basic discoveries in electronic "tunnelling" and superconductivity (1960); shared 1973 Nobel Physics Prize for the discoveries.

1933 President Franklin Roosevelt ordered all private gold holdings surrendered to the Federal Reserve Bank.

1936 Tornadoes ripped through five Southern states, killing 421.

1949 Fire in an Effingham, IL, hospital killed 77 persons.

1982 Supreme Court in 5–4 decision held that seniority systems outlawing discrimination based on race or sex are legal.

1987 An interstate highway bridge on the New York Thruway collapsed near Amsterdam, NY, sending at least three cars and a tractor trailer plunging into Schoharie Creek 80 feet below; about a half dozen persons were killed.

1989 Colin L. Powell, Army general, who served as deputy and national security advisor, became first black chairman of Joint Chiefs of Staff.

1991 Commuter plane carrying 23 people including former Texas senator, John G. Tower, crashed near Brunswick, GA, killing all aboard.

2000 Lee Petty, who became the dominant figure in auto racing in the 1940s and founded the Petty dynasty that continued to figure centrally in NASCAR racing beyond the end of the century, died at age 86.

2005 The two Mars Rovers that landed in January 2004, designed for only three months usage, remain operational; NASA approves up to 18 additional months of exploration in light of their unexpected longevity.

6

1712 Slaves in New York revolted; ended with six committing suicide, 21 were executed.

1745 William Dawes, who rode with Paul Revere to alert the colonists, born in Boston (died 1799).

1785 John Pierpont, Unitarian clergyman remembered for writing "Jingle Bells," born in Litchfield, CT (died 1866).

1789 Senate was organized with nine of its 22 members present; named John Langdon of New Hampshire as the first president pro tem; counted electoral votes which made George Washington president and John Adams vice president (Washington had received all 69 votes cast for president, Adams 34 of 69 for vice president.)

1802 Thomas W. Gilmer, public official, born in Gilmerton, VA; governor of Virginia (1840–41); as Navy Secretary (1844), he was killed when a gun exploded aboard the *Princeton* when President Tyler and his cabinet took a trip on the Potomac.

1805 Alexander E. Hosack, surgeon who was one of first to use ether in major surgery, born in New York City; a pioneer in urology (died 1871).

1810 Edmund H. Sears, Unitarian clergyman who wrote hymn, "It Came Upon a Midnight Clear," born in Sandisfield, MA (died 1876).

1823 Joseph Medill, owner of *Chicago Tribune* (1874–99), born in St. John, New Brunswick; an original member of Civil Service Commission; a founder, Republican Party (died 1899).

1830 Joseph Smith organized the Church of Jesus Christ of Latter Day Saints (Mormons) in Fayette, NY.

1832 Black Hawk War began when Sac and Fox Indians sought to recover their ceded lands in Wisconsin Territory and Illinois; ended August 2.

1841 John Tyler sworn in as president in the Indian Queen Hotel in Washington, the first vice president to succeed to the presidency because of the death of the chief executive.

1854 William Strickland, architect, died at about 67; outstanding exponent of Greek revival in United States; did marble sarcophagus of Washington at Mt. Vernon.

1858 Presidential proclamation declared Mormon Government in Utah in rebellion; six days later, Col. Thomas L. Kane, a friend of the Mormons, arrived in Salt Lake City to mediate the dispute.

1862 Two-day battle of Shiloh (TN) began; one of fiercest battles of the war; Confederate Gen. Albert S. Johnston was killed; Confederates retreated; Union lost 13,700 of 63,000 troops, Confederates 11,000 of 40,000.

1864 Convention began in New Orleans to prepare Louisiana constitution; adopted July 23, including a provision abolishing slavery.

1865 Confederate forces under Gen. Robert E. Lee, en route to Farmville, VA, were attacked by Union troops at Sayler's Creek.

1866 Lincoln Steffens, reform journalist with *McClure's* and *American* magazines, born in San Francisco; wrote *The Shame of the Cities* (died 1936).

1866 Grand Army of the Republic organized in Decatur, IL, by Dr. Benjamin F. Stephenson.

1874 Harry Houdini, escape artist, born in Appleton, WI; noted for escapes from shackles, ropes, handcuffs, and locked containers (died 1926).

1884 Walter Huston, stage/screen actor, born in Toronto; starred in films (*Treasure of Sierra Madre, Dodsworth*) and stage (*Knickerbocker Holiday*) (died 1950).

1890 Anthony H.G. Fokker, plane designer, born of Dutch parents in Indonesia; designed German World War I planes; later trimotor planes for American long distance flights (North Pole, Atlantic, Pacific) (died 1939).

1892 Donald W. Douglas, founder (1920), president, Douglas Aircraft Co., born in Brooklyn (died 1981).

1892 Lowell J. Thomas, radio news commentator and author, born in Woodington, OH; wrote numerous travel books (died 1981).

1893 Mormon Tabernacle in Salt Lake City, under construction 40 years, was completed.

1896 Widowed former president, Benjamin Harrison, married a widow, Mary S.L. Dimmick, in New York City.

1903 Mickey (Gordon S.) Cochrane, baseball player/manager, born in Bridgewater, MA; one of greatest catchers (Philadelphia 1925–33), managed Detroit (1934–37); named to Baseball Hall of Fame (died 1962).

1903 Harold E. Edgerton, developer of high speed stroboscopic photography, born in Fremont, NE; applied to various scientific uses.

1909 Robert E. Peary, on his fourth try, may have led his team to the North Pole; team included Matthew Henson and four Eskimos.

1917 United States formally declared war on Germany.

1920 Edmond H. Fischer, biochemist at U. of Washington, born in Shanghai; shared 1992 Nobel Physiology/Medicine Prize.

1927 Gerry (Gerald J.) Mulligan, saxophone player/band leader, born in New York City; also a composer and arranger (died 1996).

1928 James D. Watson, biochemist, born in Chicago; shared 1962 Nobel Physiology/Medicine Prize for determining structure of deoxyribonucleic acid (DNA).

1929 Andre Previn, pianist, composer, and conductor, born in Berlin; with Houston, London and Pittsburgh orchestra, guest conductor worldwide.

1931 Scottsboro Case began in Scottsboro, AR, in which nine black youths were tried for allegedly raping two white girls; eight were sentenced to death, one to life imprisonment; verdict overturned by Supreme Court; three subsequent trials resulted in convictions and ensuing reversals; none ever executed.

1936 Tornado in Gainesville, GA, killed 203 persons.

1937 Merle Haggard, country music singer, born in Bakersfield, CA.

1965 *Early Bird I*, first commercial satellite, launched by NASA for Comsat Corp.

1968 HemisFair 68 opened in San Antonio, TX; world's fair marked 200th birthday of city.

1987 Dow Jones industrial average passed 2,400 mark for first time, reaching 2,405.54.

1992 Sam Walton, cofounder of Wal-Mart chain of stores, died at 74.

1998 Dow Jones industrial average closed over 9,000 for the first time.

2001 In third-largest bankruptcy filing in U.S. history, California-based electricity provider Pacific Gas and Electricity had $9 billion in debts, which were increasing $300 million a month.

2004 *Horticulture* became one of a small elite group of magazines with latest issue: reached its 100th year; began in 1904 as a trade journal, became the magazine of the Massachusetts Horticultural Society in 1923, and decades later was converted into a national publication for those with such interests.

7

1640 Louis Hennepin, Recollet friar and missionary, born in Flanders; explored much of middle America with LaSalle (died 1705).

1666 Gurdon Saltonstall, colonial official, born in Haverhill, MA; governor of Connecticut (1707–24); influenced chartering of Yale College, locating it in New Haven (died 1724).

1775 Francis C. Lowell, industrialist, born in Newburyport, MA; built first complete American cotton spinning, weaving mill at Waltham, MA (1812–14); Lowell, MA, named for him (died 1817).

1780 William Ellery Channing, religious leader, born in Newport, RI; Congregational clergyman (Federal St. Church 1803–42), champion of liberal wing which became the Unitarian Church; called the apostle of Unitarianism; founder, American Unitarian Association (1825) (died 1842).

1786 William R. de Vane King, Vice President (1853), born in Sampson County, NC; elected in 1853 but died of tuberculosis before serving; represented Alabama in Senate (1819–44, 1848–53); minister to France (1844–46).

1788 Rufus Putnam and party of settlers of the Ohio Company established the first settlement in the Northwest Territory at what is now Marietta, OH.

1798 President John Adams signed act establishing the Mississippi Territory, which included the present state of Alabama.

1818 Spanish fort at St. Marks, FL, captured by troops under Gen. Andrew Jackson.

1859 Jacques Loeb, biophysiologist with various American universities, born in Mayen, Germany; developed tropism theory to account for certain instincts and behaviors, pioneered in artificial parthenogenesis and in analysis of egg fertilization (died 1924).

1860 Will K. Kellogg, founder of W.K. Kellogg Co., cereal manufacturer, born in Battle Creek, MI; worked in sanitarium with brother and developed cereals (died 1951).

1862 Treaty signed by United States and Great Britain to suppress slave trade.

1862 Island #10, an important Confederate port on Mississippi River, fell to Union forces; about 7,000 prisoners and stores taken.

1868 Convention adopted new constitution for Virginia; ratified April 18.

1869 William H. Walker, industrial chemist, born in Pittsburgh; known for producing art glass, stainless steel, research in cellulose and petroleum technology (died 1934).

1869 David G. Fairchild, botanist, born in East Lansing, MI; explored world for plants for introduction to United States (died 1954).

1873 John J. McGraw, baseball player/manager, born in Truxton, NY; managed New York (N) (1902–32), winning 10 pennants, three World Series; named to Baseball Hall of Fame (died 1934).

1893 Irene Castle, dancer, born in New Rochelle, NY; with husband, Vernon, helped popularize the one-step, turkey trot, Castle walk; also popularized bobbed hair (died 1969).

1893 Allen W. Dulles, public official, born in Watertown, NY; chief, Office of Strategic Services (OSS) in Switzerland and Germany; deputy director (1951–53), director (1953–61), Central Intelligence agency (CIA) (died 1969).

1893 Colorado granted full suffrage to women.

1896 Benny (Benjamin) Leonard, world lightweight boxing champion (1917–25), born in New York City (died 1947).

1897 Walter Winchell, columnist/radio commentator, born in New York City; began gossip column (1922), did weekly radio show (1930–50) (died 1972).

1908 Frank E. Fitzsimmons, president, Teamsters Union (1966–81), born in Jeannette, PA (died 1981).

1911 Melvin Calvin, chemist, born in St. Paul, MN; awarded 1961 Nobel Chemistry Prize for establishing chemical steps of photosynthesis process (died 1997).

1911 Accident in anthracite coal mine in Throop, PA, killed 72 miners.

1915 Billie Holiday, jazz singer, born in Baltimore; gained international reputation for her jazz-blues style (died 1959).

1922 Naval (Oil) Reserve #3, Teapot Dome, secretly leased to Harry F. Sinclair by Interior Secretary Albert B. Fall; Sinclair reassigned it to Mammoth Oil Co. for $160 million in stock; on April 25, Elk Hills naval reserve secretly leased to Edward L. Doheny.

1927 Television demonstrated successfully for first time with a picture of Commerce Secretary Herbert Hoover in Washington being shown in New York City.

1939 Francis F. Coppola, film director, born in Detroit; wrote, directed, produced *The Godfather* and its sequel; also wrote, directed *Apoca-*

lypse Now; wrote screenplays (*Patton*, *Finian's Rainbow*, *The Great Gatsby*).

1941 The USO (United Service Organization) formed by presidential order; included the Salvation Army, YMCA, YWCA, Catholic Community Service, Jewish Welfare Board, and Travelers Aid.

1978 President Carter announced that production of a neutron bomb would be deferred.

1980 United States broke diplomatic relations with Iran, following the taking of American hostages in Teheran.

2001 Cincinnati, OH, hit by days of rioting after white policeman killed an unarmed black resident; city manager resigns on May 2 as result.

2004 Environmental Protection Agency reported that eight prominent national parks suffered from unhealthy levels of smog: most in California (Joshua Tree, Kings Canyon, Sequoia, and Yosemite); others scattered around country: Arcadia (Maine), Great Smoky Mountains (North Carolina/Tennessee), Rocky Mountains (Colorado), and Shenandoah (Virginia).

8

1726 Lewis Morris, colonial leader, born in Bronx County, NY; member of Continental Congress, a signer of Declaration of Independence (died 1798).

1732 David Rittenhouse, pioneer astronomer/surveyor, born near Germantown, PA; built observatory and transit telescope, the first in America; invented collimating telescope; first director, U.S. Mint (1792–95) (died 1796).

1826 Henry Clay and John Randolph fought a harmless duel over the latter's charge of a deal between Clay and John Quincy Adams over election in the House.

1830 Mexican Congress enacted law prohibiting slavery and the further settlement of Texas by American citizens.

1832 Howell E. Jackson, associate justice, Supreme Court (1893–95), born in Paris, TN; represented Tennessee in Senate (1881–86) (died 1895).

1850 William H. Welch, developer of first American pathological laboratory at Bellevue Hospital (1879), born in Norfolk, CT; a founder, Johns Hopkins Hospital and Medical School, dean (1893–1916); director, Johns Hopkins School of Hygiene and Public Health (1918–26) (died 1934).

1857 Saucona Iron Co., predecessor of Bethlehem Steel Co., formed in Bethlehem, PA.

1869 Harvey W. Cushing, brain surgeon, born in Cleveland; with Johns Hopkins and Brigham hospitals (died 1939).

1886 Margaret Ayer Barnes, author (*Years of Grace*), born in Chicago; co-author of several plays (*Age of Innocence*, *Jenny*) (died 1967).

1892 Richard J. Neutra, architect who introduced international style to America, born in Vienna; his architectural approach called "biorealism" (died 1970).

1893 Mary Pickford, early screen actress called America's "sweetheart," born in Toronto; films included (*Tess of the Storm Country*, *Rebecca of Sunnybrook Farm*) (died 1979).

1897 Louis Skidmore, architect, born in Laurenceburg, MO; partner in firm which pioneered in design and constructed Air Force Academy (died 1962).

1898 E(dgar) Y. (Yip) Harburg, lyricist for hit shows (*Finian's Rainbow*, *The Wizard of Oz*), born in New York City (died 1981).

1903 Andrew Carnegie gave $250,000 to Cleveland for branch libraries.

1911 Mine disaster at Littleton, AL, claimed 128 lives.

1912 Sonja Henie, world champion figure skater (1927–37), born in Oslo; Olympic gold medalist (1928, 1932, 1936) (died 1969).

1913 President Wilson appeared before a special session of Congress to urge tariff reductions; personal appearance was first for a president since 1800.

1913 The 17th Amendment, ordering popular election of U.S. senators, ratified.

1918 Betty (Elizabeth B.) Warren Ford, wife of President Ford, born in Chicago.

1918 National War Labor Board established with former President Taft and Frank P. Walsh as co-chairmen.

1935 Works Progress (later Project) Administration (WPA) began, creating a national works program, headed by Harry L. Hopkins; eight-year program employed more than 8.5 million persons on 1.4 million projects costing about $11 billion; resulted in 650,000 miles of highways, 125,000 public buildings, 8,000 parks, 850 airports, and construction and repair of 124,000 bridges.

1949 United States, Great Britain, and France agreed to establish West German Republic.

1952 President Truman ordered seizure of nation's steel mills to avert a strike; seizure ruled illegal by Supreme Court June 2.

1974 Hank Aaron hit his 715th home run in Atlanta, beating Babe Ruth's long-standing lifetime mark of 714.

1988 Executive Presbytery of the Assemblies of God Church in Springfield, MO, defrocked television evangelist Jimmy Swaggart for admitted sins after he refused to stop preaching for a year; Swaggart resigned from the Assemblies saying that a year's absence would destroy his ministry.

1998 Tornadoes began and in two days killed 39 in Alabama, Georgia, and Mississippi.

2001 Black golfer Tiger Woods set new record: won fourth straight major golf tournament.

2002 *New York Times* won an unprecedented seven Pulitzer prizes, raising total won to 88.

9

1585 Second expedition sent out by Sir Walter Raleigh, under Sir Richard Grenville, leaving settlers at Roanoke Island, NC.

1597 John Davenport, founder of New Haven Colony (1638), was baptized; with Theophilus Eaton, he helped draw up a code of laws; pastor of First Church, New Haven (1638–68), First Church, Boston (1668–70) (died 1670).

1682 Sieur de LaSalle reached mouth of Mississippi River, took possession of entire area for France, naming it Louisiana.

1738 Rufus Putnam, Revolutionary War officer, born in Sutton, MA; an organizer of Ohio settlement company, a founder of Marietta, OH, first organized settlement in Northwest Territory; a judge, Northwest Territory (1790–96); U.S. Surveyor General (1796–1803) (died 1824).

1823 Lorenzo S. Coffin, railroad safety promoter, born in Alton, NH; led successful campaign to require automatic coupling and handbraking (died 1915).

1830 Eadweard J. Muybridge, motion picture pioneer, born in Kingston, England; invented zoopraxiscope, which took and reproduced pictures of animals' locomotion (died 1904).

1855 New York enacted statewide prohibition; declared unconstitutional in 1856.

1862 Charles H. Brent, Episcopal prelate, born in Newcastle, Canada; chief of chaplains, American Expeditionary Force in World War I (died 1929).

1865 Henry H. Kitson, sculptor known for

historical figures (*The Minute Man* in Lexington, MA), born in Huddersfield, England (died 1947).

1865 Gen. Robert E. Lee surrendered to Gen. U.S. Grant at Appomattox Court House, VA, in the farmhouse of William McLean, ending Civil War; Grant and Lee met at 11 A.M.; Grant received the surrender of about 28,000 men; Confederate soldiers were paroled to go home; officers were permitted to keep their sidearms, and were allowed to keep their private horses and mules.

1865 Charles P. Steinmetz, electrical inventor, born in Breslau, Germany; helped make alternating current commercially feasible; developed lightning arrestors for high powered transmission lines; patented more than 100 inventions (died 1923).

1867 Senate approved treaty purchasing Alaska from Russia for $7.2 million.

1868 Benjamin R. Curtis, a counsel for President Andrew Johnson, made opening defense speech in Senate impeachment trial.

1883 Charles H. Bonesteel, World War II general, born in Ft. Sidney, NE; commander, American forces in Iceland (1941–42), Allied commander, Iceland (1942) (died 1964).

1888 Sol Hurok, impresario who brought greatest performing artists to United States for 65 years, born in Pogar, Russia (died 1974).

1893 Charles E. Burchfield, water color artist (*Black Iron, Edge of Town, Freight Cars Under a Bridge*), born in Ashtabula Harbor, OH (died 1967).

1898 Curly (Earl L.) Lambeau, founder, coach, Green Bay Packers football team (1919–49), born in Green Bay, WI (died 1965).

1898 Paul Robeson, singer and actor, born in Princeton, NJ; starred on stage (*Emperor Jones, Porgy and Bess*); numerous concert tours; social activist and civil rights leader; screen actor (1930/40s) (died 1976).

1899 James S. McDonnell, Jr., founder (1939), chairman (1939–67), McDonnell Aircraft Co., born in Denver; merged with Douglas Aircraft, chairman (1967–80) (died 1980).

1903 Gregory Pincus, biologist who helped develop the oral contraceptive (the pill), born in Woodbine, NJ (died 1967).

1905 J. William Fulbright, legislator, born in Summer, MO; president, U. of Arkansas (1939–41); represented Arkansas in House (1943–45) and Senate (1945–74); chairman, Senate Foreign Relations Committee; initiated the Fulbright scholarships (died 1995).

1910 Abraham A. Ribicoff, legislator and public official, born in New Britain, CT; represented Connecticut in House (1949–53) and Senate (1963–81) and served as governor (1954–61); Secretary of Health, Education and Welfare (1961–62) (died 1998).

1912 Children's Bureau created in Department of Commerce and Labor; Julia Lathrop first director.

1914 Several American sailors from the USS *Dolphin* were arrested in Tampico by Mexican troops; Americans demanded an apology, which was refused.

1917 Eddystone ammunition plant in Chester, PA, destroyed by an explosion, killing 122 persons.

1919 John P. Eckert, co-inventor of computer, born in Philadelphia; with John Mauchly, invented the electronic computer, of which the third model was the Univac (died 1995).

1926 Hugh M. Hefner, founder, publisher, *Playboy* magazine (1953), born in Chicago; headed number of related enterprises (1959).

1939 Marian Anderson gave concert on steps of the Lincoln Memorial after being denied use of Constitution Hall in Washington.

1942 American and Filipino troops began abandonment of Bataan Peninsula to Japanese, with 37,000 taken prisoner; some escaped to Corregidor.

1945 An American Liberty ship exploded in the Bari, Italy, harbor; 360 were killed, 1,730 injured.

1947 Tornadoes in Texas, Oklahoma, and Kansas killed 169 persons.

1963 Winston Churchill granted honorary American citizenship.

1965 Houston Astrodome opened.

1996 James W. Rouse, developer of new "cities" (Columbia, Reston) and shopping malls, died at 81.

2000 Dead at 78, Robert Komer served as director of America's failed non-military "pacification" efforts in Vietnam.

2002 Lawyer Lynne Stewart indicted on charges of passing messages from her convicted terrorist client (bomber of World Trade Center in 1993) to outside associates.

10

1606 First charter of Virginia issued by King James, providing for incorporation of the London Company, which established first permanent English colony at Jamestown, and the Plymouth Company.

1644 William Brewster, colonial leader, died at 77; arrived on the *Mayflower*, a leader in the church and public affairs management in Plymouth.

1664 Delegates from all New Netherlands localities met in New Amsterdam to seek protection against the English.

1780 George Armistead, War of 1812 officer who successfully defended Ft. McHenry in Baltimore Harbor against the British, born in New Market, VA (died 1818).

1790 President Washington signed first patent act.

1794 Matthew C. Perry, naval officer/diplomat, born in Newport, RI; pioneer advocate of naval steamships, established first naval engineering corps, gunnery school; led fleet to Japan, negotiated treaty (1854) opening country to Western trade (died 1858).

1806 Leonidas Polk, Episcopal prelate/educator, born in Raleigh, NC; missionary bishop to Southwest (1838), bishop of Louisiana (1841); a founder, U. of the South, Sewanee, TN; Confederate general, killed at Pine Mountain (1864).

1806 Horatio Gates, Revolutionary officer, died at 78; credited with victory over Burgoyne at Saratoga, although Schuyler and Arnold were primarily responsible; defeated at Camden, SC (1780); friends tried unsuccessfully to put him in Washington's place (the Conway cabal).

1810 Benjamin H. Day, founder of first penny daily newspaper (*New York Sun* 1833), born in West Springfield, MA (died 1889).

1816 Second Bank of the United States chartered after nation was without a central bank for five years.

1817 John C. Robinson, Union general, born in Binghamton, NY; saw action at Fredericksburg, Chancellorsville, Gettysburg (where his statue stands on the battlefield), and Spotsylvania, where he lost a leg (died 1897).

1827 Lew(is) Wallace, Union general, born in Brookville, IN; served in Mexican and Civil wars and on military court which tried Lincoln conspirators; governor of New Mexico Territory (1878–81); minister to Turkey (1881–85); author (*Ben Hur*) (died 1905).

1832 Mary A. Eastin, niece of President Jackson, was married in White House to Lucien J. Polk.

1833 David M. Gregg, Union general, born

in Huntingdon, PA; commanded cavalry on Union right wing at Gettysburg, turning back Confederate attempts to turn flank (died 1916).

1835　Henry Villard, industrialist/publisher, born in Speyer, Germany; headed, Northern Pacific Railroad (1881–84), board chairman (1888–93); organized, headed, Edison General Electric Co. (1888–91); had controlling interest in *New York Post, Nation* (1881) (died 1900).

1838　Frank S. Baldwin, inventor of an adding machine, born in New Hartford, CT; his machine was called the arithmometer (1874), which was redesigned as the Monroe calculator (died 1925).

1841　*New York Tribune* began publication under Horace Greeley.

1845　Pittsburgh almost completely destroyed by fire.

1847　Joseph Pulitzer, publisher often called father of modern American journalism, born in Mako, Hungary; owner, publisher, *St. Louis Post Dispatch* (1878), *New York World* (1883); represented New York in House (1885–87); his will established Columbia School of Journalism (1912), Pulitzer prizes (1917) (died 1911).

1861　Massachusetts Institute of Technology (MIT) incorporated.

1866　Society for the Prevention of Cruelty to Animals (SPCA) organized by Henry Bergh.

1868　George Arliss, stage/screen actor, born in London; starred in many films (*Disraeli, Green Goddess*) (died 1946).

1879　John D. Hertz, founder, head of rental car service (1924), born in Ruttka, Hungary (later Czechoslovakia); also founder, head, Chicago Yellow Cabs (1915) (died 1961).

1882　Frances Perkins, first woman cabinet officer, born in Boston; New York State Industrial Commissioner (1929–33); Secretary of Labor (1933–45); member, U.S. Civil Service Commission (1946–53) (died 1965).

1885　Bernard F. Gimbel, merchant, born in Vincennes, IN; with store which bore his name (1907–66), president (1927–53), board chairman (1953–66) (died 1966).

1903　Clare Boothe Luce, playwright/diplomat, born in New York City; plays included *The Women* and *Kiss the Boys Goodbye*; with magazines (*Vogue, Vanity Fair*) (1930–34); represented Connecticut in House (1943–47); ambassador to Italy (1953–56), to Brazil (1959) (died 1987).

1910　Eddy (Edwin F.) Duchin, pianist and orchestra leader, born in Cambridge, MA (died 1951).

1917　Robert B. Woodward, chemist, born in Boston; awarded 1965 Nobel Chemistry Prize for work in chemical synthesis (died 1979).

1927　Marshall W. Nirenberg, biochemist, born in New York City; with National Institutes of Health; shared 1968 Nobel Physiology/Medicine Prize for studies of genetic code.

1941　President Franklin Roosevelt announced agreement with Denmark for American military bases in Greenland.

1942　"Death march" of American and Filipino prisoners began from Bataan; at least 5,200 Americans died.

1945　Allied troops liberated the Buchenwald concentration camp.

1963　Nuclear submarine *Thresher* lost in North Atlantic with 129 men aboard.

1996　President Clinton vetoed bill banning late-term abortions, saying the relatively few such abortions were important to a vulnerable number of women.

1997　U.S. District Court held Line-Item Veto Act of 1996 unconstitutional; would give president power to veto individual items in a large spending bill; Supreme Court dismissed the challenge June 26.

1998　Viagra, a drug that treats impotence, went on sale; in first three months, about four million prescriptions were written for the drug.

1998　Mary F. Hulman, chairman of Indianapolis Speedway since 1977, died at 93; she was the widow of Tony Hulman, who acquired the track in 1945.

2000　Announcement: new co-host of *Today* show, Katie Couric, to receive reported $10 million a year.

2003　"Amber Alert" system passed by both houses of Congress; effort to assure prompt and widespread circulation of news of missing children.

11

1711　William Rudolph, a leading Virginia planter, died at about 60; attorney general for the Crown in Virginia (1674–98); a founder, College of William & Mary.

1713　Treaty of Utrecht signed ending Queen Anne War.

1780　British began siege of Charleston, SC; city surrendered May 13.

1794　Edward Everett, public official, born in Dorchester, MA; represented Massachusetts in

House (1825–35) and Senate (1853–54) and served as governor (1835–39); minister to England (1841–45); Secretary of State (1852–53); president, Harvard U. (1846–49); gave two-hour dedication speech at Gettysburg National Cemetery at time of Lincoln's address (died 1865).

1852 Adrian C. Anson, baseball player/manager (mostly with Chicago NL), born in Marshalltown, IA; had .339 batting average with more than 3,000 hits in 27 years; named to Baseball Hall of Fame (died 1922).

1859 Enoch H. Crowder, Selective Service director in World War I, born in Edinburg, MO (died 1932).

1861 Gen. P.G.T. Beauregard demanded surrender of Ft. Sumter; refused by Union Maj. Robert Anderson, fort commander; later Anderson agreed to evacuation of fort by the 15th; was notified at 3:30 A.M. April 12 that bombardment would begin in an hour.

1862 Ft. Pulaski, commanding approach to Savannah, GA, captured by Union troops.

1862 Charles Evans Hughes, chief justice, Supreme Court (1930–41), born in Glens Falls, NY; served New York as governor (1906–10); associate justice, Supreme Court (1910–16); 1916 Republican presidential candidate; Secretary of State (1921–25) (died 1948).

1865 President Lincoln spoke from White House balcony to a crowd celebrating end of Civil War; talked of reconciliation, reconstruction in what turned out to be his last public address.

1879 Frank T. Hines, Army general and public official, born in Salt Lake City; supervised transporting two million American troops to and from Europe (1918–19); director, Veterans Bureau (1923–30), administrator of Veterans Administration (1930–45); ambassador to Panama (1945–48) (died 1960).

1893 Dean G. Acheson, Secretary of State (1949–53), born in Middletown, CT; author (*Present at the Creation*) (died 1971).

1893 The first ambassador to the United States, Sir Julian Pauncefort of Great Britain, presented his credentials to President Cleveland.

1898 President McKinley sent message to Congress on events in Cuba which justified intervention.

1899 Percy L. Julian, chemist who did much to promote use of soy products, born in Montgomery, AL (died 1975).

1900 Navy purchased its first submarine, equipped with an internal combustion engine and an electric motor; designed by John P. Holland.

1913 Oleg Cassini, fashion designer, born in Rome; began career designing costumes for Paramount Pictures, then went on his own.

1921 Iowa enacted first state tax on cigarettes.

1930 Nicholas Brady, Secretary of the Treasury (1988–93), born in New York City; represented New Jersey in Senate (1982).

1941 Office of Price Administration (OPA) created with Leon Henderson as the first administrator.

1947 Jackie Robinson of Brooklyn Dodgers became first black baseball player in the major leagues.

1951 President Truman relieved Gen. Douglas MacArthur from post of UN commander and commander of American forces in Japan and Far East for his constant criticism of American war policy; succeeded by Gen. Matthew B. Ridgway.

1953 Department of Health, Education and Welfare began operations with Oveta Culp Hobby as first secretary; divided into separate departments, Education, and Health and Human Services, in 1979.

1965 Elementary and Secondary Education Act passed, providing large-scale direct federal aid to elementary and secondary schools, a historic breakthrough in American education.

1965 Thirty-seven tornadoes ripped across six Midwestern states, leaving 242 persons dead, 2,500 injured, and $250 million in damage.

1968 President Lyndon Johnson signed Civil Rights Act, designed to end discrimination in the rental and sale of homes and apartments.

1973 The Mississippi River reached the highest flood stage in 30 years, devastating parts of nine states.

1988 Preliminary 164-page pastoral letter distributed to American Catholic bishops discussing sexism in the church; letter was third of three letters, one on peace being issued in 1983 and one on the economy in 1986; a final draft of the sexism letter will be voted on.

1996 A seven-year-old girl trying to become the youngest pilot flying across the United States was killed, along with her father and flight instructor, when the plane crashed in Wyoming.

2003 Last of six United Airlines unions agreed to benefit and wage cuts in effort to save carrier: machinists sacrifice $349 million and pilots $1.1 billion a year.

12

1724 Lyman Hall, public official, born in Wallingford, CT; member of Continental Congress (1775–80), signer of Declaration of Independence; served as governor of Georgia (1783), where he practiced medicine (died 1798).

1755 *Connecticut Gazette*, first newspaper in state, published in New Haven by James Parker.

1770 Townshend duties on various imports were altered to limit them to tea; at the same time, the Quartering Act, which required colonists to pay for quartering British troops, was allowed to expire.

1776 Convention of North Carolina colonists authorized its delegates to Continental Congress to vote for independence, the first colony to do so.

1777 Henry Clay, legislator, born in Hanover County, VA; represented Kentucky in House (1811–14, 1815–21, 1823–25), serving as Speaker every year but 1821, and in Senate (1806–07, 1810–11, 1831–42, 1849–52); Secretary of State (1825–29); drafted Missouri Compromise, laid groundwork for Pan-Americanism (died 1852).

1779 Spain by secret Treaty of Aranjuez joined France in the war against Great Britain, but did not recognize American independence.

1791 Francis P. Blair, newsman, born in Abingdon, VA; published *Congressional Globe*, predecessor of the *Congressional Record*; a founder, Republican Party (died 1876).

1804 George W. Jones, public official, born in Vincennes, IN; led efforts to create Wisconsin and Iowa territories; a first Iowa senator (1845–49) (died 1896).

1811 Group of colonists under John Jacob Astor founded the first American settlement in the Pacific Northwest — Astoria.

1818 American flag in its present form, designed by Samuel C. and Mary Reid, was flown over the Capitol for first time.

1831 U. of Alabama founded at Tuscaloosa.

1831 Grenville M. Dodge, railroad engineer, born in Danvers, MA; chief engineer, Union Pacific Railroad (1866–70); supervised building more than 10,000 miles of railroad, including linkup at Promontory Point, UT (died 1916).

1838 John S. Billings, physician and librarian, born in Switzerland County, IN; while in Army, expanded library of Surgeon General; designed Johns Hopkins Hospital; chief librarian, New York Public Library (1896–1913) (died 1913).

1844 Secretary of State John C. Calhoun signed Treaty of Annexation with Texas but Senate refused (35 to 16) to ratify treaty on June 8.

1853 Charles S. Bradley, inventor of a rotary converter, born in Victor, NY; also developed process for producing aluminum and for fixation of atmospheric hydrogen (died 1929).

1857 John T. Underwood, founder of Underwood Typewriter Co. (1895), born in London (died 1935).

1859 Frank E. Miller, physician who originated "vocal art-science," a method of voice production, born in Hartford, CT (died 1932).

1861 Civil War began as South Carolina troops fired on Ft. Sumter beginning at 4:30 A.M.; Union forces surrendered the following day.

1862 First official regiment of black troops organized by Gen. David Hunter; the regiment, composed of former slaves, was disbanded a short time later.

1865 Both Mobile and Montgomery, AL, surrendered to Union troops.

1874 William B. Bankhead, legislator, born in Moscow, AL; represented Alabama in House (1916–40), serving as majority leader (1934–36) and Speaker (1936–40) (died 1940).

1900 President McKinley signed act to establish civil government in Puerto Rico, effective May 1.

1904 Lily Pons, coloratura soprano, born in Draguignan, France; appeared in many operas and concert stage (died 1976).

1908 Chelsea, MA, was destroyed by fire, leaving 10,000 homeless.

1913 Lionel Hampton, drummer and vibraphone player/orchestra leader, born in Birmingham, AL.

1927 Rock Springs, TX, struck by a tornado which killed 74 persons.

1933 President Franklin Roosevelt named Ruth Bryan Rohde minister to Denmark and Iceland, the first American woman minister to a foreign country.

1934 Theodore Cahill, inventor of an electric typewriter, died at 67; also developed devices for heat engines, composing machines, and wireless telephony.

1937 Supreme Court sanctioned the power of Congress to regulate labor relations of persons engaged in interstate commerce in case of *NLRB v. Jones & Laughlin*.

1945 President Franklin Roosevelt died suddenly in Warm Springs, GA, of a cerebral hemorrhage at 63; Vice President Truman took oath of office as president in the Cabinet Room of the White House from Chief Justice Harlan F. Stone.

1945 Tornadoes struck Oklahoma and Arkansas killing 102 persons.

1947 David Letterman, television personality, born in Indianapolis.

1957 Vince Gill, country music singer, born in Norman, OK.

1980 Protesting the Soviet invasion of Afghanistan, the U.S. Olympic Committee voted not to participate in the Olympic Games scheduled for Moscow.

1981 First manned space shuttle, *Columbia*, successfully took off with John W. Young and Robert L. Crippen aboard; orbited earth 36 times in 54 hours, 22 minutes, landing successfully at Edwards Air Force Base, CA, on April 14.

1983 Chicago elected its first black mayor, Harold Washington, a former Illinois representative in the House.

1984 Two astronauts, John Van Hoften and George Nelson, aboard space shuttle *Challenger*, repaired a damaged solar maximum observatory which had been inoperative four years.

1985 Senator Jake Garn of Utah became first congressional observer to ride into space as a crew member of the shuttle *Discovery* launched from Cape Canaveral.

2000 Prominent British actor Anthony Hopkins obtained U.S. dual-citizenship.

2001 President Bush endorsed major new privacy protection for medical records, but implied further adjustments in provisions might be necessary.

2005 Forty-two-year veteran of covering outdoors recreational and related matters, Ed Neal, died at 90; regarded as one of the best and most productive writers in the field.

2006 Governor Mitt Romney signed into law legislation that provided virtually universal health insurance for people of Massachusetts as of July 2007; 500,000 uncovered affected; those who can pay for it but refuse would have to pay state tax surcharge.

13

1710 Jonathan Carver, author of first popular American travel book (Travels in Interior Parts of America), born in Weymouth, MA (died 1789).

1721 John Hanson, first "president," born in Charles County, MD; presiding officer of first Continental Congress (1781–82) under Articles of Confederation (died 1783).

1743 Thomas Jefferson, third president (1801–09), born in what is now Albemarle County, VA; member, Continental Congress (1775, 1776, 1783–85); author of Declaration of Independence; served Virginia as governor (1779–81); minister to France (1785–89); first Secretary of State (1790–94); Vice President (1797–1801); instrumental in founding U. of Virginia (1819) (died 1826).

1772 Eli Terry, clock maker, born in South Windsor, CT; established assembly line in first American clock factory; developed a perfected wooden clock with Seth Thomas, which dominated industry for years (died 1852).

1795 James Harper, cofounder of family publishing business (1825), born in Newtown, NY (died 1869).

1823 Sabato Morais, rabbi of Philadelphia congregations (1851–97), born in Leghorn, Italy; a founder, Jewish Theological Seminary, New York City (1886–97) (died 1897).

1832 Shadrach Bond, public official, died at 59; represented Illinois Territory as its first delegate to Congress (1812–14), later was state's first governor (1818–22).

1846 Pennsylvania Railroad chartered.

1851 Robert Abbe, first American surgeon to use radium in cancer treatment, born in New York City (died 1928).

1852 Frank W. Woolworth, originator of 5-and-10 cents stores, born in Rodman, NY; first store in Utica, NY (1879), failed; tried again in Lancaster, PA, which was successful; by 1900 there were 59 stores; by 1919, more than 1,000; built Woolworth Building, New York City (1913), then the world's tallest building (792 feet) (died 1919).

1859 Henry T. Allen, World War I general who commanded 90th Division in France, born in Sharpsburg, KY; headed occupation forces in Germany (1919) (died 1930).

1861 Maj. Robert Anderson and his federal troops surrendered to South Carolina troops after 34-hour bloodless bombardment of Ft. Sumter.

1865 Gen. William T. Sherman's troops took Raleigh, NC, from Confederate control.

1866 Butch Cassidy, outlaw and bank robber, born in Beaver, UT, as Robert L. Parker (died 1909).

1870 Metropolitan Museum of Art in New York City incorporated.

1873 John W. Davis, public official, born in Clarksburg, WV; represented West Virginia in House (1911–13); Solicitor General (1913–18);

ambassador to Great Britain (1918–21); 1924 Democratic presidential candidate (died 1955).

1874 Anson P. Stokes, Episcopal clergyman, born in New York City; canon residentiary, National Cathedral, Washington, DC (1924–39); secretary, Yale U. (1899–1921) (died 1958).

1875 Ray Lyman Wilbur, educator/public official, born in Boonesboro, IA; president, Stanford U. (1916–43), chancellor (1943–49); Secretary of Interior (1929–33) (died 1949).

1886 Albert W. Stevens, balloonist who made first photo of earth's curvature (1930), born in Belfast, MD; also photographed moon's shadow on earth during a solar eclipse (died 1949).

1890 Frank Murphy, associate justice, Supreme Court (1940–49), born in Harbor Beach, MI; mayor of Detroit (1930–33); governor-general, commissioner, Philippine Islands (1933–36); Michigan governor (1936–38); attorney general (1939–40) (died 1949).

1896 Ira C. Eaker, World War II Air Force general, born in Field Creek, TX; led first American heavy bomber attack on Germany (August 17, 1942); headed, 8th Air Force (1942–44), Mediterranean Allied Air Force (1944–45) (died 1988).

1907 Harold E. Stassen, perennial candidate for Republican presidential nomination, born in West St. Paul, MN; governor of Minnesota (1939–43); president, U. of Pennsylvania (1948–53).

1909 Eudora Welty, author (*Delta Wedding, The Ponder Heart, The Golden Apples*), born in Jackson, MS.

1918 Fire in a Norman OK, state hospital killed 38 persons.

1919 Madalyn O'Hair, atheist, born in Pittsburgh; led successful campaign to ban prayer in public schools.

1928 An explosion killed 40 persons in a dance hall in West Plains, MO.

1941 Michael S. Brown, U. of Texas scientist, born in New York City; shared 1985 Nobel Physiology/Medicine Prize for work on receptors that trap, absorb bloodstream particles with cholesterol.

1943 President Franklin Roosevelt dedicated the Jefferson Memorial in Washington on the 200th anniversary of Jefferson's birth.

1970 Apollo 13 mission developed serious problems about 200,000 miles from earth, when oxygen tanks and service modules exploded; completed mission around the moon and returned in the lunar module; splashed down successfully April 17.

1992 About 250 million gallons of water from the Chicago River leaked into underground tunnels of Loop buildings shutting them down; caused by a breach in the roof of a freight tunnel under the river.

1997 Twenty-one-year-old Tiger (Eldrick) Woods became youngest winner of Masters golf tournament, setting records with a low of 270 strokes and winning margin of 12 strokes; became first African-American to win one of the four major tournaments.

2003 Ginny Capicchioni became first woman to play in indoor National Lacrosse League; plays 12 minutes as goalkeeper in final game of season for the New Jersey Storm against the Vancouver Ravens.

2004 Michael Phelps received the prestigious New York Athletic Club's 2003 Sullivan Award as America's best amateur athlete.

2005 Eric Rudolph pleads guilty to 1996 Olympics bombing as well as attacks on abortion clinics; in exchange for plea he escapes execution and faces life in prison.

14

1528 Pamphilo de Narvaez, Spanish explorer, landed near Tampa with about 400 colonists, marched north to Apalachee (near present Tallahasee); unable to find gold, they set sail for Mexico.

1614 Pocahontas, legendary savior of Capt. John Smith, was married to John Rolfe, who is credited with introducing tobacco growing (1612); marriage brought peace to Jamestown colony.

1789 Charles Thomson, secretary of Congress, arrived at Mt. Vernon to notify George Washington of his election as first president.

1792 First apportionment act increased the number of members in House to 105, one for every 33,000 inhabitants.

1796 Benjamin L.E. de Bonneville, explorer, born in Paris; explored much of northwestern United States; served in both the Mexican and Civil wars (died 1878).

1802 Horace Bushnell, Congregational clergyman considered father of American religious liberalism, born in Bantam, CT; served church in Hartford (1833–61) (died 1876).

1810 Justin S. Morrill, legislator, born in Strafford, VT; represented Vermont in House (1855–67) and Senate (1867–98); author of Land Grant College Act, which led to numerous state agricultural and mechanical colleges (died 1898).

1813 Junius Spencer Morgan, founder of family financial business, born in West Springfield, MA; headed, J.P. Morgan & Co. (1864–90) (died 1890).

1818 Office of Surgeon General created.

1820 Maturin M. Ballou, founder, first editor, *Boston Globe*, born in Boston (died 1895).

1842 Adna R. Chaffee, Army officer, born in Orwell, OH; served in Civil and Spanish-American wars; led American relief expedition in Boxer Rebellion in China (died 1914).

1861 John J. Carty, telephone pioneer, born in Cambridge, MA; chief engineer, New York Telephone Co. (1888–1907), ATT (1907–19); had numerous inventions for telephone and switchboard use (died 1932).

1865 President Lincoln was fatally wounded at 10:15 P.M. by John Wilkes Booth, a Shakespearian actor; president was seated in a box in Ford's Theater watching the play, *Our American Cousin*, when he was shot from behind; he died at 7:22 the next morning in the home of William Peterson, across the street from the theater.

1865 Union flag was raised over Ft. Sumter in Charleston Harbor, four years and a day after the Civil War began there.

1874 Josiah Warren, social reformer, died at about 76; a member of the Owen Socialist community in New Harmony, IN, he later set up own community on Long Island, which operated 1850–62; considered founder of American philosophical anarchism; invented process for making stereotype plates easily and cheaply.

1878 George M. Holley, producer of first practical motorcycle (1899), born in Port Jervis, NY; founder, head, Holley Motor Co.; also a major supplier of carburetors (died 1963).

1879 James Branch Cabell, author of popular novels (*Jurgen*), born in Richmond, VA (died 1958).

1894 Thomas A. Edison's kinetoscope (motion picture) shown in public for first time.

1910 President Taft threw out first ball in baseball season opener in Washington; the first president to do so.

1912 Chauncey Starr, engineer who pioneered in design, development of nuclear reactors, born in Newark, NJ.

1917 Committee on Public Information established by executive order, with George Creel, a newspaper editor, in charge; office disbanded after war.

1917 Marvin J. Miller, executive director of Baseball Players Association (1966–82), born in New York City; increased ballplayer's annual salary from $19,000 to more than $240,000.

1939 President Franklin Roosevelt, in letter to Adolf Hitler, appealed for peace; a similar message went to the King of Italy.

1940 Julie Christie, screen actress (*Dr. Zhivago, Darling, Shampoo*), born in Assam, India.

1941 Pete Rose, baseball player/manager (Cincinnati, Philadelphia NL), born in Cincinnati; all-time leader in base hits (4,256); banned from baseball (1989) for gambling activities.

1959 Taft Memorial Bell Tower in Washington, DC, dedicated in honor of Sen. Robert A. Taft.

1966 President Lyndon Johnson dedicated a statute of Lincoln while in Mexico City; reaffirmed support of Alliance for Progress.

1988 Dow Jones industrial average fell 101.46 points after government announced a $13.8 billion deficit in February, the largest since October.

1988 Blast outside a GI club in Naples killed at least five people, wounded 15, including several American soldiers.

1998 Maurice Stans, Commerce Secretary (1969–72), died at 90.

1998 Eight members of the self-proclaimed Republic of Texas were convicted of fraud charges.

2000 Both Dow Jones industrial average (down 617.78 points, over 5 percent) and Nasdaq composite index (down 355.49, nearly 10 percent) had largest one-day point drops in their histories; Standard & Poor's 500 index down 83.95 (nearly 6 percent).

2001 To protect passengers in case of heart attack, FAA required airlines to carry defibrillators aboard aircraft.

15

1632 George Calvert, the first Lord Baltimore, died at about 53, shortly before charter creating Maryland as part of Virginia territory was approved; grant transferred to his son, Cecelius.

1638 New Haven, CT, founded by Theophilus Eaton and the Rev. John Davenport.

1715 Temassee Indians, incited by Spaniards, attacked South Carolina settlers, killing 400.

1741 Charles Willson Peale, foremost American portrait painter, born in Queen Anne County, MD; best known for paintings of George Washington, who sat for him many times; founded first art museum in Philadelphia (died 1827).

1775   British grenadiers and light infantry-men in Boston assigned special training, arousing suspicion of coming events.

1782   Eleazar W. Ripley, War of 1812 general, born in Hanover, NH; represented Louisiana in House (1835–39) (died 1839).

1783   Congress ratified preliminary articles of peace, officially ending American Revolution; treaty signed in Paris, September 3, formally ratified by Congress January 14, 1784.

1786   Walter Channing, physician/educator, born in Newport, RI; first professor of obstetrics and medical jurisprudence, Harvard Medical School; dean (1819–47) (died 1876).

1789   *Gazette of the United States*, a pro-administration newspaper, established, with John Fenno editor.

1791   Alexander Garden, Scottish-born naturalist, died at 61; collected botanical, mineral, and zoological specimens; gardenia named for him.

1813   Gen. James Wilkinson led American forces in taking Spanish fort at Mobile; occupied Mobile District of West Florida to the Perdido River.

1814   John L. Motley, diplomat/historian, born in Dorchester, MA; historian of the Dutch; minister to Austria (1861–67), to Great Britain (1869–70) (died 1877).

1817   New York State legislature authorized construction of the Erie Canal; created a canal board.

1821   Catesby ap Roger Jones, Confederate naval officer who commanded the *Merrimac* in its battle with the *Monitor*, born in Selma, AL (died 1877).

1843   Henry James, author (*Daisy Miller*, *The American*), born in New York City but spent most of his life abroad (died 1916).

1850   San Francisco incorporated by California's first legislature.

1859   William B. Parsons, engineer who designed, built first units of New York City subways (1899–1904), born in New York City; built East River Tunnel (1904); chief engineer, Cape Cod Canal (1905–14) (died 1932).

1861   President Lincoln issued proclamation that declared an "insurrection" existed; called on states for 75,000 three-months volunteers.

1865   Vice President Andrew Johnson sworn in as president in his suite at Kirkwood House in Washington, three hours after the death of President Lincoln.

1869   Deming Jarves, pioneer glass manufac-turer, died at 79; manufactured pressed glass known as Sandwich Glass at his factory in Sandwich, MA.

1881   Hugh H. Burnett, pioneer soil scientist, born in Wadesboro, NC; known as the father of soil conservation, he was first director, Soil Conservation Service (died 1960).

1889   A. Philip Randolph, labor and civil rights leader, born in Crescent City, FL; organizer, president, Brotherhood of Sleeping Car Porters (1925–68); an organizer of march on Washington (1963) (died 1979).

1889   Thomas Hart Benton, artist who painted realistic portraits of ordinary Midwestern people, born in Neosho, MO; did murals for Missouri State Capitol, Truman Library (died 1975).

1892   General Electric Co. established by merger of Edison General Electric Co. and Thomas Houston Electric Co.

1894   Bessie Smith, one of greatest blues singers, born in Chattanooga, TN (died 1937).

1902   Samuel K. Hoffman, propulsion engineer who pioneered in developing rocket engines, born in Williamsport, PA.

1910   The 13th Census reported a population of 91,972,266.

1912   Steamer *Titanic* sank on its maiden voyage after hitting an iceberg in the North Atlantic; 1,513 of its 2,340 passengers perished, including John Jacob Astor, Isidor Straus and his wife, George D. Widener, Benjamin Guggenheim.

1920   Niccolo Sacco, 29, a shoe factory worker, and Bartolomeo Vanzetti, 32, a fish peddler, both radicals, were accused of killing two men in a payroll holdup at Slater & Morrill shoe factory in South Braintree, MA; found guilty in 1921; despite appeals and worldwide protests, they were executed August 23, 1927.

1922   Leonard Baskin, sculptor and noted graphic artist, born in New Brunswick, NJ.

1933   Roy Clark, country music singer and musician, born in Meherrin, VA; starred on television classic (*Hee Haw*).

1940   The 16th Census reported population of 131,669,275 and the center of population two miles southeast of Carlisle, IN.

1950   The 17th Census reported population of 150,697,361 (including Alaska and Hawaii); center of population was three miles northeast of Louisville, IL.

1952   President Truman signed formal peace treaty with Japan officially ending World War II.

1959   Secretary of State John Foster Dulles resigned because of an incapacitating illness; died

May 4; Christian A. Herter named to the post April 18.

1964 Chesapeake Bay Bridge Tunnel, 17.6 miles long between the Eastern Shore of Virginia and Norfolk, opened.

1986 American naval planes and ships bombed "terrorist" targets in Libya.

2002 IRS began levying $500 fine on anyone filing for "reparations" for slave era ancestors who did not voluntarily withdraw claim; over 100,000 such nonexistent credits applied for in 2000 and 2001 with over $30 million erroneously granted.

2002 Byron White, member of U.S. Supreme Court, 1962–1993, died of complications produced by pneumonia.

2004 Bad news from Environmental Protection Agency to 474 counties in 31 states: air quality falls below federal requirements; California tops list with 36 failing counties.

2006 Pioneer race driver Louise Smith died at 89; won 38 races in career beginning in mid–1940s; in 1999 became first woman in the International Motorsports Hall of Fame.

16

1588 French force under Dominique de Gourges recaptured Ft. Carolina (San Mateo) at the mouth of St. James River in Florida; slaughtered all captives in retaliation for Spanish massacre of French settlers in 1565.

1683 William Leete, colonial leader, died at 70; a founder and town clerk of Guilford, CT (1639–62); deputy governor, New Haven Colony (1669–76), governor (1676–83).

1787 First American play (Royall Tyler's *Contrast*) produced by an American professional company staged in John St. Theater, New York City.

1789 George Washington, notified two days earlier of his election as president, set out from Mt. Vernon for New York, arriving April 23; writing in his diary, he stated: "I bade adieu to Mt. Vernon, to private life, and to domestic felicity, and with a mind oppressed with more anxious and painful sensations than I have words to express, set out for New York ... with the best disposition to render service to my country in obedience to its call, but with less hope of answering its expectations."

1806 Hugh H. Toland, surgeon who founded a medical college which became part of U. of California, born in Guilders Creek, SC; known for operations on clubfoot, strabismus (died 1880).

1856 Albert B. Dick, inventor of a mimeograph, born in Bureau County, IL; invented machine (about 1887), then founded, headed A.B. Dick Co. (died 1934).

1857 Henry S. Pritchett, astronomer, born in Fayette, MO; superintendent, Coast and Geodetic Survey (1897–1900); president, MIT (1900–06); president, Carnegie Foundation for Advancement of Teaching (1906–30) (died 1939).

1861 North Carolina state troops seized Forts Caswell and Johnston.

1862 Confederate Congress passed bill for compulsory military service for all white men 18 to 35; amended September 1862 to 18 to 45, and in February 1864 to 17 to 50.

1862 President Lincoln signed act abolishing slavery in the District of Columbia; average compensation to slave holders by government was $300.

1863 Admiral David D. Porter led Union fleet of seven ironclads, three steamers, and ten barges past the Vicksburg batteries during the night.

1867 New York legislature created free state public school system.

1867 Wilbur Wright, aviation pioneer, born in Millville, IN; with brother, Orville, made historic flights at Kitty Hawk, NC, after first experimenting with kites and gliders (died 1912).

1868 South Carolina voters ratified a new constitution during a two-day vote.

1889 Charles Chaplin, screen actor/producer, born in London; starred in many early films (*The Kid*, *The Gold Rush*, *City Lights*, *Modern Times*) (died 1977).

1890 Billy DeBeck, cartoonist (*Barney Google*, *Snuffy Smith*), born in Chicago (died 1942).

1890 Donald F. Jones, agricultural researcher who made hybrid corn commercially feasible, born in Hutchinson, KS (died 1963).

1903 Paul Waner, baseball player considered one of greatest hitters (Pittsburgh), born in Harrah, OK; named to Baseball Hall of Fame (died 1965).

1924 Henry Mancini, pianist and composer, born in Cleveland; wrote several hits ("Moon River," "Days of Wine and Roses," "Dear Hearts") and some film scores (*The Pink Panther*, *The Glenn Miller Story*, *Breakfast at Tiffany's*) (died 1994).

1929 Senate confirmed former Vice President Charles G. Dawes as ambassador to Great Britain.

1947 Most of Texas City, TX, destroyed by

explosion of French vessel *Grandcamp* in the harbor; 516 killed.

1947 Karim Abdul-Jabbar, basketball player, born in New York City as Lew Alcindor; starred at UCLA, Los Angeles Lakers; all-time leading scorer in National Basketball Association.

1953 Fire in a Chicago metalworking plant caused 35 deaths.

1966 Gala concert marked final performance at Metropolitan Opera House before moving to new home in Lincoln Center.

1996 President Clinton began three-day visit to Japan and South Korea, meeting with their leaders and signing agreements on joint security.

2000 Abram Chayes died at 77; during Cuban missile crisis in 1972, he authored the legal paper establishing the basis for the naval quarantine of the island.

2001 Environmentalists feared Bush would roll back extended wetlands protection ordered by predecessor's appointees; instead, EPA decided to leave the rules in effect.

17

1524 Giovanni de Verrazano, a Florentine navigator for the French, arrived in New York Bay and Hudson River, then proceeded to Narragansett Bay.

1741 Samuel Chase, associate justice, Supreme Court (1796–1811), born in Princess Anne, MD; member of Continental Congress (1774–78, 1784, 1785), signer of Declaration of Independence; while justice, impeached because of trial conduct (1799), acquitted (died 1811).

1743 John Page, colonial leader, born in Gloucester County, VA; represented Virginia in House (1789–97) and as lieutenant governor (1776–79) and governor (1802–05) (died 1808).

1763 *Georgia Gazette*, first newspaper in state, published in Savannah by James Johnson.

1770 Mahlon Dickerson, public official, born in Hanover Neck, NJ; served New Jersey as governor (1815–17) and in Senate (1817–33); Navy Secretary (1834–38) (died 1853).

1820 Alexander Cartwright, baseball pioneer often considered father of modern game, born in New York City; organized team which played in first game (1846) (died 1892).

1824 United States and Russia signed treaty agreeing to 54°40' line as southernmost limit of its territorial claims, withdrew restrictions against Bering Sea fishing.

1826 New York granted charter to Mohawk & Hudson Railroad, which later became New York Central.

1837 J(ohn) P. Morgan, financier who helped form U.S. Steel, General Electric, born in Hartford, CT; founder, present-day J.P. Morgan & Co. (1895); generous philanthropist (died 1913).

1838 Massachusetts passed law forbidding the retail sale of spirituous liquors.

1842 Charles H. Parkhurst, Presbyterian clergyman and reformer, born in Framingham, MA; attacked political corruption, organized vice in sermon (February 14, 1892) which aroused New York City and led to Lexow investigation, defeat of Tammany, and election of a reform administration (died 1933).

1849 William R. Day, associate justice, Supreme Court (1903–22), born in Ravenna, OH; Secretary of State (1898), led American commission to arrange peace with Spain (died 1923).

1859 Willis Van Devanter, associate justice, Supreme Court (1910–37), born in Marion, IN (died 1941).

1859 Walter C. Camp, football coach and originator of All-America teams selection, born in New Britain, CT; All-America selections began 1889; influential in shaping football rules; devised "daily dozen," series of simple calisthenics (died 1925).

1861 Virginia seceded from Union by secret legislative vote of 88 to five, which was later ratified by popular vote (128,884 to 32,134); Gov. John Letcher immediately seized Harpers Ferry arsenal and Norfolk Navy Yard.

1861 Lewis Nixon, naval architect and shipbuilder, born in Leesburg, VA; designed various battleships; operated shipbuilding firm in Elizabeth, NJ (died 1940).

1868 Mark L. Bristol, naval officer in Spanish-American and World War I, born in Glassboro, NJ; high commissioner to Turkey (1919–27); commander, Asiatic Fleet (1927); chairman, Navy General Board (1930–32) (died 1939).

1870 Roy Stannard Baker, author who wrote essays under name of David Grayson (*Adventures in Contentment*), born in Lansing, MI; magazine editor, wrote authorized biography of President Wilson (died 1946).

1871 Texas legislature approved creation of Texas A&M College.

1874 Clarence H. Mackay, who completed trans-Pacific cable (1903), born in San Francisco; owner, head, Commercial Cable Co. and Postal Telegraph (died 1938).

1879 Albert S. Howell, photographic equipment manufacturer, born in West Branch, MN; a founder, Bell & Howell Co. (1907) (died 1951).

1882 President Arthur asked Congress for a levee system for Mississippi River, which had made 85,000 homeless in March.

1890 Harry Plotz, bacteriologist, who developed protective vaccine against typhus, born in Paterson, NJ; investigated cause of measles, worked on developing a serum; studied viral diseases (died 1947).

1897 Thornton A. Wilder, author (*The Bridge of San Luis Ray, Woman of Andros*) and playwright (*Our Town, The Skin of Our Teeth, The Matchmaker*—which later became *Hello, Dolly!*), born in Madison, WI (died 1975).

1916 American Academy of Arts & Letters founded in 1904 was incorporated.

1918 William Holden, screen actor (*Bridge on the River Kwai, Stalag 17, Born Yesterday*), born in O'Fallon, IL.

1919 Josiah C. Cady, architect, died at 82; designed original Metropolitan Opera House, American Museum of Natural History.

1961 Bay of Pigs invasion of Cuba by 1,200 anti–Castro exiles was crushed; they had been trained, armed, and directed by Americans.

1973 President Nixon authorized new investigation into growing Watergate case with the appointment of special prosecutor, Archibald Cox.

1989 House Ethics Committee unanimously charged Speaker James C. Wright with 69 violations of House rules, the first time a Speaker was charged; committee found him guilty of improperly accepting gifts and evading limits on outside income.

1991 Dow Jones industrial average finished above 3000 for first time (3004.26).

1993 Federal grand jury found two Los Angeles police officers guilty of violating the civil rights of motorist Rodney King in 1991; they were later sentenced to 2½ years in prison; two other officers were acquitted.

2003 Robert C. Atkins, cardiologist and creator of the widely popular high-protein Atkins Diet, died at 72.

2003 Earl King (b. 1934) died at 69. New Orleans singer and guitarist; his "Come On" is better known under the title "Let the Good Times Roll"; wrote various Mardi Gras standards.

2004 Last Confederate Funeral held for bodies of those recovered in 2000 from sunken Confederate submarine *H.L. Hunley;* 10,000 attended in period civilian and military attire.

2006 Rabbi Arthur Hertzberg passed away at 84; civil rights leader and authority on Jewish history.

18

1644 Opechancanough began two-year war against the Virginians.

1689 Armed uprising in Boston forced the unpopular governor, Sir Edmund Andros, to take refuge in fort; later arrested and jailed for a year, then returned to England.

1775 Paul Revere, William Dawes, and Samuel Prescott spread word of the coming of British troops; Revere was captured near Lexington, later released; Dawes had to turn back; Prescott went on to Concord to warn Samuel Adams and John Hancock.

1799 John Y. Mason, legislator and public official, born in Greenville County, VA; represented Virginia in House (1831–37); Attorney General (1845–46), Navy Secretary (1844–45, 1846–49); minister to France (1854–59) (died 1859).

1803 James Madison named minister plenipotentiary to England.

1806 Congress passed Non-Importation Act, excluding many British articles because of raids against American shipping, impressment of seamen.

1831 New York University chartered.

1847 Gen. Winfield Scott led American troops to victory at Battle of Cerro Gordo.

1853 Vice President William R. King died at 67 at his home near Caluba, AL.

1857 Clarence S. Darrow, defense lawyer, born in Kinsman, OH; defended Eugene W. Debs in Pullman strike case, the Leopold-Loeb murder case in Chicago, the Scottsboro case; opposed William Jennings Bryan in Scopes "monkey" trial in Tennessee (died 1938).

1862 Successful six-day campaign began to move naval forces up the Mississippi River to New Orleans.

1864 Richard Harding Davis, best known, most influential newsman of his day, born in Philadelphia; correspondent in six wars; author (*Ranson's Folly, The Dictator*) (died 1916).

1865 Confederate troops under Gen. Joseph E. Johnston surrendered to Union troops led by Gen. William T. Sherman near Raleigh, NC.

1882 Leopold Stokowski, conductor, born in London; led symphonies in Cincinnati (1909–12),

Philadelphia (1914–36), New York (1944–45); formed American Symphony Orchestra (1962) (died 1977).

1892 Eugene J. Houdry, inventor of catalytic cracking process for making gasoline, born in Dumont, France (died 1962).

1902 Menachem M. Schneerson, rebbe (spiritual head) of Lubavich Hasidim (1951–94), born in Nikolayev, Russia; one of most important figures in American and world Jewry (died 1994).

1905 George H. Hitchings, research scientist, born in Hoquiam, WA; shared 1988 Nobel Physiology/Medicine Prize for helping develop drugs to fight leukemia, malaria, gout, herpes, and bacterial infections (died 1998).

1906 Earthquake struck San Francisco at about 5:12 A.M., followed by fires which razed more than four miles of the city; nearly 500 died.

1916 President Wilson sent ultimatum to Germany after an unarmed French channel vessel, *Sussex*, was torpedoed March 24, with four Americans injured; Wilson threatened to sever diplomatic relations unless submarine warfare changed.

1917 Woman's suffrage went into effect in Rhode Island and Michigan.

1938 President Franklin Roosevelt pardoned Dr. Francis E. Townsend, originator of an old age pension plan; Townsend had been found guilty of contempt of Congress and sentenced to 30-day prison term.

1940 Joseph L. Goldstein, Texas U. scientist, born in Sumter, SC; shared 1985 Nobel Physiology/Medicine Prize for work on receptors that trap and absorb bloodstream particles that contain cholesterol.

1942 Sixteen B-25s led by Col. James H. Doolittle, bombed Tokyo, the first Allied air attack on Japan.

1942 President Franklin Roosevelt issued an executive order creating the War Manpower Commission; terminated September 19, 1945.

1944 Ernie Pyle, war correspondent, killed by enemy gunfire on island of Ie Shima.

1950 Postmaster General Jesse M. Donaldson ordered a cut in residential mail deliveries to once a day.

1978 Senate approved 68–31 legislation to turn over the Panama Canal to Panama by the year 2000.

1983 American embassy in Beirut was bombed; 17 Americans killed.

1986 Titan 34-D rocket carrying a secret military payload blew up shortly after liftoff from the Vandenberg Air Force Base in California.

1987 Richard Wilbur, 66, was named the second poet laureate of America, succeeding Robert Penn Warren.

1988 Presidential panel on airline safety recommended making the Federal Aviation Administration an independent agency, headed by a new safety "czar."

2001 Records of the 22 million immigrants who entered U.S. through Ellis Island between 1892 to 1942 became accessible via Internet beginning today.

19

1720 William Burnet appointed governor of New York and New Jersey, and then Massachusetts, serving until his death in 1729.

1721 Roger Sherman, colonial leader, born in Newton, MA; a Connecticut legislator, he was only person to sign all important colonial documents — Articles of Confederation, Articles of Association, Declaration of Independence, the Constitution; co-author of Connecticut Compromise at Constitutional Convention, which created the modern Congress; represented Connecticut in House (1789–91) and Senate (1791–93) (died 1793).

1775 Battles of Lexington and Concord occurred, marking start of American Revolution; colonists had been alerted to planned British attack on Concord supply depot; British, headed by Maj. John Pitcairn, arrived at Lexington at dawn, were met by 70 Minute Men under Capt. John Parker; sporadic fighting went on all day along Lexington-Concord-Boston road; casualties were 73 British killed, 174 wounded, 26 missing; 93 Americans killed, wounded, or missing.

1782 Holland recognized independence of America, received John Adams as minister; followed by a loan of $2 million (June 11) and treaty of commerce (October 8).

1791 William O. Butler, Army general in Mexican War, born in Jessamine County, KY; 1848 Democratic vice presidential candidate (died 1880).

1832 Lucretia Rudolph Garfield, wife of President Garfield, born in Hiram, OH (died 1918).

1836 Augustus D. Juilliard, merchant and philanthropist, born at sea to French parents; bequeathed bulk of fortune to provide musical education for promising students (died 1919).

1850 Clayton-Bulwer Treaty between United

States and Great Britain ratified; designed to relieve tensions over Central America and to make it possible for private enterprise to build and operate an isthmian canal.

1861 Mob of Southern sympathizers attacked a Massachusetts militia regiment marching through Baltimore; four soldiers and 12 civilians killed.

1861 President Lincoln proclaimed a blockade of Confederate ports in South Carolina, Georgia, Alabama, Florida, Mississippi, Louisiana, and Texas.

1861 John G. Hibben, president, Princeton U. (1912–32), born in Peoria, IL; logic and psychology professor (1887–1912) (died 1933).

1865 May Robson, stage/screen actress (*Strange Interlude*, *Lady for a Day*), born in New South Wales, Australia (died 1942).

1865 Funeral services were held for President Lincoln in Washington; burial services were held in Springfield, IL, May 4.

1868 Paul P. Harris, founder of Rotary International in Chicago February 23, 1905, born in Racine, WI (died 1947).

1892 Gasoline-driven automobile demonstrated by its inventors, Charles A. and J. Frank Duryea in Springfield, MA.

1897 First Boston Marathon, from Boston to Hopkinton, was run.

1912 Glenn T. Seaborg, chemist, born in Ishpeming, MI; shared 1951 Nobel Chemistry Prize for discovery of plutonium; chairman, Atomic Energy Commission (1961–71).

1917 First American shots in World War I fired by American steamer *Magnolia* when it repulsed a submarine attack.

1919 Merce Cunningham, dancer and choreographer, born in Centralia, WA; developed new forms of abstract dance called "choreography by chance."

1932 Andrea Mead (Lawrence), champion skier who won 1952 Olympic gold medal, born in Rutland, VT.

1933 President Franklin Roosevelt announced the United States was going off the gold standard; Congress ratified move June 5.

1951 Gen. Douglas MacArthur, relieved of his command by President Truman, addressed a joint session of Congress.

1956 Grace Kelly, screen actress, married Prince Rainier III, ruler of Monaco, and retired from the screen.

1967 Nineteen Western Hemisphere nations signed declaration in Uruguay for formation of a Latin American common market; President Lyndon Johnson signed for the United States.

1988 Milwaukee Mayor Henry W. Maier left office after serving for 28 years, the longest tenure of any big city mayor.

1989 A 16-inch gun on the battleship *Iowa* exploded during a routine test firing north of Puerto Rico, killing 47 crewmen.

1993 A compound outside Waco, TX, where the Branch Davidian cult was holding off federal law enforcement officials, was destroyed by fire; 72 residents died; four agents of the Bureau of Alcohol, Tobacco and Firearms were killed February 28 in a raid on the compound.

1995 A bomb exploded outside the Oklahoma City Federal Building killing 169 persons, injuring more than 400; 200 nearby buildings were damaged.

1997 Rising floodwaters forced 100,000 to flee their homes in the upper Midwest and Canada; floods were caused by winter snows three times the normal volume.

2002 Yale adopted policy of providing extra financial assistance to its students who could not receive federal help due to prior criminal conviction(s); 50,000 lost federal money between 1998 and 2002; Hampshire and Swarthmore colleges already had similar policy.

2006 Two studies published by American Medical Association said that mercury amalgam dental fillings were verifiably safe for at least seven years; critics worry over longer-term effect.

2006 Scott Crossfield, one of the handful of pilots to fly the pioneer X-planes that paved the way for the American space program, died in small plane accident at 84; in November 1953 he set a new world speed record of 1,320 mph, a record that only held till December when Chuck Yeager topped it at 1,612 mph.

20

1676 Bacon's Rebellion began when Nathaniel Bacon led the frontiersmen of Virginia against the Indians because the governor refused to act.

1735 Richard Henderson, frontiersman, born in Hanover County, VA; with Daniel Boone, he built Boonesboro, a first Kentucky settlement; later established Nashville (died 1785).

1777 A New York convention adopted a state constitution.

1812 Vice President George Clinton died in

Washington at 73, the first vice president to die in office.

1836 Wisconsin Territory created.

1842 John M. Farley, Catholic Archbishop of New York (1902–18), born in County Armagh, Ireland; named cardinal 1911 (died 1918).

1842 Daniel C. French, sculptor best known for the seated Lincoln in Lincoln Memorial, born in Exeter, NH; also sculpted Minute Man in Concord, MA, and John Harvard in Harvard U. yard (died 1931).

1861 Robert E. Lee resigned his command in the U.S. Army; accepted command of Virginia Confederate forces; named a general June 18.

1867 John M. Bozeman, pioneer who blazed new trail (1863) through the Rockies, was killed by Indians at 32; his trail was between Yellowstone and Gallatin Rivers to Virginia City.

1868 Georgia citizens ratified a new state constitution adopted by convention.

1882 Holland M. ("Howlin' Mad") Smith, World War II Marine Corps general, born in Seale, AL (died 1967).

1894 Harold Lloyd, screen comedian (*The Freshman, Kid Brother, Movie Crazy*), born in Burchard, NE (died 1971).

1898 Congress adopted a joint resolution authorizing use of Army and Navy to bring about Cuban independence; helped start Spanish-American War.

1905 Harold S. Marcus, merchant who headed Nieman-Marcus stores (1950–72), born in Dallas.

1914 The House (323–29) and Senate (72–13) authorized President Wilson to take necessary actions in the wake of the Tampico, Mexico, incident when American sailors were jailed.

1920 John P. Stevens, associate justice, Supreme Court (1975–), born in Chicago.

1933 Executive order by President Franklin Roosevelt ended the export of gold; formally the nation went off the gold standard June 5.

1943 President Franklin Roosevelt conferred with Mexican President Avila Camacho at Monterey, Mexico, on cooperation during and after the war.

1961 President Kennedy said the United States would not "abandon" Cuba to Communists.

1971 Supreme Court ruled that busing could be used to achieve desegregation in dual school systems in the South.

1983 President Reagan signed Social Security amendments which placed new federal

employees under the system beginning January 1, 1984, gradually increasing the eligibility age from 65 to 66 by 2009 and to 67 by 2027.

1984 Mabel Mercer, jazz singer, died at 84; Leonard Bernstein called her "the eternal guardian of elegance in the world of popular song."

1988 Supreme Court ruled that Congress is free to tax all interest on state and local government bonds, overruling an 1895 precedent ruling.

1988 Supreme Court ruled 4–3 that alcoholism is "willful misconduct" and that the Veterans Administration could deny disability and other benefits to veterans disabled by the condition.

2000 Announcement of discovery of a rare fossilized dinosaur heart in South Dakota.

2001 American Baptist missionary Veronica Bowers and her baby killed as Peruvian Air Force, working in tandem with CIA personnel, downed their plane; thought they were drug dealers.

2003 Ruth Hale (b. 1908) died; occasionally an actress, but better known as the founder of community theaters and author of more than 70 plays.

2005 New York Stock Exchange entered world of electronic trading by agreeing to purchase Archipelago Holdings.

2005 Bankruptcy Reform Act signed by President Bush; first major changes in over a quarter century: included larger costs for filers and made it more difficult for many to totally eliminate debt.

21

1649 Maryland enacted the Toleration Act, designed to remove charge that the colony was intolerant of Protestants, repealed by Assembly in 1654.

1775 Lord Dunmore, Virginia governor, ordered all gunpowder in Williamsburg magazine removed; this was done to place it under greater security, he said, and it would be returned.

1775 Alexander Anderson, engraver who made first American wood engravings, born in New York City (died 1870).

1778 Thomas McAuley, a founder (1835) and first president (1836–40) of Union Theological Seminary, born in Coleraine, Ireland (died 1862).

1789 John Adams took office as the first vice president.

1801 Robert F.W. Allston, who made rice

cultivation on marshland possible, born in All Saints Parish, SC; developed a system of embankments and drainage ditches for rice growing; governor of South Carolina (1856–58) (died 1864).

1809   Robert M.T. Hunter, legislator, born in Essex County, VA; represented Virginia in House (1837–43, 1845–47), serving as Speaker (1839–41), and in Senate (1847–61); Confederate Secretary of State (1861–62) (died 1887).

1818   Henry W. Shaw, author known as Josh Billings, born in Lanesboro, MA (died 1885).

1828   *Webster's Dictionary* (two volumes) published.

1832   Abraham Lincoln enlisted to serve in Black Hawk War; discharged July 10.

1836   Mexican forces led by Gen. Antonio Santa Anna, who was captured, were defeated at San Jacinto by Texans under Sam Houston; Texas thus won its independence.

1838   John Muir, who led efforts to create national parks, born in Dunbar, Scotland; promoted federal conservation laws which led to Sequoia and Yosemite parks (died 1914).

1855   First railroad train crossed the Mississippi River's first bridge, which connected Rock Island, IL, and Davenport, IA.

1870   Edwin S. Porter, inventor who worked with Edison, born in Connellsville, PA; helped develop motion picture camera; made first story film (*The Life of an American Fireman* 1899) for Edison (died 1941).

1882   Percy W. Bridgman, physicist, born in Cambridge, MA; awarded 1946 Nobel Physics prize for development of high pressure chambers to study matter at extreme pressure (died 1961).

1898   Spain broke off diplomatic relations with the United States.

1915   Anthony Quinn, screen actor (*Zorba the Greek, Viva Sapata*), born in Chihuahua, Mexico.

1917   Nebraska legislature enacted woman suffrage and statewide prohibition laws.

1918   San Jacinto and Hemet in California were destroyed by an earthquake.

1930   Fire in the Ohio State Penitentiary in Columbus resulted in 320 deaths.

1945   Seventh Army captured Nuremberg, Germany.

1955   American occupation of Germany; troops remained on a contractual basis.

1958   A midair plane collision near Las Vegas killed 49 persons.

1962   First American world's fair in 22 years — the Century 21 Exposition — opened in Seattle.

1985   Forty-four persons died in a fire in a Philadelphia movie theater.

1986   Supreme Court ruled 5–4 that a person suing a news organization for libel must prove the damaging statements were false "on matters of public concern"; overturned several statutes which put burden of proof on news organizations.

1993   U.S. Holocaust Memorial Museum in Washington, DC, opened.

1995   Timothy McVeigh, 27, who was stopped by police north of Oklahoma City shortly after the federal building bombing April 19, was charged in the bombing.

2006   First quarter Ford report released: went from $1.21 billion profit in first quarter 2005 to $1.19 billion loss in current year; largely result of cost of plant closures and reduced sales.

22

1669   Richard Mather, colonial religious leader, died at 72; teacher at Dorchester, MA, church; a leader of Congregationalism; co-author of Bay Psalm Book.

1688   Jonathan Dickinson, Presbyterian clergyman who obtained charter for college that became Princeton, born in Hatfield, MA; received charter for College of New Jersey (later Princeton), its first president (1746–47) (died 1747).

1711   Eleazar Wheelock, founder of Hanover, NH, and Dartmouth College (1769), born in Windham, CT (died 1779).

1729   Michael Hillegas, first treasurer of United States (1777–89), born in Philadelphia (died 1804).

1759   James Freeman, first American Unitarian clergyman, born in Charleston, MA; a lay reader in King's Chapel, New York City, he was refused ordination because of his revisions in *Book of Common Prayer*; ordained as a Unitarian (1787) making King's Chapel the first American Unitarian church; Freeman served until 1826 (died 1835).

1774   When a private consignee tried to land a load of tea in New York City, Sons of Liberty disguised themselves as Indians, dumped tea into harbor; similar incidents occurred in Boston, Annapolis, Greenwich, NJ.

1786   Amos Lawrence, who with his brothers developed textile manufacturing, born in Groton, MA (died 1852).

1793   President Washington issued a neutrality proclamation declaring the United States was at peace with both Great Britain and France; warned citizens to abstain from any act of hostility against any belligerents.

1801 Elijah C. Bridgman, Congregational clergyman who was first American missionary (1830) to China, born in Belchertown, MA (died 1861).

1818 Cadwallader C. Washburn, founder of Washburn Crosby & Co. flour millers, born in Livermore, ME; represented Wisconsin in House (1855–61, 1867–71) and served as its governor (1872–74); donated observatory to U. of Wisconsin (died 1882).

1831 Alexander M. McCook, Union general who served at Shiloh, Murfreesboro, Chickamauga, born in Columbiana County, OH (died 1903).

1832 Julius Sterling Morton, originator of Arbor Day, born in Adams, NY; secretary of Nebraska Territory (1858–61); Agriculture Secretary (1893–97); Arbor Day observed on his birthday (died 1902).

1842 Alexander Kohut, a founder, Jewish Theological Seminary, New York City (1887), born in Feligyhaza, Hungary (died 1894).

1854 Senate ratified the Gadsden Purchase as the United States acquired from Mexico 45,535 sq. mi. of territory in southern Arizona and New Mexico for $10 million.

1874 Ellen (A.G.) Glasgow, popular novelist (*Barren Ground, Vein of Iron, The Descendants*), born in Richmond, VA (died 1945).

1876 Ole Edvart Rolvaag, author and educator, born in Norway; taught at St. Olaf College (1905–31); gained fame for *Giants in the Earth*, an epic of immigrant life on the South Dakota plains (died 1931).

1884 Otto Rank, psychoanalyst, born in Vienna; a disciple of Freud, he broke with him on the basic theory (died 1939).

1887 James Norman Hall, co-author with Charles Nordhoff of novels (*Mutiny on the Bounty, Pitcairn Island, Botany Bay*), born in Colfax, IA (died 1951).

1889 Unassigned land in Indian Territory (Oklahoma) opened to white settlement by a run for homestead claims by more than 50,000 settlers.

1898 President McKinley ordered a blockade of Cuban ports.

1898 First shots of Spanish-American War fired off Key West, FL, when the American ship *Nashville* captured the Spanish ship *Buena Ventura*.

1904 J. Robert Oppenheimer, physicist who was instrumental in developing atomic bomb, born in New York City; headed Los Alamos, NM, atomic laboratory (1943–45); chairman, Atomic Energy Commission advisory board (1947–53); director, Institute for Advanced Study, Princeton U. (1947–66) (died 1967).

1909 Rita Levi-Montalcini, medical researcher at Washington U. (in 1950s), born in Turin, Italy; shared 1986 Nobel Physiology/Medicine Prize for discovery of key proteins that control body growth.

1914 American Marines landed at Vera Cruz, Mexico; seized customs house, prevented landing of German munitions; brought nations to brink of war, which was averted by mediation of Argentina, Brazil, and Chile.

1916 Yehudi Menuhin, child prodigy violinist, born in New York City; on concert stage since 1937.

1922 Charles Mingus, major jazz musician of 1950/60s, born in Nogales, AZ; one of first to exploit bass as a solo instrument (died 1979).

1936 Glen Campbell, country music singer and entertainer, born in Billstown, AR; recorded many hits ("Wichita Lineman," "Galveston").

1937 Jack Nicholson, screen actor (*One Flew Over the Cuckoo's Nest, Terms of Endearment, Prizzi's Honor*), born in Neptune, NJ.

1944 Allied troops landed at Hollandia, New Guinea.

1954 Televised hearings into alleged Communist infiltration of Army were begun by Sen. Joseph R. McCarthy of Wisconsin; ended June 17.

1964 President Lyndon Johnson dedicated the Federal Pavilion at the World's Fair in New York City.

1970 The first "Earth Day" observed as millions of Americans participated in anti-pollution demonstrations.

1992 A plane carrying American and Dutch sky divers crashed on takeoff at Perris, CA; 16 died, six seriously injured.

1993 Alabama Gov. Guy Hunt convicted of a felony violation of state ethics law and was removed from office.

2000 In bitterly controversial move, federal immigration agents forcibly seized Cuban child Elian Gonzalez in middle of night from temporary home in Miami to return him to father in Communist Cuba.

2001 Robotic arm attached to International Space Station; built by Canadians for the international effort.

23

1541 Francisco Vasquez de Coronado and his men left the Southwest, traveled across the Texas Panhandle and Oklahoma into eastern Kansas, then returned.

1662 Charter granted by Charles II to John Winthrop on behalf of the Colony of Connecticut.

1731 William Williams, colonial merchant, born in Lebanon, CT; member of Continental Congress (1776–78, 1783, 1784), a signer of Declaration of Independence (died 1811).

1775 Massachusetts Provincial Congress authorized raising 13,000 men, named Artemus Ward as commander-in-chief, and appealed to other colonies for aid; by May 20, Rhode Island, New Hampshire, and Connecticut agreed to send 9,500 men.

1778 John Paul Jones raided British shipping in Whitehaven (England) harbor.

1784 Continental Congress enacted plan introduced by Thomas Jefferson for the territory between the Ohio and Mississippi Rivers; one of two proposals not accepted stated: "That after the year 1800 there shall be neither slavery nor involuntary servitude in any of the states."

1789 George Washington arrived in New York City for his inauguration; escorted to the first presidential mansion at One Cherry St. (Cherry and Queen streets).

1791 James Buchanan, 13th president (1857–61), born near Mercersburg, PA; represented Pennsylvania in House (1821–31) and Senate (1835–45); minister to Russia (1832–34), to Great Britain (1853–56); Secretary of State (1845–49) (died 1868).

1803 Adin Ballou, religious leader/social reformer, born in Cumberland, RI; formed splinter Universalist group, helped form Hopedale Community, a self-contained religious society, near Milford, MA (1841–59) (died 1890).

1813 Stephen A. Douglas, legislator, born in Brandon, VT; represented Illinois in House (1843–47) and Senate (1847–60); debated with Lincoln in 1858 senatorial campaign, ran against him for the presidency (1860) (died 1861).

1834 Chauncey M. Depew, legislator and renowned wit and speaker, born in Peekskill, NY; president, New York Central Railroad (1885–99); represented New York in Senate (1899–1911) (died 1928).

1831 Elbert E. Farman, Egyptologist, born

in New Haven, NY; served in Egypt many years as consul general, made vast collection of antiquities which he donated to Metropolitan Museum of Art; given Cleopatra's Needle for New York City's Central Park (died 1911).

1838 *Great Western*, first steamboat built for transatlantic service, arrived in New York from Bristol, which it had left April 8.

1839 James B. Hammond, inventor of a new style typewriter, born in Boston; made his machine in 1880 (died 1913).

1840 Henry A. House, inventor of a buttonhole machine, born in Brooklyn; also developed other attachments to sewing machines and a steam-engine driven horseless carriage (died 1930).

1844 Sanford G. Dole, first governor of Hawaii Territory (1900–03), born in Honolulu; president, Republic of Hawaii (1894–98) (died 1926).

1852 Edwin Markham, poet (*The Man with the Hoe*), born in Oregon City, OR (died 1940).

1853 Winthrop M. Crane, paper manufacturer in family business (from 1870), born in Dalton, MA; served Massachusetts as governor (1900–03) and in Senate (1904–14) (died 1920).

1856 Arthur T. Hadley, president, Yale U. (1899–1921), born in New Haven, CT; expert on railroad economics; taught at Yale (1883–99) (died 1930).

1859 First Colorado newspaper, *Rocky Mountain News*, began publication in Denver; William N. Byers was publisher.

1862 Alexis F. Lange, a leader in junior high school and junior college movements, born in Lafayette County, MO (died 1924).

1868 Popular vote in North Carolina ratified new state constitution which had been adopted by convention March 16.

1880 Carl L. Norden, inventor of bomb sight, born in Semarang, Java (died 1965).

1895 Frank Borzage, film director/producer (*Farewell to Arms, Seventh Heaven, Humoresque*), born in Salt Lake City (died 1962).

1896 Edison Vitascope, projecting motion pictures on large screen, had world premiere at Koster and Biel's music hall, 34th St. and Herald Square, New York City.

1897 Lucius D. Clay, World War II Army general, born in Marietta, GA; administrator of American occupied zone in Germany (1945–49) (died 1978).

1898 President McKinley issued call for 125,000 volunteers for war with Spain.

1899 Vladimir Nabokov, novelist (*Lolita*), born in Leningrad (died 1977).

1913 Mine disaster at Finleyville, PA, claimed 96 lives.

1921 Warren E. Spahn, all-time great left-handed pitcher who won 363 games (Boston N, Milwaukee N), born in Buffalo, NY; named to Baseball Hall of Fame.

1928 Shirley Temple (Black), most famous child screen star, born in Santa Monica, CA; delegate to UN General Assembly (1969–70), chief of protocol (1976–77).

1940 Fire in Natchez, MS, dance hall resulted in 198 deaths.

1968 United Methodist Church officially formed with merger of the Methodist Church (10.3 million members) and Evangelical United Brethren Church (750,000 members).

1993 Cesar Chavez, leader of farm laborers union, died at 66.

2001 Commander Scott D. Waddle, captain of American submarine that accidentally sank Japanese trawler in February, received official reprimand and voluntarily left Navy service.

2002 Long-time presidential adviser Karen Hughes announced return to Texas from Washington; plans to continue consultations from home.

24

1676 Simon Willard, colonial leader, died at 71; a founder of Concord (1635); member, Massachusetts General Court (1654–76); commanded colonial troops in King Philip's War (1675).

1704 First issue of an American continuous news periodical, the *Boston News Letter*, published by John Campbell, Boston postmaster; continued until 1776.

1766 Robert B. Thomas, founder/editor, *Farmer's Almanac* (1792–1846), born in Grafton, CT (died 1860).

1784 Peter V. Daniel, associate justice, Supreme Court (1841–60), born in Stafford County, VA (died 1860).

1800 Congress passed act moving the seat of government to Washington, DC.

1800 Library of Congress founded by purchase of $5,000 worth of books (152 works in 740 volumes); library was to be operated "as may be necessary for the use of Congress."

1820 Congress enacted the land law, ending the credit system of the 1800 law and reducing price of public land from $2 to $1.25 an acre.

1846 Mexican force ambushed 63 American troops near Matamoras; two days later, Gen. Zachary Taylor informed Washington that "hostilities may now be considered as commenced."

1856 Isaac Gimbel, cofounder, first president of Gimbel Bros. department store, born in Vincennes, IN (died 1931).

1862 Adm. David G. Farragut successfully ran his fleet by Confederate forts on lower Mississippi River in the dark, cutting them off from New Orleans, which was occupied by Union troops under Gen. Benjamin F. Butler.

1874 John R. Pope, architect, born in New York City; designed Constitution Hall and National Gallery of Arts in Washington (died 1937).

1876 Charles M. Manly, considered first modern aircraft engineer, born in Staunton, VA; designed light five-cylinder radial gasoline engine for planes; held about 50 patents on power generation (died 1927).

1879 Oris P. Van Sweringen, who with his brother developed Shaker Heights, a Cleveland suburb, born in Wooster, OH; controlled, operated many railroads (died 1936).

1882 Tony (Anthony F.) Sarg, creator of marionette shows, born in Coban, Guatemala; made many marionettes (died 1942).

1898 Spain declared war on the United States.

1898 Russell H. Varian, physicist known for work in microwaves, electronics, born in Washington, DC; co-inventor of Klystron, UHF resonator (died 1959).

1904 Willem KeKooning, noted abstract expressionist artist, born in Rotterdam, Netherlands (died 1997).

1905 Robert Penn Warren, poet/novelist, born in Todd County, KY; remembered for novel, *All the King's Men*; first American poet laureate (1986) (died 1989).

1917 President Wilson signed Liberty Loan Act, authorizing sale of $2 billion in 3½ percent convertible gold bonds by public subscription.

1934 Shirley MacLaine, screen actress (*Sweet Charity, Irma la Douce, Terms of Endearment*), born in Richmond, VA.

1942 Barbra Streisand, singer/actress on stage and screen, born in New York City; starred on stage (*Funny Girl*) and screen (*The Way We Were, Yentl*); recording star.

1945 American Third Army liberated the Dachau concentration camp.

1956 Alaska voters approved a constitution for the Territory.

1980 Military mission to rescue American hostages in Iran was aborted because of equipment failure; eight men were killed, much equipment lost.

1981 President Reagan ended ban on American grain sales to Soviet Union, which had been in effect 15 months.

1983 Supreme Court held 8–1 that Internal Revenue Service could deny tax exemptions to private schools that practiced racial discrimination.

1988 Explosion and fire aboard submarine, USS *Bonefish*, left 18 sailors injured, three missing.

1995 Another mail bombing attributed to the Unabomber occurred when Gilbert Murray, California Forestry Association president, was killed in Sacramento.

1997 Senate ratified Chemical Weapons Treaty, making United States the 75th country to approve elimination of all chemical weapons by year 2007.

2006 Moshe Teitelbaum (b. 1914) died at 91 after leading largest single Hassidic community in world, in New York City, since 1980; believed that Jews could rightly establish a state in Palestine only after Messiah comes and that Zionism is fundamentally wrong for that reason.

25

1769 Sir Marc I. Brunel, engineer who won design competition for the Capitol, born in Hacqueville, France; his design not used, another used for economy; built Thames tunnel (died 1849).

1776 James Madison elected to Virginia state convention; served on committee which drafted state constitution, adopted June 29.

1777 British troops began three-day raid on Connecticut towns; burned Danbury (April 27); stopped at Ridgefield by Benedict Arnold with 600 men.

1781 Battle of Hobkirk's Hill, near Camden, SC, resulted in a virtual standoff; British retreated, burning Camden on the way.

1798 Patriotic song, "Hail Columbia," composed by Joseph Hopkinson, first sung in a Philadelphia theater.

1812 General Land Office, designed to handle public lands, created as bureau in the Treasury Department; moved to Interior Department 1849.

1838 Steamer *Moselle* exploded on Ohio River near Cincinnati killing 100 persons.

1854 Charles S. Tainter, inventor of various sound recording instruments, born in Watertown, MA; inventions included the Gramophone and Dictaphone (died 1940).

1861 Edwin R.A. Seligman, economist, born in New York City; helped formulate income tax base, banking system for Federal Reserve; a founder, American Economic Association (died 1939).

1873 Howard R. Garis, author of *Uncle Wiggily* series of children's books, born in Binghamton, NY (died 1962).

1880 Michael Fokine, dancer/choreographer, born in Leningrad; directed Diaghilev's Russian ballet, own American company (died 1942).

1898 Congress declared war on Spain, saying the war had been in effect since April 21.

1900 Wolfgang Pauli, physicist, born in Vienna; first to explain behavior of some atomic particles and postulate existence of neutrino; awarded 1945 Nobel Physics Prize for that work (died 1958).

1906 William J. Brennan, associate justice, Supreme Court (1956–90), born in Newark, NJ (died 1997).

1908 Edward R. Murrow, newsman, born in Greensboro, NC; with CBS (1936–61), gaining fame with broadcasts from London during World War II; starred in own shows (*See It Now*, *Person to Person*); director, U.S. Information Service (1961–64) (died 1965).

1909 William L. Pereira, architect (Los Angeles Museum of Art, Houston Center), born in Chicago (died 1985).

1918 Ella Fitzgerald, a leading jazz singer, born in Newport News, VA (died 1996).

1944 George Herriman, cartoonist (*Krazy Kat*), died at 64; his cartoon (1910–44) was first written and drawn for adult appreciation.

1945 Organizational meeting of United Nations began in San Francisco with 50 nations attending; ended June 26.

1946 Railroad collision near Chicago resulted in 45 deaths.

1953 James D. Watson, American biologist, and Francis C.H. Crick, British biologist, succeeded in making three-dimension molecular model of DNA (deoxyribose nucleic), a major discovery; shared 1962 Nobel Physiology/Medicine Prize.

1959 St. Lawrence Seaway opened.

1962 United States resumed nuclear testing near Christmas Island, largest atoll in the Pacific, following Russian refusal to sign an atomic testing accord.

1990 Space shuttle *Discovery* successfully deployed the $1.5 billion Hubble space telescope.

1996 With only about five months left in fiscal year, Congress approved a spending bill for the rest of the year, which the president signed.

1997 Federal District Court in Greensboro, NC, held that the FDA had the power to regulate the distribution, sale, and use of tobacco products.

2000 National Park Service banned snowmobiles in bulk of its parks and other facilities.

2001 President George W. Bush reaffirmed traditional U.S. commitment to defend Taiwan if it is attacked by China.

26

1598 Expedition of Juan de Onate reached the Rio Grande River and then (May 4) the site of El Paso.

1607 Three vessels of the London Company, under command of Christopher Newport, arrived in Chesapeake Bay off Cape Henry, enroute to settling in Virginia; erected a cross (April 29) at Cape Henry; elected Edward M. Wingfield (1586–1613) as first governor, deposed him in September.

1702 Proprietors of West and East Jersey surrendered governmental authority to the Crown and the colony became a royal colony, governed by New York's governor until 1738.

1718 Esek Hopkins, sea captain who was commander of the Continental Navy (1775–78), born in Scituate, RI; had difficulties in equipping, manning few available ships; censured and dismissed (died 1802).

1727 Samuel Cranston, colonial governor of Rhode Island (1698–1727), died at 68.

1783 Seven thousand Loyalists sailed from New York to Nova Scotia or England.

1785 John James Audubon, ornithologist and artist, born in Haiti; his *Birds of America* considered a masterpiece (died 1851).

1822 Frederick Law Olmsted, pioneer landscape architect, born in Hartford, CT; designed Central and Prospect Parks in New York City, South Park in Chicago, U.S. Capitol grounds, and Boston park system (died 1903).

1828 Martha F. Finley, author of Elsie Dinsmore stories under name of Martha Farquaharson, born in Chillicothe, OH (died 1909).

1830 Benjamin F. Tracy, often called the father of the American Navy, born in Oswego, NY; as Navy Secretary (1889–93), increased number of battleships, raised service standards (died 1915).

1830 Senate began impeachment hearing of James Peck, U.S. district judge in Missouri, for holding a critic in contempt of court; acquitted January 31, 1831.

1831 New York State abolished imprisonment for debt, effective March 1, 1832.

1834 Charles F. Brown, humorist under name of Artemus Ward, born near Waterford, ME (died 1867).

1854 Massachusetts Emigrant Aid Society (later known as New England Emigrant Aid Co.) organized by Eli Thayer to promote settlement of anti-slavery groups in Kansas; founded Lawrence and other communities in three year history.

1865 Thirty-seven thousand Confederate soldiers surrendered at Hillsborough, NC.

1865 John Wilkes Booth, assassin of President Lincoln, was shot and killed in a tobacco barn between Port Royal and Bowling Green, VA.

1871 Hutchinson I. Cone, naval officer in Spanish-American War, born in Brooklyn; commanded naval aviation forces (1917–18) (died 1941).

1889 Leonard T. Troland, inventor of multicolor process for motion pictures, born in Norwich, CT; chief engineer, Technicolor Motion Picture Corp.; also conducted important experiments in vision (died 1932).

1891 Paul G. Hoffman, automaker/public official, born in Chicago; president, Studebaker Corp. (1935–53), board chairman (1953–56); director of Marshall Plan (1948–50); president, Ford Foundation (1951–55); administrator, UN Development Program (1966–72) (died 1974).

1893 Anita Loos, author (*Gentlemen Prefer Blondes*), born in Sisson, CA (died 1981).

1897 Cass Canfield, publisher (Harper & Bros. chairman 1927–61), born in New York City.

1900 Charles F. Richter, geophysicist who developed method of measuring earthquakes' severity (Richter scale), born in Butler County, OH (died 1985).

1907 Tercentenary Exposition opened in Jamestown, VA, with President Theodore Roosevelt present.

1908 Dave Tough, leading drummer of 1930/40s, born in Oak Park, IL (died 1948).

1914 Bernard Malamud, author (*The Fixer, The Tenant, Dubin's Lives*), born in New York City (died 1986).

1917 I(eoh) M. Pei, architect (L'Enfant Plaza,

National Art Gallery in Washington), born in Canton, China.

1933 Arno A. Penzies, astrophysicist, born in Munich; shared 1978 Nobel Physics Prize for work in cosmic microwaves radiation.

1936 Carol Burnett, entertainer/comedienne on screen and television, born in San Antonio, TX.

1939 President Franklin Roosevelt issued executive order for purchase of 571 military aircraft; asked for immediate construction of new naval bases.

1944 Montgomery Ward & Co., defying National Labor Relations Board orders, was seized by federal troops.

1952 Destroyer *Hobson* sank after colliding with aircraft carrier *Wasp* during Atlantic maneuvers; 176 men lost.

1983 National Commission on Excellence in Education issued report calling American elementary and secondary education "mediocre"; recommended a number of steps for improvement.

1984 President Reagan began six-day visit to China.

1991 Tornadoes in Kansas and Oklahoma killed 23 persons.

1996 Four-day auction of about 5,900 items owned by Jacqueline Kennedy Onassis and put up for sale by her children, ended in New York City; the items brought in more than $34 million.

2000 David Merrick died; producer of 88 Broadway shows including *42nd Street* and *Hello Dolly!*

2002 U.S. Agriculture Department accused California of having highest rate of food stamps being issued erroneously of any state in nation; double U.S. average; could cost state $20 million or more.

2006 National Archives study announced. Good news: since 1995 over 1 billion pages of "secret" U.S. documents made available to public, more than a four-fold increase of total from 1980–1994; bad news: reclassification to "secret" being done sloppily and inconsistently with over a third being unquestionably unjustified.

27

1584 An expedition organized by Sir Walter Raleigh sailed for the New World; the expedition, commanded by Sir Richard Grenville and Ralph Lane, landed on Roanoke Island in July.

1686 Gov. Thomas Dongan officially signed a charter for New York City.

1773 British Parliament, in effort to help near-bankrupt East India Co., removed all duties on tea exported to the American colonies; however, the three-penny import tax in America was retained; the improved position enabled East India to undersell its competitors.

1791 Samuel F.B. Morse, telegraph inventor, was born in Charlestown, MA; a portrait painter (1815–37), he was a founder, first president, National Academy of Design (1826–42); Congress voted (1843) $30,000 for an experimental telegraph line from Washington to Baltimore, which was built by Ezra Cornell; Morse sent first message May 24, 1844; involved in long litigation before he was recognized as the rightful telegraph developer (died 1872).

1805 Small force led by Capt. William Eaton, American consul at Tunis, and Lt. Presley O'Bannon, aided by shelling from three American brigs, captured Dorna in Tripoli; led Pasha of Tripoli to sue for peace.

1813 American troops burned York (now Toronto), including the governor's residence and assembly house; American commander, Gen. Zebulon Pike, was killed in an explosion of a magazine during the assault; city was abandoned May 2.

1822 Ulysses S. Grant, 18th president (1868–76), born in Pt. Pleasant, OH; Union general who led all Union forces toward end of Civil War (died 1885).

1838 Fire in Charleston, SC, destroyed $3 million in property.

1846 President Polk signed joint resolution authorizing him to notify Great Britain that joint occupation of Oregon was to be terminated; a year's notice required.

1846 Charles J. Van Depoele, inventor who demonstrated feasibility of electric trolleys, born in Lichtervelde, Belgium; had more than 200 patents on electrical items (died 1892).

1854 River steamer *Sultana* exploded near Memphis and sank, 1,450 persons died.

1854 Benjamin N. Duke, tobacco company founder (American Tobacco Co.), born in Durham, NC; with brother, founded company which he headed (1890–1929); large benefactor of Trinity College, Durham, which became Duke U. (died 1929).

1861 Maryland legislature voted 53–13 against secession.

1861 President Lincoln extended blockade of

Confederate ports to include Virginia and North Carolina.

1865 Cornell U. in Ithaca, NY, chartered.

1870 Collapse of a building in Richmond, VA, resulted in 61 deaths, 12 injured.

1878 Frank Gotch, probably greatest American professional wrestler, born in Humboldt, NE; lost only six of 196 matches (died 1917).

1893 Norman Bel Geddes, designer, born in Adrian, MI; involved in 200 operas, stage and screen plays as designer, producer, or director; foremost proponent of streamlining; designed Futurama at New York World's Fair (1939) (died 1958).

1896 Rogers Hornsby, baseball player with all-time batting average high (.424 in 1924), born in Winters, TX; lifetime batting average of .358; named to Baseball Hall of Fame (died 1963).

1896 Wallace H. Carothers, research chemist who developed neoprene, born in Burlington, IA; director, DuPont Research Lab (1926–37); did basic research on nylon (died 1937).

1897 Grant's Tomb in New York City dedicated by President McKinley.

1898 Ludwig Bemelmans, illustrator and author (*Madeline* books), born in Meran, Austria (now Italy) (died 1962).

1898 American fleet bombarded fortifications at Matanzas, Cuba.

1904 Arthur F. Burns, economist/diplomat, born in Stanislau, Austria; chairman, Federal Reserve Board (1970–78); ambassador to West Germany (1981–85) (died 1987).

1917 Mine disaster at Hastings, CO, killed 121 persons.

1938 Earl Anthony, professional bowling's first million dollar prize winner, born in Kent, WA; won Professional Bowling Association tournament six times, American Bowling Congress master champion (1977, 1984).

1941 President Franklin Roosevelt outlined a drastic economic program designed to combat inflation.

1950 Calvin Simmons, first black conductor of a major orchestra (Oakland Symphony 1979), born in San Francisco (died 1982).

1975 Saigon was shelled and imperiled by approaching Communist forces; President Ford ordered the helicopter evacuation of remaining Americans.

1978 Scaffolding inside a cooling tower at site of a nuclear power plant at Willow Island, WV, collapsed killing 51 workers, including 11 members of one family.

1981 Gerald R. Ford Library at Ann Arbor, MI, dedicated.

1981 Former Vice President Spiro T. Agnew ordered by a Maryland judge to pay $247,735 to the state to compensate for the bribes and kickbacks he received while governor and vice president.

1991 More than 70 tornadoes slashed through seven states, killing at least 28, including 18 in Andover, KS; thousands left homeless.

1997 Conference held in Philadelphia to boost volunteerism, with President Clinton and former presidents Ford, Carter, and Bush on hand; Gen. Colin Powell was general chairman.

2000 Dying at 93, Elmer Gertz was famous for his defenses of accused killers, from the 1924 Nathan Leopold-Richard Loeb case to Jack Ruby's killing of Lee Harvey Oswald. In the first case he obtained a parole; in the latter a reversal of the conviction.

28

1758 James Monroe, fifth president (1817–25), born in Westmoreland County, VA; member of Continental Congress (1783–86), represented Virginia in Senate (1790–94) and served as governor (1797–1802, 1810–11); minister to France (1794–96), to Great Britain (1803–07); Secretary of State (1811–17), War Secretary (1814–15) (died 1831).

1788 Maryland legislature by 63–11 vote ratified Constitution to enter Union as the seventh state.

1815 Andrew J. Smith, Union general, born in Bucks County, PA (died 1897).

1817 United States and Great Britain signed the Rush-Bagot Treaty, limiting armaments on the Great Lakes, providing for an unfortified American-Canadian border; ratified by Senate April 16, 1818.

1849 *Minnesota Pioneer*, first newspaper in state, published in St. Paul.

1865 Bertram G. Goodhue, architect, born in Pomfret, CT; designed Nebraska State Capitol, West Point Chapel, National Academy of Science (died 1924).

1878 Lionel Barrymore, stage/screen actor, born in Philadelphia; films included *You Can't Take It with You*, *Rasputin*; starred in *Dr. Kildare* television series; portrayed Scrooge in annual radio *Christmas Carol* reading (died 1954).

1914 Mine disaster claimed 181 lives at Eccles, WV.

1917 Robert Anderson, playwright (*Tea and Sympathy, I Never Sang for My Father*), born in New York City.

1930 James A. Baker, III, public official, born in Houston, TX; Secretary of State (1989–92), Treasury Secretary (1985–88), White House chief of staff (1981–85).

1941 A dim-out, 15 miles deep along the Atlantic Coast was put in effect to combat submarine attacks.

1945 President Truman addressed opening session of United Nations in San Francisco by telephone.

1950 Jay Leno, television entertainer, born in New Rochelle, NY.

1980 Cyrus Vance resigned as Secretary of State in protest against the aborted attempt to free the American hostages in Iran.

1988 About 60 persons were injured, three critically, in a midair explosion of a plane flying from Hilo to Honolulu; pilot landed plane safely.

2001 American multimillionaire Dennis Tito became first commercial "tourist" to go into orbit; paid the Russians $20 million for his almost eight-day stay in orbit.

2005 *Science* magazine documented creature not vanished after all: ivory-billed woodpecker, one of six American birds believed gone extinct at some point since late 1800s, found in Cache River National Wildlife Refuge, Arkansas.

29

1745 Oliver Ellsworth, chief justice, Supreme Court (1796–99), born in Windsor, CT; delegate to Continental Congress (1777–84); co-author of Connecticut Compromise which resulted in present Congress structure; represented Connecticut in Senate (1789–96) (died 1807).

1759 John Adlum, grape grower who developed the Catawba grape, born in York, PA; a pioneer in American grape growing (died 1836).

1792 Matthew Vassar, founder, endower of Vassar College (1861), born in Norfolk, England (died 1868).

1795 Lorrin Andrews, Congregational missionary to Hawaii, born in East Windsor, CT; translated Bible into Hawaiian, published first Hawaiian newspaper (1834) (died 1868).

1814 American sloop *Peacock* captured British brig *Epervier* and $120,000 in specie off the Florida coast.

1815 Abram Duryée, Union general who led regiment of Zouaves in Civil War, born in New York City; served city as police commissioner (1874–84) (died 1890).

1820 Henry W. Allen, Confederate general and Louisiana governor (1861–64), born in Prince Edward County, VA (died 1866).

1860 Lorado Taft, one of first American sculptors to work on large designs, born in Elmwood, IL; did *Fountain of Time* in Chicago and *Columbus Fountain* (died 1936).

1862 New Orleans surrendered to Union naval force under Adm. David G. Farragut and Union troops under Gen. Benjamin Butler.

1863 William Randolph Hearst, publisher of newspaper, magazine chain, born in San Francisco; represented New York in House (1903–07) (died 1951).

1870 Harrison P. Eddy, engineer who led American development of water purification and sewage treatment, born in Millbury, MA (died 1937).

1872 Forest R. Moulton, astronomer who with Thomas C. Chamberlin propounded spiral nebulae hypothesis, born in LeRoy, MI (died 1952).

1877 Thomas A. Dorgan (TAD), sports cartoonist, commentator (*New York Journal* 1900–29), born in San Francisco (died 1929).

1880 Jonas Lie, artist (*Wind Swept, Brooklyn Bridge, A New York Canyon*), born in Moss, Norway (died 1940).

1885 Frank J. Fletcher, World War I and II naval officer, born in Marshalltown, IA; commander in battles of Coral Sea, Midway (died 1973).

1885 Wallingford Riegger, composer of avant garde 20th Century music, born in Albany, GA (died 1961).

1893 Harold C. Urey, chemist, born in Walkerton, IN; awarded 1934 Nobel Chemistry Prize for discovery of heavy hydrogen, research on other isotopes and structures of atoms and molecules (died 1981).

1899 Duke (Edward K.) Ellington, pianist/composer/conductor, born in Washington, DC; remembered for "Mood Indigo," "Satin Doll," "Black, Brown & Beige" (died 1974).

1899 Labor wars in Idaho silver mines culminated in dynamiting the Bunker Hill and Sullivan concentrator in Wardner.

1904 Russ Morgan, trombonist and band leader, born in Scranton, PA (died 1969).

1931 Robert A. Gottlieb, editor/publisher, born in New York City; editor-in-chief, Simon &

Schuster and Knopf; president, A.A. Knopf (1973–87); editor, *The New Yorker* (1987–92).

1932 Radio serial, *One Man's Family*, written by Carleton E. Morse, began; ran through 3,256 episodes, ending May 8, 1959.

1936 Zubin Mehta, orchestra conductor (New York, Los Angeles philharmonics), born in Bombay.

1955 Gustav Egloff, chemist, died at 69; developed multiple-coil process for cracking crude oil to increase high octane gasoline yield, method of making rubber from butane gas.

1957 Congress enacted first Civil Rights Act since Reconstruction.

1975 American civilians were evacuated from Saigon as Communist forces completed takeover of South Vietnam.

1986 Council of Bishops of the United Methodist Church unanimously voted for "clear and unconditional" opposition to the use of nuclear weapons.

1988 American warships in the Persian Gulf allowed to protect neutral shipping under attack, according to rules announced by President Reagan.

1988 Senate by a vote of 87 to four approved a $1 billion anti–AIDS program.

1992 Four Los Angeles policemen were acquitted of assault on motorist Rodney King; touched off two days of rioting, looting, and arson in southcentral Los Angeles; 58 persons were killed, more than 600 injured, nearly 4,000 arrested.

1997 Mike Royko, popular Chicago newspaper columnist, died at 64.

2001 Census Bureau reported that whites are now a minority in almost half of country's largest cities.

2003 In toughest state law yet adopted to curb mass mail computer "spam," Virginia made it a felony subject to jail time to engage in fraudulent activities connected with the practice.

2004 Last Oldsmobiles completed (500 in all), ending the production of a car company that dated to 1897.

2006 John Kenneth Galbraith, liberal economist and adviser to presidents, died at 97; author of 33 works and one of the most widely read scholars in his field.

30

1492 Privileges and prerogatives granted Columbus by Spanish rulers, Ferdinand and Isabella, making possible his exploration.

1771 Hosea Ballou, an early leader of Universalist church, born in Richmond, NH; founder, editor, *Universalist Magazine* (1819–28), the first Universalist periodical; author (*Treatise on the Atonement*) (died 1852).

1789 George Washington inaugurated as first president on the balcony of Federal Hall (Wall and Broad Streets), New York City; oath administered by Robert R. Livingston, chancellor of New York State; Washington delivered first inaugural address in the Senate chamber in Federal Hall.

1798 Navy Department created by Congress; Benjamin Stoddert named first secretary.

1803 Napoleon signed the sale of Louisiana Territory to United States for 60 million francs (approximately $15 million); doubled area of United States by adding 828,000 sq. mi. of land.

1812 Louisiana admitted as 18th state in the Union.

1821 College of Detroit became U. of Michigan.

1822 Hannibal W. Goodwin, Episcopal clergyman who invented photographic film (1887), born in Taughannock, NY; received patent after long litigation (1898) (died 1900).

1823 Henry O. Houghton, founder of Riverside Press (1852) and publishing firm bearing his name, born in Sutton, VT; publisher became Houghton Mifflin (1880) (died 1895).

1832 William Bucknell, fur trader and explorer, died at about 42; blazed Santa Fe trail from Franklin, MO, to Santa Fe, NM, which became main commercial route to Southwest.

1858 Mary Scott L. Dimmick Harrison, second wife of President Benjamin Harrison, born in Honesdale, PA (died 1948).

1879 Stanley B. Resor, president, J. Walter Thompson ad agency (1916–55), born in Cincinnati; board chairman (1955–61) (died 1962).

1888 John Crowe Ransom, poet/editor, born in Pulaski, TN; at Vanderbilt U. (1914–37), Kenyon College (1937–58); editor, *Kenyon Review* (1939–58) poems included *Poems About God, Chills and Fever* (died 1974).

1888 President Cleveland nominated Melville W. Fuller as chief justice of the Supreme Court; confirmed by Senate July 20.

1900 Territory of Hawaii created.

1900 Casey (John L.) Jones, engineer of Cannonball Express, crashed his train into a stopped freight train near Vaughn, MS; legendary hero of railroading.

1901 Simon Kuznets, economist who devised

Gross National Product measure, born in Kharkov, Russia; awarded 1971 Nobel Economics Prize (died 1985).

1904　President Theodore Roosevelt opened Louisiana Purchase Exposition in St. Louis.

1916　Claude E. Shannon, mathematician who founded information theory, born in Gaylord, MI; theory used in computer development, communications.

1927　Bituminous mine accident at Everettville, WV, killed 97 persons.

1933　Willie Nelson, country music singer/ composer, born in Abbott, TX.

1939　New York World's Fair opened by President Franklin Roosevelt.

1948　Organization of American States (OAS), composed of 21 Western Hemisphere republics, formed in Bogota, Colombia; ratified by nations in December.

1970　President Nixon announced that American troops were being sent into Cambodia to eliminate Communist staging and communications areas.

1973　Three top presidential aides — H.R. Haldeman, John D. Ehrlichman, and John W. Dean — and Attorney General Richard Kleindienst resigned amid charges of White House cover-up efforts in the Watergate case.

1975　The last Americans were evacuated from the embassy in Saigon, virtually bringing the Vietnam War to an end.

1975　South Vietnam announced its unconditional surrender to the Vietcong.

1986　Supreme Court unanimously dismissed a case seeking to defend an Illinois law regulating and restricting abortions.

1995　President Clinton announced that trade with Iran will be halted to protest Iran's funding of terrorism and its plans to obtain nuclear weapons.

1996　National Football League owners approved the move of Houston Oilers to Nashville for the 1998 season.

1997　Seven armed separatists who proclaimed themselves the Republic of Texas were arrested after a siege; their leader, Richard McLaren, gave up two days later.

2000　At least 200,000 pro-gay rights demonstrators held rally on National Mall, Washington, DC; some estimates went far higher; their first massive Washington rally since 1993.

2003　Midland Steel Products closed after over a century of operation; last U.S.-owned manufacturer of auto and truck frames in America.

MAY

1

1528 Pamphilo de Narvaez with 300 men began march across Florida; reached Indian town near present Tallahassee; built boats, then sailed in September along Gulf Coast, past the Mississippi River; boats swept out to sea and lost.

1562 Huguenot colonists led by Jean de Ribaut entered St. John's River (FL) and built Ft. Charles on present Parris Island.

1637 Towns of Hartford, Wethersfield, and Windsor united in a self-governing confederation under the name of Connecticut.

1691 Representatives from Massachusetts, Plymouth, Hartford, and New York met in New York City to plan attacks on Montreal and Quebec.

1737 Elias Dayton, formed what became Evangelical Church, born in Pottstown, PA; formed new movement which was not recognized, named it Evangelical Association (later Church); Albright College in Reading, PA, named for him (died 1808).

1764 Benjamin H. Latrobe, designer of buildings and first American municipal water system (Philadelphia), born in Fulneck, England; designed Capitol south wing and Capitol rebuilding after British burning in 1814 (died 1820).

1780 John McKinley, associate justice, Supreme Court (1837–52), born in Culpeper County, VA; represented Alabama in House (1832–36) and Senate (1826–30, 1836–37) (died 1852).

1784 State legislature created U. of New York.

1796 Junius Brutus Booth, one of greatest tragedy actors, born in London; starred in numerous Shakespearian plays (died 1852).

1825 George Inness, painter of Hudson River School (*Delaware Water Gap*, *Peace and Plenty*), born in Newburgh, NY (died 1894).

1830 Mary H. Jones, labor leader known as "Mother Jones," born in Cork, Ireland; a prominent speaker and organizer (died 1930).

1832 Capt. Benjamin de Bonneville led a wagon train from Ft. Osage on the Missouri River to the Columbia River, starting a three-year exploration of the West.

1841 First emigrant train with 47 persons left Independence, MO, for California.

1845 Fourteen conferences of Methodist Church met in Louisville, organized Methodist Episcopal Church, South, after a dispute over slavery.

1847 Cornerstone laid for Smithsonian Institution in Washington, DC.

1847 Henry Demarest Lloyd, first journalistic "muckraker," born in New York City; wrote about the railroads, oil industry in *Chicago Tribune* and *Atlantic Monthly* (died 1903).

1852 Calamity Jane, frontierswoman, born as Martha Jane Burke in Princeton, MO; a companion of Wild Bill Hickok and a sharpshooter (died 1903).

1853 Jacob Gordon, leading American Yiddish playwright, born in Mirgorod, Russia; produced more than 30 original plays (died 1909).

1863 Four-day battle of Chancellorsville (VA) began; Confederate Gen. Stonewall Jackson fatally wounded accidentally by his own men, died May 10; one of greatest battles ended inconclusively; South lost 1,665 killed, 9,000 wounded; Union losses about 17,000.

1863 Union troops under Gen. U.S. Grant launched series of victories at Ft. Gibson, which put them outside Vicksburg, MS; other victories were at Grand Gulf, Raymond, Jackson, Champion Hill, Big Black River Bridge.

1865 President Andrew Johnson issued an

executive order to create military commission to try the Lincoln assassins.

1871 Supreme Court, with two new members, reversed ruling of February 7, 1870, and made legal tender of treasury notes issued before enabling legislation was passed.

1873 First American penny postcard issued.

1880 Albert D. Lasker, advertising executive and philanthropist, born in Freiburg, Germany; owner, Lord & Thomas ad agency (1908–42); chairman, U.S. Shipping Board (1921–23); helped endow Chicago U. medical research, public health (died 1952).

1884 Work began on Home Insurance Building in Chicago, considered the first American skyscraper; completed in fall of 1885.

1888 John F. O'Hara, Catholic Archbishop of Philadelphia (1951–60), born in Ann Arbor, MI; president, Notre Dame U. (1934–39); elevated to cardinal 1958 (died 1960).

1892 Howard Barlow, musical conductor of "Voice of Firestone" radio show, born in Plain City, OH (died 1972).

1893 Columbia Exposition in Chicago opened by President Cleveland.

1894 "Coxey's Army" of 500 arrived in Washington, DC, from Massilon, OH, to plead for work programs for unemployed; Leader Jacob S. Coxey arrested for trespassing.

1895 Leo Sowerby, composer/organist, born in Grand Rapids, MI; organist, St. James Episcopal Church, Chicago (1927–62); composed *Canticle of the Sun* (died 1968).

1896 J. Lawton Collins, World War II Army general at Guadalcanal and in Europe, born in New Orleans (died 1987).

1896 Mark W. Clark, World War II Army general, born in Madison Barracks, NY; commanded American ground forces in Europe (1942), in North Africa, Italy (1943–44), in Austria (1945–47); commanded, UN Korean forces (1952–53) (died 1984).

1898 Spanish fleet of ten vessels destroyed or captured by Americans in Manila Harbor.

1898 Eugene R. Black, president, World Bank (1949–62), born in Atlanta (died 1992).

1900 Explosion of blasting powder in coal mine at Scofield, UT, killed 200.

1901 Pan American Exposition opened in Buffalo, NY; ran until November 2.

1909 Walter Reed General Hospital in Washington, DC, opened.

1909 Kate Smith, singer known as the first lady of radio, born in Greenville, VA (died 1986).

1911 Supreme Court ordered dissolution of Standard Oil Co. and American Tobacco Co., which were found to be monopolies.

1915 American oil tanker *Gulflight* torpedoed by German submarine off the Scilly Islands during battle between the submarine and a British patrol; two Americans died.

1918 Jack Paar, host of *Tonight Show* (1957–62), born in Canton, OH.

1923 Joseph Heller, author (*Catch 22*) born in New York City.

1925 (Malcolm) Scott Carpenter, second astronaut to make orbital flight, born in Boulder, CO.

1931 Empire State Building in New York City opened.

1937 Congress by joint resolution recapitulated earlier neutrality legislation and strengthened it, giving larger discriminatory power to the president.

1943 Federal Government took over all Eastern coal mines because of strike by 530,000 miners; Union President John L. Lewis ended strike May 2.

1960 The 18th Census reported a population of 179,323,175.

1970 American population climbed over the 200 million mark in the 19th Census with a total of 203,302,031; center of population had moved to five miles east of Mascoutah, IL.

1971 Amtrak, a unified rail passenger system, began operations.

1972 Eisenhower Center, including the library, in Abilene, KS, dedicated.

1982 World's Fair opened in Knoxville, TN, with President Reagan on hand.

1998 Eldridge Cleaver, former leader of Black Panther Party, died at 62.

2001 FBI director Louis J. Freeh announced June departure to end eight years of service in post.

2001 In 1963 four black children murdered by bomb in Birmingham, AL, church; today Thomas E. Blanton, Jr., convicted of the deaths.

2003 More than 400 tornadoes documented during first 11 days of month; doubled previous record.

2

1740 Elias Boudinot, colonial leader, born in Philadelphia; represented New Jersey in Continental Congress (1777–78, 1781–84) and House

(1789–95); director, U.S. Mint (1795–1805) (died 1821).

1776 France and Spain agreed to provide funds for arms for the Americans; this done through fictitious companies.

1806 Edwin B. Morgan, pioneer in express business, born in Aurora, NY; first president, Wells Fargo & Co. (1852); a founder, U.S. Express Co. (1854); a major stockholder, *New York Times* (died 1881).

1837 Henry M. Robert, author of *Robert's Rules of Order* (1876), born in Robertville, SC; military engineer, built defenses of Washington (1861); chief of engineers (1901) (died 1923).

1847 Hugh J. Chisholm, helped form International Paper Co. (1898) and its president (1899–1910), born in Niagara Falls, Ontario (died 1912).

1865 Clyde Fitch, popular playwright (*Nathan Hale, The Climbers, Truth, Barbara Frietchie*), born in Elmira, NY (died 1909).

1866 Jesse W. Lazear, medical researcher, born in Baltimore County, MD; member of Walter Reed Commission, recovered after allowing himself to be bitten by an infected mosquito; later (1900) died after an accidental bite; helped prove that yellow fever is transmitted by mosquitoes.

1868 John Moody, financial analyst, born in Jersey City, NJ; founder, *Moody's Manual of Railroads & Corporation Securities (1900), Moody's Magazine (1905), Moody's Analyses of Investments (1909)* (died 1958).

1871 Francis P. Duffy, Catholic chaplain with American troops in Mexico (1917) and Europe (1917–18); served Church of Our Savior, New York City (died 1932).

1875 Owen J. Roberts, associate justice, Supreme Court (1930–45), born in Philadelphia; a prosecutor in Teapot Dome scandal; dean, U. of Pennsylvania Law School (1948–51) (died 1955).

1879 James F. Byrnes, legislator/jurist, born in Charleston, SC; represented South Carolina in House (1911–25) and Senate (1931–41) and served it as governor (1951–55); director, Office of Economic Stabilization (1942–43), Office of War Mobilization (1943–45), Secretary of State (1945–47); associate justice, Supreme Court (1941–42) (died 1972).

1887 Vernon B. Castle, dancer with wife, Irene, born in Norwich, England; they originated dances (one-step, turkey trot, castle walk); killed in plane crash (1918).

1890 President Benjamin Harrison signed an act creating Oklahoma Territory.

1895 Lorenz Hart, lyricist with Richard Rodgers (*Pal Joey, Babes in Arms, Boys from Syracuse, Present Arms*), born in New York City (died 1943).

1897 Norma Talmadge, screen actress (*DuBarry, Camille, Graustark*), born in Brooklyn (died 1957).

1903 Benjamin M. Spock, pediatrician whose book *Baby and Child Care* sold more than 50 million copies, born in New Haven, CT; active opponent of Vietnam War, nuclear weapons (died 1998).

1904 Bing (Harry L.) Crosby, singer/screen actor and most popular entertainer, born in Tacoma, WA; films included *White Christmas, Going My Way, High Society*, a number of *Road* pictures (died 1977).

1923 First transcontinental nonstop airplane flight begun by two Air Corps lieutenants; took 26 hours, 50 minutes to complete 2,516-mile flight from New York to San Diego.

1948 Larry Gatlin, country music singer/composer, born in Seminole, TX.

1972 Fire in Sunshine silver mine in Kellogg, ID, killed 91 persons.

1974 Former Vice President Spiro Agnew disbarred by Maryland Court of Appeals as a result of his *nolo contendere* plea in 1973 on tax evasion charges.

1985 E.F. Hutton, one of nation's largest brokerages, pleaded guilty to 2,000 federal charges of checking account manipulations.

1988 Supreme Court ruled 6–2 that manufacturers may agree with retailers to stop supplying discount stores so long as they do not agree on prices or price levels.

1988 United Methodist Church general conference in St. Louis refused by vote of 676–293 to allow the ordination of practicing homosexuals.

1996 Baseball game in Seattle ended when an earthquake measuring 4.8 on Richter scale rumbled through the Kingdome; no damage or injuries.

1997 White House and Congress announced agreement to achieve a balanced budget by year 2002; House approved May 21, Senate May 23.

1997 Labor Department reported that unemployment dropped to 4.9 percent in April, the lowest for any month since 1973.

2001 Congressional negotiators struck a deal with the White House on next fiscal year budget: expenditures to increase just under 5 percent.

2002 By unanimous vote, U.S. International

Trade Commission accepted claim that Canadian lumber industry was dumping softwood in U.S. at less than legitimate market price: assert de facto subsidy since bulk of product comes from provincial controlled forests that charge less than privately owned forests in U.S.; American builders protest decision: Canadian product superior for key building tasks.

2002 Second month of a nationwide protest against alleged pro-Palestinian and anti–Israel bias among major U.S. newspapers — charge pro-Israel demonstrations ignored to cover opposing side and slanted language used to make Palestinians look better; targets include *Los Angeles Times, San Francisco Chronicle,* and *New York Times; LA Times* lost 1,000 subscribers in April alone.

3

1765 First medical school in United States (College of Philadelphia) organized by Drs. John Morgan and William Shippen, Jr.; later became U. of Pennsylvania School of Medicine.

1802 Washington incorporated as a city with a mayor to be named by the president.

1843 William L. Wilson, Postmaster General (1895–97) who inaugurated rural free delivery, born in Middlebury, VA (now WV); represented West Virginia in House (1883–95) (died 1900).

1844 Wilbur O. Atwater, educator who set up first state agricultural extension station (1875), born in Johnsburg, NY; founder, director, Department of Agriculture Experiment Stations (1888–1907); developed caloric content of foods which are still in use (died 1907).

1849 Jacob A. Riis, journalist/reformer, born in Ribe, Denmark; with *New York Times* and *New York Sun* (1877–99), where his exposés led to improvements in schools, housing, recreational facilities; author (*How the Other Half Lives, Children of the Poor, Children of the Tenements*) (died 1914).

1851 Fifth great fire in San Francisco caused $12 million property loss with destruction of 1,500 homes.

1871 Henry S. Graves, forester, born in Marietta, OH; director, Yale Forestry School (1900–10), dean (1922–39); chief, U.S. Forest Service (1910–20) (died 1951).

1886 Railroad strikers and strike breakers fought at McCormick Harvesting Machine Co., Chicago; six men were killed; a meeting the following day resulted in the Haymarket Square riot.

1890 Benjamin Fairless, president, U.S. Steel Co. (1938–52), born in Pigeon Run, OH (died 1962).

1906 Mary Astor, screen actress (*Dodsworth, Little Women, The Maltese Falcon*), born in Quincy, IL (died 1987).

1913 William M. Inge, playwright (*Come Back, Little Sheba; Bus Stop; Dark at the Top of the Stairs*), born in Independence, KS (died 1973).

1916 Treaty signed by Haiti and United States for American control of the island; American forces occupied Haiti until 1930.

1917 First American squadron of destroyers, commanded by Adm. William S. Sims, arrived in Queenstown, Ireland.

1917 Alaska territorial legislature appropriated $60,000 to start U. of Alaska in Fairbanks.

1919 Pete Seeger, folk singer and composer ("Where Have All the Flowers Gone," "If I Had a Hammer," "Kisses Sweeter Than Wine"), born in New York City.

1933 Steve Weinberg, physicist, born in New York City; shared 1979 Nobel Physics Prize for establishing analogy between electromagnetism and the "weak" interactions of subatomic particles.

1936 Joan Collins, television actress (*Dynasty*), born in London.

1959 Unitarian and Universalist churches voted to merge.

1968 President Lyndon Johnson announced the United States and North Vietnam had agreed to meet in Paris May 10 for preliminary talks to end the war.

1983 National Conference of Catholic Bishops approved pastoral letter condemning the nuclear arms race, called for halt in development, production, and deployment of nuclear weapons.

1986 An unmanned Delta rocket lost power after liftoff at Cape Canaveral, was destroyed after it veered out of control.

1988 Special grand jury in Philadelphia cleared Mayor W. Wilson Goode and all others involved of criminal liability for death and destruction resulting from 1985 fire and deaths of radical group MOVE members.

2000 Cardinal John O'Connor of New York died at 80; generally considered most respected Roman Catholic senior churchman in the United States.

2001 President George W. Bush promised more local input into future plans that would restrict commercial use of national forests and parks.

2003 New Hampshire's state symbol "The

Old Man of the Mountain"— photographed by thousands each year — crumbled as bad weather finally overcame its rocky strength.

2004 The *Gay and Lesbian Atlas* went on sale with most recent statistical data and estimates concerning homosexual population in U.S.: Highest proportion of same-sex couples of all ages living together is in San Francisco but the highest proportion of gay senior couples is in North Dakota; gay men have higher income levels than lesbians; homosexual couples with children usually do not live in areas with high proportion of gays without children.

2006 Coca-Cola and Pepsi-Cola pledged to remove all sodas containing sugar from schools by 2009.

4

1493 Pope Alexander VI issued bill of demarcation (Inter caetera) following Columbus' discovery of America, setting a demarcation line between Spanish and Portuguese territories.

1626 Peter Minuit arrived on Manhattan Island to set up Dutch colony of Nieuw Amsterdam; became director of the New Netherlands.

1776 Rhode Island legislature renounced allegiance to the Crown; declared independence.

1778 Continental Congress ratified treaty of alliance with France, first and only such treaty ever made by United States; also a treaty of commerce, amity.

1796 William H. Prescott, historian of conquest of Mexico and Peru, born in Salem, MA (died 1859).

1796 Horace Mann, who revolutionized American education, born in Franklin, MA; first secretary, Massachusetts Board of Education (1837–47); instrumental in creating first American normal school (1839); represented Massachusetts in House (1849–52); president, Antioch College (1853–59) (died 1859).

1820 Julia Gardner Tyler, second wife of President Tyler, born in Gardner's Island, NY (died 1889).

1821 Gordon McKay, inventor of shoemaking machinery, born in Pittsfield, MA; his inventions included a heeler and lasting nailer, which revolutionized industry (died 1903).

1822 President Monroe signed act providing diplomatic relations with independent Latin American nations.

1826 Frederick E. Church, artist of Hudson River School, born in Hartford, CT (died 1900).

1851 Large part of St. Louis burned with a loss of $15 million in property.

1852 William L. McLean, publisher (*Philadelphia Bulletin* 1895–1931), born in Mt. Pleasant, PA (died 1931).

1860 Abraham L. Erlanger, theater manager, born in Buffalo, NY; a founder, Theater Syndicate (1896), which monopolized American theater in early 1900s (died 1930).

1862 Yorktown, VA, evacuated by Confederates, occupied by Union troops under Gen. George McClellan after a month-long siege.

1864 Gen. William T. Sherman and his Union troops began march to the sea.

1872 First professional league baseball game played at Ft. Wayne, IN, with home team beating Cleveland 2–0.

1872 Harold Bell Wright, popular novelist (*The Shepherd of the Hills, The Winning of Barbara Worth*), born in Rome, NY (died 1944).

1872 Alexander M. Palmer, Attorney General (1919–21) who led raids during "red scare," born in Moosehead, PA; represented Pennsylvania in House (1909–15); Alien Property Custodian (1915–19) (died 1936).

1874 Frank Conrad, instrumental in developing first radio station (KDKA, Pittsburgh, November 1920), born in Pittsburgh (died 1941).

1886 Peaceful meeting of railroad strikers in Haymarket Square, Chicago, became violent when police arrived to disperse crowd; bomb thrown, killing seven policemen, four strikers, and wounding 60; eight anarchists later found guilty of bombing.

1886 John A. Holabird, architect, born in Evanston, IL; designed several Chicago buildings (Palmolive, Daily News, Board of Trade) (died 1945).

1889 Francis J. Spellman, Catholic Archbishop of New York (1939–67), born in Whitman, MA; Bishop of New York (1933–39), elevated to cardinal 1946 (died 1967).

1891 First interracial hospital, Provident, opened in Chicago.

1916 In response to several protests, Germany promised not to sink ships without warning, but refused to abandon submarine attacks.

1928 Betsy (Elizabeth E.) Rawls, a leading golfer of 1950/60s, born in Spartanburg, SC; won women's U.S. Open four times, LPGA championship twice, named to LPGA Hall of Fame.

1930 Roberta Peters, operatic soprano (*Rigoletto, The Magic Flute*), born in New York City.

1970 Four students at Kent State U. in Ohio

were killed by Ohio National Guardsmen during an anti–Vietnam demonstration on campus.

1974 Expo '74 opened in Spokane.

1980 Department of Health, Education and Welfare became the Department of Health and Human Services; Education was spun off to become separate department.

1987 Supreme Court by 7–0 ruling said states may force Rotary clubs to admit women to membership, opening the way to breaking down barriers of male-only organizations.

1988 Chemical plant in Henderson, NV, that manufactured fuel for space shuttles was leveled by four explosions; 25 of 200 people in the plant were missing.

1989 Federal jury found Oliver L. North guilty of shredding documents, accepting an illegal gratuity, and helping obstruct Congress in the Iran-Contra affair; acquitted of nine other charges; conviction appealed.

1989 Space shuttle *Atlantis*, which blasted off from Cape Canaveral, launched the Magellan space probe to map surface of Venus.

1997 FBI reported that a "catastrophic mechanical failure" was the most likely cause of the TWA 800 airliner crash in July 1996.

2000 Most widespread wildfire in New Mexico history: What began as a controlled burn burst out of bounds and destroyed over 46,000 acres; Los Alamos National Laboratory endangered.

2004 Former Vice President Al Gore and other investors announced purchase of NewsWorld International cable network; intend to reorient it to cater to an audience in their twenties; deny any political agenda will guide its programming.

2005 Colonel David H. Hackworth dies of cancer at 74; youngest captain in Korean War; "the best battalion commander I ever saw in the U.S. Army" (General Creighton Abrams); winner of 91 medals; resigned from service after arguing on television that troop training for Vietnam was thoroughly inadequate and that officers did not have the foggiest idea how to fight guerrillas, thereby producing an unwinnable war.

5

1682 Frame of Government for Pennsylvania drawn up by William Penn; provided for a governor, council, and assembly to be elected by the freeholders; a cumbersome mechanism, it was replaced by the Charter of Privileges (1701).

1749 George Washington received his surveyor's license from the College of William & Mary.

1775 Benjamin Franklin returned to Philadelphia after ten years in England; elected to Continental Congress May 6.

1778 Baron Friedrich Wilhelm von Steuben, German officer who fought with Americans, named inspector general of Continental Army.

1796 William Pennington, New Jersey governor (1837–43), born in Newark; represented New Jersey in House (1859–61), serving as Speaker (died 1862).

1809 Frederick A.P. Barnard, organizer of a women's college (1883) now named for him, born in Sheffield, MA; with U. of Mississippi (1856–61) and Columbia College (1864–69), where he organized women's college (died 1889).

1811 John W. Draper, developed first successful daguerreotype (1840), born in Liverpool, England; a founder (1850), president, New York U. Medical School (died 1882).

1814 George M. Mowbray, pioneer oil refiner, born in Brighton, England; produced first refined oil (1859) at Titusville, PA; made many improvements in explosives, produced nitroglycerin for manufacturing (died 1891).

1827 Andrew Johnson and Eliza McCardle were married in Greeneville, TN.

1830 John B. Stetson, opened hat factory (1865) in Philadelphia which became world's largest, born in Orange, NJ (died 1906).

1832 Hubert H. Bancroft, historian of western America, born in Granville, OH; edited 39-volume history; turned over 60,000 volume library to U. of California (died 1918).

1838 George H. Hammond, meat packer who pioneered in transporting meat in refrigerator cars, born in Fitchburg, MA; Hammond, IN, named for him (died 1886).

1839 Felix Agnus, Union general and publisher, born in Lyons, France; business manager, *Baltimore American* (1869–83), publisher (1883–1920); founder, publisher *Baltimore Star* (1908–20) (died 1925).

1843 Reginald H. Fitz, physician who named appendicitis and proposed surgery for it, born in Chelsea, MA (died 1913).

1847 American Medical Association founded by 250 delegates from more than 40 medical societies and 28 colleges in Philadelphia; named Nathaniel Chapman first president.

1861 Peter C. Hewitt, electrical engineer, born in New York City; invented a mercury-vapor lamp rectifier, discovered basic principle of vacuum tube amplifier (died 1921).

1862 Battle of Williamsburg (VA) resulted in a Confederate retreat toward Richmond to prevent a Union takeover; Union forces occupied city May 6.

1864 Three-day indecisive Battle of Wilderness in Virginia began; cost Union about 18,000 casualties, including 2,200 killed; Confederate casualties about 11,000.

1890 Christopher D. Morley, author (*Kitty Foyle, Parnassus on Wheels, Thunder on the Left*), born in Haverford, PA (died 1957).

1899 Freeman F. Gosden, played Amos in *Amos 'n' Andy* radio show, born in Richmond, VA (died 1982).

1903 James Beard, cooking expert and author of cookbooks, born in Portland, OR (died 1985).

1910 Ninety miners died in an accident in a Palos, AL, mine.

1913 Tyrone Power, screen actor (*In Old Chicago, Alexander's Ragtime Band, The Razor's Edge*), born in Cincinnati (died 1958).

1915 Marines landed in Santo Domingo; occupation continued until 1924.

1915 Alice Faye, screen actress (*In Old Chicago, Little Old New York, Alexander's Ragtime Band*), born in New York City (died 1998).

1921 Arthur Schawlow, physicist, born in Mt. Vernon, NY; shared 1981 Nobel Physics Prize for work in developing laser spectroscopy technique, an inventor of laser beams.

1925 John T. Scopes, high school teacher, was arrested in Dayton, TN, for violating state law forbidding teaching evolution; indicted May 25.

1941 President Franklin Roosevelt issued an executive order for increased production of heavy bombers; set goal of 50 per month by March 1943, compared with production of nine per month.

1942 Sugar rationing began.

1942 Tammy Wynette, country music singer, born in Red Bay, AL (died 1998).

1951 United States and Iceland entered into a defense agreement by which United States undertook defense of Iceland and was permitted to build and maintain a major air base.

1960 American U-2 spy plane, piloted by Francis Gary Powers, was shot down over Russia; Powers was jailed.

1961 First American spaceman, Alan B. Shepard, Jr., rocketed 116.5 miles up in a two-orbit trip which took 15 minutes, 27 seconds.

1961 Congress raised minimum wage from $1 to $1.25 an hour over a two-year period.

1980 The Rev. Robert Drinan, the only priest in Congress, was barred from seeking reelection to his Massachusetts House seat by the Superior General of the Society of Jesus (Jesuits), of which Drinan was a member.

1988 Fire and explosion rocked a Shell Oil refinery in Norco, LA, injuring 42 persons and leaving six missing; 2,500 residents of area were evacuated.

1991 Carnegie Hall in New York City celebrated its 100th birthday with two gala concerts.

6

1606 John Norton, Puritan clergyman, born in Hertfordshire, England; served pastorates in Ipswich and Boston (1638–63), active in persecuting Quakers in state; composed first Latin book in the colonies (on church government) (1648) (died 1663).

1626 Peter Minuit bought Manhattan Island from the Man-a-Hat-a Indians for $24 worth of trinkets.

1635 John Haynes (1594–1654) chosen governor of Massachusetts; moved to Connecticut, becoming first governor under the Fundamental Laws (1639 and alternate years until his death).

1710 Richard Bland, who published earliest colonial defense against taxation by British, born in Berkeley, VA; the defense (1766) was "An Inquiry Into the Rights of the British Colonies" (died 1776).

1743 Seth Warner, Revolutionary War general, born in Roxbury, CT; with Arnold and Allen at Ticonderoga; led Vermont troops at Crown Point and Bennington (died 1784).

1748 Peleg Wadsworth, colonial leader, born in Hiram, ME; laid out defenses of Roxbury and Dorchester Heights (1775); represented Massachusetts in House (1793–1807) (died 1829).

1776 British reinforcements forced Americans to abandon siege of Quebec; began retreat from Canada, which ended in Ticonderoga in July.

1789 Georgia convention adopted a new state constitution, effective in October.

1806 Chapin A. Harris, cofounder, dean, of first dental college in world, born in Pompey, NY; wrote standard dental surgery text; help found Baltimore College of Dental Surgery (1840) (died 1860).

1808 William Strong, associate justice, Supreme Court (1870–80), born in Somers, CT;

represented Pennsylvania in House (1847–51) (Died 1895).

1814 British troops from Kingston, Canada, attacked and destroyed fort at Oswego, NY.

1830 Abraham Jacobi, founder of American pediatrics, born in Hartum, Germany; specialist in children's diseases (died 1919).

1835 James Gordon Bennett issued first number of four-page penny newspaper (*New York Herald*, one cent per copy, $3 per year); declared policy: "We shall support no party, be the agent of no faction or coterie, and care nothing for any election..."

1843 Stirling Yates, admiral who headed U.S. Fleet (1904–05), born in Baltimore; commander, Philippine squadron (1903–04) (died 1929).

1849 Wyatt Eaton, portrait painter, born in Phillipsburg, Canada, to American parents; a founder, Society of American Artists, president (died 1896).

1853 Philander C. Knox, Secretary of State (1909–13) who initiated "dollar diplomacy," born in Brownsville, PA; represented Pennsylvania in Senate (1904–09, 1917–21); Attorney General (1901–04) (died 1921).

1856 Robert E. Peary, discoverer of North Pole, born in Cresson, PA; Navy rear admiral, began Arctic exploration (1886); discovered pole on fourth try (April 6, 1909) (died 1920).

1858 Samuel B. McCormick, college president, born in Westmoreland County, PA; president, Coe College (1897–1904), Western U. of Pennsylvania (1904–20), which he moved to Pittsburgh and developed into major university (died 1928).

1861 Arkansas legislature voted 69–1 to secede from the Union.

1870 A(madeo) P. Giannini, founder (1904) of bank which became Bank of America, born in San Jose, CA; founded, Transamerica Corp. (1928) (died 1949).

1870 John T. McCutcheon, editorial cartoonist (*Chicago Tribune* 1903–45), born in Tippecanoe County, IN (died 1949).

1871 Richard B. Moore, chemist who supervised first American production of radium, born in Cincinnati; with Bureau of Mines (1912–23), surveyed Colorado radium deposits; pioneer in urging use of helium in balloons (died 1931).

1875 William D. Leahy, White House chief of staff during World War II, born in Hampton, IA; chief of naval operations (1937–39); ambassador to Vichy, France (1940–42) (died 1959).

1882 Chinese Exclusion Act passed, prohibiting immigration of Chinese laborers for ten years; restriction extended, until it finally became permanent.

1888 Emanuel Celler, who represented a New York district in House for 50 years (1922–72), born in Brooklyn.

1895 Rudolph Valentino, silent screen actor (*The Sheik, Blood and Sand*), born in Castellaneta, Italy (died 1926).

1896 Samuel P. Langley demonstrated his "aerodrome" over the Potomac River; each time the miniature steam engine with wings sustained itself for 1½ minutes, traversing a distance of more than a mile.

1898 Assistant Navy Secretary Theodore Roosevelt resigned to become a lieutenant colonel in the cavalry (Rough Riders).

1898 Daniel F. Gerber, introducer of strained baby foods, born in Fremont, MI; president, Gerber Products Co. (1945–64) (died 1974).

1902 Harry L. Golden, author (*Only in America, For 2¢ Plain*), born in New York City; editor, publisher, *The Carolina Israelite* (died 1981).

1913 Carmen Cavallero, pianist and orchestra leader, born in New York City.

1914 Randall Jarrell, poet/novelist (*The Lost World, Blood for a Stranger, Little Friend, Little Friend*), born in Nashville, TN (died 1965).

1915 Orson Welles, actor, director, producer, born in Kenosha, WI; starred in *Citizen Kane* on screen; founder, Mercury Theater, whose realistic radio broadcast of imaginary Martian invasion (1938) created panic (died 1985).

1915 Theodore H. White, author of "making of a president" books, born in Boston; served as foreign correspondent (died 1986).

1931 Willie Mays, baseball player (New York N, San Francisco), born in Fairfield, AL; named to Baseball Hall of Fame.

1933 Supreme Court invalidated Railroad Retirement Act.

1933 Barbara Aronstein Black, first woman to head a major private law school, born in New York City; dean of Columbia Law School since 1986.

1935 Works Progress Administration (WPA) began operations.

1937 German zeppelin *Hindenburg* destroyed by fire at the tower mooring at Lakehurst, NJ; 36 died in blaze.

1942 Island fort of Corregidor fell to Japanese after holding out for four months.

1984 William A. Egan, first governor of Alaska (1959), died at 69; a leader in the Alaska statehood movement.

1991 United States ended occupation of southern Iraq as United Nations troops took control of the nine-mile wide demilitarized zone.

1996 William E. Colby, director of the CIA (1973–76), died at 76.

1997 President Clinton and the Mexican president signed an agreement for broader mutual effort to fight drug trafficking; two days later he met in Costa Rica with leaders of Central America and Caribbean nations; on May 10, he attended a summit of Caribbean leaders.

2002 Due to concern that anti–American bias would result in unjust prosecution of U.S. nationals, State Department announced the country's rejection of International Court jurisdiction.

2006 Lillian Gertrud Asplund (b. 1906) died, and with her the last living individual with personal recall of any of the events surrounding the sinking of the *Titanic*; five when it happened, she remembered being passed into a lifeboat for escape for the rest of her life.

7

1738 George Whitefield, Methodist evangelist, arrived in Savannah from England.

1774 William Bainbridge, commander of the *Constitution* (Old Ironsides) during War of 1812, born in Princeton, NJ (died 1833).

1784 Thomas Jefferson named a minister plenipotentiary to join Benjamin Franklin and John Adams to negotiate treaties with foreign powers.

1789 First presidential inaugural ball held in Assembly Room on lower Broadway in New York City.

1794 Edward Delafield, founder, first president, American Ophthalmological Society (1864), born in New York City; specialized in eye diseases.

1800 Territory of Indiana created by dividing the Northwest Territory.

1833 Abraham Lincoln named postmaster of New Salem, IL, at $55 a year, plus franking privilege, exemption from military and jury duty; served for three years.

1836 Joseph G. Cannon, legislator, born in New Garden, NC; represented Illinois in House (1873–91, 1893–1913), serving as Speaker (1903–11); Speaker's power reduced (1910) after he

was accused of autocratic methods of control (died 1926).

1862 Tennessee legislature voted to secede from Union; ratified June 8 by popular vote of 104,019 to 47,238.

1862 Senate began impeachment proceedings against West H. Humphreys, U.S. District Court judge in Tennessee; charged with aiding the rebellion; found guilty, removed.

1870 Marcus Loew, movie industry pioneer, born in New York City; theater owner and movie producer (died 1927).

1879 California voters ratified their new state constitution adopted by convention.

1892 Archibald MacLeish, poet (*New Found Land, JB, The Fall of the City*), born in Glencoe, IL; Librarian of Congress (1939–44) (died 1982).

1894 Francis Brennan, first American dean of the Sacred Rota in Rome (1958–67), born in Shenandoah, PA; the Rota is Catholic church's highest court of appeals (died 1968).

1901 Gary Cooper, screen actor (*Sergeant York, Farewell to Arms, Mr. Deeds Goes to Town*), born in Helena, MT (died 1961).

1906 Congress authorized Alaska to have a delegate in the House.

1909 Edwin H. Land, inventor of Polaroid cameras, film, born in Bridgeport, CT; founder, president, Polaroid Corp. (1937–91) (died 1991).

1913 Simon Ramo, chief scientist for American intercontinental ballistics program, born in Salt Lake City.

1914 Eleanor R. Wilson, daughter of President and Mrs. Wilson, was married in the White House to Secretary of the Treasury William G. McAdoo.

1915 British steamer *Lusitania* sunk off Irish coast by German submarine, with a loss of 1,200 lives, including 128 Americans, among them Elbert Hubbard, author/publisher; Charles Frohman, theatrical producer, and Alfred G. Vanderbilt.

1933 John Unitas, star football quarterback (Baltimore 1956–72), born in Pittsburgh.

1942 Two-day Battle of the Coral Sea began; resulted in American fleet diverting Japanese invasion of Port Moresby on New Guinea.

1943 Bizerte in North Africa captured by American Second Corps.

1945 Germans surrendered to the Allies at 2:41 A.M. in the "little red schoolhouse" in Reims, France, Gen. Eisenhower's headquarters.

1957 John F. Kennedy awarded Pulitzer Prize for biography (*Profiles in Courage*).

1984 American Vietnam War veterans reached out-of-court settlement with several chemical companies in class action suit relating to herbicide Agent Orange.

1992 Michigan became 38th state to ratify what became 27th Amendment to the Constitution, which bars Congress from voting itself immediate pay raises; amendment was first proposed by James Madison in 1789.

1995 Two days of tornadoes in southern Oklahoma and northern Texas killed 23 persons.

1998 Daimler Benz AG and Chrysler Corp. announced plans to merge in a transaction valued at $40 billion.

2000 Douglas Fairbanks, Jr., died at 90, after a long movie career in which he starred in 75 feature films.

2001 U.S. resumed spy plane flights in international airspace off China; had been temporarily suspended after earlier collision of Chinese fighter with an American aircraft.

2004 Energy Secretary Spencer Abraham reacted to repeated security problems at Lawrence Livermore National Lab, one of leading U.S. nuclear research facilities: All plutonium should be removed to assure against theft; proposal comes at a time when Laboratory executives had requested permission to double the amount on the premises.

2005 Former Congressman Peter Rodino (Democrat, New Jersey) died at 95; had chaired Watergate investigation hearings that ultimately resulted in President Richard Nixon resigning office.

8

1541 Expedition of Hernando de Soto reached Mississippi River, probably at lower Chickasaw Bluffs, becoming the first Europeans to do so.

1639 William Coddington, who split with Anne Hutchinson after they founded Pocasset (later Portsmouth), founded Newport; the two Rhode Island colonies joined in 1640.

1778 Sir Henry Clinton arrived to succeed Sir William Howe as British commander.

1779 Spain declared war against Great Britain.

1795 Post Office Department established by Congress.

1821 William H. Vanderbilt, financier, born in New Brunswick, NJ; inherited family fortune; became president, New York Central Railroad (1877–83); had other large railroad holdings; donated $100,000 to erect Cleopatra's Needle in Central Park (died 1885).

1829 Lewis M. Gottschalk, pianist/composer (*Tremolo Etude, Bamboula, Last Hope*), born in New Orleans (died 1889).

1845 Virginia Baptist Foreign Missionary Society called for a convention in Augusta, GA, where 293 delegates from nine states organized the Southern Baptist Convention; Dr. W.B. Johnson of South Carolina named president.

1846 Oscar Hammerstein I, inventor of a cigar maker, born in Stettin, Germany; made fortune with many other inventions; built Manhattan Opera House, which was bought out by the Metropolitan Opera House (died 1919).

1846 Gen. Zachary Taylor led American troops to victory over Mexicans in two-day battle at Palo Alto, forcing the Mexicans to retreat to Matamoras.

1855 John W. Gates, financier known as "Bet a Million Gates," born in West Chicago, IL; formed, headed, American Steel & Wire Co.; president, Illinois Steel Co. (died 1911).

1861 Confederate Congress authorized army enlistments for the war.

1864 Two engagements at Spotsylvania Court House (Battles of the Wilderness) raged over four days, without decision, many casualties; Grant reportedly said: "I propose to fight it out along this line if it takes all summer."

1867 Convention in Annapolis completed new Maryland constitution; ratified September 18.

1869 James R. Angell, a founder of functional psychology, born in Burlington, VT; president, Yale U. (1921–37) (died 1949).

1871 United States and Great Britain signed treaty submitting the *Alabama* claims to international arbitration; United States awarded (1872) $15.5 million for damages by Confederate vessel.

1882 Peter J. McGuire, founder of Carpenters Union, recommended creation of a "Labor Day."

1884 Harry S Truman, 33d president (1945–53), born in Lamar, MO; represented Missouri in Senate (1935–45); elected Vice President (1945), succeeding to presidency on death of President Franklin Roosevelt (died 1972).

1893 Francis Ouimet, golfer who did much to popularize game in United States, born in Brookline, MA (died 1967).

1895 Fulton J. Sheen, Catholic Bishop of

Rochester (1966–69), born in El Paso, IL; auxiliary bishop of New York (1951–66); popular radio, television personality (died 1979).

1895 Edmund Wilson, critic (*The New Yorker*) and author (*Memoirs of Hecate County*), born in Red Bank, NJ (died 1972).

1899 Friedrich A. von Hayek, economist, born in Vienna; shared 1974 Nobel Economics Prize.

1910 Mary Lou Williams, all-time great jazz pianist, composer, born in Pittsburgh (died 1981).

1926 Rida Young, librettist, died at 51; wrote many musical comedies (*Naughty Marietta, Maytime*); wrote words for "Mother Machree."

1937 Thomas Pynchon, author (*V, The Crying of Lot 49*), born in Glen Cove, NY.

1940 Peter B. Benchley, author (*Jaws, The Deep*), born in New York City.

1944 First eye bank established at New York Hospital in New York City.

1984 American Presbyterian minister Benjamin Weir kidnapped in West Beirut, Lebanon; released September 9, 1985.

1987 Former Senator Gary Hart of Colorado dropped out of race for Democratic presidential nomination after revelation about his secret association with an actress-model; blamed press and campaign excesses for his action.

1991 William H. Webster, CIA director for four years, resigned; succeeded in November by Robert M. Gates.

1998 Tobacco industry settled its fourth state lawsuit, this time with Minnesota; four defendant companies agreed to pay $6.1 billion over 25 years to the state and $469 million over five years to Blue Cross/Blue Shield of Minnesota.

1998 Labor Department reported that April unemployment had declined to 4.3 percent, the lowest level in 28 years.

1998 Jennings Randolph, West Virginia legislator (House 1933–46, Senate 1958–85), died at 96.

9

1712 Carolina colony separated into North and South Carolina.

1746 Theodore Sedgwick, legislator, born in West Hartford, CT; represented Massachusetts in Continental Congress (1785–88), in House (1789–96, 1799–1802), serving as Speaker (1799–1801), and in Senate (1796–99); served on Massachusetts Supreme Court (1802–13) (died 1813).

1775 Jacob J. Brown, War of 1812 general who led troops to victory at Chippewa and Lundy Lane, born in Bucks County, PA (died 1828).

1781 British surrendered Pensacola and all of West Florida to the Spanish.

1785 James J. Espy, called the "storm king" for developing theory of storms, born in Westmoreland County, PA; served with War and Navy Departments, laid groundwork for telegraphic weather bulletins (died 1860).

1800 John Brown, antislavery leader, born in Torrington, CT; led raid on Harpers Ferry (WV), intended as a signal for a general insurrection of slaves; held arsenal for a day, then his band was overpowered by federal troops under Robert E. Lee; convicted of treason, hanged (1859); became martyr of antislavery cause.

1813 American troops under Gen. William Henry Harrison withstood attacks of British at Ft. Meigs, opposite present Maumee, OH.

1828 Charles H. Cramp, shipbuilder who developed family business into America's largest, born in Philadelphia; president of firm (1879–1903) (died 1913).

1832 Fifteen Seminole chiefs ceded their Florida lands to the United States.

1846 American troops routed a Mexican force of 6,000 at Resaca de la Palma.

1850 Edward Weston, inventor of cadmium cell, born in London; cell was adopted as official standard of electromotive force; developed manufactured dynamo-electrical machinery (died 1936).

1882 Henry J. Kaiser, shipbuilder and auto manufacturer, born in Canajoharie, NY; his company built large dams (Bonneville, Grand Coulee), housing, ships in record time in World War II; produced the Kaiser, Frazer and inexpensive Henry J automobiles (died 1967).

1892 Brehon B. Somerville, World War II Army general, born in Little Rock, AR; chief of Army Service Forces (1942–46) (died 1955).

1895 Richard Barthelmess, screen actor (*Only Angels Have Wings, The Spoilers*), born in New York City (died 1963).

1909 Gordon Bunshaft, architect (Lever Building, New York City), born in Buffalo, NY (died 1990).

1916 Germany apologized for the *Sussex* incident (April 18), ending crisis.

1918 Mike Wallace, television personality, born in Brookline, MA; with Columbia Broadcasting System (*Sixty Minutes* 1963–98).

1918 Orville L. Freeman, Secretary of Agriculture (1961–69), born in Minneapolis; governor of Minnesota (1955–61).

1926 First polar flight made by then Lt. Comm. Richard E. Byrd and Floyd Bennett over North Pole, making the 1,360-mile round trip from Spitzbergen in 15½ hours.

1927 Arkansas and Missouri struck by tornadoes, killing 92.

1928 Pancho (Richard A.) Gonzales, tennis great who held world's professional singles, doubles titles for 12 years (died 1995).

1974 House Judiciary Committee began impeachment hearings against President Nixon.

1980 Freighter *Summit Venture* rammed the Sunshine Skyway bridge over Tampa Bay, collapsing one of the twin highway spans; 35 persons were killed.

1982 President Reagan proposed two-step plan to reduce nuclear weapons and a meeting with Leonid Brezhnev in June; meeting later set for June 29, in Geneva.

1996 Scientists found a protein which might open new important lines of research in fight against AIDS.

2001 In conclusion vigorously rejected by many, psychiatrist Robert Spitzer argued that at least a proportion of gays can successfully adopt heterosexual lifestyle.

2003 Former Senator Russell B. Long died; served Louisiana as Democratic U.S. Senator from 1948–87; had distinction of being only individual to serve in a Senate seat previously occupied by both his father and mother.

2005 *The 2005 Urban Mobility Report* from the Texas Transportation Institute (based on the most recent, 2003 data) reported that the worst congestion was found in Los Angeles (93 wasted hours above a normal commute time) and San Francisco and the nearby Bay Area cities (72 wasted hours yearly); estimated nationwide cost: 3.7 billion hours and 2.3 billion gallons of fuel.

10

1730 George Ross, colonial leader, born in New Castle, DE; member of Continental Congress (1774–77), a signer of Declaration of Independence (died 1779).

1755 Robert Gray, discoverer of Gray's Harbor, OR, and Columbia River, born in Tiverton, RI; discoveries were foundation for American claims to Oregon (died 1806).

1755 George Washington named an aide to British Gen. Edward Braddock.

1773 Tea Act went into effect, giving the nearly bankrupt East India Co. an advantage in selling tea to the colonies.

1775 Force of 83 men under Ethan Allen surprised garrison of 42 British at Ft. Ticonderoga, NY, which surrendered to Allen upon his demand "in the name of the great Jehovah and the Continental Congress."

1775 Second Continental Congress met in Philadelphia, approved an appeal written by John Jay asking Canada to join American colonies; John Hancock was named president after Peyton Randolph resigned May 24.

1776 Massachusetts House of Representatives resolved that each town should meet and instruct its representatives "whether if the honorable Congress should, for the Safety of said Colonies, declare them Independent of the Kingdom of Great Britain, then the said Inhabitants will solemnly engage with their Lives and Fortunes to Support the Congress in the Measure."

1776 John Adams and Richard Henry Lee introduced a resolution to the Continental Congress calling on the colonies to adopt "such government as shall ... best conduce to the happiness and safety of their constituents in particular and America in general."

1779 British force of 2,500, brought in by ship from New York, occupied, then destroyed Portsmouth and Norfolk, Va.

1783 Society of the Cincinnati, oldest hereditary military society in North America, founded by American Revolutionary army officers; George Washington was the first president general.

1789 Jared Sparks, editor and educator, born in Willington, CT; owner, editor, *North American Review*; published diplomatic correspondence of Revolution, writings of Washington, Franklin, and ten volumes of American biographies; president, Harvard U. (1849–53) (died 1866).

1797 First vessel of new navy, the *United States*, launched in Philadelphia.

1800 Congress passed land act, hoping to stimulate sales of public lands by use of credit; system encouraged speculation, made collections difficult; abandoned in 1820.

1800 Charles Knowlton, birth control advocate, born in Templeton, MA; wrote *Fruits of Philosophy*, birth control tract, for which he was jailed for three months in Cambridge (died 1850).

1802 Horatio Allen, supervised construction and operated first American-made locomotive, born in Schenectady; president, Erie Railroad (1843); consulting engineer for Brooklyn Bridge (died 1890).

1813 Montgomery Blair, Postmaster General (1861–64), who introduced free city delivery, born in Franklin County, KY; also started postal money orders and railway post office (died 1883).

1823 John Sherman, public official, born in Lancaster, OH; represented Ohio in House (1855–61) and Senate (1861–77, 1881–97); Secretary of Treasury (1877–81), Secretary of State (1897–98) (died 1900).

1832 William R. Grace, founder of shipping company in South American trade, born in Queenstown, Ireland; mayor of New York City (1880–82, 1884–86) (died 1904).

1837 Panic of 1837 began when New York banks suspended specie payments, an action followed by other banks, after cotton prices fell almost 50 percent; ensuing depression lasted six years, with the South and West most affected.

1841 James Gordon Bennett, Jr., who succeeded his father as editor of *New York Herald*, born in New York City; sent Stanley to find Livingstone in Africa (1869–71); financed several explorations; established Paris edition of *Herald* (died 1918).

1849 Astor Place riot in New York City occurred when a mob of partisans of American actor Edwin Forrest tried to seize English actor William Macready on his farewell appearance; a riot ensued resulting in 22 dead, 36 injured.

1862 Confederates evacuated Norfolk, VA; Union troops occupied city.

1865 Jefferson Davis, Confederate president, captured by Union troops near Irwinville, GA; imprisoned for two years at Ft. Monroe, VA.

1865 Presidential proclamation announced that "armed resistance to the authority of the Government in the insurrectionary states may be regarded at an end."

1866 Henry M. Blossom, playwright (*Checkers, The Yankee Consul, The Red Mill*), born in St. Louis (died 1919).

1866 American Equal Rights Society formed in New York City.

1869 Central Pacific and Union Pacific railroads joined at Promontory Point, UT, forming first transcontinental railroad.

1872 Women who seceded from National Woman Suffrage Association while meeting in New York City nominated Victoria Claflin Woodhull for president, the first woman presidential candidate; group took name of Equal Rights Party.

1876 Alexander Graham Bell, speaking before the American Academy of Arts & Sciences in Boston, announced and demonstrated the newly-invented telephone.

1876 First American major international exposition opened in Fairmount Park, Philadelphia by President Grant; marked the American centennial.

1886 Francis P. Biddle, Attorney General (1941–45), born in Paris (died 1968).

1888 Max Steiner, composer of movie scores (*Gone with the Wind, Caine Mutiny, The Treasure of Sierra Madre*), born in Vienna (died 1971).

1899 Fred Astaire, screen actor/dancer, born in Omaha; starred in many musicals (*Top Hat, Easter Parade, Roberta, Holiday Inn*) (died 1987).

1899 Dimitri Tiomkin, composer of film musical scores (*Lost Horizon, Duel in the Sun, High Noon, The Great Waltz*), born in Russia (died 1979).

1902 David O. Selznick, movie producer (*Gone with the Wind, The Prisoner of Zenda, Tom Sawyer*), born in Pittsburgh (died 1965).

1908 Carl B. Albert, legislator, born in McAlester, OK; represented Oklahoma in House (1946–79), serving as Speaker (1971–76).

1916 First Mother's Day observed in Philadelphia and Grafton, WV.

1916 Milton Babbitt, pioneer in field of electronically-produced music, born in Philadelphia; composer (*Composition for Synthesizer, Vision and Prayer*).

1917 Gen. John J. Pershing appointed commanding general of American Expeditionary Force, effective May 26.

1925 Stephen Bechtel, Jr., chief executive officer of international construction firm (Bechtel Group), born in Oakland, CA.

1930 Adler Planetarium, first American public planetarium, opened in Chicago.

1934 Dust storms began in Midwest, the aftermath of wartime over-plowing.

1939 Methodist Episcopal Church, Methodist Church South, and Methodist Protestant Church completed a merger in Kansas City into the Methodist Church.

1939 Museum of Modern Art in New York City dedicated.

1943 Richard G. Darman, Budget Director (1989–93), born in Charlotte, NC; served as presidential assistant (1981–85).

1945 Point system for the discharge of enlisted men was announced.

1950 President Truman signed act creating the National Science Foundation.

1957 Phil(ip) Mahre, world class skier who

won Olympic gold medal for slalom, born in White Pass, WA; won seven World Cup medals for various events.

1968 Peace talks began in Paris between United States and North Vietnam.

1987 IBM researchers announced they have produced ceramic material able to handle much greater amount of electric current, opening way for new generation of high-speed computers, new medical instruments, and efficient power generation and storage.

1995 Second suspect in the Oklahoma City federal building bombing, Terry Nichols, was charged in the bombing.

2000 Federal Trade Commission announced a deal with five large music companies, withdrawing antitrust lawsuit in exchange for anticipated cut in CD prices.

2000 FDA permitted saline breast implants to be marketed once again after seven years of ban due to what had been believed to be possible health complications.

2002 Robert Hanssen, who collected $1.4 million for spying for Russia during much of his 25 years with the FBI, was sentenced to life in prison after apologizing for his conduct; sentence was in accord with plea agreement that exchanged full cooperation and revelation of all he knew in exchange for avoiding death penalty.

2004 Segregation-era murder victim Emmett Till was 14 years of age (1955); discovery of additional evidence caused Justice Department to reopen case today.

2006 Seventeen-year executive editor of *New York Times* A. M. Rosenthal died at 84; winner of Pulitzer prize.

11

1647 Peter Stuyvesant arrived in New Amsterdam to take control of Dutch colonial government from William Kieffer.

1682 General Court of Massachusetts repealed laws against observing Christmas and capital punishment for returning Quakers.

1690 English colonists, led by Sir William Phips, captured Port Royal, Nova Scotia, headquarters for French privateers which raided colonial shipping; this was one of major engagements of King William's War.

1769 Thomas Jefferson was elected to Virginia House of Burgesses; re-elected five times, serving until 1775.

1779 John Hart, a signer of Declaration of Independence, died at about 68; a New Jersey farmer, he was at 65 the oldest signer.

1791 Capt. Robert Gray entered the Columbia River, which he named after his ship.

1816 American Bible Society was formed in New York City.

1835 Convention began in Detroit to adopt state constitution; acted June 29; ratified November 2; included provision prohibiting slavery.

1836 First Iowa newspaper, *DuBuque Visitor*, published by John King.

1846 Message by President Polk to Congress led to declaration of war against Mexico two days later; he stated that "Mexico has ... shed American blood upon American soil"; House voted 174–14 with 20 abstentions in favor of war, the Senate 40–2 with three abstentions.

1852 Charles W. Fairbanks, Vice President (1905–09), born near Unionville Center, OH; represented Indiana in Senate (1897–1905) (died 1918).

1854 Ottmar Mergenthaler, inventor of the linotype, born in Hachtel, Germany; his machine resulted in upsurge of publishing (died 1899).

1854 Albion W. Small, a leader in establishing sociology as an American academic subject, born in Buckfield, ME (died 1926).

1858 Minnesota admitted into Union as 23d state.

1862 The *Merrimac*, Confederate ironclad vessel, was blown up by her commander off the Virginia coast to prevent its capture by Union forces.

1864 Union cavalry, led by Gen. Philip Sheridan, was checked at Yellow Tavern, north of Richmond, VA; Confederate Gen. J.E.B. Stuart was killed.

1880 George E. Haynes, sociologist and civil rights leader, born in Pine Bluff, AR; cofounder, first director, National Urban League (1910–16); organized social science department, Fisk U. (1910–12); first black to receive Ph.D. at Columbia U. (1912) (died 1960).

1881 Theodore von Karman, physicist who founded Aerojet General (1942), born in Budapest; director, Guggenheim Jet Propulsion Laboratory (1930); did research for Bell X-1, first plane to break sound barrier (died 1963).

1884 Alma Gluck, lyric opera/concert soprano, born in Bucharest (died 1938).

1885 King (Joseph) Oliver, pioneer jazz cornetist and band leader, born in Abend, LA; led first black jazz group to make recordings (died 1938).

1888   Irving Berlin, composer of many of the greatest popular songs, born in Temun, Russia; his 800 songs included "White Christmas," "Easter Parade," "God Bless America," "Alexander's Ragtime Band," "Always," "All Alone" (died 1989).

1891   Henry Morgenthau, Jr., public official, born in New York City; Secretary of Treasury (1934–45); author of Morgenthau Plan for disarming Germany; editor, *American Agriculturist* (1922–33) (died 1967).

1893   Martha Graham, teacher and choreographer who was one of most influential in dance, born in Pittsburgh (died 1991).

1894   Pullman Co. workers in Chicago went on strike for higher pay with the cooperation of workers on railroads which rented Pullman cars; all railroads were shut down by June 30.

1894   Ellsworth Bunker, diplomat, born in Yonkers, NY; ambassador to India (1956–61), to South Vietnam (1967–73); helped negotiate Panama Canal treaty (1977–78) (died 1984).

1895   William G. Still, first black American to conduct a major American symphony (Los Angeles 1936), born in Woodville, MS; composed numerous orchestral works (died 1979).

1897   Robert E. Gross, major aircraft manufacturer, born in Boston; bought Lockheed Aircraft Corp. (1932) for $40,000; developed it into a major company; introduced jet power for commercial aviation, developed Polaris missile (died 1961).

1905   Tornado hit Snyder, OK, killing 100 persons.

1910   Glacier (MT) National Park established.

1912   Phil Silvers, stage/television entertainer, born in New York City; starred on stage (*Top Banana, High Button Shoes*) and television (*Phil Silvers Show*) (died 1985).

1918   Richard P. Feynman, physicist, born in New York City; shared 1965 Nobel Physics Prize for development of relativistic theory of quantum electrodynamics (died 1988).

1935   An executive order created the Rural Electrification Administration (REA) to finance electricity production and distribution in rural areas not served by private utilities.

1943   American amphibious forces landed on Attu Island, off Alaska, and in 19 days of heavy fighting secured the island.

1946   Robert K. Jarvik, developer of first complete artificial heart, born in Midland, MI.

1950   President Truman dedicated the Grand Coulee Dam on Columbia River in Washington.

1953   Tornadoes hit Waco and San Angelo, TX; 124 killed, more than 500 injured.

1973   Charges against Daniel Ellsberg, who leaked the Pentagon Papers to the *New York Times*, were dismissed because of "conduct of the government" in the case.

1995   More than 170 nations at the United Nations agreed to extend in perpetuity the treaty on nonproliferation of nuclear weapons.

1996   A Valujet DC-9 crashed into the Florida Everglades near Miami, killed all 110 aboard.

1998   SBC Communications Inc. said it will acquire Ameritech Corp.; the $70 billion merger would result in largest local telephone service provider in U.S.

2000   Ford conceded that its SUVs had significant safety problems that must be remedied.

2003   The *New York Times* printed major self-critical examination: admits that its reporter Jayson Blair had managed to publish at least three dozen partially faked stories without being caught and fired; calls the failure in editorial oversight "a low point" in paper's history.

2006   Floyd Patterson (b. 1938) died at 71; made boxing history in 1960 when he became first man to recapture world heavyweight champion title after losing it; won 55 professional matches, tied 1, and lost 8 over two decades.

12

1621   Edward Winslow and Susanna Fuller White were married in the first Plymouth Colony wedding.

1775   Small American force under Lt. Col. Seth Warner seized Crown Point, NY.

1780   After a 45-day siege, Charleston, SC, surrendered to British troops under Sir Henry Clinton; was heaviest American defeat of war, with the loss of 5,000 troops and four vessels.

1789   Tammany Society founded in New York City as a patriotic association; soon became a political organization.

1806   James Shields, public official, born in Altamore, Ireland; served as governor of Oregon Territory (1849); represented Illinois (1849–55), Minnesota (1858–59) and Missouri (1879) in Senate (died 1879).

1809   Robert C. Winthrop, legislator, born in Boston; represented Massachusetts in House (1840–50), serving as Speaker (1847–49), and in Senate (1850–51) (died 1894).

1822 James L. Orr, legislator, born in Craytonville, SC; represented South Carolina in House (1849–59), serving as Speaker (1857–59); served state as governor (1865–68); minister to Russia (1872–73) (died 1873).

1850 Henry Cabot Lodge, legislator, born in Boston; represented Massachusetts in House (1887–93) and Senate (1893–1924); as chairman of Foreign Affairs Committee, led successful fight against American participation in League of Nations (died 1924).

1859 Lillian Nordica, operatic soprano, born in Farmington, ME; sang at the Met (1896–1907) and on concert stage (died 1914).

1864 Renewed Battle of Spotsylvania Court House (the third Battle of the Wilderness) resulted in some advances by Union troops.

1866 William T. Manning, Episcopal Bishop of New York (1921–46), born in Northampton, England; rector, Trinity Church, New York City (1908–21) (died 1949).

1868 Al Shean, comedy entertainer of Gallagher & Shean team, born in Dornum, Germany (died 1949).

1879 Ben Lear, World War II general, born in Hamilton, Canada; commander, 2d Army (1940–43) (died 1966).

1880 Lincoln Ellsworth, explorer, born in Chicago; flew over North Pole with Amundsen and Nobile in dirigible (1926), over South Pole (1935); made transatlantic submarine exploration (1931) (died 1951).

1895 William F. Giauque, chemist, born in Niagara Falls, Canada; awarded 1949 Nobel Chemistry Prize for research in thermodynamics (died 1982).

1898 Louisiana constitution adopted, effective September 1.

1900 Mildred H. McAfee, first director, WAVES (1942–46), born in Parkville, MO; president, Wellesley College (1936–49) (died 1994).

1906 (William) Maurice Ewing, oceanographer, born in Lockney, TX; contributed major portion of our knowledge of submarine topography (died 1974).

1925 Yogi (Lawrence P.) Berra, baseball player/manager (New York AL and NL), born in St. Louis, MO; named to Baseball Hall of Fame.

1929 Burt Bacharach, film scores composer (*Alfie, What's New Pussycat?, Butch Cassidy and the Sundance Kid*), born in Kansas City, MO; also scored plays (*Promises, Promises*) and wrote popular songs ("Walk on By," "What the World Needs Now").

1933 Agricultural Adjustment Act passed in effort to provide temporary relief for farmers, to rehabilitate agriculture; functions later assumed by Department of Agriculture.

1933 Federal Emergency Relief Act signed, setting up $500 million national relief program, directed by Harry Hopkins.

1936 Frank P. Stella, a leader in "minimal" art movement, born in Malden, MA; artist with exclusive interest in color, structure.

1943 President Franklin Roosevelt and Prime Minister Winston Churchill met for two weeks in the White House to discuss European war plans.

1949 Soviets abandoned their blockade of Berlin after 13 months.

1962 American naval and ground forces ordered to Laos.

1982 Braniff Airways was first major airline to file for bankruptcy, suspend operations.

1987 Doctors in Baltimore successfully transplanted a human heart from a living donor into another human, then transplanted a heart and lungs from an accident victim to the original heart donor.

2001 Popular singer Perry Como died at 88; had a weekly entertainment program that spanned 1948–63; known in the post–World War II era for his relaxed but effective delivery of a wide variety of songs.

2002 Former President Jimmy Carter became first serving or past American chief executive to visit Cuba since the Communist revolution of 1959; those favoring trip considered it opportunity to encourage constructive new talks with Fidel Castro, while those criticizing it saw it as giving credibility to a repressive regime barely able to function economically.

2003 New rules to require airlines to assume weight of 190 pounds for each passenger, a ten-pound increase.

2006 Blow to intra-party zealots: Nancy Pelosi, House Democratic leader, told her caucus that if they win a majority in fall elections neither censure nor impeachment of President Bush will be on her agenda.

13

1729 Henry W. Stiegel, glassmaker who founded Manheim, PA, born in Cologne, Germany; established glass factory (1764), producing glassware which became collectors' items (1785).

1742 Manasseh Cutler, Congregational clergyman and botanist, born in Killingly, CT; served Ipswich Hamlet (now Hamilton), MA (1771–1823); prepared account of New England flora; organized Ohio Co. to colonize Ohio River Valley, helped draft ordinance to govern area (died 1823).

1774 Gen. Thomas Gage arrived in Boston as governor of Massachusetts and commander-in-chief of army; at same time, Boston town meeting called for new economic sanctions against Great Britain.

1813 John S. Dwight, publisher, editor *Journal of Music* (1852–81), born in Boston; he influenced American musical education, taste; helped organize Boston Philharmonic Society (1865) (died 1893).

1846 President Polk signed declaration of war against Mexico.

1851 Convention in Annapolis adopted new Maryland state constitution; ratified by people June 4.

1857 Arthur W. Savage, inventor and founder, Savage Arms Co. (1895), born in Jamaica; invented a dirigible, torpedo, improvements in rifle magazine (died 1938).

1861 Great Britain declared its neutrality in Civil War but recognized rights of Confederacy as a belligerent.

1864 Union troops under Gen. William T. Sherman began series of battles at Resaca, GA, on their way to Atlanta.

1864 First soldier (a Confederate prisoner) buried in Arlington National Cemetery.

1883 George N. Papanicolaou, developer of pap smear test (1928), born in Comi, Greece; with Cornell U. Medical School (1937–49); his test ignored until 1940 (died 1962).

1889 Theodore Roosevelt appointed to Civil Service Commission by President Benjamin Harrison; reappointed by President Cleveland; served until 1895.

1893 Alvin A. ("Shipwreck") Kelly, flagpole sitter, born; spent 20,613 hours atop high perches, with record 1,177 hours on Atlantic City Steel Pier flagpole in 1930 (died 1952).

1908 White House Conservation Conference began at call of President Theodore Roosevelt; direct outgrowth was National Conservation Commission headed by Gifford Pinchot.

1908 Navy Nurses Corps created by Congress.

1914 Joe Louis, world heavyweight boxing champion (1937–49), born in Lexington, AL (died 1981).

1954 St. Lawrence Seaway Development Corp. established to develop, operate, and maintain the Seaway between Montreal and Lake Erie within the United States.

1984 Stanislaus M. Ulam, Polish-born mathematician who was a key figure in development of hydrogen, atomic bombs, died at 75; developed the Monte Carlo analysis, the use of random numbers to predict the result of chain reactions.

1985 Philadelphia police bombed a house containing members of a radical group (MOVE) after they refused to come out; the bomb touched off a fire which resulted in 11 deaths and destruction of 61 row houses.

1992 Three American astronauts went outside the space shuttle *Endeavor* and retrieved a wayward stranded communications satellite.

2003 California Secretary of State Kevin Shelley announced he would sponsor legislation to permit President George Bush's name to go on 2004 ballot in state; because of scheduled date for Republican National Convention he would not be the official candidate of the party in time to qualify for the California ballot.

2005 Latest round of proposed base closings listed 33 major facilities. Included were Naval Shipyard (Portsmouth, Maine) and Naval Submarine Base (New London, Connecticut); estimated savings ultimately $5.5 billion yearly.

2005 Stanford mathematics professor George B. Dantzig passed away at 90; remembered for three major scientific breakthroughs: linear programming, the Decomposition Principle, and the Simplex Algorithm.

2005 San Francisco Archbishop William Levada appointed to highest Vatican position ever held by an American, prefect of the Congregation for the Doctrine of the Faith; though conservative and acceptable to traditionalist Catholics, he had successfully run an archdiocese considered one of most liberal in nation.

14

1602 Exploration led by Bartholomew Gosnold landed at Cape Cod, which he named; attempt at settlement in area failed.

1634 Massachusetts Bay Company established representative form of government.

1737 Samuel H. Parsons, Revolutionary general, born in Lyme, CT; headed Connecticut divisions, fought at Long Island (died 1789).

1752 Timothy Dwight, president, Yale U. (1795–1817), born in Northampton, MA; chaplain to Army at West Point (1777–79) (died 1817).

1769 Land expedition led by Capt. Rivera y Moncada and Father Juan Crespi arrived at San Diego; second expedition under Gaspar de Portola and Father Junipero Serra arrived in July.

1785 John Adams named minister to England, serving until 1788.

1787 Constitutional Convention, scheduled to start in Philadelphia, unable to organize until May 25 because of late-arriving delegates.

1801 Pasha of Tripoli declared war on United States because of refusal to increase tribute payments; war lasted until June 4, 1805.

1804 Lewis and Clark Expedition set out from St. Louis on a two-year transcontinental exploration, which ended September 23, 1806.

1812 West Florida incorporated into Mississippi Territory by Congress.

1836 Treaty signed by Texas and Mexico, following the Texan victory at San Jacinto; captured Gen. Santa Anna pledged to secure Texas recognition but this was repudiated by Mexican government.

1843 Henry O. Walker, muralist (Library of Congress), born in Boston (died 1929).

1852 Louise C. Adams, widow of President John Quincy Adams, died in Washington at 77.

1852 Alton B. Parker, jurist, born in Cortland, NY; served New York state courts (1889–1904); Democratic presidential candidate (1904) (died 1926).

1863 Union troops under Gen. U.S. Grant captured Jackson, MS, enroute to Vicksburg.

1867 Jefferson Davis, former Confederate president, released on parole from Ft. Monroe, VA, after nearly two years imprisonment.

1880 Bertie C. Forbes, founder, editor, *Forbes Magazine*, born in New Deer, Scotland; author of several books on business, finance (died 1954).

1889 South Dakota voters adopted a state constitution.

1897 Sidney Bechet, all-time great soprano saxophonist, born in New Orleans (died 1959).

1898 Zutty (Arthur J.) Singleton, pioneered New Orleans style of jazz drumming, born in Bunker, LA; played with most great bands (1920–60) (died 1975).

1900 Supreme Court ruled that inheritance tax levied under War Revenue Act of 1898 was constitutional.

1913 Rockefeller Foundation chartered by New York legislature "to promote the well-being of mankind throughout the world."

1930 Carlsbad (NM) National Park established.

1942 Women's Army Auxiliary Corps (WAAC), later the Women's Army Corps (WAC), created; more than 65,000 women enlisted in about a year.

1948 President Truman announced that United States had accorded *de facto* recognition of Israel government; Israel's creation as an independent nation was proclaimed the same day.

1973 *Skylab*, the first American space station, was launched by a Saturn 5 rocket.

1975 President Ford ordered an all-out attack to recover American cargo vessel *Mayaguez* seized in Cambodia; operation successful but at cost of 15 Marine lives.

1990 Love Canal neighborhood in Niagara Falls, NY, was considered safe enough from chemical contamination to permit people to return to their homes.

15

1702 Queen Anne War began when England declared war on France.

1775 Continental Congress, meeting in Philadelphia, resolved to put colonies in state of defense against the British; recommended establishment of state governments.

1776 Virginia Convention instructed its delegates to offer a resolution to the Continental Congress for colonial independence.

1780 People of Kentucky and Illinois counties of Virginia petitioned Continental Congress to form them into separate states.

1788 James Gadsden, who made land purchase from Mexico, born in Charleston, SC; as minister to Mexico (1853–54) purchased 45,535 sq. mi. of land for $10 million, what is now southern Arizona and New Mexico (died 1858).

1796 David Austin, Congregational clergyman who predicted Second Coming for the day, told his Elizabeth, NJ, congregation after an all-day wait that "My Lord delayeth His coming."

1802 Isaac R. Trimble, Confederate general, born in Culpeper County, VA; served in Shenandoah Valley and at Gettysburg, where he was captured (died 1888).

1820 President Monroe signed Slave Trade Act, providing death penalty for those convicted of such trade, which was declared piracy.

1820 Congress granted new charter to Washington, DC, providing for popular election of its mayor.

1855 Louis Bamberger, founder of Bamberger department stores (1892), born in Baltimore; stores now part of Macy's; founded Station WOR, New York City (1922) and Institute for Advanced Study, Princeton U. (1933) (died 1944).

1856 Lyman F. Baum, author of children's stories (*The Wizard of Oz*), born in Chittenango, NY (died 1919).

1860 Ellen L. Axson Wilson, first wife of President Wilson, born in Savannah, GA (died 1914).

1862 Department of Agriculture created by Congress, headed by a commissioner; elevated to Secretary and a Cabinet member February 9, 1888.

1862 The *Alabama*, a British-built Confederate warship, launched in Liverpool; sank, captured, or burned more than 60 Union vessels.

1864 Union troops under Franz Sigel were turned back at New Market, VA, by Confederate force under J.D. Breckenridge; battle featured a gallant charge by four companies of cadets from Virginia Military Institute.

1864 Gen. William T. Sherman led Union troops to victory at Resaca, GA, then went on to Rome, GA, a Confederate supply center.

1869 National Woman Suffrage Association formed by Lucy Blackwell Stone.

1870 Henry L. Doherty, organized, headed, Cities Service Co. (1910–39), born in Columbus, OH (died 1939).

1887 John H. Hoover, World War I naval officer, born in Seville, OH; headed Caribbean command (1942) (died 1970).

1890 Katherine Anne Porter, novelist (*Flowering Judas*; *Pale Horse, Pale Rider*; *The Leaning Tower*), born near San Antonio, TX (died 1980).

1902 Richard J. Daley, mayor of Chicago (1955–76), born in Chicago; Democratic political leader (died 1976).

1904 Clifton Fadiman, literary critic (*The New Yorker* 1933–43), born in New York City; master of ceremonies, *Information Please* radio show (1933–48).

1905 Robert S. Abbott published the first issue of the *Chicago Defender*, which soon became the leading Negro newspaper.

1911 Supreme Court upheld decree of Circuit Court against Standard Oil Co. of New Jersey, which was declared a monopoly and a combination in restraint of trade; ordered its dissolution.

1915 Paul A. Samuelson, economist, born in Gary, IN; awarded 1970 Nobel Economics Prize for efforts to raise scientific analysis in economic theory; author (*Foundations of Economic Analysis*).

1918 Airmail service between Washington and New York City began.

1918 Eddy Arnold, country music singer, born in Henderson, TX.

1928 Flood Control Act signed, appropriated $325 million for ten-year flood control program in Mississippi Valley.

1929 Poisonous fumes from burning X-ray films killed 125 persons in Crile Hospital Clinic in Cleveland.

1933 Ruth Bader Ginsburg, associate justice, Supreme Court (1993–), born in New York City; served as a Circuit Court judge (1980–93).

1937 Madeleine K. Albright, first woman Secretary of State (1997–), born in Prague, Czechoslovakia; American ambassador to United Nations (1993–97).

1942 Gas rationing began in 17 Eastern states.

1966 More than 10,000 antiwar protestors demonstrated against Vietnam War at the White House.

1969 Associate Justice Abe Fortas resigned from Supreme Court amid criticism for accepting a fee from Louis E. Wolfson, who was jailed for stock manipulation.

1970 Two women generals, the first in American history, were named by President Nixon.

1972 Gov. George C. Wallace of Alabama was shot at a political rally in Laurel, MD; he was paralyzed from the waist down, ending his bid for the Democratic presidential nomination; Arthur H. Bremmer, 21, was sentenced to 63 years imprisonment August 4 for the shooting.

1972 Island of Okinawa was returned to Japan.

1980 Maxie Anderson and his son, Kris, completed first nonstop trip across North America in a 75-ft. high helium-filled balloon; trip took four days.

1988 Twenty-seven persons were killed in a head-on collision between a pickup truck and a church bus returning from an outing near Carrollton, KY.

1995 Dow Corning Corp. filed for bankruptcy protection, claiming to be overwhelmed by hundreds of thousands of lawsuits filed against it by women who used silicone breast implants; $4.25 billion had been set aside by the industry to handle claims.

2000 Supreme Court decided 5–4 that rape, domestic brutality, and similar evils are properly matters to be prosecuted under state rather than federal law.

2001 Federal Reserve adopted fifth interest rate cut of the year to spur weakening economy: ½ point.

16

1631 Fur trading post established by William Clayborne on Kent Island in the Chesapeake Bay (near Annapolis).

1769 Virginia House of Burgesses passed set of resolutions unanimously asserting that the right of taxation of Virginians lay with the governor and provincial legislature, that the colony had the right to petition the Crown for redress of grievances, and that Virginians must be tried in Virginia.

1780 Loammi Baldwin, considered father of American civil engineering, born in Woburn, MA; his work included the 79-mile Union Canal, Charleston, MA; Norfolk (VA) Navy drydocks (died 1838).

1797 President John Adams sent first war message to Congress; did not ask for declaration of war against France but recommended military preparations.

1801 William H. Seward, Secretary of State (1861–69) best remembered for purchase of Alaska from Russia ("Seward's Folly"), born in Florida, NY; served New York as governor and represented it in Senate (1849–61) (died 1872).

1804 Elizabeth P. Peabody, educator who opened first American kindergarten in Boston (1860), born in Billerica, MA (died 1894).

1812 American frigate *President* defeated British sloop off Sandy Hook.

1824 Levi P. Morton, Vice President (1889–93), born in Shoreham, VT; represented New York in House (1879–81) and served it as governor (1895–96); minister to France (1881–85) (died 1920).

1824 Edmund Kirby-Smith, Confederate general, born in St. Augustine, FL; headed Trans-Mississippi forces; last Confederate leader to surrender (June 2, 1865) (died 1893).

1827 Norman J. Colman, first Secretary of Agriculture (1889), born near Richfield Springs, NY; editor, *Colman's Rural World* (1865–1911); commissioner of agriculture (1885–89) (died 1911).

1831 David E. Hughes, inventor of microphone, born in London; also invented induction balance, electromagnet; developed improved printing telegraph (died 1900).

1832 Philip D. Armour, meat packer who headed Armour & Co. (1875–1901), born in Stockbridge, NY; responsible for utilizing waste products, introduction of refrigeration, preparation of canned meats; founder (1893), Armour Institute of Technology (died 1901).

1859 Cyrus Hall McCormick, first president, International Harvester Co. (1902–19), board chairman (1919–35), born in Washington, DC (died 1936).

1861 Irving W. Colburn, inventor of process for fabricating continuous sheets of flat glass, born in Fitchburg, MA (died 1917).

1868 Senate, sitting on the impeachment of President Andrew Johnson, voted 35–19 on Article XI, the first impeachment article to be considered; vote was one short of necessary two-thirds; article dealt with the president's removal of Secretary Stanton, veto of reconstruction acts.

1874 Ashfield Reservoir dam above Williamsburg, MA, collapsed, inundating the Mill River Valley; more than 100 persons died.

1882 Ogden M. Reid, editor and publisher, *New York Tribune* (1913–47), born in New York City; added the *New York Herald* (1924) (died 1947).

1886 Douglas Southall Freeman, editor and historian, born in Lynchburg, VA; editor, *Richmond News Leader* (1915–49); author (*R.E. Lee, Lee's Lieutenants, George Washington*) (died 1953).

1886 Peter L. Jensen, whose pioneering work made fidelity communications possible, born in Stubbekobing, Denmark (died 1961).

1892 Manton S. Eddy, World War II general, born in Chicago (died 1962).

1902 Jan W. Kiepura, operatic tenor known as the "Polish Caruso," born in Sosnowiec, Poland (died 1966).

1905 Henry Fonda, stage and screen star (*Grapes of Wrath, Mr. Roberts, On Golden Pond*), born in Grand Island, NE (died 1982).

1910 Bureau of Mines established, effective July 1.

1911 Margaret Sullavan, screen actress (*Dinner at Eight, Stage Door*), born in Norfolk, VA (died 1960).

1912 Studs L. Terkel, author of many books based on tape-recorded interviews, born in New York City; works include *Hard Times*; *Working*; *Division Street*; *America*.

1913 Woody (Woodrow) Herman, saxophone player and orchestra leader (from 1936), born in Milwaukee (died 1987).

1918 Espionage Act passed by Congress strengthening June 1917 Act; drastically enforced by Attorney General Alexander M. Palmer; freedom of speech and press disappeared temporarily.

1919 Liberace (Wladzin Valentino), pianist and orchestra leader, born in West Allis, WI; noted for flamboyant dress, candelabra on piano (died 1987).

1920 Former Vice President Levi Morton (1889–93) died in Rhinebeck, NY, on his 96th birthday.

1929 First Oscars presented by the American Academy of Motion Picture Arts and Sciences in Hollywood.

1938 Fire in the Terminal Hotel in Atlanta resulted in 35 deaths.

1957 Joan Benoit (Samuelson), America's foremost female distance runner, born in Cape Elizabeth, ME; won first women's marathon in 1984 Olympics and other major races.

1971 Cost of first class postage increased to eight cents.

1988 Supreme Court ruled 6–2 that police without warrants may search garbage bags and other refuse containers that people leave outside their homes.

1997 President Clinton in White House ceremony apologized for the "Tuskegee Study of Untreated Syphilis in the Negro Male" conducted between 1932 and 1972 by the Public Health Service.

2005 By 5–4 vote U.S. Supreme Court opened wine market to out-of-state wineries; wherever in-state wineries have right to send by mail, out-of-state ones now have the right as well; illegal to discriminate against outsiders.

17

1733 British Parliament enacted Molasses Act, placing heavy duties on importation of rum and molasses from the French West Indies to the colonies; effect never felt because law was not enforced.

1741 John Penn, colonial leader, born in Caroline County, VA; member of Continental Congress (1775–80), a signer of Declaration of Independence (died 1788).

1760 John Greenwood, pioneer dentist, born in Boston; reputed inventor of foot-power drill, springs to hold artificial plates in place, use of porcelain for artificial teeth (died 1819).

1792 New York Stock Exchange organized at Merchants Coffee house.

1837 *Baltimore Sun* founded by Arunah S. Abell.

1846 Mexican troops evacuated Matamoras on the Rio Grande; the Mexican city then became American headquarters.

1849 Fire in St. Louis destroyed 400 buildings and 27 ships; serious cholera epidemic followed.

1864 Harry Chandler, publisher, *Los Angeles Times* (1885–1942), born in Landaff, NH; developed paper to million-plus circulation (died 1944).

1875 Joel E. Spingarn, publisher and civil rights leader, born in New York City; a founder, Harcourt, Brace & Co. (1919); a founder, National Association for the Advancement of Colored People (NAACP), president (1930–39) (died 1939).

1875 First Kentucky Derby held at Churchill Downs in Louisville with *Aristides* the winner, Oliver Lewis was the jockey.

1877 Former President Grant sailed from Philadelphia on a round-the-world trip.

1884 Territory of Alaska created; while really a district, it was run as a territory, which it became August 24, 1912; laws of Oregon were extended to Alaska.

1912 Archibald Cox, original special prosecutor in Watergate investigation, born in Plainfield, NJ; fired as prosecutor by President Nixon October 20, 1973; Solicitor General (1961–65).

1914 Stewart Alsop, syndicated newspaper columnist, born in Avon, CT (died 1974).

1923 Fire in a Camden, SC, school killed 76.

1928 Congress established an airmail rate of five cents per ounce.

1946 Government seized the railroads to avert a strike; threat ended May 25.

1954 Supreme Court handed down the historic *Brown v. Board of Education* decision, unanimously ruling that racial segregation in public schools is unconstitutional because it violates the 14th Amendment guaranteeing equal protection of the laws.

1973 Senate Watergate Committee began nationally-televised hearings.

1982 President Reagan formally proposed a constitutional amendment permitting organized prayer in public schools.

1982 Supreme Court ruled 6–3 that a law barring sex discrimination in federally-aided education applies to employees as well as students.

1987 Memorial service held in Mayport, FL, the home port of the guided-missile frigate *Stark*, which was hit by an Iraqi missile in Persian Gulf, killing 37 American sailors.

2000 Two suspects arrested on murder charges stemming from 1963 Birmingham, AL, church bombing and resulting four deaths.

2001 Average fuel mileage for new vehicles in U.S. declined to 21-year low of 24.5 mpg.

2004 First government-recognized homosexual marriages occur in Massachusetts.

2004 Tony Randall (b. 1920) died; broke into radio in 1940s playing Reggie on the series *I Love a Mystery*; personified the fussy house-perfect Felix Unger in the television series *Odd Couple*.

18

1631 General Court of Massachusetts decreed that "no man shall be admitted to the body politic but such as are members of some of the churches within the limits" of the Colony.

1653 Rhode Island enacted the first law against slavery.

1769 Virginia House of Burgesses, dissolved by Governor Botetourt, met informally in the Raleigh Tavern, adopted the Virginia Association, a non-importation agreement which was widely copied.

1815 James B. Francis, hydraulic engineer who invented widely-used water turbine, born in Southleigh, England (died 1893).

1834 Sheldon Jackson, missionary who was first superintendent of public instruction in Alaska, born in Minaville, NY; responsible for creating many Alaska schools (died 1909).

1842 Dorr Rebellion began in Rhode Island when supporters of Thomas W. Dorr made an unsuccessful attempt to seize a state arsenal; Dorr and his followers had set up their own government in northwestern Rhode Island; Dorr was tried, sentenced to life imprisonment (1844); released a year later.

1846 American troops under Gen. Zachary Taylor occupied Matamoras.

1862 Josephus Daniels, journalist and diplomat, born in Washington, NC; editor, *Raleigh News and Observer* (1894–1933); Secretary of Navy (1913–21); ambassador to Mexico (1933–41) (died 1948).

1873 Sime Silverman, editor of *Variety* (1905–33), born in Cortland, NY (died 1933).

1881 Josiah Henson, Methodist clergyman who was born a slave, died at 92; reputedly the prototype of Uncle Tom in Harriet Beecher Stowe's book.

1883 Walter A. Gropius, architect/educator, born in Berlin; founder, director, Bauhaus School of Architecture in Weimar, Germany; professor, chairman, Harvard Graduate School of Design (1938–52) (died 1969).

1889 Thomas Midgely, chemist who discovered anti-knock properties of tetraethyl lead (1922), born in Beaver Falls, PA; vice president, Ethyl Gasoline Corp. (1923–44) (died 1944).

1891 Arthur J. Altmeyer, public official, born in DePere, WI; chairman, Social Security Board (1937–46), director, Social Security Administration (1946–53) (died 1972).

1892 Ezio Pinza, operatic basso and actor, born in Rome; had outstanding 22-year career in opera; starred in musicals (*South Pacific, Fanny*) (died 1957).

1897 Frank Capra, movie director (*It Happened One Night, Mr. Deeds Goes to Town, You Can't Take It with You, Lost Horizon*), born in Palermo, Sicily (died 1991).

1901 Vincent Du Vigneaud, biochemist, born in Chicago; awarded 1955 Nobel Chemistry Prize for work on pituitary hormones (died 1976).

1902 Tornado killed 114 persons and injured 250 in Goliad, TX.

1902 Meredith Willson, musicals composer (*The Music Man, The Unsinkable Molly Brown*), born in Mason City, IA (died 1984).

1904 Jacob K. Javits, legislator, born in New York City; served New York as Attorney General (1954–56) and in House (1947–52) and Senate (1957–80) (died 1986).

1906 Forest fires in two days devastated 200 square miles in northern Michigan, destroyed eight towns and villages; after being extinguished, fires started again and destroyed another 200 square miles.

1908 The motto, "In God We Trust," was restored to American coins.

1912 Perry Como, popular singer and entertainer, born in Canonsburg, PA.

1917 President Wilson signed Selective Service Act, calling for registration of 21- to 30-year-old men.

1917 President Wilson issued an executive order sending one division to France, which landed at St. Nazaire June 26.

1918 Explosion in an Oakdale, PA, chemical plant resulted in 193 deaths.

1927 An explosion in Bath School in Lansing, MI, killed 38.

1933 Tennessee Valley Authority created, undertaking a broad program of economic and social reconstruction; Arthur E. Morgan, Antioch College president, was chairman.

1936 Supreme Court held the Bituminous Coal Conservation Act of 1935 unconstitutional.

1943 United Nations Conference on Food and Agriculture began in Hot Springs, VA; resulted in formation of UN Food & Agriculture Organization.

1944 Allied forces captured Cassino, Italy.

1946 Reggie Jackson, baseball player best remembered for hitting three consecutive home runs in a World Series game (1978), born in Wyncote, PA; homers for New York Yankees were on consecutive pitches; named to Baseball Hall of Fame.

1980 Mt. St. Helens, volcano in southwest Washington, erupted violently after being dormant for 123 years; resulted in 26 deaths and 46 missing; erupted periodically after that but less violently.

1987 Supreme Court unanimously ruled that Jews, Arabs, and others who suffer discrimination based on their "ancestry" are protected under statutes barring racial discrimination; also ruled that military employees killed or injured while on duty as a result of a civilian employee's negligence may not sue the government.

2000 General Assembly of Georgia voted to remove Confederate flag from dome of capitol and fly it elsewhere on grounds.

2004 Long-lasting collision between White House and Senate Democrats over judicial nominees yielded to a compromise: 25 of 32 to be approved; president to avoid "recess appointments" of such individuals when Congress not in session.

19

1643 Delegates from Plymouth, Connecticut, New Haven, and Massachusetts Bay colonies met in Boston, created the New England Confederation, which lasted until 1684; Rhode Island was excluded.

1749 Ohio Company, formed by group of Virginia planters, acquired 500,000 acres south of and along the Ohio River for fur trading and settlement.

1774 About 1,000 persons erected a pole 45 feet high in Farmington, CT, "consecrated to the shrine of liberty," and a copy of the Boston Port Act was burned.

1777 Button Gwinnett, 42-year-old colonial leader, died of wounds suffered in a duel; represented Georgia in Continental Congress (1776–77) and a signer of Declaration of Independence.

1795 Johns Hopkins, financier who endowed university and hospital bearing his name, born in Anne Arundel County, MD (died 1873).

1796 Congress passed first national game law.

1813 Tompkins H. Matteson, historical painter (*Spirit of '76, First Sabbath of the Pilgrims, Washington's Inaugural*), born in Peterboro, NY (died 1884).

1828 President John Quincy Adams signed protective tariff act considered unjust in South, called the "tariff of abominations."

1828 William Henry Harrison appointed first minister to Colombia by President John Quincy Adams; recalled (1829) by President Jackson.

1857 John J. Abel, pharmacologist who isolated insulin in crystalline form and adrenalin, born in Cleveland (died 1938).

1863 Two unsuccessful assaults begun at Vicksburg by Union troops under Gen. U.S. Grant; Union force then settled down for a siege.

1864 Carl E. Akeley, naturalist and sculptor, born in Clarendon, NY; led expeditions for Field Museum and American Museum of Natural History; developed large habitat animal groups, new taxidermy methods; invented naturalist's motion picture camera, cement gun for sculpting (died 1926).

1877 Tom M. Girdler, a founder (1929), chief executive, Republic Steel (1930–56), born in Clark County, IN; president, Jones & Laughlin Steel (1928–30) (died 1965).

1886 Manley O. Hudson, international lawyer, born in St. Peters, MO; with Harvard U. Law School (1923–54); member, Permanent Court of Arbitration (1933–45), Permanent Court of International Justice (1936–45) (died 1960).

1888 William H. Simpson, commanding general, Ninth Army (1944–46), born in Weathersford, TX (died 1980).

1898 Alan F. Guttmacher, physician called the father of American birth control, born in Baltimore (died 1974).

1902 An accident in a bituminous coal mine at Coal Creek, TN, claimed 184 lives.

1917 Herbert Hoover appointed food controller by President Wilson; became food administrator August 10 when the food and fuel control legislation was signed.

1921 President Harding signed first immigration quota act, restricting immigration to a maximum three percent of any nationality in a year.

1924 Soldiers bonus enacted over President Coolidge's veto; original bonus was a 20-year endowment policy against which veterans could borrow; cash bonus payments authorized in 1936, based on $1.25 per day of overseas service, $1 for American service.

1925 Malcolm X, first "national minister" of Black Muslins, born in Omaha as Malcolm Little; suspended (1964), formed own sect (Organization of Afro-American Unity); assassinated 1965.

1928 Mine disaster at Mather, PA, killed 195 persons.

1934 James Lehrer, television news reporter (*MacNeill-Lehrer Report*), born in Wichita, KS.

1935 David Hartman, entertainer (*Good Morning America* 1975–87), born in Pawtucket, RI.

1940 Frank (Francisco A.) Lorenzo, head of Texas Airlines, born in New York City; he later acquired Continental, Eastern, and Peoples airlines.

1950 Munitions barges in South Amboy, NJ, exploded; 30 persons were killed.

1986 President Reagan signed Firearms Owner Protection Act, loosening firearms curbs of 1968 Gun Control Act.

1988 Carlo Lehder Rivas, reputed Colombian leader of a huge drug ring, was convicted by a jury in Jacksonville, FL.

1994 Jacqueline Kennedy Onassis, widow of President Kennedy, died at 64.

2004 Trial began of first U.S. GI accused of refusing Iraq duty and desertion during combat tour; convicted on May 21 and sentenced to one-year imprisonment.

20

1663 William Bradford, pioneer printer, born in Barnwell, England; helped found first American paper mill (1690); crown printer (1693–1742); official printer of New Jersey (1703–33); printed first American legislative proceedings, first New York paper money (1709), first American Book of Common Prayer, first newspaper in New York (Gazette 1725) (died 1752).

1690 Portland, ME (then called Casco), destroyed by French and Indians.

1691 James Blair was sent to England to obtain charter for the College of William & Mary in Charlottesville; became first president (1693–1743).

1750 Stephen Girard, banker, born in Bordeaux, France; founded bank in Philadelphia (1812), which took over business of Bank of the United States; created the Second Bank of the United States (1816); bequeathed funds to found Girard College for "poor, white, male orphans" (died 1831).

1759 William Thornton, designed the Capitol (with some modifications), born in the Virgin Islands; also designed Octagon House in Washington (died 1828).

1768 Dolley (Dorothea) Todd Madison, wife of President Madison, born in what is now Guilford County, NC; a legendary Washington hostess (died 1849).

1774 British Parliament passed Massachusetts Government Act to take "the executive power from the hands of the democratic part of government; town meetings to be held only with permission of government"; also passed Administration of Justice Act which made it possible to move trials to England.

1808 Thomas D. Rice, pioneer minstrel showman, born in New York City (died 1860).

1818 William G. Fargo, express company leader, born in Pompey, NY; helped form two companies which later became American Express Co., president (1868–81); organized Wells Fargo (1852), president (1870–72) (died 1881).

1825 Antoinette L.B. Blackwell, first ordained woman minister (Congregational), born in Henrietta, NY; active worker for abolition, temperance, woman's rights (died 1921).

1826 Potter Palmer, merchandising pioneer, born in Albany; with two partners opened Chicago dry goods store which revolutionized merchandising and later became Marshall Field & Co. (1881); built the Palmer House (died 1902).

1843 Albert A. Pope, founder of American bicycle industry, born in Boston; began producing automobiles (1890) (died 1909).

1851 Emile Berliner, inventor of many items including a microphone, gramophone, born in Hanover, Germany; also invented acoustic tile, a rotating cylinder internal combustion engine, a flat "platter" phonograph record (died 1929).

1861 Confederacy voted to move its capital from Montgomery, AL, to Richmond, VA; move made in June.

1861 North Carolina seceded from Union, but convention would not submit question for popular ratification.

1862 Homestead Act went into effect, providing settlers farms of 160 acres of surveyed public land after five years of continuous residence and payment of $26–$34 fee, or $1.25 an acre, after six months' residence.

1883 Edwin G. Nourse, first chairman, Council of Economic Advisors (1946–49), born in Lockport, NY (died 1974).

1890 Allan Nevins, biographer/historian (*Ordeal of the Union*), born in Camp Point, IL; with Columbia U. (1928–58) (died 1971).

1891 Earl R. Browder, Communist leader, born in Wichita, KS; secretary-general, American Communist Party (1930–45), expelled as a "right deviationist" (died 1973).

1899 John M. Harlan, associate justice, Supreme Court (1955–71), born in Chicago (died 1971).

1908 James Stewart, screen actor (*The Philadelphia Story, Harvey, Mr. Smith Goes to Washington*), born in Indiana, PA (died 1997).

1914 Representatives of Argentina, Brazil, and Chile began month-long unsuccessful meeting to resolve American-Mexican differences.

1926 President Coolidge signed Air Commerce Act, placing civil aviation under control of the Commerce Department.

1927 Charles A. Lindbergh began successful nonstop solo flight across Atlantic Ocean from New York to Paris; took 33 hours, 39 minutes in his plane, *Spirit of St. Louis.*

1932 Amelia Earhart became first woman to fly solo across Atlantic from Newfoundland to Ireland in approximately 15 hours.

1939 Transatlantic airmail service from New York began.

1941 Office of Civilian Defense created by executive order; terminated June 30, 1945.

1985 FBI arrested John A. Walker, Jr., retired Navy warrant officer, for passing secrets to Russia; two other family members and a friend also were arrested.

1988 A woman opened gunfire at a school in Winnetka, IL, killing an eight-year-old pupil, wounding four others; police later found her dead in a nearby house, apparently a suicide.

1993 President Clinton signed the "motor-voter" bill allowing citizens to register to vote when applying for a driver's license or at other government offices.

1996 Supreme Court by 6–3 vote struck down a Colorado state constitutional amendment that excluded homosexuals from civil rights protections.

1996 President Clinton announced he would authorize renewal of most-favored nation trade status for China; action provides lower export tariffs on trade to United States.

2002 In rejection of May 14 plea of former President Jimmy Carter to remove Cuban trade embargo, President Bush reaffirmed it would continue; internal democratic reforms must occur in Cuba first before any change.

2002 Stephen Jay Gould, prominent paleontologist and popularizer of evolutionary theory, died of cancer; best-known for his attacks on creationism and, within the evolutionary scientific community, for his advocacy of the controversial scenario of punctuated equilibrium (rapid evolutionary leaps forward separated by lengthy eras in which minimal or no change occurs).

2005 First "All Atheist Weekend" conference held in San Francisco in effort to attempt to unify atheist movements and encourage them to become political activists in behalf of their cause.

2006 In unprecedented action, FBI raided Congressman William Jefferson's office in Washington, DC investigation of alleged bribe taking.

21

1542 Hernando de Soto died after a voyage from Oklahoma down the Arkansas River to its mouth.

1690 John Eliot, English missionary known as the apostle of the Indians, died at 86; he published an Indian language catechism (1653), the Bible (1661–63), the first Bible published in North America.

1755 Alfred Moore, associate justice of Supreme Court (1799–1804), born in New Hanover County, NC (died 1810).

1796 Reverdy Johnson, public official and diplomat, born in Annapolis; defense attorney in Dred Scott case; represented Maryland in Senate (1845–49, 1863–68); Attorney General (1849–50); minister to Great Britain (1868–69) (died 1876).

1798 Benjamin Stoddert became first Secretary of the Navy.

1832 First national nominating convention of Democratic Party opened in Baltimore; unanimously endorsed President Jackson for second term.

1855 Massachusetts enacted stringent personal liberty act, which virtually nullified Fugitive Slave Act; arose from the capture and return of a slave in 1854.

1855 Edmund J. James, educator, born in Jacksonville, IL; president, Northwestern U. (1902–04), U. of Illinois (1904–20); founder, first president, American Academy of Political and Social Science (1890–1901) (died 1925).

1856 Civil war broke out in Kansas between pro- and anti-slavery forces; Lawrence was sacked by pro-slavery group, which was answered three days later by massacre at Pottawatomie, led by John Brown; temporary peace reached September 15.

1862 Edwin P. Christy, originator of Christy Minstrels (1842), died at 47; originally called the Virginia Minstrels.

1862 Congress passed legislation providing for education of black children in Washington.

1867 Frances Densmore, foremost authority on American Indian songs, born in Red Wing, MN (died 1957).

1868 John L. Hines, World War I Army officer, born in White Sulphur Springs, WV; served in France and Philippines; Army chief of staff (1924); commander, Philippines Department (1930–32) (died 1968).

1872 Richard Bennett, actor/producer (*Charley's Aunt, The Royal Family, The Barker*), born in Cass County, IN (died 1944).

1874 Nellie Grant, daughter of President and Mrs. Grant, married in White House to Algernon C.F. Sartoris of British legation.

1878 Glenn H. Curtiss, aviation pioneer, born in Hammondsport, NY; invented aileron; won trophy for first one-mile public airplane flight in America (1908); won $10,000 prize for Albany-New York flight in two hours 51 minutes (1910); developed hydroplane; supplied planes to Allies in World War I; developed Navy flying boat, which made first Atlantic crossing (1919) (died 1930).

1881 American Red Cross originated with Clara Barton as president.

1898 Armand Hammer, head of Occidental Petroleum (1957–90), born in New York City; noted art collector; instrumental in US-USSR trade negotiations (died 1990).

1901 Horace Heidt, bandleader of 1930/40s, born in Alameda, CA (died 1986).

1902 Marcel Breuer, architect and pioneer furniture designer, born in Pecs, Hungary; designed, HUD, Health and Human Services buildings in Washington, Whitney Museum in New York City, UNESCO Headquarters in Paris (died 1981).

1904 Fats (Thomas) Waller, pianist and orchestra leader, born in New York City; composer ("Honeysuckle Rose," "Ain't Misbehavin'") (died 1943).

1916 Harold Robbins, author (*The Dream Merchants, The Carpetbaggers, The Betsy*), born in New York City (died 1997).

1917 About 2,000 buildings in Atlanta burned, with damage estimated at $5 million.

1917 Raymond Burr, television actor (*Perry Mason*), born in New Westminster, British Columbia (died 1993).

1941 American merchant vessel *Robin Moor* sunk by a German submarine without warning in the South Atlantic.

1944 Janet Dailey, popular author, born in Storm Lake, IA.

1968 Nuclear submarine *Scorpion* lost near the Azores, with 99 aboard.

1969 President Nixon nominated Warren E. Burger as chief justice of the Supreme Court; confirmed June 23.

1980 President Carter ordered evacuation of 710 families from the Love Canal area in Niagara Falls, NY, a former dump for toxic chemical waste.

1998 In Springfield, OR, a 15-year-old high school student allegedly shot his parents, then went to school and fired in cafeteria killing two students, wounding 22.

2001 In dispute over responsibility for tire failures on Ford Explorers, Firestone stopped all sales to the company.

2006 Katherine Dunham died at 96; pioneer African American choreographer of modern dance; in 1931 formed first black American modern dance company in nation.

22

1620 Louis de Frontenac, colonial official, born in St. Germain, France; governor, of New France (Canada) (1672–82, 1689–98) (died 1698).

1786 Arthur Tappan, founder of *New York Journal of Commerce* (1827), born in Northampton, MA; helped found American Missionary Association; made numerous endowments to religious organizations (died 1865).

1802 Martha Washington, widow of President Washington, died at 70 at Mt. Vernon.

1807 Trial of Aaron Burr on conspiracy charges began in Richmond, VA; acquitted October 20.

1826 Christopher C. Langdell, introduced case system of law teaching, born in New Boston, NH; dean, Harvard Law School (1870–95) (died 1906).

1843 A thousand Easterners left from Independence, MO, to settle in the Oregon territory marking the beginning of large westward migration.

1844 Mary Cassatt, impressionist artist, born in Allegheny City, PA; excelled in domestic scenes (died 1926).

1848 Democratic National Committee formed in Baltimore.

1849 Abraham Lincoln obtained patent on inflated cylinders "for buoying vessels over shoals"; never put to practical use.

1854 Congress passed Kansas-Nebraska Act, permitting states an option on slavery and nullifying the Missouri Compromise.

1856 Senator Charles Sumner of Massachusetts was physically assaulted in Senate chamber by Rep. Preston S. Brooks of South Carolina for a critical speech about his uncle, Sen. Andrew P. Butler of South Carolina; Sumner never fully recovered; House censure of Brooks failed but he resigned July 14.

1872 Amnesty Act was passed, restoring civil rights to Southern citizens, except for 500 Confederate leaders.

1891 Robert G. Sproul, president, U. of California (1930–58), born in San Francisco; (died 1975).

1902 Crater Lake (OR) National Park established.

1914 Vance O. Packard, author (*The Hidden Persuaders, The Waste Makers, The Pyramid Climbers*), born in Granville Summit, PA (died 1996).

1915 George Baker, cartoonist (*Sad Sack* in World War II), born in Lowell, MA (died 1975).

1920 Civil Service Retirement Act passed by Congress, with compulsory retirement at 70 and an annuity after 15 years service.

1927 George A. Olah, awarded 1994 Nobel Chemistry Prize, born in Budapest.

1928 T. Boone Pickens, financier known as a corporate raider, born in Holdenville, OK.

1943 Helen H. Taft, widow of President Taft, died in Washington at 82.

1946 Government seized soft coal mines; a wage increase was granted a week later on government orders.

1953 President Eisenhower signed Submerged Lands Act, which gave the federal government rights to offshore lands of the seaboard states.

1971 Lyndon Baines Johnson Library at U. of Texas dedicated by the former president.

1972 President Nixon arrived in Moscow for week of summit talks, the first visit by an American president; resulted in strategic arms pact.

1987 Saragosa, TX, a town of 350 persons, was completely wiped out by a tornado, killing 30 residents and injuring 121.

1998 Both houses of Congress approved a $216 billion transportation bill, with $173 billion for highways, $41 billion for mass transit.

2000 The Supreme Court decided by 5–4 that cable companies need not restrict sexually explicit programming to very late hours at night.

2002 71-year-old Bobby F. Cherry convicted of 1963 Birmingham, AL, church bombing; it killed four girls, provoking national outrage and major regional embarrassment at the target and its youthful victims.

2004 Hallam, Nebraska: F4 strength tornado, registered just under 2½ miles wide; believed to be nearly the widest physically feasible.

23

1609 New charter granted to Virginia settlement making the Jamestown colony independent of the Plymouth Company; grant extended 200 miles north and south of Point Comfort and "from sea to sea."

1740 John Gibson, colonial leader, born in Lancaster, PA; colonel in Continental Army, commander, Ft. Pitt (1781–82); secretary of Indiana Territory (1800–16) (died 1822).

1788 South Carolina legislature ratified Constitution by vote of 149–73, becoming the eighth state in the Union.

1788 Lewis Tappan, founder of first credit rating agency (1841), born in Northampton, MA; his agency later became Dun & Bradstreet (died 1873).

1810 Margaret Fuller, often called first American woman professional journalist and first foreign correspondent, born in Cambridgeport, MA (died 1850).

1811 First Alabama newspaper, *Mobile Centinel*, founded outside Mobile (Ft. Stoddert) by Samuel Miller and John B. Hood.

1820 James B. Eads, bridge builder and engineer who invented the diving bell, born in Lawrenceburg, IN; built fleet of armor-plated gunboats to control Mississippi River (1861), built bridge over Mississippi River at St. Louis (1867–74); designed deep water channel for Mississippi delta (died 1887).

1824 Ambrose E. Burnside, Union general who commanded Army of Potomac (1862–63), born in Liberty, IN; served Rhode Island as governor (1866–69) and in Senate (1875–81); gave name to "sideburns" which he wore (died 1881).

1830 Henry M. Teller, first Senator from Colorado (1876–82, 1885–1909), born in Granger, NY; Secretary of Interior (1882–85) (died 1914).

1840 John F. Appleby, inventor of binder for grain reapers, born in Westmoreland, NY; also invented automatic feed device for rifles (1864) (died 1917).

1861 Virginia voters approved 96,750 to 32,134 for secession from the Union.

1862 Gen. Stonewall Jackson with 18,000 men took Front Royal, VA, at start of the Shenandoah Valley campaign; took Winchester two days later.

1875 Alfred P. Sloan, with General Motors as president (1923–37), board chairman (1937–56), born in New Haven, CT (died 1966).

1883 Douglas Fairbanks, silent screen star (*The Three Musketeers, Robin Hood, The Thief of Bagdad*), born in Denver (died 1939).

1903 First automobile trip across the United States began in San Francisco; ended August 1 in New York City.

1903 Wisconsin set up first direct primary election voting system.

1908 Max Abramowitz, architect, born in Chicago; designed U.S. Embassy in Rio de Janeiro, Columbia U. Law School, and Lincoln Center Philharmonic Hall.

1908 John Bardeen, physicist who won two Nobel Physics Prizes, born in Madison, WI; shared 1956 prize for discovery of transistor and the 1972 prize for developing theory of superconductivity (died 1991).

1910 Artie Shaw, clarinetist and orchestra leader (from 1936), born in New York City.

1911 New York Public Library dedicated by President Taft.

1920 Helen O'Connell, vocalist with Jimmy Dorsey band, born in Lima, OH (died 1993).

1922 *Abie's Irish Rose*, a three-act comedy, opened in Fulton Theater, New York City; ran for 2,327 performances, then a record.

1925 Joshua Lederberg, microbiologist, born in Montclair, NJ; shared 1958 Nobel Physiology/Medicine Prize for work with genetic mechanisms.

1934 Clyde Barrow, public enemy #1 in Southwest, and his partner, Bonnie Parker, were shot to death by Texas Rangers and sheriff's deputies after a two-year robbery spree during which they killed 12 persons.

1935 Donald P. Hodel, cabinet member, born in Portland, OR; Energy Secretary (1982–85), Interior Secretary (1985–89).

1939 U.S. submarine *Squalus* sank off Portsmouth, NH; 33 of 59 aboard were rescued through diving bell.

2000 Largest airline in the world (United) announced $4.3 billion deal to purchase U.S. Airways, largest regional carrier in American Northeast.

2003 "Dewey" is born in Texas, the first deer to be successfully cloned by researchers.

24

1607 Three vessels of the London Company arrived at Jamestown, VA, 32 miles from the mouth of the James River; the 105 settlers were led by Capt. John Smith; during first seven months, famine and disease reduced colony to 32, but it was saved by the arrival of supply ships and firmer administration.

1624 Charter of London Company was revoked and Virginia became a royal colony.

1764 Boston town meeting held to protest Parliament's passage of Sugar Act, denouncing taxation without representation, and proposed united action by the colonies.

1768 Thomas Bacon, Anglican clergyman who served in Maryland and Delaware (1744–68), died at about 68; compiled laws of Maryland (1765).

1816 Emanuel Leutze, historical painter (*Washington Crossing the Delaware, Westward the Course of Empire*), born in Gmund, Germany (died 1868).

1818 Seminole War ended with capture of Pensacola by forces under Andrew Jackson.

1819 The *Savannah*, a fully-rigged sailing vessel with auxiliary steam power, left Savannah, GA; arrived in Liverpool, England, 29 days later, the first ship to use steam in the Atlantic crossing.

1844 Samuel F.B. Morse tapped out first

message on his telegraph, "What hath God wrought?" in the Supreme Court chamber in Washington and the message was received in Baltimore.

1850 Henry W. Grady, co-owner, editor, *Atlanta Constitution*, born in Athens, GA (died 1889).

1852 Maurice F. Egan, negotiated purchase of Danish West Indies (Virgin Islands), born in Philadelphia; served as minister to Denmark (1907) (died 1924).

1854 Richard Mansfield, starring actor (Shakespearean plays, *Peer Gynt, Cyrano de Bergerac*), born in Helgoland, Germany (died 1907).

1854 A fleeing slave, Anthony Burns, was arrested in Boston; protests against his return to Virginia resulted in riots, call out of troops; returned but bought out of slavery; studied at Oberlin (OH) College; became pastor of Baptist church in Canada.

1856 John Brown, anti-slavery leader, led abolitionists against pro-slavery settlers at Pottawatomie, KS, killing five.

1860 George L. Heins, architect who helped design Cathedral of St. John the Divine in New York City, born in Philadelphia (died 1907).

1860 James McK. Cattell, psychologist who did pioneer research in testing, born in Easton, PA; founder, president, Psychological Corp. (1921), concerned with practical applications of psychology; edited several scientific journals (died 1944).

1870 Benjamin N. Cardozo, associate justice, Supreme Court (1932–38), born in New York City; served on New York Court of Appeals (1917–32), chief justice (1926–32); a leading spokesman for sociological jurisprudence (died 1938).

1878 Harry Emerson Fosdick, spokesman for modern liberal Christianity, born in Buffalo, NY; professor of practical theology, Union Theological Seminary (1915–46); pastor, Riverside Church, New York City (1931–46); preached on *National Vespers*, national radio program (1926–46) (died 1969).

1883 Elsa Maxwell, noted hostess, born in Keokuk, IA (died 1963).

1883 Brooklyn Bridge over East River opened with President Arthur present.

1893 Anti-Saloon League formed in Oberlin, OH, by the Rev. H.H. Russell; the Ohio plan was copied elsewhere, served as model for Anti-Saloon League of America, formed 1895.

1895 Samuel I. Newhouse, founder, head of newspaper chain, syndicate which bears his name, born in New York City (died 1979).

1898 Helen B. Taussig, physician who helped develop operation to save "blue babies," born in Cambridge, MA; worked with Dr. Alfred Blalock on operation (died 1986).

1909 Wilbur D. Mills, legislator who represented Arkansas in House (1938–77), born in Kennett, AR; headed House Ways and Means Committee, very influential in taxation matters (died 1992).

1927 Jack (John B., Jr.) Kelly, a top American oarsman, born in Philadelphia; won Diamond Sculls at Henley (1947 1949) and American single sculls title eight times (died 1985).

1935 First night major league baseball game played at Crosley Field, Cincinnati with home team beating Philadelphia 2–1.

1937 Supreme Court upheld constitutionality of Social Security Act.

1941 Bob Dylan, musician/composer ("Blowin' in the Wind," "The Times They Are a'Changin'"), born in Duluth; composed anthems of 1960s civil rights movement.

1950 Maritime Administration established.

1954 Supreme Court, in series of decisions, outlawed segregation in tax-supported colleges, junior colleges, universities, graduate schools, public housing, and public park, recreational and entertainment facilities.

1983 Supreme Court ruled 8–1 that Internal Revenue Service could deny tax exemptions to private schools that practiced racial discrimination.

1983 The 100th anniversary of the Brooklyn Bridge celebrated with two million people looking on.

1988 President Reagan vetoed trade bill but the House voted 308 to 113 to override the veto; the Senate on June 8 upheld the veto.

1994 Denny's restaurant chain agreed to pay $54 million to settle lawsuits filed by thousands of black customers who had been refused service or forced to wait longer or pay more than white customers.

2000 By a 237–197 vote House of Representatives gave in to White House pressure to grant China on-going "normal trading privileges," thereby reducing tariffs on a permanent basis.

2001 Republican majority in U.S. Senate disappeared as James Jeffords of Vermont left party and classified self as Independent.

2002 Major poll announced of non–Roman Catholic views of Catholics by *Commonweal* magazine and the Fordham Center for American Catholic Studies: 57 percent regard reverencing of images in church as form of idol worship; 83 percent that worship of Mary gives her honor that belongs only to God; almost 75 percent that Catholics will follow dictates of church leaders regardless of what they themselves may prefer.

25

1539 Hernando de Soto arrived with 600 troops at Tampa Bay from Havana to complete the exploration of Florida.

1783 Philip P. Barbour, Supreme Court associate justice (1836–41), born in Barboursville, VA; represented Virginia in House (1814–25, 1827–30), serving as Speaker (1821–23, 1827–29) (died 1841).

1787 Constitutional Convention opened in Philadelphia when a quorum of seven states had arrived; finally 55 delegates attended; George Washington, a Virginia delegate, named president; William Jackson, secretary; convention ended September 17.

1793 First Catholic priest, Stephen T. Badin, ordained in United States by Bishop John Carroll of Baltimore.

1803 Ralph Waldo Emerson, poet and essayist (*Society and Solitude, The Conduct of Life*), born in Boston; considered a spokesman for American transcendentalism (died 1882).

1825 Daniel B. Wesson, inventor of a repeating action for rifle and pistol, born in Worcester, MA; founder, Smith & Wesson Co. (1857) (died 1906).

1835 Henry C. Potter, Episcopal Bishop of New York (1887–1908), born in Schenectady, NY; rector, Grace Church, New York City (1868–83), assistant bishop (1883–87); began construction of Cathedral of St. John the Divine (died 1908).

1844 A gasoline engine was patented by Stuart Perry.

1845 William Muldoon, an outstanding athlete of 19th Century, born in Belfast, NY; an organizer of Police Athletic League, New York City; chairman, New York State Boxing Commission (1921–23) (died 1933).

1847 John A. Dowie, founder of Christian Catholic Apostolic Church, born in Edinburgh, Scotland; founder, Zion City, north of Chicago; proclaimed himself Elijah the Restorer; deposed by revolt of followers (died 1907).

1850 State convention adopted New Mexico constitution; excluded slavery.

1862 Confederate troops under Gen. Stonewall Jackson routed Union troops at Winchester, VA.

1864 Gen. William T. Sherman's drive to Atlanta continued with the repulse of Confederate attack at New Hope Church.

1865 John R. Mott, who shared 1946 Nobel Peace Prize, born in Livingston Manor, NY; general secretary YMCA (1915–31); head U.S. council, world alliance (1926–37); founder, Foreign Missions Conference (1893), World Student Christian Federation (1895) (died 1955).

1866 Carl E. ("Bunny") Schultze, cartoonist (*Foxy Grandpa* comic strip), born in Lexington, KY (died 1939).

1878 Bill ("Bojangles") Robinson, dancer/entertainer, born in Richmond, VA; starred in many revues, vaudeville, musicals (*The Hot Mikado*) (died 1949).

1879 St. Patrick's Cathedral in New York City dedicated.

1883 Lesley J. McNair, World War I and II general, born in Verndale, MN; commander, Army Ground Forces; killed in bombing at St. Lo, France, 1944.

1886 Philip Murray, president, CIO (1940–52), born in Blantyre, Scotland; vice president, United Mine Workers (1920–42), president, United Steelworkers (1942–52) (died 1952).

1889 Igor I. Sikorsky, aviation pioneer, born in Kiev, Russia; built, flew first successful multimotor plane (1913); founder, aircraft manufacturing firm (1923) which built first transatlantic clipper, workable helicopter (died 1972).

1898 American expeditionary force of nearly 2,500 sailed from San Francisco for Manila.

1898 Bennett A. Cerf, president, Modern Library (1925–71), born in New York City; founder, president, Random House (1927–65); compiled numerous anthologies; panelist on TV's *What's My Line?* (died 1971).

1905 International Joint Commission, designed to regulate use of water at Canadian-American boundary, met for first time.

1908 Theodore Roethke, poet of childhood and old age, born in Saginaw, MI (died 1963).

1915 American steamer *Nebraska* torpedoed by German submarine off Scotland.

1917 Theodore M. Hesburgh, president, Notre Dame. U. (1952–87), born in Syracuse, NY; chairman, U.S. Civil Rights Commission (1969–72).

1921 Hal David, lyricist of numerous hit songs ("What the World Needs Now," "Alfie,"

"Raindrops Keep Falling on My Head"), born in New York City.

1921 Jack Steinberger, physicist, born in Bad Kissingen, Germany; shared 1988 Nobel Physics Prize for helping capture neutrinos in high energy beam to examine structure of atomic particles.

1926 Miles Davis, Jr., a leading musician who ushered in "cool" jazz, born in Alton, IL (died 1991).

1929 Beverly Sills, opera and concert singer (New York City Opera 1955–79), born in New York City; opera director (1979 on).

1940 President Franklin Roosevelt created Office of Emergency Management.

1950 Brooklyn-Battery Tunnel, longest in United States, opened.

1955 Tornadoes in Kansas, Missouri, Oklahoma, and Texas caused death of 115 persons.

1961 President Kennedy called for a moon project—"I believe that this nation should commit itself to achieving the goal, before this decade is out, of landing a man on the moon and returning him safely to earth."

1968 Gateway Arch in St. Louis dedicated.

1979 American Airlines DC-10 jetliner crashed on takeoff at Chicago's O'Hare Airport, killing all 272 persons aboard in the worst American air disaster.

1986 More than five million Americans joined hands in an attempt to form a human chain across the nation in Hands Across America, designed to raise money for the hungry.

1987 Former Labor Secretary Raymond J. Donovan was acquitted of grand larceny and fraud charges which forced him from office two years earlier; was first sitting Cabinet member to be indicted.

1987 Supreme Court ruled 6–3 that suspects accused of serious crimes may be held in "preventive detention" before trial if a judge determines they are a danger to the public.

1988 Reagan Administration abandoned talks with General Manuel Noriega in efforts to get him to leave Panama.

1988 President Reagan arrived in Helsinki for three days of rest on his way to Moscow summit meeting.

1990 Mark Strand, poet and short story writer, named the fourth United States poet laureate.

1992 Benno C. Schmidt, Jr., Yale U. president for six years, announced he would leave at year's end to head a program to create a private school system.

2004 Boston archdiocese to close nearly 20 percent of its Roman Catholic churches; victims of declining attendance and drop in contributions.

2006 Kenneth ("Ken") Lay, convicted for securities fraud and other misdeeds that helped destroy Enron Corporation, which he had founded and led for nearly its entire existence; faces 20–30 years imprisonment.

26

1637 Massachusetts and Connecticut colonists destroyed the Pequot Indian fort at Mystic, CT, where more than 600 Indians were killed; tribe practically annihilated near Fairfield, CT.

1780 Combined British and Indian attack on St. Louis was beaten back and British plan to take Spanish and Illinois posts was dropped.

1781 Bank of North America incorporated in Philadelphia after congressional approval.

1790 Territory southwest of Ohio river created.

1828 Samuel W. Allerton, a builder of modern Chicago, born in Armenia, NY; cofounder, Union Stock Yards, Chicago (1865); a leader in community affairs (died 1914).

1835 Edward P. Alexander, Confederate general, born in Washington, GA; directed artillery at Gettysburg (died 1910).

1836 House voted first "gag rules" which would automatically table any matter relating to slavery; repealed 1844.

1837 Washington A. Roebling, engineer who directed Brooklyn Bridge construction, born in Saxonburg, PA; bridge completed 1883 (died 1926).

1845 Samuel J. Barrows, prison reformer, born in New York City; editor, *Christian Register* (1880–96); influenced passage of first New York probation law and federal parole law (died 1909).

1864 Montana became a territory, formed out of part of Idaho Territory.

1865 Civil War hostilities ended with the surrender of Gen. Edmund Kirby-Smith and his troops to Gen. E.S. Canby at New Orleans.

1868 Senate, meeting again on President Andrew Johnson's impeachment, again voted 35–19 on two other impeachment articles, one vote short of the required two-thirds; failure to impeach resulted in resignation of War Secretary Edwin M. Stanton.

1872 Joseph Urban, architect and designer

of many sets for theaters and operas, born in Vienna; designed New School for Social Research (died 1933).

1876 Robert M. Yerkes, psychologist who developed intelligence tests for more than 1.7 million men in World War I, born in Bradysville, PA (died 1956).

1886 Al Jolson, entertainer in vaudeville and stage, born in Srednick, Russia; appeared in *The Jazz Singer*, the first talking picture, and *The Singing Fool* (died 1950).

1893 Maxwell Bodenheim, poet known as the Bard of Greenwich Village, born in Hermanville, MS; his works included *Blackguard*, *Replenishing Jessica* (died 1954).

1907 John Wayne, screen actor (*True Grit*, *Red River*, *Sands of Iwo Jima*), born in Winterset, IA (died 1979).

1907 Ida S. McKinley, widow of President McKinley, died in Canton, OH, at 59.

1909 Eugenie M. Anderson, first American woman ambassador, born in Adair, IA; ambassador to Denmark (1949–53), minister to Bulgaria (1962–64).

1917 Maj. Gen. John J. Pershing, named to command American Expeditionary Force, was ordered to France with his staff.

1920 Peggy Lee, singer/lyricist, born in Jamestown, SD; sang with Benny Goodman band (1941–43), made several films.

1939 Brent Musburger, sportscaster (CBS 1974–90, ABC 1990–), born in Portland, OR.

1951 Sally K. Ride, first American woman in space, born in Los Angeles.

1954 Explosion aboard aircraft carrier *Bennington* off Rhode Island coast killed 103 crewmen.

1972 United States and USSR signed a Strategic Arms Limitation Treaty (SALT I) in Moscow; imposed five-year freeze on testing and deployment of intercontinental ballistic missiles.

1977 Securities & Exchange Commission announced that Lockheed Corporation paid nearly $38 million in bribes and extortion abroad.

1981 Marine combat jet plane crashed on the deck of aircraft carrier *Nimitz*; 14 were killed.

1998 Supreme Court ruled 6–3 that most of Ellis Island was part of New Jersey, not New York

2004 Terry Nichols convicted by Oklahoma jury of murder for role in the 1995 bombing of the Oklahoma City Federal Building; a federal jury had rejected premeditated murder charges in an earlier trial.

2005 National survey released of worst urban roads: San Francisco, California, area headed list; estimates about 1 in 4 urban streets/highways badly in need of repairs.

27

1586 Expedition to destroy New Spain led by Sir Francis Drake; destroyed Spanish fort at St. Augustine, FL.

1774 Eighty-nine members of Virginia's House of Burgesses met in Raleigh Tavern in Williamsburg, recommended a meeting of all colonies; delegates, including Washington, Jefferson, and Patrick Henry, were asked to sound out their constituencies and meet again.

1787 First number of the *Federalist Papers* appeared; written by Alexander Hamilton, James Madison, and John Jay; *Papers* designed to get New York to ratify Constitution.

1794 President Washington nominated James Monroe as minister to France; served two years; President Jefferson renamed him in 1803, when he signed treaty for purchase of Louisiana Territory.

1794 Cornelius Vanderbilt, financier who started wealthy railroad, shipping family, born in Port Richmond, NY; built Grand Central Station in New York City; made large gifts to Central U., Nashville, which became Vanderbilt U. (died 1877).

1813 Col. Winfield Scott, assisted by American naval forces, captured Ft. George, NY; British abandoned entire Niagara Frontier to Americans.

1818 Amelia Jenks Bloomer, pioneer in social reform, born in Homer, NY; founder, *Lily* (1849–55), a paper designed for reform; wore proposed new women's costume — full-cut trousers under a short skirt, soon called a "bloomer" (died 1894).

1819 Julia Ward Howe, author of lyrics for "Battle Hymn of the Republic," born in New York City (died 1910).

1832 William R. Ware, founder of American architectural education, born in Cambridge, MA; founder, head, Columbia U. Architectural School (1881–1903) (died 1915).

1835 Charles Francis Adams, railroad reformer, born in Boston; exposed corruption of railroads, served with Massachusetts railroad commission; president, Union Pacific Railroad (1884–1900) (died 1915).

1836 Jay Gould, financier, born in Roxbury, NY; had vast railroad holdings, controlled Western Union, New York City elevated railroads (died 1892).

1837 Wild Bill (James B.) Hickok, legendary sharpshooter/ frontiersman, born in Troy Grove, IL; shot during a poker game in Deadwood, Dakota Territory (1876).

1849 Adolph Lewisohn, donor of Lewisohn Stadium to City College of New York, born in Hamburg, Germany; benefactor of many other universities (died 1938).

1861 Newport News, VA, occupied by Union troops.

1875 Fire destroyed French Catholic church in South Holyoke, MA; 120 persons died.

1878 Isadora Duncan, a founder of modern expressive dancing, born in San Francisco (died 1927).

1880 Joseph C. Grew, supervised creation of foreign service in State Department (1924–27), born in Boston; ambassador to Turkey (1927–32), to Japan (1932–41) (died 1965).

1885 Richard K. Turner, World War II admiral who was an expert in amphibious warfare, born in Portland, OR (died 1961).

1888 Frederick C. Sherman, World War II admiral, born in Port Huron, MI (died 1957).

1894 Dashiell Hammett, detective story author (*The Thin Man, The Maltese Falcon*), born in St. Mary's County, MD (died 1961).

1896 Tornado struck St. Louis killing 306 people.

1907 Rachel L. Carson, author of environmental works, born in Springdale, PA; books included *Silent Spring, The Sea Around Us, The Edge of the Sea* (died 1964).

1908 Harold J. Rome, composer of musicals (*Pins and Needles, Fanny*), born in Hartford, CT (died 1993).

1911 Hubert H. Humphrey, Vice President (1965–69), born in Wallace, SD; represented Minnesota in Senate (1949–64, 1971–78); 1968 Democratic presidential candidate (died 1978).

1912 Sam Snead, all-time career winner of 81 tournaments, born in Hot Springs, VA.

1912 John Cheever, author (*The Wapshot Chronicle, The Wapshot Scandal*), born in Quincy, MA (died 1982).

1915 Herman Wouk, author (*The Caine Mutiny, Winds of War, War and Remembrance*), born in New York City.

1918 Germans launched attack between Soissons and Reims in an effort to draw reserves away from the northern sector; reached the Marne, then repulsed.

1919 First transatlantic flight completed by U.S. Navy seaplane at Lisbon, Portugal; began May 8 at Rockaway, NY, with stops in Newfoundland and the Azores.

1923 Henry A. Kissinger, Secretary of State (1973–77), born in Furth, Germany; foreign policy advisor to President Nixon (1969–73); shared 1973 Nobel Peace Prize.

1924 Methodist General Conference lifted ban on dancing, theater attendance.

1929 Supreme Court upheld constitutionality of presidential pocket veto.

1930 John S. Barth, author of experimental allegorical novels (*The Sot Weed Factor, Giles Goat Boy*), born in Cambridge, MD.

1930 William S. Sessions, FBI director (1987–93), born in Fort Smith, AR.

1932 Bonus March made on Washington by World War I veterans who wanted their bonus paid in full.

1933 Century of Progress Exposition opened in Chicago.

1933 Securities Act passed by Congress, requiring registration of all new issues of securities with the Federal Trade Commission, along with a statement of financial condition to be available to prospective purchasers.

1935 Supreme Court held the National Industrial Recovery Act of 1933 to be unconstitutional; also declared Frazier-Lehmke Farm Bankruptcy Act unconstitutional.

1937 Golden Gate Bridge opened; completed at cost of $35 million.

1943 Office of War Mobilization established with James F. Byrnes director.

1988 Senate voted 93–5 to approve Intermediate Range Nuclear Forces Treaty between U.S. and Soviet Union, first agreement to eliminate an entire class of nuclear weapons.

1993 Dow Jones industrial average hit a new high of 3554.83.

1997 One of six tornadoes in central Texas killed 27 people in Jarrell.

2003 Supreme Court ruling declared state governments obligated to give time off under the federal Family and Medical Leave Act; 4.8 million state employees affected.

2005 Eddie Albert (b. 1906) died at 99. Appeared in almost 100 movies; had co-starring role in the television comedy series *Green Acres;* starred in an experimental television broadcast in 1936 before television was commercially available; won Bronze Star with a "V" for bravery as a Marine at Tarawa during World War II.

28

1672 Richard Nicolls, colonial administrator, died at 48; first British governor of New York (1664–68), taking over from the Dutch.

1754 George Washington, with a small band of men, surprised French troops at Great Meadows (10 miles east of present Uniontown, PA); this was first battle of French and Indian War.

1764 Edward Livingston, Secretary of State (1831–33), born in Columbia County, NY; represented New York in House, then Louisiana in House (1823–29) and Senate (1829–31); minister to France (1833–35) (died 1836).

1780 Nathaniel Chapman, founder of first American postgraduate medical school, born in Summer Hill, VA; founded Philadelphia Medical Institute (1817); first president, American Medical Association (1848) (died 1857).

1786 Louis McLane, Secretary of State (1833–34), born in Smyrna, DE; minister to England (1829–31, 1845–47); Secretary of Treasury (1831–33); president, Baltimore & Ohio Railroad (1837–47) (died 1857).

1807 (Jean) Louis Agassiz, pioneer in glaciation studies and zoology, born in Motier-en-Vully, Switzerland; professor of natural history, Harvard's Lawrence Scientific School (1848–73); founder, Harvard Museum of Comparative Zoology (died 1873).

1818 P(ierre) G.T. Beauregard, Confederate general, born in New Orleans; superintendent, West Point, at outbreak of Civil War; resigned to join Confederacy; commanded bombardment of Ft. Sumter; served at Bull Run, Shiloh; manager, Louisiana lottery (1870–88) (died 1893).

1818 *Walk-in-the-Water*, first steamboat to navigate upper Great Lakes, launched at Buffalo; built by Noah Brown; began first successful voyage under command of Capt. Job Fish August 23 between Buffalo and Detroit.

1826 Benjamin G. Brown, Missouri governor (1870–73), born in Lexington, KY; represented Missouri in Senate (1863–67); vice presidential candidate, Liberal Republican Party (1872) (died 1885).

1837 Tony (Antonio) Pastor, developer of legitimate vaudeville, born in New York City; operated several theaters (died 1908).

1888 Jim (James F.) Thorpe, considered greatest athlete of 1900–50, born in Prague, OK; won decathlon and pentathlon in 1912 Olympics but was stripped of medals for having played professional baseball (medals returned to family in 1982); played football and baseball after Olympics (died 1953).

1896 Warren Giles, president, National League (1951–70), born in Tiskilwa, IL; named to Baseball Hall of Fame (died 1979).

1917 Barry Commoner, biologist who was major advocate of environmental protection, born in Brooklyn.

1918 First American success in World War I gained when 1st Division under Gen. Robert Bullard captured and held Cantigny.

1925 Federal Judge McCormick in Los Angeles declared Elks Hill lease of oil reserve lands to private companies void because contracts were secured by fraud.

1936 Congress chartered Veterans of Foreign Wars (VFW).

1944 Rudolph Giuliani, New York City mayor (since 1995), born in New York City.

1958 Presbyterian Church in the United States of America merged with United States Presbyterian Church of North America in Pittsburgh to form United Presbyterian Church in the USA.

1977 Fire in Southgate, KY, supper club killed 164 persons.

1985 David P. Jacobsen, American director of American University Hospital, was kidnapped in Beirut; released November 2, 1986.

1997 President Clinton attended celebration of 50th anniversary of the Marshall Plan in The Hague, Netherlands.

2001 Law signed to build World War II Memorial on Washington Mall.

2003 Third-largest tax-reduction bill in American history was signed by President Bush; during ten years $350 billion to go back to taxpayers.

2006 Barry Bonds hit 715th home run, beating record of Babe Ruth; on September 23 hit 734th, breaking record of Hank Aaron.

2006 Arthur Widmer (b. 1914) died; won special lifetime-achievement Academy Award in 2005 for role in inventing what became the blue screen (that made modern special effects possible prior to computers), as well as role in creating 3-D and widescreen film format.

29

1647 Freemen from four Rhode Island towns (Providence, Portsmouth, Newport, Warwick) met in Portsmouth, drafted a constitution, which established freedom of conscience, separated church and state, provided rights to towns, and created the Providence Plantations with John Coggeshall as president.

1721   South Carolina formally incorporated as a royal colony.

1736   Patrick Henry, Virginia's first governor (1776–79, 1784–86) and colonial leader, born in Hanover County, VA; member of Continental Congress (1774–76); instrumental in adoption of Bill of Rights (first 10 amendments to Constitution) (died 1799).

1765   Patrick Henry introduced resolutions challenging the Stamp Act in Virginia's House of Burgesses and made his famed treason speech ("Caesar had his Brutus, Charles the First his Cromwell, and George the Third may profit by their example... If this be treason, make the most it"); Burgesses passed only the resolutions objecting to taxation without representation.

1787   Edmund Randolph submitted "Virginia Plan" to the Constitutional Convention, calling for a bicameral legislature, which would choose an executive, a judiciary, and a council of revision with veto power over legislation.

1790   Rhode Island, which did not participate in Constitutional Convention, ratified the Constitution by a legislative vote of 34–32, entering the Union as the 13th state.

1794   John Quincy Adams nominated as minister to Netherlands, served until 1797.

1824   Cadmus M. Wilcox, Confederate general, born in Wayne County, NC; involved in most major battles, present at Appomattox surrender (died 1890).

1825   David B. Birney, Union general who commanded troops at Gettysburg, born in Huntsville, AL (died 1864).

1826   Ebenezer Butterick, inventor of paper patterns for shirts, suits, dresses, born in Sterling, MA (died 1903).

1844   James K. Polk was nominated for president by the Democratic convention, the first "dark horse" candidate; received no votes until eighth ballot, nominated unanimously on ninth.

1848   Wisconsin entered Union as 30th state.

1859   James H. Rand, inventor of visible system of file dividers, born in Tonawanda, NY; merged (1927) with Remington firm (died 1944).

1865   President Andrew Johnson issued amnesty proclamation to all (except Confederacy leaders) who took oath to obey the Constitution.

1878   Winford L. Lewis, chemist who developed poison gas named for him (lewisite), born in Gridley, CA; captain, Army Chemical Warfare Service (1917–18) (died 1943).

1884   Bureau of Animal Industry created to conduct federal meat inspection.

1890   U. of Florida founded at Tarpon Springs.

1892   Frederick S. Faust, author under several pseudonyms including Max Brand, born in Seattle; turned out more than 500 full-length "pulps," also Dr. Kildare movie scripts (died 1944).

1898   Spanish fleet bottled up in harbor of Santiago de Cuba.

1903   Bob (Leslie T.) Hope, entertainer, screen and television performer, born in Eltham, England; did various *Road* pictures with Bing Crosby; traveled extensively to entertain American troops abroad.

1911   Supreme Court dissolved the American Tobacco Co. as an illegal combination in restraint of trade.

1917   John F. Kennedy, 35th president, born in Brookline, MA; represented Massachusetts in House (1947–53) and Senate (1953–60); assassinated in Dallas 1963.

1920   John C. Harsanyi, U. of California economist (1964–90), born in Budapest; shared 1994 Nobel Economics Prize.

1932   Veterans demanding their full bonus marched on Washington; Army troops under Gen. Douglas MacArthur broke up the march.

1938   Fay (Francis T., Jr.) Vincent, baseball commissioner (1989–92), born in Waterbury, CT.

1968   "Truth in Lending" Act signed by President Lyndon Johnson.

1969   Presidential executive order established the Council of Environmental Quality; legislation enacted, effective January 1, 1970.

1978   Cost of first class postage increased to 15 cents.

1988   Pope John Paul II named 25 new cardinals, including Archbishop James A. Hickey of Washington, DC, and Archbishop Edmund C. Szoka of Detroit.

1992   Bush Administration refused to sign international treaty designed to preserve the world's plants, animals, and natural resources issued by a 98-nation meeting in Rio de Janeiro.

1995   Margaret Chase Smith, Maine Republican who was only woman elected to both houses of Congress, died at 97.

1997   First Lt. Kelly Flinn, first woman B-52 bomber pilot, discharged from Air Force after being charged with adultery.

2001   U.S. court in New York brought in

guilty verdicts on two individuals accused of conspiring to attack American embassies in Africa in 1998.

2004 Federal World War II Memorial in Washington, DC, officially dedicated.

2004 Archibald Cox, special prosecutor for the Watergate investigation against Richard Nixon, died at 92. Nixon demanded he drop court appeal to get White House recorded conversations; facing refusal, Nixon ordered Attorney General to fire him; "Saturday Night Massacre" ensued as Nixon fired the Attorney General and then the Deputy Attorney General until he finally found someone who would do so.

30

1806 Andrew Jackson and Charles Dickinson met in a duel at Harrison's Mills, KY, over some remarks about Mrs. Jackson; Dickinson was killed, Jackson wounded.

1812 John A. McClernand, Union general, born near Hardinsburgh, KY; saw action at Ft. Donelson, Shiloh, and Vicksburg (died 1900).

1848 Treaty of Guadelupe Hidalgo officially ended war with Mexico when ratifications were exchanged.

1854 Kansas-Nebraska Act signed by President Pierce, creating two new territories, recognized principle of "squatter sovereignty," led to formation of Republican Party, and made Lincoln a national figure; bill repealed Missouri Compromise.

1862 Confederate troops evacuated Corinth, MS, retiring to Tupelo, 50 miles south.

1865 John Catron, associate justice, Supreme Court (1837–65), died at about 79.

1867 Arthur V. Davis, ALCOA president (1910–28), board chairman (1928–57), born in Sharon, MA (died 1962).

1868 First Memorial (Decoration) Day observed; Gen. John A. Logan, commander-in-chief, Grand Army of the Republic (GAR), called for decorating soldiers' graves.

1883 Ludwig Lewisohn, critic and author (*The Island Within, Upstream, Midchannel*), born in Berlin; made numerous translations from German (died 1955).

1886 Dorothy L.H.W. Eustis, guide dog training pioneer, born in Philadelphia; founder (1929), the Seeing Eye, first dog guide training school (died 1946).

1887 Alexander Archipenko, one of first to adapt cubism to sculpture, born in Kiev, Russia (died 1964).

1888 James A. Farley, Postmaster General (1933–40), born in Grassy Point, NY; Democratic national chairman (1932–40), who broke with Franklin Roosevelt over third term; chairman, New York Athletic Commission (1925–33) (died 1976).

1890 Lawrence Langner, theatrical producer who was a founder of Theater Guild (1919), born in Swansea, Wales (died 1962).

1899 Irving Thalberg, movie producer (*The Big Parade, The Good Earth, Mutiny on the Bounty*), born in Brooklyn (died 1936).

1901 Cornelia Otis Skinner, actress and author (*Tiny Garments, Dithers and Jitters*), born in Chicago (died 1979).

1901 Hall of Fame for Great Americans on New York University campus dedicated.

1903 Countee Cullen, author who had prominent role in 1920s Harlem "renaissance," born in New York City (died 1946).

1908 Aldrich-Vreeland Emergency Currency Law enacted following a "bankers panic" (1907); law gave currency greater elasticity, created National Monetary Commission to study banking system.

1909 National conference on the Negro convened, led to forming of National Association for the Advancement of Colored People (NAACP).

1909 Benny (Benjamin D.) Goodman, clarinetist known as the "king of swing," born in Chicago; led own band from 1933 on (died 1986).

1911 First Indianapolis 500 automobile race held; won by Ray Harroun.

1912 Julius Axelrod, biochemist, born in New York City; shared 1970 Nobel Physiology/Medicine Prize for studies of how nerve impulses are transmitted in the body.

1918 First American troops arrived in Italy.

1922 Lincoln Memorial in Washington, DC, dedicated.

1937 Steelworkers attempting to organize Republic Steel plant in South Chicago were fired on by police, resulting in four deaths, 84 injured.

1966 *Surveyor I* satellite launched; made first American soft landing on the moon June 2.

1998 Tornado destroyed town of Spencer, SD; killed six, injured 150.

2000 Supreme Court agreed to decide whether the Clean Air Act requires the U.S. government to take into consideration monetary costs of its decisions instead of only health repercussions.

31

1636   The Rev. Thomas Hooker and his followers reached and settled Hartford, CT.

1650   Charter granted Harvard College.

1684   Timothy Cutler, Anglican clergyman and Yale College rector (1719–22), born in Charlestown, MA; rector, Christ Church, Boston (1723–65) (died 1765).

1689   Rebellion led by Jacob Leisler, a German trader, began with capture of Ft. James (on Manhattan Island); went on sporadically for years until new governor of New England arrived March 19, 1691; Leisler and seven others sentenced to death April 1691; two were hanged May 26; others later pardoned.

1775   Frontiersmen of Charlotte, NC, adopted Mecklenburg Resolves which reputedly declared null and void all royal laws and commissions.

1790   First copyright law passed and signed.

1810   Horatio Seymour, New York governor (1853–55, 1863–65), born in Pompey Hill, NY; Democratic presidential candidate (1868) (died 1886).

1819   Walt(er) Whitman, a major American poet (*Leaves of Grass*), born in West Hills, Long Island (died 1892).

1822   First American Catholic cathedral (Cathedral of the Assumption of the Blessed Virgin Mary) dedicated in Baltimore by Archbishop Marechal.

1837   William H.F. Lee, Confederate cavalry general, born in Arlington, VA; served in Peninsula campaign, second Bull Run; represented Virginia in House (1887–91) (died 1891).

1861   Emily P. Bissell, Christmas Seal founder, born in Wilmington, DE; headed first drive to aid tubercular children (1907); designed, printed, and sold the seals (died 1948).

1862   Two-day battle of Fair Oaks (Seven Pines) outside Richmond, VA, began; Confederate force withdrew to Richmond later, lost 5,700 men, including Gen. Joseph Johnston; Union force under Gen. George McClellan lost 4,400.

1866   Secret Irish brotherhood, the Fenians, led by John O'Neill, left Buffalo to raid Canada; captured Ft. Erie, but were driven back across the Niagara River two days later.

1872   Charles G. Abbot, astrophysicist, secretary, Smithsonian Institution (1928–44), born in Wilton, NH; director, Smithsonian Astrophysical Observatory (1907–44) (died 1973).

1865   Herbert F. Leary, World War II admiral, born in Washington, DC; commander, Allied naval forces, Australian-New Zealand (1942), U.S. Pacific Fleet task force (1942) (died 1957).

1889   Johnstown, PA, covered by a flood when a dam broke, wiping out seven towns in 15 minutes and killing 2,200 persons; property worth more than $10 million destroyed.

1894   Fred Allen, entertainer on radio (1932–49), born in Cambridge, MA (died 1956).

1898   Claude E. Hooper, pioneer in radio broadcast audience analysis (Hooper ratings), born in Kingsville, OH (died 1954).

1898   Norman Vincent Peale, prominent clergyman and author (*The Power of Positive Thinking, the Art of Living*), born in Bowersville, OH; pastor, Marble Collegiate Reformed Church, New York City (1932–84) (died 1993).

1903   Floods of Kansas, Missouri, and Des Moines rivers resulted in death of 200 persons, property damage of $17 million.

1908   Don Ameche, screen actor (*The Three Musketeers, Heaven Can Wait*), born in Kenosha, WI (died 1993).

1912   Henry M. Jackson, legislator, born in Everett, WA; represented Washington in House (1941–53) and Senate (1953–83) (died 1983).

1913   The 17th Amendment, which provided for direct election of U.S. senators, became effective.

1920   Edward Bennett Williams, a prominent attorney in Washington, DC, born in Hartford, CT (died 1988).

1921   Sacco-Vanzetti trial began; both were found guilty (July 14) for the holdup slaying of two men in South Braintree, MA.

1924   Patricia Roberts Harris, public official, born in Mattoon, IL; ambassador to Luxembourg (1965–67); Secretary of Housing and Urban Development (1977–79), of Health, Education and Welfare (1979–81) (died 1985).

1926   Philadelphia Sesquicentennial Exposition opened; closed November 30.

1930   Clint Eastwood, screen actor (*Dirty Harry, Magnum Force, Coogan's Bluff*), born in San Francisco.

1931   John R. Schrieffer, physicist, born in Oak Park, IL; shared 1972 Nobel Physics Prize for theory of superconductivity.

1943   Joe Namath, football quarterback (U. of Alabama, New York Jets 1965–77), born in Beaver Falls, PA.

1955   Supreme Court ordered "all deliberate speed" in integrating public schools.

1961 President Kennedy conferred in Paris with French President de Gaulle.

1985 Series of tornadoes struck New York, Pennsylvania, Ohio, and Ontario, Canada, killing 75 persons.

1988 Nine accords were signed in Moscow by American and Russian officials during the summit meeting; two involved arms, the rest were cultural.

2003 A record 543 tornadoes verified during the month; previous record was 399 in June 1992; records began keeping close tabs only in 1950.

2003 Accused murderer caught searching for food in a supermarket dumpster: Eric R. Rudolph, accused of abortion bombings and an attack at the 1996 Olympics, was arrested on attempted burglary charges in Murphy, NC; only recognized after being brought to police station.

2005 The "Deep Throat" of the Nixon administration who repeatedly leaked information of White House involvement in Watergate and the following cover-up was finally self-revealed: W. Mark Felt, a retired top-level FBI executive.

JUNE

1

1637 Jacques Marquette, Jesuit missionary and explorer, born in Laon, France; explored much of central North America with Joliet (died 1675).

1660 Mary Dyer, English-born Quaker, hanged in Boston for sedition; she was banished in 1657 but returned twice illegally to visit jailed Quakers.

1745 James Tilton, chief of hospitals in America Revolution, born in Kent County, DE; surgeon general, U.S. Army (1813–15), setting up first clear definition of duties of medical, sanitary staffs; member, Continental Congress (1783–85) (died 1822).

1774 Boston Port Act went into effect in retribution for the Tea Party and the citizens' refusal to pay for the destroyed tea; action observed as fast day.

1779 Thomas Jefferson became second governor of Virginia, serving until 1781; succeeded Patrick Henry who had served three terms.

1781 Augusta, GA, besieged by Americans since April 16, capitulated.

1789 President Washington signed first act of Congress, which prescribed the oaths of allegiance by Congress, federal, and state officials.

1792 Kentucky ratified Constitution, entered Union as 15th state.

1796 Tennessee ratified Constitution becoming the 16th state in Union.

1801 Brigham Young, Mormon leader, born in Whitingham, VT; led Mormon Church after Joseph Smith's death (1847–77); led migration to Utah; first governor, Territory of Utah (1849–57) (died 1877).

1812 President Madison sent war message to Congress, outlining reasons for going to war with Great Britain; House voted for war (79–49) on June 4, Senate (19–13) on June 18; the grounds were impressment of American seamen, violation of American neutral rights and territorial waters, the blockade of American ports.

1813 The *Chesapeake*, commanded by Capt. James Lawrence, defeated and captured by the British frigate *Shannon*; the dying appeal of Lawrence, "Don't give up the ship," became the American Navy motto.

1814 Philip Kearny, Union general, born in New York City; killed on a scouting expedition September 1, 1862.

1825 John H. Morgan, Confederate general famed for cavalry raids, born in Huntsville, AL; killed in action near Greenville, TN, September 4, 1864.

1831 John B. Hood, Confederate general who conducted unsuccessful defense of Atlanta against Sherman, born in Owingsville, KY; lost right leg at Chickamauga (died 1879).

1833 John M. Harlan, associate justice, Supreme Court (1877–1911), born in Boyle County, KY (died 1911).

1849 Francis E. and Freelan Stanley, twin automakers, born in Kingfield, ME; they developed the Stanley Steamer, popular in 1902–17; Francis developed process for making photographic dry plates, which he sold to Kodak (1905); Francis died in 1918, Freelan 1940.

1849 Territorial government of Minnesota formed.

1855 Edward H. Angle, dentist who founded modern orthodontia, born in Herrick, PA; founded first school of orthodontia (St. Louis 1895) (died 1930).

1862 Robert E. Lee assumed command of Army of Northern Virginia.

1863 Hugo Münsterberg, pioneer in applied psychology, born in Danzig, Poland (then Germany); built experimental psychology laboratory at Harvard (died 1916).

1863 Gen. Ambrose E. Burnside ordered closure of *Chicago Times*, an anti–Lincoln newspaper; President Lincoln rescinded order June 4.

1864 Unsuccessful three-day assault on Cold Harbor, VA, began; heavy casualties on both sides, with 7,000 one day (June 3).

1868 Former President Buchanan died in Wheatland, PA, at 77.

1870 Ninth Census showed a 22.6 percent increase in population to total of 38,558,371.

1880 Tenth Census shows an increase of more than 11 million to 50,155,783; center of population had moved west to 20 miles east of Columbus, IN.

1890 Annual census report showed national population of 62,979,776.

1898 Trans-Mississippi Exposition opened in Omaha; closed October 31.

1901 John W. Van Druten, playwright (*The Voice of the Turtle*; *I Remember Mama*; *Bell, Book and Candle*; *I Am a Camera*), born in London (died 1957).

1905 Lewis & Clark Exposition opened in Portland, OR; closed October 14.

1909 Alaska-Yukon-Pacific Exposition opened in Seattle; closed October 16.

1918 Executive order issued exempting conscientious objectors from military service, assigning them to farm work or positions with Quakers.

1921 Race riots in Tulsa resulted in death of 25 white persons and 60 blacks.

1921 Nelson S. Riddle, orchestra leader and composer of much music for movies and television, born in Hackensack, NJ (died 1985).

1926 Marilyn Monroe, screen actress (*Seven Year Itch, Some Like It Hot, Bus Top, Misfits*), born in Los Angeles (died 1962).

1934 Pat (Charles E.) Boone, popular singer of 1950s, born in Jacksonville, FL.

1937 Hoover (originally Boulder) Dam went into operation, supplying electricity to Los Angeles and Southern California.

1980 The 20th Census showed population had grown to 226,504,825; center of population had moved across Mississippi River to ¼ mile west of DeSoto, MO.

1988 President Reagan and Soviet leader Mikhail Gorbachev ended their fourth summit session — the first in Moscow — by putting into force the first treaty to require destruction of nuclear weapons.

1990 Presidents Bush and Gorbachev signed an agreement to cut stockpiles of long range nuclear weapons.

2000 Tito Puente, founder of "Latin jazz," died after six decades of music making and 119 albums.

2001 Hank Ketcham died (1920–2001); in 1950 began publishing *Dennis the Menace,* on the perils created by small children, which he continued to draw until handing the series over to others in 1995.

2004 Study released: University of California at Berkeley documents that junk food such as desserts combine with caffeinated and other sugar-flavored drinks and beer to constitute over 30 percent of the typical adult American's calorie intake; sodas provide 7.1 percent by themselves.

2

1732 Martha Dandridge Custis Washington, wife of President Washington, born in New Kent County, VA (died 1802).

1773 John Randolph, colonial leader, born in Prince George County, VA; represented Virginia in House (1799–1813, 1815–17, 1819–25, 1827–29) and Senate (1825–27); minister to Russia (1830) (died 1833).

1784 New Hampshire adopted a new constitution.

1817 George H. Corliss, inventor of an improved steam engine, born in Easton, NY; founder, Corliss Steam Engine Co.; builder of largest engines (died 1888).

1845 Arthur MacArthur, Army officer who served in Mexican, Civil, and Spanish-American wars; assistant chief of staff (1906–09) (died 1912).

1863 Wilbert Robinson, baseball manager (Brooklyn 18 years), born in Bolton, MA; named to Baseball Hall of Fame (died 1934).

1884 President Cleveland was married to Frances Folsom of Buffalo in the White House.

1886 Grover Whalen, New York City's official greeter (1919–35), born (died 1962).

1890 Hedda Hopper, famed movie gossip columnist, born in Holidaysburg, PA (died 1966).

1891 Thurman W. Arnold, antitrust division head, Justice Department, born in Laramie, WY; instituted 230 suits (1938–43) (died 1969).

1904 Johnny Weissmuller, Olympics (1924, 1928) swimming gold medalist, born in Windber, PA; made many *Tarzan* pictures (died 1984).

1909 Michael Todd, stage, screen producer

(*Around the World in 80 Days*), born in Minneapolis; killed in plane crash (1958).

1941 Charles Evans Hughes resigned as chief justice of Supreme Court after serving 11 years.

1941 Lend-lease agreement signed with China.

1966 White House Conference on Civil Rights, attended by 2,400, ended.

1987 Paul A. Volcker, chairman of Federal Reserve Board for eight years, resigned; President Reagan named Alan Greenspan to succeed him.

1989 Traditional Episcopalians upset by consecration of first woman bishop in the church's history, formed the Episcopal Synod of America in a meeting in Ft. Worth, TX.

1997 Timothy McVeigh was found guilty of bombing a federal building in Oklahoma City in 1995 which killed 168 people; jurors recommended McVeigh be sentenced to death; sentence was appealed.

2001 Comedian Imogene Coca died: vaudevillian from age 12; pioneered television comedy with Sid Caesar on *Your Show of Shows*, 90 minutes each Saturday night.

2003 Federal Communications Commission by 3–2 vote rewrote rules in effect since 1975: Aoo: TV station owners may now buy more of them and simultaneously own newspapers in same cities. Some changes later modified by congressional mandate and others put on indefinite hold for reconsideration.

2004 Army indirectly extended active duty period of many ready to leave service: If their units are heading for Afghanistan or Iraq, they must stay until tour completed.

2006 Victim of leaks depicting him as a spy, nuclear scientist Wen Ho Lee promised $1.65 million by government and newspapers; newspapers had not been sued but refused to have reporters reveal their sources; to avoid revelation of sources, newspapers agreed to pay in what appeared to be unprecedented arrangement.

3

1621 Dutch West India Co. chartered by Netherlands State General to create colonies in the New World and along the African west coast.

1726 Philip William Otterbein, religious leader who helped found what became United Brethren in Christ Church, born in Dillenberg, Germany; held German Reformed pastorates in Maryland and Pennsylvania; with Martin Boehm

and others formed (1789) simple organization and a profession of faith for a new church (died 1813).

1781 Thomas Jefferson resigned as governor of Virginia; offered post of peace commissioner which he declined.

1790 Convention in South Carolina completed new state constitution.

1803 Valentine W.L. Knabe, founded piano manufacturing plant in Baltimore, born in Kreuzberg, Germany (now Poland) (died 1884).

1808 Jefferson Davis, Confederate president (1861–65), born in what is now Todd County, KY; represented Mississippi in House (1845–46) and Senate (1847–51, 1857–61); Secretary of War (1853–57) (died 1889).

1819 Thomas Ball, sculptor, born in Charlestown, MA; did many portrait busts, a life-size Daniel Webster, Lincoln and a kneeling slave (*Emancipation*) (died 1911).

1844 Garrett A. Hobart, Vice President (1897–99), born in Long Branch, NJ; served in state legislature, a Republican leader (died 1899).

1864 Ransom E. Olds, pioneer automaker, born in Geneva, OH; founder, Olds Motor Vehicles Co. (1899); founder, Reo Motor Co., president (1904–24), chairman (1924–36) (died 1950).

1869 Aristides Agramonte, bacteriologist, born in Camaguey, Cuba; served on Walter Reed Commission which discovered yellow fever was transmitted by mosquitoes; organized, headed, Louisiana State U. Medical School tropical disease department (died 1931).

1873 Otto Loewi, pharmacologist, born in Frankfurt, Germany; shared 1936 Nobel Physiology/Medicine Prize for discoveries on chemical transmission of nerve impulses; forced to turn over prize to Germany (1938) as price for emigration (died 1961).

1879 Raymond Pearl, founder of biometry (use of statistics in biology, medicine), born in Farmington, NH (died 1940).

1880 Alexander Graham Bell transmitted first wireless telephone message on his newly-invented photophone.

1899 Georg von Békésy, physiologist, born in Budapest; awarded 1961 Nobel Physiology/Medicine Prize for findings concerning the stimulation of cochlea of the ear (died 1972).

1900 Abel Green, writer/editor, *Variety* (1921–73), born in New York City (died 1973).

1904 Charles R. Drew, surgeon who developed blood banks, born in Washington, DC; directed blood plasma program in United States and Great Britain in World War II (died 1950).

1904 Jan Peerce, leading tenor in Metropolitan Opera, born in New York City; first American to sing with Bolshoi Opera (died 1984).

1906 Josephine Baker, internationally famous singer and dancer, born in St. Louis (died 1975).

1916 National Defense Act passed, expanding regular army to 175,000 (225,000 in five years); also authorized National Guard of 450,000.

1918 American Second Division helped stop German advance at Chateau-Thierry.

1926 Allen Ginsberg, poet (*Howl, Kaddish*), born in Newark, NJ; introduced "flower power" in demonstration clashes with police (1965) (died 1997).

1936 Larry McMurtry, author (*All My Friends Are Going to Be Strangers, Last Picture Show*), born in Wichita Falls, TX.

1940 Sale of surplus war material to Great Britain authorized; President Franklin Roosevelt released surplus arms, ammunition, and planes.

1942 Three-day Battle of Midway resulted in first Japanese defeat, with the loss of four aircraft carriers; Americans lost one.

1942 Japanese bombed Dutch Harbor in the Aleutians, occupied islands of Attu, Agattu, and Kiska.

1961 President Kennedy met with Russian Premier Khrushchev in Paris.

1965 Edward H. White became first American to "walk" in space during a nearly 98-hour 62-orbit flight which ended June 7.

1974 Supreme Court ruled 5–3 that women must receive equal pay for equal work.

1997 Dennis James, pioneer television announcer/talk show host, died at 71.

2000 William Simon was a major figure in the U.S. Olympic Committee as well as serving the federal government in such posts as Secretary of the Treasury; dead of complications from lung disease.

2002 Industry survey released on economic side effects of 9/11 attack: Hotel industry profits dropped 19.4 percent in 2001, worst fall since 1938; further 11 percent drop anticipated for 2002.

2004 George Tenet, seven-year CIA director veteran, announced resignation; had endured much criticism over accuracy of pre–Iraqi war intelligence data and other issues.

2004 The U.S. Energy Department, which oversees American nuclear weapons, announced that the number of deployed nukes would be reduced "almost in half" during the following eight years in conformity with a treaty signed with Russia; warheads would, however, not be destroyed and would be accessible if circumstances change.

4

1752 John E. Howard, colonial leader, born in Baltimore County, MD; served in Continental Army, Continental Congress (1784–88); represented Maryland in Senate (1796–1803) and served it as governor (1789–91) (died 1827).

1754 George Washington and his small force built Ft. Necessity, east of present Uniontown, PA; surrendered to a superior force of French troops July 3.

1805 Peace concluded between Tripoli and United States after nearly four years of fighting; tribute payments to other Barbary states continued until 1816.

1845 First American grand opera, *Leonora* by William H. Fry presented at Chestnut St. Theater in Philadelphia.

1864 Union troops under Gen. U.S. Grant sought unsuccessfully to dislodge Lee's Confederate force at Cold Harbor, VA.

1878 Frank N.D. Buchman, evangelist, born in Pennsburg, PA; director, Christian work, Penn State U. (1909–15); founded "A First Christian Fellowship" at Penn State and Moral Rearmament movement (the Oxford Group) in Great Britain (died 1961).

1878 Alla Nazimova, actress who starred in Ibsen roles, born in Yalta, Russia (died 1945).

1884 Fontaine T. Fox, Jr., cartoonist (*Toonerville Trolley* 1906–55), born in Louisville, KY (died 1964).

1896 First Ford automobile assembled in a brick work shed in Detroit.

1898 Jerauld Wright, first Allied supreme commander of NATO forces, born in Amherst, MA; led various amphibious operations.

1910 Robert B. Anderson, public official, born in Burleson, TX; Navy Secretary (1953–54), Secretary of Treasury (1957–61) (died 1989).

1911 Rosalind Russell, screen actress (*Craig's Wife, My Sister Eileen, Auntie Mame*), born in Waterbury, CT (died 1976).

1919 Robert Merrill, operatic baritone with Metropolitan Opera (1945–75), born in New York City.

1944 Rome occupied by American Fifth Army and British Eighth Army.

1985 Supreme Court struck down Alabama law permitting a minute of prayer or meditation in public schools.

2002 House and Senate Intelligence Committees began review of official handling of terrorist danger from 1986 to present.

2002 American Civil Liberties Union filed suit against American, Continental, Northwest and United Airlines arguing that Arab-appearing passengers had been removed from their flights after passing through screening and boarding due to passenger fears in wake of 9/11 attack; argue illegal discrimination manifested.

2003 Famous businesswoman and television personality Martha Stewart is charged with lying about illegal stock market transactions but not with criminal acts about the transactions themselves; resigns post as chairwoman of OmniMedia.

2006 Kelly Kulick became first woman to qualify for a guaranteed spot in all Professional Bowling Association competitions for the entire season; PBA was opened to women in 2004 after the Professional Women's Bowling Association Tour was unable to gain funding in 2003.

5

1542 Luis Moscosco, appointed by Hernando de Soto to succeed him, led expedition across Arkansas and Texas; believed to have gone west as far as Trinity River.

1762 Bushrod Washington, associate justice, Supreme Court (1798–1829), born in Westmoreland County, VA; Mt. Vernon bequeathed to him, living there from 1802 (died 1829).

1773 Boston Committee of Correspondence signed a "Solemn League and Covenant," to be effective October 1, for suspension of commerce with Great Britain.

1775 Lyman Spalding, physician who founded U.S. Pharmacopeia (1820), born in Cornish, NH; investigated yellow fever, vaccination, and hydrophobia (died 1821).

1823 George T. Angell, active worker for crime prevention and protection of animals, born in Southbridge, MA (died 1909).

1825 Jabez L.M. Curry, Confederate leader and educator, born in Lincoln County, GA; member of Confederate Congress and Army; president, Howard College (1865–68); active in efforts to promote southern education; minister to Spain (1885–88, 1902) (died 1903).

1831 Marcus J. Wright, Confederate general who compiled 70-volume record of Civil War, born in Purdy, TN (died 1922).

1840 Edward Cary, editor, *New York Times* (1871–1917), born in Albany (died 1917).

1845 Gen. Stephen Kearny began march from Ft. Leavenworth to occupy New Mexico, California.

1851 *Uncle Tom's Cabin* by Harriet Beecher Stowe began appearing in serial form in the *Washington National Era*; ran until April 1, 1852.

1854 Canadian Reciprocity Treaty signed; designed to end disputes over fishing rights in American and Canadian waters.

1877 John H. Breck, cosmetics manufacturer, born in Holyoke, MA (died 1965).

1887 Ruth F. Benedict, major contributor to cultural anthropology, born in New York City; demonstrated role of culture in individual personality formation; author (*Patterns of Culture*) (died 1948).

1917 More than nine million men registered for military service in local draft boards.

1919 Accident in anthracite coal mine at Wilkes-Barre, PA, caused 92 deaths.

1919 Congress by joint resolution approved the woman's suffrage amendment (19th), sent it to the states for ratification; earlier the House voted 304–89 in favor of the amendment, the Senate 56–25.

1920 Women's Bureau created in Department of Labor.

1933 Joint congressional resolution voided the gold clause in government obligations and private contracts; abandoning gold standard had been announced April 20 by President Franklin Roosevelt.

1934 Bill (William D.) Moyers, journalist, television reporter and commentator, born in Hugo, OK; press secretary to President Lyndon Johnson (1965–67); publisher *Newsday* (1967–70).

1942 United States declared war on Bulgaria, Hungary, and Rumania.

1942 Explosion at Elwood, IL, ordnance plant resulted in 49 deaths.

1946 Fire in Chicago's LaSalle Hotel resulted in 61 deaths.

1947 Secretary of State George C. Marshall offered plan at Harvard commencement to extend aid to European countries; Congress later authorized about $12 billion in aid over next four years.

1950 Congress enacted President Truman's Point Four program.

1968 Sen. Robert F. Kennedy was shot fatally in a Los Angeles hotel by Sirhan Sirhan; died the next morning; Sirhan was found guilty of first degree murder April 17, 1969; sentenced to death, later changed to life imprisonment.

1995 President Clinton issued his first veto of a congressional action — a rescissions bill which cut $16.4 billion from spending previously approved by Congress.

2000 In a 6–3 decision, though lacking a single rationale all would endorse, the Supreme Court upheld the right of divorced parents and single mothers to forbid visits by grandparents.

2001 Hurricane Allison had weakened to a major tropical storm when it hit Texas; $5 billion estimated damage at time.

2001 In an unprecedented situation, control of Senate passed to the Democrats, not because of winning new seats but because of defection of Republican Senator Jim Jeffords to their ranks.

2002 Justice Department announced plan to fingerprint and regularly update some 100,000 visa holders visiting/living in U.S.; returns to practices in effect 1950s-1980s; critics assail program from two directions: Some say it will target Muslims; others question competency of Immigration and Naturalization Service to administer the changes.

2003 Two *New York Times* senior editors resigned in scandal over plagiarism and factual errors not being detected.

2004 After suffering from Alzheimer's for years, former President Ronald Reagan passed away at 93.

2004 Some days the underdog wins: 136th Belmont Stakes won by 36-to-1 long shot Birdstone, removing overwhelming favorite Smarty Jones' chance of winning the Triple Crown of racing.

6

1622 Claude Jean Allouez, Jesuit missionary, born in St. Didier, France; served Great Lakes area, explored with Marquette; said to have baptized 10,000 Indians and preached to 100,000 (died 1689).

1755 Nathan Hale, Revolution martyr, born in Coventry, CT; captured behind British lines (September 21, 1776), executed as a spy; his final words were: "I only regret that I have but one life to lose for my country."

1756 John Trumbull, painter of historical scenes (*The Declaration of Independence*), born in Lebanon, CT; painted murals for Capitol rotunda, which were later removed because of the dampness of the walls (died 1843).

1764 Massachusetts Assembly asked Great Britain to repeal Sugar Act, seeking the cooperation of other colonies in the request.

1804 Louis A. Godoy, publisher of first American women's periodical (*Godoy's Lady's Book*), born in New York City (died 1878).

1809 Timothy S. Arthur, magazine editor/author (*Ten Nights in a Barroom*), born near Newburgh, NY; editor, *Arthur's Home Magazine* (died 1885).

1842 Steele MacKaye, playwright (*Hazel Kirke*), born in Buffalo, NY; established first American dramatic school at Lyceum Theater, New York City (died 1894).

1846 John Davey, tree care specialist, born in Somersetshire, England; specialized in care of ornamental trees (died 1923).

1849 Ft. Worth, TX, established when Major Ripley A. Arnold and an American cavalry troop set up an outpost.

1858 Samuel Untermyer, lawyer, born in Lynchburg, VA; instrumental in getting antitrust, Federal Reserve, and Federal Trade Commission legislation passed (died 1940).

1862 Commodore C.H. Davis' Union vessels destroyed a Confederate fleet and took over Memphis.

1874 Sanford L. Cluett, shirt and collar maker (Cluett, Peabody), born in Troy, NY; invented Sanforizing process, named for him (died 1968).

1902 Jimmie Lunceford, saxophonist and orchestra leader, born in Fulton, MS; band active 1929–47 (died 1947).

1904 Oregon adopted direct primary election for party nominations.

1904 National Tuberculosis Association organized in Atlantic City.

1912 Mt. Katmai in Alaska erupted, resulting in formation of the Valley of the Ten Thousand Smokes.

1918 American Marines launched attack on German positions in Belleau Wood, near Chateau Thierry; took positions three weeks later.

1918 Edwin G. Krebs, biochemist who shared 1992 Nobel Physiology/Medicine Prize, born in Lansing, IA.

1933 National Employment System Act went into effect creating the U.S. Employment Service.

1934 Securities and Exchange Commission

established with power to regulate trading in securities.

1941 Louis Chevrolet, auto designer and racer, died at 63; worked with General Motors designing first Chevrolet (1911); main interest was racing.

1944 Allied troops landed on Cherbourg Peninsula in France; about 175,000 men landed along a 60-mile front in Normandy, with 4,500 ships and 9,000 aircraft involved; Allied casualties were about 10,000.

1944 Philip A. Sharp, biologist, shared 1993 Nobel Physiology/Medicine Prize, born in Kentucky.

1946 President Truman nominated former Treasury Secretary Frederick M. Vinson as chief justice of Supreme Court; confirmed June 20.

1949 President Truman established office of U.S. High Commissioner for Germany, naming John J. McCloy to the post.

1983 James E. Casey, founder of United Parcel Service (UPS) (1907), died at 95.

1989 House Speaker James C. Wright resigned; Majority Leader Thomas S. Foley of Washington named to the post.

1995 MLS (Major League Soccer) to open regular 32-game season in April 1996 with ten-team outdoor league.

1998 President Kim Dae Jung of South Korea began nine-day tour of U.S.; met President Clinton June 9.

2001 Forty-year smoker of Philip Morris' Marlboro brand received $3 billion jury award in damages.

2003 Justice Department rejected holding of gay pride month event at the agency though such had been held in past; gay advocates condemned it as discriminatory; opponents of observance argued that it would provide improper legitimacy to the lifestyle.

2005 U.S. Supreme Court decision: federal laws prohibiting use of medical marijuana valid even if state laws permit such usage.

7

1494 Spain and Portugal signed Treaty of Tordesillas establishing a line of demarcation in the New World, 370 leagues west of Cape Verde.

1629 Charter of 31 articles of freedom and exemptions by Dutch West India Co. established privileges and patron land ownership in the New World settlement.

1652 General Court of Massachusetts set up a mint in Boston with first issue the "pine tree shilling"; John Hull was first mintmaster.

1712 Pennsylvania passed law forbidding importation of Africans.

1740 Alexander Spotswood, Virginia leader, died at about 64; lieutenant governor (1710–20), ran colony because governor was not present; developed Williamsburg as capitol, built Governor's Palace and Wren Building of College of William & Mary.

1745 Lindlay Murray, called the father of English grammar, born in Dauphin County, PA; author of *English Grammar* (1795), which sold almost one million copies (died 1826).

1776 Richard Henry Lee of Virginia made a motion in Continental Congress that "these united colonies are, and of right ought to be, free and independent states; that they are absolved from all allegiance to the British crown, and that all political connection between them and the State of Great Britain is, and ought to be, totally dissolved..." also called for foreign alliances and creation of a confederation of the colonies.

1776 American troops under Gen. John Sullivan were defeated at Three Rivers, between Quebec and Montreal, by a British force under Gen. Guy Carleton.

1824 Alfred Pleasanton, Union general, born in Washington, DC; served at Antietam, Fredericksburg, and Chancellorsville; commanded cavalry at Gettysburg (died 1897).

1843 Susan E. Blow, started first American public kindergarten (St. Louis 1873), born in St. Louis (died 1916).

1845 John F. Goucher, benefactor of Baltimore Women's College, born in Waynesburg, PA; was president of the college, renamed Goucher College (1919) (died 1922).

1854 First American YMCA began in Buffalo, NY.

1894 Alexander P. DeSeversky, aeronautical engineer, born in Tiflis, Russia; president, Seversky Aircraft Corp. (1931–39); invented various aviation devices, including a bomb sight (died 1974).

1896 Robert S. Mulliken, chemist/physicist, born in Newburyport, MA; awarded 1966 Nobel Chemistry Prize for research on bond holding atoms together in a molecule.

1896 Vivien Kellems, businesswoman who was outspoken opponent of alleged unfair taxation, born in Des Moines, IA (died 1975).

1897 George Szell, concert pianist/conductor (Berlin State Opera, Metropolitan Opera, Cleveland Symphony), born in Budapest (died 1970).

1909 Peter W. Rodino, Jr., legislator, born in Newark, NJ; represented New Jersey in House (1949–89); chairman, House Judiciary Committee, which conducted impeachment proceedings against President Nixon.

1909 Jessica Tandy, actress, winner of Oscar as best actress in *Driving Miss Daisy*, born in London; starred in many plays (*A Streetcar Named Desire, The Fourposter, The Gin Game*) (died 1994).

1917 Gwendolyn Brooks, poet (*A Street in Bronzeville, Annie Allen*), born in Topeka, KS; first black woman to receive a Pulitzer Prize.

1917 Twenty delegates from Lions Club nationwide met in Chicago to form Lions International.

1920 Supreme Court upheld constitutionality of both the Volstead Act and 18th Amendment, declared state laws authorizing light wines and beer were invalid, and held that Congress had authority to define intoxicating liquors.

1928 Charles Strouse, composer of stage musicals (*Bye Bye Birdie, Golden Boy, Applause, Annie*), born in New York City.

1979 President Carter approved development of the MX missile.

1996 Max Factor, cosmetics manufacturer, died at 91.

2000 Federal judge ordered Microsoft divided into two companies for antitrust violations; solution recommended by U.S. Justice Department and 17 state attorneys general.

2006 U.S. Senate defeated Constitutional amendment to ban same-sex marriages by 49–48.

8

1633 Dutch bought land from the Indians and erected Ft. Good Hope where Hartford, CT, now stands.

1748 William Few, colonial leader, born near Baltimore; represented Georgia in Continental Congress (1780–82, 85–88) and in Senate (1789–93); member of Constitutional Convention (died 1828).

1765 Massachusetts House of Representatives, which had approved resolution by James Otis, sent circular letter to other colonies calling for a meeting in October in New York "to consult together on the present circumstances of the colonies..."; principal topic was to be the Stamp Act, which was to go into effect November 1.

1780 Robert McCormick, inventor of grist mill and hydraulic machine (1830), born in Rockbridge County, VA; experimented unsuccessfully with threshing, reaping machines (died 1846).

1781 Benjamin Franklin, John Jay, and John Adams named commissioners to negotiate peace with Great Britain.

1783 Thomas Sully, artist, born in Horncastle, England; painted more than 2,600 works, mostly portraits, some historical scenes (died 1872).

1786 Samuel R. Betts, judge renowned for decisions in admiralty law, born in Richmond, MA; served 41 years in U.S. District Court, Southern New York (died 1868).

1806 George Wythe, colonial leader, died at 80; served as Virginia judge, taught many lawyers, including Thomas Jefferson; America's first law professor (College of William & Mary); member of Continental Congress (1775–77); signer of Declaration of Independence.

1813 David D. Porter, Union naval officer, born in Chester, PA; served in Civil War, commanding mortar fleet at New Orleans and Vicksburg; superintendent, Naval Academy (1865–69) (died 1891).

1838 George M. Sternberg, pioneer bacteriologist, born in Otsego County, NY; Surgeon General (1893–1902), began Army Medical School, the Nurses' and Dental Corps (died 1915).

1845 Former President Jackson died at 78 in the Hermitage near Nashville.

1847 Ida Saxton McKinley, wife of President McKinley, born in Canton, OH (died 1907).

1848 Franklin M. King, agricultural scientist who invented cylindrical tower silo, born in Whitewater, WI (died 1911).

1861 Tennessee voters approved secession from the Union 104,913 to 47,238.

1862 Battle of Cross Keys occurred near Harrisonburg, VA, when 6,500 Confederates under Gen. R.S. Ewell turned back 12,000 Union troops under Gen. John C. Fremont.

1862 Richard M. Bissell, insurance executive who formed Aetna and Connecticut insurance companies, born in Chicago; president, Hartford Insurance Co. (1913–41); a founder, Chicago Symphony Orchestra (1891) (died 1941).

1869 Frank Lloyd Wright, noted architect, born in Richland Center, WI; disciple of organic architecture; designed Tokyo's Imperial Hotel, only building to withstand 1923 earthquake, and

Guggenheim Museum, New York City (died 1959).

1872 President Grant signed act making Post Office an executive department.

1877 Robert F. Wagner, legislator, born in Hesse-Nassau, Germany; represented New York in Senate (1927–49); introduced Social Security, National Labor Relations Act, Railway Pension Act, 1937 housing law (died 1953).

1905 President Theodore Roosevelt urged Japanese and Russians to end their war, invited them to peace conference in Portsmouth, NH, which they accepted.

1908 President Theodore Roosevelt created National Conservation Commission, with Gifford Pinchot as chairman.

1913 (James) Walter Kennedy, commissioner, National Basketball Association (1963–75), born in Stamford, CT (died 1977).

1915 William Jennings Bryan resigned as Secretary of State because of disagreement with presidential policy on *Lusitania* sinking; succeeded by Robert Lansing.

1917 Byron R. (Whizzer) White, associate justice, Supreme Court (1962–93), born in Ft. Collins, CO; an All-American football player at Colorado U.

1917 Metal mine disaster at Butte, MT, killed 163 persons.

1918 Robert Preston, stage/screen actor, born in Newton Highlands, MA; starred in *The Music Man* on stage.

1936 Kenneth G. Wilson, Cornell U. physicist, born in Waltham, MA; awarded 1982 Nobel Physics Prize for describing how pressure and temperature change structure of matter.

1939 President Franklin Roosevelt greeted King George VI and Queen Mary on their visit to United States, the first by a British sovereign.

1953 Tornadoes hit southern Michigan, northwestern Ohio, and Massachusetts over a two-day period, killing 229.

1956 President Eisenhower, fully recovered from a heart attack, suffered an attack of ileitis; operated on successfully June 9.

1972 Congress enacted a bill for federal aid to college and university students and a $2 billion allocation to help elementary and secondary schools desegregate.

1992 William B. McGowan, chairman of MCI communications, died at 64; his lawsuit led to breakup of the ATT system.

2000 Further manufacture of pesticide chlorpyrifos banned by Environmental Protection Agency after 30 years on the market and widespread usage; reason: major health dangers documented.

2001 In reversal of past assumptions about heart attacks, scientists report partial regrowth of damaged heart muscle is possible.

2006 Texas Congressman Tom DeLay resigned from Congress due to accusations of campaign finance violations and corruption charges against his close associates; had been majority leader till previous year and one of the most important figures in obtaining and maintaining a Republican majority in the House of Representatives.

9

1768 Samuel Slater, textile manufacturer who launched American cotton industry, born in Derbyshire, England; manufactured fine cotton thread (died 1835).

1772 Irate Rhode Islanders attacked and burned the customs schooner *Gaspee* when it ran aground while pursuing a vessel near Providence.

1785 Sylvanus Thayer, called the father of the Military Academy, born in Braintree, MA; West Point superintendent (1817–33) (died 1872).

1786 Alexander McDougall, Revolutionary general, died at 54; a founder of Sons of Liberty in New York; took part in battles at White Plains, Germantown; commanded, West Point after Benedict Arnold's departure.

1791 John Howard Payne, actor/playwright, best remembered for lyrics for "Home, Sweet Home," from his opera, *Clari*, born in New York City; wrote about 60 plays (died 1852).

1851 Charles J. Bonaparte, public official, born in Baltimore; Secretary of Navy (1905–06), Attorney General (1906–09), launching many antitrust suits including American Tobacco Co.; a founder, president, National Municipal League (1894) (died 1921).

1861 U.S. Sanitary Commission, forerunner of Red Cross, organized by War Secretary.

1863 Battle of Brandy Station (VA), greatest cavalry battle of the Civil War, occurred when Gen. Joseph Hooker tried to determine whether Confederate forces were moving northward.

1868 Edward F. McGlachlin, Army officer in Spanish-American War and World War I, born in Fond du Lac, WI; commander, 1st Division (1918–19) and 7th Division (1919–21) (died 1946).

1893 Cole Porter, composer of musicals

(*Anything Goes, Panama Hattie, Kiss Me Kate, DuBarry Was a Lady, Can-Can*), born in Peru, IN (died 1964).

1893 S(amuel) N. Behrman, playwright (*Biography, No Time for Comedy, Fanny*), born in Worcester, MA (died 1973).

1893 Three floors of Ford Theater in Washington, DC, collapsed during reconstruction work, killing 22 persons, injuring 68.

1895 Robert F. DeGraff, publisher who founded Pocket Books (1939), born in Plainfield, NJ (died 1981).

1899 Jim Jeffries knocked out Bob Fitzsimmons in 11th round in Coney Island for heavyweight boxing championship.

1900 Fred Waring, orchestra leader/choral director, born in Tyrone, PA; his chorus, The Pennsylvanians, appeared regularly from 1923 on (died 1984).

1901 George Price, cartoonist who helped modernize magazine cartoons, born in Coylesville, NJ (died 1995).

1902 Woodrow Wilson unanimously elected president of Princeton U. by the trustees; served until 1910, when he became New Jersey governor.

1902 First automatic vending restaurant (Horn & Hardart) opened at 818 Chestnut St., Philadelphia.

1916 Robert S. McNamara, public official, born in San Francisco; executive with Ford Motor Co. (1946–60); Secretary of Defense (1961–68); president, World Bank (1969–81).

1916 Les Paul, guitarist with Mary Ford, born in Waukesha, WI.

1930 Ben Abruzzo, balloonist who crossed both Atlantic and Pacific Oceans, born in Rockford, IL (died 1985).

1941 Federal troops took over North American Aviation Co. in Ingleside, CA, because strike there was hurting defense production.

1953 Worcester, MA, and vicinity were struck by tornadoes causing 90 deaths.

1959 First American ballistic missile submarine (*George Washington*) launched at Groton, CT.

1972 Flash flood at Rapid City, SD, caused 237 deaths, $160 million in damage.

1978 Larry Holmes defeated Ken Norton in 15 rounds in Las Vegas to win world heavyweight boxing title.

1986 Supreme Court ruled 5–3 to invalidate Reagan Administration "Baby Doe" ruling requiring hospitals to treat, feed severely handicapped infants on the grounds that refusing treatment was a form of discrimination.

10

1586 Starving colonists at Roanoke Island, NC, were rescued by Sir Francis Drake and returned to England.

1661 Massachusetts Bay Colony issued declaration of liberties which indicated that English laws were not binding on the colonies.

1735 John Morgan, pioneer physician, born in Philadelphia; founded Philadelphia College of Surgeons, U. of Pennsylvania Medical College (1765); chief medical officer during Revolution (1775–77) (died 1789).

1753 William Eustis, public official and legislator, born in Cambridge, MA; represented Massachusetts in House (1801–05, 1820–23) and served it as governor (1823–25); Secretary of War (1809–13), resigning under criticism of the war's conduct; minister to Holland (1814–18) (died 1825).

1775 James Barbour, legislator and public official, born in Barboursville, VA; represented Virginia in Senate (1815–25) and served as its governor (1812–15); Secretary of War (1825–28); minister to Great Britain (1828–29) (died 1842).

1775 Continental Congress accepted John Adams' proposal that forces defending Boston be accepted as the Continental Army; four days later it voted to raise six companies of riflemen in Pennsylvania, Maryland, and Virginia; named committee to draft rules of administration of the Army.

1776 Continental Congress named committee to prepare Declaration of Independence, consisting of Thomas Jefferson, John Adams, Benjamin Franklin, Roger Sherman, and Robert R. Livingston; brought in draft June 28.

1810 Benjamin S. Ewell, Confederate officer and educator, born in Washington, DC; after Civil War, he rebuilt burned buildings of College of William & Mary in Williamsburg, kept charter in force by ringing bell periodically; finally got government help and school reopened in 1888 (died 1894).

1814 James W. Nye, Nevada pioneer, born in DeRuyter, NY; first and only Nevada territorial governor (1861–64), one of first Nevada senators (1864–73) (died 1876).

1816 Convention opened in Corydon, IN, which later adopted state constitution; slavery was prohibited.

1835 Rebecca Fulton, first woman U.S. senator, born near Decatur, GA; appointed by Georgia governor October 3, 1922, served until November 22 (died 1930).

1849 David Lubin, fruit grower who organized growers to work on fruit growing problems, born in Poland; also organized an international institute of agriculture (died 1919).

1850 Convention of nine slave states in Nashville called for extending the Missouri Compromise line west to the Pacific; second convention in November denounced the Compromise, asserted the right to secession.

1861 Small Union force from Ft. Monroe, VA, defeated by Confederate troops as it tried to capture a battery; this was first battle of Civil War.

1862 Mrs. Leslie Carter, actress sometimes called America's Sarah Bernhardt, born in Lexington, KY; starred in many plays (*Zaza*, *La Tosca*) (died 1937).

1864 Confederate Congress authorized use of men between 17 and 18 and 45 to 50 for military service.

1865 Frederick A. Cook, polar explorer, born in Callicon Depot, NY; with early Peary polar expeditions, claimed to have reached North Pole April 21, 1908, before Peary; claim rejected after investigation (died 1940).

1887 Harry F. Byrd, public official and legislator, born in Winchester, VA; represented Virginia in Senate (1933–65) and served as governor (1926–30) (died 1966).

1891 Al Dubin, noted lyricist, born in Zurich, Switzerland; wrote many hits ("Tip Toe Through the Tulips," "42nd Street," "Shuffle Off to Buffalo," "Anniversary Waltz," "Lullaby of Broadway") (died 1945).

1897 New state constitution went into effect in Delaware.

1898 Marines made first landing in Cuba, coming ashore at Guantanamo Bay.

1901 Frederick Loewe, composer of musicals (*Brigadoon, Camelot, My Fair Lady*), born in Berlin; also wrote score for movie *Gigi* (died 1988).

1903 Clyde R. Beatty, wild animal trainer, born in Chillicothe, OH (died 1965).

1906 Christian Science Cathedral in Boston dedicated.

1915 Saul Bellow, author (*Adventures of Augie March, Herzog, Henderson, The Rain King*), born in Lachine, Canada; awarded 1976 Nobel Literature Prize.

1920 Federal Power Commission established; ended October 1, 1977, with functions transferred to Department of Energy.

1921 Bureau of Budget created in Treasury Department; became part of Office of Management and Budget (1970).

1922 Judy Garland, singer/screen actress (*Wizard of Oz, A Star is Born, Babes in Arms*), born in Grand Rapids, MN (died 1969).

1933 F. Lee Bailey, criminal lawyer who represented Dr. Sam Shepard, Capt. Medina in My Lai trial, Boston Strangler, Patty Hearst, born in Waltham, MA.

1935 Alcoholics Anonymous founded by William G. Wilson and Dr. Robert Smith in New York.

1940 President Franklin Roosevelt, speaking at U. of Virginia, called for speedy American defense and help for those opposing force.

1967 Joseph E. Ritter, Catholic Archbishop of Indianapolis (1944–46) and St. Louis (1946–61), died at 76; named a cardinal 1961.

1971 President Nixon lifted 21-year embargo on trade with Communist China.

1974 President Nixon began first Middle East tour by an incumbent president.

1980 Supreme Court ruled unanimously that a zoning ordinance which limits development in the name of conservation does not necessarily violate the constitutional rights of affected property owners.

1983 Presbyterian Church (USA) formed in Atlanta by merger of United Presbyterian Church in the U.S.A. and the Presbyterian Church in the U.S. after a split of 122 years over the question of slavery and the Civil War.

1993 The *New York Times* will acquire the *Boston Globe* in a $1.1 billion merger.

2002 Supreme Court decides 9–0 that it does not violate the Americans with Disabilities Act to refuse to hire a disabled individual if that impairment makes the job dangerous.

11

1741 Joseph Warren, physician who rode with Paul Revere to warn colonists, born in Roxbury, MA; killed at the Battle of Bunker Hill June 17, 1775.

1796 Nathaniel Gorham, colonial leader, died at 58; member, Massachusetts Board of War (1778–81), Continental Congress (1782–83, 1785–87), its president (1786); member of Constitutional Convention (1787).

1805 Detroit leveled by fire, leaving only one building standing.

1823 James L. Kemper, Confederate general who led right wing of Pickett's charge at Gettysburg, born in Madison County, VA (died 1895).

1850 People of Kentucky ratified their state constitution.

1859 Famous Comstock lode of silver discovered in Six Mile Canyon, NV.

1879 Ralph Pulitzer, publisher, born in St. Louis; president, Press Publishing Co., which published the *New York World* (1911–30) (died 1939).

1880 Jeannette Rankin, first woman member of Congress, born near Missoula, MT; represented Montana in House (1917–19, 1941–43), cast vote against war both in 1917 and 1941 (the only dissenting vote) (died 1973).

1886 David B. Steinman, bridge engineer who built more than 40 bridges world wide, born in New York City; his bridges include George Washington and Triborough, New York City; Thousand Islands over the St. Lawrence (died 1960).

1913 Vincent T. Lombardi, football player/coach, born in New York City; played with Fordham U., New York Giants; coached Giants, Green Bay, Washington (died 1970).

1913 Risë Stevens, opera/concert mezzosoprano, born in New York City; sang at Metropolitan from 1938, such roles as Mignon and Carmen.

1918 American planes made first air raid, dropping bombs on railroad station at Dommary-Barancourt, near Metz.

1938 Johnny VanderMeer, Cincinnati Reds left hander, pitched 3–0 no-hit game against Boston Braves; four days later, he pitched a 5–0 no-hitter against Brooklyn.

1942 Gen. Dwight D. Eisenhower named commander of European Theater of Operations.

1947 Sugar rationing ended.

1956 Joe (Joseph C.) Montana, football quarterback (Notre Dame U; San Francisco, Kansas City 1979–96), born in Monongahela, PA; completed 3,409 passes for 40,551 yards, 273 touchdowns; led 49ers to four Super Bowl wins.

1958 Clarence DeMar, marathoner who won Boston Marathon seven times between 1911 and 1930, died at 70.

1985 Karen Ann Quinlan, 31, died after more than ten years in a state of being irreversibly comatose; parents received court permission years before to disconnect respirator.

1989 The Rev. Jerry Falwell, founder of Moral Majority, announced official disbanding of the religious right's political lobbying group because it had achieved its goals of keeping the United States from moving farther to the left.

1990 Supreme Court ruled 5–4 that a new law forbidding the burning or defacement of the American flag was unconstitutional.

2001 Today Timothy McVeigh executed by lethal injection; blew up federal building in Oklahoma City, April 19, 1995.

2003 David Brinkley, anchor and co-anchor of network news broadcasts for decades, died at 82.

2004 First presidential funeral since 1973, as ceremonies held in Washington, DC, and body of Ronald Reagan is then interred in California.

2005 After a career of controversial behavior both in and out of the ring, heavyweight champion Mike Tyson ended final match by conceding it to opponent before beginning of seventh round.

12

1775 Governor Thomas Gage of Massachusetts Bay Colony issued proclamation offering to pardon all rebels except Samuel Adams and John Hancock if they would lay down their arms and "return to their duties of peaceable subjects."

1776 Continental Congress named committee to prepare Articles of Confederation and Perpetual Union; plan submitted July 12.

1776 Virginia Convention adopted bill of rights drafted by George Mason, which had wide influence in the United States and later in France.

1792 Convention at Newcastle adopted state constitution and established the state name of Delaware.

1806 John A. Roebling, developed machinery and process for making wire rope, born in Muhlhausen, Germany; used the wire rope in building suspension bridges; made preliminary plans for Brooklyn Bridge, but died before construction was completed (died 1869).

1820 Constitution of Missouri adopted by convention in St. Louis; ratified by the people January 6, 1821; provided for legislation to prevent free blacks and mulattoes from settling in state.

1833 James B. Weaver, presidential candidate, born in Dayton, OH; represented Iowa in House (1879–81, 1885–89); candidate of Greenback-Labor Party (1880) and People's Party (1892), winning 22 electoral votes and more than one million popular votes (died 1912).

1837 Samuel W. Abbott, pioneer in public health movement, born in Woburn, MA; used demographic studies (died 1904).

1838 President Van Buren signed act establishing Territory of Iowa.

1859 Thomas J. Walsh, legislator, born in Two Rivers, WI; represented Montana in Senate (1912–33); chairman of Teapot Dome investigation; nominated for Attorney General (1933), but died before confirmation.

1864 Frank M. Chapman, ornithologist who founded, edited, *Bird-Lore*, born in Englewood, NJ; chairman, Ornithology Department, American Museum of Natural History (1920–42) (died 1945).

1871 Victor D. Brenner, sculptor who designed first portrait coin (Lincoln penny), born in Shavli, Russia (died 1924).

1874 Charles L. McNary, legislator, born near Salem, OR; represented Oregon in Senate (1917–44), minority leader (1933–44); Republican vice presidential candidate (1940) (died 1944).

1877 Thomas C. Hart, World War II admiral, born in Davison, MI; commander, Asiatic Fleet (1939–42), combined Allied fleet (1942); superintendent, Naval Academy (1931–34); represented Connecticut in Senate (1945–47) (died 1963).

1893 John B. Hodge, World War II general, born in Golconda, IL (died 1963).

1899 Fritz A. Lipmann, biochemist, born in Königsberg, Germany (now Russia); shared 1953 Nobel Physiology/Medicine Prize for studies of living cells; discovered coenzyme A, a basic catalyst in animal metabolism (died 1986).

1905 Arthur S. Flemming, educator and public official, born in Kingston, NY; director, Office of Defense Mobilization (1952–57), Secretary of Health, Education & Welfare (1958–61); president, U. of Oregon (1961–68); member, Commission on Civil Rights (1974–81) (died 1996).

1906 Meatpacking companies (Armour, Swift, Cudahy, Nelson Morris) found guilty of violating Elkins Act, fined $15,000 each for accepting rebates.

1915 David Rockefeller, banker, Chase Manhattan Bank (from 1995–), born in New York City.

1922 Ed Wynn staged first radio broadcast of a Broadway production (*The Perfect Fool*); the first broadcast with a studio audience.

1924 George H.W. Bush, 41st president (1989–93), born in Milton, MA; served as Vice President (1981–89); represented Texas in Senate (1967–71), UN ambassador (1971–72), China liaison officer (1974–75), CIA director (1976–77).

1924 Gun turret exploded on USS *Mississippi* off San Pedro, CA; 48 men killed.

1937 Pan-American Exposition opened in Dallas; closed October 31.

1939 National Baseball Hall of Fame dedicated at Cooperstown, NY.

1941 President Franklin Roosevelt nominated Associate Justice Harlan F. Stone for Chief Justice of the Supreme Court; confirmed June 27.

1942 President Franklin Roosevelt made radio appeal for scrap rubber campaign; more than 300,000 tons were collected between June 15 and 30.

1944 Big Bend (TX) National Park established.

1963 Medger Evers, field secretary for NAACP, shot to death from ambush in front of his home in Jackson, MS.

1968 President Lyndon Johnson addressed UN General Assembly in New York City shortly after it approved (95–4) the Nuclear Nonproliferation Treaty.

1971 Tricia (Patricia) Nixon, daughter of President and Mrs. Nixon, was married in the White House Rose Garden to Edward R.F. Cox.

1981 Major league baseball players went on strike over free agent policy; strike ended August 9.

1987 The PTL (Praise the Lord) television ministry filed for reorganization under the federal bankruptcy code, blaming the "chaotic mismanagement" of founder Jim Bakker for piling up $70 million in debts.

1997 President Clinton appointed an advisory board on race issues, chaired by historian John Hope Franklin.

2000 Justice Department settled dispute with former President Richard Nixon's estate over records seized after his resignation; government to pay $18 million in compensation.

2001 George W. Bush made first presidential visit to Europe; stressed need for an anti-missile defense for the Western nations.

2002 New rules of the Accreditation Council for Graduate Medical Education limit hospital residents to 80-hour work week, 24-hour work shift; rules to take effect in summer 2003.

2005 Earthquake registers 5.2 with epicenter 20 miles from Palm Springs, CA.

2006 West Virginia Senator Robert Byrd set new longevity service record for Senate; reelected eight times.

13

1784 Henry Middleton, colonial leader, died at 67; member of Continental Congress (1774–76), its president (1774–75).

1786 Winfield Scott, highest ranking military man between Revolution and Civil War, born near Petersburg, VA; general-in-chief of Army (1841–61); commanded American troops in Mexican War; 1852 Whig presidential candidate (died 1866).

1792 William A. Burt, invented a typographer, forerunner of typewriter, born in Worcester, MA; also invented a solar compass, equatorial sextant (died 1858).

1793 Commerce with France suspended as relations worsened.

1854 Bradley A. Fiske, inventor, born in Lyons, NY; among his inventions were an electric range finder, electric ammunition hoist, torpedo plane (died 1942).

1858 Explosion aboard the steamship *Pennsylvania* in Mississippi River near Memphis killed 160 persons.

1868 The 14th Amendment enacted, forbidding any state from depriving any person of life, liberty, or property without due process of law.

1868 Wallace C.W. Sabine, founder of architectural acoustics, born in Richwood, OH (died 1919).

1872 Daniel W. Adams, Confederate general, died at 52; saw action at Chickamauga.

1879 Robert E. Wood, merchant, born in Kansas City, MO; with Montgomery Ward (1919–24), Sears (1924–54), president and board chairman (1928–54); founder, All State Insurance Co. (died 1969).

1880 Vincent Rose, bandleader (1900–40s) and composer ("Avalon," "Whispering," "Blueberry Hill"), born in Palermo, Sicily (died 1944).

1888 President Cleveland signed act establishing Department of Labor to be headed by a commissioner, effective June 30.

1894 Mark VanDoren, poet and critic, born in Hope, IL; literary editor, *The Nation* (1924–28), film critic (1935–38); prolific poet (died 1972).

1903 Red (Harold) Grange, football player known as the "Galloping Ghost," born in Folksville, PA; starred at U. of Illinois, Chicago Bears (1925–35) (died 1991).

1911 Louis Walter Alvarez, physicist and co-developer of ground-controlled radar to permit all-weather plane landings, born in San Francisco; awarded 1968 Nobel Physics Prize for study and discovery of "resonance" particles (died 1988).

1913 Ralph Edwards, television performer and producer, born in Merino, CO.

1915 Don Budge, tennis player, born in Oakland, CA; one of few to win "grand slam" (America, Australian, British, French singles) in one year (1938).

1917 First American division embarked for France; arrived June 25.

1924 Torsten N. Wiesel, medical researcher, born in Upsala, Sweden; shared 1981 Nobel Physiology/Medicine Prize for study of brain's function in vision.

1933 Home Owners Loan Corp. (HOLC) established to refinance non-farm mortgages; loans were made on about a million mortgages by June 1936.

1935 Jim Braddock defeated Max Baer in 15 rounds in New York City to become world heavyweight boxing champion.

1942 Office of War Information (OWI) created by consolidating Office of Facts & Figures, Office of Governmental Reports, and Coordinator of Information; abolished August 31, 1945.

1943 Office of Strategic Services (OSS) established with William J. Donovan director; designed to engage in intelligence operations; terminated October 1, 1945; forerunner of Central Intelligence Agency (CIA).

1946 "Major" Edward Bowes, radio personality, died at 82; originated amateur hour.

1967 President Lyndon Johnson nominated Thurgood Marshall to the Supreme Court, the first black named to the court; confirmed August 30.

1968 Chief Justice Earl Warren submitted his resignation from the Supreme Court.

1971 *New York Times* began publishing what came to be known as the Pentagon Papers, classified information on American-Indochina involvement; other papers followed suit; Supreme Court by 6–3 vote upheld right to publish June 30.

1989 President Bush vetoed legislation to raise hourly minimum wage to $4.55; had asked raising limit to $4.25 an hour.

1996 The Montana antitax, antigovernment group, the Freemen, surrendered to federal agents after a nearly three months standoff.

2001 With CIA director George Tenet as mediator, Palestinians and Israel embraced ceasefire proposal.

2003 State of Maine promised to have low-cost health insurance policy available for all residents by 2009.

2005 U.S. Senate apologized for never passing anti-lynching law during the segregation era.

2005 Singer Michael Jackson acquitted on all child molestation and abuse charges; jury had deliberated some 30 hours scattered over 7 days.

14

1639 Fundamental Articles of New Haven, CT, were adopted; prepared by Theophilus Eaton and the Rev. John Davenport.

1665 Thomas Willett became first mayor of New York City.

1716 Peter Harrison, first American architect, born in York, England; designed King's Chapel in Boston, Christ Church in Cambridge (died 1775).

1775 Continental Congress passed resolution authorizing formation of Continental Army of 20,000 — ten companies of expert riflemen; marks birthday of present Army.

1777 Continental Congress resolved that American flag be "thirteen stripes alternate red and white, that the Union be stars white in a blue field..."

1801 Heber C. Kimball, Mormon leader, born in Sheldon, VT; one of the 12 original Mormon apostles (1836); a chief advisor to Brigham Young; lieutenant governor, State of Deseret (Utah) (1849–68) (died 1868).

1805 Robert Anderson, Union officer who commanded Ft. Sumter when it was attacked by Confederates starting Civil War, born near Louisville, KY (died 1871).

1810 Ward Hunt, associate justice, Supreme Court (1873–82), born in Utica, NY (died 1886).

1811 Harriet Beecher Stowe, author of *Uncle Tom's Cabin*, born in Litchfield, CT; outstanding book of the time (died 1896).

1820 John Bartlett, compiler of well-known *Familiar Quotations*, born in Plymouth, MA (died 1905).

1846 Americans raised flag of the California Republic at Sonoma, which they had captured from the Mexicans June 11.

1855 Robert M. LaFollette, public official and legislator, born in Primrose, WI; represented Wisconsin in House (1885–91) and Senate (1906–25); launched Teapot Dome investigation; governor of Wisconsin (1900–06); 1924 Progressive Party presidential candidate (died 1925).

1862 John U. Nef, pioneer chemist, born in Herisan, Switzerland; investigated bivalent carbons, fulminates, mechanism of organic reactions (died 1915).

1862 John J. Glennon, Catholic Archbishop of St. Louis (1903–46), born in County Meath, Ireland (died 1946).

1868 Karl Landsteiner, pathologist, born in Vienna; with Rockefeller Institute, discovered four types of human blood (1900), helping make transfusions safe; awarded 1930 Nobel Physiology/Medicine Prize for that work (died 1943).

1884 John McCormack, operatic tenor (Metropolitan, Chicago operas), born in Athlone, Ireland; noted for roles in *Faust*, *La Boheme*, *Madama Butterfly* (died 1945).

1889 Samoan Treaty signed in Berlin, placing islands under joint control of United States, Great Britain, and Germany, with a fueling station for American fleet.

1895 Louis Finkelstein, president/chancellor, Talmud Jewish Theological Seminary (1940–72), born in Cincinnati (died 1991).

1898 American expeditionary force of 17,000 sailed from Tampa for Cuba.

1900 Territory of Hawaii established.

1906 Margaret Bourke-White, photographer (*Life* magazine 1936–69), born in New York City (died 1971).

1909 Burl Ives, folk singer and screen actor (*Cat on a Hot Tin Roof*, *The Big Country*), born in Hull, IL; made numerous records (died 1995).

1934 Max Baer knocked out Primo Carnera in 11 rounds in Long Island City for world heavyweight boxing championship.

1941 President Franklin Roosevelt ordered freezing of all German and Italian assets in the United States.

1943 Supreme Court ruled that school children could not be compelled to salute the flag if the ceremony conflicted with their religion; case was brought by Jehovah's Witnesses.

1947 President Truman formally signed peace treaties with Italy, Hungary, Rumania, and Bulgaria.

1958 Eric Heiden, ice skater who won five gold medals in 1980 Olympics, born in LaCrosse, WI.

1972 Environmental Protection Agency announced near-total ban on use of DDT, effective December 31, 1972.

1985 Terrorists seized TWA plane between Athens and Rome with 104 Americans aboard; one American was killed before all passengers were released by June 30.

1988 Howard H. Baker, Jr., former Tennessee senator, resigned as White House chief of staff after 16 months service; succeeded by Kenneth M. Duberstein.

1989 Rep. Richard A. Gephardt of Missouri elected House majority leader, Rep. William H. Gray, III, of Pennsylvania majority whip.

1989 Queen Elizabeth II of Great Britain made former President Reagan an honorary knight.

2000 (Robert) Trent Jones, Sr., designed or redesigned over 500 golf courses; dead at 93.

2004 In an 8–0 decision the Supreme Court upheld the words "under God" in pledge of allegiance; five of votes, however, stressed that the plaintiff lacked legal standing to bring the suit.

2005 Heritage Foundation study asserted that voluntary vows of sexual chastity among teenagers often work, contradicting two earlier analyses working from the same source data that came to the opposite conclusion.

15

1649 First trial for witchcraft held in Charlestown, MA; Margaret Jones found guilty and executed.

1752 Benjamin Franklin, flying a kite in a thunderstorm, proved that lightning is electricity.

1767 Rachel Donelson Jackson, wife of President Jackson, born in Halifax County, VA (died 1828).

1773 Asher Benjamin, pioneer architect, born in Greenfield, MA; wrote number of guides which influenced American architecture (died 1845).

1775 George Washington unanimously appointed commander-in-chief of the colonial armies by the Continental Congress; Washington accepted the next day, saying he would serve without salary, keeping track of his expenses.

1776 New Hampshire legislature adopted declaration of independence, instructing its delegates to the Continental Congress to vote for such action.

1787 William Paterson submitted the "New Jersey Plan" to the Constitutional Convention, calling for retention of the Confederation but giving Congress the power to tax, to regulate foreign and interstate commerce, and to name a plural executive and Supreme Court.

1800 Nation's capital moved from Philadelphia to the District of Columbia.

1804 The 12th Amendment was ratified; required separate electoral votes for president and vice president.

1805 William B. Ogden, railroad president and first mayor of Chicago, born in Walton, NY; served as mayor 1837; president, Chicago & Northwestern Railroad (1859–68); first president, Union Pacific Railroad (1862–63) (died 1877).

1826 Charles B. Smith, humorist under pseudonym of Bill Arp, born in Lawrenceville, GA (died 1903).

1833 Edward M. McCook, Union General of cavalry, born in Steubenville, OH; minister to Hawaii (1866–69), governor of Colorado Territory (1869–75) (died 1909).

1834 N.J. Wyeth began construction of first Idaho settlement, Ft. Hall on Snake River.

1836 Arkansas entered Union as the 25th state.

1836 George L. Shoup, first governor of Idaho Territory (1889) and state (1890), born in Kittaning, PA; first Idaho senator (1890–1901) (died 1904).

1845 President Polk ordered Gen. Zachary Taylor to the Rio Grande to protect Texas in case Mexico declared war.

1846 Oregon Treaty signed by President Polk after it was ratified by Senate, fixing boundary between United States and British North America along 49th parallel, ending 50 years of boundary dispute.

1849 Former President Polk died in Nashville at 53.

1850 Willard Richards published first Utah newspaper, the *Deseret News*, in Salt Lake City.

1861 Union troops occupied Harpers Ferry, WV, after Confederate force retreated to Winchester, VA.

1861 Ernestine Schumann-Heink, one of greatest opera singers, born in Lieben, Austria (now Czechoslovakia) (died 1936).

1863 Confederate force defeated Union troops at Winchester, VA.

1863 Confederate cavalry raided Chambersburg, PA.

1864 Arlington National Cemetery established.

1864 Gen. U.S. Grant led unsuccessful four-day assault on Petersburg, VA, losing more than 7,500 men; began siege which lasted nine months.

1869 Massachusetts appointed Board of Railroad Commissioners, the first state railroad law.

1879 Samuel C. Lind, inventor of electroscope for radium measurement, born in McMinnville, TN; originator of ionization theory of chemical effect of radium rays (died 1965).

1881 William McFee, author (*Casuals of the Sea, The Harbourmaster, Derelicts*), born in London (died 1966).

1887 Malvina Hoffman, sculptor, born in New York City; executed bronzes of 101 racial types for the Field Museum (died 1966).

1894 Robert Russell Bennett, composer who orchestrated all Rodgers and Hammerstein musicals, born in Kansas City, MO (died 1981).

1902 Erik H. Erickson, psychologist who introduced concept of "identity crisis," born in Frankfurt, Germany (died 1994).

1903 Barney Oldfield became first man to drive an automobile at 60 miles per hour.

1904 Steamer *General Slocum* burned in New York's East River, 1,021 died; passengers were on an excursion from St. Mark's German Lutheran Church.

1910 David Rose, orchestra leader and composer (*Holiday for Strings*), born in London (died 1990).

1914 Saul Steinberg, cartoonist and illustrator (mostly in *The New Yorker*), born in Rimnicu-Sarat, Rumania.

1915 Thomas H. Weller, biologist, born in Ann Arbor, MI; shared 1954 Nobel Physiology/Medicine Prize for work on isolating polio virus.

1916 Herbert A. Simon, economist, born in Milwaukee; awarded 1978 Nobel Economics Prize for pioneering research in decision-making process in economic organizations.

1916 Marshall Field IV, head of Field Enterprises, born in New York City; editor, publisher, *Chicago Sun-Times* (1949–65), *Chicago Daily News* (1958–65) (died 1965).

1917 Espionage Act signed by President Wilson, called for 20 years in prison and up to $10,000 fine for aiding the enemy, obstructing recruiting, or refusal to serve.

1923 Erroll Garner, jazz pianist and composer ("Misty"), born in Pittsburgh (died 1977).

1924 President Coolidge signed bill making American-born Indians citizens.

1929 Agricultural Marketing Act enacted by congress to aid farm price stability.

1934 Great Smoky Mountains (NC) National Park established.

1934 National Guard Act signed by President Franklin Roosevelt making the Guard part of the Army in wartime or national emergency.

1937 Waylon Jennings, country music singer, born in Littlefield, TX.

1939 Mixed Claims Commission found Germany guilty of two explosions in 1916 and 1917 (Black Tom Island and Kingsland, NJ) but Germany never paid the $55 million damage award.

1944 American troops landed on Mariana Islands; Saipan taken July 9, Guam on August 10, and Tinian, August 11.

1944 First B-29 Superfortress raid on Japan hit Yawata on Kyushu Island.

1946 President Truman proposed to Congress that the Army and Navy departments be merged into a single Department of Defense.

1982 Supreme Court ruled 5–4 that illegal aliens must have access to free education.

1993 John B. Connally, former Texas governor, died at 76; was riding with President Kennedy when he was killed by rifle fire in Dallas in 1963.

2001 During summit conference preliminaries with Russian president Putin, President Bush strongly advocated expansion of NATO to East European countries formerly in the Eastern Bloc.

16

1775 George Washington accepted the commission as commanding general of the Continental Army, saying "...yet I feel great distress from a consciousness that my abilities may not be equal to the extensive and important task..."

1775 Continental Congress created office of Engineer of the Continental Army.

1778 British troops under Gen. Henry Clinton began evacuating Philadelphia.

1779 Sir Francis Bernard, colonial governor, died at 67; served as governor of New Jersey (1758–60) and Massachusetts (1760–69), a period described as "among the most turbulent."

1804 Alvin Adams, express business pioneer, born in Andover, VT; founder (1854) of Adams Express Co., which absorbed several companies (died 1877).

1834 Wesley Merritt, Spanish-American War Army general, born in New York City; superintendent, West Point (1882–87); commander, American forces in Philippines (1898), helped capture Manila (died 1910).

1858 Abraham Lincoln, nominated by Illinois Republicans in Springfield for the Senate, made the famous speech in which he said: "A house divided against itself cannot stand. I believe this government cannot endure permanently half slave and half free. I do not expect the Union to be dissolved; I do not expect the house to fall; but I do expect it will cease to be divided. It will become all one thing, or all the other."

1868 *Atlanta Constitution* began publication.

1889 Nelson Doubleday, founder/head of publishing firm, born in Brooklyn (died 1949).

1890 Stan Laurel, half of first great movies comedy team (Laurel and Hardy), born in Ulverston, England (died 1965).

1892 Raymond Rubicam, cofounder, chief executive officer, Young & Rubicam advertising agency (1923–44), born in Brooklyn (died 1978).

1902 George C. Simpson, paleontologist and one of world's foremost authorities on evolutionary theory, born in Chicago; with American Museum of Natural History (1928–59).

1902 Barbara McClintock, geneticist, born in Hartford, CT; awarded 1981 Nobel Physiology/Medicine Prize for pioneer work in genetic mechanisms (died 1992).

1903 Helen Traubel, principal Wagnerian soprano of Metropolitan Opera (1939–53), born in St. Louis (died 1972).

1916 Hank (Angelo) Luisetti, college basketball star who revolutionized game with one-handed shot, born in San Francisco.

1917 Katherine Graham, newspaper executive, born in New York City; publisher, *Washington Post* (1968–78), board chairman (from 1973).

1925 Fifty persons died in a railroad accident at Hackettstown, NJ.

1933 Emergency Railroad Transportation Act became effective; provided for reorganization of the industry under a federal administrator.

1933 Congress enacted National Industrial Recovery Act, providing for federal control of nation's entire industrial structure through codes; the NRA, directed by Gen. Hugh Johnson, affected 500 industrial fields, 22 million employees; act also created Public Works Administration under Interior Secretary Harold L. Ickes, which eventually spent more than $4 billion on 34,000 public works projects; act held unconstitutional, NRA terminated January 1, 1936.

1933 President Franklin Roosevelt signed Banking Act of 1933 creating the Federal Deposit Insurance Corp., guaranteeing bank deposits up to $5,000.

1933 Farm Credit Act went into effect, reorganizing agricultural credit.

1933 Navy Department was allocated $238 million for 32 new vessels.

1938 Joyce Carol Oates, author (*By the North Gate, With Shuddering Fall*), born in Lockport, NY.

1944 American air offensive began against the Japanese by B-29 bombers.

1976 American ambassador to Lebanon, Francis E. Maloy, Jr., and an aide were killed by unidentified gunmen.

1978 President Carter and Gen. Omar Herrera signed treaties in Panama City which would turn over the Panama Canal to Panama in the year 2000.

1980 Supreme Court ruled 5–4 that biological organisms can be patented under federal law.

1992 Presidents Bush and Yeltsin announced agreement to sharply reduce stocks of long-range missile warheads and to eliminate all multiple warhead land-based missiles.

1995 Salt Lake City was selected as site for the 2002 Winter Olympics.

17

1579 Sir Francis Drake, preying on Spanish shipping and settlements along Pacific coast, anchored in San Francisco Bay; took possession of area in the name of Queen Elizabeth I.

1673 Louis Joliet, Father Pere Marquette, and five others reached Mississippi River at Prairie du Chien, WI.

1745 Louisburg, French fortress on Cape Breton Island, fell to American and English forces under William Pepperell after a six-weeks siege.

1746 Joseph Winston, Revolutionary officer and legislator, born in Louisa County, VA; represented North Carolina in House (1793–95, 1803–07); Winston (now Winston-Salem) named for him (died 1815).

1751 Joshua Humphreys, architect who designed, supervised construction of War of 1812 naval vessels, born in Haverford, PA (died 1838).

1768 Isaac Parker, Massachusetts Supreme Court chief justice (1814–30), born in Boston; helped establish Harvard Law School, where he taught (1816–30) (died 1830).

1774 Massachusetts House of Representatives, meeting in Salem, approved resolution by Samuel Adams for "a meeting of committees from the several colonies ... to consult upon the present state of the colonies ... and to deliberate and determine upon wise and proper measures to be by them recommended ... and for the recovery and establishment of just rights and liberties, civil and religious, and the restoration of union and harmony between Great Britain and the colonies..."

1775   Battle of Bunker Hill, which was mostly fought on adjoining Breed's Hill, took place, with 1,600 Americans and six cannons, led by Col. William Prescott, holding off two charges by British troops; Prescott reportedly commanded "don't fire till you see the whites of their eyes;" Americans then retreated toward Cambridge on the third charge because of dwindling ammunition; British won position at cost of 1,054 casualties; Americans lost about 100 dead, 267 wounded, 30 prisoners.

1777   Gen. John Burgoyne and 7,700 British troops began move south from St. Johns; objective was to meet British troops moving east along the Mohawk River and north along the Hudson River.

1778   Clash occurred between French and British naval units, officially marking the start of hostilities between the two countries.

1778   Continental Congress, in response to British request for peace conference, said it would only negotiate for withdrawal of the British and American independence.

1791   Abel P. Upshur, public official, born in Northampton County, VA; Secretary of Navy (1841–43), Secretary of State (1843–44); killed with several other cabinet members and legislators February 28, 1844, when a gun exploded on a Navy vessel during an inspection.

1824   Bureau of Indian Affairs established as a subsidiary of War Department.

1825   Bunker Hill Monument cornerstone laid by Marquis de Lafayette; ceremony was addressed by Daniel Webster.

1837   Charles Goodyear obtained patent for the manufacture of rubber tires.

1843   Bunker Hill Monument dedicated by President Tyler, with Daniel Webster giving the address.

1855   Richard A. Canfield, gambling house operator on 44th Street, New York City, born in New Bedford, MA; his establishment called the Monte Carlo of America; forced to close (1902) (died 1914).

1856   First Republican presidential nominating convention opened in Philadelphia; named John C. Fremont as the candidate.

1860   Charles Frohman, theater manager and producer responsible for evolution of the star system, born in Sandusky, OH; died in sinking of the *Lusitania* (1915).

1863   Travelers Insurance Co., first accident insurance company, chartered in Hartford.

1867   John R. Gregg, inventor of a popular shorthand system, born in Rockcorry, Ireland (died 1948).

1871   James W. Johnson, civil rights leader who helped found the NAACP, born in Jacksonville, FL; served as its first secretary (1916–30) (died 1938).

1872   World's Peace Jubilee and International Music Festival opened in Boston; one event included a chorus of 20,000 and an orchestra of 2,000, including church bells, cannons, and Boston firemen banging out the "Anvil Chorus" on anvils; Patrick S. Gilmore was the conductor.

1882   Igor Stravinsky, composer who led futurist group in modern music, born in Oranienbaum, Russia; composer of ballets (*Le Sacre du Printemps*, *Petrouchka*), operas (*Le Rossignol*), much other music (died 1971).

1902   Sammy Fain, popular songs composer ("Love Is a Many-Splendored Thing," "That Old Feelin,'" "Dear Hearts and Gentle People"), born in Chicago (died 1989).

1902   Congress passed Newlands Reclamation Act, which provided for government construction of irrigation works from the sale of public lands in 16 western states.

1904   Ralph Bellamy, stage/screen actor (*Sunrise at Campobello*, *Detective Story*, *State of the Union*), born in Chicago (died 1991).

1907   Charles Eames, furniture designer who helped design the contour-molded chair, born in St. Louis (died 1978).

1914   John Hersey, author (*A Bell for Adano*, *Hiroshima*, *The Wall*), born in Tientsin, China (died 1993).

1917   Dean Martin, screen actor and entertainer, born in Steubenville, OH; starred in numerous films, television shows (died 1995).

1919   Kingman Brewster, president, Yale U. (1963–71), born in Longmeadow, MA; ambassador to Great Britain (1977–81).

1928   Amelia Earhart became first woman to fly the Atlantic Ocean, when she was a passenger on a 20-hour flight from Newfoundland to Burry Port, Wales.

1942   *Yank*, the Army magazine, first issued.

1943   Newt(on L.) Gingrich, legislator, born in Harrisburg, PA; represented Georgia in House (1979–98), serving as Speaker (1995–98).

1946   Barry Manilow, popular singer and composer ("Mandy," "I Write the Songs," "Can't Smile Without You"), born in New York City.

1963   Supreme Court ruled 8–1 that laws requiring recitation of the Lord's Prayer or Bible verses in public schools are unconstitutional.

1971 United States and Japan signed treaty returning Okinawa Island to the Japanese; captured by Americans during World War II.

1972 Five men were arrested by Washington police for breaking into Democratic national headquarters in the Watergate Building, starting the entire Watergate scandal.

1986 President Reagan announced that Warren Burger, Supreme Court chief justice for 17 years, was retiring and Associate Justice William Rehnquist was being nominated to succeed him; Senate confirmed Rehnquist September 17.

1987 Bernard H. Goetz acquitted of attempted murder by a New York City jury in the subway shooting of four men he said were going to rob him; he was convicted of a felony for carrying an unlicensed revolver.

1996 Mel Allen, baseball radio announcer, died at 83 after a long illness.

1996 Valujet Airlines, operator of a plane that crashed in Florida in May killing 110 passengers, voluntarily suspended operations.

1998 Senate defeated $516 billion tobacco bill which would have increased cost of cigarettes and was aimed at reducing smoking by teenagers.

2001 Governor Rick Perry of Texas vetoed ban on mentally retarded murderers being executed; defenders of decision argued that juries were already under guidelines requiring such matters to be taken into consideration in deciding punishment.

2002 Supreme Court threw out by 8–1 decision a local ordinance that demanded a solicitation permit for door-to-door religious or other solicitations: violates freedom of speech right.

18

1778 British, feeling threatened by a French blockade, evacuated Philadelphia; 3,000 Tories accompanied the troops to New York City.

1798 Naturalization Act amended to require 14 years residence (had been five) and notice of intention five years before application; repealed April 14, 1802, and original 1795 act reenacted.

1798 Rep. Robert G. Harper of South Carolina gave the historical toast of "millions for defense but not one cent for tribute" at a dinner for John Marshall, envoy to France, in Philadelphia.

1802 Henry Durant, a founder, first president, U. of California, born in Acton, MA; instrumental in getting a charter for California college (1855), which became university in 1868; served as president 1870–72 (died 1875).

1812 Congress completed its declaration of war against Great Britain.

1850 Cyrus H.K. Curtis, publisher, born in Portland, ME; established *Ladies Home Journal* (1876), headed Curtis Publishing Co. which issued the *Journal, The Country Gentleman, Saturday Evening Post*; also owned *Philadelphia Public Ledger, New York Post* (died 1933).

1854 Edward W. Scripps, publisher, born near Rushville, IL; cofounder, *Cleveland Penny Press* (1878), added other papers (St. Louis, Cincinnati) to form first newspaper chain; cofounder, Scripps McRae League (now Scripps Howard) and United Press (died 1926).

1857 Henry C. Folger, Standard Oil Co. president (1911–23), chairman (1923–28), born in New York City; donated major Shakespeare collection, building to Washington, DC (died 1930).

1877 James Montgomery Flagg, painter, illustrator, born in Pelham Manor, NY; best remembered for Uncle Sam recruiting poster, "I want you" (died 1960).

1886 Alexander Wetmore, ornithologist noted for work on American birds, born in North Freedom, WI; secretary, Smithsonian Institution (1945–52) (died 1978).

1896 Philip Barry, playwright (*The Animal Kingdom, Holiday, Here Come the Clowns, The Philadelphia Story*), born in Rochester, NY (died 1949).

1906 Kay Kyser, orchestra leader, born in Rocky Mount, NC (died 1985).

1907 Jeannette McDonald, singer/screen actress (*The Merry Widow, Naughty Marietta*), born in Philadelphia; starred with Nelson Eddy (died 1965).

1910 Mann-Elkins Act passed, placing telephone, telegraph, cable, and wireless companies under the Interstate Commerce Commission.

1913 Sylvia Porter, syndicated financial columnist, born in Patchogue, NY (died 1991).

1918 Jerome Karle, chemist, born in New York City; awarded 1985 Nobel Chemistry Prize for developing mathematical techniques for use of X-ray crystallography in body chemistry.

1918 Franco Modigliano, economist at MIT, born in Rome, Italy; awarded 1985 Nobel Economics Prize for work on effect of household savings on financial markets.

1924 George L. Mikan, first "big man" in professional basketball, born in Joliet, IL; considered greatest player of 1900–50 era.

1926 Allan R. Sandage, astronomer, co-discoverer of quasar (quasi-stellar radio source), born in Iowa City, IA.

1932 Dudley R. Herschbach, chemist, born in San Jose, CA; shared 1986 Nobel Chemistry Prize for helping create first detailed understanding of chemical reactions.

1941 Los Angeles and other southern California cities began receiving water from the $200 million Colorado Aqueduct on the Colorado River.

1942 Manhattan District organized for producing an atomic bomb, with Gen. Leslie R. Groves in charge.

1953 Air Force Globemaster crashed near Tokyo, killing 129 persons.

1979 SALT II agreement, limiting nuclear weapons, signed in Vienna by President Carter and Soviet leader Leonid Brezhnev; Senate failed to ratify pact.

1982 Army Gen. John W. Vessey, Jr., became chairman of Joint Chiefs of Staff.

1983 Space shuttle *Challenger*, with five crew members, launched at Cape Canaveral, FL; made perfect landing in Mojave Desert June 24; crew included first American woman astronaut, 25-year-old Sally K. Ride.

1987 Charles Glass, an American journalist, kidnapped in Beirut, Lebanon; set free several weeks later.

1990 During U.S. Open golf tournament in Rochester, NY, four golfers shot holes-in-one on the sixth hole in the space of less than two hours; there had never been more than one ace on a single hole and only 21 in all since 1895.

1991 Wellington Webb became first black elected mayor of Denver.

2001 President Putin of Russia responded to U.S. anti-missile plans: if built, Russia would increase and modernize its supply of missiles carrying multiple warheads.

2006 U.S. Episcopal Church appointed Katharine Jefferts Schori as first female presiding bishop.

19

1619 English Separatist group living in Holland received a patent in name of John Wyncop, an English clergyman, for a colony within the Virginia Company; later merged with another group.

1754 Intercolonial Albany Congress began at call of British Board of Trade to conciliate the Iroquois; meetings ended July 11.

1773 Patsy Custis, 17-year-old stepdaughter of George Washington, died from one of her recurring "fits."

1781 Gen. Nathanael Greene and his troops failed to dislodge British from Fort 96, SC.

1793 Joseph E. Sheffield, merchant, born in Southport, CT; endowed scientific school named for him at Yale (1854) (died 1882).

1812 President Madison issued proclamation declaring war against Great Britain.

1816 William H. Webb, shipbuilder, born in New York City; endowed Webb Institute of Naval Architecture at Glen Cove, NY (died 1899).

1826 Charles L. Brace, a founder/executive secretary of Children's Aid Society (1853–90), born in Litchfield, CT (died 1890).

1846 First recorded baseball game played in Hoboken, NJ, with New York Knickerbockers losing to New York Club 23–1.

1856 Elbert Hubbard, author who founded Roycroft Shop in East Aurora, NY, born in Bloomington, IL; the shop revived old handicrafts; publisher, *The Philistine* (1895–1915) and *The Era* (1908–15) magazines; author of *A Message to Garcia*; died in sinking of the *Lusitania* (1915).

1862 Slavery abolished in territories of the United States.

1863 William A. Brady, actor and producer of more than 250 plays, born in San Francisco (died 1950).

1864 The *Alabama*, a British-built Confederate cruiser which preyed on Union shipping, was destroyed by the USS *Kearsage*, a Union warship, off the French coast.

1876 Raymond L. Ditmars, reptile curator, Bronx Zoo (1899–1942), born in Newark, NJ; made important contributions to study of snakes (died 1942).

1878 Niece of President Hayes, Emily Platt, was married in White House to Col. Russell Hastings.

1881 Jimmy (James J.) Walker, famous and popular mayor of New York City (1926–32), born in New York City (died 1946).

1885 Bartholdi's Statue of Liberty, presented by the French people, arrived in New York City in crates.

1886 William Howard Taft was married to Helen Herron in Cincinnati.

1896 Wallis Warfield, socialite who became wife of Duke of Windsor, born in Blue Ridge Summit, PA; Windsor renounced the crown to marry her (died 1986).

1902 Guy Lombardo, leader of Royal Canadians orchestra for 50 years, born in London, Canada (died 1977).

1903 Lou (Henry Louis) Gehrig, baseball player who played (then) record 2,130 consecutive games (New York AL), born in New York City (died 1941).

1910 Paul J. Flory, physical chemist, born in Sterling, IL; awarded 1974 Nobel Chemistry Prize for developing analytic methods to study properties, structure of long-chain molecules.

1910 Abe Fortas, associate justice, Supreme Court (1965–69), born in Memphis, TN; nominated for chief justice but accusations of bribery forced him to request withdrawal of nomination (died 1982).

1914 Lester Flatt, pioneer country/western singer, guitarist with Earl Scruggs, born in Overton County, TN (died 1979).

1920 American Federation of Labor, meeting in Montreal, endorsed the League of Nations.

1934 National Archives created; placed under General Services Administration (1949).

1934 National Labor Relations Board created by joint resolution, replacing the National Labor Board.

1938 Railroad accident at Saugus, MT, killed 47 persons.

1944 Battle of the Philippines Sea resulted in the Japanese loss of three aircraft carriers and about 200 planes.

1953 Julius and Ethel Rosenberg, convicted as spies, were electrocuted in Sing Sing Prison after President Eisenhower turned down clemency plea.

1972 Tropical Storm Agnes moved from Florida to New York over a nine-day period with heavy rains and floods; Pennsylvania hit the hardest; 177 persons were killed and $3 billion in damage resulted from storm.

1977 Catholic Bishop John Neumann of Philadelphia, known for his development of parochial schools, was canonized — the first American male to achieve sainthood.

1987 Supreme Court by 7–2 vote struck down as "establishment of religion" a 1981 Louisiana law that required any public school teaching the theory of evolution to give equal time to the view of divine creation as a science.

1997 The play *Cats* staged its 6,138th performance, putting it ahead of *A Chorus Line* as the longest running Broadway show in history.

2000 By a decisive 6–3 vote, U.S. Supreme Court ruled that even voluntary student-initiated prayer before athletic contests unconstitutional.

2003 McDonald's, one of the largest single buyers of meat for fast-food purposes, ordered suppliers to begin to move to use of antibiotics only for disease-control purposes rather than to boost animal weight; its European operations had ordered the step in 2000.

2006 With murders hitting 53 in current year and 5 teenagers murdered two days earlier in worst single shooting incident in over a decade, Mayor Ray Nagin of hurricane-crippled New Orleans conceded he could not handle the situation; asked for troops; Governor dispatched 60 state police and 100 National Guard.

20

1658 Thomas Brattle, church leader and Harvard U. treasurer (1693–1713), born in Boston; chief organizer, Brattle St. Church; differed with Mather, condemned Salem witchcraft trials (died 1713).

1675 King Philip of the Wampanoag Indians attacked Swansea, touching off King Philip War, which ended August 12, 1676.

1732 James Edward Oglethorpe received charter to settle between the Savannah and Altamaha Rivers; charter granted liberty of conscience to all except Catholics.

1756 William R. Davie, colonial leader who was instrumental in codification of colonial laws, born in Egremont, England; governor of North Carolina (1798–99), involved in cession of Tennessee to the Union and founding of North Carolina U. (died 1820).

1774 More than 8,000 persons attended meeting in Philadelphia to oppose closing of Boston's port; marked start of Philadelphia revolutionary movement.

1778 Pierre Lacléde, fur trader who founded St. Louis (1764), died at about 54; headed St. Louis until civil government formed.

1782 Continental Congress established first great seal of the United States, featuring an American eagle, which remained through other changes.

1807 President Thomas Jefferson refused to appear as a witness in Aaron Burr's treason trial.

1823 Jesse L. Reno, Union General at Manassas and Chantilly, born in Wheeling, WV; killed at South Mountain September 14, 1862.

1824 John L. Morgan, Confederate general, born in Athens, TN; represented Alabama in Senate (1877–1907) (died 1907).

1832 Benjamin H. Bristow, first Solicitor General (1870–72), born in Elkton, KY; Secretary of Treasury (1874–76) (died 1896).

1837 David J. Brewer, associate justice, Supreme Court (1889–1910), born in what is now Izmir, Turkey, to American missionary parents (died 1910).

1841 Samuel F.B. Morse received patent for the telegraph.

1844 Francis E. Warren, known as the father of reclamation, born in Hinsdale, MA; governor, Wyoming Territory (1885–86, 1889–90) and the state (1890); represented state in Senate (1890–93, 1895–1929) (died 1929).

1858 Charles F. Murphy, head of Tammany Hall (1902–24) and political leader, born in New York City (died 1924).

1858 Charles W. Chesnutt, considered first American black novelist (*The Conjure Woman, The Colonel's Dream*), born in Cleveland (died 1932).

1860 Alexander Winton, automaker who built first big cars (1897), born in Grangemouth, Scotland (died 1932).

1863 West Virginia entered the Union as the 35th state.

1868 Helen M. Shepard, philanthropist who endowed American Hall of Fame at New York U., born in New York City (died 1938).

1874 Territorial government for District of Columbia abolished by Congress, replaced by a commission form of government.

1878 Arthur E. Morgan, chairman, Tennessee Valley Authority (1933–38), born in Cincinnati; dismissed by President Franklin Roosevelt after he refused to substantiate charges against other authority members; president, Antioch College (1920–36) (died 1975).

1883 Royal E. Ingersoll, World War II admiral, born in Washington; commander-in-chief, Atlantic Fleet (1942–43), Western Sea Frontier (1944) (died 1976).

1898 Guam occupied by American forces, led by Capt. Henry Glass of the USS *Charleston.*

1903 Glenna C. Vare, golfer who dominated women's golf in 1920s, born in New Haven, CT (died 1989).

1905 Lillian Hellman, playwright (*The Children's Hour, The Little Foxes, The Watch on the Rhine*), born in New Orleans (died 1984).

1909 Errol Flynn, screen actor (*Robin Hood, Virginia City, Elizabeth and Essex*), born in Hobart, Tasmania (died 1959).

1921 Rep. Alice Robertson of Oklahoma presided over House of Representatives for 30 minutes, the first woman to do so.

1924 Chet (Chester B.) Atkins, country music guitarist, born in Luttrell, TN; record company executive.

1924 Audie Murphy, most decorated World War II soldier, born near Kingston, TN; received Congressional Medal of Honor; killed in plane crash (1971).

1926 Eucharistic Congress of Catholic Church opened near Chicago; attracted about a million persons.

1927 Geneva Naval Conference involving United States, Great Britain, and Japan opened; ended in a stalemate.

1941 Congress was notified of the sinking by a German submarine of the first American merchant ship, the *Robin Moor.*

1943 Race riots began in Detroit; 34 died before riot was put down by federal troops.

1945 Anne Murray, popular singer, born in Springhill, Nova Scotia.

1947 Everglades (FL) National Park established.

1950 Lionel Richie, composer and singer, born in Tuskegee, AL.

1956 Venezuelan Super Constellation crashed in Atlantic Ocean off Asbury Park, NJ, killing 74 persons.

1972 Howard D. Johnson, developer of restaurant and motor lodge chain, died at about 76; his chain was largest food distributor after the Army and Navy.

1984 Supreme Court ruled unanimously that the Federal Aviation Administration (and by implication all federal agencies) may not be sued for damages or mistakes that contribute to disasters.

1995 Southern Baptist Convention, America's largest Protestant denomination and one founded largely in defense of slavery, overwhelmingly approved resolution on racial reconciliation that repents of racism and asks forgiveness from all Afro-Americans.

1997 Four major American tobacco companies and several states' attorneys general agreed on a settlement that would cost companies $368.5 billion; requires approval of Congress and the Clinton administration.

2002 Utah lost before Supreme court (5–4): Census did not utilize a prohibited procedure in 2000 that cost the state a congressional representative.

2002 Supreme Court prohibited death penalty for mentally retarded by 6–3.

21

1639 Increase Mather, Congregational clergyman, born in Dorchester, MA; pastor, Boston Second Church (1664–1723); president, Harvard U. (1685–1701); his Cases of Conscience Concerning Evil Spirits (1693) is credited with ending the witchcraft trials (died 1723).

1774 Daniel D. Tompkins, Vice President (1817–25), born in what is now Scarsdale, NY; served New York as governor (1807–17) (died 1825).

1779 Spain formally declared war on Great Britain, but refused to recognize American independence or pledge to fight until such independence was attained, as the French had done.

1788 New Hampshire, by a legislative vote of 57–46, ratified the Constitution and became the ninth state; its ratification made the Constitution operative.

1810 Zachary Taylor and Margaret M. Smith were married near Louisville, KY.

1831 George W. Nichols, music and art promoter, born in Tremont, ME; largely responsible for Cincinnati's development as a musical center; founder, first president, Cincinnati College of Music (1879–85) (died 1885).

1832 Joseph H. Rainey, first black to serve in the House of Representatives, born in Georgetown, SC; represented South Carolina (1870–79) (died 1887).

1834 Patent granted Cyrus H. McCormick for a grain reaper, the first successful automatic cutting machine.

1850 Daniel C. Beard, American Boy Scout founder, born in Cincinnati; served as national scout commissioner (1910–41) (died 1941).

1860 Congress authorized the post of Signal Officer, marking the start of the Army Signal Corps; Maj. Albert J. Myer was first Signal Officer.

1880 Arnold L. Gesell, pioneer in child development studies, born in Alma, WI; director, Yale Clinic of Child Development (1911) (died 1961).

1882 Rockwell Kent, artist and author, born in Tarrytown Heights, NY; known for landscapes, wood engraving, and lithography; author (*Wilderness, Voyaging N by E*) (died 1971).

1887 Norman L. Bowen, pioneer in experimental petrology, born in Kingston, Canada; made valuable contributions to optical glass industry (died 1956).

1888 Ralph H. Upson, aeronautical engineer, born in New York City; designed first successful metal-clad airship; made major contributions to wing design (died 1968).

1890 Lewis H. Brereton, pioneer Air Force officer, born in Pittsburgh; held various World War II commands (9th Air Force, Allied airborne forces in Western Europe) (died 1967).

1892 Reinhold Niebuhr, most influential theologian of 20th Century, born in Wright City, MO; proposed Christian realism that recognized the persistence of evil, and the egotism and pride of nations and other social groups (died 1971).

1894 Democratic silver convention held in Omaha; 1,000 delegates voted for a free-coinage plank in the platform.

1898 Donald Culross Peattie, botanist and author of popular nature stories, born in Chicago (died 1964).

1911 Supreme Court ordered dissolution of DuPont de Nemours Co. as a combination in restraint of trade.

1912 Mary T. McCarthy, author (*The Group, Vietnam, Memories of a Catholic Girlhood*), born in Seattle (died 1989).

1923 Judy Holliday, screen actress remembered for her role in *Born Yesterday*, born in New York City (died 1965).

1923 First presidential radio broadcast made by President Harding, whose speech dedicating Francis Scott Key Memorial in Baltimore was broadcast over WEAR (now WFBR).

1927 Carl B. Stokes, the first black mayor of a major American city, born in Cleveland, which he headed 1967–71 (died 1996).

1932 Jack Sharkey defeated Max Schmeling in 15 rounds in New York City to win world heavyweight boxing championship.

1933 Great Lakes-Gulf waterway opened with the arrival of barges in Chicago from New Orleans.

1934 National Mediation Board established.

1940 Richard M. Nixon married Thelma C. (Pat) Ryan in Riverside, CA.

1961 President Kennedy opened a plant in Freeport, TX, for the conversion of salt water to fresh water.

1973 In five separate cases, all decided by 5–4 votes, the Supreme Court set rules for the suppression of pornography.

1978 Air Force Gen. David C. Jones was named chairman of the Joint Chiefs of Staff.

1982 Federal jury after four days of deliberation found John W. Hinckley, Jr., not guilty by reason of insanity in the shooting of President Reagan and three others.

1982 Supreme Court by 7–2 decision ruled that the 1871 Civil Rights Act permitted individuals to sue state and local officials and agencies directly in federal courts.

2003 Maynard Jackson died (b. 1938); served three times as Atlanta's mayor, the first black American to do so.

2004 Under FBI and state legislative investigation for alleged corruption, Connecticut governor John Rowland resigned.

2004 *SpaceShipOne* with Michael Melvil at the controls became first private craft to enter the edges of space; on October 4 won $10-million award for making the flight twice in a week.

2006 U.S. Episcopal Church urged membership to avoid appointing any more openly gay to post of bishop, but declined to ban the practice; Archbishop of Canterbury responded on June 27 by recommending that national Episcopal churches that ordain openly homosexual leaders be given a secondary status in the Anglican communion.

22

1793 First extensive canal in the United States, the Middlesex Canal, was started to connect the Merrimac River and Woburn; completed 1808.

1807 American frigate *Chesapeake* stopped by British frigate *Leopard* off the Virginia coast, the British claiming four men aboard were British deserters; the American commander, James Barron, refused to permit search of vessel, the British fired and killed three, wounded 18, and removed the four men.

1837 Arthur Gilman, developed Radcliffe College (1893), born in Alton, IL; instrumental in getting instruction for women at Harvard (1879), leading to Radcliffe (died 1909).

1854 Connecticut passed prohibition law (with a few minor exceptions); repealed 1872.

1870 Congress passed act creating the Department of Justice, with the Attorney General at its head.

1888 Alan Seeger, poet ("I Have a Rendezvous with Death"), born in New York City (died 1916).

1888 Harold H. Burton, associate justice, Supreme Court (1945–58), born in Jamaica Plain, MA; reform mayor of Cleveland (1935–40); represented Ohio in Senate (1941–45) (died 1964).

1898 Erich Maria Remarque, author (*All Quiet on the Western Front*), born in Osnabruck, Germany (died 1970).

1903 Carl Hubbell, baseball pitcher (New York N 1928–43) who won 253 games, born in Carthage, MO; named to Baseball Hall of Fame (died 1988).

1906 Anne Morrow Lindbergh, widow of Aviator Charles Lindbergh, born in Englewood, NJ; author of several popular books (*North to the Orient*; *Listen! the Wind*).

1910 Katherine Dunham, dancer and choreographer, born in Chicago; first to organize black troupe of professional caliber.

1912 Progressive Party organized by disgruntled Republicans; at its August 5 convention it nominated Former President Theodore Roosevelt for president, Hiram Johnson of California for vice president.

1918 An empty troop train crashed into a circus train near Ivanhoe, IN; 68 persons were killed.

1921 Joseph Papp, founder, producer of New York Shakespeare Festival, the Public Theater, born in New York City (died 1991).

1921 Gower Champion, dancer and choreographer/director of musicals (*Bye, Bye Birdie*; *Hello, Dolly!*; *The Happy Time*), born in Geneva, IL (died 1980).

1922 Herrin (IL) Massacre occurred when several hundred striking coal miners forced non-union workers operating the mine to surrender; ordered to run for their lives and more than 20 were killed.

1922 Bill Blass, fashion designer, born in Ft. Wayne, IN.

1937 Joe Louis knocked out Jim Braddock in eighth round at Chicago to win world heavyweight boxing championship; he was youngest (23) to win the crown.

1943 Eighth Air Force made its first large-scale daylight raid on the Ruhr.

1944 GI Bill of Rights (Servicemen's Readjustment Act) was signed, providing benefits for World War II veterans.

1949 Ezzard Charles, after retirement of Joe Louis, defeated Joe Walcott in 15 rounds in Chicago to gain world heavyweight boxing championship.

1949 Meryl Streep, screen actress (*Kramer vs. Kramer*, *Out of Africa*), born in Summit, NJ.

1970 President Nixon signed an extension of the 1965 Voting Rights Act lowering the voting age to 18.

2003 Gladys Heldman dead at 81; founder of *World Tennis* magazine; played a pivotal role in creating professional women's tennis.

2003 Largest hailstone ever photographed (7 inches wide) recovered in Aurora, Nebraska; previous record: 5.7 inches at Coffeyville, Kansas, September 3, 1970.

2004 Happy publisher: Former President Bill Clinton's *My Life* sold over 500,000 copies on first day of issue.

23

1780 Advance of British troops was checked by Americans under Gen. Nathanael Greene at Springfield, NJ; British crossed to Staten Island, thus ending war in New Jersey.

1791 John Jones, surgeon who published first surgical textbook in the colonies (1775), died at 62; personal physician to Benjamin Franklin, attended Washington.

1803 Jason Lee, Methodist missionary who worked with Indians in Oregon, born in Stanstead, Canada; helped organize white settlement near Salem; influential in establishing Oregon provisional government (died 1845).

1845 Texas Congress in special session voted for annexation by the United States.

1875 Carl Milles, sculptor (*The Meeting of the Waters* in St. Louis), born in Lagga, Sweden; also did sculptures in Rockefeller Center (died 1955).

1876 Irvin S. Cobb, journalist and author (*Judge Priest* books), born in Paducah, KY; worked on several newspapers, magazine; wrote screen plays (died 1944).

1894 Alfred C. Kinsey, zoologist who directed massive study of sexual behavior which shattered many myths, born in Hoboken, NJ; founder, Institute for Sex Research, Indiana U. (1942) (died 1956).

1906 Congress authorized $25,000 a year for presidential travel expenses; increased to $40,000 in 1948.

1913 William P. Rogers, Secretary of State (1969–73), born in Norfolk, NY; was Attorney General (1958–61).

1927 Bob Fosse, choreographer and producer (*Pippin, Damn Yankees, Sweet Charity, Dancin', Cabaret* [movie]), born in Chicago (died 1987).

1931 Wiley Post and Harold Gatty began successful round-the-world flight in the *Winnie Mae*; took eight days, 15 hours, 51 minutes.

1936 Richard D. Bach, author (*Jonathan Livingston Seagull*), born in Oak Park, IL.

1938 Civil Aeronautics Act signed, creating the Civil Aeronautics Authority to supervise all but military aviation.

1940 Wilma Rudolph, athlete who won three gold medals in 1960 Olympics, born in St. Bethelehem, TN (died 1994).

1943 James Levine, musical director of Metropolitan Opera (1975–), born in Cincinnati.

1944 Tornadoes struck Ohio, Pennsylvania, West Virginia, and Maryland, causing 150 deaths.

1947 Congress passed over President Truman's veto the Taft-Hartley Act, which limited the conduct of unions in labor-management disputes, banned the closed shop, called for 60 days notice before striking, forbade union contributions to political campaigns.

1967 Senate voted 92–5 to censure Sen. Thomas J. Dodd of Connecticut for using political funds for personal benefit.

1967 President Lyndon Johnson and Soviet Premier Aleksei Kosygin began meetings at Glassboro (NJ) State College; agreed to avoid crises that might lead to war.

1998 Maureen O'Sullivan, screen actress, died at 87.

2003 Affirmative action giving minorities an advantage in college entrance upheld by 5–4 Supreme Court ruling so long as concept applied as but one of varied factors; in separate case declared that giving such a person an automatic 20 points in determining admissibility unconstitutional because minority status sole criterion.

2005 In narrow 5–4 decision, U.S. Supreme Court upheld validity of local government's eminent domain right to seize private property for resale to companies that will develop it in a manner to increase tax revenues.

2006 After record-setting 5½ years service as Secretary of Transportation under Presidents Clinton and Bush, Norman Mineta announced resignation; first Japanese-American to hold post; had been Secretary of Commerce in last year of President Bill Clinton's Administration.

24

1497 John Cabot, Italian-born English explorer, sighted land, probably in the vicinity of Cape Breton or Newfoundland; went on to sail southeast, possibly reaching Maine.

1564 Huguenot colonists from France, led by René de Laudonniére, arrived at St. John's River (FL) and built Ft. Caroline.

1700 Samuel Sewall published "The Selling of Joseph," a tract condemning slavery.

1729 Edward Taylor, Puritan clergyman and poet, died at about 87; considered finest poet of colonial America.

1771 E(leuthére) I. DuPont, industrialist who formed beginnings of vast company, born in Paris, France; established gunpowder plant (1802) near Wilmington, DE (died 1834).

1788 Thomas Blanchard, inventor of lathe, born in Sutton, MA; invention paved way for machine tools (died 1864).

1797 John J. Hughes, Catholic Archbishop of New York (1850–64), born in County Tyrone, Ireland; bishop of New York (1842–50); founded St. John's College (1841), which became Fordham U.; began construction of St. Patricks' Cathedral (1858) (died 1864).

1803 Matthew Thornton, Irish-born physician and legislator, died at 89; member of Continental Congress (1776–78); a signer of Declaration of Independence.

1811 John A. Campbell, associate justice, Supreme Court (1853–61), born in Washington, GA; resigned from court to become Assistant War Secretary for Confederacy (1862–65) (died 1889).

1813 Henry Ward Beecher, prominent Congregational clergyman, born in Litchfield, CT; served Plymouth Church in Brooklyn (1847–87); opponent of slavery and favored woman's suffrage; charged with adultery (1874), sensational six months trial ended in hung jury; exonerated by two church bodies (died 1887).

1839 Gustavus F. Swift, founder, head of meat packing firm, born near Sandwich, MA; helped develop refrigerated car (died 1903).

1842 Ambrose G. Bierce, author (*The Devil's Dictionary*), born in Meigs County, OH; disappeared while with Pancho Villa in Mexico (1914).

1858 George von L. Meyer, public official and diplomat, born in Boston; ambassador to Italy (1900–05), to Russia (1905–07); Postmaster General (1907–09), Navy Secretary (1909–13) (died 1918).

1863 Hiram Brundage published first newspaper in Wyoming, *Daily Telegraph*, at Ft. Bridger.

1872 Frank W. Crowninshield, editor of various magazines, including *Vanity Fair* (1914–35), born in Paris of American parents (died 1947).

1883 Victor F. Hess, physicist, born in Schloss Waldstein, Austria; shared 1936 Nobel Physics Prize for discovery of cosmic radiation (died 1964).

1885 Woodrow Wilson was married to Ellen Louise Axson in Savannah, GA.

1895 Jack Dempsey, world heavyweight boxing champion (1919–26), born in Mansassa, CO (died 1983).

1898 First land battle in Cuba occurred at Las Guasimas.

1900 Gene Austin, top recording artist of 1920s ("My Blue Heaven"), born in Gainesville, TX (died 1972).

1908 Former President Cleveland died at Princeton, NJ, at 71.

1915 Norman Cousins, author and editor (*Saturday Review* 1940–78), born in Union City, NJ (died 1990).

1916 John Ciardi, poet and critic, born in Boston; poetry editor, *Saturday Review* (1956–75), author of verse translations of Dante's *Inferno* (died 1986).

1916 William B. Saxbe, Attorney General (1974–75), born in Mechanicsburg, OH; represented Ohio in Senate (1969–74); ambassador to India (1975–77).

1918 About 27,000 American troops began two-day attack on Belleau Wood; this first major action resulted in complete possession of area.

1941 President Franklin Roosevelt promised aid to Soviet Russia.

1945 George E. Pataki, New York governor (since 1995), born in Peekskill, NY.

1947 Gen. Dwight D. Eisenhower named president of Columbia U.; took over after retiring from Army; installed October 11.

1948 Russians halted all land and water traffic between Western Zone of Germany and Berlin, touching off the Berlin Airlift which began June 26.

1949 President Truman, in special message to Congress urged program of technical assistance to underdeveloped areas, in what became known as the Truman Doctrine, enacted June 5, 1950.

1950 Plane crashed into Lake Michigan killing 58 persons.

1975 A jet liner crashed near Kennedy Airport, New York City; 113 killed.

1982 Supreme Court ruled 8–1 that federal and state officials are entitled only to "qualified immunity" from civil damage suits arising from their official acts, not "absolute immunity" enjoyed by the President.

1982 Supreme Court ruled 5–4 that no president may be sued for damages for any official action that he takes while in office.

1993 House voted 280–150 to halt construction of the Superconducting Supercollider, the $11 billion proton smasher in Texas.

1996 Supreme Court ruled 8–1 that law enforcement officials had the right to seek criminal penalties against a defendant and to seize the same person's property.

1998 AT&T announced it would acquire Tele-Communications Inc., a cable television company, in a transaction valued at $37.3 billion.

2002 Major change in U.S. Middle East policy: Yasir Arafat must be removed from authority before a Palestinian state can be given diplomatic recognition.

2004 In a 5–4 ruling Supreme Court decided that its rejection of the death penalty option in certain states did not apply to those who had been so sentenced prior to the decision.

25

1773 Eliphalet Nott, president of Union College (1804–66), born in Ashford, CT; invented a base-burning stove using anthracite coal (died 1866).

1788 Virginia's convention, with anti–Constitution forces led by Patrick Henry and those in favor by James Madison, ratified the Constitution 89–79, becoming the tenth state of the Union.

1831 President Jackson named Martin Van Buren minister to Great Britain; the Senate (January 25, 1832) rejected the nomination by Vice President Calhoun's tie-breaking vote.

1837 Charles T. Yerkes, street railway owner (Chicago), born in Philadelphia; his bequest to U. of Chicago (1892) made Yerkes Observatory possible (died 1905).

1842 Reapportionment Act passed; called for district election of congressmen.

1862 The "Seven Days Battles" around Richmond began; Confederate troops under Gen. Robert E. Lee forced Union forces to retreat to Harrison's Landing; considered one of fiercest battles of the war; although it was considered a Union victory, Gen. McClellan was unable to take Richmond.

1865 Robert Henri, painter who was a leader of the modernist "Ashcan" school of artists, born in Cincinnati (died 1929).

1868 President Andrew Johnson signed act

providing an eight-hour work day for laborers and workmen in government employ.

1874 Rose C. O'Neill, originator and designer of Kewpie dolls, born in Wilkes-Barre, PA (died 1944).

1876 Gen. George Custer made his last stand at Little Bighorn River in the Black Hills, when he attacked a large Indian force under Sitting Bull; Custer and his 266 men were annihilated by the Indians.

1886 Henry H. (Hap) Arnold, commander of Air Force (1941–45), born in Gladwyne, PA; awarded trophy for 30-mile flight (1912); commanded Army Alaskan flight (1934); chief, Army Air Corps (1938); built world's largest air force during war (died 1950).

1886 James F. McIntyre, Catholic Archbishop of Los Angeles (1948–79), born in New York City; named cardinal 1953 (died 1979).

1887 George Abbott, actor and producer more than 60 years, born in Forestville, NY; wrote or co-authored many musicals (*Three Men on a Horse, The Boys from Syracuse, On Your Toes*) (died 1995).

1889 Lucy W. Hayes, wife of President Hayes, died in Fremont, OH, at 57.

1890 Edwin L. James, managing editor, *New York Times* (1915–50), born in Irvington, VA (died 1951).

1892 Strike began at Carnegie Steel in Homestead, PA, by the Amalgamated Association of Steel and Iron Workers; mills closed June 30.

1906 Stanford White, prominent architect, was shot to death in New York City by Harry K. Thaw, wealthy playboy, who was jealous of White's earlier friendship with Mrs. Thaw.

1910 Postal Savings Bank system established, effective January 3, 1911; closed March 28, 1966.

1911 William H. Stein, biochemist, born in New York City; shared 1972 Nobel Chemistry Prize for pioneering studies of enzymes.

1917 First American troops arrived in France.

1938 Fair Labor Standards Act signed, raising minimum wage of those in interstate commerce from 25 to 40 cents, limiting hours to 44 per week, plus time and a half for overtime; also prohibited use of children under 16.

1941 President Franklin Roosevelt issued executive order establishing the first Fair Employment Practices Committee; this was forerunner of state fair employment practice laws.

1950 North Korean force of 100,000 invaded the Republic of Korea at several points.

1957 United Church of Christ was formed

by union of the Evangelical and Reformed Church and the Congregational Christian Church; to be effective July 4, 1961.

1982 Secretary of State Alexander M. Haig resigned; succeeded by George P. Schultz.

1985 Explosion in a fireworks plant in Hallett, OK, killed 21 persons.

1986 Supreme Court ruled 6–3 that libel suits brought by public figures should be dismissed before trial in the absence of "clear and convincing" evidence of malice.

1987 Supreme Court ruled 5–4 that military personnel cannot sue the government or superior officers for damages, even in cases of gross and deliberate violations of their constitutional rights; it also held that military personnel may be court-martialled for crimes unrelated to their service.

1992 President Bush signed bill which ended dispute that shut down rail freight lines and threatened commuter service; bill called for 20-day cooling off period with binding arbitration to follow if necessary.

1996 Bomb exploded at a military complex near Dhahran in Saudi Arabia, killing 19 American servicemen, wounding several hundred people.

1997 President Clinton approved air-quality standards that tightened limits on soot and ground-level ozone.

1997 Supreme Court struck down 1993 Religious Freedom Restoration Act intended to prevent all government agencies from intruding on religious practices.

1998 Supreme Court ruled unconstitutional the 1996 Line Item Veto Act which permitted a president to eliminate specific items in spending or tax bills.

1998 President Clinton arrived in China, met with President Jiang Zemin June 27.

2001 U.S. Supreme Court ruled 7–2 that right to publish print copies of an individual's writings does not automatically cover the right for the publisher to reprint them on the Internet.

2001 With similar measures proposed in 40 states, New York became the first to pass legislation banning use of cell phones while driving.

2002 U.S. second-largest long-distance telephone company WorldCom admits $3.8 billion overstatement of revenue during preceding five quarters; as more information became available scandal grew even larger.

2003 Last openly segregationist governor of Georgia, Lester Maddox, died at 87.

2006 Political analysis: Number of vets in Congress at post–World War II low: only 25 percent of House, 31 percent of Senate.

2006 The great giveaway: Warren Buffett announced he would give 83 percent of his $44 billion in investments to the Bill & Melinda Gates Foundation.

26

1703 Thomas Clap, Yale U. rector (1740–45), president (1745–66), born in Scituate, MA (died 1767).

1741 John Langdon, colonial legislator, born in Portsmouth, NH; member, Continental Congress (1775–76, 1783); "president" of New Hampshire (1785), governor (1788, 1805–09, 1810–11); represented state in Senate (1789–1801), serving as first president pro tem (1789) (died 1819).

1742 Arthur Middleton, colonial leader, born in Charleston, SC; member of Continental Congress (1776–78, 1781–83), a signer of Declaration of Independence (died 1787).

1778 Battle of Monmouth (now Freehold), NJ, began; Americans and British each suffered about 360 casualties; Americans turned back British, who returned to New York City.

1784 Spain closed Mississippi River to navigation by Americans.

1819 Abner Doubleday, credited with inventing, naming baseball while in school in Cooperstown, NY, born in Ballston Spa, NY (died 1893).

1833 Harvard U. conferred honorary LLD degree on President Jackson, which was strongly opposed by an alumnus and former president, John Quincy Adams, who considered it a disgrace to confer the honor "upon a barbarian who could not write a sentence of grammar and could hardly spell his name."

1844 President Tyler, widowed two years earlier, married Julia Gardiner in New York City; the first president to be married while in office.

1845 John McTammany, inventor of a mechanical player piano and voting machine, born in Glasgow, Scotland (died 1915).

1858 Federal troops established post in Cedar Valley on Utah Lake by arrangement with Brigham Young; the Mormon rebellion ended and Gov. Alfred Cumming took office June 30.

1862 Gen. Robert E. Lee struck at Union forces in Mechanicville, VA, during the Seven Days Battles; Confederates withdrew to Richmond July 2, ending the Peninsula Campaign.

1863 Confederate troops under Gen. Jubal

Early arrived at Gettysburg, PA; took York, PA, the next day.

1865 Bernard Berenson, foremost authority on Renaissance art, born in Biturmansk, Lithuania (died 1959).

1885 Edwin C. Ernst, radiologist, born in St. Louis; known for diagnoses, treatment by X-ray and radium applications (died 1969).

1888 Lee Simonson, a founder, director, Theater Guild (1919–40), born in New York City; designed sets for many Broadway hits (died 1967).

1891 Sidney C. Howard, playwright (*The Silver Cord*, *Salvation*, *The Late Christopher Bean*), born in Oakland, CA (died 1939).

1892 Pearl S. Buck, author (*The Good Earth*, *Sons*, *House of Earth*), born in Hillsboro, WV; awarded 1938 Nobel Literature Prize (died 1973).

1894 Jeanne Eagels, actress remembered for role of Sadie Thompson in *Rain*, born in Kansas City, MO (died 1929).

1900 Army commission headed by Dr. Walter Reed was named to investigate yellow fever in Cuba; experiments resulted in discovery that the disease is spread by mosquitos.

1901 Stuart Symington, first Secretary of Air Force (1947–50), born in Amherst, MA; represented Missouri in Senate (1953–76) (died 1988).

1902 William P. Lear, founder, president, Lear Aviation Co., born in Hannibal, MO; built navigation aids, lightweight automatic pilot (died 1978).

1911 Edward H. Levi, president, U. of Chicago (1968–75), born in Chicago; Attorney General (1975–77).

1914 Babe (Mildred E.) Didrikson Zaharias, one of greatest women athletes, born in Port Arthur, TX; 1932 Olympic gold medalist; three times U.S. Open golf champion (1948, 1950, 1954) (died 1956).

1929 Jules Feiffer, syndicated political and social cartoonist, born in New York City; with *Village Voice* (from 1956).

1934 Evangelical & Reformed Church formed by union of the Evangelical Synod of North America and Reformed Church in the United States.

1935 President Franklin Roosevelt established National Youth Administration, providing work relief and employment programs for the 16–25 age group; also part-time employment for needy students; program ended July 12, 1943.

1936 Merchant Marine Act went into effect, creating the Maritime Commission; became Maritime Administration 1950.

1944 American forces captured Cherbourg, France.

1945 President Truman witnessed signing of charter of United Nations in San Francisco.

1948 Berlin Airlift began in effort to get around the Russian blockade.

1952 Immigration and Naturalization Act passed, removing the last racial and ethnic barriers to naturalization.

1958 Mackinac Straits Bridge in Michigan dedicated.

1959 St. Lawrence Seaway dedicated at Montreal by President Eisenhower and Queen Elizabeth II.

1961 Greg LeMond, only American winner of the Tour de France cycling event (1986, 1989, 1990), born in Los Angeles.

1968 Island of Iwo Jima returned to Japan after nearly 23 years occupation.

1977 Fire in the Columbia, TN, jail killed 42 persons.

1980 House created the Synthetic Fuels Corporation to speed development of alternate energy sources; passed by Senate June 19.

1986 House, for first time in three years, approved request from President Reagan for military aid to the Contras in Nicaragua; effective October 1.

1987 Supreme Court ruled 5–4 that government regulators have limited power to grant public access to private property; authority limited to restricting use of private land without paying the owners.

1987 Supreme Court Justice Lewis F. Powell, Jr., resigned after 15 years service.

1991 Coroner in Louisville, KY, at the request of author doing book on former President Zachary Taylor, exhumed parts of the body, which were to determine if he had been poisoned; found president had died of natural causes.

1996 Supreme Court ruled 7–1 that women cannot be barred from state-supported military college.

1997 Supreme Court by 7–2 ruling extended free speech to the Internet; also by unanimous ruling, Court upheld New York and California laws making physician-assisted suicide a crime.

2000 President Clinton praised two scientific research teams as their leaders came to the White House to announce completion of first preliminary version of the entire contents of the over 3.1 billion parts of the human genetic code.

2001 In reversal of stance taken since 1890s, meeting of 550 Reform rabbis in Monterey, California, endorsed propriety of such ancient Jewish rituals as circumcision, but stopped short of requiring them for conversion.

2003 In *Stogner v. California,* U.S. Supreme Court repudiated prosecution for child molestation of those whose actions did not occur within the existing time frame of the statute of limitations; states can not expand prosecutable time frame after the incidents have occurred. Considered, in part, a backlash against "false memory" syndrome prosecutions.

2003 South Carolina politician Strom Thurmond died at 100; had established record for length of Senate service; during career had been elected to Senate as Democrat, Independent, and Republican.

27

1542 Juan Cabrillo (Rodriguez) sailed along coast of California, discovered San Diego Bay (September 28), Catalina Island (October 7), Drake's Bay (November 16).

1691 Province of Maryland, following a great deal of unrest, became a royal province, with Sir Lionel Copley as first royal governor; restored to proprietor, Charles Calvert, the fourth Lord Baltimore, 1715.

1696 Sir William Pepperell, first colonist to receive a baronetcy for leading successful attack on Cape Breton Island, born in Kittery Point, ME; chief justice, Massachusetts Superior Court (1730–59) (died 1759).

1776 Thomas Hickey, an Army guard, was hanged in New York City for plotting to kidnap George Washington and turn him over to the British.

1777 Gen. John Burgoyne, advancing from Canada, reached Crown Point, NY.

1787 Thomas Say, called the father of descriptive entomology in America, born in Philadelphia (died 1834).

1809 John Quincy Adams named minister to Russia.

1820 Ignaz A. Pilat, landscape gardener, born in St. Agatha, Austria; laid out Central Park in New York City following plans of Frederick Law Olmsted and Calvert Vaux (died 1870).

1823 Dorman B. Eaton, leader in creating civil service, born in Hardwick, VT; chairman, National Civil Service Commission (1873–75); drafted Civil Service Act (1883); chairman, Civil Service Commission (1883–86) (died 1899).

1832 Cholera epidemic began in New York City; took 400 lives before ending in October.

1844 Mob of men with blackened faces stormed jail in Carthage, IL, and murdered Mormon Church founder, Joseph Smith, and his brother, Hyrum.

1846 Henry E. Abbey, first manager, Metropolitan Opera House, New York City (1883–96), born in Akron, OH; managed many stars (died 1896).

1850 Lafcadio Hearn, author known for his books on Japan, born in Santa Maura Island, Greece (died 1904).

1862 Gen. George B. McClellan abandoned siege of Richmond, began retreat.

1863 Confederate troops under Gen. Robert E. Lee encamped at Carlisle, PA.

1864 Gen. William T. Sherman and his Union troops were beaten back at Kenesaw Mountain, GA, by Confederates under Gen. J.E. Johnston; Union losses were 3,000.

1870 Frank R. Lillie, son of an escaped slave known for poetry (*Majors and Minors, Lyrics of Lowly Life*), born in Dayton, OH (died 1906).

1874 John Golden, playwright (*Turn to the Right, Lightnin,' Susan and God*), born in New York City; composer of "Poor Butterfly" (died 1955).

1880 Helen Keller, blind author and lecturer on behalf of blind, born in Tuscumbia, AL; lost sight and hearing in illness at 19 months (died 1968).

1884 President Arthur signed act creating Bureau of Labor in Department of the Interior.

1893 Panic of 1893 was touched off when New York City stock market crashed in wake of dwindling gold reserves, tariffs, and depletion of surplus.

1899 Juan T. Trippe, founder, first president, Pan American Airways (1927–68), born in Seabright, NJ (died 1981).

1901 Merle S. Tuve, geophysicist who developed radiowave exploration of ionosphere, born in Canton, SD.

1905 Industrial Workers of the World (IWW) organized in Chicago.

1913 Willie Mosconi, 14 times world pocket billiards champion (1941–57), born in Philadelphia (died 1993).

1927 Robert J. Keeshan, television's Captain Kangaroo, born in Lynbrook, NY; began playing Clarabelle on *Howdy Doody Show.*

1930 H. Ross Perot, billionaire who twice ran for president (1992, 1996) as an independent, born in Texarkana, TX.

1934 President Franklin Roosevelt signed Railway Labor Act, which upheld rights of workers to organize and bargain, created national railroad adjustment board.

1942 FBI Director J. Edgar Hoover announced arrest of eight Nazi saboteurs who had landed from submarines on the Long Island and Florida coasts.

1946 Sally Priesand, first American woman ordained as a rabbi (1972), born in Cleveland.

1950 President Truman announced that in keeping with UN resolution calling for immediate halt to North Korean invasion which began two days earlier, he had ordered American air and sea forces to give Korean Republican Army support and cover.

1957 Louisiana and Texas were struck by Hurricane Audrey and a tidal wave, leaving 531 dead or missing.

1959 Vice President Nixon and Queen Elizabeth II of Great Britain dedicated the $650 million St. Lawrence Hydroelectric Power Project at Massena, NY.

1980 President Carter signed bill calling for draft registration by 19- and 20-year-old men.

1989 Federal appeals court overturned Lyn Nofziger's conviction for illegal lobbying because of ambiguities in conflict of interest law; had been a presidential aide, then a private lobbyist.

1990 Major flaws in light-gathering mirrors of the Hubble space telescope were discovered; flaws may cripple its ability to view depths of the universe.

1991 Justice Thurgood Marshall, first and only black on the Supreme Court, announced his retirement after 24 years.

1997 Supreme Court in 5–4 ruling invalidated a provision of 1993 Brady gun control act requiring local officials to check backgrounds of prospective handgun buyers.

2000 Massive fire began that destroyed almost 200,000 acres in Washington, including much of the area where radioactive waste stored at the Hanford, Washington, nuclear site.

2000 Proposed purchase of WorldCom by Sprint for $129 billion received roadblock: Justice Department sued to block transaction out of concern that consumer service and cost gains achieved since the breakup of AT&T might be fatally compromised.

2001 Comedian Jack Lemmon died at 76; successful dual career in both movies and television.

2002 *New England Journal of Medicine* published what was regarded as definitive study of relationship of birth control pill and breast cancer: no linkage; 80 percent of U.S. women use the pill for short or extended periods of time.

2003 "Do Not Call List" authorized by Federal Trade Commission to become effective in October; telemarketers prohibited from contacting those on list.

2005 Supreme Court divided 5–4 in opposite directions in two Ten Commandments on government property cases: A public display in Kentucky crosses permissible church-state boundary, court argues, while engraved copy on monument in Texas does not.

28

1742 William Hooper, colonial leader, born in Boston; member of Continental Congress (1774–77), a signer of Declaration of Independence (died 1790).

1776 Troops under William Moultrie beat off a heavy British attack on a fort of sand and palmetto logs on Sullivans Island in Charleston harbor; all British ships were damaged and suffered 200 casualties; fort later named in Moultrie's honor.

1776 Convention in Maryland authorized its congressional delegation to unite in declaring independence of the colonies.

1778 Battle of Monmouth (now Freehold), NJ, ended in standoff; later, British slipped away to New York.

1794 National Capitol Commission, through a misunderstanding, dismissed French architect, Stephen Hallett; his design was second but he had been retained to revise plans of William Thornton.

1814 American sloop *Wasp* destroyed a British sloop near the English Channel.

1836 Former President Madison died in Montpelier, VA, at 85.

1858 Otis Skinner, one of greatest character actors, born in Cambridge, MA; performed many Shakespearean roles and *Kismet, Sancho Panza* (died 1942).

1862 Admiral David Farragut's fleet sailed past Confederate batteries at Vicksburg during the night.

1863 Gen. George E. Meade named commander of Army of the Potomac.

1873 Alexis Carrel, surgeon, born in Ste. Fayles-Lyon, France; awarded 1912 Nobel Physiology/Medicine prize for work on vascular ligature and grafting of blood vessels and organs; developed early "artificial heart" medicine (died 1944).

1876 Oley Speaks, concert baritone and composer ("Sylvia," "On the Road to Mandalay," "When the Boys Come Home"), born in Canal Winchester, OH (died 1948).

1891 Carl Spaatz, World War II Air Force general, born in Boyertown, PA; chief, strategic bombing force, Germany (1944), Japan (1945); first Air Force chief of staff (1947) (died 1974).

1894 President Cleveland signed act creating Labor Day — the first Monday in September — as a legal national holiday.

1902 Richard Rodgers, composer of many hit musicals, born in New York City; wrote with Lorenz Hart *Connecticut Yankee, Present Arms, Jumbo, Babes in Arms, Boys from Syracuse, Pal Joey*; with Oscar Hammerstein, II, wrote *Oklahoma, Carousel, South Pacific, The King and I, Flower Drum Song, The Sound of Music* (died 1979).

1906 Marie Goeppert-Mayer, physicist, born in Kattowitz, Germany (now Poland); shared 1963 Nobel Physics Prize for research on structure of atom (died 1972).

1918 Chemical Warfare Service created in the Army.

1919 Treaty of Versailles signed by Germany and the Allies, formally ending World War I and providing for League of Nations.

1919 Harry Truman and Bess (Elizabeth V.) Wallace were married in Independence, MO.

1927 Two Army Air Corps pilots — Lts. Lester J. Maitland and Albert F. Hegenberger — made first successful flight from San Francisco to Honolulu.

1934 National Housing Act signed, creating the Federal Housing Administration (FHA) to insure loans for construction and repair of homes.

1937 Civilian Conservation Corps (CCC) created; liquidated June 30, 1943.

1939 Regular transatlantic passenger air service began, with 22 persons aboard Pan-Am clipper which flew from Pt. Washington, NY, to Lisbon.

1940 Congress passed Alien Registration Act, directed toward eliminating subversive activities, which were causing concern on the eve of war; about five million registered between August 27 and December 26.

1941 Office of Scientific Research and Development created by executive order.

1959 Railroad tank cars at Meldrin, GA, exploded, killed 25 persons.

1962 Lutheran Church in America founded by consolidation of the United Lutheran Church in America, the Augustana Evangelical Lutheran Church, and Finnish Evangelical Lutheran Church.

1978 Supreme Court by 5–4 vote refused to allow a firm quota system in affirmative action plans, ordered the admission of Alan P. Bakke to U. of California medical school; Bakke, a 38-year-old white, contended he had been a victim of reverse discrimination.

1988 Navy Capt. William E. Norden, 51-year-old American military attache in Athens, was killed by a car bomb.

1988 Justice Department filed suit to oust senior leadership of International Brotherhood of Teamsters, charging that the union had made a pact with organized crime; called for court-appointed trustee to oversee new elections for 1.7 million members.

1992 University of Pittsburgh surgeons implanted a baboon liver in a terminally-ill patient; he lived two months.

1995 Plans to impose 100 percent tariffs on Japanese luxury cars by United States were dropped when agreement reached opening Japanese markets to American automobiles and parts.

1997 Boxing championship fight between Evander Holyfield and Mike Tyson was ended when Tyson was disqualified for biting off a piece of Holyfield's right ear.

2000 U.S. Supreme Court ruled 5–4 that states can not ban late-term "partial-birth abortions"; effectively rejects such legal prohibitions found in 31 states.

2000 By 5–4, U.S. Supreme Court upheld right of Boy Scouts to ban homosexuals from being scout leaders; critics attack ruling as legalizing bigotry, defenders as reconfirming the right of private voluntary organizations to set their own moral criteria for membership and leadership.

2001 A unanimous Supreme Court threw out Massachusetts' wide ban on tobacco advertising; health risks inadequate to justify.

2002 New federal anthrax policy: All soldiers going into a region where it might be used by an enemy to be inoculated; over half of vaccine supply to be stored stateside for emergency civilian use.

2003 By 6–3, U.S. Supreme Court declared unconstitutional state laws prohibiting sexual relations between those of the same gender; reverses its 1986 5–4 decision in opposite direction; directly applies to Texas law but implicitly repudiates all 13 remaining such statutes.

2004 Supreme Court decided by 6–3 that since Guantánamo Bay, Cuba, is American-controlled territory the right of habeas corpus applies to terror war detainees imprisoned there.

2006 U.S. Senate fell one vote short of Constitutional amendment to ban flag burning in 66–34 vote.

29

1541 Hernando de Soto crossed Mississippi River into Arkansas near Sunflower Landing.

1565 Pedro Menéndes de Avilés sailed from Cadiz, Spain, with royal orders to destroy the French colonies in Florida.

1721 Johann Kalb (Baron de Kalb), German officer who fought with the Americans, born in Hüttendorf; mortally wounded in action at Camden, SC, August 16, 1780.

1721 John Ettwein, leader of Moravian American church (1784–1802), born in Freudenstadt, Germany; his official church correspondence is treasure of American historical information (died 1802).

1767 Townshend Acts enacted by Parliament, imposing new taxes on colonies, effective November 1; import duties to be levied on glass, lead, paints, paper, and tea; widespread nonimportation followed.

1776 Virginia adopted state constitution for which Thomas Jefferson wrote preamble.

1830 John Q.A. Ward, first American-trained sculptor, born near Urbana, OH; did many outdoor works, equestrian statues (died 1910).

1832 Luigi Palma de Cesnola, Union general and archaeologist, born in Rivarolo, Italy; served in Shenandoah campaign; American consul in Cyprus (1865–76), where he launched vast archaeological project; his collection purchased by Metropolitan Museum of Art, of which he became director (1879–1904) (died 1904).

1852 John B. McMaster, author of eight-volume history of American people, born in Brooklyn; pioneered in showing influence on national evolution of social and economic forces (died 1932).

1858 George W. Goethals, Army engineer who directed Panama Canal construction, born in Brooklyn; governor, Canal Zone (1914–17) (died 1928).

1861 William J. Mayo, cofounder with brother of Mayo Clinic (1915), born in Leseur, MN (died 1939).

1863 James Harvey Robinson, organizer, New School of Social Research, New York City (1919–21), born in Bloomington, IN; pioneered new methods and content of history teaching (Columbia 1892–1918) (died 1936).

1865 William E. Borah, legislator who represented Idaho in Senate (1907–40), born in Fairfield, IL; chairman, Senate Foreign Relations committee (1924–40); opposed League of Nations, World Court (died 1940).

1868 George E. Hale, astronomer, born in Chicago; organized, directed, Yerkes Observatory (1895–1905), director of Mt. Wilson Observatory (1905–23); invented spectroheliograph (1889) (died 1938).

1890 Robert Laurent, sculptor who influenced modern American sculpture, born in Concarneau, France (died 1970).

1901 Nelson Eddy, singer and screen actor (with Jeannette McDonald) in *Rose Marie, Maytime, Naughty Marietta*, born in Providence, RI (died 1967).

1906 Mesa Verde (CO) National Park established.

1906 President Theodore Roosevelt signed act creating Bureau of Immigration and Naturalization.

1906 Congress authorized preparation of plans for a lock canal in Panama.

1908 Leroy Anderson, composer ("Syncopated Clock," "Fiddle Faddle"), born in Cambridge, MA (died 1975).

1910 Frank H. Loesser, composer of musicals (*Guys and Dolls, Most Happy Fella*), born in New York City; also wrote hit song, "Praise the Lord and Pass the Ammunition" (died 1969).

1925 Earthquake destroyed downtown Santa Barbara, CA; suffered $20 million loss.

1933 Primo Carnera knocked out Jack Sharkey in sixth round in New York City to win world heavyweight boxing championship.

1938 Olympic (WA) National Park established.

1949 United States removed the last of its troops from Korea.

1954 Oprah Winfrey, talk show hostess, born in Kosciusko, MS.

1956 Federal Aid Highway Act signed, inaugurating the $33 billion interstate highway system.

1966 American planes began bombing Hanoi area of Vietnam.

1972 Supreme Court ruled that journalists have no right to withhold confidential information from grand juries.

1972 Hurricane Agnes struck eastern United States in ten-day storm which resulted in 118 deaths.

1982 President Reagan signed extension of Voting Rights Act of 1965 with stronger provisions against discrimination.

1982 Arms control talks between United States and Soviet Russia began in Geneva.

1988 Supreme Court ruled 7–1 upholding the power of independent counsels to prosecute illegal acts by high-ranking government officials.

1988 Supreme Court ruled that children testifying in sexual abuse cases must confront their alleged abusers "face to face," put in doubt were laws in 26 states which shield children from possible trauma in such confrontations.

1995 Shuttle *Atlantis* docked with Russian space station *Mir*; remained coupled until July 4; Norman E. Thagard, American astronaut who had been on *Mir* since March and two Russian astronauts relieved by another pair, returned on the *Atlantis*.

1995 Lana Turner, movie actress and legendary "sweater girl," died at 75.

1995 The Unabomber sent the *New York Times* and *Washington Post* a 35,000 word manifesto, promising to stop killings if they published it; papers did so September 19.

2000 California Supreme Court by 6–1 upheld as constitutional the first American state's ban of military-style assault weapons; critics argued law discriminatory by permitting equally dangerous weaponry to be sold.

2000 Former San Jose, California, mayor Norman Mineta nominated by President Clinton to be Secretary of Commerce; first Japanese-American to hold that level post.

2001 National Japanese-American Memorial opens near National Mall in Washington DC; honors those Japanese-Americans who fought for country during World War II and those who were interned.

2006 Supreme Court ruled 5–3 that there was no legal authority for trying Guantánamo-held accused terrorists before military tribunals.

30

1632 Charter for Maryland (lands north of Potomac River) granted to George Calvert, the first Lord Baltimore; charter was not issued until after his death and his son, Cecil Calvert, became first proprietor; charter set out the area between the Potomac River and 40° north.

1768 Elizabeth Kortright Monroe, wife of President Monroe, born in New York City (died 1830).

1812 First interest bearing Treasury notes authorized.

1815 The Dey of Algiers signed treaty agreeing to release all American prisoners and ending molestation of American commerce; treaty came after American fleet destroyed several Algerian raiding parties and sailed into Algiers harbor.

1819 William A. Wheeler, Vice President (1877–81), born in Malone, NY; represented New York in House (1861–63, 1869–77) (died 1887).

1841 President Tyler signed act for relief of widow of former President William Henry Harrison; the $25,000 was first presidential widow pension.

1855 William B. Caperton, commander in chief, Pacific Fleet (1916–19), born in Spring Hill, TN; involved in Vera Cruz and Caribbean operations (1915–16) (died 1941).

1859 Charles Blondin, French tightrope walker, crossed Niagara River below the Falls on a tightrope.

1864 President Lincoln signed Internal Revenue Act increasing income tax to 5 percent on incomes of $601 to $4,999, to 10 percent on incomes over $10,000.

1865 Trial of eight persons involved in Lincoln assassination began before a military commission; all were found guilty (John Wilkes Booth was killed earlier during his escape attempt).

1879 Walter Hampden, actor best remembered for his role of Cyrano de Bergerac which he played about 1,000 times, born in Brooklyn; also did *The Admirable Crichton* (died 1955).

1882 Charles J. Guiteau, convicted murderer of President Garfield, was executed in Washington.

1900 Pier fire in Hoboken, NJ, killed more than 300 persons, did $4.6 million damage.

1903 Mine disaster at Hanna, WY, killed 169 persons.

1905 William Zeckendorf, head of Webb & Knapp, international realtors (1942–65), born in Paris, IL (died 1976).

1906 Pure Food and Drug Act and Meat Inspection Act were signed by President Theodore Roosevelt.

1911 Czeslaw Milosz, author, born in Sateiniai,

Poland (now Lithuania); awarded 1980 Nobel Literature Prize; among works was *The Captive Mind.*

1917 Lena Horne, singer and actress (*Cabin in the Sky, Stormy Weather*), born in New York City.

1918 Eugene V. Debs, Socialist leader, arrested in Cleveland, OH, for interfering with military recruiting; sentenced to ten years.

1921 Former President Taft appointed chief justice of Supreme Court by President Harding; resigned because of ill health February 3, 1930.

1924 Federal grand jury in Washington indicted Albert B. Fall, Harry F. Sinclair, Edward L. Doheny and his son for bribery and conspiracy to defraud the government in connection with Teapot Dome oil leases.

1926 Paul Berg, biochemist, born in New York City; shared 1980 Nobel Physiology/Medicine Prize for pioneering research in genetic engineering.

1938 President Franklin Roosevelt laid cornerstone for Federal Building at New York World Fair.

1942 Robert D. Ballard, oceanographer who led successful exploration of *Titanic* wreck (1985–86), born in Wichita, KS; headed Deep Sea Submergence Laboratory at Woods Hole (MA) Oceanographic Institution.

1943 Executive order officially ended Works Project Administration (WPA), which in eight years employed more than 8.5 million persons on more than 1.4 million projects costing $11 billion.

1950 President Truman authorized Gen. Douglas MacArthur to use American ground forces to assist in halting North Korean aggression.

1951 Fifty persons were killed in crash of an airliner north of Denver.

1956 Midair collision of two airliners over the Grand Canyon killed 128 persons.

1957 Hurricane Audrey swept from Texas to Alabama in five days causing 390 deaths.

1966 Mike Tyson, world heavyweight boxing champion (1987–90), born in New York City; after three years in prison, reclaimed WBA and WBC titles; lost WBA title in 1996.

1971 Supreme Court by 6–3 vote refused to bar newspapers from publishing the Pentagon Papers.

1982 Equal Rights Amendment (ERA) failed when three legislatures refused to approve the amendment before the midnight deadline; 38 states were needed to ratify.

1989 Energy Department acknowledged for first time that a weapons production plant could harm its neighbors, promised to pay $73 million to settle claims of up to 24,000 neighbors of the Feeds Materials Production Center in Fernald, OH.

1998 Remains of the "Unknown Soldier" buried in Arlington Cemetery were identified by use of new DNA testing and returned to family for burial.

2000 General Assembly of the Presbyterian Church (USA) voted 268–251 to ban ministers from conducting holy union rites for homosexual and lesbian couples; proposal requires approval of majority of church's 171 presbyteries to go into effect.

2001 During his third hospitalization for heart problems since the November 2000 election, Vice President Cheney becomes first vice president to receive a pacemaker.

2001 Chet Atkins died (1924–2001); winner of 13 Grammy Awards, he became prominent both as songwriter and as performer; considered a pivotal player in modernizing country music and creating the "Nashville sound."

2002 "The Quest for Immortality" collection of Egyptian antiquities began nationwide tour at National Gallery of Art in Washington, DC; largest collection ever sent to U.S.

2002 First-class stamps increased to $.37, a 3-cent jump.

JULY

1

1725 Comte de Rochambeau, French general in American Revolution, born in Vendome; commanded French troops at Yorktown (1781) (died 1807).

1769 Gaspar de Portola arrived in present-day San Diego, where he established a presidio; considered founder of San Diego.

1795 President Washington nominated John Rutledge as Supreme Court chief justice, presided until December 15; not confirmed by Senate; had served as associate justice (1789–91).

1802 Gideon Welles, a founder of *Hartford Press*, born in Glastonbury, CT; Secretary of Navy (1861–69); also helped found Republican Party (died 1878).

1805 Michigan Territory established.

1817 Samuel L. Mather, developed iron ore deposits at Lake Superior, born in Middletown, CT; president, treasurer, Cleveland Iron Mining Co. (1869–90) (died 1890).

1818 Josiah Gorgas, Confederate general, born in Dauphin County, PA; chief of ordnance for Confederate forces; despite difficulties maintained steady flow of arms and ammunition (died 1883).

1819 John M. Brannan, Union general who saw action at Chickamauga, Missionary Ridge, born in Washington, DC (died 1892).

1833 Alfred T.A. Torbert, Union general who commanded cavalry in Sherman's army, born in Georgetown, DE (died 1880).

1840 Sixth Census reported American population had grown to 17,069,453, with the center of population south of Clarksburg, WV.

1847 First adhesive postage stamps went on sale (5¢ Benjamin Franklin, 10¢ George Washington).

1854 Albert B. Hart, editor of American history series (*Epochs of America*, *American Nation*), born in Clarksville, PA (died 1943).

1858 Willard L. Metcalf, painter of New England scenes (*Family of Birches*, *Icebound*, *Twin Birches*), born in Lowell, MA (died 1925).

1862 Pacific Railway Act passed providing assistance for a northern route transcontinental railroad (became Union Pacific); about 45 million acres were provided and $60 million loaned.

1862 President Lincoln signed act establishing office of Commissioner of Internal Revenue.

1862 Congress passed an anti-polygamy act.

1862 David White, paleobotanist and geologist, born in Palmyra, NY; with U.S. Geological Survey (1886–1935), developed theory of carbon ratio, which helped found petroleum industry (died 1935).

1862 Confederate troops under Gen. Robert E. Lee were defeated at Malvern Hill, VA, by Union troops under Gen. George McClellan; Confederates lost about 5,500 men.

1863 Three day battle of Gettysburg began; battle touched off when small detached forces met accidentally outside Gettysburg; a decisive victory for Union and considered turning point of war; Union losses were 23,000, Confederates about 28,000.

1863 Missouri convention adopted an ordinance that slavery should cease in state July 4, 1870.

1877 Benjamin O. Davis, first black Army general, born in Washington, DC (died 1970).

1880 Abraham Levitt, founder of construction firm which built much post–World War II housing, born in Brooklyn (died 1962).

1882 Susan Glaspell, author/playwright (*Alison's House*), born in Davenport, IA (died 1948).

1892 James M. Cain, author of suspense fiction (*The Postman Always Rings Twice*, *Double Indemnity*), born in Annapolis, MD (died 1977).

1893 President Cleveland was secretly operated on for cancer of the upper jaw aboard a yacht anchored in Long Island Sound; remained secret until 1917, when the doctor who performed the operation revealed story.

1893 Walter F. White, secretary of NAACP (1931–55), born in Atlanta; was assistant secretary (1918–29) (died 1955).

1898 Americans took fortified ridge village of El Caney and San Juan Hill, commanding heights overlooking Santiago, Cuba; Theodore Roosevelt commanded the Rough Riders at San Juan Hill.

1899 Gideons International organized by three traveling men to distribute Bibles in hotels, motels, hospitals, and penal institutions.

1899 World's first juvenile court opened in Chicago.

1899 Charles Laughton, screen actor (*Henry VIII, Mutiny on the Bounty, Ruggles of Red Gap*), born in Scarborough, England (died 1962).

1902 Territorial government created for Philippine Islands, with Filipinos becoming Philippine citizens and the start of partial self-government.

1902 William Wyler, movie director (*Mrs. Miniver, Ben Hur, The Best Years of Our Lives*), born in Mulhouse, France (died 1981).

1902 Permanent census office created.

1914 Prohibition went into effect in West Virginia.

1915 Statewide prohibition went into effect in Alabama.

1916 Olivia de Havilland, screen actress (*Gone with the Wind, The Heiress*), born in Tokyo.

1916 Dwight D. Eisenhower and Mamie G. Doud were married in Denver.

1918 Sugar rationing went into effect; allowing two pounds per person a month.

1921 President Harding appointed Gen. John J. Pershing as chief of staff.

1926 Robert W. Fogel, U. of Chicago economist, born in New York City; shared 1993 Nobel Economics Prize.

1929 Robert M. Hutchins, dean of Yale Law School, became fifth president of U. of Chicago; at 30, he was youngest major university head.

1929 Gerald M. Edelman, biochemist, born in New York City; shared 1972 Nobel Physiology/Medicine Prize for research on chemical structure and nature of antibodies.

1939 President Franklin Roosevelt by executive order consolidated 24 units and established the Federal Security Agency, the Federal Works Agency, and the Federal Loan Agency; the Security Agency was abolished April 11, 1953, Works June 30, 1949, and Loan June 30, 1947.

1941 Mammoth Cave (KY) National Park established.

1941 Alfred G. Gilman, pharmacologist who shared 1994 Nobel Physiology/Medicine Prize, born in New Haven, CT.

1943 Pay-as-you-go income tax went into effect.

1946 First peacetime atomic bomb test conducted on Bikini Atoll in the Pacific.

1949 General Services Administration (GSA) established to manage government property and records.

1961 Hawaii Volcanoes and Haleakala (Hawaii) national parks established.

1961 Carl Lewis, Olympic track gold medalist, born in Birmingham, AL; won nine gold medals in four Olympics (1984–96).

1964 Michigan's fourth constitution went into effect.

1966 Medicare, government program designed to pay part of medical expenses of those over 65, went into effect as part of Social Security Administration.

1968 United States, Russia, and Great Britain were among the signers of a nuclear nonproliferation treaty limiting the spread of nuclear material and technology to nonnuclear nations.

1970 Office of Management and Budget created.

1971 U.S. Postal Service, the reorganized Post Office Department, began operations.

1971 The 26th Amendment lowering the voting age to 18 went into effect.

1971 ACTION created as an independent agency for administering volunteer service programs (Peace Corps, VISTA, Foster Grandparents, Retired Senior Volunteer Program, Senior Companion Program, National Center for Service Learning).

1973 Centers for Disease Control established in Atlanta.

1974 Air Force Gen. George S. Brown became chairman of Joint Chiefs of Staff.

1981 United Auto Workers rejoined the AFL-CIO after a 13-year split over policy.

1986 Four-day program of concerts, tall ships, ethnic festivals, and fireworks began to commemorate 100th anniversary of the Statute of Liberty; statue underwent two years of restoration.

1987 President Reagan nominated Judge

Robert H. Bork of U.S. Circuit Court of Appeals to succeed Lewis F. Powell, Jr., on Supreme Court; nomination was rejected.

1988 President Reagan signed legislation expanding Medicare to help remove the threat of catastrophic illness.

1988 Pentagon halted payments on nine military programs costing more than $1.2 billion because they may have been tainted by Defense Department fraud and bribery scandal.

1996 Supreme Court by 7–2 vote ruled that Federal Government had broken its contract with savings and loans when Congress changed accounting rules and in effect pushed many savings and loans into insolvency.

1996 Twelve members of the paramilitary group Freeman were arrested in Phoenix (AZ) area thwarting a plot to bomb seven government buildings.

2000 Dead of heart attack at 79, Walter Matthau carved out a lengthy Broadway and movie career; most remembered for his comedy roles, including *The Odd Couple*.

2003 Fox Movie Channel halted its showing of the 1930s Charlie Chan mysteries because of protests over a white man playing the hero and stereotypes in the stories from the era when the films were made.

2004 Ending an almost seven-year, 2.2 billion-mile journey, the Cassini spacecraft goes into orbit around Saturn; first photographs are clearest ever images of planet's rings.

2004 Marlon Brando died at 80 (1924–2004). One of top Hollywood stars during the 1950s, perhaps best remembered for the early film *On the Waterfront* (1954) and his 1970s portrayal of a gangster kingpin in *The Godfather*.

2005 Sandra Day O'Connor announced intent to resign from Supreme Court as soon as replacement chosen; opens door for potential ideological realignment.

2

1759 Nathan Read, inventor and engineer, born in Warren, MA; designed multitubular steam boiler, double-acting steam engine, chain wheel device to propel boats, machine for cutting and heading nails; represented Massachusetts in House (1800–3) (died 1849).

1776 Gen. William Howe and about 10,000 men landed unopposed on Staten Island; joined by a strong fleet and 150 transports under Lord Richard Howe; garrison grew to 32,000 by August.

1776 Continental Congress voted for independence by vote of 12–0, with New York abstaining because it lacked instructions; Congress discussed Declaration of Independence and approved it without discussion two days later.

1776 New Jersey adopted its constitution.

1777 Gen. John Burgoyne and his British troops began siege of Ft. Ticonderoga; Americans abandoned it July 6.

1777 Week-long convention at Windsor adopted the name of Vermont and a state constitution which forbade slavery; applied for admission to union of colonies.

1798 Former President Washington nominated as lieutenant colonel and commander-in-chief of American armies by President John Adams; confirmed by Senate.

1807 President Jefferson issued proclamation ordering British warships to leave American territorial waters.

1810 Robert A. Toombs, Confederate Secretary of State, born in Wilkes County, VA; represented Georgia in House (1845–53) and Senate (1853–61); fled to England (1865–67) to escape arrest (died 1885).

1812 Peter Gansevoort, Revolutionary officer, died at 63; commanded troops at Ft. George (1776) and Ft. Schuyler (1777), during British siege.

1819 Lucius J. Knowles, inventor of a steam pump, born in Hardwick, MA; improved and manufactured a loom (died 1884).

1840 Francis A. Walker, president, MIT (1881–97), born in Boston; served as Union general (rising from private); chief, Bureau of Statistics (1869–71), supervised 1870 and 1880 census; studies on wages and profits influenced economic theory (died 1897).

1850 Robert Ridgway, bird curator, U.S. National Museum (1880–1929), born in Mt. Carmel, IL; in charge of Smithsonian bird collection (1869–80) (died 1929).

1853 Frederick T. Gates, philanthropy advisor to John D. Rockefeller, born in Maine, NY; instrumental in getting Rockefeller endowment for U. of Chicago, helped establish Rockefeller Foundation (died 1929).

1855 Clarence W. Barron, owner of Dow Jones, including *Wall St. Journal*, born in Boston; perfected financial news reporting; founder, editor, *Barron's Weekly* (died 1928).

1862 Morrill Act which granted public land

to states for industrial and agricultural education, passed by Congress and signed by President Lincoln; amounted to about 13 million acres of land.

1862 President Lincoln issued proclamation calling for 300,000 volunteers for three years service.

1864 Gen. Jubal Early led his Confederate troops into Winchester, VA, enroute to Washington, DC; occupied Martinsburg, WV.

1872 George W. Mundelein, Catholic Archbishop of Chicago (1915–39), born in New York City; named cardinal 1924 (died 1939).

1881 President Garfield was shot and fatally wounded by Charles J. Guiteau in a Washington railroad station; president died September 19; the mentally unstable Guiteau was a disappointed office-seeker.

1890 Sherman Antitrust Act signed by President Benjamin Harrison, the first federal act which attempted to regulate trusts; law was so general and ambiguous that the courts had to decide many points.

1894 Lewis W. Douglas, public official, born in Bisbee, AZ; represented Arizona in House (1927–33); Budget Director (1933–34); deputy administrator, War Shipping Board (1942–44); ambassador to Great Britain (1947–50) (died 1974).

1894 Attorney General Richard Olney got an injunction against American Railway Union, whose strike against the Pullman Co. affected all railroads; union defied injunction and federal troops were sent in to help operate the trains.

1898 Anthony C. McAuliffe, World War II general commanding at Bastogne, born in Washington, DC; remembered for his answer of "Nuts!" to German surrender demand (died 1975).

1906 Hans A. Bethe, physicist, born in Strasbourg, then in Germany; awarded 1967 Nobel Physics Prize for contributions to knowledge concerning energy production of stars.

1908 Thurgood Marshall, first black associate justice, Supreme Court (1967–91), born in Baltimore; NAACP legal services director (1938–61); judge, U.S. Court of Appeals (1961–65); Solicitor General (1965–67) (died 1993).

1912 First American dirigible, the *Akron*, exploded 2,000 feet over Atlantic City, NJ, five were killed.

1915 Bomb exploded in Senate reception room; had been placed by Eric Muenter, alias Frank Holt, a German instructor at Cornell U.; no one was injured.

1917 First regular convoy of merchant ships

sailed for Europe from Norfolk, VA; German submarine attack two days later was beaten off.

1917 More than 100 blacks were killed or wounded in two-day riot in East St. Louis, IL; touched off by importation of blacks as strikebreakers.

1918 Explosives at Split Rock, NY, blew up, causing 50 deaths.

1918 Robert W. Sarnoff, president, RCA Corp. (1955–75), born in New York City (died 1997).

1926 Army Air Corps created.

1932 Franklin D. Roosevelt set a precedent by appearing at Democratic national convention in Chicago to accept presidential nomination — "I pledge myself to a new deal for the American people."

1937 Amelia Earhart (Putnam) and co-pilot Fred Noonan disappeared while on a flight near Howland Island in the Pacific.

1937 Richard Petty, auto racing all-time winner of NASCAR races (200), born in Randleman, NC; won Daytona 500 six times, NASCAR champion five times.

1939 John Sununu, New Hampshire governor (1983–87), born in Havana, Cuba; served as White House chief of staff for President Bush.

1955 Sen. Lyndon B. Johnson, majority leader, suffered a heart attack; did not return to Senate until December.

1964 President Lyndon B. Johnson signed Civil Rights Act, which included provisions for public accommodations and equal employment opportunities.

1965 Equal Employment Opportunity Commission became operational.

1982 Supreme Court ruled 8–0 that the NAACP cannot be held liable financially for losses of white merchants during seven-year boycott in Claiborne County, MS.

1985 Agreement reached to hold American-Russian summit meeting in Geneva November 19 and 20.

1994 USAir jetliner trying to abort landing during a thunderstorm crashed into a home near Charlotte, NC; 37 were killed.

1998 Bud Selig, who served for a time as de facto baseball commissioner, was named the ninth baseball commissioner.

2001 President Bush endorsed only limited drilling for natural gas and oil in the Gulf of Mexico, reducing area by 75 percent from 6 million acres to 1.5 million; retreat from earlier and broader proposal apparently encouraged by Jeb Bush, his brother, the governor of Florida.

2002 Steve Fossett succeeded in sixth effort to circle the earth nonstop — in a balloon.

2004 John C. Murphy (b. 1919), cartoonist, died; drew the *Prince Valiant* comic strip from 1970-March 2004.

3

1731 Samuel Huntington, colonial leader, born in Windham, CT; member of Continental Congress (1776–84), its president (1779–81, 1783), signer of Declaration of Independence; Connecticut governor (1786–96) (died 1796).

1738 John S. Copley, first great American portrait painter, born in Boston (died 1815).

1754 George Washington and 400 men were defeated at Ft. Necessity (Great Meadows, PA) by a French force of 900; formally surrendered July 4.

1775 George Washington took formal command of Continental Army of 14,500 men at Cambridge, MA.

1778 Settlers in Wyoming Valley of Pennsylvania attacked by British, aided by Tories and Indians; many massacred; event was called "the surpassing horror of the Revolution."

1814 American troops under Gen. Jacob Brown captured Ft. Erie, Canada, and pushed on to the Chippewa River.

1819 A first American savings bank (Bank for Savings) opened in New York City.

1844 Treaty of Wanghia signed with China, the first treaty of peace, amity, and commerce with China.

1844 Dankmar Adler, architect, born in Langfeld, Germany; partner of Louis Sullivan, did many buildings in Chicago, St. Louis (died 1900).

1878 George M. Cohan, actor/playwright/composer, born in Providence; acted in many plays which he wrote and produced (*Little Johnny Jones*, *45 Minutes from Broadway*, *Get-Rich-Quick Wallingford*); among his songs were "Mary's a Grand Old Name," "I'm a Yankee Doodle Dandy," "You're a Grand Old Flag," "Give My Regards to Broadway," "Over There" (died 1942).

1879 Alfred Korzybski, founder of general semantics, born in Warsaw, Poland; author of *Science and Sanity* (died 1950).

1890 Idaho admitted to Union as 43rd state.

1898 Spanish fleet destroyed and 600 men killed when fleet tried to run American blockade of Santiago de Cuba harbor.

1900 John Mason Brown, drama critic and author (*To All Hands*, *Daniel Boone*), born in Louisville, KY (died 1969).

1902 President Theodore Roosevelt issued proclamation of peace and amnesty for the Philippines.

1915 J.P. Morgan acting as agent for British government on war contracts, was slightly wounded by Eric Muenter at Glen Cove, NY; Muenter, who had bombed Senate reception room the previous day, committed suicide in jail three days later.

1930 Pete Fountain, Dixieland clarinetist and orchestra leader, born in New Orleans.

1935 Harrison H. (Jack) Schmitt, astronaut who piloted Apollo 17 lunar module on 1972 mission, born in Santa Rita, NM; represented New Mexico in Senate (1977–83).

1964 Army Gen. Earle G. Wheeler became chairman of Joint Chiefs of Staff.

1970 Navy Adm. Thomas H. Moorer became chairman of Joint Chiefs of Staff.

1974 President Nixon signed limited nuclear agreements in Moscow.

1988 American vessel *Vincennes* in the Persian Gulf mistakenly shot down an Iranian passenger plane, thinking it was a hostile attack plane; all 290 persons aboard were killed.

1989 Supreme Court by 5–4 vote left intact the *Roe v. Wade* 1973 ruling establishing the constitutional right to abortion, but encouraged states to cut back sharply on that right; court ruled that states may require doctors to determine whether a fetus at least 20 weeks old is "viable" or capable of surviving outside the womb.

2001 First artificial heart to operate solely within human body successfully implanted by Louisville, Kentucky, surgeons.

2003 Labor Department reported that in June U.S. unemployment hit 6.4 percent, a nine-year high.

2005 Gaylord Nelson, founder of Earth Day, died at 89; three-term Senator and Wisconsin governor.

4

1584 Expedition sent out by Sir Walter Raleigh arrived off coast of North Carolina, landing at Roanoke Island.

1752 Proprietary colony of Georgia became a royal colony as original 21-year charter expired.

1776 Continental Congress unanimously adopted the Declaration of Independence in

Philadelphia; publicly proclaimed July 8 (New York did not vote approval until July 9 when instructions arrived).

1778 George Rogers Clark led Americans to victory at British post of Kaskaskia, IL; followed up with victories at other Illinois posts resulting in Virginia legislature organizing area as Illinois County in October.

1789 First tariff law enacted, imposing import duties "for the encouragement and protection of manufacturers."

1802 United States Military Academy at West Point formally opened.

1804 Nathaniel Hawthorne, author (*The Scarlet Letter, Twice Told Tales, House of Seven Gables*), born in Salem, MA (died 1864).

1816 Fort Dearborn, at what is now Chicago, rebuilt to replace fort destroyed four years earlier.

1817 Work begun on Erie Canal with ground-breaking at Rome, NY; completed 1825.

1819 Edward R. Squibb, founder of pharmaceutical laboratory which became E.R. Squibb & Sons (1892), born in Wilmington, DE; original lab founded in Brooklyn 1858 (died 1900).

1819 Territorial government of Arkansas created.

1825 Groundbreaking ceremonies held in Newark, OH, for 308-mile Ohio Canal between Cleveland and Portsmouth on the Ohio River; completed 1828.

1826 Two former presidents died the same day—Thomas Jefferson at Monticello at 83 and John Adams in Quincy, MA, at 90; shortly before he died, Adams said: "Thomas Jefferson still survives"; actually he had died a few hours earlier.

1826 Stephen C. Foster, composer of numerous classic songs, born near Pittsburgh; his songs include "My Old Kentucky Home," "Massa's in the Cold, Cold Ground," "O Susanna," "Old Black Joe," "Old Folks at Home," "Camptown Races" (died 1864).

1827 Slavery abolished in New York State under provisions of an 1817 law.

1828 Baltimore & Ohio Railroad begun with cornerstone laying near Baltimore, with the last surviving signer of Declaration of Independence, Charles Carroll, laying first stone; this was first American public railroad.

1828 President John Quincy Adams broke ground for the Chesapeake & Ohio Canal in Georgetown (Washington, DC).

1828 James J. Pettigrew, Confederate general led left wing of Pickett's charge at Gettysburg,

born in Lake Scuppernong, NC; mortally wounded in retreat from Gettysburg (1863).

1831 Former President Monroe died in New York City at 73.

1831 Treaty concluded with France settling claims for depredations of American shipping during Napoleonic wars; French paid 25 million francs, Americans 1.5 million.

1832 "America" was first sung publicly at Park St. Church in Boston.

1836 Territorial government of Wisconsin established.

1836 State of Illinois began building a canal to connect Mississippi River and Lake Michigan; panic of 1837 temporarily halted work; opened April 23, 1848.

1840 Independent federal treasury system created with subtreasuries in New York City, Boston, Charleston, and St. Louis.

1845 Texas voters in convention in Austin approved annexation by United States; action ratified by referendum October 13.

1846 Rebellious Californians, the so-called Bear Flaggers, held victory celebration in Sonoma and declared California independent; the next day they created a military organization, with Col. John C. Fremont commander.

1847 James A. Bailey, circus owner who merged with P.T. Barnum in 1882, born in Detroit (died 1906).

1848 President Polk laid cornerstone of the Washington Monument.

1850 Clayton-Bulwer Treaty ratified; called for United States and Great Britain to refrain from occupying any part of Central America; replaced by Hays-Pauncefort Treaty in 1902.

1851 President Fillmore laid cornerstone for south House extension of the Capitol; completed in November 1867.

1861 Francis B. Crocker, instrumental in establishing American electrical standards, born in New York City (died 1921).

1861 Congress met in special session at call of President Lincoln, who described steps taken in the war, asked for additional powers.

1862 Confederate cavalry under Gen. J.H. Morgan began three weeks of raiding along the Louisville & Nashville Railroad in Tennessee and Kentucky.

1863 Gen. John C. Pemberton led 30,000 Confederate troops in surrendering besieged Vicksburg to Gen. U.S. Grant; gave Union control of Mississippi River.

1863 Gen. Robert E. Lee and his Confederate troops began retreat from Gettysburg, retiring to a position west of Hagerstown, MD, before returning to Virginia.

1866 Fire in Portland, ME, destroyed 1,500 buildings.

1867 Stephen T. Mather, first director, National Park Service (1917–29), born in San Francisco; established, coordinated national park system and principles for their use and preservation (died 1930).

1872 Calvin Coolidge, 30th president (1923–29), born in Plymouth, VT; assumed office August 2, 1923, on death of President Harding; served as mayor of Northampton, MA (1910–11), governor of Massachusetts (1916–19) (died 1933).

1874 Steel bridge over Mississippi River at St. Louis opened.

1881 Tuskegee Institute opened with 30 students and Booker T. Washington as principal.

1883 Rube (Reuben L.) Goldberg, cartoonist remembered for complicated machine cartoons, born in San Francisco; also drew the *Boob McNutt* cartoon (died 1970).

1884 United States received the Statute of Liberty as gift from the French people.

1885 Louis B. Mayer, movie executive who developed Metro-Goldwyn-Mayer, born in Minsk, Russia; began with small New England movie chain; then went into production (died 1957).

1889 Five constitutional conventions began — North Dakota, South Dakota, Montana, Washington, and Idaho.

1894 Republic of Hawaii established.

1895 Irving Caesar, one of the greatest song lyricists ("Tea for Two," "I Want to Be Happy," "Crazy Rhythm"), born in New York City (died 1996).

1898 Gertrude Lawrence, stage actress (*Pygmalion, The King and I, Private Lives, Lady in the Dark*), born in London (died 1952).

1898 Wake Island captured by American force.

1900 Louis Armstrong, trumpeter, singer and orchestra leader, born in New Orleans; known as "Satchmo" (died 1971).

1901 Abe Saperstein, founder of Harlem Globetrotters basketball team (1927), born (died 1966).

1902 William Howard Taft appointed governor general of Philippine Islands by President McKinley as military rule of islands ended.

1903 President Theodore Roosevelt sent first message on the Pacific cable to Philippines.

1911 First Workmen's Compensation Act went into effect in New Jersey.

1911 Mitch(ell) Miller, popular choral director and recording company executive, born in Rochester, NY.

1917 First government aviation training field opened in Rantoul, IL.

1918 American shipyards launched 95 ships on this day.

1918 Twin columnist sisters — Ann Landers and Abigail Van Buren (Dear Abbie) — born in Sioux City, IA, as Esther P. (Landers) and Pauline E. (Abbie) Friedman.

1919 Jack Dempsey defeated Jess Willard in four rounds in Toledo to win world's heavyweight boxing championship.

1921 Gerard Debreau, economist with U. of California, born in Calais, France; awarded 1983 Nobel Economics Prize for work on how prices operate to balance production and consumption.

1927 Neil Simon, playwright (*The Odd Couple, Sweet Charity, The Sunshine Boys, Prisoner of Second Avenue, Last of the Red Hot Lovers*), born in New York City.

1940 Franklin D. Roosevelt Library in Hyde Park, NY, dedicated by him.

1942 American Air Force crews participated in British raid on the Netherlands, the first American air operation in Europe.

1946 United States gave independence to the Philippine Islands by executive proclamation, recognizing the Republic of Philippines.

1950 President Eisenhower issued proclamation making Hawaii the 50th state.

1960 The 50-star American flag was raised for the first time at 12:01 A.M. at Ft. McHenry National Monument in Baltimore.

1966 President Lyndon Johnson signed act creating the American Revolution Bicentennial Commission.

1967 Freedom of Information Act went into effect to make government information more readily available; withholding of information required the government to prove its sensitivity.

1976 Americans celebrated 200th anniversary with events of all kinds; President Ford visited Independence Hall in Philadelphia, the site of the Declaration signing, and New York City, with its "tall ships" parade.

1992 World's largest gathering of "tall ships" in a century appeared in New York Harbor to salute Independence Day and the 500th anniversary of Columbus' voyage.

1997 American spacecraft, the Mars *Pathfinder*,

landed on Mars; later began sending back pictures and rock analyses.

1997 Charles Kuralt, CBS newsman and author noted for his "On the Road" series, died at 62.

2005 *Deep Impact* mission completed after six-month space journey: hit comet and photographed results.

5

1756 William Rush, first American-born sculptor, born in Philadelphia; also known for carved ship figureheads; a founder, Pennsylvania Academy of Fine Arts (died 1833).

1776 Patrick Henry became Virginia's first governor.

1779 British troops ravaged the Connecticut coast, taking New Haven, Fairfield, and Norwalk.

1794 Sylvanus Graham, food reformer who advocated use of whole wheat, born in West Suffield, CT; also urged use of coarsely-ground flour (graham flour) (died 1851).

1801 David G. Farragut, Union naval officer who led capture of Mississippi River and Mobile Bay, born near Knoxville, TN; held special ranks of vice admiral (1864), admiral (1866); reputedly said at Mobile: "Damn the torpedoes, full speed ahead" (died 1870).

1810 P(hineas) T. Barnum, showman, born in Bethel, CT; opened American museum of curios, exhibited General Tom Thumb, brought Jenny Lind to American for concert tour; joined (1882) with James A. Bailey to form world's largest circus (died 1891).

1814 Battle of Chippewa Falls, near Niagara Falls, took place, resulting in British withdrawal; however, failure of American naval forces at Sacketts Harbor, NY, to cooperate with land forces made American withdrawal necessary.

1841 William C. Whitney, Secretary of Navy (1885–89), born in Conway, MA; a leader in New York City street railway system; prominent in horse racing (died 1904).

1843 Oregon settlers, meeting in Champoeg, adopted constitution for provisional government to serve until United States could take over.

1860 Robert Bacon, financier who helped establish U.S. Steel, Northern Securities, born Jamaica Plain, MA; partner in J.P. Morgan & Co. (1894–1903); Secretary of State (1909); ambassador to France (1909–12) (died 1919).

1865 Secret Service established.

1867 James M. Wayne, associate justice, Supreme Court (1835–67), died at 87.

1879 Dwight F. Davis, public official, born in St. Louis; War Secretary (1925–29), governor general, Philippines (1929–32); donor of cup for international tennis competition (died 1945).

1879 Wanda Landowska, pianist and composer, born in Warsaw, Poland (died 1959).

1888 Herbert S. Gasser, physiologist, born in Platteville, WI; shared 1944 Nobel Physiology/Medicine Prize for work on functions of nerve fibers (died 1963).

1890 Frederick L. Allen, editor (*Harpers* 1941–54), born in Boston; author of *Only Yesterday, Since Yesterday* (died 1954).

1891 John H. Northrop, biologist and chemist, born in Yonkers, NY; shared 1946 Nobel Chemistry Prize for preparing enzyme, virus proteins in pure form.

1894 Gov. John P. Altgeld of Illinois protested the sending of federal troops July 3 by President Cleveland to Pullman strike in Chicago; he argued that state and local authorities could handle situation; arrival of troops broke strike.

1902 Henry Cabot Lodge, legislator, born in Nahant, MA; represented Massachusetts in Senate (1937–44, 1947–53); chief, UN mission (1953–60); Republican vice presidential candidate (1960); ambassador to South Vietnam (1963–64, 1965–67) (died 1985).

1918 Excursion steamer *Columbia* sank in Illinois River near Peoria with the loss of 200 persons.

1935 Congress passed National Labor Relations Act — the Wagner Act — for the peaceful settlement of labor disputes.

1944 Mine accident at Belmont, OH, caused death of 66.

1945 Gen. Douglas MacArthur announced recapture of Philippine Islands.

1988 The 69th General Convention of Episcopal Church, meeting in Detroit, unanimously approved antidiscrimination resolution to protect AIDS sufferers.

1989 Federal Judge Gerhard A. Gesell fined Oliver L. North $150,000 for his crimes in the Iran-Contra case; placed him on probation for two years, ordered him to perform 1,200 hours of community service; had been convicted of destroying official documents, giving false statements, and accepting an illegal gift.

1991 National League awarded franchises to Denver and Miami; to begin baseball play in 1993.

1996 Hurricane Bertha began its week long passage through the Virgin Islands; came ashore near Jacksonville, NC; 12 persons were killed, damages estimated at $270 million.

2002 Baseball legendary left fielder Ted Williams died; lifetime record: 521 home runs; served as Marine pilot during World War II and Korea.

2004 Due to likely size of legal awards to victims of priestly child abuse, Roman Catholic Archdiocese of Portland, Oregon, filed for bankruptcy.

2006 Ken Lay died of heart attack while awaiting sentencing for fraud charges surrounding the collapse of Enron; irony: some stockholders outraged he had avoided jail time by dying.

6

1699 Captain Kidd, a pirate, seized in Boston; sent to England where he was hanged 1701.

1736 Daniel Morgan, Revolutionary general who commanded troops in North Carolina, born in Hunterdon County, NJ; led victory over British at Cowpens (died 1802).

1747 John Paul Jones, Revolutionary naval officer, born in Kirkbridge, Scotland; commanded the *Bonhomme Richard* in fierce battle with the British *Serapis* (September 21, 1779); scored many victories over British; credited with quote: "I have not yet begun to fight" (died 1792).

1759 John Barney, Revolutionary naval officer, born in Baltimore County, MD; commanded large flotilla which tried to stop British march on Washington; then joined land forces at Bladensburg, MD; wounded and captured (died 1818).

1766 Alexander Wilson, ornithologist whose seven volume *American Ornithology* is considered a classic, born in Paisley, Scotland (died 1813).

1768 Johann C. Beissel, German-born founder of the Dunkers, died at 78; organized (about 1730) the "Solitary Brethren of the Community of Seventh-Day Baptists" (Dunkers) at Ephrata, PA; composer of many hymns which influenced American hymnology.

1775 Second Continental Congress adopted a declaration of causes and necessity of taking up arms, drafted by John Dickinson and Thomas Jefferson, which said in part: "We are reduced to the alternative of choosing an unconditional submission to the tyranny of irritated ministers, or resistance by force. The latter is our choice. We have counted the cost of this contest, and find nothing so dreadful as voluntary slavery... Our cause is just... Our union is perfect..."

1777 Gen. John Burgoyne with 8,000 British troops captured Ft. Ticonderoga, which had been abandoned by American troops under Gen. Arthur S. St. Clair.

1785 Congress created currency system devised by Robert Morris and Gouverneur Morris, with the dollar as its unit and a decimal ratio.

1790 Congress passed act for a federal city in a 10-mile square on the Potomac River after 1800; until then Philadelphia would be the capital.

1798 Philo P. Stewart, cofounder, Oberlin (OH) College (1833), born in Sherman, CT; invented the Oberlin cookstove (died 1868).

1800 Alonzo Potter, Episcopal Bishop of Pennsylvania (1860–65), born in Dutchess County, NY; established hospital (1860) and divinity school (1863) in Philadelphia (died 1865).

1831 Daniel C. Gilman, first president, Johns Hopkins U. (1875–1901), born in Norwich, CT; president, U. of California (1872–75), Carnegie Foundation (1901–04), National Civil Service Reform League (1901–07) (died 1908).

1832 John B. Gordon, Confederate general at Antietam, Chancellorsville, Spotsylvania, born in Upson County, GA; served Georgia as governor (1886–90) and in Senate (1873–80, 1891–97) (died 1904).

1854 Meeting in Jackson, MI, attended by former Whigs, Democrats, and Free Soilers, resulted in formation of Republican Party.

1869 Agoston Haraszthy de Mokesa, pioneer grape grower, died at about 57; a Hungarian grower, he introduced in California the Tokay, Zinfandel, and Shiras grapes (1849).

1869 Virginia ratified its new constitution, which recognized equal civil rights.

1875 Roger W. Babson, economist who pioneered use of charts in forecasting business trends, born in Gloucester, MA; founder of statistical organization, Babson Institute, and Webber College (for women) for sound business training (died 1967).

1876 Harry F. Sinclair, founder of Sinclair Oil Co., president (1916–49), born in Wheeling, WV; involved in Teapot Dome scandals, indicted but acquitted of conspiracy to defraud (1928); guilty of contempt of court and Congress (1929), served three months (died 1956).

1884 Harold S. Vanderbilt, involved in family's railroad empire, born in Oakdale, NY; won yachting's America's Cup three times, developed contract bridge (died 1970).

1890   Leo Friedlander, sculptor of equestrian groups at Memorial Bridge, Washington, DC, born in New York City; did sculpture at RCA Building entrance (died 1966).

1892   Jack Yellen, lyricist ("Ain't She Sweet," "Wonder What's Become of Sally," "Happy Days Are Here Again"), born in Razcki, Poland (died 1991).

1892   Strike at Carnegie Steel plant in Homestead, PA, erupted into violence; seven guards and 11 strikers and spectators were shot to death; violence began with arrival of Pinkerton detectives; National Guard arrived soon thereafter.

1894   Federal troops, ordered July 3 by President Cleveland, arrived in Chicago to protect the mails and interstate commerce affected by Pullman strike; the strike was broken in a week.

1896   James S. Love, developer of Burlington Industries Inc. (1923), born in Cambridge, MA; company first manufacturer of rayon (died 1962).

1897   Ralph S. Damon, airline executive (Curtiss-Wright, TransWorld Airlines), born in Franklin, NH (died 1956).

1920   Franklin D. Roosevelt, Assistant Secretary of Navy, nominated for vice presidency by Democratic national convention.

1921   Nancy Davis Reagan, wife of President Reagan, born in New York City.

1925   Merv Griffin, singer and television emcee/host of talk show, born in San Mateo, CA.

1932   Cost of first class postage increased to three cents.

1933   First major league All-Star baseball game held in Chicago, with the American League winning 4–2.

1944   Stampede at circus fire in Hartford, CT, resulted in 168 killed and 193 injured.

1944   Part of a railroad train plunged into a gorge near High Bluff, TN, 35 died.

1946   Sylvester Stallone, screen star best known for his *Rocky* and *Rambo* films, born in New York City.

1948   President Truman announced start of Berlin Airlift to circumvent blockade of the city by Russia.

1953   (Irene) Temple Bailey, author (*Glory of Youth, Trumpeter Swan, Enchanted Ground*), died.

1957   Harry S Truman Library dedicated in Independence, MO.

1960   President Eisenhower issued proclamation reducing import quotas of Cuban sugar by 95 percent in answer to Castro's "deliberate policy of hostility" to United States.

1994   Fourteen firefighters died near Glenwood Springs, CO, when they were surrounded by forest fires; fires raged in 11 states in July.

2001   In return for escaping death penalty, former FBI agent Robert P. Hanssen pleaded guilty to spying for Russia; charges included betraying to Soviets identity of nine double agents.

2003   William Straus died at 88; refugee from Nazi Germany who pioneered the first organic dairy farm in western U.S.; promoted environmentally friendly farming.

2006   In major setback for same-sex marriage advocates, the highest court in New York (the Court of Appeals) ruled that there was nothing inherently discriminatory in limiting marriage to heterosexual couples: It is a question to be decided by the legislature and not by the courts. Georgia Supreme Court upheld voter-approved ban on such marriages same day.

7

1540   Francisco Vasquez de Coronado, who led force into New Mexico to capture the "Seven Cities of Cibola," captured first city (Hawikuh, which became Granada-Cibola); explored areas north and east before returning to Mexico.

1586   Thomas Hooker, liberal Puritan leader, born in Leicestershire, England; helped found Hartford and frame the Fundamental Orders, which long served Connecticut as a constitution (died 1647).

1742   Gen. James Oglethorpe led force to victory over the Spanish in Battle of Bloody Marsh on St. Simons Island, GA.

1768   Philip S. Physick, known as father of American surgery, born in Philadelphia; one of first to use animal ligature in surgery, leaving them in the tissues to be absorbed; developed number of useful surgical instruments (died 1837).

1798   Congress repealed treaties with France, terminating the alliance, and for next two years an undeclared naval war followed.

1846   Naval forces under Commodore John D. Sloat went ashore at Monterey, raised the American flag, and proclaimed California part of the United States.

1849   T(heophil) Mitchell Prudden, pathologist who was first to make diphtheria antitoxin in United States, born in Middlebury, CT (died 1924).

1860 Abraham Cohan, founder, editor *Jewish Daily Forward* (1902–51), born in Vilna, Poland; author of *Rise of David Levinsky* and *Yekl* (died 1951).

1864 First North Dakota newspaper, *Frontier Scout*, published by S.C. Winegar at Ft. Union.

1865 Four persons were hanged for participation in conspiracy to kill President Lincoln — David E. Herold, Lewis Paine, George A. Atzerodt, Mrs. Mary E.J. Surrat; four others were imprisoned.

1890 Harry A. Noyes, chemist who developed food freezing process, born in Marlboro, MA (died 1970).

1898 Congress by joint resolution annexed the Hawaiian Islands.

1899 George Cukor, movie director (*Little Women, My Fair Lady, A Star Is Born, Philadelphia Story*), born in New York City (died 1983).

1906 Satchel (Leroy R.) Paige, baseball pitcher who may have pitched in more than 2,000 games in over 20 years, born in Mobile, AL; named to Baseball Hall of Fame (died 1982).

1907 Robert A. Heinlein, foremost American science fiction writer, born in Butler, MO; his works include *Farmer in the Sky, Stranger in a Strange Land* (died 1988).

1911 Gian Carlo Menotti, opera composer (*Amahl and the Night Visitors, The Medium, The Consul, The Telephone*), born in Cadegliano, Italy.

1917 Lawrence F. O'Brien, commissioner, National Basketball Assn. (1975–84), born in Springfield, MA; Postmaster General (1965–68); chairman, National Democratic Committee (1968–72) (died 1990).

1917 Emma Goldman and Alexander Berkman sentenced to two years imprisonment and fined $10,000 for impeding registration in military draft; Supreme Court upheld decision.

1927 Doc (Carl H.) Severinsen, trumpeter and orchestra leader, born in Arlington, OR; musical director, *Tonight Show* for many years.

1941 American forces occupied Iceland at invitation of Icelandic government.

1946 Jimmy Carter and Rosalynn Smith were married in Plains, GA.

1946 Pope Pius XII announced canonization of Frances Xavier Cabrini (Mother Cabrini), the first American citizen to become a saint.

1947 Commission on Organization of the Executive Branch of Government — the Hoover Commission — created; recommendations (April 1, 1949) led to Reorganization Act of 1949.

1978 Solomon Islands became independent after having been an American protectorate since World War II.

1987 Kiwanis International ended 72-year men-only policy by an overwhelming vote of its 8,200 clubs to admit women.

1994 Tropical Storm Alberto caused flooding in vicinity of Macon, GA; at least 17 were killed.

8

1657 Abraham DePeyster, colonial official who held almost every city and colony post, born in New Amsterdam (New York City) (died 1728).

1758 British force defeated at Ticonderoga by the French under Montcalm.

1776 Declaration of Independence, adopted four days earlier, published and proclaimed publicly in Philadelphia; (John Adams wrote: "...the bells rung all day and almost all night").

1778 French fleet, commanded by Comte d'Estains, arrived off the Delaware Capes, later off Sandy Hook, blockading the British for nearly two weeks; then sailed for Rhode Island.

1779 Spain authorized her subjects in Louisiana to capture English posts on the Mississippi River.

1779 Fairfield, CT, burned by the British and Hessians.

1826 Benjamin H. Grierson, Union officer who led cavalry raids in South, born in Pittsburgh; later, as a general, he fought against the Indians (died 1911).

1839 John D. Rockefeller, founder, president, Standard Oil Co. (1870–1911), born in Richford, NY; endowed four charitable corporations — Rockefeller Foundation, General Education Board, Laura Spellman Rockefeller Memorial, and Rockefeller Institute for Medical Research (died 1937).

1862 Ella Reeve Bloor, a founder of American Communist Party, born on Staten Island, NY (died 1951).

1868 *Daily New Mexico* published, the first newspaper in state.

1869 William Vaughn Moody, playwright (*The Great Divide, The Faith Healer*), born in Spencer, IN (died 1910).

1872 Joseph M. Flint, surgeon who organized first mobile hospital for troops in France, born in Chicago; professor at U. of California (1901–07), Yale (1907–21) (died 1944).

1872 Harry von Tilzer, popular composer ("Wait Till the Sun Shines, Nellie," "I Want a Girl Just Like the Girl," "In the Evening by the Moonlight"), born in Detroit (died 1946).

1881 Mantis J. Van Sweringen, railroad executive who helped develop Shaker Heights, a Cleveland suburb, born in Wooster, OH; bought Nickel Plate Railroad (1916), later bought others, at one time controlling 21,000 miles of railroad (died 1935).

1882 Percy A. Grainger, pianist and composer ("Country Garden"), born in Melbourne, Australia (died 1961).

1889 John L. Sullivan won world heavyweight boxing championship from Jake Kilrain in Richburg, MS; this was last bare knuckle prize fight.

1891 Warren G. Harding was married to Florence K. DeWolfe in Marion, OH.

1896 William Jennings Bryan delivered his "Cross of Gold" speech in favor of silver coinage at Democratic national convention in Chicago, saying: "You shall not press down upon the brow of labor, this crown of thorns; you shall not crucify mankind upon a cross of gold"; nominated for president by convention.

1899 David E. Lilienthal, public official, born in Morton, IL; with Tennessee Valley Authority (1933–46), chairman (1941–46); chairman, Atomic Energy Commission (1946–50) (died 1981).

1900 George Antheil, concert pianist and ultra-modern composer (*Ballet Mécanique, Transatlantic, Archipelago*), born in Trenton, NJ (died 1959).

1906 Philip C. Johnson, architect known for functionalist glass-steel buildings, born in Cleveland; his buildings include the Seagram Building and New York State Theater in New York City.

1907 George W. Romney, president, American Motors (1954–62), born in Chihuahua, Mexico, to American parents; governor of Michigan (1963–69); secretary of Housing & Urban Development (1969–73) (died 1995).

1908 Nelson A. Rockefeller, Vice President (1974–77), born in Bar Harbor, ME; Assistant Secretary of State (1944–45), Undersecretary of HEW (1952–56); governor of New York (1958–73) (died 1979).

1914 Billy Eckstine, a leading singer of 1940/50s, born in Pittsburgh (died 1993).

1931 Roone Arledge, radio/television executive, born in Forest Hills, NY; head of American Broadcasting Co. sports, news operations.

1937 Roald Hoffman, chemist, born in Zloezow, Poland; shared 1981 Nobel Chemistry Prize for work in developing quantum mechanics rules which allow chemists to predict outcome of chemical reactions.

1950 Gen. Douglas MacArthur named commander-in-chief of UN troops in Korea.

1957 Grace A. Coolidge, widow of President Coolidge, died in Northampton, MA, at 78.

1976 Former President Nixon was disbarred by Appellate Division, New York State Supreme Court on charges of obstructing justice in the Watergate investigation.

1997 Senate Governmental Affairs Committee began hearings on fund-raising practices during the 1994 and 1996 elections.

1998 Tentative agreement reached by Dow Chemical Corp. and lawyers for 170,000 women who claimed they were made ill by Dow's silicone breast implants; settlement gives $3.2 billion to the woman (from $12,000 to $60,000 each).

1998 Four leaders of Montana Freemen were convicted in Billings, MT, for conspiring to defraud four banks.

2000 *Harry Potter and the Goblet of Fire,* the fourth book of an extremely popular children's series (but which simultaneously enjoyed a large adult readership), was released to the public; broke 3,000,000 in sales within 48 hours — highest figure then on record for any book.

2003 Researchers reported first major increase in high blood pressure since the 1960s: about one-third of Americans now suffer from it; officials concerned because heart attacks and strokes often occur as result; suspect increase in American weight level may be to blame.

2006 At 88 June Allyson died; had been popular actress in movies of 1940s and 1950s.

9

1577 Thomas W. De La Warr, colonial administrator, born in England; named first governor and captain general of Virginia colony (1610–11); returned to England to seek aid for colony, died while returning to Virginia (1618).

1677 Sir William Berkeley, colonial governor, died at 71; served as governor of Virginia (1642–76).

1750 Thomas Posey, Revolutionary officer at Saratoga and Stony Point, born in Fairfax County, VA; represented Louisiana in Senate (1812–13) and served Indiana Territory as governor (1813–16) (died 1818).

1755 Gen. Edward Braddock, who arrived from England with 1,450 men, was defeated by the French and Indians in Battle of the Wilderness on the Monongahela River; Braddock was mortally wounded; retreat led by George Washington, commander of 450 colonial troops; British lost nearly 1,000 men.

1766 Jacob Perkins, inventor of machine that cut and headed nails and tacks in one operation (c. 1790), born in Newburyport, MA; developed steel plates for printing bank notes, postage stamps (died 1849).

1793 Five-day constitutional convention ended in Windsor, completing Vermont's constitution; adopted by legislature November 2, 1796.

1802 Thomas Davenport, inventor of first commercially successful electric motor (1843), born in Williamsport, VT (died 1851).

1819 Elias Howe, inventor of first practical sewing machine (1846), born in Spencer, MA (died 1867).

1828 Claus Spreckels, known as the "sugar king," founded what became California Sugar Co., born in Lamstedt, Germany; developed sugar plantation in Hawaii (died 1908).

1832 President Jackson named first Commissioner of Indian Affairs, part of the War Department until 1849.

1846 American troops under Commodore John B. Montgomery occupied San Francisco.

1847 Edwin J. Houston, electrical engineer co-inventor of arc lighting system (1881), born in Alexandria, VA (died 1914).

1850 President Taylor died of coronary thrombosis at 66 in the White House after serving little more than a year.

1856 Daniel Guggenheim, head of American Refining & Smelting Co. (1905–19), born in Philadelphia; founder, Guggenheim Foundation (died 1930).

1856 Nikola Tesla, electrician and inventor of electrical items, born in Smiljan, Yugoslavia (then Austria); inventor of motors, generators, transformers, Tesla coil, a system of arc lighting, wireless system of communication and power transmission, devices that made alternating current practical (died 1943).

1858 Franz Boas, establisher of modern structure of anthropology, born in Minden, Germany; with Columbia U. (1896–1942) (died 1942).

1858 Richard A. Ballinger, Interior Secretary (1909–11), born in Boonesboro, IA; target of criticism and investigation of Alaska coal land claims; cleared, then resigned (died 1922).

1863 Port Hudson, MS, untenable after fall of Vicksburg, fell to Union troops after six-weeks siege.

1864 Confederate troops under Gen. Jubal A. Early crossed Potomac River into Maryland, met Union force at Monocacy, near Frederick, and held in check.

1868 The 14th Amendment, which protects a citizen's rights, was ratified.

1870 Charles Hayden, banker who founded Hayden, Stone & Co., born in Boston; gave $150,000 for equipment for New York City planetarium named for him (died 1937).

1877 Bell Telephone Co. formed, succeeding Bell Patent Association, the first telephone company.

1878 Hans V. Kaltenborn, newspaper and radio correspondent, born in Milwaukee; on air 102 times in 18 days during the Munich crisis (died 1965).

1881 Samuel L. Rothafel, theater operator known as "Roxy," born in Stillwater, MN; remembered for Radio City Music Hall and development of precision dancers (the Rockettes) (died 1936).

1887 Samuel Eliot Morison, official American naval historian, born in Boston; prepared 15 volume history of Navy in World War II; author of *Admiral of the Ocean Sea, John Paul Jones* (died 1976).

1894 Dorothy Thompson, syndicated columnist, foreign correspondent, born in Lancaster, NY; wife of Sinclair Lewis (1928–42) (died 1961).

1897 Albert C. Wedemeyer, World War II general who commanded American forces in China (1944–46), born in Omaha, NE (died 1989).

1908 Paul Brown, football coach (Cleveland Browns 1948–62, Cincinnati Bengals 1968–76), born in Norwalk, OH (died 1991).

1911 John A. Wheeler, physicist, born in Jacksonville, FL; received 1968 Enrico Fermi Award for his work in nuclear fission.

1918 Railroad accident at Nashville, TN, caused 101 deaths.

1947 O(renthal) J. Simpson, football player (U. of Southern California, Buffalo Bills (1969–77), born in San Francisco; was center of trial in murder of his wife and a friend, found not guilty.

1956 Tom Hanks, screen actor who won best acting Oscars in 1993 (*Philadelphia*) and 1994 (*Forrest Gump*), born in Oakland, CA.

1982 Pan American Boeing 727 crashed after takeoff from Kenner, LA; killed 145 persons on the plane, eight on the ground.

1996 Melvin Belli, prominent defense attorney, died at 88.

1997 Major television networks, except National Broadcasting Co., agreed on a revised and expanded television ratings system.

1998 Senate passed bill reforming the way the Internal Revenue Service operates; had been approved by the House June 25.

2002 Rod Steiger died at 77; both as supporting actor and leading man, he carved out a unique niche through powerful characterizations in both early television (1948–1953) and then in the movie industry.

2003 Acting on a proposal first presented to it in 1994, Food and Drug Administration announced the requirement for trans fat to be listed as part of snack foods' nutritional level; believed to be more dangerous to health than saturated fat.

2004 Isabel Sanford (b. 1917), died; played "Weezy" Mills Jefferson, the wife, in the 11-year television series *The Jeffersons;* first black woman to win Emmy Award for best actress in a comedy series.

10

1754 Delegates from New England, New York, Pennsylvania, and Maryland, meeting in Albany, approved "Plan of Union" (mostly written by Benjamin Franklin), which called for a union of all colonies, except Georgia and Nova Scotia, under a president-general, appointed and paid by the Crown, and a council; the plan was rejected by the colonies and Great Britain.

1761 George Clinton, governor of New York (1743–53), died at 75.

1792 George M. Dallas, Vice President (1845–49), born in Philadelphia; represented Pennsylvania in Senate (1831–33); minister to Russia (1837–39), to Great Britain (1856–61); Dallas, TX, named for him (died 1864).

1795 President Washington issued first presidential amnesty, or pardon, to all people involved in the Whiskey Rebellion on their signing oath of allegiance to United States.

1821 Christopher C. Augur, Union general who commanded defense of Washington, DC (1863), born in Kendall, NY; also served in Mexican War (died 1898).

1825 Richard King, developer of world's largest ranch in Texas, born in Orange County, NY; at time of his death, ranch was 600,000 acres; eventually grew to million acres (died 1885).

1832 President Jackson vetoed bill to recharter Second Bank of the United States, which became a major issue in his reelection campaign; bank had existed 20 years; federal funds were withdrawn in September and placed in state banks.

1834 James A.M. Whistler, artist best known for his *Portrait of My Mother*, born in Lowell, MA; spent most of his life in Europe (died 1903).

1839 Adolphus Busch, founder, head, Anheuser Busch Co. (1861), born in Mainz, Germany; pioneered in pasteurization of beer, making long-distance unrefrigerated shipping possible (died 1913).

1850 Vice President Millard Fillmore sworn in as president on death of President Taylor.

1867 Finley Peter Dunne, writer remembered for his sketches of an Irish bartender, Mr. Dooley, born in Chicago (died 1936).

1875 Mary N. Bethune, founder of school for black girls in Daytona, FL, born in Mayesville, SC; merged her 19-year-old school in 1923 with Cookman Institute to form Bethune-Cookman College, which she headed (1932–42, 1946–47); founder, National Council of Negro Women (1937) (died 1955).

1888 Graham McNamee, radio announcer/master of ceremonies in 1930s, born in Washington, DC (died 1942).

1889 Julia G. Tyler, widow of President Tyler, died in Richmond, VA, at 69.

1890 Wyoming became the 44th state.

1891 Rexford G. Tugwell, governor of Puerto Rico (1941–46), born in Sinclairville, NY; member of Roosevelt "brain trust" (died 1979).

1894 Jimmy McHugh, popular composer ("I Can't Give You Anything but Love," "I Feel a Song Coming On," "Coming in on a Wing and a Prayer"), born in Boston (died 1969).

1897 John Gilbert, silent screen leading man, born in Logan, UT (died 1936).

1902 Maurice N. Eisendrath, president Union of American Hebrew Congregations (1946–73), born in Chicago (died 1973).

1902 Johnstown, PA, was scene of a bituminous coal mine accident which killed 112.

1907 Federal Government filed suit against 65 corporations and 27 persons of the American Tobacco Co. as a combination in restraint of trade.

1919   Senate began consideration of Versailles Treaty and League of Nations; voted down initially November 19; turned down again March 19, 1920.

1920   David Brinkley, television newsman, born in Wilmington, NC; with NBC (1951–81) with Chet Huntley and John Chancellor, then ABC (1982–97).

1920   Owen Chamberlain, physicist, born in San Francisco; shared 1959 Nobel Physics Prize for demonstrating existence of anti-proton.

1925   Scopes Trial, which challenged teaching of evolution in school, began in Dayton, TN, pitting Clarence Darrow for the defense against prosecution team which included William Jennings Bryan; trial ended July 25 with conviction of teacher, John T. Scopes; Bryan died a day after the trial.

1932   Jerry Herman, musicals composer (*Hello, Dolly!, Mame*), born in New York City.

1943   Arthur Ashe, first black star in men's tennis, born in Richmond, VA; Wimbledon champion (1975), captain of U.S. Davis Cup team (died 1993).

1943   Combined American, British, and Canadian amphibious forces invaded Sicily; ended successfully August 17 at cost of 7,400 American casualties.

1947   Arlo Guthrie, folk singer and composer, born in New York City.

1962   *Telstar I* relayed first transmission of television signals between the United States and Europe.

1985   Gunmen in Beirut kidnapped Thomas Sutherland, a dean of American University.

2002   Discovery of wreckage of PT-109 announced; boat sunk while skippered by future president John F. Kennedy.

11

1681   A concession to province of Pennsylvania was issued by William Penn to regulate land sales and grants, and to deal with Indian relations.

1767   John Quincy Adams, sixth president (1825–29), born in Braintree (now Quincy), MA; represented Massachusetts in Senate (1803–8) and House (1831–48); minister to Netherlands (1794–96), to Germany (1796–1801), to Russia (1809–11), to Great Britain (1815); chief negotiator after War of 1812; Secretary of State (1817–25) (died 1848).

1774   Sir William Johnson, British superintendent of Indian affairs (1755–74), died at 59.

1782   British evacuated Savannah, which they had held since December 29, 1778.

1792   British evacuated posts west of the Alleghenies and Detroit was occupied by Capt. Moses Porter and 65 American soldiers.

1798   Marine Corps was established.

1804   Aaron Burr fatally wounded Alexander Hamilton in a duel at Weehawken, NJ; duel brought on by Hamilton's derogatory remarks during Burr's campaign for New York governor; Hamilton reportedly said Burr was "a dangerous man ... who ought not to be trusted with the reins of government"; Hamilton died the next day.

1806   James Smith, a signer of Declaration of Independence, died at 87.

1813   Gen. Peter B. Porter led Americans in defeating British in attack on Black Rock section of Buffalo, NY.

1831   Henry C. Timken, inventor of tapered roller bearing, born near Hamburg, Germany; invented special type of carriage spring (1877) and the bearing (1898); founded Timken Roller Bearing Axle Co. (1898) (died 1909).

1836   Specie circular issued by Treasury Secretary Levi Woodbury, which stemmed violent speculation in public lands and revealed the unsoundness of many small banks.

1838   John Wanamaker, founder of one of first major department stores (1869), born in Philadelphia; store was first to advertise, offer full refunds; Postmaster General (1889–93) (died 1922).

1861   George W. Norris, legislator, born in Sandusky County, OH; represented Nebraska in House (1903–13) and Senate (1914–43); opposed American entry into World War II; leader in forming Tennessee Valley Authority (died 1944).

1862   President Lincoln named Gen. Henry Halleck as general-in-chief of Union forces, replacing Gen. George McClellan.

1864   Confederate troops under Gen. Jubal A. Early reached within six miles of Washington, DC, but retreated during the night.

1878   President Hayes removed Chester A. Arthur from post of Collector of the Port of New York.

1881   Clarence Budington Kelland, author who created character of Scattergood Baines, born in Portland, MI (died 1964).

1890   President Benjamin Harrison signed act authorizing bridge across Hudson River to connect New York and New Jersey.

1892   Armed union miners expelled nonunion miners and fought pitched battle at the lead and silver mines at Coeur d'Alene, ID; trouble continued until 1905.

1899 E(lwyn) B. White, author (*Stuart Little*, *Charlotte's Web*, *Trumpet of the Swan*), born in Mt. Vernon, NY; long-time writer for *The New Yorker* (died 1985).

1915 Colin Kelly, first American World War II hero, born in Madison, FL; piloted disabled bomber into a Japanese vessel after his crew bailed out (1941).

1920 Yul Brynner, screen actor (*The King and I*), born on Sakhalin Island, Japan (died 1985).

1927 Theodore H. Maiman, physicist who built first laser, born in Los Angeles; founder, president, Laser Video Corp., Korad Corp.

1932 Nat(haniel W.) Niles, pioneer American figure skater, died in Boston at 45; won American men's title (1918, 1925, 1927) and with Theresa W. Blanchard won the pairs title nine times.

1936 President Franklin Roosevelt dedicated the Triborough Bridge in New York City.

1955 Air Force Academy accepted the first class of 306 cadets at an interim site at Lowery Air Force Base, CO.

1979 An orbiting unmanned space vehicle, *Skylab*, disintegrated over Australia and the Indian Ocean.

2001 In Washington state's North Cascades area, four firefighters died fighting 2,500-acre fire.

2006 Homeland Security's database of possible terrorist targets resulted in odd statistics: Indiana headed list with 8,591 potential targets; New York had only 5,687 and California 3,212; list included certain flea markets and petting zoos.

12

1808 *Missouri Gazette* was published by Joseph Charles in St. Louis, the first paper west of the Mississippi; later became St. Louis Republican.

1817 Henry David Thoreau, one of the great figures in American literature, born in Concord, MA; author of *Walden* and *A Week on the Concord and Merrimack Rivers* (died 1862).

1821 Daniel H. Hill, Confederate general who served in Peninsular Campaign, Antietam, and Chickamauga, born in York District, SC (died 1889).

1840 Benjamin Altman, founder of department store, born in New York City; opened small dry goods store (1865), which became B. Altman & Co.; donated large art collection to Metropolitan Museum of Art (died 1913).

1843 Joseph Smith, Mormon leader, announced in Nauvoo, IL, that a divine revelation sanctioned practice of polygamy; announcement caused bitter feelings among both Mormons and non–Mormons.

1849 Dolley Madison, widow of President Madison, died at 81 in Washington, DC.

1854 George Eastman, camera inventor, born in Waterville, NY; perfected method for making photographic dry plates (1880) and flexible film (1884); invented Kodak, first low-priced readily-available camera (1888); founder, Eastman School of Music, Rochester, NY (died 1932).

1871 Riot involving Irish Catholics and Protestants in New York City killed 52

1895 R. Buckminster Fuller, developer of geodesic dome, born in Milton, MA; also had several Dymaxion inventions (died 1983).

1895 Oscar Hammerstein, II, lyricist of popular songs and musicals, born in New York City; songs include "Rose Marie," "Sunny," "Who," "My Blue Heaven"; musicals were *Show Boat*, *New Moon*, *Oklahoma*, *Carousel*, *South Pacific*, *The King and I*, *The Flower Drum Song*, *The Sound of Music* (died 1960).

1895 Kirsten Flagstad, soprano in Wagnerian operas, born in Evanger, Norway (died 1962).

1908 Milton Berle, entertainer who was first television superstar, born in New York City; known as Uncle Miltie.

1913 Willis E. Lamb, Jr., physicist, born in Los Angeles; shared 1955 Nobel Physics Prize for work on hydrogen spectrum.

1917 Andrew N. Wyeth, one of most popular painters of his time, born in Chadds Ford, PA.

1925 Roger B. Smith, chief executive officer, General Motors (1981–90), born in Columbus, OH.

1934 Van (H. Levan) Cliburn, concert pianist who won International Tschaikvsky Piano Competition (1958), born in Shreveport, LA.

1937 Bill Cosby, comedian who was first black to star in television series, born in Philadelphia.

1967 Black riots in Newark, NJ, began, lasting five days during which 26 were killed, 1,500 injured, and 1,000 arrested; considerable damage to property.

1974 John D. Ehrlichman, presidential aide, and three others were found guilty of conspiring to violate civil rights of Dr. Lewis Fielding, psychiatrist to man who leaked Pentagon Papers, by breaking into his office.

1980 Richard Queen, an American hostage held at embassy in Teheran, was released because of poor health.

1989 President Bush addressed the Hungarian Parliament in Budapest, the first American president to do so.

1994 Employees of United Airlines were able to gain economic control of company.

2004 U.S. reduced acceptable LDL cholesterol levels by roughly 30 percent.

2005 The "father of affirmative action," former presidential adviser Arthur Fletcher, died at 80.

13

1729 John Parker, commander of Minute Men at Lexington in start of Revolution, born in Lexington, MA; reputedly told his men: "Stand your ground. Don't fire unless fired upon. But if they mean to have a war, let it begin here" (died 1775).

1753 William Penn Academy in Philadelphia chartered; later became the U. of Pennsylvania.

1787 Continental Congress adopted the Northwest Ordinance, setting up a government for the area north of the Ohio River and west of New York, guaranteeing freedom of religion, support for schools, no slavery; the ordinance stated: "Religion, morality, and knowledge, being necessary to good government and the happiness of mankind, schools and the means of education shall forever be encouraged."

1814 José S. Alemany, first Catholic Archbishop of San Francisco (1853–84), born in Vich, Spain; missionary bishop to Southwest (died 1888).

1815 James A. Seddon, Confederate Secretary of State (1862–65), born in Fredericksburg, VA (died 1880).

1821 Nathan Bedford Forrest, Confederate cavalry general, born in Bedford County, TN (died 1877).

1824 James I. Waddell, Confederate naval officer who commanded the *Shenandoah* which raided American shipping in Pacific, born in Pittsboro, NC (died 1886).

1857 Franklin H. Martin, founder, American College of Surgeons, born in Jefferson County, WI; founder, editor, *Surgery, Gynecology and Obstetrics* (died 1935).

1862 Gen. Nathan Bedford Forrest led 2,000 Confederate troops in capture of Murfreesboro, TN.

1863 Union troops captured Yazoo City, MS.

1863 Four days of draft riots began in New York City, resulting in about 75 deaths; rioters protested provision allowing money payments in place of military service; payments ended in 1864.

1864 John Jacob Astor, IV, businessman who increased family fortune with vast New York City real estate holdings, born in New York City; died in sinking of *Titanic* (1912).

1865 Editorial by Horace Greeley in *New York Tribune* used expression, "Go west, young man, go west"; he later gave credit for phrase to J.L.B. Soule, who had used it in 1851 in the *Terre Haute* (IN) *Express*.

1886 Edward J. Flanagan, founder of Boys Town, born in Roscommon, Ireland; founded Home for Boys near Omaha, NE (1917), which later became Boys Town (died 1948).

1890 Tornado caused drowning deaths of 100 persons at Lake Pepin, MN.

1901 Mickey (Edward P.) Walker, welterweight (1922–26) and middleweight (1926–31) boxing champion, born in Elizabeth, NJ (died 1981).

1912 Senate declared seat of William L. Lorimer of Illinois vacant after a two-year investigation of bribery charges.

1913 Dave Garroway, television personality who started the *Today* show, born in Schenectady (died 1983).

1917 Executive order called 678,000 men into military service from among those who had registered earlier.

1935 Jack Kemp, football quarterback and political figure, born in Los Angeles; after pro football career, he served New York in House and then as Secretary of Housing & Urban Development; 1996 Republican vice presidential candidate.

1977 A 25-hour power failure struck New York City area, leading to extensive looting; 3,776 looters were arrested, property damages estimated at $135 million.

1985 President Reagan underwent successful surgery on the abdomen at Bethesda Naval Medical Center; returned to White House July 20.

1994 R.H. Macy & Co. and Federated Department Stores Inc. agreed on a merger to create one of nation's largest department store chains — 460 stores, sales of $13.5 billion.

1995 President Clinton accepted report of Defense Base Closure Commission proposing to close 19 bases and consolidate 26 others.

2000 Former war foes U.S. and (North) Vietnam agree to virtually unrestricted trade.

2001 In Washington, DC, mother gave birth to septuplets (seven children); only third known occurrence in world.

2006 As result of massive pro-undocumented/illegal alien rallies and the accompanying controversy over the treatment of such, a Pew Hispanic Center national survey indicated that for first time most Latinos (58 percent) felt that Hispanics were working together in a common cause.

14

1782 Jesse D. Elliott, War of 1812 naval officer second in command to Perry, born in Hagerstown, MD; captured two British brigs on Lake Erie, the first American success of the war (died 1845).

1832 President Jackson signed Tariff Act amending the 1828 act, but it was still not satisfactory to the South.

1839 John C. Gray, a leading authority on real property law, born in Brighton, MA; cofounder, *American Law Review* (1866) (died 1915).

1853 Commodore Matthew C. Perry received by Japanese Lord of Toda and negotiated treaty opening Japan to American commerce.

1853 First American world fair — Exhibition of Industry of All Nations — opened in new Crystal Palace in New York City with President Pierce on hand.

1855 New Hampshire enacted a prohibition law.

1857 Frederick L. Maytag, appliance manufacturer who founded Maytag Co. (1909), born in Elgin, IL (died 1937).

1860 Owen Wister, author (*The Virginian*), born in Philadelphia; his book helped establish the cowboy as an American hero (died 1938).

1865 Arthur Capper, Kansas governor (1915–19) and served it in Senate (1919–49), born in Garnett, KS; editor, publisher, *Topeka Daily Capital*, several agricultural magazines (died 1951).

1870 Congress approved annual pension of $3,000 to Mary Todd Lincoln, widow of President Lincoln.

1883 First class of rabbis was ordained in United States after graduating from Hebrew Union College in Cincinnati.

1898 Albert D. Chandler, public official and baseball commissioner (1945–51), born in Corydon, KY; known as "Happy," served Kentucky as governor (1935–39, 1955–59) and in Senate

(1939–45); named to Baseball Hall of Fame (died 1991).

1903 Irving Stone, author (*Lust for Life*, *The Agony and the Ecstasy*, *The President's Lady*), born in San Francisco (died 1989).

1904 Isaac B. Singer, Yiddish author (*The Family Moskat*, *The Magician of Lublin*, *The Manor*), born in Radzymin, Poland; awarded 1978 Nobel Literature Prize (died 1991).

1906 William H. Tunner, Air Force general who directed Berlin airlift, born in Elizabeth, NJ (died 1983).

1912 Woody (Woodrow W.) Guthrie, folk singer and composer of more than 1,000 songs about American life, born in Okemah, OK (died 1967).

1913 Gerald A. Ford, 38th president (1974–77), born in Omaha as Leslie L. King, Jr., and assumed name of stepfather after his adoption; represented Michigan in House (1949–73); appointed Vice President (1973) on resignation of Spiro T. Agnew, became president on resignation of President Nixon.

1920 Bella Abzug, a leader of feminist movement, born in New York City (died 1998).

1927 John Chancellor, television newsman with NBC (1960–82), born in Chicago; director, Voice of America (1966–67) (died 1996).

1938 Howard Hughes completed record round-the-world flight in three days, 19 hours, 14 minutes, 28 seconds.

1986 One hundred sixty American soldiers arrived in Bolivia to help fight against production of cocaine.

2000 Florida jury awarded nationwide record of $144.8 billion punitive damages in class-action lawsuit over health harm to 500,000 Florida smokers.

15

1704 August G. Spangenberg, founder of Moravian Church in North America, born in Kletzenberg, Germany; Moravian bishop 1735–62, then returning to Germany (died 1792).

1779 Clement Clark Moore, author best known for the ballad, "'Twas the night before Christmas...," born in New York City; helped found General Theological Seminary, New York City (1819) (died 1863).

1779 Gen. Anthony Wayne led 1,200 men in night bayonet attack on Stony Point, NY, a fort along the western shore of the Hudson River; captured all 700 British troops, dismantled the fort.

1796   Thomas Bulfinch, author (*Mythology, The Age of Fable*), born in Newton, MA; (died 1867).

1802   Robert Aitken, Scottish-born printer, died at 68; his major accomplishment according to Library of Congress catalog was "the Aitken Bible, the first complete English Bible printed in America, and the only one authorized and approved by Congress to this day (June 1902)."

1813   British fleet arrived in Potomac River.

1850   Maria Frances Xavier Cabrini, first American saint, born in Lodigiano, Italy; founder, Missionary Sisters of the Sacred Heart (1880); came to America 1889, naturalized; canonized 1946 (died 1917).

1900   Thomas Francis, Jr., physician who conducted evaluation of Salk polio vaccine test, born in Gas City, IN (died 1969).

1901   Truman B. Douglass, clergyman who led unification of Congregational and Evangelical and Reformed denominations into the United Church of Christ (1957), born in Grinnell, IA (died 1969).

1903   Walter D. Edmonds, author (*Rome Haul, Drums Along the Mohawk*), born in Boonville, NY (died 1998).

1913   Augustus O. Bacon of Georgia became first senator elected by popular vote.

1918   Three-day German attack began in the fourth battle of Champagne; turned back by 85,000 American and French troops.

1921   R. Bruce Merrifield, chemist, born in Ft. Worth, TX; awarded 1984 Nobel Chemistry Prize for synthesizing peptide and protein molecules.

1922   Leon N. Lederman, physicist, born in New York City; shared 1988 Nobel Physics Prize for helping capture neutrinos in a high-energy beam to examine the structure of atomic particles.

1933   Wiley Post began round-the-world solo flight of 15,596 miles, which took seven days, 18 hours, 49½ minutes.

1946   Linda Ronstadt, popular singer, born in Tucson, AZ.

1952   First successful transatlantic helicopter flight started at Westover Air Force Base in Massachusetts; ended July 31 at Prestwick, Scotland.

1975   United States and Soviet Russia began Apollo-Soyuz space mission; the two spacecraft linked up in space two days later and orbited together for two days.

1988   The 17-man General Executive Board of the Teamsters Union elected William J. McCarthy as the new president, succeeding the late Jackie Presser; board by one vote rejected Presser's handpicked candidate, Secretary-Treasurer Weldon Mathis.

1995   *Newsday*, 10-year-old New York City newspaper, published its final issue; the parent Long Island edition *Newsday* will continue.

2004   To permit Medicare coverage, serious overweight now defined by it as an "illness."

16

1681   Sieur d'Pierre Iberville, French explorer of Louisiana, born in Montreal, Canada; established first French settlement in Louisiana, at what is now Biloxi, and later at Mobile (1698) (died 1706).

1741   Vitus Bering, a Danish sea captain in the service of Russia, sighted the volcano of St. Elias in what is now Alaska; later landed at Kodiak.

1769   Spanish Franciscan missionary, Junipero Serra, founded a mission at San Diego, the first European settlement in California.

1769   Edmund Fanning, sea captain called the Pathfinder of the Pacific, born in Stonington, CT; discovered islands named for him (died 1841).

1782   Treaty signed with France setting the amount owed by the United States ($7,037,037) to be repaid annually for 12 years, beginning in 1785.

1787   Constitutional Convention accepted the Connecticut compromise, which created the present congressional structure — equal representation in Senate, lower house based on population.

1790   President Washington signed act setting Philadelphia as seat of government from 1790 to 1800, during which a federal city was to be created along the Potomac River.

1798   Public Health Service began with legislation authorizing Marine hospitals to care for American merchant seamen.

1821   Mary Baker Eddy, founder of Christian Science Church, born in Bow, NH; as an invalid she sought many types of healing, founded the spiritual, metaphysical system known as Christian Science; wrote *Science and Health*, explaining the system; founded the *Christian Science Monitor* (1883) (died 1910).

1829   Robert B. Potter, Union general who saw action at Fredericksburg, Vicksburg, born in Schenectady, NY (died 1887).

1845   Theodore N. Vail, first president, American Telephone & Telegraph Co. (1885–89,

1907–19), born in Minerva, OH; general superintendent, railway mails; general manager, Bell Telephone Co. (1878–87) (died 1920).

1863 After one-week siege, Jackson, MS, was evacuated by Confederate troops.

1874 Joseph L. Goldberger, Public Health Service physician who discovered nature of and cure for pellagra, born in Austria (died 1929).

1874 Henry S. Tucker, Episcopal presiding bishop (1937–46), born in Warsaw, VA; Bishop of Virginia (1927–46) (died 1959).

1877 Ivy L. Lee, developer of public relations as a profession, born in Cedartown, GA; served Democratic National Committee, Pennsylvania Railroad, John D. Rockefeller (died 1934).

1877 Bela Schick, pediatrician who developed test for susceptibility to diphtheria, born in Boglar, Hungary; chief pediatrician, Mt. Sinai Hospital, New York City (died 1967).

1880 Kathleen Norris, author (*The Rich Mrs. Burgoyne, Mother, Saturday's Child, The Sea Gull*), born in San Francisco (died 1966).

1881 Louis F. Bachrach, photographer who headed Bachrach Inc. (1915–55), born in Baltimore (died 1963).

1882 Mary Todd Lincoln, widow of President Lincoln, died in Springfield, IL, at 63.

1898 Santiago, with a garrison of 24,000, surrendered, virtually ending the Spanish-American War.

1903 Carmen Lombardo, vocalist with Guy Lombardo band, born in London, Canada (died 1971).

1907 Barbara Stanwyck, screen and television actress, born in New York City (died 1990).

1911 Ginger (Virginia) Rogers, screen actress who starred in musicals with Fred Astaire, born in Independence, MO (died 1995).

1935 First automatic parking meter installed in Oklahoma City.

1945 First atomic bomb, produced in Los Alamos, NM, successfully exploded at Alamagordo, NM.

1946 Bureau of Land Management created in Interior Department by consolidating the General Land Office and Grazing Service.

1967 Fire in state prison at Jay, FL, resulted in 37 deaths.

1997 Dow Jones industrial average passed 8000 for first time with a record-high closing of 8038.88.

1998 Dow Jones industrial average closed over 9300 for first time; reached 9337.97.

2004 Double blow to nuclear research at Los Alamos National Laboratory: installation essentially closed down today until review of both security and safety procedures completed; July 26, Energy Department suspended classified research at location.

17

1744 Elbridge Gerry, Vice President (1813–14), born in Marblehead, MA; member of Continental Congress (1776–81, 1782–85), signer of Declaration of Independence; represented Massachusetts in House (1789–93) and served it as governor (1810, 1811); his name is associated with politicized boundary lines (gerrymandering) (died 1814).

1745 Timothy Pickering, Secretary of State (1795–1800), born in Salem, MA; Continental Army quartermaster general (1781–83), adjutant general (1777–78); Postmaster General (1791–95), War Secretary (1795); represented Massachusetts in Senate (1803–11) and House (1813–17) (died 1829).

1752 Gabriel Johnston, governor of North Carolina (1734–52), died at 53.

1754 King's (later Columbia) College opened in New York City.

1763 John Jacob Astor, fur trader and financier, born in Waldorf, Germany; entered American fur trade (1784), founded Astoria, OR (1811) as a trading post; monopolized Mississippi and upper Missouri valleys fur trade; invested heavily in New York City real estate (died 1848).

1768 Stephen T. Badin, first Catholic priest ordained in United States (1793), born in Orleans, France; spent 26 years riding among settlements in Kentucky; about 1832, acquired land on which Notre Dame U. was founded 10 years later (died 1853).

1812 Combined British and Indian task force took garrison at Mackinac, where Lakes Huron and Michigan join.

1856 Railroad wreck near Philadelphia killed 66 children on an outing.

1864 Union troops under Gen. William T. Sherman crossed Chattahoochee River, eight miles from Atlanta.

1864 James R. Gilmore, unofficial representative of President Lincoln, met with Confederate President Jefferson Davis in Richmond to discuss terms for ending war; conference failed because Union would not recognize Confederacy independence.

1889 Erle Stanley Gardner, author of popular Perry Mason mystery series, born in Malden, MA (died 1970).

1899 James Cagney, screen actor (*Yankee Doodle Dandy, Mr. Roberts*), born in New York City (died 1986).

1916 Federal Farm Loan Act went into effect, providing long-term credit, set up 12 farm loan banks; members of Loan Board named July 27.

1938 Douglas ("Wrong Way") Corrigan flew the Atlantic Ocean from Brooklyn to Dublin despite lack of permission; claimed he thought he was flying to Los Angeles (died 1995).

1944 Explosion of ammunition dumps at Port Chicago, CA, killed 322 persons.

1945 President Truman, Prime Minister Winston Churchill (later Clement Atlee), and Premier Stalin met until August 2, in Potsdam, Germany, to discuss postwar European problems.

1948 Delegates from 13 Southern states formed the Dixiecrats in Birmingham and nominated J. Strom Thurmond for president.

1955 Disneyland opened in Anaheim, CA.

1975 Three American astronauts (Tom Stafford, Donald K. Slayton, Vance Brand) in an Apollo spacecraft linked up with a Soviet Soyuz spacecraft 140 miles above the earth, exchanged visits with the two Soviet cosmonauts.

1981 Two skywalks in Hyatt Regency Hotel in Kansas City, MO, collapsed, killing 113.

1984 George M. Low, Austrian-born educator and space scientist with NASA, died at 58; directed planning for first manned moon landing and walk; president, Rensselaer Polytechnic Institute.

1986 LTV Corporation, second largest steel company, filed for bankruptcy, the largest industrial company ever to file for bankruptcy in United States.

1987 Dow Jones industrial average closed above 2500 (2510.04) for first time as bull market continued.

1990 Dow Jones industrial average closed at new high of 2999.75.

1995 Five-day heat wave in Middle West and Northeast resulted in at least 500 deaths.

1996 TWA jetliner traveling from New York City to Paris exploded and crashed into Atlantic Ocean off Long Island, killing all 230 persons aboard.

2001 FBI reported 184 laptops and 449 firearms unaccounted for in its offices.

2006 Mickey Spillane died at 88; best-selling detective novelist; literary critics often hated his books, but public bought over 100 million of them.

18

1543 Survivors of the DeSoto expedition, led by Luis Moscosco, arrived at Tampa Bay more than four years after it left there.

1663 Charter granted to Rhode Island guaranteed religious freedom regardless of "differences of opinions in matters of religion."

1670 Spain and England signed Treaty of Madrid in which Spain recognized the right of England to her colonies in the Caribbean and in America.

1757 Royall Tyler, jurist and playwright, born in Boston; chief justice, Vermont Supreme Court (1807–13); wrote *The Contrast*, the first professionally-produced play written by an American (died 1826).

1768 John Dickinson's patriotic ballad, "Song for American Freedom," printed in the *Boston Gazette*.

1775 Second Continental Congress recommended establishment of Committees of Safety in all colonies to carry on functions of government.

1854 Tom L. Johnson, inventor of coin farebox for street cars, born near Georgetown, KY; represented Ohio in House (1891–95), mayor of Cleveland (1901–9); had street railway interests in Indianapolis and Cleveland (died 1911).

1861 Samuel W. Stratton, physicist who served as first director, Bureau of Standards, born in Litchfield, IL; president, Massachusetts Institute of Technology (1923–30) (died 1931).

1864 President Lincoln sent Horace Greeley to meet with Confederate peace commissioners in Niagara Falls, Ontario; effort unsuccessful.

1886 Simon B. Buckner, Jr., World War II general, born in Munfordville, KY; commandant, West Point (1933–36); commanding general, Alaska (1940–44); headed Okinawa invasion, killed in action (1945).

1890 Charles Erwin Wilson, president, General Motors (1941–52), born in Minerva, OH; GM vice president (1929–40); Secretary of Defense (1953–57) (died 1961).

1896 Patrick A. O'Boyle, Catholic Archbishop of Washington (1948–73), born in Scranton, PA; named cardinal 1967.

1906 Clifford Odets, playwright (*Waiting for Lefty, Golden Boy*), born in Philadelphia (died 1963).

1911 Hume Cronyn, actor (*High Tor*, *The Fourposter*, *The Gin Game*), born in London, Canada.

1913 Red (Richard) Skelton, entertainer on screen and television, born in Vincennes, IN (died 1997).

1918 Second battle of the Marne began with about 85,000 American troops taking part in battle which was war's turning point; battle and major German offensive ended August 6.

1921 John H. Glenn, Jr., first American astronaut to orbit earth (1962), born in Cambridge, OH; represented Ohio in Senate (1974–98).

1929 Dick Button, World and Olympic figure skating champion, born in Englewood, NJ; won Olympic golds (1948, 1952), world champion (1948–52).

1935 Tenley Albright, first American woman to win Olympic medal in figure skating (1956), born in Newton Centre, MA; won American title (1951–56), world championship (1953, 1955).

1944 American troops captured St. Lo, the French road center connecting Normandy and Brittany.

1947 Presidential Succession Act signed, providing that House Speaker and Senate President Pro Tem succeed to the presidency before cabinet members.

1951 Joe Walcott knocked out Ezzard Charles in seventh round in Pittsburgh to win world heavyweight boxing championship.

1955 President Eisenhower attended five-day Geneva Conference with British, French, and Russian leaders.

1969 Car driven by Sen. Edward M. Kennedy of Massachusetts plunged off a bridge on Chappaquidick Island, MA; 28-year-old secretary, Mary Jo Kopechne, was found drowned in the car.

1984 Gunman killed 21 persons in and near a McDonald's restaurant in San Ysidro, CA; the gunman was shot and killed by police.

1988 James C. McKay, independent prosecutor, reported that Attorney General Edward Meese, III, had probably broken the law in his personal finances management, but he largely exonerated him of wrongdoing in two major government scandals; McKay said he would not bring criminal charges.

2005 General William Westmoreland died at 91; after successful World War II and Korean career, commanded all U.S. forces in Vietnam, 1964–68.

2006 A Pew Internet and American Life Project studying self-identified computer "bloggers" (estimated 12 million adults nationwide with 57 million readers) revealed wider variety of ages and fewer literary pretensions than often believed.

19

1782 New York proposed a convention of states to amend the Articles of Confederation; Congress did not act on the proposal.

1806 Alexander D. Bache, physicist who was superintendent, U.S. Coast Survey (1843–67), born in Philadelphia; first president, National Academy of Sciences (1863) and Girard College(1836); an incorporator of Smithsonian Institution (died 1867).

1808 John Paterson, Revolutionary War general throughout war, died at 64; represented New York in House (1803–05).

1814 Samuel Colt, inventor, manufacturer of revolving breech pistol, born in Hartford, CT; plant opened in mid–1830s, made extensive use of assembly line techniques (died 1862).

1823 George H. Gordon, Union general throughout the war, born in Charlestown, MA; raised regiment at start of war (died 1886).

1845 Fire in New York City resulted in property loss of $6 million.

1846 Edward C. Pickering, astronomer who pioneered in photometric and spectroscopic techniques, born in Boston; director, Harvard Observatory (1876–1919) (died 1919).

1848 First women's rights convention held in Seneca Falls, NY, involving such persons as Sarah and Angelina Grimké, Lucretia Mott, and Elizabeth Cady Stanton; issued declaration of sentiments and resolutions.

1860 Lizzie A. Borden, charged with ax murder of her parents (August 4, 1892), born in Fall River, MA; acquitted after sensational trial; gave rise to popular chant of the day: "Lizzie Borden took an ax/And gave her mother 40 whacks/When she saw what she had done/She gave her father 41" (died 1927).

1865 Charles H. Mayo, who with brother founded what became Mayo Clinic, born in Rochester, MN; they formed staff of St. Mary's Hospital, Rochester; their $2.8 million gift helped it become the Mayo Clinic (died 1939).

1876 Joseph Fielding Smith, Mormon leader who headed Council of Twelve of the church (1951–72), born in Salt Lake City (died 1972).

1885 Malcolm Muir, president, McGraw Hill, Inc. (1928–37) and creator of *Business Week* (1929), born in Glen Ridge, NJ; publisher/editor-in-chief, *Newsweek* (1937–61) (died 1979).

1891 Paul V. McNutt, public official, born in Franklin, IN; governor of Indiana (1933–37); high commissioner, Philippines (1937–39, 1945–46), then ambassador (1946–47); chairman, War Manpower Commission (1942–45) (died 1955).

1921 Rosalyn Yalow, medical physicist, born in New York City; shared 1977 Nobel Physiology/Medicine Prize for research on role of hormones in body chemistry.

1922 George S. McGovern, 1972 Democratic presidential candidate, born in Avon, SD; represented South Dakota in House (1957–60) and Senate (1963–77).

1944 American 5th Army captured Leghorn, Italy.

1967 Midair collision of Piedmont Boeing 727 and Cessna 310 near Hendersonville, NC, killed 82 persons.

1977 Two days of flooding in Johnstown, PA, resulted in 68 deaths.

1984 Democratic National Convention in San Francisco nominated New York Representative Geraldine A. Ferraro as its vice presidential candidate, the first woman to be named a candidate by a major party.

1989 United Airlines DC-10 crashed while making emergency landing at Sioux City, IA, airport; 111 died, 187 survived.

1993 President Clinton dismissed FBI Director William S. Sessions after a harsh internal ethics report on his conduct; Louis J. Freeh named to succeed him.

1996 Summer Olympic Games opened in Atlanta.

2000 Americans with Disabilities Act was passed in July 1990, yet survey released today indicated only 56 percent of those covered who are capable of work and desire to do so have either full- or part-time job; figure for nondisabled: 80 percent.

2005 Judge John Roberts nominated to replace Sandra Day O'Connor on Supreme Court; before confirmation, Chief Justice William Rehnquist dies and Roberts is nominated to take that seat instead.

20

1591 Anne Hutchinson, religious liberal, baptized in Alford, England; preached salvation by individual intuition of God without regard for church; banished from Massachusetts (1637), settled in Rhode Island; finally massacred by Indians (1643).

1605 Samuel de Champlain, on his second of 11 trips to eastern Canada, landed at Nanset Sound on Cape Code.

1629 Samuel Skelton named pastor of first church in Massachusetts at Salem; church was constituted August 6, by 30 persons.

1663 Samuel Stone, Puritan clergyman, died at 61; purchased site of Hartford, CT, from Indians (1636), settled there, serving as minister (1636–63).

1749 George Washington named official surveyor of Culpeper County, VA.

1789 First federal navigation act passed, imposing a duty on ship tonnage.

1832 Alexander L. Holley, builder and designer of steel plants, born in Lakeville, CT; brought Bessemer process to United States and improved it; began first American Bessemer operation in Troy, NY (1865); built many steel plants (died 1882).

1838 (John) Augustin Daly, drama critic and playwright (*Under the Gaslight*, *The Red Scarf*, *Divorce*), born in Plymouth, NC; also adapted many plays from French and German (died 1899).

1864 Fighting began around Atlanta (Peach Tree Creek) and ended with Confederate evacuation of the city (September 1).

1869 Joseph W. Byrns, legislator, born in Cedar Hill, TN; represented Tennessee in House (1909–36), serving as majority leader (1932–35) and Speaker (1935–36) (died 1936).

1880 Egyptian obelisk "Cleopatra's Needle" placed in Central Park, New York City.

1890 Theda Bara, screen actress who starred as a "vamp" in silent films, born in Cincinnati (died 1955).

1894 Wiley B. Rutledge, Jr., associate justice, Supreme Court (1943–49), born in Cloverport, KY; justice, Court of Appeals (1939–43) (died 1949).

1917 Drawing for first military draft held to determine order of service.

1920 Elliott L. Richardson, public official, born in Boston; Secretary of HEW (1970–73), Attorney General (1973), Secretary of Defense (1973).

1922 Alan S. Boyd, first Secretary of Transportation (1966–69), born in Jacksonville, FL; chairman, Civil Aeronautics Board (1961–65); became chief executive officer, Amtrak (1971).

1933 Gen. Hugh S. Johnson proclaimed the Blue Eagle as emblem of the National Recovery Administration (NRA) and industrial recovery; discontinued September 5, 1935, following invalidation of the compulsory code system.

1969 Neil A. Armstrong, in flight of *Apollo XI*, became first man to set foot on the moon at 4:17:40 EDT, quickly followed by Edwin E. (Buzz) Aldrin.

1976 An unmanned *Viking I* spacecraft successfully landed for first time on Mars.

1990 William J. Brennan resigned from Supreme Court after 34 years service.

1993 The body of Vincent Foster, deputy White House counsel, found in a park outside Washington, DC; autopsy indicated he had committed suicide.

1995 Board of Regents of U. of California voted 14–10 to stop admitting students, hiring faculty, and awarding contracts on the basis of race or sex.

2006 U.S. Senate voted 98–0 to extend Voting Rights Act, which otherwise would have expired.

21

1667 Peace of Breda signed, ending the second Anglo-Dutch War (1664–67) and confirmed British possession of New Netherlands (New York).

1742 John C. Symmes, Revolutionary officer who served Monmouth and Short Hills, born in Southhold, NY; member, Continental Congress (1785–86); founded colony centered around present Cincinnati (died 1814).

1802 David Hunter, Union general who was commander, Department of South (1862), born in Washington, DC; president of commission which tried Lincoln assassination collaborators (died 1886).

1817 Joseph K. Barnes, surgeon general (1862–82), born in Philadelphia; attended two presidents on their death beds (Lincoln and Garfield) (died 1883).

1824 Stanley Matthews, associate justice, Supreme Court (1881–89), born in Cincinnati; represented Ohio in Senate (1877–79) (died 1889).

1826 Mahlon Loomis, inventor of numerous electrical devices, born in Oppenheim, NY; pioneered wireless telegraphy experiments, developed kaolin process to make artificial teeth (died 1886).

1838 John R. Brooke, Union general who served at Fredericksburg, Chancellorsville, Gettysburg, and Cold Harbor, where he was severely wounded, born in Montgomery County, PA; also served in Spanish-American War; military governor, Puerto Rico and Cuba (1899) (died 1926).

1860 Chauncey Olcott, wrote and sang "My Wild Irish Rose," born in Buffalo, NY; introduced song, "Mother Machree" (died 1932).

1860 Edward J. Hanna, Catholic Archbishop of San Francisco (1915–35), born in Rochester, NY (died 1944).

1861 First battle of Bull Run (near Manassas, VA) fought, with Union Army led by Gen. Irvin McDowell, routed in several hours by Confederate force under Gens. Joseph E. Johnston and Stonewall Jackson; Union losses were 2,900, Confederate 2,000.

1864 Francis Folsom Cleveland, wife of President Cleveland, born in Buffalo, NY (died 1947).

1867 Vanguard of westward-bound Mormons reached Salt Lake City; rest of migration arrived two days later, now celebrated by Mormons as Day of Deliverance.

1881 George F. Dick, who with wife, Gladys, isolated scarlet fever germ and developed serum, born in Ft. Wayne, IN (died 1967).

1885 Frances Parkinson Keyes, author (*Crescent Carnival, Fielding's Folly*), born in Charlottesville, VA (died 1970).

1899 Ernest Hemingway, author (*Farewell to Arms, For Whom the Bell Tolls, The Old Man and the Sea*), born in Oak Park, IL; awarded 1954 Nobel Literature Prize (died 1961).

1899 Hart Crane, poet remembered for "White Buildings" and "The Bridge," born in Garrettsville, OH (died 1932).

1920 Isaac Stern, one of greatest violinists, born in Kreminiecz, Russia.

1930 Congress in special session ratified London Naval Treaty, which had been signed April 22 by United States, Great Britain, France, Italy, and Japan; became effective January 1, 1931; expired December 31, 1936.

1930 Veterans Administration established as an independent agency.

1945 Senate approved American membership in United Nations Food & Agriculture Organization.

1946 Kenneth Starr, independent counsel who led investigation of President Clinton, born in Vernon, TX.

1956 President Eisenhower participated in three-day conference of 18 American republics in

Panama City; conference issued declaration calling for solution of economic problems.

1959 World's first atomic-powered merchant ship, the *Savannah*, launched in Camden, NJ.

1976 Mysterious ailment, "Legionnaire's Disease," killed 29 persons who attended a four-day convention in Philadelphia.

1987 Two Kuwaiti oil tankers were re-registered as American ships, the first of 11, as part of an administration plan to provide naval escorts for Kuwaiti oil shipments through the Persian Gulf.

2000 Special counsel for government cleared Justice Department of any legal responsibility for fiery deaths at end of Branch Davidian cult siege in Texas in 1993; ten-month study denied reports that besiegers had used flammable tear gas.

2002 WorldCom filed Chapter 11 bankruptcy; amount set new record, being twice as large as that of Enron seven months earlier.

2006 IRS to cut 157 lawyer-auditors (almost half) from its staff that audits high-income individuals in areas such as estate and gift taxes; civil service regulations prohibit them from being transferred to regular income tax audits.

22

1585 The first attempt to colonize Roanoke Island, NC, was made with the arrival of 117 colonists; the attempt ended 1586, but another was made in 1587; the colony was left unprovided because of the Spanish War; colony was never found and became the legendary "lost colony"; the first child to be born to English parents in America, Virginia Dare, was born there August 18, 1587.

1620 Thirty Pilgrims from Scrooby, England, who had taken refuge in Holland, left Leyden for England to emigrate to America under the leadership of William Brewster.

1686 Gov. Thomas Dongan granted a city charter to Albany by which the city obtained all vacant and unappropriated lands within its limits; Peter Schuyler was first mayor.

1796 Moses Cleaveland, leading a party of 46 men from the Connecticut Land Co., arrived at mouth of the Cuyahoga River; laid out a plan for what later became the city of Cleveland.

1849 Emma Lazarus, poet, born in New York City; best remembered for her lines from "The New Colossus" which were inscribed on the pedestal of the Statue of Liberty — "Give me your tired, your poor..." (died 1887).

1861 Gen. George B. McClellan assumed command of the Department of Washington and Northeast Virginia.

1861 Congress enacted law calling for enlistment of 500,000 volunteers for a six months period to not more than three years; three days later, the period of enlistment was changed to service "during the war."

1862 President Lincoln informed his cabinet that he planned to free slaves on New Year's Day 1863; gave them a draft of the Emancipation Proclamation.

1878 Ernest Ball, composer ("Mother Machree," "When Irish Eyes Are Smiling"), born in Cleveland (died 1927).

1882 Edward Hopper, artist of contemporary life (*Early Sunday Morning, Nighthawks*), born in Nyack, NY (died 1967).

1888 Selman A. Waksman, microbiologist, born in Priluki, Russia; awarded 1953 Nobel Physiology/Medicine Prize for co-discovery (1952) of streptomycin (died 1973).

1889 Morris Fishbein, physician and editor (*AMA Journal* (1924–49), born in St. Louis; served as assistant editor (1913–24) (died 1976).

1891 Ely Culbertson, bridge expert, born in Poiana de Verbilao, Rumania to American parents; invented bridge system; editor, *Bridge World Magazine* (1929–55) (died 1955).

1893 Karl A. Menninger, psychologist who was a cofounder of Menninger Clinic in Topeka, KS; cofounder with father, Charles F., and brother, William C. (died 1990).

1898 Stephen Vincent Benét, poet and author (*John Brown's Body, The Devil and Daniel Webster*), born in Bethlehem, PA (died 1943).

1898 Alexander Calder, sculptor who developed mobiles and stabiles, born in Philadelphia (died 1976).

1905 Severe yellow fever epidemic began in New Orleans, ended in October with about 3,000 cases and about 400 deaths.

1911 Prohibition in Texas was defeated by 6,000 votes out of 462,000 cast.

1913 Tex (Charles B.) Thornton, president (1953–61), chairman (1953–81) of Litton Industries, born in Haskell, TX (died 1981).

1916 Bomb exploded in San Francisco during Preparedness Day parade killing nine persons and injuring 40; Thomas Mooney and Warren K. Billings were eventually found guilty and sentenced; pardoned in 1939.

1918 President Wilson issued proclamation placing telephone and telegraph systems under government control; placed under postmaster August 1.

1922 Jason Robards, Jr., actor (*The Iceman Cometh, A Moon for the Misbegotten, A Thousand Clowns*), born in Chicago.

1923 Robert J. Dole, legislator, born in Russell, KS; represented Kansas in House (1961–69) and Senate (1969–96); Senate majority leader (1994–96); Republican presidential nominee (1996), vice presidential nominee (1976).

1932 Federal Home Loan Bank Act went into effect, creating a five-man Home Loan Bank Board and discount banks, designed to reduce foreclosures, stimulate residential construction.

1934 John Dillinger, gangster, was gunned down by law officers in front of Biograph Theater in Chicago, ending a string of robberies and 16 murders.

1943 American 7th Army took Palermo, Sicily.

1944 Monetary and financial conference ended three weeks of meetings in Bretton Woods, NH; attended by 44 nations and resulted in creation of International Monetary Fund and International Bank for Reconstruction and Development.

1963 President Kennedy signed act to help states provide capital improvements for research in agricultural experiment stations.

2004 9/11 Commission issued its report of failures leading up to the attacks on that date and recommendations to alter and repair intelligence and other functions to prevent a repetition.

23

1764 James Otis' pamphlet, "The Rights of the British Colonies Asserted and Proved," published in Boston.

1816 Charlotte S. Cushman, actress who starred on American (1835–58) and English (1845–49) stages, born in Boston (died 1876).

1834 James Gibbons, Catholic Archbishop of Baltimore (1877–1921), born in Baltimore; Bishop of Richmond (1872–77); founder, first chancellor, Catholic U., Washington DC (1889) (died 1921).

1848 Richard F. Pettigrew, South Dakota pioneer who served state as one of its first senators (1889–1901), born in Ludlow, VT (died 1926).

1863 Samuel H. Kress, cofounder with brother of S.H. Kress dime store chain, born in

Cherryville, PA; established foundation to purchase art works for museums (died 1955).

1865 Edward T. Sanford, associate justice, Supreme Court (1923–30), born in Knoxville, TN; a justice, U.S. District Court (1908–23) (died 1930).

1873 James E. (Sunny Jim) Fitzsimmons, horse trainer who saddled 2,275 winners (1907–63), born in Brooklyn (died 1966).

1877 Colby M. Chester, first president, General Foods (1929–35), born in Annapolis, MD (died 1965).

1885 Former President Grant died in Mt. McGregor, near Saratoga, NY, at 63.

1888 Raymond T. Chandler, author of detective novels (*The Big Sleep, Farewell My Lovely, The Lady in the Lake*), born in Chicago (died 1959).

1888 Gluyas Williams, magazine cartoonist, born in San Francisco; illustrated works of Robert Benchley (died 1982).

1901 Ben Hibbs, editor, *Saturday Evening Post* (1942–61), born in Fontana, KS (died 1975).

1906 Vladimir Prelog, chemist, born in Sarajevo, Yugoslavia; shared 1975 Nobel Chemistry Prize for research on structure of biological molecules (antibiotics, cholesterol).

1926 Robert M. Adams, archaeologist and anthropologist who was secretary of Smithsonian Institution (1984–94), born in Chicago; director, U. of Chicago Oriental Institute (1981–82), U. of Chicago provost (1982–84).

1947 The Amvets, founded in Kansas City, MO, in 1944, chartered by Congress.

1967 Week-long riots began in Detroit, resulting in more than 40 deaths, 1,000 injuries, destruction of 5,000 homes; 4,700 paratroopers and 8,000 National Guardsmen sent in to quell rioting.

2000 Justice Department released 1999 statistics: record 4.5 million men and women either paroled or placed on probation; 24 percent had been jailed for drug crimes and 18 percent for drunken driving offenses.

2001 U.S. taxpayers began to receive $300–$600 special tax rebates from IRS; economists commonly suspect it will help faltering U.S. economy by increasing private spendable income.

2002 Bush signed measure to store radioactive waste at Yucca Mountain in Nevada; state challenges wisdom and safety of decision.

2003 James E. Davis, member of the New York City governing council, murdered by political foe inside City Hall's council chambers.

24

1608 Capt. John Smith began a six-weeks exploration of Chesapeake Bay.

1679 New Hampshire made a royal colony.

1696 Benning Wentworth, first royal governor of New Hampshire (1741–64), born in Portsmouth, NH (died 1770).

1701 Antoine Cadillac, French governor of Louisiana (1713–16), founded Ft. Pontchartrain du Detroit, which later became the city of Detroit.

1758 George Washington elected to Virginia House of Burgesses from Frederick County; marked his entry into politics; election campaign cost him 39 pounds, six shillings for 130 gallons of rum, wine, beer, and cider.

1766 Pontiac, chief of Ottawa Indians and leader of war against colonial outposts, signed peace treaty in Oswego, NY.

1796 John M. Clayton, Secretary of State (1849–50), born in Dagsboro, DE; represented Delaware in Senate (1829–36, 1845–49, 1853–56); negotiated treaty for neutralized canal across Panama (died 1856).

1798 John A. Dix, public official, born in Boscawen, NH; represented New York in Senate (1845–49) and as governor (1873–75); Secretary of Treasury (1861); minister to France (1866–69) (died 1879).

1803 Alexander J. Davis, architect, born in New York City; one of most successful exponents of Greek revival style (U. of North Carolina Assembly Hall, VMI buildings) (died 1892).

1822 Benn Pittman, shorthand expert and inventor of electromechanical process of relief engraving, born in Trowbridge, England; came to United States to teach shorthand system invented by his brother; founded Photographic Institute (died 1910).

1829 Lewis Miller, improver of agricultural machinery and cofounder, Chautauqua movement, born in Greentown, OH (died 1899).

1847 Brigham Young led the Mormons into the Great Salt Lake valley.

1855 William H. Gillette, playwright and actor noted for his role as Sherlock Holmes, born in Hartford, CT (died 1937).

1858 Abraham Lincoln challenged Stephen A. Douglas to a series of debates in their race for the Senate; Lincoln lost when Illinois legislature selected Douglas by a vote of 54–46.

1862 Former President Van Buren died in Kinderhook, NY, at 79.

1866 Tennessee readmitted to the Union by joint resolution of Congress.

1876 Jean Webster, author (*Daddy Long Legs, Dear Enemy,* the *Patty* series), born in Fredonia, NY (died 1916).

1880 Ernest Bloch, composer and educator, born in Geneva, Switzerland; composed (*Macbeth; A Lyric Drama; America, a Symphony*); founder, director, Cleveland Music Institute (1920–25), San Francisco Music Conservatory (1925–30) (died 1959).

1892 Thomas H. Jones, sculptor best known for the Tomb of the Unknown Soldier in Arlington Cemetery, Washington, DC, born in Buffalo, NY (died 1969).

1898 Amelia Earhart, aviatrix who was first woman to fly Atlantic Ocean as passenger (1928) and as pilot (1932), born in Atchison, KS; lost on round-the-world flight in 1937.

1905 Remains of John Paul Jones, which had been found buried in France, were placed in a tomb at the Naval Academy, Annapolis.

1913 Britton Chance, biophysicist who pioneered in study of rapid biologic reactions, born in Wilkes-Barre, PA.

1914 Kenneth B. Clark, psychologist whose work on race relations helped bring about Supreme Court school desegregation ruling, born in Panama Canal Zone.

1915 Excursion steamer *Eastland* capsized at its dock in Chicago River as it was starting on trip with 2,572 passengers, 844, mostly women and children, were drowned.

1916 John D. MacDonald, author (*The Executioners, Key to the Suite, Condominium*), born in Sharon, PA (died 1986).

1929 Kellogg-Briand Pact, renouncing war as an instrument of national policy, formally proclaimed; later ratified by 63 nations.

1931 Fire in a Pittsburgh home for aged resulted in 48 deaths.

1935 Pat(rick) Oliphant, editorial cartoonist, born in Adelaide, Australia.

1953 Former President Hoover named chairman of the Commission of Government Operations (the second Hoover Commission) by President Eisenhower; commission functioned until June 30, 1955.

1974 Supreme Court by 8–0 vote ruled that President Nixon had to turn over 64 White House tapes to the Watergate special prosecutor.

1998 Two U.S. Capitol police officers were killed by a gunman at the Capitol; Russell E. Weston, Jr., was charged with the murders.

2002 Roman Catholic bishops appointed Gov. Frank Keating (Oklahoma) to head a committee of lay Catholics to review cases of purported clerical abuse of minors.

2005 Texan Lance Armstrong retired from the Tour de France as he brought in his seventh consecutive win in the race.

25

1729 After more than 35 years as a proprietary colony torn by unrest and dissension, North Carolina became a royal colony.

1750 Henry Knox, Revolutionary War general who was first Secretary of War (1785–94), born in Boston (died 1806).

1759 British troops took Ft. Niagara from the French.

1775 Anna Symmes Harrison, wife of President William Henry Harrison, born in Morristown, NJ (died 1864).

1814 Battle of Lundy's Lane near Niagara Falls, Ontario, was claimed as a victory by both the Americans and British.

1817 First newspaper in Michigan, *Detroit Gazette*, founded by John F. Sheldon and Ebenezer Reed.

1823 Benjamin T. Roberts, Methodist clergyman who was expelled from church because of his criticism, born in Gowanda, NY; became first general superintendent, Free Methodist Church (1860–93), which he founded after his expulsion (died 1893).

1824 Richard J. Oglesby, public official, born in Oldham County, KY; served Illinois as governor (1865–73, 1885–89) and in Senate (1873–79); was Union general in Civil War (died 1899).

1830 John Jacob Bausch, cofounder, president, Bausch & Lomb Optical Co. (1853), born in Suessen, Germany (died 1926).

1840 Carroll D. Wright, educator and statistician, born in Dumbarton, NH; first commissioner, Bureau of Labor (1885–1905); first president, Clark U. (1902–09); president, American Statistical Association (1897–1909) (died 1909).

1840 Flora A. Darling, cofounder, Daughters of the American Revolution (DAR), born in Lancaster, NH (died 1910).

1844 Thomas Eakins, considered one of America's greatest realistic painters, born in Philadelphia; among his works were *The Chess Players* and *The Gross Clinic* (died 1916).

1853 David Belasco, producer and playwright (*Girl of the Golden West, May Blossom; Laugh, Clown, Laugh*), born in San Francisco (died 1931).

1856 Charles Major, author who wrote under name of Sir Edwin Cuskoden (*When Knighthood Was in Flower, Dorothy Vernon of Haddon Hall*), born in Indianapolis (died 1913).

1857 Frank J. Sprague, "father" of electrical traction, born in Milford, CT; invented train control systems, various motors; co-inventor third rail system; founder, Sprague Electric Railway & Motor Co. (1884) which constructed first modern trolley system (Richmond, VA); his electric elevator company designed, installed high speed automatic elevators, which helped make tall buildings practical (died 1934).

1868 Territory of Wyoming created out of parts of the Dakotas, Utah, and Idaho.

1870 Maxwell F. Parrish, painter and illustrator, born in Philadelphia; best known for illustrations of *Mother Goose in Prose* and the *Knickerbocker History of New York* (died 1966).

1894 Walter Brennan, screen actor in about 100 films and on television (*The Real McCoys*), born in Lynn, MA (died 1974).

1898 American occupation of Puerto Rico began; forces led by Gen. Nelson A. Miles.

1915 American steamship *Leelanaw* sunk by a German submarine off Scotland.

1927 Stanley Dancer, a leading harness racing driver and first to top $1 million in winnings, born in New Egypt, NJ; won Hambletonian four times.

1952 Puerto Rico became first overseas American commonwealth; President Truman signed Puerto Rico Constitution Act.

1954 Walter Payton, football player who is all-time leading ground gainer, born in Columbia, MS; starred with Chicago Bears (1975–88).

1956 Italian Liner *Andrea Doria* sank off Nantucket Island after a collision; 52 perished, 1,600 persons saved.

1963 United States, Great Britain, and Soviet Russia agreed on limited nuclear test ban treaty, barring all but underground testing; ratified by Senate September 24.

1987 Commerce Secretary Malcolm Baldrige was killed in a horse riding accident while practicing for a rodeo in northern California.

2000 George W. Bush announced family friend Richard B. Cheney would run as his vice presidential nominee in November election.

2000 The final initial segment of the joint

American-Russian International Space Station arrived in orbit and parts were linked; parts to form the core living quarters for an eventual expanded facility.

2005 Major trade union split: Service Employees International Union (1.8 million members) and Teamsters (1.4 million) split with AFL-CIO, saying the organization had failed to reverse the major drop in union membership.

2006 Carl Brashear died; first black master diver in U.S. Navy history; successfully (and against much opposition) was able to maintain certification for continued diving after losing bottom part of leg in accident during retrieval of nuclear warhead.

26

1739 George Clinton, Vice President (1805–12), born in Little Britain, NY; member, Continental Congress (1775–76); governor of New York (1777–95, 1801–4) (died 1812).

1774 Freeholders of Albermarle County, VA, adopted resolutions drafted by Thomas Jefferson, urging non-importation of British goods, with certain philosophical principles of relations of the colonies and Parliament.

1775 Post Office Department created by Continental Congress, which named Benjamin Franklin as Postmaster General.

1777 British troops under Gen. Barry St. Leger began siege of Ft. Stanwix, now part of Rome, NY.

1784 Charles Morris, naval officer sometimes called the Navy's statesman because of his administrative skill, born in Woodstock, CT; with Board of Navy Commissioners 13 years (died 1856).

1788 New York legislature, by vote of 30–27, ratified the Constitution, with Alexander Hamilton leading the pro-ratification forces; entered union as the 11th state.

1790 House voted 34–28 with three abstentions to assume the debts of states up to $21,500,000.

1796 George Catlin, artist who concentrated on the American Indians, born in Wilkes-Barre, PA (died 1872).

1797 John Quincy Adams and Louise Catherine Johnson were married in London.

1799 Isaac Babbitt, inventor of journal box (1839) to be lined with an alloy which became known as Babbitt metal, born in Taunton, MA;

cast the first brass cannon in United States (died 1862).

1805 Constantine Brumidi, painter known for his frescoes in the Capitol, born in Rome (died 1880).

1822 Orange Judd, agricultural editor (*American Agriculturist* 1856–83), born near Niagara Falls, NY; responsible for establishing first agricultural experiment station (Wesleyan U.); also edited, *Prairie Farmer* (1884–88) (died 1892).

1848 John D. Archbold, prominent in development of Standard Oil, born in Leesburg, OH; president, Standard Oil of New Jersey (1911–16) (died 1916).

1856 William Rainey Harper, first president, U. of Chicago (1891–1906), born in New Concord, OH; was a professor of religion (died 1906).

1858 Ella Boole, prohibitionist, born in Van Wert, OH; president, National Women's Christian Temperance Union (WCTU) (1925–33), international WCTU (1931–47) (died 1952).

1858 Edward M. House, advisor to President Wilson, born in Houston (died 1938).

1862 George B. Cortelyou, first secretary, Department of Commerce & Labor (1903–04), born in New York City; Postmaster General (1905–07), Secretary of Treasury (1907–09); president, New York Consolidated Gas Co., which became Con Edison (1909–35) (died 1940).

1874 Serge Koussevitsky, conductor, Boston Symphony (1924–49), born in Vyshni Vdochek, Russia; founder of Berkshire Festival (1937) (died 1951).

1887 Reuben L. Kahn, immunologist who developed blood serum test for diagnosis of syphilis, born in Kovno, Lithuania (now Russia) (died 1979).

1893 George Grosz, expressionist painter, born in Berlin; his paintings, which attacked corruption and decadence of German society, were condemned by Nazis (died 1959).

1898 Spanish Government, through the French, asked for American peace terms, which were communicated two days later.

1903 Estes Kefauver, legislator, born near Madisonville, TN; represented Tennessee in House (1937–49) and Senate (1949–63), where he conducted televised hearings on crime; Democratic vice presidential candidate (1956) (died 1963).

1906 Gracie Allen, comedienne who teamed with husband, George Burns, on radio and in movies, born in San Francisco (died 1964).

1941 Philippines armed forces were nationalized by executive order, with Gen. Douglas MacArthur named commander-in-chief of American Far East forces.

1947 Congress passed the National Security Act which unified the armed forces under a Secretary of Defense; created the National Security Council.

1948 President Truman signed executive order ending racial segregation in the armed forces.

1989 President Bush signed legislation ending a half-century of federal price controls on natural gas.

1990 President Bush signed the Americans with Disabilities Act, which will guarantee disabled access to jobs, transportation, public accommodations, and communication.

2000 John Tukey, inventor of such pervasively used computer terminology as *software* and *bit*, died at 85.

2004 Democratic National Convention began; Senator John Kerry accepted nomination for president.

2004 Justice Department reported that number of imprisoned had reached record 6.9 million; about 3.2 percent of U.S. adults.

2005 First in nation used-car buyer protection: California Gov. Arnold Schwarzenegger signed into law a measure allowing buyers to purchase a two-day right-to-return on all vehicles.

27

1690 Protestant Association under John Goode seized St. Mary's, capital of Maryland, in revolt against the proprietary government.

1752 Samuel Smith, Revolutionary War officer and commanded defense of Baltimore in War of 1812, born in Carlisle, PA; represented Maryland in House (1793–1803, 1816–22) and Senate (1803–15, 1835–38), serving as president pro tem (1805–8) (died 1839).

1753 John Warren, physician who was cofounder of Harvard Medical School (1782), born in Roxbury, MA; first Harvard professor of anatomy and surgery; a founder, president, Massachusetts Humane Society (died 1815).

1770 Robert Dinwiddie, lieutenant governor of Virginia (1751–58), died at 77; sent George Washington to protect the Ohio region against French; tried unsuccessfully to get colonial cooperation for this protection.

1777 Two best-known foreign officers to serve with Americans in Revolution arrived in Philadelphia — 20-year-old Marquis de Lafayette and "Baron" Johnann de Kalb; both were commissioned major generals.

1789 Department of Foreign Affairs created by Congress and President Washington; changed to Department of State September 15, 1789.

1818 Eben N. Horsford, industrial chemist who developed process for making condensed milk, baking powder, born in Moscow, NY (died 1893).

1852 George F. Peabody, banker and educator, born in Columbus, GA; director, General Education Board; treasurer, Southern Education Board — both Rockefeller philanthropies; Peabody Award for broadcasting excellence named in his honor (died 1938).

1853 Cyrus L.W. Eidlitz, architect (New York Times Building, Buffalo Public Library, Chicago's Dearborn Station), born in New York City (died 1921).

1866 Atlantic cable brought to Newfoundland by Cyrus W. Field, opening telegraphic communication with Great Britain.

1867 Walter A. Sheaffer, fountain pen manufacturer who founded, headed Sheaffer Pen Co. (1913–38), born in Bloomfield, IA (died 1946).

1868 Alaska organized as a territory.

1870 Bertram B. Boltwood, scientist who made important contributions to knowledge of radioactivity, born in Amherst, MA; discovered element ionium (died 1927).

1882 Congress passed act awarding $50,000 pension to Lucretia Garfield, widow of President Garfield.

1889 Bruce Bliven, editor, *New Republic* magazine (1923–55), born in Emmettsburg, IA (died 1977).

1905 Leo Durocher, baseball player (New York A, St. Louis NL)/manager (Brooklyn, New York NL, Chicago NL), born in West Springfield, MA; named to Baseball Hall of Fame (died 1991).

1922 Norman Lear, television producer/director (*All in the Family*, *The Jeffersons*, *Maude*, *Sanford and Son*), born in New Haven, CT.

1947 Housing & Home Finance Agency, predecessor of Department of Housing & Urban Development, created; ended with start of HUD September 5, 1965.

1948 Peggy Fleming, 1968 world and Olympic figure skating champion, born in San Jose, CA.

1953 Armistice signed at Panmunjon, ending hostilities in Korea.

1974 House Judiciary Committee voted in

favor of first impeachment article on President Nixon; favored second article July 29, third July 30; full House by 412–3 vote accepted committee report without debate.

1995 President Clinton signed revised rescissions bill which cut $16.3 billion in previously-approved spending; earlier bill vetoed because of cuts in education, training, and environmental spending.

1995 Three large industrial unions — auto workers, steelworkers, and machinists — voted to merge into one union by year 2000.

1995 Korean War Memorial in Washington, DC, dedicated.

1996 A pipe bomb exploded in Centennial Park in downtown Atlanta, killing one person; did not interfere with Olympic Games.

2001 Scientific embarrassment at Lawrence Berkeley National Laboratory in California: Laboratory concedes that the 1999 claim of discovering two new superheavy elements was erroneous; scientific data had been misinterpreted.

2003 Bob Hope dead at 100; radio and movie entertainer; had entertained multiple generations of troops from World War II through the 1990 Persian Gulf War.

2004 Five past leaders of Holy Land Foundation that provided charitable assistance to Palestine, charged with using organization as a front to channel $12 million to terrorists.

28

1746 Thomas Hayward, colonial jurist, born in St. Luke's Parish, SC; member of Continental Congress (1776–78), signer of Declaration of Independence (died 1809).

1751 Joseph Habersham, Postmaster General (1795–1801), born in Savannah, GA; member of Continental Congress (1785–86) (died 1815).

1767 James A. Bayard, legislator, born in Philadelphia; represented Delaware in House (1797–1803) and Senate (1805–13); important worker in getting House to elect Thomas Jefferson president; one of three negotiators of Treaty of Ghent ending War of 1812 (died 1815).

1778 Charles Stewart, commander of the *Constitution* in War of 1812, born in Philadelphia; senior flag officer (1859–62) (died 1869).

1795 Edwin A. Stevens, manager of Camden & Amboy Railroad (1830–65), born in Hoboken, NJ; inventor of a plow; endowed Stevens Institute of Technology (died 1868).

1809 Ormsby M. Mitchel, astronomer who did much to popularize subject, born in Morganfield, KY; taught at Cincinnati College (1836–59); Union general, died of yellow fever (1862).

1840 Edward D. Cope, paleontologist who discovered about 1,000 species of extinct vertebrates in United States, born in Philadelphia; owner, editor, *American Naturalist* (1878–97) (died 1897).

1859 Convention approved Nevada's constitution; popular vote ratified action September 7.

1859 Ballington Booth, founder, Volunteers of America (1896), born in Yorkshire, England; headed Salvation Army operations in United States (1887–96), but resigned after disagreement with his father, Army founder William Booth (died 1940).

1868 The 14th Amendment went into effect, guaranteeing that a citizen's rights would not be abridged.

1868 Burlingame Treaty between United States and China signed, provided for free immigration between the two nations.

1881 John G. Machem, founder (1936) of fundamentalist Presbyterian Church of America, born in Baltimore (died 1937).

1887 Marcel Duchamp, painter whose work stimulated 20th Century art trends, born in Blainville, France (died 1968).

1901 Harry Bridges, president, International Longshoremen's Union, born in Melbourne, Australia (died 1990).

1901 Rudy (Hubert P.) Vallee, popular singer considered the original crooner, born in Island Pond, VT (died 1986).

1907 Earl S. Tupper, developer of Tupperware, born in Berlin, NH; developed party approach to marketing product (died 1983).

1907 William D. Haywood acquitted of 1905 murder of former Idaho Governor Stuenenerg for lack of corroborative evidence.

1915 Charles H. Townes, physicist, born in Greenville, SC; shared 1964 Nobel Physics Prize for developing maser and principles of producing high-intensity radiation.

1915 President Wilson ordered military occupation of Haiti; order restored by August 1, puppet government set up; Haiti became semi-protectorate for ten years.

1929 Jacqueline Kennedy Onassis, widow of President Kennedy and Aristotle Onassis, born in Southampton, NY (died 1994).

1932 President Hoover ordered Army to

remove bonus marchers who refused to leave after Senate (June 17) defeated the bonus bill; two marchers were killed in skirmishes with Washington police; Gen. MacArthur led troops.

1943 Bill (William W.) Bradley, star college and professional basketball player, born in Crystal City, MO; represented New Jersey in Senate (1979–96).

1945 Jim (James R.) Davis, cartoonist (*Garfield*), born in Marion, IN.

1945 Army B-25 bomber crashed into Empire State Building, 13 were killed.

1945 Senate approved United Nations charter 89–2.

1965 President Lyndon Johnson announced troop buildup in Vietnam, sending an additional 50,000 troops to bring total to 125,000.

1977 First Alaska oil moved by 800-mile pipeline from Prudhoe Bay to Valdez.

1984 Olympic Games began in Los Angeles.

1998 Bell Atlantic Corp. announced it planned to absorb GTE Corp.; combined they would control a third (63 million) of nation's local telephone access links.

2003 Public relations breakthrough: Newest issue of *Bride* magazine — oldest and widest circulating magazine of its type — features major article on gay marriages.

29

1786 First newspaper west of the Alleghenies, Pittsburgh Gazette, established by John Scull and Joseph Hull, two young Philadelphia printers.

1796 Walter Hunt, inventor of numerous items, born in Martinburg, NY; inventions include a restaurant steam table, knife sharpener, sewing machine (failed to apply for patent), fountain pen, safety pin (which he sold for $400), disposable paper collar (died 1859).

1797 Daniel Drew, speculator and stock manipulator, born in Carmel, NY; as cattleman, was said to have watered cattle on way to slaughter, giving rise to term stock watering; his benefactions made possible founding of Drew Theological Seminary, Madison, NJ (1866) (died 1879).

1805 Hiram Powers, sculptor who did busts of many notables and other works (*Greek Slave, Fisher Boy*), born near Woodstock, VT (died 1873).

1806 Horace Abbott, iron manufacturer for railroads and ships, born in Sudbury, MA; output included armor plate for the *Monitor* and other ironclads (died 1887).

1825 George H. Pendleton, a leader in creation of civil service, born in Cincinnati; represented Ohio in House (1857–65) and Senate (1879–85); minister to Germany (1885–89) (died 1889).

1859 Convention in Wyandotte approved Kansas constitution, which forbade slavery but restricted suffrage to white males; ratified October 4.

1861 Alice H. Lee Roosevelt, first wife of President Theodore Roosevelt, born in Chestnut Hill, MA (died 1884).

1869 Booth Tarkington, author (*Penrod, Seventeen, Alice Adams, The Magnificent Ambersons*), born in Indianapolis (died 1946).

1877 (Charles) William Beebe, naturalist who descended to the then (1934) record depth (3,028 ft.) in a bathysphere which he invented, born in Brooklyn; director of ornithology and scientific research, New York Zoological Society (died 1962).

1878 Don(ald R.O.) Marquis, newspaper columnist (*New York Sun, New York Tribune* 1912–25), born in Walnut, IL; creator of "Archy and Mehitabel" (died 1937).

1887 Sigmund Romberg, operetta composer (*Blossom Time, The Student Prince, Desert Song, Maytime*), born in Szeged, Hungary (died 1851).

1892 William Powell, screen actor (*The Thin Man, Life with Father, Mr. Roberts*), born in Pittsburgh (died 1984).

1898 Isidor I. Rabi, physicist, born in Rymanow, Austria; invented atomic molecular beam magnetic resonance method for observing spectra in radio-frequency range; awarded 1944 Nobel Physics Prize for work on magnetic movement of atomic particles (died 1988).

1899 United States signed Hague Peace Convention for pacific settlement of disputes and various other international matters.

1910 Heinz L. Fraenkel-Courat, biochemist, born in Breslau, Germany; worked on relationship between protein structure and biological activity.

1914 Marcel Bich, creator of Bic Pen Co. in United States to produce pens and lighters, born in Turin, Italy.

1918 Edwin G. O'Connor, author best known for *The Last Hurrah*, born in Providence, RI (died 1968).

1920 First transcontinental airmail service began (New York to San Francisco).

1926   Don Carter, outstanding bowler of 1950s, born in Miami, FL.

1935   Thomas E. Dewey appointed special prosecutor in New York State to lead drive against crime.

1957   Ratification completed for American participation in International Atomic Energy Agency.

1958   National Aeronautics & Space Administration (NASA) established.

1967   Fire and explosion aboard the carrier *Forrestal* off Vietnam killed 134.

1974   Former Treasury Secretary John Connally indicted in milk-support bribery scandal; acquitted April 17, 1975.

1986   Federal jury in New York City awarded only $1 in damages to U.S. Football League, which had sued the National Football League.

1994   Senate confirmed Judge Stephen G. Breyer to succeed Harry Blackmun on the Supreme Court.

1998   Costly 54-day strike against General Motors by two UAW locals came to an end; strike affected 27 GM plants, idling nearly 200,000 workers.

2001   For decades Vieques (part of Puerto Rico) utilized for Navy practice bombing; Puerto Ricans by more than two-thirds vote today insist it be ended; vote not legally binding on U.S. government.

2005   Astronomers from California Institute of Technology announce finding of new planet-like object beyond Pluto.

30

1609   Samuel de Champlain, on his third trip to Canada, voyaged up the Richelieu River and entered the lake named for him.

1619   House of Burgesses convened in Virginia, the first representative assembly in the New World; convened by Gov. George Yeardley; met until August 6.

1630   The first church in Boston was organized in Charlestown, with John Wilson as teacher; transferred to Boston 1632.

1777   Gen. John Burgoyne and his British troops occupied Ft. Edward, NY, in their drive to split New York State.

1822   William T. Adams, author known as Oliver Optic, born in Bellingham, MA; wrote about 120 books, 1,000 stories for boys; was school teacher in Boston (1846–65) (died 1897).

1831   Helen T. Blavatsky, cofounder of Theosophical Society, born in Ekaterinoslav, Russia; with Henry S. Olcott founded society (1875); set up official journal, *The Theosophist*; many of her so-called miracles were demonstrated to be frauds (died 1891).

1855   James E. Kelly, sculptor of American historical figures, born in New York City (died 1933).

1857   Thorstein B. Veblen, economist and author (*The Theory of the Leisure Class*, *The Theory of Business Enterprise*), born in Cato, WI; founder, editor, *Journal of Political Economy* (1892–1905) (died 1929).

1863   Henry Ford, pioneer automaker, born in Greenfield, MI; founder, president, Ford Motor Co. (1903–19, 1943–45); introduced Model T and became world's largest auto producer; introduced profit sharing (1914); chartered *Peace Ship* to Europe in effort to end World War I; built Henry Ford Hospital, Detroit (died 1947).

1864   Part of Confederate defenses of Petersburg, VA, was blown up, but failure to follow up cost Union force 3,000 men and continuation of six weeks siege for another seven-and-a-half months.

1866   Riot broke out in New Orleans as a constitutional convention was assembling; police fired on mob, killing or wounding more than 200.

1880   Robert R. McCormick, editor, publisher, *Chicago Tribune* (1920–55), born in Chicago (died 1955).

1880   Max(imilian J.) Hirsch, dean of American thoroughbred trainers, born in Fredericksburg, TX; trained many winners, including triple-crown winner, *Assault* (died 1969).

1889   Vladimir Zworykin, electronics engineer who developed first practical television system, born in Murom, Russia; with RCA (1929–45); his system invention (1938), made practical the electron microscope (1939) (died 1951).

1889   Emanuel Haldeman-Julius, author, publisher of Little Blue Books (biographies, how-to books), born in Philadelphia (died 1951).

1890   Casey (Charles D.) Stengel, baseball player (New York NL)/manager, born in Kansas City, MO; managed New York AL to ten pennants and seven World Series wins; first manager, New York Mets; named to Baseball Hall of Fame (died 1975).

1896   Railroad accident at Atlantic City, NJ, caused 60 deaths.

1907   First elections held in the Philippines; legislature convened October 16 for first time.

1916 Explosion and fire in munitions plant at Black Tom Island, NJ, destroyed $22 million worth of property; sabotage suspected but no evidence found.

1932 Olympic Games opened in Los Angeles.

1940 Act of Havana approved unanimously by 21 republics of Pan American Union, permitting the takeover of European colonies in Western Hemisphere if endangered by aggression; signed by President Franklin Roosevelt October 10.

1941 Paul Anka, singer and composer ("My Way," "She's a Lady," "You're Having My Baby"), born in Ottawa, Canada.

1942 President Franklin Roosevelt signed act establishing the Women Appointed for Voluntary Emergency Service (WAVES), the women's branch of the Navy.

1942 Commerce Secretary Harry L. Hopkins was married to Mrs. Louise Gill Macy in the White House.

1952 The 4.4 mile Chesapeake Bay Bridge near Annapolis, MD, opened.

1965 Medicare Act signed by President Lyndon Johnson in Independence, MO; former President Truman, who first recommended it in 1954, was on hand.

1991 Commission recommended closure of 34 American military bases, with 48 others to be realigned; Congress and the President later approved.

1997 Dow Jones industrial average closed above 8,200 for the first time; had closed over 7,000 on February 13 and over 8,000 July 16.

31

1653 Thomas Dudley, governor of Massachusetts (1634, 1640, 1645, 1650), died at 77; had served as deputy governor 13 times; helped found Cambridge, as governor had signed charter for Harvard College.

1763 James Kent, jurist whose decisions helped create American system of equity, born in Putnam County, NY; first law professor, Columbia (1793); New York Supreme Court justice (1798–1804), chief justice (1804–23); chancellor Court of Chancery (1814–23) (died 1847).

1771 Anthony Kohlman, Jesuit priest, born in Kaiserberg, Germany; as administrator, New York diocese (1808–14), he won lawsuit to keep confessional information confidential; led state to pass legislation (1828) protecting the confessional (died 1835).

1775 Continental Congress rejected Lord North's plan for reconciliation.

1789 Customs Service established.

1793 Thomas Jefferson submitted his resignation as Secretary of State, effective December 31, over policy differences with Alexander Hamilton and President Washington.

1803 John Ericsson, engineer who developed screw propeller for ships, born in Värmland Province, Sweden; built the *Monitor* for Union Navy; made many improvements in steam machinery, launched new era in naval engineering (died 1889).

1804 First newspaper in Indiana Territory, *Indiana Gazette*, founded in Vincennes by a Kentucky printer, Elihu Stout.

1813 British troops captured Plattsburgh, NY; swept American shipping off Lake Champlain.

1813 American troops recaptured York (Toronto); again abandoned city.

1816 George H. Thomas, Union general known as the Rock of Chickamauga, born in Southampton County, VA; commanded Army of the Cumberland (died 1870).

1822 Abram S. Hewitt, cofounder, Cooper & Hewitt, developer of first American open hearth furnaces (1862), born in Haverstraw, NY; the furnaces produced first American steel; represented New York in House (1874–79, 1881–86); mayor of New York City (1887–88) (died 1903).

1856 Harold C. Ernst, bacteriologist with Harvard Medical School (1885–1922), born in Cincinnati; established first diphtheria antitoxin laboratory (died 1922).

1859 Theobald Smith, pathologist who developed a theory of immunization, born in Albany, NY; worked on cause and nature of infections and parasitic diseases (died 1934).

1864 Edward N. Hurley, originator, developer of pneumatic tool industry, born in Galesburg, IL; chairman, Federal Trade Commission (1913–17); chairman, U.S. Shipping Board (1917–19) (died 1933).

1867 S(ebastian) S. Kresge, head of dime store chain (1907–66), born in Bald Mount, PA (died 1966).

1875 Former President Andrew Johnson died near Jonesborough, TN, at 66.

1882 Herbert E. Ives, pioneer in television and wire transmission of pictures, born in Philadelphia; invented first practical artificial daylight lamp (died 1953).

1899 Robert T. Stevens, industrialist who headed J.P. Stevens & Co. (1929–42, 1955–69), born; Army Secretary (1953–55) (died 1983).

1912 Milton Friedman, economist, born in New York City; awarded 1976 Nobel Economics Prize for work in consumption analysis and monetary history and theory.

1917 American oil steamer *Montano* torpedoed by a German submarine off Irish coast, 24 men lost.

1919 Curt(is) Gowdy, sports broadcaster (NBC), born in Green River, WY.

1919 Telephone and telegraph lines were returned to private ownership; had been under government control for a year.

1921 Whitney M. Young, Jr., executive director, National Urban League (1961–71), born in Lincoln Ridge, KY (died 1971).

1936 Elizabeth Dole, Secretary of Transportation (1983–87) and Labor (1989–91), born in Salisbury, NC; president, American Red Cross.

1940 Railroad accident at Cuyahoga Falls, OH, killed 43 persons.

1948 Idlewild International Airport dedicated by President Truman; renamed Kennedy Airport in 1963.

1973 Delta jetliner crashed in fog while landing at Boston's Logan Airport; 89 killed.

1975 Turkey refused to allow the U.S. to reopen bases there.

1989 Islamic militants announced in Beirut that they had hanged Marine Corps Lt. Col. William R. Higgins, an American hostage since February 1988.

1991 An Amtrak passenger train derailed near Camden, SC, and crashed into freight cars; seven persons were killed, 125 injured.

1991 Presidents Bush and Gorbachev signed a Strategic Arms Reduction Treaty (START 1) to reduce offensive arms by 30 percent over seven years.

1994 UN Security Council authorized a United States-led invasion and occupation of Haiti if sanctions fail to remove its military government.

1995 Walt Disney Co. will buy Capital Cities/ABC for $19 billion, the companies announced in the second largest corporate takeover.

1996 House approved Welfare Reform Bill, which the Senate had approved the day before; the bill, signed by President Clinton in August, provides welfare through block grants to the States.

2001 Expanding potential farming land: genetically modified tomato revealed by University of California (at Davis) scientists that can grow in salty water and salty soils.

2001 Poul Anderson (1926–2001) passed away; major mover in modern science fiction from late 1940s to his death; winner of seven Hugos and three Nebulas (the genre's highest awards).

AUGUST

1

1539 Hernando de Soto began march from Tampa into Florida and wintered near Pensacola Bay.

1768 Boston merchants agreed not to import British goods as protest against the Townshend measures; within a few weeks, the example was followed by other Massachusetts communities and New York.

1769 Spanish expedition under Gaspar de Portola and Father Juan Crespi reached what is now Los Angeles, calling it Our Lady Queen of Angels.

1770 William Clark, co-leader of Lewis and Clark Expedition (1804–6), born in Caroline County, VA; governor of Missouri Territory (1813–21) (died 1838).

1774 Virginia House of Burgesses adopted series of resolutions drafted by Thomas Jefferson calling for non-importation of British goods and "to oppose by all just and proper means every injury to American rights"; this led to dissolution of the House and delegates met in Raleigh Tavern.

1778 John C. Warren, cofounder, Massachusetts General Hospital (1821), born in Boston; dean, Harvard Medical School (1816–18) (died 1856).

1779 Francis Scott Key, author of poem that became "The Star Spangled Banner," born in what is now Carroll County, MD; wrote his poem after watching British bombardment of Ft. McHenry in Baltimore Harbor and saw American flag still flying; the poem was put to tune of British drinking song ("To Anacreon in Heaven") (died 1843).

1781 Lord Charles Cornwallis, with about 7,500 troops, set up headquarters in Yorktown, VA, from which to campaign against Americans.

1791 George Ticknor, educator who popularized modern language studies at Harvard (1819–35), born in Boston; a founder, Boston Public Library (1852) (died 1871).

1793 Yellow fever epidemic struck Philadelphia, lasting until November 9; killed about 4,000 persons.

1794 Federal Society of Journeymen Cordwainers (Shoemakers), the nation's first labor union, organized in Philadelphia.

1800 Second Census reported the American population to be 5,308,483.

1815 Richard Henry Dana, author remembered for *Two Years Before the Mast*, born in Cambridge; admiralty lawyer who wrote standard manual of maritime law (died 1882).

1818 Maria Mitchell, first American woman astronomer (Vassar College 1865–89), born in Nantucket, MA (died 1889).

1819 Herman Melville, author (*Moby Dick, Omoo, Typee*), born in New York City (died 1891).

1830 Fifth Census reported population of 12,866,020.

1843 Robert Todd Lincoln, Secretary of War (1881–85), born in Springfield, IL; minister to Great Britain (1889–93); president, Pullman Co. (1897–1911) (died 1926).

1873 First cable car put into service on Clay St. hill in San Francisco.

1875 Ernest T. Weir, steel manufacturer, born in Pittsburgh; a founder, president, Weirton Steel Co. (1909); a founder, National Steel Co. (died 1957).

1876 Colorado admitted to Union as the 38th state.

1878 Eva Tanguay, entertainer remembered for her theme, "I Don't Care," born in Marbleton, Canada; starred in musical comedies (died 1947).

1887 John C.H. Lee, World War II general

who headed supply services in Europe, born in Junction City, KS (died 1958).

1894 Benjamin Mays, president, Morehouse College (1940–67), born in Epworth, SC (died 1984).

1907 Army organized an aeronautical division in Signal Corps, with one officer (Capt. Charles D. Chandler) and two enlisted men.

1916 Prohibition law signed by Utah governor.

1921 Jack Kramer, tennis champion, born in Las Vegas, NV; won American singles (1946–47), Wimbledon (1947); organized professional players tour.

1929 James H. Billington, Librarian of Congress since 1987, born in Bryn Mawr, PA.

1933 Dom DeLuise, comedian and screen actor, born in New York City.

1943 Low-level American air raid made on oil refineries of Ploesti, Rumania.

1946 President Truman signed law creating five-member Atomic Energy Commission (now Nuclear Regulatory Commission) and providing assistance to private research in atomic energy.

1946 Congress enacted Fulbright Act, which provided for use of money received from the sale of war surplus to Allied governments for financing cultural and educational interchange.

1950 American citizenship and limited self-government granted to Guam, which the United States received from Spain in 1898.

1958 First class postage increased to four cents an ounce.

1966 Charles Starkweather, 25, barricaded himself in tower at U. of Texas in Austin and shot and killed 13 persons, wounded 31 others, before being killed by police; earlier he had killed his wife and mother.

1976 Flash flood in Colorado River canyon killed 139 persons and did extensive damage.

1995 Westinghouse Electric Corporation announced that it will buy Columbia Broadcasting System for about $5 billion.

2000 SETI, an organization dedicated to the use of electronic technology to listen for possible extraterrestrial signals, announced receipt of $12.5 million seed money to begin developing a radiotelescope complex to further the effort; when completed, would permit simultaneous monitoring of a dozen stars.

2005 President George W. Bush circumvented Democratic refusal to vote on John Bolton as new U.S. ambassador to the U.N. by appointing him to post while Congress was in recess; appointment good through January 2007.

2006 MTV celebrates 25th anniversary, pioneer youth-oriented music cable channel.

2006 Balance of power on Kansas State Board of Education again shifted; previous 6–4 majority against evolution alone being taught becomes 6–4 in favor.

2006 The tax that refused to die finally died: The IRS had been collecting an excise tax on all long-distance phone calls since 1898; after losing five cases before federal appeal courts that the "add-on" was invalid, the Treasury Department gave up its efforts to maintain this tax source.

2

1567 Dominique de Gourges set sail from Bordeaux, France, to avenge the destruction of French colonies in Florida; in May 1568, he burned the Spanish forts and killed the settlers.

1754 Pierre C. L'Enfant, city planner who designed layout of Washington, DC, born in Paris; after serving with Continental Army, he renovated New York City Hall for the Congress as Federal Hall (1787); expense of his work in Washington led to his dismissal (1792); the excellence of his work was recognized and carried out (1801) (died 1825).

1776 Declaration of Independence formally signed by 54 delegates to Continental Congress.

1790 Results of First Census announced as 3,929,214 persons, including 697,697 slaves and 59,557 free blacks.

1819 Convention in Huntsville adopted Alabama constitution.

1832 Sauk and Fox Indians were defeated at Battle of Red Axe, midway between Prairie du Chien and LaCrosse, WI; Black Hawk War virtually ended.

1832 Henry S. Olcott, cofounder, first president, Theosophical Society (1875–1907), born in Orange, NJ; editor, *Theosophist* (1888–1907) (died 1907).

1835 Elisha Gray, inventor of numerous telephone, telegraph devices, born near Barnesville, OH; cofounder, Gray & Barton, which became Western Electric Co.; claimed invention of telegraph but a long patent battle settled by Supreme Court in favor of Alexander Graham Bell (died 1901).

1845 American troops under Gen. Zachary Taylor arrived in Corpus Christi, TX.

1865 Irving Babbitt, cofounder of modern humanistic movement, born in Dayton, OH; taught at Harvard U. (1894–1933) (died 1933).

1871 John Sloan, artist of landscapes and portraits, born in Lock Haven, PA; also did magazine illustrations (died 1951).

1876 Wild Bill Hickok was killed in a Deadwood, SD, saloon by Jack McCall, while playing poker; Hickok was holding two pairs (aces and 8s), now known as a "dead man's hand."

1880 Arthur G. Dove, considered the first American abstract artist, born in Canandaigua, NY (died 1946).

1892 Jack L. Warner, cofounder with brothers of major film company (1923), born in London, Canada; Warner Bros. introduced first talking picture (died 1978).

1894 Westbrook Pegler, sports writer and syndicated columnist, born in Minneapolis (died 1969).

1905 Myrna Loy, screen actress (*The Thin Man, The Best Years of Our Lives, Broadway Bill*), born in Helena, MT (died 1993).

1909 Army purchased its first heavier-than-air machine from the Wright brothers.

1909 Lincoln penny issued by the Philadelphia mint, replacing the Indian head.

1911 Harriet Quimby was licensed as first American woman airplane pilot.

1912 Senate by vote of 51–4 extended principle of the Monroe Doctrine to Asiatic powers by blocking the sale of 400,000 acres in Lower California to a Japanese syndicate; action based on feeling the land had potential military value.

1918 State of war began between United States and Russia; American affairs in Russia were put in hands of a Swedish consul general.

1923 U.S. Steel Co. adopted an eight-hour day; had been 12 hours.

1923 President Harding, 55, died in San Francisco enroute from Alaska; succeeded by Vice President Calvin Coolidge.

1924 James A. Baldwin, author (*Go Tell It on the Mountain, Nobody Knows My Name*), born in New York City (died 1987).

1924 Carroll O'Connor, actor who starred as Archie Bunker in television series, *All in the Family*, born in New York City.

1927 President Coolidge announced his non-candidacy for reelection; "I do not choose to run for president in 1928."

1939 Albert Einstein, in a letter to President Franklin Roosevelt, alerted him to the opportunity for developing an atomic bomb.

1939 Hatch Act was passed, forbidding "pernicious" political action by federal workers and office holders.

1985 Delta Air Lines jumbo jet crashed during landing at Dallas-Ft. Worth Airport during storm killing 132 persons.

1998 Shari Lewis, noted puppeteer for 40 years, died at 65.

2000 Republican National Convention opened; nominates later in week George W. Bush for president and Dick (Richard) Cheney for vice president.

2001 Senate voted unanimously (98–0) to approve Robert Mueller as new FBI director.

2005 CAFTA (Central America Free Trade Agreement) signed by President Bush; removed bulk of trade restrictions between U.S. and six Central American nations; considered logical next step by NAFTA proponents.

2005 President Bush endorsed idea that school students should be exposed to both evolutionary and "intelligent design" concepts of human ancestry; remarks spark indignation by those insisting that only evolution should be taught in public schools.

3

1492 Christopher Columbus and his three ships (Nina, Pinta, Santa Maria) set sail from Palos, Spain, for "China."

1777 British Gen. Barry St. Leger led his troops to victory at Ft. Stanwix on the Mohawk River, but vacated the fort (August 22) on hearing of colonial reinforcements; moved to Oswego.

1780 Benedict Arnold, at his own request, took command of the West Point fort.

1785 First Episcopal ordination held in the United States, that of the Rev. Ashbel Baldwin, at Middletown, CT.

1795 Treaty of Greenville signed by Gen. Anthony Wayne and 90 Indian leaders, ending the fighting in Ohio; Indians ceded 25,000 sq. mi. of what is now southeast Indiana and southern Ohio.

1808 Hamilton Fish, Secretary of State (1869–77), born in New York City; represented New York in House (1843–45) and Senate (1851–57), and served as its governor (1849–50) (died 1893).

1811 Elisha G. Otis, elevator developer, born in Halifax, VT; devised automatic safety appliance for elevators; patented a steam elevator

(1861), the foundation for Otis elevator business (died 1861).

1814　British advance across the Niagara River to Buffalo checked at Black Rock by Morgan's Rifles.

1821　Uriah S. Stephens, an organizer of Garment Cutters Union (1862), born in Cape May, NJ; a founder, Knights of Labor (1869) (died 1882).

1824　William B. Woods, associate justice, Supreme Court (1880–87), born in Newark, OH (died 1887).

1836　Greene V. Black, dentist whose method for filling teeth is still used, born in Winchester, IL; developed silver amalgam (1895) for fillings (died 1915).

1841　Francis Delafield, pathologist who founded Association of American Physicians (1886), its first president, born in New York City; coauthor of pathology textbook (1911) (died 1915).

1846　Iowa state constitution, approved by convention in May, was ratified; included a clause prohibiting slavery.

1846　Samuel M. Jones, manufacturer known as "Golden Rule" Jones for his enlightened employee practices, born in Beddgelert, Wales; mayor of Toledo (1897–1904) (died 1904).

1855　Henry C. Bunner, first editor, *Puck Magazine*, born in Oswego, NY (died 1896).

1884　Louis Gruenberg, pianist and opera composer (*Green Mansions, Emperor Jones, Jazz Suite*), born in Litovsk, Russia (died 1964).

1886　Russell C. Westover, cartoonist (*Tillie the Toiler*), born in Los Angeles (died 1966).

1900　Ernie Pyle, noted World War II correspondent, born in Dana, IN; killed by sniper fire in the Pacific in 1945.

1904　Albert Halper, novelist (*Union Square, The Foundry, The Chute, Sons of the Fathers*), born in Chicago.

1909　Walter Van Tilburg Clark, author of short stories, novels (*The Oxbow Incident, Track of the Cat*), born in East Oreland, ME (died 1971).

1918　Japan and the United States announced plans for joint intervention in Siberia; American troops landed at Vladivostok August 4.

1921　Richard Adler, composer of musicals (*Pajama Game, Damn Yankees*), born in New York City.

1923　Vice President Calvin Coolidge was sworn in as president by his father, a justice of the peace, in Plymouth Notch, VT, following the death of President Harding.

1924　Leon M. Uris, author (*Exodus, Battle Cry, Mila 18, QB VIII, Trinity*), born in Baltimore.

1926　Tony Bennett, popular singer in concerts, clubs, and television, born in New York City.

1941　Martha Stewart, homemaking adviser, entrepreneur, born in Nutley, NJ.

1949　National Basketball League and Basketball Association of America merged to form National Basketball Association.

1958　*Nautilus*, nuclear-powered submarine under command of William R. Anderson, became first to cross under Arctic ice of the North Pole.

1981　Federal air traffic controller (Professional Air Traffic Controllers Organization) began nationwide strike after rejecting government's final offer; most of the 12,000 were fired and replaced.

1984　Stock market staged an unprecedented rally as more than 236 million shares changed hands on the New York Stock Exchange (rising 36 points), beating the previous day's record of 172.8 million shares; more than 696 million shares were traded during the week.

2004　In first voter test of acceptability of homosexual marriage to general population, Missouri changed its constitution to bar it.

4

1735　Trial of New York editor, Peter Zenger, ended in acquittal; he was arrested November 17, 1734, on charge of libel; Philadelphia lawyer Andrew Hamilton established the principle of freedom of the press for which the New York Council gave him franchises of the city for "his learned and generous defense of the rights of mankind and the liberty of the press."

1789　Congress authorized first federal bond issue to fund domestic, state debt.

1790　Congress authorized creation of Revenue Cutter Service and Coast Guard, with ten vessels for the collection of revenue.

1816　Russell Sage, financier and wholesale grocer, born in Oneida County, NY; represented New York in House (1853–57); after his death (1906), his widow endowed the Russell Sage Foundation with $10 million.

1817　Frederick T. Frelinghuysen, Secretary of State (1881–85), born in Millstone, NJ; represented New Jersey in Senate (1866–69, 1871–77) (died 1885).

1823　Oliver P. Morton, Indiana governor

(1861–67) and Senator (1867–77), born in Salisbury, IN (died 1877).

1837   Texas petitioned Congress for annexation to United States; refused August 25.

1858   Charles S. Palmer, inventor of basic process for cracking oil to get gasoline (1900), born in Danville, IL; sold rights to Standard Oil (1916) (died 1939).

1860   Obed Hussey, inventor, manufacturer of a grain reaper (1834–58), died at 68.

1861   Jesse W. Reno, inventor of a moving stairway (1892), born in Ft. Leavenworth, KS (died 1947).

1865   John Flanagan, sculptor of monumental clock in Library of Congress, born in Newark, NJ (died 1952).

1874   Chautauqua Movement began at Lake Chautauqua, near Jamestown, NY, with a two-weeks instructional course in Sunday School management by John H. Vincent, a Methodist clergyman, and Lewis Miller of Akron, OH; started popular programs which spread widely and rapidly.

1914   President Wilson declared American neutrality in World War I; offered American mediation to the warring nations.

1916   United States bought the Danish West Indies (now Virgin Islands) from Denmark for $25 million; ratified by Senate September 7.

1919   Walter B. Wriston, banker, born in Middletown, CT; executive vice president, First National City Bank (now Citibank), New York City (1960–67), president (1967–70), board chairman (1970–85).

1944   Railroad accident near Stockton, GA, killed 47 persons.

1945   President Truman signed Bretton Woods Act, which authorized United States to participate in UN Food and Agricultural Organization.

1947   Puerto Rico given right to elect its own governor by popular vote.

1963   Representatives of United States, Soviet Russia, and Great Britain signed Nuclear Test Ban Treaty, prohibiting the testing of nuclear weapons in space, above ground, or under water.

1964   Three white civil rights workers were found murdered and buried in an earthen dam on a farm near Philadelphia, MS.

1964   President Lyndon Johnson announced American air attacks on North Vietnam oil storage and PT boat bases in retaliation for attacks on American destroyers in Gulf of Tonkin.

1977   President Carter signed legislation cre-

ating Department of Energy, effective October 1, with James R. Schlesinger as first secretary.

2000   Roman Catholic archdiocese of San Francisco fired all teenage rectory workers to avoid any danger of allegations of sexual abuse in the future.

2003   By 6–1 vote, California Supreme Court upheld the validity of some 20,000 gay/lesbian adoptions; decision covers most commonly used procedure and those not officially registered as partners with the state.

5

1749   Thomas Lynch, Jr., colonial leader, born in Winyah, SC; member of Continental Congress (1776–77) and signer of Declaration of Independence; lost at sea (1779).

1774   George Washington elected a delegate to Continental Congress.

1819   John Bidwell, who led first party of settlers overland from Missouri River to California (1841), born in Chautauqua County, NY (died 1900).

1858   First successful Atlantic cable laid; Queen Victoria and Secretary of State James Buchanan exchanged congratulations August 16; cable broke down September 1, not restored to proper functioning until after Civil War (1866).

1859   Thomas B. Osborne, biochemist, born in New Haven, CT; known especially for his investigations of vegetable proteins, discovery of vitamin in cod liver oil (died 1929).

1861   President Lincoln signed an income tax bill — 3 percent on incomes in excess of $800.

1864   Admiral David Farragut began Union takeover of Mobile Bay from Confederate forces; during this engagement, Farragut reputedly said, "Damn the torpedoes, full speed ahead."

1867   President Andrew Johnson asked for resignation of Secretary of War Edwin M. Stanton; he refused and was suspended (August 12), removed February 12, 1868.

1867   Jacob Ruppert, owner of Rupper Brewery, New York City (1914–39), born in New York City (died 1939).

1875   Clare M. Briggs, cartoonist (*When a Feller Needs a Friend*, and *Mr. and Mrs.*), born in Reedsburg, WI (died 1930).

1875   Malin Craig, Army chief of staff (1935–39), born in St. Joseph, MO; served in Spanish-American War and World War I (died 1945).

1879 Thomas Holcomb, Marine Corps commandant (1936–43), born in New Castle, DE; minister to Union of South Africa (1944–48) (died 1965).

1882 Hugh S. Johnson, director, NRA (National Recovery Act) (1933–34), born in Ft. Scott, KS; originated, supervised, conscription program, World War I (died 1942).

1886 Bruce Barton, advertising executive and author (*The Man Nobody Knows, The Book Nobody Knows*), born in Robbins, TN; headed advertising firm (Batton, Barton, Durstine, Osborne 1918–67); represented New York in House (1937–41) (died 1967).

1889 Conrad P. Aiken, novelist and poet, born in Savannah, GA; poetry included *Earth Triumphant, Brownstone Ecologues*; his novels included *The Voyage, Great Circle, Conversation* (died 1973).

1905 President Theodore Roosevelt met with Russian and Japanese peace commissioners in Oyster Bay, NY; conference began August 9, in Portsmouth, NH.

1906 Wasily Leontief, economist, born in Leningrad; with Harvard U. (1931–75); awarded 1973 Nobel Economics Prize for developing input-output analysis used in economic planning (died 1993).

1906 John Huston, movie director (*The Maltese Falcon, Treasure of Sierra Madre, Key Largo, The African Queen*), born in Nevada, MO (died 1987).

1914 Bryan-Chamoco Treaty signed, granting United States exclusive right to build an interoceanic canal in Nicaragua.

1914 Railroad accident at Tipton Falls, MO, cost 43 lives.

1917 National Guard was transferred into U.S. Army.

1926 First talking picture, a series of short features, shown at the Warner Theater, New York City.

1930 Neil A. Armstrong, astronaut who was first man to land on moon (1969), born in Wapakoneta, OH; as he stepped on moon, he said, "That's one small step for man, one giant leap for mankind."

1933 National Labor Board established with Sen. Robert F. Wagner of New York chairman to decide collective bargaining disagreements.

1962 Marilyn Monroe, screen actress, died in Hollywood after an overdose of sleeping pills.

1982 House by 204–202 vote rejected an immediate freeze of American and Russian nuclear arsenals; accepted a call for cuts to be followed by a freeze.

1988 James A. Baker, III, resigned as Treasury Secretary to take over Republican presidential campaign of Vice President George Bush, effective August 17; succeeded by Nicholas F. Brady, Wall St. investment banker.

2000 President Clinton vetoed major marriage tax reduction on grounds of amount of government revenue to be lost.

2003 First openly avowed homosexual became a bishop in the U.S. Episcopal Church; V.G. Robinson endorsed by bishops' vote of 62–45.

1736 *Virginia Gazette,* first newspaper in Virginia, published in Williamsburg by William Parks.

1774 Ann Lee, founder of the American Shakers, landed in New York from England with eight followers.

1777 Bloody battle of Oriskany, NY, near Ft. Stanwix, occurred when 860 American troops were ambushed; both sides claimed victory; Gen. Nicholas Herkimer, 49, was mortally wounded.

1788 Draft of proposed constitution submitted to the Constitutional Convention by a five-man committee; debate went on until September 15.

1810 William D. Ticknor, founder of a leading American publishing house, born in Lebanon, NH; published *Atlantic Monthly* and major American and English authors (died 1864).

1811 Judah P. Banjamin, Confederate Secretary of War, of State, born in St. Thomas, West Indies; represented Louisiana in Senate (1852–61); went to England after Civil War; served as Queen's Counsel (1872–83) (died 1884).

1819 Samuel P. Carter, commandant, Naval Academy (1870–73), born in Elizabethton, TN; had distinction of serving as Union army general (1861–63) then as an admiral with various naval commands (died 1891).

1828 Andrew T. Still, founder of osteopathy, born in Jonesboro, VA; founded, American School of Osteopathy, Kirksville, MO (1894) (died 1917).

1861 Edith K. Carow Roosevelt, second wife of President Theodore Roosevelt, born in Norwich, CT (died 1948).

1864 Union naval forces captured all positions around Mobile Bay, occupied Ft. Gaines.

1867 James M. Loeb, banker and philanthropist, born in New York City; founder, Loeb Classical Library (died 1933).

1874 James T. Shotwell, international relations expert who helped set up United Nations, born in Strathroy, Canada (died 1965).

1889 George C. Kenney, commander of Allied air forces in South Pacific (1942–45), born in Yarmouth, Nova Scotia; commander, Strategic Air Command (1945–48) (died 1977).

1893 Louella O. Parsons, first American movie columnist, born in Freeport, IL; column widely syndicated (died 1972).

1895 Francis W. Reichelderfer, chief, U.S. Weather Bureau (1938–63), born in Harlan, IN (died 1983).

1899 Ezra Taft Benson, president, Mormon Church (1985–94), born in Whitney, ID; Secretary of Agriculture (1953–61) (died 1994).

1904 Hank (Henry P.) Iba, basketball coach whose teams won 767 games in 41 years, born in Easton, MO; coached U.S. Olympic team three times (died 1993).

1905 Clara Bow, screen actress known as the "It" girl of the 1920s, born in New York City (died 1965).

1908 Helen H. Jacobs, woman tennis star of 1920/30s, born in Globe, AZ; was American singles champion (1932–35), Wimbledon (1935) (died 1997).

1911 Lucille Ball, screen and television actress (*I Love Lucy, The Lucy Show*), born in Jamestown, NY (died 1989).

1914 Ellen L. Wilson, first wife of President Wilson, died in White House at 54.

1917 Robert Mitchum, screen actor (*The Longest Day, Ryan's Daughter*) and television (*Winds of War*), born in Bridgeport, CT (died 1997).

1926 Gertrude Ederle, 20, became first woman to swim English Channel, going from Cap Gris-Nez, France to Dover, England, in 14 hours, 31 minutes.

1928 Andy Warhol, painter who led pop art movement of 1960s, born in Pittsburgh; film director (*The Chelsea Girls, Mr. Hustler*) (died 1987).

1930 Joseph F. Crater, New York Supreme Court judge, disappeared in New York City and no trace was ever found of him.

1945 Atomic bomb dropped on Hiroshima, Japan, by an American plane, killing thousands; this was first use of atomic energy in wartime.

1965 President Lyndon Johnson signed Voting Rights Act.

1996 NASA Administrator Daniel Golden said there was evidence pointing to possible existence of life beyond earth; said reputed evidence contained in a 4.5 lb. meteorite that reportedly originated on Mars more than four billion years ago.

1997 Dow Jones industrial average closed at all-time high of 8259.31.

2001 Census Bureau estimated that 11.2 percent of all Americans now foreign born (highest percentage since 1930). State figures of foreign-born: California, 25.9 percent; New York 20.4 percent; Florida, Hawaii, New Jersey—about 17 percent each.

2002 Bush signed bill giving him authority to negotiate trade pacts; Congress surrenders authority to revise text, can only vote treaties up or down; surrenders authority to alter them.

2006 BP (British Petroleum) began closing Alaska pipeline due to discovery of massive corrosion problems, cutting U.S. production of oil by 8 percent; later attempts to keep a drastically limited amount flowing through the pipeline.

7

1726 James Bowdoin, colonial leader, born in Boston; delegate to Constitutional Convention, governor of Massachusetts (1785–87); Bowdoin U. named for him (died 1807).

1742 Nathanael Greene, Revolutionary War general, born in what is now Warwick, RI; Army Quartermaster General (1778–80), resigned after congressional criticism; headed Army of the South (1780–82) (died 1786).

1789 War Department created with Gen. Henry Knox as first secretary; took office September 12.

1794 President Washington issued proclamation ordering end of Whiskey Rebellion, riots in western Pennsylvania against excise tax on whiskey; called on four states for 15,000 militia to quell riots; created first presidential commission to study problem; riots ended in September.

1826 Robert G. Dun, headed mercantile agency (R. G. Dun & Co.), born in Chillicothe, OH; company merged with Bradstreet Co. (1933) to form Dun & Bradstreet; publisher, *Dun's Review*, a business weekly (from 1893) (died 1900).

1839 John F. Dryden, who established what became Prudential Insurance Co. (1875), born in Farmington, ME; headed both the Prudential

Friendly Society and Prudential Insurance (1881–1912); represented New Jersey in Senate (1902–07) (died 1911).

1856 Lew Dockstader, minstrel who was a leading comedian of his time, born in Hartford, CT (died 1924).

1858 Charles R. Crane, industrialist and diplomat, born in Chicago; president, Crane Co., valves and fittings maker (1912–14); on special mission to Russia (1917), minister to China (1920–21) (died 1939).

1861 Hampton, VA, burned by Confederate troops.

1861 James B. Eads, St. Louis engineer, received federal contract to build seven ironclad boats.

1885 Billie Burke, stage and screen actress, born in Washington, DC; films included *Dinner at Eight, The Wizard of Oz, Father of the Bride* (died 1970).

1887 Carl E. Wickman, formed company which became Greyhound Corp. (1930), born in Varnhus, Sweden; Greyhound president (1930–46), chairman (1946–51) (died 1954).

1890 Elizabeth G. Flynn, American Communist leader, born in Concord, NH; imprisoned (1951–53), died in Moscow 1964.

1900 First Davis Cup tennis matches began at Longview Cricket Club in Boston, with United States team defeating an English team five matches to none.

1904 Ralph J. Bunche, United Nations official, born in Detroit; awarded 1950 Nobel Peace Prize for mediating the Palestine War (1948–49) (died 1971).

1904 Train wreck at Eden, CO, killed 96 persons.

1912 Former President Theodore Roosevelt, denied the Republican presidential nomination, accepted nomination of Progressive (Bull Moose) Party.

1918 Alice Wilson, niece of President Wilson, married to the Rev. Isaac S. McElroy, Jr., in White House with the groom's father officiating.

1927 International Peace Bridge at Buffalo, NY, dedicated by Vice President Dawes and the Prince of Wales.

1942 Garrison (Gary E.) Keillor, author and story teller (*Lake Wobegon*), born in Anoka, MN.

1942 Marines landed on Guadalcanal, where fighting went on for six months.

1944 American 3rd Army reached Brest, France.

1953 Refugee Relief Act passed admitting escapees from Communist aggression into the United States on an emergency basis outside regular quotas.

1964 Congress passed Tonkin Resolution, authorizing presidential action in Vietnam after North Vietnamese boats reportedly attacked American destroyers.

1982 New Jersey Governor Kean signed bill reinstating death penalty in state.

1985 Agreement was reached ending two-day strike of professional baseball players.

1989 Rep. Michael Leland of Texas and 15 others died when their plane crashed into a mountain in Western Ethiopia enroute to a refugee camp; Leland was chairman of House Select Committee on Hunger.

1990 Operation Desert Shield forces left for Saudi Arabia to defend that country following the invasion of Kuwait by Iraq.

1998 Bombs exploded minutes apart outside the United States embassies in Nairobi, Kenya and Dar-es-Salaam, Tanzania; 224 persons, including 12 Americans, were killed.

2000 Announcement of first Jew to ever run for vice president on a major party ticket; Al Gore promises that Senator Joseph Lieberman of Connecticut will be his choice.

2001 In what is regarded as largest cash advance for an unwritten nonfiction work, former President Clinton received $10 million for his memoirs.

2001 In first nationwide study, the *American Journal of Public Health* found that teenagers in same-sex relationships attempted suicide twice as often as heterosexual teens; earlier studies on more limited samples had indicated a possibly even higher rate.

2005 Peter Jennings died of lung cancer; at age 26 he served two years as ABC anchor for evening news; returning to that post in 1983, he remained in it till his death.

8

1672 Dutch fleet shelled New York City, starting third Anglo-Dutch War, and the English settlers quickly capitulated; Esopus and Albany also were occupied by August 15.

1763 Charles Bulfinch, architect, born in Boston; architect of national Capitol (1817–30), designed state capitols of Massachusetts, Connecticut, and Maine (died 1844).

1779 Benjamin Silliman, Yale's first chemistry professor and a founder of its Medical School, born in Trumbull, CT (died 1864).

1799 Nathaniel B. Palmer, first person to sight Antarctica (November 18, 1820) though he did not land, born in Stonington, CT; Palmer Peninsula named for him (died 1877).

1814 American and British peace commissioners met without reaching a solution in Ghent, Belgium; Americans were Henry Clay, John Quincy Adams, Albert Gallatin, James A. Bayard, and Jonathan Russell.

1814 Esther H. Morris, suffragette, born in Tioga County, NY; instrumental in winning suffrage for women in Wyoming, the first state to do so; first American woman justice of the peace (South Pass City, WY, 1870–74) (died 1902).

1819 Charles A. Dana, editor and publisher, born in Hinsdale, NH; editor, *New York Tribune* (1847–62); owner/editor, *New York Sun* (1868–97); coeditor, 16-volume *New American Cyclopedia* (died 1897).

1822 George Stoneman, Union general who served throughout the South, born in Busti, NY; governor of California (1883–87) (died 1894).

1839 Nelson A. Miles, Army officer who served in Civil and Spanish-American wars, born in Westminster, MA; commander, U.S. Army (1895) (died 1925).

1857 Henry Fairfield Osborn, head of American Museum of Natural History (1908–33), born in Fairfield, CT; museum's curator of vertebrate paleontology (died 1935).

1866 Matthew A. Henson, accompanied Peary on all North Pole explorations, born in Charles County, MD; planted flag on pole (1909) (died 1955).

1879 Robert H. Smith, cofounder, Alcoholics Anonymous (1935), born in St. Johnsbury, VT (died 1950).

1884 Sara Teasdale, poet ("Rivers to the Sea," "Love Song," "Dark of the Moon," "Strange Victory"), born in St. Louis (died 1933).

1887 Oliver E. Buckley, research director, Bell Laboratories (1933–40), president (1940–52), born in Sloan, IA (died 1959).

1890 Daughters of the American Revolution (DAR) organized in Washington, DC.

1890 Pauline Lord, screen actress (*Anna Christie, Ethan Frome*), born in Hanford, CA (died 1950).

1896 Marjorie Kinnan Rawlings, author (*The Yearling*), born in Washington, DC (died 1959).

1900 Hurricane smashed into Puerto Rico, killing about 2,000 persons.

1900 Victor Young, band leader and composer ("Sweet Sue," "Street of Dreams," "My Foolish Heart"), born in Chicago (died 1956).

1901 Ernest O. Lawrence, physicist, born in Canton, SD; awarded 1939 Nobel Physics Prize for his invention of the cyclotron, which accelerated advances in nuclear physics (died 1958).

1902 Welton D. Becket, architect who designed Los Angeles Music Center, born in Seattle (died 1969).

1908 Arthur J. Goldberg, United Nations ambassador (1965–68), born in Chicago; general counsel, CIO; Secretary of Labor (1961–62); associate justice, Supreme Court (1962–65) (died 1990).

1937 Dustin Hoffman, screen actor (*Kramer vs. Kramer, The Graduate, Tootsie*), born in Los Angeles.

1942 Four heavy cruisers, three American, lost in Battle of Savo Island.

1945 President Truman signed United Nations charter; ratified by Senate.

1945 Allies signed agreement creating International War Crimes Tribunal.

1998 Ravens football stadium in Baltimore opened.

2000 Confederate submarine *H.L. Hunley* brought to surface by archaeological recovery team; sank during Civil War.

2002 By 3–1 vote, Federal Communications Commission required all new televisions to be able to receive digital signals by 2007; critics protest result could be up to $250 higher price per set.

2005 In an effort to revive the once flourishing but now depressed sports player card trading market, the Major League Baseball Players Association announced that only two companies would receive permission to issue cards showing players; market had been flooded with wide variety of competing collections.

2006 The Federal Reserve ended an unprecedented series of 17 consecutive interest rate increases — the longest in its history — by retaining rates at the same 5.25 percent level.

9

1619 Sir Thomas Dale, colonial administrator, died at about 40; marshal of Virginia, issued rigorous code to cope with colonists' "laziness and insubordination"; his tenure (1611–16) called "the five years of slavery."

1673 Anthony Colve became governor of New York City, which had been captured by a Dutch squadron; governed until February 19, 1674, when news arrived of the end of hostilities between England and Holland; New York was returned to the British.

1680 An Indian revolt drove Spanish settlers out of New Mexico for 10 years; 400 colonists were killed, Santa Fe was sacked (August 15).

1733 James Clinton, Revolutionary War general who served at Montreal, Yorktown, born in Orange County, NY (died 1812).

1757 Settlers surrendered Ft. William Henry at southern end of Lake George, NY; British garrison was massacred by Indians, the fort burned August 10.

1793 Solomon L. Juneau, fur trader who founded Milwaukee and its first mayor (1846), born near Montreal (died 1856).

1809 William B. Travis, commander of the Americans in the Alamo siege and died with them (1836), born near Red Banks, SC.

1812 Egbert P. Judson, inventor of first blasting explosives, born in Syracuse, NY; his invention was suitable for railroad construction (died 1893).

1813 First American blackout occurred when St. Michaels, MD, received report of an impending British shelling; women, children, and older persons were evacuated; British overshot darkened town.

1814 Gen. Andrew Jackson concluded treaty with Creek Indians, ending year-long war; Creeks gave up two-thirds of their territory to United States.

1818 Capt. James Biddle, representing President Monroe, claimed northwest Oregon trading post of Astoria as American territory; founded in 1811, it was taken by British in 1813; restored to United States October 6, 1818.

1819 William T.G. Morton, first dentist to use ether in extractions, born in Charlton, MA; first used 1846 (died 1868).

1827 William M. Stewart, Senator who wrote 15th Amendment, born in Galen, NY; represented Nevada in Senate (1864–75, 1887–1905); his amendment holds that race is no bar to voting rights (died 1909).

1829 First American-made locomotive pulled a train on new railroad at Honesdale, PA; driven by Horatio Allen, Delaware & Hudson Railroad engineer and designer of the locomotive.

1842 Webster-Ashburton Treaty signed, fixing the American-Canadian border in Maine and Minnesota.

1848 Former President Van Buren nominated for president by Free Soil Party meeting in Buffalo; received 191,263 popular votes but no electoral votes.

1862 Confederate forces defeated Union troops at Cedar Mountain, GA.

1896 Leonide Massine, dancer and choreographer, born in Moscow; was with many companies, including Ballet Russe, New York City Ballet (died 1979).

1898 Spain accepted peace terms ending Spanish-American War; treaty called for Spain to relinquish Cuba, cede Puerto Rico and a Ladrone island to United States, and for United States to occupy Manila until the Philippines decision was made in another treaty.

1905 Russian-Japanese peace conference began in Portsmouth, NH.

1910 Mayor William J. Gaynor of New York City was severely wounded by a discharged city employee; never fully recovered, died 1913.

1911 William A. Fowler, astrophysicist, born in Pittsburgh; shared 1983 Nobel Physics Prize for "a complete theory of the formation of the chemical elements in our universe" (died 1995).

1916 Lassen (CA) National Park established.

1921 Veterans Bureau established to administer all veterans affairs; Col. Charles R. Forbes named director.

1928 Robert J. Cousy, basketball star (Holy Cross U., Boston Celtics), born in New York City.

1945 Second atomic bomb was dropped by American plane, this time on Nagasaki, Japan.

1965 Explosion of a missile silo killed 53 at Searcy, AR.

1974 President Nixon resigned, the first president to do so; succeeded by Vice President Gerald R. Ford.

1988 First baseball game under the lights was played in Wrigley Field, Chicago, the first time in 74 years; only remaining unlighted field; game scheduled for previous day but rained out.

1989 President Bush signed $159 billion rescue package for savings and loan industry; designed to clean up most heavily indebted savings and loans; created the Resolution Trust Corp.

1991 U.S. Attorney General Dick Thornburgh resigned to run for Pennsylvania Senate seat; succeeded by William P. Barr.

1995 Jerry Garcia, singer/guitarist with the rock group, The Grateful Dead, for 30 years, died at 53.

2001 President Bush endorsed federally funded stem cell research, but insisted the funds not be used to destroy new embryos to create the cells.

2002 U.S. government decided that that National Environmental Policy Act only applied to strictly territorial waters a few miles out and not to the broader "exclusive economic zone" which covers out to 200 miles; would permit sonar testing and other activities that some environmentalists argue are dangerous to sea creatures.

2005 Space shuttle *Discovery* landed at 5:12 A.M. in California in first American manned space launch since the *Columbia* disaster; only three shuttles left: *Discovery, Atlantis,* and *Endeavor;* shuttles essential if International Space Station to be completed.

2006 Department of Homeland Security warned that, unless a Microsoft patch for a security hole in their software was promptly installed, its absence could result in massive damage being inflicted on vital parts of America's computer-driven economic structure.

2006 Discoverer of the radiation belts surrounding the earth (which are named after him), Dr. James van Allen passed away at 91 of a heart attack.

10

1622 Council for New England granted John Mason and Sir Ferdinando Gorges a patent for all land between the Merrimack and Kennebec Rivers in Maine.

1674 William Vesey, Anglican rector of Trinity Church, New York City (1697–1746), born in Braintree, MA; Vesey Street in New York City named for him (died 1746).

1753 Edmund J. Randolph, colonial official, born in Williamsburg, VA; member of Continental Congress (1779–82) and Constitutional Convention (1787); served Virginia as governor (1786–88); U.S. Attorney General (1789–94), Secretary of State (1794–95); chief counsel for Aaron Burr in his treason trial (1807) (died 1813).

1781 Robert R. Livingston of New York named first Secretary of Foreign Affairs, serving until 1783.

1790 The *Columbia*, commanded by Capt. Robert Gray, arrived in Boston, completing first round-the-world voyage by an American vessel; began October 1, 1787.

1806 Arunah S. Abell, founder, editor, publisher, *Baltimore Sun* (1837–87), born in East Providence, RI; also founded *Philadelphia Public Ledger* (1836) (died 1888).

1814 John C. Pemberton, Confederate general, born in Philadelphia; commanded Vicksburg when it fell to Union troops under General Grant (died 1881).

1815 William H. Fry, composer of first publicly-performed American-written grand opera (*Leonora*), born in Philadelphia (died 1864).

1821 Jay Cooke, financier, born in Sandusky, Ohio; when his Northern Pacific Railroad failed, it precipitated the panic of 1873; also had successful mining operations in Utah (died 1905).

1821 Missouri entered Union as 24th state.

1843 Joseph McKenna, associate justice, Supreme Court (1898–1925), born in Philadelphia; represented California in House (1885–1902); Attorney General (1897–98) (died 1926).

1846 Smithsonian Institution established by Congress after ten-year fight led by former president John Quincy Adams to accept an endowment from a Britisher, James Smithson, "to found at Washington under the name of Smithsonian Institution, an establishment for the increase and diffusion of knowledge among men."

1849 Horace Fletcher, nutritionist, born in Lawrence, MA; a pioneer student of nutrition; Fletcherism and fletcherize became part of American language (died 1919).

1861 Confederate troops defeated Union force at Wilson's Creek, MO, as part of the internal battle over secession; Union Gen. Nathaniel Lyon was killed.

1868 Paul M. Warburg, banker, born in Hamburg, Germany; with Kuhn, Loeb; helped plan national banking reorganization (1907–14), member of first Federal Reserve Board (1914–18); gained prominence by warning of 1929 stock market crash seven months before it occurred (died 1932).

1874 Herbert C. Hoover, 31st President (1929–33), born in West Branch, IA; chairman, Belgian relief campaign (1915–19); American food administrator (1917–18); Secretary of Commerce (1921–28) (died 1964).

1887 A hundred people were killed in Chatsworth, IL, and hundreds more injured when a burning bridge collapsed under weight of a crossing train.

1900 Philip Levine, immunologist, born in Russia; first to recognize the Rh factor in blood (died 1987).

1900 Norma Shearer, screen actress (*Smilin'*

Through, Strange Interlude, The Women, The Barretts of Wimpole Street), born in Montreal (died 1983).

1914 First members of Federal Reserve Board sworn in; Charles A. Hamlin of Boston was chairman.

1917 Food and Fuel Control Act went into effect, empowering the president to set food and fuel prices and license producers and distributors.

1928 Eddie (Edwin J.) Fisher, popular singer, born in Philadelphia.

1965 President Lyndon Johnson signed $7.5 billion housing bill with a rent subsidy provision.

1972 Herbert Hoover Library in West Branch, IA, dedicated.

1977 American and Panamanian negotiators reached agreement in principle to turn over the Panama Canal to Panama by year 2000.

1987 Dow Jones industrial average climbed nearly 44 points to close above 2600 (2635.84) for first time.

1988 President Regan signed bill providing reparation payments of $20,000 to each Japanese-American interned during World War II; the tax-free payments will be made to 60,000 survivors of the internment.

1988 Space shuttle *Discovery* main engines successfully test fired after a series of delays; plans went ahead for first space flight since the January 28, 1986, explosion of shuttle *Challenger*.

1989 President Bush announced that he would name Gen. Colin L. Powell, former national security advisor, as chairman of Joint Chiefs of Staff, the first black in that post.

1993 Judge Ruth Bader Ginsburg sworn in as Supreme Court justice.

1993 President Clinton signed bill reducing federal budget deficits by $496 billion over five years.

1995 President Clinton endorsed proposed Food & Drug Administration regulations aimed at curbing smoking by young people.

2002 Federal government adopted first nationwide privacy policy to protect confidentiality of medical records; critics react with concern whether the privacy safeguards (especially in regard to computer systems) are strong enough.

2005 End of 115-year-old oil company: Unocal Corp. shareholders voted to agree to purchase by Chevron for $17.9 billion; attempt by partly Communist-owned China National Offshore Oil Corp. for a higher $18.5 billion had ignited bitter U.S. controversy before it withdrew bid a week earlier.

2006 After British arrested two dozen individuals in reported plot to blow up airliners on way to the United States, U.S. Homeland Security raised flight security alert to highest (red) level for the first time for all flights from that country; Raised to second-highest level for all other flights, domestic and foreign.

11

1760 Philip Embury (1728–73), first Methodist clergyman in the United States, arrived in New York City; founded Wesley Chapel (the first John St. Church) in 1768.

1766 Several persons were bayoneted by troops in New York City while trying to rebuild a Liberty Pole; probably first blood shed for American liberty.

1777 Gen. John Burgoyne, in need of supplies, sent 700 men to Bennington, VT; they were routed by Americans led by Gen. John Stark on August 16.

1787 *Kentucky Gazette* founded in Lexington by surveyor, John Bradford; this was first newspaper in state.

1807 David R. Atchison, legislator, born in Frogtown, KY; represented Missouri in Senate (1843–55), serving as president pro tem 16 times; some felt he was president for one day (March 4, 1849), which would have been inauguration day for Zachary Taylor, who waited to be sworn in on Monday, March 5; a city in Kansas and county in Missouri named for him (died 1886).

1833 Robert G. Ingersoll, lawyer and popular proponent of agnosticism, born in Dresden, NY; served as Illinois attorney general (1867–69) (died 1899).

1841 Burt G. Wilder, zoologist noted for studies of animal brains, born in Boston; with Cornell U. (1867–1910) (died 1925).

1847 Benjamin R. Tillman, legislator popularly known as "Pitchfork Ben," born in Edgefield County, SC; served South Carolina as governor (1890–94) and represented it in Senate (1895–1918) (died 1918).

1862 Carrie Jacobs Bond, composer ("A Perfect Day," "Just a-Wearyin' for You," "I Love You Truly"), born in Janesville, WI (died 1946).

1865 Gifford Pinchot, first professional American forester, born in Simsbury, CT; director, Forest Service (1898–1910); founder, Yale School of Forestry, professor (1903–36); served Pennsylvania as governor (1923–27, 1931–35) (died 1946).

1867 Joseph M. Weber, part of Weber and Fields vaudeville comedy team, born in New York City; was a theater manager (died 1942).

1880 Forty persons died in railroad accident at Mays Landing, NJ.

1881 Caroline C. Fillmore, second wife and widow of President Fillmore, died in Buffalo, NY, at 67.

1905 Erwin Chagaff, biochemist who launched modern era of biochemical genetics, born in Vienna.

1921 President Harding formally invited Great Britain, France, Italy, and Japan to discuss arms reduction and limitations.

1921 Alex P. Haley, author of popular *Roots*, born in Ithaca, NY; book gave rise to television series (died 1992).

1925 Carl T. Rowan, syndicated columnist, born in Ravenscroft, TN; ambassador to Finland (1963); head, U.S. Information Agency (1964).

1925 Mike Douglas, television host, born in Chicago; at one time, was a singer in big band era; host of a talk show.

1933 Jerry Falwell, founder, head, Moral Majority, born in Lynchburg, VA.

1955 Two Flying Boxcars collided in midair over Germany; 66 killed.

1964 Congress approved War on Poverty (Office of Economic Opportunity); all programs were taken over in 1973 by existing departments.

1965 Six days of rioting in Watts section of Los Angeles began; resulted in 34 deaths, more than 1,000 injuries, and fire damage of $175 million.

1975 United States vetoed admission into United Nations of North and South Vietnam.

1980 Week-long Hurricane Allen swept through Caribbean and Texas claiming 272 lives.

1988 Senate unanimously confirmed Richard L. Thornburgh, former Pennsylvania governor, as Attorney General, succeeding Edwin Meese; sworn in August 13.

1988 President Reagan signed $3.9 billion drought relief measure to aid stricken farmers hit by the worst drought in 50 years.

1994 Major league baseball players went on strike after the day's games principally because of the owners' attempt to impose a cap on overall teams salary levels.

1997 President Clinton became first president to use line item veto power; vetoed three provisions of a bill.

1998 British Petroleum PLC announced it would merge with Amoco Corp.; the $54.3 billion merger would be the largest in the oil industry.

2002 Sixth-largest American carrier, U.S. Airways, filed for bankruptcy.

2006 Mike Douglas died at 81; during career, the pioneer talk-show host of 21 years did some 6,000 90-minute shows.

12

1658 A "rattle-watch" of eight men, the first police force, established in New Amsterdam.

1676 King Philip of Narragansett Indians killed by an Indian friend of the colonists and the war against New England colonists ended.

1778 Storm prevented an engagement of French and British fleets off Newport, RI; the French fleet and 4,000 troops sailed August 22 to Boston for repairs.

1781 Robert Mills, first American-born architect, born in Charleston, SC; served as architect of public buildings, designing the Treasury, Post Office, and Washington Monument (died 1855).

1791 Timothy Pickering named first Postmaster General, taking office August 19.

1846 Richard K. Fox, publisher, *Police Gazette* (1877–1922), born in Belfast (died 1922).

1852 Michael J. McGivney, Catholic priest who was principal founder of Knights of Columbus (1882), born in Waterbury, CT (died 1890).

1856 James B. Brady, financier known as "Diamond Jim," born in New York City; salesman for railroad supply house (1879), became successful financier (died 1917).

1859 Katherine L. Bates, author of lyrics for patriotic hymn, "America the Beautiful," born in Falmouth, MA; English professor, Wellesley College (1891–1925) (died 1929).

1862 Julius Rosenwald, with Sears Roebuck (1895–1932), born in Springfield, IL; was vice president (1895–1910), president (1910–25), chairman (1925–32); set up $40 million fund for welfare of mankind; presented Chicago with Museum of Science and Industry (1929) (died 1932).

1867 President Andrew Johnson suspended Edward M. Stanton as Secretary of War.

1867 Edith Hamilton, popularizer of classical literature in United States, born in Dresden, Germany (died 1963).

1876 Mary Roberts Rinehart, novelist (*The Circular Staircase, Tish, The Breaking Point*), born in Pittsburgh (died 1958).

1877 James W. Wadsworth, legislator, born

in Geneseo, NY; represented New York in Senate (1915–25) and House (1933–51) (died 1952).

1880 Christy (Christopher) Mathewson, baseball pitcher (New York NL) who won 372 games, born in Factoryville, PA; one of first five named to Baseball Hall of Fame (died 1925).

1881 Cecil B. DeMille, movie director and producer of first full length movie (*The Squaw Man*), born in Ashfield, MA; produced many hits (*Ten Commandments*, *The King of Kings*, *Cleopatra*, *The Crusades*) (died 1959).

1882 George W. Bellows, a leading realist painter and lithographer, born in Columbus, OH; did sports and war scenes (*Stag at Sharkeys*, *Up the Hudson*, *Polo Game at Lakewood*) (died 1925).

1882 Vincent Bendix, inventor of automobile starter, born in Moline, IL; first mass producer of four-wheel brakes (died 1945).

1895 Lynde D. McCormick, World War II admiral, born in Annapolis, MD; involved in Coral Sea and Midway battles; commander, Atlantic Fleet (1951–52), Allied Atlantic commander, NATO (1952–54); president, Naval War College (1954–56) (died 1956).

1897 Otto Struve, astronomer who discovered interstellar matter, born in Kharkov, Russia (died 1963).

1898 Protocol signed ending the Spanish-American War.

1902 International Harvester Co. incorporated in New Jersey with $120 million capitalization.

1919 Michael Kidd, dancer and choreographer (*Finian's Rainbow*, *Guys and Dolls*, *Can-Can*), born in New York City.

1927 Mstislav Rostropovitch, cellist and conductor (Washington National Symphony since 1977), born in Baku, Russia.

1960 *Echo I*, first passive communications satellite, launched.

1970 Postal reform measure signed, creating an independent U.S. Postal Service, thus relinquishing government control after almost 200 years.

1988 Outgoing Attorney General Edwin Meese, III, announced establishment of a new system of "special counsels" to investigate wrongdoings by members of Congress.

1997 Hudson Foods, Inc., announced it was recalling 20,000 lbs. of beef after some people in Colorado became ill after eating Hudson hamburgers; subsequent recalls brought total recall to 25 million pounds.

2000 Loretta Young died; had own TV series from 1953 to 1961 and acted in over 100 films.

2004 James McGreevey announced resignation as governor of New Jersey as of August 15; although married, admitted he had had an affair with a male; charges he was threatened with blackmail; lawyer of lover says governor had been guilty of sexual harassment instead.

2005 State of emergency declared by New Mexico governor Bill Richardson in several counties bordering Mexico: combination of drug smuggling, violent crime, and flood of illegal immigrants blamed.

13

1751 Academy and College of Philadelphia, founded by Benjamin Franklin, opened; later merged into U. of Pennsylvania.

1788 James McGready (1758?–1817), Presbyterian clergyman, licensed to preach; inspired revivalist movement in Logan County, KY (1797–99), which swept through South and West.

1812 The *Essex*, commanded by Capt. David Porter, captured British sloop *Alert*.

1818 Lucy Blackwell Stone, women's rights leader, born near West Brookfield, MA; helped organize national women's rights convention in Worcester, MA (1850); founder, American Woman's Suffrage Association (1869); founder, coeditor, *Woman's Journal* (1872–93) (died 1893).

1839 Michael A. Corrigan, Catholic Archbishop of New York (1885–1902), born in Newark, NJ; Bishop of Newark (died 1902).

1844 Constitution framed by New Jersey convention, restricting the ballot to "white male citizens," ratified by the people.

1846 American troops under Commodore Robert E. Stockton and Capt. John C. Fremont defeated Mexican defenders of Los Angeles; Mexicans re-took city later, holding it until January 10, 1847.

1849 Lenora M.K. Berry, labor leader, born in Ireland; headed woman's department, Knights of Labor; active in temperance, women's rights movements (died 1930).

1851 Felix Adler, educator and reformer, born in Alzey, Germany; founder, Society of Ethical Culture (1876), a non-religious association for ethical improvement (died 1933).

1860 Annie Oakley, frontierswoman and sharpshooter, born in Darke County, OH; starred in Buffalo Bill's Wild West Show (died 1926).

1867 George B. Luks, artist and cartoonist, born in Williamsport, PA; among his works were *The Wrestlers, Little Madonna, Woman and Black Cat*; created comic strip, *The Yellow Kid* (died 1933).

1895 Bert Lahr, stage and screen actor (*The Wizard of Oz*), born in New York City (died 1967).

1897 Detlev W. Bronk, physiologist who founded biophysics, born in New York City; head of Rockefeller Institute (1953–68) (died 1975).

1898 American troops occupied Manila after nearly a year's siege and a one-day assault.

1899 Alfred J. Hitchcock, movie director and producer, born in London; master of suspense films and radio/television shows (*The 39 Steps, The Lady Vanishes, Rear Window, Suspicion, Vertigo, Dial M for Murder*) (died 1980).

1906 Racial violence in Brownsville, TX, resulted in death of one white man; 167 black soldiers from nearby Ft. Brown were dishonorably discharged on circumstantial evidence without a trial; action reversed in 1972 clearing men of the guilty verdict.

1912 Ben (William B.) Hogan, considered one of three greatest golfers of 1900–50 era, born in Dublin, TX (died 1997).

1912 Salvador E. Luria, biologist, born in Turin, Italy; shared 1969 Nobel Physiology/Medicine Prize for work on genetic structure of viruses (died 1991).

1920 George Shearing, popular blind jazz pianist and composer, born in London.

1958 Malcolm Lockheed, founder of what became Lockheed Aircraft, died at about 71; designed hydraulic and auto braking systems.

1986 Senate voted 53–47 to approve President Reagan's request for $100 million to aid the Nicaraguan Contras; approved by House in June.

2003 Governor Gray Davis of California discovered number of opponents he would face in October in effort to remove him from office: 134 rivals certified for the ballot.

2004 In a season that would pummel Florida with multiple large-scale hurricanes, Charley (category 4) hit the state with damage then estimated at $15 billion.

2006 As of today, 51 U.S. state and territorial governors had signed a joint protest to Congress urging it to reject, in House-Senate Conference, a House proposal that would permit president to unilaterally federalize national guard in national emergencies.

14

1607 Two ships of Plymouth Company arrived at Popham Beach on the Sagadahoc (lower Kennebec) River in Maine; settlers built a fort, other buildings, but venture was abandoned September 1608, when the colony failed because of illness and factionalism.

1734 Thomas Sumter, Revolutionary officer and legislator, born near Charlottesville, VA; served in South Carolina campaigns; represented state in House (1789–93, 1797–1801) and Senate (1801–10) (died 1832).

1755 Virginia legislature appointed George Washington a colonel in Virginia regiment and commander-in-chief of Virginia forces protecting the frontier against the French and Indians.

1756 After a four-day siege, Oswego, NY, surrendered to French troops under Gen. Louis J. de Montcalm; fort was destroyed.

1773 Peter B. Porter, War of 1812 general, born in Salisbury, CT; served at Chippewa, Lundy's Lane, and Ft. Erie; represented New York in House (1809–13, 1815–16); Secretary of War (1828–29) (died 1844).

1776 Convention opened in Annapolis to prepare Maryland's constitution, which was proclaimed November 8.

1819 First Texas newspaper, *Texas Republican*, published in Nacogdoches.

1848 Territory of Oregon established.

1860 Ernest Thompson Seton, naturalist and author (*Biography of a Grizzly*), born in South Shields, England; chief scout, Boy Scouts of America (1910–15) (died 1946).

1863 Ernest L. Thayer, author remembered for ballad, "Casey at the Bat," born in Lawrence, MA (died 1940).

1869 Daniel C. Jackling, revolutionized copper mining by developing method of removing low-grade ore, born in Appleton, MO (died 1956).

1886 Arthur J. Dempster, physicist who built first mass spectrometer, born in Toronto (died 1950).

1891 Sarah C. Polk, widow of President Polk, died in Nashville at 87.

1892 C. Bromley Oxnam, Methodist bishop who headed World Council of Churches (1948–54), born in Sonora, CA; a founder, National Council of Churches (1950) (died 1963).

1899 Whit Burnett, cofounder, editor, *Story Magazine* (1931), born in Salt Lake City (died 1973).

1900 Siege of foreign legations, including American, in Peking was raised by 5,000 troops, ending the Boxer Rebellion, an anti-foreign Chinese uprising; siege began June 17 and 231 foreigners and many Chinese Christians were killed.

1918 Anna Held, stage and vaudeville comedienne, died at 45.

1923 Accident in a bituminous coal mine at Kemmerer, WY, claimed 99 lives.

1925 Russell W. Baker, syndicated *New York Times* columnist, born in Loudon County, VA.

1935 Social Security Act signed by President Franklin Roosevelt.

1941 Atlantic Charter issued by President Franklin Roosevelt and Prime Minister Winston Churchill following three-day meeting at sea off Newfoundland declaring their joint peace aims.

1945 Japanese government surrendered, bringing World War II to a close.

1947 Danielle Steel, popular author (*Crossings, Changes, Secrets*), born in New York City.

1947 Domestic airmail rate reduced to five cents per ounce, effective October 1.

1959 Magic (Earvin) Johnson, basketball player (Los Angeles), born in Lansing, MI; NBA most valuable player three years; retired 1991 after testing positive to AIDS; returned briefly in 1992 and 1996.

1964 Federal Employees Salary Act raised salary of vice president from $35,000 to $43,000.

1967 Floods damaged most buildings in Fairbanks, Alaska, with a loss of $200 million.

1969 World's largest mint opened in Philadelphia.

1974 Forty year ban on private gold transactions lifted.

1994 Woodstock's 25th anniversary celebration in Saugerties, NY, ended in a sea of mud and trash and wide disorder.

1995 The Citadel, all-male South Carolina military school, admitted Sharon Faulkner to cadet corps after exhausting all legal efforts to bar her; however, four days after her entry, she dropped out because of harshness of opening days.

2000 Democrats opened their national convention; nominated Al Gore for president and Joseph Lieberman for vice president.

2002 Religious backlash: After July decision of Big Brothers/Sisters to require all affiliates to accept homosexual mentors, moral conservatives withdrew endorsement of group and argued that policy provides new opportunities for implicit/explicit sexual propaganda for the lifestyle; only handful of 490 affiliates protest requirement.

2003 Worst electrical failure in U.S. history affected sections of Canada and American Midwest and Northeast; 50 million plunged into darkness.

2006 Six-term Rep. Bob Ney of Ohio (Republican) withdrew from Congressional reelection race due to reputed connections with Jack Abramoff, convicted of lobbying corruption; Ney denied wrongdoing.

15

1675 Nicholas Eaton, colonial administrator, died at 82; "president" of Rhode Island (1650–51), 1654), deputy governor (1666–69, 1670–71), governor (1672–74).

1694 Treaty signed at Albany by representatives of Massachusetts, Connecticut, New York, and New Jersey and the Iroquois tribe.

1765 Andrew Oliver, the Boston Stamp Act agent, resigned; before the effective date of the Act (November 1), all agents had resigned.

1790 John Carroll consecrated as first American Catholic bishop at Lulworth Castle, England; served the Baltimore diocese.

1812 Garrison at Ft. Dearborn (site of Chicago) was massacred by Indians after it evacuated the post, which was burned the next day.

1814 Gen. Andrew Jackson assumed command of American troops at New Orleans.

1817 Mississippi convention adopted state constitution; later ratified by legislature.

1824 John S. Chisum, frontiersman who at one time was the cattle "king" with world's largest cattle herd (100,000), born in Hardeman County, TN (died 1884).

1846 The *Californian*, published by Robert Semple and Walton Colton in Monterey, was first newspaper in state.

1855 Walter Hines Page, ambassador to Great Britain (1913–18), born in Cary, NC; founder, editor, *The World's Work* (1900–13); editor, *Atlantic Monthly* (1895–98) (died 1918).

1859 Charles A. Comiskey, owner of Chicago White Sox baseball team (1900–31), born in Chicago; played for about 11 years; named to Baseball Hall of Fame (died 1931).

1860 Florence K. DeWolfe Harding, wife of President Harding, born in Marion, OH (died 1924).

1879 Ethel Barrymore, stage star of numerous plays, born in Philadelphia; among her hits were *A Doll's House, Alice-Sit-by-the-Fire, The Constant Wife*) (died 1959).

1880 J(acob) J. Shubert, theatrical producer, born in Syracuse, NY; with brothers, were important figures in the theater (died 1963).

1881 Richard S. Reynolds, founded (1919) U.S. Foil Co. which became Reynolds Aluminum, born in Bristol, TN (died 1955).

1887 Edna Ferber, author (*So Big, Show Boat, Cimarron, Giant*), born in Kalamazoo, MI; coauthor of several plays (*Royal Family, Dinner at Eight, Stage Door*) (died 1968).

1888 Albert Spalding, a leading violinist of his day, born in Chicago (died 1953).

1896 Sheldon Glueck, criminologist, born in Warsaw; with wife, Eleanor, made pioneering studies of criminal character and behavior (died 1980).

1896 Gerty Theresa Cori, biochemist, born in Prague; shared 1947 Nobel Physiology/Medicine Prize with husband, Carl F., for work on animal starch metabolism (died 1957).

1904 Bill Baird, puppeteer who led 20th Century revival of puppetry, born in Grand Island, NE (died 1987).

1912 Julia Child, cooking expert, born in Pasadena, CA; author of several cookbooks, popular television performer, columnist.

1914 Panama Canal formally opened to traffic; took seven years to build at cost of $336,500,000; Panama Railroad steamer, *Ancon*, took nine hours to pass through.

1919 President Wilson vetoed act repealing daylight savings time; veto was overridden by Congress August 20.

1922 Lukas Foss, composer and orchestra conductor (Buffalo 1963–71, Brooklyn 1971–81, Milwaukee 1981–), born in Berlin.

1924 Phyllis S. Schlafly, women's leader who staunchly opposed Equal Rights Amendment, born in St. Louis.

1935 Aviator Wiley Post and entertainer Will Rogers died in a crash of Post's plane in Alaska.

1935 Vernon E. Jordan, Jr., civil rights leader who headed National Urban League (1972–81), born in Atlanta.

1944 American 7th Army invaded southern France and drove up the Rhone Valley.

1945 Gasoline and fuel oil rationing ended.

1953 Navy Admiral Arthur W. Radford became chairman of Joint Chiefs of Staff.

1957 Air Force Gen. Nathan F. Twining named chairman of Joint Chiefs of Staff.

1971 Cost of Living Council created by executive order; abolished July 1, 1974; President Nixon began sweeping new economic program, imposing wage and price controls and a rent freeze; also devalued dollar by cutting its tie with gold.

1988 Republican national convention opened in New Orleans; nominated Vice President Bush for president, Indiana Senator Daniel Quayle for vice president.

2003 With Proposition 13 now 25 years old, Californians still debate its consequences: proponents speak of how its drastic curb on real estate assessment increases made it possible for thousands to stay in their homes; opponents bemoan lost tax revenue.

2006 Wal-Mart announced first quarterly loss since 1996; major causes: closing all stores in Germany and Korea and high energy prices.

2006 Hazelton, Pennsylvania, sued over ordinance to fine landlords renting to illegal immigrants and deny business licenses to their employers.

16

1777 Gen. John Stark led 1,600 New Hampshire and Vermont troops to victory near Bennington, VT; routing British troops seeking supplies for Burgoyne's army.

1780 British troops under Lord Charles Cornwallis withstood American attack on Camden, SC, inflicting heavy losses on Americans (800–900 dead, 1,000 captured); Baron Johann de Kalb fighting with Americans fatally wounded.

1782 John Adams named minister plenipotentiary to Holland.

1784 Nathan Hale, owner, editor, *Boston Advertiser* (1814–54), born in Westhampton, MA; a founder, *North American Review* (1815), *Christian Examiner* (1824) (died 1863).

1789 Amos Kendall, business manager for Samuel F.B. Morse and the telegraph, born in Dunstable, MA; Postmaster General (1835–40), a founder, Gallaudet College (died 1859).

1798 Mirabeau N. Lamar, Republic of Texas vice president (1836), president (1838–41), born in Warren County, GA; minister to Nicaragua, Costa Rica (1857–59) (died 1859).

1802 Isaac Adams, inventor of power printing press, born in Rochester, NH; press used primarily for book printing in 19th Century (died 1883).

1811 George Jones, a founder, *New York Times* (1851), born in Poultney, VT; directed fight against Tweed Ring in New York City (died 1891).

1812 American force of 2,500 surrendered Detroit to British-Indian force of 1,300; Gen. William Hull surrendered fort without firing a shot, fearing an Indian massacre of women and children (including his daughter and grandchildren); British force led by Gen. Isaac Brock.

1824 Marquis de Lafayette, at invitation of President Monroe, visited United States, staying nearly 16 months.

1828 Joseph B. Carr, Union general at Bull Run, Richmond, Petersburg, and Gettysburg, born in Albany, NY; held center of Union line at Gettysburg (died 1895).

1851 William H. Harvey, economist who advocated bimetallism, born in Buffalo, WV; 1932 Liberal candidate for president (died 1936).

1854 Duncan Phyfe, Scottish-born cabinetmaker, died at 76; his first furniture shop on what is now Fulton St., New York City, turned out his neoclassical style furniture.

1862 Amos Alonzo Stagg, football coach who introduced the huddle, man-in-motion, end-around play, born in West Orange, NJ; coached U. of Chicago (1892–1933), U. of the Pacific (1933–46) (died 1965).

1865 Dennis J. Dougherty, Catholic Archbishop of Philadelphia (1918–51), born in Girardville, PA (died 1951).

1868 Bernarr Macfadden, publisher and physical culturist, born near Mill Spring, MO; published several newspapers, magazines (*True Confessions, True Story, Photoplay*) (died 1955).

1879 James F. Bell, first president, General Mills (1928–34), chairman (1934–47), born in Philadelphia (died 1961).

1882 Harvard Annex, which later became Radcliffe College, chartered.

1884 Hugo Gernsback, inventor of improved dry battery, born in Luxembourg; as a publisher, helped establish science fiction (died 1967).

1892 Hal (Harold R.) Foster, cartoonist (*Prince Valiant*), born in Halifax (died 1982).

1894 George Meany, president, AFL-CIO (1955–79), born in New York City; president, New York State Federation of Labor (1934–39); secretary-treasurer, AFL (1940–52), president (1952–55) (died 1980).

1896 Gold was discovered on Bonanza Creek and the Klondike River in Canadian Northwest Territory; gold rush followed (1897–99), when about 100,000 headed for area.

1904 Wendell M. Stanley, virologist, Rockefeller Institute (1931–48), born in Ridgeville, IN; shared 1946 Nobel Chemistry Prize for preparing enzymes, virus proteins in pure form (died 1971).

1930 Frank Gifford, football player (U. of Southern California, New York Giants), born in Santa Monica, CA; became television sportscaster.

1949 General Omar N. Bradley became first chairman of Joint Chiefs of Staff.

1987 Great Basin National Park near Baker, NV, dedicated; first new park in 15 years.

1987 Northwest Airlines jetliner crashed after takeoff from Detroit airport, killing 154 persons.

2005 Arizona governor Janet Napolitano became second state chief executive officer to declare state of emergency in several counties bordering Mexico: combination of drug smuggling, violent crime, and flood of undocumented immigrants blamed.

2005 New U.S. Forest Service estimate of the dollar value of recreational lands reduced by 90 percent, from $111 billion to $11 billion; figures based upon survey of forest admissions (200 million in 2002, for example) and estimate that each visit produces about $46 revenue in or near the forests; environmentalists prefer higher estimates to reduce danger of logging.

2006 Consumers began to return up to 4.1 million Sony laptop batteries that might catch fire after Dell Computer announced recall on previous day; recall extended to 1.8 million batteries in Apple computers on August 24.

17

1590 Sir John White arrived at Roanoke Island, NC, and found no trace of the colonists he left there July 22, 1585; fate of "Lost Colony" never determined.

1786 Davy Crockett, frontiersman, born in Greene County, TN; represented Tennessee in House (1827–31, 1833–35); was killed with defenders of the Alamo in 1836.

1799 Convention in Frankfort adopted Kentucky state constitution.

1803 Capt. John Whistler and a company of soldiers arrived in Chicago area to build Ft. Dearborn; fort was destroyed in 1812, rebuilt 1816.

1804 Barbara Heck, Irish-born Methodist known as the "mother" of American Methodism, died at 70; helped organize first Methodist church in United States (New York City 1765).

1807 Robert Fulton's steamboat, *Clermont*, began its trip on Hudson River; completed round trip from New York to Albany in 62 hours.

1859 John F. Queeny, founder, Monsanto Chemical Co. (1901), born in Chicago (died 1933).

1864 Charles H. Cooley, who helped found sociology in United States, born in Ann Arbor, MI (died 1929).

1864 Edward W. Eberle, chief of naval operations (1923–27), born in Denton, TX; as commander of the *Oregon*, he directed dash around Cape Horn to participate in battle of Santiago in Spanish-American War (died 1929).

1866 Julia Marlowe, stage star in Shakespearian and other roles, born in Caldbeck, England; starred with husband, Edward H. Sothern (died 1950).

1868 Gene Stratton Porter, popular novelist (*Freckles, Girl of the Limberlost, The Harvester*), born in Wabash County, IN (died 1924).

1887 Marcus Garvey, founder, Universal Negro Improvement Association, first important black movement, born in Jamaica (died 1940).

1887 Samuel A. Stritch, Catholic Archbishop of Milwaukee (1930–39), of Chicago (1939–46), born in Nashville, TN; Bishop of Toledo (1921–30); first American named to Rome curia (1958); elevated to cardinal (1946) (died 1958).

1890 Harry L. Hopkins, headed Federal Emergency Relief Administration (1933–38), born in Sioux City, IA; Secretary of Commerce (1938–40); director, Lend Lease Administration (1941); special assistant to President Franklin Roosevelt (died 1946).

1892 Mae West, stage and screen actress who was sex symbol of early 1930s, born in Brooklyn; among her films was *Diamond Lil* (died 1980).

1896 Leslie R. Groves, general who headed Manhattan Project, which developed atomic bomb (1942–47), born in Albany, NY (died 1970).

1903 Joseph Pulitzer gave $1 million to establish the School of Journalism at Columbia U.

1915 Flooding at Galveston, TX, caused 275 deaths.

1918 George S. Brown, Air Force general who was chairman of Joint Chiefs of Staff (1974–78), born in Montclair, NJ (died 1978).

1918 Judge Kenesaw M. Landis in Chicago found 100 leaders of IWW (Industrial Workers of the World) guilty of conspiracy against prosecution of the war.

1943 Week-long conference between President Franklin Roosevelt and Prime Minister Winston Churchill began in Quebec.

1961 United States and 19 Latin American nations, meeting in Uruguay, signed Alliance for Progress put forth by President Kennedy March 13.

1969 Two-day Hurricane Camille hit Gulf Coast, leaving at least 300 dead and damage exceeding $300 million; resulted in torrential rains in West Virginia and Virginia, causing floods and killing about 50 persons.

1978 Three Albuquerque, NM, men (Ben Abruzzo, Max Anderson, Larry Newman) began first successful crossing of the Atlantic Ocean in a balloon, flying the 3,107 miles from Presque Isle, ME, to Paris in 137 hours, six minutes.

1988 United States exploded a nuclear device under the Nevada desert with Soviet Russian scientists monitoring an American test for first time.

1988 A Pakistan C-130 plane exploded shortly after takeoff from Islamabad, killing Pakistan President Zia, American Ambassador Arnold L. Raphel, Brig. Gen. Herbert M. Wasson, chief American defense representative in Pakistan, and 34 others.

1996 Reform Party nominated Ross Perot, the Texas billionaire, for president.

2003 Public safety officials from around U.S. spoke out concerning how widespread use of cellular telephones repeatedly encroaches on emergency frequencies, garbling transmissions, resulting in delayed response; problems reported in at least 27 states.

2006 An ACLU lawsuit gained its first victory as Federal Judge Anna Digs Taylor of Detroit upheld its claim that National Security Agency wiretaps without a warrant were illegal even in cases of terrorism.

18

1587 Virginia Dare was born, the first English child born in the United States; she was part of the colony on Roanoke Island, NC, which disappeared.

1774 Meriwether Lewis, coleader of Lewis & Clark Expedition (1804–06), born in Albemarle County, VA; served as private secretary to President Jefferson, who named him to explore lands of the Louisiana Purchase; selected William Clark as co-leader (died 1809).

1795 President Washington signed Jay Treaty with Great Britain.

1803 Nathan Clifford, associate justice, Supreme Court (1858–81), born in Rumney, NH; represented Maine in House (1839–43); Attorney General (1846–48) (died 1881).

1807 Charles Francis Adams, diplomat, born in Boston; represented Massachusetts in House

(1858–61); minister to Great Britain (1861–68), keeping the British neutral during the Civil War; edited works and memoirs of his presidential father and grandfather (died 1886).

1818 William F. Barry, artillery commander in Sherman's march to the sea, born in New York City; organized, headed, Artillery School, Ft. Monroe, VA (1867–77) (died 1879).

1834 Marshall Field, merchant, born near Conway, MA; partner in dry goods store which became Marshall Field & Co., of which he was president (1881–1906); store became world's largest dry goods firm; donated land for U. of Chicago site; gave funds for Columbian Museum at Chicago's World Fair (1893), which is now Field Museum of Natural History (died 1906).

1846 Col. Stephen Kearny and an American force occupied Santa Fe and declared New Mexico annexed to the United States.

1847 Robley D. Evans, commanded American fleet in 1907 round-the-world trip, born in Floyd, VA; perfected long distance signal light (died 1912).

1852 Margaret S. Taylor, widow of President Taylor, died near Pascagoula, MS, at 63.

1867 Thomas E. Donnelley, developed family firm into major printing company, born in Chicago (died 1955).

1871 Gus Edwards, entertainer and composer ("School Days," "By the Light of the Silvery Moon"), born in Hohensaliza, Germany (died 1945).

1873 Otto A. Harbach, librettist (*The Firefly*; *Kid Boots*; *Sunny*; *No, No, Nanette*; *Roberta*; *Rose Marie*; *The Desert Song*), born in Salt Lake City (died 1963).

1890 Maurice Podoloff, engineered merger of basketball leagues into the National Basketball Association, serving as NBA commissioner (1949–63), born (died 1955).

1917 Caspar W. Weinberger, Defense Secretary (1981–88), born in San Francisco; Secretary of Health, Education & Welfare (1973–75); publisher, *Fortune* (1988–).

1920 Nineteenth Amendment, giving women the right to vote, ratified with the approval of Tennessee, which later rescinded the action; amendment considered ratified August 26.

1927 Rosalynn Smith Carter, wife of President Carter, born in Plains, GA.

1934 Roberto Clemente, baseball player (Pittsburgh), born in Carolina, Puerto Rico; named to Baseball Hall of Fame (died 1972).

1934 Rafer Johnson, winner of 1960 Olympics decathlon, born in Hillsboro, TX.

1937 Robert Redford, screen actor (*All the President's Men*, *Butch Cassidy and the Sundance Kid*, *The Sting*), born in Santa Monica, CA.

1938 President Franklin Roosevelt and Canadian Prime Minister Mackenzie King dedicated the Thousand Islands Bridge over the St. Lawrence River.

1941 President Franklin Roosevelt and Canadian Prime Minister Mackenzie King agreed to set up a permanent joint defense board to defend northern half of continent.

1941 President Franklin Roosevelt signed legislation extending military service to 18 months; House approved 203–202, Senate 45–30.

1955 Hurricane Diane ravaged six northeastern states, causing 180 deaths and $457 million in property damage.

1956 Alexander Graham Bell Museum opened in Baddeck, Nova Scotia, where he spent his summers for 35 years.

1969 Three-day music concert took place near Bethel, NY; the affair, known as Woodstock, attracted about 300,000 young people.

1987 Dow Jones industrial average rose 15.14 points to top the 2700 mark (2700.57) for first time.

1993 Dow Jones Industrial Average reached a new high of 3604.86.

2003 For the first time ever the complete *Enola Gay* B-29 that dropped the first atomic bomb on Hiroshima went on public display; restoration to original condition took ten years and $1 million.

2006 As further indication of the decline of the American automobile industry, Ford announced plans to cut fourth-quarter production 21 percent (168,000 vehicles); General Motors had announced a 7 to 8 percent reduction.

19

1751 Samuel Prescott, who accompanied Paul Revere and William Dawes on ride to alert colonists to British advance, born in Concord, MA; was captured by British (1777) and died in Halifax that year.

1779 American troops under Capt. Henry ("Light Horse Harry") Lee made successful surprise raid on fort at Paulus Hook (now part of Jersey City).

1785 Seth Thomas, clockmaker, born in Wolcott, CT; associated with Eli Terry and Silas

Hoadley; formed own company in 1812 (died 1859).

1793 Samuel G. Goodrich, author who wrote under name of Peter Parley, born in Ridgefield, CT; turned out more than 100 children's stories (some done by staff members); founder, Robert Merry's Museum (1841–50) (died 1860).

1800 James Lenox, donor of land and books to found Lenox Library in New York City (1870), born in New York City (died 1880).

1812 The *Constitution* ("Old Ironsides"), under command of Capt. Isaac Hull, destroyed British frigate *Guerriere*, off Nova Scotia.

1814 Gen. Robert Ross led a landing of British troops at Benedict, MD, about 50 miles southeast of Washington, DC.

1848 Letter published in *New York Herald* revealed discovery of gold in California.

1851 Charles E. Hires, developer of root beer, born near Bridgeton, NJ (died 1937).

1856 Gail Borden received patent for "the concentration of milk," this condensed milk was beginning of various instant foods.

1853 Henry I. Cobb, architect, born in Brookline, MA; designed Newberry Library, Chicago; Pennsylvania State Capitol; American U. buildings, Washington, DC (died 1931).

1862 *New York Tribune* published letter by Horace Greeley, the "Prayer of 20 Million," in which he said, "all attempts to put down the rebellion and at the same time uphold its inciting cause are preposterous and futile."

1870 Bernard Baruch, financier and banker, born in Camden, SC; chairman, War Industries Board (1918–19), various other boards in both World Wars; developed plan for development, control of atomic energy (died 1965).

1871 Orville Wright, aviation pioneer, born in Dayton, OH; with brother made first successful flights in motor-powered plane at Kitty Hawk, NC, December 17, 1903 (died 1948).

1873 Fred Stone, a popular comedian of his day (*The Wizard of Oz*, *Lightnin'*), born near Longmont, CO (died 1959).

1877 Tom (Thomas T.) Connolly, legislator, born in McLennan County, TX; served Texas in House (1916–28) and Senate (1928–53) (died 1963).

1878 Manuel L. Quezon, first president of Commonwealth of Philippines (1935–41), born in Luzon (died 1944).

1893 Alfred Lunt, actor who co-starred with wife, Lynn Fontanne, born in Milwaukee; among their 27 plays were *The Guardsman*, *Design for Living*, *Taming of the Shrew* (died 1977).

1902 Ogden Nash, humorous poet (*Hard Lines, I'm a Stranger Here Myself, Good Intentions, The Face Is Familiar*), born in Rye, NY (died 1971).

1903 James G. Cozzens, novelist (*Guard of Honor, By Love Possessed*), born in Chicago (died 1978).

1906 Philo T. Farnsworth, engineer who developed an early television system, born in Beaver, WA; held more than 300 patents in electronics (died 1971).

1914 President Wilson, in message to the Senate, appealed for neutrality in World War I; had proclaimed such neutrality August 4.

1919 Malcolm S. Forbes, publisher of family magazine (*Forbes*), born in New York City; also a noted balloonist (died 1990).

1931 Willie Shoemaker, jockey who won more than 7,000 horse races, born in Fabens, TX; rode in more than 24,000 races.

1946 Bill (William J.) Clinton, 42nd President (1993–), born in Hope, AR; served as Arkansas Attorney General (1976) and governor (1978–80, 1982–92).

1960 Francis Gary Powers, pilot of an American U-2 spy plane shot down over Russia (May 5, 1960), was convicted of espionage and sentenced to 10 years imprisonment.

1974 Rodger P. Davies, ambassador to Cyprus, killed by a sniper in Nicosia.

1988 Eight insolvent Texas savings and loans associations merged into one institution by Federal Home Loan Bank Board; the $2.5 billion bailout was largest in thrift industry.

1997 Strike against UPS (United Parcel Service) by the Teamsters Union settled after two weeks stoppage which cost UPS an estimated $600 million in revenue.

2000 Natural gas pipeline exploded near Carlsbad, New Mexico, killing 11 individuals.

2006 In an effort to "diversify" both geographically and racially the impact of the traditional first presidential caucus (Iowa) and primary (New Hampshire), the Democrats moved South Carolina and Nevada to the first two weeks in January of the 2008 election cycle.

20

1745 Francis Asbury, Methodist leader, born near Birmingham, England; missionary to American colonies (1771); a leader in forming American Methodist Episcopal Church (1779–84);

consecrated as superintendent (1784); assumed title of bishop (1785), ruling the church until his death in 1816.

1764 Samuel L. Mitchill, physician and educator, born in North Hempstead, NY; professor, Columbia U. (1792–1801); an organizer, vice president, Rutgers Medical College (1826–30); a founder, editor, *Medical Repository* (1797–1820); represented New York in House (1801–04, 1810–13) and Senate (1804–09) (died 1831).

1781 American and French armies set out from New York to capture Cornwallis and his British troops in Virginia.

1785 Oliver Hazard Perry, commander of American naval forces in Lake Erie which defeated British (1813), born in South Kingston, RI (died 1819).

1794 Gen. Anthony Wayne led American troops to victory over Indians in Battle of Fallen Timbers at the Maumee Rapids (near present Toledo), ending 40 years warfare with Indians in Northwest Territory.

1832 Thaddeus S.C. Lowe, pioneer aeronaut and inventor, born in what is now Riverton, NH; balloonist with meteorological interests, serving as chief of Army's aeronautics section (1861–65); invented ice machine (1865), coke oven (died 1913).

1833 Benjamin Harrison, 23rd President (1889–93), born in North Bend, OH; represented Indiana in Senate (1881–87) (died 1901).

1834 Francis R.T. Nicholls, first Louisiana governor after Reconstruction (1877), born in Donaldsonville, LA; Confederate general who lost left arm at Winchester, left foot at Chancellorsville; Louisiana chief justice (1892–1912) (died 1912).

1842 Senate ratified Webster-Ashburton Treaty settling Canadian-American boundary.

1847 Gen. Winfield Scott and his troops defeated Mexican army at Churubusco, four miles south of Mexico City; earlier in the day, they had taken Heights of Contreras.

1860 Henry T. Rainey, legislator, born near Carrollton, IL; represented Illinois in House (1902–34, except 1921–23), serving as Speaker (1933–34) (died 1934).

1861 Convention in Wheeling of pro-Union Virginians called for creating new state to be called Kanawha; ratified by popular vote of 18,862 to 514.

1866 President Andrew Johnson issued proclamation declaring the insurrection and civil war at an end.

1873 Eliel Saarinen, architect who planned development of Canberra, Australia, born in Rantasalmi, Finland; designed League of Nations in Geneva (died 1950).

1879 Ralph Budd, president of Burlington and Great Northern railroads, born in Waterloo, IA; introduced streamlined trains (died 1962).

1881 Edgar A. Guest, poet (*Home [It Takes a Heap o' Livin']*) and columnist, born in Birmingham, England; wrote daily "Breakfast Table Chat" for *Detroit Free Press* (died 1959).

1886 Paul (J.O.) Tillich, influential theologian of his time in North America, born in Starzeddel, Germany (died 1965).

1905 Jack (Weldon J.) Teagarden, noted jazz trombonist and band leader, born in Vernon, TX; played with Red Nichols, Paul Whiteman (died 1964).

1910 Eero Saarinen, noted architect, born in Kirkkonummi, Finland; designed TWA Terminal at Kennedy Airport; Dulles Airport Terminal, Washington; St. Louis Arch; Beaumont Theater in Lincoln Center (died 1961).

1913 Roger W. Sperry, psychobiologist, born in Hartford, CT; with Caltech; shared 1981 Nobel Physiology/Medicine Prize for work on determining the role played by each side of the brain (died 1994).

1924 Dawes Plan, a method of German reparation payments, adopted; plan was worked out by group of experts led by Charles G. Dawes; plan replaced by Young Plan May 17, 1930.

1974 House, without debate, voted 412–3 to accept three articles of impeachment of President Nixon recommended by its Judiciary Committee.

1988 Federal jury in New York ruled that the Hunt brothers — Nelson Bunker, William H., and Lamar — conspired in attempt to corner world silver market a decade ago; ordered to pay more than $130 million in damages to Minpeco, S.A.

1991 Hurricane Bob hit the Eastern seaboard, killing two; cut power to millions of homes and businesses; caused flooding from North Carolina to Maine.

1996 An increase in the minimum wage from $4.25 to $4.75 an hour was enacted, effective October 1; wage would again be increased September 1, 1997 to $5.15 an hour.

2003 Computer sex-offender database loophole documented: California reported that of 80,746 individuals on list, some 23,000 had addresses a year or more out-of-date; 14,000 had five-year-old addresses; convicted had not updated their location when they moved.

2006 Pulitzer prize-winning Associated Press photographer Joe Rosenthal died at 94; produced one of the most remembered World War II photographs: raising of U.S. flag on Iwo Jima.

21

1783 Thomas Garrett, wealthy abolitionist, born in Upper Darby, PA; in 40 years, helped about 300 runaway slaves escape; blacks in Wilmington, where he lived, called him "our Moses" (died 1871).

1796 Asher B. Durand, cofounder of Hudson River School of landscape painting, born near Newark, NJ; cofounder, National Academy of Design (died 1886).

1796 James Lick, philanthropist, born in Fredericksburg, PA; gave $700,000 for a "powerful telescope, superior to and more powerful than any telescope ever yet made"; it became basis for Lick Observatory on Mt. Hamilton, CA (died 1876).

1822 John Fritz, who helped revolutionize American steel industry, born in Chester, PA; general superintendent, chief engineer, Bethlehem Steel Co. (died 1913).

1831 Slave insurrection, led by Nat Turner in Southampton County, VA, resulted in massacre of 55 whites and eventually more stringent laws for slaves.

1843 William Pepper, physician who founded first American teaching hospital (1874), nursing school, born in Philadelphia; with U. of Pennsylvania Medical School (1868–94); provost, U. of Pennsylvania (1880–94); a founder, Wharton School of Finance, Philadelphia Free Library (died 1898).

1854 Frank A. Munsey, founder, publisher, *Argosy Magazine* (1896), *Munsey's Magazine* (1899), born in Mercer, ME; at one time, owned *New York Sun, New York Telegram* (died 1925).

1858 Lincoln-Douglas debates began in Ottawa, IL, with about 12,000 on hand; continued to October 15 in seven Illinois cities — Ottawa, Freeport, Jonesboro, Charleston, Galesburg, Quincy, and Alton.

1863 Civil War in Missouri and Kansas culminated with raid on Lawrence, KS, when a band led by a Confederate guerilla captain, William C. Quantrill, killed 150 men and wounded 30 others in what has been called "the most atrocious act of the Civil War."

1865 Convention in Jackson, MS, adopted ordinance outlawing slavery.

1878 American Bar Association organized in Saratoga, NY.

1896 Roark Bradford, author (*Old Man Adam an' His Children, John Henry*), born in Lauderdale County, TN; his *Old Man Adam* was adapted into play *Green Pastures* (died 1948).

1904 Count (William) Basie, pianist and orchestra leader, born in Red Bank, NJ; led orchestra for more than 40 years (died 1984).

1917 President Wilson fixed price of bituminous coal, then two days later, anthracite; named Harry A. Garfield fuel administrator.

1928 Commerce Secretary Herbert C. Hoover resigned to run for president.

1936 Wilt(on) Chamberlain, basketball player who scored 31,491 points, born in Philadelphia; starred with San Francisco, Philadelphia, Los Angeles; averaged 30.1 points per game in his career.

1938 Kenny Rogers, country music singer, born in Houston; sang with several groups (New Christy Minstrels, First Edition) before becoming soloist.

1944 Dumbarton Oaks Conference opened in Washington, DC, to draw up basic proposals for a postwar organization to succeed the League of Nations.

1945 Executive order by President Truman terminated Lend-Lease program, which in five years supplied $50.6 billion in aid to foreign nations.

1959 Hawaii became 50th state.

1974 President Ford nominated Nelson Rockefeller for appointment to the vacant vice presidency.

1996 President Clinton signed bill which would allow workers who changed jobs to maintain their insurance.

2000 San Francisco, California, became the 51st locality in the nation to require a higher minimum wage than that set by the federal government: $9 initially, to rise in a year to $10.

22

1607 Bartholomew Gosnold, explorer and colonizer, died of malaria in Jamestown, VA, at about 37; explored New England coast, naming Cape Cod, Martha's Vineyard (after his daughter); vice admiral of fleet which settled Jamestown, a site he opposed.

1777 British Gen. Barry St. Leger, hearing that an American force under Benedict Arnold was on the way to relieve Ft. Stanwix, retreated to Oswego and eventually Montreal, leaving stores and weapons and Gen. Burgoyne without help.

1778 James K. Paulding, author of humorous pieces and defense against English criticism, born in Putnam County, NY; Secretary of Navy (1838–41) (died 1860).

1787 John Fitch successfully launched his first steamboat on the Delaware River, with members of the Constitutional Convention looking on.

1802 John I. Blair, a founder, Delaware, Lackawanna and Western, and Union Pacific railroads, born near Belvidere, NJ; at one time was president of 16 lines (died 1899).

1807 Aaron Burr tried in Richmond on charges of having levied war against the United States and planning to invade Mexico; acquitted September 1.

1814 Joshua Barney's flotilla of boats on the Patuxent River was unable to stop the British fleet nearing Washington.

1834 Samuel P. Langley, aeronautical pioneer, born in Roxbury, MA; secretary, Smithsonian Institution (1887–1906); experimented with heavier-than-air aircraft, constructed models which successfully flew 3,000 and 4,200 ft. (1896), the first flights of mechanically-propelled heavier-than-air machines (died 1906).

1848 Ulysses S. Grant and Julia Boggs were married in St. Louis.

1848 Melville S. Stone, founder, owner, *Chicago Daily News* (1875–88), born in Hudson, IL; general manager, Illinois Associated Press (1893), national manager (1900–23) (died 1929).

1851 Yacht *America* won cup offered by the Royal Yacht Society of England in a race around the Isle of Wight; cup was presented to New York Yacht Club; this was first of the America's Cup races.

1864 Robert L. Howze, Army commander of 38th Division in France (1918), born in Overton, TX; commanded Army of Occupation in Germany (1918–19); also served in Spanish-American War (died 1926).

1867 Charles F. Jenkins, inventor of motion picture projector (1895), born near Dayton, OH; also invented a conical paper cup, an early automobile starter, many other devices (died 1934).

1868 Ernest R. Graham, architect, born in Lowell, MI; designed Equitable and Flatiron buildings, New York City; Union Station, Washington; Field Museum and Wrigley Building, Chicago (died 1936).

1868 Willis R. Whitney, General Electric

Research Laboratory director (1900–28), GE vice president of research (1928–41), born in Jamestown, NY (died 1958).

1878 Edward Johnson, director, Metropolitan Opera House (1935–50), born in Guelph, Canada (died 1959).

1893 Dorothy Parker, author and poet (*Enough Rope, Not So Deep as a Well, Here Lies, Sunset Guns*), born in West End, NJ (died 1967).

1893 Tropical storm began an eight-day move from the Caribbean up the East Coast, killing 1,000 persons; Charleston, SC, severely damaged.

1920 Denton A. Cooley, heart surgeon who was a founder of Texas Heart Institute, born in Houston.

1920 Ray D. Bradbury, science fiction author (*The Martian Chronicles, The Illustrated Man, Fahrenheit 451*), born in Waukegan, IL.

1934 H. Norman Schwartzkopf, commanding general, Desert Storm operation, born in Trenton, NJ.

1978 Congress passed constitutional amendment to give District of Columbia full voting rights in Congress; requires ratification by three-fourths of state legislatures.

1996 Congressional legislation to reform welfare signed by President Clinton; states would establish own welfare programs using federal grants.

1997 Federal official ordered new election of Teamsters Union president because more than $220,000 in illegal contributions were used in electing Ron Carey in December 1996.

1998 Tropical Storm Charley lashed parts of Texas for two days; resulted in much damage, 20 deaths.

2005 In three separate California Supreme Court decisions, court expanded gay rights by ruling that same-sex couples are entitled to the same rights and obligations after separation as heterosexual couples in regard to children born during their period of being together.

23

1751 John Fenno, founder, editor, Gazette of the United States (1789–98), born in Boston (died 1798).

1761 Jedidiah Morse, considered father of American geography, born in Woodstock, CT; pastor, First Congregational Church, Charlestown, MA (1789–1819); author of first American geography book (*Geography Made Easy*), which went into 25 editions; also wrote *Elements of Geography* and *American Gazeteer* (died 1826).

1775 King George III issued proclamation declaring American colonies in rebellion and ordered suppression of the rebellion.

1826 Francis Wayland, dean of Yale Law School (1873–1903), born in Boston (died 1904).

1843 Mexican President Santa Anna notified United States that Mexico would "consider equivalent to a declaration of war against the Mexican Republic the passage of an act of the incorporation of Texas in the territory of the United States."

1869 Edgar Lee Masters, author (*The Spoon River Anthology*), born in Garnett, KS (died 1950).

1879 The Church of Christ, Scientist, chartered by Mary Baker Eddy.

1883 Jonathan M. Wainwright, World War II general, born in Walla Walla, WA; defended Bataan, Corregidor and became Japanese prisoner (1942–45) (died 1953).

1887 Alvin Hansen, considered greatest economist of New Deal, born in Viborg, SD (died 1975).

1888 Morris L. Ernst, general counsel, American Civil Liberties Union (1929–54), born in Uniontown, AL; successful in getting release of James Joyce's *Ulysses* for American publication (died 1976).

1890 Aubrey W. Williams, executive director, NYA (National Youth Administration) (1935–43), born in Springville, AL (died 1965).

1905 Ernie Bushmiller, cartoonist (*Nancy*), born in New York City (died 1982).

1912 Gene Kelly, dancer and screen actor (*Cover Girl, On the Town, Singing in the Rain*), born in Pittsburgh (died 1996).

1921 Kenneth J. Arrow, economist, born in New York City; shared 1972 Nobel Economics Prize for work on theory of general economic equilibrium.

1921 Charles Lee Brown, president (1977–78), chairman (1979 on), American Telephone & Telegraph, born in Richmond, VA; reorganized ATT after court-ordered divestiture of the Bell companies.

1924 Robert M. Solow, economist who was awarded 1987 Nobel Economics Prize, born in New York City.

1926 Rudolph Valentino, silent screen idol, died in New York City at 31.

1927 Niccola Sacco and Bartolomeo Vanzetti were executed in Charlestown, MA, for alleged killing of two men in a Massachusetts payroll holdup despite six-year worldwide campaign for their release; vindicated July 19, 1977, by a proclamation of the Massachusetts governor.

1931 Hamilton O. Smith, microbiologist, born in New York City; shared 1978 Nobel Physiology/Medicine Prize for studies of the specificity of restriction enzymes.

1944 French troops recaptured Marseilles.

1982 Environmental Protection Agency proposed new rules to reduce lead in gasoline at a faster rate than had been scheduled.

1988 President Reagan signed landmark trade bill designed to battle trade deficit by streamlining the machinery for imposing import curbs and expanding job training.

1996 President Clinton approved regulations aimed at curbing the sale of tobacco products to young people.

1997 John C. Kendrew, biochemist who shared 1962 Nobel Chemistry Prize, died at 80.

2001 In order to avoid violating existing treaties, President Bush announced intention to eventually withdraw from 1972 antiballistic missile agreement.

2004 University of California at Berkeley rated number one state-run college; ranked 21st in combined public-private institution list.

24

1624 Sir Francis Wyatt, who had been Virginia governor under the London company, was named the first royal governor by James I, serving for two years, then again 1639–41.

1706 Charleston, SC, withstood attack by French and Spanish privateers.

1795 James W. Wallack, Shakespearian actor and cofounder of Wallack's Theater in New York City, born in London (died 1864).

1810 Theodore Parker, Unitarian clergyman and a leader in antislavery agitation, born in Lexington, MA; his liberality led him to found new Congregational Society; was member of secret committee aiding John Brown's raid on Harpers Ferry (died 1860).

1814 Gen. Robert Ross led 4,500 British troops over 6,000 American militia under Gen. William Winder at Bladensburg, MD; British went on the next day to burn the Capitol, White House, and Library of Congress in Washington in retaliation for burning of York (Toronto) April 27, 1813.

1823 John Newton, Union general who served in most major engagements, born in Norfolk, VA; chief, Army Engineers (1884–86); New York City public works commissioner (1886–88); president, Panama Railroad Co. (1888–95) (died 1895).

1835 Lyman R. Blake, inventor of a form of shoe that could be sewn and machine to sew soles on uppers, born in South Abington, MA (died 1883).

1846 Henry Gannett, known as father of American mapmaking, born in Bath, ME; headed, U.S. Board of Geographical Names (1890–1910); a founder, National Geographic Society (died 1914).

1847 Charles F. McKim, architect, born in Chester County, PA; designer, Boston Public Library, old Madison Square Garden, Penn Station, White House restoration (died 1909).

1848 Fire aboard liner *Ocean Monarch* off coast of Wales killed 200 Americans.

1857 Panic of 1857 began when New York City branch of Ohio Life Insurance & Trust Co. of Cincinnati failed; over speculation in wheat belt real estate and railroad construction triggered the 18-month depression.

1886 William F. Gibbs, director of mass production of American cargo ships in World War II, born in Philadelphia (died 1967).

1890 Duke Kahanamoku, best swimmer in world between 1912 and 1928, born in Honolulu; held every record in distances up to a half mile (died 1968).

1895 Richard J. Cushing, Catholic Archbishop of Boston (1944–70), born in Boston; was world's youngest archbishop at the time of his elevation (died 1970).

1898 Albert Claude, microbiologist, born in Luxembourg; shared 1974 Nobel Physiology/Medicine Prize for fundamental discoveries in anatomy of cells; developed centrifuge method for separating cells (died 1983).

1898 Malcolm Cowley, American literary critic and author (*Exile's Return, Think Back on Us*), born in Belsano, PA (died 1989).

1912 Panama Canal Act passed, exempting vessels of American coast-wise trade from payment of canal tolls; protested by Great Britain; President Wilson asked for and received change eliminating the exemption.

1912 Congress created domestic parcel post system.

1921 Peace treaty with Austria signed in Vienna.

1925 Shirley Hufstedler, first Secretary of Education (1979–81), born in Denver; was a California jurist.

1949 North Atlantic Treaty Organization (NATO) established, agreeing that "an armed attack against one or more of them shall be considered an attack against them all"; countries included United States, Canada, and 10 European nations.

1954 Congress passed the Communist Control Act which outlawed the Communist Party; signed by President Eisenhower.

1960 Cal(vin E.) Ripken, Jr., Baltimore baseball player who set new consecutive game record, born in Havre de Grace, MD; in 1995, he broke Lou Gehrig's long-standing record of 2,130 consecutive games.

1989 Dow Jones industrial average reached record high of 2734.64.

1989 *Voyager 2* spacecraft passed the planet Neptune 3,048 miles above its north pole after a 12-year 4.4 billion miles journey.

1989 Under an agreement between Pete Rose and the baseball commissioner, Rose was permanently banished from baseball, pending an appeal after one year; Rose had been accused of betting on baseball but the agreement stated Rose would not be found formally guilty of betting.

1992 Hurricane Andrew struck the Bahamas, South Florida, and the Gulf Coast; storm killed about 20 persons; Homestead Air Force Base was destroyed, $1 billion worth of crops were damaged, and total estimated damage was about $15 billion.

2000 Vicente Fox, president-elect of Mexico, visited U.S. and argued that the Mexican-American border should be considered only a line on a map; Vice President Al Gore reported as regarding the idea as "clearly problematic."

2000 Unanimous California Supreme Court put sharp restrictions on right of companies to require arbitration of disputes with employees; when arbitration does occur company must pay all costs and employees must be able to gain same monetary damages as if they had sued.

2004 EPA reported mercury-contaminated fish now found in all states except Alaska and Wyoming; a rise from 44 states in first such study in 1993.

25

1540 Hernando de Alarcon, Spanish explorer who sailed up the Gulf of California, arrived in the Colorado River and proceeded to approximately the junction of the Gila, Williams, and Colorado rivers.

1783 Samuel C. Reid, designer of present American flag, born in Norwich, CT; a War of 1812 naval officer, he and his wife made flag which first flew over the Capitol April 12, 1818 (died 1861).

1799 Andrew J. Donelson, aide and secretary to President Jackson, born near Nashville; reared at the Hermitage by Jackson; negotiated treaty of annexation with Texas Republic (1844–45), minister to Prussia (1846–49); vice presidential candidate (1856) (died 1871).

1819 Allan Pinkerton, founder of first American private detective agency in Chicago (1850), born in Glasgow; guarded President-elect Lincoln on trip to Washington inauguration; organized Secret Service (1861–62); prominent in lessening disorders in union strikes (died 1884).

1822 Gardiner G. Hubbard, founder, first president, National Geographic Society (1888–97), born in Boston; a principal backer of Alexander Graham Bell, a developer of commercial telephone use; a founder, *Science* (1883) (died 1897).

1825 Henry W. Birge, Union general at Port Hudson and Red River campaigns, born in Hartford, CT (died 1888).

1828 Robert Trimble, associate justice, Supreme Court (1817–28), died at 51.

1836 Bret (Francis Bret) Harte, author (*The Luck of Roaring Camp, The Outcasts of Poker Flat*), born in Albany, NY (died 1902).

1837 Calvin M. Woodward, pioneer in manual training high school development (St. Louis 1880), born in Fitchburg, MA (died 1914).

1850 Bill (Edgar W.) Nye, writer of humorous articles for *Laramie* (WY) *Boomerang* and *New York World*, born in Shirley, ME (died 1896).

1862 William C. Proctor, president of Proctor & Gamble (1907–34), born in Glendale, OH; one of first to give employees half day off on Saturdays, provided profit-sharing (died 1934).

1867 James W. Gerard, ambassador to Germany (1913–17), born in Geneseo, NY (died 1951).

1880 Joshua L. Cowen, inventor of toy electric train (1900), born in New York City; headed Lionel Corp. (1940–65) (died 1965).

1912 Ted Key, cartoonist (*Hazel*), born in Fresno, CA.

1913 Walter C. Kelly, cartoonist (*Pogo*), born in Philadelphia.

1916 Frederic C. Robbins, microbiologist, born in Auburn, AL; shared 1954 Nobel Physiology/Medicine Prize for his work on polio virus.

1916 National Park Service established in the Interior Department.

1918 Leonard Bernstein, composer and conductor, born in Lawrence, MA; compositions include *Candide, On the Town, West Side Story* and various symphonies, operas, ballets; conductor, New York Philharmonic (1958–69) (died 1990).

1919 George C. Wallace, Alabama governor (1962–66, 1970–78, 1983–87), born in Clio, AL; presidential candidate of American Independent Party (1972); shot and paralyzed at rally near Washington, DC (died 1998).

1921 Peace treaty with Germany signed in Berlin formally ending World War I as of July 2.

1927 Althea Gibson, first black woman tennis player to win singles, doubles at Wimbledon, Forest Hills (1957–58), born in Silver, SC.

1930 Sean Connery, actor in James Bond movies, born in Edinburg, Scotland.

1931 Cecil D. Andrus, Interior Secretary (1977–81), born in Hood River, OR; governor of Idaho (1970–77, 1987–95).

1944 Allied troops entered Paris.

1954 Hurricane Carol swept East Coast for six days, killing 68, causing $500 million in property damage.

1958 Congress provided pensions of $10,000 to presidential widows (increased to $20,000 in 1971), to presidents $25,000 and up to $50,000 for office space, help (raised to $69,630 and $96,000).

1967 George Lincoln Rockwell, leader of American Nazi Party, was shot to death by another party member in Arlington, VA.

1981 *Voyager 2*, an unmanned spacecraft, transmitted pictures of Saturn as it passed within 63,000 miles of the planet.

1997 Florida became second state (after Mississippi) to settle its liability suit against five tobacco companies, which agreed to pay state $11.3 billion to cover health costs related to tobacco use.

2000 Carl Banks died at 99; veteran comic book illustrator for Disney Company and inventor of Scrooge McDuck.

2004 White House report to Congress shifted blame for any global warming to human-produced sources; in past had stressed difficulty in putting primary blame on any one cause.

26

1765 Agitation over the forthcoming Stamp Act resulted in raid in Boston in which records of vice-admiralty court were burned; the home of currency comptroller was ransacked, and home and library of Chief Justice Thomas Hutchinson was looted.

1784 Stephen McCormick, inventor of a cast-iron plow with detachable parts, born in Auburn, VA (died 1875).

1791 John Fitch received patent for steamboat on which he had been working since 1785; launched successfully 1787.

1817 U. of Michigan established in Detroit by state legislature.

1818 Illinois adopted its state constitution at a convention in Kaskaskia; included a clause prohibiting slavery.

1835 An address developed by a committee of the Democratic nomination in Baltimore was published in *Washington Globe*, which was equivalent of party's first platform.

1842 Start of federal fiscal year changed from January 1 to July 1.

1844 John W. Burgess, educator called father of American political science, born in Cornersville, TN; with Columbia U. (1890–1912) (died 1931).

1857 National Teachers Association organized in Philadelphia; became National Education Association in 1870.

1867 Robert W. Moton, educator who succeeded Booker T. Washington as head of Tuskegee Institute (1915–35), born in Amelia County, VA; head, Hampton Institute, VA (1890–1915) (died 1940).

1872 James Couzens, general manager, Ford Motor Co. (1903–15), born in Chatham, Canada; mayor of Detroit (1919–22); represented Michigan in Senate (1922–36); endowed Michigan Children's Fund with $12 million (died 1936).

1872 Joseph T. Robinson, Arkansas governor (1913) and served it in House (1903–13) and Senate (1913–37), born in Lonoke, AR; Democratic vice presidential candidate (1928) (died 1937).

1873 Lee DeForest, electrical engineer sometimes called father of radio, born in Council Bluffs, IA; had more than 300 inventions, including triode electron tube; made many contributions to wireless communication; installed first high-powered Navy radio station; exhibited sound movies (1923) (died 1961).

1874 Zona Gale, author (*Miss Lulu Bett, Faint Perfume*), born in Portage, WI (died 1938).

1882 James Franck, physicist and biochemist, born in Hamburg, Germany; shared 1925 Nobel Physics Prize for discovery of laws governing impact of electrons on atoms (died 1964).

1884 Earl Derr Biggers, author of Charlie Chan stories and *Seven Keys to Baldpate*, born in Warren, OH (died 1933).

1886 Jerome C. Hunsaker, organizer of first American aeronautical college course (MIT 1914), born in Creston, IA; designed NC-4 flying boat which flew the Atlantic (1919) (died 1984).

1901 Maxwell D. Taylor, World War II commander of 101st Airborne Division, born in Keytesville, MO; chairman, Joint Chiefs of Staff (1962–64); ambassador to South Vietnam (1964–65) (died 1987).

1904 Christopher Isherwood, author of Berlin stories which formed basis for play, *Cabaret*, born in Cheshire, England (died 1986).

1906 Albert B. Sabin, developer of vaccine for polio prevention, born in Bialystok, Russia; his attenuated virus vaccine (1959) used widely through world (died 1993).

1913 Keokuk Dam, largest dam in world, opened across Mississippi River.

1921 Ben(jamin C.) Bradlee, executive editor, *Washington Post* (1968–91), born in Boston.

1935 Geraldine A. Ferraro, first woman major party national candidate (Democratic 1984 Vice Presidential candidate), born in Newburgh, NY; represented New York in House.

1935 United Auto Workers, meeting in its first convention, chartered by AFL.

1942 Wendell Willkie began his round-the-world fact-finding tour as a presidential special envoy.

1988 Federal jury in Newark, NJ, acquitted 20 reputed mob figures of racketeering charges ending what may be the nation's longest federal criminal trial — 21 months.

1998 Frederick Reins, who shared in the 1995 Nobel Physics Prize, died at 80.

2001 U.S. surgeon general Dr. David Satcher released study indicating "striking disparities" in availability of mental health assistance to ethnic/racial minorities; language barrier and cultural stereotypes (both positive and negative) often get in way.

2004 Private survey of government secrecy practices indicated that over 14 million documents classified in 2003 (no figures available from CIA), while 43.1 million were declassified — a drastic increase in documents prohibited to the public and major decrease in those released.

2004 U.S. Census reported that 45 million Americans lacked health insurance; the new high pushed percentage of uncovered to 15.6 percent.

27

1637 Charles Calvert, governor of Maryland (1661–75), born in London; proprietor of colony (1675–1715) (died 1715).

1640 Henry Dunster chosen first president of Harvard College just three weeks after arriving from England, where he had been curate of Bury.

1640 Plantation agreement drawn up by inhabitants of Providence, in which they covenanted, among other things, "to hould forth liberty of conscience."

1741 Joseph Reed, colonial leader, born in Trenton, NJ; served George Washington as military secretary; member, Continental Congress (1777–78); president, Pennsylvania supreme executive council (1778–81) (died 1785).

1749 James Madison, president, College of William & Mary (1777–1812), born near Staunton, VA; first Episcopal bishop of Virginia (1790) (died 1812).

1776 Convention in New Castle adopted name of Delaware State, chose Dover as its capital, and adopted a constitution, effective September 21, 1776.

1776 In Battle of Long Island, a large British force routed Americans, inflicting 1,500 casualties on 5,000-man force; Americans withdrew while British were preparing for siege of Brooklyn Heights.

1796 Sophia Smith, endowed Smith College in Northampton, MA, born in Hatfield, MA; bequeathed inherited fortune to found college (opened 1875) (died 1870).

1805 Sallie Chapman Law, known as the mother of the Confederacy, born in Wilkes County, NC; organized, managed hospitals in South during Civil War (died 1894).

1809 Hannibal Hamlin, Vice President (1861–65), born in Paris Hill, ME; represented Maine in House (1843–47) and Senate (1848–61, 1869–81) and served state as governor (1857); minister to Spain (1881–82) (died 1891).

1824 Hiram G. Berry, Union general who was killed at Chancellorsville May 3, 1863, born in Rockland, ME.

1832 Black Hawk was surrendered by Winnebago Indians, with whom he had taken refuge, to the Indian agency at Prairie du Chien, WI, ending brief Black Hawk War.

1839 Emory Upton, Union general who served in Tennessee, Alabama, and Georgia, born near Batavia, NY; wrote on military tactics and history (died 1881).

1845 Texas convention approved state constitution; ratified by voters October 13.

1857 James J. Keane, Catholic Archbishop of Dubuque, IA (1911–29), born in Joliet, IL (died 1929).

1858 Second Lincoln-Douglas debate held in Freeport, IL, and featured statement by Douglas that slavery could be introduced or excluded by the people of an area.

1859 World's first commercially-productive oil well drilled by Edwin L. Drake at Titusville, PA; struck oil at 69½ ft., producing about 25 barrels a day.

1864 John Buchanan published first newspaper in Montana, *Montana Post*, in Virginia City.

1865 James H. Breasted, archaeologist and a leading Orientalist, born in Rockford, IL; with U. of Chicago (1894–1935), led numerous expeditions to Egypt and Mesopotamia (died 1935).

1865 Charles G. Dawes, Vice President (1925–29), born in Marietta, OH; Comptroller of Currency (1897–1901); first American budget director (1921); developed plan for German reparation payments after World War I; ambassador to Great Britain (1929–32); chairman, Reconstruction Finance Corp. (RFC) (1932); shared 1925 Nobel Peace Prize (died 1951).

1871 Theodore Dreiser, novelist (*Sister Carrie*, *An American Tragedy*, *The Titan*, *The Genius*), born in Terre Haute, IN (died 1945).

1876 Eugene G. Grace, Bethlehem Steel president (1913–46), chairman (1946–48), born in Goshen, NJ (died 1960).

1877 Lloyd C. Douglas, novelist (*The Magnificent Obsession*, *White Banners*, *The Robe*) born in Columbia City, IN (died 1951).

1882 Samuel Goldwyn, movie producer who helped form Metro-Goldwyn-Mayer (MGM), born in Warsaw, Poland; an independent producer for many years (died 1974).

1890 Man Ray, painter and photographer, born in Philadelphia as Emmanuel Radinski; cofounder of "da-da" group; developed rayograph ("cameraless photography" — objects placed on photographic paper, then exposed) (died 1976).

1908 Lyndon B. Johnson, 36th President

(1963–69), born near Stonewall, TX; represented Texas in House (1937–49) and Senate (1949–61); Vice President (1961–63), succeeding to presidency on death of President Kennedy (died 1973).

1913 Martin A. Kamen, biochemist who discovered carbon-14 isotope, born in Toronto; the isotope is a basic tool in biochemical, archaeological research.

1915 Walter Heller, chairman, Council of Economic Advisors (1961–64), born in Buffalo, NY (died 1987).

1915 Norman F. Ramsey, Harvard U. physicist who shared 1989 Nobel Physics Prize, born in Washington, DC.

1917 President Wilson replied to August 1 note from Pope, rejecting the peace overture because negotiations were worthless until a German people's government was created.

1929 Ira Levin, novelist (*Rosemary's Baby*, *The Boys from Brazil*), born in New York City; also playwright (*No Time for Sergeants*).

1935 Federal Theater Project organized under the Works Progress Administration to provide employment for theater artists.

1950 President Truman ordered Army to seize the railroads to prevent a general strike; roads were returned to private owners in 1952.

1975 Ohio Gov. James Rhodes and 27 Ohio National Guardsmen were exonerated of blame in shooting 13 Kent State students, four of whom died, in a May 1970 anti–Vietnam demonstration.

1988 More than 50,000 marchers reenacted the Rev. Martin Luther King, Jr., march with 150,000 civil rights activists 25 years ago in Washington, DC.

1996 Democratic national convention in Chicago nominated President Clinton and Vice President Gore for re-election.

2002 Report showed reversal of past pattern: In 1980 143,000 black males in jail/prison and 463,700 in college ; in 2000 those imprisoned outnumbered those in university studies by 791,600 to 603,032. Imprisoned category, however, covers a wider age range than that in higher education.

28

1565 Spanish settlers under Pedro Menéndes des Avilés landed at St. Augustine, FL; city founded September 8.

1609 Henry Hudson in the *Half Moon*, searching for the Northwest Passage, anchored in Delaware Bay.

1728 John Stark, Revolutionary War general, born in Londonderry, NH; served at Bunker Hill, Trenton, Princeton; led troops to victory at Bennington, VT (died 1822).

1774 Elizabeth Ann Seton, first American-born Catholic saint, born in New York City; founder, first superior, Sisters of Charity (1809–21); founder, St. Joseph's College, Emmettsburg, MD; canonized 1975 (died 1821).

1818 Jean Baptiste Point duSable, Haitian-born pioneer called the father of Chicago, died at about 73; built first house on Chicago site, opened first trading post in 1770s.

1823 James Oliver, inventor of process to make hard-faced plows, born in Liddesdale, Scotland; headed plow works (1869–1908) (died 1908).

1830 Locomotive *Tom Thumb*, built by Peter Cooper, tested on the Baltimore & Ohio Railroad.

1831 Lucy W. Webb Hayes, wife of President Hayes, born in Chillicothe, OH (died 1889).

1841 Bernhard Listemann, violinist who founded (1875) club which developed into Boston Philharmonic Orchestra, born in Schlotheim, Germany; concertmaster, Boston Symphony Orchestra (1881–85) (died 1917).

1861 Combined Union land and sea attack on Forts Clark and Hatteras on North Carolina coast resulted in Union takeover.

1862 Irving Hale, World War I general who founded Veterans of Foreign Wars (VFW), born in North Bloomfield, NY (died 1930).

1867 Midway Islands occupied in the name of United States by Capt. William Reynolds of the USS *Lackawanna*.

1878 George H. Whipple, first dean, U. of Rochester Medical School, born in Ashland, NH; shared 1934 Nobel Physiology/Medicine Prize for discovery of liver therapy against anemia (died 1976).

1893 Joseph T. McNarney, commander of American forces in Europe and military governor of Germany (1945–47), born in Emporium, PA; deputy supreme commander, Mediterranean area in World War II (died 1972).

1897 Louis Wirth, sociologist who pioneered in urban problems, born in Gemünden, Germany (died 1952).

1899 Charles Boyer, movie actor who starred in many films (*Algiers, Gaslight, Arch of Triumph*), born in Figeac, France (died 1978).

1908 Roger T. Peterson, ornithologist who wrote many bird field guides, born in Jamestown, NY (died 1996).

1910 Tjalling C. Koopmans, Yale economist, born in s'Graveland, Netherlands; shared 1975 Nobel Economics Prize for work in mathematics as it bears on production efficiency (died 1985).

1914 Richard Tucker, operatic tenor (*Aida, Pagliacci, La Boheme*), born in New York City; with Metropolitan Opera (1945–75) (died 1975).

1963 About 200,000 persons demonstrated peacefully in Washington to support blacks' demands for equal rights; highlight of event was speech by the Rev. Martin Luther King, Jr.—"I have a dream that this nation will rise up and live out the true meaning of its creed—'We hold these rights to be self-evident; that all men are created equal.'"

1964 Ten days of race rioting broke out in Philadelphia; more than 500 persons were injured, 350 arrested.

1988 Nearly 70 persons were killed or died later of injuries when three Italian Air Force jets collided during air show at U.S. Air Force Base in West Germany.

1994 Viacom Inc. agreed to sell Madison Square Garden and New York Knicks and Rangers teams to partnership of Cablevision Systems and ITT corporations for $1.075 billion.

1995 Chase Manhattan and Chemical Banking corporations announced merger in deal valued at $10 billion.

1997 California began to enforce anti-affirmative action measure approved by voters; bars state from race or gender-based preferences in school admissions, public hiring, and contracting.

2000 The Anti-Defamation League rebuked Sen. Joseph Lieberman, Democratic vice presidential candidate and a Jew, for his "overt expressions" of faith and labeled his language as "contrary to the American ideal."

2005 Livermore National Laboratory proud of its recent acquisition of BlueGene/L, world's fastest computer: 360 trillion calculations a second.

29

1629 Administration of Massachusetts Bay Co. transferred from England to America; John Winthrop chosen governor of colony in October.

1776 Men of John Glover's "amphibious" force ferried 9,000 men from Long Island, where they were under British fire, across the East River to New York City.

1779 American expedition led by Gens. John Sullivan and James Clinton defeated force of 1,500 Tories and Indians at Newtown, NY (near present Elmira), ending raids on western Pennsylvania and New York settlements.

1780 Richard Rush, public official and diplomat, born in Philadelphia; Comptroller of Treasury (1811–14), Attorney General (1814–17), Secretary of State (1817), Treasury Secretary (1825–29); minister to Great Britain (1817–25), to France (1847–49) (died 1859).

1802 John Galloway, lawyer who opposed efforts at independence, died at 72; unsuccessful in first Continental Congress to create imperial legislature, rather than independence; went to England, spokesman for Loyalists.

1809 Oliver Wendell Holmes, author and poet, born in Cambridge, MA; wrote *The Autocrat of the Breakfast Table* and several well-known poems (*The Chambered Nautilus, Old Ironsides, Last Leaf*) (died 1894).

1811 Henry Bergh, founder of SPCA (American Society for Prevention of Cruelty to Animals) (1866), born in New York City; headed SPCA (1866–88); also a founder American Society for Prevention of Cruelty to Children (1875) (died 1888).

1814 Alexandria, VA, saved from destruction by British fleet by paying more than $100,000 worth of tobacco, naval stores, and merchandise.

1829 Patrick A. Feehan, first Catholic Archbishop of Chicago (1880–1902), born in County Tipperary, Ireland; Bishop of Nashville (1865–80) (died 1902).

1857 Charles J. Glidden, developed world's first telephone exchange (Lowell, MA 1877), born in Lowell; his system developed rapidly, sold it to Bell; also interested in automobiles, aviation (died 1927).

1862 Second two-day Battle of Bull Run began and Union troops under Gen. John Pope withdrew to Washington, with losses of 14,000; Confederates under Gen. Stonewall Jackson lost 9,100; Union Gen. Philip Kearny killed in the battle.

1876 Charles F. Kettering, developer of automobile self-starter, born near Loudonville, OH; helped form what is now Delco; president, General Motors Research Corp. (1920–47) (died 1958).

1899 Lyman L. Lemnitzer, World War II general who headed American, UN forces in Far East (1955–57), born in Honesdale, PA; chairman, Joint Chiefs of Staff (1960–63); supreme commander, NATO forces (1963–69) (died 1988).

1899 George V. Denny, Jr., moderator of "Town Meeting of the Air" (1932–52), born in Washington, NC (died 1959).

1915 Ingrid Bergman, screen actress (*Casablanca, Intermezzo, Joan of Arc, Gaslight*), born in Stockholm (died 1982).

1916 Organic Act of the Philippine Islands passed, greatly enlarging self-government, promised independence as soon as stable government organized.

1920 Charlie Parker, a founder of "bop" music and its leading exponent, born in Kansas City, KS; a jazz saxophonist and composer (died 1955).

1921 Peace treaty signed with Hungary in Budapest declaring World War ended July 2.

1924 Dinah Washington, jazz blues singer known as queen of the blues, born in Tuscaloosa, AL (died 1963).

1935 Railroad Retirement Board created to administer railroad retirement and unemployment insurance programs.

1935 "Labor Day storm" in southern Florida began, lasting nearly two weeks, with 40 persons killed; winds were estimated at 150–200 mph over Florida Keys.

1938 Peter Jennings, ABC television news anchor (from 1983), born in Toronto.

1958 Michael Jackson, one of most popular singers/entertainers of early 1980s, born in Gary, IN.

1960 Hurricane Donna began, raking entire Eastern Seaboard with 140 mph winds for nearly two weeks; caused 148 deaths.

1986 Three Lutheran bodies approved plan to merge into one denomination — the Evangelical Lutheran Church in America — on January 1, 1988; merger involves Lutheran Church in America, American Lutheran Church, and Association of Evangelical Lutheran churches.

2000 Center for Medicinal Cannabis Research announced it will be funded by $3 million from State of California to scientifically investigate the possible medical benefits of marijuana usage.

2002 Verifying decades-long suspicion of its presence, divers accidentally discovered Japanese miniature sub sunk at Pearl Harbor on December 7, 1941.

2004 New York City assembled unprecedented large police and associated forces to assure Republican National Convention not disrupted by demonstrators or terrorists; 10,000 police directly involved with 27,000 in reserve.

2005 Decreasing from a dread category 5 status to a category 3, Hurricane Katrina made landfall in Louisiana and Mississippi and inflicted a massive $100 billion in damage.

30

1781 French fleet, commanded by Admiral Fancoise de Grasse, arrived in Yorktown, VA, with 3,000 troops.

1794 Stephen W. Kearny, Army officer who led in capture of New Mexico and helped win California, born in Newark, NJ (died 1848).

1813 One of bloodiest Indian massacres in American history occurred at Ft. Mims, AL, about 35 miles north of Mobile, in which about 250 persons were killed; marked beginning of Creek War.

1817 John Williams, presiding bishop of Episcopal Church (1887–99), born in Deerfield, MA; president, Trinity College (1848–53); a founder, dean, Berkeley Divinity School, Middletown, CT (1854–99) (died 1899).

1820 George F. Root, founder, New York Normal Institute (1853) to train music teachers, born in Sheffield, MA; composer of hymns ("The Shining Shore," "The Battle Cry of Freedom," "Tramp, Tramp, Tramp, the Boys Are Marching," "Just Before the Battle, Mother") (died 1895).

1821 Cornelius H. Delamater, engineer who built first iron boats and first steam engines used in United States, born in Rhinebeck, NY; built engines for the *Monitor* and first successful submarine (1881) (died 1889).

1822 Rowland H. Macy, founder of dry goods store which became Macy's department store (1858), born on Nantucket Island, MA (died 1877).

1834 Convention in Nashville adopted Tennessee constitution; ratified by popular vote in March 1835.

1837 Ellen L. Herndon Arthur, wife of President Arthur, born in Culpeper Court House, VA (died 1880).

1869 First journey down Colorado River, through the Grand Canyon, completed by Maj. John Wesley Powell and nine men; the 900-mile trip from Green River, WY, to the Grand Wash Cliffs began May 24.

1893 Huey P. Long, Louisiana governor known as the "Kingfish" (1928–32), born in

Winnfield, LA; represented state in Senate (1932–35); assassinated in Louisiana state Capitol (1935).

1896 Raymond Massey, actor, born in Toronto; starred in films (*Scarlet Pimpernel, Abe Lincoln, East of Eden*) and several plays (*Idiot's Delight, Abe Lincoln in Illinois*) (died 1983).

1900 Franklin C. Fry, Lutheran leader, born in Bethlehem, PA; president, United Lutheran Church (1944–62), Lutheran World Federation (1957–63), American Lutheran Church (1962–68) (died 1968).

1901 Roy Wilkins, NAACP official, born in St. Louis; executive secretary (1955–64), executive director (1965–80) (died 1981).

1901 John Gunther, foreign correspondent and author of series of *Inside* books, born in Chicago (died 1970).

1904 Charles E. (Chip) Bohlen, diplomat, born in Clayton, NY; ambassador to Russia (1953–57), to Philippines (1957–59), to France (1962–68) (died 1974).

1907 John W. Mauchly, physicist who was co-inventor of electronic computer, born in Cincinnati (died 1980).

1907 Shirley Booth, screen actress (*Come Back, Little Sheba*), born in New York City; also starred as *Hazel* on television (died 1992).

1909 Joan Blondell, screen actress (*A Tree Grows in Brooklyn, Footlight Parade*), born in New York City (died 1979).

1912 Edward M. Purcell, physicist, born in Taylorville, IL; shared 1952 Nobel Physics Prize for measurement of magnetic fields in atomic nuclei (died 1997).

1918 Ted (Theodore S.) Williams, considered one of greatest hitters in baseball (Boston AL), born in San Diego; named to Baseball Hall of Fame.

1918 William D. Haywood and 14 other IWW (Industrial Workers of the World) members were sentenced to 20 years in prison, $20,000 fines, for violating the Espionage Act; 80 others received lesser sentences.

1930 Warren Buffett, financier/businessman, born in Omaha, NE.

1954 Hurricane Carol struck northeastern United States, caused 68 deaths.

1961 President Kennedy named Gen. Lucius D. Clay as his personal representative in West Berlin, with the rank of ambassador.

1962 A "hot line" was installed connecting Washington, DC, and Moscow, permitting quick exchanges by the heads of state.

1983 Eighth space shuttle flight took off from Cape Canaveral, FL, returned safely September 5; featured first flight by an American black astronaut, Guion S. Bluford II.

1998 Hurricane Bonnie off the southeastern coast struck parts of Virginia and North Carolina; did considerable damage, three were killed.

2001 Ashley Martin became first female both to play and score points as a kicker in a Division I college football team, that of Jacksonville State University.

2004 Republican National Convention opened its meeting in New York City; George W. Bush and Richard (Dick) Cheney renominated.

2004 Astronomer Fred Whipple passed away at 97; invented the now popular "dirty snowball" (i.e., a pile of icy materials) explanation for comets.

31

1778 British fleet brought Gen. Clinton's army to Rhode Island; raided shipping and towns in area.

1800 John Blair, one of the original associate justices of Supreme Court (1789–96), died at 68; represented Virginia in Constitutional Convention (1787).

1822 Galusha A. Grow, legislator, born in Ashford, CT; represented Pennsylvania in House (1850–63, 1894–1903) and served as Speaker (1861–63) (died 1907).

1847 Convention approved Illinois constitution; ratified by popular vote March 6, 1848.

1874 Edward Lee Thorndike, leader in experimental psychology, born in Williamsburg, MA; pioneered in measurement of learning, intelligence (died 1949).

1885 Dubose Heyward, author of *Porgy* and *Mamba's Daughters*, born in Charleston, SC; also wrote libretto for *Porgy and Bess* (died 1949).

1886 Earthquake felt over a 1,000-mile area in the southeast; 90 percent of Charleston, SC, damaged, 57 were killed and property worth $5 million destroyed.

1893 Clifton B. Cates Marine Corps commandant (1948–52), born in Tiptonville, TN (died 1970).

1897 Fredric March, stage and screen actor, born in Racine, WI; stage roles included *The Skin of Our Teeth, Long Day's Journey into Night* and movies were *Dr. Jekyll and Mr. Hyde, Best Years of Our Lives, Inherit the Wind* (died 1975).

1897 Patent issued to Thomas A. Edison for a motion picture camera.

1903 Arthur Godfrey, radio and television entertainer, born in New York City; a leader in entertainment in 1940/50s (died 1983).

1903 First automobile (Packard) crossed the country (San Francisco to New York) under its own power; took 52 days.

1908 William Saroyan, novelist (*My Name Is Aram*, *The Human Comedy*) and playwright (*The Time of Your Life*, *My Heart's in the Highlands*), born in Fresno, CA (died 1981).

1918 Alan Jay Lerner, playwright and lyricist (*Paint Your Wagon*, *Brigadoon*, *My Fair Lady*, *Camelot*), born in New York City (died 1986).

1935 Frank Robinson, baseball player/manager, born in Beaumont, TX; first to be named most valuable player in both leagues, first black major league manager (Cleveland 1975); named to Baseball Hall of Fame.

1942 Bethesda Naval Medical Center dedicated by President Franklin Roosevelt, who helped draft plans for the center.

1945 Itzhak Perlman, concert violinist, born in Tel Aviv, Palestine.

1955 Edwin Moses, Olympics 400-meters hurdles gold medalist (1976, 1984), born in Dayton, OH; won 122 consecutive races (1977–87).

1969 Rocky Marciano, retired world heavyweight boxing champion, died in a plane crash.

1983 Russian planes shot down a Korean Air Lines plane which had drifted over Soviet territory on the island of Sakhalin; all 269 persons aboard died, including 52 Americans (September 1, American time).

1988 Delta Boeing 727 jetliner crashed on takeoff at Dallas-Ft. Worth airport; 13 persons died, but 94 miraculously survived.

1998 Dow Jones industrial average dropped 512.61 points to reach annual low of 7,539.07; was the second biggest one-day drop.

2000 Republican-backed repeal of estate tax vetoed by President Clinton: "fails the test of fairness and fiscal responsibility."

2002 Lionel Hampton died at 94; known as a powerful and energetic band-leader and for his vibraphone playing, he entertained audiences from 1930s to 1990s and introduced many up-and-coming jazz, rhythm-and-blues, and rock-and-roll musicians to a wider audience.

2004 During July and August, worst Alaskan wildfires ever: over 5 million acres scourged.

2005 Cindy Sheehan (mother of soldier killed in Iraq) temporarily ended anti-war demonstrations outside Crawford, Texas, ranch of President Bush; wide publicity given to her protests both then and later.

2006 Summer (June 1-August 31) ended with second-highest average temperature since 1895: 74.5; summer heat killed 200; late heavy rains in some regions still left 40 percent of nation with moderate to severe drought conditions. The year 1936 was marginally hotter.

2006 Housing market hit during August: For first time in 11 years, sale price of existing homes fell; sales of such homes down 12.6 percent from previous year.

2006 For second straight month August trade deficit hit an all-time monthly high: July was $68 billion; August $69.9 billion.

SEPTEMBER

1

1646 A synod of Congregational churches met in Cambridge "to discuss, dispute, and cleare up ... such questions of church government and discipline ... as they shall thinke needful and meete"; at the third session, August 1648, they adopted the Cambridge Platform, which formulated relations between church and state; ratified by the congregations 1651.

1655 Governor Peter Stuyvesant led a force to capture Ft. Trinity (New Castle) and Ft. Christina (September 15), putting the Swedish colony (Delaware) under Dutch rule.

1774 British troops from Boston seized cannon and powder at Charlestown and Cambridge to use for fortifying Boston Neck.

1779 French fleet of 35 ships arrived off Georgia.

1785 Peter Cartwright, Methodist clergyman, born in Amherst County, VA; major figure in religious development of the West (died 1872).

1791 Lydia H.H. Sigourney, widely read poet ("How to Be Happy," "Pocahontas," "The Faded Hope"), born in Norwich, CT (died 1865).

1795 James Gordon Bennett, founder, editor, *New York Globe* (1832), *New York Herald* (1835–67), born in Keith, Scotland; developed many new journalistic procedures (died 1872).

1807 Aaron Burr acquitted after a month-long treason trial in Richmond; he then went into exile in Europe to avoid further prosecutions (for murder of Hamilton in New York and New Jersey, for treason in Ohio, Kentucky, Louisiana and Mississippi).

1814 British fleet entered Penobscot Bay and at the cost of one man took all of Maine east of the Penobscot River.

1815 Peace was made with Indians of the Northwest at a council in Detroit.

1821 William Becknell led a wagon train from Independence, MO, to Santa Fe, opening the Santa Fe Trail.

1822 Hiram R. Revels, first black elected to Senate (Mississippi 1870–71), born in Fayetteville, NC; president, Alcorn A&M (1871–74, 1876–1901) (died 1901).

1826 Alfred E. Beach, inventor of shield for tunneling under ground, born in Springfield, MA; built a tunnel in New York City (1869), launching underground transportation (died 1896).

1849 Elizabeth Harrison, leader in kindergarten movement, born in Athens, KY; founder, president, teachers' training school (1887–1920) (died 1927).

1850 Convention in Monterey began consideration of California state constitution; adopted October 13, ratified November 13; contained clause barring slavery.

1854 Cornerstone laid for first railroad bridge across Mississippi River, between Rock Island, IL, and Davenport, IA.

1864 Gen. John B. Hood and his Confederate troops evacuated Atlanta, moved to Lovejoy's Station, 30 miles southeast, to protect Andersonville and its 34,000 prisoners.

1869 Cleveland Abbe, director of Cincinnati Observatory, began issuing weather reports, preceding the start of U.S. Weather Bureau in 1871.

1875 Edgar Rice Burroughs, creator of *Tarzan* about whom he wrote 23 books, born in Chicago (died 1950).

1877 Rex E. Beach, author of Alaskan adventure novels (*The Barrier, Flowing Gold*), born in Atwood, MI (died 1949).

1892 Leverett Saltonstall, Massachusetts governor (1939–44) and senator (1944–67), born in Chestnut Hill, MA (died 1979).

1894 Forest fire near Hinckley, MN, burned more than 160,000 acres, killing 418 persons.

1898 Jimmy Hatlo, cartoonist ("They'll Do It Every Time," "Little Iodine"), born in Providence, RI (died 1963).

1904 Joe Venuti, first great jazz violinist, born at sea near New York City (died 1978).

1907 Walter P. Reuther, president, United Auto Workers (1946–70), CIO (1952–55), born in Wheeling, WV (died 1970).

1909 Dr. Frederick Cook announced he had reached the North Pole April 21, 1908 (Peary reached the Pole April 6, 1909); Cook's proof was considered insufficient.

1915 Germany accepted limitations on submarine warfare demanded by United States.

1923 Rocky (Rocco) Marciano, world heavyweight boxing champion (1952–56), born in Brocton, MA; retired undefeated after 49 fights; died in plane crash 1969.

1933 Conway Twitty, country music singer and composer, born in Friarspoint, MS (died 1993).

1937 President Franklin Roosevelt signed Wagner-Steagall Act establishing U.S. Housing Authority in Interior Department to make low interest 60-year loans to local agencies, providing 10 percent of the funds for slum clearance and housing projects.

1961 United States, Australia, and New Zealand signed mutual security pact.

1961 TWA Constellation crashed near Hinsdale, IL, shortly after takeoff in Chicago, killing 78 persons.

1965 Economic Development Administration established by the Commerce Secretary to help in economic development of areas with severe unemployment.

1972 Bobby Fischer became first American to win world chess championship defeating Boris Spassky of Soviet Russia.

1985 Wreckage of ocean liner *Titanic*, which sank in 1912 carrying 1,500 to their death, was found by an American-French search team.

1988 Federal Communications Commission announced guidelines to bring high definition television to United States in 1990s, providing pictures twice as clear as they are now and improved sound.

1995 Rock-and-Roll Hall of Fame inaugurated in Cleveland.

1997 Federal minimum hourly wage rate rose to $5.15 an hour from $4.75.

2001 China agreed to drop objections to U.S. antimissile project in exchange for U.S. no longer protesting increase in Chinese military strength.

2004 Sexual assault charges against basketball superstar Kobe Bryant dismissed when accuser declined to testify; Bryant insisted that the sex was consensual, not forced.

2005 U.S. to start requiring its citizens to show passports whenever returning to country from either Mexico or Canada.

2005 Multinational group of 67 scientists reported in *Nature* magazine that chimpanzees share with humans identical or virtually identical 96 percent of 3 billion genes; major divergences in 35 million DNA segments.

2006 Pentagon released report that highest priority of U.S. forces in Iraq now that of preventing country from falling into civil war.

2006 Antimissile test launch from Vandenberg Air Force Base, California; hits mock-attack missile 100 miles high at 18,000 mph; development program has cost over $100 billion.

2

1630 Massachusetts Bay Colony governor met for first time with his assistants.

1765 Henry Bouquet, British officer who was instrumental in crushing Indian rebellion under Pontiac (1763), died at 46; served in expedition against Ft. Duquesne, became colonial citizen.

1789 Treasury Department established with Alexander Hamilton the first secretary, effective September 11.

1831 William P. Frye, Maine legislator, born in Lewiston, ME; served in House (1871–81) and Senate (1881–1911), where he was president pro tem (1896–1911) (died 1911).

1837 James H. Wilson, Union general who commanded cavalry in Tennessee and Georgia, born in Shawneetown, IL; second in command of Americans at Boxer Rebellion in China (died 1925).

1839 Henry George, economist who advocated single-tax plan, born in Philadelphia; would place entire tax burden on land; author *Progress and Poverty* (died 1897).

1850 Eugene Field, newspaper columnist and author of children's poems ("Wynken, Blinken and Nod," "Little Boy Blue"), born in St. Louis (died 1895).

1850 Albert G. Spalding, cofounder of sporting goods firm, born in Ogle County, IL; named to Baseball Hall of Fame (died 1915).

1855 Hoke Smith, Interior Secretary (1893–96), born in Newton, NC; owner, *Atlanta Journal* (1887–1900); served Georgia as governor (1907–09) and in Senate (1911–21) (died 1931).

1864 Union troops under Gen. William T. Sherman occupied Atlanta after its evacuation the previous day.

1866 Hiram W. Johnson, California governor (1911–17), born in Sacramento, CA; also served state in Senate (1917–45); 1912 Progressive Party vice presidential candidate (died 1945).

1869 Hiram P. Maxim, inventor of firearm silencer and electrical instruments, born in Brooklyn; also made some automobile improvements (died 1936).

1885 Many of the 400 Chinese imported to work in Union Pacific Railroad coal mines were killed during an attack by 200 American miners.

1901 Adolph F. Rupp, U. of Kentucky basketball coach (1930–77), born in Halstead, KS; teams won 879 games, four national championships (died 1977).

1914 Convention signed with Panama defining boundaries of Panama Canal Zone, giving United States control over harbor waters at Colon and Ancon.

1916 Adamson Act passed by Congress at President Wilson's request providing for an eight-hour day for railroad workers (had been 10) without reducing their wages; effective January 1, 1917.

1917 Cleveland Amory, social historian (*The Proper Bostonians*), born in Nahant, MA; active conservationist (died 1998).

1919 Communist Party of America organized in Chicago.

1937 Peter V. Ueberroth, baseball commissioner (1984–89), born in Chicago; president, Los Angeles Olympics Organizing Committee (1982–84).

1945 Japanese signed surrender document aboard the USS *Missouri* in Tokyo Bay.

1947 Treaty of Rio de Janeiro, a defense pact, signed by 19 American nations, with President Truman on hand for final session; conference began August 15.

1948 Terry Bradshaw, football player (Pittsburgh 1970/80s), born in Shreveport, LA; led team to four Super Bowl championships.

1952 Jimmy Connors, tennis player who won U.S. singles title five times and Wimbledon twice, born in East St. Louis, IL.

1974 Federal standards for private pension plans were adopted.

1988 PTL movement founder Jim Bakker submitted $165 million plan to buy back television ministry assets; had been ousted in 1987 after a sex scandal; Bakker unable to produce $3 million letter of credit which would have secured the deal.

1998 Allen Drury, author (*Advise and Consent*), died at 80.

2005 Bob Denver, popular television central character of *Gilligan's Island* television series, died of cancer; though program only ran three seasons, it became a mainstay of viewing for younger children for decades.

3

1609 Henry Hudson aboard the *Half Moon* arrived in New York harbor, sailed up the river named for him to Albany.

1783 Final peace treaty ending American Revolution signed in Paris by John Adams, John Jay, and Benjamin Franklin for United States and representatives of Great Britain, France, Spain, and Holland.

1803 Prudence Crandall, who opened school for black girls in Canterbury, CT (1831), born in Hopkinton, RI; school led to prosecution (1833), intensifying racial conflict; moved to Illinois (died 1890).

1811 John H. Noyes, founder of Oneida Community (1848) in central New York, born in Brattleboro, VT; formed society (1836) to restore early Christian communism; Oneida Community flourished, became known for silverware; fled to Canada to avoid prosecution for adultery (died 1886).

1820 George Hearst, mining executive and newspaper publisher, born in Franklin County, MO; developed numerous successful mining enterprises; publisher, *San Francisco Examiner* (1880–91); represented California in Senate (1886–91) (died 1891).

1833 First issue of *New York Sun* published, the first penny paper in New York, with Benjamin H. Day as publisher.

1855 Battle of Ash Hollow (NE) occurred when 1,200 troops under Gen. W.S. Harney defeated Little Thunder and his Sioux Indians; attack was designed to punish Sioux for Grattan massacre on the California trail.

1856 Louis H. Sullivan, considered father of modernist architecture, born in Boston; co-designer, Auditorium Theater, Chicago; designed Wainwright Building, St. Louis; Transportation Building at 1893 World Fair (died 1924).

1860 Edward A. Filene, successful merchant, born in Salem, MA; developed family dry goods and clothing store applying scientific management principles; promoted employees' welfare, originated bargain basement; founder, Twentieth Century Fund (died 1937).

1861 James Hartness, invented flat turret lathe and other machines, born in Schenectady; invented turret equatorial telescope, screw thread comparator (died 1934).

1895 First professional football game played in Latrobe, PA, with the Latrobe YMCA defeating the Jeannette (PA) Athletic Club 12–0.

1901 Ted (Edwin H.) Patrick, editor, *Holiday* (1946–64), born in Rutherford, NJ (died 1964).

1905 Carl D. Anderson, physicist, born in New York City; shared 1963 Nobel Physics Prize for discovery of positron and ability to produce it artificially (died 1991).

1907 Loren C. Eiseley, anthropologist who headed U. of Pennsylvania anthropology department (1947–59), born in Lincoln, NE; curator of Early Man Museum (died 1977).

1910 Dorothy Maynor, concert and opera soprano, born in Norfolk, VA (died 1939).

1912 Ohio voters ratified their new constitution; an amendment proposing woman suffrage was defeated.

1913 Alan Ladd, screen actor (*Shane, The Great Gatsby*), born in Hot Springs, AR (died 1964).

1925 Navy dirigible *Shenandoah* broke up over Akron, OH; 14 died.

1926 Anne Jackson, screen actress who with husband, Eli Wallach, formed one of finest American acting teams, born in Allegheny, PA.

1939 German submarine sank British passenger liner *Athenia* off the northwest Irish coast with a loss of 112 lives, including 28 Americans.

1940 United States transferred 50 over-age destroyers to Great Britain in exchange for naval and air bases in Newfoundland, Bermuda, the Bahamas, Jamaica, St. Lucia, Trinidad, Antigua, and British Guiana.

1942 Allied troops crossed Straits of Messina from Sicily to invade Italy.

1944 Allied troops liberated Brussels.

1976 Spacecraft *Viking II* landed on Mars.

1991 Fire in a chicken processing plant in Hamlet, NC, killed 25 persons, injured 40.

2002 Third-largest American trucking business, Consolidated Freightways, filed for bankruptcy and completely closed its operations; affects 300 service centers and 15,500 employees.

2003 According to Census Bureau, U.S. foreign-born population now larger than population of Canada, over 33 million.

2004 After shortness of breath and chest pain, former President Bill Clinton checked into hospital; major artery blockages found; heart bypass surgery scheduled.

2004 Government announcement: Major 17 percent Medicare premium increase to go into effect in 2005.

2005 U.S. Supreme Court Chief Justice William H. Rehnquist died at 80 after 33 years on Court.

4

1781 Los Angeles founded by 12 families on instructions of the Spanish governor.

1802 Marcus Whitman, medical missionary, born in Rushville, NY; served Indians in Pacific Northwest; instrumental in securing Oregon for United States; he, and his wife, and 12 others were killed by Cayuse Indians November 29, 1847.

1803 Sarah Childress Polk, wife of President Polk, born in Murfreesboro, TN (died 1891).

1804 Thomas U. Walter, Architect of Capitol who designed, supervised construction of wings and Capitol dome, born in Philadelphia (died 1887).

1810 Donald McKay, developer and builder of clipper ships, born in Nova Scotia; the vessels were the fastest of early 1850s (died 1880).

1846 Daniel H. Burnham, architect who supervised construction of Chicago World Fair (1893), born in Henderson, NY; active in city planning (Chicago, Washington, Cleveland, San Francisco, Manila); designed many buildings (Montauk, Chicago; Flatiron, New York City; Union Station, Washington) (died 1912).

1847 *Santa Fe Republican* issued, the first English newspaper in New Mexico.

1848 Richard R. Bowker, founder, editor, *Library Journal* (1876–1926), born in Salem, MA; founder, American Library Association; editor, *Publishers Weekly* (1884–1926) (died 1933).

1863 Union troops occupied Knoxville, TN, which had been evacuated.

1864 Atlanta's civilian population ordered to leave city.

1866 Simon Lake, builder of first successful gas engine submarine, (1897), born in Pleasantville, NJ (died 1945).

1875 Rollin Kirby, editorial cartoonist, born

in Galva, IL; worked for *New York World* and *World-Telegram* (1913–39) and *New York Post* (1939–42) (died 1952).

1876 George P. Day, founder, head, Yale U. Press (1908–59), born in New York City; treasurer, Yale U. (1910–42) (died 1959).

1886 Geronimo, Apache chief, surrendered.

1906 Max Delbrück, an innovator of molecular biology, born in Berlin; shared 1969 Nobel Physiology/Medicine Prize for study of mechanism of virus infection in living cells (died 1981).

1908 Richard Wright, author (*Native Son, Black Boy, The Outsider*), born near Natchez, MS; wrote first influential protest novel by a black writer (died 1960).

1913 Stanford Moore, biochemist with Rockefeller U., born in Chicago; shared 1972 Nobel Chemistry Prize for pioneering studies in enzymes (died 1982).

1917 First American was killed in France by bombs dropped on Army Base Hospital #5 at Dannes-Camiers.

1917 Henry Ford, II, auto manufacturer, born in Detroit; chief executive officer, Ford Motor Co. (1945–80) (died 1987).

1918 American troops landed in Archangel, Russia; along with other Allied troops they were assigned to protect ports.

1918 Paul Harvey, ABC network news reporter and commentator (beginning 1944), born in Tulsa, OK.

1918 Billy Talbert, tennis player who won several championships in 1950s, born in Cincinnati; captain, American Davis Cup team (1952–57).

1949 Tom Watson, golfer who won U.S. Open (1982), Masters twice, and British Open five times, born in Kansas City, MO.

1951 Transcontinental television inaugurated when President Truman spoke at the Japanese peace treaty conference in San Francisco.

1957 Arkansas National Guardsmen, called out by Gov. Orval Faubus, barred nine black students from entering all-white high school in Little Rock; after a court order and arrival of federal troops, students entered September 24.

1960 Hurricane Donna began eight-day sweep from Caribbean through eastern United States, killing 148 persons.

1961 President Kennedy signed act creating Agency for International Development.

1971 Jet airliner crashed into a mountain near Juneau, Alaska, killing 111 persons.

1982 Fire in a Los Angeles apartment house killed 24 persons.

5

1774 First Continental Congress assembled in Carpenter's Hall (Chestnut St. between 3rd and 4th), Philadelphia; drew up declaration of rights and grievances; 12 colonies sent 56 delegates to the meeting; 10 resolutions adopted October 14 setting forth rights of the colonists, among time to "life, liberty and property" and of the provincial legislatures to exclusive power of lawmaking "in all cases of taxation and internal policy;" 13 parliamentary acts since 1763 were declared to violate American rights; Georgia was only colony not represented; Peyton Randolph of Virginia presided over Congress, which met until October 26.

1781 British fleet of 19 ships under Admiral Thomas Graves engaged French fleet at entrance to Chesapeake Bay; British were beaten, disabled, and forced to return to New York, leaving waters off Yorktown under French control.

1795 Peace treaty signed with Algiers, costing $992,463.25 and an agreed annual tribute of $27,500.

1804 William A. Graham, Secretary of Navy (1850–52), born in Lincoln County, NC; served North Carolina as governor (1845–49); Whig candidate for vice president (1852) (died 1875).

1813 American brig *Enterprise* defeated English brig *Boxer* off Monhegan Island, ME.

1833 George H. Hartford, developer of successful food chain (Great Atlantic & Pacific), born in Augusta, ME; took over A&P 1869 (died 1917).

1835 John G. Carlisle, Secretary of Treasury (1893–97), born in what is now Kenton County, KY; represented Kentucky in House (1877–90), serving as Speaker (1888–89), and Senate (1890–93) (died 1910).

1836 Frank Abbott, dentist who invented many dental operating devices, born in Shapleigh, ME; many devices still in use (died 1897).

1856 Thomas E. Watson, Georgia legislator (House 1891–93, Senate 1921–22), born near Thomson, GA; Populist nominee for vice president (1896), for president (1904) (died 1922).

1874 Nap(oleon) Lajoie, baseball player (Cleveland) (1896–1916), born in Woonsocket, RI; lifetime batting average .338; named to Baseball Hall of Fame (died 1959).

1877 Crazy Horse, 28-year-old Sioux Indians chief, was killed while resisting imprisonment; led Ogalala tribe in Battle of Little Big Horn in which Custer and his men were wiped out.

1879 Frank B. Jewett, president, Bell Telephone Laboratories (1925–44), born in Pasadena, CA (died 1949).

1880 James W. Bryce, a pioneer in applying electronics to business machines, born in New York City; with IBM (from 1917); held more than 500 patents (died 1949).

1882 First Labor Day parade held in New York City.

1897 Arthur C. Nielsen, market researcher who pioneered in television programs ratings, born in Chicago (died 1980).

1902 Darryl F. Zanuck, longtime movie producer, starting with *The Jazz Singer* with Al Jolson, born in Wahoo, NE (died 1979).

1905 Russian and Japanese representatives signed peace treaty in Portsmouth, NH, ending their war; President Theodore Roosevelt was mediator.

1912 John M. Cage, Jr., modernist musical composer, born in Los Angeles (died 1992).

1916 Frank G. Yerby, novelist (*The Foxes of Harrow, The Vixens, Price's Castle, Beaton Row*), born in Augusta, GA (died 1992).

1921 Jack J. Valenti, president, Motion Picture Association of America (from 1966), born in Houston; special assistant to President Lyndon Johnson (1963–66).

1927 Paul Volcker, chairman, Federal Reserve Board (1979–88), born in Cape May, NJ; president, Federal Reserve Bank, New York (1975–79).

1929 Bob Newhart, entertainer, born in Oak Park, IL; popular television personality and comedian of 1960–90s.

1939 United States declared its neutrality in World War II and a proclamation by President Franklin Roosevelt prohibited export of arms to belligerents.

1975 President Ford was unharmed when a Secret Service agent grabbed a pistol aimed at the president by Squeakey (Lynette) Frome.

1996 Three Muslim radicals were convicted of plotting to blow up 23 American airliners over the Pacific Ocean.

1997 Arizona Gov. Fife Symington resigned after a federal jury found him guilty of fraud in actions prior to his election.

2004 Category 2 hurricane Frances hit Florida with damage estimated at the time at $8.9 billion.

2005 John Roberts nominated to be new Chief Justice of Supreme Court; had originally been selected to take place of Sandra Day O'Connor.

2006 Chevron test well in Gulf of Mexico indicated largest oil find in generation: potential of 750,000 barrels a day by 2012.

2006 AbioCor artificial heart approved by FDA for extreme cases of heart failure when patient ineligible for heart transplant; two-pound purely internal implant is powered by external power source (without wire connections); test recipients survived for up to 17 months.

6

1513 Vasco Nunez de Balboa started from Antigua de Darien to find "the other sea" described by Indians; crossed the Isthmus and discovered Pacific Ocean September 25.

1628 Company of colonists with John Endecott as governor arrived at Salem, beginning permanent settlement of Massachusetts Bay Colony.

1711 Henry M. Muhlenberg, called the father of Lutheranism in America, born in Einbeck, Germany; as missionary to America, he organized United Lutheran Church (1748) (died 1787).

1757 Marquis de Lafayette, French general who fought with Americans, born; became an intimate associate of George Washington; served at Brandywine, Valley Forge, Yorktown (died 1834).

1781 New London, CT, was plundered and burned by the British.

1782 Martha Jefferson, wife of President Jefferson, died at Monticello at 33.

1805 Horatio Greenough, sculptor who developed theory of functionalism, born in Boston; did sculpture of George Washington (now in Smithsonian) and The Rescue (in the Capitol) (died 1852).

1811 James M. Gilliss, founder of Naval Observatory, born in Washington (died 1865).

1819 William S. Rosecrans, Union general who drove Confederates out of what became West Virginia, born in Kingston, OH; headed Army of the Mississippi, Missouri; minister to Mexico (1868–69); represented California in House (1881–85); Register of the Treasury (1885–93) (died 1898).

1821 Alvin P. Hovey, Union general credited with victory at Vicksburg, born near Mt. Vernon, IN; represented Indiana in House (1887–89) and served as its governor (1889–91); minister to Peru (1865–70) (died 1891).

1842 Melville E. Ingalls, founder, president of railroad which became the Big Four (1880–

1905), born in Harrison, ME; president, Chesapeake & Ohio Railroad (1888–1900) (died 1914).

1860 Jane Addams, social worker who helped found Hull House in Chicago, born in Cedarville, IL; head of Hull House (1889–1935); president, International Congress of Women (1919); shared 1931 Nobel Peace Prize (died 1935).

1861 General Grant led Union troops in occupying Paducah, KY.

1864 Convention in Annapolis adopted Maryland constitution, calling for abolition of slavery; ratified by popular vote October 12–13; effective November 1.

1869 Coal mine disaster at Avondale, PA, resulted in 108 deaths.

1873 Howard E. Coffin, cofounder, vice president, Hudson Motor Car Co. (1909–30), born near West Milan, OH; founder, president, National Air Transport Inc. (1925–28), which later became United Airlines (died 1937).

1875 Arthur Train, lawyer who wrote legal stories, many of which featured fictional Ephraim Tutt, born in Boston (died 1945).

1876 Boardman Robinson, painter and illustrator, born in Somerset, Nova Scotia; painted murals in Radio City, Justice Department; a pioneer political cartoonist (died 1952).

1878 Henry Seidel Canby, editor, *Saturday Review of Literature* (1924–36), born in Wilmington, DE; author (*The Age of Confidence, Alma Mater, American Estimates*) (died 1961).

1888 Joseph P. Kennedy, first chairman, Securities & Exchange Commission (1934–35), born in Boston; chairman, Maritime Commission (1937); ambassador to Great Britain (1937–40) (died 1969).

1890 Claire L. Chennault, commander, American Air Force in China (1942–45), born in Commerce, TX; founder, Flying Tigers (died 1958).

1891 John Charles Thomas, operatic baritone, born in Meyersdale, PA (died 1960).

1893 John W. Bricker, Ohio governor (1939–45) and Senator (1947–59), born in Madison County, OH; Republican vice presidential candidate (1944) (died 1986).

1899 "Open door" policy in China announced by Secretary of State John Hay.

1899 Billy Rose, producer and composer, born in New York City; songs included "Barney Google," "That Old Gang of Mine," "Me and My Shadow," "Without a Song," "Paper Moon"; produced *Jumbo*, the Aquacade, *Carmen Jones* (died 1966).

1901 President McKinley was shot while at Pan American Exposition in Buffalo by a 28-year-old anarchist, Leon F. Czolgosz; president died eight days later.

1901 Ernst Weber, pioneer in developing microwave communications equipment, born in Vienna; president, Microwave Research Institute (1957–69).

1943 Part of the Congressional Limited was derailed near Philadelphia, 79 persons were killed.

1954 President Eisenhower announced the United States had joined with five other nations to form an agency to investigate peacetime uses of atomic energy; the nations were Great Britain, Canada, France, Australia, and South Africa.

1978 Talks began at Camp David between President Carter, Egyptian President Sadat, and Israeli Prime Minister Begin to achieve a Mideast accord.

1985 DC-8 jetliner crashed on takeoff at Milwaukee Airport, killing all 31 persons aboard.

1990 Preliminary census figures showed Detroit may drop out of top ten cities of more than one million; city has lost half of its population in past 40 years.

1995 Cal Ripken, Jr., Baltimore shortstop, played in his 2,131st consecutive baseball game, breaking the 2,130 game record set by New York Yankee Lou Gehrig in 1939.

1996 Hurricane Fran came ashore at Cape Fear, NC, and caused 34 deaths and more than $3.2 billion damage in North Carolina, Virginia and several other states.

2001 Justice Department (and the 18 states supporting its lawsuit) agreed to drop demand that Microsoft be broken up as punishment for abusing its role as dominant operating system (Windows) provider.

2002 For only second time in its history in Washington, DC, both houses of Congress meet in ceremonial session in New York City; purpose: to honor emergency workers and dead of September 11, 2001 World Trade Center bombing.

7

1630 Court of assistants, sitting at Charlestown, MA, ordained that the new settlement across the Charles River be known as Boston, after Boston in Litchfield.

1664 British troops captured New Amsterdam from the Dutch, renamed it New York; Dutch recaptured it in August 1673, but ceded it to the British in November 1674.

1727 William Smith, first provost of U. of Pennsylvania (1755–91), born in Aberdeen, Scotland; teacher, Academy & Charitable School, Philadelphia, which became U. of Pennsylvania (1754) (died 1803).

1729 William Burnet, governor of New York and New Jersey (1720–27) and Massachusetts (1727–29), died at 41.

1737 Arthur Middleton, led South Carolina movement to overthrow proprietary control (1719), died at 56; served as acting governor during absence of crown representative (1725–31).

1749 René Auguste Chouteau, a founder of St. Louis, born in New Orleans; active fur trader (died 1829).

1783 William Lawrence, organizer of first company to manufacture woolen goods in Lowell, MA (c. 1825), born in Groton, MA (died 1848).

1815 Howell Cobb, governor of Georgia (1851–52) and served it in House (1843–51, 1855–57) being Speaker (1849–50), born in Jefferson County, GA; Secretary of Treasury (1857–60); was a Confederate general in Civil War (died 1868).

1819 Thomas A. Hendricks, Vice President (1885), born near Zanesville, OH; represented Indiana in House (1851–55) and Senate (1863–69) and served state as governor (1872); commissioner, U.S. General Land Office (1855–59); served as vice president only from March 4 to November 25, dying in office.

1829 Ferdinand V. Hayden, instrumental in establishing Yellowstone National Park, born in Westfield, MA; served with U.S. Geological Survey (1872–86) (died 1887).

1840 Luther C. Crowell, inventor of square-bottomed paper bag, born on Cape Cod, MA; produced machinery for bagmaking; improved printing press (died 1903).

1846 Regents of Smithsonian Institution met for first time and named Joseph Henry as first secretary; served until 1878.

1860 Grandma (Anna M.) Moses, well known "primitive" painter, born in Greenwich, CT (died 1961).

1862 Confederate troops under Gen. Robert E. Lee occupied Frederick, MD; had expected Union force to evacuate Harpers Ferry, WV; when they did not, Lee split his forces.

1863 Union troops captured Ft. Wagner in Charleston Harbor.

1867 J(ohn) P. Morgan, banker, born in Irvington, NY; headed family firm, acted as agent for Allied governments in floating large American loans during World War I; donated art collection to Metropolitan Museum of Art, New York City (died 1943).

1871 U. of Nebraska opened.

1873 Carl L. Becker, historian at Cornell U. (1917–45), born in Lincoln Township, IA; author of *Our Great Experiment in Democracy, Progress and Power* (died 1945).

1875 Edward F. Hutton, founder/chairman, E. F. Hutton & Co. (1904–62), born in New York City; founder, Freedoms Foundation (1949) (died 1962).

1892 Jim Corbett beat John L. Sullivan in 21 rounds in New Orleans for world's heavyweight boxing championship; the first title fight using padded gloves.

1900 Taylor Caldwell, novelist (*Dynasty of Death, The Eagles Gather, This Side of Innocence*), born in Manchester, England (died 1985).

1908 Michael E. DeBakey, pioneer in developing procedures for heart surgery and transplants, born in Lake Charles, LA.

1909 Elia Kazan, stage and screen director and author, born in Istanbul; his stage plays were *The Skin of Our Teeth, Death of a Salesman, Cat on a Hot Tin Roof*; screen plays were *On the Waterfront, Gentleman's Agreement*; wrote *The Arrangement*.

1914 James A. Van Allen, physicist who specialized in high altitude research, born in Mt. Pleasant, IA; discovered magnetosphere or Van Allen radiation belts around the earth (1958).

1916 United States Shipping Board created.

1917 American transport *Minnehaha* was sunk by a submarine off Irish coast; 48 persons lost.

1918 John A. Swearingen, Jr., president/chairman, Indiana Standard Oil (1958–83), born in Columbia, SC.

1923 (Mae) Louise Suggs, golfer who had 50 career victories, born in Atlanta; won Women's Open (1948, 1952) and LPGA (1957); named to LPGA Hall of Fame.

1924 Daniel K. Inouye, first elected representative of Hawaii, born in Honolulu; first American of Japanese ancestry to serve in Congress, representing Hawaii in Senate (since 1963).

1936 Buddy (Charles) Holly, singer and guitarist who was major influence on early rock-and-roll music, born in Lubbock, TX (died 1959).

1943 Fire in Gulf Hotel in Houston claimed 55 lives.

1965 Three-day hurricane, Betsy, hit Gulf

Coast states, killing 80 (mostly in New Orleans) and causing estimated $1.3 billion damage.

1979 Week-long Hurricane David swept north from the Caribbean over eastern United States; 1,100 casualties reported for storm.

1988 Securities & Exchange Commission accused Drexel Burham Lambert Inc. of extensive fraud, with Michael Milken, head of its "junk-bond" financing division, as the principal target.

1992 Fay Vincent resigned as baseball commissioner after three years to avoid a legal battle.

1995 Sen. Robert Packwood of Oregon resigned from Senate after an Ethics Committee recommended his expulsion because of sexual misconduct, influence peddling, and obstruction of justice.

2004 Number of U.S. military casualties in Iraq hit 1,000.

2006 Formal command control over Iraqi armed forces passed to local government by U.S.

2006 U.S. House of Representatives voted 264–146 to prohibit slaughter of horses for their meat; would close three U.S. plants and save 90,000 horses a year; critics argue that the horses would generally have been killed anyway due to age or disability.

8

1565 First American Catholic parish organized in St. Augustine, FL.

1685 Thomas Fleet, founder, publisher, *Boston Evening Post* (1735–58), born in Shropshire, England (died 1758).

1779 French naval force with 6,000 men led by Adm. Comte d'Estaing arrived off Savannah from the West Indies.

1781 American troops under Gen. Nathanael Greene and Francis Marion inflicted heavy losses on British at Eutaw Springs, SC, forcing their withdrawal to Charleston.

1815 Alexander Ramsey, Secretary of War (1879–81), born near Harrisburg, PA; governor of Minnesota as a territory (1849–53) and state (1859–63) and represented it in Senate (1863–75) (died 1903).

1828 Margaret Olivia Sage, philanthropist who used $70 million fortune inherited from her husband, Russell, to found foundation named for him, born Syracuse, NY; foundation created to improve American social and living conditions; her vast philanthropies attributed to her efforts to counteract her husband's reputation as a "skinflint" (died 1918).

1828 Joshua L. Chamberlain, Union general who led defense of Little Round Top at Gettysburg, born in Brewer, ME; won Congressional Medal of Honor for his actions; served Maine as governor (1866–70); president, Bowdoin College (1871–73) (died 1914).

1829 Seth M. Brown, Confederate general at Vicksburg and Richmond, born in Fredericksburg, VA (died 1900).

1860 Lake Michigan excursion ship, *Lady Elgin*, collided with a lumber ship; 300 persons were killed.

1872 George H. Dern, Secretary of War (1933–36), born in Dodge County, NE; served Utah as governor (1925–32); co-inventor of Holt-Dern ore roaster (died 1936).

1873 David O. McKay, president, Mormon Church (1951–70), born in Huntsville, UT (died 1970).

1887 Jacob L. Devers, World War II general who headed invasion of southern France, born in York, PA; commander, Army ground forces (1945–49) (died 1979).

1889 Robert A. Taft, legislator called "Mr. Republican," born in Cincinnati; represented Ohio in Senate (1939–53) (died 1953).

1892 Pledge of allegiance to the flag appeared in the juvenile periodical, *The Youth's Companion*; written by Assistant Editor Francis Bellamy.

1896 Howard Dietz, lyricist for musical shows (*Three's a Crowd, Little Show, Merry-Go-Round*), born in New York City (died 1983).

1900 Flood and tidal wave hit Galveston, TX, with a loss of 6,000 lives and property loss of $15 million; storm with 100 mph winds raged for 14 days.

1920 Transcontinental airmail service established between New York and San Francisco.

1922 Sid Caesar, entertainer who was an early television star (*Show of Shows*), born in Yonkers, NY.

1934 Fire aboard steamer *Morro Castle* off New Jersey coast resulted in 137 deaths.

1935 Huey Long, Louisiana senator and former governor, was fatally wounded in Baton Rouge by Dr. Carl A. Weiss; died two days later.

1943 Italy surrendered to Allies; on October 13, it declared war on Germany.

1951 Japanese peace treaty signed in San Francisco by United States, Japan, and 47 other nations.

1954 Southeast Asia Treaty Organization

(SEATO) formed in Manila by United States, Great Britain, France, Australia, New Zealand, the Philippines, Pakistan, and Thailand.

1971 John F. Kennedy Center opened in Washington, DC.

1974 President Ford issued an unconditional pardon to former President Nixon for all crimes he "committed or may have committed" while president.

1982 Founder William S. Paley announced his resignation as chairman of Columbia Broadcasting System, effective April 20, 1983; returns in 1986 with major company reorganization.

1982 Agreement announced for merger of American Lutheran Church, Association of Evangelical Lutheran Churches, and Lutheran Church in America to form single church of 5.5 million members.

1988 Angelo B. Giamatti, president of National League, named baseball's seventh commissioner, effective April 1, 1989; succeeded Peter Ueberroth who did not seek to be renamed.

1998 Mark McGwire of St. Louis Cardinals hit his 62nd home run of the season, surpassing the record set by Roger Maris in 1961.

1998 Dow Jones industrial average made its largest daily increase of 380.53 to close at 8,020.78.

2003 Harvey Milk High School opens in Greenwich Village, New York City, with 7 teachers and 72 students; first public high school in nation designed for gay, bisexual, and transgender students; moral conservatives indignant at implicit approval of lifestyle involved; some liberals concerned it may be a form of segregating such individuals from mainstream.

2004 Dan Rather of CBS News released purported letter of President Bush's National Guard commander claiming he received special preference on multiple occasions; massive furor as skeptics jump on apparent internal indications that documents not written at that time; on September 20 Rather reluctantly concedes genuineness had not been vindicated, but refuses to admit it was a forgery.

9

1675 New England Confederation declared war on Wampanoag Indians (the King Philip War); fighting lasted until August 1676 (two years longer in Maine), with the death of one out every 16 men of military age, a cost of 90,000 pounds, and destruction of 12 towns.

1711 Thomas Hutchinson, royal governor of Massachusetts (1771–74) whose actions hastened revolution, born in Boston; colonial chief justice when Stamp Act was upheld, resulting in his home being burned by a mob (1765); went to England to live, died there in 1780.

1721 Edmund Pendleton, colonial leader, born in Caroline County, VA; headed Virginia Committee of Safety; first Speaker, Virginia House of Delegates and helped revise state laws; first president, Virginia Supreme Court of Appeals (1779–1803) (died 1803).

1741 Russian explorers landed on Adak Island in Aleutians.

1747 Thomas Coke, first American Methodist superintendent (1784), born in Brecon, Wales; returned to England soon after appointment, making frequent trips to America (died 1814).

1753 George Logan, physician who went to France (1798–99) to improve relations, born near Germantown, PA; Congress passed Logan Act forbidding a private citizen from carrying on diplomatic relations; represented Pennsylvania in House (1801–07) (died 1821).

1789 House, at urging of James Madison, recommended to states adoption of 17 amendments to the Constitution suggested during ratification process; Senate reduced number to 12 and submitted them for ratification September 25.

1789 William C. Bond, first director, Harvard Observatory (1839–59), born in Portland, ME; directed construction of the observatory (died 1859).

1791 Commission in charge of setting up new seat of government decided to call area Territory of Columbia, and the capital, Washington.

1814 Royal E. House, inventor of teletype machine (1846), born in Rockland, VT, invented other electrical devices (died 1895).

1823 Joseph Leidy, laid foundation for American vertebrate paleontology, born in Philadelphia; wrote standard text on anatomy (died 1891).

1841 President Tyler vetoed Second Bank bill on grounds of unconstitutionality; had been passed to replace the repealed sub-treasury system; efforts to override veto failed.

1850 Victor F. Lawson, owner, *Chicago Daily News* (1876–1925), first penny newspaper in Midwest, born in Chicago; pioneered in developing foreign news service; published *Chicago Record-Herald* (1881–1914) (died 1925).

1850 California admitted to Union as the 31st state.

1850 Congress created Territory of New Mexico and Territory of Utah.

1863 Gen. William Rosecrans' Union troops entered Chattanooga, which had been evacuated by Confederates.

1874 William D. Mitchell, Attorney General (1929–33), born in Winona, MN; Solicitor-General (1925–29); chief counsel for congressional investigation of Japanese attack on Pearl Harbor (1945) (died 1955).

1884 American Historical Association organized in Saratoga, NY.

1887 Alf(red M.) Landon, governor of Kansas (1932–36), born in West Middlesex, PA; Republican presidential candidate (1936) (died 1987).

1889 Preston Dickinson, pioneer in modern art in United States, born in New York City (died 1930).

1890 Marriner S. Eccles, chairman, Federal Reserve Board (1936–48), born in Logan, UT; member of board (1934–36) (died 1977).

1893 First child of a president born in White House was Esther, second child of President and Mrs. Cleveland.

1895 American Bowling Congress organized.

1898 Frankie Frisch, baseball player (New York NL and St. Louis NL), born in New York City; named to Baseball Hall of Fame (died 1973).

1899 C(yrus) R. Smith, president, American Airlines, born in Minerva, TX; Commerce Secretary (1968–69).

1918 French and American troops launched attack in Argonne.

1919 Boston police went on strike; National Guard sent in and strike was broken.

1921 Floods in San Antonio caused 250 deaths and property damage of $3 million.

1957 Congress passed Civil Rights Act, the first of its kind since Reconstruction days; created Civil Rights Commission, provided for federal enforcement of constitutional civil rights.

1965 Department of Housing and Urban Development created, effective November 9; Robert C. Weaver, the first secretary, sworn in January 17, 1966.

1969 Collision of a passenger jet and a light plane near Indianapolis killed 86 persons.

1986 American educator Frank Herbert Reed was kidnapped in West Beirut.

1990 Ellis Island in New York harbor reopened as the Ellis Island Immigration Museum.

1990 Presidents Bush and Gorbachev, meeting in Helsinki, pledged to reverse Iraq's conquest of Kuwait even if peaceful means fail.

1992 Quentin N. Burdick, who represented North Dakota in Senate for past 32 years, died at 84.

1998 Independent Counsel Kenneth Starr reported to House Judiciary Committee "substantial and credible information" that President Clinton had lied under oath, obstructed justice, and abused powers of his office.

2001 Walter Jinotti, biomedical engineer, died at 74; in 1982 invented a method of determining pollen level that was adopted by Associated Press; in 1987 he invented a method that could determine the level in only 20 minutes.

2004 Edward Teller, "the father of the hydrogen bomb" and pioneer nuclear researcher, died at 95.

10

1608 John Smith assumed presidency of the Jamestown council.

1736 Carter Braxton, colonial leader, born in Newington, VA; member, Continental Congress (1775–76, 1777–83, 1785) and signer of Declaration of Independence (died 1797).

1787 John J. Crittenden, Attorney General (1841, 1850–53), born near Versailles, KY; represented Kentucky in Senate (1817–19, 1835–41, 1842–48, 1855–61) and served state as governor (1848–50) (died 1863).

1794 Blount College, which became U. of Tennessee, chartered.

1806 William Crompton, coinventor of improved weaving loom, born in Lancashire, England (died 1891).

1813 Oliver Hazard Perry led American naval forces to victory over British in Battle of Lake Erie; Americans captured two ships, two brigs, one schooner, one sloop; British abandoned Detroit; Perry sent his classic message: "We have met the enemy and they are ours."

1832 Randall L. Gibson, Confederate general and legislator, born in Woodford County, KY; represented Louisiana in House (1875–83) and Senate (1883–92); instrumental in founding Tulane U. (died 1892).

1833 President Jackson announced the government would not continue to use the Second Bank of the United States as a depository; funds would be deposited in 23 state banks.

1836 Joseph Wheeler, known for his efforts to achieve reconciliation of north and south, born near Augusta, GA; commanded cavalry units in

Confederate Army and in Spanish-American War; represented Alabama in House (1881–1900) (died 1906).

1839 Isaac K. Funk, founded publishing company which became Funk & Wagnalls, born in Clifton, OH; editor, *Literary Digest* (1890–1912), *Standard Dictionary, Jewish Encyclopedia* (died 1912).

1839 C(harles) S. Peirce, originator of pragmatic philosophy in United States, born in Cambridge, MA (died 1914).

1842 Letitia Tyler, wife of President Tyler, died in White House at 51; the first First Lady to die there.

1846 Patent issued to Elias Howe for first practical sewing machine.

1863 Little Rock captured by Union troops.

1874 Mark Sullivan, popular columnist and commentator, born in Avondale, PA; author of *Our Times, The Education of an American* (died 1952).

1885 Carl Van Doren, English professor (Columbia U. 1911–30) and author (*Benjamin Franklin, Mutiny in January, The Great Rehearsal*) (died 1950).

1886 Hilda Doolittle, poet under name of "HD," born in Bethlehem, PA; works include "Sea Garden," "Hymen," "Red Shoes for Bronze" (died 1961).

1892 Arthur H. Compton, physicist, born in Wooster, OH; shared 1927 Nobel Physics Prize for discovery of change in wave length of scattered X-rays, discovered electrical nature of cosmic rays (died 1962).

1894 United Daughters of the Confederacy (known as UDC in South) organized in Nashville.

1895 Melville J. Herskovitz, anthropologist, born in Bellefontaine, OH; made major contributions to role of individual in culture, and African and Afro-American ethnology (died 1963).

1908 John A. Barr, chairman, Montgomery Ward (1955–64), born in Akron, IN; dean, Northwestern U. Graduate Business School (1964–75) (died 1979).

1919 General Pershing led First Division in parade on New York's Fifth Avenue.

1924 N.F. Leopold, Jr., and R.A. Loeb were convicted of murder of Robert Franks in Chicago after sensational trial in which they were defended by Clarence Darrow; sentenced to life imprisonment.

1929 Arnold Palmer, first golfing millionaire, born in Youngstown, PA; won Masters tournament four times.

1934 Roger Maris, baseball player who hit record 61 home runs in one season (1961), born in Hibbing, MN (died 1985).

1963 President Kennedy federalized Alabama National Guard to halt delay of school integration by Gov. George C. Wallace.

1965 George Baker, better known as Father Divine, died at about 88; organized Peace Mission movement in New York and Philadelphia areas, calling for communal living with a strict moral code; movement died quickly after his death.

1993 President Clinton and his health task force, headed by Mrs. Clinton, proposed plan to guarantee health insurance for all Americans while expanding federal power to control private medical care spending.

2004 United Jewish Communities released results of three-year study: first drop in American Jewish population since 1800; insufficient number of children being born to maintain current size; 47 percent marry non-Jews.

2006 A 6.0 magnitude earthquake hit 260 miles SW of Tampa, Florida; most severe in Southeastern United States in three decades, but produced minimal damage.

11

1776 Fruitless peace conference held between Americans and British on Staten Island; Benjamin Franklin, John Adams, and Edmund Rutledge conferred with Lord Howe, but there was no progress when British demanded revocation of Declaration of Independence.

1777 British defeated Americans at Brandywine, giving them control of Philadelphia, which they occupied September 26; Americans lost about 1,000 men; the Marquis de Lafayette was slightly wounded.

1786 Delegates from Virginia, Pennsylvania, New Jersey, Delaware, and New York met in Annapolis and adopted an invitation to other states for a meeting next May to revise Articles of Confederation; other state delegates had failed to arrive in time for meeting.

1789 First Secretary of Treasury, Alexander Hamilton, named by President Washington.

1789 President Washington signed act establishing federal salaries — president $25,000, vice president $5,000, chief justice $4,000, associate justices $3,500, State and Treasury secretaries $3,500, War Secretary $3,000.

1814 American naval forces in Plattsburgh Bay on Lake Champlain routed a larger British force, ending British efforts to invade New York; American fleet commanded by Capt. Thomas MacDonough; British land force retreated to Canada.

1821 Erastus F. Beadle, publisher who originated dime novels, born in Pierstown, NY; novels included those about *Deadwood Dick, Nick Carter*, the forerunners of modern paperbacks (died 1894).

1833 William H. Hatch, legislator who helped provide foundation for agricultural research, born near Georgetown, KY; represented Missouri in House (1875–95), whose legislation also helped getting cabinet status for Department of Agriculture (died 1896).

1838 John Ireland, Catholic Archbishop of St. Paul (1888–1918), born in Burnchurch, Ireland; influential in establishing Catholic U. in Washington (1889); considered greatest American churchman of his time (died 1918).

1844 Nelson O. Nelson, successful manufacturer of plumbing, building supplies, born in Norway; introduced profit-sharing (1896), which he advocated to reconcile differences between capital and labor (died 1918).

1850 Jenny Lind, the "Swedish nightingale," began American concert tour at Castle Garden, New York City; gave 91 concerts, the last on June 9, 1851.

1852 First Washington newspaper, *Columbian*, published in Olympia by James W. Wiley and Thornton F. Mcelroy.

1854 William Holabird, architect who established skeleton method of skyscraper building, born in Dutchess County, NY; some of his designs, all in Chicago, were Cook County Building, and City, Congress, LaSalle, and Sherman hotels (died 1923).

1861 Kentucky legislature demanded that Confederate forces, which had seized Columbus, KY, withdraw; a week later, legislature created military force to ensure withdrawal.

1862 O. Henry, short story writer, born in Greensboro, NC, as William S. Porter; columnist, *New York World*; author of *The Gift of the Magi, The Furnished Room* (died 1910).

1877 Rosika Schwimmer, pioneer advocate of world government, born in Budapest; convinced Henry Ford to sponsor peace ship to end World War I (died 1948).

1884 Harvey Fletcher, physicist who headed group which developed binaural, stereophonic sound, born in Provo, UT (died 1981).

1893 World Parliament of Religions opened in conjunction with Columbia Exposition in Chicago.

1896 Robert S. Kerr, cofounder, Kerr-McGee Oil Co., born in Ada, OK; served Oklahoma as governor (1943–47) and represented it in Senate (1949–63) (died 1963).

1902 Jimmie Davis, country music singer who was Louisiana governor (1944–48), born in Quitman, LA.

1913 Paul "Bear" Bryant, football coach whose teams won more than 330 games in 39 years, born in Kingsland, AR; spent 26 years as Alabama U. coach (died 1983).

1926 Ten days of hurricanes began in Florida and Alabama; ended with 243 deaths.

1937 Robert L. Crippen, astronaut on two-man team which made first successful space shuttle flight (1981), born in Beaumont, TX; later commanded 1983 and 1987 flights.

1941 "Shoot-on-sight" policy announced by President Franklin Roosevelt after torpedo attack on American destroyer *Greer* near Iceland; warned that German and Italian vessels entering American defensive waters did so at their own risk.

1944 President Franklin Roosevelt and Prime Minister Winston Churchill met in Quebec to discuss postwar problems in Germany.

1944 First Army units crossed German border north of Trier.

1961 Passenger train rammed a Pennsylvania National Guard train near Newcomerstown, OH, killing 33.

1972 Bay Area Rapid Transit system (BART), linking Oakland and San Francisco, went into operation.

1982 Army helicopter carrying five crewmen and 39 members of an international parachuting team crashed at Mannheim, West Germany, killing all aboard.

1985 Pete Rose of Cincinnati Reds set new major league record of 4,192 career base hits, surpassing Ty Cobb's record set in 1928.

1986 Dow Jones industrial average plunged 86.61 points in busiest session in New York Stock Exchange history when a record 237.6 million shares changed hands; stocks dropped another 34.17 points the next day, ending a week when the average fell 141.03 points.

2001 Approximately 3,000 Americans died when terrorists seized four airliners and crashed them into the two towers of the World Trade Center in New York City, the Pentagon in Arlington, Virginia, and a field near Shanksville, Pennsylvania.

2002 Johnny Unitas — widely regarded as the best quarterback in NFL history and as the spark that ignited the League's popularity — died of a heart attack while exercising; threw touchdown passes in 47 consecutive games, setting a record no one has ever come near to equaling.

12

1687 John Alden, a founder of Danbury, MA, died at about 88; influential member of Plymouth Colony, remembered for proposing to Priscilla Mullens on behalf of shy Miles Standish.

1775 Continental Congress reconvened and for first time all 13 colonies were represented; Georgia sent delegation for first time.

1776 Gen. George Washington evacuated American troops from Manhattan to avoid being trapped; set up fortifications on Harlem Heights.

1788 Alexander Campbell, a cofounder of Disciples of Christ Church (1827), born in County Antrim, Ireland; denied a Baptist license at Brush Run, PA (1813), he became an itinerant preacher; founder, president, Bethany College, WV (1840–66) (died 1866).

1789 Henry Knox was named first Secretary of War by President Washington.

1806 Andrew H. Foote, Union navy commander of upper Mississippi River operations, born in New Haven, CT; an ardent temperance advocate, he ended daily liquor ration on American ships (1862) (died 1863).

1811 James Hall, geologist who began study of American stratigraphy, born in Hingham, MA; first president, Geological Society of America (died 1898).

1812 Richard M. Hoe, inventor of rotary printing and web presses, born in New York City; developed many other items which led to modern newspaper press (died 1886).

1814 British began unsuccessful attack on Baltimore, including shelling Ft. McHenry, which led Francis Scott Key to write poem which later became "The Star Spangled Banner."

1818 Richard J. Gatling, inventor of first practical machine gun, born in Hartford County, NC; also invented steam plow, sowing machine (died 1903).

1825 Ainsworth R. Spofford, librarian of Library of Congress (1864–97), born in Gilmantown, NH (died 1908).

1839 John J. Keane, Catholic Archbishop of Dubuque, IA (1900–11), born in Balyshannon,

Ireland; Bishop of Richmond, VA (1878–89); first rector, Georgetown U., Washington, DC (1889–97) (died 1918).

1862 Confederate troops began siege, bombardment of Harpers Ferry, WV; took city September 15.

1869 National Prohibition Party organized in Chicago.

1876 Harry C. Stutz, automaker and cofounder, head Stutz Car Co. (1913–19), born near Ansonia, CT; producers of popular Stutz Bearcat (died 1930).

1877 Frederick H. Koch, a leader in American folk playwrighting and theater group organizer, born in Covington, KY; with U. of North Carolina (1918–44) (died 1944).

1880 Henry L. Mencken, author and editor, born in Baltimore; coeditor, *Smart Set, American Mercury* (1924–33); author of *Prejudices, The American Language, Treatise on the Gods* (died 1956).

1888 Grover C. Loening, pioneer aircraft engineer, born in Bremen, Germany of American parents; chief aeronautical engineer, Army Air Corps (1914–15); headed two aircraft companies (1917–38); invented strut-braced monoplane, an amphibian plane (died 1976).

1891 Arthur Sulzberger, publisher, *New York Times* (1935–61), born in New York City; with *Times* from 1919 to 1968 (died 1968).

1893 Lewis B. Hershey, Army general who headed Selective Service System (1941–70), born in Steuben County, IN (died 1977).

1898 Ben(jamin) Shahn, artist of urban life, born in Kaunas, Lithuania; worked with Diego Rivera on "Man at the Crossroads" in New York's Rockefeller Center (died 1969).

1913 Jesse (James C.) Owens, track star who won four gold medals in 1936 Olympics, born in Danville, AL (died 1980).

1918 Battle of St. Mihiel began, the first distinctly American operation; involved 550,000 American troops; victory gained September 16, at cost of 7,000 American casualties; removed German threat of long-standing.

1918 Eugene V. Debs convicted in Cleveland of violation of Espionage Act; sentenced September 14 to 10 years imprisonment.

1922 American Episcopal Church voted to delete word "obey" from marriage service.

1924 Tom Landry, football player (New York) and coach (Dallas 1960–89), born in Mission, TX.

1925 President Coolidge named National

Aircraft Board, headed by Dwight W. Morrow, to investigate government's role in aviation.

1928 Five-day hurricane moved from the Caribbean to Florida, killing 4,000 persons, 1,836 of them in Florida.

1931 George Jones, country music singer, born in Saratoga, TX.

1940 Explosion at the Hercules Powder plant in Kenvil, NJ, killed 55 persons.

1944 American troops entered Germany, crossing between Eupen and Trier.

1953 John F. Kennedy and Jacqueline Lee Bouvier were married in Newport, RI.

1959 *Luna 2*, an unmanned spacecraft, became first to land on the moon.

1964 Canyonlands (UT) National Park established.

1965 Hurricane Betsy ended five day attack on Gulf Coast states, 74 died.

1986 Joseph Cicippio, an accountant at American U., abducted from West Beirut campus.

1988 Environmental Protection Administration study recommended that every house in the United States should be tested for radon.

1989 David N. Dinkins, Manhattan borough president, defeated three-term Mayor Edward L. Koch in the Democratic primary for mayor; subsequently became city's first black mayor.

2000 Selma, Alabama, selected first black mayor (James Perkins, Jr.) by ousting mayor of 35 years, Joseph J. Smitherman.

2003 At 71, singer-songwriter Johnny Cash died; received 11 Grammy Awards; over 1,500 songs recorded.

2005 Hurricane Katrina evacuation embarrassment: Louisiana officials report 45 previously unknown bodies found in Memorial Hospital, New Orleans; unknown number of them died during and after the hurricane.

2005 FEMA (Federal Emergency Management Agency) chief Michael Brown resigned after prolonged criticism of federal response to Hurricane Katrina; insists he's being blamed for mistakes and misjudgments of others.

2006 U.S. government survey of 850 previous studies conceded that many veterans of the first Persian Gulf War came home with various medical problems, but denied that there is any set of characteristics that can be classified as a distinct "Gulf War Syndrome"; critics fear implicit message of excusing nontreatment of those who do not fall into accepted health diagnoses.

13

1635 Massachusetts General Court banished Roger Williams from Salem but authorized him to stay over the winter; he fled (January, 1636) for fear of deportation and founded Provincetown (June, 1636).

1755 Oliver Evans, builder of first American high pressure steam engine, born near Newport, DE; called the Watt of America (died 1819).

1761 Caspar Wistar, author of first American textbook on anatomy, born in Philadelphia; flower genus *Wisteria* named for him (died 1818).

1777 Gen. John Burgoyne led his British troops to an encampment at Saratoga, NY.

1788 With nine states having ratified the Constitution, Congress established New York City as the capital, set January 7, 1789, as the date for the appointment of presidential electors, who would ballot on February 4, 1789, and scheduled first meeting of new Congress for March 4, 1789.

1789 First loan to United States government negotiated by Alexander Hamilton with New York banks.

1803 John Barry, the nation's first Navy commodore, died at 58; was a naval hero of Revolution.

1813 John Sedgwick, Union general at Antietam, Chancellorsville, and Gettysburg, born in Cornwall, CT; killed by a sniper at Spotsylvania May 9, 1864.

1814 Francis Scott Key, an attorney detained aboard a ship in Baltimore harbor because of British shelling of Ft. McHenry, wrote a poem which later became "The Star Spangled Banner"; British abandoned effort and withdrew to Halifax.

1817 John M. Palmer, Illinois governor (1869–73), born in Scott County, KY; as Union general he served at Chickamauga, Atlanta; presidential candidate of National or Gold Democrats Party (1896) (died 1900).

1826 Anthony J. Drexel, founder, Drexel Institute of Technology, Philadelphia, born in Philadelphia; co-owner, *Philadelphia Ledger* (died 1893).

1841 The Cabinet, except Secretary of State, resigned because of President Tyler's veto of the Second Bank bill, the so-called Fiscal Corporation Act.

1847 Americans using scaling ladders captured Chapultepec, which commanded eastern approaches to Mexico City.

1851 Walter Reed, military surgeon who headed study of yellow fever, born in Belroi, VA; Washington Army hospital named for him (died 1902).

1857 Milton S. Hershey, founder of chocolate company in Lancaster, PA (1893), born in Derry Township, PA; city of Hershey developed around plant; founder, Hershey Industrial School for orphan boys (died 1945).

1860 John J. Pershing, commander-in-chief, American Expeditionary Force (1917–19), born in Linn County, MO; served in Philippines, commanded force sent into Mexico to capture Pancho Villa; Army chief of staff (1921–24) (died 1948).

1863 Cyrus Adler, religious leader, born in Van Buren, AR; first president, Dropsie College for Hebrew & Cognate Learning, Philadelphia (1908–40); president, Jewish Theological Seminary, New York City (1915–40); American Jewish Historical Society organizer (1892), president (1898–1940); editor, *Jewish Encyclopedia, American Jewish Yearbook* (died 1940).

1866 Adolf Mayer, a foremost psychiatrist, born in Niederweningen, Switzerland; headed Phipps Psychiatric Clinic, Johns Hopkins (1910–41) (died 1950).

1874 Arnold Schönberg, a foremost composer of modern music (*Pelleas and Melisande, Pierrot Lunaire*), born in Vienna; to America (1934), taught at UCLA (died 1951).

1876 Sherwood Anderson, poet and novelist (*Winesburg, Ohio; Poor White; Dark Laughter*), born in Camden, OH (died 1941).

1880 Jesse L. Lasky, pioneer movie maker, born in San Jose, CA; helped make *The Squaw Man* (with DeMille and Goldwyn), the first American feature length film; made more than 1,000 films (died 1958).

1883 Lewis E. Lawes, warden of Sing Sing (NY) prison (1919–40), born in Elmira, NY (died 1947).

1886 Alain L. Locke, first American black student to receive Rhodes Scholarship, born in Philadelphia; with Howard U. philosophy department (1912–53), chairman (1918–53) (died 1954).

1911 Bill Monroe, country music singer who developed bluegrass style, born in Rosine, KY (died 1996).

1926 Andrew F. Brimmer, first black member of Federal Reserve Board (1966), born in Newellton, LA.

1928 Floods at Lake Okeechobee, FL, caused 2,000 deaths.

1960 Act of Bogota was announced to provide for social and economic reform in Latin America with American help.

1971 More than 1,000 state troopers and police stormed Attica (NY) prison, ending four-day rebellion; nine hostages and 28 convicts killed in the assault.

1982 ICC authorized merger of Missouri Pacific and Western Pacific railroads with the Union Pacific to create third largest American railroad.

1989 Fay Vincent, deputy baseball commissioner, named commissioner to succeed A. Bart Giamatti, who died suddenly September 1.

1994 President Clinton signed Crime Control and Prevention Act which provided for 100,000 more police officers, expanded federal death penalty applying to about 60 crimes, and banned 19 types of semiautomatic weapons.

1994 Small plane crashed onto White House lawn killing the pilot identified as a Maryland truck driver; President and family were not at home at the time.

2000 FAA announced that rudder system on Boeing 737s were potentially dangerous and must be replaced; 737s outnumber all rival types of aircraft in use.

2005 After two weeks of finger-pointing between federal, state, and local officials for the botched evacuation and immediate recovery efforts in New Orleans after Hurricane Katrina, President Bush conceded that the responsibility on the national level was ultimately his.

2006 Former Texas governor Ann Richards died of esophageal cancer; first woman to win a top tier of state government position in 50 years when twice elected state treasurer in 1982 and 1986; then elected governor in 1990; major Democratic powerhouse both before and after she held office.

14

1638 John Harvard, 31-year-old Congregational clergyman, at his death bequeathed his 260-volume library and half his $2,000 estate for a college; Newton (Cambridge) selected as site (March 13, 1639); school named for him.

1741 Robert Eden, governor of Maryland (1768–76), born in Durham, England (died 1784).

1742 James Wilson, associate justice, Supreme Court (1789–98), born in Carskerdon,

Scotland; member, Continental Congress (1775–76, 1782–83, 1785–87) and Constitutional Convention (1787), a signer of Declaration of Independence; first law professor, U. of Pennsylvania (1790–98) (died 1798).

1778 Continental Congress named Benjamin Franklin minister to France.

1813 James R. Wood, a renowned surgeon who helped found Bellevue Hospital, New York City, born in Mamaroneck, NY; chief surgeon, Bellevue; helped add medical school and nation's first nurses training school to hospital; introduced first hospital ambulance service (died 1882).

1819 Henry J. Hunt, Union general who was artillery chief at Gettysburg, born in Detroit; headed artillery for Army of Potomac (died 1889).

1846 George B. Selden, inventor of a gasoline motor, born in Clarkson, NY; sold rights to motor to auto manufacturers on a royalty basis; Ford challenged payments, winning protracted litigation (died 1922).

1847 Force of 11,000 Americans occupied Mexico City after taking city protected by 30,000 troops.

1860 Hamlin Garland, author (*A Son of the Middle Border*, *A Daughter of the Middle Border*), born in West Salem, MA (died 1940).

1867 Charles Dana Gibson, creator of "Gibson Girl," born in Roxbury, MA; also author of *The Education of Mr. Pipp*, *The Americans* (died 1944).

1872 Final decision of Geneva Arbitration Tribunal awarded $15.5 million to United States from Great Britain for damages caused by Confederate vessel *Alabama*, which was built in Britain.

1883 Margaret H. Sanger, family planner who set up first birth control clinic (1916), born in Corning, NY; founder, National Birth Control League (1914), which became Planned Parenthood Foundation (1942) (died 1966).

1887 Karl T. Compton, physicist, president, MIT (Massachusetts Institute of Technology) (1930–48), born in Wooster, OH; physics professor, Princeton (1919–30) (died 1954).

1887 Stanley (Stanislaus) Ketchel, probably best middleweight boxer, born in Grand Rapids, MI; won 46 of his 61 bouts by knockouts; was shot and killed in Springfield, OH, in 1910.

1892 Ben Moreel, commander of Seabees in World War II, born in Salt Lake City; board chairman, Jones & Laughlin Steel Co. (1947–58) (died 1978).

1896 John R. Powers, model agency pioneer, born in Easton, PA; founded first model agency in 1921.

1898 Hal B. Wallis, movie producer (*Little Caesar*, *Green Pastures*, *Casablanca*, *Rose Tattoo*), born in Chicago (died 1986).

1901 Vice President Theodore Roosevelt sworn in as president on death of President McKinley, eight days after he was shot; oath administered by U.S. District Judge John R. Hazel in the Ansley Wilcox home in Buffalo, NY.

1910 Bernard A. Schriever, Air Force general who headed intercontinental ballistics missile program (1954–66), born in Berlin.

1915 Statewide prohibition adopted by popular vote in South Carolina.

1920 Lawrence Klein, economist awarded 1980 Nobel Economics Prize for development of economic models, born in Omaha, NE.

1940 Congress approved first peacetime draft for military service.

1944 American forces invaded Palau Islands, taking Peleliu and Augaur.

1959 Congress passed Griffin-Landrum Act, designed to protect rights of individual union members against "dictatorial, ironfisted" union officials' actions and to ensure free and democratic secret ballot elections.

1975 Elizabeth Ann Seaton, first native-born American to be beatified (1962), was canonized.

1984 First successful transatlantic solo balloon flight began at Caribou, ME, with Joe W. Kittinger the pilot; landed near Savona, Italy, September 17.

1993 Israel and Jordan signed agreement in Washington establishing an agenda for negotiations to end 45 years of mutual hostility.

1994 Remainder of regular baseball season, the playoffs, and World Series were cancelled because of the players' strike.

1995 Dow Jones industrial average passed the 4800 mark (4801.80) for first time.

1996 Troops from United States and other countries began monitoring peace accord between three warring factions in Bosnia and Herzegovina.

1997 An American C-141 cargo plane collided with a German plane off South Africa with the loss of the 33 in both planes.

1998 World Com, Inc., purchased MCI Communications in a $43.4 million deal in the third largest telecommunications merger in U.S. history.

2000 Blood advisory panel for the FDA voted 7–6 to maintain 15-year-old policy of prohibiting males who had ever had sex with another male from giving blood due to AIDS danger; alternatives to require a one- or five-year gap before giving blood rejected.

2001   President Bush visited ruins of collapsed World Trade Center in New York and praised rescue effort.

2006   FDA urged Americans to avoid eating frozen spinach due to contamination from E. coli that had resulted in hospitalizations and deaths; by October 6, 199 cases reported with 102 hospitalized and three deaths.

2006   Segway recalled all its one-person self-balancing electric scooters made since 2002 for software update; cited danger of accidentally going into reverse.

15

1655   Indians attacked New Amsterdam, Pavonia, and Staten Island, killing 101 Dutch settlers in three days and taking 150 prisoners.

1752   English troupe, including Lewis Hallam, presented *The Merchant of Venice* in Williamsburg, VA, the first professional theatrical production in the colonies; marked the beginning of American theater.

1776   British troops under Gen. William Howe occupied New York City.

1789   James Fenimore Cooper, first important American novelist (*Last of the Mohicans, The Deerslayer, The Spy, The Pathfinder*), born in Burlington, NJ (died 1851).

1794   James Madison and Dolley Danbridge Payne Todd were married at Harewood in Jefferson County, VA.

1795   Zachariah Allen, inventor of first hot-air house heating system (1821), born in Providence, RI; also invented automatic steam-engine cutoff (1834) (died 1882).

1835   Richard Olney, Attorney General (1893–95) and Secretary of State (1895–97), born in Oxford, MA; directed policy for settling Venezuela boundary dispute with Great Britain (died 1917).

1835   First newspaper in Kansas, *Kansas Weekly Herald*, published in Leavenworth by William H. Adams.

1857   William Howard Taft, 27th President (1909–13), born in Cincinnati; Solicitor General (1890–92), U.S. Circuit Court judge (1892–1900); first civil governor, Philippines (1901–04), Secretary of War (1904–08); constitutional law

professor, Yale (1913–21); chief justice, Supreme court (1921–30) (died 1930).

1857   Brigham Young ordered Utah troops to repel the "invasion" of troops sent by the president to replace him as governor.

1862   Confederate troops under Gen. Stonewall Jackson captured Harpers Ferry, WV, and 10,700 Union troops and much equipment; surrender included garrisons at Winchester, VA, and Martinsburg, WV.

1865   Convention in Charleston, SC, repealed the secession ordinance; abolished slavery four days later.

1876   Frank E. Gannett, head of newspaper chain named for him, born in Bristol, NY (died 1957).

1876   Bruno Walter, orchestra conductor (Vienna, Los Angeles, New York, Minneapolis), born in Berlin; conducted Salzburg Festival (1925–38) (died 1962).

1882   Arthur D. Whiteside, president, Dun & Bradstreet (1930–52), born in East Orange, NJ.

1883   U. of Texas opened in Austin.

1887   U.S. Constitution centennial celebration began in Philadelphia.

1889   Robert C. Benchley, critic/author and screen actor, born in Worcester, MA; his books include *From Bed to Worse, My Ten Years in a Quandary*; remembered for movie short, *The Treasurer's Report* (died 1945).

1903   Roy Acuff, country music singer, born in Maynardsville, TN (died 1992).

1906   Rosy (Emmett) O'Donnell, commander-in-chief, Pacific Air Force during World War II, born in New York City (died 1971).

1914   Creighton Abrams, commanding general in Vietnam (1968–72), born in Springfield, MA; Army chief of staff (1972–74) (died 1974).

1918   Austro-Hungarian government suggested an "unofficial" peace conference; idea rejected by President Wilson.

1928   Cannonball (Julian) Adderley, jazz saxophonist, born in Tampa, FL (died 1975).

1928   Bryce Canyon (UT) National Park established.

1929   Murray Gell-Mann, physicist, born in New York City; awarded 1969 Nobel Physics Prize for contributions and discoveries about classification of elementary particles and their interaction.

1950   American Marines made amphibious landing on Womi Island, which dominates Inchon Harbor in Korea; Inchon later was taken.

1958 Train plunged into bay near Bayonne, NJ; 48 people died.

1959 Soviet Premier Khrushchev began 12-day visit to United States.

1961 Dan(iel C.) Marino, Miami football quarterback, born in Pittsburgh; by 1997 had become all-time leader in yards passing (51,636) and touchdown passes (369).

1963 Negro church in Birmingham bombed; four black girls were killed, 20 injured; racial rioting followed.

1969 Congress raised salary of vice president from $43,000 to $62,500.

1982 Senate, by vote of 47–46, killed proposal which would impose severe restrictions on a woman's right to have an abortion.

1988 Hurricane Gilbert, after raking Jamaica, the Caymans, and the Yucatan Peninsula, struck Texas and adjoining Mexico, leaving about 20 dead and more than 500,000 homeless, mostly in Mexico; flooding affected Mexican area resulting in drowning about 100 persons.

1995 National Basketball Association owners voted 24–5 to approve new collective bargaining agreement with the players, ending a lockout which began July 1.

1997 Two popular diet drugs were taken off the market after FDA findings that the drugs could cause heart ailments.

2006 U.S. Treasury set record for one day's corporate and individual tax receipts: $85.8 billion; previous record was September 15, 2005 — $71 billion.

16

1620 The *Mayflower* set sail from Plymouth, England, with 101 persons (56 adults, 31 children, 14 indentured servants) and a crew of 48; voyage took 65 days, during which one passenger died, two children were born.

1671 Capt. Thomas Batts crossed the Blue Ridge Mountains, starting from the present Petersburg, VA; discovered falls of the Great Kanawha River.

1672 Anne D. Bradstreet, poet and first important American woman writer, died at about 60; among her works was *The Tenth Muse*.

1766 Samuel Wilson, meat packer, born in Arlington, MA; inspector of meat sold to Army in War of 1812; he stamped "U.S." on it for "United States," but it was commonly said to stand for "Uncle Sam," which is what Wilson was called (died 1854).

1776 Continental Army under Gen. Washington repulsed British in Battle of Harlem.

1803 Orestes A. Brownson, editor (*Brownson's Quarterly Review*), an influential publication, born in Stockbridge, VT (died 1876).

1804 Squire Whipple, invented a truss used in bridge building, born in Hardwick, MA; the trapezoidal-shaped truss was called the Whipple truss (died 1888).

1822 Charles Crocker, financier and railroad builder, born in Troy, NY; helped form Central Pacific Railroad, which joined Union Pacific at Promontory Point, UT; merged Central Pacific into Southern Pacific, of which he was president (1871–88) (died 1888).

1823 Francis Parkman, foremost historian of his time (*The Oregon Trail, France and England in North America*), born in Boston (died 1893).

1832 George W.C. Lee, president, Washington & Lee U. (1871–97), born in Ft. Monroe, VA; served on Jefferson Davis' staff in Civil War (died 1913).

1838 James J. Hill, Great Northern Railway president (1882–1907), chairman (1907–12), born in Rockwood, Canada; helped develop iron ore deposits at Mesabi Range, MN (died 1916).

1852 Clarence Lexow, headed New York legislative investigation which uncovered corruption in New York City, born in Brooklyn (died 1910).

1875 James C. Penney, developer, board chairman (1916–46) of 1,500-store chain, born in Hamilton, MO; began as store clerk (1895) at $2.27 a month (died 1971).

1877 Jacob Schick, razor inventor, manufacturer, born in Des Moines, IA; invented magazine razor (1923), first successful electric razor (1924) (died 1937).

1883 Francis B. Davis, Jr., U.S. Rubber Co. president (1929–42), chairman (1929–49), born in Ft. Edward, NY (died 1962).

1893 Albert Szent-György, biochemist, born in Budapest; awarded 1937 Nobel Physiology/ Medicine Prize for work on biological combustion; isolated Vitamin C (died 1986).

1893 Cherokee Strip, more than six million acres between Kansas and Oklahoma, opened to settlers; about 90,000 persons took part in wild scramble for land; eight were killed, many injured.

1893 Earl Carroll, theatrical producer of musicals and his annual *Varieties*, born in Pittsburgh (died 1948).

1899 Samuel Spewack, playwright with wife of many hits (*Spring Song; Boy Meets Girl; Kiss Me, Kate*), born in Russia (died 1971).

1914   Allen Funt, creator, host of television's *Candid Camera* program in 1950s, born in New York City.

1919   Congress granted national charter to American Legion.

1920   Bomb exploded in Wall St. at noon, killing 35, injuring 100.

1924   Lauren Bacall, stage and screen actress, born in New York City; films included *The Big Sleep* and *Key Largo*, starred in *Applause* on stage.

1926   Robert Schuller, television evangelist and clergyman, born in Alton, IA.

1927   Peter Falk, stage/screen actor (*Prisoner of Second Avenue*), born in New York City; starred on television in *Colombo*.

1940   President Franklin Roosevelt signed Selective Training and Service Act, the first peacetime military draft; all men 21 to 36 were required to register.

1942   Dennis W. Conner, three times winning skipper of America's Cup yachting race (1980, 1987, 1988), born in San Diego, CA; also losing skipper twice.

1943   Lae in New Guinea captured by American and Australian troops.

1966   New Metropolitan Opera House in Lincoln Center, New York City, opened with an American opera specially commissioned for the occasion — Samuel Barber's *Antony and Cleopatra*.

1989   Hurricane Hugo began its six-day journey from the Caribbean through southeastern United States; 504 persons died.

1994   President Clinton sent former President Carter, Gen. Colin L. Powell, and Sen. Sam Nunn of Georgia to make final diplomatic attempt to have Haiti's military leaders step down.

1995   Hurricane Marilyn smashed into St. Thomas in the Virgin Islands, destroying 80 percent of its houses, killing at least eight.

1997   Helen Jepson, opera star of 1930/40s, died at 92.

2004   Category 3 hurricane Ivan did $14.2 billion damage (contemporary estimate) as it hit Alabama and Florida.

2006   *Death of a President* received the Fipresci (critics') Award at the Montreal Film Festival; pseudo-documentary showed assassination of sitting President George Bush; defenders speak of how it forces consideration of American anti–Arab bias; critics wonder whether it is an incitement to murder.

17

1607   First American jury trial held in Jamestown, VA, when the deposed governor, Edward M. Wingfield, was found guilty of slandering Capt. John Smith, who was awarded 200 pounds, and John Robinson, who received 100 pounds.

1656   Massachusetts enacted severe law against Quakers, calling for their imprisonment at hard labor until shipped out; later (October 14) set fine of 40 shillings per hour for harboring Quakers; every Quaker coming into the jurisdiction after punishment would suffer loss of one ear, for second offense loss of the other ear, for third offense having tongue "bored through with a hot iron."

1730   Friedrich von Steuben, Revolutionary general, born in Magdeburg, Germany; was inspector general with task of training Army (died 1794).

1776   The Presidio, around which San Francisco grew, founded by Jose Moraga, a lieutenant of Juan de Anza, Spanish officer and explorer.

1779   Langdon Cheves, Speaker of House (1814–15) while representing South Carolina (1810–15), born in Abbeville District, SC; headed United States Bank (1819–22) (died 1857).

1787   Constitutional Convention, with 39 in favor and three abstentions, approved final draft of Constitution to be submitted to states for ratification; three abstainers (Gerry of Massachusetts, Randolph and Mason of Virginia) wanted another convention for amendments.

1796   President Washington issued his farewell address after completing two terms; he deplored dangers of a party system, counseled that public credit be cherished, advised steering clear of permanent foreign alliances; not delivered as a speech but published September 19 in *Philadelphia Daily American Advertiser*.

1800   Frank Buchanan, planned Naval Academy, of which he was first superintendent (1845–47), born in Baltimore; commanded Confederate fleet in Mobile Bay, captured 1864 (died 1874).

1825   Lucius Q.C. Lamar, associate justice, Supreme Court (1888–93), born in Putnam County, GA; represented Mississippi in House (1857–60, 1873–77) and Senate (1877–85); Secretary of Interior (1885–88) (died 1893).

1854   David D. Buick, founder, head, Buick Manufacturing Co. (1902–06), born in Arbroth,

Scotland; went into debt developing auto, manufacture of which he lost control of (died 1929).

1855 Cornerstone laid for Boston Public Library.

1862 Battle of Antietam or Sharpsburg (MD) occurred with no decisive result; Confederates under Gen. Robert E. Lee withdrew on the 18th; battle considered significant because it stopped one of greatest threats to Washington, caused Great Britain and France to postpone their decision to intervene, and was "the bloodiest single day" of war; nearly 5,000 killed, 19,000 wounded.

1869 Ben Turpin, screen actor best known for his cross-eyed expression in films (1907–40), born in New Orleans (died 1940).

1883 William Carlos Williams, poet who was one of leading 20th-century literary figures, born in Rutherford, NJ (died 1963).

1900 J(ohn) Willard Marriott, founder, president of restaurant/hotel chain named for him (1928–64), born in Marriott, UT; was board chairman (1964–85) (died 1986).

1900 Martha Ostenso, author (*Wild Geese*), born in Bergen, Norway (died 1963).

1907 Warren E. Burger, chief justice, Supreme Court (1969–86), born in St. Paul, MN (died 1995).

1907 State constitution adopted by voters of Oklahoma, including prohibition.

1908 First aviation casualty occurred at Ft. Myer, VA, when a plane went out of control when the propeller blade broke; Lt. Thomas Selfridge was killed, Orville Wright was seriously injured.

1909 Edward N. Cole, General Motors president (1967–74), born in Marne, MI (died 1977).

1911 First transcontinental flight (New York to Pasadena) began; Calbraith B. Rogers made 68 hops in 49 days to cover the 3,390 miles; flying time 82 hours.

1923 Hank Williams, singer and composer (*Your Cheatin' Heart, Jambalaya*), born in Georgiana, AL; a leader of early country music (died 1953).

1926 Hurricane near Miami caused 370 deaths, thousands of injuries; made about 50,000 people homeless and caused $100 million in property damage.

1927 George Blanda, football player (Chicago, Houston, Oakland), born in Youngwood, PA; scored 2,022 points in 26-year career as quarterback, place kicker.

1930 Hoover Dam (originally Boulder Dam) dedicated at Las Vegas, NV.

1931 Anne Bancroft, stage actress (*Two for the Seesaw, The Miracle Worker*), born in New York City.

1934 Maureen Connolly, tennis star of early 1950s, born in San Diego, CA; career ended when she suffered a crushed leg in a horseback riding accident (1954) (died 1969).

1947 Freedom Train dedicated in Philadelphia before 33,000 mile tour.

1951 Jimmy Yancey, musician credited with originating boogie-woogie piano style, died at 57.

1959 Great Lakes steamer *Notonic* caught fire at Toronto pier, killing about 130.

1983 Humberto S. Medeiros, Catholic Archbishop of Boston (1970–83), died at 67; named cardinal in 1973.

1997 About 100 countries agreed to ban production or use of land mines; U.S. did not sign treaty; President Clinton pointed out that giving up land mines would jeopardize American troops in Korea.

2002 Thanks to the Hubble Space Telescope, a third category of black hole was discovered in space.

2002 Study released commonly regarded as most reliable survey of current religious membership in U.S.: *Religious Congregations & Membership: 2000* indicated a decade growth among Mormons (Church of Jesus Christ of Latter-Day Saints) of 19.3 percent; Christian Churches/Churches of Christ, 18.6 percent; Assemblies of God, 18.5 percent; Roman Catholic Church, 16.2 percent. More liberal churches losing membership: United Church of Christ loses 14.8 percent of members; Presbyterian Church, USA, 11.6 percent.

2003 Richard Grasso lost a vote of confidence of the directors of the New York Stock Exchange 13–7 and resigned as chairman; had been enduring weeks of criticism over revelation of yearly $140 million pay/benefits.

18

1679 New Hampshire set up as separate province with a government vested in a president and council appointed by the King and an assembly chosen by the people.

1726 Nathaniel Folsom, colonial leader, born in Exeter, NH; member of Continental Congress (1774–75, 1777–80); led New Hampshire state militia (1775) and was president of its constitutional convention (1783) (died 1790).

1733 George Read, colonial leader, born near North East, MD; member, Continental Congress (1774–77) and Constitutional Convention (1787); a signer of Declaration of Independence; represented Delaware in Senate (1789–93) and served as its chief justice (1793–98) (died 1798).

1777   As British troops moved on the city, the Liberty Bell was moved from Philadelphia to Zion Reformed Church in Allentown; returned a year later.

1779   Joseph Story, associate justice, Supreme Court (1811–45), born in Marblehead, MA; represented Massachusetts in House (1808–09); a pioneer in organizing, directing teaching at Harvard Law School; author of famous series of commentaries (1832–45) (died 1845).

1793   President Washington laid cornerstone for southeast portion of the Capitol.

1796   Hosea Ballou, a founder, first president, Tufts College (1854–61), born in Guilford, VT; held various pastorates (died 1861).

1804   Walter L. Newberry, endowed reference library (Newberry) in Chicago, born in South Windsor, CT (died 1868).

1812   Herschel V. Johnson, governor of Georgia (1853–57), born in Burke County, GA; Democratic vice presidential candidate (1860) (died 1880).

1848   Lucien Howe, ophthalmologist who wrote New York law requiring prophylactic drops in newborn babies' eyes (1890), born in Standish, ME; a founder, Harvard ophthalmology laboratory (1926) and Buffalo Eye & Ear Infirmary (1896) (died 1928).

1850   Congress passed Fugitive Slave Act, which supplemented and amended earlier (1793) act for handling fugitives from justice and runaway slaves.

1851   Henry J. Raymond and George Jones founded *New York Times*.

1857   John H. Clarke, associate justice, Supreme Court (1916–22), born in Lisbon, OH (died 1945).

1859   Gilbert M. Hitchcock, founder, publisher, *Omaha World-Herald* (1885–89), born in Omaha; represented Nebraska in House (1903–05, 1907–11) and Senate (1911–23) (died 1934).

1870   Clark Wissler, curator, American Museum of Natural History (1906–41), born in Wayne County, IN; author of ethnology classic, *The American Indian* (died 1947).

1873   Firm of Jay Cooke & Co. failed; many other investment firms went under the next day, touching off Panic of 1873; New York Stock Exchange closed for ten days; depression lasted until 1878.

1886   Powel Crosley, founder of Crosley Corp., president (1921–45), born in Cincinnati;

owner, Cincinnati Reds baseball team (1934–61) (died 1961).

1895   Cotton States & International Exposition opened in Atlanta; closed December 31.

1905   Claudette Colbert, screen actress (*It Happened One Night*), born in Paris (died 1996).

1905   Greta Garbo, screen actress (*Anna Christie, Anna Karenina, Camille, Ninotchka*), born in Stockholm (died 1990).

1905   Agnes DeMille, dance director and choreographer, born in New York City (died 1993).

1907   Edwin M. McMillan, physicist, born in Redondo Beach, CA; shared 1951 Nobel Chemistry Prize for co-discovery of transuranium elements; devised improvements in cyclotron.

1947   Department of Defense created, consolidating the Navy, War, and Air Force departments into one agency.

1986   Transportation Department announced approval of purchase of Eastern Airlines for $676 million by Texas Air, which earlier had agreed to purchase People Express.

1990   Atlanta selected to host the 1996 Summer Olympics Games.

1994   Agreement reached in Haiti for the return of President Jean-Bertrand Aristide and departure of military leaders; American troops arrived September 19 to control airfields and ports.

1996   President Clinton issued executive order creating the Grand Staircase–Escalante National Monument in southern Utah.

1997   Media executive Ted Turner announced he would donate $1 billion over ten years to benefit United Nations agencies.

2000   Announcement of $80 million gift to renovate National Museum of American History.

2002   A three-member panel of the Ninth U.S. Circuit Court of Appeals reinstated right of Burmese to sue American Unocal Corp. on grounds that they knowingly permitted and encouraged slavery, assault and rape, and murder by the soldiers protecting their pipeline. Suit invokes an 18th-century American law permitting such lawsuits for incidents that happen abroad.

2003   A category 2 hurricane at landfall, Isabel did widespread flood and water damage through the mid–Atlantic states with estimated (at time) damage of $3,370,000,000.

2006   Iranian-American Anousheh Ansari became first female space tourist as she headed to the International Space Station aboard a Russian Soyuz launch vehicle; cost: $20 million.

19

1650 Treaty of Hartford settled boundary between New Netherlands (New York) and Connecticut.

1676 Jamestown, VA, burned by Nathaniel Bacon and planters in their war with Gov. William Berkeley, who refused to act against marauding Indians; the rebellion ended when 30-year-old Bacon died of fever October 26.

1727 *Maryland Gazette*, first newspaper in state, began publication in Annapolis.

1737 Charles Carroll, colonial leader, born in Annapolis; member of Continental Congress (1776–78) and signer of Declaration of Independence; a first Maryland senator (1789–92); an original director, Baltimore & Ohio Railroad (died 1832).

1739 Andrew Pickens, Revolutionary general who served at Cowpens and led capture of Augusta, GA, born near Paxtang, PA; represented South Carolina in House (1793–95) (died 1817).

1775 American force under Col. Benedict Arnold left Newburyport, MA, on expedition to capture Canada; reached the St. Lawrence River November 9; another American force under Gen. Richard Montgomery followed the Lakes George-Champlain route; met Arnold at Quebec December 2; joint American assault December 31 failed.

1777 First battle of Bemis Heights (or Freeman's Farm) resulted in Gen. Burgoyne's return to camp to await reinforcements which never showed up; technically Bemis Heights was a British victory.

1780 John H. Cocke, a founder, planner of U. of Virginia, born in Surry County, VA; served on University Board of Visitors for 33 years (died 1866).

1782 British and American peace negotiators began talks in Paris.

1792 William B. Astor, known as the landlord of New York City because of vast real estate holdings, born in New York City; built Astor Library, addition (died 1875).

1804 Elling Eielsen, founder of Evangelical Lutheran Church of America (1846), born in Voss, Norway (died 1883).

1824 William Sellers, founder, head of machine tool works, born in Delaware County, PA; proposed standard system of screw threads, adopted by federal government (1868) (died 1905).

1829 Gustav Schirmer, who formed, headed music publishing company (1855–93), born in Königsee, Germany (died 1893).

1835 Ethan A. Hitchcock, first American ambassador to Russia (1898), born in Mobile, AL; Secretary of Interior (1898–1907), did much to enlarge forest reserves and withdraw mineral lands from exploitation (died 1909).

1859 John F. Jameson, historian who led successful drive for creation of National Archives, born in Somerville, MA; a founder, *American Historical Review* editor (1895–1901, 1905–28) (died 1937).

1862 Confederate troops under Gen. Sterling Price were defeated by Union troops led by Gen. William Rosecrans at Iuka, MS; prevented two Confederate forces from joining.

1863 Two-day battle of Chickamauga Valley, GA, outside Chattanooga, began; Confederate troops under Gen. Braxton Bragg drove Union troops under Gen. William S. Rosecrans into Chattanooga, which was virtually besieged until reinforcements arrived; Confederates lost 18,450 men, Union 16,170.

1864 Gen. Philip Sheridan and his Union troops defeated Confederates at Winchester, VA; three days later, Union troops won again at Fisher's Hill and Cedar Creek, driving Confederates from Shenandoah Valley.

1872 Key Pittman, who represented Nevada in Senate (1913–40), born in Vicksburg, MS; an effective spokesman for silver interests (died 1940).

1876 Vera C.S. Cushman, organizer of YWCA (Young Women's Christian Association) (1906), born in Ottawa, IL (died 1946).

1881 President Garfield died in Elberon, NJ, at 49 as the result of the July 2 shooting.

1899 Royal B. Lord, World War II general who invented portable steel emplacement, portable cableway, born in Worcester, MA (died 1963).

1905 Leon Jaworski, special prosecutor in Watergate case (1973–74), born in Waco, TX (died 1982).

1906 President Theodore Roosevelt issued proclamation extending eight-hour day to all government workers.

1907 Lewis F. Powell, Jr., associate justice, Supreme Court (1972–87), born in Suffolk, VA (died 1998).

1927 Harold Brown, Secretary of Defense (1977–81), born in New York City; Secretary of Air Force (1965–69); president, California Institute of Technology (1969–77).

1936 Al Oerter, holder of unmatched Olympic record of four consecutive gold medals in one sporting event (discus throw) (1956–68), born in New York City.

1940 Paul Williams, composer of popular music (*We've Only Just Begun*, *Rainy Days and Mondays*), born in Omaha, NE.

1957 First underground nuclear explosion occurred at Nevada testing grounds.

1967 Martin Block, most popular disc jockey of 1930/40s, died in New York City.

1988 Senate approved free trade agreement with Canada, which the president signed, clearing the way for America's part in phasing out tariffs on $131 billion in goods crossing the border; Canadian Parliament still must act.

1989 Appellate Division of New York State Supreme Court returned America's Cup to United States, overturning an earlier lower court decision awarding it to New Zealand; appeal is planned.

2000 Senate approved 83–15 China trade bill; approved in May by House: China's trade status to become permanent rather than reviewed yearly.

2005 Post-hurricane disaster nerves: Faced with approaching tropical storm Rita and under pressure not to risk another flood disaster in New Orleans, Mayor Ray Nagin urged evacuation of those who had returned to the city.

20

1565 Spanish forces under Pedro Menéndes de Avilés destroyed the Huguenot settlement in Ft. Caroline at mouth of St. John's River (FL), putting to death almost the entire garrison, "not as Frenchmen, but as Lutherans"; Spanish renamed fort San Mateo.

1676 Edward Randolph, a special agent of the Crown, submitted first of two reports in which he found that Massachusetts was not enforcing the Navigation Acts, was putting English citizens to death for their religious views, denying the right of appeal to the Privy Council, and refusing the oath of allegiance; his report resulted in forfeiture of the colony's charter (1684).

1809 Sterling Price, governor of Missouri (1853–57), born in Prince Edward County, VA; Confederate general who saw action in Missouri, Arkansas, Texas (died 1867).

1810 Joseph Harrison, engineer who devised new principle in locomotive boiler construction, born in Philadelphia; manufactured locomotive boilers (died 1874).

1820 George W. Morgan, minister to Portugal (1858–61), born in Washington County, PA; as Union general he served with Gens. Buell and Sherman; represented Ohio in House (1867–73) (died 1893).

1820 John F. Reynolds, Union general who was killed in first-day action at Gettysburg (July 1, 1863), born in Lancaster, PA; had seen action at Fredericksburg, Chancellorsville.

1829 Albert J. Myer, organizer of a signal corps for Army (1861), born in Newburgh, NY; founded, supervised, Weather Service as part of his signal corps (1870–80); Ft. Myer, VA, named for him (died 1880).

1833 David R. Locke, writer under name of Petroleum V. Nasby, born in Vestal, NY; gained fame for satirical writing against slavery (died 1888).

1849 George B. Grinnell, founder of Audubon Society (1886), born in Brooklyn; original promoter of Glacier National Park; an expert on Plains Indians folklore; editor, *Forest and Stream* (1876–1911) (died 1938).

1850 Congress passed act abolishing slave trade in Washington; effective January 1, 1851.

1850 Congress abolished flogging in Navy.

1853 Elisha G. Otis installed first safety elevator in New York City.

1861 Herbert Putnam, librarian of Library of Congress (1899–1939), born in New York City (died 1955).

1865 Constitutional convention in Alabama repealed secession ordinance; abolished slavery two days later.

1878 Upton B. Sinclair, author of muckraking novels (*The Jungle*, *Oil!*, *King Coal*), born in Baltimore; also wrote 11-volume Lanny Budd series; Socialist candidate for Congress and president several times (died 1968).

1881 Vice President Arthur took oath of office as president in his New York City home (123 Lexington Ave.) at 2 A.M., following President Garfield's death.

1884 Maxwell E. Perkins, editor with Scribner's publishers, born in New York City; developed such authors as F. Scott Fitzgerald, Ernest Hemingway, Thomas Wolfe (died 1947).

1885 Jelly Roll (Ferdinand) Morton, musician considered one of the inventors of jazz, born in New Orleans; composed "King Porter Stomp," "Jelly Roll Blues" (died 1941).

1902 Church fire in Birmingham, AL, killed 115 persons.

1913 S. Dillon Ripley, secretary, Smithsonian Institution (1964–84), born in New York City.

1917 Red (Arnold J.) Auerbach, basketball coach (1950–66)/general manager (1967–84), Boston Celtics, born in New York City.

1946 President Truman requested resignation of Commerce Secretary Henry A. Wallace because of an earlier speech criticizing American policy toward Russia.

1963 President Kennedy, speaking to UN General Assembly, called for better American-Soviet cooperation and a joint expedition to the moon.

1977 United States and Canada agreed to build 3,700-mile natural gas pipeline from Alaska to the lower 48 states.

1984 American Embassy annex in Beirut bombed by an explosives-filled truck, 23 killed.

1988 Lauro F.M. Cavazos, president of Texas Tech University, confirmed and sworn in as Secretary of Education, the first Spanish-American cabinet member; succeeded William J. Bennett, who resigned.

1995 American Telephone & Telegraph Co. announced biggest corporate breakup ever, splitting into three separate companies for communications services, communications equipment, and computers.

1998 Cal Ripken, Jr., Baltimore Oriole shortstop, ended his record-breaking streak of playing in consecutive ballgames at 2,632.

2000 End of the six-year "Whitewater" business endeavor probe; Special Prosecutor Robert W. Ray reports no evidence uncovered that would justify his prosecuting either President Clinton or his wife.

2001 U.S. demanded that Taliban in Afghanistan close all terrorist camps and give Osama bin Laden to U.S. for punishment; Taliban refuses.

2006 California filed lawsuit against six major automobile manufacturers including Ford and General Motors, arguing that they should be financially liable for the pollution their vehicles produce and their contribution to global warming and environmental degradation.

21

1595 Juan de Onate appointed Spanish governor of New Mexico; commissioned to explore and settle area.

1645 Louis Joliet, explorer of much of the Great Lakes and Mississippi Valley, born in Beaupre, Canada; first sighted Mississippi River in 1673 (died 1700).

1737 Francis Hopkinson, colonial leader and author of political satires against British, born in Philadelphia; member, Continental Congress (1776) and signer of Declaration of Independence (died 1791).

1776 Fire, either accidental or set, burned much of New York City's business district.

1776 Delaware adopted its state constitution and became a political unit; had been known as the "three lower counties" of Pennsylvania.

1776 Nathan Hale was captured by British and hanged as spy the next day; at the hanging, Hale said: "I only regret that I have but one life to lose for my country."

1779 Spanish troops overpowered a British garrison at Baton Rouge; controlled area for next 20 years.

1780 Benedict Arnold, commander of West Point garrison, met with British Major John André at Joshua Hett Smith's house on west bank of Hudson River near Haverstraw to deliver plans of the fort; André was captured near Tarrytown by American troops two days later and Arnold fled to the British September 25.

1784 First successful American daily newspaper, *Pennsylvania Packet and General Advertiser*, published by John Dunlap; later merged with the *North American*.

1788 Margaret Smith Taylor, wife of President Taylor, born in Calvert County, MD (died 1852).

1855 Samuel Rea, Pennsylvania Railroad president (1912–25), born in Hollidaysburg, PA; rose from rodman (1871) to president (died 1929).

1856 Illinois Central Railroad completed from Chicago to Cairo.

1867 Henry L. Stimson, Secretary of State (1929–33), born in New York City; was Secretary of War twice (1911–13, 1940–45); Governor General, Philippines (1927–29) (died 1950).

1885 H(arold) T. Webster, cartoonist noted for "The Timid Soul" (Caspar Milquetoast) and "Life's Darkest Moments," born in Parkersburg, WV (died 1952).

1893 First American gasoline-powered automobile built by Charles E. and J. Frank Duryea.

1893 Frank Willard, cartoonist ("Moon Mullins"), born in Anna, IL (died 1958).

1926 Donald A. Glaser, physicist, born in Cleveland; awarded 1960 Nobel Physics Prize for invention of "bubble chamber" to study sub-atomic particles.

1931 Larry Hagman, television actor (*Dallas*, *I Dream of Jeannie*), born in Ft. Worth, TX.

1938 A New England hurricane resulted in 680 deaths, $400 million damage.

1965 Water Quality Act passed by Congress to meet problems of water pollution and shortages.

1981 Senate by 99–0 vote confirmed Sandra Day O'Connor as first woman Supreme Court justice; she took her seat September 25.

1982 Football players struck against the National Football League, the first in-season strike in 61 years; ended November 16.

1982 President Reagan signed bill freeing intercity bus industry from many regulations governing routes and fares.

1989 School bus with 83 students was rammed by a truck and plunged 40 feet into a water-filled pit near Alton, TX; 19 students were killed, one died later.

2001 In response to economic concerns raised by success of terrorist attacks in New York and Washington, stock market plummeted 14 percent; second biggest drop in its history.

2003 After eight years photographing and sending scientific data back to Earth concerning Jupiter and its moons, the *Galileo* mission was intentionally destroyed by plunging it into the atmosphere of Jupiter; reason: to assure that Earth-originated bacteria could not contaminate future findings in the region.

2005 U.S. Centers for Disease Control and Prevention issued most extensive study of human exposure to dangerous substances yet done: although lead level down, most Americans carry residue of dozens of toxic substances and pesticides.

2005 With the mammoth Hurricane Katrina disaster only weeks behind, Hurricane Rita became a category 5 hurricane and up to a million Texas coastal and near-coastal residents began a precautionary evacuation further inland.

2006 Space shuttle *Atlantis* successfully landed at Cape Canaveral after 12-day mission to install first new construction on the International Space Station in 3½ years: 17½-ton addition included large solar panels to produce electricity.

22

1711 Tuscarora Indian War began with massacre of settlers along the Chowan and Roanoke Rivers in North Carolina.

1768 Delegates from 26 Massachusetts towns met in Boston to draw up statement of grievances.

1788 A group of New Jersey colonists reached their Ohio lands and founded Losantiville, later renamed Cincinnati.

1789 Act passed to provide compensation for members of Congress—$6 for every day of the session and mileage.

1789 Office of Postmaster General created as branch of Treasury Department in which Samuel Osgood was named September 26; Postmaster General became member of the Cabinet March 9, 1829, and the Post Office became an executive department June 8, 1872.

1807 William Cramp, founder of shipbuilding company named for him (1830), born in Philadelphia; company president (1830–79) (died 1879).

1827 John G. Parke, Union general who served at Antietam, Fredericksburg, Vicksburg, Petersburg, born near Coatesville, PA (died 1900).

1853 Hugh L. Scott, Army chief of staff (1914–17), born in Danville, KY; served in Indian campaigns, became negotiator with various tribes (died 1934).

1862 President Lincoln issued preliminary Emancipation Proclamation; formal document issued January 1, 1863.

1870 Arthur Pryor, bandmaster, born in St. Joseph, MO; started with John Philip Sousa, then formed own band (died 1942).

1895 Paul Muni, screen actor (*Louis Pasteur*, *The Good Earth*, *Emile Zola*), born in Lemberg, Austria (died 1967).

1901 Charles B. Huggins, physician, born in Halifax, Nova Scotia; shared 1966 Nobel Physiology/Medicine Prize for discovery of role of hormones in treating cancer of prostate (died 1997).

1906 Race riots in Atlanta left 21 persons dead; city was placed under martial law.

1914 Prohibition law enacted in Virginia, effective November 1, 1916.

1918 American troops took over the Argonne Forest.

1919 Steel strike for union recognition began at Gary (IN) U.S. Steel plant; ended in failure January 8, 1920.

1922 Chen Ning Yang, physicist, born in Hopei, China; with Institute for Advanced Study, Princeton U. (1944–65); shared 1967 Nobel Physics Prize for disproving principle of conservation of parity.

1942 David J. Stern, commissioner, National Basketball Association (since 1984), born in New York City.

1966 United States offered to stop bombing North Vietnam if Hanoi would match the de-escalation; offer made to UN General Assembly.

1973 Dallas–Ft. Worth Airport dedicated.

1973 Henry Kissinger sworn in as Secretary of State, becoming the first naturalized citizen to hold the post.

1975 Second assassination attempt on President Ford made in San Francisco; Sara Jane Moore, a police and FBI informer, was apprehended.

1987 National Football League players went on strike but team owners said they would continue playing with non-strikers after a one-week halt; strike abandoned after four weeks.

1989 Hurricane Hugo with 135 mph winds struck Charleston, SC, after wreaking havoc on Virgin Islands and Puerto Rico; more than 20 killed in Caribbean; about 12 in South Carolina; damage estimated in the billions.

1993 Part of an Amtrak train fell off a 12-ft. high trestle into a bayou, 15 miles north of Mobile, AL, killing 47 persons; train caught fire, trapping sleeping passengers; trestle had been struck 15 minutes earlier by a line of towed barges.

1995 Time Warner, Inc., and Turner Broadcasting System announced plans to merge.

1996 Dorothy Lamour, screen actress who starred in "Road" pictures, died at 81.

2006 Wal-Mart began test program in 65 Tampa Bay Florida area stores to sell 291 generic medicines at $4 for a 30-day supply (versus typical $10-$30); hopes to roll out program to all of Florida in January 2007 and expand to many other states the same year.

2006 Patricia C. Dunn, chair of the board of Hewlett-Packard Company and considered one of most influential women in nation, resigned post in scandal over illegal actions in attempting to ferret out company sources secretly providing information to newspapers.

23

1728 Mercy Otis Warren, colonial writer called the mother of the American Revolution, born in Barnstable, MA; held a political salon during pre–Revolutionary days; wrote two anti–Tory plays, a three-volume history of Revolution (died 1814).

1745 John Sevier, governor of temporary state of Franklin (1785–88) and first governor of Tennessee (1796–1801, 1803–09), born in New Market, VA; represented state in house (1789–91, 1811–15) (died 1815).

1777 John Paul Jones, commander of the *Providence*, captured or burned ten prize vessels.

1779 American troops, with help of French fleet, made unsuccessful siege of Savannah; French fleet left for Europe October 9.

1779 John Paul Jones in *Bonhomme Richard* led American squadron of six ships into battle with British convoy, led by the *Serapis*, off English coast; the *Bonhomme Richard* bested the *Serapis*; during fierce battle, Jones reputedly said, "I have not yet begun to fight."

1780 Major John André, adjutant general of British Army, captured while trying to return to British lines after having met with Benedict Arnold two days earlier; had incriminating West Point plans with him.

1786 John England, Catholic Bishop of Charleston, SC (1820–42), born in Cork, Ireland; founded first American Catholic newspaper, *U.S. Catholic Miscellany* (died 1842).

1800 William H. McGuffey, author of the famed *McGuffey Readers*, born in Washington County, PA; the *Readers* were standard texts in 19th Century American schools (died 1873).

1806 Lewis and Clark Expedition ended with return to St. Louis; started out May 14, 1804.

1816 Elihu B. Washburne, Secretary of State (1869), born in Livermore, ME; represented Illinois in House (1853–69), minister to France (1869–77) (died 1887).

1823 James Black, prohibitionist and first presidential candidate of Prohibition Party (1872), born in Lewisburg, PA (died 1893).

1830 Elizabeth K. Monroe, wife of President Monroe, died at Oak Hill, VA, at 62.

1833 President Jackson removed William J. Duane as Treasury Secretary for refusing to withdraw federal funds from the National Bank; funds withdrawn by his successor October 1.

1838 Victoria Claflin Woodhull, founder of Equal Rights Party (1872) and its presidential candidate, born in Homer, OH (died 1927).

1845 Knickerbocker Club, the first baseball team, organized in New York City by Alexander J. Cartwright.

1852 William S. Halsted, surgeon who developed local anesthesia (1885), born in New York City; performed first successful blood transfusion (1881), set up first school of surgery, Johns Hopkins Hospital (1890) (died 1922).

1867 John A. Lomax, folk song collector, born in Goodman, MS; first curator, Archives of

American Folk Songs, Library of Congress (1932–48) (died 1948).

1884 Adna R. Chaffee, Jr., organizer of Army's first mechanized brigade, born in Junction City, KS; assigned to develop armored forces (1938) (died 1941).

1884 Eugene Talmadge, Georgia governor (1932–36, 1940–42, 1946), born in Forsyth, GA; noted for flamboyant tactics (died 1946).

1889 Walter Lippmann, columnist and author (*A Preface to Politics, A Preface to Morals, The Good Society*), born in New York City (died 1974).

1892 First Christian Science Church organized in Boston by Mary Baker Eddy and 12 followers.

1897 Walter Pidgeon, screen actor (*Mrs. Miniver, Madame Curie*), born in East St. John, Canada (died 1984).

1899 Tom C. Clark, associate justice, Supreme Court (1949–67), born in Dallas, TX; Attorney General (1945–49) (died 1977).

1899 Louise Nevelson, famed for large abstract wood sculptures (*Sky Cathedral*), born in Kiev, Russia (died 1988).

1901 Trial of Leon F. Czolgosz, assassin of President McKinley, began in Buffalo, NY; lasted only eight hours 26 minutes; in 34 minutes jury returned verdict of guilty.

1915 Clifford G. Shull, physicist who shared 1994 Nobel Physics Prize, born in Pittsburgh.

1920 Mickey Rooney, screen actor (*Andy Hardy* series), stage and television actor, born in New York City.

1926 Gene Tunney beat Jack Dempsey in ten rounds in Philadelphia for world heavyweight boxing championship.

1930 Ray Charles, blind pianist and composer of jazz and pop music, born in Albany, GA.

1949 Bruce Springsteen, singer and entertainer, born in Freehold, NJ.

1952 Rocky Marciano knocked out Jersey Joe Walcott in 13th round in Philadelphia for world heavyweight boxing championship.

1966 Congress passed legislation raising minimum wage to $1.40 an hour, effective February 1, 1967, and to $1.60 an hour February 1, 1968.

1987 Stock prices rose 75.23 points, a record-breaking one-day gain.

1988 House approved and sent to President Reagan tightened curbs on textile, apparel, and shoe imports; President Reagan vetoed bill September 28, calling it "protectionism at its worst"; House failed to override veto.

1988 Former Presidential Advisor Michael K. Dever given suspended three-year prison term and fined $100,000 for lying to a congressional committee and grand jury about his lobbying after leaving the White House.

2000 Though serving as both assistant secretary of state and an ambassador to Finland, Carl Rowan was most known for his writings concerning white-black relations; dead at 75.

24

1654 With surrender of Ft. Orange (now Albany) by the Dutch to the British, the village of Beverwyck was renamed Albany.

1755 John Marshall, chief justice, Supreme Court (1801–35), born near Germantown, VA; his Court tenure exerted profound influence on legal, judicial history; represented Virginia in House (1799–1800), Secretary of State (1800–01) (died 1835).

1789 Federal Judiciary Act passed, creating American judicial system, much as it is today; established Supreme Court and Office of Attorney General (Edmund Randolph).

1789 John Jay named first chief justice of Supreme Court, confirmed September 26; continued to act as Secretary of State until Thomas Jefferson returned from France (March 22, 1790); first associate justices named were James Wilson, John Rutledge, William Cushing, John Blair, and Robert H. Harrison.

1827 Henry W. Slocum, Union general who commanded extreme right at Gettysburg, born in Delphi, NY; represented New York in House (1869–73, 1883–85) (died 1894).

1837 Mark (Marcus A.) Hanna, political leader, born in New Lisbon, OH; headed McKinley presidential campaign; chairman, Republican National Committee; represented Ohio in Senate (1897–1904) (died 1904).

1843 Adam W. Wagnalls, publisher who helped found Funk & Wagnalls Co., born in Lithopolis, OH (died 1924).

1862 Governors of 16 states met in Altoona, PA, and approved President Lincoln's Emancipation Proclamation.

1869 "Black Friday" panic in securities market occurred when gold prices fell from 163½ to 133 when James Fisk, Daniel Drew, and Jay Gould tried to corner market.

1890 Mormon Church ended polygamy with a manifesto which called on Mormons to "refrain from contracting any marriage forbidden by the law of the land."

1890 Allen J. Ellender, who represented

Louisiana in Senate (1937–72), born in Montegut, LA (died 1972).

1891 William F. Friedman, considered world's greatest cryptologist, born in Kishinev, Russia; devised first solution for the rotor cipher machine (died 1969).

1895 André H. Cournand, physiologist, born in Paris; shared 1956 Nobel Physiology/Medicine Prize for discoveries concerning heart catheterization, pathological changes in circulatory system (died 1988).

1896 F. Scott Fitzgerald, author who was spokesman for lost generation and Jazz Age, born in St. Paul, MN; works include *The Great Gatsby, This Side of Paradise, Tender Is the Night* (died 1940).

1899 George F. Doriot, credited with creating American professional business management corps, born in Paris; industrial management professor, Harvard (1926–66).

1900 Ham(mond E.) Fisher, cartoonist ("Joe Palooka"), born in Wilkes-Barre, PA (died 1955).

1905 Severo Ochoa, biochemist with NYU Medical School, born in Luarca, Spain; shared 1959 Nobel Physiology/Medicine Prize for discoveries related to compounds within chromosomes (died 1993).

1907 John F. Dunning, pioneer experimenter in neutrons, born in Shelby, NE; with Naval Research Office (1946–75); first to demonstrate fission of uranium 235 (1940) (died 1975).

1930 John W. Young, astronaut who was pilot of first space shuttle (1981), born in San Francisco; made six space flights, taking part in first two-man flight (1952).

1936 Jim Henson, creator of the Muppets for *Sesame Street* and own program, born in Greenville, MS (died 1990).

1955 President Eisenhower suffered a "moderate" heart attack in Denver.

1957 President Eisenhower sent federal troops to Little Rock, AR, to preserve order and to allow black students to enter an all-white high school.

1962 Fifth Circuit Court of Appeals ordered U. of Mississippi to admit James H. Meredith, a black student.

1988 Massachusetts Episcopal Diocese elected first female bishop in 450-year history of Anglican Church; election of the Rev. Barbara C. Harris could result in some problems.

1997 United States and Russia signed Comprehensive Test Ban Treaty which would outlaw nuclear weapons tests and other nuclear explosions; signed by 146 nations, but only ratified by eight (U.S. and Russia not yet ratified).

1998 Hurricane Georges began its assault on the Caribbean, including Puerto Rico, the Florida Keys, and the Gulf Coast; more than 600 were killed in the Caribbean; mass evacuations in the American areas held death toll to 41.

1998 National Basketball Association cancelled 24 exhibition games as its lockout of the players and inability to agree on contract continued.

2005 Hurricane Rita hit Texas and Louisiana as a category 3 hurricane and left estimated $9.43 billion damage behind.

25

1493 Christopher Columbus sailed from Cadiz, Spain, on his second voyage with a fleet of 17 ships and 1,500 men; arrived in Lesser Antilles November 3; named island on which he landed Dominica.

1513 Vasco Nunez de Balboa discovered the Pacific Ocean after crossing Panama Isthmus.

1690 First American newspaper, *Publick Occurrences Both Foreign and Domestick*, issued in Boston by Benjamin Harris, with the announcement it would be published once a month or oftener "if any glut of occurrences happen"; it was suppressed four days later.

1758 Christopher Sower, printer and publisher, died at 65; published German edition of Bible, one of first in America.

1775 Ethan Allen, hero of Ticonderoga, and 38 men were captured by British in campaign against Montreal; not released until 1778.

1789 First amendments to the Constitution, the Bill of Rights, were submitted to states for ratification; 12 amendments submitted, 10 ratified.

1807 Alfred L. Vail, telegraph pioneer, born in Morristown, NJ; partner of Samuel F.B. Morse in telegraph production; worked with Ezra Cornell in building first telegraph line (Baltimore to Washington) (died 1859).

1823 Thomas J. Wood, Union general at Chickamauga, Missionary Ridge, born in Munfordville, KY (died 1906).

1832 William L. Jenney, who designed what may have been first skyscraper, born in Fairhaven, MA; designed first tall building using steel as a building material (Home Insurance Bldg., Chicago 1884) (died 1907).

1841 James M. Bailey, sometimes called first

newspaper columnist, born in Albany, NY; wrote for *Danbury* (CT) *News* (died 1894).

1843 Melville R. Bissell, inventor of carpet sweeper, born in Hartwick, NY; manufactured sweeper (died 1889).

1843 Thomas C. Chamberlin, geologist who was co-developer of spiral nebulae theory of earth's origin, born in Mattoon, IL; specialized in study of glacial deposits and their evidence of past climatic conditions; founder, editor, *Journal of Geology* (1893–1922) (died 1928).

1846 Mexicans surrendered Monterey to American troops under Gen. Zachary Taylor.

1847 Vinnie Hoxie, sculptor of full-length marble statue of President Lincoln in Capitol rotunda, born in Madison, WI (died 1914).

1855 William S. Benson, first chief of naval operations (1915–19), born in Macon, GA (died 1932).

1866 Thomas H. Morgan, zoologist and biologist, born in Lexington, KY; awarded 1933 Nobel Physiology/Medicine Prize for discoveries on hereditary function of chromosomes; first native-born American, first non-physician to win this prize (died 1945).

1890 Sequoia (CA) National Park established.

1897 William C. Faulkner, novelist who was awarded 1949 Nobel Literature Prize, born in New Albany, MS; works include *A Fable*; *The Reivers, Sanctuary; Absalom, Absalom*, and the Snopes family series (died 1962).

1899 James M. Landis, public official, born in Tokyo of American parents; member, Federal Trade Commission (1933–34), Securities & Exchange Commission (1934–37); director, Civil Defense (1942–43); minister to Middle East (1943–44); dean, Harvard Law School (1937–46) (died 1964).

1903 Mark Rothko, artist who pioneered abstract expressionism, born in Dvinsk, Russia (died 1970).

1905 Red (Walter W.) Smith, syndicated sports columnist, born in Green Bay, WI (died 1982).

1925 Submarine *S-51* sank after colliding with a steamer off Block Island; 37 men perished.

1926 Ford Motor Co. introduced eight-hour day, five-day work week.

1931 Barbara Walters, radio and television personality, born in Boston; with *Today* show, then became first woman anchor of a national television news show (ABC 1976).

1956 First transatlantic telephone cable went into operation.

1961 President Kennedy proposed to UN General Assembly a series of steps leading to eventual nuclear disarmament.

1962 Sonny Liston knocked out Floyd Patterson in first round in Chicago to win world heavyweight boxing championship.

1978 Two planes collided over San Diego, killing 144 persons.

1988 The Rev. Juniperro Serra, founder of California missions, beatified by Pope John Paul II in the Vatican.

1988 Supreme Court refused to stop a Flint, MI, woman from having an abortion that her estranged husband had sought to prevent.

1995 Ross Perot said he is forming a new Independent Party that will field a presidential candidate in 1996.

2000 Senate appropriated $7.8 billion in effort to save fragile Everglades, Florida, ecosystem from environmental changes.

2001 Census Bureau report: poverty rate lowest in decades in 2000, shrank to 11.3 percent; critics argue that numbers indicate those who are poor, though, actually have become even poorer. Official poverty level for an individual, $8,794; for four-person family, $17,603.

2004 Hurricane Jeanne brought category 3 winds to Florida as it did $6.9 billion damage (contemporary estimate).

2006 *Business Week* issue of September 25 reported that since 2001 U.S. economy added 1.6 million new jobs in the health-care field (including the pharmaceutical and insurance industries) and 900,000 in home-building industry (including mortgage brokers and real estate agents), but no numerical growth in other fields; information industry (telecommunications, Web businesses, software, semiconductors) lost over 1.1 million jobs.

26

1651 Francis D. Pastorius, who laid out Germantown, PA, in 1683, and led party of German Friends to town, born in Sommerhausen, Germany (died 1720).

1774 John Chapman, better known as Johnny Appleseed, born in Leominster, MA; ranged over Ohio River Valley planting and pruning apple trees (1800–10) (died 1825).

1776 Continental Congress named Silas Deane, Benjamin Franklin, and Thomas Jefferson to negotiate treaties of commerce and amity with

European countries; Jefferson declined and was replaced by Arthur Lee.

1777 British under Generals William Howe and Charles Cornwallis occupied Philadelphia and Germantown; Congress fled to Lancaster and later to York.

1781 Andrew Lewis, who led British to victory over Indians at Pt. Pleasant (1774), died at 61; his victory resulted in peace with Indians early in Revolution; was general in Continental Army.

1787 Protestors led by Daniel Shay confronted Massachusetts militia at Springfield and began sporadic fighting until insurgents were routed in 1788; rebellion kept Massachusetts legislature from imposing direct tax, to lower court fees, and to exempt clothing and tools of one's trade, and household goods from debt process.

1789 President Washington named Thomas Jefferson as first Secretary of State; John Jay, who had been named first Supreme Court chief justice, handled State duties until Jefferson returned from France in March 1790; President also named Edmund Randolph as Attorney General, Samuel Osgood as Postmaster General.

1810 Southern expansionists captured Baton Rouge, proclaimed independent state of South Florida.

1813 Gen. Wade Hampton led American troops from Plattsburgh to Montreal; another force under Gen. James Wilkinson sailed Lake Ontario to St. Lawrence River.

1831 First American third party, Anti-Masonic Party, held first convention in Baltimore, nominating William Wirt for president.

1841 Stephen B. Elkins, War Secretary (1891–93), born in Perry County, OH; represented New Mexico in House (1872–77) and West Virginia in Senate (1895–1911); founded Elkins, WV (died 1911).

1844 First newspaper in Oklahoma, *Cherokee Advocate* (printed in English and Cherokee), published in Tahlequa by William P. Ross.

1862 Arthur B. Davies, painter and printmaker, born in Utica, NY; organized "Ashcan School" exhibit, a revolt of young American artists (1908), and its follow-up the Armory Show (1913) (died 1928).

1874 Oakes Ames, with Harvard Botanical Garden (1899–1922), director (1910–22), born in North Easton, MA; donated his 57,000 specimen orchid herbarium to Harvard (died 1950).

1874 Lewis W. Hine, photographer who originated photo story, born in Oshkosh, WI (died 1940).

1888 T(homas) S. Eliot, author and poet who was a major figure in 20th-century literature, born in St. Louis; lived in England most of his life; his work (*The Waste Land, Prufrock and Other Observations*) brought him 1948 Nobel Literature Prize (died 1965).

1888 James Frank Dobie, Texas folklorist (*Coronado's Children, Apache Gold and Yanqui Silver*), born in Live Oak County, TX (died 1964).

1891 Charles Munch, musical conductor of symphonies (Boston 1949–62), born in Strasbourg, France (died 1968).

1898 George Gershwin, composer of many classics, hit shows, born in Brooklyn; shows included *Porgy and Bess, Girl Crazy, Of Thee I Sing* and the classic "Rhapsody in Blue" (died 1937).

1901 Ted Weems, bandleader of 1920/30s, born in Pitcairn, PA (died 1963).

1909 William H.G. France, Sr., stock car pioneer who founded NASCAR (1948), born; built Daytona (FL) and Talladega (AL) speedways (died 1992).

1914 Federal Trade Commission Act went into effect, which according to President Wilson was "to make men in a small way of business as free to succeed as men in a big way, and to kill monopoly in the seed."

1918 Meuse-Argonne offensive began, designed to cut the main supply lines of German army; involved 1.2 million troops, suffered 120,000 casualties; ended November 11.

1919 President Wilson suffered a paralytic stroke in Pueblo, CO, while on a speaking tour to promote the League of Nations and Versailles Treaty; was left virtually incapacitated for remainder of his term.

1925 Marty Robbins, country music composer and singer, born in Glendale, AZ (died 1983).

1940 Presidential proclamation banned export of scrap iron and steel to any nation outside the Western Hemisphere, except Great Britain.

1947 Lynn Anderson, country music singer, born in Grand Forks, ND.

1950 American troops recaptured Seoul from the North Koreans.

1972 American Museum of Immigration opened at base of Statue of Liberty.

1983 Australian yacht, *Australia II*, beat an American boat, *Liberty*, off Newport, RI, to win America's Cup, which had not been lost by an American in 132 years.

1986   President Reagan vetoed bill applying economic sanctions against South Africa; the House overrode veto September 29, the Senate on October 2.

1991   Four men and four women, crew of *Biosphere 2*, entered giant airtight greenhouse in Arizona desert for two-year experiment in living in self-contained miniature world.

1993   Eight participants emerged from *Biosphere 2* in Arizona desert after two-year stay.

1994   Senate Majority Leader George Mitchell abandoned efforts to get a health-care reform bill through Congress this term.

1996   Astronaut Shannon Lucid ended 188-day stay in space, longer than any other American; most of the time was spent in Russian space station *Mir*.

1996   Senate failed to override presidential veto of a bill which would have banned late-term abortions.

2006   Iva Toguri died at 90; as "Tokyo Rose" (nickname given her and others in West but one not actually used by her) she was one of almost a dozen women doing anti–American propaganda broadcasts from Japan during World War II; due to having American citizenship she was prosecuted and jailed after the war in spite of opposition by General Douglas MacArthur and his staff; pardoned in 1977.

2006   Bernard J. Ebbers, 65, began de facto life imprisonment of 25 years; punishment for his role in $11 billion accounting fraud at WorldCom Inc.; was founder of company.

27

1514   Ponce de Leon received patent from Spanish crown to settle "the islands of Bimini and Florida," but on arriving the following February was attacked by natives and mortally wounded.

1722   Samuel Adams, colonial leader, born in Boston; tax collector of Boston (1756–64); member, Massachusetts legislature (1765–74); led agitation which brought on Boston Tea Party; member, Continental Congress (1774–81) and signer of Declaration of Independence; lieutenant governor, Massachusetts (1789–93), governor (1794–97) (died 1803).

1732   James Franklin, half-brother of Benjamin Franklin, published first Rhode Island newspaper, *Rhode Island Gazette*, in Newport.

1774   Continental Congress voted non-intercourse (non-importation, export, or consumption) with Great Britain, set up committee to carry out this resolution; adopted and signed October 20.

1777   Fifth Continental Congress met for one day at Lancaster, PA.

1779   John Adams named minister plenipotentiary to negotiate treaties of peace and commerce with Great Britain.

1809   Raphael Semmes, commander of Confederate sea raider, *Alabama*, born in Charles County, MD; the vessel destroyed 64 ships before being sunk off British coast by Union warship, *Kearsage* (died 1877).

1830   Treaty of Dancing Rabbit Creek ended all Choctaw Indian claims to land in Mississippi and provided for their removal west of the Mississippi.

1840   Thomas Nast, editorial cartoonist (*Harper's Weekly* 1862–86), born in Landau, Germany; invented political symbols of the donkey and elephant, campaigned against Tweed Ring (died 1902).

1840   Alfred T. Mahan, president, Naval War College (1886–89, 1892–93), born in West Point, NY (died 1914).

1846   Edward N. Westcott, banker and author, whose *David Harum* book became a play and movie, born in Syracuse, NY (died 1898).

1855   Joy Morton, founder, president, Morton Salt Co. (1885–1934), born in Detroit; founder, Morton Arboretum, Lisle, IL (died 1934).

1861   Edwin H. Anderson, librarian of New York Public Library (1913–34), born in Zionsville, IN; helped found Columbia U. library school (died 1947).

1887   James D. Dole, founder of Hawaiian pineapple industry, born in Jamaica Plains, MA; founded Hawaiian Pineapple Co. (1901) (died 1958).

1896   Sam(uel J.) Ervin, Jr., chairman, Senate Watergate Committee (1973–74), born in Morganton, NC; represented North Carolina in House (1946–47) and Senate (1954–75) (died 1985).

1898   Vincent M. Youmans, composer of light operas and hit songs, born in New York City; among his songs were "Tea for Two," "Sometimes I'm Happy," "Without a Song," "Rise 'n Shine" (died 1946).

1915   Gasoline tank car exploded in Ardmore, OK, killing 47 persons.

1919   Charles H. Percy, president, Bell & Howell Co. (1948–64), born in Pensacola, FL; represented Illinois in Senate (1966–84).

1939 Kathy (Kathrynne A.) Whitworth, winner of most women's golf tournaments (88), born in Monahans, TX; named to LPGA Hall of Fame.

1964 Warren Commission released report concluding that Lee Harvey Oswald was solely responsible for assassination of President Kennedy.

1975 Hurricane Eloise ended its two-week assault on Caribbean area and northeast United States; 71 persons were killed.

1979 Department of Health, Education and Welfare divided into two departments — Health and Human Services, headed by Patricia R. Harris, and Education, with Shirley Hufstedler named secretary December 6.

1985 General Synod of United Church of Christ declared its ecumenical partnership with Christian Church (Disciples of Christ).

1986 Senate approved 74–23 most comprehensive changes in federal income tax system since World War II; House approved measure 292–136.

1988 Reports circulated that carbon testing of material in Shroud of Turin proved it was made in 14th century, could not be burial cloth of Christ as claimed.

1988 New York State health officials declared it safe for hundreds of former residents to return to Love Canal in Niagara Falls, NY; had been declared disaster area ten years earlier because of chemical contamination.

1995 Treasury Department announced the United States will issue new $100 note, redesigned to incorporate many new anti-counterfeiting features.

2003 Donald O'Connor died at 78; vaudevillian, movie actor, comedian and dancer won every major acting-related award except the Oscar; best remembered for his co-starring roles with Francis the mule and for his outstanding performance in the musical classic, *Singin' in the Rain.*

2005 Change to Win Federation created from seven labor unions in effort to create a rival to the AFL-CIO and increase the size of the unionized American workforce.

2006 With its contract with Venezuelan-controlled Citgo coming to its scheduled end, 7-11 announced it would market its own brand; Venezuelan leader Hugo Chavez had denounced President Bush as a devil and drunk at UN, fueling proposals to boycott Citgo.

28

1542 Spanish explorers Juan Rodriguez Cabrillo and Bartolomé Ferrelo, searching for a direct route to the East Indies through Spanish waters, arrived at a Pacific coast port which they named San Miguel; they were in fact at what is now San Diego and had discovered California.

1765 Ship *Diligence* arrived in Cape Fear River with stamped paper for North Carolina, but was prevented from landing by armed colonists.

1774 Continental Congress turned down by one vote plan of Joseph Galloway of Pennsylvania to give American colonists something approaching dominion status as a solution for home rule.

1776 Convention adopted Pennsylvania state constitution.

1781 Yorktown, VA, encircled by 9,000 American and 7,800 French troops beginning a siege of three weeks.

1788 Continental Congress voted to transmit draft of a new constitution to the states for ratification; would become operative when nine states ratified.

1813 British evacuated Detroit after American victory (September 10) in Battle of Lake Erie made their position untenable.

1839 Frances E.C. Willard, temperance crusader, born in Churchville, NY; president, Women's Christian Temperance Union (1879–98) and World WCTU (1891) (died 1898).

1840 George W. Peck, publisher, *Milwaukee Sun,* born in Henderson, NY; his popular *Peck's Bad Boy* stories appeared in that paper (died 1916).

1850 President Fillmore appointed Brigham Young governor of Territory of Utah.

1856 Kate Douglas Wiggin, author remembered for *Rebecca of Sunnybrook Farm* and *Mother Carey's Chickens,* born in Philadelphia (died 1923).

1863 Frederick W. MacMonnies, sculptor (Nathan Hale in New York City, Columbian Fountain in Chicago), born in Brooklyn (died 1937).

1887 Avery Brundage, active in national, international amateur athletics, born in Detroit; president, U.S. Olympic Association (1929–53), International Olympic Committee (1952–72) (died 1975).

1892 Thomas Parran, Jr., Surgeon General (1936–48), born in St. Leonard, MD; with Public Health Service (1917–30); a leader in efforts to control, eradicate venereal diseases (died 1968).

1893 Marshall Field, III, founder, publisher, *Chicago Sun* (now *Sun–Times*), (1941), born in Chicago; organized philanthropic Field Foundation (died 1956).

1895 Wallace K. Harrison, architect, born in

Worcester, MA; led design of United Nations Building, Rockefeller Center, Trylon and Perisphere in 1939 World Fair, Metropolitan Opera House in Lincoln Center (died 1981).

1901 William S. Paley, Columbia Broadcasting System president (1928–46), chairman (1946–83), born in Chicago (died 1990).

1902 Ed(ward V.) Sullivan, newspaper columnist and host of popular television variety show, born in New York City (died 1974).

1902 Al(fred G.) Capp, cartoonist ("Lil Abner") born in New Haven, CT (died 1979).

1913 Alice Marble, tennis player who won American and Wimbledon singles in 1930s, born in Plumas County, CA (died 1990).

1918 Fifth Liberty Loan drive opened; closed October 19 with subscriptions of nearly $7 billion.

1920 Grand jury in Chicago indicted eight White Sox baseball players on charges of "throwing" 1919 World Series.

1924 Two of four Army Air Service planes reached Seattle, completing an around-the-world flight; made 57 stops in 175 days.

1937 President Franklin Roosevelt dedicated Bonneville Dam on the Columbia River.

1940 National Airport in Washington dedicated by President Franklin Roosevelt.

1987 Earthquakes struck southern California doing considerable damage, which was increased by a major aftershock on September 30.

1994 Presidents Clinton and Yeltsin signed agreement at the White House to speed destruction of American and Russian nuclear weapons.

2000 FDA approved prescription usage of RU-486 to end pregnancies.

2004 A 6.0 magnitude earthquake hit seven miles from Parkfield in central California; this stretch of the San Andreas fault endured earlier earthquakes four times in the twentieth century (1901, 1922, 1934, 1966) and at least twice in the nineteenth (1857 and 1881).

2006 Before an indignant House Energy and Commerce subcommittee, former chairman of the board of Hewlett-Packard, Patricia C. Dunn, repeatedly insisted that the methods used to investigate news leaks from her organization had been fully legal so far as she knew and insisted similar activities almost certainly carried out widely in business world; hostile interrogators stressed the illegality and deceit of some of the methods she states she was unaware of but financed.

29

1780 Major John André, British officer, found guilty by a court martial headed by Gen. Nathanael Greene; hanged October 2; an aide to Sir Henry Clinton, he dealt with Benedict Arnold for plans of West Point.

1789 Congress established 1,000-man U.S. Army.

1789 President Washington signed first federal appropriations act — $639,000 to defray expenses in 1789.

1829 Giles A. Smith, Union general who served at Vicksburg and with Sherman on march through Carolinas, born in Jefferson County, NY (died 1876).

1831 John M. Schofield, commanding general of Army (1888–95), born in Gerry, NY; West Point superintendent (1876–81), Secretary of War (1868–69) (died 1906).

1838 Henry H. Richardson, architect (Harvard U. buildings, Marshall Field Building, Chicago), born in St. James Parish, LA (died 1886).

1859 Hermann M. Biggs, pioneer in preventive medicine, born in Trumansburg, NY; introduced diphtheria toxin in United States (1894) (died 1923).

1892 Elmer L. Rice, playwright (*Street Scene, Counsellor At-Law, The Adding Machine*), born in New York City (died 1967).

1895 Joseph B. Rhine, parapsychologist, born in Waterloo, PA; with Duke U. (1927–65), Institute of Parapsychology, Durham, NC; author of *Extra Sensory Perception* (died 1980).

1901 Enrico Fermi, physicist who helped build first sustained nuclear chain reaction (December 2, 1942), born in Rome; awarded 1938 Nobel Physics Prize for production of neutron bombardment and for discovery of effectiveness of slow neutrons in producing radioactivity (died 1954).

1906 Greer Garson, screen actress (*Mrs. Miniver*), born in County Dow, Ireland (died 1996).

1908 Gene Autry, western singer and screen actor, born in Tioga, TX; made 82 pictures, wrote more than 250 songs; owner, California Angels baseball team (died 1998).

1913 Stanley Kramer, screen director, producer (*High Noon, Caine Mutiny, Death of a Salesman, Guess Who's Coming to Dinner*), born in New York City.

1915 Hurricanes in Louisiana claimed 500 lives.

1915 Oscar Handlin, influential in field of social history, born in New York City; noted for work on American immigration (*The Uprooted*).

1927 Tornado struck St. Louis killing 90 persons, injuring 1,500; destroyed 5,000 buildings and caused $50 million damage.

1931 James W. Cronin, physicist, born in Chicago; shared 1980 Nobel Physics Prize for groundbreaking research on the Big Bang theory of the universe's origin.

1941 American and British officials met in Moscow with Russians and agreed to send Russia large amounts of war materials.

1948 Bryant Gumbel, co-host of *Today* show (1982–97), born in New Orleans.

1982 Cyanide placed in Tylenol capsules caused death of seven persons in Chicago area; killer was not found.

1986 Soviets freed American journalist Nicholas Daniloff, who had been held in Moscow for allegedly spying; a day later, Gennadi Zakharov, a Soviet UN employee, pleaded no contest to a spying charge in New York City and was freed to return to Russia.

1987 The Rev. Pat (M.G.) Robertson announced he would resign his Southern Baptist ordination and give up leadership of multimillion dollar religious broadcasting empire to pursue campaign for Republican presidential nomination.

1988 Space shuttle *Discovery* lifted off successfully at Cape Canaveral, FL, in first American space shot since tragic *Challenger* disaster in January 1986, when the capsule blew up after liftoff killing all seven aboard; landed successfully October 3, at Edwards Air Force Base, CA.

1992 Two sightseeing helicopters collided over Niagara Falls; one crashed, killing four persons.

1998 Tom Bradley, first black mayor of Los Angeles (1973–93), died at 80.

2005 John Roberts sworn in as youngest Chief Justice of U.S. Supreme Court in over 200 years; 17th to hold post.

2006 U.S. Senate passed 80–19 the previously approved House legislation to erect a 700-plus mile border fence between Mexico and U.S.; Mexico intends to strongly protest the decision.

2006 Florida Representative Mark Foley resigned from Congress over reported sexually suggestive and explicit computer correspondence with underage male page who had worked for him; checks himself into alcoholic rehab center shortly afterwards.

30

1762 Nathan Smith, founder of medical schools at Yale, Bowdoin, and U. of Vermont, born in Rehoboth, MA (died 1829).

1774 Continental Congress resolved to recommend that no American products be exported after September 10, 1775, unless the grievances of the colonies were resolved before then.

1777 Sixth Continental Congress met in York, PA; adjourned June 27, 1778.

1800 Treaty of Morfontaine, commonly known as the Convention of 1800, was agreed on, superseding the 1778 treaties with France; released the United States from its defensive alliance with France.

1803 Sylvester Marsh, builder of inclined railway to top of Mt. Washington, NH, born in Compton, NH; invented special engine design, cog rail, atmospheric brake for the railway (died 1884).

1809 William Henry Harrison, governor of Indiana Territory, concluded treaty with several Indian tribes in Ft. Wayne, IN, by which United States bought three million acres on Wabash and White Rivers; condemned by Tecumseh, Shawnee chief, who demanded return of the land.

1819 Thomas Jordan, founder, editor, *Financial and Mining Record* (1870–92), born in Luray, VA; Confederate general who was chief of staff for Gen. Beauregard (died 1895).

1861 William Wrigley, Jr., founder, president, chewing gum company (1891–1932), born in Philadelphia; owner, Chicago Cubs baseball team (died 1932).

1864 Percy L. Howe, pioneer in dental research, born in North Providence, RI; demonstrated relationship of oral and bodily health (died 1950).

1870 Thomas W. Lamont, banker with J.P. Morgan & Co. (1911–48), born in Claverack, NY; board chairman (1943–48) (died 1948).

1875 Fred Fisher, composer of popular hits, born in Cologne, Germany of American parents; among his hits were "Come, Josephine, in My Flying Machine," "Peg o' My Heart," "Dardanella," "Chicago" (died 1942).

1882 World's first hydroelectric plant began operations on Fox River at Appleton, WI.

1882 Charles L. Lawrence, aeronautical engineer who designed first air-cooled aeronautical engine, born in Lenox, MA (died 1950).

1886 William Langer, governor of North Dakota (1932–40) after a court fight, born near Everest, ND; also represented state in Senate (1940–59) (died 1959).

1892 Leaders of Amalgamated Association of Iron and Steel Workers on strike against Carnegie Homestead plant were arrested on charges of treason against Pennsylvania.

1895 Lewis Milestone, movie director (*The Front Page, All Quiet on the Western Front, Mutiny on the Bounty*), born in Chisinau, Russia (died 1980).

1924 Truman Capote, author (*In Cold Blood, Breakfast at Tiffany's, Other Voices Other Rooms*), born in New Orleans (died 1984).

1928 Elie Wiesel, author (*Night Dawn, The Accident*), born in Sughet, Rumania; awarded 1986 Nobel Peace Prize.

1930 Dad (C.M.) Joiner tapped the great East Texas oil field for the first time, making Dallas the oil center of the area.

1935 First American opera, *Porgy and Bess*, written by George Gershwin, opened in Boston.

1943 Merchant Marine Academy in Kings Point, NY, dedicated.

1948 Edith K.C. Roosevelt, widow of President Theodore Roosevelt, died in Oyster Bay, NY, at 87.

1952 Cinerama, a three-film strip process, opened in New York City; stimulated interest in wide screens.

1953 President Eisenhower nominated Earl Warren as chief justice of Supreme Court; confirmed October 5.

1966 Hurricane Inez completed its six-day swing from the Caribbean to Mexico, striking Florida enroute; storm claimed 293 lives.

1976 Congress overrode presidential veto on $50 billion appropriations bill for social services, including manpower, education, and health projects.

1993 Gen. Colin J. Powell ended his four-year term as chairman of the Joint Chiefs of Staff; succeeded by Gen. John M. Shalikashvili.

1998 Bank America Corp. merged with Nation's Bank Corp. in a $61.6 billion stock transfer; resulted in largest American bank.

2002 West Coast ports close in retaliation for work slowdown; ports move almost $300 billion of cargo yearly.

2005 After spending 85 days in jail for refusal to testify to a grand jury about her sources for a CIA leak story, Judith Miller of the *New York Times* broke her silence and testified.

2006 Louisiana became the 12th state to modify its Constitution to prohibit state and local government from using eminent domain to buy private property for resale to business for economic development to increase state/local tax income.

OCTOBER

1

1730 Richard Stockton, colonial leader, born in Princeton, NJ; member, Continental Congress (1776), signer of Declaration of Independence (died 1781).

1732 Library Company began operating in Philadelphia with arrival of books from England; subscription library had been founded by Benjamin Franklin in November 1731.

1746 John P.G. Muhlenberg, Revolutionary general and legislator, born in Trappe, PA; served at Stony Point and Yorktown; represented Pennsylvania in House (1789–91, 1793–94, 1799–1801) and Senate (1801) (died 1807).

1768 Two regiments of British soldiers arrived in Boston from Halifax to enforce customs laws.

1781 James Lawrence, War of 1812 naval officer, born in Burlington, NJ; commanded the *Chesapeake* against the British *Shannon* June 1, 1813; though mortally wounded, he rallied his men saying, "Don't give up the ship"; a phrase which became the Navy slogan.

1799 Rufus Choate, eminent trial lawyer described as one "who made it safe to murder," born in Essex, MA; represented Massachusetts in House (1831–34) and Senate (1841–45) (died 1859).

1800 Secret treaty of San Ildefonso signed, whereby Spain returned Louisiana to France.

1804 William C.C. Claiborne formally installed as territorial governor of Louisiana.

1812 Territory of Missouri created.

1813 Caroline C. McIntosh Fillmore, second wife of President Fillmore, born in Morristown, NJ (died 1881).

1820 Fourth Census reported American population to be 9,638,453.

1826 Benjamin B. Hotchkiss, inventor of a machine gun, magazine rifle, born in Watertown, CT (died 1885).

1832 Caroline L. Scott Harrison, first wife of Benjamin Harrison, born in Oxford, OH (died 1892).

1832 Henry C. Work, composer of popular songs ("Come Home Father" [a temperance song], "Grandfather's Clock," "Marching Through Georgia"), born in Middletown, CT (died 1884).

1849 Convention in Frankfort adopted new Kentucky state constitution.

1849 Michael H. DeYoung, cofounder (1865), editor (1880–1925) of *San Francisco Chronicle*, born in St. Louis (died 1925).

1850 David R. Francis, ambassador to Russia (1916–18), born in Richmond, KY; served Missouri as governor (1889–93), Interior Secretary (1896–97) (died 1927).

1860 Eighth Census reported population of 31,443,321 and population center had moved to 20 miles south of Chillicothe, OH.

1881 William E. Boeing, founder Boeing Airplane Co. (1916), born in Detroit (died 1956).

1889 North Dakotans voted to adopt their constitution, including prohibition.

1890 President Benjamin Harrison signed act transferring the Weather Bureau to the Department of Agriculture.

1890 Yosemite (CA) National Park established.

1891 Stanford U. opened in Palo Alto, CA.

1893 Faith C. Baldwin, popular novelist (*Face Toward the Spring, Many Windows, New Girl in Town*), born in New Rochelle, NY (died 1978).

1899 William A. Patterson, president (1934–63), chief executive officer (1963–80), United Air Lines, born in Honolulu (died 1980).

1903 First World Series played between Boston Red Sox and Pittsburgh Pirates; Pittsburgh won first three games but Boston won series.

1904 Vladimir Horowitz, concert pianist, born in Kiev, Russia.

1908 Henry Ford introduced the Model T, priced at $850.

1910 *Los Angeles Times* offices bombed, 21 employees were killed and building demolished; three union men were later found guilty.

1914 Daniel J. Boorstin, librarian of Library of Congress (1975–87), born in Atlanta; author (*The Americans*).

1917 Second Liberty Bond issue of $3.8 billion in 4 percent convertible gold bonds was authorized.

1920 Walter Matthau, screen actor (*The Odd Couple, Fortune Cookie, Sunshine Boys*), born in New York City.

1920 Charles Ponzi, Boston speculator, indicted on 86 counts of using the mails to defraud.

1924 William Rehnquist, chief justice, Supreme Court (since 1986), associate justice (1972–86), born in Milwaukee.

1929 Jimmy (James E.) Carter, 39th President (1977–81), born in Plains, GA; served Georgia as governor (1970–74).

1935 Julie Andrews, stage (*My Fair Lady*) and screen actress (*Mary Poppins, Sound of Music*), born in Walton, England.

1942 First American jet flight took place when a Bell XP-59A, powered by two turbojet engines, flew at Edwards Air Force Base, CA.

1945 Rod(ney C.) Carew, baseball player (Minnesota, Los Angeles) born in Gaton, Panama; named to Baseball Hall of Fame; considered one of greatest hitters.

1955 The *Forrestal*, first of new class of aircraft carriers, commissioned; has displacement of about 60,000 tons, flight deck of more than 800 feet.

1960 Army Gen. Lyman L. Lemnitzer named chairman of Joint Chiefs of Staff.

1960 Connecticut General Assembly abolished county governments; necessary county functions transferred to state.

1961 Roger Maris of New York Yankees hit his 61st home run of season, breaking the old season record of 60 set by Babe Ruth nearly 40 years earlier.

1962 Army Gen. Maxwell D. Taylor became chairman of Joint Chiefs of Staff.

1962 James Meredith became first black student at U. of Mississippi after 3,000 troops put down riots.

1965 Administration on Aging created; functions later transferred to the Human Development Office.

1979 Panama took control of the Panama Canal Zone.

1983 Job Training Partnership Act of 1984 went into effect, replacing the Comprehensive Employment & Training Act (CETA), with training programs focusing primarily on the private sector.

1984 Labor Secretary Raymond J. Donovan indicted in New York City on charges of participation in scheme to defraud New York Transit Authority; took leave of absence from cabinet; acquitted in 1987.

1985 Navy Adm. William J. Crowe, Jr., became chairman of Joint Chiefs of Staff.

1986 President Carter Memorial Library dedicated in Atlanta.

1992 Senate approved START I (Strategic Arms Reduction Treaty), which had been signed July 31, 1991.

1995 Ten Muslims convicted in New York City of conspiracy to conduct a terrorist campaign, including bombings and assassinations.

1997 Army Gen. Henry H. Shelton became chairman of Joint Chiefs of Staff.

2

1656 Connecticut passed law to fine and banish Quakers.

1755 Hannah Adams, first American woman professional writer, born in Medfield, MA; among her works were *Truth and Excellence of the Christian Religion, History of the Jews* (died 1831).

1780 British Major John André hanged as a spy in Tappan, NY, for dealings with Benedict Arnold.

1782 Charles Lee, Revolutionary general, died at 51; captured by British and while prisoner gave British plans for defeating Americans; exchanged, put in charge of attack on Monmouth; began retreat instead; court martialled, dismissed from Army (1780).

1788 Continental Congress moved unceremoniously from rooms in New York's City Hall so that the building could be renovated for new federal government.

1819 George W. Getty, Union general distinguished for defense of Suffolk (1863), born in Washington, DC; served with Army of the Shenandoah (1864), the Potomac (1865) (died 1901).

1830 Charles Pratt, cofounder of crude oil refining company, born in Watertown, MA; became Standard Oil executive after company was sold; benefactor, founder, Pratt Institute, Brooklyn, for training artisans, draftsmen (died 1891).

1831 E(dwin) L. Godkin, founder, editor, *The Nation* (1865–81), born in Mayne, Ireland; editor, *New York Post* (1883–1900), into which *The Nation* had been merged (died 1902).

1835 First battle of Texas Revolution occurred in Gonzales, where Texans successfully refused to surrender a cannon to 100 Mexican soldiers.

1865 Connecticut voted against Negro suffrage.

1867 Theodore F. Green, Rhode Island governor (1932–36) and represented it in Senate (1936–60), born in Providence; was (then) oldest man to serve in Congress (died 1966).

1871 Cordell Hull, Secretary of State (1933–44), called the father of the United Nations, born in Byrdstown, TN; awarded 1945 Nobel Peace Prize; represented Tennessee in House (1907–21, 1923–31) and Senate (1933–44) (died 1955).

1874 Edwin H. Crump, political boss of Memphis area, born in Holly Springs, MS; Memphis mayor (1910–16, 1940) (died 1954).

1877 Carl T. Hayden, legislator, born in what is now Tempe, AZ; represented Arizona in House (1912–27) and Senate (1927–69), serving as president pro tem (1957–69) (died 1972).

1879 Wallace Stevens, insurance executive and poet (*Harmonium, Ideas of Order, Man with the Blue Guitar*), born in Reading, PA (died 1955).

1885 Ruth Bryan Rohde, first woman named to head American diplomatic post, born in Jacksonville, IL; named minister to Denmark (1933–36); represented Florida in House (1919–23) (died 1954).

1889 First Pan-American Conference opened in Washington.

1891 Arizona territorial legislature adopted a constitution.

1895 Groucho (Julius H.) Marx, screen and television actor with brothers, born in New York City (died 1977).

1895 Bud (William) Abbott, comedian, half of Abbott and Costello team, born in Asbury Park, NJ (died 1974).

1901 Charles S. Draper, pioneered in developing navigational guidance systems for ships, planes, rockets, born in Windsor, MO (died 1988).

1909 Alex(ander G.) Raymond, cartoonist (*Flash Gordon, Rip Kirby*), born in New Rochelle, NY (died 1956).

1919 James M. Buchanan, economist, born in Murfreesboro, TN; awarded 1986 Nobel Economics Prize for pioneering development of new methods for analyzing economic and political decision-making.

1942 Office of Economic Stabilization created; James F. Byrnes named director.

1967 Thurgood Marshall sworn in as first black Supreme Court justice.

1968 North Cascades (WA) and Redwood (CA) National Parks established.

1970 Plane carrying Wichita State U. football team crashed at Silver Plume, CO; 29 died.

1985 Screen actor Rock Hudson died at 59 in Los Angeles; his death from AIDS gave publicity to the disease and a strong impetus to efforts for fund-raising to find a cure.

1988 Catholic Archdiocese of Detroit announced recommendations to close 43 of Detroit's 112 churches serving 10,000 parishioners because of low membership and high operating costs; closings scheduled for June 1989.

1991 Apple Computer and IBM Corp. signed contract to create an alliance in computers and software.

3

1656 Miles Standish, colonial leader, died at about 72; arrived on *Mayflower*, served as military defender of colony, treasurer for nine years, and on governor's council for 29 years.

1724 Herman Husbands, leader of the Whiskey Rebellion in Western Pennsylvania, born probably in Cecil County, MD; tried, condemned to death, but later pardoned (died 1793).

1777 James Jackson, one of first physicians to introduce vaccination against smallpox (1800), born in Newburyport, MA (died 1867).

1784 Ithiel Town, architect, born in Thompson, CT; designed state capitols in Indiana, North Carolina, the New Haven and Trinity churches, Customs House in New York City (died 1844).

1789 President Washington issued proclamation establishing Thanksgiving Day; first one observed November 26.

1790 John Ross, half-breed Cherokee leader who was chief of United Cherokee Nation (1839–66), born near Lookout Mountain, TN (died 1866).

1800 George Bancroft, Secretary of Navy (1845–46) who established Naval Academy, born in Worcester, MA; minister to Great Britain (1846–49), to Germany (1867–74); author of ten-volume American history (died 1891).

1802 George Ripley, Unitarian theologian who helped organize experimental Brook Farm community in Massachusetts, born in Worcester, MA; literary critic, *New York Tribune* (1849–80) (died 1880).

1803 John Gorrie, physician who devised method of treating malaria in a cool room, born in Charleston, SC; eventually built machine (c. 1842) to cool room, probably first mechanical refrigerating device (died 1855).

1804 Townsend Harris, first American consul general to Japan (1855–59), minister (1859), born in Sandy Hill, NY; negotiated commercial treaty with Japan; a founder, City College of New York (died 1878).

1823 Benjamin F. Stephenson, founder of Grand Army of Republic (GAR) (1866), born in Wayne County, IL; Union regimental surgeon (1861–64) (died 1871).

1854 William C. Gorgas, physician who did much to control yellow fever during Panama Canal construction, born near Mobile, AL; chief sanitary officer, Havana (1898–1902), Panama Canal Commission (1904–13); Army Surgeon General (1914–16) (died 1920).

1862 Gen. William S. Rosecrans led his Union troops to victory over Confederates under Gen. Earl Van Dorn at Corinth, MS.

1872 Fred Clarke, baseball player/manager (Pittsburgh), born in Winterset, IA; named to Baseball Hall of Fame (died 1960).

1892 U. of Idaho, chartered in 1889, opened.

1899 Gertrude Berg, radio and television actress/writer (The Goldbergs series), born in New York City (died 1966).

1900 Thomas C. Wolfe, novelist (*Look Homeward, Angel*; *The Web and the Rock*; *You Can't Go Home Again*), born in Asheville, NC (died 1938).

1910 Convention began in Santa Fe to adopt New Mexico constitution.

1922 First woman to serve in the U.S. Senate, Mrs. Rebecca L. Fulton, appointed by Georgia governor to fill a vacancy; served until November 22.

1925 Gore Vidal, author (*Myra Breckenridge, Burr, 1876, Kalki*), born in West Point, NY.

1941 Chubby Checker, entertainer, born as Ernest Evans in Philadelphia; helped popularize the twist, a dance craze of the early 1960s.

1951 Bobby Thomson, New York Giants, hit a home run with two men on base in bottom of ninth inning to beat Brooklyn 5–4 and give the Giants the pennant; Giants were 13½ games behind August 11 and wound up season tied with Brooklyn, then won two of three play-off games.

1962 Explosion in New York Telephone Co. building in New York caused 23 deaths.

1965 National origins quota system of immigration abolished.

1970 National Oceanic and Atmospheric Administration (NOAA) formed by combining Weather Service, Ocean Survey, and Marine Fisheries services.

1987 Sweeping new free trade agreement between United States and Canada announced; would eliminate all tariffs between the two countries by 1999; needs approval of Canadian Parliament and U.S. Congress.

1994 Mike Espy resigned as Secretary of Agriculture under pressure from White House following disclosure that large poultry producer gave his girlfriend a $1,200 college scholarship.

1995 O.J. Simpson, football star and sportscaster, found not guilty of the murder of his wife and another person after a trial which began January 24.

2000 First debate between presidential candidates Al Gore and George W. Bush.

2004 Janet Leigh died; although appearing in many movies during the 1940s and 1950s and in made-for television films in the 1970s, her brief appearance in *Psycho* and its famous shower death scene (1960) resulted in an Academy Award nomination.

2005 Bush nominated White House counsel Harriet Miers as replacement for Sandra Day O'Connor on Supreme Court; after extended criticism of her talents and abilities by both conservatives and liberals, she withdrew on October 27.

2005 Alastair G.W. Cameron, head of the Harvard University Astronomy Department (1976–82), died at 80; one of major pioneers of the now popular scenario that the moon was created as result of the impact of a Mars size planet with the earth; impact created fragments that ultimately coalesced into the moon.

2006 A leading conservative newspaper, the *Washington Times,* called for immediate resignation of Republican Speaker of the House of Representatives Dennis Hastert for inadequate pursuit of sexual harassment allegations against Florida Congressman Mark Foley; called for interim replacement by Rep. Henry Hyde, who was in his final term in Congress.

2006 Nobel Physics Prize won by John Mather and George Smoot of U.S. for work providing evidence for Big Bang theory of universe's origin; Andrew Fire and Craig Mellon win at same time for medical breakthrough in "turning off" genes from functioning, opening door for potential cure of diseases such as cancer.

4

1777 About 1,000 Americans were lost in audacious attack on British headquarters in Germantown, PA, in effort to free Philadelphia; attack abandoned.

1809 Robert C. Schenck, legislator, born in Franklin, OH; represented Ohio in House (1843–51, 1863–71); minister to Brazil (1851–53), to Great Britain (1871–76); was Union general in Civil War (died 1890).

1810 Eliza McCardle Johnson, wife of President Andrew Johnson, born in Leesburg, TN (died 1876).

1812 American troops defeated British at Ogdensburg, NY.

1822 Rutherford B. Hayes, 19th President (1877–81), born in Delaware, OH; represented Ohio in House (1865–67) and served it as governor (1867–71, 1875–76); became president in disputed election with Samuel J. Tilden; resolved by 15-member electoral commission (died 1893).

1858 Michael I. Pupin, physicist who invented multiplex telegraphy, born in Idvor, Hungary (now Yugoslavia); at Columbia U. (1901–31); improved coil for long-distance telephony (died 1935).

1861 Frederic Remington, painter of animals, American West scenes, born in Canton, NY (died 1909).

1861 Walter Rauschenbusch, Baptist theologian who founded Society of Jesus, which became Brotherhood of the Kingdom, born in Rochester, NY; with Rochester Seminary (1897–1918); a leader in social interpretation and application of Christianity (died 1918).

1862 Edward Stratemeyer, publisher and author under own name and several pseudonyms, born in Elizabeth, NJ; turned out several series of youth books (*The Rover Boys, Tom Swift, The Hardy Boys, The Bobbsey Twins*) (died 1930).

1871 U. of Alabama at Tuscaloosa reorganized and opened.

1879 Edward M. East, geneticist whose work led to development of hybrid corn, born in DuQuoin, IL (died 1938).

1884 Damon Runyon, journalist and author (*Blue Plate Special, Guys and Dolls*), born in Manhattan, KS; wrote several screenplays (*Lady for a Day, Little Miss Marker*) (died 1946).

1890 John Kelly, Sr., winner of Olympic single (1920) and double sculls (1920, 1924), born in Philadelphia (died 1960).

1893 Walter A. Maier, religious leader who was regular speaker on popular weekly Lutheran hour (1930–50), born in Boston (died 1950).

1895 Buster (Joseph F.) Keaton, silent screen comedian, born in Piqua, KS; master of deadpan (died 1966).

1905 Calvin Coolidge and Grace Anna Goodhue were married in Burlington, VT.

1918 Shell loading plant in Morgan, NJ, exploded, leveling several nearby villages and killing 90 persons.

1918 Germany and Austria asked President Wilson to "take steps for restoration of peace" and to notify other belligerents of the request.

1922 Malcolm Baldrige, Secretary of Commerce (1981–87), born in Omaha, NE; died in a horse riding accident (1987).

1924 Charlton Heston, screen actor (*Ben Hur, Julius Caesar*), born in Evansville, IL.

1945 Gen. Douglas MacArthur, directing military occupation of Japan, issued orders restoring civil liberties, freeing political prisoners, and abolishing the secret police.

1959 *Luna 3*, an unmanned satellite, was first to circle moon and send back pictures of the far side.

1965 Pope Pius VI arrived in New York City to deliver a peace message to United Nations; later conferred with President Lyndon Johnson.

1974 Joseph H. Hirschhorn Museum and Sculpture Garden opened in Washington.

1995 Pope John Paul II arrived in Newark for his fourth visit since 1978.

1997 Thousands of Christian men met in Washington to reaffirm their faith in God and pledge to help restore nation and preserve family structure; rally organized by group called Promise Keepers.

2000 Announcement: Library of Congress to receive record $60 million from John W. Kluge, a telecommunications entrepreneur.

2002 Hurricane Lili (category 1 storm) made landfall; estimated damage of $860 million.

2002 John Walker Lindh, Californian and

member of Taliban military who was captured in Afghanistan, sentenced to 20 years imprisonment; apologizes for his bad judgment; escapes potential life imprisonment.

2002 First international meeting of the National Center on Disaster Psychology and Terrorism begins in Palo Alto, California; mental health efforts traditionally aimed at individuals; in light of 9/11 terrorist attack professionals in field felt need to share ideas on how to handle situations when massive numbers are simultaneously affected by disaster.

2004 Astronaut Gordon Cooper died at 77; spent 222 hours in space: flew "Faith 7" Project Mercury Mission (May 1963), command pilot Gemini 5 mission, on which he became first person to have taken two space flights (August 1965); served as backup pilot (Gemini 12) and backup commander Apollo X.

2006 After the Dow Jones average edged to an all-time high October 3, today it jumped a dramatic 123.19 points to 11,850.53.

5

1609 John Smith, burned in a powder explosion, deposed from presidency of the Jamestown council and sent back to England.

1703 Jonathan Edwards, regarded as greatest theologian of American Puritanism, born in East Windsor, CT; pastor of Northampton Church (1729–50) and dismissed over argument on church admission standards; led revival (1734–35) that spread through Connecticut and paved way for later tours by George Whitefield; president, College of New Jersey (later Princeton) (1757–58) (died 1758).

1748 Benjamin Moore, Episcopal Bishop of New York (1801–16), born in Newtown, NY; president, Columbia U. (1801–11) (died 1816).

1751 James Iredell, one of original Supreme Court associate justices (1790–99), born in Lewes, England; attorney general of North Carolina (1779–81) (died 1799).

1774 Assembly of Massachusetts met in Salem despite ban on such meetings; named Committee of Safety empowered to call out militia and promote military organization.

1784 Dutch Reformed Church Synod established first American theological seminary in New York City; later became the New Brunswick (NJ) Theological Seminary.

1787 Thomas Stone, colonial leader, died at 44; member of Continental Congress (1775–78) and signer of Declaration of Independence.

1804 Robert P. Parrott, inventor of a rifle, first American rifled cannon, born in Lee, NH; his guns were used by Union forces in Civil War (died 1877).

1813 American troops under Gen. William Henry Harrison overtook and defeated retreating British-Indian forces near Thamesville, Canada; Tecumseh killed in the battle, resulting in collapse of Indian confederacy and its alliance with British.

1818 Connecticut convention adopted state constitution; ratified by popular vote.

1822 Moses Sperry Beach, invented device for feeding newsprint into presses from a roller, born in Springfield, MA; owner, *New York Sun* (1852–68); his device made it possible for first time to print on both sides of paper at one time (died 1892).

1824 Henry Chadwick, sportswriter who did much to promote professional baseball, born in Exeter, England; worked on several New York City papers; edited, published annual official baseball guide; named to Baseball Hall of Fame (died 1908).

1829 Chester Alan Arthur, 21st President (1881–85), born in Fairfield, VT; collector, Port of New York (1871–78); elected vice president, serving from March 4 to September 19, 1881, when he became president at death of President Garfield (died 1886).

1848 Edward L. Trudeau, physician who specialized in tuberculosis, born in New York City; founded Trudeau Sanitarium in Adirondacks (1884), Saranac Laboratory (1894), first American laboratory devoted to tuberculosis (died 1915).

1860 Gov. William H. Gist of South Carolina wrote confidential letter to each cotton state governor, informing him that if Abraham Lincoln was elected, South Carolina would call a secession convention.

1869 Frank H. Hitchcock, Postmaster General (1909–13), who initiated parcel post, airmail, and postal savings, born in Amherst, OH (died 1935).

1877 Three-day battle of Bear Paws Mountain in Idaho ended when Chief Joseph surrendered to Col. Nelson A. Miles ending Nez Perce War.

1879 (Francis) Peyton Rous, physiologist with Rockefeller Institute (1910–45), born in Baltimore; shared 1966 Nobel Physiology/Medicine

Prize for discovery of tumor-producing viruses; first to isolate cancer-causing virus (died 1970).

1882   Robert H. Goddard, physicist known as father of modern rocketry, born in Worcester, MA; with Clark U. (1914–43), he engaged in rocket research for reaching high altitudes (died 1945).

1892   Two of the notorious Dalton brothers were killed in an attempted bank robbery in Coffeyville, KS; another was captured.

1895   Walter Bedell Smith, World War II general who was chief of staff to Gen. Eisenhower, born in Indianapolis; ambassador to Russia (1946–49); director, CIA (1950–53); Undersecretary of State (1953–54) (died 1961).

1902   Ray A. Kroc, founder, president, McDonald's fast-food chain (1955–68), born in Chicago; chain's board chairman (1968–84) (died 1984).

1908   Joshua Logan, director, producer of hit plays (*Mr. Roberts, South Pacific, Fanny*), born in Texarkana, TX; also in films (*Picnic, Bus Stop*) (died 1988).

1910   St. Patrick's Cathedral in New York City dedicated by New York Archbishop John M. Farley.

1931   Clyde Pangborn and Hugh Herndon, Jr., arrived at Wenatchee, WA, from near Tokyo, becoming first to fly nonstop across the Pacific.

1986   C-123-K cargo plane carrying supplies to the Contras was shot down by Nicaraguan soldiers; two Americans died in crash; a third, Eugene Hasenfus of Marinette, WI, was captured; he was later sentenced to 30 years imprisonment but was pardoned by Nicaraguan President Daniel Ortega.

1995   Hurricane Opal did considerable damage along Gulf Coast; killed 15 persons.

2000   Only vice presidential debate of this election year held between candidates Dick Cheney and Joseph Lieberman.

2001   First of series of anthrax attacks during month delivered by mail; four dead as result by end of October.

2004   Vaccination scandal: Half of U.S. flu vaccine facing destruction; manufacturer lost its license to make product due to safety concerns.

6

1622   Piscataqua, NH, at mouth of Piscataqua River, settled by three Plymouth merchants.

1767   (Johann Christian) Gottlieb Graupner, musician who organized Boston Philharmonic Society (c. 1810), the first regular American concert orchestra, born in Verden, Germany (died 1836).

1777   Sir Henry Clinton began advance up Hudson River to help Burgoyne at Saratoga; captured Forts Clinton and Montgomery, seven miles below West Point.

1779   Nathan Appleton, industrialist who made significant contribution to American textile industry, born in Ipswich, NH (died 1861).

1809   John W. Griffiths, designer of the "clipper ship," born in New York City (died 1882).

1846   George Westinghouse, inventor of air brake and automatic signaling system, born in Central Bridge, NY; also developed system for wide distribution of electric power; founder (1886), Westinghouse Electric Co. to produce dynamos, transformers (died 1914).

1848   Allan McL. Hamilton, pioneer American neurologist, born in Brooklyn (died 1919).

1857   Joseph T. Dickman, commander, Third Army in Germany (1918–19), born in Dayton, OH; led Third Division (1917–18) (died 1927).

1859   Frank A. Seiberling, founder (1898) Goodyear Tire & Rubber Co., born in Summit County, OH; lost control (1921), then founded Seiberling Rubber Co. (died 1955).

1862   Albert H. Beveridge, author of four-volume biography of John Marshall, born in Highland County, OH; represented Indiana in Senate (1899–1911) (died 1927).

1866   Reginald A. Fessenden, inventor of high frequency alternator, born in Milton, Canada of American parents; worked with Edison; his alternator led to first radio broadcast of voice and music (died 1932).

1867   George H. Lorimer, editor, *Saturday Evening Post* (1899–1937), born in Louisville, KY; raised circulation from 1,800 to three million (died 1937).

1876   American Library Association organized in Philadelphia.

1884   Naval War College established by Navy Department in Newport, RI, first institution of its kind, with Commodore Stephen B. Luce as first president.

1888   Clarence C. Little, conducted research on cancer inheritance, born in Brookline, MA; head, Jackson Laboratory, and managing director, American Society for Control of Cancer (1929–56) (died 1971).

1905 Helen Wills (Roark), tennis champion (American singles seven times, Wimbledon eight times in 1920/30s), born in Centerville, CA (died 1998).

1906 Janet Gaynor, screen actress (*Seventh Heaven, A Star Is Born*), born in Philadelphia (died 1984).

1927 *The Jazz Singer* with Al Jolson opened in New York City, the first part-talking picture.

1938 United States sent strong protest to Japan following 1937 invasion of China, which violated the Open Door policy.

1955 Airliner crashed near Laramie, WY, killing 46 persons.

1978 Congress extended deadline for ratification of the Equal Rights Amendment by 39 months.

1979 Pope John Paul II was first pope ever received in White House.

1987 Senate Judiciary Committee voted to recommend to full Senate that nomination of Robert H. Bork to the Supreme Court be rejected; Senate turned down nomination by 58–42 vote.

1987 Stock prices plunged 91.55 points on Dow Jones industrial average to 2,548.63, the largest one-day decline.

2000 William P. Bundy, adviser on Far Eastern affairs to three American presidents, passed away at 83.

2006 Microsoft released planned final pre-release version of its new Windows Vista operating system for widespread testing; previous test version tried by 3 million users; general release scheduled for January 2007.

7

1727 William S. Johnson, president, Columbia College (1787–1800), born in Stratford, CT; member, Continental Congress (1784–87); represented Connecticut in Senate (1789–91) (died 1819).

1728 Caesar Rodney, "president" of Delaware (1778–82), born in Dover, DE; member, Continental Congress (1774–76, 1777–78); signer of Declaration of Independence (died 1784).

1746 William Billings, first professional American musical composer, born in Boston; published first of six collections (1770) (died 1800).

1756 *New Hampshire Gazette*, first newspaper in state, published in Portsmouth by Daniel Fowle.

1763 Great Britain issued proclamation forbidding colonial settlements beyond the Allegheny Mountains to appease Indians.

1765 Stamp Act Congress, with 28 delegates, began more than two weeks deliberation in New York City; passed resolutions opposing the tax October 19; attending were delegates from all colonies except Virginia, New Hampshire, North Carolina, and Georgia.

1777 Second battle of Bemis Heights near Saratoga, NY, resulted in defeat of Gen. John Burgoyne and his British troops by Americans under Benedict Arnold, who was severely wounded; Burgoyne retreated to Saratoga.

1777 Francis Nash, Revolutionary general, was killed in action at 35; Nash County, NC, and Nashville, TN, named for him.

1780 British force of 1,100 led by Maj. Patrick Ferguson was trapped and defeated atop King's Mountain on the Carolinas' border by a force of 1,900 frontiersmen.

1792 George Mason, colonial statesman, died at 67; drew up non-importation resolution following enactment of Stamp Tax and Townshend duties; also wrote most of Virginia's constitution; opposed U.S. Constitution, refused to become one of Virginia's first senators.

1821 Richard H. Anderson, Confederate general at Antietam, Gettysburg, born in Statesburg, SC (died 1879).

1826 Quincy tramway, first American railway, completed, running three miles from Quincy, MA, to tidewater on Neponset River.

1826 William B. Bate, Tennessee governor (1882–86) and Senator (1886–1905), born in Sumner County, TN; Confederate general at Shiloh and Murfreesboro (died 1905).

1833 Margaret Fox, spiritualist who made public appearances throughout United States and Europe, born in Bath, Canada; with sister, Katherine, encouraged stories that spirits knocked at their Wayne County, NY, home; fostered spiritualism and an investigation of it (died 1893).

1842 Bronson C. Howard, playwright (*Saratoga, Shenandoah, Aristocracy*), born in Detroit (died 1908).

1849 James Whitcomb Riley, poet of Hoosier dialect (*When the Frost Is on the Punkin', The Old Swimmin' Hole*), born in Greenfield, IN (died 1916).

1856 John W. Alexander, portrait painter, muralist (*Evolution of the Book* in Library of Congress), born in Allegheny, PA (died 1915).

1858 Charles F. Marvin, chief, U.S. Weather Bureau (1913–34), born in Putnam, OH (died 1943).

1865 Constitutional convention in Raleigh, NC, repealed secession ordinance; two days later abolished slavery.

1866 Martha M. Berry, founder of schools for underprivileged back country children, born near Rome, GA; considered (in 1931) one of 12 greatest American women (died 1942).

1888 Henry A. Wallace, vice president (1941–45), born in Adair County, IA; edited farm magazines (1910–33); Secretary of Agriculture (1933–40); Secretary of Commerce (1945–46); Progressive Party presidential candidate (1948) (died 1965).

1898 Alfred F. Wallenstein, orchestra conductor (New York Philharmonic (1929–36), Los Angeles Symphony (1943–56), born in Chicago (died 1983).

1905 Andy Devine, character actor who appeared in more than 300 movies (1928–77), born in Flagstaff, AZ (died 1977).

1907 Helen C. MacInnes, suspense novels author (*Assignment in Brittany, North from Rome, Decision at Delphi, Prelude to Terror*), born in Glasgow, Scotland (died 1985).

1911 Vaughn Monroe, orchestra leader and singer ("Racing with the Moon"), born in Akron, OH (died 1973).

1916 German submarine *U-53* entered Newport, RI, harbor, sank six merchant vessels off Nantucket Island on the next day, three more on the following day.

1970 President Nixon asked for cease-fire in Southeast Asia; turned down.

2002 Hubble Space Telescope discovery announced: Tentatively named "Quaoar" and over half the size of Pluto, the object circles the sun every 288 years; largest size solar system area discovery since that of Pluto itself.

2003 Actor Arnold Schwarzenegger gained decisive victory in California governorship race; incumbent Gray Davis repudiated by voters in mid-term.

2006 "Star Trek" soars higher than any one had imagined: In first studio-sanctioned auction of material from the five TV series and ten movies, three-day sale ended with take of over $7 million. Top price: the 78-inch *Enterprise-D* from *Next Generation* brought $576,000; top costume price: $144,000 for a space suit worn by Dr. McCoy in the original television series.

2006 Christening of USS *George H.W. Bush,* latest and last of the Nimitz class aircraft carriers to be added to the American fleet.

8

1609 John Clarke, a founder of Rhode Island, born in Westhorpe, England; a pioneer in American religious liberty (died 1676).

1720 Jonathan Mayhew, Congregational clergyman whose preaching began movement to Unitarianism, born in Chilmark, MA; served West Church, Boston (1747–66) (died 1766).

1810 James W. Marshall, co-discoverer of gold, born in Hunterdon County, NJ; a California pioneer, he made discovery January 24, 1848, while building sawmill for John Sutter; launched gold rush (died 1885).

1838 John M. Hay, private secretary for Abraham Lincoln (1860–65), born in Salem, IN; wrote ten-volume biography of Lincoln; ambassador to Great Britain (1897–98); Secretary of State (1898–1905) (died 1905).

1840 Hawaii's first written constitution completed, including such innovations as a popularly elected legislature.

1846 Elbert H. Gary, a leading organizer, U.S. Steel Co. (1901) of which he was board chairman (1903–27), born in Wheaton, IL; president, Federated Steel Co. (1898–1901) (died 1927).

1851 Hudson River Railroad opened between New York City and Albany.

1862 Confederate troops attacked Perryville, KY; no clear-cut winner but Confederates abandoned Kentucky.

1869 J. Frank Duryea, cofounder with brother of Duryea Motor Wagon Co., born in Canton, IL; won first automobile race (1895 Chicago) (died 1967).

1869 Former President Franklin Pierce died in Concord, NH, at 64.

1871 Great Chicago fire, which burned 17,450 buildings and killed 250 persons, started in a barn at 137 DeKoven St. and lasted 27 hours; loss was estimated at $196 million, left 100,000 homeless.

1871 Week-long forest fire began in Michigan and Wisconsin, destroyed a wide area, killed about 1,200 persons, 600 of them in Peshtigo, WI.

1890 Eddie (Edward V.) Rickenbacker, aviator who was a World War I ace (credited with downing 26 planes), born in Columbus, OH; Eastern Air Lines general manager (1935–38), president (1938–63); crashed in Pacific Ocean

(1942) on special mission for government; rescued after three weeks on a raft (died 1973).

1912 John W. Gardner, Secretary of Health, Education & Welfare (1965–68), born in Los Angeles; president, Carnegie Corporation, Carnegie Foundation for Advancement of Teaching (1955–64); director, National Urban Coalition; helped organize, headed, Common Cause (1970).

1914 Dr. Simon Flexner announced success in isolating and transmitting germ of infantile paralysis.

1918 President Wilson, replying to German-Austrian request for peace talks, demanded the evacuation of occupied territory as first condition for armistice; agreed (October 23) to submit matter to other governments.

1941 Jesse L. Jackson, founder, executive director, Operation PUSH (since 1971), born in Greenville, NC; founder, national director, Operation Breadbasket (1966–71).

1941 Office of Lend-Lease Administration created by executive order.

1956 Don Larsen of New York Yankees pitched only perfect World Series game, allowing no one to reach first base and facing only 27 batters, beating Brooklyn 2–0.

1965 President Lyndon Johnson underwent gallbladder operation in Bethesda Naval Center.

1974 Franklin National Bank of New York City failed, the largest bank failure in American history.

1988 Five-day "siege of Atlanta" ended with 450 arrests of persons trying to block entrance to abortion clinics; periodic picketing began in July, more than 1,100 protestors were jailed.

1990 Drs. E. Donnall Thomas and Joseph E. Murray shared 1990 Nobel Physiology/Medicine Prize for their pioneering work in transplantation.

1996 Mignon G. Eberhart, popular mystery story author, died at 90.

1996 Canadian-born American William Vickery shared 1996 Nobel Economics Prize; three days later he died suddenly.

1998 House, along party lines, authorized its Judiciary Committee to inquire into possible impeachment of President Clinton.

2001 New Department of Homeland Security received its first head: Tom Ridge, previously governor of Pennsylvania, sworn in; agency to coordinate fight against terrorism.

9

1700 Yale College chartered by General Court and established in Saybrook, CT.

1779 American and French troops unsuccessful in trying to capture Savannah; Count Casimir Pulaski wounded in battle and died two days later.

1782 Lewis Cass, governor, Michigan Territory (1813–31) and represented state in Senate (1849–57), born in Exeter, NH; Secretary of War (1831–36), of State (1857–60); Democratic presidential nominee (1848) (died 1866).

1822 George Sykes, Union general who was at Gettysburg, born in Dover, DE (died 1880).

1830 Harriet G. Hosmer, most successful sculptress of her day, born in Watertown, MA (died 1908).

1837 Francis W. Parker, a founder of progressive elementary education, born in Bedford, NH; founder, director, U. of Chicago School of Education (1901) (died 1902).

1839 Winfield S. Schley, Spanish-American War admiral, born in Frederick County, MD; directed destruction of Spanish fleet as it tried to flee Santiago, Cuba; involved in later controversy over who was credited with the victory (he or Adm. William T. Sampson) (died 1911).

1858 First overland mail stage from San Francisco reached St. Louis after 23 days, four hours; opposite stage which left at same time reached San Francisco October 10 after 24 days, 20 hours, 35 minutes.

1860 Leonard Wood, governor-general, Philippines (1921–27), born in Winchester, NH; Spanish-American War general who organized Rough Riders; governor of Cuba (1900–03); Army chief of staff (1910–14) (died 1927).

1863 Gamaliel Bradford, wrote many biographies (Lee, Civil War generals, Darwin), born in Boston (died 1932).

1863 Edward W. Bok, editor-in-chief, *Ladies Home Journal* (1889–1919), born in Den Helder, Netherlands; author (*The Americanization of Edward Bok*) (died 1930).

1871 Elizabeth S. Kingsley, inventor of double crostic puzzle, born in Brooklyn (died 1957).

1873 Charles R. Walgreen, founder, developer of drugstore chain named for him, born near Galesburg, IL (died 1939).

1884 Martin E. Johnson, photographer who with wife, Osa, photographed African wildlife, born in Rockford, IL (died 1937).

1888 Washington Monument opened to the public.

1890 Aimee Semple McPherson, best known woman evangelist of her day, born in Ingersoll, Canada; founder, Church of the Foursquare

Gospel, Los Angeles, serving as its minister (1923–44) (died 1944).

1899 (Charles) Bruce Catton, historian (*Mr. Lincoln's Army, Glory Road, A Stillness at Appomattox*), born in Petoskey, MI; editor, *American Heritage* (1954–59) (died 1978).

1903 Walter F. O'Malley, president (1950–70)/owner, Brooklyn/Los Angeles baseball team (1957–79), born in New York City (died 1979).

1910 Forest fires in northern Minnesota destroyed six towns, killing 400 persons, and causing about $100 million in property losses.

1940 John Lennon, singer/composer member of the Beatles, born in Liverpool, England; shot to death outside his New York City apartment (1980).

1941 Trent Lott, Senate majority leader (from 1996), born in Grenada, MS; represented Mississippi in Senate.

1982 President Reagan suspended Poland's 22-year most favored nation trade status in response to Poland's outlawing of Solidarity trade union.

1984 President Reagan signed law providing that Social Security Administration may not terminate disability benefits on basis that disability no longer existed unless beneficiary has medically improved and is able to work.

1985 Cruise ship *Achille Lauro* highjacked in Mediterranean; one American was killed before ship was retaken.

1986 Senate by 87–10 vote found U.S. District Judge Harry Claiborne guilty on three impeachment charges; had been found guilty by a court but drew his judicial salary until impeached.

1989 Two cancer researchers at U. of California Medical School in San Francisco, Dr. J. Michael Bishop and Dr. Harold E. Varmus, awarded 1989 Nobel Physiology/Medicine Prize; other awards given Yale professor Sidney Altman and Thomas Cech of Colorado U. for chemistry; Norman F. Ramsay of Harvard and Hans Dehmelt of U. of Washington for physics.

1995 An Amtrak train was detailed southwest of Phoenix, AZ, as a result of sabotage; one crew member was killed, about 100 injured.

1996 Three American scientists shared 1996 Nobel Physics Prize — David M. Lee and Robert C. Richardson of Cornell U. and Douglas C. Osterhoff of Stanford U.; two Americans shared Chemistry Prize — Robert F. Curl, Jr., and Richard E. Smalley, both of Rice U.

2005 Louis Nye (b. 1913), died of cancer at 92; comedian who appeared in various roles in a wide variety of comedy television series.

10

1615 Unsuccessful six-day siege begun of an Iroquois stronghold, probably on Lake Onondaga, by the Hurons aided by Samuel de Champlain.

1738 Benjamin West, a leading American and English painter, born near Springfield, PA; charter member of Royal Academy (1768), president (1792–1820); historical painter to George III (died 1820).

1758 Jean Pierre Chouteau, fur trader who established first permanent white settlement in Oklahoma (1796), born in New Orleans; settlement near present Salina (died 1849).

1770 Benjamin Wright, called father of American engineering, born in Wethersfield, CT; chief engineer, Erie Canal construction (died 1842).

1775 Sir William Howe succeeded Gen. Thomas Gage as commander-in-chief of British Army in America.

1777 Hezekiah Niles, editor, *Niles Weekly Register* (1811–36), very influential newspaper of the time, born in Chester County, PA; editor, *Baltimore Post* (1805–11) (died 1839).

1780 Continental Congress adopted policy on western lands ceded to the central government by any state.

1790 American troops led by Gen. Josiah Harmar were defeated by a force of Ohio Indians near Ft. Wayne, touching off five-year war in Northwest Territory.

1795 Samuel Fraunces, owner of famed Fraunces Tavern in New York City (1770–89), died at about 73; site of Washington's farewell to his officers; household steward to Washington (1789–94).

1828 Samuel J. Randall, House Speaker (1876–81) who codified and strengthened Speaker's power, born in Philadelphia; represented Pennsylvania in House (1863–90) (died 1890).

1831 Henry Mason, piano manufacturer who with Emmons Hamlin founded Mason & Hamlin Organ Co. (1854), born in Brookline, MA (died 1890).

1845 U.S. Naval Academy at Annapolis formally opened as Naval School; became known as the Academy in 1850; founded by Navy Secretary George Bancroft.

1861 Maurice B. Prendergast, painter who was a leader of art radicals, born in Roxbury, MA; known for Boston street scenes, life in Venice (died 1924).

1862 Confederate Gen. J.E.B. Stuart led his troops in capture of Chambersburg, PA, destroyed stocks and took usable stores; returned to Virginia.

1863 Alanson B. Houghton, Corning Glass Works president (1910–18), board chairman (1918–41), born in Cambridge, MA; represented New York in House (1919–22); ambassador to Germany (1922–25), to Great Britain (1925–29) (died 1941).

1888 Forty-five persons died in a railroad accident at Mud Run, PA.

1892 Earl E. Dickson, adhesive bandage inventor, born in Grandview, IN (died 1961).

1897 Elijah Muhammad, Black Muslim leader, born near Sandersonville, GA, as Elijah Poole; headed Black Muslims (1934–75) (died 1975).

1900 Helen Hayes, stage (*Victoria Regina, Harriet*) and screen actress (*Airport, Sin of Madelon Claudet, Arrowsmith*), born in Washington, DC (died 1993).

1903 Vernon Duke, musicals composer (*Cabin in the Sky*), born in Pskov, Russia; also composed ballets for Serge Diaghilev (died 1969).

1908 Johnny Green, composer of many popular songs ("Body and Soul"), born in New York City.

1911 California adopted women's suffrage.

1918 Thelonius S. Monk, jazz composer and pianist who was a founder of "bop," born in Rocky Mount, NC (died 1982).

1924 James D. Clavell, author (*Taipan, Shogun*), born in England.

1934 Antiwar treaty of non-aggression and conciliation signed by Argentina, Chile, Brazil, Mexico, Paraguay, Uruguay, and United States in Rio de Janeiro.

1951 Congress passed Mutual Security Act, which continued military and economic aid programs, marking new emphasis on military rather than economic aid.

1960 *Courier 1-B*, first successful active communications satellite, launched.

1973 Vice President Spiro T. Agnew resigned; pleaded *nolo contendere* (no contest) to tax evasion charges; given three years probation, $10,000 fine.

1997 Major tobacco companies agreed to settlement of class-action suit brought against them by 60,000 present and former flight attendants, who claimed second-hand smoke in planes caused them to get cancer and other diseases.

1997 International Campaign to Ban Land Mines and its coordinator, Jody Williams of Putney, VT, awarded 1997 Nobel Peace Prize.

1998 Clark Clifford, adviser to several presidents, died at 91.

2000 New Hampshire Chief Justice David Brock acquitted on four impeachment charges.

2003 Faced with a Florida prosecutor's apparent determination to find grounds to prosecute him for illegally obtaining prescriptions, the 600-station, 20-million listener, number one talk-show host Rush Limbaugh admitted on the air that continued back pain was the root of his problem — that an operation had not cured it and the search for relief had caused him to become addicted; announces he would be entering a rehabilitation facility.

2004 Christopher Reeve, who had been paralyzed in a horse-riding accident after great success playing Superman in big-budget films, died at 52.

11

1614 United Netherland Company formed by Amsterdam merchants to settle "New Netherlands" between 40° and 45° N; charter expired January 1, 1618.

1759 Mason L. Weems, known as Parson Weems the author, born in Anne Arundel County, MD; known for the life of George Washington including the account of the cherry tree (died 1825).

1776 Battle of Valcour Island began when American fleet took up position between Valcour Island and western shore of Lake Champlain to halt British fleet; British defeated Americans in two-day battle but had to withdraw (November 3) to Canada because of the delay and lateness of the season.

1779 Gen. (Count) Casimir Pulaski died of wounds received two days earlier in siege of Savannah; a distinguished Polish officer who served with Americans.

1835 Theodore Thomas, orchestra conductor (New York, Chicago), born in Esens, Germany; conducted Chicago Symphony (1891–1905) (died 1905).

1841 Louis Kempff, admiral in charge of

American naval forces in China during Boxer Rebellion, born in Belleville, IL (died 1920).

1844 Henry J. Heinz, a founder of F. & J. Heinz Co. (1876), born in Pittsburgh; firm became H.J. Heinz Co., food products producer, of which he was president (1905–19); coined slogan "57 varieties" (died 1919).

1855 James Gayley, who invented bronze cooling plate for blast furnace walls, born in Lock Haven, PA; with Carnegie and U.S. Steel; also developed dry air blast and other steelmaking improvements (died 1920).

1863 Harry A. Garfield, president, Williams College (1908–34), born in Hiram, Ohio; U.S. fuel administrator (1917–18) (died 1942).

1872 Harlan F. Stone, chief justice, Supreme Court (1941–46), born in Chesterfield, NH; dean, Columbia Law School (1910–24); Attorney General (1924–25); associate justice, Supreme Court (1925–41) (died 1946).

1881 Stark Young, drama critic (*New Republic, Theatre Arts*), born in Como, MS; author (*So Red the Rose, Heaven Trees*) (died 1963).

1882 Robert N. Dett, one of first composers to use Negro folk tunes in classical work, born in Drummondville, Canada; directed Hampton Institute choir (1913–43) (died 1943).

1884 Eleanor Roosevelt Roosevelt, wife of President Franklin Roosevelt, born in New York City; set many precedents as First Lady; became magazine columnist; chairman, UN Commission on Human Rights (1946–53) (died 1962).

1890 Daughters of the American Revolution organized in Washington, DC.

1897 Willie (William F.) Hoppe, probably greatest billiards player of all time, born in Cornwall-on-Hudson, NY; won 51 titles between 1906 and 1952 (died 1959).

1897 Nathan F. Twining, World War II general who directed air war against Japan, born in Monroe, WI; chairman, Joint Chiefs of Staff (1957–60) (died 1982).

1897 Joseph Auslander, poet (*The Unconquerables*), born in Philadelphia; translated *Fables of LaFontaine* and the *Sonnets of Petrarch* (died 1965).

1906 Charles F. Revson, a founder, president (1932–62), board chairman (1962–75), Revlon Inc., world's largest cosmetics and fragrance firm (died 1975).

1910 Joseph W. Alsop, Jr., syndicated newspaper columnist, born in Avon, CT (died 1989).

1918 Jerome Robbins, choreographer who staged many ballets, films, plays (*West Side Story*,

Fiddler on the Roof), born in New York City (died 1998).

1928 *Graf Zeppelin*, commanded by Dr. Hugo Eckener, began flight from Friedrichhafen, Germany, to Baltimore, New York, and Lakehurst, NJ, with 20 passengers and crew of 40; took approximately 111 hours for 6,300-mile trip.

1939 President Franklin Roosevelt named advisory committee on uranium after learning about possibility of an atomic bomb.

1942 Battle of Cape Esperance in Solomon Islands began; Japanese lost an aircraft carrier and four destroyers.

1968 George White, producer/director of *George White's Scandals* (1919–39), died in Hollywood at about 80.

1984 Astronaut Kathryn D. Sullivan became first American woman to walk in space.

1986 President Reagan and Soviet leader Mikhail Gorbachev began meetings in Reykjavik, Iceland; reached virtual agreement on missiles limitations, but failed because of disagreement over "Star Wars," missile defense system.

1988 World's largest private bank, Bank of Credit & Commerce International of Luxembourg, nine of its officers, and 75 others were indicted in Washington on charges of laundering more than $32 million in cocaine proceeds for the Colombia Medellín cartel.

2000 Second presidential debate between candidates Bush and Gore.

2006 First American indicted for treason since World War II: Adam Yehiye Gadahn, 28, formerly of California and now known in al-Qaeda circles as "Azzam the American," accused of making propaganda videos for the terrorist organization.

2006 Microsoft released unprecedented 26 patches for its Windows systems; fixes were delayed in distribution today by failures in the company's own networking system.

12

1492 Land was sighted from the *Pinta*, one of three vessels in Christopher Columbus' fleet seeking China; land was probably Watling's Island in the Bahamas; later renamed San Salvador.

1710 Jonathan Trumbull, colonial official, born in Lebanon, CT; held various state posts, including Connecticut governor (1769–84); one of first to foresee possible independence from Great Britain; Washington is said to have referred to him as Brother Jonathan, which became phrase describing typical American (died 1785).

1769 Horace H. Hayden, cofounder of first dental school in world (Baltimore 1840), born in Windsor, CT (died 1844).

1775 Lyman Beecher, Presbyterian clergyman (Boston 1826–32), Cincinnati (1832–42), born in New Haven, CT; president, Lane Theological Seminary, Cincinnati (1832–52); accused of heresy by conservative foes, acquitted by synod (died 1863).

1776 Gen. William Howe moved his main British force from New York City to Westchester, sought unsuccessfully to cut off American retreat to New Jersey.

1803 Alexander T. Stewart, founder (1823) of what became New York's largest dry goods store, born in Lisburn, Ireland; store later acquired by John Wanamaker (died 1876).

1813 Lyman Trumbull, legislator who introduced resolution that became 13th Amendment abolishing slavery, born in Colchester, CT; served Illinois in Senate (1855–73) (died 1896).

1815 William J. Hardee, Confederate general at Shiloh and Missionary Ridge, born in Camden County, GA; wrote popular tactics manual (*Hardee's Tactics*) (died 1873).

1837 Treasury notes totaling $10 million authorized to relieve economic distress brought on by the Panic of 1837.

1840 Helena Modjeska, actress on American stage (from 1877), born in Cracow, Poland; specialized in serious and Shakesperean roles (died 1909).

1841 Joseph O'Dwyer, pioneer in diphtheria treatment, born in Cleveland; successfully used intubation (to prevent asphyxiation) and serum in diphtheria (died 1898).

1846 Louis E. Levy, inventor who made photoengraving possible, born in Stenowitz, Austria; invented photochemical etching process and co-invented an etched glass screen for making halftones (died 1919).

1858 Isaac N. Lewis, inventor of military weapons, born in New Salem, PA; invented artillery position finder, a machine gun, and originated modern artillery corps organization adopted by Army (1902) (died 1931).

1860 Elmer A. Sperry, inventor of more than 400 items and founder, president, Sperry Gyroscope Co. (1910–29), born in Cortland, NY; best known inventions are gyrocompass, various gyrocontrols, high-intensity arc searchlight (died 1930).

1860 William L. Sibert, Army engineer in Panama Canal construction, born in Gadsden, AL; organized, directed, Army Chemical Warfare Service (1918–20) (died 1935).

1874 Abraham A. Brill, known as the father of American psychoanalysis, born in Kanczuga, Austria (now Poland); translated works of Jung and Freud (died 1948).

1875 Rutherford B. Hayes elected governor of Ohio.

1876 New constitution for North Carolina ratified by popular vote.

1889 Perle Mesta, foremost unofficial hostess in Washington, DC, in 1940s, born in Sturgis, MI; envoy to Luxembourg (1949–53); served as model for Irving Berlin's musical, *Call Me Madam* (died 1975).

1906 Joe (Joseph E.) Cronin, president, American League (1959–73), born in San Francisco; player/manager (Washington, Boston A); named to Baseball Hall of Fame (died 1984).

1932 Dick Gregory, entertainer and leader in various civil rights movements, born in St. Louis.

1935 Luciano Pavarotti, operatic tenor, born in Modena, Italy.

1954 Four-day hurricane, Hazel, killed 99 persons in United States, 594 in Haiti, and 85 in Canada.

1973 Rep. Gerald R. Ford of Michigan became first appointed vice president under 25th Amendment; succeeded Spiro T. Agnew who resigned; Ford sworn in December 6.

1988 Developer Donald Trump agreed to buy Eastern Airlines' Northeast shuttle for about $350 million; renamed Trump Shuttle.

1997 President Clinton began week-long visit to three South American countries.

1997 John Denver, popular singer/composer, died in crash of his light plane in California.

2000 Seventeen American sailors killed on USS *Cole* while refueling in Yemen as result of terrorist bomb attack; vessel towed home to U.S. on October 26.

2002 Ray Conniff (born 1916), bandleader, passed away. Throughout his career he emphasized an easy listening style of music that gained a dedicated audience; though this was in decline in his last decades, in his prime in the 1950s and 1960s he turned out 25 albums in a row that hit the "top 40 LPs" list of the day.

2003 Democratic efforts to stall Congressional reapportionment measure in Texas—even by collectively leaving the state to make a vote impossible—finally overcome by Republicans;

new districts designed to assure new seats for Republicans.

2003 Bill ("Willie") Shoemaker (b. 1931) died at 71; jockey who won 8,833 races in career and first jockey to break $100 million winnings in career.

2006 Genetic Savings and Clone, the first company to provide cloned animals for pet owners as replacements for their deceased pets, closed its doors; in spite of reducing its charge from $50,000 per animal to $32,000, it had been unable to find a market, cloning only two animals in six years.

13

1754 Mary L.H. McCauley, better known as Molly Pitcher the Revolutionary heroine, born near Trenton, NJ; she brought water to artillerymen at battle of Monmouth; when her husband was overcome by heat, she took over his gun (died 1832).

1775 U.S. Navy founded when Congress created the Continental Navy of the American Revolution by authorizing fitting out two ships of ten guns each; increased to four ships October 30.

1792 Cornerstone of the original White House laid; President John Adams became the first occupant in 1800.

1812 American force making a premature attack on Queenston Heights in Canada was defeated with loss of 1,000 men; British Gen. Isaac Brock was killed.

1826 LaFayette C. Baker, chief of U.S. Secret Service (1862–68), born in Stafford, NY; led in capture of John Wilkes Booth after Lincoln assassination (died 1868).

1843 B'nai B'rith, Jewish fraternal society, founded.

1857 Minnesotans ratified their state constitution; slavery prohibited.

1862 John R. Commons, a developer of unemployment insurance system, born in Hollandsburg, OH; economist with U. of Wisconsin (1904–32) (died 1945).

1864 Union troops surrendered Dalton, GA, to Confederates led by Gen. John B. Hood.

1886 Two-day storm along Gulf of Mexico and floods in Texas took 147 lives.

1890 Conrad Richter, author of books on frontier life, westward expansion, born in Pine Grove, PA; among his works were *The Trees, The Town, The Fields* (died 1968).

1892 Pennsylvania National Guardsmen were withdrawn from Homestead after 95 days; had guarded Carnegie steel mill against strikers; violence renewed October 20, strike ended November 20.

1908 Church of the Nazarene organized by merging group of small religious bodies at a meeting in Pilot Point, TX.

1909 Herbert L. Block, editorial cartoonist better known as Herblock, born in Chicago; with *Washington Post* (since 1946); widely syndicated.

1910 Art Tatum, internationally-famed jazz pianist, born in Toledo (died 1956).

1917 Burr Tillstrom, puppeteer (*Kukla, Fran and Ollie* show on television), born in Chicago (died 1985).

1918 Three days of forest fires in Minnesota and Wisconsin killed about 1,000 persons, did $100 million in damage.

1932 President Hoover laid cornerstone for new Supreme Court Building.

1938 Elzie C. Segar, cartoonist (*Popeye*), died at 43.

1942 Art Garfunkel, singer/composer ("Mrs. Robinson," "Scarborough Fair," "Bridge Over Troubled Waters"), born in New York City; teamed with Paul Simon in 1960s.

1962 Jerry Rice, football wide receiver (San Francisco) who by 1997 had become all-time leader in touchdowns and touchdown pass receptions, born in Starkville, MS.

1970 Senate by 60–5 vote rejected findings and recommendations of Commission to Study Obscenity and Pornography; publicly rejected by President Nixon October 24.

1978 President Carter signed Civil Service Reform Act, first major revision in federal employment code since 1883.

1988 President Reagan signed welfare reform bill calling for government to provide additional training and support while welfare recipients must find jobs.

1989 Dow Jones industrial average fell 190.58 points to 2,569.26, the second largest daily loss; market recovered much of the loss in several days.

1998 National Basketball Association cancelled first two weeks of regular season because of continuing lockout; first time a work stoppage caused cancellations.

2000 Gus Hall died after a long career in the U.S. Communist Party, including running for president four times under its banner.

2002 Stephen Ambrose died; although writing on various other periods as well, he was most remembered as a historian of the invasion of Europe in World War II.

2006 Unlawful Internet Gambling Enforcement Act signed by President Bush that effectively prohibited all U.S. Internet gambling—an estimated $6 billion yearly—by prohibiting banks from clearing checks to such places and credit card companies from processing payments; first Internet site had been established in 1995; opposition to such gambling fueled by moral objections and concern over unscrupulous companies.

2006 Air America Radio, a self-avowed liberal oriented radio network, filed for bankruptcy after two years of broadcasting; $4.3 million assets; $20.2 million debts.

14

1644 William Penn, founder of American Quakerism and Pennsylvania, born in London; served as trustee to manage West Jersey colony in America, had important role in framing its charter (1677); inherited father's large financial claim against Charles II for which he received grant of what became Pennsylvania (1681); prepared frame of government, laid out Philadelphia, made treaties with Indians (died 1718).

1696 Thomas Johnson, leader of Church of England in colonies, born in Guilford, CT; first president, King's (later Columbia) College (1754–63) (died 1772).

1734 Francis Lightfoot Lee, colonial leader, born in Westmoreland County, VA; member, Virginia House of Burgesses (1758–76); member, Continental Congress (1775–79), signer of Declaration of Independence (died 1797).

1765 Town of Braintree, MA, adopted instructions against Stamp Act which were written by John Adams in his first venture into Massachusetts politics; widely copied throughout state.

1773 Thomas Jefferson appointed surveyor of Albemarle County by College of William & Mary.

1774 Continental Congress adopted declaration of the rights of the colonies.

1814 Jean Baptiste Lamy, Catholic Archbishop of Santa Fe (1875–85), born in Lempdes, France; missionary to Southwest, Bishop of Santa Fe (1853–75); commemorated in Willa Cather's *Death Comes for the Archbishop* (died 1888).

1842 Croton Aqueduct, providing water for New York City, opened.

1857 Joseph R. Lamar, associate justice, Supreme Court (1911–16), born in Elbert County, GA (died 1916).

1857 Elwood Haynes, inventor of a one-cylinder automobile (July 4, 1894), born in Portland, IN; automobile produced with help of Apperson brothers and is now in Smithsonian; manufactured cars until 1920; discovered various alloys (tungsten chrome steel, chromium and nickel, cobalt and chromium, cobalt, chromium and molybdenum); patented stainless steel (1919) (died 1925).

1863 Union troops under Gen. George Meade repulsed Confederate attack led by Gen. A.P. Hill at Bristoe Station, VA, ending another threat to Washington, DC.

1866 Charles F. Hughes, naval officer who was operations chief, U.S. battle fleet, born in Bath, ME; served with British in North Sea (1917–18) (died 1934).

1873 Ray C. Ewry, winner of eight gold medals in track events in Olympics (1900, 1904, 1908), born in Lafayette, IN (died 1937).

1876 Henry A. Ironside, evangelist known as archbishop of fundamentalism, born in Toronto; pastor, Moody Memorial Church, Chicago (1930–48) (died 1951).

1890 Dwight D. Eisenhower, 34th President (1952–60), born in Denison, TX; Allied commander in Europe, World War II; Army chief of staff (1954–58); president, Columbia U. (1948–50); commander, NATO forces (1950–52) (died 1969).

1892 Sumner Welles, Undersecretary of State who laid foundation for American good neighbor policy (1933–43), born in New York City (died 1961).

1894 Maurice Pate, first executive director, UNICEF (1947–65), born in Pender, NE (died 1965).

1894 E(dward) E. Cummings, poet whose work featured unorthodox typography and experimental approaches, born in Cambridge, MA (died 1962).

1896 Lillian Gish, early screen actress (*Birth of a Nation*, *Orphans in the Storm*), born in Springfield, OH (died 1993).

1906 Hannah Arendt, political scientist/author (*On Revolution*, *Eichmann in Israel*), born in Hanover, Germany (died 1975).

1910 John R. Wooden, basketball coach (UCLA 1948–78), born Martinsville, IN; teams won ten national championships.

1912 Former President Theodore Roosevelt

shot in the chest by a fanatic (John N. Scrank) in Milwaukee; bullet lodged near right lung fracturing a rib; Roosevelt went on to speaking engagement; assailant adjudged insane.

1916 First Professional Golfers Association (PGA) tournament held in Mt. Vernon, NY; won by John Barnes.

1916 C(harles) Everett Koop, Surgeon General (1982–89), born in New York City.

1941 Lanham Act signed, authorizing $150 million for defense housing.

1943 Eighth Air Force raided Schweinfurt, Germany ball-bearing plants.

1947 Air Force Maj. Charles E. Yeager broke sound barrier in a Bell X-1 rocket plane at Muroc, CA.

1949 Eleven American Communist Party leaders convicted after nine-months trial for conspiracy to overthrow government; ten sentenced to five years, one to three years; Supreme Court upheld convictions June 4, 1951.

1953 Clarence Saunders, founder of Piggly Wiggly (1916) grocery chain, died at 72; stores were prototype of modern supermarkets.

1973 President Nixon ordered by Court of Appeals to turn over tapes to U.S. District Court Judge John J. Sirica in Watergate investigation; President Nixon unsuccessfully offered a summary of the tapes.

1983 New translation of Bible readings to eliminate reference to God as solely male announced by National Council of Churches.

1987 Dow Jones industrial average took record-breaking drop of 85.46 points for a loss of 3.81 percent of the market's value.

1988 Court documents discussed at a congressional hearing revealed that government knew for decades that nuclear weapons plants near Fernald, OH, near Cincinnati, were releasing thousands of tons of waste into atmosphere, endangering thousands of workers and area residents.

1996 Archer Daniels Midland Co. agreed to pay fine of $100 million for conspiring with competitors to fix prices of two agricultural products.

1996 Dow Jones industrial average passed the 6,000 mark (6,010) for first time.

2003 Contingency planning for worst case situation: Defense Department analyst produces *An Abrupt Climate Change Scenario and Its Implications for U.S. National Security* (dated October 2003): extreme change could produce both droughts with accompanying famine and simultaneous major flooding in other parts of the world — circumstances posing high prospect of igniting regional wars.

2006 Freddy Fender dead of lung cancer; after recording his first hits in Spanish, he carved out a successful English language career in Tex-Mex style country music.

2006 The first openly homosexual member of Congress, Gerry Studds, died at 69; had been censured by House of Representatives for having had sex with a congressional page but went on to win repeated reelections.

15

1770 Baron de Botetourt (Norbonne Berkeley), colonial governor of Virginia (1768–70), died at 52.

1818 Irvin McDowell, Union general in both battles of Bull Run, born in Columbus, OH (died 1885).

1829 Asaph Hall, astronomer with Naval Observatory (1862–91), born in Goshen, CT; discovered two satellites of Mars (1877) (died 1907).

1830 Helen Hunt Jackson, poet/author (*Ramona*), born in Amherst, MA (died 1885).

1858 William S. Sims, admiral who headed World War I naval operations, born in Port Hope, Canada; promoted convoy system (died 1936).

1872 Edith B. Galt Wilson, second wife of President Wilson, born in Wytheville, VA (died 1961).

1873 Henry F. Ward, Methodist clergyman who headed American Civil Liberties Union (1920–40), born in London; with Union Theological Seminary (from 1918); chairman, American League for Peace & Democracy (1930–40) (died 1966).

1878 Edison Electric Light Co., first electric company, incorporated in New York City; began supplying power in 1882.

1881 Lena M. Phillips, founder (1919), National Federation of Business & Professional Women's Clubs, born in Nicholasville, KY; served Federation as executive secretary (1919–23), president (1926–29); founder, International Federation of Business & Professional Women (1930) (died 1955).

1881 P(elham) G. Wodehouse, author of 90+ novels, mostly farces about English gentry, born in Guildford, England; creator of Jeeves the butler (died 1975).

1883 Robert L. Ghormley, commander of Allied naval forces in South Pacific (1942), born in Portland, OR (died 1958).

1886 Jonas W. Ingram, commander, South Atlantic Force (1942–44), Atlantic Fleet (1944–45), born in Jeffersonville, IN (died 1952).

1899 William C. Menninger, psychiatrist who with brother and father founded Menninger Clinic, neuropsychiatric center in Topeka, KS (died 1966).

1900 Mervyn Leroy, film director (*The Wizard of Oz*), born in San Francisco (died 1987).

1906 Alicia Patterson, founder, editor/publisher, *Newsday* (1940–63), born in Chicago (died 1963).

1908 John K. Galbraith, economist, born in Iona Station, Canada; editor, *Fortune* (1943–48); ambassador to India (1961–63); chairman, Americans for Democratic Action (1967–69); author (*The Great Crash, The Affluent Society*).

1914 Clayton Antitrust Act signed, replacing the Sherman Act and strengthening federal antimonopoly laws.

1917 Arthur M. Schlesinger, Jr., historian and speechwriter for President Kennedy, born in Columbus, OH; cofounder, Americans for Democratic Action (1947); author (*The Age of Jackson, Robert Kennedy and His Times*).

1917 American destroyer *Cassin* torpedoed off south Irish coast.

1920 Mario Puzo, author best known for *The Godfather*, born in New York City.

1924 Lee A. Iacocca, president, Ford Motor Co. (1970–78), born in Allentown, PA; chief executive officer, Chrysler Corporation (1979–93).

1948 Gerald R. Ford and Elizabeth B. Warren were married in Grand Rapids, MI.

1966 Guadelupe Mountains (TX) National Park established.

1968 Department of Transportation created by combining eight elements from other departments; began operations April 1, 1967, with Alan S. Boyd as secretary.

1991 Ronald H. Coase, U. of Chicago economist, awarded the 1991 Nobel Economics Prize.

1991 Long controversial hearings on confirmation of Clarence Thomas for the Supreme Court ended with Senate approval 52–48.

1997 During preceding week, seven Americans shared or won Nobel prizes — Paul D. Boyer shared Chemistry, Robert C. Merton and Myron S. Scholes shared Economics, Jody Williams, coordinator of ban land mines campaign, shared Peace; Steven Chu and William D. Phillips shared Physics, and Stanley B. Prusiner awarded Physiology/Medicine Prize.

1998 Congress and President Clinton agreed on $1.7 trillion 1999 budget with the surplus going toward protecting Social Security.

2001 Scientific stumbling block to dealing with anthrax attacks in U.S. received greater public attention: no quick way to quickly and definitively diagnose whether an individual has been exposed; even electronic "sniffers" only work well when large amount is released into atmosphere.

2004 Federal Drug Administration ordered that all antidepressant drugs carry a conspicuous warning that they may cause suicidal thoughts and attempted suicide among those who are adolescents and younger.

2006 In strongest earthquake to hit Hawaii since 1983, a 6.7 hit just north-northwest of Kailua-Kona (Hawii Island) with aftershocks registering as high as 5.8 (U.S. Geological Survey estimates); widespread power outrages throughout the island chain, affecting 95 percent on Oahu.

16

1649 Maine government passed act granting all Christians the right to form churches provided "they be orthodox in judgment and not scandalous in life."

1701 Yale U. founded in Killingworth, CT, as the Collegiate School by Congregationalists dissatisfied with the growing liberalism at Harvard.

1754 Morgan Lewis, New York governor (1804–07), chief justice (1801–04), born in New York City; served in both Revolution and War of 1812 (died 1844).

1758 Noah Webster, dictionary compiler and author, born in West Hartford, CT; his *American Spelling Book* helped standardize American spelling, grammar; worked 20 years on the *American Dictionary of the English Language*; a founder, Amherst College (died 1843).

1760 Jonathan Dayton, legislator, born in what is now Elizabeth, NJ; member, Continental Congress (1787–89); represented New Jersey in House (1791–99) serving as Speaker (1795–99) and in Senate (1799–1805); a founder of Dayton, OH (died 1824).

1775 Falmouth (now Portland, ME) burned by the British, reacting to American privateer raids on British shipping.

1777 British troops under Gen. Henry Clinton burned Esopus (now Kingston), NY, but felt too insecure to push farther north to meet Burgoyne's force near Saratoga; returned to New York City for reinforcements.

1835 William R. Shafter, general in Civil and Spanish-American wars, born in Kalamazoo County, MI; commanded expeditionary force to Cuba (1898) (died 1906).

1851 Frederick H. Gillett, legislator, born in Westfield, MA; represented Massachusetts in House (1893–1925), serving as Speaker (1919–25) and in Senate (1925–31) (died 1935).

1855 Abraham Lincoln, speaking in Peoria, made his first public denunciation of slavery.

1859 John Brown and 17 men raided Harpers Ferry (WV) federal arsenal; site retaken by federal troops under (then) Col. Robert E. Lee two days later; Brown tried, executed December 2; raids further aroused national slavery passions.

1861 Charles A. Platt, painter of New England scenes, born in New York City; helped design Freer Art Gallery (died 1933).

1875 U. of Provo founded by Brigham Young in Utah; later became Brigham Young U.

1880 Frank Aydelotte, president Swarthmore College (1921–40), born in Sullivan, IN; introduced Oxford Plan of teaching at Swarthmore; director, Institute of Advanced Study, Princeton (1940–47) (died 1956).

1885 Will(iam) Harridge, president, American League (1931–58), born in Chicago; named to Baseball Hall of Fame (died 1971).

1888 Eugene O'Neill, playwright who was awarded 1936 Nobel Literature Prize, born in New York City; wrote many hit plays—*Emperor Jones, Anna Christie, Desire Under the Elms, Strange Interlude, Mourning Becomes Electra, The Iceman Cometh* (died 1953).

1891 Mob in Valparaiso, Chile, attacked American sailors from cruiser *USS Baltimore*; two were killed, several wounded.

1893 Carl L. Carmer, novelist (*Stars Fell on Alabama, Listen for a Lonesome Drum, Genesee Fever*), born in Cortland, NY (died 1976).

1898 William O. Douglas, associate justice, Supreme Court (1939–76), born in Maine, MN; chairman, Securities & Exchange Commission (1936–39); author (*Of Men and Mountains, A Living Bill of Rights*) (died 1980).

1899 Dismal Swamp Canal opened; original survey made by George Washington.

1916 First birth control clinic opened at 46 Amboy St., Brooklyn, by Margaret Sanger and others.

1940 More than 16 million men 21 to 36 registered for military training and service.

1946 Price controls on meat were lifted.

1962 Tamara McKinney, only American woman skier to win overall Alpine World Cup Championship (1984), born.

1973 First black mayor of a major southern city, Maynard Jackson, was elected in Atlanta.

1973 Secretary of State Henry Kissinger shared 1973 Nobel Peace Prize.

1987 Stocks plummeted 108.36 points on Dow Jones industrial average when a record-breaking 338.4 million shares were traded.

1987 First Lady Nancy Reagan underwent successful modified radical mastectomy.

1987 Eighteen-month-old Jessica McClure was successfully removed from an abandoned well shaft in Midland, TX, after 57½ hours of mass effort to get her out of shaft into which she tumbled while playing.

1988 Pakistani government said sabotage was cause of August 17 crash near Islamabad which took the life of Pakistan President Zia, American Ambassador Arnold Raphel, and 10 top Pakistani generals.

1990 Nobel Economics Prize for 1990 was shared by Harry M. Markowitz of Baruch College, William F. Sharpe of Stanford U., and Merton H. Miller of U. of Chicago.

1991 Dow Jones industrial average rose to record high 3,061.71; a month later (November 15) it dropped 120 points to 2,943.20.

1995 Hundreds of thousands of black men gathered in Washington, DC, for the Million Man March organized by Nation of Islam leader, Louis Farrakhan; march designed to demonstrate responsible personal behavior.

2000 Massive "Family Rally" held in Washington, DC, by the Rev. Farrakhan, head of Nation of Islam.

2002 Federally imposed election guidelines for states approved by Senate 92–2; House had approved earlier 357–48.

2003 Feminist Patricia Ireland removed as leader of YWCA (Young Women's Christian Association) after less than six months service; conservative critics argued that she was irresponsibly radical and supported policies in contradiction to traditional YWCA principles and goals.

2006 New York lawyer Lynne Stewart sentenced to 28 months imprisonment for helping smuggle messages of convicted terrorist client to outside followers.

17

1691 New royal charter issued to Massachusetts, including Maine and Plymouth in colony; called for crown-appointed governor, a council elected by General Court, subject to governor's veto, the substitution of a property requirement for voting instead of religion, royal review of legislation, appeals to King.

1760 Anne Parrish, founder of industry house to employ needy women (1795), born in Philadelphia; this was first American charitable organization for women (died 1800).

1777 Gen. John Burgoyne and 5,700 British troops surrendered at Saratoga after being surrounded by American forces and left without British reinforcements.

1780 Richard M. Johnson, Vice President (1837–41), born near Louisville, KY; elected by Senate when no vice presidential candidate received majority of electoral votes; represented Kentucky in House (1807–19, 1829–37) and Senate (1819–29) (died 1850).

1781 Lord Charles Cornwallis, commanding an encircled British force at Yorktown, began negotiations for surrender.

1803 John Quincy Adams took his seat in Senate, serving until 1808.

1829 Delaware River–Chesapeake Bay Canal opened.

1851 Thomas Fortune Ryan, financier involved in New York transportation and banks, born in Nelson County, VA; an organizer, American Tobacco Co. (died 1928).

1859 Childe Hassam, leading American exponent of impressionistic painting, born in Boston; known for scenes of New York City life (died 1935).

1864 Robert Lansing, Secretary of State (1915–20), born in Watertown, NY; resigned at request of President Wilson, who accused him of holding unauthorized cabinet meetings during his (Wilson's) illness (died 1928).

1880 Charles H. Kraft, cofounder of cheese (now foods) company (1909), born in Ft. Erie, Canada; pioneer in developing blended and pasteurized cheese (died 1952).

1886 Ernest W. Goodpasture, virologist and pathologist who made notable contributions to understanding infectious diseases, born in Montgomery County, TN (died 1960).

1895 Doris Humphrey, choreographer and pioneer in American modern dance, born in Oak Park, IL (died 1958).

1902 Nathanael West, author of surrealistic satires, born in New York City; remembered for *Miss Lonelyhearts* and *The Day of the Locust* (died 1940).

1909 Cozy (William R.) Cole, one of greatest jazz percussionists, born in East Orange, NJ (died 1981).

1915 Arthur Miller, playwright (*Death of a Salesman, The Crucible, A View from the Bridge*), born in New York City.

1917 Transport *Antilles* torpedoed and sunk with loss of 70 persons.

1918 Rita Hayworth, screen actress (*Cover Girl, Pal Joey, My Gal Sal*), born in New York City (died 1987).

1930 Jimmy Breslin, newspaper columnist/author (*The Gang Who Couldn't Shoot Straight*), born in New York City.

1931 Al Capone was found guilty in Chicago Federal Court of income tax evasion, sentenced to 11 years in prison.

1933 Albert Einstein arrived to make his home in Princeton, NJ.

1933 Commodity Credit Corporation organized to stabilize and protect farm income and prices, to help maintain balanced and adequate agricultural supplies.

1941 U.S. destroyer *Kearny* torpedoed off Iceland by a German submarine, 11 died.

1966 Twelve New York City firefighters were killed fighting a fire.

1977 Supreme Court ruled that Concorde, a supersonic plane, could land in New York City's Kennedy Airport, ending 19-month legal battle.

1979 President Carter approved legislation creating Department of Education; Department of Health, Education and Welfare renamed Department of Health and Human Services.

1986 Congress approved measure which virtually eliminated mandatory retirement at age 70; President Reagan later signed bill.

1988 United States and the Philippines concluded agreement to guarantee American military use of strategic air and naval bases in the islands through 1991 in exchange for $962 million in American aid.

1989 Earthquake measuring 6.9 on Richter scale hit San Francisco Bay area at 5:04 P.M. Pacific time; at least 60 persons were killed, most by collapse of upper deck of two-tier Interstate 880 in Oakland; 1,000 injured, sustained billion dollars damages; scheduled World Series game in San Francisco's Candlestick Park cancelled; none of 60,000 in ballpark injured.

1990 The 1990 Nobel Physics Prize was shared by Drs. Richard E. Taylor, Jerome I. Friedman, and Henry J. Kendall; Chemistry Prize awarded to Dr. Elias J. Corey.

1996 Civil trial against O.J. Simpson, former football star, got under way; Simpson had been acquitted of murdering his former wife and a friend; civil trial brought by victims' families seeking damages.

2000 Third and final presidential debate between candidates Bush and Gore held in St. Louis, Missouri.

2005 In major cost-cutting move to keep the company solvent, General Motors and United Auto Workers concurred on $1 billion cut in health benefits yearly.

2006 Census Bureau estimate: U.S. population hit 300 million at around 7:46 A.M. today; hit 200 million 39 years before, 100 million 91 years previously; U.S. only industrialized nation to have major population growth.

2006 President Bush signed into law the Military Commissions Act to permit accused terrorists to be tried before military tribunals and to clarify what types of interrogation methods would be permitted; opponents argued that it would allow excessively harsh questioning techniques; no right of habeas corpus to apply to internees.

18

1595 Edward Winslow, Plymouth Colony governor (1633, 1636, 1644), born in Droitwich, England; arrived on Mayflower (died 1655).

1631 Michael Wigglesworth, clergyman whose poem *The Day of Doom* (1662) was first American best seller, born in Yorkshire, England (died 1705).

1748 Treaty of Aix-la-Chappelle (Aachen, Germany) ended War of Succession (King George's War); Louisburg on Cape Breton Island returned to France.

1774 Delegates to first Continental Congress adopted a Continental Association pledging that their colonies would (1) cease all importation from Great Britain, (2) totally discontinue slave trade, (3) institute non-consumption of British products and various foreign luxury products, and (4) embargo all exports to Britain, Ireland, and West Indies; this is sometimes considered the first true American Union.

1776 Thaddeus Kosciusko, Polish officer, commissioned a colonel of engineers in the Con-

tinental Army; distinguished himself at Ticonderoga and Saratoga.

1787 Robert L. Stevens, invented the T-rail for railroads, still in use, born in Hoboken, NJ; built the *Maria*, fastest sailing ship for about 20 years (died 1856).

1812 Francis H. Smith, first president, Virginia Military Institute (1839–89), born in Norfolk, VA; Confederate Army officer (died 1890).

1818 Edward O.C. Ord, Union general at Corinth and Vicksburg, born in Cumberland, MD; held various postwar military commands (died 1883).

1824 Allen B. Wilson, patented a sewing machine (1850), born in Willet, NY; machine manufactured by Nathaniel Wheeler (died 1888).

1831 Thomas Hunter, organized first evening high school (New York City 1866), born in Ardglass, Ireland; organized, headed, Normal College, New York City (1870–1906), later named for him (died 1915).

1839 Thomas B. Reed, House Speaker (1889–90, 1895–99), born in Portland, ME; represented Maine in House (1877–99); responsible for rules which enhanced Speaker's power to speed legislation of majority (died 1902).

1844 Harvey W. Wiley, called father of Food & Drug Administration, born in Kent, IN; chief chemist, Agriculture Department (1883–1912), established methods and philosophy of food analysis (died 1930).

1847 Henry O. Havemeyer, who helped found, headed American Sugar Refining Co. (1891), born in New York City; company produced half of America's sugar; donated vast art collection to Metropolitan Museum of Art (died 1907).

1867 Control of Alaska transferred from Russia to United States in ceremonies at Sitka.

1875 Henry E. Yarnell, commander of Atlantic Fleet (1936–39), born near Independence, IA; held various other commands (died 1959).

1876 U. of Oregon opened in Eugene.

1878 James Truslow Adams, historian (*The Founding of New England, Epic of America, The March of Democracy*), born in Brooklyn (died 1949).

1882 Charles M.A. Stine, holder of numerous chemical patents with DuPont (from 1907), born in Norwich, CT; among the patents were propellant powder, high explosives, dyes, artificial leather, paint (died 1954).

1889 Fannie Hurst, author (*Imitation of Life, Humoresque, Anitra's Dance, Stardust, Lummox*), born in Hamilton, OH (died 1968).

1896 Nat Holman, basketball player/coach, born in New York City; star of original Celtics team, which won 720 of 795 games (1921–30); coach, CCNY (1950–52, 1955–60) (died1955).

1921 Senate ratified separate treaties concluding peace with Germany, Austria, and Hungary.

1927 George C. Scott, screen actor (*Patton, Dr. Strangelove, Hindenburg*), born in Wise, VA.

1931 Herbert W. Chilstrom, first bishop of Evangelical Lutheran Church, born in Litchfield, MN; church formed by merger of Lutheran denominations.

1935 Earthquake occurred near Helena, MT, doing considerable damage.

1939 Mike Ditka, college and professional football player, born; coach of Chicago Bears (1982–93), New Orleans (1997).

1956 Martina Navratilova, considered one of world's greatest women tennis players, born in Prague, Czechoslovakia.

1982 Bess Truman, widow of President Truman, died in Independence, MO, at 98.

1988 Congress passed bill changing Veterans Administration into 14th cabinet department, effective in Spring 1989; President Reagan signed measure October 26.

1988 Most cigars and possibly some pipe and loose tobacco will carry cancer warning labels as result of agreement reached by tobacco manufacturers to end California lawsuit.

1989 Space shuttle *Atlantis* lifted off from Cape Canaveral, FL, and hours later released the nuclear-powered Galileo probe to Jupiter.

1996 Morey Amsterdam, television comedian remembered for the Dick Van Dyke show, died at about 81.

2000 Julie London died at 74; actress and popular singer during the 1950s.

19

1630 A general court, the first in New England, met in Boston.

1748 Martha W. Skelton Jefferson, wife of President Jefferson, born in Charles City County, VA (died 1782).

1765 Stamp Act Congress, meeting in New York City, issued resolutions opposing the tax.

1774 Counterpart of the Boston Tea Party occurred in Annapolis harbor when a tea ship, *Peggy Stewart*, was burned by the colonists.

1779 Thomas C. Brownell, Episcopal Bishop of Connecticut (1819–65), born in Westport, MA; presiding bishop (1852–65); first president, Trinity (then Washington) College (1823–31) (died 1865).

1781 British force of 8,000 men under Lord Charles Cornwallis, surrounded by American and French troops at Yorktown, VA, surrendered; defeated force marched out from Yorktown at 2 P.M. with their colors cased and bands playing an old British march (*The World Turned Upside Down*); British fleet, learning of surrender, returned to New York.

1834 Francis C. Barlow, New York attorney general who launched prosecution of Tweed ring, born in Brooklyn (died 1896).

1848 Samuel Guthrie, chemist who discovered chloroform, died at 66; invented percussion priming powder with a punch lock to explode it, replacing flintlock muskets; devised process for fast conversion of potato starch into sugar.

1861 William J. Burns, founder of private detective agency with branches throughout country (1909), born in Baltimore; director, Bureau of Investigation (now FBI) (1921–24) (died 1931).

1863 John H. Finley, New York State education commissioner (1921–37), born in Grand Ridge, IL; president, Knox College (1892–99), City College of New York (1903–13); editor-in-chief, *New York Times* (1937–38) (died 1940).

1864 Battle of Cedar Creek, 60 miles west of Washington, won by Union troops, ending Confederate control of Shenandoah Valley.

1871 Walter B. Cannon, pioneer in X-ray observation, born in Prairie du Chien, WI; professor, Harvard Medical School (1900–42); discovered a substance (sympathin) which causes stimulation of certain organs (died 1945).

1885 Charles E. Merrill, a founder, partner, Merrill Lynch brokerage, born in Green Cove Springs, FL; founder, Safeway Stores, *Family Circle* magazine (died 1926).

1895 Lewis Mumford, architectural critic/author (*The Culture of Cities, The Urban Prospect, The City in History*), born in Flushing, NY (died 1990).

1901 Arleigh A. Burke, World War II admiral known as "31-knot Burke," born near Boulder, CO; chief of naval operations (1955–59).

1910 Subrahmanyan Chandrasekhar, astrophysicist with U. of Chicago, born in Lahore, India; shared 1983 Nobel Physics Prize for work on evolution of stars (died 1995).

1922 Jack Anderson, newspaper columnist, born in Long Beach, CA; took over *Washington*

Merry Go Round column on death of Drew Pearson (1969).

1943 Secretary of State Cordell Hull, British Foreign Secretary Anthony Eden, and Soviet Foreign Commissar Vyacheslaw Molotov met in Moscow to discuss political and military matters, including opening a second front.

1962 Evander Holyfield, three times world heavyweight boxing champion (1990–92, 1993–94, 1996–99), born.

1973 Arab oil-producing nations imposed ban on oil exports to United States after the outbreak of Arab-Israeli war; lifted March 18, 1974.

1982 John Z. DeLorean, prominent automaker, arrested in Los Angeles; charged with drug possession; accused of scheme to sell enough drugs to shore up his ailing auto company; eventually acquitted.

1987 Selling panic pushed Dow Jones industrial average down record 508 points, draining more than $500 billion from value of stocks, a 22.6 percent loss of value.

1993 House again voted down continuing construction of the Superconducting Supercollider; two days later, project was killed officially.

1994 Martha Raye, screen comedienne, died at 78.

2006 After registering nine record closing daily numbers in little more than two weeks, the Dow Jones ended the day at a historically unprecedented 12,012 points.

2006 The Court of Appeals, New York's highest judicial body, ruled 6–0 that church-related social welfare agencies that carry health insurance must include birth control and similar coverage even when the religion believes it is a grievous sin to use it; critics argue that it provides judicial precedent for churches to have to fund abortions through its medical coverage.

2006 Wal-Mart announced $4-per-prescription program would immediately be expanded to 14 more states; Target announces same day it will match the offer in the 12 states where the two chains compete.

20

1629 John Winthrop elected first governor of Massachusetts Bay Colony as settlers were getting ready to sail from England.

1674 James Logan, chief justice, Pennsylvania Supreme Court (1731–39), born in County Armagh, Ireland; came to America (1699) as secretary to William Penn; held various provincial posts (died 1751).

1783 Continental Congress voted to meet alternately in Annapolis and Trenton until a permanent site was selected.

1803 Senate by 24–7 vote ratified treaty with France transferring Louisiana to the United States; President Jefferson authorized the takeover October 30.

1812 Austin Flint, founder, professor, Buffalo (NY) Medical College (1847–61), born in Petersham, MA; founder, Bellevue Medical college (1861); a pioneer in heart research (died 1886).

1816 James W. Grimes, Iowa governor (1854–58) and senator (1859–69), born in Deering, NH; stricken by apoplexy during President Andrew Johnson impeachment trial, he was carried into Senate and cast deciding vote to prevent impeachment (died 1872).

1818 Convention of 1818, sequel to Treaty of Ghent, signed in London, agreeing on American fishing rights and the American-Canadian boundary.

1825 Daniel E. Sickles, Union general at Chancellorsville and Gettysburg, where he lost his right leg, born in New York City; military governor of Carolinas (1865–67); minister to Spain (1869–75); represented New York in House (1857–61, 1893–95) (died 1914).

1853 Benjamin Harrison was married to Caroline L. Scott in Oxford, OH.

1859 John Dewey, pioneer in progressive education, born in Burlington, VT; author of *School in Society, How We Think, Democracy and Education* (died 1952).

1874 Charles Edward Ives, composer known for polytonal harmonies, unusual rhythms, born in Danbury, CT (died 1954).

1884 Bela Lugosi, stage and screen actor known for horror films (*Dracula, Frankenstein*), born in Lugos, Hungary (died 1956).

1889 Benjamin T. Babbitt, inventor who held more than 100 patents, died at 80; among them were soap processes, an ordnance projector, steam boilers, and pumps.

1890 Sherman Minton, associate justice, Supreme Court (1949–56), born in Georgetown, IN; represented Indiana in Senate (1935–41); judge, U.S. Circuit Court of Appeals (1941–49) (died 1965).

1891 Samuel F. Bemis, historian of American diplomacy, born in Worcester, MA; author of two-volume study of John Quincy Adams (died 1973).

1895 William W. Wurster, architect who designed San Francisco projects—Ghirardelli Square and Golden Gate Project, born in Stockton, CA (died 1973).

1900 Wayne L. Morse, represented Oregon in Senate (1945–69), born in Madison, WI; dean, U. of Oregon law school (died 1974).

1905 Manfred B. Lee, author who with Frederic Dannay formed team which was Ellery Queen, mystery writer, born in New York City (died 1971).

1913 Grandpa (Marshall L.) Jones, country music personality and singer, born in Niagara, KY (died 1998).

1925 Art Buchwald, syndicated humorous columnist, born in Mt. Vernon, NY.

1931 Mickey Mantle, baseball player (New York Yankees) who hit 536 career home runs, born in Spavinaw, OK; named to Baseball Hall of Fame (died 1995).

1944 An explosion of huge liquid gas tanks in Cleveland resulted in a fire which raged through a 50-block area, killing 135, injuring 215.

1947 House Committee on Un-American Activities began hearings on alleged Communism in Hollywood; resulted in ten indictments for contempt of Congress.

1964 Former President Hoover died in New York City at 90.

1973 Watergate Special Prosecutor Archibald Cox fired by President Nixon when Cox threatened to seek judicial ruling that the president was violating a court order to turn over tapes; Attorney General Elliott Richardson resigned rather than fire Cox, Deputy Attorney General Donald Ruckelshaus was fired for refusing to do so.

1976 Ferry and tanker collided in Mississippi River near Luling, LA; 77 persons died.

1979 John F. Kennedy Library in Boston dedicated.

1990 Senate confirmed nomination of David H. Souter of New Hampshire to fill a vacancy on the Supreme Court.

2004 Baseball history in the American League Championship Series: in previous 25 cases when a team was ahead 3–0 in the Series, it proceeded to win the championship; for the first time ever the Red Sox broke that tradition by winning four consecutive games for the title after losing the first three.

2006 U.S. Supreme Court upheld right of Arizona to require photo identification to vote in that fall's election; voters had approved measure in 2004; Court argued that it is premature for courts to void the measure so close to election day without clearest evidence that it should be done.

2006 Surprise and consternation hit New York City as spokesperson announced that unexpected additional human remains from the 9/11 terrorist attack had been found; city to renew search in the other "manholes" at the site similar to the one where the fragments were located; a number of surviving family members demanded that all construction be stopped until absolutely certain everything had been located.

21

1692 Gov. Benjamin Fletcher of New York also was commissioned as governor of Pennsylvania.

1736 William Shippen, chief of medical department, Continental Army (1777–81), born in Philadelphia; founder, president, College of Physicians, Philadelphia (1805–08) (died 1808).

1776 Concord, MA, called for a convention to prepare a state constitution.

1776 George Washington withdrew his troops from New York City to White Plains.

1776 George Izard, War of 1812 general, born in Richmond, England; resigned from army (1815) after criticism for failing to push advantage over British at Canadian border; governor, Arkansas Territory (1825–28) (died 1828).

1785 Henry M. Shreve, who established practica-bility of steam navigation on Mississippi River, born in Burlington County, NJ; Shreveport, LA, named for him (died 1851).

1797 *Constitution* ("Old Ironsides") launched in Boston; active in war with Tripoli and War of 1812.

1808 Samuel F. Smith, Baptist clergyman, wrote music for "America," born in Boston; hymn writer ("The Morning Light is Breaking") (died 1895).

1855 Howard H. Russell, congregational clergyman who was a founder, first general superintendent, Anti-Saloon League of America (1895–1903), born in Stillwater, MN (died 1946).

1861 Battle of Ball's Bluff (near Leesburg, VA) resulted in a Confederate victory.

1868 Earthquake struck San Francisco causing $3 million in damage.

1876 Ding (Jay N.) Darling, editorial cartoonist (*Des Moines Register, New York Tribune*), born in Norwood, MI (died 1962).

1877 Oswald T. Avery, geneticist who paved

way for genetic engineering with studies of cell structures, born in Halifax, Nova Scotia (died 1955).

1879 After many fruitless experiments, Thomas A. Edison succeeded in making an incandescent lamp wherein a loop of carbonized cotton thread glowed in a vacuum for more than 40 hours.

1891 Ted (Edwin M.) Shawn, dancer who formed Denishawn Dancers with wife, Ruth St. Denis, born in Kansas City, MO; founder, Jacob's Pillow Dance Festival (died 1972).

1892 Columbian Exposition in Chicago dedicated; opened to public May 1, 1893.

1897 Yerkes Observatory at Williams Bay near Lake Geneva, WI, opened and dedicated; built for U. of Chicago by Charles T. Yerkes.

1917 Dizzy (John B.) Gillespie, jazz trumpeter and arranger known as creator and king of bop, born in Cheraw, NC (died 1993).

1944 Aachen was captured, the first sizable German city taken by the Allies.

1976 Congress repealed Homestead Act of 1862 for all states except Alaska because there was no longer any public land suitable for cultivation.

1986 American writer Edward Austin Tracy kidnapped in Beirut.

1987 Confidence returned to Wall St. after Dow Jones industrial average rose 186.84 points.

1988 Deposed President Ferdinand Marcos of the Philippines and his wife were indicted by a federal grand jury in New York City on racketeering charges for buying Manhattan real estate with hundreds of millions of dollars allegedly embezzled from their government; also charged with defrauding American financial institutions of more than $165 million.

1991 Wind-driven fires in the hills above Oakland, CA, killed 24 persons, destroyed about 1,000 structures.

1995 Maxene Andrews, one of the singing Andrews sisters, died at 79.

22

1693 Thomas Fairfax, owner of 5.2 million acres between the Potomac and Rappahannock Rivers in Virginia, born in Kent, England; lived there from 1745 until his death in 1781; George Washington surveyed his holdings in Shenandoah Valley.

1738 James Manning, first president, Brown U. (1765–91), born in Piscataway, NJ; also a founder of the school (died 1791).

1746 Charter granted for College of New Jersey (later Princeton) to Jonathan Dickinson, a leading Presbyterian of his time; was first president of the college which opened in Newark in May 1747.

1775 Peyton Randolph, president of first two Continental Congress sessions (1774, 1775), died at about 54.

1780 John Forsyth, Secretary of State (1834–41), born in Fredericksburg, VA; represented Georgia in House (1813–18, 1823–27) and Senate (1818–19, 1829–34) and served it as governor (1827–29); minister to Spain (1829–33) (died 1841).

1813 Charles Scott, commander of Virginia troops in Revolution, died at about 74; served with Washington in Braddock's campaign against French and Indians (1755); served Kentucky as governor (1808–12).

1821 Collis P. Huntington, railroad builder, president (Southern Pacific 1890–1900), born in Harwinton, CT; joined Central Pacific with Union Pacific at Promontory Point, UT (died 1900).

1832 Leopold Damrosch, founder, conductor, New York Oratorio Society (1873) and New York Symphony Society (1878), born in Posen, Poland; conducted first American performance of Wagner's major operas at the Met (died 1885).

1836 Sam Houston, who received 80 percent of vote, took oath of office as president of the independent Republic of Texas.

1873 Stephen M. Babcock, dairying pioneer who developed (1890) test for milk's butterfat content, born in Bridgewater, NY (died 1931).

1854 James A. Bland, minstrel song composer ("Carry Me Back to Old Virginny," "Oh Dem Golden Slippers," "In the Evening by the Moonlight"), born in Flushing, NY (died 1911).

1875 Sons of the American Revolution (SAR) organized in San Francisco.

1879 David H. Knott, formed, owned Knott Hotels Corp. (1927), born in Orange, NJ; had 35 hotels and restaurants (died 1954).

1881 Clinton J. Davisson, physicist, born in Bloomington, IL; shared 1937 Nobel Physics Prize for discovery of diffraction of electrons by crystals (died 1958).

1882 Newell C. Wyeth, artist and illustrator of children's books, born in Needham, MA (died 1945).

1883 First national horse show held in Madison Square Garden, New York City.

1883 Metropolitan Opera House, costing

about $1,732,000, opened with a performance of Gounod's *Faust*.

1884 George W. Hill, president, American Tobacco Co. (1925–46), born in Philadelphia; devised unique Lucky Strike cigarette promotions (died 1946).

1887 John Reed, journalist and radical, born in Portland, OR; with Pancho Villa in Mexico and participated in Russian 1917 October revolution, writing *Ten Days That Shook the World*; indicted for sedition but escaped to Russia where he died (1920); buried in the Kremlin.

1889 John L. Balderston, playwright (*Berkeley Square*) and screenwriter, born in Philadelphia (died 1954).

1890 Joseph N. Welch, attorney who served as special Army counsel in McCarthy televised hearings (1954), born in Primghar, IA (died 1960).

1896 Charles G. King, chemist known for isolation, synthesis of Vitamin C, born in Entiat, WA; also worked on enzymes and synthetic fats.

1900 Edward R. Stettinius, Secretary of State (1944–45) and first American UN delegate (1945–46), born in Chicago; president, U.S. Steel (1939); Lend-Lease administrator (1941–43), Undersecretary of State (1943–44) (died 1949).

1903 George W. Beadle, geneticist, born in Wahoo, NE; shared 1958 Nobel Physiology/Medicine Prize for discovering how genes transmit hereditary characteristics; president, U. of Chicago (1960–68) (died 1989).

1905 Karl G. Jansky, engineer whose research led to radio astronomy, born in Norman, OK; worked with Bell Research on static (died 1950).

1907 Panic of 1907 begun by failure of Knickerbocker Trust Co. copper market actions; Westinghouse Electric went into receivership, Pittsburgh Stock Exchange closed, several banks failed; loans by J.P. Morgan & Co. and the Treasury Department checked the panic; crisis ended in December.

1907 Jimmy (James E.) Foxx, baseball player (Philadelphia AL, Boston AL) with career batting average of .325 and 534 home runs, born in Sudlersville, MD; named to Baseball Hall of Fame (died 1957).

1913 Mine explosion in Dawson, NM, killed 263 persons.

1913 Robert Capa, photographer with *Life* magazine, Magnum Photo, born in Budapest; covered various World War II battlefronts (died 1954).

1914 Constance Bennett, screen actress of 1940s (*Lady with a Past, Topper*), born in New York City (died 1965).

1917 Alien Property Custodian established to handle American assets of an enemy or an ally of an enemy; functions moved (1934) to Justice Department.

1922 Joan Fontaine, screen actress (*Rebecca, Suspicion*), born in Tokyo.

1925 Robert Rauschenberg, artist whose "combine paintings" founded pop art and neo–Dada movements of 1950s, born in Port Arthur, TX.

1938 Chester F. Carlson discovered xerography, producing a dry image without a chemical reaction, in Rochester, NY; his Haloid Corp. founded in 1957, later became Xerox.

1962 Soviet missile buildup in Cuba revealed by President Kennedy; naval and aerial quarantine of Cuba begun; crisis ended October 28, quarantine ended November 20.

1965 Highway Beautification Act signed, providing for reduced federal highway assistance to states that do not control billboards and junkyards along highways.

1979 Shah of Iran flew to New York City for cancer treatments.

1990 President Bush vetoed civil rights bill which would have reversed six recent Supreme Court decisions which civil rights organizations claimed had weakened anti-discrimination laws.

1995 Commemorating United Nations 50th anniversary, President Clinton called for a crackdown on international crime, including terrorism and drug smuggling.

23

1750 Thomas Pinckney, colonial leader, born in Charleston, SC; served South Carolina as governor (1787–89) and represented it in House (1797–1801); minister to Great Britain (1792–95), to Spain (1795–96); unsuccessful Federalist vice presidential candidate (1796) (died 1828).

1817 James W. Denver, Union general who was governor of Kansas Territory (1857–58), born in St. Louis County, MO; represented California in House (1855–57); Denver, CO, named for him (died 1892).

1827 Orville J. Victor, originator of the "dime novel" (c. 1860), born in Sandusky, OH; organized, trained, directed stable of writers to grind out such books (died 1910).

1831 Basil L. Gildersleeve, promoter of classical studies in America, born in Charleston, SC; founder, editor, *American Journal of Philology* (1880–1920) (died 1924).

1835 Adlai E. Stevenson, Vice President (1893–97), born in Christian County, KY; represented Illinois in House (1875–77, 1879–81); Assistant Postmaster General (1885–89) (died 1914).

1838 Francis H. Smith, engineer, artist/author (*Col. Carter of Cartersville*; *Caleb West, Master Diver*), born in Baltimore (died 1915).

1850 First national women's rights convention held in Worcester, MA.

1869 John W. Heisman, football coach at nine colleges (1892–1927), born; annual college football trophy named for him (died 1936).

1871 Edgar J. Goodspeed, helped prepare *Revised Standard Version of the New Testament*, born in Quincy, IL; chairman, New Testament Department, U. of Chicago (1923–37) (died 1962).

1873 William D. Coolidge, inventor of ductile tungsten and tube for production of X-rays, born in Hudson, MA; with General Electric (died 1975).

1875 Gilbert N. Lewis, chemist first to isolate heavy hydrogen isotope, born in Weymouth, MA; developed various theories (atomic, valence, photon) (died 1946).

1876 Paul P. Cret, architect (Folger Library and Federal Reserve in Washington, DC), born in Lyon, France (died 1945).

1895 Clinton P. Anderson, Agriculture Secretary (1945–48), born in Centerville, SD; represented New Mexico in Senate (1949–73) (died 1975).

1899 Bernt Balchen, pilot for numerous flights over poles, including first over South Pole (1929), born in Tveit, Norway (died 1973).

1905 Felix Bloch, physicist, born in Zurich, Switzerland; shared 1952 Nobel Physics Prize for work in measurement of magnetic fields in atomic nuclei (died 1938).

1906 Gertrude Ederle, first woman to swim English Channel (1925), born in New York City.

1917 American troops saw their first action on the Western front in the Toul sector.

1925 Johnny Carson, emcee of *Tonight* television show (1962–92), born in Corning, IA.

1934 Jean Piccard and his wife, Jeannette, flew from Michigan to Ohio in a balloon which reached an altitude of more than 57,000 feet.

1944 Three-day Battle of Leyte Gulf resulted in major defeat for Japanese navy, which lost two battleships, four aircraft carriers, nine cruisers, and nine destroyers.

1946 Opening session of UN General Assembly in Flushing Meadows, Long Island, was addressed by President Truman.

1966 President Lyndon Johnson attended seven-nation Manila Conference, which ended October 25; he pledged to "continue our military and other efforts ... as long as may be necessary ... until aggression is ended" in South Vietnam.

1983 Bomb-filled truck smashed through barriers at the Marine compound at the Beirut Airport, killing 241 Americans.

1998 Palestinian leader Yasser Arafat and Israeli Prime Minister Benjamin Netanyahu signed new peace agreement in Washington, following series of meetings arranged by President Clinton.

2001 Apple Computer announced it would shortly start shipping the iPod at $399 each; apparatus holds 65 hours of audio.

2004 Opera baritone Robert Merrill died at 87 while watching World Series on television; performed over 500 times with the New York Metropolitan Opera over three decades.

2006 Only two business days after breaking into uncharted Dow Jones industrial highs, a triple-digit leap took the stock market yet further, to 12,117.

2006 Jeffrey K. Skilling, sentenced to 24 years in prison for his role as CEO in Enron scandal that cost employees over a billion dollars in retirement benefits and investors even larger sums.

2006 IBM sued Amazon.com alleging patent infringement, arguing that pivotal technology used by the e-retailer utilized procedures patented by IBM as far back as 1980s.

24

1776 Presbytery of Hanover petitioned the Virginia Assembly for religious liberty and removal of taxes to support the Anglican Church.

1781 George Washington's report of victory at Yorktown was read to Continental Congress, whose members went in procession to nearby Dutch Lutheran Church to give thanks.

1788 Sarah J. Buell Hale, editor, born in Newport, NJ; editor (1828–37) of *Ladies Magazine*, which became *Godey's Lady's Book*, editing it 1837–77 (died 1879).

1808 John Sartain, engraver who introduced pictorial illustration to American periodicals, born in London (died 1897).

1830 Belva A.B. Lockwood, feminist who was first woman attorney to appear before Supreme

Court, born in Royalton, NY; presidential nominee, National Equal Rights Party (1884, 1888) (died 1917).

1855 James S. Sherman, vice president (1909–12), born in Utica, NY; represented New York in House (1887–91, 1893–1909) (died 1917).

1861 First transcontinental telegraph line completed; first telegram received by President Lincoln from Sacramento, CA.

1871 Riot in Los Angeles against Chinese by a mob resulted in hanging of 15 and shooting of six.

1887 George W. Borg, a founder, auto parts firm (Borg Warner) (1928), born in West Burlington, IA; helped develop disc auto/truck clutch (died 1960).

1889 Arde Bulova, developer of family watch business, born in New York City; standardized many watchmaking procedures (died 1958).

1899 Gilda Gray, dancer known as "Queen of the Shimmy," born in Cracow, Poland (died 1959).

1904 Moss Hart, playwright and director, born in New York City; coauthor (with George S. Kaufman) of *Once in a Lifetime, You Can't Take It with You, The Man Who Came to Dinner*; (with Kurt Weill and Ira Gershwin) *Lady in the Dark*; (with Irving Berlin) *Face the Music*; librettist for *As Thousands Cheer* and *Jubilee*; director, *My Fair Lady* and *Camelot* (died 1961).

1931 George Washington Bridge over Hudson River opened.

1933 Wages and Hours Act went into effect, setting up minimum wage and maximum weekly hours.

1945 United Nations came into formal existence when the Soviet Union deposited its ratification, bringing total to 29 nations.

1949 Cornerstone laid for United Nations headquarters in New York City.

1962 President Kennedy issued proclamation demanding that Russia dismantle its military bases in Cuba and withdraw its armaments; Russia agreed to do so a few days later.

1976 Fire in a Bronx, NY, social club claimed the lives of 25 persons.

1985 President Reagan, addressing United Nations General Assembly on its 40th anniversary, asked the Soviet Union to join the United States in seeking settlements of five regional disputes involving Soviet-supported regimes.

1998 Mary S. Calderone, physician and influential advocate of sex education, died at 94.

2000 $237 billion federal budget surplus announced.

2002 The "Beltway Snipers" arrested after series of killings and shootings in Washington, DC, and surrounding areas that began October 2.

2002 Harry Hay (born 1912) died; arguably founder of gay rights movement in U.S.: the Mattachine Society that he helped form in 1950 was the first such advocacy group to survive.

2005 Hurricane Wilma rolled over Florida (category 3 at landfall) and did estimated $14.43 billion in damage.

2005 Rosa Parks, civil rights pioneer, passed away at 92; her refusal to yield a bus seat to a white person in the 1950s sparked more than a year-long boycott of Birmingham, AL, bus system; event regarded as one of pivotal events launching the civil rights revolution in the South.

2005 President Bush nominated Ben Bernanke of Princeton to replace long-serving Alan Greenspan as chairman of the Federal Reserve.

25

1741 Russian explorers, led by Vitus Bering, discovered Kiska Island in the Aleutians.

1764 John Adams and Abigail Smith were married in Weymouth, MA.

1811 Carl F.W. Walther, Lutheran leader, born in Langenschursdorff, Germany; cofounder, president, Concordia Theological Seminary (1854–87); president, Missouri Synod (1846–50, 1864–78) (died 1887).

1812 U.S. frigate *United States* captured British frigate *Macedonian* off Madeira Islands.

1850 Southern Rights Association formed in South Carolina to resist the anti-slavery states.

1859 Chester A. Arthur and Ellen L. Herndon were married in New York City.

1866 Gilbert Patten, author of adventure stories under name of Burt L. Standish, born in Corinna, ME; remembered for *Frank Merriwell* series (died 1945).

1873 John N. Willys, owner, president, Willys-Overland Auto Co. (1907–25), born in Canandaigua, NY; a bicycle manufacturer originally; ambassador to Poland (1930–32) (died 1935).

1887 Supreme Court, in Wabash Railroad case, ruled that states do not have the power to regulate interstate traffic.

1888 Richard E. Byrd, aviator and explorer, born in Winchester, VA; with Floyd Bennett, became first to fly over North Pole (1926); flew over South Pole (1929), made several Antarctic expeditions (1928–30, 1933–35) (died 1957).

1890 Floyd Bennett, aviator who was pilot for Byrd (above) on first flight over North Pole, born near Warrensburg, NY (died 1928).

1891 Charles E. Coughlin, Catholic priest who opposed New Deal economics, born in Hamilton, Canada; his opposition carried on weekly radio program and publication, *Social Justice*, which was banned from mails; church imposed silence on him (1942) (died 1979).

1892 Caroline L. Harrison, wife of President Benjamin Harrison, died in White House at 60.

1902 Woodrow Wilson inaugurated as president of Princeton U.

1902 Henry Steele Commager, historian with New York U., Columbia, born in Pittsburgh; author (*The Blue and the Gray, Era of Reform*); coauthor (*The Growth of the American Republic*) (died 1998).

1904 Arshile Gorky, a leading art expressionist in United States, born in Khorkum Vari, Turkey (died 1948).

1912 Minnie Pearl (Sarah O.C. Cannon), country entertainer, born in Centerville, TN (died 1996).

1914 John Berryman, a major American poet of his time (*Homage to Mistress Bradstreet*), born in McAlester, OK (died 1972).

1924 Bobby (Robert W.) Brown, baseball player (New York AL), born in Seattle; president, American League (1984–92).

1926 U. of California at Los Angeles (UCLA) dedicated.

1929 Albert B. Fall found guilty of accepting bribe in Teapot Dome scandal while Interior Secretary; sentenced to one year, $100,000 fine.

1930 Hannah H. Gray, first woman president of a major American university (U. of Chicago 1978), born in Heidelberg, Germany.

1941 Helen Reddy, singer/screen actress, born in Melbourne, Australia.

1946 Forest fire destroyed most of Bar Harbor, ME; damaged Acadia National Park.

1948 Dan Gable, champion wrestler and coach (Iowa U.) born in Waterloo, IA; 1972 Olympic gold medal in wrestling; his Iowa wrestlers won 11 Big Ten titles (1977–87) without losing a match.

1983 American troops landed on island of Grenada in West Indies in effort to halt a Cuban buildup and to protect American students on the island; area was secured within a few days.

1995 AFL-CIO convention elected John J. Sweeney as its new president, succeeding Lane Kirkland, who retired in August.

2001 Windows XP went on sale; first major update of Microsoft's computer operating system since Windows 95; Microsoft to spend $200 million promoting product.

2002 U.S. Senator Paul Wellstone perished in small plane accident with wife and daughter, throwing the campaign for his seat — election day less than two weeks away — into confusion at a time when Democrats had only a one-seat majority in the Senate.

2004 Medical trouble on highest court: It was announced that Chief Justice William Rehnquist has thyroid cancer and is receiving treatment.

2004 The Congressional Gold Medal, the U.S.' highest award for civilians, awarded to Dr. Martin Luther King, Jr., and his wife, Coretta Scott King.

2006 The New Jersey Supreme Court unanimously ruled that the current marital system violated the right of homosexuals to equal treatment; by 4–3 vote, the justices permit legislature to choose between expanding the right to marry to them or creating the functional equivalent through civil unions; the 3-judge minority wished to require the legislature to accept the marriage option.

26

1757 Charles Pinckney, a most important contributor to Constitutional Convention, born in Charleston, SC; served South Carolina as governor (1788–92, 1796–98, 1806–10) and represented it in Senate (1798–1801) and House (1818–20); minister to Spain (1801–06) (died 1824).

1774 Massachusetts Committee of Safety created with John Hancock as chairman.

1825 The 363-mile-long Erie Canal opened; canal boat *Seneca Chief* left Buffalo with Gov. DeWitt Clinton on board; arrived in New York City November 4; canal cost $7 million and cut travel time by a third, shipping costs by 90 percent.

1831 John W. Noble, Interior Secretary (1889–93), born in Lancaster, OH; was a Union general (died 1912).

1832 Convention adopted Mississippi constitution; ratified by general election.

1854 Charles W. Post, cereal maker who developed Postum, born in Springfield, IL; also manufactured various cereals (died 1914).

1861 Richard D. Sears, tennis champion and one of first seven named to Tennis Hall of Fame, born in Boston; won national amateur singles (1881–87) and doubles (1882–87); president, U.S. Lawn Tennis Association (1887–88) (died 1943).

1863 Ellsworth M. Statler, hotel chain founder (1905), born in Somerset County, PA; chain later taken over by Hilton Hotels (died 1928).

1876 H(enry) B. Warner, screen director and actor (*King of Kings, Lost Horizon, Sorrell and Son*), born in London (died 1958).

1877 Max Mason, president, U. of Chicago (1925–28), Rockefeller Foundation (1929–36), born in Madison, WI; invented several submarine detection devices (died 1961).

1881 Big shootout at OK Corral occurred as the Espy brothers and Doc Holiday had a showdown with Clanton gang; shootout actually occurred in alley near corral.

1894 John S. Knight, founder, head of newspaper chain bearing his name, born in Bluefield, WV (died 1981).

1899 Judy (William J.) Johnson, outstanding Negro League baseball player, born in Snow Hill, MD; named to Baseball Hall of Fame.

1910 John J. Krol, Catholic Archbishop of Philadelphia (1961–88), born in Cleveland; elevated to cardinal 1967 (died 1996).

1911 Mahalia Jackson, gospel singer, born in New Orleans; her singing linked religious and secular music (died 1972).

1932 Charles E. Ashburner, America's first city manager, died at 62; an independent consultant and contractor, he completed repairs to a Staunton, VA, dam at a fifth of a local contractor's estimate; council created new position of city manager; in three years (1908–11), he defined and set standards for position.

1942 First battle of Solomon Islands resulted in heavy Japanese fleet losses and American aircraft carrier *Hornet* was sunk.

1949 Minimum wage legislation raised the wage from 40 cents an hour to 75 cents.

1993 Clinton Administration cancelled plans for trade sanctions against Japan after Tokyo agreed to open public sector construction market to international competition.

1997 Chinese President Jiang Zemin began nine-day visit to United States; met President Clinton in Washington October 29.

2000 Last game of World Series: New York Yankees beat and seal series victory over New York Mets, 4 games to 1; first time since 1956 that both teams came from New York City.

2001 President Bush signed Patriot Act into law; intended to consolidate and expand anti-terrorist activities of federal government.

2005 Chicago White Sox won World Series for first time since 1917.

2006 Arson set 42,000-acre Esperanza forest fire near Cabazon, CA, killed four firefighters immediately, with fifth dying of burns a few days later; suspected arsonist later arrested and charged with arson and murder and suspected of setting as many as ten other fires.

27

1659 In keeping with the Massachusetts law making it a capital offense for a Quaker to return after banishment, two Quakers — William Robinson and Marmaduke Stevenson — were hanged on the Boston Common.

1749 Jared Ingersoll, colonial legislator, born in New Haven, CT; member of Continental Congress (1780–81) and Constitutional Convention (1787); Pennsylvania attorney general (1790–99, 1811–17); Federalist vice presidential candidate (1812) (died 1822).

1763 William Maclure, considered father of American geology, born in Ayr, Scotland (died 1840).

1787 First of 77 essays signed by "Publius," supporting proposed Constitution, appeared in New York newspapers; later (with additional essays) they were collected as *The Federalist Papers*; most (about 51) were written by Alexander Hamilton, 28 by James Madison, five by John Jay.

1793 Eliphalet Remington, firearms manufacturer and later (c. 1856) expanded into implements, born in Suffield, CT; began manufacturing in Ilion, NY, then Springfield, MA (died 1861).

1795 Thomas Pinckney, minister to Spain, negotiated Treaty of San Lorenzo with Spain, establishing boundaries of Florida and Louisiana, and gave Americans right of free navigation on Mississippi River.

1795 Samuel R. Hall, Congregational clergyman, founder of first American normal school (Concord, VT 1823), born in Croydon, NH; his school was teachers' training school (died 1877).

1800 Benjamin F. Wade, Senate president

pro tem who would have become president if President Andrew Johnson had been impeached, born in Feeding Hills, MA; represented Ohio in Senate (1851–69) (died 1878).

1810 President Madison issued proclamation taking possession of West Florida, from the Mississippi to Perdido River, as part of Louisiana Purchase.

1811 Isaac M. Singer, sewing machine manufacturer, born in Pittstown, NY; improved and patented an existing sewing machine (1851); by 1860, was world's foremost sewing machine manufacturer (died 1875).

1811 Stevens T. Mason, first governor of Michigan (1835–40), born in Loudon County, VA (died 1843).

1822 George B. Armstrong, credited with developing railway mail service, born in County Armagh, Ireland (died 1871).

1827 Albert Fisk, who invented special form of bridge truss, born in Lauterbach, Germany; built some of America's longer railroad bridges; standardized freight rates, virtually founding railroad economics as a science (died 1897).

1828 Jacob D. Cox, Secretary of Interior (1869–70), born in Montreal to American parents; served Ohio as governor (1866–68); dean, Cincinnati Law School (1881–97); president, U. of Cincinnati (1885–89) (died 1900).

1837 Whitelaw Reid, editor, *New York Tribune* (1872–1905), born near Xenia, OH; minister to France (1889–92), ambassador to Great Britain (1905–12) (died 1912).

1838 John D. Long, Secretary of Navy (1897–1902), born in Buckfield, ME; served Massachusetts as governor (1880–82) and represented it in House (1883–89) (died 1915).

1841 American brig *Creole*, carrying a cargo of slaves, sailed from Hampton Roads to New Orleans; slaves mutinied, killing one white crew member and forcing mate to take ship to the Bahamas; British freed all slaves except the actual revolt participants.

1858 Theodore Roosevelt, 26th President (1901–09), born in New York City; led Rough Riders in Cuba during Spanish-American War; member, U.S. Civil Service Commission (1889–95); assistant secretary of Navy (1897–98); elected vice president (1900), succeeding to presidency on death of President McKinley; awarded 1906 Nobel Peace Prize (died 1919).

1864 Ironclad Confederate ram *Albemarle* was sunk in Plymouth (NC) harbor by a Union raiding party led by Lt. William B. Cushing.

1869 Steamer *Sultana* exploded on Mississippi River near Memphis, killing 1,450.

1870 Roscoe Pound, dean, Harvard Law School (1916–36), born in Lincoln, NE; dean, U. of Nebraska Law School (1903–07); also a botanist of note (died 1964).

1873 James J. Davis, Secretary of Labor (1921–30), born in Tredegar, Wales; represented Pennsylvania in Senate (1930–44); director-general, Loyal Order of Moose (1906–21) (died 1947).

1874 Owen D. Young, board chairman, General Electric (1922–39, 1942–44), born in Van Hornesville, NY; a leader in developing German reparations plan (died 1962).

1880 Theodore Roosevelt and Alice H. Lee were married in Brookline, MA.

1882 Mary Josephine Rogers, founder of Maryknoll Sisters, born in Roxbury, MA (died 1955).

1904 First New York City subway opened, running from City Hall to 145th St. on the West Side.

1919 President Wilson vetoed Volstead prohibition endorsement bill; veto overridden the same day by the House and on October 28, by the Senate.

1922 Ralph Kiner, baseball player (Pittsburgh) who had .369 career batting average and was home run leader seven seasons, born in Santa Rita, NM; named to Baseball Hall of Fame.

1923 Roy Lichtenstein, pioneer in "comic strip" paintings and "pop" style, born in New York City (died 1997).

1925 Warren Christopher, Secretary of State (1993–97), born in Scranton, ND; deputy Secretary of State (1977–81).

1972 Consumer Product Safety Commission created.

1992 Roger Miller, popular singer/composer ("King of the Road"), died at 56.

1997 Stock market, affected by economic problems in Southeast Asia, dropped 554 points, the largest single-day drop in Dow Jones history.

2001 Largest ever gift to an American university: California Institute of Technology received $600 million from Gordon Moore, cofounder of Intel Corp.

2003 Eight simultaneous fires ignited 500,000 acres; historically, one of California's largest conflagrations.

2004 U.S.' Cassini space probe neared Titan, a moon of Saturn, and took first ever close-up photographs and scientific readings; results puzzled scientists as they were significantly different from anything expected; Cassini scheduled for 45 more flybys during following four years.

2005 The National Academy of Sciences and National Science Teachers Association prohibited Kansas from using its materials because it says state overemphasizes possible difficulties with evolutionary reconstructions and does not explicitly rule out any supernatural role in human development.

2006 Improbable winners: St. Louis Cardinals beat Detroit Tigers and won the World Series; no team had ever won it with fewer regular season victories (83); lost 10 of last 14 games; got into play-offs at all only because another team lost last game of its season; first Cardinals victory since 1982.

28

1586 Francis West, governor of Virginia (1627–29), born in England; commander at Jamestown (1612) (died 1634).

1636 Harvard College founded by an act of Massachusetts General Court, which granted 400 pounds toward a school or college to be built at Newtown (Cambridge).

1766 Leading New York City citizens signed agreement banning purchase of English goods until Stamp Act was repealed; followed (October 31) by 200 New York City merchants, 400 Philadelphia merchants in November, 250 Boston merchants December 6.

1767 In wake of Townshend Acts, imposing import duties, a Boston town meeting drew up list of British goods not to be purchased after December 31; similar action followed in Providence, Newport, and New York City.

1776 British troops under Gen. William Howe attacked Americans led by George Washington at White Plains, NY; British captured key hill positions but Americans slipped away while British awaited reinforcements.

1786 Isaac Sears, New York merchant who seized arsenal and customhouse on hearing of battle at Lexington, holding city until American army arrived, died at about 56; moved to Boston, from which he sent out privateers to prey on British shipping.

1798 Levi Coffin, anti-slavery leader known as president of the underground railway, born in New Garden City, NC (died 1877).

1801 Henry Inman, one of most prominent first-generation American-trained artists, born in Utica, NY (died 1846).

1808 Horace Smith, who with Daniel B. Wesson invented, manufactured revolvers, born in Cheshire, MA (died 1893).

1818 Abigail Adams, wife of President John Adams, died in Quincy, MA, at 73.

1836 Homer D. Martin, landscape artist who was among first Americans to use impressionism in his work, born in Albany, NY (died 1897).

1847 J. Walter Thompson, founder, head (1878–1916) of one of nation's leading advertising agencies, born in Pittsfield, MA (died 1928).

1858 Henry Koplik, pediatrician who paved way for diagnosis of measles, born in New York City; established first American milk depot to provide milk for poor infants (died 1927).

1865 Convention in Tallahassee repealed Florida's secession ordinance; abolished slavery November 6.

1869 Joseph B. DeLee, obstetrician who founded Chicago Lying-In Hospital (1895) and Chicago Maternity Center (1932), born in Cold Spring, NY (died 1942).

1875 Gilbert H. Grosvenor, president, National Geographic Society (1920–66), born in Istanbul to American parents; editor, *National Geographic Magazine* (1899–1954) (died 1966).

1886 Statue of Liberty, which arrived dismantled in 214 packing cases from France and then erected on Bedlow (now Liberty) Island, dedicated by President Cleveland.

1893 Carter H. Harrison, five-term Chicago mayor, was assassinated by P.E. Prendergast, a disappointed office seeker.

1896 Howard H. Hansen, director, Eastman School of Music (1924–64), born in Wahoo, NE (died 1981).

1907 Edith Head, fashion designer for movies, born in Los Angeles (died 1981).

1914 Jonas E. Salk, developer of polio vaccine (1954), born in New York City; director, Salk Institute of Biological Studies (1963–95) (died 1995).

1916 American steamship *Lanso* sunk by a German submarine off Portugal.

1925 Courtmartial of Col. Billy Mitchell of Air Service began; an outspoken critic of Army policies, he was found guilty December 17, sentenced to suspension from rank, command, and duty; resigned February 1, 1926.

1926 Bowie Kuhn, baseball commissioner (1969–83), born in Takoma Park, MD.

1941 Office of Lend-Lease Administration created with Edward R. Stettinius as director.

1946 Atomic Energy Commission established with David E. Lilienthal as first chairman; later became Nuclear Regulatory Commission.

1949 Bruce Jenner, 1976 Olympic decathlon winner, born in Mt. Kisco, NY.

1955 Bill (William H.) Gates, head of Microsoft, world's largest computer software company, born in Seattle, WA.

1986 Formal 100th birthday observance of the Statue of Liberty held.

2005 Lewis ("Scooter") Libby, chief of state to the vice president, indicted for reputedly lying to investigators and grand jury; investigation centered on who leaked allegedly secret identity of a Washington-based CIA agent to press but indictments do not concern that matter.

2005 Dr. Richard Smalley, a leading figure in the emerging field of nanotechnology, died of cancer at 62; discovered "buckyballs" in 1985, opening up a new field of chemical research and development.

2006 Red Auerbach died at 89 after repeated major illnesses; considered among the handful of top basketball coaches of the 20th century; invented and popularized key elements in the playing of the modern professional form of the sport.

29

1652 Massachusetts Bay Colony, in defiance of Parliament, declared itself an independent commonwealth.

1784 Robert Hoe, founder (1823), R. Hoe & Co. printing press manufacturer, born in Leicestershire, England (died 1833).

1796 Charles Lynch, colonial judge whose name is associated with "lynching," died at 60; as a judge in Bedford County, VA, he never sentenced anyone to death.

1819 Convention in Portland adopted Maine constitution; ratified by people in town meetings December 6.

1828 Thomas F. Bayard, first ambassador to Great Britain (1893–97), born in Wilmington, DE; Secretary of State (1885–89); represented Delaware in Senate (1869–84) (died 1898).

1831 Othniel C. Marsh, first American paleontology professor, born in Lockport, NY; his many discoveries of fossils of extinct horses and pterodactyl contributed to evolutionary theory (died 1899).

1832 James Gordon Bennett published first

issue of *New York Globe*, a two-cents morning newspaper.

1860 Gen. Winfield Scott advised President Buchanan that certain national forts in the South be garrisoned to avoid their seizure by "insurgents"; advice turned down lest it further excite South.

1865 Charles H. Ingersoll, with brother, founded company (1892) which made and sold inexpensive watches, born in Delta, MI.

1870 Robert B. Owens, credited with discovery of alpha rays, born in Anne Arundel County, MD; invented an electromagnetic system for guiding ships and planes (died 1940).

1884 Several hundred Protestant clergymen met with presidential candidate James G. Blaine in New York City to assure him of their support; the Rev. Samuel D. Burchard of Hudson St. Presbyterian Church said, "We are Republicans and don't propose to leave our party and identify ourselves with the party whose antecedents are rum, Romanism, and rebellion"; remarks were later attributed to Blaine and were said to have cost him the election.

1891 Fanny Brice, stage comedienne who played Baby Snooks on radio (1936–51), born in New York City; also known for song "My Man" (died 1951).

1901 Leon F. Czolgosz, convicted slayer of President McKinley, electrocuted in Auburn (NY) State Prison.

1919 International Labor Organization (ILO) held its first meeting in Washington; Albert Thomas named director general.

1920 Benjamin Benacerraf, pathologist with Harvard Medical School, born in Caracas, Venezuela; shared 1980 Nobel Physiology/Medicine Prize for discoveries of how genetic makeup determines body's response to infection and cancer.

1921 William H. Mauldin, cartoonist who created World War II characters, Willie and Joe in *Stars & Stripes*, born in Mountain Park, NM; later editorial cartoonist.

1925 Zoot (John H.) Sims, saxophonist and clarinetist, born in Inglewood, CA (died 1985).

1929 Stock market crash began, bringing on worst American depression; stock losses in ensuing two years estimated at $50 billion.

1940 First draft numbers selected in Washington following the registration of more than 16 million men.

1947 Frances F. Cleveland, widow of President Cleveland, died in Baltimore at 83.

1966 National Organization of Women (NOW) formed.

1969 Supreme Court ruled unanimously that school districts must end segregation "at once" and operate integrated systems "now and hereafter."

1974 Former President Nixon underwent surgery to prevent blood clot in leg from entering his lungs.

1990 United Nations warned Iraq of unspecified measures if it did not withdraw from Kuwait.

1991 Governors of nine Eastern states and the District of Columbia agreed to adopt California's program for cleaner cars to fight smog.

1998 John Glenn, 77, returned to space as a crew member of the *Discovery* nine-day flight; conducted tests on effect of space on older persons; Glenn was first American astronaut to orbit earth in 1962.

2001 U.S. Justice Department announced 1,000 individuals detained on suspicion of terrorist activities since 9/11 attack.

2002 U.S. Environmental Protection Agency data showed miles per gallon continued to shrink: had peaked in 1988; for 2003 new models just being released it had shrunk by 6 percent to 20.1 MPG. .

2006 Major storm brought widespread winds of 50 mph and higher throughout Northeastern region; Mount Washington (New Hampshire) had 100 mph sustained winds with gusts of 114 — and 11 inches of snow.

2006 After a month of student protests and a rejection of the hiring decision by the faculty (82 percent–18 percent), the Board of Trustees reversed itself and rejected Jane Fernandes as next president of Gallaudet University (Washington, DC), America's leading school for the deaf.

30

1683 A Charter of Liberties was enacted by delegates from New York City, Albany, Schenectady, Esopus (Kingston, NY), Martha's Vineyard, Nantucket, and Pemaquid (eastern Maine) which called for meeting at least once in three years and its approval would be required for imposing taxes; originally approved by Duke of York but disapproved in 1687.

1735 John Adams, second President (1797–1801), born in Quincy, MA; defended British soldiers accused of murder in Boston Massacre;

member, Continental Congress (1774–78), a signer of Declaration of Independence; commissioner to France (1778–79), minister to Netherlands (1780–85); helped negotiate peace treaty ending Revolution; became first elected vice president (1789) (died 1826).

1768 First American Methodist chapel (42 John St., New York City) dedicated.

1807 James S. Wadsworth, commander of divisions at Fredericksburg and Gettysburg, born in Geneseo, NY; mortally wounded at Battle of the Wilderness (1864); founder, Free Soil Party.

1829 John Rogers, sculptor noted for groups (*The Slave Auction*, Civil War scenes), born in Salem, MA (died 1904).

1840 William G. Sumner, one of first, most influential American sociology teachers (Yale U. 1872–1910), born in Paterson, NJ; advocated free trade, sound currency, development of big business; author (*Folkways*) (died 1910).

1857 Gertrude Atherton, popular novelist (*The Conqueror, Black Oxen*), born in San Francisco (died 1948).

1862 Gen. William S. Rosecrans named commander of Army of the Ohio, replacing Gen. D.C. Buell; unit renamed Army of the Cumberland.

1865 Convention in Milledgeville repealed Georgia's secession ordinance; abolished slavery November 4.

1873 Emily Post, who wrote novels, books on design, and best known for work on etiquette, born in Baltimore; etiquette book written 1922, wrote syndicated column (died 1960).

1875 Missouri's state constitution ratified by popular vote; effective November 30.

1877 Herbert W. Hoover, founder of Hoover Suction Sweeper Co. (1910), born in North Canton, OH; company's president (1922–48), board chairman (1948–54) (died 1954).

1882 William F. Halsey, World War II admiral, born in Elizabeth, NJ; commander, Allied naval forces, South Pacific (1942–44), Third Fleet (1944–45); helped turn Battle of Leyte Gulf into overwhelming Allied victory (died 1959).

1883 Bob Jones, evangelist who founded Bob Jones U. (Greenville, SC), born in Dale County, AL; toured world as evangelist, radio evangelist (died 1968).

1885 Ezra L. Pound, poet who influenced American and English literature, born in Hailey, ID; lived in Italy as an expatriate; works include *Cantos, Personae, Exultations* (died 1972).

1886 Zoe Akins, poet and playwright (*The*

Old Maid), born in Humansville, MO (died 1958).

1888 Alan G. Kirk, World War II admiral, born in Philadelphia; commanded amphibious invasion of Sicily and naval forces in Normandy landing; ambassador to Belgium (1946–49), to Soviet Russia (1949–52) (died 1963).

1894 Charles Atlas, physical culturist who developed successful mail order fitness program, born in Italy; developed self into model (died 1972).

1895 Dickinson W. Richards, helped develop technique of cardiac catheterization, born in Orange, NJ; technique opened new era in heart research; shared 1956 Nobel Physiology/Medicine Prize for the development.

1912 Vice President James S. Sherman died in Utica, NY, at 57.

1914 Marion Ladewig, considered best woman bowler of all time, born in Grand Rapids, MI; won seven women's all-star titles; woman bowler of year (1950–54, 1957–59, 1963).

1918 Allied representatives met in Paris, drew up conditions for an armistice.

1928 Daniel Nathans, biologist, born in Wilmington, DE; shared 1978 Nobel Physiology/Medicine Prize for discovery of application of restriction enzymes to problems of molecular genetics.

1938 Radio dramatization by Orson Welles and his Mercury Theater of *War of the Worlds* created a nationwide scare.

1941 U.S. destroyer *Reuben James* was torpedoed and sunk off Ireland; 100 of crew lost.

1972 President Nixon signed amendment to Social Security Act to provide additional $5.3 billion for the elderly.

1972 Railroad accident in Chicago killed 45 persons.

1988 Kraft, Inc., agreed to a $13.1 billion buyout by Philip Morris Cos., Inc., in the biggest merger ever between two non-oil American companies.

2000 Steve Allen died; creator of the first late-night television show, *The Tonight Show,* and hosted it for its first two years.

2006 Unwanted distinction: Based upon 2005 crime statistics, St. Louis, MO, now the worst crime-afflicted city in nation after for years in the top ten; a 20 percent jump in violent crime from previous year took city to the top of the list.

31

1740 William Paca, governor of Maryland (1782–85), born near Abingdon, MD; member of Continental Congress (1774–79) and signer of Declaration of Independence (died 1799).

1754 Charter of College of the Province of New York signed by Gov. James DeLancey of New York; school later became King's College, then Columbia.

1783 Fourth convention in New Hampshire framed constitution acceptable to the people, effective June 1, 1784; contained clause forbidding slavery.

1791 *National Gazette,* an anti-administration newspaper, established with Philip Freneau as editor.

1800 *National Intelligencer,* a most quoted newspaper, began publishing in Washington, DC.

1801 Theodore D. Woolsey, president, Yale U. (1846–71), born in New York City (died 1889).

1803 The *Philadelphia,* while helping blockade port of Tripoli, ran aground on a reef and was captured.

1816 Philo Remington, president, Remington Co. (1861–89), born in Litchfield, NY; firearms company branched into agricultural equipment and typewriters (died 1889).

1826 Joseph R. Hawley, Union general who became Connecticut governor (1866), born in Stewartville, NC; represented Connecticut in House (1872–75) and Senate (1881–1905) (died 1905).

1827 Richard M. Hunt, architect who helped found American Institute of Architects, born in Brattleboro, VT; designed many mansions, main part of Metropolitan Museum of Art, National Observatory in Washington, Fogg Museum at Harvard (died 1895).

1830 Andrew J. Aikens, developer of ready-to-print newspaper page (1864) which became Western Newspaper Union, born in Barnard, VT (died 1909).

1831 Rudolf Eickemeyer, inventor with about 150 patents, born in Altenbamberger, Germany; among his inventions were a hat-making machine that revolutionized the industry, a differential gear for mowing/reaping machines, many electrical machines and devices (died 1895).

1831 Daniel Butterfield, Union general who composed bugle call, *Taps,* born in Utica, NY; served at Gettysburg and with Sherman's March to the Sea (died 1901).

1860 Juliette G. Low, founder, president (1915–20) of Girl Scouts, born in Savannah, GA; originally known as Girl Guides (1912), became Girl Scouts (1913) (died 1927).

1863 William G. McAdoo, secretary of treasury (1913–18), born near Marietta, GA; president, Hudson & Manhattan Railroad; first chairman, Federal Reserve Board (1917–19); represented California in Senate (1933–38) (died 1941).

1864 Nevada admitted to the Union as the 36th state.

1867 Ed(ward J.) Delahanty, baseball player who was first to win batting championship in both leagues, born in Cleveland; named to Baseball Hall of Fame (died 1903).

1869 William A. Moffett, naval officer who served at battles of Manila Bay (1898) and Vera Cruz (1914), born in Charleston; headed Bureau of Aeronautics (1921–33) (died 1933).

1873 International Peace Bridge across the Niagara River between Buffalo, NY, and Ft. Erie, Canada, completed.

1875 Eugene I. Meyer, first president, organizer, World Bank (1946), born in Los Angeles; owner of *Washington Post* (1933 on) (died 1959).

1900 Ethel Waters, popular blues singer and actress (*A Member of the Wedding*), born in Chester, PA (died 1977).

1900 Cal Hubbard, member of college and professional football and baseball halls of fame, born in Keytesville, MO; after football career, served as American League baseball umpire (1936–51) (died 1977).

1902 Wilbur Shaw, automobile racer who won Indianapolis 500 race three times (1937, 1939, 1940), born; pioneered use of crash helmets (died 1954).

1930 Michael Collins, astronaut who piloted first manned lunar mission (1969), born in Rome, Italy.

1931 Dan(iel) Rather, television newsman, anchor of CBS News from 1981 on, born in Wharton, TX; had served as CBS White House correspondent.

1940 National Institutes of Health in Bethesda, MD, dedicated.

1950 Jane Pauley, co-host of the *Today* show (1976–89), born in Indianapolis.

1963 Fire in State Fairgrounds Coliseum in Indianapolis resulted in 74 deaths.

1994 An American Eagle flight crashed in a field near Roselawn, IN, killing 68 persons.

2003 Presidential adviser to several presidents, including Kennedy and Clinton, Richard E. Neustadt died at 84; long-time Harvard professor and author of *Presidential Power* (1960; revised 1990).

2004 Fannie Mae, largest financier of U.S. home mortgages, put new rule in effect: it will no longer purchase loans that include a binding arbitration requirement in lender-purchaser disputes; agency fears it compromises purchasers' rights and imposed buried-in-fine-print details that go unnoticed.

2005 Samuel A. Alito, Jr., nominated as replacement for retiring Supreme Court Justice Sandra Day O'Connor; with 15 years service on the Third Circuit Court of Appeals (Philadelphia), the conservative choice has more judicial experience than any nominee since Benjamin Cardozo in 1932.

2006 Hubble rescue mission approved by NASA in policy reversal: The greatly successful space telescope was in need of major repairs; shuttle mission to fix had been scuttled in 2004 over safety concerns.

NOVEMBER

1

1642 Jean Nicolet, French explorer who was first European to reach Lake Michigan (1634), died at 44.

1678 William Coddington, governor of Aquidneck, RI (1674–75, 1678), died at 77; protested Massachusetts persecution of Anne Hutchinson and moved to Rhode Island.

1757 (Johann) George Rapp, founder of Harmonites sect, born in Iptinger, Germany; sect founded towns of Harmony in Pennsylvania and Indiana; colony successful until 1903 (died 1847).

1764 Stephen Van Rensselaer, president, Erie Canal Commission (1825–39), born in New York City; founder, Rensselaer Polytechnic Institute (RPI) (1824); represented New York in House (1822–29) where he cast deciding vote to make John Quincy Adams president (1824); served state as lieutenant governor (1795–1801) (died 1839).

1765 Stamp Act went into effect.

1767 Great Britain modified trade laws, reducing the three-penny duty on foreign molasses imported by the colonists to one penny on all molasses; export duties on British West Indies sugar were removed.

1776 Continental Congress authorized a lottery to raise $5,000 for military purposes.

1784 Continental Congress began its session in Trenton, NJ; continued for a year.

1800 President John Adams took up residence in the White House, the first president to do so; in a letter to his wife, he wrote, "I pray Heaven bestow the best of blessings on this house and all that shall hereafter inhabit it. May none but wise and honest men ever rule under this roof."

1808 John Taylor, president of Mormon Church (1880–87), born in Milnthrope, England; forced into exile because of his polygamy (1884–87) (died 1887).

1815 Crawford W. Long, reputedly the first surgeon to use ether in surgery, born in Danielsville, GA (died 1878).

1818 James Renwick, architect who revived Gothic design, born in New York City; among his works were Grace Church, St. Patrick's Cathedral, CCNY, all in New York City; Smithsonian Institution and Corcoran Art Gallery in Washington, DC (died 1895).

1830 Former President John Quincy Adams elected to House from the Plymouth, MA, district, serving until his death in 1848.

1835 Second Seminole War began; continued intermittently for seven years.

1844 Convention at Iowa City approved the Iowa constitution.

1852 Louisiana residents ratified their state constitution which had been adopted by a convention in Baton Rouge in July.

1860 Boies Penrose, Republican boss of Pennsylvania (1904–21), born in Philadelphia; represented Pennsylvania in Senate (1897–1921) (died 1921).

1861 Gen. George B. McClellan named commander-in-chief of Union Army; also became general-in-chief of Army with retirement of Gen. Winfield Scott.

1871 Stephen Crane, author best known for *The Red Badge of Courage*, born in Newark, NJ (died 1900).

1880 Grantland Rice, sportswriter (*New York Herald Tribune* and widely syndicated), born in Murfreesboro, TN (died 1954).

1880 Sholem Asch, author of biblical novels (*The Nazarene, The Apostle, Moses, Mary*), born in Kutno, Poland (died 1957).

1890 Mississippi constitution adopted by convention, effective January 1, 1891.

1897 New Library of Congress opened.

1900 The 12th Census reported gain of more than 13 million people in a decade to 75,994,575.

1918 Railroad wreck in Malbone St. tunnel in Brooklyn killed 92 persons.

1932 Al Arbour, hockey coach who led New York Islanders to four Stanley Cup titles (1980–83), born.

1941 Rainbow Bridge over the Niagara River at Niagara Falls opened.

1949 Helen Hokinson, cartoonist who featured middle-aged matrons and club members, died in an airplane crash at 56; cartoons usually in *The New Yorker*.

1949 Two planes collided over Washington; 55 persons died.

1950 Assassination attempt made on President Truman in Washington by two Puerto Rican nationalists; one was killed, as was a White House guard, Leslie Coffelt.

1952 First hydrogen device was exploded at Eniwetok Atoll in the Pacific.

1955 United Air Lines DC-6 exploded, crashed at Longmont, CO, killing 44; explosion caused by a bomb planted in plane.

1973 Leon Jaworski of Texas named Special Watergate Prosecutor succeeding Archibald Cox, who had been fired by President Nixon.

1977 American membership in the International Labor Organization (ILO) was terminated at the direction of the president; United States had been a member since 1934.

1979 Mamie Eisenhower, widow of President Eisenhower, died in Washington at 82.

1981 Cost of first-class postage rose to 20 cents.

1982 Bowie Kuhn deposed as baseball commissioner when five National League teams voted not to renew his contract.

2006 Music publisher Buddy Killen died at 73; had played major role in launching careers of Dolly Parton and others, played backup music for groups, and wrote several hundred songs that were hits when recorded.

2006 Pulitzer prize-winning William Styron died at 81; wrote *Confessions of Nat Turner*.

2

1734 Daniel Boone, legendary frontiersman, born near Reading, PA; made numerous trips to Kentucky, guiding settlers there (1775), erected fort on site of what is now Boonesboro (died 1820).

1760 Lewis R. Morris, represented Vermont in the House (1797–1803), where his vote was key to election of Jefferson as president, born in Scarsdale, NY; on 36th ballot in Jefferson-Burr contest in House, Morris withheld his vote turning election to Jefferson (died 1825).

1772 At call of Samuel Adams, a Boston town meeting created 21-man standing Committee of Correspondence to communicate Boston's position to other communities and "to the World"; James Otis was chairman; other colonies formed similar committees and by February 1774 only North Carolina and Pennsylvania were without such groups.

1790 Jacob R. Hardenbergh, Dutch Reformed clergyman helped found Queens (later Rutgers) College (1766), died at 54; was president (1786–90).

1791 U. of Vermont chartered; opened in Burlington 1800.

1795 James K. Polk, 11th President (1845–49), born in Mecklenburg County, NC; represented Tennessee in House (1825–39), serving as Speaker (1835–39); also served state as governor (1839–41) (died 1849).

1802 John Thompson, founder of New York City banks, born in Peru, MA; founded First National Bank, of which he was president (1863–73), and Chase National Bank (1877) (died 1891).

1810 Andrew A. Humphreys, chief, Army Engineers (1866–79), born in Philadelphia; led survey of Mississippi delta (1850–51, 1857–61); Union general through Civil War (died 1883).

1865 Warren G. Harding, 29th President (1921–23), born in Morrow County, OH; represented Ohio in Senate (1915–21); died in San Francisco (1923) enroute to Washington from an Alaska visit.

1869 Voters in New York ratified new constitution, but refused to waive property qualification of black men.

1880 Thomas A. Edison demonstrated first direct current underground power transmission system.

1885 Harlow Shapley, director, Harvard Observatory (1921–52), born in Nashville, MO; astronomer at Mt. Wilson Observatory (1914–21) (died 1972).

1885 Winthrop A. Aldrich, president, board chairman, Chase National Bank (1933–53), born in Providence, RI; ambassador to Great Britain (1953–57) (died 1974).

1886 Florida ratified its new constitution.

1889 North Dakota entered Union as the 39th state and South Dakota as the 40th.

1897 Dennis King, actor in musicals (*Rose Marie, Vagabond King, Three Musketeers*), born in Coventry, England (died 1983).

1897 Richard B. Russell, governor of Georgia (1931–33) and served state in Senate (1933–71), born in Winder, GA (died 1971).

1908 Bunny (Roland B.) Berigan, trumpeter and leader in 1930s swing era, born in Hilbert, WI (died 1942).

1913 Burt Lancaster, screen actor (*Elmer Gantry, The Bird Man of Alcatraz, The Killers*), born in New York City (died 1994).

1917 Postage rates went from two to three cents for first-class mail; postcards from one to two cents.

1920 Public radio broadcasting began at Station KDKA in Pittsburgh, providing the first election results; first regular evening broadcasts began November 30.

1922 Barber B. Conable, Jr., president, World Bank (1986–91), born in Warsaw, NY; represented New York in House (1965–85).

1923 Billy (William) Haughton, a leading harness-race driver, born in Gloversville, NY; won Hambletonian four times, ranks fourth in races won (4,910) and purses earned ($40.2 million) (died 1986).

1932 Melvin Schwartz, physicist, born in New York City; shared 1988 Nobel Physics Prize for helping capture neutrinos in a high-energy beam to examine the structure of atomic particles.

1939 Congress enacted and President Franklin Roosevelt signed an amended neutrality law to permit belligerents to purchase and remove, at their own risk, war materials.

1948 President Truman reelected in a major political upset over New York Governor Thomas E. Dewey.

1962 President Kennedy announced that Soviet missile bases in Cuba were being dismantled and "progress is now being made toward restoration of peace in the Caribbean."

1972 Bureau of Indian Affairs Building in Washington was invaded by 500 American Indians who were protesting Bureau policies.

1983 President Reagan signed bill designating the third Monday in January as a national holiday honoring the Rev. Martin Luther King, Jr.

1986 David P. Jacobsen, an American hostage in Beirut, was released.

2001 New statistics released: Unemployment rose in October to 5.6 percent — highest figure in five years.

2004 In spite of election-day exit polling pointing to opposite result, Bush won reelection and expanded Republican majorities in House and Senate.

2006 Microsoft and Novell, Inc., agreed to make Windows and open source Linux system work together on same computer systems; will permit OpenOffice to run on Windows systems without compatibility problems.

2006 The Rev. Ted Haggard, President of the National Association of Evangelicals, one of nation's leading Christian conservative religious leaders (often considered a moderate within their ranks), resigned after charges of drug use and homosexual relations with a male "escort"; denied sex and asserted had not actually used drugs though had purchased them and been "tempted" to use; accuser admitted he had gone public, in part, in order to discredit opposition to homosexual rights proposals.

3

1620 Council of New England incorporated in Plymouth, England, "for the planting, ruling, ordering, and governing New England in America."

1623 Dutch West India Co. authorized sending five to six families to start a settlement in New Netherland.

1723 Samuel Davies, Presbyterian clergyman who helped found the Hanover Presbytery (1765), born in New Castle County, DE; raised funds in England for the College of New Jersey (later Princeton), of which he was president (1759–61) (died 1761).

1741 William Irvine, Revolutionary general, born in Enniskillen, Ireland; captured in Canadian expedition (1776), exchanged (1778); commander, Ft. Pitt, Pittsburgh (1781–1803) (died 1804).

1757 Robert Smith, Secretary of State (1809–11), born in Lancaster, PA; served as Secretary of Navy (1801–09) (died 1842).

1762 Secret Treaty of Ildefonso between Spain and France called for transfer to Spain of Louisiana Territory west of the Mississippi River.

1775 St. John's, Canada, under siege since September 6 by 1,000 American troops, surrendered to Gen. Richard Montgomery; Canadian expedition designed to prevent British invasion from the north.

1793 Stephen F. Austin, Texas colonizer,

born in Wythe County, VA; carried out colonization plan of father; directed colony's government, maintained peace and order; imprisoned in Mexico City (1833–34) for advocating Texas independence (died 1836).

1794 William Cullen Bryant, co-owner, co-editor, *New York Evening Post* (1829–78), born in Cummington, MA; poet remembered for *Thanatopsis* and *To a Waterfowl* (died 1878).

1816 Jubal A. Early, Confederate general who led raid in Shenandoah Valley (1864), born in Franklin County, VA; remained a rebel, never taking oath of allegiance to United States after the war (died 1894).

1834 Charles L. Fleischmann, founder of yeast manufacturing firm, born in Budapest (died 1897).

1841 Isabella M. Alden, author of books for juveniles (the *Pansy* books), born in Rochester, NY (died 1930).

1845 Edward D. White, chief justice, Supreme Court (1910–21), associate justice (1894–1910), born in LaFourche Parish, LA; known for "the rule of reason" in antitrust cases (died 1921).

1854 Jokichi Takamine, chemist who developed starch-digesting enzyme for distilling industry, born in Takaoa, Japan; isolated adrenalin from supra-adrenal gland (died 1922).

1879 Vihjalmur Stefansson, Arctic explorer who learned and taught how humans can live in cold regions, born in Arnes, Canada (died 1962).

1884 Joseph W. Martin, House Speaker (1947–49, 1953–55), born in North Attleboro, MA; represented Massachusetts in House (1925–67) (died 1968).

1887 Nat Fleischer, outstanding boxing authority and founder, editor, *Ring Magazine* (1922–72), born in New York City; wrote many books on boxing (died 1972).

1891 William McKinley elected governor of Ohio.

1897 Idaho amended its constitution to permit woman suffrage.

1900 First automobile show opened in New York City's Madison Square Garden.

1903 Julian P. Boyd, historian who edited Jefferson's papers, born in Converse, SC; associated with Princeton U. (died 1980).

1903 Walker Evans, first photographer to have an exhibition in Museum of Modern Art (1938), born in St. Louis; associate editor, *Fortune* (1945–65) (died 1975).

1909 James Reston, reporter, columnist *New York Times* (1939–95), born in Clydebank, Scotland (died 1995).

1918 Bob Feller, baseball pitcher (Cleveland) who led American League in strikeouts seven times, born in Van Meter, IA; named to Baseball Hall of Fame.

1933 Michael S. Dukakis, governor of Massachusetts (1975–79, 1983–87), born in Brookline, MA; 1988 Democratic presidential nominee.

1949 Larry Holmes, world heavyweight boxing champion (1978–85), born in Cuthbert, GA.

1979 Ku Klux Klan members killed five demonstrators at an anti–Klan rally in Greensboro, NC.

1992 Carol Moseley-Braun of Illinois became first black woman elected to U.S. Senate.

1992 Arkansas Gov. Bill Clinton elected president, defeating President Bush's effort to be reelected; Senator Al Gore, Jr., of Tennessee elected vice president.

1997 Between November 3 and 12, Iraq prevented UN inspectors from doing their job; Russia worked out an accord which allowed inspections to resume November 20.

1998 Democrats picked up five seats in the House in the congressional election in which Republicans expected to increase their margin in the House.

2000 Total land burned by forest fires from January 1–November 3: 7.2 million acres, worst hit areas were in western states.

2006 Economic good news announcement: jobless rate dropped to 4.4 percent in October, lowest rate in five years.

4

1493 Christopher Columbus, on his second voyage, arrived at the Leeward Islands in the West Indies and explored Puerto Rico.

1732 Thomas Johnson, first governor of Maryland (1777–79), born in Calvert County, MD; member of Continental Congress (1774–77); associate justice, Supreme Court (1791–93) (died 1819).

1791 American force led by Gen. Arthur St. Clair virtually wiped out by Indians at Ft. Wayne, IN; two-thirds of the 900 men were killed or wounded; St. Clair resigned his Army command (1792).

1794 James Monroe, minister to France, effected release of Thomas Paine from a Paris prison, where he had been held for about a year on a technicality.

1796 Treaty of Peace, Friendship, and Navigation signed with Tripoli.

1809 Benjamin R. Curtis, associate justice, Supreme Court (1851–57), born in Watertown, MA; wrote one of two dissenting opinions in Dred Scott case; served as counsel for President Andrew Johnson in impeachment trial (died 1874).

1810 John Allen, dentist who perfected type of denture still in use (1851), born in Broome County, NY; founded Ohio College of Dental Surgery and New York College of Dentistry (died 1892).

1813 British offered to negotiate peace with United States.

1816 Stephen J. Field, associate justice, Supreme Court (1863–97), born in Haddam, CT; his decisions were important in developing constitutional law (died 1899).

1833 William P. Hepburn, legislator instrumental in enactment of Pure Food & Drug Act, born in Wellsville, OH; represented Iowa in House (1881–87, 1893–1909); Solicitor of the Treasury (1889–93) (died 1916).

1837 James Douglas, brought about reforms in mining and metal industries, born in Quebec; president, Copper Queen Consolidated Mining Co. in Arizona; Douglas, AZ, named for him (died 1918).

1841 Benjamin F. Goodrich, founder of tire company bearing his name (1876), born in Ripley, NY (died 1888).

1841 First migrant wagon train from Missouri reached California.

1842 Abraham Lincoln and Mary Todd were married in Springfield, IL.

1862 Richard J. Gatling received patent for his multiple-barreled rapid-fire gun.

1874 Sewell L. Avery, president, Montgomery Ward (1931–55), born in Saginaw, MI; resisted federal attempts to take Ward property (1944), carried bodily from his office (died 1960).

1876 James E. Fraser, sculptor who designed Indian head nickel, 1919 Victory medal, born in Winona, MN; did numerous busts, monuments (died 1953).

1879 Will Rogers, author and entertainer, born in Oologaw, OK; starred in numerous films, stage revues, Wild West shows; a syndicated columnist (died 1935).

1881 Denver was made permanent capital of Colorado.

1884 New constitution for Montana ratified by popular vote.

1906 Bob Considine, war correspondent, syndicated columnist with Hearst papers for nearly 40 years, born in Washington, DC (died 1975).

1916 Walter L. Cronkite, anchor for *CBS Evening News* (1962–81), born in St. Joseph, MO.

1918 Art Carney, screen actor (*Harry and Tonto, The Odd Couple*) and television (*The Honeymooners*), born in Mt. Vernon, NY.

1931 Buddy (Charles) Bolden, legendary creator of jazz in New Orleans at turn of century, died at about 63.

1948 American-born T.S. Eliot awarded 1948 Nobel Literature Prize.

1979 Iranian militants seized American Embassy in Teheran and took more than 66 hostages; demanded that Shah be returned to Iran; most Americans held until January 20, 1981.

1982 Secretary Richard S. Schweiker of Department of Health & Human Services approved regulations requiring tamper-proof packaging on almost all non-prescription drugs.

1988 President Reagan signed bill ratifying an international treaty banning genocide which was drafted 40 years ago; Wisconsin Senator William Proxmire made 3,300 daily speeches over 19 years urging American ratification.

1990 Defense Department to call up major combat units from reserves to join American force in Persian Gulf area; at least 100,000 troops will join the 150,000 already there.

2001 After winning the last three World Series in a row, the New York Yankees were defeated by the Arizona Diamondbacks, a team that had not even existed five years earlier.

2003 Call for broadening appeal of Democratic Party or catering to racism? Howard Dean, candidate for Democratic nomination for president and later chairman of the Democratic National Committee, insisted in debate that he wished to be "the candidate for guys with Confederate flags in their pickup trucks." By following day outrage causes him to apologize for any "pain" the remark may have inadvertently caused.

5

1639 Massachusetts General Court named Richard Fairfield of Boston as postmaster general to care for letters "brought from beyond the seas or to be sent thither" and to receive a penny for each.

1732 John Glover, leader of "amphibious" forces, born in Salem, MA; led Americans in ferrying Gen. Washington and his men across

Delaware River and 9,000 men across the East River from Long Island to escape British (died 1797).

1733 (John) Peter Zenger began publication of *New York Weekly Journal*, which eventually became the object of a precedent-setting trial.

1742 Sir John Johnson, organizer of Tories and Indians for raids on Americans in Mohawk and Schoharie valleys during Revolution, born in Johnstown, NY (died 1830).

1757 Joseph Anderson, first Comptroller of Treasury (1815–36), born in White Marsh, PA; represented Tennessee in Senate (1797–1815), serving as president pro tem (1804–05) (died 1837).

1779 Washington Allston, considered first important American landscape painter, born in Waccamaw, SC (died 1843).

1781 John Hanson, Maryland delegate to Continental Congress, elected "President of the United States in Congress assembled"; in effect the Congress presiding officer, but sometimes considered the first president.

1791 *Knoxville Gazette* founded nearly a year before the city at what is now Rogersville, TN, by George Roulstone and Robert Ferguson; this was first Tennessee newspaper.

1792 Isaac Toucey, Attorney General (1848–49), Secretary of Navy (1857–61), born in Newtown, CT; represented Connecticut in House (1835–39) and Senate (1852–57) and state as governor (1846–47) (died 1869).

1814 Ft. Erie, Canada, abandoned and blown up by Americans, ending American attempts to capture Canada; Americans withdrew across river to Buffalo.

1818 Ben(jamin F.) Butler, leader of impeachment movement against President Andrew Johnson, born in Deerfield, NH; Union general who led land forces in capturing New Orleans; served as governor of Massachusetts (1882–84) and represented state in House (1867–75, 1877–79) (died 1893).

1832 William W. Averell, inventor of system of asphalt paving and insulating conduits for electrical wires, born in Cameron, NY; Union cavalry general (died 1900).

1850 Michigan voters ratified state constitution; proposal for Negro suffrage defeated.

1850 Ella Wheeler Wilcox, author of syndicated daily poem, born near Madison, WI; poems collected in more than 20 volumes (*Drops of Water, Poems of Passion, Sweet Danger*) (died 1919).

1855 Eugene V. Debs, labor and political leader, born in Terre Haute, IN; national secretary, Brotherhood of Locomotive Firemen (1880–97); led strike against Pullman Co. (1894), arrested, served six months for contempt; organized Social Democratic Party (1897), its presidential candidate five times (1900–20); indicted for violating 1918 Espionage Act, sentenced to ten years, released 1921 (died 1926).

1857 Ida M. Tarbell, magazine editor and author, born in Erie County, PA; editor, *McClure's Magazine* (1896–1906); associate editor, *American Magazine* (1906–15); wrote history of Standard Oil Co., which led to federal investigation and eventual dissolution of company (died 1914).

1862 George A. Ball, developer of glass canning jar (1884), born near Greensburg, OH (died 1955).

1863 James W. Packard, automaker who with brother founded Packard Electric Co. (1890), born in Warren, OH; designed motor car (1899), president, Packard Motor Car Co. (1902–15) (died 1928).

1869 Nicholas Longworth, Speaker of House (1925–31), born in Cincinnati; represented Ohio in House (1903–13, 1915–31); married Alice, daughter of President Theodore Roosevelt, in White House (1906) (died 1931).

1872 Boss (William M.) Tweed, who controlled New York City and plundered its treasury, convicted and sent to jail.

1879 Will R. Hays, movie "czar" (1922–45), born in Sullivan, IN; chairman, Republican National Committee (1918–21); postmaster general (1921–22); president, Motion Pictures Producers & Distributors (1922–45) (died 1954).

1885 Will(iam J.) Durant, author (*Story of Civilization, The Story of Philosophy, The Mansions of Philosophy*), born in North Adams, MA (died 1981).

1893 Raymond F. Loewy, industrial designer, born in Paris; specialized in product design, packaging, transportation, and buildings (died 1986).

1894 Beardsley Ruml, author of federal income tax withholding system (1943), born in Cedar Rapids, IA (died 1960).

1895 Charles MacArthur, playwright (*Lulu Belle, Salvation*) and coauthor (with Ben Hecht) (*The Front Page, Twentieth Century*), born in Scranton, PA (died 1956).

1895 George B. Selden granted patent for a "road engine," the first American patent for a gasoline-driven car.

1912 Roy Rogers, television and screen actor, born in Cincinnati; formed musical group, "Sons of the Pioneers"; former owner of fast-food restaurant chain named for him (died 1998).

1918 Allies agreed to accept President Wilson's 14 points as basis for peace discussions.

1920 Douglas C. North, educator and economist who shared 1993 Nobel Economics Prize, born in Cambridge, MA.

1921 Proclamation issued creating November 11 as Armistice Day.

1930 Mine disaster at Millfield, OH, killed 79 persons.

1943 Senate by an 85–5 vote approved idea of a postwar international organization.

1946 New Jersey adopted a new constitution, first change since 1844.

1953 President Eisenhower empowered New York State Power Authority to develop with Canada the St. Lawrence River hydroelectric project.

1982 Women became full-fledged firefighters in New York City with the graduation of 11 women and 103 men from its Fire Academy.

1987 President Reagan's second nominee to Supreme Court, Douglas H. Ginsburg, admitted he smoked marijuana in 1960/70s; a few days later, he asked that his nomination be withdrawn.

1990 Rabbi Meir Kahane, leader of anti–Arab movement in Israel, assassinated by a gunman during a conference in a New York City hotel.

1994 Former President Reagan, 83, announced he was suffering from Alzheimer's disease.

1994 George Foreman at 45 became the oldest heavyweight boxing champion, defeating Michael Moorer; Foreman had been champion in 1973–74.

2002 Republicans enlarged majority edge in House of Representatives seats; regained Senate majority.

2003 Mass murderer Gary Ridgway pled guilty to killing 48 women (with high proportion of prostitutes and runaways) during the 1980s in Washington state; escapes death penalty by fully providing all information he remembered; known as the "Green River Killer" because of where he regularly dumped bodies; defied psychiatric profile by being both married and holding down a job.

6

1643 A general court composed of two deputies each from four Connecticut towns (New Haven, Stamford, Guilford, Milford) adopted a Frame of Government, established the Mosaic law as the basis for its legal system.

1752 George Washington was appointed district adjutant with rank of major of Virginia by Gov. Robert Dinwiddie; his first military appointment.

1758 John Adams admitted to practice law before the Supreme Court in Boston.

1789 The Catholic See of Baltimore created, with John Carroll as first bishop.

1822 Gordon Granger, Union general who served throughout war with especial distinction at Chickamauga, born in Jay, NY (died 1876).

1832 Joseph Smith, president of an offshoot of original Mormon Church — Reorganized Latter Day Saints Church (1860–1914) — opposed to polygamy, born in Kirtland, OH (died 1914).

1841 Nelson W. Aldrich, chairman, National Monetary Commission which led to formation of Federal Reserve System, born in Foster, RI; represented Rhode Island in House (1878–81) and Senate (1881–1911) (died 1915).

1851 Charles H. Dow, who with Edward D. Jones founded the *Wall St. Journal* (1882), born in Sterling, CT; paper inaugurated publication of an average from the daily market price of selected securities (the Dow Jones) (died 1902).

1854 John Philip Sousa, composer and bandmaster known as the "march king," born in Washington, DC; directed U.S. Marine Band (1880–92), then his own band; wrote 140 marches ("Stars and Stripes Forever," "Semper Fidelis"), ten comic operas (*El Capitan, The Bride-elect*) (died 1932).

1861 James Naismith, originator of basketball, born in Almonte, Canada; developed game while physical education instructor at Springfield (MA) YMCA (1891) (died 1939).

1869 First intercollegiate football game played at New Brunswick, NJ, with Rutgers defeating Princeton 6–4.

1886 Gus(tav G.) Kahn, lyricist ("Ain't We Got Fun," "My Buddy," "Toot, Toot, Tootsie," "I'll See You in My Dreams," "Chloe"), born in Coblenz, Germany (died 1941).

1887 Walter Johnson, baseball pitcher (Washington) who won 414 games (1907–27), born in Humboldt, KS; one of first five named to Baseball Hall of Fame (died 1946).

1888 Taylor Spink, editor, *Sporting News* (1914–62), born in St. Louis (died 1962).

1890 Henry K. Sherrill, presiding bishop, American Episcopal Church (1946–58), born in Brooklyn (died 1980).

1892   Harold W. Ross, founder, editor, *The New Yorker* (1925–51), born in Aspen, CO (died 1951).

1893   Edsel B. Ford, president, Ford Motor Co. (1919–43), born in Detroit (died 1943).

1896   Fibber McGee, radio entertainer, born in Peoria, IL, as Jim Jordan; with wife, Molly, had popular show in 1930s (died 1988).

1903   United States recognized Panama's independence from Colombia.

1916   Ray Conniff, musician who led a choral group, born in Attleboro, MA.

1917   New York voters adopted woman suffrage constitutional amendment; Ohio voters turned it down.

1921   James Jones, author (*From Here to Eternity*), born in Robinson, IL (died 1977).

1922   Accident in bituminous coal mine at Spangler, PA, killed 77 persons.

1928   Franklin D. Roosevelt elected governor of New York; reelected in 1930.

1931   Mike Nichols, television comedian (with Elaine May) and stage/screen director, born in Berlin; stage plays included *The Odd Couple*, *Plaza Suite*, *The Gin Game*; screen plays included *Who's Afraid of Virginia Woolf*, *The Graduate*.

1934   Nebraska adopted a unicameral legislature.

1985   Hurricane Juan ended ten-day attack of southeast United States with 97 deaths.

1991   Washington state voters turned down term limits proposal which would have thrown out its entire House delegation in 1994; limits also would have applied to Senate and governor.

1995   Cleveland Browns football team to move to Baltimore next year, Art Modell, franchise owner, announced.

2000   F.D.A. announced that PPA (phenylpropanolamine) would be banned from medicines due to stroke danger; companies immediately began to pull affected products from store shelves.

2003   Federal Partial-Birth Abortion Ban Act, which had been twice vetoed by President Clinton, signed into law by President Bush; by end of day federal judges in both New York and San Francisco banned its implementation in most of country on grounds of possible unconstitutionality under current Supreme Court guidelines.

7

1637   Anne Hutchinson was sentenced to banishment from the colony by the Massachusetts General Court for her religious opinions; allowed to remain until March.

1731   Robert Rogers, frontiersman, born in Methuen, MA; headed Rogers Rangers, raiders during French & Indian War; later imprisoned on charges of espionage, escaped and organized Queens Rangers; defeated at White Plains, fled (1780) to England (died 1795).

1763   Benedict J. Flaget, Catholic bishop of "The Wilderness," born in Contournant, France; served area between Alleghenies and Mississippi River (1810–50) (died 1850).

1785   Continental Congress began new session in New York; ended November 3, 1786; reopened three days later in final session under confederation.

1800   Platt R. Spencer, originator, teacher of Spencerian style of penmanship, born in Fishkill, NY; author of numerous penmanship books (died 1864).

1811   Battle of Tippecanoe occurred after unsuccessful negotiations with Shawnee chief, Tecumseh; Americans suffered heavy losses but battle considered victory because of repulsing Indian attackers; Americans led by William Henry Harrison.

1814   American troops under Gen. Andrew Jackson captured Pensacola, FL, from British.

1832   Andrew D. White, first president, Cornell U. (1868–85), born in Homer, NY; minister to Germany (1879–81), to Russia (1892–94); ambassador to Germany (1897–1902) (died 1918).

1835   Texas convention made provisional declaration of independence from Mexico, demanding self-rule; organized provisional government November 13.

1837   Elijah P. Lovejoy, abolitionist editor (*The Alton Observer*), was shot and killed by mob at Alton, IL; known as "the martyr abolitionist."

1860   Gov. Joseph E. Brown of Georgia recommended to his legislature that a convention be called to consider secession; January 16 set for convention.

1861   Battle of Belmont (MO), Gen. Grant's first Civil War battle and first defeat, occurred; attack on Belmont designed to keep Gen. Leonidas Polk and his troops from aiding Confederates in Missouri.

1862   President Lincoln relieved Gen. George B. McClellan of command of Army of the Potomac; replaced him with Gen. Ambrose E. Burnside.

1864   George L. Hartford, who helped develop

Atlantic & Pacific grocery chain, born in Brooklyn (died 1957).

1864   Eleanor M. (Cissie) Patterson, owner, publisher of *Washington Herald, Washington Times*, born in Chicago; also had interest in *Chicago Times, New York Daily News* (died 1948).

1868   Royal S. Copeland, sponsor of much food and drug legislation, born in Dexter, MI; president, New York City Board of Health (1918–23); represented New York in Senate (1923–38) (died 1938).

1876   Presidential election resulted in Democratic candidate, Samuel J. Tilden, getting popular vote margin of 350,000; however, returns were disputed in Florida, Louisiana, South Carolina, and Oregon; without these, Tilden was one electoral vote short of election; resolved by an electoral commission in favor of Rutherford B. Hayes by one electoral vote.

1882   Grover Cleveland elected governor of New York.

1886   Chester Barnard, president, USO (United Service Organizations) (1942–45), which provided entertainment for military personnel, born in Malden, MA (died 1961).

1893   Colorado adopted woman suffrage by popular vote.

1906   Eugene Carson Blake, Presbyterian clergyman who headed National Council of Churches (1954–57), born in St. Louis; general secretary, World Council of Churches (1966–72) (died 1985).

1908   New York Circuit Court ruled against American Tobacco Co., holding it was a trust and combination in restraint of trade.

1915   Italian liner *Ancona* sunk without warning by an Austrian submarine; 27 Americans were among 272 victims.

1916   American steamship *Columbian* sunk by a German submarine off Spain.

1918   Billy (William F.) Graham, who conducted evangelistic missions throughout the world, born in Charlotte, NC.

1920   Max Kampelman, chief arms control negotiator (1983–90), born in New York City.

1922   Al Hirt, jazz trumpeter and orchestra leader, born in New Orleans.

1950   Hawaii voters ratified their state constitution.

1962   Eleanor Roosevelt, widow of President Franklin Roosevelt, died in New York City at 78.

1967   John Nance Garner, former vice president (1933–41), died in Uvalde, TX, at 98.

1967   First two black mayors of major cities

elected — Carl B. Stokes in Cleveland, OH, and Richard G. Hatcher in Gary, IN.

1967   Corporation for Public Broadcasting created.

1990   Staten Island residents voted overwhelmingly to form a commission to study how to secede from New York City.

1996   Space shuttle, the Mars Environmental Survey Pathfinder, successfully launched, the first of 13 Mars shots scheduled for the next decade.

1996   Baseball owners voted 18–12 against a proposed five-year labor agreement with the players association.

2000   Presidential race victory hinged on who won Florida, where the vote difference between George W. Bush and Al Gore was paper thin as the next day dawned; Bush remains winner after bitter recount battles in various Florida counties and a court case that goes all the way to the U.S. Supreme Court.

2004   Howard Keel, the singing hero of varied movie musicals of the 1940s and 1950s including *Kiss Me Kate* (1953) and *Seven Brides for Seven Brothers* (1954), died of colon cancer. As musicals began to disappear, he made a successful transition into action and war films in the 1960s.

2006   Election day for one-third of U.S. Senate and all of House of Representatives; by sunrise next morning Democrats had gained at least an 8-seat majority in House and the control of the Senate was still up in the air as two seats were too close to decide from initial returns (ultimately they brought a Democratic victory in that chamber as well); Democratic sweep overturned Republican seats in all regions of country and ideological inclinations.

2006   Arizona rejected state constitutional ban on same-sex marriages while Colorado, Idaho, South Carolina, South Dakota, Tennessee, Virginia, and Wisconsin adopted them; proponents of such bans attributed Arizona defeat to inclusion of a prohibition of domestic partner arrangements as well.

8

1701   Charter of Liberties, prepared by William Penn, adopted; remained Pennsylvania's constitution until Revolution; called for a unicameral legislature, with laws being prepared by the governor with consent of the Assembly.

1725   *New York Gazette*, first newspaper in

New York province, published by William Bradford.

1731 Library Company of Philadelphia founded by Benjamin Franklin; a subscription library it opened with arrival of books from England in 1732.

1732 John Dickinson, "penman" of the Revolution, born in Talbot County, MD; wrote declaration of rights and grievances of Stamp Act Congress; active in Continental Congress (1774–80) and Constitutional Convention; sought conciliation with England; voted against Declaration of Independence (died 1808).

1772 William Wirt, Attorney General (1817–29) who was involved in many precedent-setting cases, born in Bladensburg, MD; presidential candidate, Anti-Masonic Party (1831) (died 1834).

1813 Gen. Andrew Jackson led Americans to victory in Battle of Talladega (AL) against Creek Indians.

1821 George H. Bissell, oil industry pioneer, born in Hanover, NH; founder, head, Pennsylvania Rock Oil Co. (1854), which drilled first successful oil well in Titusville, PA (1859) (died 1884).

1830 Oliver O. Howard, a founder, president, Howard U., Washington, DC (1869–73), born in Leeds, ME; Union general who commanded Sherman's right wing on March to the Sea; headed, Freedmen's Bureau (1865–72) (died 1909).

1836 Milton Bradley, games manufacturer, born in Vienna, ME; invented successful game (Checkered Game of Life), manufactured kindergarten materials (died 1911).

1837 Mt. Holyoke College founded by Mary Lynn at South Hadley, MA.

1838 Rufus W. Peckham, associate justice, Supreme Court (1895–1909), born in Rensselaerville, NY (died 1909).

1848 George W. Gould, invented bifocal lens glasses, born in Auburn, ME; compiled several medical dictionaries (died 1922).

1861 USS *San Jacinto*, commanded by Capt. Charles Wilkes, stopped British steamer and removed James M. Mason and John Slidell, Confederates en route to England; imprisoned in Ft. Warren, MA, until December 26.

1864 Gen. George B. McClellan, Lincoln's unsuccessful opponent for presidency, resigned from army.

1869 Joseph F. Rutherford, president, Jehovah's Witnesses (1916–42) born in Boonville, MO; imprisoned (1917–19) for counseling people to be conscientious objectors (died 1942).

1871 Robert W. Bingham, publisher, *Louisville Courier-Journal, Times,* born in Orange County, NC; ambassador to Great Britain (1933–37) (died 1942).

1883 Charles Demuth, painter who was key figure in introducing cubist technique to United States, born in Lancaster, PA (died 1935).

1889 Montana admitted to Union as 41st state.

1897 Dorothy Day, organized hospitality houses for urban poor, born in New York City; journalist, publisher, *Catholic Worker* (died 1980).

1898 Theodore Roosevelt elected governor of New York.

1900 Margaret Mitchell, author of *Gone with the Wind,* her only book, born in Atlanta (died 1949).

1909 Katharine Hepburn, stage, screen, television actress, born in Hartford, CT; among her roles were *The Philadelphia Story, The African Queen, The Lion in Winter, Guess Who's Coming to Dinner, On Golden Pond.*

1910 Washington state constitutional amendment provided woman suffrage.

1910 Mine disaster at Delagua, CO, killed 79 persons.

1910 Franklin D. Roosevelt elected to New York Senate.

1933 Harry L. Hopkins named head of Civil Works Administration, created to place four million unemployed on public works projects; agency spent $933 million on 190,000 projects; terminated March 1934.

1942 Angelo Cordero, jockey who was third in career purses and fourth in victories, born in San Juan, Puerto Rico; rode Kentucky Derby winner three times, Preakness twice, Belmont once.

1942 American and British forces landed in French North Africa, under command of Gen. Dwight D. Eisenhower; took Casablanca, Oran, and Algiers.

1966 Edward W. Brooke, Republican from Massachusetts, became first black popularly elected to U.S. Senate; first to serve there in 85 years.

1982 Fire in county jail in Biloxi, MS, killed 29 persons.

1984 Space shuttle *Discovery* launched at Cape Canaveral, FL; during eight-day mission it captured two stray communications satellites.

1988 Vice President George Bush elected president, defeating Massachusetts Governor Michael S. Dukakis, becoming the first sitting vice president since Martin Van Buren (1836) to be elected president.

1994 Republicans won a majority in both houses of Congress for first time since 1952.

1996 Erskine Bowles, 51-year-old Charlotte, NC, investment banker, named to succeed Leon Panetta as White House chief of staff; headed Small Business Administration (1993–94) and was deputy chief of staff (1994–95).

2000 Ruth J. Simmons became first black American to head an Ivy League university, taking over the presidency of Smith College.

2001 Postal Service requested $5 billion from Congress to pay for costs of dealing with discovery of anthrax mail and to compensate for revenues lost due to reduced mail use after September 11 terrorist attacks; say alternative is to cut services, increase rates.

2005 Latest installment in on-going dispute between evolutionists and creationists and intelligent design advocates in Kansas: by 6–4, Board of Education required that high school students must be grounded in evolutionary concepts but also be exposed to challenges to the dogma and possible alternatives; how standards to be specifically applied left up to 300 local school systems.

2006 With handling of Iraq war/occupation a major theme of the Democratic sweep to power in mid-term elections the previous day, Defense Secretary Donald Rumsfeld resigned, effective upon approval of a successor; had served six years in post and had held it earlier under President Ford as well.

9

1724 John Thomas, Revolutionary general, born in Marshfield, MA; in command at Roxbury, captured Dorchester Heights, forcing British evacuation of Boston; commanded operations at Quebec; died of smallpox June 2, 1776.

1731 Benjamin Banneker, finished planning of Washington, DC, after Pierre L'Enfant was dismissed, born in Ellicott, MD; published annual almanac (1791–1802) (died 1806).

1793 William Maxwell, Kentucky printer, established *Centinel of the North-Western Territory* in Cincinnati.

1795 Josiah Tattnall, naval officer in War of 1812 and Mexican War, born in Savannah, GA; in Confederate navy, commanded the *Virginia* (the former *Merrimac*), which he sank to prevent

its capture, and coastal defenses of Virginia, Georgia, and South Carolina (died 1871).

1801 Gail Borden, considered father of instant food industry, born in Norwich, NY; developed method of condensing milk (1856), formed what later became Borden Co.; invented a meat biscuit, a variety of juice concentrates (died 1874).

1802 Elijah P. Lovejoy, abolitionist editor (Alton, IL), born in Albion, ME; killed by mob while protecting his Alton paper November 7, 1837.

1824 First presidential election in which popular vote was tabulated gave Andrew Jackson 152,901 votes, John Quincy Adams 114,023, Henry Clay 47,217, and William H. Crawford 46,979.

1825 A(mbrose) P. Hill, Confederate general killed in action at Petersburg, VA, in 1865, born in Culpeper, VA; initiated attack that began battle of Gettysburg.

1833 Sally Louisa Tompkins, only woman commissioned by Confederate Army, born in Matthews County, VA; known as Captain Sally, she turned her Richmond home into a hospital (died 1916).

1853 Stanford White, architect who helped design old Madison Square Garden and Washington Arch (New York City), born in New York City (died 1906).

1857 Oregon constitution ratified by popular vote.

1858 John M. Carrère, architect, born in Rio de Janeiro of American parents; among his designs were Carnegie Institution, Senate and House office buildings, New York Public Library (died 1911).

1865 Frederick Funston, Spanish-American War general, born in New Carlisle, OH; captured Filipino guerrilla leader, Emilio Aguinaldo; commanded force which captured Vera Cruz (1914) (died 1917).

1872 Richest quarter of Boston burned in three-day fire, destroying 767 buildings, with an estimated value of $75 million, and killing 14 persons.

1873 Marie Dressler, stage/screen actress (*Min and Bill, Tugboat Annie, The Late Christopher Bean*), born in Coburg, Canada (died 1934).

1874 Albert F. Blakeslee, botanist who demonstrated that chemicals could interfere with genetic mechanism, born in Geneseo, NY (died 1954).

1881 Herbert F. Kalmus, a developer of

Technicolor process of moviemaking, born in Chelsea, MA; president, Technicolor Inc. (1922–63) (died 1963).

1886 Ed Wynn, comedian who starred on stage (*The Perfect Fool*) and radio (*Texaco Fire Chief*), born in Philadelphia (died 1966).

1898 Leonard Carmichael, secretary, Smithsonian Institution (1952–64), born in Germantown, PA; credited with modernizing institution (died 1973).

1906 President Theodore Roosevelt made inspection trip of Panama, first president to leave country while in office; also visited Puerto Rico November 21.

1906 Muggsy (Francis J.) Spanier, cornetist and leader in Dixieland jazz, born in Chicago (died 1967).

1908 Bernard Kilgore, executive with *Wall St. Journal* (1929–67), born in Albany, IN; president of paper (1945–67) (died 1967).

1911 Lincoln Memorial National Park in Hodgenville, KY, dedicated by President Taft.

1915 R. Sargent Shriver, first director of Peace Corps (1960–65) and War on Poverty (1964–68), born in Westminster, MD; ambassador to France (1968–70); Democratic vice presidential candidate (1972).

1917 Florence Chadwick, long-distance swimmer, born in San Diego; swam English Channel both ways (August 8, 1950), Catalina Channel, the Bosporus, Straits of Gibraltar (died 1995).

1918 Spiro T. Agnew, vice president (1969–73), born in Baltimore; governor of Maryland (1966–68); resigned vice presidency amid charges of illegal financial dealings; pleaded no contest to federal income tax evasion charges (died 1996).

1918 President Wilson named Herbert Hoover to represent United States in organization of European food relief; distributed about 46 million tons (1918–20).

1918 Kaiser Wilhelm of Germany abdicated.

1918 German delegates given terms of armistice by Gen. Ferdinand Foch in Compiègne Forest near Rethonde.

1934 Carl Sagan, a science popularizer (*The Dragons of Eden, Broca's Brain*), born in New York City; provided valuable insight into origin of life in earth's primeval environment (died 1996).

1935 The CIO (Congress of Industrial Organizations) established.

1943 Agreement signed in White House by 44 nations to create the United Nations Relief & Rehabilitation Administration (UNRRA).

1965 Power failure lasting 13½ hours blacked out northeastern United States and southeastern Canada; New York City was hardest hit.

1965 Department of Housing & Urban Development began operations; Robert C. Weaver named first secretary January 18, 1966.

1996 Evander Holyfield, former heavyweight boxing champion, defeated Mike Tyson with an 11th-round technical knockout to regain the WBA title, which he had held 1990–92 and 1993–94.

2003 New first for women: Association of American Medical Colleges reported that for 2003 academic year, more women than men seeking medical training; year also represented reversal of six-year decline in total enrollments in programs.

2004 Second-term post-election Cabinet reshuffle began: John Ashcroft out at Justice Department and Donald Evans out as Secretary of Commerce; more follow in future weeks.

2004 As part of its "Big Fat Lie" campaign against misleading and fraudulent weight-loss products, the Federal Trade Commission announced lawsuits against six companies marketing such goods to the public.

2005 Face-off before a joint session of two Senate committees: Top executives of five largest oil companies attempted to justify their vast and skyrocketing profits at a time when prices were putting crimp in consumers' pocketbooks; pointed to high rate of reinvestment of profits in new production and how windfall profits taxes had been tried in the past.

2006 Veteran black television journalist Ed Bradley died at 65 of leukemia; winner of 16 Emmy Awards; had been on staff of CBS news' *60 Minutes* for 26 years.

2006 Eleven million bottles of 500 mg strength acetaminophen recalled by manufacturer; affected varying labels for several years' production run; small metal fragments discovered.

10

1674 Dutch occupation of New York City, which began in August 1673, ended after the signing of the Treaty of Westminster.

1766 Queens College (which later became Rutgers) at New Brunswick, NJ, chartered.

1775 Continental Congress created the Marine Corps by authorizing two battalions of Marines.

1776 John Paul Jones, commanding two ships (*Providence* and *Alfred*) captured many

British prizes in a three-week raid off Nova Scotia.

1792 Samuel Nelson, associate justice, Supreme Court (1845–72), born in Hebron, NY; with New York Supreme Court (1831–45), chief justice (1837–45) (died 1873).

1801 Samuel G. Howe, founder, director of what became Perkins School for the Blind, Boston (1832–76), born in Boston; founded first school for mentally-retarded (died 1876).

1808 Osage Treaty signed with Indians ceding nearly all of present Missouri and Arkansas, north of the Arkansas River.

1821 New York State convention adopted new constitution which abolished requirement of property ownership for voting.

1827 Alfred H. Terry, Union general at Bull Run, Port Royal, Ft. Fisher, Richmond, and Petersburg, born in Hartford, CT (died 1890).

1843 Former President John Quincy Adams delivered oration at cornerstone laying of Mt. Adams Astronomical Observatory near Cincinnati, the first American observatory.

1860 South Carolina legislature called for a convention in Columbia December 17 to consider secession.

1865 Capt. Henry Winz, a commander of Andersonville (GA) Confederate prison, was hanged following a trial by a military commission; subsequent investigations questioned legality of the action.

1867 Alexander P. Moore, owner, *New York Daily Mirror, Boston Advertiser* (1928–30), born in Pittsburgh; editor, *Pittsburgh Leader* (1904–28); ambassador to Spain (1923–25), to Peru (1928–30) (died 1930).

1869 Wayne B. Wheeler, general/national superintendent, Anti-Saloon League (1898–1915), born in Trumbull County, OH; claimed authorship of 18th Amendment (died 1927).

1871 Henry M. Stanley, *New York Herald* correspondent, found the missionary, Dr. David Livingstone, at Lake Tanganyika in Africa, and offered the famous greeting, "Dr. Livingstone, I presume."

1871 Winston Churchill, author of historical novels (*Richard Carvel, The Crisis, The Crossing*), born in St. Louis (died 1947).

1874 Donald B. MacMillan, explorer who was with Peary (1908–09) and led other expeditions (1913–37), born in Provincetown, MA (died 1970).

1879 Vachel Lindsay, poet (*General William Booth Enters Heaven, Congo, Abraham Lincoln Walks*), born in Springfield, IL (died 1931).

1893 John P. Marquand, novelist (*The Late George Apley, Wickford Point, H.M. Pulham Esq.*), born in Wilmington, DE; also wrote the Mr. Moto series of short stories (died 1960).

1896 John K. Northrop, cofounder, chief engineer, Lockheed Aircraft Corp. (1927), born in Newark, NJ; formed Avion Corp. (1927), Northrop Corp. (1938) (died 1981).

1909 Johnny Marks, composer best known for "Rudolph the Red-Nosed Reindeer," born in Mt. Vernon, NY (died 1985).

1913 Karl J. Shapiro, critic, poet ("Person, Place, Thing," "The Place of Love"), born in Baltimore; poetry consultant, Library of Congress (1946–47).

1914 Port of Houston symbolically opened to international commerce when President Wilson pushed a button in the White House.

1988 Energy Department announced that Texas had been selected as the site of the $4.4 billion superconducting super-collider over six other states; site, 35 miles south of Dallas, will if constructed be the largest scientific instrument ever built — a 53-mile-long racetrack-shaped tunnel.

2002 In response to repeated embarrassing scientific misrepresentation of test results, the U.S. physicists' American Physical Society issued a new and more detailed set of ethical responsibilities and guidelines for future publications.

2003 World Trade Organization ruled that U.S. steel tariffs violated international trade agreements; ruling automatically authorized retaliatory charges on American imports into Europe.

2003 Faced with a perceived failure in his momentum toward Democratic presidential nomination, Senator John Kerry of Massachusetts replaced Jim Jordan as campaign manager with Mary Beth Cahill, a pro-choice activist with Emily's List and once chief of staff for Senator Edward Kennedy.

2006 Russia and U.S. agreed to terms under which U.S. would support Russian admission to World Trade Organization; currently Russia the only major economic power not within it.

2006 Jack Palance died at 87; veteran star who carved out a distinctive niche as movie villain; perhaps most remembered as the bully in *Shane* (1953) and for his Academy award winning supporting role in the comedy *City Slickers* (1992).

11

1647 Massachusetts enacted a law requiring a community with 50 householders to maintain a school and every town with 100 householders to maintain a grammar school.

1771 Ephraim McDowell, pioneer in abdominal surgery, born in Rockbridge County, VA; performed first recorded American ovarian surgery (1809) (died 1830).

1776 Maryland convention adopted a state constitution.

1778 Cherry Valley Massacre occurred at an outpost 46 miles west of Albany when Butler's Rangers and Indians under Joseph Brant attacked, killing 30 and taking 71 prisoners, burning all the buildings and killing all cattle.

1781 Cyrus Alger, designed first cylinder stove and first gun with rifled barrel, born in West Bridgewater, MA; produced ammunition in War of 1812 (died 1856).

1799 Charles S. Bent, fur trader who with his brothers built Bent's Fort in Colorado, born in what is now Charleston, WV; served as civil governor of New Mexico (1846–47) (died 1847).

1811 Ben McCulloch, Confederate general who was killed at Battle of Pea Ridge, AR, born in Rutherford County, TN; served as a scout in Mexican War (died 1862).

1813 American force defeated by Canadian troops 90 miles north of Montreal; campaign against Montreal abandoned.

1831 Nat Turner, leader of rebellion of Virginia slaves which resulted in death of 55 whites, was hanged.

1836 Henry M. Alden, editor, *Harper's Magazine* (1863–1919), born near Darby, VT (died 1919).

1858 James A. Garfield and Lucretia Rudolph were married in Hiram, OH.

1859 Samuel Insull, president, Chicago Edison Co., later Consolidated Edison, born in London; was private secretary to Thomas A. Edison; vice president, Edison General Electric (1889–92); tried for fraud on holding companies, stock transactions, acquitted (died 1938).

1864 George W. Crile, surgeon who as a founder, director, Cleveland Clinic Hospital (1921), born in Chilo, OH; contributed much to the study of shock from surgery (died 1943).

1872 Maude Adams, noted actress (*Little Minister, L'Aiglon, Peter Pan*), born in Salt Lake City; played Peter Pan about 1,500 times (died 1963).

1872 Frederick A. Stock, conductor, Chicago Symphony Orchestra (from 1905), born near Cologne, Germany; general music director, Chicago's World Fair (1933) (died 1942).

1874 James L. Kraft, with brother founded J.L. Kraft Brothers & Co. (1909), born in Ft. Erie, Canada (died 1953).

1875 Vesto M. Slipher, director, Lowell Observatory (1901–52), born near Mulberry, IN; directed research which led to discovery of the former planet Pluto (died 1969).

1885 Stanford University founded in California, opened 1891.

1885 George S. Patton, World War II general who headed armies in North Africa, Sicily, and western Europe, born in San Gabriel, CA; served in Mexico and World War I; first man detailed to tank corps (1917) (died 1945).

1889 Washington admitted to Union as the 42nd state.

1893 Clarence D. Chamberlin, pilot of record 3,911-mile nonstop flight from Roosevelt Field, NY, to Germany in 42 hours, 31 minutes (1927), born in Denison, IA (died 1976).

1897 Gordon W. Allport, psychologist at Harvard (1930–67), born in Montezuma, IN; developed concept of personality which dealt with real, present problems rather than searching for childhood trauma (died 1967).

1899 Pat O'Brien, screen actor (*The Front Page, The Last Hurrah, Knute Rockne*), born in Milwaukee (died 1983).

1900 Hugh D. Scott, Jr., Republican leader (1969–76), born in Fredericksburg, VA; represented Pennsylvania in House (1941–45, 1947–59) and Senate (1959–76) (died 1994).

1901 New Alabama constitution adopted by popular vote.

1918 Armistice signed at 5:00 A.M. bringing World War I to a close as the Germans agreed to terms; firing ended at 11:00 A.M. at the fronts.

1921 Burial ceremony held at the site of the Tomb of the Unknown Soldier in Arlington Cemetery with President Harding on hand.

1922 Kurt Vonnegut, Jr., author (*Player Piano, Slaughterhouse Five, The Sirens of Titan*), born in Indianapolis.

1932 Tomb of the Unknown Soldier in Arlington National Cemetery dedicated by War Secretary Patrick J. Hurley.

1968 Vote to merge the Methodist Church and the Evangelical United Brethren Church was ratified; the new United Methodist Church, the largest American Protestant church, will combine ten million Methodists and 750,000 Evangelical UB members.

1984 President Reagan dedicated the Vietnam Veterans Memorial in Washington.

1985 Mormon Church elected Ezra Taft Benson, 80, as president, succeeding Spencer Kimball.

1987 President Reagan nominated Federal Appeals Judge Anthony M. Kennedy to fill Supreme Court vacancy; he was third nominee for the post; confirmed by Senate February 3, 1988.

2001 Mark McGwire announced retirement from baseball after 16 seasons in the major leagues He hit 583 home runs and in 1998 set a new record of 70 home runs in a season. Repeated serious injuries convinced him he could no longer deliver the kind of quality play needed to justify his new $30 million two-year contract.

2002 Microsoft's Bill Gates to give $100 million to fight spread of AIDS.

2002 The nuclear power industry's internal watchdog group, the Institute of Nuclear Power Operations, released report to all its members warning them that there was evidence that at least some locations were so pressed to meet energy production expectations that necessary safety precautions were being neglected.

12

1655 Sir Francis Nicholson, colonial administrator, born near Richmond, England; lieutenant governor of New England Dominion (1688) and Virginia (1690–92); governor, Maryland (1694–98), Virginia (1698–1705), South Carolina (1720–25) (died 1728).

1751 Margaret Corbin, Revolutionary heroine who took over husband's gun at Ft. Washington after he was killed (1776), born in Franklin County, PA; she was completely disabled; granted lifetime pension (died 1800).

1770 Joseph Hopkinson, U.S. district judge (1828–42) who wrote patriotic song, "Hail Columbia," born in Philadelphia; represented Pennsylvania in House (1815–19) (died 1842).

1790 Letitia Christian Tyler, first wife of President Tyler, born in New Kent County, VA (died 1842).

1815 Elizabeth Cady Stanton, who organized women's rights convention in Seneca Falls, NY (1848), born in Johnstown, NY; worked 40 years with Susan B. Anthony; first president, National Woman Suffrage Association (1869–90), American Woman Suffrage Association (died 1902).

1825 George Munro, one of leading publishers of "dime" novels and weekly *Fireside Compan-*

ion (1866–96), born in West River, NC (died 1896).

1831 Eli H. Janney, inventor of automatic railway car coupler (1868), born in Loudon County, VA (died 1912).

1846 Samuel Theobald, ophthalmologist who introduced using boric acid for eye diseases, born in Baltimore; a founder, Baltimore Eye, Ear & Throat Dispensary, hospital (died 1930).

1864 Gen. William T. Sherman sent his final message before starting the next day on 32-day "March to the Sea," during which he would be out of touch.

1877 Warren R. Austin, delegate to the UN (1947–53), born in Highgate, VT; represented Vermont in House (1931–46) (died 1962).

1880 Harold R. Stark, admiral in command of European waters (1942–45), born in Wilkes-Barre, PA; chief of naval operations (1939–42) (died 1972).

1886 Joseph N. Pew, Jr., board chairman, Sun Oil Co. (1947–63), born in Pittsburgh; Pennsylvania Republican leader (died 1963).

1889 DeWitt Wallace, cofounder with wife of *Reader's Digest* (1922), born in St. Paul, MN; *Digest* publisher (died 1981).

1908 Harry A. Blackmun, associate justice, Supreme Court (1970–84), born in Nashville, IL.

1920 Jo Stafford, singer with Tommy Dorsey band, born in Coalinga, CA.

1921 Armaments conference began in Washington, continued to February 6, 1922; major powers agreed to curtail naval construction, outlaw poison gas, restrict submarine attacks on shipping, and respect integrity of China.

1927 Holland Tunnel under Hudson River between New York City and Jersey City opened to traffic.

1929 Grace Kelly, screen actress (*County Girl, High Society*), born in Philadelphia; married Prince Rainier of Monaco (1956) (died 1982).

1936 San Francisco–Oakland Bridge opened.

1940 Two-day blizzard raged through Midwest and northeastern United States; 144 persons died.

1942 Three-day naval battle of Guadalcanal assured American success in land fighting on the island; Japanese lost two battleships, a cruiser, two destroyers, ten transports; Americans lost two cruisers, seven destroyers.

1942 Kaiser Shipyards, which built 1,460 ships during World War II, set construction record on the *Robert E. Peary*, which was launched 4½ days after keel was laid.

1968 Sammy Sosa, baseball player, born; passed the Roger Maris home run record of 61 in 1998, just after it was broken by Mark J. McGwire.

1980 Unmanned spacecraft, *Voyager I*, came within 77,000 miles of Saturn, transmitting valuable data back to earth.

1981 First successful nonstop balloon crossing of Pacific Ocean completed; crew composed of Ben Abruzzo, Larry Newman, Rocky Aoki, and Ron Clark.

1987 American Medical Association told nation's doctors that they cannot refuse to treat people infected with the AIDS virus.

1997 Two more Islamic militants were convicted for their part in the 1993 bombing of the World Trade Center in New York City; earlier four others were convicted.

2001 American Airlines flight 587 was leaving JFK International in NYC when engines and tail fin came off; resulting crash killed all 260 aboard.

2003 Penny Singleton (b. 1908) died at 95; played Blondie in 28 movies (between 1938 and 1950) based on the comic strip of the same name and did voice of Jane Jetson in the *Jetsons* animated cartoon series on television; in 1969 became president of American Guild of Variety Artists, thereby becoming first female to head an AFL-CIO union.

2004 Murder of Laci Peterson and her unborn child had received widespread national publicity since her disappearance in late December 2002; today her husband, Scott, was convicted of first-degree murder for Laci's death and second-degree for the child's; faces death penalty.

13

1644 Massachusetts Bay General Court banished all Baptists from the colony.

1775 Americans under Gen. Richard Montgomery occupied Montreal, which had been abandoned by the British; occupation lasted until June 15, 1776.

1807 Lt. Zebulon B. Pike sighted a peak in Colorado, which was later named for him.

1809 John A.B. Dahlgren, naval officer who developed much ordnance, born in Philadelphia; he developed 11-inch (Dahlgren) gun; reorganized, equipped naval ordnance yard in Washington, DC (died 1870).

1813 Allen G. Thurman, legislator, born in Lynchburg, VA; represented Ohio in House (1845–47) and Senate (1869–81); Democratic vice presidential candidate (1888) (died 1895).

1814 Joseph Hooker, Union general who commanded Army of Potomac (1863), born in Hadley, MA; served with Gens. George Thomas and William T. Sherman (died 1879).

1833 Edwin T. Booth, a foremost actor of his day, noted for his Hamlet, born near Bel Air, MD (died 1893).

1834 Peter A.B. Widener, businessman active in meat and street railway businesses, born in Philadelphia; left large art collection to Philadelphia; founder, Crippled Children's Training School (died 1915).

1838 Joseph Fielding Smith, president, Mormon Church (1901–18), born in Far West, MO; strengthened church organization and fostered friendly relations with non–Mormons (died 1918).

1843 Mt. Rainier in Washington erupted.

1850 California voters ratified their constitution, which had been adopted earlier by a convention.

1853 John Drew, actor who starred in many plays with Maude Adams and Ada Rehan, born in Dublin (died 1927).

1856 Louis D. Brandeis, associate justice, Supreme Court (1916–34), born in Louisville, KY; first to use economic and sociological data to buttress legal arguments; was special counsel for the people in numerous wage-hour cases (died 1941).

1864 James Cannon, Jr., Methodist bishop who was a leader of Anti-Saloon League of America, born in Salisbury, MD; active opponent of Alfred E. Smith's candidacy for president (1928) (died 1944).

1864 Arthur Fairbanks, director, Museum of Fine Arts, Boston (1907–25), born in Hanover, NH; fine arts professor, Dartmouth U. (1928–33) (died 1944).

1866 Abraham Flexner, made major study of American medical education (1910), which became basis for modern medical education, born in Louisville, KY; organizer, director, Institute for Advanced Study, Princeton (1930–39) (died 1959).

1872 Louis G. Hupp, pioneer who with his brother produced the Hupmobile beginning in 1909, born (died 1961).

1893 Edward A. Doisy, biochemist who shared 1943 Nobel Physiology/Medicine Prize for analysis of Vitamin K, born in IL (died 1986).

1898 Earl Sande, premier jockey of 1920s, born in Groton, SD; his mounts included Man o' War (died 1968).

1900 Samuel K. Allen, developer of first nuclear physics laboratory (U. of Chicago 1935–41), born in Chicago; was part of group which developed first successful chain reaction (died 1965).

1909 Fire in a Cherry, IL, mine killed 259 miners.

1938 Francis Xavier (Mother) Cabrini was beatified; later became first American citizen proclaimed a Catholic saint.

1942 Draft age lowered to 18, with deferments limited to war industries, agriculture, hardship cases, and clergy.

1982 Vietnam War Memorial unveiled in Washington, DC; two black granite walls listed names of all 57,939 Americans who died in the war.

1986 President Reagan acknowledged an 18-month "secret diplomatic initiative" involving the shipment of "small amounts of defensive weapons and spare parts" to Iran, but denied any trade of arms for hostages.

1995 President Clinton vetoed congressional resolutions designed to keep government running for rest of the month because they would have increased premiums for Medicare. Failure to pass appropriations led to furlough of 770,000 federal employees, 1.9 million continued to work. Impasse resolved in a continuing resolution November 20 and furloughed employees returned.

1996 Alma Kitchell, pioneer radio singer who hosted first radio talk shows in 1930s and 1940s, died at 103; also hosted first television cooking show (1947).

2000 America's large public pension group — the $170 billion California Public Employees Retirement Fund — decided to base future investments not only on potential revenue generation but also the recipient country's environmental, worker, and human-rights records.

2001 President Bush announced foreigners accused of terrorism to be tried before military tribunals.

2002 No more fuel exports to North Korea: Country admitted it was researching and trying to build nuclear bombs.

2003 Roy S. Moore, Chief Justice of Alabama, removed from post by ethics board; group cited, among other things, refusal to remove large monument with Ten Commandments on them in obedience to federal court instructions.

14

1765 Robert Fulton, inventor of a practical submarine and developer of steamboat, born in Lancaster County, PA; invented submarine (1800), with torpedoes (1805); his steamboat *Clermont* (1807) made New York–Albany round-trip in 62 hours; invented machine for sawing marble, for spinning flax, for weaving hemp into rope (died 1815).

1784 Samuel Seabury consecrated by nonjuring Jacobite bishops of Episcopal Church in Scotland as first American Episcopal bishop; English bishops had refused to do so.

1785 Convention of State of Frankland (later Tennessee) met in Greenville and adopted its constitution; John Sevier named governor.

1803 Jacob Abbott, founder, Mt. Vernon School for Girls, Boston (1829), born in Hallowell, ME; author of juvenile stories (28 volumes of *Rollo* books, 36 volumes of *Harper's Story* books) (died 1879).

1819 Christopher Rodgers, Union naval officer and Naval Academy superintendent (1874–78), born in Brooklyn; commander-in-chief, Pacific Squadron (1878–80) (died 1892).

1820 Anson Burlingame, minister to China (1861–67), born in New Berlin, NY; responsible for treaty (1868) establishing reciprocal rights of citizens of both countries; represented Massachusetts in House (1855–61) (died 1870).

1828 James B. McPherson, Union commander of the Army of Tennessee, born near Clyde, OH; killed by skirmishers near Atlanta (1864).

1850 Jesse W. Fewkes, ethnologist with Bureau of American Ethnology (1895–1928), born in Newton, MA; worked with Hopi Indians, collecting thousands of artifacts and assuring preservation of Hopi pueblos, cliff dwellings (died 1930).

1861 Frederick J. Turner, historian (*Rise of the New West*, *The Frontier in American History*), born in Portage, WI; developed theory that American civilization was outgrowth of political and environmental forces, that frontier had large influence on development (died 1932).

1863 Leo H. Baekeland, inventor of photographic paper and synthetic resin named Bakelite, one of first plastics used widely, born in Ghent, Belgium (died 1944).

1864 Gen. William T. Sherman set out with 60,000 men from Atlanta on March to the Sea, cutting a 60-mile swath along 300 miles, destroying virtually everything in his path.

1871 Ernest K. Coulter, an organizer of New York Children's Court (1902–12), born in Columbus, OH; founder of Big Brother movement (1900); general manager, Society for Prevention of Cruelty to Children (1914–36) (died 1952).

1881 Trial of Charles Jules Guiteau, accused of assassinating President Garfield, began in Washington, DC; found guilty November 25.

1889 Nellie Bly, newspaper reporter, began her record-breaking round-the-world trip; finished in 72 days, six hours, 11 minutes, 14 seconds.

1896 Mamie G. Doud Eisenhower, wife of President Eisenhower, born in Boone, IA (died 1979).

1897 John Steuart Curry, painter and muralist (Interior, Justice departments, Kansas Capitol), born in Dunavant, KS (died 1946).

1900 Aaron Copland, composer of ballets (*Billy the Kid, Appalachian Spring*) and movie scores (*Of Mice and Men, Our Town, The Red Pony, The Heiress*), born in Brooklyn (died 1990).

1904 Dick Powell, screen and television actor, born in Mt. View, AR (died 1963).

1908 Joseph R. McCarthy, whose investigative methods gave rise to term "McCarthyism," born in Grand Chute, WI; represented Wisconsin in Senate (1947–57); censured by Senate 1954 (died 1957).

1930 Edward H. White, II, first astronaut to walk in space, born in San Antonio, TX; killed with two others in capsule fire (1967).

1937 Congress of Industrial Organizations (CIO) established in Pittsburgh by delegates to convention of Committee of Industrial Organizations; John L. Lewis named president.

1955 Daniel J. Tobin, president of Teamsters Union (1907–52), died at 80.

1970 Plane carrying Marshall University football team and staff crashed near Kenova, WV; 75 persons killed.

1972 Dow Jones industrial average closed above 1,000 for first time.

1988 Transportation Department ordered wide range of drug testing for more than four million transportation workers, including random testing; most transportation companies were ordered to have comprehensive testing programs operating by December 1989.

1996 Catholic Cardinal Joseph Bernardin, Archbishop of Chicago for 14 years, died of cancer at 68.

1998 Planned air strikes on Iraq for interfering with UN inspections were called off at the last moment as Iraq agreed to cooperate.

2000 Robert Trout dead at 91; known for "live as it happens" coverage of events on radio and television at a time when that approach to journalism was uncommon.

2001 Red Cross received $543 million to help victims of 9/11 attack but later said part of it would go elsewhere; today it pledges entire amount to go to New York.

2002 Nancy Pelosi (Democrat) became first female House of Representatives party leader.

2006 The U.S. Conference of Catholic Bishops issued a policy guideline welcoming homosexuals since the "inclination" was not itself sinful; on the other hand such individuals should share their status only with family and close friends and cannot receive communion if engaging in actual gay sexual liaisons.

15

1637 Massachusetts General Court ordered that Harvard College was "to bee at Newtowne" (later renamed Cambridge).

1753 George Washington and small party left for Ft. Le Boeuf, about 12 miles south of Erie, PA, to maintain friendly relations with Indians of Six Nations, locate sites for forts, and carry a message to French asking them to leave what was considered British territory; message delivered December 12, but French refused to leave.

1777 Small American forces holding two New Jersey forts along Hudson River (Mifflin and Mercer) evacuated the positions after three weeks of British shelling.

1777 Continental Congress adopted the "Articles of Confederation and Perpetual Union" after a year of intermittent debates; states did not complete ratification until March 1, 1781.

1797 Thurlow Weed, editor, *Albany Evening Journal* (1830–62) and political leader of state, born in Greene County, NY (died 1882).

1805 Lewis and Clark Expedition reached mouth of the Columbia River.

1807 Peter H. Burnett, first governor of California (1849–51), born in Nashville, TN (died 1895).

1807 James H. Hammond, legislator and governor of South Carolina (1842–44), born in Newberry District, SC; represented state in House (1835–36) and Senate (1857–60); remembered for his 1858 taunt of northern sympathizers — "You dare not make war on cotton ... Cotton is king!" (died 1864).

1846 Tampico, Mexico, captured by American troops.

1854 First Nebraska newspaper, *Nebraska Palladium*, published in Belleview by Thomas Morton.

1863 Four Union divisions under Gen. William T. Sherman arrived in Chattanooga, TN.

1873 Sara Josephine Baker, pediatrician who organized first government child hygiene bureau (New York City 1908–23), born in Poughkeepsie, NY; brought child death rate to lowest of any large city (died 1945).

1880 Ralph C. Browne, inventor, born in Salem, MA; developed electrical system, mechanism for North Sea mine barrage in World War I, portable X-ray apparatus, an airlift mine pump (died 1960).

1881 Franklin P. Adams, columnist known as F.P.A., born in Chicago; *The Conning Tower* column appeared 1922–41; regular panelist on *Information Please* radio program (died 1960).

1881 Conference of labor organizations began in Pittsburgh; ended with formation of the Federation of Organized Trades and Labor Unions; merged with American Federation of Labor (1896).

1882 Felix Frankfurter, associate justice, Supreme Court (1939–62), born in Vienna; law professor at Harvard (1914–39) (died 1965).

1887 Marianne C. Moore, poet (*What Are Years?*, *Observations*, *Nevertheless*), born in St. Louis, MO (died 1972).

1887 Georgia O'Keeffe, painter of desert scenes and symbolic abstractions, born in Sun Prairie, WI (died 1986).

1891 W. Averell Harriman, government official, born in New York City; with family railroad, shipping businesses; Lend–Lease coordinator (1941–43); ambassador to Russia (1943–46), to Great Britain (1946); secretary of commerce (1946–48); governor of New York (1954–58); ambassador at large (1961, 1965–75) (died 1986).

1891 (W.) Vincent Astor, financier and social reformer, born in New York City; headed corporation publishing *Newsweek* (died 1959).

1892 James F. Stevens, author of *Paul Bunyan* stories, born in Albia, IA (died 1971).

1896 Street lights in Buffalo, NY, were switched on by power from Niagara Falls, 20 miles away; the first long-distance electric transmission.

1900 Carnegie Institute of Technology founded by Andrew Carnegie in Pittsburgh; opened 1905.

1906 Curtis E. LeMay, World War II Air Force general, born in Columbus, OH; headed bomber groups in Europe, China; commander, Strategic Air Command (1957–61); chief of staff, Air Force (1961–65) (died 1990).

1906 United States sued Standard Oil Co. of New Jersey and 70 other corporations and partnerships, and seven persons including John D. Rockefeller, under Sherman Antitrust Act.

1929 Edward Asner, television actor (*Mary Tyler Moore Show*, *Lou Grant* series), born in Kansas City, MO.

1935 Commonwealth of the Philippines inaugurated under the presidency of Manuel Quezon.

1969 About 250,000 persons took part in an anti–Vietnam demonstration march in Washington.

1987 Continental DC-9 crashed on takeoff from the Denver airport killing 28 people aboard and injuring 54 persons.

1994 Federal Reserve Board raised two key short-term interest rates by 0.75 percentage points; this led banks to raise their prime rate from 7.75 percent to 8.5 percent.

1995 Dow Jones industrial average passed the 4,900 mark for the first time.

1996 Texaco settled a two-year-old lawsuit brought by 1,400 current and former employees charging the company with favoring whites in promotions and raises; company to pay $520 million in settlement.

1998 Civil rights leader Kwame Ture, formerly known as Stokely Carmichael, died at 57.

2000 New charitable foundation to be nation's seventh biggest: Intel cofounder Gordon Moore contributed $5 billion to be used for research and other activities, with an emphasis on the type of projects that would often be overlooked by government.

2002 The second movie in an on-going series, *Harry Potter and the Chamber of Secrets,* was released to American audiences.

2003 Mitchell Paige died at 85 of congestive heart failure; received U.S.' highest military award, the Medal of Honor, for actions on Guadalcanal during World War II; out of some 40 million who served in American wars only 3,408 given; spent years exposing those falsely claiming the award.

2005 Penalty for steroid use agreed to by baseball players' association: 50-game suspension the first time there is a failed drug test; 100 the second; lifetime ban the third.

2006 The Marine Toys for Tots Foundation that gives thousands of presents to the needy each Christmas had rejected the offer for 4,000 new talking Jesus dolls on grounds that they might offend non–Christians; after receiving intense criticism the group reversed itself— not on grounds that the policy was now believed to be wrong but that "we realized it's a lot less time-consuming to find homes for the dolls than it is to answer media and complaints."

16

1753 James McHenry, private secretary to George Washington (1778–80) and Lafayette (1780–81), born in County Antrim, Ireland; member of Continental Congress (1783–86), Constitutional Convention (1787), War Secretary (1796–1800); fort in Baltimore harbor named for him (died 1816).

1764 Return J. Meigs, Postmaster General (1814–23), born in Winchester, KY; served Ohio as its first chief justice (1803–04) and governor (1810–14); represented state in Senate (1808–10) (died 1824).

1776 British under Gen. William Howe captured Ft. Washington, NY, taking nearly 3,000 prisoners.

1821 Emmons Hamlin, who with Henry Mason manufactured pianos and organs, born in Rome, NY (died 1885).

1823 Henry G. Davis, Democratic vice presidential candidate (1904), born in Baltimore (died 1916).

1873 W(illiam) C. Handy, composer of various "blues" (St. Louis, Beale St., Memphis), born in Florence, AL (died 1958).

1876 Alabama constitution ratified by popular vote.

1889 George S. Kaufman, coauthor of numerous plays (*The Man Who Came to Dinner, You Can't Take It with You, Once in a Lifetime, Dinner at Eight*), born in Pittsburgh (died 1961).

1896 Lawrence M. Tibbett, operatic baritone who sang at Metropolitan Opera from 1923 on, born in Bakersfield, CA; also appeared in several movies (died 1960).

1899 Mary Margaret McBride, conductor of daytime radio talk shows (1934–54), born in Paris, MO (died 1976).

1905 Eddie (Albert Edwin) Condon, guitarist and bandleader who promoted Dixieland music, born in Goodland, IN (died 1973).

1907 Oklahoma entered Union as the 46th state.

1909 Burgess Meredith, stage actor (*High Tor, Winterset*) and screen actor (*Of Mice and Men, Advise and Consent*), born in Cleveland (died 1997).

1914 Federal Reserve System inaugurated with opening of 12 Federal Reserve banks.

1917 President Wilson issued proclamation requiring registration of enemy aliens, forbidding them in the District of Columbia, the Panama Canal Zone, and waterfront areas.

1933 United States recognized Soviet Russia and established diplomatic relations.

1946 Evangelical United Brethren Church organized by union of the Evangelical Church and the Church of the United Brethren in Christ.

1982 Strike of National Football League players ended after eight weeks.

1995 Houston Oilers announced that the team would move to Nashville, TN, in 1998; subject to approval of National Football League.

2000 President Bill Clinton became first American chief executive to visit Hanoi, Vietnam; Richard Nixon had visited Saigon in 1969.

2000 Amtrak began utilizing its high-speed 150 mph Acela Express on the Boston-Washington run.

2001 First cinematic version of the best-selling book series hit the big screen in America to enthusiastic crowds: *Harry Potter and the Sorcerer's Stone.*

2004 First female black Secretary of State: Condoleezza Rice to move from National Security Adviser into the post.

2004 NASA's unmanned X43 scramjet broke jet speed record unofficially, at Mach 9.6 (c. 6,500 mph).

2004 Reed Irvine died at 82; founder of Media in Accuracy, which for 35 years had relentlessly pressed televised and print media over reportage it believed to be liberally biased and/or inaccurate.

2006 Clear Channel Communications agreed to be bought out for $18.7 billion — conditional on no better offer being made by December 7; Clear Channel either owns outright or runs 1,150 radio stations, making it the largest chain in nation.

2006 Nobel-winning economist Milton Friedman died at 94; created what became the "Chicago school of economics."

2006 Although she would not take the post until the new Democratic majority takes control of the House of Representatives in January 2007, Nancy Pelosi of California was unanimously selected by current Democratic House members to become the next Speaker of the House, the first woman to occupy the post. In stunning setback immediately after selection, her strongly backed choice for the new Majority leader of the party was rejected by 149–86, with Steny H. Hoyer selected over John P. Murtha.

17

1734 Peter Zenger, editor of the *New York Weekly Journal*, was arrested for criticizing the administration.

1764 Indian war led by Chief Pontiac ended with their surrender on the Muskingum River in the Ohio Territory.

1788 Seth Boyden, inventor and manufacturer, born in Foxborough, MA; developed process for making patent leather (1819), malleable cast-iron (1826), sheet iron, a hat-shaping machine; manufactured locomotives and stationary engines (died 1870).

1790 Solyman Brown, founder of American dentistry as an organized profession, born in Litchfield, CT (died 1876).

1800 Congress convened in Washington, DC, for first time.

1835 Frederick Leypoldt, publisher/editor, *Library Bulletin* (1868–73) which became *Publishers Weekly* (1873), born in Stuttgart, Germany; a founder, publisher, *Library Journal* (died 1876).

1863 Two-weeks siege of Knoxville, TN, begun by Confederate troops; ended when they retreated before approaching Union troops.

1865 William M. Burton, introduced process for getting gasoline by cracking petroleum (1913), born in Cleveland (died 1954).

1877 Frank P. Lehm, aviation pioneer, born in Mansfield, OH; pilot of first Army airship, balloon; headed air service of 2nd Army (1918–19); organized, commanded Air Corps Training Center (1926–30) (died 1963).

1878 Hans Zinsser, an expert in infectious diseases, born in New York City; at Harvard Medical School, helped develop immunization against some typhus fevers (died 1940).

1878 Grace Abbott, a leading advocate of child labor laws, born in Grand Island, NE; chief, Child Labor Division, Children's Bureau (1921–34) (died 1939).

1881 Samuel Gompers led in forming the Federation of Organized Trades and Labor Unions, forerunner of American Federation of Labor.

1888 Donald M. Nelson, chairman, War Production Board (1942–44), born in Hannibal, MO; with Sears Roebuck (1912–42), executive vice president (1939–42) (died 1959).

1902 Eugene P. Wigner, physicist, born in Budapest; shared 1963 Nobel Physics Prize for research on structure of atom and its nucleus, helped construct first atomic reactor (1942) (died 1995).

1904 Paul Cadmus, artist (*The Fleet's In*, *Greenwich Village Cafeteria*, *Coney Island*), born in New York City.

1904 Isamu Noguchi, sculptor ("kouros") and furniture designer, born in Los Angeles (died 1989).

1904 William H. Hastie, first black federal judge (1937), born in Knoxville, TN; governor of Virgin Islands (1946–49) (died 1976).

1930 Robert B. Mathias, Olympic decathlon champion (1948, 1952), born in Tulare, CA; represented California in House (1967–75).

1934 Lyndon B. Johnson and Claudia Alta (Ladybird) Taylor were married in San Antonio, TX.

1982 Marie L. Garibaldi sworn in as first woman judge on the New York State Supreme Court.

1993 House approved NAFTA (North American Free Trade Agreement) by 234–200 vote; three days later Senate approved 61–38.

1998 Inspection of Iraq military sites was resumed by UN inspectors.

1998 Federal Reserve Board reduced short-term interest rates by a quarter percentage point (5.0 to 4.75); it was the third cut in seven weeks.

2003 The powerful American Association of Retired People endorsed Bush's proposed medicine program for senior citizens; considers it best that can be accomplished at the time.

2006 Former football coaching giant Bo Schembechler died after filming a television program; as coach of Michigan Wolverines, had a 194–48–5 record; career figures were 234–65–8.

2006 Ruth Brown died at 78; "the girl with a tear in her voice" as she was widely known, was top black woman recording artist in the early years of the 1950s; her songs turned Atlantic Records into a massive player in the recording business; added to the Rock and Roll Hall of Fame in 1993.

2006 The FDA officially reversed its 14-year

prohibition of silicone breast implants to improve physical appearance, convinced that prior health concerns had been drastically overstated.

18

1618 Charter of privileges, orders, and laws granted Virginia settlers, giving them a voice in their government.

1787 King's Chapel in Boston, the first Anglican church in New England, became the first American Unitarian church with the ordination of James Freeman, who had been refused Anglican ordination because of his revisions of the Book of Common Prayer.

1799 Joseph Dixon, pioneer in industrial use of graphite, born in Marblehead, MA (died 1869).

1801 John Butterfield, an organizer of express companies, born in Berne, NY; merged his express company with two others to form American Express Co. (1850); organized Wells, Fargo & Co. (1852) to carry overland mail west of St. Louis (died 1869).

1810 Asa Gray, foremost American botanist of mid-1800s, born in Sauquoit, NY; professor of natural history, Harvard (1842–73); major early American supporter of Charles Darwin (died 1888).

1820 Nathan B. Palmer in sloop *Hero* discovered peninsula extending from the Antarctic continent; peninsula later named for him.

1824 Franz Sigel, Union general at Pea Ridge and second Bull Run, born in Sinsheim, Germany (died 1902).

1828 John A.J. Creswell, Postmaster General (1869–74), born in Port Deposit, MD; launched great improvements in postal service (died 1891).

1834 Henry L. Higginson, banker who founded Boston Symphony Orchestra (1881), born in New York City; financed orchestra 1881–1918 (died 1919).

1841 Paul J. Pelz, architect who was co-winner of design competition for Library of Congress (1873), born in Seitendorf, Germany; designed buildings for Georgetown U., U. of Virginia (died 1918).

1847 Revised constitution of New York adopted and ratified.

1857 Rose M. Knox, cofounder of gelatin company (1890), president (1908–47), born in Mansfield, OH (died 1950).

1860 James E. Sullivan, founder of Amateur Athletic Union (AAU) (1888), born in New York City; director, 1904 Olympic Games in St. Louis (died 1914).

1861 Josiah K. Lilly, president, Eli Lilly & Co. (1898–1932), board chairman (1932–48), born in Greencastle, IN (died 1948).

1867 William J. Flynn, chief, U.S. Secret Service (1912–17), born in New York City; director, bureau of investigation, Justice Department (1919–21), predecessor of FBI (died 1928).

1870 Dorothy Dix, advice to lovelorn columnist, born in Montgomery County, TN, as Elizabeth Gilmer; began column in New Orleans (1896), widely syndicated from 1901 (died 1951).

1874 National Women's Temperance Union organized in Cleveland, with Mrs. Anna Wittenmeyer of Philadelphia as president, Miss Frances E. Willard of Chicago, corresponding secretary.

1874 Clarence S. Day, Jr., author of autobiographical books which formed basis for play *Life with Father*, born in New York City (died 1935).

1880 Actress Sarah Bernhardt made her first American appearance at Booth Theater in New York City.

1883 Four standard time zones were established by the railroads.

1885 Forrest (Phog) Allen, college basketball coach for 48 years with 746 career wins, born (died 1974).

1886 Former President Arthur died in New York City at 57.

1886 Charles Edward Wilson, General Electric president (1940–42, 1944–50), born in New York City; vice chairman, War Production Board (1942–44) (died 1972).

1886 James S. Kemper, founder, Lumbermen's Mutual Casualty Co. (1912) and Kemper Group, born in Van Wert, OH (died 1980).

1889 Amelita Galli-Curci, coloratura soprano with Metropolitan Opera from 1920, born in Milan, Italy (died 1963).

1899 Eugene Ormandy, concert violinist and conductor (Minneapolis Symphony 1931–36, Philadelphia from 1936), born in Budapest (died 1985).

1901 Second Hay-Pauncefort Treaty between United States and Great Britain signed, recognizing exclusive right of U.S. to construct, regulate, and manage any isthmian canal; ratified December 16.

1901 George H. Gallup, founder, American Institute of Public Opinion (1935) to conduct polls, born in Jefferson, IA (died 1984).

1903 United States concluded a treaty with Panama for construction of a canal; provided for a lease of ten-mile strip across isthmus in perpetuity for ten million dollars and an annual fee of $250,000 beginning nine years after ratification; Senate ratified treaty February 23, 1904.

1906   George Wald, biologist who shared 1967 Nobel Physiology/Medicine Prize for work on Vitamin A and the eye, born in New York City (died 1997).

1909   Johnny Mercer, author of many hit song lyrics, born in Savannah, GA; among the hits were "Blues in the Night," "Accentuate the Positive," "Lazy Bones," "Moon River," "Days of Wine and Roses," "Satin Doll," "Black Magic" (died 1976).

1922   Stanley Cohen, researcher at Vanderbilt Medical School, born in New York City; shared 1986 Nobel Physiology/Medicine Prize for discovery of key proteins that control body growth.

1923   Alan B. Shepard, Jr., first American astronaut in suborbital space flight (May 5, 1961), born in East Derry, NH; fifth man on the moon (1971) (died 1998).

1942   Linda Evans, television actress (*Dynasty*), born in Hartford, CT.

1963   Fire in the Surfside Hotel in Atlantic City, NJ, claimed 25 lives.

1978   Rep. Leo J. Ryan of California and four other Americans were shot to death as they prepared to leave Guyana by members of the Peoples Temple; soon thereafter more than 900 members of the Temple were murdered or committed suicide.

1987   Iran-Contra House-Senate Committee in final report stated that President Regan bears "ultimate responsibility" for Iran-Contra affair because he allowed a "cabal of zealots" to seize control of policy and bypass the law. "The Iran initiative succeeded only in ... improperly generating funds for the Contras and other covert actions ... damaging relations between the executive and Congress and engulfing the president in one of the worst credibility crises of any administration in U.S. history."

1994   Tropical Storm Gordon pounded Caribbean area and Florida for ten days, resulting in 800 deaths.

1996   Harold J. Nicholson, high-ranking CIA officer, charged with selling top secrets to the Russians.

1997   The FBI concluded its investigation of the July 1996 crash of TWA flight 800 off Long Island; ruled out criminal sabotage as a possible cause.

2001   Conoco Inc., and Philips Petroleum Company agreed to combine to become third-largest U.S. oil company; ConocoPhillips to be worth $35 billion.

2003   Massachusetts Supreme Judicial Court declared that restriction of marriage to heterosexuals violated the state's constitution; legislature given six months to change law or have court impose its own standards.

2005   The motion picture version of *Harry Potter and the Goblet of Fire* (fourth in on-going cinematic adaptations) was released to American theaters.

2006   New Mexico State Fairgrounds evacuated after police found two radioactive objects, one of which was initially mislabeled a potential bomb; criminal investigation initiated as to source and purpose.

19

1493   Puerto Rico discovered by Christopher Columbus on his second voyage.

1752   George Rogers Clark, frontiersman who was governor of Illinois Territory, born near Charlottesville, VA; led in conquering territory (1779–83) (died 1818).

1794   Jay's Treaty of commerce, navigation, and amity signed in London by Lord Grenville, British foreign minister, and John Jay, acting secretary of state; resolved question of control of the northwest posts.

1811   John A. Winslow, Union naval commander of *Kearsage* when it destroyed the Confederate raider *Alabama* (1864), born in Wilmington, NC (died 1873).

1831   James A. Garfield, 20th President (1880–81), born in Cuyahoga County, OH; represented Ohio in House (1863–80); fatally wounded in a Washington, DC, railroad station July 2, 1881, died September 19.

1832   South Carolina legislature protested the 1828 and 1832 national tariffs.

1834   Franklin Pierce and Jane M. Appleton were married in Amherst, MA.

1835   Fitzhugh Lee, one of ablest Confederate cavalry officers, born in Fairfax County, VA; commanded a corps in Spanish-American War (died 1905).

1862   Billy (William A.) Sunday, professional baseball player (1883–90) who became successful evangelist, revivalist, born in Ames, IA (died 1935).

1863 President Lincoln delivered immortal two-minute speech dedicating the Gettysburg, PA, battlefield as a national cemetery; principal address by Edward Everett lasted two hours.

1875 Hiram Bingham, discoverer of Inca ruins, Machu Picchu, born in Honolulu; served Connecticut as governor (1924–25) and in Senate (1925–33) (died 1956).

1887 James B. Sumner, biochemist who shared 1946 Nobel Chemistry Prize for preparing enzymes, virus proteins in pure form, born in Canton, MA (died 1955).

1899 Allen Tate, biographer (Robert E. Lee, Stonewall Jackson, Jefferson Davis) and poet (*Ode to the Confederate Dead, Winter Sea*), born in Clarke County, KY (died 1979).

1905 Tommy Dorsey, trombonist and noted orchestra leader, born in Shenandoah, PA (died 1956).

1912 George E. Palade, biologist, born in Jassy, Rumania; shared 1974 Nobel Physiology/Medicine Prize for contributions to understanding the inner workings of living cells.

1915 Earl W. Sutherland, Jr., biochemist who shared 1971 Nobel Physiology/Medicine Prize for research on how hormones work, born in Burlingame, KS (died 1974).

1919 Senate rejected the Versailles Treaty and League of Nations after a debate which began July 10.

1919 Zion (UT) National Park established.

1921 Roy Campanella, baseball player (Brooklyn) whose career was cut short by paralyzing auto accident, born in Philadelphia; named to Baseball Hall of Fame (died 1993).

1934 Larry King, radio/television interviewer, born in New York City.

1936 Dick Cavett, television talk show host and interviewer, born in Gibbon, NE.

1938 Ted (Robert E.) Turner, sports and television executive, born in Cincinnati; owner, Atlanta baseball and basketball teams and cable television network; won 1977 America's Cup yacht race.

1942 Calvin Klein, fashion designer, born in New York City.

1963 Former President Eisenhower rededicated the national cemetery at Gettysburg, PA, 100 years after its dedication by President Lincoln.

1974 President Ford conferred in Tokyo with the Japanese prime minister and Emperor of Japan, first incumbent president to visit Japan.

1979 Iran released 13 African American, non–U.S.-citizens, and women hostages who were being held in the American Embassy.

1985 President Reagan and Soviet General Secretary Mikhail Gorbachev met in Geneva for five hours over two days; no substantive agreements were reached.

1985 Largest civil judgment in American history ($10.53 billion) was assessed against Texaco Inc. by a state court jury in Houston, TX; recipient of the judgment would be Pennzoil Co.

1990 Presidents Bush and Gorbachev and the leaders of 20 other nations signed an arms control treaty to destroy non-nuclear weapons.

1992 Dorothy Kirsten, opera singer, died at 82.

1996 A commuter plane landing at Quincy, IL, collided with a private plane taking off, killing 13 people in both planes.

1997 Bobbi McCaughey, 29, a seamstress, gave birth to septuplets in Des Moines, IA; the four boys and three girls were said to be surprisingly healthy.

2003 Chairman of the Congressional Hispanic Caucus and several sympathetic non-members in Congress insisted that same generous admission rights to U.S. be bestowed on Mexicans that were currently enjoyed by Canadians; insist anything else is unjustified discrimination.

2006 In Hanoi, Vietnam, President Bush signed agreement with President Vladimir Putin of Russia to permit Russia to enter WTO; on same day held talks (separately) with both Putin and President Hu Jintao (People's Republic of China) in attempt to gain support for strong actions to block Iranian development of nuclear weaponry.

20

1726 Oliver Wolcott, colonial leader, born in Windsor, CT; member, Continental Congress (1775–78, 1780–84), signer of Declaration of Independence; led Connecticut troops during Revolution; served state as lieutenant governor (1787–96) and governor (1796–97) (died 1797).

1733 Philip J. Schuyler, colonial leader, born in Albany, NY; member, Continental Congress (1775, 1778–81); represented New York in Senate (1789–91, 1797–98); a founder, Union College (died 1804).

1776 British under Lord Charles Cornwallis captured Ft. Lee, NJ, but Americans under Gen. Nathanael Greene escaped.

1776   Gen. Washington began a successful retreat across the Hudson River to New Jersey.

1811   Construction began on Cumberland Road connecting Cumberland, MD, and Wheeling, WV; road later extended and became main route for settlers of the West.

1817   First Seminole War began; ended May 24, 1818, with capture of Pensacola, FL.

1819   First Arkansas newspaper, *Arkansas Gazette*, published in Arkansas Post by William E. Woodruff.

1837   Lewis E. Waterman, developer (1884) and manufacturer of an improved fountain pen, born in Decatur, NY (died 1901).

1855   Josiah Royce, important American exponent of absolute idealism, born in Grass Valley, CA; author of *The Religious Aspect of Philosophy* (died 1916).

1866   Kenesaw M. Landis, first baseball commissioner (1921–44), born in Millsville, OH; a U.S. district judge (1905–21); named to Baseball Hall of Fame (died 1944).

1867   Patrick J. Hayes, Catholic Archbishop of New York (1919–38), born in New York City; named a cardinal 1924 (died 1938).

1869   Clark C. Griffith, baseball pitcher (Chicago AL, New York AL) who won 240 games, born; co-owner, president (Washington 1920–55); named to Baseball Hall of Fame (died 1955).

1873   William W. Coblentz, physicist who pioneered in infra-red spectrophotometry, born in North Lima, OH; founder, Radiometry Section, National Bureau of Standards; a major figure in setting international radiation standards (died 1962).

1874   James M. Curley, mayor of Boston 16 years between 1914 and 1950, born in Boston; served Massachusetts as governor (1934–36) and represented state in House (1911–14, 1942–46); he was the model for the hero of *The Last Hurrah* (died 1958).

1878   Claude G. Bowers, historian (*Jefferson and Hamilton, The Tragic Era*), born in Hamilton County, IN; ambassador to Spain (1933–39), to Chile (1939–53) (died 1958).

1884   Norman M. Thomas, Socialist Party leader who was its presidential candidate five times (1928–48), born in Marion, OH; a founder, American Civil Liberties Union (1920) (died 1968).

1887   Earnest A. Hooton, who laid foundation for American physical anthropology, born in Clemansville, WI; author (*Up From the Apes, Why Men Behave Like Apes*) (died 1954).

1889   Edwin P. Hubble, astronomer at Mt. Wilson Observatory (1919–53), born in Marshfield, MO; studied nebulae (died 1953).

1900   Chester Gould, cartoonist (*Dick Tracy*), born in Pawnee, OK (died 1985).

1909   U.S. Circuit Court of Appeals held Standard Oil Co. of New Jersey to be an illegal corporation and ordered its dissolution.

1917   American troops participated in Allied offensive which broke through the Hindenburg Line.

1925   Robert F. Kennedy, Attorney General (1961–64), born in Brookline, MA; represented New York in Senate (1965–68); assassinated in Los Angeles while campaigning for presidential nomination (1968).

1945   President Truman appointed Gen. Dwight D. Eisenhower as Army chief of staff, Admiral Chester W. Nimitz as chief of naval operations.

1945   International War Crimes Tribunal began trial of 24 top Nazi leaders in Nuremberg; 18 were convicted.

1967   National Commission on Product Safety created.

1968   Explosion and fire in a Mannington, WV, coal mine killed 78 miners.

1974   Justice Department filed civil antitrust suit against American Telephone & Telegraph Co. (ATT).

1988   Mother Katherine Drexel, a Philadelphia nun, was beatified by Pope John Paul II; born to wealth she took a vow of poverty, founded (1891) Sisters of the Blessed Sacrament for Indians and Colored People.

1992   United States and European Community (except France) reached compromise agreement after six years negotiations on reducing farm subsidies, clearing the way for a broader trade agreement.

1993   Senate endorsed the North American Free Trade Agreement (NAFTA); endorsed earlier by the House; agreement effective January 1, 1994.

1996   Dow Jones industrial average climbed above 6,400 (6,430.02), the tenth record close in 11 sessions.

1998   Russia launched the first section of the international space station which will be built by the United States and 15 other nations.

2003   Centers for Disease Control syphilis statistics for 2002 released: 85 percent increase among white males from previous year; estimated 40 percent increase among gays; San Francisco jumped from sixth worst rate to first.

2006 In largest pedestrian death toll from a single car accident, 10 had been killed and 63 injured in California when an elderly driver smashed through the Santa Monica Farmers' Market; today, now 90 and asserting physical inability to attend any but two hours of the trial and any of the sentencing, the man was sentenced to five years probation.

2006 Unanimous California Supreme Court decision that freedom of speech protected the reprinting of articles that might be considered libelous; any legal vulnerability as to accuracy and reliability solely that of the source that wrote the original statement or article.

21

1620 Pilgrim leaders aboard the *Mayflower*, anchored off what is now Provincetown, MA, drafted a compact signed by 41 adults which set up "a civil body politic" to frame "just and equal laws"; named John Carver as governor.

1729 Josiah Bartlett, first governor of New Hampshire (1793–94), born in Amesbury, MA; signer of Declaration of Independence; state Superior Court associate justice (1782–88), chief justice (1788–90); "president" of New Hampshire (1790–92) then governor (died 1795).

1785 William Beaumont, made study (1833) considered greatest contribution to gastric digestion knowledge, born in Lebanon, CT; studied digestive process on patient whose stomach was exposed by a gunshot wound (died 1853).

1789 North Carolina's legislature ratified Constitution by 194–77 vote, making it the 12th state in the Union.

1806 Charles Merriam, founder, head, G & C Merriam Co. (1832), born in West Brookfield, MA; published textbooks, dictionaries (died 1887).

1812 Ft. Niagara, NY, fired on by British from Fts. George and Newark.

1818 Lewis H. Morgan, called the father of American anthropology, born near Aurora, NY; studied American Indian culture (died 1881).

1834 Frederick Weyerhaeuser, called the "lumber king," born in Niedersaulheim, Germany; acquired vast timber holdings in U.S. (died 1914).

1835 Hetty (Henrietta H.) Green, a feared Wall St. operator and reputedly America's richest woman in early 1900s, born in New Bedford, MA; inherited fortune from her father (died 1916).

1847 The *Phoenix* sank off Sheboygan, WI, taking 146 lives, 127 of them immigrants arriving from the Netherlands.

1867 Vladimir N. Ipatieff, chemist who determined structure of isoprene, the basic rubber molecule, born in Moscow; developed process for making low-grade gasoline into high octane (died 1952).

1883 William F. Lamb, architect remembered for his work on Empire State Building, born in Brooklyn (died 1952).

1887 Thomas A. Edison announced invention of the phonograph; exhibited the device on November 28.

1891 Edward Ellsberg, inventor of underwater torch for cutting steel, born in New Haven, CT; improved methods for dehydrating and dewaxing lubricating oil, and of cracking crude oil for manufacture of anti-knock gasoline.

1899 Vice President Garrett A. Hobart died in Paterson, NJ, at 55.

1904 Coleman Hawkins, creator of tenor saxophone for jazz, born in St. Joseph, MO (died 1968).

1907 Jim Bishop, author noted for hour-by-hour accounts of noted events, born in Jersey City, NJ; books include *The Day Lincoln Was Shot, The Day Christ Died, The Day Kennedy Was Shot* (died 1987).

1920 Stan(ley F.) Musial, baseball player (St. Louis NL) who was batting champion seven times, most valuable player three, born in Donora, PA; named to Baseball Hall of Fame.

1924 Florence K. Harding, widow of President Harding, died in Marion, OH, at 64.

1942 Alcan Highway to Alaska opened.

1943 Larry Mahan, outstanding rodeo performer, born in Brooke, OR; won World Champion All-Around Cowboy title (1966–71, 1973) and twice bull-riding champion.

1964 Verrazano Narrows Bridge over New York Harbor opened.

1979 Mob attacked American Embassy in Islamabad, Pakistan, killing four persons.

1980 Fire in MGM Grand Hotel in Las Vegas claimed 87 lives.

1995 Dow Jones industrial average passed 5,000 for the first time.

2006 New high in stock value for both Google ($500 a share) and Apple Computer ($88.60).

2006 Filmmaker Robert Altman died at 81; had directed such hits as *MASH.*

22

1643 Sieur de LaSalle, explorer, born in Rouen, France; traversed the Mississippi River, claiming the territory for France (died 1687).

1704 First independent assembly of Delaware met in New Castle, ceasing to be the "lower counties of Pennsylvania."

1744 Abigail Smith Adams, wife of President John Adams, born in Weymouth, MA; a noted letter writer whose work was published posthumously (died 1818).

1754 Abraham Baldwin, a founder, first president, U. of Georgia (1798), born in Guilford, CT; represented Georgia in Continental Congress (1789), in House (1789–98) and Senate (1799–1807) (died 1807).

1791 John W. Jones, Speaker of House (1843–45), born near Amelia Court House, VA; represented Virginia in House (1835–45) (died 1848).

1795 William Henry Harrison and Anna T. Symmes were married in North Bend, OH.

1800 Linn Boyd, Speaker of House (1851–55), born in Nashville, TN; represented Kentucky in House (1835–37, 1839–55); elected Kentucky lieutenant governor (1859), but died before taking office.

1819 Joseph Seligman, founder of international banking house, born in Baiersdorf, Germany; aided Union cause by marketing bonds abroad; member of Committee of 70 which exposed Tweed Ring (died 1880).

1837 Adelbert R. Buffington, co-inventor of disappearing gun carriage, born in Wheeling, WV (died 1922).

1840 William Robinson, inventor of automatic electric signaling system, born in Tyrone, Ireland; his system was basis for all modern automatic block signaling systems (died 1921).

1842 Mt. St. Helens in Washington erupted.

1847 Mexican government notified United States it had appointed commissioners to negotiate peace.

1856 Heber J. Grant, president of Mormon Church (1918–45), born in Salt Lake City (died 1945).

1858 William Stanley, inventor of electrical equipment (transformer, two-phase motors, generators), born in Brooklyn (died 1916).

1868 John Nance Garner, Vice President (1933–41), born in Red River County, TX; represented Texas in House (1903–33), serving as Speaker (1931–33) (died 1967).

1898 Sarah G. Blanding, president, Vassar College (1946–64), born in Lexington, KY (died 1984).

1899 Hoagy (Hoagland H.) Carmichael, pianist and composer, born in Bloomington, IN; songs include "Stardust," "Rockin' Chair," "Georgia on My Mind," "Lazy River" (died 1981).

1900 Wiley Post, aviator who twice flew around the world, born in Grain Saline, TX; plane crash in Alaska (1935) killed him and passenger, Will Rogers.

1902 David J. McDonald, president of United Steelworkers (1952–65), born in Pittsburgh (died 1979).

1917 National Hockey League formed.

1922 Mine accident at Dolomite, AL, killed 90 miners.

1935 The *China Clipper* left Alameda, CA, in first trans–Pacific airmail flight; arrived in Manila seven days later.

1943 President Franklin Roosevelt, Prime Minister Winston Churchill, and Chinese President Chiang Kai-shek met in Cairo to discuss war in Asia and the Pacific; meeting lasted four days.

1943 Billie Jean King, tennis champion (American, Wimbledon singles five times in 1960s/70s), born in Long Beach, CA.

1950 Standing commuter train was struck by another train at Richmond Hill, NY, killing 79 persons.

1963 President Kennedy was shot and killed by a sniper in Dallas, TX; Gov. John B. Connally was wounded; Lee Harvey Oswald was charged with the shooting; Vice President Lyndon B. Johnson was sworn in as president aboard Air Force One at Love Field, Dallas by U.S. District Judge Sarah T. Hughes.

1998 The nation's murder rate reached its lowest level in 30 years as serious crime reported in 1997 declined for the sixth consecutive year.

2000 Vice President-elect Dick Cheney had minor heart attack; bounced back rapidly.

2001 Massachusetts scientists at Advanced Cell Technology reported first cloning of cows.

2004 Twenty-four-year anchor of *CBS Evening News* Dan Rather announced he would resign those duties March 9, 2005; his pre-election embracing of an apparently forged anti–Bush document had led to furious demands for his removal on grounds of partisan bias.

23

1726 Edward Bass, first Episcopal bishop of Massachusetts (1797–1803), born in Dorchester,

MA; rector at Newburyport, MA (1752–97) (died 1803).

1749 Edward Rutledge, colonial leader, born in Charleston, SC; member of Continental Congress (1774–77) and signer of Declaration of Independence; governor of South Carolina (1798–1800) (died 1800).

1765 Twelve county judges of Frederick, MD, became first American jurists to repudiate the British Stamp Act.

1804 Franklin Pierce, 14th President (1853–57), born in Hillsboro, NH; represented New Hampshire in House (1833–37) and Senate (1837–42) (died 1869).

1817 William C.C. Claiborne, first governor of Louisiana (1812–16), died at 52; governor of Mississippi Territory (1801–03) and Territory of Orleans (1804–12).

1818 James Vick, who developed largest American mail order seed business, born in Chichester, England; his experiments in cross-breeding, gardening exerted wide influence (died 1882).

1852 Vermont enacted a prohibition law.

1855 Frank F. Fletcher, World War I admiral, born in Oskaloosa, IA; inventor of Fletcher breach mechanism and gun mounts (died 1928).

1859 Joseph A. Holmes, first director, U.S. Bureau of Mines (1910–15), born in Laurens, SC; popularized slogan "Safety first" (died 1915).

1859 Billy the Kid, outlaw, born in New York City as William H. Bonney; most notorious outlaw of American Southwest (died 1881).

1863 Three-day Battle of Missionary Ridge (or Lookout Mountain), near Chattanooga, began; Union victory led by Gen. U.S. Grant made possible drive through Georgia to the sea and division of the South; Confederate losses were 8,684, Union about 6,000.

1878 Ernest J. King, who headed combined World War II American fleet, born in Lorain, OH; architect of Allied sea victory (died 1956).

1887 Boris Karloff, actor in various monster screen roles, born in London (died 1969).

1889 Alexander M. Patch, World War II general who commanded 7th Army in invasion of southern France, born in Ft. Huachuca, AZ (died 1945).

1927 Otis Chandler, publisher, *Los Angeles Times*, from 1960, born in Los Angeles.

1928 Jerry (Jerold L.) Bock, composer of musicals (*Fiorello*, *Fiddler on the Roof*), born in New Haven, CT.

1942 SPARS (Semper Paratus Service), the women's branch of the Coast Guard, created.

1945 Food rationing, except sugar, ended.

1963 Fire in the Golden Age Nursing Home in Fitchville, OH, killed 63 persons.

1974 President Ford and Soviet leader Leonid Brezhnev conferred in Vladivostok on offensive nuclear weapons.

1992 Three days of tornadoes in the South and Midwest resulted in 26 deaths.

1994 Eric Hawkins, pioneering choreographer of American dance, died at 85.

1998 America Online, Inc., announced it will acquire Internet pioneer, Netscape Communications, Inc.

2002 Longshoremen and Pacific port operators agreed to new six-year West Coast contract; at its worst, the lengthy negotiations had been hit with an 11-day lockout at 29 ports which had been broken by President Bush on October 7 by invoking Taft-Hartley Act to reopen facilities.

2006 Anita O'Day, sometimes called "the Jezebel of Jazz" due to her drug and other problems, died at 87; considered one of handful of top artists in her field of music; actively entertained from 1940s for over a half century.

2006 Gerald M. Boyd, first black to hold city editor and managing editor posts (among several others) at the *New York Times*, died of lung cancer; had resigned after a reporter had successfully faked parts of many stories without being detected by management.

24

1713 Junipero Serra, Franciscan missionary, born in Mallorca, Spain; set up first European settlement in San Diego (1769), called the apostle of California (died 1784).

1726 Pelatiah Webster, publicist who wrote first proposal (1783) for a United States, born in Lebanon, CT; his work was "A Dissertation on the Political Union of the Thirteen United States of North America" (died 1795).

1784 Zachary Taylor, 12th President (1849–50), born in Orange County, VA; commanded Army of Rio Grande in Mexican War; captured Monterey, defeated Mexicans at Buena Vista (1846), ending the war (died 1850).

1807 Joseph Brant, Mohawk Indian chief, died at 65; commanded Indians working with British during Revolution; responsible for Cherry Valley massacre (1778), ravaged Mohawk Valley; settled in Canada after the war.

1818 David H. Agnew, brilliant medical lecturer and surgeon, born in Lancaster County, PA; with U. of Pennsylvania (1870–89), chief medical consultant when President Garfield was mortally wounded (1881) (died 1892).

1832 South Carolina convention passed ordinance to nullify Federal Tariff Act, which placed duties on foreign imports; called for refusal to make payments after February 1, 1833; legislature ratified Act November 27.

1841 Richard Croker, Tammany Hall leader (from 1862) and New York City political boss (1886–1902), born in County Cork, Ireland; moved to Ireland (1903) to live (died 1922).

1844 Charles V. Gridley, Spanish-American War admiral, born in Logansport, IN; immortalized in command by Admiral Dewey — "You may fire when ready, Gridley!" (died 1898).

1849 Frances H. Burnett, author of children's books (*Little Lord Fauntleroy*), born in Manchester, England (died 1924).

1853 Bat (William B.) Masterson, frontier sheriff, born in Iroquois County, IL; sheriff in Ford County, KS; assisted Wyatt Earp in Tombstone, AZ (1880–1902); sports writer, *New York Morning Telegraph* (1902–21) (died 1921).

1859 Cass Gilbert, architect, born in Zanesville, OH; designed Minnesota State Capitol, St. Louis Library, Woolworth Building, Supreme Court (died 1934).

1868 Scott Joplin, ragtime pianist, composer ("Maple Leaf Rag," opera *Tremonisha*), born in Texarkana, TX (died 1917).

1869 National woman's suffrage convention held in Cleveland; organized Woman's Suffrage Association.

1871 National Rifle Association organized in New York City.

1876 Hideyo Noguchi, bacteriologist who made significant findings in etiology of syphilis, paresis, born in Inawashiron, Japan (died 1928).

1876 Walter B. Griffin, architect who won international design competition for Canberra, Australia, born in Maywood, IL; supervised construction (1913–21) (died 1937).

1877 Alben W. Barkley, Vice President (1949–53), born in Graves County, KY; represented Kentucky in House (1913–27) and Senate (1927–49, 1955–56) (died 1956).

1888 Dale Carnegie, public speaking teacher, born in Maryville, MO; created Institute for Effective Speaking & Human Relations; author of *How to Win Friends and Influence People* (died 1955).

1890 George E. Stratemeyer, Air Force general who commanded China-Burma-India area (1943–45), born in Cincinnati (died 1969).

1911 Joe (Joseph M.) Medwick, baseball player (St. Louis NL) who had lifetime batting average of .324, born in Carteret, NJ; named to Baseball Hall of Fame (died 1975).

1912 Garson Kanin, playwright (*Born Yesterday*), born in Rochester, NY; screen director (*Diary of Anne Frank, Funny Girl*).

1922 Colorado River compact signed by representatives of seven states to control use of river water.

1925 William F. Buckley, Jr., founder, editor, *National Review*, from 1955 on, born in New York City; columnist, author (*God and Man at Yale, Serving the Queen, Stained Glass*).

1926 Tsung-Dao Lee, physicist with Columbia U. (1953 on), born in Shanghai; shared 1957 Nobel Physics Prize for work concerning the parity laws of physics.

1938 Oscar Robertson, basketball star (Cincinnati U.; Cincinnati, Milwaukee pro teams), born in Charlotte, TN.

1940 Paul Tagliabue, commissioner, National Football League (1989–2006), born in Jersey City, NJ.

1944 Dan Glickman, Secretary of Agriculture since 1995, born in Wichita, KS.

1963 Lee Harvey Oswald, accused assassin of President Kennedy, was shot and killed in the Dallas city jail by Jack Ruby, a Dallas nightclub owner; Ruby was sentenced to death March 14, 1964, but a new trial was ordered after appeal; Ruby died before the new trial in 1967.

1965 An explosion at the Keokuk, IA, armory killed 20 people.

1987 United States and Russia resolved their remaining differences over a new treaty banning medium- and shorter-range missiles; U.S. will dismantle 364 cruise and Pershing 2 missiles deployed in Europe and the Soviet Union will dismantle 553 SS-20 and SS-4 missiles over a three-year period.

1988 President Reagan announced he would veto a comprehensive ethics bill because it was "flawed, excessive and discriminatory"; had passed House 347–7 and by a voice vote in Senate.

1998 Union Camp Corp. and International Paper Co. announced plans to merge.

1998 Tobacco industry and states reached tentative agreement for a $206 billion settlement of pending suits by the states; 12 states are expected to agree.

2003 More freedom for cell phone consumers began today: Federal Communications Commission mandated changes now effective, including right to keep same cell phone number when changing carriers and to move landline number to cell phone usage.

2005 Pat Morita (b. 1932) died at 72; probably the most well-known Japanese-American actor, having had some 200 film and television appearances, most notably as Arnold, a diner owner on the TV series *Happy Days,* and as the karate mentor in the film *The Karate Kid.*

2006 "Black Friday" (the day after Thanksgiving which traditionally marks when retailers start to turn a profit for the year) began Christmas shopping season with an impressive start: A survey of 45,000 mall-based stores found sales up 6 percent over previous year; a second survey, however, estimated number of shoppers declined by a million from previous year but found that those who went out spent more.

2006 Robert McFerrin, Sr., died at 85 as result of a heart attack; first black male to be made a member of New York Metropolitan Opera; provided the singing voice for Sidney Poitier in motion-picture version of *Porgy and Bess.*

25

1757 Henry B. Livingston, associate justice, Supreme Court (1806–23), born in New York City (died 1823).

1758 John Forbes led British troops to victory over French at Ft. Duquesne, later renamed Pittsburgh.

1758 John Armstrong, Secretary of War (1813–14), born in Carlisle, PA; represented New York in Senate (1800–02, 1803–04); minister to France (1804–10) (died 1843).

1783 Last of British troops left New York City.

1816 Lewis M. Rutherford, who made first telescope designed for celestial photography, born in Morrisania, NY (died 1892).

1817 John Bigelow, co-editor, co-owner, *New York Post* (1848–61), born in Malden, NY; minister to France (1861–66), while there discovered original manuscript of Benjamin Franklin's autobiography (died 1911).

1835 Andrew Carnegie, steel industry leader and philanthropist, born in Dunfermline, Scotland; owner, Homestead Steel Works (1888) and controlled seven other companies, consolidating them into Carnegie Steel Co. (1899); merged with U.S. Steel (1901) and retired; distributed wealth to libraries, education, international peace (died 1919).

1835 Arthur Sewall, builder of full-rigged and steel sailing vessels, born in Bath, ME; Democratic vice presidential nominee (1896) (died 1900).

1846 Carry A. Nation, temperance leader, born in Garrard County, KY; argued that with Kansas a prohibition state, any citizen had right to destroy places selling intoxicants; armed with a hatchet, she went on wrecking sprees (died 1911).

1855 Paul Starrett, headed construction firm which built the Flatiron and Empire State buildings in New York City, born in Lawrence, KS (died 1957).

1862 Ethelbert W. Nevin, composer known for *The Rosary* and *Mighty Lak a Rose*, born in Edgeworth, PA (died 1901).

1867 Senate Judiciary Committee resolved that President Andrew Johnson "be impeached for high crimes and misdemeanors."

1869 Ben(jamin B.) Lindsey, who created headed, first American juvenile court (Denver 1900–27), born in Jackson, TN; also created new conciliation court (Los Angeles 1939), advocated family court, companionate marriages (died 1943).

1874 Joe Gans, considered greatest lightweight boxing champion (1902–08), born in Baltimore (died 1910).

1893 Joseph Wood Krutch, editor, *The Nation* (1924–53), born in Knoxville, TN; professor, Columbia U. (1936–52) (died 1970).

1896 Virgil G. Thompson, composer of scores for film documentaries (*The Plow that Broke the Plains, The River, Louisiana Story*), born in Kansas City, MO; music critic, *New York Herald Tribune* (1940–54) (died 1989).

1899 William R. Burnett, novelist (*Little Caesar, The Asphalt Jungle*), born in Springfield, OH (died 1982).

1913 Jessie W. Wilson, daughter of President and Mrs. Wilson, married in White House to Francis B. Sayre.

1914 Joe (Joseph P.) DiMaggio, baseball player (New York AL) who set record of hitting safely in 56 consecutive games, born in Martinez, CA; named to Baseball Hall of Fame (died 1999).

1915 Ku Klux Klan revived by William J. Simmons of Atlanta.

1926 National Broadcasting Co. went on air with 24 radio stations.

1939 Martin Feldstein, chairman, Council of Economic Advisors (1981–84), born in New

York City; economist with Harvard U. (from 1967).

1950 Eighteen Communist Chinese divisions launched surprise attack on Korea.

1957 President Eisenhower suffered a stroke; made a speedy recovery, returning to duty December 9.

1986 President Reagan announced resignation of National Security Advisor John M. Poindexter and dismissal of his aide, Lt. Col. Oliver North; announced that inquiry disclosed that some proceeds of arms sales to Iran had gone into a Swiss bank account to finance military aid to the Nicaraguan Contras.

1998 Dr. Jack Kevorkian, advocate of assisted suicide, was charged with first-degree murder for the nationally-televised euthanizing of a terminally ill man.

1998 Flip Wilson, who became the first black host of a top television variety show, died at 64.

2002 Largest federal reorganization in half century: Legislation to create new Department of Homeland Security signed into law; cabinet-level agency to have 170,000 employees.

2002 National Governors Association study: 24 states facing huge $50 billion plus deficit; California alone hits $12 billion.

26

1727 Artemus Ward, Revolutionary War general, born in Shrewsbury, MA; assumed command of troops after Lexington and directed siege of Boston until Gen. Washington arrived; member, Continental Congress (1780–81) and represented Massachusetts in House (1791–95) (died 1800).

1783 Continental Congress began holding sessions in the Maryland State House in Annapolis; continued until June 3, 1784.

1789 Thanksgiving celebrated as national holiday for first time.

1791 First cabinet meeting held as President Washington met with the secretaries of war, state, and treasury, and the attorney general.

1792 Sarah Moore Grimké, active worker in abolitionist and women's rights movements, born in Charleston, SC; with sister, became Quakers (died 1873).

1807 William S. Mount, first native-born painter to specialize in painting scenes of everyday life, born in Setauket, NY (died 1868).

1828 William H. Sylvis, a founder, president, National Labor Union (1868–69), born in Indiana County, PA (died 1869).

1832 Mary E. Walker, women's rights activist, born in Oswego, NY; served as nurse with Union Army (1861–64), wearing men's clothes to attract attention to women's rights (died 1919).

1857 Edward C. Potter, sculptor of animals (the lions at New York Public Library entrance), born in New London, CT (died 1923).

1861 Convention in Wheeling adopted West Virginia state constitution.

1876 Willis H. Carrier, founder, president, Carrier Corp. (1915–31), born in Angola, NY; Carrier board chairman (1931–43) (died 1950).

1883 President Arthur attended unveiling of statue of Washington on steps of Sub-Treasury Building in New York City.

1894 Norbert Wiener, mathematician with MIT 42 years and developer of cybernetics, born in Columbia, MO; his development led to much modern automation (died 1964).

1895 William G. Wilson, cofounder, Alcoholics Anonymous (1935), born in East Dorset, VT; with wife, founded Al-Anon for spouses of alcoholics, Alateen for their children (died 1971).

1912 Eric Sevareid, newspaper, television reporter and commentator, born in Velva, ND (died 1992).

1922 Charles M. Schulz, cartoonist (*Peanuts*), born in Minneapolis.

1924 George Segal, sculptor known for life-size tableaux, born in New York City.

1975 President Ford announced that the federal government would help New York City meet its financial obligations and avoid defaulting on its loans.

1996 Baseball club owners approved five-year agreement with the players' association, reversing their turndown of November 6; pact calls for revenue sharing by the clubs and inter-league play.

2000 Final election results certified in Florida, giving Bush victory by 537 votes; Gore threatens court fight over the outcome.

2002 President Bush signed Terrorism Risk Insurance Act; in case of future attacks, U.S. government would reimburse private insurance carriers a maximum of $100 billion to cover losses.

27

1703 James DeLancey, chief justice, New York Supreme Court (1733–60), born in New York City; heard Peter Zenger case (died 1760).

1746 Robert R. Livingston, as New York State Chancellor (1777–1801) administered oath of office to President Washington, born in New York City; member, Continental Congress (1775–78, 1779–81, 1784–85); first American secretary of foreign affairs (1781–83); minister to France (1801–04); aided Robert Fulton in building steamboat (died 1813).

1806 President Jefferson issued proclamation warning citizens of the Aaron Burr conspiracy to set up separate nation west of the Alleghenies.

1843 Cornelius Vanderbilt, headed various railroad companies, born in Staten Island, NY; bequeathed $1.5 million to Yale U.; with brothers, endowed Vanderbilt Clinic at Columbia U. (died 1899).

1848 Henry A. Rowland, first physics professor, Johns Hopkins U. (1875–1901), born in Honesdale, PA; invented concave grating for spectroscope, determined mechanical equivalent of heat (died 1901).

1857 Alfred Cumming named Utah governor by President Buchanan, who proclaimed territory in rebellion.

1857 S. Adolphus Knopf, specialist in treating tuberculosis, born in Halle, Germany; founder, New York City and national tuberculosis associations (died 1940).

1870 Joseph S. Mack, truck manufacturer, born in Mt. Cobb, PA; with brothers, founded wagon company (1889), built first successful gas-powered truck, bus (1900) (died 1953).

1874 Charles A. Beard, historian who helped found New School for Social Research, born in Knightstown, IN; noted for economic interpretation of American institutional development; with wife, Mary, wrote *The Rise of American Civilization* (died 1948).

1881 Thomas I. Parkinson, president, Equitable Life Assurance Society (1927–53), born in Philadelphia (died 1959).

1893 Richard K. Sutherland, chief of staff, American–Far East forces (1941–45), born in Hancock, MD; chief of staff, Philippine military mission (1938–41) (died 1966).

1901 Army War College established in Washington, DC, as an officers' postgraduate school; Gen. Tasker H. Bliss named president.

1901 Ted (Edward B.) Husing, pioneer radio announcer of 1920s, born in New York City (died 1962).

1903 Lars Onsager, physical chemist, born in Oslo, Norway; awarded 1968 Nobel Chemistry Prize for development of equations in thermodynamics (died 1976).

1909 James Agee, author (*A Death in the Family*) and screenwriter (*The African Queen*), born in Knoxville, TN (died 1955).

1912 David Merrick, theatrical producer, born in St. Louis; hits include *Fanny*; *Gypsy*; *Becket*; *Carnival*; *Oliver*; *Hello, Dolly!*; *I Do, I Do*; *Promises, Promises*.

1917 Bob Smith, created and starred in *Howdy Doody*, popular children's television show, born in Buffalo, NY (died 1998).

1963 President Lyndon Johnson, in an address to Congress, pledged to continue the late President Kennedy's policies and urged action on civil rights and tax cuts.

2001 Not exempt: 7–2 U.S. Supreme Court decision held that gambling taxes apply to casinos and other gambling on Indian tribal territory.

2006 U.S. Supreme Court threw out, without comment, the request to reinstate a $10.1 billion Illinois verdict against Philip Morris. Illinois Supreme Court had done so earlier on grounds that regardless of whether "light" and "low tar" cigarettes deserve the label or are safer, the Federal Trade Commission had approved the use of such terminology.

2006 Department of Homeland Security issued proposed new rules for 60-day public comment before adoption or rejection: businesses with a large number of invalid social security numbers (common among illegal immigrants) to have to verify genuineness of numbers or let employees go; following day news released that the probable next head of the House Homeland Security Committee threatened Cintas Corp. (country's largest uniform manufacturer) with possible prosecution if any workers terminated for having such invalid identifications.

28

1773 First ships carrying tea arrived in Boston Harbor.

1777 John Adams named commissioner to France.

1777 British troops occupied Rhode Island.

1792 Nathan Lord, president, Dartmouth College (1828–63), born in South Berwick, ME (died 1870).

1795 United States bought peace from Algiers and Tunis by paying $800,000, supplying a frigate, and paying an annual tribute of $25,000.

1831 John W. Mackay, miner who gained control of richest part of Comstock Lode, born in Dublin; cofounder, Commercial Cable Co. (1883), which laid two submarine cables to Europe; founder, Postal Telegraph Co. (1886) in unsuccessful effort to break Western Union monopoly (died 1902).

1837 John W. Hyatt, discoverer of fundamental principles in making celluloid, born in Starkey, NY; also found process for solidifying hard woods, invented a water filter and purifier (died 1920).

1857 Benjamin K. Rachford, physician who did important research in digestion, born in Alexandria, KY; started Babies Milk Fund in Cincinnati (1909) (died 1929).

1866 David Warfield, star actor in early 1900s (*The Auctioneer, Music Master*), born in San Francisco (died 1951).

1866 Henry Bacon, architect of various memorials including the Lincoln Memorial in Washington, DC, born in Watseka, IL (died 1924).

1866 John Barrett, director-general, Pan American Union (1907–20), born in Grafton, VT; served in several Latin American countries (died 1938).

1868 Robert S. Abbott, founder, editor, *Chicago Defender*, born on St. Simons Island, GA (died 1940).

1873 Frank Phillips, cofounder, Phillips Petroleum, president (1917–47), born in Scotia, NE (died 1950).

1894 Brooks Atkinson, drama critic on *New York Times* for 31 years, born in Melrose, MA; war correspondent in World War II (died 1984).

1895 Jose Iturbi, concert pianist and conductor for several musicals, films, born in Valencia, Spain (died 1980).

1895 First automobile race was held in Chicago, with J. Frank Duryea winning the 54-mile race driving at 7½ mph.

1903 J. Howard McGrath, Attorney General (1949–52), born in Woonsocket, RI; served Rhode Island as governor (1940–45) and in the Senate (1945–49) (died 1966).

1904 James O. Eastland, who represented Mississippi in Senate (1941–78), born in Doddsville, MS.

1908 Explosion and cave-in at Marianna Mine in Monongahela, PA, killed more than 100 persons.

1909 Rose Bampton, operatic soprano with Metropolitan Opera from 1932 on, born in Cleveland.

1919 American-born Lady Nancy Astor elected to House of Commons from Plymouth, the first woman ever elected to Parliament.

1942 Coffee rationing began.

1942 A Boston nightclub, Cocoanut Grove, burned, killing 498 persons.

1943 Teheran Conference between President Franklin Roosevelt, Prime Minister Winston Churchill, and Premier Joseph Stalin began; ended four days later with agreement for the invasion of France.

1950 Russell A. Hulse, physicist at Princeton U. who shared 1993 Nobel Physics Prize, born in New York City.

1964 *Mariner 4*, an unmanned satellite, photographed the surface of Mars and studied the Martian atmosphere.

1982 Space shuttle with a crew of six, including for first time western European scientists, took off from Cape Canaveral; made numerous scientific experiments, landed at Edwards Air Force Base, CA, December 8.

1993 Garry Moore, popular television game show host, died at 78.

1995 President Clinton signed $6 billion highway funding bill which also ended the federal 55 mph speed limit established in 1974; states now have right to set own limits.

2000 U.S. Supreme Court by 6–3 forbids police stops designed primarily to discover banned drugs.

2001 U.S. signed contract with British firm to buy 155 million doses of smallpox vaccine; due to be supplied during following year and will boost emergency reserve to enough to vaccinate entire population if needed; cost: $428 million.

2006 Film clips from a new picture about the birth of Jesus were banned yesterday from Chicago's annual Christkindlmarket festival; Chicago's executive director of special events argued that it would be "insensitive" to the feelings of non–Christians to permit them to be shown; today grounds were shifted to it being a "commercial message" provided by a profit-making motion-picture company; also insisted it was advice rather than an order.

29

1727 Ezra Stiles, president of Yale (1778–95) and considered most learned man of his time, born in North Haven, CT; pastor, Second Congregational Church, New Haven (1755–76) (died 1795).

1729 Charles Thomson, secretary of Continental Congress (1774–89), born in County Derry, Ireland; leader of Philadelphia opposition to British policies (died 1824).

1760 French surrendered Detroit to English troops under Maj. Robert Rogers.

1773 New York Sons of Liberty adopted resolutions against tax on tea and exclusive right of East India Co.; warned that anyone selling, buying, or transporting such tea "shall be deemed an enemy to the liberties of America."

1799 Amos Bronson Alcott, a leader of New England transcendentalists, born in Wolcott, CT; founded several innovative schools (died 1888).

1802 Convention in Chillicothe ratified the Ohio constitution, including a clause prohibiting slavery.

1811 Wendell Phillips, president, Anti-Slavery Society (1865–70), born in Boston; also advocated penal reform prohibition and woman suffrage (died 1884).

1816 Morrison R. Waite, chief justice, Supreme Court (1874–88), born in Lyme, CT (died 1888).

1832 Louisa May Alcott, author best remembered for *Little Women*, born in Germantown, PA (died 1888).

1864 Sand Creek massacre occurred in Kiowa County, CO, when more than 100 Indians were killed by American cavalrymen led by Col. John M. Chivington.

1876 Joseph E. Davies, ambassador to Russia (1936–38) and author (*Mission to Moscow*), born in Watertown, WI; commissioner of corporations (1913–15); Federal Trade Commission chairman (1915–16), vice chairman (1916–18) (died 1958).

1890 First Army-Navy football game played at West Point with Navy the winner 20–0.

1895 Busby Berkeley, choreographer noted for large-scale, spectacular dances in numerous films, stage musicals, born in Los Angeles (died 1976).

1908 Adam Clayton Powell, Jr., first black city councilman in New York City (1941–44), born in New Haven, CT; represented New York in House (1945–67, 1969–71); pastor, Abyssinian Baptist Church, New York City (1936–71) (died 1972).

1923 Frank Reynolds, television newsman with ABC (1963–83), born in East Chicago, IN; evening news anchor (1978–82) (died 1983).

1929 Richard E. Byrd, with Bernt Balchen as pilot, became first to fly over South Pole.

1950 National Council of Churches formed by 29 major American Protestant churches and four Eastern Orthodox churches.

1963 President Lyndon Johnson named investigating commission into assassination of President Kennedy; Supreme Court Chief Justice Earl Warren named chairman.

1988 George Mitchell, Senator from Maine (1984–94), named majority leader succeeding Senator Robert Byrd of West Virginia.

1990 UN Security Council authorized United States and its allies to expel Iraq from Kuwait by force if Iraq forces are not withdrawn by January 15, 1991.

1991 Dust storm near Coalinga, CA, covered a highway causing a pileup of about 100 motor vehicles; 12 persons were killed, about 150 injured.

1992 United States closed the Subic Bay Naval Base in the Philippines after nearly 100 years in operation.

1995 President Clinton in London endorsed a peace agreement reached in Northern Ireland; he became first president to visit there (November 30–December 1).

1997 Coleman Young, first black mayor of Detroit, serving record 20 years (1974–93), died at 79.

2006 U.S. government agreed to pay $2 million for misidentifying the fingerprint of an Oregon resident as that of an individual involved in the Madrid, Spain, train bombings of 2004; arrested and held until Spanish police identified print as someone else's; case raises controversial question of how often similar prints are mistakenly identified as identical.

30

1723 William Livingston, first governor of New Jersey (1776–90), born in Albany, NY; member, Continental Congress (1774–76) and delegate to Constitutional Convention (1787) (died 1790).

1725 Martin Boehm, cofounder, United Brethren Church (1789), born in Lancaster County, PA; consecrated bishop of Mennonite Church (1759) but excluded from Mennonite communion because of his liberal views (died 1812).

1729 Samuel Seabury, first American Episcopal bishop (1784), born in Groton, CT (died 1796).

1782 Provisional treaty of peace signed by the American colonies and Great Britain in Paris.

1810 Oliver F. Winchester, developer of the Winchester rifle about 1866, born in Boston (died 1880).

1819 Cyrus W. Field, a leader in paper business, born in Stockbridge, MA; promoted first American submarine transatlantic cable, which worked briefly (1858), then achieved success in 1866 (died 1892).

1829 First Welland Canal, connecting Lakes Erie and Ontario, opened.

1835 Mark Twain, author of many classics, born in Florida, MO, as Samuel M. Clemens; works included *Tom Sawyer, Huckleberry Finn, The Innocents Abroad, A Connecticut Yankee in King Arthur's Court, Life on the Mississippi* (died 1910).

1858 Charles A. Coolidge, architect, born in Boston; among his designs were Harvard Medical School, Chicago Public Library and Art Institute, Rockefeller Institute in New York City (died 1936).

1864 Union troops under Gen. George H. Thomas turned back Confederate troops under Gen. John Hood at Franklin, TN; Confederate Gen. Patrick R. Cleburn was killed.

1869 Mississippi ratified its new constitution, which had been rejected in 1868.

1869 Texas voters ratified their new constitution.

1908 Root-Takahira agreement reached in an exchange of notes between Secretary of State Elihu Root and Japanese Ambassador Takahira; called for Japanese confirmation of the Open Door policy in China.

1911 Standard Oil Co. of New Jersey went out of existence as each subsidiary company assumed control of its own affairs in keeping with court-ordered dissolution.

1915 Henry Taube, foremost American inorganic chemist, born in Saskatchewan, Canada; awarded 1983 Nobel Chemistry Prize for work in mechanism of electron transfer reactions, especially in metal complexes.

1915 An explosion at a Dupont plant near Wilmington, DE, killed 31 persons; believed to have been caused by sabotage.

1917 Rainbow Division, representing every state, arrived in France.

1924 Shirley A. Chisholm, first black woman popularly elected to Congress, born in New York City; represented New York in House (1969–82).

1926 Andrew V. Schally, medical researcher, born in Wilno, Poland; shared 1977 Nobel Physiology/Medicine Prize for research in role of hormones in body chemistry.

1929 Dick Clark, television personality and producer, born in Mt. Vernon, NY.

1942 First war loan drive began, resulting in sale of nearly $13 billion in bonds between November 30 and December 23.

1956 Floyd Patterson knocked out Archie Moore in fifth round in Chicago to become world heavyweight boxing champion.

1984 Basis for merger of nine Protestant denominations was reached by the Consultation of Church Union after 22 years of effort; denominations are the African Methodist Episcopal, African Methodist Episcopal Zion, Disciples of Christ, Christian Methodist, Episcopal, International Council of Community Churches, Presbyterian, United Methodist, and United Church of Christ.

1993 Brady Bill, which provides for required five-day waiting period to buy a gun, was signed into law by President Clinton.

1996 Tiny Tim (Herbert Khanry), singer famed for his falsetto singing ("Tiptoe through the tulips..."), died at about 64.

1998 Exxon and Mobil announced plans to merge into what would be the world's largest corporation.

2005 Official Atlantic hurricane season hit highest ever record with Hurricane Epsilon: 25 named storms, with 14 developing into hurricanes; record grows to 27 named storms with Zeta on December 30.

2006 The year when pessimism went wrong: After widely expressed fears that it would be another horrible year for foul weather, the hurricane season ended today with only five tropical storms rising to the level of hurricane. New records: no tropical storms during October (last happened in 2002), only one hurricane entered Gulf of Mexico (a low figure last reached in 1997), no category 4 or 5 hurricanes (last occurred in 1997).

2006 Microsoft's new Windows operating system, Vista, officially released; will come pre-installed on new computers only in early 2007; survey of major companies indicates that half of their computers do not have the computing power to run Vista.

DECEMBER

1

1741 Samuel Kirkland, missionary who worked with Iroquois Indians, born in Norwich, CT; instrumental in keeping Six Nations Indians neutral during Revolution; founded Hamilton Oneida Academy (1793), which became Hamilton College (1812) (died 1808).

1763 Patrick Henry, arguing Parson's Cause case, challenged the authority of the Crown to disallow colonial statutes.

1777 Baron Friedrich von Steuben, Prussian military officer, arrived in Portsmouth, NH, offered his services to American army.

1810 Census reported the American population at 7,239,881 and the center of population 40 miles northwest of Washington.

1814 Gen. Andrew Jackson and his troops arrived in New Orleans to defend it against British.

1824 Electoral College met to cast presidential votes: Andrew Jackson 99, John Quincy Adams 84, William H. Crawford 41, Henry Clay 37; no candidate having received a majority of the 261 votes, decision was turned over to House of Representatives which elected Adams president, John C. Calhoun, vice president.

1826 William Mahone, Confederate general at Malvern Hill and Bull Run, born in Southampton County, VA; represented Virginia in Senate (1881–87) (died 1895).

1834 President Jackson in annual message to Congress reported that the national debt had been eliminated.

1845 President Polk in his message to Congress claimed Oregon for the United States.

1850 Seventh Census reported rise of 36 percent in United States population to 23,191,876.

1872 Gerard Swope, president, General Electric (1922–40, 1942–44), born in St. Louis; first president, International General Electric (1919) (died 1957).

1879 Lane Bryant, founder of clothing store chain bearing her name, born in Lithuania as Lena Himmelstein; pioneered in merchandising maternity, stout women's clothing (died 1951).

1886 Jefferson Caffery, diplomat, born in Lafayette, LA; ambassador to Cuba (1934–37), to Brazil (1937–44), to France (1944–49), to Egypt (1949–55) (died 1974).

1886 Rex Stout, author of Nero Wolfe mysteries, born in Noblesville, IN (died 1975).

1896 Ray Henderson, composer of popular songs ("That Old Gang of Nine," "Bye, Bye, Blackbird," "Five Foot Two, Eyes of Blue"), born in Buffalo, NY (died 1970).

1899 Robert H.W. Welch, Jr., founder, John Birch Society (1958), born in Chowan County, NC; associated with family candy business until 1957 (died 1985).

1909 First Christmas savings club opened by Carlisle (PA) Trust Co.

1911 Walter Alston, baseball manager (Brooklyn, Los Angeles NL 1954–75), born in Butler County, OH; named to Baseball Hall of Fame (died 1984).

1912 Minoru Yamasaki, architect (New York City's World Trade Center), born in Seattle (died 1986).

1913 First drive-in gas station was opened by Gulf Refining Co. in Pittsburgh.

1913 Mary Martin, singer and actress (South Pacific, Peter Pan, I Do, I Do), born in Weatherford, TX (died 1990).

1918 First American troops returned from Europe, landed in New York City.

1925 Martin Rodbell, biochemist with National Institutes of Health who shared 1994 Nobel Physiology/Medicine Prize, born in Baltimore, MD.

1935 Woody (Heywood) Allen, writer and movies director (*What's New, Pussycat?, Sleeper, The Front, Annie Hall, Zelig*), born in New York City.

1936 President Franklin Roosevelt addressed opening session of Inter-American Conference for Maintenance of Peace in Buenos Aires.

1939 Lee Trevino, first golfer to win American, Canadian, and British Opens in same year (1971), born in Dallas, TX.

1942 Nationwide gasoline rationing went into effect.

1945 Bette Midler, screen actress and singer, born in Paterson, NJ.

1955 Rosa Parks refused to give her seat on a Montgomery, AL, bus to a white man; touched off major boycott led by the Rev. Martin Luther King, Jr., and an eventual Supreme Court decision outlawing segregation on buses.

1956 Virgin Islands National Park established.

1958 Parochial school in Chicago burned, killing 90 children and three teachers.

1969 First draft lottery since World War II was held in New York City.

1974 A TWA 727 crashed during a storm at Upperville, VA; 92 persons were killed.

1988 President Reagan vowed not to pardon former aide Oliver L. North but he ruled out releasing sensitive documents for North's defense; action could force dismissal of the major charges against North, former National Security Advisor John M. Poindexter and two other defendants in the Iran-Contra Affair.

1994 Senate, by 76–24 vote, followed House approval of the GATT Treaty (General Agreement on Tariffs and Trades), which provided for free trade; President Clinton signed bill December 8.

1997 A 14-year-old boy, Michael Carneal, killed three girls and injured five others at Heath High School in West Paducah, KY, during a prayer meeting before school.

2

1738 Richard Montgomery, colonial Army general who was killed at siege of Quebec (December 31, 1775), born in Dublin.

1823 Monroe Doctrine enunciated, opposing European intervention in Western Hemisphere; doctrine contained in President Monroe's annual message to Congress, stating in part, "The American continents, by the free and independent conditions which they have assumed and maintained, are henceforth not to be considered a subject for future colonization by any European powers."

1832 Convention in Dover adopted a revised Delaware constitution.

1832 John Carbutt, photographer, born in Sheffield, England; devised new gelatin-covered dry plate, introduced orthochromatic plate, giving correct color value in photography (died 1905).

1844 The gag rules, which were adopted by the House between 1836 and 1840, were repealed; rules were designed to forbid considering any petitions relating to slavery.

1863 Jane M.A. Pierce, wife of President Pierce, died in Andover, MA, at 57.

1863 Charles Ringling, with four brothers, began first circus (1884), born in McGregor, IA; bought out other units and by 1907 had America's leading circus (died 1926).

1863 Thomas Crawford's bronze sculpture, *Freedom*, placed atop the Capitol dome.

1864 Carl Van Anda, managing editor, *New York Times* (1904–32), born in Georgetown, OH (died 1945).

1866 Harry T. Burleigh, singer and composer, born in Erie, PA; soloist, St. George's Episcopal Church, New York City, 52 years; with choir of Temple Emanu-El, New York City, 25 years; first to arrange about 100 Negro spirituals (died 1949).

1884 Ruth Draper, world-renowned monologist, born in New York City (died 1956).

1885 George R. Minot, medical researcher, born in Boston; shared 1934 Nobel Physiology/ Medicine Prize for discovery of liver therapy for anemia (died 1950).

1886 Widowed Theodore Roosevelt was married to Edith K. Carow in London.

1893 William Gaxton, stage and screen actor (*A Connecticut Yankee, 50 Million Frenchmen*), born in San Francisco (died 1963).

1895 Jesse Crawford, organist featured at Paramount Theater, New York City, born in Woodland, CA (died 1962).

1895 Daughters of the American Revolution (DAR) chartered by Congress.

1906 Peter C. Goldmark, developer of color television, born in Budapest; also developed first commercially-successful long-playing record (1948) (died 1977).

1912 Supreme Court ruled that merger of Union Pacific and Southern Pacific railroads constituted a combination in restraint of trade; merger dissolved.

1924   Alexander M. Haig, Army general, commander of NATO forces (1974–79), born in Philadelphia; aide to President Nixon (1969–74), secretary of state (1981–82).

1925   Julie Harris, actress (*Member of the Wedding, Forty Carats, I Am a Camera, The Belle of Amherst*), born in Grosse Pointe Park, MI.

1930   Gary S. Becker, awarded 1992 Nobel Economics Prize, born in Pottsville, PA.

1942   Enrico Fermi, Arthur Compton, and their colleagues succeeded in achieving a controlled chain reaction of uranium under the Stagg Field stands at U. of Chicago; marked the beginning of the Atomic Age.

1954   Senate by 67–22 vote cited Wisconsin Sen. Joseph R. McCarthy for contempt of the Senate elections subcommittee, for the abuse of its members, and insults to the Senate during the Army televised hearings.

1970   Environmental Protection Agency came into being as 13 administrative units from other agencies were combined.

1980   Three Alaska national parks were created: Katemai, Kenai Fjords, and Lake Clark across the Cook Inlet from Archangel; also Mt. McKinley National Park was renamed Denali National Park.

1982   First permanent artificial heart was implanted in a human being — 61-year-old Barney Clark — at U. of Utah Medical Center; Clark lived about three months.

1988   United Nations General Assembly voted overwhelmingly to move its sessions from New York City to Geneva after Secretary of State George Shultz denied a visa for PLO Chairman Yasser Arafat to speak at the UN's New York meeting.

1992   UN Security Council agreed to let the United States lead an international military force to Somalia to protect deliveries of food and medicine; U.S. to send 28,000 troops in four stages.

1993   Space shuttle *Endeavor* launched on 11-day mission during which the Hubble space telescope was repaired.

1998   Former Agriculture Secretary Mike Espy was cleared of all 30 charges against him, ending four-year $17-million corruption investigation.

2001   Enron Corp. filed for bankruptcy; largest corporate bankruptcy in U.S. history.

2004   First female poet laureate died at 83; Mona Van Duyn had also won Pulitzer prize.

2005   North Carolina executed Kenneth L. Boyd, the 1,000th person so punished since the Supreme Court reconsidered its prohibition of the death penalty and decided to permit it again in 1976.

2006   Giant drug manufacturer Pfizer pulled the plug on its next-generation cholesterol drug torcetrapib (designed to raise good cholesterol) while in massive 15,000-person, multi-year drug tests; cause: concern over heart complications and death; program ended on a Saturday night and as recently as Thursday firm had been holding major meeting with investors lauding the potential of the drug.

3

1677   About 4,000 tobacco farmers in Albemarle colony of Carolina issued a manifesto justifying the rebellion against selling tobacco through New England; rebellion, led by John Culpeper and George Durant, ended two years later without settlement.

1755   Gilbert C. Stuart, renowned portrait painter, born in North Kingston, RI; best known for various portraits of George Washington and an unfinished Athenaeum head of Washington (died 1828).

1789   Virginia ceded ten square miles of land to Congress for a seat of government.

1807   David Alter, physicist who made possible spectroscopic determination of chemical nature of gases, born in Westmoreland County, PA (died 1881).

1807   Gamaliel Bailey, editor of *National Era* in Washington (1847–59) which serialized *Uncle Tom's Cabin*, born in Mt. Holly, NJ; editor of *Cincinnati Philanthropist* (1835–47), first anti-slavery journal in West (died 1859).

1809   Samuel Adler, rabbi who helped lay foundation for Reformed Judaism, born in Worms, Germany; helped revise the prayer book; rabbi, Emanu-El Congregation (died 1891).

1818   Illinois admitted to the Union as the 21st state.

1826   George B. McClellan, Union general who was replaced as commander of Army of the Potomac (1862) because of his over-cautiousness, born in Philadelphia; 1864 Democratic presidential nominee; governor of New Jersey (1878–81) (died 1885).

1833   Oberlin Collegiate Institute in Oberlin, OH, opened as first American coeducational college.

1838 Cleveland Abbe, pioneer weather forecaster, born in New York City; director, Cincinnati Observatory (1868), where he began issuing weather reports; joined Weather Bureau at its organization (1871); retired 1916 (died 1916).

1838 Convention in St. Joseph adopted Florida's constitution.

1842 Ellen H. Richards, an organizer, first president, American Home Economics Association (1908), born in Dunstable, MA; instructor, MIT (1884–1911) (died 1911).

1842 Charles A. Pillsbury, became world's largest flour miller by 1889, born in Warner, NH; invested in small flour mill (1869); introduced new methods and grew (died 1889).

1857 Carl Koller, ophthalmologist who introduced cocaine as a local anesthetic in eye operations (1884); launched use of local anesthesia in other operations (died 1944).

1863 Confederate Gen. James Longstreet began retreat from Knoxville, TN, ending siege, as Union force under Gen. William T. Sherman approached.

1868 Treason trial of Jefferson Davis, Confederate president, began in Richmond; after unconditional amnesty proclamation, the charges were dropped February 25, 1869.

1870 George H. Denny, president, chancellor, U. of Alabama (1912–55), born in Hanover County, VA; president, Washington & Lee U. (1902–11) (died 1955).

1871 Newton D. Baker, secretary of war (1916–21), born in Martinsburg, WV; mayor of Cleveland (1912–16); member, Permanent Court of Arbitration at The Hague (1928–36) (died 1937).

1873 Atwater Kent, founder, head of leading radio manufacturing company of 1920s, born near Burlington, VT (died 1949).

1892 Julius Ochs Adler, executive vice president, general manager, *New York Times* (1935–55), born in Chattanooga, TN (died 1955).

1903 John von Neumann, mathematician with Institute for Advanced Study, Princeton (1933–57), born in Budapest; built mathematical analyzer which sped development of hydrogen bomb (died 1957).

1912 Senate began impeachment hearings of Robert W. Archibald, associate judge, Commerce Court; charged with collusion with coal mine owners and railroad officials; found guilty January 13, 1913, on five of 13 counts; removed from bench.

1930 Andy Williams, popular singer of stage and television, born in Wall Lake, IA.

1974 Spacecraft *Pioneer II* passed the planet Jupiter on its course for Saturn.

2000 The first African-American woman to win a Pulitzer (*Annie Allen*, 1950), Gwendolyn Brooks died at 83.

4

1585 John Cotton, headed Congregationalism in colonies, born in Derby, England; opposed democratic institutions; responsible for expulsion of Anne Hutchinson, Roger Williams (died 1652).

1674 Jacques Marquette and two companions caught by onset of winter, built cabin on site of Chicago, the first white men to live there.

1682 First Pennsylvania assembly met at Upland (now Chester); incorporated Delaware settlements into Pennsylvania, adopted a code, naturalized settlers already there.

1730 William Moultrie, Revolutionary general who commanded defense of Sullivan's Island (now Ft. Moultrie) in Charleston Harbor, born in Charleston, SC; defended city in 1779; served South Carolina as governor (1785–87, 1794–96); a British prisoner (1780–82) (died 1805).

1736 Thomas Godfrey, author of first American full-length play (*The Prince of Parthia*) produced on a professional stage, born in Philadelphia (died 1763).

1783 Gen. George Washington took leave of his officers at Fraunces Tavern, New York City, saying, "With a heart full of love and gratitude, I now take leave of you. I most devoutly wish that your latter days may be as prosperous and happy as your former ones have been glorious and honorable."

1833 American Anti-Slavery Association organized in Philadelphia and a constitution written, primarily by William Lloyd Garrison.

1860 George A. Hormel, founder, president, Hormel & Co. (1882–1928), born in Buffalo, NY; produced first American canned hams (died 1946).

1861 Lillian Russell, actress and singer, the feminine ideal of her age, born in Clinton, IA (died 1922).

1865 Luther H. Gulick, a cofounder of Camp Fire Girls, born in Honolulu; director, Springfield (MA) YMCA school, cooperated with James Naismith in developing basketball (died 1918).

1867 The Grange (formally the Patrons of Husbandry) organized to protect farmers' interests.

1867 Charles A. Herty, chemist who invented method of turpentine orcharding, born in Milledgeville, GA; also developed method of determining oil in cottonseed products and process of making white paper from young southern pine trees (died 1938).

1875 William "Boss" Tweed, convicted of swindling New York City of about $200 million, was helped to escape from jail and flee to Cuba.

1880 Gar(field) Wood, racing boat builder and racer, born in Mapleton, IA; credited with building the Navy PT boat (died 1971).

1882 Nine-man congressional tariff commission, after six months study, recommended substantial tariff reductions.

1895 Arthur Murray, dancing teacher who with wife organized 450 dance schools, born in New York City (died 1991).

1895 New constitution adopted by a South Carolina convention, effective January 1, 1896.

1897 Robert Redfield, anthropologist with U. of Chicago (1927–58), born in Chicago; author (*Tepotzlan, Peasant Society and Culture, The Little Community*) (died 1958).

1903 Frank D. Merrill, who headed Merrill's Marauders against Japanese in Burma during World War II, born in Hopkinton, MA.

1905 Munro Leaf, writer and illustrator, born in Hamilton, MD; wrote *Grammar Can Be Fun, Manners Can Be Fun, The Story of Ferdinand, Wee Gillis*) (died 1976).

1908 Alfred D. Hershey, geneticist and virologist, born in Owosso, MI; shared 1969 Nobel Physiology/Medicine Prize for discoveries on the genetic structure of viruses (died 1997).

1915 Henry Ford and delegation of peace advocates sailed from New York on the *Oscar II*, chartered by Ford, "to try to get the boys out of the trenches and back to their homes by Christmas" and end the war; Ford left the delegation December 22 in Christiana and returned home.

1922 Deanna Durbin, singer and screen actress, born in Winnipeg, Canada; popular star of 1930/40s.

1923 Maria Callas, soprano who sang 43 leading roles in more than 500 performances in the world's opera houses, born in New York City (died 1977).

1924 John C. Portman, Jr., architect who designed Peachtree Center in Atlanta, born in Walhalla, SC; also designed several Hyatt-Regency House hotels.

1928 Senate ratified Kellogg-Briand peace pact with only one dissenting vote (Blaine of Wisconsin).

1943 Second Cairo conference began with President Franklin Roosevelt, Prime Minister Winston Churchill, and President Ismet Inonu of Turkey present; ended December 6.

1963 Use of English in United States in place of Latin for parts of the Catholic mass and sacraments approved by Ecumenical Council.

1980 Fire in Stouffer Inn in Harrison, NY, killed 26 persons.

1984 Four hijackers seized a Kuwaiti plane enroute to Pakistan and held 161 hostages on the ground at Teheran Airport until Iranian security men stormed plane December 9; two Americans were shot to death before the rescue.

1991 Charles Keating, chairman of a California savings and loan, convicted on 17 counts of securities fraud; prosecution claimed Keating induced 17,000 investors to buy $250 million in uninsured bonds.

1996 National commission recommended changing the way the cost-of-living index is calculated; changes could result in lowering national deficit and reduce increases in Social Security, retirement, and pension benefits tied to index changes.

2003 President Bush retreated on steel tariffs to protect American industry; after adverse World Trade Organization ruling, agrees to remove them rather than face retaliatory tariffs.

2006 NASA announced it intended to establish a permanent international moon base research center by 2024.

2006 Faced with the inability to get majority confirmation from the Senate even after a recess appointment, John Bolton handed in his resignation as U.S. ambassador to the U.N.; his pointed and sharp rhetoric had won him both defenders for vigorously upholding American interests and critics for annoying potential allies.

5

1775 Siege of Quebec begun by American troops under Gen. Richard Montgomery.

1776 Phi Beta Kappa, first American fraternity, founded at College of William & Mary in Williamsburg, VA.

1777 First New Jersey newspaper, *New Jersey Gazette*, published in Burlington by Isaac Collins.

1779 John Sergeant, who represented Pennsylvania in House (1815–23, 1827–29, 1837–41), born in Philadelphia; national Republican vice presidential candidate (1832) (died 1852).

1782 Martin Van Buren, eighth president (1837–41), born in Kinderhook, NY; vice president (1833–37), secretary of state (1829–31); served New York as governor (1828) and in Senate (1821–28) (died 1862).

1786 George Washington appointed as one of seven Virginia delegates to a proposed convention of states in Philadelphia.

1792 Electors selected by the states reelected President Washington and Vice President John Adams; Washington received 132 votes (one from Vermont, two from Maryland did not vote), Adams received 77 votes, George Clinton 50.

1796 Andrew Jackson took his seat in House of Representatives, first member from Tennessee; served until 1797, when he was elected to Senate, serving four months (1797–98) and again in 1823–25.

1803 Thomas J. Rusk, a leader in Texas' fight for independence, born in Pendleton District, SC; first chief justice, Texas Supreme Court (1840); represented state in Senate (1846–57) (died 1857).

1805 Michael B. Menard, fur trader who developed city of Galveston (1836), born in LaPrairie, Canada; Menard County, TX, named for him (died 1856).

1831 Former President John Quincy Adams took his seat in House as a representative from Massachusetts, serving until 1848.

1839 George A. Custer, Army general who with his men was slain at Battle of Little Big Horn (June 25, 1876), born in New Rumley, OH; battle became known as "Custer's Last Stand."

1841 Marcus Daly, developer of Anaconda Copper Co. in Butte, MT, born in Ireland (died 1900).

1848 President Polk's annual message confirmed the discovery of gold in California and gave impetus to the gold rush.

1876 Conway Theater in Brooklyn burned; about 295 persons died.

1879 Clyde V. Cessna, builder of first cantilever plane (1927) and founder, head of Cessna Co., born in Hawthorne, IA (died 1954).

1896 Carl F. Cori, biochemist, born in Prague; shared 1947 Nobel Physiology/Medicine Prize with his wife, Gerty; they discovered course of catalytic conversion of glycogen (died 1984).

1901 Walt(er E.) Disney, developer of animated movie cartoons, born in Chicago; produced many hit films (*Snow White, Fantasia, Mary Poppins*); created theme parks (Disney World, Disneyland) (died 1966).

1901 Grace Moore, soprano star of opera, stage, and screen, born in Slabtown, TN; killed in plane crash in Copenhagen, January 26, 1947.

1902 J. Strom Thurmond, "Dixiecrat" presidential candidate (1948) receiving 39 electoral votes, born in Edgefield, SC; served South Carolina as governor (1946–48) and in the Senate (1955–2003) as the only successful write-in candidate.

1904 Arnold Gingrich, founder, publisher, *Esquire* magazine, born in Grand Rapids, MI (died 1976).

1906 Otto Preminger, movie director (*Forever Amber, Exodus, Anatomy of a Murder, Advise and Consent*), born in Vienna (died 1986).

1933 The 21st Amendment, repealing the 18th (Prohibition) Amendment, went into effect.

1946 President Truman appointed a Committee on Civil Rights to recommend "more adequate and effective means and procedures for the protection of the civil rights of the people of the United States"; asked for legislation February 2, 1948, on its recommendations; a law was enacted September 9, 1957.

1953 Tornado in Vicksburg, MS, killed 38 persons.

1955 American Federation of Labor and Congress of Industrial Organizations merged to form the AFL-CIO with 15 million members.

1974 Hazel Wightman, early tennis star, died at 88; won numerous titles between 1910 and 1930.

1984 American Medical Association called for an end to both professional and amateur boxing because of its danger to health.

1988 Jim Bakker, former president of PTL television ministry, indicted on 24 federal charges of fraud and conspiracy, as were several of his associates; the TV evangelist resigned in 1987 amid a sex and hush money scandal.

1996 President Clinton announced he will nominate Madeleine Albright, UN ambassador (1993–96), to become secretary of state in 1997, the first woman to occupy that office.

1997 Labor Department reported unemployment declined to 4.6 percent in November, the lowest since October 1973.

2003 The only two U.S. makers of flu vaccine reported that their entire supply had been distributed, leaving many wondering whether there might be a shortfall later in flu season.

2006 New York City Board of Health invoked its power today to ban all trans fats in foods served in city restaurants; frying in trans fats oils illegal as of July 2007; all use prohibited in July 2008; ban challenged on legal grounds (product is legal under FDA rules) and practical ones (difficulty in implementing in only 18 months).

6

1637 Sir Edmund Andros, colonial governor (New York (1674) and New England (1686), born on Guernsey Island, off England; his rule was resented and ignored; colonists rebelled (1688), jailed him, then sent him back to England; governor of Virginia (1692–97) (died 1714).

1683 Gov. Thomas Dongan granted charter to New York City, which set up a government consisting of a mayor, six aldermen, six common councillors; charter officially signed April 27, 1686.

1752 Gabriel Duval, associate justice, Supreme Court (1811–36), born in Prince Georges County, MD; first Comptroller of Treasury (1802–11) (died 1844).

1776 Kentucky established as a county of Virginia.

1790 James Monroe took his seat as senator from Virginia, serving until 1794.

1823 (John) Eberhard Faber, who set up first American pencil factory (1861), born in Stein, Germany; first to put eraser on pencil (died 1879).

1830 Naval Observatory established in Washington, DC.

1833 John S. Mosby, Confederate cavalry commander (Mosby's Rangers), born in Edgemont, VA (died 1916).

1836 Charles F. Chandler, who invented flushing toilet water closet and refused to patent it in public interest, born in Lancaster, MA; president, New York City Board of Health (1867–84) (died 1925).

1840 Richard H. Pratt, who organized non-reservation Indian school which became Carlisle (PA) Indian Industrial school, born in Rushford, NY; was principal of Carlisle (1879–1904) (died 1924).

1847 Abraham Lincoln took his seat in House of Representatives.

1859 Edward H. Sothern, Shakespearean actor, born in New Orleans (died 1933).

1859 Herbert M. Lord, U.S. budget director (1922–29), born in Rockland, ME; Army finance director (1918–22) (died 1930).

1863 Atlee Pomerene, special prosecutor in Teapot Dome investigation (1924), born in Berlin, OH; represented Ohio in Senate (1911–23) (died 1937).

1863 Charles M. Hall, who invented method of producing pure aluminum by electrolysis (1886), born in Thompson, OH; his company later became Alcoa (died 1914).

1864 President Lincoln appointed Salmon P. Chase as chief justice, Supreme Court; confirmed same day; served until 1873.

1865 The 13th Amendment, abolishing slavery, was ratified.

1867 Karl T.F. Bitter, sculptor who directed sculpture at various world's fairs, born in Vienna; his four figures (*Architecture, Sculpture, Painting, Music*) are at front entrance to Metropolitan Museum of Art (died 1915).

1867 Convention in Alabama framed a new constitution.

1872 William S. Hart, silent screen cowboy star of 1920s, born in Newburgh, NY (died 1946).

1883 Thomas E. Braniff, founder of airline (1930) named for him, born in Salina, KS (died 1954).

1884 Washington Monument completed; dedicated February 1885.

1886 (Alfred) Joyce Kilmer, poet best remembered for "Trees," born in New Brunswick, NJ (died 1918).

1887 Lynn Fontanne, actress who with husband, Alfred Lunt, formed most famous American theater couple, born in London; they starred in *The Guardsman, Design for Living, The Taming of the Shrew* (died 1983).

1889 Jefferson Davis, president of the Confederacy, died in New Orleans at 81.

1889 Robert W. Woodruff, Coca-Cola president (1923–39), board chairman (1939–55), born in Columbus, GA; made Coca-Cola a household word (died 1985).

1896 Ira Gershwin, lyricist who wrote lyrics for brother George's music, and others, born in New York City; lyricist for stage (*Lady in the Dark*) and screen (*Cover Girl, A Star Is Born*) (died 1983).

1898 Alfred Eisenstadt, photojournalist who developed technique of the picture story, born in Dinschau, Germany (died 1995).

1904 President Theodore Roosevelt in annual message to Congress developed corollary to Monroe Doctrine — "as much as we do not permit

European intervention in Latin American affairs, America must preserve order and protect life and property in those countries"; later led to intervention in some countries.

1907 Coal mine explosion at Monogah, WV, resulted in 361 deaths.

1916 American aviation volunteers formed the Lafayette Escadrille to help the Allies; with American entry into the war, it became the 103rd Pursuit Squadron.

1917 American destroyer *Jacob Jones* was torpedoed and sunk by a German submarine off the English coast.

1920 Dave Brubeck, pianist and composer who was a leading force in contemporary jazz, born in Concord, CA.

1921 Otto Graham, football player (Northwestern U., Cleveland 1946–55)/coach (Washington, Coast Guard Academy), born in Waukegan, IL.

1941 Project begun by Office of Scientific Research and Development to study feasibility of building an atomic bomb.

1949 Leadbelly (Huddie Ledbetter), legendary folk singer and 12-string guitar player, died at about 64.

1973 Rep. Gerald Ford of Michigan sworn in as vice president, the first to take that office under the 25th Amendment.

1977 Longest coal strike in American history began; ended March 25, 1978.

1979 Shirley M. Hufstedler, California jurist, was named first Secretary of Education; served until 1981.

1988 Soviet leader Mikhail Gorbachev arrived in New York City to address the UN General Assembly on December 7; lunched with President Reagan and Vice President (and President-elect) George Bush.

1994 Treasury Secretary Lloyd Bentsen resigned after two years in the post; Robert Rubin, chairman of National Economic Council, succeeded him.

1995 President Clinton vetoed a congressional seven-year budget bill touching off a continuing battle through the month; a partial government shutdown began December 16 and lasted 21 days.

1996 Federal Trade Commission approved the purchase by Boeing Co. of Rockwell International's aerospace/weapons business.

1997 In a runoff election, Houston voters elected a black mayor for the first time — Lee Brown.

2000 Werner Klemperer, actor best known for his role as Col. Wilhelm Klink on television's popular *Hogan's Heroes*, dead at 80.

2002 Philip Berrigan, ex-Roman Catholic priest, who destroyed draft board records as a form of anti–Vietnam war protest, died at 79 of cancer; regarded as heroic by sympathizers and as dangerously naïve or seditious by foes.

2006 Major meeting of NASA officials reported that latest analysis of Mars Global Surveyor photographs suggested presence of freshly formed water, undermining persistent past analysis of officials that such photographs should not be interpreted in that manner.

2006 The Committee on Jewish Law and Standards of Conservative Judaism endorsed reports permitting ordination of homosexuals to be rabbis as well as same-sex commitment ceremonies, but retained prohibition on anal sex; such rulings are considered authoritative but not necessarily the only proper analysis of Jewish tradition, leaving the door open to disputes over the matter at affiliated Jewish institutions.

7

1672 Richard Bellingham, colonial governor (Massachusetts 1641, 1654, 1665–72), died at about 80; was lieutenant governor (1635, 1640, 1653, 1655–65).

1787 Delaware legislators unanimously ratified the Constitution, becoming the first state in the Union.

1804 Noah H. Swayne, associate justice, Supreme Court (1862–81), born in Frederick County, VA (died 1884).

1818 Henry Peterson, editor, *Saturday Evening Post* (1846–74), born in Philadelphia (died 1891).

1835 James K. Polk, a member of the House from Tennessee for ten years, was elected Speaker, serving until 1839.

1841 Michael Cudahy, who formed, headed own meat company (1890–1910), born in County Kilkenny, Ireland; a partner in Armour & Co. (1875–90) (died 1910).

1842 New York Philharmonic Orchestra presented its first concert.

1850 Solomon Schechter, founder, United Synagogue of America (1913), born in Focsani, Rumania; president, Jewish Theological Seminary (1902–15) (died 1915).

1862 Union troops were victorious at Prairie Grove, AR.

1863   Richard W. Sears, organizer of Sears Roebuck (1893), born in Stewartville, MN; president (1893–1909); acquired shipment of abandoned watches, sold them by mail; hired Alvah C. Roebuck to repair them (died 1914).

1866   Edwin H. Hughes, senior bishop of Methodist Church (1932–50), born in Moundville, WV; became a bishop in 1908 (died 1950).

1867   House by a 108–57 vote turned down Judiciary Committee 5–4 recommendation to impeach President Andrew Johnson.

1873   Willa S. Cather, author (*O Pioneers, My Ántonia, Death Comes for the Archbishop*), born in Winchester, VA; an editor, *McClure's Magazine* (1905–12) (died 1947).

1874   Blacks in Vicksburg, MS, attacked the courthouse in attempt to prevent the ouster of a sheriff; 75 blacks were killed before attack ended.

1879   Rudolf Friml, pianist and composer of operettas (*The Firefly, Rose Marie, The Vagabond King*), born in Prague (died 1972).

1883   Edmund E. Day, president, Cornell U. (1937–51), born in Manchester, NH; founder, dean of first business administration school (Michigan U. 1924–27) (died 1951).

1888   Heywood Broun, syndicated columnist (*It Seems to Me*), born in Brooklyn; wrote for several New York newspapers; a founder, American Newspaper Guild (died 1939).

1905   Gerard F. Kuiper, astronomer known for discoveries and theories of solar system, born in Haren Karspell, Netherlands (died 1973).

1915   Eli Wallach, stage actor (*The Rose Tattoo, Teahouse of the August Moon*) and on screen (*The Magnificent Seven, The Misfits*), born in New York City.

1917   Congress passed joint resolution declaring war on Austria-Hungary.

1941   Japanese launched surprise attack on Pearl Harbor in Hawaii and on other Pacific islands, destroying or damaging 19 warships, 150 planes, and killing 2,400 persons; attacks also launched on Philippines, Guam, Midway, Hong Kong, and Malay Peninsula.

1946   Fire in Winecoff Hotel in Atlanta killed 120 persons, injured 100.

1956   Larry Bird, basketball player (Boston Celtics) for 13 seasons, born in French Lick, IN; scored 21,791 points in 897 games; NBA most valuable player in 1984, 1986.

1987   Pacific Southwest Airlines commuter jet crashed near Harmony, CA, killing all 44 persons aboard.

1987   Soviet leader Mikhail S. Gorbachev arrived in Washington to sign treaty scrapping some medium- and short-range missiles; signing occurred December 9.

2004   IBM sold off its personal computer business to Chinese firm Lenovo for $1.75 billion; withdrew from industry it had created, though retaining 18.9 percent interest; purchase makes Lenovo third-largest PC maker, behind Dell and Hewlett-Packard.

2006   Last official gathering of Pearl Harbor survivors at the site of the attack; reason: rapidly diminishing numbers, advanced age, and growing physical limitations; about 400 attended.

2006   Jeane J. Kirkpatrick died; wrote *Political Woman*, first major analysis of women in contemporary politics (1974); U.S. representative at U.N. (1981–85); syndicated columnist (1986–97).

8

1765   Eli Whitney, cotton gin inventor, born in Westboro, MA; invented the gin (1793), operated factory to manufacture muskets (1801) using interchangeable parts (died 1825).

1801   President Jefferson's first annual message to Congress was sent in written form, breaking the precedent of personal appearance; written messages continued to 1913.

1812   Henry V. Poor, editor, *American Railroad Journal* (1849–62), born in Andover, ME; published railroad manuals, handbook of investment securities (died 1905).

1816   August Belmont, developer of own banking firm, born in Alzei, Germany; consul general for Austria in America (1844–50); minister to the Netherlands (1853–57); noted art collector, race horse owner (*Man O' War*) (died 1890).

1828   Clinton B. Fisk, founder of Fisk University for blacks (1867), born in Western New York; was a Union general in Civil War (died 1890).

1831   James Hoban, designed and supervised construction of original White House (1792–1800) and its replacement (1815–29), died at 69.

1839   Alexander J. Cassatt, president, Pennsylvania Railroad (1899–1906), born in Pittsburgh; built Penn Station, New York City (died 1906).

1841   James H. Logan, producer of the loganberry, born in Rockville, IN; served California Superior Court (1880–92) (died 1928).

1856 Henry T. Mayo, World War I admiral who commanded Atlantic Fleet (1916–19), born in Burlington, VT (died 1937).

1858 Henry P. Huse, admiral who commanded American naval forces in Europe (1920–22), born in West Point, NY (died 1942).

1858 Alfred H. Cowles, a pioneer in electric smelting, born in Cleveland; founder (1885) Electric Smelting & Aluminum Co. (died 1929).

1859 William H. O'Connell, Catholic Archbishop of Boston (1907–44), born in Lowell, MA; bishop of Portland, ME (1901–06); named cardinal 1911 (died 1944).

1861 William C. Durant, auto manufacturer, born in Boston; organized, headed, Durant Dort Carriage Co., world's largest buggy maker; organized Buick Motor Co. (1905), General Motors (1908), president (1916–20); founder, Durant Motor Co. (1921) (died 1947).

1863 President Lincoln issued proclamation of amnesty and reconstruction of seceding states; no state actually restored under this plan.

1879 Louisiana's new constitution, adopted in April, ratified by popular vote; capital was moved from New Orleans to Baton Rouge.

1885 Kenneth Roberts, historical novelist (*Rabble in Arms, Arundel, Oliver Wiswell, Northwest Passage*), born in Kennebunk, ME (died 1957).

1886 American Federation of Labor (AFL) organized in Columbus, OH, by 25 labor groups representing 150,000 members.

1888 Fiske Kimball, architect known for restoration of historical houses, born in Newton, MA; involved in restoring Monticello and member of board which planned reconstruction of Colonial Williamsburg, construction of Rockefeller Center (died 1955).

1889 Hervey Allen, author best known for *Anthony Adverse*, born in Pittsburgh (died 1949).

1891 Percy L. Crosby, cartoonist (*Skippy*), born in Brooklyn (died 1964).

1894 James Thurber, author and cartoonist, born in Columbus, OH; cartoonist for *The New Yorker*; among his writings were *The Secret Life of Walter Mitty, My Life and Hard Times, Fables of Our Time* (died 1961).

1913 Delmore Schwartz, poet and short story author (*In Dreams Begin Responsibilities, The World Is a Wedding, Summer Knowledge*), born in New York City (died 1966).

1925 Sammy Davis, Jr., entertainer and actor, born in New York City; starred on stage (*Mr. Wonderful, Golden Boy*) and screen (*Porgy and Bess, Sweet Charity*) (died 1990).

1941 Congress declared war on Japan within 33 minutes in the wake of the Pearl Harbor attack; Jeannette Rankin, Montana representative, cast lone vote against the declaration; she also voted against war in 1917.

1947 Thomas Cech, Colorado U. chemist who shared 1989 Nobel Chemistry Prize, born in Chicago.

1953 President Eisenhower, speaking to the UN General Assembly, proposed the launching of an international "atoms for peace" program through an international atomic energy agency.

1980 Former Beatle John Lennon was shot and killed outside his New York City apartment by a former psychiatric patient.

1988 It was a bad day for American fliers — five were killed when a helicopter crashed in northern Honduras during a training exercise, five others when a DC-7 from the U.S. Agency for International Development was shot down over Mauritania, and an American pilot and at least three others when an Air Force plane crashed in Ramscheid, West Germany, during a training flight.

1991 The *Dallas Times Herald* ceased publication.

1992 American Marines landed at Mogadishu launching the United Nations food mission in Somalia.

1998 The *Endeavor* spacecraft carried U.S.-made portion of the planned space station into orbit to join the Russian portion.

1998 A power outage in a 49–square-mile area including San Francisco brought city to standstill for about seven hours.

1998 The Supreme Court ruled that police cannot search people and their cars after ticketing drivers for minor violations.

2001 Betty Holberton (1917–2001) passed away; one of six individuals who programmed ENIAC (Electronic Numerical Integrator and Computer), the forerunner of the modern computer; headed committee that created COBOL, first program capable of being run on multiple computers.

2003 President Bush signed law that would establish a Medicare drug benefit to begin in 2006.

9

1561 Sir Edwin Sandys, founder of the Virginia colony, born in England; assisted in obtaining a charter for the Mayflower (died 1629).

1776 British force under Gen. Henry Clinton captured Newport, RI.

1848 Joel Chandler Harris, author remembered for his *Uncle Remus* stories, born in Putnam County, GA (died 1908).

1879 Benjamin D. Foulois, pioneer aviator who established Air Force (1910), born in Washington, CT; chief, Army Air Corps (1931–35) (died 1967).

1886 Clarence Birdseye, inventor of process for freezing food, born in Brooklyn; founder of what later became General Foods Corp.; also invented an infrared heat lamp (died 1956).

1898 Emmett Kelly, circus clown known as Weary Willie, born in Sedan, KS (died 1979).

1902 Lucius M. Beebe, syndicated columnist on cafe society, born in Wakefield, MA; publisher, *Territorial Enterprise*, Virginia City, NV (1950–60) (died 1966).

1906 Freddy Martin, bandleader of 1930/40s, born in Cleveland.

1907 First Christmas seals went on sale in Wilmington, DE.

1911 Lee J. Cobb, actor remembered for his role of Willy Loman in *Death of a Salesman*, born in New York City (died 1976).

1912 Thomas P. (Tip) O'Neill, Speaker of House (1977–87), born in Cambridge, MA; represented Massachusetts in House (1953–87) (died 1994).

1917 L. James Rainwater, physicist, born in Council, ID; shared 1975 Nobel Physics Prize for theory that some atomic nuclei are asymmetrical, not spherical (died 1986).

1918 Kirk Douglas, screen actor (*Spartacus, The Glass Menagerie, Seven Days in May*), born in Amsterdam, NY.

1919 William N. Lipscomb, physical chemist, born in Cleveland; awarded 1976 Nobel Chemistry Prize for work on structure bonding mechanisms of boranes.

1932 Bill Hartack, jockey who rode five Kentucky Derby winners, born in Colver, PA.

1958 John Birch Society, an anti–Communist organization, formed by Robert H.W. Welch, Jr., a retired candy manufacturer; named for an American captain killed by Chinese Communists in 1945.

1962 Petrified Forest (AZ) National Park established.

1967 Lynda Bird Johnson, daughter of President and Mrs. Lyndon Johnson, was married in the White House to Charles S. Robb.

1994 Dr. Jocelyn Elders, the outspoken U.S. surgeon general, resigned at the request of President Clinton.

1998 Crew of *Endeavor* space shuttle attached antennas to the space station being built nearly 250 miles above the earth. The American- and Russian-built chambers will form the basis for the international space station.

1998 Iraq refused to allow UN arms inspectors to enter the ruling party headquarters in Baghdad.

2001 Two days after being forced out of last major stronghold in Afghanistan, Taliban declared defeated.

2003 A 4.5 earthquake hit 30 miles SW of Richmond, Virginia; strongest in 30 years in state.

2006 Space shuttle *Discovery* launched at 8:47 P.M. in first American nighttime space launch since 2003; astronauts scheduled to rewire key space station components and to install first permanent power system.

2006 Martin Nordell died at 91; the illustrator had created both the popular *Green Lantern* hero and comic book and the advertising industry's "Pillsbury Doughboy."

10

1607 Capt. John Smith left Jamestown, VA, and ascended the Chickahominy River to get provisions; he was captured by Indians and according to legend was saved by Pocahontas, daughter of the Indian chief, Powhatan.

1741 John Murray, father of Universalist Church in America, born in Alton, England; set up pastorate in Independent Church of Christ in Gloucester, MA (1779–83), the Universalist Society, Boston (1793–1809) (died 1815).

1783 Henry Leavenworth, Army commander in southwest, born in New Haven, CT; fort and city named for him (died 1834).

1785 Daniel Appleton, cofounder of family publishing house (1838), born in Haverhill, MA (died 1849).

1787 Thomas H. Gallaudet, founded first free school for deaf in Hartford (1817), born in Philadelphia; school principal (1817–30); Gallaudet College in Washington named for him (died 1851).

1795 Matthias W. Baldwin, founded what later became Baldwin Locomotive Works (1832), born in Elizabethtown, NJ (died 1866).

1813 Zachariah Chandler, Interior Secretary (1875–77), born in Bedford, NH; represented

Michigan in Senate (1855–75, 1879); a founder of Republican Party (died 1879).

1817 Mississippi admitted to Union as the 20th state.

1830 Emily Dickinson, one of America's foremost poets, born in Amherst, MA; her work was published posthumously (died 1886).

1832 President Jackson issued proclamation to people of South Carolina saying that their acts nullifying the 1828 and 1832 tariffs were "incompatible" with the existence of the Union and "an impractical absurdity."

1851 Melvil Dewey, founder, director, New York State Library School (1887–1906), born in Adams Center, NY; director, New York State Library (1889–1906); originated decimal classification system; founder, American Library Association (died 1931).

1859 Frederick U. Adams, inventor of many street-lighting devices, born in Boston; also invented many railroad rolling stock devices (died 1921).

1864 Gen. William T. Sherman and his Union troops arrived in Savannah, after a 300-mile march to the sea; took Ft. McAllister three days later.

1869 Territory of Wyoming passed a woman's suffrage law.

1883 Alfred Kreymborg, poet ("Mushrooms," "Less Lonely," "Manhattan Men") and coeditor *American Caravan*, a literary miscellany (1927–31), born in New York City (died 1966).

1886 Horace B. Liverwright, cofounder, president, Boni and Liverwright publishers (1918–30) (died 1933).

1890 Edward J.H. O'Brien, editor of *The Best Short Stories* (1915–40) and a British version (1921–40), born in Boston (died 1941).

1896 First intercollegiate basketball game played in New Haven, with Wesleyan defeating Yale 4–3.

1898 Treaty of Paris concluded with Spain, formally ending Spanish-American War; Spain ceded Puerto Rico, Guam, and the Philippines to the United States for $20 million, relinquished all claim and title to Cuba, and assumed $400 million Cuban debt; ratified by Senate February 6, 1899.

1906 Walter H. Zinn, physicist who developed first breeder reactor (1951), born in Kitchener, Canada.

1906 President Theodore Roosevelt awarded 1906 Nobel Peace Prize for his role in ending Russo-Japanese War; first American to win the Peace Prize.

1911 Chet (Chester R.) Huntley, newsman who teamed with David Brinkley (1956–70), born in Cardwell, MT (died 1974).

1913 Morton Gould, conductor and composer of musicals (*Billion Dollar Baby*) and ballets (*Fall River Legend*), born in Philadelphia (died 1996).

1917 Boys Town, 11 miles west of Omaha, NE, founded by the Rev. Edward J. Flanagan.

1920 President Wilson awarded the 1919 Nobel Peace Prize.

1926 Vice President Charles G. Dawes shared the 1925 Nobel Peace Prize.

1934 Howard M. Temin, molecular biologist, born in Philadelphia; shared 1975 Nobel Physiology/Medicine Prize for research on process by which a virus can change the genetic makeup of a cell.

1941 Japanese landed on Luzon in the Philippines.

1948 UN General Assembly adopted the Universal Declaration of Human Rights, drafted by its Commission on Human Rights, headed by Mrs. Eleanor Roosevelt.

1971 Farm Credit Administration established.

1985 Supreme Court ruled 5–4 against the use in court of self-incriminating evidence against a defendant that was obtained by stealth without counsel being present for the defendant.

1997 Boston Red Sox baseball team signed Cy Young Award-winning pitcher Pedro Martinez to a record-setting six-year $75 million contract.

2004 Former New York City Police Commissioner Bernard Kerik withdrew as nominee for Secretary of Homeland Security; official reason: non-payment of taxes for housekeeper-nanny; critics were posed to attack his accumulation of $6.2 million through stock options in recent years as well.

2004 National Center for Health Statistics issues latest survey of juvenile sexual behavior: Sexually active individuals had dropped to 46 percent from 55 percent (1995): more females (47 percent), however, now active than males (46 percent); 91 percent of males claim to use some form of contraception and 83 percent of females.

2004 Chiron Corporation confirmed receipt of Food and Drug Administration letter demanding more information on how it was correcting faults at its Liverpool manufacturing plant; half of 2004 U.S. flu vaccine had to be destroyed due to contamination.

2005 Richard Pryor, black comedian who

gained widespread popularity across racial lines at a time when the phenomenon was new, died at 65 of a heart attack.

11

1586 John Mason, a founder of New Hampshire, born in King's Lynn, England; cofounder of company which settled on Piscataqua River (died 1635).

1620 Pilgrims sighted what is now Plymouth and created a settlement there December 25, calling it New Plymouth.

1750 Isaac Shelby, first governor of Kentucky (1792–96, 1812–16), born in Washington County, MD; Revolutionary general who led defeat of British at King's Mountain (died 1826).

1775 Governor Dunmore of Virginia, who placed the colony under martial law and began to raise an army, was decisively defeated by mixed force of 900 Virginians and North Carolinians at Great Bridge, VA.

1816 Indiana admitted to the Union as the 19th state.

1818 Jerome I. Case, inventor of a threshing machine (1844), born in Williamstown, NY; manufactured agricultural machinery (died 1891).

1824 Jonathan Letterman, Army surgeon who reorganized field medical service, born in Canonsburg, PA; introduced ambulance service for battlefield casualties (died 1872).

1833 Albert G. Ellis and John V. Suydam published first Wisconsin newspaper, *Green Bay Intelligencer.*

1876 Ada Louise Comstock, president, Radcliffe College (1923–43), born in Moorhead, MN; dean, Smith College (1912–23) (died 1973).

1882 Fiorello H. LaGuardia, mayor of New York City (1933–45), born in New York City; represented New York in House (1917–19, 1923–33); director, Office of Civilian Defense (1941–42); director-general, UNRRA (United Nations Relief & Rehabilitation Administration) (1946) (died 1947).

1882 Bijou Theater in Boston became first theater lighted by Edison's incandescent lights for a performance of Gilbert & Sullivan's *Iolanthe.*

1886 Victor McLaglen, screen actor (*The Informer, What Price Glory?, The Quiet Man*), born in London (died 1959).

1890 Mark Tobey, painter whose work is described as "white-line" or "white writing," born in Centerville, WI; work a synthesis of Oriental brushwork and American abstractionism (died 1976).

1892 John A. Larson, psychiatrist who invented the polygraph (lie detector) (1921), born in Nova Scotia.

1896 Women's suffrage went into effect in Idaho.

1903 Marine Corps formally occupied Guantanamo, naval station ceded by Cuba to the United States.

1905 Pare Lorentz, documentary film maker (*The Plow That Broke the Plains, The River*), born in Clarksburg, WV.

1922 Second agreement made by which Secretary Albert Fall leased the Elks Hills Naval Oil Reserve in California to E.M. Doheny, an oil executive.

1934 Fire in the Hotel Kerns in Lansing, MI, killed 34 persons.

1941 Germany and Italy declared war on the United States, which in turn declared war on Germany.

1941 Japanese captured Guam.

1982 Chemical storage tank exploded at Union Carbide plant near Destrehan, LA; 20,000 people were evacuated as a precaution.

1982 Seven largest black denominations representing 65,000 churches and 20 million Christians established Congress of National Black Churches.

1985 General Electric Co. agreed to buy RCA Corp. for $6.28 billion, the biggest corporate merger outside the oil industry.

1986 A. Bartlett Giamatti, 48-year-old president of Yale U. (1977–86), became president of the National (baseball) League.

1992 Fierce snowstorm lashed New York metropolitan area, destroying more than 12,000 homes.

1994 Mail bomb exploded in North Caldwell, NJ, killing Thomas Mosser; the death was linked to the serial bomber called the Unabomber.

1997 International global warming conference in Japan reached tentative agreement for reduction in using fossil fuels.

1997 Microsoft Corp. ordered to stop requiring computer makers to distribute its Internet browsing program.

1998 House Judiciary Committee approved three articles of impeachment of President Clinton based on grounds of perjury; a fourth article was approved the next day.

2006 Environmental Protection Agency

adopted new standards for calculating new car mileage; purpose to produce numbers closer to what occurs in real-life driving situations; estimated drop of 8 percent for highway driving and 12 percent for city/urban driving.

12

1745   John Jay, chief justice, Supreme Court (1789–94), born in New York City; member, Continental Congress (1774–79); drafted New York's first constitution (1777), serving state as its first chief justice (1777–78) and governor (1795–1801); secretary of foreign affairs (1784–89) (died 1829).

1776   Continental Congress, fearing British attack on Philadelphia, moved its sessions to Baltimore.

1786   William L. Marcy, secretary of state (1853–57), born in Sturbridge, MA; represented New York in Senate (1831–33) and served it as governor (1833–39); war secretary (1845–49); coined phrase "spoils system" ("To the victor belong the spoils of the enemy") (died 1857).

1787   Pennsylvania legislators ratified Constitution by vote of 46–23, making it the second state of the Union.

1791   Bank of the United States, created February 25, 1791, opened for business in Philadelphia.

1805   William Lloyd Garrison, founder, editor, *The Liberator* (1831–66), born in Newburyport, MA; a founder, American Anti-Slavery Society, president (1843–65) (died 1879).

1805   Henry Wells, cofounder of express company merged into American Express Co. (1850), which he headed (1850–65), born in Thetford, VT; organized Wells Fargo (1852) to operate in the West (died 1878).

1806   Isaac Leeser, rabbi and editor, born in Westphalia, Germany; rabbi of two Philadelphia synagogues (1829–68); founder, editor, *The Occidental and American Jewish Advocate* (1843–68); founder, Maimonides College (1868) (died 1868).

1830   Joseph O. Shelby, Confederate cavalry general, born in Lexington, KY (died 1897).

1843   William P. Dillingham, author of Senate bill which set immigration quotas for 40 or more years, born in Waterbury, VT; represented Vermont in Senate (1900–23) and served it as governor (1888–90) (died 1923).

1846   Treaty of New Granada (Colombia) signed, conveying the right of way to the United States to cross the Isthmus of Panama and guaranteeing neutrality of the isthmus and sovereignty of New Granada.

1849   Peter F. Collier, founder, publisher, *Colliers Weekly* (1896–1909), born in County Carlow, Ireland; entered publishing business (1877) (died 1909).

1864   Arthur Brisbane, syndicated editorial columnist in about 1,000 papers, born in Buffalo, NY; editor, *New York Evening Journal* (1897–1921) (died 1936).

1864   Paul E. More, essayist and cofounder of modern humanism, born in St. Louis; wrote 11 volumes of essays (died 1937).

1866   Edward A. Ross, a founder of American sociology, born in Virden, IL; with U. of Wisconsin (1906–37) (died 1951).

1876   First prohibition amendment to Constitution proposed by Rep. Henry W. Blair of New Hampshire.

1878   Rachel Crothers, playwright (*The Three of Us, Susan and God, Nice People*), born in Bloomington, IL; an organizer, American Theater Wing, which operated stage door canteens (died 1958).

1881   Arthur Garfield Hays, general counsel, national director, American Civil Liberties Union (1912–54), born in Rochester, NY (died 1954).

1881   Harry M. Warner, president, Warner Bros. (1923–56), born in Krasnosielce, Poland (died 1958).

1893   Edward G. Robinson, screen actor (*Little Caesar, Brother Orchid, Five-Star Final*), born in Bucharest (died 1973).

1910   President Taft nominated Associate Justice Edward D. White as chief justice of the Supreme Court; confirmed by Senate same day.

1912   Henry Armstrong, boxer who held three boxing championships simultaneously (featherweight, welterweight, lightweight) (1937–38), born in Columbus, MS (died 1988).

1913   First crossword puzzle, by Arthur Wynne, published in *New York World*.

1915   Frank Sinatra, popular singer and screen actor (*From Here to Eternity, Pal Joey*), born in Hoboken, NJ (died 1998).

1923   Bob Barker, television emcee (*The Price Is Right*), born in Darrington, WA.

1927   Robert Noyce, invented the integrated circuit and founded several high-tech companies, born in Burlington, IA (died 1989).

1928   Helen Frankenthaler, artist whose work was transitional between abstract expressionism and color field painting, born in New York City.

1932   Bob (Robert E.L.) Pettit, star basketball player (Louisiana State U.; St. Louis Hawks), born in Baton Rouge, LA; first player to break 20,000 point barrier, scoring 20,880 in career.

1937   Japanese bombers, while on attack on China, sank American gunboat *Panay* and three Standard Oil supply ships, 27 miles above Nanking on the Yangtze River; Japan accepted responsibility, made a formal apology later in the month, and paid indemnities.

1985   DC-8 jetliner carrying 284 homebound American soldiers and eight crew members crashed on takeoff after refueling at Gander, Newfoundland; all killed.

1985   President Reagan signed Gramm-Rudman balanced-budget law which set progressively lower federal deficit targets for FY 1986 through 1991; called for automatic federal spending cuts if targets are not met.

1990   Education Secretary Lauro F. Cavazo resigned under pressure; replaced by Lamar F. Alexander.

1998   Lawton Chiles, Florida governor and senator, died at 68.

2000   U.S. Supreme Court ruled 5–4 that the existing deadline of that night for recounting of disputed presidential ballots must be honored, thereby eliminating any chance of further counts reversing the paper-thin Bush victory in Florida, which gave him the electoral votes to win the presidency.

13

1810   Clark Mills, sculptor who did first American equestrian statue (Gen. Jackson facing the White House), born in Onondaga County, NY; statue also was first large bronze cast in United States; did many busts (died 1883).

1816   First American savings bank, Provident Institution for Savings, in Boston, incorporated; opened February 25, 1819.

1818   Mary Todd Lincoln, wife of President Lincoln, born in Lexington, KY (died 1882).

1835   Phillips Brooks, Episcopal Bishop of Massachusetts (1891–93), born in Boston; rector, Trinity Church, Boston (1869–91); wrote "O Little Town of Bethlehem" (died 1893).

1837   William Lyon McKenzie, Canadian insurgent leader of unsuccessful raid on Toronto, set up provisional government on Navy Island; surrendered January 13, 1838, imprisoned for 18 months for violating American neutrality.

1844   John H. Patterson, developer of National Cash Register Co., born in Dayton, OH; bought National Manufacturing Co. (1884), which he developed into NCR (died 1922).

1856   A.(bbot) Lawrence Lowell, president, Harvard U. (1909–33), born in Boston; had great impact on education (died 1943).

1857   Lucius W. Nieman, editor, part owner, *Milwaukee Journal*, born in Bear Creek, WI; endowed Nieman Fellowships for journalism at Harvard (died 1935).

1862   Battle of Fredericksburg (VA) occurred between 122,000 Union troops under Gen. A.E. Burnside and 78,000 Confederate troops under Gen. Robert E. Lee; massed attack failed, Union forces withdrew; Gen. Burnside was replaced by Gen. Joseph Hooker.

1863   Mason M. Patrick, chief of Air Service (1918–19) and Army Air Service (1921–27), born in Lewisburg, WV (died 1942).

1886   Roy S. Durstine, partner in advertising agency (BBDO — Batton, Barton, Durstine and Osborn) (1918–39), born in Jamestown, ND (died 1962).

1887   Alvin C. York, most decorated World War I American soldier, born in Pall Mall, TN; awarded Congressional Medal of Honor for capturing German machine gun nest and 90 men (died 1964).

1890   Marc(us C.) Connelly, playwright, coauthor (*Dulcy, Merton of the Movies, Beggar on Horseback*), author (*Green Pastures*), born in McKeesport, PA (died 1980).

1897   Drew Pearson, syndicated columnist with Robert Allen (1932–42), alone (1942–69), producing *Washington Merry-Go-Round*, born in Evanston, IL (died 1969).

1899   Harold K. Guinzburg, cofounder, Viking Press and founder of Literary Guild (1926), born in New York City (died 1961).

1915   Ross MacDonald, author of mystery novels featuring Lew Archer, detective, born in Las Gatos, CA, as Kenneth Millar (died 1983).

1920   George Shultz, Secretary of State (1982–89), born in New York City; Secretary of Labor (1968–70), director, Office of Management & Budget (1970–72); Secretary of Treasury (1972–74).

1921   Four-power treaty involving Pacific possessions was signed by United States, Great Britain, France, and Japan; effective August 17, 1923.

1923   Philip W. Anderson, physicist, born in Indianapolis; shared 1977 Nobel Physics Prize for work underlying computer memories, electronic devices.

1925 Dick Van Dyke, actor (*Bye Bye Birdie*—stage, *Mary Poppins*—screen, and television), born in West Plains, MO.

1977 A DC-3 crashed after takeoff at Evansville, IN; 29 were killed.

1979 Supreme Court ordered dismissal of suit by 24 congressmen challenging the president's termination of a defense treaty with Taiwan.

1988 Quadrennial Commission on Executive, Legislative and Judicial Salaries recommended 50 percent pay increase for Congress, federal judges, and other top federal officials; proposal approved by president but disapproved by Congress; compromise pay increases subsequently passed.

1994 American Eagle commuter plane crashed on approach to Raleigh-Durham, NC, airport; 15 persons were killed.

1995 Dow Jones industrial average closed at an all-time high of 5,216.47.

1997 Seventy members of World Trade Organization (including United States) agreed to open their banking, insurance, and securities markets to outside firms (U.S. already open).

2000 Al Gore conceded the presidential victory to his opponent after considering whether to contest the presidential vote count on the floor of Congress.

2001 President Bush formally withdrew country from Anti-Ballistic Missile Treaty to permit development and testing of antimissile weapons; withdrawal went into effect six months later.

2002 Cardinal Bernard Law of Boston resigned post; had been widely blamed for not being active enough in stopping child sexual abuse by priests — his actions considered a "cover-up" by critics.

2004 Oracle Corp. bought PeopleSoft for $10.3 billion after 18 months of wrangling and dispute; creates the world's second-biggest maker of business applications software.

14

1715 Thomas Dongan, governor of New York (1682–88), died at 81.

1773 Large number of Bostonians met to discuss the arrival of a ship loaded with tea; voted to ask owner to send ship and tea back to England.

1774 Ft. William and Mary in Portsmouth (NH) harbor captured by 400 men, probably the first blow for independence.

1775 Philander Chase, presiding Episcopal bishop (1843–52), born in Cornish, NH; frontier bishop (Ohio 1819–31, Illinois 1835); founder, Kenyon College (1824) (died 1852).

1777 Thomas Conway appointed major general against George Washington's recommendation; Conway led conspiracy (Conway Cabal) to supplant Washington with Horatio Gates; plot discovered, Conway resigned.

1779 James Madison elected to Continental Congress, the youngest delegate; served until 1786.

1780 Judah P. Spooner and Timothy Green, IV, published first newspaper in Vermont, the *Vermont Gazette and Green Mountain Post-Boy*, in Westminster.

1782 British evacuated Charleston, SC, after more than two years occupation.

1790 Alexander Hamilton proposed creation of a national bank; approved by Senate and House, signed by President Washington (February 25, 1791).

1794 Erastus Corning, a founder, first president, New York Central Railroad, born in Norwich, CT; mayor of Albany (died 1872).

1799 George Washington, after a ride in snow and rain around his estate, developed acute laryngitis; after being bled, he died at Mt. Vernon at 67; President John Adams asked Americans to wear crepe on their left arm for 30 days in his memory; eulogized in Congress by Henry Lee as "first in war, first in peace, first in the hearts of his countrymen."

1801 Joseph Lane, Oregon Territory governor (1848–50) and one of state's first senators (1859–61), born in Buncombe County, NC; general in Mexican War (died 1881).

1814 Battle of Lake Borgne preceded battle for New Orleans, with the British clearing the western approach to city and skirting its fortifications; British delayed attack on New Orleans because of their heavy losses, thus providing time for an organized defense.

1819 Alabama admitted to Union as the 22nd state.

1829 John M. Langston, president, Virginia Normal and Collegiate Institute (1885–97), born in Louisa, VA; minister to Haiti (1877–85) (died 1897).

1856 Louis Marshall, lawyer involved in many civil rights and labor cases, born in Syracuse, NY; a founder, Jewish Welfare Board; chairman, American Jewish Relief Committee during World War I (died 1929).

1884 Jane Cowl, actress (*Lilac Time, Smilin' Through, Within the Law, Common Clay*), born in Boston (died 1950).

1885 Brock Pemberton, theatrical director and producer (*Miss Lulu Bett, Strictly Dishonorable, Kiss the Boys Goodbye, Harvey*), born in Leavenworth, KS (died 1950).

1894 Eugene V. Debs sentenced to six months in prison for contempt of court during the Pullman strike, other leaders given three months.

1896 James H. Doolittle, Air Force general who led air raid on Tokyo (1942), born in Alameda, CA; commanded Air Force in North Africa invasion; commander, 9th Air Force in Europe (1944) (died 1993).

1902 Julia D. Grant, widow of President Grant, died in Washington at 76.

1904 Chicago Orchestra Hall opened with a concert conducted by Theodore Thomas.

1904 Senate began impeachment hearings against District Judge Charles Swayne of Florida for incompetence and corruption; acquitted February 27, 1905.

1909 Edward L. Tatum, geneticist, born in Boulder, CO; shared 1957 Nobel Physiology/Medicine Prize for discovering how genes transmit hereditary characteristics (died 1975).

1911 Spike (Lindley A.) Jones, leader of orchestra which featured unusual arrangements and sound effects, born in Long Beach, CA (died 1965).

1919 Shirley Jackson, short story writer ("The Lottery," "Life Among the Savages"), born in San Francisco (died 1965).

1920 Congress, as part of its naval appropriations bill, asked the president to call an international naval conference.

1934 Charlie Rich, country and Western singer, born in Forrest City, AR; known as the "Silver Fox"; made many hit recordings (died 1995).

1946 John D. Rockefeller, Jr., gave $8.5 million toward purchase of New York City property for the United Nations headquarters.

1965 Connecticut voters ratified their new state constitution by vote of 178,432 to 84,129.

1988 President Reagan, in a surprising reversal, authorized "a substantive dialogue" with the PLO (Palestine Liberation Organization); three weeks earlier a visa was denied PLO leader Yasser Arafat to come to the United States because the PLO was involved in terrorism.

1997 Iranian president Mohammad Khatani called for talks with the United States, changing his country's nearly 20-year-old anti–American attitude.

1998 President Clinton began trip to Israel to strengthen the earlier Palestinian-Israeli accord.

2001 Two Chicago area Islamic charities had all assets frozen by U.S. government; had received $8.5 million contributions previous year; U.S. fears groups a conduit for money to al-Qaeda terrorists.

2005 Largest U.S. trade deficit on record for October: $68.9 billion.

2006 Breast Cancer Conference in San Antonio, Texas, reported startling drop in latest available breast cancer statistics: 7 percent overall drop from 2002 to 2003 — largest one-year decline ever; in 2002 federal study linked hormone replacement therapy with increase in cancer and use of therapy dropped dramatically; cause-effect relationship between drop in use and drop in cancer rate assumed highly probable.

2006 Red Sox signed Japanese pitcher Daisuke Matsuzaka with a guaranteed $52 million over six-year contract; paid his home team $51.1 million merely for right to negotiate with him; career average: 108 victories and 60 losses; 1,355 strikeouts.

2006 Ahmet Ertegun, cofounder of Atlantic Records, died after two weeks in a coma; introduced and helped popularize a wide variety of modern musical talent to American audiences, including Ray Charles, Aretha Franklin, Rolling Stones, and Bette Midler.

15

1689 James Blair appointed ecclesiastical representative of Bishop of London in Virginia; founded College of William & Mary (1693), serving as its first president (1693–1743).

1770 Thomas Jefferson commissioned lieutenant of Albemarle County and "Chief Commander of all His Majesty's Militia, Horse and Foote" in that county.

1778 Maryland refused to ratify Articles of Confederation until the rights to western territories were clarified.

1791 Bill of Rights — the first ten amendments to the Constitution — went into effect after ratification by the states.

1795 Senate by 14–10 vote rejected nomination of John Rutledge for Supreme Court chief justice because of his speech opposing the Jay Treaty before his nomination.

1814 Hartford Convention began considering revisions in Constitution; ended January 5, 1815, with statement declaring that states had a right to protect their own best interests; set up committee to negotiate with the federal government but disbanded after the victory at New Orleans and the Treaty of Ghent.

1831 Franklin B. Sanborn, arranger of financing for John Brown's raid on Harper's Ferry, born in Hampton Falls, NH; narrowly avoided prosecution (died 1917).

1835 Mexican government abolished all local rights in Texas.

1836 Fire destroyed the Post Office and Patent Office buildings in Washington.

1837 George B. Post, architect who pioneered in skyscraper building, born in New York City; introduced elevators in buildings, using iron floor beams, supplying steam heat in buildings; among his buildings were City College of New York, New York Stock Exchange, the Wisconsin Capitol (died 1913).

1846 John E. Pillsbury, with U.S. Coast Survey (1875–91), making a study of Gulf Stream, born in Lowell, MA (died 1919).

1848 Edwin H. Blashfield, artist of murals in Library of Congress dome (*Evolution of Civilization*), born in New York City (died 1936).

1855 Kansas ratified its state constitution; prohibited slavery.

1861 Charles E. Duryea, automobile pioneer, born near Canton, IL; with brother, J. Frank, organized Duryea Motor Wagon Co. (1895), sold first car (1896); inventor of spray carburetor (1892), first to use pneumatic tires on cars (1893) (died 1938).

1863 Arthur D. Little, chemical engineer who devised various processes (chrome tanning, electrolytic manufacture of chlorates, artificial silk, gas), born in Boston; superintendent of first American mill producing sulphite wood pulp (died 1935).

1864 Union troops under Gens. George Thomas and John M. Schofield, routed Confederates under Gen. John B. Hood in two-day battle before Nashville.

1877 John T. McNicholas, Catholic Archbishop of Cincinnati (1925–50), born in County Mayo, Ireland (died 1950).

1888 Maxwell Anderson, playwright (*Eliza-beth the Queen, High Tor, Key Largo, Winterset, Anne of the Thousand Days*), born in Atlantic, PA (died 1959).

1890 Sitting Bull, 56-year-old Sioux chief who led his tribe against Americans, died after being shot in a scuffle with Indian police at Standing Rock (SD) reservation.

1892 J. Paul Getty, oil industry leader, who built family business into a vast company (1956), born in Minneapolis (died 1976).

1908 U.S. Circuit Court issued final decree against the tobacco trust, American Tobacco Co. et al. and restrained the combined companies from interstate and foreign trade.

1913 Muriel Rukeyser, poet of social and political themes (*Orpheus, Waterlily Fire, Elegies*), born in New York City (died 1980).

1938 President Franklin Roosevelt spoke at groundbreaking ceremonies for Jefferson Memorial in Washington.

1944 Plane in which Glenn Miller, orchestra leader, was a passenger disappeared on a flight from England to France.

1965 Walter M. Schirra, Jr., and Thomas P. Stafford completed first space rendezvous when their Gemini capsule joined with that of Frank Borman and James A. Lovell, Jr.

1967 Silver Bridge over Ohio River, connecting Pt. Pleasant, WV, and Kanauga, OH, collapsed; 46 persons were killed.

1976 *Argo Merchant* ran aground off Nantucket Island, resulting in a 7.7 million gallon oil spill.

2006 Capital punishment put on hold in two states: in California a federal judge was concerned that lethal injection was being done in a way to violate Constitutional prohibition of cruel and unnatural punishment; in Florida, Governor Jeb Bush suspended executions until an investigation could be made of why, two days earlier, the needles carrying the lethal drugs weren't inserted into veins properly and a second dose was required to complete the execution.

16

1773 Boston Tea Party took place as 50 to 60 colonists disguised as Mohawk Indians dumped 342 chests of tea from the vessel, Dartmouth, into the harbor to protest the import duty on tea.

1792 Abbott Lawrence, manufacturer who with two brothers founded textile industry in

Lawrence, MA, born in Groton, MA; represented Massachusetts in House (1835–40); minister to Great Britain (1849–52) (died 1855).

1811 Earthquake centered near New Madrid, MO, resulted in an area of 30,000 square miles sinking from five to 15 feet; listed among the greatest known earthquakes in history.

1817 John S. Carlile, a leader in creating West Virginia, which he represented in the Senate (1861–65), born in Winchester, VA; represented Virginia in House (1855–57) (died 1878).

1828 John Beatty, Union general at Murfreesboro, Lookout Mountain, and Knoxville, born near Sandusky, OH; represented Ohio in House (1868–73) (died 1914).

1830 John F. Hartranft, governor of Pennsylvania (1873–79), born near Pottstown, PA; was a Union general in Civil War (died 1889).

1833 Seaman A. Knapp, developer of rice growing in Louisiana, born in Schroon Lake, NY (died 1911).

1835 The "great fire" in New York City destroyed 700 buildings in the heart of the city, causing $20 million in property damage.

1844 Helen F.G. Villard, head of Women's Peace Society (1919–28), born in Boston; a founder of NAACP (died 1928).

1846 Mormon Battalion, enroute from New Mexico to California, captured Tucson.

1846 Convention in Madison framed a Wisconsin state constitution; rejected by a referendum in April 1847.

1854 Joseph Fels, founder, Fels-Naphtha (Soap) Co., born in Halifax Court House, VA; championed single-tax program (died 1914).

1854 Austin M. Knight, commander, Asiatic Fleet (1917–18) and president, Naval War College (1913–17), born in Ware, MA (died 1927).

1857 Edward E. Barnard, photographed Milky Way with wide-angle cameras opening a new astronomical field of study, born in Nashville; discovered first new satellite of Jupiter since Galileo (died 1923).

1857 New chamber for the House of Representatives completed in Capitol.

1863 George Santayana, philosopher and author (*The Life of Reason, The Sense of Beauty, The Last Puritan*), born in Madrid; professor at Harvard U. (1889–1912) (died 1952).

1863 Ralph A. Cram, supervising architect, Princeton U. (1907–29), born in Hampton Falls, NH; helped plan buildings for West Point, Rice Institute, Cathedral of St. John the Divine (died 1942).

1868 Benevolent and Protective Order of Elks organized in New York City.

1877 Artur Bodanzky, conductor, Metropolitan Opera Company (1915–39), born in Vienna (died 1939).

1901 Margaret Mead, anthropologist with American Museum of Natural History (1926–69), born in Philadelphia; author (*Coming of Age in Samoa, Sex and Temperament*) (died 1978).

1907 Fleet of 16 American battleships began world cruise to demonstrate American naval strength; returned February 21, 1909.

1918 Colorado governor signed a statewide prohibition law; prohibition went into effect in Nevada.

1934 John A. Jacob, president and chief executive officer, National Urban League (1982–1994), born in Trout, LA.

1941 French liner *Normandie* in New York Harbor taken over by U.S. Navy.

1943 Collision of two railroad streamliners near Lumberton, NC, resulted in death of 73.

1944 Battle of the Bulge began as Germans tried to sever American lines in the Belgium-Luxembourg area; turned back by Christmas Day.

1951 Plane plunged into Elizabeth River after takeoff from Elizabeth (NJ) Airport; 56 persons were killed.

1960 Midair collision of two airliners over New York City resulted in 134 deaths.

1963 President Lyndon Johnson signed bill setting up $1.2 billion construction program for college classrooms, laboratories, and libraries.

1974 Presidents Ford and d'Estaing of France completed two days of meetings on energy and gold policies on the island of Martinique.

1988 Lyndon H. Larouche, Jr., political maverick, convicted on 13 counts of tax- and mail-fraud conspiracy for cheating the IRS and his supporters; a perennial presidential candidate, Larouche faces maximum penalty of 65 years in prison and fines totaling $3.25 million.

1988 Ambassador Robert H. Pelletreau, Jr., and four representatives of the Palestine Liberation Organization met in Tunis for 90 minutes in a historic meeting of the two sides.

1998 U.S. opened attack on military installations and suspected weapons sites in Iraq; Great Britain also took part. The attack resulted from Iraq's refusal to allow UN inspections of sites.

1998 House Republicans postponed a vote on impeachment articles set for December 17, because of the action in Iraq.

1998 Owens Corning announced the company will pay $1.2 billion to settle 90 percent of the lawsuits it faces from individuals exposed to asbestos.

2000 President-elect Bush announced retired General Colin Powell to become Secretary of State; first African American to hold post.

2000 Tornado hit Englewood, Alabama; 11 deaths.

2001 Generous but not all used: In blood drives after September 11 terrorist attacks, Red Cross collected 928,293 pints of blood; 49,860 pints destroyed because hospitals did not need it all.

2004 Financial Accounting Standards Board, which sets the accounting standards for the industry, ordered that, as of varying dates in the following year, stock options must be deducted as expenses on all companies' profit-and-loss calculations; change to hit Silicon Valley's computer-related industries the hardest.

2004 Second large "Silicon Valley" computer industry merger in less than a week: computer security software manufacturer Symantec Corp. buys Veritas Software, a firm emphasizing storage of data; $13.5 billion deal to create one of five largest software companies in world.

2005 Joseph L. Owades died at 86. Pioneer post–Prohibition beer maker; trained many of America's top brewmasters; created Samuel Adams Boston Lager and invented the first "light beer."

2006 First successful launch from the Mid-Atlantic Regional Spaceport, Wallops Island, Virginia; two satellites put into orbit; facility shares property used by NASA for over 13,000 suborbital launches over past decades.

17

1540 Hernando DeSoto reached Mississippi River; remained until April 25, 1541.

1623 Plymouth Colony established trial by jury.

1734 William Floyd, colonial leader, born in Brookhaven, NY; member, Continental Congress (1774–77, 1778–83), signer of Declaration of Independence; represented New York in House (1789–91) (died 1821).

1748 James M. Varnum, Revolutionary War general at Forts Mercer and Mifflin on the Delaware, born in Dracut, MA; member, Continental Congress (1780–82, 1786–87) (died 1789).

1754 George Washington leased Mt. Vernon

from his half-brother's widow at an annual rent of 15,000 lbs. of tobacco; inherited estate in 1761.

1758 Nathaniel Macon, Speaker of House (1801–07) and Senate president pro tem (1826–27), born in what is now Warren County, NC; represented North Carolina in House (1791–1815) and in Senate (1815–28) (died 1837).

1762 Pliny Earle, inventor of wool-and-cotton carding machinery, born in Leicester, MA (died 1832).

1777 France recognized the independence of the 13 American colonies.

1792 South Carolina enacted law prohibiting importation of slaves; amended December 18, 1817, repealed December 16, 1818.

1797 Joseph Henry, physicist and first secretary, director, Smithsonian Institution (1846–78), born in Albany, NY; developed first electromagnet, primitive versions of telegraph, electric motor; unit of induction, "henry," named for him (died 1878).

1807 John Greenleaf Whittier, a founder, editor, *Atlantic Monthly*, born in Haverhill, MA; poet ("Ichabod," "Barbara Fritchie") (died 1892).

1815 John Bapst, founder Boston College (1858), born in Laroche, Switzerland (died 1887).

1817 Henry R. Worthington, developer of direct steam pump (1859), born in New York City; invented duplex steam feed pump (died 1880).

1824 Thomas S. King, Unitarian clergyman (Boston 1848–60, San Francisco 1860–64), born in New York City; helped save California for the Union cause (died 1864).

1835 Alexander Agassiz, zoologist who developed, headed Calumet, Hecla copper mines, born in Neuchatel, Switzerland; curator, Harvard Museum of Cooperative Zoology (1874–85), director (1902–10) (died 1910).

1860 James H. McGraw, publisher of technical magazines (McGraw-Hill 1916–48), born in Panama, NY (died 1948).

1861 Arthur E. Kennelly, electrical engineer who established units, standards adopted internationally, born in Bombay, India (died 1939).

1866 Supreme Court in Milligan case held that no branch of government has power to suspend writ of habeas corpus where the courts are open.

1892 Edwin J. Cohn, chemist with Harvard (1912–53), born in New York City; did much work on fractionating blood (died 1953).

1894 Arthur Fiedler, founder, conductor, Boston Pops Orchestra (1930–79), born in Boston (died 1979).

1903 Wilbur and Orville Wright demonstrated first motor-driven airplane at Kitty Hawk, NC, with Orville first flying 120 feet in 12 seconds; Wilbur then went 852 feet in 59 seconds.

1903 Erskine Caldwell, author (*Tobacco Road, God's Little Acre*), born in White Oak, GA; collaborated with photographer-wife, Margaret Bourke-White on several pictorial books (died 1987).

1906 William McM. Martin, Jr., first salaried president, New York Stock Exchange (1938–41), born in St. Louis; chairman, Federal Reserve Board (1951–70); director, Export-Import Bank (1945–50).

1908 Willard F. Libby, physicist, born in Grand Valley, CO; awarded 1960 Nobel Chemistry Prize for using carbon-14 to measure time in archaeology and geology (died 1980).

1927 Submarine S-4 sank after colliding with a Coast Guard destroyer off Provincetown, MA; all 40 men aboard were lost.

1941 Rear Admiral Chester Nimitz replaced Admiral Huband Kimmel as commander-in-chief of American Pacific Fleet.

1944 Three American destroyers sank during a typhoon in the Philippines Sea; 790 lives lost.

1985 President Reagan vetoed a bill which would have limited American imports of textiles.

1992 President Bush and the heads of Canada and Mexico signed copies of the North American Free Trade Agreement (NAFTA) in their respective capitals.

1998 Attack on Iraqi military targets was intensified. Congress voiced its support of the presidential decision to attack Iraq.

2000 Teamsters in Detroit approved new contract, ending a 5½ year newspaper strike.

2001 Although not a cure for the common cold, scientists in Chicago announced a medicine that reduces its potency and duration.

2004 Intelligence Reform and Terrorism Act of 2004 signed into law by president; most comprehensive reorganization of intelligence gathering in decades.

2006 Revolt within U.S. Episcopal Church: Two large historic Virginia congregations that came into existence prior to the American Revolution seceded from U.S. Episcopal control along with at least five smaller parishes; they put themselves under the Convocation for Anglicans in North America, an organizational subsidiary of the Episcopal Church of Nigeria. Local churches upset by "liberal" theological drift in U.S. church and appointment of openly gay Episcopal bishop in 2003.

18

1680 Josiah Winslow, governor of Plymouth Colony (1673–80), died at about 51; was the first native-born governor.

1776 North Carolina convention adopted state constitution; named Richard Caswell governor.

1787 New Jersey convention unanimously ratified Constitution, becoming the third state in the Union.

1789 Virginia consented to separation of Kentucky counties from its jurisdiction.

1813 British captured Ft. Niagara at Niagara Falls in a surprise attack.

1819 Isaac T. Hecker, Catholic priest who was principal founder of Paulist Fathers and its superior (1858–88), born in New York City; founder, *Catholic World* (1865), *Young Catholic* (1870); organized Catholic Publication Society (1870) (died 1888).

1820 Alabama legislature chartered state university at Tuscaloosa.

1835 Lyman Abbott, Congregational clergyman and editor, born in Roxbury, MA; with *Illustrated Christian Weekly* (1876), coeditor, *Christian Union* (1876–81), editor-in-chief (1881–99); author (*Theology of an Evolutionist, The Spirit of Democracy*) (died 1922).

1858 *Territorial Enterprise*, first newspaper in Nevada, published by William L. Jernegen and Alfred James.

1860 South Carolina convention in Charleston adopted secession ordinance and declared itself an independent commonwealth; formally adopted by legislature December 20.

1861 Edward A. MacDowell, composer (*Indian Suite, Woodland Sketches, Sea Pieces*), born in New York City (died 1908).

1864 Samuel F. Cadman, Congregational clergyman who was first radio minister, born in Wellington, England; president, Federal Council of Churches of Christ (1924–28) and its radio minister (1928–36) (died 1936).

1872 William H. Standley, chief of naval operations (1933–37), born in Ukiah, CA; ambassador to Russia (1942–43) (died 1963).

1881 Gladys Dick, physician who with husband, George F., made important discoveries about scarlet fever, born in Pawnee City, NE (died 1963).

1886 Ty(rus R.) Cobb, probably greatest offensive baseball player, born in Narrows, GA; career batting average of .367 with 4,191 hits in 33 years, mostly with Detroit; one of first five named to Baseball Hall of Fame (died 1961).

1888 Robert Moses, headed New York state and New York City park commissions (1924–64), born in New Haven, CT; president, New York World's Fair (1964–65) (died 1981).

1890 Edwin H. Armstrong, radio pioneer who developed FM (frequency modulation) radio transmission, born in New York City; also invented superheterodyne circuit, basic to modern radio, radar, television (died 1954).

1895 Anti-Saloon League founded in Washington, DC.

1898 Fletcher Henderson, influential jazz arranger and orchestra leader, born in Cuthbert, GA (died 1952).

1904 George Stevens, movies director (*Gunga Din, A Place in the Sun, Shane, Giant, Diary of Anne Frank*), born in Oakland, CA (died 1975).

1913 Ray Meyer, DePaul basketball coach (1942–85), born in Chicago.

1915 Widowed President Wilson married a widow, Mrs. Edith B. Galt, in Washington, DC.

1916 Betty Grable, screen actress who was the World War II pin-up girl, born in St. Louis (died 1973).

1916 President Wilson suggested peace negotiations to World War I belligerents; Central Powers and Turkey suggested no peace terms but asked for a meeting in a neutral country; Allies asked for reparations, return of conquered areas, and freedom for Czechs and Slavs.

1939 Dr. Harold E. Varmus, who shared 1989 Nobel Physiology/Medicine Prize for his cancer research, born in Oceanside, NY.

1941 Office of Defense Transportation created by executive order.

1947 Steven Spielberg, movie producer (*ET, Raiders of the Lost Ark*), born in Cincinnati.

1958 *Score* satellite launched, becoming first to transmit voice messages from space.

1964 President Lyndon Johnson announced a new sea-level canal would be constructed in Central America or Colombia; a new treaty was proposed to Panama to replace 1903 pact.

1972 President Nixon ordered resumption of bombing over North Vietnam.

1998 House of Representatives began debating the four articles of impeachment passed by its Judiciary Committee.

1998 U.S. and British attacks on Iraqi military targets continued; Russia denounced the attacks.

2002 Creator of Black Entertainment Television purchased NBA expansion team to be based in Charlotte, NC; Robert Johnson becomes first black owner of major professional sports franchise.

2006 Robert Gates sworn in to replace Donald H. Rumsfeld as Secretary of Defense; Rumsfeld served second longest of any man in post, falling just nine days short of Robert McNamara's record; consensus opinion: forced out of office to calm public resentment at inability of American forces to decisively gain upper hand in occupation of Iraq.

2006 Federal government presented proposed rules to drive Medicaid medicine costs down: Studies indicate that current system pays up to 35 percent over drug cost given mass buyers in private industry; the program, administered by the individual states, to restructure payment rules to encourage purchase of generics when available.

2006 Pioneer television cartoonist Joe Barbera died; with William (Bill) Hanna, created and popularized such 1960s hits as *Huckleberry Hound, Yogi Bear,* and *Scooby-Do.* As studio cartoonists the two created *Tom and Jerry* for MGM in the 1930s.

19

1675 New England troops led by Gen. Josiah Winslow in the "Great Swamp Fight" captured the Narragansett fort with more than 1,000 Indians killed or captured.

1714 John Winthrop, who established first American experimental physics laboratory (1746), born in Boston; did important astronomy research at Harvard (1738–79) (died 1779).

1732 *Poor Richard's Almanac* published in Philadelphia for first time by Benjamin Franklin.

1753 John Taylor, pioneer in crop rotation, born in Caroline County, VA; represented Virginia in Senate (1792–94, 1803, 1822–24) (died 1824).

1776 Thomas Paine published first issue of "American Crisis," in which he stated: "These are the times that try men's souls..."

1777 Gen. Washington and his troops established winter headquarters in Valley Forge, PA.

1779 Council of Pennsylvania conducted a

court-martial of Benedict Arnold on two trivial charges brought by Philadelphia permitting the entry of unauthorized vessels into port and using state wagons to transport private property; court directed a reprimand by the commander-in-chief.

1813 After British captured Ft. Niagara the previous day, they burned villages of Youngstown, Lewiston, and Manchester.

1814 Edwin M. Stanton, Secretary of War (1862–67) whose dismissal led to impeachment proceedings against President Andrew Johnson, born in Steubenville, OH; Attorney General (1860–61); when impeachment failed, he resigned (May 1868); named to Supreme Court (1869) but died before he could take his seat.

1817 James J. Archer, Confederate general who served at Manassas, Antietam, and Gettysburg, born in Hartford County, MD; captured at Gettysburg and died soon after his release in 1864.

1846 Ambrose Swasey, inventor of a range and position finder, born in Exeter, NH; cofounder, Warner & Swasey (1881), makers of machine tools, astronomical instruments (died 1937).

1849 Henry C. Frick, a leader in consolidation which resulted in U.S. Steel Co. (1901), born in West Overton, PA; chairman, Carnegie Steel Co. (1899–1900); endowed Frick Museum of Art, New York City (which once was his home) (died 1919).

1852 Albert A. Michelson, who headed physics department, U. of Chicago (1892–1931), born in Strelno, Germany; established speed of light; first American awarded Nobel Physics Prize (1907) for spectroscopic and meteorologic investigations (died 1931).

1865 Minnie Maddern Fiske, actress who popularized Ibsen plays in United States, born in New Orleans (died 1932).

1869 George H. Doran, founded publishing company (1907) which merged with Doubleday (1927) to form Doubleday, Doran & Co., born in Toronto (died 1956).

1888 Fritz Reiner, orchestra conductor (Cincinnati 1922–31, Pittsburgh 1938–48, Chicago 1953–62), born in Budapest (died 1963).

1890 State University of Oklahoma founded in Norman; opened 1892.

1894 Ford Frick, New York sportswriter who served as baseball commissioner (1951–65), born in Wawaka, IN; named to Baseball Hall of Fame (died 1978).

1901 Oliver H.P. LaFarge, author (*Laughing Boy*), born in New York City; president, American Association of Indian Affairs (1933–42, 1948–63) (died 1963).

1903 George Snell, scientist, born in Bradford, MA; shared 1980 Nobel Physiology/Medicine Prize for discoveries of how genetic makeup determines body's response to infection and cancer development.

1907 Mine explosion at Jacob's Creek, PA, killed 239 miners.

1920 David H. Susskind, host of syndicated television show and producer, born in New York City (died 1987).

1929 William Safire, columnist, *New York Times*, born in New York City; presidential assistant (1969–73).

1941 Office of Censorship, headed by Byron Price, created by executive order.

1943 William C. DeVries, who headed team which placed first Jarvik-7 heart into a human being (1982), born in New York City.

1945 President Truman named Eleanor Roosevelt, widow of President Franklin Roosevelt, to American UN delegation; she later headed UN Human Rights Commission.

1950 Gen. Dwight D. Eisenhower appointed supreme commander of European defense by NATO ministers; resigned May 30, 1952, to accept Republican presidential nomination.

1960 Fire aboard aircraft carrier *Constellation*, under construction in Brooklyn Navy Yard, killed 50 and injured 150, doing $50 million damage.

1967 President Lyndon Johnson began weeklong round-the-world trip, including stops in Australia, Thailand, South Vietnam, Pakistan, Italy, and the Azores.

1974 Nelson A. Rockefeller confirmed and sworn in as vice president.

1984 United States withdrew from UNESCO (United Nations Educational, Scientific & Cultural Organization) because of agency's mismanagement and politicization.

1987 Texaco Inc. and Pennzoil Co. signed final settlement designed to end their $10.3 billion lawsuit and close most costly legal battle in American history.

1992 Dana Andrews, movie actor, died at 83.

1998 House of Representatives, voting close to partisan lines, approved two of four articles of impeachment; Article 1, approved 228–206, accused President Clinton of perjury; Article 2, approved 221–212, accused President of witness tampering and obstruction of justice; President said he will not resign.

1998   Rep. Bob Livingston of Louisiana, during Clinton impeachment debate, announced he would not assume speakership and will resign his seat; action came two days after he admitted to having extramarital affair.

1998   Operation Desert Fox, the attack on Iraq, ended; mission declared a success.

2000   Shift in Federal Reserve priorities to avoid potential recession as that becomes a more serious perceived danger than that of inflation.

2001   Comcast bought AT&T cable television, making it largest cable company in nation.

2006   Labor Department released startling November inflation numbers: expected .5 percent jump turned out to be a full 2 percent (30-year high); experts expected "core" price index which excludes volatile food and energy to have .2 percent increase but it soared 1.3 percent (passing any increase in last quarter century).

20

1606   Colonists set sail from England to Virginia in three ships.

1686   Sir Edmund Andros arrived in Boston to assume leadership of New England government and to organize a Dominion of New England (to include New York, New Jersey, and Pennsylvania) for more effective military operations in the event of war with France and for better enforcement of Navigation Acts.

1744   Joshua Clayton, served as "president" of Delaware (1789–92) and its first governor (1792–96), born in Cecil County, MD (died 1798).

1776   Third Continental Congress opened in Baltimore.

1783   Virginia ceded western lands to central government opening way for Maryland to ratify the Articles of Confederation.

1803   United States took formal possession of Louisiana after its purchase, with William C.C. Claiborne, Mississippi Territory governor, representing the United States and Pierre Clement de Laussat the French.

1812   Sacagawea, Indian interpreter, died at about 25; she was only woman to accompany Lewis and Clark Expedition.

1813   Samuel J. Kirkwood, Interior Secretary (1881–82), born in Harford County, MD; served Iowa as governor (1860–64, 1876–77) and represented it in Senate (1866–67, 1877–81) (died 1894).

1832   Robert Y. Hayne, South Carolina governor, issued counter-proclamation to President Jackson's nullification proclamation; called for a general convention of states to consider federal-state relations.

1860   South Carolina seceded from Union, stating that "the union now subsisting between South Carolina and other states, under the name of 'United States of America' is hereby dissolved."

1862   Confederate troops captured Union supply base at Holly Springs, MS, destroying large quantity of supplies.

1864   Gen. William T. Sherman's Union troops took over Savannah, completing eight-months march to the sea; Confederate troops retreated to Charleston, SC.

1867   William W. "Pudge" Heffelfinger, legendary football player, born in Minneapolis; starred for Yale (1888–91), named to its all-time team (died 1954).

1868   Harvey S. Firestone, Firestone Tire & Rubber Co. organizer (1900), president (1903–32), chairman (1932–38), born in Columbiana, OH; promoted rubber growing in the Philippines and South America (died 1938).

1876   Walter S. Adams, director of Mt. Wilson Observatory (1923–46), born in Syria to American missionary parents; developed method of determining distance of a star from earth by comparing its luminosity to its apparent brightness (died 1956).

1879   Earle Ovington, first American airmail pilot (1911), born in Chicago; invented various electrical appliances, including high-frequency apparatus (died 1936).

1881   Branch W. Rickey, baseball manager, club president (Brooklyn, St. Louis NL, Pittsburgh) born in Stockdale, OH; instituted "farm" system; brought first black player (Jackie Robinson) into major leagues; named to Baseball Hall of Fame (died 1965).

1884   William G. Mennen, president, Mennen & Co. (toiletries) (1916–65), born in Newark, NJ (died 1968).

1899   John J. Sparkman, Alabama legislator (House 1936–46 and Senate 1946–78), born in Hartselle, AL; 1952 Democratic vice presidential candidate (died 1985).

1900   Ted Fio Rito, bandleader and composer (*King for a Day; Laugh, Clown*), born in Newark, NJ (died 1971).

1901   Robert J. Van de Graaff, nuclear physicist known for development of high-voltage electrostatic generator, born in Tuscaloosa, AL (died 1967).

1904 Irene Dunne, screen actress (*The Awful Truth*, *Life with Father*), born in Louisville, KY (died 1990).

1930 President Hoover signed $116 million Emergency Construction Act to aid the unemployed and the $45 million Drought Relief Act.

1941 Admiral Ernest King named commander-in-chief of American naval forces.

1945 Senate by 65–7 vote and House by 344–15 passed the United Nations Participation Act, making the United States a member.

1952 Air Force plane crashed on takeoff at Larson Air Force Base, Moses Lake, WA; 87 were killed.

1967 Weeklong blizzard raged through southwestern United States, killed 51.

1989 Invasion force of about 20,000 American troops overthrew regime of Gen. Manuel A. Noriega in Panama; Noriega went into hiding for several days, then sought refuge in Vatican mission in Panama City; surrendered to American drug agents January 3, 1990, and flew to Miami to stand trial on drug charges; Panama Canal traffic halted for one day by the invasion, first closing in 175 years.

1998 A Houston woman, 27-year-old Nkem Chukwu, delivered seven children—five girls, two boys; another child, a girl, born December 8; first known surviving set of octuplets.

2000 President Bill Clinton approved government regulations to severely reduce auto and truck emissions during following decade.

2002 Republican Governor of Alaska Frank Murkowski had resigned U.S. Senate seat to run for governorship; today, as governor, appoints his daughter as replacement Senator.

2002 Trent Lott resigned as Senate Republican Majority leader due to backlash at his praise of Strom Thurmond in speaking of the segregationist period of Thurmond's life.

21

1624 Charter of Swedish West India Co. granted to William Usselinx under which a colony was established on the Delaware River.

1719 *Boston Gazette*, third American newspaper, began publication under William Brocker; lasted until 1798.

1740 Arthur Lee, who arranged French help for Continental Army, born in Westmoreland County, VA; made several other foreign missions (died 1792).

1790 Samuel Slater began production in Pawtucket, RI, in first American cotton mill, using new cotton cording and spindle mill machinery.

1837 Joseph G. McCoy, pioneer cattleman who helped open Chisholm Trail, born in Sangamon County, IL; began driving cattle from Texas to Abilene, KS (died 1915).

1860 Henrietta Szold, founder, president, Hadassah, American Women's Zionist Organization (1916–26), born in Baltimore (died 1945).

1866 Fetterman Massacre occurred near Ft. Kearny, WY, when 90 American soldiers under Capt. William J. Fetterman were massacred by Sioux Indians.

1876 Alfred I. DuPont, president, DuPont Co. (1919–26), born in Wilmington, DE (died 1963).

1890 Herman J. Muller, geneticist with Indiana U. (1945–67), born in New York City; awarded 1946 Nobel Physiology/Medicine Prize for work on hereditary effects of X-rays on genes (died 1967).

1891 John W. McCormack, Speaker of House (1962–71), born in Boston; represented Massachusetts in House (1928–71), majority leader (1940–41) (died 1980).

1892 Walter Hagen, one of three best golfers of 1900–50 era, born in Rochester, NY; won British (four times), American (two) and French Opens in 1920s (died 1969).

1895 Eric Johnston, U.S. Chamber of Commerce national director (1924–41), president (1942–45), born in Washington, DC; president, Motion Picture Producers & Distributors (1945–52) (died 1963).

1918 Donald T. Regan, Treasury Secretary (1981–85), White House chief of staff (1985–87), born in Cambridge, MA; was chairman, Merrill Lynch & Co.

1926 Joe (Joseph) Paterno, football coach at Penn State U. since 1966, born in New York City; teams won nearly 300 games.

1928 President Coolidge signed legislation for construction of Boulder Dam; construction began September 17, 1930; completed 1936; renamed Hoover Dam.

1935 Phil Donahue, host of televised national talk show, born in Cleveland.

1937 Jane Fonda, screen actress (*Klute*, *Coming Home*, *On Golden Pond*), born in New York City; social activist, physical fitness authority.

1944 Bastogne besieged by German force; siege lifted December 26.

1951 Explosion and fire in a West Frankfort, IL, coal mine took 119 lives.

1954 Chris Evert (Lloyd), tennis player who won 157 championships in 1970–80s, born in Ft. Lauderdale, FL.

1959 Florence Griffith Joyner, winner of three Olympic gold medals (1988) in track events, born.

1979 Congress approved $1.5 billion in federal loan guarantees to financially strapped Chrysler Corp.

1988 Drexel Burnham Lambert, Inc., agreed to plead guilty to six federal felony counts and pay $650 million fine to settle biggest securities fraud case in history.

1988 Pan American 747, Flight 103, enroute from London to New York City exploded in midair over Lockerbie, Scotland, killing all 259 aboard and 11 on the ground; a week later investigators determined that a bomb in a suitcase was the cause.

2006 National Institute on Drug Abuse released a survey of some 50,000 eighth, tenth, and twelfth graders that indicated illegal drug use down a dramatic 23 percent since 2001; only 14.9 percent admitted using such substances; on the other hand usage of over-the-counter medicines or prescription drugs for recreational purposes had grown significantly.

22

1696 James E. Oglethorpe, British general who led formation of Georgia colony and founded Savannah, born in London; received charter 1732, accompanied first group of immigrants (1733–34), returning in 1735–36 and 1738–43 (died 1785).

1719 First Pennsylvania newspaper, *American Weekly Mercury*, published in Philadelphia by Andrew Bradford and John Copson.

1727 William Ellery, colonial leader, born in Newport, RI; member, Continental Congress (1776–81, 1783–85), signer of Declaration of Independence; chief justice, Rhode Island (1785) (died 1820).

1775 Esek Hopkins named commander-in-chief of colonial fleet and captains (John Paul Jones then a first lieutenant); Hopkins faced many difficulties, relieved of command 1778.

1789 Levi Woodbury, associate justice, Supreme Court (1845–51), born in Francestown, NH; Secretary of Navy (1831–34), of Treasury (1834–41); represented New Hampshire in Senate (1825–31, 1841–45) and served as its governor (1823–25) (died 1851).

1807 Congress passed Embargo Act, the first designed to bring warring powers (Great Britain and France) to terms and end severe effects on American commerce; proved unenforceable and withdrawn March 1, 1809.

1821 Josiah B. Grinnell, founder of Grinnell, IA (1854), and instrumental in planning Grinnell college, born in New Haven, CT; represented Iowa in House (1863–67) (died 1891).

1823 Thomas W.S. Higginson, Unitarian clergyman active in anti-slavery movement, born in Cambridge, MA; colonel of first black regiment (1862–64); biographer (Longfellow, Whittier) (died 1911).

1826 James S. Negly, Union general at Murfreesboro, born in East Liberty, PA (died 1901).

1828 Rachel Jackson, wife of President Jackson, died in Nashville at 61.

1842 Joseph B. Bloomingdale, cofounder of department store, born in New York City; instituted ten-hour work day and half day off per week (died 1904).

1843 Prentiss Ingraham, author of about 700 adventure "dime" novels, born in Adams County, MS; many of the novels were about his friend, Buffalo Bill (died 1904).

1852 Opie Read, founder, editor of humorous journal *Arkansas Traveler* (1883–91), born Nashville; author of adventure stories (died 1939).

1856 Frank B. Kellogg, awarded Nobel Peace Prize (1929) as coauthor of Kellogg-Briand peace pact, born in Potsdam, NY; successful federal prosecutor of antitrust cases (died 1937).

1862 Connie Mack, baseball manager of Philadelphia AL (1901–51), born as Cornelius McGillicuddy; team won nine pennants, five world championships; named to Baseball Hall of Fame (died 1956).

1869 Edwin Arlington Robinson, poet (*The Town Down the River, Merlin, Lancelot, Tristram*), born in Head Tide, ME (died 1935).

1869 Bainbridge Colby, secretary of state (1920–21), born in St. Louis (died 1950).

1883 Edgard Varese, a leading experimenter in composing 20th-century music, born in Paris (died 1965).

1885 Deems Taylor, composer (*Peter Ibbetson, The King's Henchman, Jurgen*), born in New York City; music critic and radio commentator of New York Philharmonic broadcasts (died 1966).

1901 Andre Kostelanetz, famed for radio

broadcasts of orchestra music from 1928 on, born in Leningrad; conductor of Boston Symphony (died 1980).

1903 Haldan K. Hartline, biophysicist who shared 1967 Nobel Physiology/Medicine Prize for work on human eye, born in Bloomsburg, PA (died 1983).

1911 Grote Reber, astronomer who built first radio telescope (1937), born in Wheaton, IL; pioneer in radio astronomy, mapped sources of light and low frequency.

1912 Claudia Alta Taylor (Ladybird) Johnson, wife of President Lyndon Johnson, born in Karnack, TX.

1919 About 250 alien radicals were deported.

1922 James C. Wright, Jr., Speaker of House (1987–89), born in Ft. Worth, TX; represented Texas in House (1955–89).

1941 Amended Selective Service Act signed, extending military service to those between 20 and 44, with registration for all men between 18 and 64.

1944 Steve (Stephen N.) Carlton, baseball pitcher (mostly St. Louis NL, Philadelphia NL), who won 329 games and had 4,136 strikeouts, born in Miami; won Cy Young Award four times and named to Baseball Hall of Fame.

1977 Explosion in grain elevator in Westwego, LA, caused death of 35 persons.

1993 Wal-Mart announced it will discontinue the sale of handguns in its 2,000 department stores.

2005 Presidential $1 Coin Act became law and provided for all presidents to be depicted on the coins; four new ones to be issued each year.

2006 Praised two years previously when she became the first lesbian fire chief in a major city, Bonnie Bleskachek was demoted today and had her pay reduced by $40,000 by 8–5 Minneapolis, Minnesota, City Council vote; she had been accused by three female and one male firefighter of sexual harassment and discrimination and had vigorously opposed the accusations. Decision was a compromise between retaining her in current post and concern over a lawsuit if fired.

2006 Population growth estimated by Census Bureau (2000 vs. July 1, 2006); major up states include: Nevada (24.9 percent), Arizona (20.2 percent), Georgia (14.4 percent), Utah (14.2 percent), Idaho (13.3 percent), Texas (12.7 percent), North Carolina (10.1 percent); only two states decline: Louisiana (-4.1 percent) and North Dakota (-1.0 percent).

23

1770 Demetrius A. Gallitzin, first Catholic priest ordained and trained in United States, born in The Hague, Netherlands; served as missionary in western Pennsylvania (died 1840).

1775 Royal proclamation issued closing American colonies to all commerce, effective March 1, 1776.

1778 Col. Archibald Campbell led 3,500 British troops to mouth of Savannah River; six days later they dispersed small American force holding the city.

1783 Gen. George Washington appeared before Congress in Annapolis to resign his commission and "to take leave of all the employments of public life."

1784 Continental Congress, which had been meeting in Trenton, NJ, voted to move to New York City until a permanent capital was ready; Congress named commission to lay out a federal district on the banks of the Delaware.

1788 Maryland legislature ceded ten square miles of land to Congress for a seat of government.

1805 Joseph Smith, Mormon Church founder, born in Sharon, VT; began having visions (1820) telling him the church of Christ had been withdrawn from earth and he was to restore it; received golden plates (1827) which he translated into *The Book of Mormon*; founded church April 6, 1830, at Fayette, NY; moved church successively to Ohio, Missouri, and Illinois; arrested and jailed, then pulled from Illinois jail by non–Mormon mob, killed June 27, 1844.

1814 Advance guard of 2,400 British troops landed seven miles below New Orleans; turned back by American attack.

1823 Traditional Christmas story written by Clement C. Moore ("Twas the night before Christmas...") appeared anonymously in Troy, NY, *Sentinel*.

1833 Charles B. Richards, engineer who invented first steam-engine indicator suitable for high-speed engines, born in Brooklyn; invented machine for testing strength of metals; professor, Sheffield Scientific School, Yale U. (1884–1909) (died 1919).

1850 Oscar B. Straus, Secretary of Commerce & Labor (1906–09), born in Otterberg, Germany; minister to Turkey (1887–89, 1898–1900, 1906–10); member, Permanent Court of Arbitration (1902–06) (died 1926).

1853 William H. Moody, associate justice, Supreme Court (1906–10), born in Newbury, MA; Secretary of Navy (1902–04), Attorney General (1904–06); represented Massachusetts in House (1895–1902) (died 1917).

1856 James B. Duke, with brother, developed American Tobacco Co. which he headed (1890–1911), born in Durham, NC; large donor to Trinity college, which became Duke U. (died 1925).

1860 Harriet Monroe, founder, editor, *Poetry Magazine* (1912–36), born in Chicago (died 1936).

1861 British presented note demanding release of James M. Mason and John Slidell, Confederate diplomats who were seized aboard a British ship; British called seizure an "affront to the British flag and a violation of international law"; United States agreed, released men December 26.

1864 George H. Parker, one of first American experimental zoologists, born in Philadelphia (died 1955).

1867 Sarah B. Walker, businesswoman known as "Madam C.J. Walker," born in Delta, LA; developed formula for straightening tightly-curled hair; became one of first women millionaires (died 1919).

1872 John C. Marin, painter (*Sunset Casco Bay, Lower Manhattan from the River*), born in Rutherford, NJ (died 1953).

1873 (Robert) Burns Mantle, edited annual collection of "best plays" (1919–47), born in Watertown, NY; drama critic, *New York Daily News* (1922–45) (died 1948).

1876 Edwin T. Meredith, magazine publisher (*Successful Farming, Better Homes & Gardens*), born in Avoca, IA; secretary of agriculture (1920–21) (died 1928).

1900 Otto Soglow, cartoonist ("The Little King"), born in New York City (died 1973).

1913 President Wilson signed Owens-Glass Federal Reserve Act, which established Federal Reserve System, first comprehensive reorganization of national banking system since 1863.

1918 José Greco, one of greatest Spanish-type dancers, born in Montorio nei Frentani, Italy.

1939 Myron C. Taylor, industrialist, named personal representative of President Franklin Roosevelt to the Vatican and Pope Pius XII.

1941 Wake Island fell to the Japanese.

1947 Bill (William H.) Rodgers, one of best marathoners, born in Hartford, CT; won Boston and New York races four times each, set records in 10-mile and 25-kilometer distances.

1970 North tower of World Trade Center in New York City topped out, making it the tallest (1,350 ft.) building in world.

1982 Senate broke a filibuster and approved five cents a gallon gas tax and a truck user fee increase to finance highway repairs and transit projects; House approved December 7.

1985 President Reagan notified Congress of decision to observe the unratified SALT II Treaty, which was due to expire December 31.

1986 *Voyager*, piloted by Dick Rutan and Jeana Yeager, completed nonstop, around-the-world flight without refueling, landing at Edwards Air Force Base, CA, after flight of nearly 26,000 miles in nine days, three minutes, 44 seconds.

1998 Iraq refused to allow entry by UN observers monitoring its border with Kuwait.

2000 Billy Barty dies: Founder of the advocacy association, "Little People of America"; acted in many motion pictures and television programs.

2001 Passenger on flight to U.S. subdued over the Atlantic as he attempted to set fire to shoes with explosives in them.

2002 Senator Bill Frist of Tennessee (Republican) became first Senate majority leader ever elected by voice vote during a conference telephone call.

2003 First confirmed U.S. case of "Mad Cow Disease" appeared in Washington state.

2006 Former Republican Senator Robert Stafford died at 93; played pivotal role in pushing through the "Stafford loan" program that now provides federal college tuition assistance to 14 million Americans.

24

1737 Silas Deane, who obtained help from France in Revolution and enlisted services of Lafayette, Pulaski, and Steuben, born in Groton, CT; member, Continental Congress (1774–76) (died 1789).

1745 William Paterson, associate justice, Supreme Court (1793–1806), born in County Antrim, Ireland; one of first senators from New Jersey (1789–90) and served state as attorney general (1776–83) and governor (1790–92) (died 1806).

1745 Benjamin Rush, who wrote first American chemistry textbook and helped found Pennsylvania Medical School, born near Philadelphia; member, Continental Congress (1776–77), signer of Declaration of Independence; treasurer of the mint (1797–1813) (died 1813).

1772 Barton W. Stone, a founder of Disciples of Christ Church, born near Port Tobacco, MD (died 1844).

1782 French Army, which had been fighting with Americans in Revolution for two-and-a-half years, sailed for home.

1802 Horace Green, first American physician to specialize in diseases of throat, air passages, born in Chittenden, VT (died 1866).

1809 Kit (Christopher) Carson, guide for expeditions of Fremont (1840s) and a scout in Mexican War, born in Madison County, KY (died 1868).

1814 Treaty of Ghent signed by negotiators in London, bringing War of 1812 to a close; included return of captured territory and creation of commissions to decide disputed boundaries.

1821 William P. Poole, librarian who launched *Index to Periodical Literature*, born in Salem, MA; librarian in Boston (1852–69), Cincinnati (1872–73), Chicago (1874–94) (died 1894).

1851 Fire in Library of Congress did extensive damage, destroying 35,000 of the 55,000 books (including two-thirds of the 6,500 purchased from Thomas Jefferson).

1863 James H. McRae, commanded 78th Division (1918–19), Philippine Department (1924–26), Second Corps area (1926–27), born in Lumber City, GA (died 1940).

1865 Ku Klux Klan formed as a social club by six young Confederate veterans in Pulaski, TN.

1873 American temperance movement began when Eliza Trimble Thompson of Hillsboro, OH, led 70 women from a prayer meeting to outside a saloon, and pleaded for owner to close it; visited 12 others on succeeding days; movement spread elsewhere.

1877 Thomas A. Edison applied for patent for his newly invented phonograph.

1881 Charles W. Cadman, student of Indian songs and composer (*The Land of the Misty Water*, *The Garden of Death*), born in Johnstown, PA; also wrote cantata (*The Vision of Sir Launfall*), operettas, operas (died 1946).

1885 Paul Manship, sculptor known for Prometheus fountain in Rockefeller Center, New York City, born in St. Paul, MN (died 1966).

1887 Lucrezia Bori, lyric soprano with Metropolitan Opera (1912–36), born in Valencia, Spain (died 1960).

1893 Harry Warren, hit songs composer (*42nd Street*, *Lullaby of Broadway*, *Shuffle Off to Buffalo*, *Chattanooga Choo-Choo*, *September in the Rain*), born in Brooklyn (died 1981).

1905 Howard R. Hughes, machine tool company owner who branched into aviation, movies, born in Houston; produced movies (*Hell's Angels*, *The Outlaw*); owned much of Las Vegas "strip"; became a recluse (died 1976).

1906 Reginald A. Fessenden, developer of high-frequency alternator, made first radio broadcast of voice and music from his station in Brant Rock, MA.

1907 John F. Cody, Catholic Archbishop of New Orleans (1964–65), of Chicago (1965–82), born in St. Louis; named cardinal 1967 (died 1982).

1914 Robert E. Cushman, Jr., Marine Corps commandant (1972–75), born in St. Paul, MN (died 1985).

1921 President Harding pardoned Eugene V. Debs and 23 others convicted under wartime espionage and other laws; effective December 25, 1921.

1929 Fire in White House destroyed interior and contents of executive offices; official papers were saved; President Hoover operated out of Executive Office Building next door until April 25, 1930.

1930 Robert Joffrey, founder, Joffrey Ballet (1956) and American Ballet Center (1953–65), which he directed, born in Seattle (died 1988).

1943 Gen. Dwight D. Eisenhower designated supreme commander, Allied Expeditionary Forces.

1951 *Amahl and the Night Visitors* by Gian-Carlo Menotti broadcast for first time, repeated on television annually.

1965 Holiday truce began in Vietnam along with a 37-day suspension of American bombing.

1988 Lower house of Canadian Parliament voted final approval to U.S.-Canadian free trade agreement which over a ten-year period will create largely free market of 270 million people; Canadian Senate approved, December 30; American Congress had approved earlier; went into effect January 1, 1989.

1992 President Bush granted pardons to six former Reagan Administration officials who were convicted of or faced charges in Iran-Contra affair, including former Defense Secretary Caspar W. Weinberger.

1998 Snow and freezing rain in much of the nation caused numerous fatal storm-related accidents and thousands were affected by power outages.

25

1709 John Peter Miller, Dutch Reformed clergyman who headed Dunkers (German Seven-Day Baptists), born in Zweikirchen, Germany; headed Dunkers in Ephrata, PA (1768–96); Congress retained him to translate Declaration of Independence into several languages (died 1796).

1724 First building of Church of England opened in American colonies in Stratford, CT, by the Rev. Samuel Johnson.

1756 Samuel DeWitt, cartographer for Continental Army, born in Wawarsing, NY; New York State surveyor general (1784–1834) (died 1834).

1776 Gen. George Washington led famed crossing of ice-clogged Delaware River to surprise the British in Trenton, NJ.

1784 Sixty clergymen met in Baltimore to form American Methodist Church; Francis Asbury and Thomas Coke unanimously elected superintendents; group adopted English discipline, liturgy, prayer book, hymns, and 24 articles of religion prepared by John Wesley.

1793 Edward T. Taylor, chaplain of Boston's Seamen's Bethel (1829–71), born in Richmond, VA (died 1871).

1810 Lorenzo L. Langstroth, invented movable frame beehive which revolutionized bee industry, born in Philadelphia; developed methods for large-scale honey production (died 1895).

1813 John Roach, sometimes called "father" of American iron shipbuilding, born in County Cork, Ireland; built marine engines and iron steamships (died 1887).

1817 Samuel Sloan, president, Delaware, Lackawanna & Western Railroad (1867–99), chairman (1899–1907), born in Lisburn, Ireland (died 1907).

1817 Gilbert C. Van Camp, food products executive who built first cold-storage warehouse and originated process of canning foods, born in Brookville, IN (died 1900).

1821 Clara Barton, founder of American Red Cross and its first president (1882–1904), born in Oxford, MA; worked five years to get American signature on Geneva agreement (died 1912).

1829 Patrick S. Gilmore, bandleader and composer (*When Johnny Comes Home Again*), born in Dublin (died 1892).

1830 South Carolina Canal and Railroad Co. (now part of Southern Railway), initiated scheduled service on first six-mile line from Charleston; its steam locomotive, *Best Friend*, was first to pull string of cars in United States.

1837 Zachary Taylor led Americans to victory over Seminoles near Lake Okeechobee, FL, in second Seminole War.

1851 Herman Fresch, chemist who devised methods which led to founding of American sulphur mining industry, born in Guildorf, Germany; developed method for desulphurizing crude oil and hot water smelting process for extracting sulphur (died 1914).

1865 Evangeline C. Booth, Salvation Army American commander (1904–34) and world leader (1934–50), born in London (died 1950).

1868 President Andrew Johnson issued proclamation of unconditional pardon and amnesty to all concerned in the "insurrection."

1870 Helena Rubinstein, cosmetics manufacturer, born in Cracow, Poland (died 1965).

1886 Kid (Edward) Ory, leading exponent of New Orleans jazz and composer (*Muskrat Ramble*), born in LaPlace, LA (died 1973).

1887 Conrad Hilton, hotel chain founder (1946), born in San Antonio, NM; Hilton Hotels owned 125 units worldwide at his death in 1979.

1888 David Lawrence, founder, editor, *U.S. News & World Report* (1933) and syndicated columnist, born in Philadelphia (died 1973).

1889 Lila Bell Wallace, cofounder with husband, DeWitt, of *Readers Digest* (1921), born in Vinden, Canada (died 1984).

1893 Robert L. Ripley, cartoonist who developed widely syndicated *Believe It or Not* feature (1918), born in Santa Rosa, CA (died 1949).

1899 Humphrey Bogart, screen actor (*The Maltese Falcon, Casablanca, Treasure of Sierra Madre, The African Queen*), born in New York City (died 1957).

1904 Gladys Swarthout, mezzosoprano with Metropolitan Opera (1929–45) and screen actress, born in Deepwater, MO (died 1969).

1907 Cab(ell) Calloway, orchestra leader and "hi-de-ho" singer, born in Rochester, NY; performed in several stage and screen productions (died 1994).

1924 Rod Serling, television playwright (*Twilight Zone* series, *Patterns, Requiem for a Heavyweight*), born in Syracuse, NY (died 1975).

1948 Barbara Mandrell, country music singer and television performer, born in Houston.

1998 Three balloonists trying to make first nonstop round-the-world flight of a balloon had to abandon the flight in the Pacific Ocean near Hawaii because of changing weather conditions.

2000 U.S. had a Christmas day partial eclipse of the moon.

2005 Charles Socarides (b. 1922), died; American psychiatrist who fought a rearguard action after 1973 against the new dominant opinion of his profession that homosexuality should be regarded as acceptable sexual behavior; claimed to have changed the sexual patterns of a significant minority of individuals from same-sex orientation to opposite-sex.

2006 Frank Stanton died at 98; headed CBS for over a quarter-century; played pivotal role in expanding the network in both its radio and early television days; invented first reliable method of calculating size of a radio listening audience.

2006 James Brown, "Godfather of Soul," died at 73; radically redirected the nature of dance music for entertainers who followed.

26

1738 Thomas Nelson, governor of Virginia (1781), born in Yorktown, VA; a signer of Declaration of Independence (died 1789).

1776 Battle of Trenton fought after 2,400 American troops crossed icy Delaware River at night and surprised about 1,400 Hessians, capturing 918 and killing 30, while suffering only five casualties.

1812 British began blockade of Chesapeake and Delaware bays; later extended to mouth of Mississippi River and ports of New York, Charleston, Port Royal, and Savannah; eventually included New England.

1817 President Monroe assigned Gen. Andrew Jackson to command troops against Seminole Indians.

1820 Dion Boucicault, actor and playwright with great influence on 19th-century American theater, born in Dublin; among his plays were *The Octoroon* and *The Colleen Bawn* (died 1890).

1825 President John Quincy Adams accepted invitation to send delegates to a congress of American nations in Panama, provoking long arguments in Congress, which finally approved; action was too late because one delegate had died, the other arrived after the congress had adjourned.

1837 George Dewey, admiral who led American naval forces to victory in Manila Bay (May 1, 1898), born in Montpelier, VT (died 1917).

1837 Morgan G. Bulkeley, first president, Aetna Life (1879–1922) and National (baseball) League (1876), born in East Haddam, CT; served Connecticut as governor (1889–93) and in Senate (1905–11); named to Baseball Hall of Fame (died 1922).

1844 James L. Reid, developer of leading American variety of corn (Reid's yellow dent), born near Russellville, OH; organized seed business (died 1910).

1859 Robert H. Ingersoll, maker of $1 watches (1892) of which he sold more than 70 million by 1919, born in Delta, MI; developed mail order business in rubber stamps, switching to watches (died 1928).

1860 Federal troops, sufficient to man only one of three forts in Charleston Harbor, were moved to Ft. Sumter to avoid a clash; vacated Ft. Moultrie occupied by South Carolina troops.

1891 Henry V. Miller, author remembered for *Tropic of Cancer* and *Tropic of Capricorn*, born in New York City (died 1980).

1908 Jack Johnson knocked out Tommy Burns in 14th round in Sydney, Australia, to win world heavyweight boxing championship.

1917 Proclamation by President Wilson placed all railroads under government control; Treasury Secretary William G. McAdoo appointed director general of railroad administration; roads returned to owners March 1, 1920.

1921 Steve Allen, originator of *Tonight* television show (1950) and composer of about 2,000 songs, born in New York City.

1935 Shenandoah (VA) National Park established.

1947 Blizzard in New York City and northeastern United States caused 55 deaths.

1972 Former President Truman died in Independence, MO, at 88.

1990 The 1990 Census showed a population of 249,632,692, an increase of more than 23 million in a decade.

1990 Gary Kasparov retained world chess title, winning the 22nd game against Anatoly Karpov in New York City.

1998 Iraq said it would fire on U.S. and British warplanes patrolling the no-fly zones in Iraq.

1998 President Clinton called on Congress to enact stricter drunken-driving laws.

2000 Jason Robards, Jr., died at 78; considered one of all-time great actors both on Broadway and in film, with two best-supporting role Oscars to his credit.

2001 Good news for diabetics: Sugar consumption limits loosened by American Diabetes Association.

2002 Record lottery winner: Andrew J. Whittaker, Jr., of West Virginia; takes $113.4 million immediately rather than $314.9 million long-term payout.

2004 Reggie White, renowned NFL player who was twice NFL Defensive Player of the Year, died at 43.

2006 Gerald R. Ford, 38th U.S. President, died at 93; America's only unelected president: Had been selected by Richard Nixon as replacement for resigned Vice President Spiro Agnew and was voted into office by Congress; defeated when ran in next presidential election.

27

1771 William Johnson, associate justice, Supreme Court (1804–34), born in Charleston, SC (died 1834).

1797 Charles Hodge, Presbyterian clergyman and one of most important American religious figures of 19th Century, born in Philadelphia; author of *Systematic Theology* (died 1878).

1798 William W. Corcoran, founder of Corcoran Art Gallery in Washington, DC, born in Washington; donated own collection and large sums of money to museum (died 1888).

1829 Hinton R. Helper, author of anti-slavery book which contributed to start of Civil War, born in what is now Davie County, NC; his book (*The Impending Crisis of the South, and How to Meet It*) sold 100,000 copies in North (died 1909).

1864 Peyton C. March, World War I general who reorganized war department as chief of staff (1918–21), born in Easton, PA (died 1955).

1881 Donald D. Brace, who headed Harcourt Brace publishers (1942–48), born in West Winfield, NY (died 1955).

1883 Cyrus S. Eaton, once clerk to John D. Rockefeller and active in Cleveland utilities, born in Pugwash, Nova Scotia; a founder, Republic Steel Co. (1930) (died 1979).

1892 Cornerstone laid for Cathedral of St. John the Divine in New York City.

1896 Louis Bromfield, novelist (*The Green Bay Tree, Early Autumn*), born in Mansfield, OH; scientific agriculturist (Malabar Farm) (died 1956).

1896 Arch Ward, *Chicago Tribune* sports editor who started baseball's All-Star Game (1933), born (died 1955).

1904 Marlene Dietrich, screen actress (*The Blue Angel, Algiers*), born in Berlin (died 1992).

1906 Oscar Levant, pianist and composer (*The American Way* and other musicals), born in Pittsburgh; appeared in several movies, panelist on *Information Please* radio show (died 1972).

1915 William H. Masters, physician, who with wife specialized in human sexuality problems, born in Cleveland; they wrote several books on subject.

1941 Rationing began, starting with tires; ended late in 1945, except for sugar; at its peak there were 13 programs in effect.

1943 Army took over all American railroads to prevent a strike; returned to private management January 18, 1944.

1968 Frank Borman, James A. Lovell, Jr., and William A. Anders completed first flight to the moon, sending back pictures of the moon's surface.

1992 American jet shot down an Iraqi warplane after Iraqi jets breached the allied-imposed no-fly zone in southern Iraq.

1998 Justice Department reported there were nearly 35 million crimes against people in 1997, a drop of 37 million from 1996.

2000 President Bill Clinton appointed first African-American to U.S. Court of Appeals based in Richmond, Virginia.

2002 Ninth U.S. Circuit Court of Appeals upheld a 2000 federal law prohibiting any "substantial burden on religious exercise" of prisoners unless it can be justified on grounds of maintaining jail security; ruling permits Muslim religious meetings on Friday and six-inch beards.

2006 Dow Jones stock market hit unprecedented closing high of 12,510.57; 22nd new high since October 1.

2006 Massachusetts Supreme Court unanimously ruled that it could not force the state legislature to vote on a proposed gay marriage ban (prerequisite for it being submitted to the voters for consideration) but that its refusal to decide one way or another on the matter represented "indifference to, or defiance of, its constitutional duties."

28

1714 George Whitefield, evangelist who preached in the colonies (1740, 1744–48, 1769), sparking a religious revival, born in Gloucester, England; founder of Calvinistic Methodists after he broke with the Wesleys over predestination (died 1770).

1789 Thomas Ewing, first Secretary of Interior (1849–50), born in what is now West Liberty, WV; represented Ohio in Senate (1831–37, 1850–51); Secretary of Treasury (1841) (died 1871).

1825 James Wilkinson, Army officer who commanded forces on Canadian frontier (1813), died at 68; involved in Conway Cabal and forced to resign Army commission; implicated in Aaron Burr's conspiracy, but acquitted.

1832 Vice President Calhoun resigned over nullification dispute and tariffs; returned by South Carolina to Senate the following year.

1832 St. Louis U., first university west of the Mississippi, chartered.

1835 President Jackson nominated Roger B. Taney for Supreme Court chief justice after John Marshall's death; confirmed by Senate March 15, 1836.

1835 American force of 112 wiped out (four survived) when Indians ambushed it near Tampa Bay at start of Florida war; known as Dade Massacre, after troop leader, Maj. Francis L. Dade.

1846 Iowa admitted to Union as the 29th state.

1856 Woodrow Wilson, 28th President (1913–21), born in Staunton, VA; professor, president, Princeton U. (1902–10), governor of New Jersey (1910–12); a leader in forming League of Nations; awarded 1919 Nobel Peace Prize (died 1924).

1873 William D. Harkins, nuclear chemist who predicted existence of neutron and deuterium, born in Titusville, PA; his research basic to nuclear fission process (died 1951).

1890 Russell L. Maxwell, World War II general who commanded American troops in North Africa (1942), born in Oakdale, IL (died 1968).

1896 Roger H. Sessions, composer of operas (*Trial of Lucullus, Montezuma*), chamber music and concertos, born in Brooklyn (died 1985).

1900 Ted (Theodore A.) Lyons, baseball pitcher (Chicago AL) who won 260 games in 21 years, born in Lake Charles, LA; named to Baseball Hall of Fame (died 1986).

1902 Mortimer J. Adler, editor, *Encyclopedia Brittanica, Annals of America*, born in New York City; organized Great Books program, U. of Chicago; founder, Institute of Philosophical Research.

1905 Earl ("Fathah") Hines, pianist and orchestra leader who had great influence on development of swing, born in Duquesne, PA (died 1983).

1905 Charlie Weaver, popular television performer, born in Toledo, OH, as Cliff Arquette (died 1974).

1929 Owen Bieber, president, United Auto Workers (1983–95), born in North Dorr, MI.

1933 John Y. Brown, restaurateur and investor in Kentucky Fried Chicken chain, born in Lexington, KY; governor of Kentucky (1979–83).

1961 Edith B. Wilson, widow of President Wilson, died in Washington at 89.

1981 President Reagan imposed sanctions on Soviet Union for its role in the Polish crackdown on independent labor unions.

1998 U.S. warplanes fired on Iraqi antiaircraft guns 250 miles north of Baghdad after they fired on Western aircraft patrolling the no-fly zone.

2000 Census Bureau reported a 13.2 percent rise in U.S. population since the last census, resulting in a new figure of 281,421,906 residents.

2004 Feminist activist and intellectual Susan Sontag died of leukemia at 71; author of 17 works of fiction and nonfiction; wrote and directed a variety of screenplays.

2006 Spc. Dustin R. Donica of Spring, Texas, became the 3,000th U.S. military casualty during Iraq war and ensuing occupation; more military dead during this December than any previous month in Iraq.

29

1778 Savannah, GA, captured by 3,500 British troops.

1780 John Adams named minister to Holland.

1800 Charles Goodyear, developer of vulcanization process basic to rubber manufacture, born in New Haven, CT; bought patent rights to sulphur treatment process from N.M. Haywood, developed own process, founded rubber company (died 1879).

1805 Asa Packer, developer, head, Lehigh Valley Railroad, born in Groton, CT; endowed Lehigh U. (died 1879).

1808 Andrew Johnson, 17th President (1865–69), born in Raleigh, NC; represented Tennessee in House (1845–53) and Senate (1857–62, 1875) and served state as governor (1853–57); elected vice president and became president on death of President Lincoln (died 1875).

1812 USS *Constitution* captured British frigate *Java* off Brazil.

1813 Combined British and Indian force crossed Niagara River and burned Black Rock and Buffalo in reprisal for American burning of Newark in Canada (December 10).

1835 Treaty approved which provided for removal of Cherokees and other tribes of the South to a reservation west of the Mississippi River in return for land, the expense of the move, and $5 million.

1837 Party of Canadian militia crossed Niagara River, boarded small American steamboat *Caroline*, which was suspected of carrying supplies to Canadian insurgents; vessel set afire, cast adrift; one American killed.

1845 Texas admitted to Union as the 28th state.

1862 Union troops were defeated at Chickasaw Bluffs, MS, in an unsuccessful effort to get to Vicksburg.

1871 Meyer London, a founder, American Socialist Party (1899–1901), born in Suwalki Province, Poland; represented New York in House (1915–19, 1921–23), (died 1926).

1876 Railroad bridge collapsed in a snowstorm at Ashtabula, OH; 92 died.

1879 Capt. Billy (William) Mitchell, air power advocate, born in Nice, France, of American parentage; court-martialed for outspoken views, convicted, sentenced to five years suspension; resigned from service (1926) (died 1936).

1891 Joyce C. Hall, founder with brother of greeting card business (1910) in Kansas City, MO, born in David City, NE; by 1968 Hallmark Cards, which he headed (1913–66), was world's largest greeting card business (died 1982).

1902 Argentine Foreign Minister Luis M. Drago enunciated policy which said that collection of financial claims in Western Hemisphere by force would violate the Monroe Doctrine; policy arose out of dispute over unpaid Venezuelan debts, which later went to arbitration.

1907 Robert C. Weaver, first Secretary of Housing & Urban Affairs (1966–69) and first black to serve in Cabinet, born in Washington, DC (died 1997).

1937 Mary Tyler Moore, television actress (Dick Van Dyke and her own shows), born in New York City.

1946 Lafitt Pincay, leading jockey in career purse earnings ($116.1 million) and second in career victories, born in Panama City, Panama; outstanding jockey five times.

1970 President Nixon signed Occupational Safety & Health Act, authorizing the setting of federal standards.

1972 Eastern Airlines Lockheed Tristar crashed on approach to Miami Airport, killing 101 persons.

1994 Dow Jones industrial average ended year at 3,833.43.

1995 President Clinton signed bill that abolishes the 108-year-old Interstate Commerce Commission, effective January 1, 1996.

1995 Dow Jones industrial average closed at 5117.12.

2000 Final Cabinet nominees of President-elect Bush announced.

2006 Federal Communications Commission approved AT&T's purchase of Bell South for $85 billion, to create largest telecommunications company in U.S.; effectively reunites much of company broken up by federal government in 1984, but now it has variety of major competitors that did not exist then.

30

1784 Stephen H. Long, explorer of upper Mississippi Valley and Rocky Mountains, born in Hopkinton, NH (died 1864).

1794 Christian Metz, religious leader who led 800 German settlers in forming what became Amana Community, born in Neuwied, Germany; original settlement in Ebenezer, NY (1842–54) was the Community of True Inspiration, becoming Amana when it moved to Iowa (died 1867).

1819 John W. Geary, first mayor of San Francisco (1851–52), born in Westmoreland County, PA; served in both Mexican and Civil wars; military governor of Savannah; governor of Pennsylvania (1867–73) (died 1873).

1844 Charles A. Coffin, founder of General Electric Co. (1892) by merging two companies, born in Somerset County, ME; was GE president (1892–1913) and board chairman (1913–22) (died 1926).

1847 John P. Altgeld, controversial governor of Illinois (1890–96), born in Nieder Selters, Germany; protested President Cleveland's sending troops to control Pullman strike; pardoned agitators involved in Haymarket riot (1886) (died 1902).

1851 Asa G. Candler, developer of Coca-Cola, its president (1887–1916), born in Carroll County, GA; mayor of Atlanta (1917–18) (died 1929).

1852 Rutherford B. Hayes and Lucy Ware Webb were married in Cincinnati.

1853 Gadsden Purchase signed, calling for United States to pay $10 million to Mexico for 29,640 square miles of land in southern New Mexico and Arizona to straighten out American-Mexican border; purchase negotiated by James Gadsden, minister to Mexico.

1860 President Buchanan refused to meet commissioners from South Carolina, which had voted to secede December 20; advised them by letter that Ft. Sumter, SC, would be defended.

1860 South Carolina troops seized federal arsenal in Charleston.

1862 During night of December 30–31, the Union ironclad *Monitor* went down in a gale off Cape Hatteras, NC; four officers and 12 men drowned.

1863 William H. Park, authority on public health aspects of diphtheria, pneumonia, tuberculosis, and poliomyelitis, born in New York City (died 1939).

1867 Simon Guggenheim, capitalist and philanthropist who founded Guggenheim Foundation, born in Philadelphia; represented Colorado in Senate (1907–13) (died 1941).

1869 Noble Order of Knights of Labor organized in Philadelphia by garment cutters union.

1873 Alfred E. Smith, governor of New York (1918–20, 1922–28), born in New York City; 1928 Democratic presidential candidate (died 1944).

1880 Alfred Einstein, a world authority on musicology, born in Munich, Germany (died 1952).

1898 Vincent Lopez, pianist and orchestra leader, born in Brooklyn (died 1975).

1899 American Telephone & Telegraph Co. formed.

1900 Clarence L. Barnhart, coeditor of several dictionaries (*Thorndike-Barnhart*), born in Plattsburgh, MO (died 1993).

1903 Fire in Iroquois Theater in Chicago's Loop took 602 lives, mostly from smoke, suffocation, and panic.

1905 Former Idaho Gov. Frank Steunenberg was killed; a former miner, found guilty of the murder, claimed killing was ordered by union (Western Federal of Miners); "Big Bill" Haywood, union secretary, and other officers were tried, acquitted.

1906 Railroad accident in Washington, DC, claimed 53 lives.

1935 Sandy (Sanford) Koufax, one of greatest left-handed pitchers (Brooklyn) who threw four no-hit games, born in New York City; named to Baseball Hall of Fame.

1935 Marian Anderson, one of world's great contraltos, made her New York debut.

1969 President Nixon signed most far-reaching tax reform bill in American history; was expected to lower taxes by five percent and remove nine million low-income Americans from the tax rolls.

1988 President Reagan and President-elect Bush were subpoenaed as defense witnesses in criminal trial of retired Lt. Col. Oliver L. North in Iran-Contra affair.

1996 Lew Ayres, famed screen actor, including the Dr. Kildare series, died at 88.

1998 U.S. warplanes hit three Iraqi military targets as President Hussein continued to defy the no-fly zone in southern Iraq.

2004 Artie Shaw, last surviving superstar of the swing era in music, passed away at 94; had been outstanding composer, clarinetist, and bandleader; abandoned public performing at height of abilities in 1954 due to frustration at admirers' resistance to his constantly moving on to yet another musical challenge; turned to writing instead.

31

1775 About 1,000 American troops led by Benedict Arnold and Gen. Richard Montgomery besieging Quebec since January 5, were defeated in an attack on the city; Gen. Montgomery was killed; siege continued through winter; Americans finally evacuated area June 15.

1781 Bank of North America, first national bank, founded by Robert Morris and chartered by Congress; had been approved May 26, 1781.

1783 Thomas Macdonough, War of 1812 naval officer who defeated British in Battle of Lake Champlain (1814), born in New Castle County, DE (died 1825).

1808 John Nixon, president, Bank of North America (1792–1808), died at 75; led Philadelphia guard in battles at Amboy and Princeton; an organizer of Bank of Pennsylvania (1780).

1815 George G. Meade, commander, Army of the Potomac (1863–65), born in Cadiz, Spain; led Union troops at Gettysburg (died 1872).

1851 Henry C. Adams, pioneer in public finance, relation of government and industry, born in Davenport, IA; economist at Michigan U. (1886–1921) (died 1921).

1853 Tasker H. Bliss, first commandant, Army War College (1903–05), born in Lewisburg,

PA; chief of staff during World War I, transforming small peacetime army into huge war machine (died 1930).

1857 King (Michael J.) Kelly, legendary baseball player who was subject of fans' chants of "slide, Kelly, slide," born; named to Baseball Hall of Fame (died 1894).

1860 John T. Thompson, co-inventor of Thompson submachine gun, born in Newport, KY (died 1940).

1862 Four-day Battle of Stone River (near Murfreesboro, TN) began as a Confederate victory; unable to hold gains, retreated; sometimes considered a turning point in war; each army had 1,200 casualties.

1864 George W. Ritchey, astronomer who invented various instruments, born in Tuppers Plains, OH; invented fixed vertical universal type of reflecting telescope, cellular type of optical mirrors, designed, built 40-inch reflecting telescope at Naval Observatory (died 1945).

1867 Valcour Aime, builder of first American sugar refinery, died at 69.

1870 Thomas H. Connally, chief of American League baseball umpires (1931–54), born in Manchester, England; named to Baseball Hall of Fame (died 1961).

1880 George C. Marshall, Army chief of staff with major responsibility for American troops in World War II, born in Uniontown, PA; awarded 1953 Nobel Peace Prize for promoting Marshall Plan as Secretary of State (1947–50); Secretary of Defense (1950–51) (died 1959).

1884 Stanley F. Reed, associate justice, Supreme Court (1938–57), born in Mason County, KY; Solicitor General (1935–38) (died 1980).

1884 Elizabeth Arden, cosmetics leader, born in Ontario, Canada; founder, owner of company bearing her name; operated 100 beauty salons (died 1966).

1904 Nathan Milstein, regarded as leading violin interpreter of concertos, born in Odessa, Russia (died 1992).

1905 Jule Styne, composer of musical comedies (*High Button Shoes*, *Gentlemen Prefer Blondes*, *Gypsy*, *Funny Girl*), born in London (died 1994).

1918 Statewide prohibition went into effect in Montana.

1943 John Denver, singer and composer ("Leaving on a Jet Plane," "Rocky Mountain High"), born in Roswell, NM; screen actor (*Oh God*) (died 1997).

1944 Crash of two sections of Pacific Limited near Ogden, Utah, resulted in 50 deaths.

1972 Roberto Clemente, baseball player (Pittsburgh 1955–72), died in a plane crash at 38.

1975 Cost of first-class postage rose to 13 cents.

1986 Fire in Dupont Plaza Hotel in San Juan, Puerto Rico, killed 96 persons.

1988 Federal Home Loan Bank Board expected to sell 222 insolvent savings and loan associations at year's end.

1991 Dow Jones industrial average ended year at record 3,168.83 level.

1996 Dow Jones industrial average closed at 6,448.27, a 26 percent advance over a year ago.

2000 Alan Cranston, Senator best known for his advocacy of nuclear disarmament while California's U.S. Senator, died at 86.

2000 Library of Congress analysis: Total world sales of military weaponry to other nations hit $36.9 billion in 2000; U.S. arms manufacturers had $18.6 billion in sales, followed distantly by Russia ($7.7 billion) and France ($4.1 billion).

2001 Apparent new record for ex-president speech-making: Bill Clinton's financial disclosure records indicate he earned $9.2 million during year in speeches and lectures given around the world.

2002 Wall Street ended 2002 with third consecutive yearly decline in prices; had not happened previously since the Great Depression.

2002 Census Bureau statistics: 10 percent growth in American businesses, 1997–2002; minority increases: black-owned, 45 percent; Hispanic, 31 percent; Asian, 24 percent; total percentage of minority owned of all businesses: about 18 percent.

2004 Of all U.S. childbirths this year, 11 percent were for a fourth or later child, up from 10 percent in 1995.

2005 October 2006 analysis of latest 2005 census survey data: percentage of married couples (whether with or without children) slid to 49.7 percent of the population from 52 percent five years ago; causes: major ones include more unmarried couples living together and more older individuals without mates.

2006 2006 was the year "pay for listening" satellite radio services took off: the rival systems XM Satellite Radio jumped listeners 30 percent (to about 7.8 million radios) and Sirius Satellite Radio 80 percent (to about 6 million).

2006 Associated Press/AOL mid–December poll results released on American views of what will happen in 2007: 70 percent expect major natural disaster, 60 percent terrorist attack, 25 percent the return of Jesus.

INDEX

Years shown as two digits are 1900s.